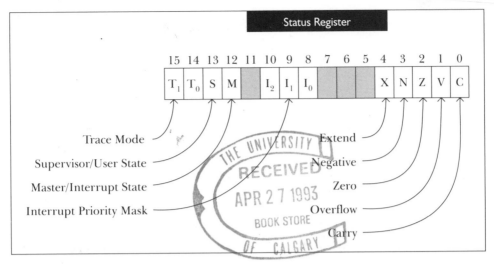

Status Register

15	14	13	12	11	10	9	8	7	6	5	4	3	2	1	0
T_1	T_0	S	M		I_2	I_1	I_0				X	N	Z	V	C

Trace Mode
Supervisor/User State
Master/Interrupt State
Interrupt Priority Mask

Extend
Negative
Zero
Overflow
Carry

Effective Addressing Mode Categories

Addressing Mode	Mode	Register	Assembler Syntax
Data Register Direct	000	Register	Dn
Address Register Direct	001	Register	An
Address Register Indirect	010	Register	(An)
Address Reg Indirect with Postincrement	011	Register	(An)+
Address Reg Indirect with Predecrement	100	Register	–(An)
Address Reg Indirect with Displacement	101	Register	(d16,An)
Address Reg Indirect with Index (8-Bit Displacement)	110	Register	(d8,An,Rn)
Absolute Short	111	000	xxx.W
Absolute Long	111	001	xxx.L
PC with Displacement	111	010	(d16,PC)
PC with Index (8-Bit Displacement)	111	011	(d8,PC,Rn)
Immediate	111	100	#<data>
Address Reg Indirect with Index (Base Displacement)	110	Register	(bd,An,Rn)
PC with Index (Base Displacement)	111	011	(bd,PC,Rn)
Memory Indirect Pre-Indxed	110	Register	([bd,An,Rn],od)
Memory Indirect Post-Indexed	110	Register	([bd,An],Rn,od)
PC Memory Indirect Pre-Indexed	111	011	([bd,PC,Rn],od)
PC Memory Indirect Post-Indexed	111	011	([bd,PC],Rn,od)

MC68000 Data Structures

7 **Byte** 0

15 **Word** 0
MSB	LSB

31 **Long Word** 0
MSW	LSW

31   24 23 **24-Bit Address** 0
	Address

Exception Priorities for the MC68000 Family

Group Priorty	Priority within the Group
0	Reset
1	Address error Bus error
2	BKPT #n, CHK, CHK2
	Divide by zero, Format
	Trap #n; TRAPV
3	Illegal instruction A-line
	F-line, Privilege violation

ASSEMBLY LANGUAGE AND SYSTEMS PROGRAMMING FOR THE M68000 FAMILY

ASSEMBLY LANGUAGE AND SYSTEMS PROGRAMMING
for the
M68000 FAMILY

SECOND EDITION

William Ford
University of the Pacific

William Topp
University of the Pacific

D. C. HEATH AND COMPANY
Lexington, Massachusetts   Toronto

Address editorial correspondence to:

D. C. Heath
125 Spring Street
Lexington, MA 02173

Cover: Jean Bailey
Appendixes A, B, and E © 1989 by Motorola, Inc.

Publisher simultaneously in Canada.

Printed in the United States of America.

International Standard Book Number: 0-669-28199-9

Library of Congress Catalog Number: 92-70594

10 9 8 7 6 5 4 3 2 1

To all those who helped make this book a reality and to our children who make it a necessity.

PREFACE

The assembly language and systems programming applications for the Motorola 68000 family of microprocessors constitute the focus of this comprehensive text. These processors are used in a variety of PC systems and peripheral devices. Their sophisticated instruction set provides a powerful set of addressing modes, and a well-designed assembly language is available for solving even the most complex problems. Developers that use one of the 68000 processors for applications require programmers to have a detailed understanding of its assembly language and architecture.

The first seven chapters contain the majority of the basic syntax and instructions for the MC68000 assembly language. Chapters 8–11 cover the key application areas, including extended arithmetic operations, string handling routines and I/O code conversion, high-level language code constructs and the runtime environment, and data structures. The material in the first seven chapters along with selected topics from the applications in Chapters 8–11 is suitable for a one-semester course in assembly language programming. Chapters 12–14 introduce I/O programming, exception processing, interrupts, and advanced applications of assembly language to systems programming. The advanced material in these chapters could be combined with the run-time systems sections in Chapter 10 to support courses in programming languages, systems programming, operating systems, microcomputers and computer organization. In addition, the accessible writing style and the well-placed presentation of detail make the text suitable for self-study and allow instructors to assign supplemental reading as necessary.

This second edition is completely up-to-date. Each chapter begins by describing the MC68000 assembly language and adds a separate section on the MC68020/30/40 processors. The format allows the instructor to select as much of the information as he or she desires. The material on the MC68020/30/40 processors details their architecture, addressing modes, data types, and additional instructions. Chapter 15, Advanced M68000 System Topics, gives detailed information on cache memory and coprocessing.

Throughout the text, examples and complete programs are used extensively to illustrate concepts, instructions, and addressing modes. They provide the reader with hands-on experience using the MC68000 processor, its assembly language, and applications. Beginning with Chapter 8, the reader is introduced to libraries of routines to use in applications and to illustrate the use of include files and separately linked code files in assembly language.

The Macintosh is a leading computer using the M68000 family of processors. This text adds detailed notes for the Macintosh user without detracting from a study of the MC68000. The text gives a detailed description of the Macintosh run-time system and how it affects assembly language programming. A series of programs compare and contrast programming algorithms on the Macintosh and a system supporting absolute addressing. To further support Macintosh users we have written the Macintosh Assembly System (MAS), a complete assembly system with editor and source-level debugger running MC68020/30/40 code. This system is discussed with the text support materials.

The book highlights assembly language routines for I/O programming, string handling, extended arithmetic operations, floating point numbers, and code conversion. The routines are bundled in libraries. Chapter 9 provides a complete library of I/O programming routines. The library assumes the existence of low-level operating system calls to implement character input and output. This main library implements numerical and character stream I/O and can be used with system redirection. Chapter 12 introduces an I/O library for a standalone system. The primitive input and output routines, assumed in Chapter 9, are written for a standalone system. These routines, combined with the numerical and character I/O routines, provide a library for a standalone system. The book also includes an interrupt-driven I/O driver with buffering and flow control. Appendix D lists the various routines.

This book can be used to explore fundamental topics in systems programming, among them high-level language run-time environments, the construction of I/O drivers, memory management, concurrent programming, and coprocessing. The MC68881 floating-point coprocessor is introduced in detail and includes a floating-point I/O library. The MC68030 MMU (Memory Management Unit) is presented with a complete application.

CHAPTER DESCRIPTIONS

Chapters 1–7 present the basics of the M68000 family of processors, including their architecture and organization. The chapters introduce standard Motorola assembly language syntax and operations, the main instructions, and addressing modes. The organization and instruction set for the MC68020/30/40 processors is covered in a separate section in each chapter. This section features detailed examples and programs. For readers using these processors, the text and the special sections on the MC68020/30/40 processors will provide a complete overview of these systems. Chapter 15, which introduces coprocessors, includes a technical presentation of material relevant only to the MC68020/30/40 processors.

Chapter 1 introduces high-level language, assembly language, and machine language code. A brief history of the M68000 family of processors is featured.

Chapter 2 covers the binary and hexadecimal number systems and the arithmetic used in assembly language programming. Readers unfamiliar with these topics will need to study the concepts and examples because this material is fundamental to the rest of the book.

Chapter 3 discusses the basic architecture of the MC68000. The machine code format for instructions, including opcode words and extension words, is covered. The architecture of the MC68020/30/40 processors is introduced.

Chapter 4 begins a study of Motorola assembly language programming. Topics include an overview of the structure of a program, an introduction to addressing modes and basic assembly language instructions, and a description of the I/O library routines. A discussion of common syntax and run-time errors is also presented.

Chapter 5 introduces control structures for assembly language programming using the branch instructions. Algorithms to implement high-level language conditionals and loop structures are covered. A separate section focuses on the concept of branch offsets and machine code. The chapter introduces the MC68000 bit handling instructions and the beginning of advanced application programs that mark each subsequent chapter.

Chapter 6 uses the concept of array access to cover the remaining MC68000 addressing modes. PC relative modes introduce position independent code. These modes and A5-relative addressing describe the Macintosh code structure and run-time environment. Two addressing modes available on the MC68020/30/40 processor are introduced.

Chapter 7 discusses assembly language subroutines. Parameter passing using registers and the stack is covered. High-level language subroutine calls are a major topic in Chapter 10. However, the LINK/UNLK instructions and stack frame are introduced in this chapter to support good assembly language program design.

Chapters 8–11 focus on major applications areas for assembly language. Concepts are implemented by writing separate subroutines that are grouped in libraries and included in or linked into applications. The reader may choose from among a variety of applications, depending on his or her interest. Each of the chapters may be read independently.

Chapter 8 considers extended 64-bit arithmetic operations for signed numbers. Number operations are also available for binary coded decimal (BCD) integers. An optional section introduces IEEE floating-point numbers, along with a library of routines to demonstrate floating-point number handling.

The MC68020/30/40 processors introduce bit field operations that permit extended bit tests and extension. These are used to simplify some of the floating-point routines. MC68020/30/40 extended instructions for multiplication, division, and BCD arithmetic are presented.

Chapter 9 explores a variety of topics on string handling and ASCII-binary code conversions. A library for null-terminated strings is developed. A data conversion library is used to develop a complete keyboard/screen I/O library. The chapter concludes with a brief treatment of data encryption.

Chapter 10 covers selected topics in the high-level language run-time environment. The chapter focuses on code generated by a compiler to implement high-level language constructs. It includes a discussion of jump tables, high-level language stack frames, recursion, reentrant code, and position-independent code. The MC68020/30/40 memory indirect modes are introduced, along with applications to jump tables.

Chapter 11 selects classical topics from data structures, including stacks, queues, linked lists, and trees. Each structure contains a package of operators that load, update, and retrieve data.

Chapters 12–15 apply to courses in systems programming. Topics in these chapters include I/O programming, exception processing, peripheral device interrupts, process handling, the coprocessor interface, and memory management using a MMU.

Chapter 12 treats I/O programming on a stand-alone system. The chapter provides an overview of hardware components and programming details for an ACIA, timer, and PIA. Application programs running on a Motorola Educational Computer Board (ECB) illustrate the use of the MC6850 ACIA and the MC68230 PIA/Timer. A standalone I/O package is fully developed.

Chapter 13 introduces exception processing. The MC68000 exceptions are defined, and relevant exception service routines are used in a series of test programs. In particular, a complete program to perform single stepping of a program running in user mode is presented. MC68020/30/40 exception processing is treated in detail, including a description of the dual trace bits, master/interrupt stack pointers, and extended stack frame.

Chapter 14 completes the discussion of exception processing with a study of interrupt processing. It assumes a careful reading of topics in Chapters 12 and 13. MC68020/30/40 interrupt processing is included. Complete programs include an interrupt driven I/O driver with flow control and I/O buffering and a transmit interrupt printer driver.

Chapter 15 is a capstone chapter covering advanced assembly language and systems programming topics. The chapter features topics that apply primarily to the MC68020/30/40 processors. The concept of process switching introduces the topic of concurrent programming and the resulting problems of mutual exclusion. A significant program is presented to illustrate the concepts. Techniques for manipulating the cache are explored with a programming example. The M68000 Coprocessor Interface is discussed. Then the MC68881/68882 floating-point coprocessors are presented in detail with complete programs and a library for floating point I/O. The MC68020/30/40 processors support bus fault recovery. The entire bus fault recovery process is described, along with a complete program implementing software recovery from a fault. The chapter presents the MC68030 on-chip memory management unit with an application program.

CHAPTER ORDER

Chapters 1–7 cover the basic topics of assembly language programming. These concepts are integral to understanding the book. The chapters provide the reader with sufficient background to program a system with absolute addressing or a system using base relative addressing (Macintosh). Chapters 8–12 may be covered independently. Chapter 13 uses the I/O library developed in Chapter 12. Chapters 14–15 require a complete reading of Chapters 12 and 13. An interested reader can focus on MC68020/30/40 instructions and syntax. Each chapter introduces concepts common to the MC68000 and the MC68020/30/40 systems. A separate section isolates instructions, addressing modes, and concepts peculiar to the newer processors. These sections use the same format as the rest of the book and contain a number of examples and complete programs. Chapter 15 focuses predominantly on MC68020/30/40 topics.

SUPPORT MATERIALS

With only minor exceptions, the *M68000 Family Resident Structured Assembler Reference Manual* defines the assembly language syntax used in this book. The *M68000 Family Programmer's Reference Manual* defines the instruction set used in this book.

The *Instructor's Guide* offers teaching tips for each chapter, transparency masters and answers to all written exercises. The guide features complete programs with run-time output for most of the programming exercises and is available from the publisher.

Also available to instructors is the SMC68000 Absolute Assembler, which models a hypothetical SMC68000. The machine allows students to write small assembly language programs using the restricted Motorola instructions introduced in Chapter 3 and to execute the assembled machine code in a well-defined run-time environment. You may choose a version of the SMC68000 package running on a Macintosh, a UNIX 4.2, or System V system, or a DOS-PC system. All are available on one 3 1/2-inch disk. For information, contact D. C. Heath.

For Macintosh users, the Macintosh Assembly System (MAS) Version 2.0, offers an integrated programming environment that includes a comprehensive editor, a 68020/30/40 assembler with include files and projects, a run-time support environment and a full-featured source-level debugger. The distribution includes all of the text programs. For information, contact D. C. Heath.

A complete 68020 assembler written in C and running under 4.2BSD or System V UNIX is available. A distribution includes all of the text programs. The software can be ported to any system by rewriting the file which generates the object code format for a specific machine. To purchase the software at a nominal cost, contact William Topp at Ramsoft, 456 S. Regent Stockton, CA 95204 (billt@uop.edu).

ACKNOWLEDGMENTS

The authors have been supported by friends, students, and colleagues in the preparation of the book. The University of the Pacific has generously provided resources and support to complete the project. D. C. Heath offered a superb team of professionals who handled the book from manuscript to final production. We are especially grateful to acquisitions editor Carter Shanklin, editorial assistant Heather Monahan, designer Cornelia Boynton, and production editors Bryan Woodhouse and Ron Hampton.

Greg Winters of Gasboy Development, Kirkland, Washington, has been a valuable technical consultant for the text. He is an author of the UNIX MC68020 assembler that also is used in the Motorola Assembly System (MAS).

Students have offered valuable criticism for the first edition by giving us explicit feedback or unsolicited blank stares. We have incorporated their suggestions and those of colleagues using the first edition.

Our reviewers offered invaluable guidance for the revision. As critics and supporters of our work, they provided detailed comments on both the content and the pedagogical approach. We took most of their recommendations into account in this revision. Special thanks go to Dana Lasher at University of North Carolina, Raleigh; Dr. Frank Merat, Case Western Reserve University; Calvin J. Ribbens, Virginia Polytechnic Institute; and Norman Wright, Brigham Young University.

Motorola Semiconductor has been most cooperative in providing documentation. The educational division under Fritz Wilson continues to support universities enthusiastically.

William Ford
William Topp

C O N T E N T S

Chapter 3 | **MACHINE ORGANIZATION AND PROGRAMMING**   **59**

Chapter 6 | **ARRAYS AND STACKS**   **211**

Chapter 13 | **EXCEPTION PROCESSING**

Chapter 14 | PERIPHERAL DEVICE INTERRUPTS   733

CHAPTER 1

INTRODUCTION

You probably began your study of computers by learning how to use languages such as Pascal. You built your knowledge of algorithms, practiced the discipline of writing programs, and became familiar with the run-time environment of your computer system. This high-level language background forms the basis for building skills that apply to assembly language programming. In studying assembly language, you will become familiar with the architecture and instruction set of the underlying computer and understand how high-level language constructs are implemented. In the process, you will master the computer as a tool for solving increasingly complex problems.

This text introduces the Motorola family of processors, including the MC68000, MC68020, MC68030, and MC68040 processors. The primary goal of this text is the careful presentation of Motorola assembly language for these processors. The text includes many complete programs to help you understand the language. In most cases, these programs are independent of the run-time environment of the host operating system. In some cases, however, you must make programming adjustments in the host system in order to run your programs in a specific environment. For example, Macintosh programs require the use of relative addresses. When necessary, programs include notes to indicate special system requirements.

|1.1| COMPUTERS AND COMPUTER LANGUAGES

To use a particular computer, you must provide program code that ultimately defines a series of machine instructions. You can write this code in a high-level language, in the intermediate symbolic code of assembly language, or directly in machine language.

FIGURE 1.1   The MC68030 Chip in the M68000 Family (Courtesy Motorola)

High-Level Languages

We refer to languages such as Pascal, C, and Ada as **high-level languages**. They permit the user to write programs with English-like statements and common mathematical symbols. A program called a **compiler** reads the user's **source code** (high-level language) and converts it into the machine language that the computer recognizes. The modern approach to computer programming is to use a high-level language whenever possible. It relieves the user of system-dependent details, greatly speeds up program development time, and provides more readable and maintainable programs. The following example of a Pascal function illustrates high-level language programming. We will also use the code to demonstrate assembly language and machine language programming. The function is passed a parameter N. The sum $5 + 5 + 5 + \cdots + 5 + 5$ is the return value $N * 5$.

```
FUNCTION TOTAL (N : INTEGER)
VAR
     SUM : INTEGER;
     I   : INTEGER;
```

```
BEGIN
     SUM := 0;
     FOR I := 1 TO N DO BEGIN
         SUM := SUM 5;
     TOTAL := SUM;
END;
```

Machine Language

Modern compilers translate high-level language source code into **machine code**, which consists of sequences of 0's and 1's. Machine code specifies the operation, its size, and its access to data for the specific computer system in use. For example, the statement "SUM := SUM + 5" uses the MC68000 machine instruction "add the integer value 5 to the memory address SUM." Assume that the variable SUM corresponds to memory address 8.

High-Level Language Statement

$$SUM := SUM + 5$$

Action: Add the 32-bit value 5 to the variable SUM and store the result in SUM.

Machine Code

0000 0110 1011 1001	Machine instruction: add a number to contents in memory
0000 0000 0000 0000 0000 0000 0000 0101	The number to add is 5
0000 0000 0000 0000 0000 0000 0000 1000	The address in memory is 8

Assembly Language

Machine language programming was the earliest mode of programming a computer. It allows direct access to the instruction set and internal registers of the central processing unit (CPU). However, it is too tedious and inefficient to be practical. At the other end of the spectrum, high-level language programs are relatively easy to write, but they result in compiled code that is usually both larger and less efficient than programmer-generated, machine language code. From the early days of computer languages, programmers perceived the need to access machine instructions using a more symbolic and natural representation. **Assembly language** programming grew out of this need. In it, machine operations are represented by

FIGURE I.2   A Motorola Development System (Courtesy Motorola)

mnemonic codes (such as ADD and MOVE) and symbolic names that specify memory addresses. The following examples illustrate equivalent assembly language code for some of the high-level language statements in the Pascal function TOTAL. You know that a FOR LOOP first initializes a counter and then compares the counter with the upper bound. The following list describes both the Pascal and assembly language code. Assume the count I is stored in register D1 and the upper bound N is stored in register D2.

High-Level Language Construct	Pascal Statement	MC68000 Assembly Language Code
Assignment statement	SUM := SUM + 5	ADDI.L #5,SUM
Initialize a variable	I := 1	MOVEQ #1,D1
Comparison test	I <= N	CMP.L D1,D2

For the interested reader, the function TOTAL is given as a complete MC68000 assembly language subroutine. The details necessary to understand the assembly language code are introduced in Chapters 2–7. With that background, you can read most MC68000 assembly language programs and freely explore the systems and high-level language programming applications found in Chapters 8–15.

```
            XDEF            TOTAL                     ; SUBROUTINE DECLARATION

TOTAL

; PARAMETERS ARE DEFINED RELATIVE TO A6
; PARAMETER N IS AT OFFSET 8 RELATIVE TO A6

            LINK            A6, #0
            CLR.L           D0                        ; SUM IS STORED IN D0;
            MOVEM.L         D1[D2,-(SP)               ; SAVE SYSTEM REGISTERS ON STACK
            MOVE.L          (8,A6),D2                 ; ASSIGN UPPER BOUND N TO D2
            MOVEQ           #1,D1                     ; ASSIGN COUNT 1 TO REGISTER D1
            CMP.L           D1,D2                     ; COMPARE I AND N
            BLT             SET_RETURN                ; IF N < I, SETUP RETURN OF 0
LOOP:
            ADDI.L          #5,D0
            ADDI.L          #1,D1                     ; INCREMENT THE COUNTER I
            CMP.L           D1,D2                     ; COMPARE I AND N
            BGE             LOOP                      ; IF N >= I, LOOP AGAIN
SET_RETURN:
            MOVEM.L         (SP)+,D1-D2               ; RESTORE SYSTEM REGISTERS
            UNLK            A6
            RTS                                       ; RETURN

            END
```

From High-Level Language to Execution

A high-level language such as Pascal can be run on different computer systems because the language is supported by a variety of compilers that translate the relatively standard Pascal syntax into machine language code. A system utility called the **linker** merges the compiled machine code with library modules to produce an executable code file. At run time, a **loader** copies the code file into memory and launches the program. Figure 1.3 illustrates the process from compilation to code execution.

Assembly language programming follows a pattern similar to high-level language programming. A program called an **assembler** reads the source code and converts it to machine code. The process is a relatively simple translation, because assembly language code has a one-to-one correspondence with blocks of machine code. Assembly language programming allows the user to access internal system registers and instructions not available in a high-level language. It also enables the code to be optimized for speed and size.

Assemblers can be divided into two categories: resident assemblers and cross assemblers. A **resident assembler** translates symbolic code to machine code for the same computer. A **cross assembler** produces machine code for another type of computer (see Figure 1.4). You can then download the

FIGURE 1.3   Process of Compilation to Code Execution

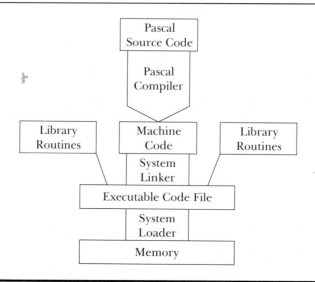

code to the machine and run it. This text assumes that you are using a resident assembler, but you may use a cross assembler, if necessary.

1.2 | WHY STUDY ASSEMBLY LANGUAGE?

The obvious benefits of high-level languages restrict the widespread use of assembly language programming. Nevertheless, there are a number of good reasons for taking the time to master at least one assembly language.

Learning assembly language teaches you how a computer works. The process of working with a computer on its own terms allows you to understand such things as computer arithmetic, machine registers, and the rudiments of bus architectures and input/output (I/O) programming. Knowing such concepts makes it easier for you to use your computer more effectively.

Systems programming is the discipline of designing and implementing the software that enables people to use a particular system. This includes writing editors, compilers, assemblers, system utilities, and the operating system itself. Anyone who wants to master computer organization or systems programming must understand assembly language programming. Applying assembly language to systems programming is a major theme in this text.

Assembly language has practical applications in a number of areas of

FIGURE 1.4   Cross-Assembled Code

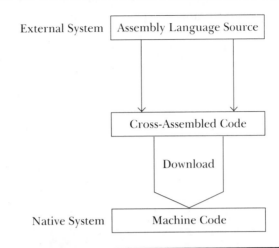

computer programming. Every computer system has a number of peripheral devices such as terminals, printers, and disk drives. Often it is more efficient to use assembly language to communicate with these devices. Also, you may encounter cases in which no high-level language construct will permit you to produce a specific type of machine-language sequence, so you must write short sequences of assembly language to do the job. This frequently occurs when you are writing the kernel of an operating system.

Another reason for considering assembly language is efficiency. Using code that is essentially at machine level provides complete control of the system. A carefully written assembly language program usually outperforms a corresponding high-level language program in both execution speed and storage requirements. Of course, an assembly language program using a poorly written algorithm may not be as efficient as a high-level language program using a well-written algorithm. Program development and maintenance time for an assembly language program is still greater than the time required for a high-level language program. Thus, programmers generally use assembly language only when greater efficiency is mandated or when storage limitations dictate. For instance, search routines typically use assembly language code for pattern matching. Today, assembly language instructions in an application program are greatly simplified when **in-line assembly language code** is included. A compiler allows the user to insert blocks of assembly language instructions within the high-level language code. The compiler uses variables within assembly language instructions and translates the instructions into machine code. The use of in-line code enables the programmer to efficiently link assembly language code with the high-level language code.

Modern high-level languages provide a mechanism for subroutine calls and parameter passing that is best understood by studying equivalent assembly language programming details. The same high-level languages have a variety of conditional and loop constructs whose implementation can be understood by looking at the equivalent assembly language code. You can better understand compiler-generated code and structured high-level language constructs by writing assembly language programs.

Many programming systems use **integrated environments**. That is, a large executive program handles a number of different tasks such as entering and editing source code, generating machine code, executing a pro-

FIGURE 1.5   Motorola's 68040 Microprocessor (Courtesy Motorola)

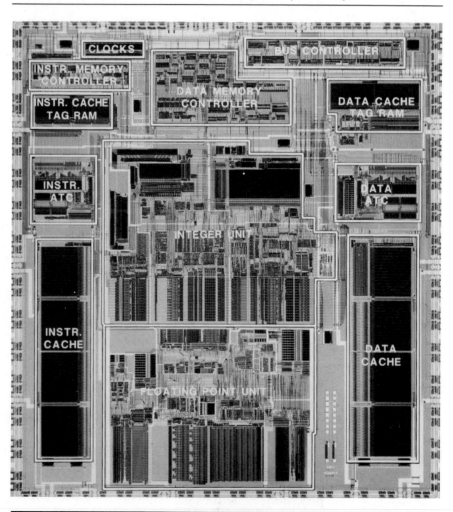

gram within a run-time support environment, and debugging. Examples include Turbo Pascal and the Macintosh Assembly System (MAS). To program an integrated environment, you must understand the system stack and dynamic memory allocation. You can use this understanding to create a run-time environment that starts program execution and monitors program status. Many of the principles of a run-time environment are covered in this text.

1.3 | THE MOTOROLA M68000 FAMILY OF MICROPROCESSORS

A **microprocessor** is a collection of circuits packaged on a small silicon chip. A microprocessor contains the basic instruction logic for a computer and the circuitry to interact with an external environment. Microprocessors are a relatively new product in the history of computers. In 1970, Intel Company developed the Intel 4004 chip, which became the processor for a 4-bit computer used to control a printing calculator. In 1972, Intel produced the 8008 chip, an 8-bit processor. As the market grew, other companies also introduced microprocessor chips. The result today is a substantial number of microprocessors with complex architectures operating at increasingly higher speeds.

Motorola Corporation, one of the leaders in the development of microprocessors in the 1970s, introduced two successful 8-bit processors: the MC6800 and MC6809. The chips used two 8-bit accumulators and allowed limited 16-bit arithmetic. At the same time, Motorola released a number of peripheral-device interfaces to support the MC6800 processor. Motorola was the first to offer a family of systems, coordinating processors and support devices. Today, most vendors market a family of chips and devices, not a single processor.

When the 6800 chips were being designed, some members of the Motorola engineering team joined MOS Tech and helped create the successful 6502 processor. The chip was similar to the 6800 and captured a large market share. Several computer companies, including Apple, Commodore, and Atari, selected the 6502/6800 processors for their systems.

The early microprocessors were relatively slow and difficult to program, especially in high-level languages. In the late 1970s, 16- and 32-bit processors revolutionized the microcomputer industry. They had the power to perform at speeds previously available only on mainframe systems. The larger instruction set, extended arithmetic operations, and extended addressing modes created systems resembling those of large (mainframe) computers.

The Motorola 68000 is a member of this next generation of processors, providing for 16-bit data transfer and 32-bit operations. Other members of the family include the MC68010 and MC68012 processors that allow the

FIGURE 1.6 Macintosh II System

computer to be a *virtual machine*. Programmers can use these two processors to simulate a large computer system with a range of peripheral devices not actually present on the system. The processors also are effective in the design of new software for developmental systems.

The MC68000 processor has 32-bit internal registers. Although the processor supports only a 24-bit address bus and a 16-bit data bus, the register size accommodated the development of the MC68020, which is a full 32-bit processor having both a 32-bit address bus and a 32-bit data bus. The MC68020 processor was introduced in 1984 and provides high-speed co-processing and additional process-control instructions. The processor has a greatly expanded instruction set that can be effectively used to optimize compiler code. In rapid order, Motorola released newer versions of their 32-bit processors. In 1987, the MC68030 processor upgraded the 68020 and provided increased speed, cache memory, and an onboard memory management unit. The MC68040 introduced new instructions and has an onboard floating-point coprocessor.

The development of new processors in the M68000 family will likely include more onboard memory and device chips to support throughput. It is unlikely that data and address bus size will increase, because most applications can work within the current precision and new technology (graphics screens and the like) can be developed effectively on the newer systems.

Motorola is developing a family of reduced instruction-set computer (RISC) chips that should command a significant market share in computer systems of the future. A RISC chip is designed around a small set of instructions that execute in one clock cycle. In theory, a RISC system uses a great many internal registers to create relatively simple and very efficient code. Contrast this with complex instruction-set computer (CISC) systems, which include the M68000 family of processors. CISC systems have a variety of tailor-made instructions that enable some algorithms to execute very efficiently. Both types of processors will likely continue to be developed and find applications.

Several vendors in the personal computer market have adopted the M68000 family of processors. They are also extensively used in larger systems for process control and graphics devices.

The Motorola 68000 and its assembly language are a good vehicle for students to learn about computers. The instructions are flexible yet relatively simple to organize. The processor's architecture is clean and contemporary.

1.4 MC68000 SYSTEMS AND DEVICES

Personal computers, workstations, multiprocessor systems, and interface devices use the MC68000 processors. Scientific applications that require high-performance processing for graphics and artificial intelligence also use them.

Auxiliary devices are available for the MC68000 processors. Arithmetic can be performed with the MC68881/82 floating-point coprocessors. All operations perform 80-bit precision arithmetic. The coprocessor performs data conversion, and special transcendental functions are available for scientific applications.

A *memory management unit* (*MMU*) is a chip that translates logical program addresses into physical addresses in memory. Such a chip is very useful in a multiuser environment, where the many users have to relocate their logical addresses in different physical blocks of memory. The same chip also protects memory by blocking a process from accessing memory outside the space allocated to that process. This allows for efficient concurrent programming. The MC68000 processor uses the 16-bit MC68451 MMU chip. The MC68020/30/40 processors use the MC68851 paged memory management unit (PMMU), which can tie into the MC68020 coprocessor interface. As a result, the instructions and registers in the PMMU

FIGURE 1.7   The MC68040 Chip (Courtesy Motorola)

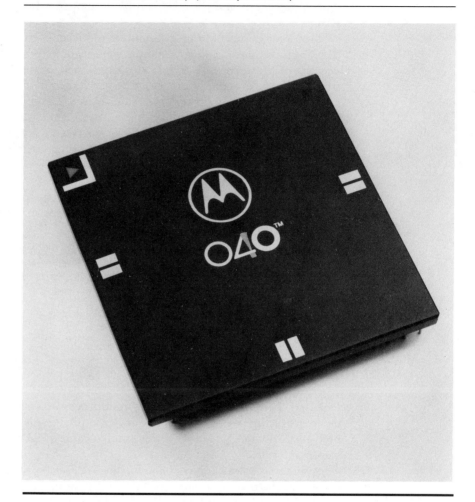

appear to be a subset of the registers and instructions in the MC68020 processor. The M68000 family was designed to use the MC6800 peripheral devices. This enabled customers to use their older devices while getting the benefit of the new processors. In the 1980s, Motorola released a series of new disk controllers and multifunctional serial and parallel interfaces. The devices joined the M68000 family of processors to give increased speed and sophistication to Motorola systems.

For most Motorola systems, the processor and auxiliary interface devices are connected on a single board. The newer members of the M68000 family have more resources on the chip. The corresponding systems have expanded onboard chip resources. The MC68020 processor combines with the MC68881 floating-point coprocessor and MC68451 memory management coprocessor. The MC68030 processor uses the MC68882 floating-point coprocessor and a memory management unit on the chip.

EXERCISES

1. Make a list of popular personal computers on the market. Find out what processor is used in each of these computers.

2. Identify the corresponding high-level language statement in the following assembly language segments.

```
(a)  MOVE       X,Y
(b)  MOVE       A,D0
     ADD        B,D0
     MOVE       D0,C
(c)  TST        A              ; TEST
     BMI        QUIT           ; BRANCH ON MINUS
(d)             MOVE       #10,D0
     COMPUTE:   JSR        PRINT_D0
                MULS       D0,D0           ; MULTIPLY
                CMP        #1000,D0        ; EVALUATE 1000 < = D0
                BLE        COMPUTE
```
   Note: What does the assembly language code print?

3. Distinguish between systems and applications programming. Give examples of each mode of programming.

4. Compiler A is written in a high-level programming language, whereas compiler B is written in assembly language.
   (a) Which compiler will be more likely to translate large programs faster?
   (b) Which compiler will be easier to maintain and extend?

5. High-level language compilers often have an option to optimize code.
   (a) What does this mean?
   (b) In general, would optimized compiler code run as quickly as assembly language code?

6. List the components of an integrated environment that you have used.

7. A compiler translates high-level language code such as Pascal to the native code of the machine. This translation may be directly to machine code or to assembly language. The latter serves as intermediate code requiring an additional translation to machine code.
   (a) Give several reasons why a translation to assembly language may be done.
   (b) Explain why moving a compiler from machine A to machine B is easier if it compiles high-level language code to assembly language first.

8. Suppose your computer monitors a series of devices. When a device requires service, the device sends an interrupt signal to the CPU. This causes the code that services the device to execute immediately. Explain why assembly language may be more appropriate for this application than a high-level language would be.

CHAPTER 2

REPRESENTATION OF DATA

Computer data is stored in memory as a sequence of 0's and 1's. Without interpretation, the binary data has no useful meaning. Only when some representation is applied to a 0-1 sequence does the data contain meaningful information. This chapter discusses representations for numbers and characters. After a brief review of decimal numbers, the binary number system (base 2) is introduced as a natural model for building numbers with computer circuitry. Then we see how the hexadecimal number system (base 16) facilitates binary-data recognition and conversion. Fixed-length numbers, both unsigned and signed, are discussed next. This leads to a discussion of two's complement representation, which is critical to the understanding of assembly language programming.

This chapter introduces the operations of two's complement addition and subtraction. A discussion of overflow follows. Next, the use of numbers to represent characters introduces the ASCII character set, which is an internationally recognized representation for characters. The chapter concludes with a brief treatment of bit operations.

MC68000 processors support other data representations, as well, including BCD integers and floating-point numbers, and these representations are introduced in Chapter 8, along with related instructions and algorithms. Multiplication and division operations are introduced in Chapter 4, along with the MC68000 instructions. Related to bit operations are both signed and unsigned shifts. The text does not introduce the shift operators until Chapter 5, when related MC68000 instructions are presented along with sample programs.

Decimal numbers provide a foundation for understanding general number systems. The decimal number system is in base 10. A set of digits (0–9) is given, along with increasing powers of 10, to form the representation of the number. Consider the decimal 1125.

$$1125_{10} = 1(10)^3) + 1(10^2) + 2(10^1) + 5(10^0)$$

A general number system writes a number in **positional notation representation** with a designated base B and a set of digits $d_0, d_1, d_2, \ldots, d_n$. A number is coded as a sequence of digits with each digit having an associated power of the base. An equivalent **expanded notation representation** also gives the value of the number. The following number N is a k-digit number.

Positional Notation Representation

$$N = d_{k-1}\, d_{k-2} \cdots d_i \cdots d_1\, d_0 \qquad (0 \le d_i \le B - 1)$$

Expanded Notation Representation

$$N = d_{k-1}\,(B^{k-1}) + d_{k-2}(B^{k-2}) + \cdots + d_i(B^i) + \cdots + d_1(B^1) + d_0(B^0)$$

Note: In this text, the two number representations will be shortened to *positional representation* and *expanded representation*, respectively.

Each number system is defined by its base, its digits, and the value of the successive powers of the base (see Table 2.1).

Nonnegative or unsigned numbers are introduced in the following sections. Representations for signed numbers are discussed in Section 2.3.

Binary Numbers

Modern digital computers use different physical attributes to represent and distinguish data. With transistor circuit logic, voltage levels can be distinguished as high or low voltage. On a dynamic memory chip, a capacitor can be charged or not. A switch can be opened or closed. These and other attributes can identify two states that represent one of two digits, 0 and 1.

TABLE 2.1   Number Systems

SYSTEM	BASE	DIGITS	POWERS
Binary	2	0,1	1,2,4,8,16,32, . . .
Octal	8	0,1,2,3,4,5,6,7	1,8,64,512,4096, . . .
Decimal	10	0,1,2,3,4,5,6,7,8,9	1,10,100,1000, . . .

The system carefully measures the attribute so that the states can be unambiguously defined. For instance, low voltage is identified with a range of voltage readings. High voltage is associated with a second range of readings. An undefined range of readings separates the low- and high-voltage levels and hence distinguishes state 0 from state 1.

Low Voltage		High Voltage
State 0		State 1

Computers use the two-state logic to store numbers in the **base 2** or **binary system**. The binary digits 0 and 1 are referred to as *bits*. The binary system uses powers of 2 (which have values 1, 2, 4, 8, 16, and so on). For instance, thirteen (13_{10}) has an expanded binary representation

$$13_{10} = 1(2^3) + 1(2^2) + 0(2^1) + 1(2^0)$$

The corresponding positional representation is $13_{10} = 1101_2$. Like decimal numbers, binary numbers in positional representation are unchanged if you add leading zeros. For instance,

$$13_{10} = 1101_2 = 01101_2 = 001101_2$$

If you add trailing zeros, however, you shift the binary digits to the left and increase the value of the number by a power of 2. For instance, shifting 1101_2 left by two digits increases its value by $4 = 2^2$.

$$110100_2 = 1(2^5) + 1(2^4) + 0(2^3) + 1(2^2) + 0(2^1) + 0(2^0)$$
$$= 1101_2 \times (2^2) = 52_{10}$$

The decimal value of a binary number is computed directly from its expanded representation; simply add up the terms in the sum. For example,

$$101010_2 = 1(2^5) + 0(2^4) + 1(2^3) + 0(2^2) + 1(2^1) + 0(2^0) = 42_{10}$$

Finding the decimal value of a binary number from its positional representation requires repeated multiplication.

Algorithm (Binary to Decimal Conversion) Let $N = d_n d_{n-1} \cdots d_1 d_0$ be a binary number in positional representation. Repeated multiplication generates the expanded representation of N. The variable S is the partial sum with initial value 0. For each step k ($k = n$ down to 0), fetch the digit d_k and update the partial sum S where

$$S = S \times 2 + d_k$$

Step n: $\quad S = 0 \times 2 + d_n$

Step n $-$ *1:* $S = S \times 2 + d_{n-1} = d_n(2^1) + d_{n-1}$

Step n $-$ *2:* $S = S \times 2 + d_{n-2} = d_n(2^2) + d_{n-1}(2^1) + d_{n-2}$

.
.
.

Step 1: $S = S \times 2 + d_1 = d_n2^{n-1} + d_{n-1}2^{n-2} + \cdots + d_22^1 + d_1$

Step 0: $S = S \times 2 + d_0 = d_n2^n + d_{n-1}2^{n-1} + \cdots + d_12^1 + d_0$

The partial sum S is decimal value of N.

EXAMPLE 2.1

Consider the binary number $N = 1101_2$ with digits $d_3 = 1, d_2 = 1, d_1 = 0, d_0 = 1$. S is initially 0. For each step in the algorithm, compute the value of S.

Step 3: $S = 0 \times 2 + d_3 = 1$

Step 2: $S = S \times 2 + d_2 = 1(2) + 1 = 3$

Step 1: $S = S \times 2 + d_1 = 3(2) + 0 = 6$

Step 0: $S = S \times 2 + d_0 = 6(2) + 1 = 13$

The final partial sum S is the value of N.

$$1101_2 = 1(2^3) + 1(2^2) + 0(2^1) + 1(2^0) = 13$$

EXAMPLE 2.2

Compute the decimal value of a binary number from the expanded representation of the number.

$$110101_2 = 1(32) + 1(16) + 1(4) + 1(1) = 53_{10}$$
$$10000110_2 = 1(128) + 1(4) + 1(2) = 134_{10}$$
$$11111_2 = 1(16) + 1(8) + 1(4) + 1(2) + 1(1) = 31_{10}$$

You can convert a decimal number to its binary equivalent "in your head" for small values. Find the largest power of 2 that is less than or equal to the number. With this starting power of 2, compute the number as a sum of decreasing powers of 2. Use the digit 1 for each term in the sum and the digit 0 as a place holder. For example,

$$35_{10} = 32 + 2 + 1$$
$$= 1(32) + 0(16) + 0(8) + 0(4) + 1(2) + 1(1)$$
$$= 100011_2$$

For larger numbers, use repeated division by 2. The successive remainders give the binary digits from right to left.

Algorithm (Decimal to Binary Conversion) Assume that the nonnegative integer N is given as a decimal number. The binary expanded representation of N has the form

$$N = d_n 2^n + d_{n-1} 2^{n-1} + \cdots + d_1 2^1 + d_0 2^0$$

where $d_0, d_1, \ldots, d_n$ are the digits in the binary positional representation of N. The algorithm solves for the successive digits.

Step 0: Divide N by 2. The remainder is d_0, and the quotient is given by N_0. The quotient includes the first n terms of the expansion.

$$N_0 = d_n 2^{n-1} + d_{n-1} 2^{n-2} + \cdots + d_1 2^0$$

Step 1: Divide N_0 by 2. The remainder is d_1, and the quotient is N_1.

$$N_1 = d_n 2^{n-2} + d_{n-1} 2^{n-3} + \cdots + d_2 2^0$$

Step k: Divide N_{k-1} by 2. The remainder is d_k, and the quotient is N_k.

$$N_k = d_n 2^{n+k-1} + d_{n-1} 2^{n-k-2} + \cdots + d_{k+1} 2^0$$

Step n: The iterative algorithm stops when the quotient $N_n = 0$. If it continued, each step would generate a leading 0 and not change the value.

The positional representation of N is $d_n d_{n-1} \cdots d_2 d_1 d_0$ where d_k is the remainder in step k.

EXAMPLE 2.3

Convert the decimal number 105 to binary using repeated division by 2.

Step 0: $2 \overline{)105}$ $\dfrac{52}{}$ R 1 $d_0 = 1$ *Step* 1: $2 \overline{)52}$ $\dfrac{26}{}$ R 0 $d_1 = 0$

Step 2: $2 \overline{)26}$ $\dfrac{13}{}$ R 0 $d_2 = 0$ *Step* 3: $2 \overline{)13}$ $\dfrac{6}{}$ R 1 $d_3 = 1$

Step 4: $2 \overline{)6}$ $\dfrac{3}{}$ R 0 $d_4 = 0$ *Step* 5: $2 \overline{)3}$ $\dfrac{1}{}$ R 1 $d_5 = 1$

Step 6: $2 \overline{)1}$ $\dfrac{0}{}$ R 1 $d_6 = 1$

The binary representation of N is

$$105 = 1101001_2$$

Hexadecimal Numbers

Binary numbers are a natural representation for numbers in a computer. They require a large number of digits, however, and this makes them cumbersome for us to use. *Hexadecimal numbers* permit easy conversion to and from binary numbers and require fewer digits in their representation.

Hexadecimal numbers are constructed from a base of 16 with digits in the range 0–15 (decimal). The first ten digits are inherited from the decimal numbers: 0, 1, 2, 3, . . . ,9. The digits from 10 to 15 are represented by A, B, C, D, E, and F. Hexadecimal numbers are commonly referred to as *hex* numbers.

Hex Digits

$A_{16} = 10_{10}$ $B_{16} = 11_{10}$ $C_{16} = 12_{10}$ $D_{16} = 13_{10}$ $E_{16} = 14_{10}$

$F_{16} = 15_{10}$

Powers of 16

$16^0 = 1$ $16^1 = 16$ $16^2 = 256$ $16^3 = 4096$ and so on

In positional-notation form, sample hex numbers are 17E, 48, and FFFF8000. Hex numbers have an expanded representation using powers of 16. By converting each hex digit to decimal and multiplying by the corresponding power of 16, the hex number is given a decimal value.

EXAMPLE 2.4

The hex number $2A3F_{16}$ has the following expanded representation:

$$2A3F_{16} = 2(16^3) + A(16^2) + 3(16^1) + F(16^0)$$

Replace each power of 16 and each hex digit by its corresponding decimal value.

$$2A3F_{16} = 2(4096) + 10(256) + 3(16) + 15$$

After multiplying the terms, the sum gives the decimal equivalent.

$$2A3F_{16} = 8192 + 2560 + 48 + 15 = 10815_{10}$$

You can convert a large number from decimal representation to hex representation by repeatedly dividing by 16. The successive remainders, written as hex digits, give the hex positional representation.

EXAMPLE 2.5

The decimal number 382 converts to hex in three steps. The remainders H_0, H_1, and H_2 are the hex digits.

Step 0: $\dfrac{23 \text{ R } 14}{16 \,)\overline{382}}$ $H_0 = E$

Step 1: $\dfrac{1 \text{ R } 7}{16 \,)\overline{23}}$ $H_1 = 7$

Step 2:

$$\begin{array}{r} 0 \ \ \text{R} \ 1 \\ 16 \overline{\smash{)}\ 1} \end{array} \qquad H_2 = 1$$

Record the hex digits from right to left: $382_{10} = 17E_{16}$.

General Number Systems

This section summarizes the main concepts of a number system. Algorithms for conversion with binary numbers are given in abstract form. In Section 2.5, they are coded in Pascal.

A number system can be designed for any base $B > 1$. Numbers are coded in positional notation with B distinct digits d_i in the range 0 to $(B - 1)$. The equivalent expanded representation uses powers of the base, B^0, B^1, B^2, B^3, ... The k digit number N has the following positional and expanded representations.

Positional Representation

$$N = d_{k-1} \, d_{k-2} \, d_{k-3} \ldots d_1 \, d_0 \qquad (0 \le d_i \le B - 1)$$

Expanded Representation

$$N = d_{k-1}(B^{k-1}) + d_{k-2}(B^{k-2}) + d_{k-3}(B^{k-3}) + \cdots + d_1(B^1) + d_0(B^0)$$

EXAMPLE 2.6

A sample of different number base values is given in both positional and expanded representation. This text emphasizes base 2 (binary), base 10 (decimal), and base 16 (hex). Exercises cover base 8 (octal), which has historical significance and is used in some programming languages.

$$\begin{array}{ll} \text{(Base 4)} & 1032_4 = 1(4^3) + 0(4^2) + 3(4^1) + 2 = 78_{10} \\ \text{(Base 8)} & 316_8 = 3(8^2) + 1(8^1) + 6 = 206_{10} \\ \text{(Base 12)} & A34_{12} = A(12^2) + 3(12^1) + 4 = 1480_{10} \\ \text{(Base 20)} & 47_{20} = 4(20^1) + 7 = 87_{10} \end{array}$$

Algorithm (Base to Binary Conversion) Conversion from binary to decimal was described earlier using repeated multiplication. The algorithm can be generalized to convert a number from any base to binary. For each step, the partial sum is multiplied by base B.

Let $B > 1$ be the base of the number system and N be a k-digit number in positional representation.

$$N = d_{k-1} \, d_{k-2} \, d_{k-3} \cdots d_1 \, d_0 \qquad (0 \le d_i \le B - 1)$$

The k-step algorithm uses repeated multiplication, which builds the equivalent expanded representation of N. Let S be the partial sum with initial value 0. For each step k, the value of S is updated.

$$S = S \times B + d_k$$

The current value of S is recorded in expanded representation.

Step $k - 1$: $S = S \times B + d_{k-1}$
                $S = d_{k-1}$

Step $k - 2$: $S = S \times B + d_{k-2}$
                $S = d_{k-1}(B^1) + d_{k-2}$

Step $k - 3$: $S = S \times B + d_{k-3}$
                $S = d_{k-1}(B^2) + d_{k-2}(B^1) + d_{k-3}$

Step 1: $S = S \times B + d_1$
                $S = d_{k-1}(B^{k-2}) + d_{k-2}(B^{k-3}) + \cdots + d_2(B^1) + d_1$

Step 0: $S = S \times B + d_0$
                $S = d_{k-1}(B^{k-1}) + d_{k-2}(B^{k-2}) + \cdots + d_1(B^1) + d_0$

The resulting value of S is the value of N.

Algorithm (Decimal to Base Conversion)   Conversion from decimal to binary was described earlier using repeated division by 2. The following generalized algorithm merely substitutes division by base B. For each step, the remainder d_i is a digit in the positional representation of the number.

$$N = d_{n-1}\, d_{n-2}\, d_{n-3} \cdots d_1\, d_0$$

Step 0: Divide N_0 by B. The remainder is the digit d_0. N_0 is the quotient used in the next step.

$$N = N_0 \times B + d_0$$

Step 1: Divide N_0 by B. The remainder d_1 corresponds to B^1.

$$N_0 = N_1 \times B + d_1$$

Step k: Divide N_{k-1} by B. The remainder d_k corresponds to B^k. The algorithm stops at step n when $N_n = 0$. The positional representation of N is

$$N = d_{k-1}\, d_{k-2}\, d_{k-3} \cdots d_1\, d_0$$

The primary reason for introducing hex numbers is their natural correspondence with binary numbers. They permit compact representation of binary data and memory addresses.

Binary-Hex Conversion

Hex digits have a 4-bit binary representation in the range 0–15. Table 2.2 lists the correspondence between hex and binary numbers.

TABLE 2.2 Hex and Binary Digits

HEX	BINARY	HEX	BINARY
0	0000	8	1000
1	0001	9	1001
2	0010	A	1010
3	0011	B	1011
4	0100	C	1100
5	0101	D	1101
6	0110	E	1110
7	0111	F	1111

To represent a binary number in hex, start at the right end of the numbers and partition the bits into groups of four, adding leading zeros to the last group on the left, if necessary. Write each group of 4 bits as a hex digit. For example,

$$1110111001_2 = 0011\ 1011\ 1001 = 3B9_{16}$$
$$111100011101110_2 = 0111\ 1000\ 1110\ 1110 = 78EE_{16}$$

To convert from a hex number to a binary number, reverse this process and write each hex digit as 4 bits. Consider the following example:

$$A789_{16} = 1010\ 0111\ 1000\ 1001 = 1010011110001001_2$$

The mathematical basis for the conversion between binary and hex numbers is derived from expanded representation in the two bases. Take, as an example, $N = 101101_2$.

$$N = \underbrace{1(2^5) + 0(2^4)}_{\text{Group 2}} + \underbrace{1(2^3) + 1(2^2) + 0(2^1) + 1(2^0)}_{\text{Group 1}}$$

The terms in Group 1 include powers of 2 less than $2^4 = 16$. The terms in Group 2 have powers of at least $2^4 = 16$. By rewriting N with powers of 16, each coefficient h_1 and h_0 appears as a binary number in the range 0–15.

$$N = [1(2^1) + 0(2^0)](16^1) + [1(2^3) + 1(2^2) + 0(2^1) + 1](16^0) = h_1 h_0$$

Record each coefficient as a hex number.

$$h_1 = 1(2^1) + 0(2^0) = 10_2 = 2_{16}$$
$$h_0 = 1(2^3) + 1(2^2) + 0(2^1) + 1(2^0) = 1101_2 = D_{16}$$

Hence, $N = 101101_2 = 2D_{16}$.

Binary Addition and Subtraction

Addition and subtraction with binary numbers follow the familiar rules for decimal numbers. Operate on the successive digits from right to left. For each digit, the following facts apply.

Binary Addition Facts

$$0 + 0 = 0 \quad 0 + 1 = 1 \quad 1 + 1 = 10_2 \quad 1 + 1 + 1 = 11_2$$

Binary Subtraction Facts

$$0 - 0 = 0 \quad 1 - 0 = 1 \quad 1 - 1 = 0_2 \quad 10_2 - 1 = 1$$

EXAMPLE 2.7

To find the sum of binary numbers, use familiar column addition and the binary addition facts. Record a carry above the adjacent digit.

```
Carry    1 1 1 1         Carry        1
         1110110                  01101
     +   1011101              +   10001
        11010011                 11110
```

EXAMPLE 2.8

To find the difference between two binary numbers, use the binary subtraction facts. For each column requiring a borrow, write the value 0, 1, or 2 above the digit to indicate the revised subtraction after the borrow occurs.

```
        12               212
     11001            110011
   -   110          -  11101
     10011            10110
```

Hex Addition and Subtraction

Addition and subtraction in the hex system involve learning basic addition and subtraction facts for the hex digits 0–F. Remember the classic "tens table"? With hex it is a "sixteens table." With practice, you can memorize these facts. Another approach is to convert the hex digits to decimal, perform the addition or subtraction, and then reconvert to hex. Consider the following examples.

Sample Hex Addition Facts

```
1.    C        12_10      2.    9         9_10
    + E      + 14_10           + D      + 13_10
              26_10                      22_10
```

To reconvert the results to hex, note that $26_{10} = 16 + 10 = A_{16}$ with a carry of 1; thus, $C + E = 1A$. $22_{10} = 16 + 6 = 6_{16}$ with a carry of 1; thus, $9 + D = 16$.

Sample Hex Subtraction Facts

1.
$$\begin{array}{r} E \\ -\ 2 \\ \hline \end{array} \qquad \begin{array}{r} 14_{10} \\ -\ 2_{10} \\ \hline 12_{10} \end{array}$$

2.
$$\begin{array}{r} 19 \\ -\ F \\ \hline \end{array} \qquad \begin{array}{r} 25_{10} \\ +\ 15_{10} \\ \hline 10_{10} \end{array}$$

The hex result in 1 is given by converting 12_{10} to C_{16}; thus, $E - 2 = C$. Similarly, the result in 2 is A.

EXAMPLE 2.9

Apply the basic hex addition and subtraction facts to solve the following problems.

$$\begin{array}{r} 1 \\ 1A \\ +2C \\ \hline 46 \end{array} \qquad\qquad \begin{array}{r} 1\ \ 1 \\ DF6D \\ +246C \\ \hline 103D9 \end{array}$$

The borrow is given in decimal.

$$\begin{array}{r} 5\ 26 \\ 6\ \ A \\ -3\ \ F \\ \hline 2\ \ B \end{array} \qquad\qquad \begin{array}{r} 26\ \ \ \ 21 \\ 2\ A\ 1\ 5 \\ -1\ C\ 0\ C \\ \hline E\ 0\ 9 \end{array}$$

2.2 | FIXED-LENGTH NUMBERS

The binary and hex numbers introduced so far have been limited to non-negative integers of unbounded size. We did not pay attention to signed numbers, nor did we consider the physical limitations of a computer. This section considers binary numbers stored in a computer and the fact that computers frequently require limiting the number of bits. This section also introduces binary representations for signed numbers.

Fixed-Length Unsigned Numbers

Computer arithmetic is performed on data stored in fixed-length memory locations. The contents in a location are viewed simply as a sequence of bits corresponding to powers of 2. The representation is referred to as the **unsigned number representation**, and its value is an unsigned number. Bit positions are referenced from right to left, beginning with bit 0. For example, with an 8-bit number, we would have

8-Bit Unsigned Binary Number

7	6	5	4	3	2	1	0

EXAMPLE 2.10

The following are 8-bit unsigned numbers with their equivalent hex and decimal representations.

BINARY	HEX	DECIMAL	
01011101	5D	93	
11111111	FF	255	(Largest possible value)
00000000	00	0	(Smallest possible value)
00110011	33	51	

Addition with fixed-length binary numbers requires special consideration, because the sum has an upper bound. With fixed-length numbers, any final carry must be discarded. This can result in an incorrect response. For example, consider a computer that stores numbers in 8 bits. The equivalent decimal addition is included to illustrate the effect of overflow with the lost carry of $2^8 = 256$.

$$11001001 = 201_{10}$$
$$+\ 01001111 = \ \ 79_{10}$$
$$\boxed{1}\ \ \ 00011000 = \ \ 24_{10} \quad \text{not } 280_{10}$$

Lost carry

Fixed-Length Signed-Magnitude Numbers

Representation of both positive and negative binary numbers using a fixed number of bits introduces some complexity. In the traditional decimal system, we use a $+$ or $-$ sign as a prefix to a number's value. The sign represents the ordering (positive or negative) of the number, and the digits represent its magnitude. The number is thus referred to as a **signed number** and the form is described as the **signed-magnitude representation**. We can store such numbers in a computer as fixed-length binary numbers by specifying a bit to represent the sign.

$$N = sb_nb_{n-1} \cdots b_1b_0 \qquad s = \begin{cases} 0 \text{ if } N \geqslant 0 \\ 1 \text{ if } N < 0 \end{cases}$$

Usually the sign is given in the leftmost or **most significant bit** of the number. In an 8-bit number, bit 7 is the **sign bit**, and the other seven bits form the magnitude, which is limited to the range 0–127.

The following numbers are recorded in 8-bit signed magnitude representation. The traditional signed decimal form is included.

$$+5 = 00000101 \qquad +60 = 00111100$$
$$-7 = 10000111 \qquad -87 = 11010111$$
$$+127 = 01111111 \qquad -127 = 11111111$$

To facilitate addition and subtraction with signed magnitude, remember the following two carefully constructed rules of signs:

Rule 1 When adding two numbers of like sign, add the two magnitudes and assign the "like sign." For example,

$$\begin{array}{llcr} \textit{Problem:} & -50 & \textit{Operation:} & 50 \\ & \underline{+ \ -25} & & \underline{+ \ 25} \\ & & & 75 \end{array}$$

$$\textit{Result:} \quad -50 \ + \ -25 = -(50 + 25) = \ -75$$

Rule 2 When adding two numbers of unlike sign, subtract the smaller magnitude from the larger magnitude and assign to the result the sign of the larger magnitude. For example,

$$\begin{array}{llcr} \textit{Problem:} & 25 & \textit{Operation:} & 50 \\ & \underline{+ \ -50} & & \underline{- \ 25} \\ & & & 25 \end{array}$$

$$\textit{Result:} \quad 25 \ + \ -50 = -(50 - 25) = \ -25$$

The signed-magnitude representation of numbers has some drawbacks for computer arithmetic. Addition and subtraction use both the sign and the magnitude in their operations. A second drawback stems from the two forms of 0.

$$+0 = 00000000 \qquad -0 = 10000000$$

A computer frequently tests for 0, and the two representations add complexity to many algorithms.

Fixed-Length Odometer Numbers

To the average user, the signed-magnitude representation of integers is commonplace, even natural. Given a choice, a user initially might want computers to use the same representation. Computers do not do this, however. Most microcomputers use a **two's complement representation**, which permits efficient storage of numbers and simplified addition and subtraction circuitry. Initially, you may find this representation unnatural and confusing. With practice, however, you should find the representation easy to manage. To assist you in understanding this concept, a new model of numbers, called **odometer numbers**, is introduced.

Odometer Number Representation

Suppose a person is sitting on an exercycle with a five-digit mileage indicator (odometer). The cycle has an initial odometer reading of 00000. When the person pedals forward, the indicator reads 00001, 00002, and so on. When he or she pedals backward, the indicator likewise moves backward. After the individual travels 1 mile, the indicator reads 99999, after another mile 99998, and so on. The odometer readings indicate the direction traveled (see Table 2.3).

A signed number is represented on a number line with magnitude and direction. A base point fixes 0. Negative values are indicated on the left by a minus sign, and positive numbers are shown on the right as unsigned numbers. With the odometer model, the value -1 corresponds to 99999, -2 corresponds to 99998, and so on.

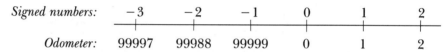

The odometer model introduces problems with its conflicting interpretation of numbers. For instance, the reading 60000 could result from pedaling forward 60,000 miles or backward 40,000 miles. Some convention is needed to give each number a unique value. One such convention would

TABLE 2.3 Odometer Readings

ODOMETER READING	DISTANCE TRAVELED
00040	40 miles forward
.	.
.	.
.	.
00002	2 miles forward
00001	1 mile forward
00000	0
99999	1 mile backward
99998	2 miles backward
.	.
.	.
.	.
99960	40 miles backward

TABLE 2.4 Odometer Number Values

ODOMETER NUMBER	DECIMAL NUMBER
49999	49999
.	.
.	.
.	.
00002	2
00001	1
00000	0
99999	−1
99998	−2
.	.
.	.
.	.
50000	−50000

split the range 00000–99999 into two parts, with numbers 00000–49999 representing positive odometer numbers and 50000–99999 representing negative odometer numbers. Table 2.4 compares the values of odometer numbers and decimal numbers.

Addition and Subtraction of Odometer Numbers

Odometer numbers can be added and subtracted as standard integers. A new set of algorithms is used.

Addition Algorithm Add the successive digits of the odometer numbers as standard decimal digits and discard any carry from the high-order digit. For example,

$$
\begin{array}{rr}
99998 & -2 \\
+\ 00003 & +\ \ 3 \\
\hline
\boxed{1}\ 00001 & 1
\end{array}
$$

Subtraction Algorithm Subtraction and addition are related as inverse operations:

$$A - B = A + (-B)$$

To subtract, add A to the negative side of B. The following example includes the equivalent signed-number subtraction for decimal integers as a comparison:

$$
\begin{array}{cc}
\textit{Signed Number} & \textit{Odometer Number} \\
\begin{array}{r}
-5 \\
-\ 3 \\
\hline
-8
\end{array}
&
\begin{array}{rcr}
99995 & & 99995 \\
-\ 00003 & \rightarrow & +\ 99997 \\
\hline
& & 99992
\end{array}
\end{array}
$$

EXAMPLE 2.11

We use the algorithms for odometer numbers to solve the following addition and subtraction problems. The signed-magnitude representation is included for comparison.

$$
\begin{array}{rl}
3 & 00003 \\
+\ -3 & +\ 99997 \\
\hline
0 & \boxed{1}\ 00000
\end{array}
\qquad
\begin{array}{rl}
-1 & 99999 \\
-\ -6 & +\ 00006 \\
\hline
5 & \boxed{1}\ 00005
\end{array}
$$

Negative Odometer Numbers

The negative of N in the odometer model corresponds to a trip of N miles in the backward direction. It is computed by subtracting N from 100,000.

$$
\text{NEG}(N) = 100000 - N = 10^5 - N
$$

The calculation of $\text{NEG}(N)$ suggests calling the odometer numbers the **ten's complement representation** of five-digit decimal numbers.

Computing $\text{NEG}(N)$ is prone to error because of the number of "borrow from zero" steps. You can use a trick that subtracts N from 99999. The result is short 1 ($99999 = 100000 - 1$), but you can remedy the shortage by adding 1 after the subtraction. This shortcut reduces the potential for error.

EXAMPLE 2.12

Consider the odometer number $N = 4500$. By definition, $\text{NEG}(N) = 100000 - 04500 = 95500$. The following calculation computes $\text{NEG}(N)$ using the "subtract from nines" algorithm.

$$
\begin{array}{rr}
& 99999 \\
- & 04500 \\
\hline
& 95499 \\
\text{add } +1 \qquad + & 00001 \\
\hline
& 95500
\end{array}
$$

The preceding concepts and algorithms are summarized as follows:

Definition Let N be a five-digit odometer number. The ten's complement of N is $100,000 - N$ and is denoted by NEG(N). It is the odometer representation of $-N$. *Note:* The number $-50,000$ is an exception. It is represented by $50,000$ and is its own ten's complement.

Algorithm For N, a five-digit odometer number, compute the ten's complement of N, denoted by NEG(N), using the following two-step process:

$$\text{NEG}(N) = (99999 - N) + 1$$

The value $99999 - N$ is called the **nine's complement** of N.

Fixed-Length Two's Complement Numbers

We can extend the concepts developed for odometer numbers to fixed-length binary numbers. The result is a new representation for binary numbers called the two's complement representation. This section focuses on 8-bit fixed-length numbers. We will generalize the results to n-bit numbers later.

The binary number represents an odometer with each digit having a value 0 or 1. When you pedal backward 1 mile, the reading is 11111111. For subsequent miles, the readings are 11111110 (2 miles backward), 11111101 (3 miles backward), and so on. The set of 8-bit binary numbers is partitioned into two disjoint classes, negative and positive integers. The negative numbers are generated by pedaling backward. Thus 11111111 represents -1, 11111110 represents -2, and so forth. The range of values for the set is -128 to $+127$. Table 2.5 gives sample values for the binary representation and the corresponding base-10 numbers.

As with odometer numbers, the two's complement representation for a negative number can be found by counting backward through the sequence 11111111, 11111110, 11111101, and so on. However, this method is tedious and impractical, and we need a more efficient algorithm.

Algorithm For 8-bit numbers, the negative of N, written $-N$, is computed by using binary subtraction from $100000000_2 = 2^8$. For example, let $N = 00000011$. The negative of N is 11111101.

$$100000000 - 00000011 = 11111101$$

Definition If N is a fixed-length 8-bit number, the negative of N is given by $2^8 - N$.

The negative of N is called the **two's complement of N** and is denoted by **2comp(N)**.

TABLE 2.5 Binary Number Values

8-BIT REPRESENTATION	DECIMAL VALUE
01111111	127
01111110	126
.	.
.	.
.	.
00000010	2
00000001	1
00000000	0
11111111	−1
11111110	−2
11111101	−3
.	.
.	.
.	.
10000010	−126
10000001	−127
10000000	−128

The representation of 8-bit numbers whose negatives are defined by $2\text{comp}(N)$ is called the 8-bit two's complement representation.

For odometer numbers, we computed the negative of N in a two-step process, using the nine's complement to eliminate potential borrowing errors. In the case of 8-bit two's complement numbers, the corresponding shortcut uses a "subtract from ones" step and the addition of a final 1.

$$2\text{comp}(N) = ((2^8 - 1) - N) + 1$$
$$= (11111111 - N) + 1$$

EXAMPLE 2.13

Consider the decimal numbers 27 and 1. The two-step process is used to compute (a) $2\text{comp}(27)$ and (b) $2\text{comp}(1)$.

(a) $27 = \quad 00011011_2$

$$
\begin{array}{r}
11111111 \\
-\ 00011011 \\
\hline
11100100 \\
+\qquad 1 \\
\hline
11100101 \ = -27_{10}
\end{array}
$$

(b) $1 = \quad 00000001_2$

$$
\begin{array}{r}
11111111 \\
-\ 00000001 \\
\hline
11111110 \\
+\qquad 1 \\
\hline
11111111 \ = -1_{10}
\end{array}
$$

In this example, the subtraction step involves subtracting each bit of N from 1. You may note that the result is predictable. If the bit of N is 0, the subtraction $1 - 0$ yields the result 1. If the bit of N is 1, the subtraction $1 - 1$ yields the result 0. Hence, the subtraction can be done by simply reversing the value of each of the binary bits in N. The result is called the **one's complement of N** and is denoted **1comp(N)**.

EXAMPLE 2.14

We compute 2comp(N) by using 1comp(N) and adding a final 1.

(a) $N = 27_{10} = 00011011$
   1comp(N) = 11100100
   2comp(N) = 11100100 + 1 = 11100101 = -27_{10}

(b) $N = 1_{10} = 00000001$
   1comp(N) = 11111110
   2comp(N) = 11111110 + 1 = 11111111 = -1_{10}

(c) $N = -27_{10} = 11100101$
   2comp(N) = 00011010 + 1 = 00011011 = 27_{10}

(d) $N = 116_{10} = 01110100$
   2comp(N) = 10001011 + 1 = 10001100 = -116_{10}

Be careful not to think of 2comp(N) as a negative number. It is just $-N$ in two's complement representation. If N is negative, 2comp(N) is a positive number.

Fixed-Length One's Complement Numbers

We use the one's complement operation to compute 2comp(N). One's complement is also a representation of an integer number. It has been used in a few computer systems and has some important applications in check-sum algorithms. Studying one's complement representation will add to your understanding of number systems and will highlight some of the advantages of two's complement numbers. The following definitions and examples apply to fixed-length 8-bit numbers.

The one's complement representation of a positive integer is the same as the signed-magnitude representation. A negative number is represented by the one's complement of the corresponding positive number. For example,

$$38 = 00100110$$
$$-38 = 11011001 = 1\text{comp}(38)$$

The range of 8-bit one's complement numbers is -127 to 127. The leftmost bit is a sign bit.

POSITIVE NUMBERS	NEGATIVE NUMBERS
01111111 = 127	10000000 = −127
01111110 = 126	10000001 = −126
.	.
.	.
.	.
00000010 = 2	11111101 = −2
00000001 = 1	11111110 = −1
00000000 = 0	11111111 = −0

A basic rule of algebra holds for one's complement representation. The negative of the negative of a number is the original number. As with signed-magnitude numbers, the two representations of 0 is a drawback. For addition and subtraction, one's complement numbers are treated as unsigned numbers. However, the carry bit requires special treatment.

One's Complement Addition   Treat each term as an unsigned number.

(a)			*(b)*		
	5	00000101		6	00000110
+	−5	+ 11111010	+	−8	+ 11110111
	0	11111111		−2	11111101

The addition rule requires adding back into the sum any carry out of the high-order bit. The step is referred to as "end around carry."

(c)			*(d)*		
	−5	11111010		127	01111111
+	−5	+ 11111010	+	−3	+ 11111100
	−10	① 11110100		124	① 01111011
		└──── 1			└──── 1
		11110101 = −10			01111100 = 124

The rule for one's complement addition requires that the numbers be added as unsigned numbers, with the carry added to the original sum. In examples (a) and (b), the carry is 0.

Both signed-magnitude and one's complement numbers have two reprsentations of 0 and require special addition rules. These problems are not found with two's complement numbers, the representation of choice for most computer systems.

N-Bit Two's Complement Numbers

We used 8-bit fixed-length numbers for examples and definitions to introduce two's complement numbers. The results are now summarized for arbitrary n-bit numbers.

1. Two's complement n-bit numbers are binary numbers of length n. The bits are numbered right to left from bit 0 to bit $n - 1$. For each bit d_i, the subscript corresponds to the power of 2 in the binary expansion.

d_{n-1}	d_{n-2}	d_{n-3}	$\cdots$	d_3	d_2	d_1	d_0

2. The range of values is -2^{n-1} to $2^{n-1} - 1$. The range is split in two parts to distinguish negative and positive numbers.

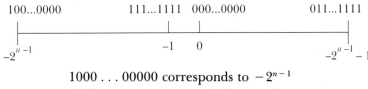

$$1000\ldots00000 \text{ corresponds to } -2^{n-1}$$
$$0111\ldots11111 \text{ corresponds to } 2^{n-1} - 1$$

3. The leftmost (high-order) bit is the sign bit. Negative numbers have a 1 in this bit. Positive numbers have a 0.

4. For a number M, the negative of M is denoted by $2\text{comp}(M)$.

$$2\text{comp}(M) = 2^n - M$$

The value $2\text{comp}(M)$ also can be computed with the more convenient algorithm

$$2\text{comp}(M) = 1\text{comp}(M) + 1$$

5. For all values M, $M + 2\text{comp}(M) = 0$. Hence $2\text{comp}(M)$ is the additive inverse of M. For all negative values of M except -2^{n-1}, $2\text{ comp}(M)$ is a positive value. Notice that $2\text{comp}(-2^{n-1}) = -2^{n-1}$.

6. The magnitude of a negative number is hidden in its representation. Typically, you associate magnitude with unsigned numbers. As an unsigned number, $111\ldots11111_2$ equals 4,294,967,295. It equals -1 as a two's complement number. You discover the magnitude of a negative number by first computing its two's complement. The result is the magnitude of the number. For instance, $2\text{comp}(111\ldots11111_2) = 000\ldots0001$. The magnitude is 1.

The two's complement representation for 16-bit numbers is particularly important in an MC68000 system. Key values are listed in Table 2.6 for future reference.

TABLE 2.6   16-Bit Two's Complement Values

BINARY NUMBER	HEX NUMBER	DECIMAL NUMBER
0111111111111111	7FFF	32767
.	.	.
.	.	.
.	.	.
0000000000000001	0001	1
0000000000000000	0000	0
1111111111111111	FFFF	−1
1111111111111110	FFFE	−2
.	.	.
.	.	.
.	.	.
1000000000000001	8001	−32767
1000000000000000	8000	−32768

Two's Complement Hex Numbers

Binary numbers can be written in hex to simplify the tedious recording of 0's and 1's in the binary representation. The definition of two's complement binary numbers also applies to hex numbers. For the definition and examples, assume 16-bit numbers. A 16-bit two's complement hex number N is written as four hex digits.

$$2\text{comp}(N) = 10000_{16} - N$$
$$1\text{comp}(N) = \text{FFFF} - N$$

EXAMPLE 2.15

For hex numbers, compute (a) 2comp(06FD) and (b) 2comp(903B) using both the definition and 1comp(N) + 1.

(a)	10000		FFFF	(b)	10000		FFFF
	− 06FD		− 06FD		− 903B		− 903B
	F903		F902		6FC5		6FC4
		+	1			+	1
			F903				6FC5

2comp(06FD) = F903   2comp (903B) = 6FC5

You can use a shortcut to compute 2comp(N) for hex numbers. Subtract the low-order digit from 16. Subtract all other digits from 15. This is an alternative to finding the one's complement and adding 1.

EXAMPLE 2.16   Redo the short problems in Example 2.15 using the simplified subtraction shortcut.

(a) $2\text{comp}(06\text{FD}) = h_3 h_2 h_1 h_0 = \text{F}903$

$$
\begin{array}{cccc}
h_0 = & 16 & h_1 = & 15 & h_2 = & 15 & h_3 = & 15 \\
& -13 & & -15 & & -6 & & -0 \\
\hline
& 3 & & 0 & & 9 & & 15 = \text{F}
\end{array}
$$

(b) $2\text{comp}(903\text{B}) = h_3 h_2 h_1 h_0 = 6\text{FC}5$

$$
\begin{array}{cccc}
h_0 = & 16 & h_1 = & 15 & h_2 = & 15 & h_3 = & 15 \\
& -11 & & -3 & & -0 & & -9 \\
\hline
& 5 & & 12 = \text{C} & & 15 = \text{F} & & 6
\end{array}
$$

Bit 15 is the sign big in a 16-bit two's complement binary number. This bit is part of the high-order hex digit. If the number is negative, the high-order hex digit is in the range 8–F. If the number is positive, the digit is in the range 0–7. For instance, 9A20 is negative and 4A20 is positive.

2.3 | TWO'S COMPLEMENT OPERATIONS

You can write a number in two's complement representation for different fixed lengths. This section introduces **sign extension**, which converts a number to a larger length but equivalent value. Such sign-extended numbers are used in many MC68000 instructions. This section also introduces the operations of two's complement addition and subtraction.

Sign Extension of Two's Complement Numbers

The concept of sign extension can be illustrated using numbers with 3, 4, and 8 bits. Table 2.7 details equivalent two's complement representations for a series of numbers.

An evident pattern emerges in the high-order bits of the three number systems. Using the odometer model, think of the systems as three separate odometers. A trip of 1 mile backward rolls the bits back to all 1's, independent of the size of the odometer. Movement forward identically changes the low-order bits on each odometer. In fact, knowing the pattern for a

TABLE 2.7 Equivalent Two's Complement Numbers

DECIMAL	3-BIT	4-BIT	8-BIT
0	000	0000	00000000
1	001	0001	00000001
2	010	0010	00000010
3	011	0011	00000011
−1	111	1111	11111111
−2	110	1110	11111110
−3	101	1101	11111101
−4	100	1100	11111100

3-bit odometer reading provides a simple transition to the pattern for readings in the larger odometers.

	3-BIT		4-BIT		8-BIT
−2	110	→	1 110	→	11111 110
3	011	→	0 011	→	00000 011

In converting from a 3-bit number to its equivalent value in a larger fixed-length representation, the high-order bit is *replicated*. This is the principle of sign extension.

Definition   Let X be a two's complement number with fixed length M. The sign extension of X with fixed length N ($M < N$) replicates the high-order bit of X in its high-order ($N - M$) bits.

EXAMPLE 2.17

Using the preceding definition, an 8-bit number is sign-extended to a 16-bit number.

8-BIT NUMBER	16-BIT SIGN-EXTENDED NUMBER
10101100	11111111 10101100
00011100	00000000 00011100

If the 8-bit number is given in hex, the replicated hex digit is F if the high-order hex digit is $8 - F$. The replicated digit is 0 if the high-order hex digit is $0 - 7$.

8-BIT NUMBER	16-BIT SIGN-EXTENDED NUMBER
9B	FF 9B
5F	00 5F

Addition and Subtraction of Two's Complement Numbers

The following rules for addition and subtraction of two's complement binary numbers use the principles introduced for the base-10 odometer numbers.

Addition Rule   Add two terms using straight binary addition. Any final carry is discarded.

$$
\begin{array}{rr}
-2 & 11111110 \\
+\ \ 3 & +\ 00000011 \\
\hline
1 & 00000001
\end{array}
\qquad
\begin{array}{rr}
-1 & 11111111 \\
+\ -1 & +\ 11111111 \\
\hline
-2 & 11111110
\end{array}
$$

Subtraction Rule   Perform the subtraction $N - M$ by computing $N + 2\text{comp}(M)$. For example,

$$
\begin{array}{rrr}
1 & 1 & 00000001 \\
-\ 2 & +\ -2 & +11111110 \\
\hline
-1 & -1 & 11111111
\end{array}
\qquad
\begin{array}{rrr}
8 & 8 & 00001000 \\
-\ 7 & +\ -7 & +11111001 \\
\hline
1 & 1 & 00000001
\end{array}
$$

Hex addition for arbitrary length numbers was introduced in Section 2.1. These rules also extend to fixed-length two's complement numbers.

EXAMPLE 2.18   Add the following 16-bit two's complement hex numbers as straight hex numbers, and discard the final carry.

$$
\begin{array}{r}
A5B6 \\
+\ 3A94 \\
\hline
E04A
\end{array}
\qquad
\begin{array}{r}
803E \\
+\ A74B \\
\hline
2789
\end{array}
\qquad
\begin{array}{r}
D67A \\
+\ 80D7 \\
\hline
5751
\end{array}
$$

In hex, you can frequently subtract $M - N$ directly using simple column subtraction of the digits. This eliminates first finding $2\text{comp}(N)$. If $M < N$, the operation $M - N$ will require a borrow for the high-order digit. The borrow corresponds to 16^4 in the definition of the two's complement:

$$M + 2\text{comp}(N) = M + (16^4 - N) = 16^4 - (M - N)$$

EXAMPLE 2.19

We subtract hex numbers using a straight column subtraction of the digits. You can obtain the same result by adding the two's complement.

	Direct Subtraction	Two's Complement Addition	
	30FC	30FC	
	$-\,0011$	$+\,\text{FFEF}$	$2\text{comp}(0011)$
	30EB	30EB	
	5F3C	5F3C	
	$-\,\text{A0F4}$	$+\,5\text{F0C}$	$2\text{comp}(\text{A0F4})$
	BE48	BE48	

2.4 | OVERFLOW: SIGNED AND UNSIGNED

Using the basic algorithms and rules presented so far, you may produce an incorrect result when you add fixed-length binary numbers. With signed numbers, the sum of two numbers of like sign may have the opposite sign, contrary to the usual rules of arithmetic. With unsigned numbers, the sum may exceed the upper limit of the fixed-length numbers. In each case, the addition produces an **overflow**. To better understand the problem, examine the number line.

Consider the addition of hex numbers $3000_{16} + 6000_{16} = 9000_{16}$.

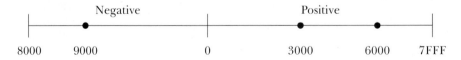

The sum of these two positive numbers exceeds the upper limit (7FFF_{16}) of positive numbers and has a result that falls in the range of negative numbers. This is called **signed overflow**. A similar overflow can occur when adding two negative numbers.

On the other hand, consider the addition of unsigned hex numbers $6000_{16} + D000_{16} = 3000_{16}$.

0	3000	6000	D000	FFFF

The sum of the two 16-bit numbers exceeds the upper limit ($FFFF_{16}$) of 16-bit unsigned numbers. The correct result 13000_{16} is truncated to 3000_{16}. This addition results in **unsigned overflow**.

Signed Overflow

Signed numbers are fixed-length binary numbers given in two's complement representation. Overflow can occur with either addition or subtraction and is identified by simple "rule of signs" tests.

Signed Addition Overflow Test

1. Overflow occurs when the sum of two numbers of like sign (positive or negative) has a result with the opposite sign.

2. Signed overflow never occurs when adding two numbers of unlike sign.

Signed Subtraction Overflow Test
Subtract $M - N$ by adding $M + 2\text{comp}(N)$. Hence, the presence of overflow is derived from test 1 and test 2 for addition.

1. Signed overflow can occur when subtracting terms with unlike signs. Overflow occurs if

$$\text{negative} - \text{positive} = \text{positive}$$
$$\text{positive} - \text{negative} = \text{negative}$$

2. Signed overflow never occurs when subtracting two numbers of like sign.

EXAMPLE 2.20

Applying the signed overflow tests, you can see when overflow occurs in the following problems:

50A3	(positive)	3826	(positive)
+6A38	(positive)	−7000	(positive)
BADB	(negative)	C826	(negative)
Overflow		No overflow	

$$\begin{array}{ll} 38A3 & \text{(positive)} \\ +A330 & \text{(negative)} \\ \hline DBD3 & \text{(negative)} \end{array} \qquad \begin{array}{ll} C839 & \text{(negative)} \\ -7000 & \text{(positive)} \\ \hline 5839 & \text{(positive)} \end{array}$$

No overflow   Overflow

The computer hardware flags the existence of signed overflow. You must simply be aware of the possibility of overflow and insert logic to respond to the flag. This topic is covered in Chapter 5 when the "Branch on Overflow" is introduced and in Chapter 13 with the "Trap on Overflow" exceptions. Table 2.8 summarizes the signed overflow tests.

Unsigned Overflow

An n-bit fixed-length binary number can represent an unsigned number in the range from 0 to $2^n - 1$. For instance,

Fixed-Length Size	Range
8-bit	0–255
16-bit	0–65535

Unsigned overflow occurs with fixed-length numbers when the sum or difference is "out of range." The following set of conditions tests for overflow in the addition and subtraction of unsigned numbers.

Unsigned Addition Overflow Test   Assume that M and N are n-bit unsigned numbers. Overflow occurs if the sum $M + N$ is greater than $2^n - 1$, the upper bound of the range of unsigned numbers. Equivalently, there is a carry of 1 out of the high-order bit.

TABLE 2.8 Signed Overflow Summary

ADDITION		POSSIBLE OVERFLOW	OVERFLOW TEST
positive + positive		Yes	Result negative
negative + negative		Yes	Result positive
positive + negative		No	
negative − positive		Yes	Result positive
positive − negative		Yes	Result negative
negative − negative		No	
positive − positive		No	

Unsigned Subtraction Overflow Test For the operation $M - N$, overflow occurs if N is greater than M. Equivalently, the operation $M - N$ requires a borrow.

EXAMPLE 2.21

Occurrences of unsigned overflow are shown for the following addition and subtraction problems. Numbers have a fixed length of 8 bits, and the corresponding decimal problem is included.

Binary numbers

127	01111111	130	10000010
-128	-10000000	$+129$	$+10000001$
-1	$11111111 = 255$	259	$00000011 = 3$
	Overflow		Overflow

Hex numbers

A3	C2	40	8A
$+47$	$+80$	$-A0$	-55
EA	42	A0	35
No overflow	Overflow	Overflow	No overflow

Application: Identifying Signed Overflow

The previous section introduced tests for signed overflow. They provide the user with simple rules to identify overflow. The computer, however, uses a different test to set an overflow flag. The computer compares carries in the high-order bit. We call this the *carry test*.

Signed Overflow Carry Test Assume M and N are two's complement numbers. The sum $M + N$ produces signed overflow if, and only if, the carry into the high-order bit is not equal to the carry out of the high-order bit.

For example, the 16-bit sum $C016 + 8016 = 402C$ involves the operation *negative + negative = positive* and produces signed overflow. The carry into bit 15 is 0 and the carry out of bit 15 is 1. With the carry test, the two carries are not equal; hence the sum produces signed overflow.

```
                   ┌──────── Carry in = 0
                   │
               1 1 0 0 0 0 0 0 . . .
               1 0 0 0 0 0 0 0 . . .
              ─────────────────────
             1 0 1 0 0 0 0 0 0 . . .
             └──────────── Carry out = 1
```

You can verify the carry test by listing all combinations of positive and negative terms. For an n-bit number, only bits $n - 1$ and $n - 2$ are given.

Case 1: Sum of two positive numbers is negative. Signed overflow occurs.

```
               ┌──────── Carry in = 1
               ↓
       0 X . . .
       0 X . . .
      ─────────────
     0 1 X . . .
     ↑
     └──────────────── Carry out = 0
```

Carry in = 1   Carry out = 0

Case 2: Sum of two negative numbers is positive. Signed overflow occurs.

```
               ┌──────── Carry in = 0
               ↓
       1 X . . .
       1 X . . .
      ─────────────
     1 0 X . . .
     ↑
     └──────────────── Carry out = 1
```

Carry in = 0   Carry out = 1

Case 3: Sum of two positive numbers is positive. No signed overflow occurs.

```
               ┌──────── Carry in = 0
               ↓
       0 X . . .
       0 X . . .
      ─────────────
     0 0 X . . .
     ↑
     └──────────────── Carry out = 0
```

Carry in = 0   Carry out = 0

Case 4: Sum of two negative numbers is negative. No signed overflow occurs.

```
               ┌──────── Carry in = 1
               ↓
       1 X . . .
       1 X . . .
      ─────────────
     1 1 X . . .
     ↑
     └──────────────── Carry out = 1
```

Carry in = 1   Carry out = 1

Case 5: The two numbers have opposite signs. No signed overflow occurs.

If carry in = 0, then carry out = 0.
If carry in = 1, then carry out = 1.

2.5 | REPRESENTING CHARACTER DATA

Computers use numbers to represent characters. No natural correspondence, however, is made between characters and numbers; hence an assignment of a number code to a character must be defined. Historically, two character code sets were used: American Standard Code for Information Interchange (ASCII) and Extended Binary Coded Decimal Interchange Code (EBCDIC). The EBCDIC representation was derived from character codes on punch cards. The code is still used on some mainframe systems. Most microcomputer systems, however, use the ASCII character set.

ASCII characters have a 7-bit code. They are usually stored in a fixed-length 8-bit number. The 2^7 = 128 different codes are partitioned into 95

TABLE 2.9 ASCII Character Set

00 NUL	01 SOH	02 STX	03 ETX	04 EOT	05 ENG	06 ACK	07 BEL
08 BS	09 HT	0A LF	0B VT	0C FF	0D CR	0E S0	0F S1
10 DLE	11 DC1	12 DC2	13 DC3	14 DC4	15 NAK	16 SYN	17 ETB
18 CAN	19 EM	1A SUB	1B ESC	1C FS	1D GS	1E RS	1F US
20 SP	21 !	22 "	23 #	24 $	25 %	26 &	27 '
28 (	29)	2A *	2B +	2C ,	2D −	2E .	2F /
30 0	31 1	32 2	33 3	34 4	35 5	36 6	37 7
38 8	39 9	3A :	3B ;	3C <	3D =	3E >	3F ?
40 @	41 A	42 B	43 C	44 D	45 E	46 F	47 G
48 H	49 I	4A J	4B K	4C L	4D M	4E N	4F O
50 P	51 Q	52 R	53 S	54 T	55 U	56 V	57 W
58 X	59 Y	5A Z	5B [	5C \	5D]	5E ^	5F _
60 `	61 a	62 b	63 c	64 d	65 e	66 f	67 g
68 h	69 i	6A j	6B k	6C l	6D m	6E n	6F o
70 p	71 q	72 r	73 s	74 t	75 u	76 v	77 w
78 x	79 y	7A z	7B {	7C		7D }	7E ~	7F DEL

TABLE 2.10 ASCII Character Ranges

ASCII CHARACTERS	DECIMAL	HEX	BINARY
Control characters	0–31	00–1F	00000000– 00011111
Blank space	32	20	00100000
Decimal digits	48–57	30–39	00110000– 00111001
Uppercase letters	65–90	41–5A	01000001– 01011010
Lowercase letters	97–122	61–7A	01100001– 01111010

printable characters and 33 control characters. The control characters define communications protocol and special operations on peripheral devices.

Table 2.9 shows the complete ASCII character set. The binary number corresponding to a character is given in hex. Appendix E lists the ASCII character set with the corresponding binary code in both hex and decimal.

The character representation designates contiguous ranges for efficient code conversion. Control characters, decimal digits, and alphabetic characters fall within well-defined ranges (see Table 2.10).

EXAMPLE 2.22

The 26 uppercase and 26 lowercase letters have ranges that begin at ASCII values 65 and 97, respectively. Corresponding letters in the alphabet differ by 32. A simple addition implements the change in case for letters.

(a) Add 32 to change a letter from uppercase to lowercase. Consider uppercase 'B'.

$$\text{Uppercase 'B'} = 66_{10} = 0100\ 0010_2$$

By adding 32, the letter 'B' is converted to lowercase.

$$\text{Lowercase 'b'} = 98_{10} = 0110\ 0010_2$$

Note: 'B' and 'b' are the second letter in their character range. The corresponding ASCII codes contain value 2 in the low-order 5 bits.

(b) Subtract 32 to change a letter from lowercase to uppercase.

$$\text{Lowercase \quad 'e'} = 101_{10} = 0110\ 0101_2$$
$$\text{Uppercase \quad 'E'} = 69_{10} \quad = 0100\ 0101_2$$

(c) ASCII digits contain the corresponding numerical value in the low-order 4 bits.

$$\text{ASCII digit '8'} = 56_{10} = 38_{16} = 0011\ 1000$$

The low-order 4 bits are $1000_2 = 8$.

Control Characters

Control characters are used with input/output (I/O) devices and data-transmission protocols. They direct cursor motion, screen clear, line insert, and special character fonts. Table 2.11 lists noteworthy control characters, along with a description of the action on a typical peripheral device.

EXAMPLE 2.23

(a) The ASCII representation for characters in the string "10 Rue Ct." is given in hex by

$$31\ 30\ 20\ 52\ 75\ 65\ 20\ 43\ 74\ 2E$$

(b) The following sequence of ASCII codes transmits to the terminal three bell characters followed by a carriage return and line feed.

$$07\ 07\ 07\ 0D\ 0A$$

Character Application: Pascal Number Conversion

Section 2.1 described algorithms to convert a number between its binary representation and a base B representation. The algorithms are now presented as Pascal I/O subroutines. The Pascal functions ORD and CHR use a few critical ASCII number facts to implement the conversion.

1. To convert the ASCII digit to the number digit, use the ORD function

$$\text{ORD}(\langle char \rangle) = \text{ASCII value of } \langle char \rangle$$

For example,

$$\text{ord ('0')} = 48 \qquad \text{ord('1')} = 49$$
$$\text{ord ('A')} = 65 \qquad \text{ord('B')} = 66$$

TABLE 2.11 Control Characters

SYMBOL	DECIMAL	HEX	MEANING
BEL	7	07	Bell—ring the bell on the terminal
BS	8	08	Backspace—backspace the screen cursor
HT	9	09	Horizontal tab—advance cursor to next tab
LF	10	0A	Line feed—advance cursor down one line
FF	12	0C	Form feed—advance printer to top of next
CR	13	0D	page Carriage return—move cursor to start of line

For the ASCII digit Char__N in the range '0'–'9', the corresponding decimal digit N is computed by

$$N = \text{ORD}(\text{Char\_}N) - \text{ORD ('0')}$$

For ASCII digit Char__N in the range 'A'–'F', the corresponding hex digit N is computed by

$$N = \text{ORD}(\text{Char\_}N) - \text{ORD ('A')} + 10$$

2. To convert the number digit to the ASCII digit, use the CHR function

$$\text{CHR}(\langle\text{value}\rangle) = \text{ASCII character for } \langle\text{value}\rangle$$

For example,

$$\text{chr}(48) = \text{'0'}$$
$$\text{chr}(65) = \text{'A'}$$

For digit N in the range 0–9, the corresponding ASCII digit Char__N is computed by

$$\text{Char\_}N = N + \text{CHR}(0)$$

For hex digit N in the range A–F, the corresponding ASCII hex digit Char__N is computed by

$$\text{Char\_}N = N + 55$$

Arbitrary Base Input: Pascal Function GETBASEVALUE

Reading a number in general base representation uses repeated multiplication by the base B. For the function, the base is passed as a parameter, and the function returns the resulting binary number. Each digit in the number is entered using READ. The input terminates at "end of line" or with a nonbase digit.

For a k-digit number, the k-step algorithm uses repeated multiplication

$$N = N \times \text{base} + \text{digitvalue}$$

which builds the equivalent expanded representation of N.

```
FUNCTION GetBaseValue (Base: integer): integer;
    VAR
        value: integer;
        ch: char;
        charvalue: ARRAY[' '. .'~'] OF integer;
BEGIN
    FOR ch := chr(32) TO chr(126) DO
        charvalue[ch] := -/;
```

```
        IF  Base  <=  10  THEN
            FOR  ch  :=  '0'  TO  chr(Base - 1 + 48)  DO
                charvalue [ch]  :=  ord(ch) - ord('0')
        ELSE  BEGIN
            FOR  ch  :=  '0'  TO  '9'  DO
                charvalue [ch]  :=  ord(ch) - ord('0');
            FOR  ch  :=  'A'  TO  chr(54 + Base)  DO
                charvalue [ch]  :=  ord(ch) - ord('A') + 10;
        END;
        value  :=  0;
        IF  NOT  eoln  THEN
            REPEAT
                read(ch);
                value  :=  value * Base + charvalue [ch];
            UNTIL  (charvalue[ch] < 0)  or  elon
        ELSE
            value  :=  0;
        readln;
        GetBaseValue  :=  value;
END;
```

Arbitrary Base Output: Pascal Procedure PUTBASEVALUE

Writing a binary number in a general base representation uses repeated division by the base B. The successive remainders are recorded as ASCII digits in the base number system and give the positional representation of the number.

The binary number N and the base $B \leq 16$ are passed as parameters. After each division step, the remainder is used as an index into the "digitvalue" array of ASCII digits. The digit is stored in the "outputstring" string. The number, written in positional notation, is output. For $N = 69$, the successive remainders for division by 5 are 4, 3, 2.

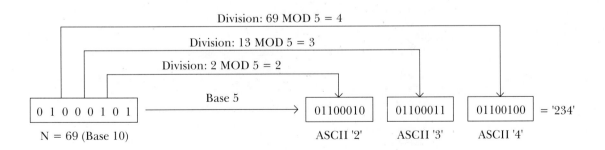

```
PROCEDURE PutBaseValue (N, Base: integer);
    VAR
        quotient: integer;
```

```
            remainder: integer;
            index: integer;
            digitvalue: STRING[16];
            outputstring: STRING[20];
            i: integer;
        BEGIN
            digitvalue := '0123456789ABCDEF';
            index := 21;
            quotient := N;
            REPEAT
                remainder := quotient MOD Base;
                index := index 1;
                outputstring[index] := digitvalue[remainder +1];
                quotient := quotient DIV Base;
            UNTIL quotient = 0;
            FOR i := index TO 20 DO BEGIN
                write(outputstring[index]);
                index := index + 1;
            END;
            writeln;
        END;
```

A program uses the two Pascal routines. For three test cases,

1. Input a base-8 number and output its base-16 representation

2. Input a base-16 number and output its base-4 representation

3. Input a base-4 number and output its base-8 representation

A run is included with input given in italic.

PROGRAM 2.1

Number
Conversion Test
Program

```
PROGRAM NumToDec (input, output);
    VAR
        N: integer;
    FUNCTION GetBaseValue (Base: integer): integer;
        . . .
    END;
    PROCEDURE PutBaseValue (N, Base: integer);
        . . .
    END;
BEGIN
    N := GetBaseValue(8);
    PutBaseValue(N, 16);
    N := GetBaseValue(16);
    PutBaseValue(N, 4);
    N := GetBaseValue(4);
    PutBaseValue(N, 8);
    readln;
END.
```

⟨Run⟩

377
FF
7FFF
13333333
1212
146

|2.6| BIT OPERATIONS

Assembly language programmers test and assign bit values. For example, you may need to test whether an integer is odd or even. The presence of a 1 in the low-order bit of the integer provides the answer. You can change a letter from uppercase to lowercase by changing bit 5 from a 0 to a 1. This has the effect of adding 32 (2^5) to the ASCII value of the letter. In a byte, bits 3–5 might identify a process number in the range 0–7. The programmer may need to assign the value 5 to this bit range.

Bit operations use a **mask**, which is a sequence of bits designed to target a set of bits in another number. Used in conjunction with a bit operation, a mask allows programmers to set or clear specific bits in the other number.

EXAMPLE 2.24

The set of target bits S and mask M are identified for each of the following 8-bit applications.

(a) Test for an odd integer. $S = \{0\}$

$$M = 00000001$$

(b) Change a character from uppercase to lowercase. $S = \{5\}$

$$M = 00100000$$

(c) Isolate bit range 3–5. $S = \{3,4,5\}$

$$M = 11000111$$

Bit operations are performed with a series of logical functions: OR, AND, NOT, and EOR. Table 2.12 defines the functions for a single bit. Motorola assembly language extends the functions to operate on pairs of corresponding bits in two n-bit numbers.

These operations are similar to high-level language logical functions NOT, OR, AND, and EOR, which operate on Boolean variables (logical values TRUE and FALSE). The bit value of 1 corresponds to the logical value of TRUE, and the bit value of 0 corresponds to the logical value of

TABLE 2.12 Bit Operations

x	y	NOT x	x OR y	x AND y	x EOR y
0	0	1	0	0	0
0	1	1	1	0	1
1	0	0	1	0	1
1	1	0	1	1	0

FALSE. The function EOR might not be familiar. It is TRUE only if the two bits differ. It answers the question, "Are M and N different?"

EXAMPLE 2.25

The 8-bit numbers $x = 1100011$ and $y = 01110110$ are used with the operations (a) x OR y, (b) x AND y, and (c) x EOR y.

(a)	x	11100011	(b)	x	11100011	(c)	x	11100011
OR	y	01110110	AND	y	01110110	EOR	y	01110110
		11110111			01100010			10010101

EXAMPLE 2.26

Store value 5 in bits 3–5 of a register R. We use two operations and masks. Initially, we use the AND function to clear bits 3–5. The value 5 is stored with the OR function. Assume the register has value 10011101.

Step 1: Let mask $M_1 = 11000111$. Put 0's in bits 3–5.

$$
\begin{array}{lll}
 & R & 10011101 \\
\text{AND} & M_1 & 11000111 \\
\hline
 & & 10000101
\end{array}
$$

Step 2: Let mask $M_2 = 00101000$. Put value 5 in bits 3–5.

$$
\begin{array}{lll}
 & R & 10000101 \\
\text{OR} & M_2 & 00101000 \\
\hline
 & & 10101101
\end{array}
$$

Note: If the bits are not cleared and bit 4 is originally 1, the OR operations sets bits 3 and 5 with the resulting value of 7.

EXAMPLE 2.27

Let $X = AC26$ and $M = FF00$. The operations (a) X and M, (b) X or M, and (c) X EOR M yield the following:

(a)	X	AC26	(b)	X	AC26	(c)	X	AC26
AND	M	FF00	OR	M	FF00	EOR	M	FF00
		AC00			FF26			5326

Notes

1. The AND operation sets the bits of X to 0 for 0 in the mask. For bits 1 in the mask, the bits of X are unchanged.

2. The OR operation sets the bits of X to 1 for 1 in the mask. For bits 0 in the mask, the bits of X are unchanged.

3. The EOR operation reverses the bits of X for 1 in the mask. For bits 0 in the mask, the bits of X are unchanged.

EXERCISES

1. Give the expanded representation for each of the following numbers. Then multiply each term and record as a decimal number.
   (a) 10110_2 (b) 302_4 (c) 4421_5 (d) 1670_8

2. Convert each of the following decimal numbers to a binary number:
   (a) 12   (b) 25   (c) 124   (d) 78   (e) 256   (f) 88   (g) 1005

3. Convert each of the following decimal numbers to a hex number:
   (a) 22   (b) 52   (c) 96   (d) 190   (e) 256   (f) 991   (g) 2000

4. Convert each of the following unsigned binary numbers to an unsigned decimal number:
   (a) 111   (b) 1011   (c) 111011   (d) 11100111   (e) 111010101

5. Convert each of the following unsigned hex numbers to an unsigned decimal number:
   (a) A06C   (b) 5FFD   (c) 2847   (d) 42FA   (e) FFFF

6. Use repeated division to convert each of the following decimal numbers to a hex number:
   (a) 89   (b) 312   (c) 705   (d) 3000   (e) 5555

7. Write the decimal number 2365 as a base 7 number.

8. The patriot records numbers only in base 1776. Use repeated multiplication to convert the number 284_{1776} to a decimal number.

9. Convert each of the following hex numbers to a binary number:
   (a) A876   (b) A8897   (c) FFFF   (d) 7896   (e) 0167   (f) 5555

10. Convert each of the following binary numbers to a hex number:
    (a) 11110010   (b) 11101101
    (c) 1111000101010101   (d) 10101010101010101

11. Octal numbers have digits 0–7. The base is 8, and powers of the base are 1, 8, 64, and so forth.

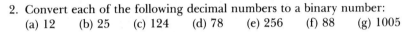

$$45_8 = 37_{10} \qquad 111_8 = 73_{10}$$

Each octal digit can be represented by a 3-bit number.

$$0 = 000 \quad 1 = 001 \quad 2 = 010 \quad 3 = 011$$
$$4 = 100 \quad 5 = 101 \quad 6 = 110 \quad 7 = 111$$

(a) Use repeated division to convert each of the following decimal numbers to its octal equivalent number:
(i) 25   (ii) 87   (iii) 48   (iv) 101

(b) Use the "shortcut grouping" to convert each of the following octal numbers to a binary number:
(i) 47   (ii) 216   (iii) 646   (iv) 17221

(c) Convert each of the following binary numbers to an octal number:
(i) 11011011   (ii) 1010011   (iii) 100100111100

(d) By using an intermediate binary number, convert each of the following numbers from hex to octal:
(i) 4F   (ii) A27   (iii) 1101   (iv) FFFF

12. Convert each number in the designated base to its decimal equivalent:
(a) $6A_{12}$ (b) 1403_5 (c) $4FB_{20}$ (d) 210210_3

13. Convert the following decimal numbers to a number in the designated base:
(a) 232 (to base 5)   (b) 1523 (to base 7)
(c) 194 (to base 3)   (d) 3721 (to base 20)

14. Perform the indicated operations for the binary numbers of arbitrary length.

(a)
$$\begin{array}{r} 111011 \\ + \quad 100111 \\ \hline \end{array}$$
(b)
$$\begin{array}{r} 110110 \\ + \quad 110110 \\ \hline \end{array}$$
(c)
$$\begin{array}{r} 1100110 \\ + \quad 1110111 \\ \hline \end{array}$$
(d)
$$\begin{array}{r} 11111111 \\ + \quad 11111111 \\ \hline \end{array}$$

(e)
$$\begin{array}{r} 11001 \\ - \quad 01101 \\ \hline \end{array}$$
(f)
$$\begin{array}{r} 100110 \\ - \quad 100010 \\ \hline \end{array}$$
(g)
$$\begin{array}{r} 0110011 \\ - \quad 0011111 \\ \hline \end{array}$$
(h)
$$\begin{array}{r} 111010101 \\ - \quad 101111111 \\ \hline \end{array}$$

15. Perform the indicated operations for the hex numbers of arbitrary length.

(a)
$$\begin{array}{r} 1235 \\ + \quad 567A \\ \hline \end{array}$$
(b)
$$\begin{array}{r} A9876 \\ + \quad FDCA0 \\ \hline \end{array}$$
(c)
$$\begin{array}{r} 555575 \\ + \quad 000F34 \\ \hline \end{array}$$
(d)
$$\begin{array}{r} 889ADFC \\ + 7776543 \\ \hline \end{array}$$

(e)
$$\begin{array}{r} A96 \\ - \quad 975 \\ \hline \end{array}$$
(f)
$$\begin{array}{r} FDA2 \\ - \quad DACB \\ \hline \end{array}$$
(g)
$$\begin{array}{r} 76543 \\ - \quad 65AC1 \\ \hline \end{array}$$
(h)
$$\begin{array}{r} B675C \\ - \quad AFFFF \\ \hline \end{array}$$

16. Perform the indicated operations on the following numbers of different bases. Assume each number has arbitrary length.

(a) Base 4
$$\begin{array}{r} 1203 \\ + \quad 2332 \\ \hline \end{array}$$
(b) Base 8
$$\begin{array}{r} 7046 \\ + \quad 2742 \\ \hline \end{array}$$
(c) Base 12
$$\begin{array}{r} A27B \\ + \quad 507A \\ \hline \end{array}$$
(d) Base 20
$$\begin{array}{r} 2H4 \\ + \quad A7C \\ \hline \end{array}$$

17. A bicycle has a three-digit odometer. Each digit is in the range 0–9. Assuming that the odometer numbers reverse direction when you pedal backward, what is the range of positive and negative numbers that can be represented by this odometer? Assuming that the odometer starts at 000 each time, find the odometer reading for trips of

(a) 10 miles backward   (b) 280 miles backward
(c) 102 miles backward   (d) 800 miles forward
The odometer reads 650. Assuming the rider pedals only forward, what are the fewest number of miles he or she travels to get that reading? What are the fewest number of miles if the rider pedals only backward?

The odometer reads 750 when the rider begins. What are the fewest number of miles the cyclist travels and what is the direction of pedaling so that the odometer will have a reading of 300?

18. Write out all possible 4-bit two's complement binary numbers and give the decimal equivalent for each number.

19. (a) Give the range of 12-bit two's complement binary numbers. Record your answer in both binary and hex.

    (b) Give the range of 20-bit two's complement binary numbers. Record your answer in both binary and hex.

20. Compute the 8-bit two's complement of each of the following binary numbers:
    (a) 00101101_2 (b) 00001011_2 (c) 00011011_2 (d) 11001010_2

21. Compute the 16-bit two's complement of each of the following hex numbers:
    (a) 48_{16} (b) $FFF4_{16}$ (c) 120_{16} (d) $AB76_{16}$
    (e) 1_{16} (f) 0_{16} (g) 8000_{16}

22. Find the 32-bit two's complement of the following hex numbers:
    (a) $0000F0B3_{16}$ (b) $A07A30D0_{16}$ (c) $C071170C_{16}$

23. Perform the following operations assuming 8-bit two's complement arithmetic:

    (a)   10110001   (b)   01101100   (c)   01111000   (d)   00001000
        + 11111010   + 01011111   − 10011001   − 01111010

24. Sign-extend each of the following 8-bit numbers to a 16-bit two's complement number:
    (a) 01111011_2 (b) 10000001_2 (c) 01100001_2

25. Sign-extend each of the following 8-bit numbers to a 16-bit hex number:
    (a) 92_{16} (b) $A8_{16}$ (c) $7F_{16}$ (d) $E0_{16}$

26. Perform the following operations on 16-bit two's complement hex numbers. Indicate (YES or NO) whether signed overflow occurs.

    (a)   80CD   (b)   80CD   (c)   FF06   (d)   7FFF
        + 1701   + 8701   + 10F1   − FFFE

    (e)   AF76   (f)   80CD   (g)   FF06   (h)   8701
        + 1701   − 8701   + AF76   − 70CD

27. Perform the following operations on the 16-bit unsigned hex numbers. In each case, indicate whether unsigned overflow occurs.

(a)	80CD	(b)	70C3	(c)	AF76	(d)	7FFF
	+ 1701		+ A80D		+ 10FA		+ FFFE

28. For 6-bit signed magnitude numbers, give the representation for each of the following decimal numbers:
    (a) 10   (b) -18 (c) 31   (d) -31
    What is the range for these numbers?

29. For 6-bit one's complement numbers, give the representation for each of the following decimal numbers:
    (a) 10   (b) -18 (c) 31   (d) -31
    What is the range for these numbers?

30. Use the addition algorithm for 8-bit one's complement numbers for each of the following:

(a)	10110001	(b)	01101100	(c)	01111000	(d)	00001000
	+ 11111010		+ 01011111		− 11011001		− 01111010

31. Determine the string corresponding to the following sequences of 7-bit ASCII codes expressed in hex:
    (a) 50   61   73   63   61   6C   27   73   20   43   48
        52   20   69   73   20   65   61   73   69   65   72
    (b) 50   41   47   45   3D   0D

32. Assume that a control character is written to the screen as ^⟨character⟩. For example, control A is ^A.
    (a) The control character ESC has ASCII value 27. What is its screen representation?
    (b) What is the ASCII value of ^T?
    (c) What is the control character corresponding to ^#?

33. Let $U = FF00_{16}$ and $V = 67AB_{16}$. Compute the 16-bit result for each of the following operations:
    (a) U AND V (b) U OR V (c) NOT U (e) U EOR V

34. Let $U = FF0C_{16}$ and $V = 1ABD_{16}$. Compute the 16-bit result for each of the following operations:
    (a) U AND V (b) U OR V (c) NOT U
    (d) NOT (U AND V)   (e) U EOR V (f) (NOT U) EOR V

35. Assume that your computer's circuitry cannot implement the NOT operation. Explain how you could implement NOT using a mask and the EOR operation. Test your conclusion on the 8-bit binary number 01001110_2.

36. Using a bit table, verify the equation

$$X \text{ EOR } Y = (\text{NOT } X \text{ AND } Y) \text{ OR } (X \text{ AND NOT } Y)$$

X	Y	NOT X AND Y	X AND NOT Y	X AND NOT Y OR NOT X AND Y	X EOR Y
0	0				
1	0				
0	1				
1	1				

37. Given a 16-bit two's complement number and no division instruction, show how you could use the bit operations to compute the remainder (Pascal MOD function) after dividing by 16. Use as a test case the result

$$23 \text{ MOD } 16 = 7$$

38. Give the mask and the bit operation for each of the following situations:
    (a) You want to toggle (turn ON then OFF) bit 3 in an 8-bit register.
    (b) Turn off bits 5 and 6 in a register.
    (c) Turn on bit 7 in a register.

CHAPTER 3

MACHINE ORGANIZATION AND PROGRAMMING

*B*ecause assembly language instructions provide direct access to most system components, some knowledge of computer organization is necessary to program effectively in assembly language. This chapter presents an overview of the structure of a computer, with emphasis on the architecture of the Motorola 68000. The key components are given with a simplified description sufficient to begin the study of assembly language programming. Chapters 12–14 describe input/output (I/O) programming and exception handling and present additional material on computer organization. The architecture of the MC68020/30/40 is introduced in Section 3.5 but is treated in detail in Chapters 13–15.

3.1 THE STRUCTURE OF A COMPUTER

Computer processing involves the flow of data among the central processing unit (CPU), memory, and I/O devices. The CPU is the command center of a system, directly accessing data from both disk, memory, and I/O interface registers. During the running of a program, both instructions and data reside in memory, making it a focal point in the processing cycle. A diagram of the flow is given in Figure 3.1.

At the code level, a computer program comprises instructions and data that reside in memory. For each instruction, the processor fetches an **operation code** from memory. The code specifies both the operation and the

FIGURE 3.1 Computer Data Flow

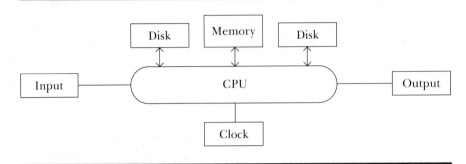

data used by the operation. The data items are stored immediately after the operation code and are called **extension words.**

Operation Code
Extension Word
Extension Word
Next Operation Code

The CPU interprets the operation code, fetches the data, and then carries out the instruction. The process just described is called an **instruction execution cycle**. Details of a cycle are described in Example 3.1. For a complete program, the cycle is repeated many times with the processor carrying out a sequence of operations that reads (fetches) data from memory and writes (stores) data to memory.

EXAMPLE 3.1

On the MC68000, the instruction

    ADD #5, 2000_{16}

directs the CPU to add 5 to the contents at memory location 2000_{16}. The instruction cycle includes fetching the operation code, fetching the data contents from location 2000_{16}, adding 5, and then storing the result in the same location. Assume that the contents at location 2000_{16} is 4039_{16}. After completing the addition, the contents are $403E_{16}$. The instruction execution cycle requires the following information.

Operation Code The 16-bit operation code is

0000011001	111001	$= 0679_{16}$

The high-order 10 bits specify an add operation with a constant term ("add a number"). The low-order 6 bits indicate that the second term (destination) is an absolute address in memory.

Extension Words   The 16-bit number 5 and the 32-bit address 2000_{16} are stored as extension words immediately after the operation code.

0679	← Operation Code
0005	← Number 5
0000	← Address 002000
2000	

During the execution cycle, the CPU carries out the addition and stores the result $403E_{16}$ in location 2000_{16}.

Before	After
4039	403E
2000	2000

This introduction gives only an overview of data flow on the MC68000. Specific details on data size, internal processor registers, and instruction codes are developed throughout the chapter.

Computer System Diagram

The components of a computer system are designed to support instruction execution. The heart of the system is the **central processing unit (CPU)**, which defines the instruction set and manages the system's interface with memory and external devices. The CPU accesses data along the **bus,** which is a set of parallel data/signal lines that allow for the transfer of data and information back and forth among the system components. Most of the communication occurs between memory and the CPU, although communication with such devices as a keyboard, monitor, and disk also use the bus. All data flow and instruction execution are synchronized by a clock that coordinates the interaction among components. Figure 3.2 is a block diagram of a basic system.

Memory

Before you can execute a program, all or part of it must be loaded into the computer's memory, which acts as a storage place for instructions and data.

FIGURE 3.2 Basic Computer System

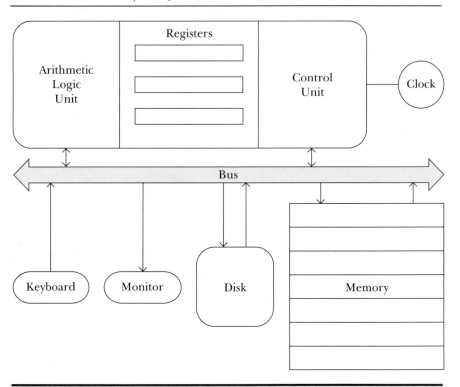

Memory consists of a sequence of addressable "locations." The contents at a location are a binary value that represents data, instructions, or the status of system devices. Memory simply holds some information that is useful to the computer.

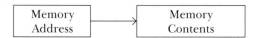

Every computer has a smallest addressable content unit, and the size of this unit is used to classify the machine. This unit may be a single bit, an 8-bit group, or a larger group. If a bit can be addressed as a separate value, the machine is **bit addressable**. If 8-bits constitute the smallest addressable unit, the machine is **byte addressable**, because a byte equals 8 bits. If 2 or more bytes are the smallest addressable unit, the machine is **word addressable**. As is the case with most microprocessors, the Motorola 68000 is a byte-addressable machine.

In a MC68000 system, memory is partitioned into a contiguous set of locations whose contents are 8-bit, or single byte, values. To the programmer, memory is an array of bytes. Figure 3.3 presents a simple view of

FIGURE 3.3 Physical View of Memory

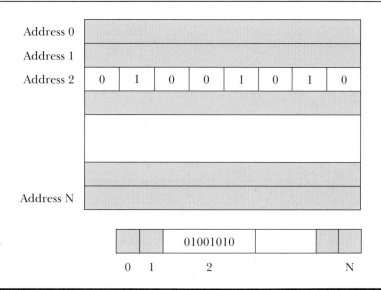

memory using both vertical and horizontal grids. Each location is identified by its address. At address 2, the byte value $4A_{16}$ is stored.

Computer programs use memory to store both instructions and data. Some programs are part of the **operating system** and reside in **read-only memory (ROM)**. The programs include routines to initialize ("boot") the system; communicate with the keyboard, screen, and disk devices; and provide the user with the ability to interface with the system. Routines in the operating system define the controlling software of the system, and the user should not inadvertently modify them. ROM memory provides the security. However, most programs use **random-access memory (RAM)**, which permits both read and write operations. Such programs change the contents in RAM locations.

ROM is usually placed on the main system board, called the **mother board**, as a separate memory chip called **programmable read-only memory (PROM)**. If the system software needs to be updated, new PROM chips are physically set on the board. The typical PROM chip also is reusable, which means that the memory contents can be magnetically erased and then the chip can be reprogrammed. Chips such as these are referred to as erasable programmable read-only memory (**EPROMs**).

 The Macintosh operating system illustrates the use of ROM. The Macintosh is a graphically based system that uses function calls to a series of routines called the **Toolbox**. The routines are organized into a series of "managers," one for each primary task in the system. For instance, the Memory Manager

FIGURE 3.4 Memory Map

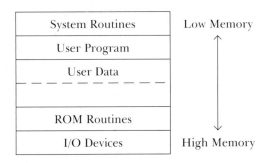

contains routines to handle memory, including the allocation of new memory for programs and the relocation of memory blocks during execution. The Menu Manager sets up the menu bar and pull-down menus, highlights menu items, identifies key equivalent menu access, and so forth. Most of the managers contain critical system routines that are stored in the Toolbox ROM. These routines, varying from 64 to 256 kilobytes (64K to 256K) in size, are the very heart of the Macintosh and cannot be changed. Additionally, some Toolbox utilities are located in RAM. These routines are typically written in assembly language for greater efficiency.

User programs must share memory space with the operating system. This sharing is made possible by assigning specific ranges of memory addresses to the system routines and the user programs. The allocation of memory is referred to as a **memory map** for the system. Figure 3.4 gives a typical memory map for a single-user system running a single application.

Computer access to a memory location is fast. The time to read or write instructions or data is measured in nanoseconds (a **nanosecond** is one-billionth of a second or 10^{-9} seconds). Typical memory access times are 80 to 120 nanoseconds (ns) per access.

Central Processing Unit

The instruction execution cycle is directed by the CPU, which can be partitioned into three functional units: the control unit, the arithmetic/logic unit, and internal registers (see Figure 3.5).

The **control unit** interprets an operation code and directs the execution of an instruction. The operation code, called the **opcode**, is loaded into an instruction register and then is decoded to identify the operation. Data transfer between the memory and external devices is initiated and monitored by the control unit. The control unit acts as an arbiter as various components of the system compete for the resources of the CPU.

FIGURE 3.5 CPU Components

Arithmetic Logic Unit	Registers	Control Unit

All computations are performed within the **arithmetic/logic unit (ALU)**, the computer's numerical calculator and logical analyzer. The ALU receives data from memory and registers, performs the calculation, and, if necessary, arranges for the result to be stored in memory.

Internal register is a general term for a storage location in the CPU. An internal register holds data and addresses while an instruction is executed. The system reserves some registers to support program execution. For example, the addresses of an operation code and extension words are maintained in a register called the **program counter** (PC). For fetch and store operations, the address of the memory location is located in a **memory address register** (MAR). For a numeric calculation, the presence of overflow, a change in algebraic sign, a carry, a borrow, and so forth is flagged by the system and stored in the **status register (SR)**. Programmers then use the flags to introduce program flow control and logical decision making.

 Computer systems generally permit access to some programmable registers for the temporary storage of data. During instruction execution, the use of registers reduces the need for time-consuming memory references to the same data and greatly increases program efficiency. The number of available registers varies greatly from system to system. The Motorola 68000 has 15 general-purpose registers and 2 stack registers that are used for subroutine and exception processing.

Clock

The activities of the CPU are synchronized by means of a **system clock**, which generates a regular pulse beat just like a ticking clock. All activities of the CPU are measured in clock cycles. Typical rates for modern microcomputers are in the range 16–40 megahertz (MHz), where

$$1 \text{ MHz} = 1 \text{ million cycles (ticks) per second}$$
$$= 1 \text{ million hertz}$$

If a CPU is running at 16 MHz, there are 16 million cycles of the clock per second. For an instruction requiring 8 clock cycles, execution time is

$$8(1/16,000,000) = 500 \text{ nanoseconds (ns)}$$
$$= 0.5 \text{ microseconds } (\mu s)$$

The Bus

The CPU communicates with memory and peripheral devices along a bus, a set of parallel data/signal lines. The bus lines transfer addresses, data, and signals that relay information on the system environment. On most computers, separate lines are allocated for each of these tasks, making it easier to divide the bus into its functional components and consider an **address bus**, a **data bus**, and a **control bus** (see Figure 3.6).

Address Bus

Each location in memory has an address that must be identified before the CPU can access its contents. The CPU communicates with a memory location by first placing the address on the address bus and then executing the read or write operation. The number of lines on the address bus determines the range of possible memory addresses. Because each line carries 1 bit of the address value, a CPU having a 16-bit address bus can access up to 2^{16} bytes of memory. The Motorola 68000 supports a 24-bit address bus with memory addresses in the range 000000_{16} to $FFFFFF_{16}$. The maximum size of memory on an MC68000 system is 2^{24} or approximately 16 million bytes of memory.

FIGURE 3.6   Bus Transfer

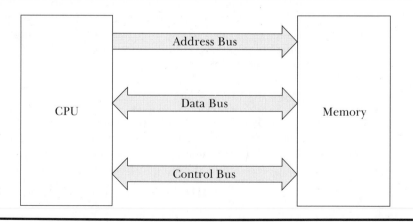

The size of memory is measured in bytes. (Remember that 8 bits equals a byte.) To simplify the measurement, however, the unit **kilobyte,** abbreviated simply as K, is frequently used.

$$1K = 2^{10} = 1024 \qquad \text{(1K is therefore approximately 1000 bytes)}$$

We use binary arithmetic to compute the size and range of memory. The size is usually given in K units, and the memory range is given in hex.

$$64K = 2^6 \times 2^{10} \text{ bytes} = 2^{16} \text{ bytes} = 16^4 \text{ bytes}$$
$$= 10000_{16} \text{ bytes}$$
$$= 65536_{10} \text{ bytes}$$

The ranges of memory addresses are:

Hex Addresses	Decimal Addresses
0000_{16}–$FFFF_{16}$	0–65535

For larger units of memory, a new unit of measure, the **megabyte,** abbreviated M, is used.

$$1M = 1K^2 = 2^{20} \text{ bytes}$$
$$= 1024^2 \text{ bytes (1M is approximately 1 million bytes)}$$

The MC68000 can address 16 megabytes (16M) of memory. That is,

$$2^{24} = 2^4 \times 2^{20} = 2^4 \times K^2 = 16M$$

Most MC68000 systems are configured with 1–8M of memory.

EXAMPLE 3.2

For memory size given in kilobytes or megabytes, we compute the valid memory address range in hex by expanding the size as a power of 16.

(a) 2 megabytes (2M)

$$2M = 2^1 \times 2^{20} = 2 \times 16^5 = 200000_{16}$$

The memory range is 000000_{16}–$1FFFFF_{16}$.

(b) 256 kilobytes (256K)

$$256K = 2^8 \times 2^{10} = 2^{18} = 2^2 \times 2^{16} = 4 \times 16^4 = 40000_{16}$$

The memory range is 000000_{16}–$03FFFF_{16}$.

Every address passed to memory by the CPU must exist. If a nonexistent address is placed on the address bus, a **bus error** is generated. For instance, in a system with 64K of main memory, a reference to memory at address $00FFFE_{16}$ is acceptable, but a reference to memory at address 010000_{16} will cause a bus error.

Data Bus

The amount of data transferred in a single memory cycle is determined by the number of lines on the data bus. For instance, under the constraint of eight lines ("width 8"), only a single byte or character can be transferred in a memory read or write cycle. Access to a 16-bit integer requires two memory cycles. The MC68000 system employs a 16-bit data bus.

Control Bus

A computer maintains signal lines to monitor the system environment. For instance, an attempt to access nonexistent memory activates a bus error signal line that permits the CPU to identify the error condition. When you turn on the power switch and the system boot process is initiated, a reset signal is sent to the CPU. Other signal lines identify requests for service from peripheral devices (interrupts) and enable the CPU to service the device. The architecture of the MC68000 control bus is discussed in Chapters 12 to 14, along with I/O programming and exception processing.

3.2 | PERIPHERAL DEVICES

A computer system must transmit data to and from its external environment. This is accomplished by means of input/output (I/O) devices. A wide variety of I/O devices are available and are described in this section. The units are commonly called **peripheral devices**. Chapter 12 covers the general principles of I/O programming.

Disk Drives

A **disk drive** is a high-capacity and moderately high-speed data storage device that augments main memory. Data is magnetically located on a flexible disk (floppy disk) or on one or more stacked rigid platters (hard disks), as shown in Figure 3.7. The disk rotates rapidly, permitting data to be accessed by a read/write head located on a movable arm similar to the arm of a phonograph.

A single disk surface consists of a series of concentric circles, called **tracks**, and the tracks are subdivided into **sectors**. A fixed number of bytes is packed on each sector (see Figure 3.8). The **sector density** (high, double, single, etc.) indicates the relative number of bytes per sector. The capacity of a disk is measured by the number of surfaces (single or two-sided), the number of tracks, the number of sectors, and the packing density (typically 512 to 1024 bytes per sector on a floppy disk).

Disk access time is measured in milliseconds (10^{-3} seconds). A typical access time might be 12–28 milliseconds (ms). A disk drive can retrieve data directly from any specified point on a disk and thus is called a **random-access device**.

FIGURE 3.7 Hard Disk

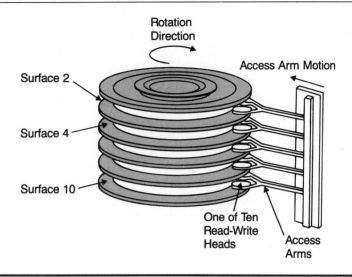

Magnetic Tape Devices

Using the same principles as a tape recorder, data is placed along the surface of a magnetic tape device (see Figure 3.9) in the order of its arrival. A tape is therefore called a **sequential device**. Any jump to a new block of data requires a time-consuming fast-forward or rewind of the tape. Thus magnetic tape is used primarily for bulk storage. Mainframe computers often use 2400-foot reels of 1/2-inch magnetic tape. Such a reel can hold the equivalent of 50,000 typed pages of text. Also in common use are 1/4-inch

FIGURE 3.8 Tracks and Sectors

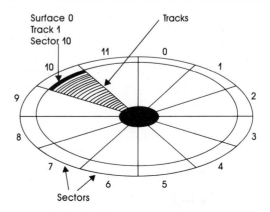

FIGURE 3.9   Magnetic Tape

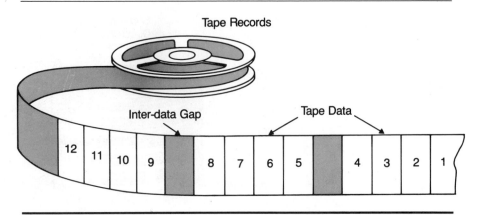

tape cartridge systems. A cartridge can hold at least 60M of data. This is the most common .type of tape backup system used with personal computers. For larger computers, an 8-millimeter tape system is available that provides high-speed backup for over 1 gigabyte (10^9 bytes) of data. The relatively slow access times for tape drives are measured in seconds.

Monitors

Modern personal computers and workstations use a **monitor** for display. A bit-mapped monitor consists of rows of small dots called **pixels**, which can be in any one of several states. We draw figures by darkening a number of pixels.

The resolution of a monitor depends on the density of pixels in dots per inch. Figure 3.10 illustrates a typical monitor. When using a bit-mapped display, you must draw everything, including text. A character is drawn in a font that specifies its shape in a given size (measured in pixels) and in a given style (plain, italic, bold, shadow, etc.). The bit-mapped approach is very flexible and allows you to deal with text in a great variety of fonts, sizes, and styles; it also allows for the integration of text and graphics in a document. Figure 3.11 shows the character 'a' and its pixel representation in the Geneva font. Note how the selective darkening of pixels forms the character. Because everything is drawn to the screen, drawing routines in a graphically based system must be highly efficient and are normally written in assembly language.

Terminals

A **terminal** (see Figure 3.12) is actually two communication devices, a keyboard and a screen, that permit data transfer to and from an external

FIGURE 3.10 Monitor

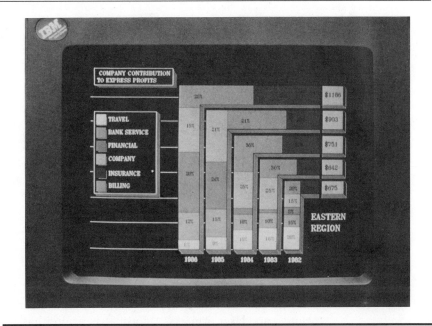

computer. Some text and graphics terminals are recognized by the industry as standards and define a protocol that the computer recognizes. Other terminals and terminal communication packages emulate one or more of the standard protocols. Terminals receive and transmit data at speeds ranging from 30 to 1920 characters per second.

FIGURE 3.11 Bit-Mapped Screen

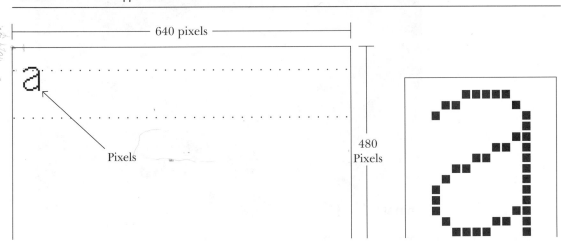

FIGURE 3.12 Terminal Device

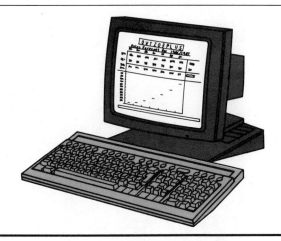

Printers

A printer is an output device only. Although many different vendors manufacture printers, there are basically two types in common use, dot-matrix printers and laser printers. A dot-matrix printer has a print head that passes across the paper. The print head contains a matrix of dots. As the print head moves across the paper, selected dots imprint on the paper to build portions of a character or graphic. These printers are cost effective and can produce typewriter-quality text. A **laser printer** provides output of

FIGURE 3.13 Laser Printer

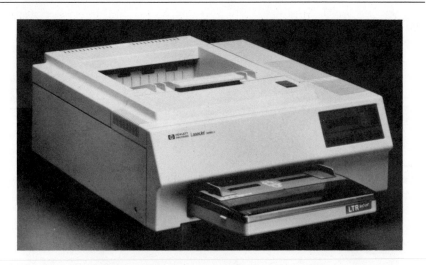

higher quality and speed. These printers are driven by an engine containing a tiny laser. The laser generates heat, which imprints toner on paper. A laser printer is similar in concept to a monitor. It uses the pixel approach to printing text and graphics. The density of the most common laser printers is 300 dots per inch (dpi). A laser printer (see Figure 3.13) is equipped with a variety of embedded fonts and can receive other fonts downloaded from the application software.

3.3 | DATA ORGANIZATION AND THE MC68000

The MC68000 possesses a 24-bit address bus and a bidirectional 16-bit data bus to transfer data between the CPU and memory. The memory address is placed on the address bus, and the data transfer is carried out using either a read bus cycle or a write bus cycle. A **read cycle** transfers data from memory to the CPU, whereas a **write cycle** transfers data from the CPU to memory. Each byte of memory has a unique 24-bit address. When transferring data to and from memory, the byte address of the location is placed on the address bus. The MC68000 is a byte-addressable machine but can transfer 2 bytes of data (called a **word**) in a single memory access. The word is referenced by the address of the first byte and is the maximum unit of data transfer on the data bus. One additional data type for the MC68000 needs to be discussed. A **long word** is a 32-bit number, consisting of four consecutive bytes. Because the MC68000 has a 16-bit data bus, the CPU must access long-word data using two 16-bit data bus cycles. A long word consists of 2 consecutive words (4 consecutive bytes) with the address of the first word defining its location in memory. With two's complement numbers, the range of a long word is

$$-2^{31} \leq N \leq 2^{31} - 1$$

The MC68000 requires that words be accessed only at even byte addresses. If word data is referenced at an odd address, the processor signals an **address error**. In cases in which only a single byte is accessed, one of the address line (A0) indicates whether it is the upper or lower byte of the corresponding word.

EXAMPLE 3.3

Assume that the 8-bit hex data 0A 4F 67 occupies 3 consecutive bytes of memory beginning at location 000500_{16}.

0A	4F	67
000500	000501	000502

- The word $0A4F_{16}$ can be accessed in a single 16-bit memory cycle. The word has address 000500_{16}.

- The byte $4F_{16}$ can be accessed in a memory cycle. The memory address 000501_{16} is placed on the address bus. Along the data bus, 8 bits are transferred.

- The 16-bit value $4F67_{16}$ at address 000501_{16} cannot be accessed in a single memory cycle because its address is odd. The access requires two 8-bit read cycles.

Data Organization in Memory

A standard bit-numbering convention specifies data in memory. On the MC68000, the **least significant bit** is 0, the next position is bit one, and so on. The **sign bit** (bit position 7 for byte data, bit position 15 for word data, bit position 31 for long-word data) is the leftmost, or most significant, bit of the byte, word, or long word. This numbering scheme is illustrated in Figure 3.14. Bits 0–7 are called the **least significant byte (LSB)** of a word, and bits 8–15 are called the **most significant byte (MSB)** of a word. In a long word, bits 0–15 are referred to as the **least significant word (LSW)**, and bits 16–31 are referred to as the **most significant word (MSW)**.

FIGURE 3.14 Byte, Word, and Long Word Data Organization

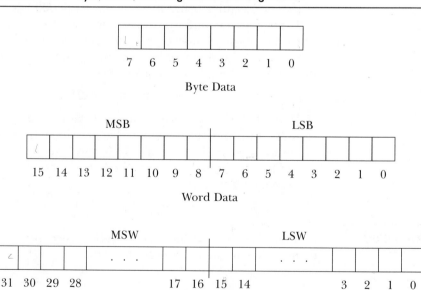

Because bit 0 corresponds to 2^0 and bit $n - 1$ corresponds to 2^{n-1}, the least significant and most significant bits in an n-bit number are also called the **low-order bits** and **high-order bits**, respectively. For a word, the LSB and MSB are referred to as the **low-order byte** and **high-order byte**, respectively; for a long word, the LSW and MSW are referred to as the **low-order word** and **high-order word**, respectively.

EXAMPLE 3.4

Assume that five memory words beginning at address 000500_{16} contain the 16-bit two's complement value for the decimal integers 2, 42, -6, 22, and -7. The data in the grid is given in hex.

0002	002A	FFFA	0016	FFF9
000500	000502	000504	000506	000508

- The integer value -7 is stored at address 000508_{16}. The LSB of the word is at address 000509_{16} and has value $F9_{16}$. The MSB is at address 000508_{16} with value FF_{16}.

- The long word beginning at address 000504_{16} has the value

$$FFFA0016_{16} = -393194_{10}$$

- The hex digits FA_{16} are the byte contents at address 000505_{16}. They are the LSB of the word $FFFA_{16}$ at address 000504_{16} and are contained in both the LSW of the long word at address 000502_{16} and the MSW of the long word at address 000504_{16}.

Data Organization in MC68000 Registers

The MC68000 has a series of system registers that are used during program execution. The registers include a 32-bit program counter (PC) that contains the address of the next instruction to be read from memory and a 16-bit status register. The MC68000 also has a set of general-purpose data and address registers that are detailed in the following sections.

The Data Registers

The MC68000 contains eight **data registers** with symbolic names D0, D1, . . . , D7. These registers provide high-speed storage for temporary data, counters, and control variables. They also hold data used in arithmetic operations. Each register contains 32 bits (a long word) of data.

Most MC68000 instructions permit byte, word, or long-word operations on a data register. Word (16-bit) operations access the LSW of the register, whereas byte (8-bit) operations access the LSB of the register. Because long-

FIGURE 3.15 MC68000 Data Registers

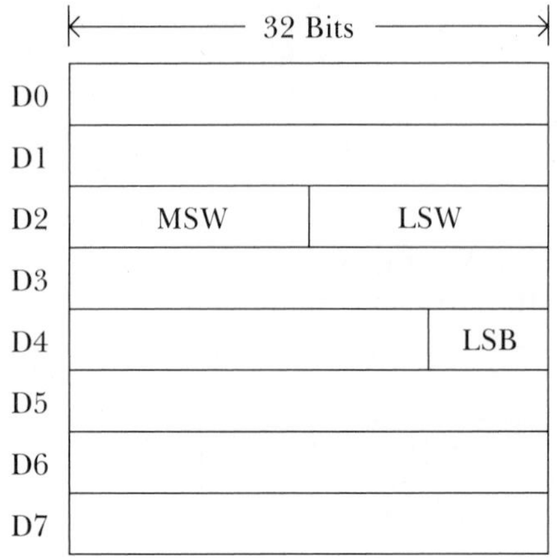

word operations are available, the MC68000 is referred to as a **32-bit processor**. The data registers are fundamental to the MC68000 because most arithmetic instructions require that at least one of the operands be located in such a register. Figure 3.15 illustrates the data registers along with a partition of the 32 bits into words and bytes.

EXAMPLE 3.5

(a) Assume that data register D1 contains the long word $0A25FF3B_{16}$.

The register is referenced by its name D1. In order to distinguish between the name of the register and the actual contents of a register, this text uses the standard Motorola convention; that is, the contents of the register are designated by enclosing the register name in parentheses. Use of the suffix ".L" indicates that all 32 bits of the register are referenced. A word reference uses the suffix ".W", and a byte reference uses a ".B" suffix. For example,

$$(D1.L) = 0A25FF3B_{16} \qquad (D1.W) = FF3B_{16} \qquad (D1.B) = 3B_{16}$$

(b) The contents of a data register are given with eight hex digits. Assume that D4 is a second data register with $(D4.L) = 7A10093A_{16}$. The addition instruction, ADD.⟨size⟩ D1, D4, allows for a byte, word, or long-word operation, depending on the size specification (B = byte, W =

word, L = long word). The computation affects only the number of bits specified by the size.

ADD.B D1, D4	*ADD.W D1, D4*	*ADD.L D1, D4*
3B	FF3B	0A25FF3B
+ 3A	+ 093A	+ 7A10093A
75	0875	84360875

$(D4.L) = 7A100975_{16}$ $(D4.L) = 7A100875_{16}$ $(D4.L) = 84360875_{16}$

The Address Registers

The MC68000 contains nine 32-bit address registers. As shown in Figure 3.16, seven of the registers A0–A6, are general-purpose registers for a programmer to access data in memory. The other registers are stack pointers used for subroutines and exception processing. The user stack pointer is introduced in Chapter 7, and the supervisor stack pointer, available to the programmer when the MC68000 operates in supervisor mode, is introduced in Chapter 13.

Because address registers are designed to process 24-bit memory addresses, special conditions are in effect. All operations on address registers are long-word operations affecting the entire 32 bits of the register. Only long-word data can be written into address registers. When word data is

FIGURE 3.16 MC68000 Address Registers

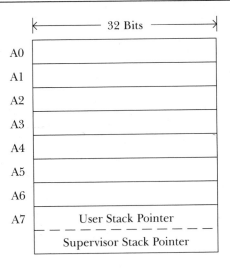

specified, it is sign-extended to 32 bits. Only the low-order 24 bits of an address are placed on the address bus.

	Sign-Extended	
Word Data	*Long Word*	*Address Reference*
$4A2F_{16}$	$00004A2F_{16}$	$004A2F_{16}$
$CF00_{16}$	$FFFFCF00_{16}$	$FFCF00_{16}$

This text uses the standard Motorola conventions to represent absolute addresses and address registers. If X is an address, simply refer to "X" when specifying the location in memory. Refer to the contents of memory at address X by enclosing the address in parentheses. You can reference an address register by its name. The contents of an address register point to a memory location and are referenced by enclosing the register in parentheses. Consider the presentations for the following data:

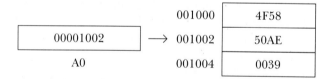

Let $X = \$001000$ be an absolute memory address. A reference to the address is given by the symbol X. The contents of memory pointed to by X is given by $(X) = \$4F58$. The register A0 contains the address $\$001002$. The name of the address register is A0. The contents of the register is $(A0) = \$001002$.

The representation of addresses and memory contents is modified for pictures. An arrow indicates that the address "points" at the memory location. Figure 3.17 illustrates the notation used in diagrams to distinguish the address from the contents in memory pointed to by the address.

FIGURE 3.17   Address Register/Memory Diagram

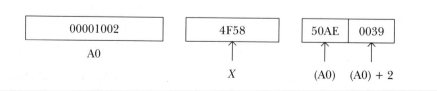

|3.4| BASIC MACHINE INSTRUCTIONS

The concept of an instruction cycle was introduced in Section 3.1. The topic is now developed using specific instructions that are selected from the MC68000 instruction set. The instructions will use standard Motorola assembly language syntax and machine code and thus will apply in Chapter 4 when assembly language programming is introduced. In order to simulate a real run-time environment, a hypothetical CPU, called the *SMC68000,* is developed to execute the instructions. The SCM68000 CPU is controlled by a small operating system that supplies simple I/O routines and supports the loading and running of executable machine code. This section focuses on machine code and illustrates instruction execution on a run-time system.

The SMC68000 System

The **SMC68000** processor contains a program counter, a status register, and a data register D0. For data transfer, the system has a 24-bit address bus and a 16-bit data bus. A memory map for the system, pictured in Figure 3.18, includes 16K of RAM in the range 0000_{16}–$3FFF_{16}$, 1K of EPROM in the address range 4000_{16}–$43FF_{16}$, and peripheral-device interface registers in the range 10000_{16}–$100FF_{16}$. The registers allow access to both a keyboard and a screen. System routines are loaded in the first 500_{16} bytes of memory, and user programs are loaded and run from an address at or above 500_{16}.

Instructions for the SMC68000 have both an assembly language format and a machine language format. The assembly language format of an instruction contains a **mnemonic** specifying the operation and **operands** spec-

FIGURE 3.18 SMC68000 Memory Map

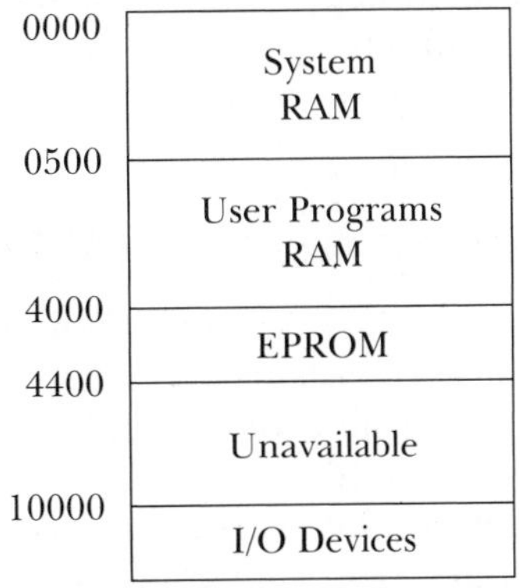

FIGURE 3.19 Machine Code Format

Opcode Word
Extension
Word(s)

ifying the data used by the operation. An operand is specified by an **addressing mode** that tells the CPU whether the data needed by the instruction is located in the data register or in a memory location. SMC6800 instructions have one or two operands.

> One-operand instruction: ⟨mnemonic⟩ ⟨operand⟩
> Two-operand instructions: ⟨mnemonic⟩ ⟨operand⟩, ⟨operand⟩

If an instruction requires two operands, the first operand is the **source**, and the second is the **destination**.

The machine code format includes a 16-bit opcode word that specifies the instruction and the addressing modes of the operands. The opcode word indicates whether each operand is a register, a constant number, or the contents of a memory location. Information on the specific constant value or the absolute memory address is placed in extension words immediately after the opcode word. The opcode word and extension words combine to form the machine code for an instruction (see Figure 3.19).

The SCM68000 system contains a small operating system in the 1K EPROM. The code, called a *monitor*, provides an interface that allows the user to load 16-bit hex values from the keyboard and begin program execution at a specified starting address. The SMC monitor reads an array of 16-bit hex numbers representing program machine code. The first number specifies the **load address** of the program. The hex numbers are loaded into RAM beginning at the load address, and then the monitor starts the code running by setting the program counter (PC) to the **starting address** of the user program.

SMC68000 Instructions

The SMC68000 supports four instructions: MOVE, ADD, SUB, and TRAP. The TRAP instruction interfaces with the operating system to provide I/O and to permit program exit back to the operating system. The instructions operate on 16-bit values and perform word operations. The instructions are introduced using both assembly language format and the corresponding machine code. The available source and destination operands are

D0	The general-purpose data register
#N	A constant number
address	A 32-bit memory address

By default, all numbers used in operands are decimal. The prefix "$" designates a hex number. The SCM68000 has a 24-bit address bus (3 bytes) but uses 32 bits to store the address. A constant number is stored as a 16-bit extension word. The opcode word for each instruction was selected from the instruction listings in the *M68000 Programmer's Reference Manual* (see Appendix B). The opcodes will apply to a MC68000 system and are developed further in Section 4.8, which covers the structure of opcodes.

MOVE Instruction

Syntax	*Machine Code*	*Assembly Language*	
	303C 〈number〉	MOVE	#N, D0
	33FC 〈number〉 〈address〉	MOVE	#N, 〈address〉
	3039 〈address〉	MOVE	〈address〉, D0
	33C0 〈address〉	MOVE	D0, 〈address〉

Action Copy the 16-bit word specified by the source operand into the location specified by the destination operand.

EXAMPLE 3.6

(*a*) MOVE $000200,D0

Machine Code   3039 0000 0200

The address $000200 is stored as a 32-bit long word in two extension words.

Action Move the 16-bit contents ($0FCD) at address $000200 into register D0.

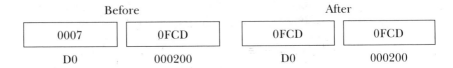

Before		After	
0007	0FCD	0FCD	0FCD
D0	000200	D0	000200

(*b*) MOVE   #14,D0

Machine Code   303C 000E

The decimal number 14 is located immediately after the opcode word as the extension word $000E.

Action Place the 16-bit value $000E in D0.

	Before		After
	0143		000E
	D0		D0

(c) MOVE   #$20,$001000

   Machine Code   33FC   0020   0000   1000

(d) MOVE   D0,$000200
   Machine Code   33C0   0000   0200

ADD and SUB Instructions

Syntax	ADDI	#N, D0	SUBI	#N, D0
	ADDI	#N, ⟨address⟩	SUBI	#N, ⟨address⟩
	ADD	⟨address⟩, D0	SUB	⟨address⟩, D0
	ADD	D0, ⟨address⟩	SUB	D0, ⟨address⟩

Action   The ADD instruction adds the 16-bit word specified by the source and the 16-bit contents specified by the destination. The result is stored in the destination.

$$\langle source \rangle + \langle destination \rangle \rightarrow \langle destination \rangle$$

The SUB instruction subtracts the contents of the source from the contents of the destination. The result is stored in the destination.

$$\langle destination \rangle - \langle source \rangle \rightarrow \langle destination \rangle$$

Machine Code		*Assembly Language*	
0640	⟨number⟩	ADDI	#N, D0
0679	⟨number⟩ ⟨address⟩	ADDI	#N, ⟨address⟩
D079	⟨address⟩	ADD	⟨address⟩, D0
D179	⟨address⟩	ADD	D0, ⟨address⟩
0440	⟨number⟩	SUBI	#N, D0
0479	⟨number⟩ ⟨address⟩	SUBI	#N, ⟨address⟩
9079	⟨address⟩	SUB	⟨address⟩, D0
9179	⟨address⟩	SUB	D0, ⟨address⟩

Note   The forms ADDI/SUBI (immediate) must be used when adding or subtracting constants. Details are provided in Chapter 4.

EXAMPLE 3.7

(a) SUB   D0,$001200

Machine Code   9179 0000 1200

Action Assume (D0.W) = $0F13 and ($001200) = $01C8. Subtract the 16-bit value in D0 from the contents at $001200. The difference, $01C8 − $0F13 = $F2B5, is stored at location $001200.

Before		After	
0F13	01C8	0F13	F2B5
D0	001200	D0	001200

(b) ADDI   #$64,D0

Machine Code   0640 0040

Action The 16-bit value $0040 is added to (D0.W). The sum $FFC8 + $0040 = $0008 is stored in D0.

Before	After
A45F FFC8	A45F 0008
D0	D0

EXAMPLE 3.8

The following machine code corresponds to SMC68000 instructions.

Instruction		Machine Code			
ADDI	#242,$003308	0679	00F2	0000	3308
SUB	$001006,D0	9079	0000	1006	

TRAP Instruction

Syntax

TRAP	#0	Halt program execution; return to monitor
TRAP	#1	Read a decimal number from the keyboard into (D0.W)
TRAP	#2	Write the value in (D0.W) to the screen as a decimal number

Action The TRAP #0 instruction halts program execution and returns control to the operating system. To prevent run-time errors, SMC68000 programs should terminate with TRAP #0.

    TRAP #1 is used for input. The decimal number typed on the keyboard is stored in the low-order word of D0.

TRAP #2 is used for output. The low-order word in D0 is printed to the screen in decimal.

Machine Code	*Assembly Language*
4E40	TRAP #0
4E41	TRAP #1
4E42	TRAP #2

Note The TRAP instructions cause the CPU to transfer control to the operating system in ROM. Technically, the trap instruction causes an "exception" to occur that interrupts normal processing and causes the processor to execute code beginning at a predefined location in memory. Upon completion of the code, program control is transferred to the instruction following the trap. After the TRAP #0 instruction, control returns to the operating system.

In Chapter 4, we introduce a library of I/O routines to use when running a program. The user can access the library with simple subroutine calls.

EXAMPLE 3.9

The following code sequence inputs a number (TRAP #1), doubles it, and then outputs the results (TRAP #2). A STOP (TRAP #0) terminates the program.

TRAP	#1	READ A NUMBER N INTO D0
MOVE	D0, $600	STORE THE NUMBER N IN LOCATION $600
ADD	$600, D0	DOUBLE THE NUMBER IN D0 = 2 ∗ N
TRAP	#2	OUTPUT THE NUMBER IN D0 TO THE SCREEN
TRAP	#0	STOP EXECUTION

SMC68000 Programs

Most readers learn principles of programming from high-level languages. Variables, assignment statements, and other constructs are the building blocks of a program. Each high-level language statement translates into one or more basic machine instructions. Assembly language code provides the equivalent of the machine code. An example illustrates these ideas. Consider the Pascal code

```
I := 79;
X := Y + I;
X := X + 18;
```

The variables I, X, and Y represent locations in memory. Assume that I corresponds to location $002000, X to location $002002, and Y to location $002004. In translating the high-level language statements into SCM68000 instructions, register D0 is used for temporary storage. D0 is referred to as a **scratch register**. A semicolon (;) introduces a comment that continues to the end of the line.

```
I := 79;
     MOVE      #79,$002000     ; "MOVE" IS AN ASSIGNMENT
X := Y + I;
     MOVE      $002000,D0      ; STORE I IN A SCRATCH REGISTER
     ADD       $002004,D0      ; ADD Y TO VALUE I IN D0
     MOVE      D0,$002002      ; ASSIGN RESULT TO LOCATION X
X := X + 18;
     ADDI      #18,$002002     ; ADD 18 TO VALUE X
```

The instructions and resulting machine code are summarized.

Instruction		Machine Code			
MOVE	#79,$002000	33FC	004F	0000	2000
MOVE	$002000,D0	3039	0000	2000	
ADD	$002004,D0	D079	0000	2004	
MOVE	D0,$002002	33C0	0000	2002	
ADDI	#18,$002002	0679	0012	0000	2002

PROGRAM 3.1

The sample SMC68000 code fragments are better understood as part of a complete program executed in a run-time environment. In the following program, the preceding Pascal statements are embedded in a program that includes variable declaration and I/O using readln and writeln. The equivalent SMC68000 assembly language code includes TRAP calls for the I/O statements. Pascal assigns memory locations to the variables and allows you to refer to these locations with symbolic names I, X, and Y. In machine language, the user must assign storage directly.

Note Throughout this text, complete assembly language programs are presented in lowercase letters. Program fragments are given in uppercase letters.

Pascal Code

```
PROGRAM smc_demo (input, output);
VAR
    i       : integer
    x, y    : integer
BEGIN
    i   :=   79;
    readln (y);
```

```
    x := y + i;
    x := x + 18;
    writeln(x);
END.
```

SMC Assembly Language Code   Assume that the SMC assembly language code uses locations $002000, $002002, and $002004 for the variables I, X, and Y, respectively.

```
    MOVE    #79,$002000
    TRAP    #1              ; READLN (Y)   INPUT INTO D0
    MOVE    D0,$002004      ; STORE D0 IN LOCATION Y
    MOVE    $002000,D0      ; FETCH VARIABLE I FOR THE ADD
    ADD     $002004,D0      ; ADD Y + I
  → MOVE    D0,$002002      ; STORE THE SUM IN X
    ADDI    #18,$002002     ; ADD 18 TO X
    TRAP    #2              ; WRITELN STATEMENT (PRINT X)
    TRAP    #0              ; HALT
```

For program execution, the machine code is loaded into memory at a particular load address. On a SMC68000 system, the load address is in user space at an address at or above $000500. Assume that the code for the sample program is loaded into memory at address $000500. Instruction opcode words and extension words are stored sequentially from this address. The following is the machine code for the program. The address of each word is included.

SMC Machine Language Code

Memory Address	Machine Code	Instruction	
000500	33FC	MOVE	#79,$002000
000502	004F		
000504	0000		
000506	2000		
000508	4E41	TRAP	#1
00050A	33C0	MOVE	D0,$002004
00050C	0000		
00050E	2004		
000510	3039	MOVE	$002000,D0
000512	0000		
000514	2000		
000516	D079	ADD	$002004,D0
000518	0000		
00051A	2004		

00051C	33C0	MOVE	D0,$002002
00051E	0000		
000520	2002		
000522	4E42	TRAP	#2
000524	4E40	TRAP	#0

The SMC68000
Instruction Execution Cycle

An instruction is executed with a sequence of memory read (fetch) and write (store) cycles. Each instruction is executed by first reading its opcode word and then, depending on the instruction, reading extension words. The specific action of the instruction may require additional read or write cycles.

The stages in an instruction execution cycle were briefly introduced in Section 3.1. Now additional details are given using two SMC68000 instructions from Program 3.1. Data transfer on the address bus and data bus illustrates a read/write cycle. Assume that the PC is set at $000510.

Instruction I: MOVE $002000,D0   (Code 3039   0000   2000)

1. The value in the PC ($000510) is put on the address bus with a request to "read" the contents of that location.

2. The 16-bit content at location $000510 is the instruction opcode word $3039. The memory hardware puts this value on the data bus and returns the value to the processor, where the control unit begins inter-

FIGURE 3.20   Instruction I—Opcode Read Cycle

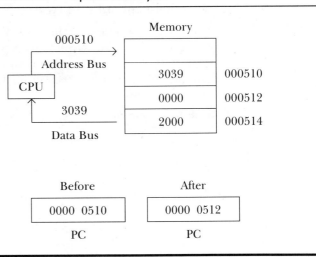

FIGURE 3.21   Instruction 1—Extension-Word Read Cycles

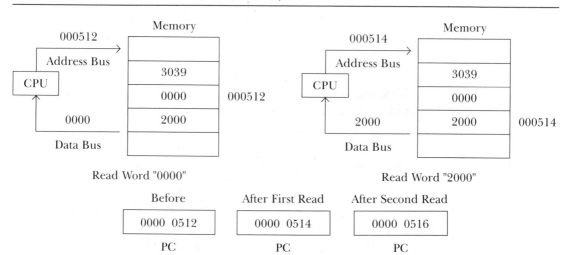

Read Word "0000"   Read Word "2000"

pretation of the instruction. On the read cycle, the control unit causes the PC to be incremented by 2, and it now points at location $000512. Figure 3.20 shows the opcode read cycle.

3. The control unit recognizes that the MOVE instruction requires a specific value for the address. This is found in the two extension words immediately following the opcode word (at locations $000512 and $000514). Two read cycles are executed. The value of the PC is increased by 2 on each cycle. The PC has the final value $000516, and the address $002000 is stored in a CPU system register. Figure 3.21 illustrates the two extension-word read cycle.

4. The actual execution of the MOVE instruction requires an additional read cycle. The address $002000 is put on the address bus with a "read" request. The contents in the memory location ($004F) are put on the data bus and stored in the register D0, as seen in Figure 3.22.

FIGURE 3.22   Instruction 1—Execution Read Cycle

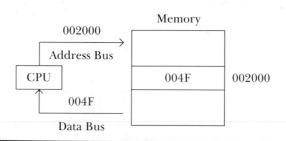

Instruction 2:   MOVE D0, $2002   (Code 33C0) 0000 2002)

1. The PC initially has the value $00051C. With three read cycles, the instruction is fetched from memory. On each read, the PC is incremented by 2. Its final value is $000522.

2. Execution of the instruction requires a write cycle. The address $002002 is put on the address bus, and the value in D0 is stored in location $002002. Figure 3.23 shows the execution write cycle, assuming that TRAP #1 reads $0055.

An instruction execution cycle always requires read cycles to fetch the opcode word and any extension words. Additional read/write cycles may be required by the specific action of the instruction.

EXAMPLE 3.10

The read and write cycles are identified for the following instructions.

ADD $1000,D0   (Code   D079 0000 1000)

Three read cycles are used for the opcode and extension words. The ADD instruction uses one read cycle to fetch the word of data from memory location $001000. No write cycle is required to store the sum in register D0.

MOVE #14,$2200   (Code   33FC 000E 0000 2200)

Four read cycles load the instruction. The MOVE instruction uses one write cycle to move the constant 14 to memory location $002200.

Technical documentation in the *M68000 8-/16-/32-Bit Microprocessor Programmer's Reference Manual* contains CPU execution times for each instruction, measured in clock cycles. You can better understand the concept of instruction timing by examining simulated times for the SMC68000 system. Instruction execution times and access times for read or write cycles are combined with clock speed to measure the total time needed to execute an

FIGURE 3.23   Instruction 2—Execution Write Cycle

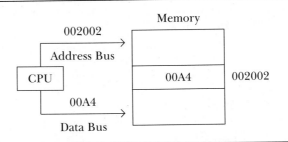

instruction. The following example uses hypothetical times to illustrate instruction timing on a SMC68000 system.

Assume that each memory read or write requires four clock cycles and that the ADD operation, using the ALU, requires two clock cycles. On a 25-MHz processor, one clock cycle is 40 nanoseconds. The following breakdown computes the total time to execute

    ADD $001000, D0

Execution Cycles	Number of Reads/Writes	Number of Clock Cycles
Read the opcode word	1	4
Read the 32-bit address $001000	2	8
Read the 16-bit contents of address $001000 into D0	1	4
Perform the ADD operation	0	2

Summary   The instruction requires four read cycles and no write cycles. It takes 18 clock cycles, or 720 nanoseconds.

Decoding SMC68000 Machine Language Instructions

The process of **disassembling** (decoding) a machine language instruction is more difficult than assembling it. The opcode word is the first word of the instruction. Its fields contain information on both the operation and operands. By decomposing its bit pattern, you can identify the assembly language instruction mnemonic and the addressing modes for the operands. The addressing modes may require additional information to access specific values or locations in memory. This information will be contained in extension words following the opcode word. Assuming that the code executes correctly, the word following the extension words will be the opcode word for the next instruction.

A segment of program machine code contains the following opcode and extension words:

    33C0   0000   1000   0479   FFFA   0000   1050

Two instructions are identified and decoded.

Instruction 1   The process of decoding a machine language instruction begins with the opcode word $33C0, which corresponds to the MOVE instruction:

MOVE D0,⟨address⟩

The address identified in the destination operand is read from the two words ($0000 1000) following the opcode word. The SMC68000 instruction is

MOVE D0, $00001000

Instruction 2 The word $0479 is the opcode of the next instruction. It corresponds to the instruction

SUBI #N,⟨address⟩

The constant N is read from the extension word ($FFFA = −6). The address is read from the next two extension words ($0000 1050). The SMC68000 instruction is

SUBI #-6, $00001050

EXAMPLE 3.13 The following code segment has the starting address $000500. Initially, (D0.W) is $01C6, and the 16-bit contents of address $001000 are $18C2.

Memory Address	Contents
000500	0440
000502	00A2
000504	D179
000506	0000
000508	1000
00050A	0479
00050C	0041
00050E	0000
000510	1000
000512	3039
000514	0000
000516	1000
000518	4E42
.	.
.	.
.	.
001000	18C2

The machine code disassembles into the following SMC68000 assembly language instructions:

Memory Address	SMC Instructions	
000500	SUBI	#162,D0
000504	ADD	D0,$001000
00050A	SUBI	#65,$001000
000512	MOVE	$1000,D0
000518	TRAP	#2

After executing the code, the 16-bit content of address $001000 is

$$01C6 - 00A2 + 18C2 - 0041 = 19A5$$

and the decimal value $6565 = 19A5_{16}$ is printed.

3.5 | MOTOROLA 68020/30/40 ORGANIZATION

The MC68020, MC68030, and MC68040 processors have advanced features that increase speed and efficiency. This section describes their internal registers and data organization. This material applies to the new MC68020/30/40 instructions and addressing modes, which are presented as topics in subsequent chapters. The advanced architectural features of the MC68020/30/40 are described in Chapter 15.

Internal Registers

The MC68020/30/40 program counter is a full 32-bit register, and the processor interfaces with a 32-bit address bus. Up to 2^{32} bytes (4 gigabytes) of memory can be addressed in the range $00000000–$FFFFFFFF.

The processor also accesses a 32-bit data bus. An instruction such as

MOVE.L $00002000,D0

fetches the 32-bit (long-word) contents from memory in a single data bus cycle. The suffix ".L" specifies a 32-bit operation.

The MC68020/30/40 supports eight general-purpose data registers, D0–D7, and ten address registers. The registers A0–A6 are used for general-purpose programming as for the MC68000. The MC68020/30/40 also has three stack pointers, one for user programs and two for the operating system. Data registers support byte, word, and long-word operations. Quad-word (64-bit) data are permitted with data registers and are used by MC68020/30/40 extended multiply and divide instructions.

Data Organization in Memory

On the MC68020/30/40, memory is byte addressable, with data specified in byte, word, and long-word units. Unlike the MC6800020/30/40, the

FIGURE 3.24 Data Units in Memory

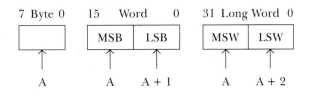

MC68020 does not require that word and long-word data be aligned on even byte boundaries. Thus address A in Figure 3.24 can be any valid memory address.

On the MC68000, all word and long-word accesses must be made at an even address. The instruction

MOVE.L #5, $1001

generates an address error on the MC68000 but is valid on the MC68020/ 30/4. Data transfer, however, is more efficient when word data are aligned on even byte boundaries and long word data are aligned at addresses that are divisible by 4.

EXAMPLE 3.14

Data bus cycles and data transfer to memory are compared for two different MOVE instructions. These examples do execute, but they would be more efficient if the data were aligned at a long word boundary. The XX tag indicates that the byte value is unchanged.

(a) MOVE.L #5,$1001

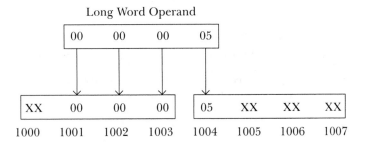

The instruction MOVE.L #5,$1001 transfers the long word in two data bus cycles.

(b) MOVE.W #5,$1003

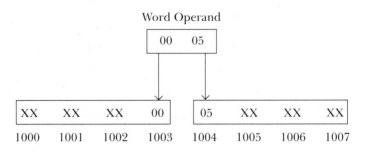

The 16-bit data transferred requires two data bus cycles.

Dynamic Bus Sizing

The MC68020/30/40 processors handle data transfers to or from 8-, 16-, or 32-bit ports. During a bus transfer cycle, the device signals how many bits it is capable of transferring in one operation. The device's capacity is known as its **port size**. When the processor is executing an instruction that requires a read of long-word data, it attempts to transfer 32 bits during the first bus cycle. If the device port size is 32 bits, the processes latches the data, and the transfer is complete. If the device port size is 16 bits, another bus cycle is run. In the case of an 8-bit device, three more bus cycles are necessary.

EXERCISES

1. Differentiate between RAM and ROM. What happens to a program in memory when the CPU power is lost? Why do vendors use ROM to hold basic system software programs?

2. A system has 256K of ROM beginning at address $80000.
   (a) Give the address range of the ROM.
   (b) Which of the following instructions would cause a run-time error? Explain.
      i. MOVE #20,$83200
      ii. MOVE $83200,D0

3. Research the following questions in a computer organization book.
   (a) How are EPROMs programmed?
   (b) How are EPROMs erased?
   (c) What are EEPROMs? What is the danger of using EEPROMs in place of EPROMs?

4. What is the meaning of each of the following system registers?
   (a) Program counter   (b) Status register   (c) Memory address register

5. Suppose a 68000-based system has a CPU clock rate of 25 MHz and an instruction takes eight clock cycles. How many microseconds does it take to execute the instruction?

6. Suppose a machine instruction of the form JMP ADDRESS causes a transfer to the instruction at ADDRESS. How do you suppose the CPU will implement this instruction?

7. The Macintosh and IBM PC (Personal Computer) systems use different bus architectures. Identify the name of a bus running on a Macintosh system and the name of a bus running on a PC system.

8. A byte-addressable system has an 18-bit address bus. What is its maximum memory capacity? What is the range of addressable bytes?

9. A byte-addressable computer system contains 512K of memory. What is the highest addressable byte of memory? If 128K of memory is added, what is the highest addressable byte?

10. The following word contents are found in consecutive memory locations:

Address	Contents
00101A	F0CE
00101C	3BAB
	07FC
	B760
	2FB3

    (a) Fill in the missing addresses.
    (b) What is the value of the long word at address $00101E?
    (c) What are the byte contents in byte $001021?
    (d) In which byte addresses can the hex digit B be found?
    (e) What are the contents of the MSB of the word at address $00101E?
    (f) List all long words that contain the hex digit 0.

11. The smallest unit the XYZ-784 CPU is capable of addressing is a byte, and it can deal directly with integers of 24 bits. Furthermore, it has a 20-bit address bus. Answer the following questions about the XYZ-784:
    (a) Classify the XYZ-784 by its type of addressing.
    (b) What is the data bus width? Classify the XYZ-784 according to its word length.
    (c) Propose a format for the storage of words and long words on the XYZ-784.
    (d) Specify the memory address range of the XYZ-784.
    (e) In kilobytes or megabytes, specify the maximum addressable memory for the XYZ-784.

12. What is the capacity of a hard disk system with 10 surfaces, 200 tracks, 9 sectors per track, and 1024 bytes per sector?

13. Investigate the 8-millimeter high-capacity tape drive that uses VCR technology. What is the primary purpose of such a drive?

14. Distinguish EGA, VGA, and Super-VGA graphics for personal computers. A Macintosh system uses bit-mapped graphics. What does this mean?

15. What is a Postscript laser printer?

16. Starting at address $1000, memory contains the following sequence of 16-bit decimal values:

$$10 \quad 221 \quad -7 \quad -18 \quad 12$$

   (a) Draw a picture of these five words, with the contents given in hex.
   (b) What is the LSB of the word at address $1004?
   (c) What are the contents of byte $1007?

17. What is the definition of the least significant word and the most significant word when dealing with a long word? Show how the integer 223 is stored in a long word.

18. On an Intel processor, the LSB of a 16-bit number is stored first followed by the MSB of the number.

LSB	MSB

Intel 16-Bit Word

For example, the number $4076 is stored as 76 40.
   (a) What is the Intel data storage of the decimal number 1024?
   (b) What is the Intel data storage of the binary number %100111010110?
   (c) The data $9C 03 is stored in consecutive bytes of memory. What is the corresponding 16-bit decimal value?

19. Data register D0 contains the 32-bit value $207B6AFA. Give the hex value for each of the following:
   (a) (D0.W)   (b) (D0.L)   (c) (D0.B)
   (d) LSB of D0   (e) MSW of D0   (d) LSW of D0

20. Distinguish uses for an address register and a data register.

21. In memory, the following data is stored in consecutive locations.

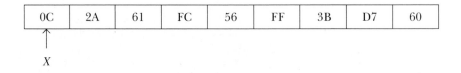

0C	2A	61	FC	56	FF	3B	D7	60

X

Assume that address register A0 is assigned the value x.
   (a) What is the 16-bit value at location (A0) + 6?
   (b) What is the 32-bit value at location (A0) + 2?
   (c) What are the offsets relative to (A0) for all words containing the hex digit F?

22. Give the machine code for each of the following MC68000 instructions:
    (a) ADDI   #30,$002000   (b) SUB D0,$002050
    (c) MOVE $003050,D0   (d) ADDI #$1000,D0

23. Give the SMC68000 assembly language instruction for the corresponding machine code.
    (a) D079   0001   0500
    (b) 0679   0032   0002   0000

24. Write the following code segment in machine language. Label each instruction with its address. The load address is to be $1000.

MOVE	$000500,D0
ADDI	#50,D0
SUB	$000502,D0
SUBI	#101,$000504

25. Decode the following machine language segment. What is the effect of the program?

Address	Instruction		
000200	3039	0000	0500
000206	9079	0000	0502
00020C	D079	0000	0504
000212	D079	0000	0506
000218	4E42		
00021E	4E40		

    .   .
    .   .
    .   .

000500	000A
000502	0007
000504	0010
000506	0025

26. Decode the following machine code into a sequence of assembly language instructions:

000500	33FC	FFF9	0000	0536
000508	3039	0000	0536	
00050E	D079	0000	0536	
000514	33C0	0000	0538	
00051A	3039	0000	0534	
000520	D079	0000	0538	
000526	33C0	0000	053A	
00052C	0679	0003	0000	053A
000534	4E40			
000536	I			
000538	J			
00053A	K			

27. Enter SMC68000 assembly language instructions for each of the following statements. Then convert the assembly language to machine code, assuming that the load address is $500.

    Statement 1: Input a number N from the keyboard.
    Statement 2: Store the number in memory location $950.
    Statement 3: Load the value $FFFF in data register D0.
    Statement 4: Subtract the number N from $FFFF in D0.
    Statement 5: Add 1 to the result in D0.
    Statement 6: Output the value in D0 to the screen.
    Statement 7: Stop program execution.

    What is the relationship between the input value N and the output value in statement 6?

28. Write the machine language code in Exercise 27 as a Pascal code segment.

29. How many read/write memory cycles are needed to execute each of the following instructions?
    (a) MOVE #1,D0   (b) MOVE   D0,$008000
    (c) ADDI #5,$002210   (d) SUB $002000,D0
    (e) MOVE $006008,D0   (f) MOVE   #5,$3300

30. Assume the existence of a memory-to-memory access instruction

    MOVE ADDRESS1,ADDRESS2

    that copies the word contents of the first address to that of the second address. Each address is a 32-bit long word. Compute the number of read and write cycles necessary to execute the specific instruction.

    MOVE.W $001000,$002000

31. If the following instruction is located at address $002000, trace the value of the PC for each stage of the instruction fetch cycle.

    SUBI.W #7,D0

32. The following instruction sequence begins at location $001000:

    33C0 0000 0500 0679 0005 0001 3500

    Disassemble the machine code and trace the value of the PC as the instructions are fetched and then executed.

33. Assume an MC68000-based system has 32K of memory. Which of the following instructions will execute without error?
    (a) 303C 8000   (b) 3039 0000 8000

34. An MC68000-based system has 48K of memory.
    (a) What is its address range? Give your answer in hex.
    (b) Indicate which of the following instructions will execute without error:
        (i) MOVE #$C000,D0   (ii) ADD $00BFFE,D0
        (iii) SUB $00C000,D0   (iv) MOVE D0,$00C004

35. State what value is in location $001004 when the following program executes to the point marked by a star (*).

Address	Instruction		
000500	3039	0000	1000
000506	D079	0000	0518
00050C	9079	0000	1002
000512	33C0	0000	0518
000518	01C2	0000	1004
→	*		
.	.		
.	.		
.	.		
001000	3200		
001002	0002		
001004	0000		

36. Convert the following machine code sequence to assembly language instructions. After executing the code, determine the contents at locations $00020A, $00020C, and register D0.

00010A	303C	000A		
00010E	33C0	0000	020A	
000114	0679	00C3	0000	020C
00011C	9079	0000	020C	
000122	0679	0AF3.	0000	020A
00012A	0640	00F8		
.	.			
.	.			
.	.			
00020A	0036			
00020C	03FA			

Initially, (D0.L) = 0000 003B.

37. Decode the following code segment and specify what will happen when it is executed. This is an example of "self-modifying" code.

Address	Contents			
000500	3039	0000	0770	
000506	D079	0000	0772	
00050C	33C0	0000	0512	
000512	0000	1000	0000	0774
000770	0600			
000772	0079			
000774	0007			

CHAPTER 4

ASSEMBLY LANGUAGE PROGRAMMING

Assembly language programming provides a method of creating instructions that are the symbolic equivalent of machine code. The syntax of each instruction is structured to allow direct translation to machine code. An assembler also permits the use of directives that support program design and documentation and the linking and loading of code.

This chapter begins a formal study of MC68000 assembly language programming. It introduces the overall program structure, specification of variables and data types, and syntax rules for program statements. Generally, the development follows the standards detailed in the *M68000 Family Resident Structured Assembler Reference Manual.* The opcode mnemonics, register names, and directives are fairly standard. Assemblers, however, permit considerable variation in symbol names (such as uppercase and lowercase letters), operand expressions, delimiters, and so forth. These variations are listed in your assembler's reference manual. This text notes some of the typical variations.

Running an assembly language program requires a program execution cycle. First, a source program is entered and edited and then read by a resident assembler. The assembler assigns values to the user-defined addresses and translates statements into machine code. A **linker** is then called to merge the code generated by the assembler with external code referenced by the program. Such external code normally resides in code libraries. When a request is made to run the program, a **loader** is called to copy the code into memory at a given starting address and to begin execution. Figure 4.1 illustrates the program execution cycle.

FIGURE 4.1   Overall Assembly Process

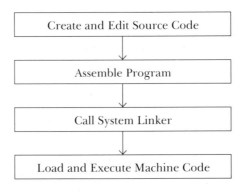

4.1 | MC68000 ASSEMBLY LANGUAGE PROGRAM STRUCTURE

Each assembly language assumes a syntax specification and a run-time environment. This section presents an overview of the rules of syntax for a standard MC68000 assembler and includes many of the language's major components. Specific rules of syntax are given later in the section. The run-time environment is discussed in the next section.

Sample MC68000 Program

The following sample program highlights the syntax of MC68000 assembly language code. An equivalent Pascal program presents variable declarations, assignment statements, and calculations. On first reading, you may not understand many of the details in the assembly language code. However, this program serves as an introduction to the general structure of an assembly language program and some of the key rules of syntax.

Note: Remember that, in this text, complete assembly language programs are presented in lowercase letters, whereas program fragments are given in uppercase letters.

PROGRAM 4.1

Sample Program

Pascal Code

```
program example (output);
var
    i,j,k : integer;
begin
    i := 75;
    j := 4;
    k := i, + j - 6;
```

```
writeln (k)
end.
```

MC68000 Code The equivalent assembly language code includes directives, comments, and symbolic addresses. Line numbers are added for reference.

```
(1)              xref        decout, newline, stop
(2)   ; program instruction section
(3)   start:     move.w      i,d0
(4)              add.w       j,d0
(5)              subi.w      #6,d0
(6)              move.w      d0,k          ;   (d0) = i + j - 6
(7)              jsr         decout
(8)              jsr         newline
(9)              jsr         stop

(10)  ; data declaration section
(11)             data
(12)  i:         dc.w        75
(13)  j:         dc.w        4
(14)  k:         ds.w        1
(15)
(16)             end
```

Key concepts are identified in each line.

1. Line (1) introduces the directive XREF. A **directive** is an instruction that tells the assembler to perform a support function such as reserving memory. The directive **XREF** permits access to the predefined executable code segments named DECOUT, NEWLINE, and STOP residing outside of the existing program. These code segments are called **external routines** and will be merged into this program's assembled code by a linker.

2. Line (2) is a full-line **comment**, whereas line (6) contains a short in-line comment describing the action of the corresponding instruction. Comments are used extensively in an assembly language program to provide documentation. In this text, they are set off by a semi-colon (;).

3. Line (3) begins with the label START. A **label** is a symbolic name for a memory address. In this case, START has a value equal to the load address of the code. A good practice is to label the first instruction of a program. The MOVE instruction contains the suffix ".W". Many Motorola instructions can operate on data of word (.W), long-word (.L), and byte (.B) sizes. In this case, the instruction moves the word (16 bits) at address I to data register D0.

4. Lines (3), (4), and (6) use symbolic addresses I, J, and K. The data size and initial values for I and J are given in the data section at lines (12) and (13). Unlike assembly language, Pascal does not allow compile-time initialization of variables, so a run-time assignment must be done.

5. Line (7) to (9) make calls to the external routines DECOUT, NEWLINE, and STOP. The routine DECOUT outputs (D0.W) in decimal, routine NEWLINE moves the cursor to the next line on the screen, and routine STOP causes an exit from the program and return to the operating system. Each procedure is called with the MC68000 JSR ("Jump to Subroutine") instruction. Each subroutine contains a return that causes the next statement after the JSR to execute.

6. Line (11) contains the DATA directive. It specifies that the lines that follow contain program data definitions.

7. Lines (12) to (14) allocate actual data space for the symbolic addresses I, J, and K that are given as labels. The directive DC.W 75 ("Define Constant") tells the assembler to initialize the word with decimal value 75. The directive DS.W 1 ("Define Storage") tells the assembler to reserve one word of uninitialized data storage.

8. Line (16) is the END directive. It signals the assembler to stop assembling instructions and interpreting directives. It must be the last statement of each MC68000 assembly language program.

MC68000 Assembly Language

Syntax

A typical assembly language program begins with directives, is followed by assembly language instructions and data declarations, and terminates with the END directive.

```
Directives
    XREF directive . . .
Assembly Language Instructions . . .
Data Section
    DATA directive
    "Define Constant" directives . . .
    "Define STORAGE" directives . . .
End Directive
```

All assemblers are line oriented; hence program syntax is defined for a line. The MC68000 assembler partitions a line into four distinct fields. In application, one or more of the fields may be empty. The following chart illustrates the fields for the instruction

```
SETUP:    MOVE.W    D0,D2    ; SET LSW OF D2
```

Label	Opcode Mnemonic	Operand(s)	Comment
SETUP:	MOVE.W	D0,D2	; SET LSW OF D2

Label Field

A label is a symbolic name for a memory address. A label field may be defined only once in the program, but it may be referenced more than once in statements and data declarations.

1. Label names begin with a letter (A–Z or a-z) and may be followed by letters, digits (0–9), or special symbols such as a period, dollar sign, hyphen, or underscore. This text uses the underscore (_) in a label name. Some assemblers permit only uppercase or lowercase letters, whereas others will internally convert letters to one of the cases and thus will not distinguish uppercase and lowercase letters.

2. With most assemblers, a label definition starts in any column and terminates with a colon. This is the convention used throughout the text. Motorola has an extended definition of labels, allowing them to start in column 1 and be terminated by a blank character.

EXAMPLE 4.1

Valid Labels
```
PRINT:    JSR    DECOUT    ; PRINT IS TERMINATED BY A COLON
COL_1     DC.W   35        ; COL_1 IS MOTOROLA STANDARD
```

Invalid Labels
```
GO OUT    ADD.W  D0,D1     ; BLANK IN THE LABEL NAME.
VALUE:    DC.W   35

VALUE:    DS.W   1         ; LABEL IS DEFINED TWICE
```

Opcode Field

The **opcode field** contains symbolic names, called mnemonics, for machine instructions and assembler directives. The MC68000 assembler supports free-format instruction input.

1. If a label definition is present, the opcode or directive can appear anywhere on the line after the label.

2. If the assembler adheres to the Motorola standard, an opcode or directive cannot begin in column 1.

EXAMPLE 4.2

```
        MOVE.W    D0,I       ; MOVE.W IS THE OPCODE
    I:  DS.W       4         ; DS DIRECTIVE IN OPCODE FIELD.
```

Operand Field

The operand field specifies the source and destination for the read and write cycles of the instruction. MC68000 instructions have zero, one, or two operands.

1. At least one blank character must separate an operand from its opcode field. When two operands are present, they must be separated by commas. Some assemblers will not allow extra spaces to separate the operands.

2. MC68000 assemblers have a variety of syntax for specifying constant data in the different number systems. Constant values are decimal by default. The Motorola standard defines the following prefixes to specify a number in the respective bases.

   Hex $ Binary %   Octal @

   Note: Some assemblers use suffixes such as H in 2000H or prefixes such as 0x to indicate hex.

3. Some assemblers permit arithmetic operations and expression evaluation within operands. Operations are often limited to addition and subtraction, although multiplication and integer division may be included. The "+", "−", and "*" operations are used in this text.

EXAMPLE 4.3

The following list shows equivalent constants in the different number systems. Leading zeros may be included in the constants.

Decimal	Binary	Octal	Hex
62	%00111110	@76	$003E
22	%10110	@26	$16

EXAMPLE 4.4

The 16-bit contents of address I + 4 is moved to (D0.W).

```
    MOVE.W    I+4,D0
```

Comment Field

The **comment field** is the last field on a line, and it provides space for program documentation. The assembler ignores the comments, but it is included in any listing of the source program. The following is standard Motorola assembler syntax.

1. The comment is separated from the previous field (usually an operand) by one or more spaces and continues to the end of the line.

2. A comment cannot occur on a line containing only a label field because the first word of the comment will be interpreted as an opcode.

3. An entire line can be treated as a comment, provided that an asterisk (*) appears in column 1. This special character prevents the first word from being treated as a label.

EXAMPLE 4.5

Standard Motorola
Comment Syntax

```
          ADD.WI,D0                THIS IS A COMMENT
START:     THIS IS AN INVALID COMMENT—NO OPCODE IS PRESENT
*  THIS WHOLE LINE IS A COMMENT.
          MOVE.W D0,I + 2         THE +2 IS A POSSIBLE ERROR
```

The instruction in the last line might not be handled as intended by a standard Motorola assembler. The space after the label "I" is a delimiter and the " +2" becomes part of a comment.

To safeguard against inadvertently creating comments, many assemblers require that a comment be accompanied by a special character. This text adopts this convention and requires that a comment begin with a semicolon. The comment continues to the end of the line.

 Several assembly systems on the Macintosh, including the Macintosh Programmer's Workshop (MPW) and the Macintosh Assembly System (MAS), have adopted the use of the semicolon comment indicator.

EXAMPLE 4.6

Comment with
Semicolon

```
          ADD.W I,D0         ; THIS IS A COMMENT·
START:  ; THIS IS A VALID COMMENT
        ; THIS WHOLE LINE IS A COMMENT.
          MOVE.W D0,I +2    ; THE +2 PRESENTS NO PROBLEM
```

Storage Allocation Directives

The MC68000 assembler provides a variety of storage allocation directives to reserve space in memory for program data. In some systems, instructions and data reside in separate segments. The **DATA directive** specifies entrance into the data segment of the program. The data storage directives occur within this segment of the program.

FIGURE 4.2   Contiguous Code and Data Space

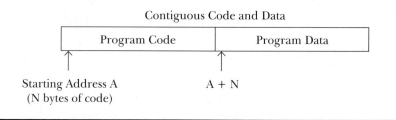

DATA Directive

Syntax   DATA

Description   The DATA directive indicates that the statements that follow allocate data for the program.

Note   Some assemblers include both DATA and CODE directives. This allows the programmer to interlace data and program statements. During code generation, the assembler writes code to the segment that was last specified by a DATA or CODE directive.

In some systems, data is placed directly after the last instruction word, as indicated in Figure 4.2.

In other systems, such as the Macintosh, data is placed in a data segment separate from the program code (see Figure 4.3). On larger systems with a memory management unit (MMU), the operating system separates instruction and data space. Memory containing the instruction code is write protected, whereas the data space is read/write.

"Define Constant" (DC) Directive

Syntax   DC.⟨size⟩   ⟨constants⟩

FIGURE 4.3   Separate Code and Data Space

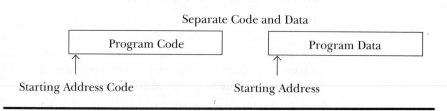

Description This directive both allocates and initializes data space with constant value(s). The data is one or more operands separated by commas. The constants can be numbers or characters enclosed in single quotation marks and the size parameter may be "B" (byte), "W" (word), or "L" (long word).

EXAMPLE 4.7

(a) I: DC.W 15,35
When the program loads, the 16-bit values $000F and $0023 are loaded into consecutive memory locations beginning at address I.

000F	0023
I	I + 2

(b) LIST: DC.L $F67CA
The constant $F67CA is stored as the long word $000F67CA at address LIST.

(c) MSG: DC.B 'THIS IS A STRING', 10
The string and the byte 10 (ASCII code for LINEFEED) are stored in 17 bytes beginning at location MSG. The DC directive allows the mix of character and numeric data.

"Define Storage" (DS) Directive

Syntax DS.⟨size⟩ ⟨count⟩

Description This directive only reserves memory locations and does not initialize the contents. The count specifies the number of reserved memory locations, and size parameters "B", "W", and "L" apply.

EXAMPLE 4.8

(a) I: DS.W 4
Allocates four words of memory beginning at address I.

(b) J: DS.L 3
        DC.W 10
Allocates three consecutive long words (12 bytes) of uninitialized memory beginning at address J. Then it loads the value 10 ($000A) in address J + 12.

Note Do not confuse "DS.W 10" with "DC.W 10". The first directive allocates ten words of memory, whereas the second directive allocates only one word of memory with initial value $000A.

"Define Constant Block" (DCB) Directive

Syntax   DCB.⟨size⟩   ⟨count⟩,⟨value⟩

Description   This directive causes the assembler to reserve a block of initialized memory, with the size of each element of the block determined by the parameter ⟨size⟩. The total number of items in the block is given by the parameter ⟨count⟩, and each data item is initialized to ⟨value⟩.

EXAMPLE 4.9

LIST: DCB.W   4, − 1

The four words beginning at address LIST are initialized to $-1 = \$FFFF$. The result is equivalent to the data constant directive

LIST: DC.W − 1, − 1, − 1, − 1

Handling Character Data

The MC68000 uses the ".B" (byte) form of an instruction to process character data. The 8-bit operations are used to deal with ASCII character codes. Use a character in an instruction by enclosing it in single quotation marks. For the DC.B directive, initialize a string by enclosing it in single quotes.

MOVE.B #'A',D0 ; STORES CHAR A (ASCII $41) IN (D0.B)

Before	After
8C07 2A00	8C07 2A41
D0	D0

ADDI.B #$20,CHAR ; CONVERTS UPPER TO LOWERCASE

Before	After
B (ASCII $42)	b (ASCII $62)
Char	Char

EXAMPLE 4.10

(a) The following are equivalent instructions:

MOVE.B #'e',D0
MOVE.B #$65,D0
MOVE.B #%01100101,D0

(b) The DC directive defines a string at location MSG.

MSG: DC.B 'INSERTING ASCII CODES INTO MEMORY'

(c) The 8-bit value 10 appends the linefeed character to the string. Note that 10 is a decimal. It is an example of the DC directive that mixes character and numeric data.

HEADER: DC.B 'HERE COMES LINEFEED', 10

If an odd number of characters are allocated with a DATA directive (DC.B or DS.B), the subsequent label has an odd address. Word or long-word instructions that access this address cause an address error, and the program terminates. MC68000 assemblers permit using the DS directive with an argument of 0 to set the location counter to an even address.

Even-Boundary Directive

Syntax   DS.W 0

Description   During the assembly process, the directive sets the value of the next label to an even-numbered address.

$$\text{Location Counter} = \text{Location Counter} \qquad \text{(if even)}$$
$$= \text{Location Counter} + 1 \quad \text{(if odd)}$$

Note Most assemblers provide a directive EVEN that is equivalent to DS.W 0. This text uses the EVEN directive in examples and programs.

EXAMPLE 4.11

Data Directives and Character Handling

(a) Assume that STR is label $002000.

```
STR:      DC.B     'ODD NUMBERS'
          EVEN     ; SETS LIST TO EVEN ADDRESS
LIST:     DS.W     10
```

The character string STR contains 11 characters. Without the use of the EVEN directive, label LIST has value $00200B, and any word or long-word access would result in an address error. The MC68020/30/40 processors would permit the access, but good programming style dictates the use of the EVEN directive when word and character data are intermixed.

(b) The following character strings are equivalent. Use 8-bit numbers and characters when defining strings.

```
DC.B   71,78,78,68      ; 'GOOD' IN ITS ASCII CODE
DC.B   'GOOD'           ; EQUIVALENT STRING
```

(c) DC.B 28,245 ; 245 IS A BYTE; NOT A PRINTABLE CHARACTER

4.2 | THE ASSEMBLING PROCESS

The preceding section introduced the structure of an assembly language program. Now we consider the process of assembling the source and loading the code file. The sample program from Section 4.1 is given in Table 4.1, along with a machine code listing. This section details the steps used by the assembler to produce the machine code.

The assembler program normally executes in a two-pass process. Pass 1 reads through the entire source program and computes the value (memory address) of each label. This step is required because, in many cases, the labels are referenced before they are defined in the program. Pass 2 rereads the program, and converts each instruction to machine code, but now with specific addresses associated with the labels. Consider the sample program.

Pass 1

The assembler assumes that the program will be loaded at address $000000. The **location counter**, a variable in the assembler program, is initialized to 0. The assembler reads each instruction and adds the length of the instruction to the location counter. The length is the number of bytes in the instruction machine code, including the opcode word and any extension words. The location counter dynamically computes the cumulative length of the program, and this is the address of the next instruction to be read. When the assembler identifies a label, the current value of the location counter is assigned as the value of the label. The label name and its value are placed in an assembler-maintained data structure called the **symbol table**. This table is used during Pass 2 to look up the value of a label when it is needed in the machine code. Table 4.2 gives the length and corresponding value of the location counter for each instruction.

The symbol table is dynamically created during Pass 1. Typically, the table contains a symbol field, a type field, and a value field. The type field

TABLE 4.1   Assembly Language and Machine Code

SOURCE LINE	RELATIVE ADDRESS	MACHINE CODE	LABEL	OPERATION	OPERANDS
1	000000			xref	decout, newline, stop
2	000000			; program instruction section	
3	000000	3039	start:	move.w	i,d0
		0000			
		0028			
4	000006	D079		add.w	j,d0
		0000			
		002A			
5	00000C	0440		subi.w	#6,d0
		0006			
6	000010	33C0		move.w	d0,k
		0000			
		002C			
7	000016	4EB9		jsr	decout
		0000			
		0000			
8	00001C	4EB9		jsr	newline
		0000			
		0000			
9	000022	4EB9		jsr	stop
		0000			
		0000			
10	000028			; data declaration section	
11	000028			data	
12	000028	004B	i:	dc.w	75
13	00002A	0004	j:	dc.w	4
14	00002C		k:	ds.w	1
15	00002E				
16	00002E			end	

		SYMBOL TABLE			
decout	000000	i	000028	j	00002A
k	00002C	newline	000000	start	000000
stop	000000				

indicates whether the label is defined locally (L) or externally (G = global). In this example, the program's four local labels are placed in the table with the value of the location counter at the time the label is encountered. The external labels DECOUT, NEWLINE, and STOP are put in the table with a value of 0 (see Table 4.3).

TABLE 4.2   Pass I: Location Counter

	MC68000 INSTRUCTION		LENGTH	LOCATION COUNTER
	xref	decout,newline	0	0 = $0
	xref	stop	0	0 = $0
start:	move.w	i,d0	6	0 = $0
	add.w	j,d0	6	6 = $6
	subi.w	#6,d0	4	12 = $C
	move.w	d0,k	6	16 = $10
	jsr	decout	6	22 = $16
	jsr	newline	6	28 = $1C
	jsr	stop	6	34 = $22
	data		0	40 = $28
i:	dc.w	75	2	40 = $28
j:	dc.w	4	2	42 = $2A
k:	ds.w	1	2	44 = $2C
	end		0	46 = $2E

Pass 2

Having constructed the symbol table in Pass 1, the assembler now rereads the program and outputs code for each statement, using the symbol table to look up the value of each label. For instance, when the assembler encounters the statement "ADD.W J,D0", it reads the opcode word ($D079) from an instruction code table while it reads the extension words for address J ($0000 002A) directly from the symbol table.

> Instruction: ADD.W   J,D0
> Machine code: D079   0000   0024

Most assemblers can produce a combined listing of the source program, the machine code, and the symbol table if you request it. Such a listing is called a **listing file.** Table 4.1 is an example of a listing file.

It is possible to construct an assembler using only one pass over the source text. Such a program is said to be a **one-pass assembler**. A symbol

TABLE 4.3   Pass I: Symbol Table

LABEL	TYPE	VALUE	LABEL	TYPE	VALUE
DECOUT	G	000000	I	L	000028
NEWLINE	G	000000	J	L	00002A
STOP	G	000000	K	L	00002C
START	L	000000			

table is maintained as before, but each entry of the table contains a pointer to a "fixup" list. This list contains the locations within the code of all undefined references to the symbol. When the symbol is defined as a label, the assembler scans the list and places the value of the symbol within the code at all the places where it was previously referenced. One-pass assemblers are more difficult to construct.

4.3 | THE RUN-TIME ENVIRONMENT

After assembling the source code, a linker is called to generate an **executable code file** in which all references to external routines are resolved. The user enters a "RUN" command to initiate program execution under the control of the operating system. The operating system begins execution by first calling a loader routine to place the program in memory and then providing input and output facilities.

Some operating systems provide multiprogramming capability that permits more than one process to share the CPU. Even systems designed for a single user can have multiprogramming capability by specifying the program as the **foreground task**. Other programs in the system are **background tasks**. The CPU gives priority status to the foreground task but shares execution cycles with background tasks when the primary task does not need system resources. On the Macintosh, the Multifinder interface is an example of a foreground/background multiprogramming system.

Operating systems designed to be accessed by more than one user are said to be **multiuser systems**. The UNIX operating system is a primary example of such a system. User access to the CPU is divided into quantums of time known as **time slices**. After completing several execution cycles, the system interrupts the program using a hardware-supplied pulse called the **timer interrupt**. It then suspends operation of the current program and begins execution of a previously suspended program. Figure 4.4 illustrates memory containing several programs. A timer interrupt causes a switch from one program to another.

With time, more programs request access to memory than can be accommodated, and all or portions of programs must be copied to disk to make room in memory. When code or data belonging to a program is swapped back into memory, it generally must occupy a new location, because the original memory is occupied. The operating system or memory management hardware must permit the code to continue execution at different memory addresses. Addresses in the machine code must be relocated to account for the new memory locations. Originally, the assembler specifies the addresses that the loader must modify when the code is placed in memory.

FIGURE 4.4 Program Time Sharing

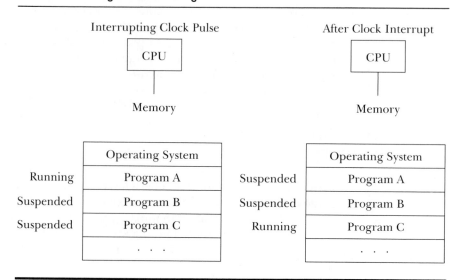

PROGRAM 4.2

Preloaded
Machine Code

The following assembly language program is given with a listing file. The load address is assumed to be $000000.

Address	Code		Source Program	
000000		XREF	STOP	
000000	33FC 0006 0000 0016	START:	MOVE.W	#6, I
000008	33FC 0005 0000 0018		MOVE.W	#5, J
000010	4EB9 0000 0000		JSR	STOP
			DATA	
000016		I:	DS.W	1
000018		J:	DS.W	1
00001A			END	

The subroutine STOP is contained in an external code file that must be appended to the main program by a linker. The linker also resolves the reference to STOP by assigning its correct address in the extension words at location $000012. We assume that the linker appends the external routines to the end of the main code file. In this case, the external STOP routine has address 00001A in the linked code file.

The operating system loads the program into memory at a load address. Assume that the address is $000500. The instruction "MOVE.W #6,I" contains a reference to an address I, which is $000016 in the preloaded code file. Similarly, address J is $000018. The addresses I and J must change to $000516 and $000518 for the program to execute correctly.

Only the addresses I and J are adjusted to compensate for the change in load address. The adjustment value, $500, is called the **relocation constant**. It is the value of the new load address. When a program is relocated, some addresses in the code file (**relocatable addresses**) are altered by adding the relocation constant. All other quantities in the program are called **absolute**. During the assembling process, the list of relocatable addresses is identified and stored in a table called the **relocation map**. This map can be used during program relocation and is also used by a linker when combining the assembled code with code from other external modules. In Program 4.3, the relocatable addresses are marked with asterisks.

	Address	Code		Source Program	
PROGRAM 4.3					
Loaded Machine Code	000500			XREF	STOP
	000500	33FC 0006 0000 0516	START:	MOVE.W	#6,I
	000508	33FC 0005 0000 0518		MOVE.W	#5,J
	000510	4EB9 0000 051A		JSR	STOP
	000516		I:	DS.W	1
	000518		J:	DS.W	1
	00051A			END	

EXAMPLE 4.12

In Program 4.2, the machine code for instruction "MOVE.W #6,I" contains both relocatable and absolute values. The address I is a relocatable value. However, the opcode word ($33FC) and the extension word ($0006) for the constant #6 are absolute values. When you load the program into memory, the address of I becomes

$$000016 + 500 = 000516$$

Many systems are equipped with a **memory management unit (MMU)**, which is a hardware device to perform address translation and memory protection. The MMU resides between the CPU and the bus, intercepting addresses and translating them to their physical address in memory. Figure 4.5 diagrams the action of an MMU. In a multiuser system, the MMU prevents one program from modifying memory belonging to another program (memory protection) by generating a bus error signal if such an attempt occurs. If an MMU is present, software relocation is not done. Chapter 15 discusses an MMU in detail.

 Another approach to relocation is used on the Macintosh. Instruction code is generated relative to the program counter, so that all labels have an address relative to the current program counter. Data values are defined relative to the address register A5. Technically, program counter and base-relative addressing is used. When a program is loaded into memory, the value of A5 is set, and individual addresses are not relocated because they are a fixed offset from the PC or A5. Base-relative code and its use on the Macintosh are covered in Chapter 6.

|4.4| INTRODUCTION TO ADDRESSING MODES

This section covers the basic MC68000 assembly language addressing modes. Chapter 3 used a limited set of the modes with the MOVE, ADD, SUB, and TRAP instructions. Their formal definition is included here along with address register modes.

On the MC68000, an instruction operand is specified by using one of 12 addressing modes. An **addressing mode** tells the CPU how to locate the data or address needed by the instruction. If data is found in memory, the associated address is called the **effective address** (⟨ea⟩) of the operand. For a register operand, the actual register is the effective address. Given the

FIGURE 4.5   Address Translation by MMU

addressing mode, the CPU computes the effective address of the operand using extension words if necessary. On the MC68020/30/40 processers, 18 addressing modes are available.

Absolute and Immediate Addressing Modes

In Chapter 3, operands for the MOVE, ADD, SUB, and TRAP instructions employed constant data and specific memory addresses. These are examples of absolute and immediate addressing modes.

Absolute Long Mode

Syntax ⟨address⟩

Description The operand is a 32-bit unsigned number that represents the effective address of the operand. The address is a constant, a label, or an expression. This mode requires two extension words containing the address as a long word.

EXAMPLE 4.13

(a) MOVE.W   I, D0
The source operand I is in absolute long addressing mode. The label I is the address of the operand and is stored as a 32-bit value in two extension words. The 16-bit contents at location I are assigned to (D0.W).

(b) ADD.W $500, D0
The source is in absolute long addressing mode with effective address $000500. The two extension words are $0000 and $0500.

(c) MOVE.W   D0, I-4
The 32-bit value of the expression I-4 is the effective address of the destination operand.

Absolute Short Mode

Syntax ⟨address⟩.W

Description The memory address is accessed as a 16-bit word and then is sign-extended to 24 bits to give the effective address of the operand. The address is stored in a single extension word.

EXAMPLE 4.14

(a) MOVE.W $1000.W, D0
The source operand is in absolute short addressing mode. The effective address is $001000. A single extension word $1000 is located after the opcode word in the instruction.

(b) ADD.L   I.W, D0
The low-order 16 bits of the symbolic address I form the extension word. For example, if I = $0001A800, the extension word is $A800.

Absolute short mode is available only for addresses in the extreme ends of the memory range. Absolute short addresses in the range $0000–$7FFF correspond to addresses in the first 32K of memory. Absolute short addresses in the range $8000–$FFFF correspond to addresses in the highest 32K of the MC68000 memory range ($FF8000–$FFFFFF). Devices called **I/0 controllers** often have addresses near the high end of memory. An instruction using absolute short mode executes faster because only one data bus cycle is necessary to fetch the address from memory. Figure 4.6 shows the range of accessible MC68000 memory locations.

FIGURE 4.6 Absolute Short Memory Address Range

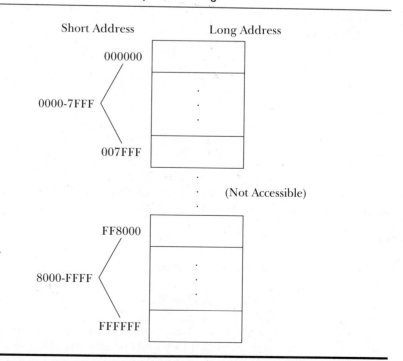

memory. Figure 4.6 shows the range of accessible MC68000 memory locations.

Most non-Macintosh assemblers generate absolute long mode by default for all addresses. Others default to absolute short mode for all addresses in the low-order 32K of memory. You should assemble a short program with a listing file to test your particular assembler. A Macintosh assembler distinguishes between constant and symbolic address. The instruction "MOVE #5, $800" is valid and causes the value 5 to be stored at address $000800. The instruction "MOVE.W D0, A" treats A as an offset to the value in register A5. The address A is not in absolute long or absolute short addressing mode. The situation is developed fully in Chapter 6.

Immediate Mode

Syntax   #N

Description   The operand is a number given in decimal, hex, or any other permitted number system. The mode is restricted to source operands. Word or byte instructions store the number in one extension word, whereas long instructions require two extension words.

EXAMPLE 4.15

(a) MOVE.W   #$452, D0
The constant $0452 is stored as the first extension word after the opcode.

(b) MOVE.L   #$452, D0
The constant $00000452 is stored as two extension words after the opcode.

(c) MOVE.L   #I, D0
Assuming that I is a label, the 32-bit value I is stored in register D0. On the Macintosh, this instruction is invalid because a label is an offset to A5 and is not an actual address.

(d) ADDI.W   #%1011, D0
The immediate data is the binary number 1011_2.

Register Direct Addressing Modes

Both data and address registers are used as operands. The associated addressing modes are referred to as **register direct modes**. Information on the mode and the register is found in the opcode word, and no extension word is required. Many MC68000 instructions require that one or both operands be register direct mode. This restriction will be highlighted as the instructions are introduced.

Data Register Direct Mode

Syntax   D*n* $(0 \leq n \leq 7)$

Description   The operand is a data register. An instruction directly accesses the data in the register, and no extension word is required.

EXAMPLE 4.16

(*a*) ADDI.W   #$6A, D6
The destination operand is data register direct mode. The immediate data $6A is added to (D6.W).

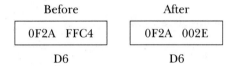

Before	After
0F2A FFC4	0F2A 002E
D6	D6

(*b*) SUB.L   D3, D1
Both operands are data register direct mode. The long word (D3.L) is subtracted from (D1.L).

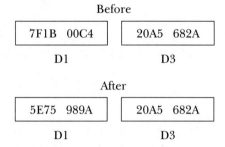

Before

7F1B 00C4	20A5 682A
D1	D3

After

5E75 989A	20A5 682A
D1	D3

Address Register Direct Mode

Syntax   A*n* $(0 \leq n \leq 7)$

Description   The operand is an address register. An instruction directly accesses the contents of the register, and no extension word is required. The content of an address register is the address of a memory location. The address register can be viewed as a pointer to a memory location.

EXAMPLE 4.17

(*a*) MOVE.L   A3, D5
The source operand is address register direct mode. The 32-bit contents of A3 are stored in data register D5.

Before		After	
072A 7B02	0001 0000	0001 0000	0001 0000
D5	A3	D5	A3

In Chapter 3, the SMC68000 instructions MOVE, ADD, ADDI, SUB, and SUBI were defined and used. In fact, these instructions are subsets of corresponding instructions on the real MC68000 and have been used throughout this chapter. Now that some addressing modes have been introduced, a formal presentation of the instructions is appropriate.

INSTRUCTION

MOVE
(Move)

Syntax   MOVE.⟨size⟩   ⟨ea⟩,⟨ea⟩

Action   The contents of the source operand are copied to the destination location.

Notes

1. All addressing modes on the MC68000 are permitted for the source operand.

2. The destination cannot be an address register, an immediate operand, or any of the PC-relative modes presented in Chapter 6. A special version of the instruction permits the user to write data into an address register.

3. The size parameter may be "B", "W", or "L".

INSTRUCTION

ADD/SUB
(Add/Subtract)

Syntax   ADD.⟨size⟩   ⟨ea⟩,D*n*   SUB.⟨size⟩   ⟨ea⟩,D*n*
            ADD.⟨size⟩   D*n*,⟨ea⟩   SUB.⟨size⟩   D*n*,⟨ea⟩
            ADDI.⟨size⟩   #N,⟨ea⟩   SUBI.⟨size⟩   #N,⟨ea⟩

Action   Each instruction executes the corresponding arithmetic operation for fixed-length binary numbers of the given size.

Notes

1. ADD and SUB require that either the source or destination operands be a data register.

2. The size parameter may be "B", "W", or "L".

3. The destination may not be an address register. Address register versions of these instructions exist for this purpose.

Address Register Instructions

Only a restricted set of instructions permits an address register destination operand. The instructions allow the user to write data into an address register.

INSTRUCTION

MOVEA
(Move Address)

Syntax   MOVEA.⟨size⟩   ⟨ea⟩,An

Action   The contents of the source operand are stored in the address register A*n*. If word data is specified, it is sign-extended before being placed in the register.

Notes

1. The destination operand must be an address register.

2. All addressing modes are permitted for the source operand.

3. The size parameter is restricted to word or long word.

EXAMPLE 4.18

(a) MOVEA.L   #STRING, A0
    The label STRING is a 32-bit number. It is stored in A0, which is initialized to point at memory address STRING. Assume a data declaration of STRING: DC.W 10, and that STRING is $00002000.

$000A	
$2000	$2002

$0000 2000
A0

(b) MOVEA.L $2000, A3
    The contents of the long word at address $002000 are stored in register A3.

$0000	$5200
$2000	$2002

$0000 5200
A3

Store the contents in A3

(c) MOVEA.W   #ALPHA, A2
    Assume that ALPHA is $8000. The word data is sign-extended to $FFFF8000 and stored in A2.

INSTRUCTION

ADDA/SUBA
Add/Subtract
Address

Syntax   ADDA.⟨size⟩   ⟨ea⟩,A*n*
           SUBA.⟨size⟩   ⟨ea⟩,A*n*

Action   The contents of the source operand are added to (or subtracted from) the contents of the address register. If word data is specified, the 16-bit contents from the source operand is first sign-extended and then the operation is performed.

Notes

1. The destination operand must be an address register.

2. Any addressing mode can be used for the source operand.

3. The size parameter is restricted to word or long word.

EXAMPLE 4.19

(a) ADDA.L   #100, A0
     The source operand is immediate mode, and the destination operand is address register direct mode. The resulting value of A0 is

(A0) = (A0) + 00000064

(b) SUBA.W   ALPHA, A1
     The 16-bit contents of ALPHA is first sign-extended to a long word. This value is subtracted from the value in the address register.

(A1) = (A1) − FFFF8C07 = 00011444

	Before	After
8C07	0000 A04B	0001 1444
ALPHA	A1	A1

Warning: This may not have been the intended result. You may have wanted address $00001444. Use .W carefully.

Using the MOVEA instruction is one way to initialize an address register. It sets the address register to the contents of the operand. The MC68000 also provides a "Load Effective Address" instruction, LEA, that sets an address register to the address of the operand. LEA is very useful in dynamic address calculations.

INSTRUCTION

LEA
(Load Effective
Address)

Syntax   LEA ⟨ea⟩, A*n*

Action   The effective address of the source operand is loaded into the specified address register.

Notes

1. The address of the source operand, not the contents of the source operand, is loaded into the register.

2. No size specification is used.

EXAMPLE 4.20

(a) LEA   ALPHA, A2
    Assume that ALPHA is address $000500 with contents $6785. The LEA instruction stores the address $000500 in register A2. This is equivalent to MOVEA.L #ALPHA,A2.

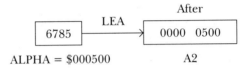

             ALPHA = $000500   A2

(b) LEA   #ALPHA, A3
    This is an invalid instruction. #ALPHA is a constant and does not represent an effective address.

EXAMPLE 4.21

Example 4.15(c) introduces the instruction "MOVE.L #I, D0". The instruction is not valid on the Macintosh because I is not assembled as an absolute long address. The following code segment is valid on the Macintosh and has the equivalent action of storing address I in D0.

    LEA I, A0
    MOVE.L A0,D0

Indirect Addressing

The MC68000 provides a series of indirect addressing modes that use the address registers. The simplest of these modes is introduced in this section. Chapter 6 introduces other indirect modes in support of array processing.

Address Register Indirect Mode

Syntax   (A*n*)

Description The operand specifies the contents of the memory location whose address is contained in A*n*. MC68000 assembly language consistently uses the "parentheses A*n*" syntax to indicate indirect reference.

EXAMPLE 4.22

Assume that BETA is a label with value $006000. The following sequence of instructions initializes address register A0 to point to address $006000 and then moves the contents of location $006000 to data register D0.

```
LEA       BETA,A0
MOVE.W    (A0),D0
```

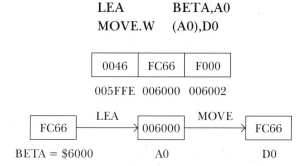

A complete program illustrates address register indirect mode and the LEA instruction. The program also introduces a simple instruction that clears (initializes to 0) a data register or a memory location.

INSTRUCTION

CLR
(Clear)

Syntax CLR.⟨size⟩ ⟨ea⟩

Action The contents at the given effective address are initialized to 0. The operand may be either a data register or a memory location.

Note The size parameter may be "B", "W", or "L".

EXAMPLE 4.23

CLR. B D3

Before	After
8C07 2A4F	8C07 2A00
D3	D3

PROGRAM 4.4

Three-Word Sum

Beginning at memory location TERM, add the contents of three consecutive 16-bit memory locations. The sum is stored at location RESULT and printed to the screen using the decimal output routine DECOUT. The input/output routines are described in the next section.

Note This sum could be computed more simply using the following sequence of statements:

ADD.W	TERM, D0
ADD.W	TERM + 2, D0
ADD.W	TERM + 4, D0

However, when loop constructs are introduced (see Chapter 5), using address register indirect mode is fully justified. The logic

ADD.W	(A0), D0
ADDA.W	#2, A0

can be repeated any number of times. In a general sum algorithm, the rather clumsy use of expressions TERM + 6, TERM + 8, and so on is not practical.

Note The authors have run the complete programs on a Macintosh system using the Macintosh Assembly System. All program listings in this text include an example of a run following the code. In a program run, any input typed by the user is set in italics. Output is given in normal type.

```
              xref        decout, newline, stop
start:
              lea         term,a0       ; assign term to (a0)
              lea         result,a1     ; assign result to (a1)
              clr.w       d0            ; set (d0) to 0
              add.w       (a0),d0       ; add 1st term
              adda.w      #2,a0         ; move (a0) to the next word
              add.w       (a0),d0       ; add 2nd term
              adda.w      #2,a0
              add.w       (a0),d0       ; add 3rd term
              move.w      d0,(a1)       ; store sum in "result"
              jsr         decout
              jsr         newline
              jsr         stop

              data

term:         dc.w        45, 29, 68
result:       ds.w        1

              end
```

⟨Run of Program 4.4⟩

|4.5| INPUT AND OUTPUT ROUTINES

To present complete programs, a series of I/O routines is used to read data from a keyboard to an MC68000 system and write data from an MC68000 system to a screen. Number routines DECOUT and HEXOUT have been used in several sample programs. This section describes the full set of routines used in this text. Routines are included for both number and character data. Your assembler should have a library of these routines that is linked to your code file. The algorithms to implement the routines are presented in Chapter 9.

TABLE 4.4 Numeric Input and Output Routines

ROUTINE	ACTION
DECIN	A 16-bit signed decimal number is read from the keyboard and stored in (D0.W.).
DECIN_LONG	A 32-bit signed decimal number is read from the keyboard and stored as a long word in (D0.L).
DECOUT	The value (D0.W) is output to the screen as a signed decimal number with two trailing blanks. The contents of D0 are preserved.
DECOUT_LONG	The long-word value (D0.L) is ouptut to the screen as a signed decimal number with two trailing blanks. The contents of D0 are preserved.
HEXIN	A hex number, up to four digits, is read from the keyboard and stored in (D0.W).
HEXIN_LONG	A hex number, up to eight digits, is read from the keyboard and stored as a long word in (D0.L).
HEXOUT	The value (D0.W) is output to the screen as four hex digits with two trailing blanks. Leading zeros are included, and the contents of D0 are preserved.
HEXOUT_LONG	The long-word value (D0.L) is output to the screen as eight hex digits with two trailing blanks. Leading zeros are included, and the contents of D0 are preserved.
NEWLINE	A new line is sent to the screen. This subroutine is equivalent to the Pascal "WRITELN;" statement.

TABLE 4.5   Character Input and Output Routines

ROUTINE	REGISTER A0	REGISTER D0	ACTION
STRIN	Address of the input buffer	Maximum number of characters to read	A character string is read from the keyboard into the buffer
STROUT	Address of the output buffer	Number of characters to print	A character string at address (A0) is output to the screen

The number routines pass data to or from data register D0 and permit the reading and writing of word and long-word data. The I/O routines in Table 4.4 support both signed decimal numbers and hex numbers.

Registers A0 and D0 are used as parameters for two I/O string-handling routines, STRIN and STROUT (see Table 4.5). In each case, a **string buffer** (block of memory) must be declared using data storage directives. The address register A0 points to the first byte of the buffer, while (D0.W) holds a character count.

EXAMPLE 4.24

Here we examine an application of STRIN and STROUT, including the use of data directives to define the string buffer.

(a) Character input: STRIN

Define a buffer to hold the characters. Be sure that the buffer is large enough to hold the maximum number of characters you expect to read. For keyboard input, 80 characters is generally sufficient.

BUFNAME: DS.B 80

Set A0 to point to the buffer, and set D0 to the maximum number of characters that may be read. The STRIN routine reads the number of characters specified in D0 or until a CR (carriage return) is entered. The CR is converted into the system's end-of-line (EOLN) character and stored in the string as the last character. On a UNIX system, the EOLN character is linefeed ($0A). On the Macintosh, the EOLN character is carriage return ($0D).

```
LEA       # BUFNAME, A0
MOVE.W    # 80, D0
JSR       # STRIN
```

The contents of register A0 are unchanged, whereas the contents of D0.W are set to the actual number of characters read. Note that the terminating newline is included in this count. For instance, with a line of input "Test Input", (D0.W) = $000B.

(b) Character output: STROUT
Application: Set A0 to point to a string of characters, and store in D0 the exact number of characters you wish to output.

```
        LEA       MSG,A0
        MOVE.W    #29,D0
        JSR       STROUT

        DATA
MSG:    DC.B      'This string has 29 characters'
```

The contents of registers A0 and D0 are not changed.

The STROUT routine implements *newline expansion.* The system's EOLN character is output as a two-character packet carriage-return (CR) and line-feed (LF). For output, the EOLN character is referred to as the *newline* character.

PROGRAM 4.5

Address Ranges

The following program demonstrates many of the I/O routines. A segment of memory starting at address "BEGINNING" and terminating at address "ENDING" is initialized using DCB directives. This range of addresses is printed using the prompt "ADDMESG".

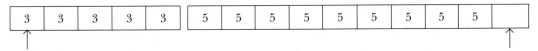

Beginning   Ending = Beginning + $0E

The user is asked to input a memory address in this range. The contents of this memory location are printed.

```
        xref    strout, hexin_long, hexout_long, decout
        xref    newline, stop
start:
        lea     addmesg,a0   ; print addresses "beginning","ending"
        move.w  #43,d0
        jsr     strout       ; output the string to the terminal
        lea     beginning,a1
        move.l  a1,d0
        jsr     hexout_long  ; output the value of "beginning"
        lea     ending,a1
```

```
            suba.w    #2,a1
            move.l    a1,d0
            jsr       hexout_long  ; output the value of "ending"
            jsr       newline
            lea       prompt,a0    ; request the address
            move.w    #42,d0
            jsr       strout
            jsr       hexin_long   ; input the address (long word)
            movea.l   d0,a1        ; a1 points at word to be displayed
            lea       result,a0    ; print result message
            move.w    #39,d0
            jsr       strout
            move.w    (a1),d0      ; print the contents at address input
            jsr       decout
            jsr       newline
            jsr       stop

            data

beginning:
            dcb.w     5,3               ; note the use of the dcb directive
            dcb.w     9,5
ending:
addmesg:
prompt:
            dc.b      'The addresses "beginning" and "ending" are '
result:
            dc.b      'Enter the address of a word in the range: '
            dc.b      'The 16 bit contents at that address is '
            even

            end
```

⟨Run of Program 4.5⟩

```
The addresses "beginning" and "ending" are 00388C74 00388C8E
Enter the address of a word in the range: 388C80
The 16 bit contents at that address is 5
```

PROGRAM 4.6

String Modification

In this program, the input routine STRIN is emphasized. A string is read from the keyboard. The program changes the first character to 'A' and the last character to 'Z'. The modified string is printed. It is assumed that the string contains at least two characters prior to the terminating newline. The number of characters read is stored in (D0.W) and is used to access the last character.

```
            xref      strin, strout, newline, stop

start:      move.w    #28,d0
            lea       prompt,a0
```

```
          jsr        strout
          lea        string, a0
          move.w     #79, d0
          jsr        strin
          move.w     d0, d1
          move.b     #'A', (a0)        ; change 1st char to 'A'
          subi.w     #2, d1            ; offset to last char is (d0.w) - 2
          adda.w     d1, a0
          move.b     #'Z', (a0)        ; change last char to 'Z'
          lea        string, a0
          jsr        strout            ; output modified string.
                                       ; (d0.w) still is the string length
          jsr        stop

          data
prompt:   dc.b       'Enter the string to modify:
string:   ds.b       80
          end
```

⟨Run of Program 4.6⟩

```
Enter the string to modify: Here is a string.
Here is a stringZ
```

4.6 LOGICAL OPERATIONS

Chapter 2 introduced the logical operations OR, AND, EOR, and NOT. The MC68000 has machine instructions to implement these operations, which are useful in applications that involve the setting of bit patterns within bytes, words, and long words. The instruction format is typical of most MC68000 instructions, permitting only a limited set of addressing modes. A data register must be used in the instructions AND, OR, and EOR, and special forms of the instructions are available for an immediate mode source operand.

INSTRUCTION	*Syntax*	OR.⟨size⟩	⟨ea⟩,Dn
		OR.⟨size⟩	Dn,⟨ea⟩
OR/AND		ORI.⟨size⟩	#N,⟨ea⟩
EOR/NOT			
The Logical		AND.⟨size⟩	⟨ea⟩,Dn
Operations		AND.⟨size⟩	Dn,⟨ea⟩
		ANDI.⟨size⟩	#N,⟨ea⟩

EOR.⟨size⟩   D*n*,⟨ea⟩
EORI.⟨size⟩   #N,⟨ea⟩

NOT.⟨size⟩   ⟨ea⟩

Action   Each instruction executes the corresponding logical operation for fixed-length binary numbers. The source operand serves as the mask, and the bits in the destination operand are changed.

Notes

1. OR and AND require that either the source or destination operands be a data register. EOR requires that the source be a data register.

2. The size parameter may be "B", "W", or "L".

EXAMPLE 4.25

(*a*) OR.W   A, D3
The instruction evaluates the logical OR of the 16-bit contents of address A with (D3.W). The result is stored in D3.

Before   After

| 0FF0 | 1234 A017 | | 1234 AFF7 |

     A   D3   D3

(*b*) ANDI.L   #$00FF00FF, (A4)
The source operand is a mask. Every other byte of the long word at address A4 is cleared.

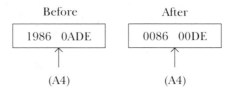

Before   After

| 1986 0ADE | | 0086 00DE |

      ↑   ↑

     (A4)   (A4)

EXAMPLE 4.26

The EOR operation is used in extended arithmetic and floating-point calculations. Assume that the sign of each number is stored as a byte in a data register. The register has value 0 if the corresponding number is positive and 1 if it is negative. The EOR operation gives the sign of the product.

$$
\begin{array}{lll}
\text{positive} \times \text{positive} = \text{positive} & \quad 0 \times 0 = 0 \\
\text{negative} \times \text{negative} = \text{positive} & \quad 1 \times 1 = 0 \\
\text{positive} \times \text{negative} = \text{negative} & \quad 0 \times 1 = 1 \\
\text{negative} \times \text{positive} = \text{negative} & \quad 1 \times 0 = 0
\end{array}
$$

The EOR operation is logically equivalent to an expression using AND, OR, and NOT. Program 4.7 demonstrates the equivalence using sample data stored in registers.

$$A \text{ EOR } B = (NOT(A) \text{ AND } B) \text{ OR } (A \text{ AND } NOT(B))$$

PROGRAM 4.7

Logical Operator EOR

1. Using HEXIN, store A and B in D0 and D1.

2. Compute A EOR B and store the result in D0.

3. Use registers D1–D4 to store components for the OR operation.

$$D1 = A \quad D3 = NOT \ A$$
$$D2 = B \quad D4 = NOT \ B$$

4. Compute (NOT A AND B) and (A AND NOT B), and combine these results using the OR operation.

```
        xref      hexin,hexout,newline,stop
start:
        jsr       hexin           ; input  b
        move.w    d0,d2           ; copy   b to d2
        move.w    d0,d4           ; copy   b to d4
        jsr       hexin           ; input  a
        move.w    d0,d1           ; copy   a to d1
        move.w    d0,d3           ; copy   a to d3

;  compute a EOR b and output the result.
        eor.w     d2,d0
        jsr       hexout

;  set registers d3 and d4 to values NOT a and NOT b
        not.w     d3
        not.w     d4
;  compute (NOT a AND b) or (NOT b AND a)
        and.w     d3,d2
        and.w     d4,d1

;  OR the two expressions and output the results
        or.w      d2,d1
        move.w    d1,d0           ; move d1 to d0 for output
        jsr       hexout
        jsr       newline
        jsr       stop

        end
```

⟨Run of program 4.7⟩

```
0f0f 8a3c
8533 8533
```

|4.7| ERRORS IN THE PROGRAMMING PROCESS

Programming in assembly language is generally more difficult than programming in a high-level language such as Pascal or FORTRAN. Assembly language requires greater attention to detail in managing data transfer between memory and the CPU. An assembler provides little or no run-time error checking. As with high-level languages, these errors are the most difficult to identify. Some systems provide code-level debuggers that trace instruction execution and output processor status information. These are useful tools in tracking down run-time errors. You probably have an external tool of this type on your system or are running an integrated assembly language programming environment that contains a debugger. This section describes some of the typical problems you will find when you enter and run an assembly language program. The goal of the examples is to establish the importance of the warning "Program in assembly language carefully."

Syntax Errors

A **syntax error** occurs when the programmer incorrectly writes a statement or improperly declares labels. Most syntax errors are identified in Pass 1 of the assembly process and are listed with relatively specific messages. Some examples follow.

Typing Error

(a) GO OUT: ADD.W   D0, D1
Blank included in the label name.

(b) MOVE.W   A D0
The comma between the operands is missing.

(c) MOV.W   A, D0
The instruction opcode is misspelled.

Definition Error

(d) JSR   DECOUT
An invalid label error occurs if DECOUT has not been defined with the XREF directive.

(e) VALUE: DC.W   35
VALUE: DS.W   1
Label is defined twice.

Invalid Instruction Error

(f) EOR.W   (A0), D2

EOR requires that the source operand be a data register. This is an invalid MC68000 instruction.

(g) MOVE.L   D2, A4

Technically, this is invalid because the MOVEA form of the instruction is required. Many assemblers recognize that the MOVE instruction has address register direct mode for the destination and thus generate code for the MOVEA instruction.

Run-time Errors

Run-time errors occur during execution of the program. They can leave the system in an unrecoverable condition (fatal error) or can produce incorrect output. Fatal errors are often easy to fix because a system debugger can identify the status of the registers, program counter, and identify instructions near the offending error. Run-time errors that are caused by a logical flaw in the algorithm can be the most difficult to diagnose.

Bus Error

An instruction attempts to reference a nonexistent memory address. The programmer may assume that more memory is present than actually exists or that a programming error has placed an incorrect value in an address register.

Illegal Instruction

The CPU reads an opcode word that does not correspond to a valid MC68000 instruction. This is often caused by jumping into data space and attempting to process an opcode word that is data. Consider the following code segment. The JMP instruction is equivalent to the high-level language "GOTO" statement.

```
          XREF       STOP

START:    MOVEA.W    COMPUTE, A0
            .
            .
            .
          JMP        (A0)           ; JUMPING INTO TROUBLE
            .
            .
COMPUTE:  ADDI.W     #$12,D0        ; THE OPCODE AT COMPUTE IS 0640
```

At START, the programmer intended to initialize A0 with the label COMPUTE. The intended instruction was

```
MOVEA.L #COMPUTE, A0
```

In that case, the JMP instruction would have caused program execution to continue at COMPUTE. However, the MOVEA instruction at START actually assigns $00000640 to the PC. This is the sign-extended opcode for the ADDI instruction. At the JMP instruction, program execution continues at location $000640. In most cases, an invalid instruction error occurs at this address, and execution aborts. In some cases, the program "accidentally" jumps to an instruction, and execution continues independent of the program logic.

Address Error

The CPU attempts to read or write a word or long word at an odd address. Failing to use "EVEN" or "DS.W 0" to set labels to an even address is a source of address errors. The MC68000 always identifies this as an error. The MC68020/30/40 identifies address errors only during an instruction fetch cycle. In the following code, an address error will occur on a MC68000 CPU.

```
           MOVE.W    I,D0
             . . .

           DATA
MSG:       DC.B      'HELLO WORLD'
I:         DC.W      77
             . . .
```

If the EVEN directive is used, no address error will occur.

```
MSG:       DC.B      'HELLO WORLD'
           EVEN
```

Insidious Error

Consider the code

```
        xref       stop, hexout

go:     move.w     $1006,d0   ; you wanted move.w #1006,D0
        add.w      j,do
        add.w.     d0,d0
        move.w     d0,i
        jsr        hexout
        move.w     #8,d0
        add.w      i,d0
        add.w      j,d0
```

```
        jsr         hexout
        jsr         stop

        data
i:      ds.w        1
j:      dc.w        $fff9
        end
```

The program has neither a syntax nor a run-time error. The code runs and produces no apparent errors. Unfortunately, it is not the program you intended to run.

The contents of the word at address $1006 are moved into D0, not the number $1006. The instruction MOVE.W #$1006, D0 was intended. Assume that the program is placed in memory at the starting address $1000 and that the contents of address $1006 are $D079, the opcode word for the "ADD.W J, D0" instruction. The number $D079 is moved into D0. After executing the code,

I contains   (D079 + FFF9) * 2 = A0E4

D0 contains   8 + A0E4 + FFF9 = A0E5

The program output is A0E4 A0E5.

4.8 | HAND-TRANSLATION OF INSTRUCTIONS

Chapter 3 introduced SMC68000 machine code for a small set of instructions, emphasizing the opcode word and extension words. The code is exactly that used by the MC68000. This chapter introduces addressing modes and additional instructions. You now have the background for a more detailed study of machine code. In the process, we will preview the Motorola documentation for instructions from Appendix B.

The MC68000 mnemonics are listed in alphabetical order. Each instruction description is divided into seven sections with accompanying specifications. Properly interpreted, the description indicates valid assembly language syntax, the resulting machine code, and the change in the processor status register caused by execution of the instruction. The LEA instruction is introduced from Appendix B as an example. Explanatory comments are given in square brackets.

INSTRUCTION

LEA
(Load Effective Address)

Operation   ⟨ea⟩ → A*n*   [Specify the action of the instruction.]

Assembler Syntax   LEA   ⟨ea⟩, A*n*

Attributes   Size = (Long)   [The data size may be only 32 bits.]

Description   The effective address is loaded into the address register A*n*. All 32 bits of the address register are affected by the instruction.

Condition Codes   Not affected   [The LSB of the status register is referred to as the condition code register (CCR). It detects the presence of an overflow and a carry in an operation and specifies whether an operation produces a 0 or negative result. The LEA instruction does not affect the condition codes.]

Instruction Format

15	14	13	12	11	10	9	8	7	6	5	4	3	2	1	0
0	1	0	0	Register An			1	1	1	Effective Address Mode			Register		

[The bit fields for the opcode word are listed. The actual opcode word is determined by using the table of valid addressing modes for the instruction.

Each addressing mode has a specific MC68000 code divided into a 3-bit MODE and 3-bit REGISTER value. Table 4.6 provides a complete list of codes. If an instruction does not permit an addressing mode for the source or destination operand, a dash ("—") replaces the code in the table in Appendix B.]

Instruction Fields

Register field: Specifies the address register that is to be loaded with the effective address.
Effective address field: Specifies the address that is to be loaded into the address register.

[All MC68000 instructions use selected bits to specify the operation, the size parameter, and the addressing modes of the operand(s). The instruction

TABLE 4.6   Addressing Mode Code and Register Values

ADDRESSING MODE	MODE	REGISTER	ADDRESSING MODE	MODE	REGISTER
Dn	000	reg #	(d,An,Rm)	110	reg #
An	001	reg #	Abs. Short	111	000
(An)	010	reg #	Abs. Long	111	001
(An)+	011	reg #	(d,PC)	111	010
−(An)	100	reg #	(d,PC,Rm)	111	011
(d,An)	101	reg #	Immediate	111	100

fields section specifies the possible modes for the source and destination operands and the location of identifying bits in the opcode word. The LEA instruction has the address register (0–7) listed in bits 9–11 and the effective address of the source in bits 0–5.]

EXAMPLE 4.27

Instruction

LEA   ARR,A5

Register Field   The destination address register is A5. The register field is 1 0 1.

Effective Address Field   The source is absolute long mode with value 1 1 1 0 0 1.

15	14	13	12	11	10	9	8	7	6	5	4	3	2	1	0	
0	1	0	0	1	0	1	1	1	1	1	1	1	0	0	1	= $4BF9

The source operand requires two extension words. The machine code for the instruction is

4 B F 9
Address ARR

EXERCISES

1. Identify and correct any syntax errors in the following:
   - (a)   ADD.W   D0;Y
   - (b)   MOVE.L   X   Y
   - (c)   ADDI.W   #5A,D0
   - (d)   GLOBAL   STOP,HEXOUT
   - (e)   LOOP: THIS IS A LABEL
   - (f)   MOVE.L   D0,#3A0F

2. Identify and correct any syntax errors in the following:
   - (a)   MOVE.B   "X",D2
   - (b)   ;   THIS IS A TWO-LINE
               COMMENT
   - (c)   DC.B   "Quit (YES or NO)"
   - (d)   DS.B   'Apt Number 7B'
   - (e)   DCB.W   7:5
   - (f)   I,J: DC.W   15

3. Seven words of data are to be stored in memory beginning at address DAT.
   - (a) Explain the action of the directive "DC.W 7".

(b) Give the define constant block directive that allocates the seven words in memory and initializes the memory to 0.

4. Indicate the number of bytes of memory allocated by the directive for each of the following:

(a)	ALPHA:	DS.L	5
(b)	BETA:	DC.B	'This is a string',10
(c)	A:	DC.L	$32

5. Use storage directives to initialize data space beginning at address "A" with the following 16-bit hex data. Convert the numbers to decimal and load the data as decimal numbers.

        0012   FFE0   000E   FFFF   0043   00A2

6. Data space is defined with storage directives. Determine the number of bytes of memory that are allocated in each of the following definitions:

(a)	A:	DC.W	15,33,0
	B:	DC.L	−5,1893
	C:	DS.W	$A
	D:	DS.L	6
(b)	LOC__1:	DCB.L	15,33
	LOC__2:	DC.B	'LIST',10,13
	LOC__3:	DS.W	@25

7. After the assembler completes Pass 1, what is the value of label C?

```
            XREF        STOP
START:      MOVE.W      #$AFFF,D0
            ADDI.W      #70,A
            SUB.W       D0,B
            JSR         STOP            ; THREE WORD-INSTRUCTION

            DATA
A:          DC.W        100
B:          DS.L        4
C:          DS.W        10
            END
```

8. Starting at label GREETING, declare the string 'GOOD EXERCISE' followed by a long-word $100A at an even byte boundary.

9. Write the following instructions, using hex for the immediate mode constant:
(a) MOVE.B   #'f', D0   (b) MOVE.B   #'[', D0

10. Rewrite each of the following instructions so that the immediate mode constant is given in hex, octal, and binary:
(a) ADDI.W   #88, (A0)   (b) SUBI.L   #37, D4

11. Compare and contrast a one-pass and a two-pass assembler.

12. Hand-assemble the following program, assuming that the program begins at address $000000 and STOP has value $100000. The opcode word for JSR is $4EB9.

```
        xref    stop
start:  move.w  #3,d0
        add.w   a,d0
        add.w   b,d0
        move.w  d0,c
        addi.w  #5,d0
        jsr     stop

        data
a:      dc.w    1
b:      dc.w    2
c:      ds.w    1
        end
```

Assuming the load address is $001000, modify the machine code.

13. Assume I and J are labels. For each instruction, indicate which quantities are absolute and which are relocatable.
(a) MOVE.W #5, D0   (b) ADDI.W #$56, D0
(c) MOVE.W D0, I   (d) MOVE.W #8, J

14. Each statement contains a syntax error. Rewrite the instruction with correct syntax.
(a) ADDI.L #4, A0   (b) ADDA.B #1, A0

15. In the instruction MOVE.W #16,D0, the constant 16 must not be relocated because it is an absolute quantity. In the following code segment, are the immediate values in the MOVE and SUBI instructions relocatable or absolute? Explain your answer carefully.

```
START:      MOVE.L   #ENDCODE,D0
            SUBI.L   #START,D0
              .
              .
              .
```

            ← Last executable instruction

```
ENDCODE:
A:          DS.W  1
              .
              .
              .

            END
```

16. Identify a syntax error in each of the following instructions:

(a)	ADDI.B	#'0,D5	(b) SUBI.W	(A3),D1
(c)	LEA	#$2000,A4	(d) ADD.L	D4,A0
(e)	ADD.B	(A2),(A3)	(f) MOVEA.L	A5,D6

17. Give the addressing mode of the operands for each of the following instructions:
    - (a) MOVE.W   #5, (A6)   (b) ADD.L   LIST,D4
    - (c) ANDI.B   #$80,D0   (d) SUB.W   A.W,D3
    - (e) MOVEA.L   T.W,A4   (f) LEA   BUF,A5
    - (g) MOVE.B   #'0',(A2)   (h) ADD.L   #LIST,D3

18. Compute the actual address placed on the address bus for each of the following absolute short addresses:
    - (a) A.W = $7EEA   (b) TABLE.W = $8666
    - (c) X.W = $FFFF   (d) BUF.W = $1000

19. The initial 32-bit contents of D0, D1, D2 are

    (D0.L) = $4567FFDD   (D1.L) = $7890EAFC   (D2.L) = $00005467

    Compute the contents of D1 after executing each instruction. The initial values should be used for each instruction.
    - (a) ADD.W   D0,D1   (b) SUB.B   D2,D1
    - (c) ADD.L   D0,D1   (d) ORI.W   #$0F66,D1
    - (e) ANDI.B   #$66,D1   (f) EORI.L   #$00FFF084,D1

20. Identify the syntax errors in the following:
    - (a) ADD.L   #6,A3   (b) EOR.B   A,D0
    - (c) LEA   #500,A2   (d) MOVEA.B   #7,A3
    - (e) ADDA.L   A4,D2   (f) ADD.W   A,B

21. The initial value of (A2) is $5000. The long word at that address is $00AA5000. Describe the action of each instruction.
    - (a) LEA $5000,A5   (b) MOVEA.W   A2,A5
    - (c) LEA   (A2),A5   (d) MOVEA.L   (A2),A5

22. Give the value of A0 after executing each of the following instructions:
    - (a) MOVEA.W #$8000, A0
    - (b) The value of A0 is initially $42B01152
        - i.   ADDA.W   #$C000,A0   ii. LEA   (A0),A0
        - iii. MOVEA.W   #$300,A0   iv. SUBA.L   #$14,A0
    - (c) Address register (A2) = $001000. The long word in memory at address $001000 is $0010A00C. What is the resulting value of A2?
        - i.   LEA   (A2),A2   ii. MOVEA.L   (A2),A2
        - iii. MOVEA.W   (A2),A2   iv. ADDA.L   (A2),A2

23. The initial value of A0 is $004000. The long-word contents at that memory address are

00F2	0052

    4000   4002

Give the value of A2 after executing each of the following instructions:

(a)	LEA	$4000,A2	(b) MOVEA.L	$4000,A2
(c)	LEA	(A0),A2	(d) MOVEA.L	#$4000,A2
(e)	MOVEA.L	(A0),A2	(f) MOVEA.L	#$A0,A2

24. Assume (D0.B) represents data in an 8-bit register. Use the logical operations to specify the register bits 0 to 7. Give your answer using a complete MC68000 instruction with an immediate mode data mask.
    (a) Clear (set to 0) bits 1, 3, and 6. Leave all other bits unchanged.
    (b) Set bits 1 and 2, and clear all other bits.
    (c) Change the value of bits 0 to 2, and leave all other bits unchanged.

25. The value of A and B are $1000 and $2000, respectively. Hand-translate each instruction. Include any extension words that may be required.

(a)	MOVE.W	#1,D0	(b) MOVEA.L	A,A3
(c)	LEA	A.W,A6	(d) MOVE.B	(A3),D1
(e)	SUBA.L	(A0),A6	(f) SUB.B	D2,D3
(g)	CLR.B	D3	(h) OR.W	D0,D1

26. Identify the difference between the following code fragments:

(a)	MOVE.L	I,D0	(b) MOVE.L	I + 2,D0
	ADDI.L	#2,D0		

27. Hand-translate the following instructions. Give the opcode word and any extension words that may be required.

(a)	LEA	$4000,A5	(b) MOVE.L	$3000.W,$4000
(c)	ANDI.L	#7,D0	(d) NOT.B	D3

28. Each of the following is the machine code for a version of the MOVE instruction. Decode each and give the assembly language form of the instruction.
    (a) 2692   (b) 1A82

29. Use a data directive to initialize an input buffer for STRIN. You enter the string "Here is a line" followed by a carriage return.
    (a) Give the directive to initialize the input buffer.
    (b) Before calling STRIN, what is the value of D0?
    (c) After calling STRIN, what is the value of D0?

30. Assume the following instructions are executed in sequential order. Give the value of D0 after each instruction.

```
MOVE.L   #$F2BCA2F6,D0
ANDI.W   #$FF0F,D0
ORI.L    #$01000000,D0
NOT.B    D0
EORI.W   #$F555,D0
```

31. Identify any run-time errors or logical errors in the following programs:

    (a)
    ```
              XREF      STOP,HEXOUT
    START:    MOVE.W    I,D0
              JSR       HEXOUT
              JSR       STOP
              DATA
    STR:      DC.B      'COUNT'
    I:        DC.W      $0010
              END
    ```

    (b)
    ```
              XREF      STOP,HEXIN__LONG,HEXOUT
    START:    LEA       I,A0
              MOVE.L    #-4,D1
              ADDA.L    D1,A0
              JSR       HEXIN__LONG
              MOVE.L    D0, (A0)
              JSR       STOP
              DATA
    I:        DS.W      10
              END
    ```

    What would happen if you entered the value START?

32. Explain the action of the following code segment:

    ```
         LEA       BUF,A0
         MOVE.W    #81,D0
         JSR       STRIN
         SUBI.W    #1,D0
         JSR       STROUT
              .
              .
              .
    BUF: DS.B      82
    ```

PROGRAMMING EXERCISES

33. Using the following data storage directives, write a program that computes the value of the word at address VALUES plus the word at address VALUES + 2 minus the word at VALUES + 4. Use address-register indirect mode to access the data values. Store the sum in location RESULT. Test your answer by writing the value using HEXOUT. Use Program 4.4 as a model.

    ```
    VALUES:   DC.W   27
              DC.W   45
              DC.W   18
    RESULT:   DS.W   1
    ```

34. Let D0 simulate a 16-bit system control register. Use the bit indices 0 to 15. The following exercises assign bit values to the register. For each exercise, input an initial value using HEXIN. Make the specified bit changes, and output the result using HEXOUT.

    (a) Set bits 2, 3, and 4 to 1 while leaving all other bits unchanged.
    (b) Clear bit 3 and the high-order byte (MSB).
    (c) Change the value for bits 0 to 3 and leave all other bits unchanged.

35. Enter a 16-bit two's complement number N using HEXIN. Echo the value of N using HEXOUT. Your code should compute the two's complement of N in each of the following three ways. For each case, test your result by outputting the value with HEXOUT.

    Method 1: Use NOT and ADDI.
    Method 2: Subtract from $FFFF and ADD 1.
    Method 3: Subtract from 216. You must use long arithmetic for this method.

36. Enter a long word using HEXIN_LONG. Copy to registers D1 and D2 the LSW and MSW of the input.

0000	LSW

D1

MSW	0000

D2

   Verify that the instructions "OR.L D2,D1" and "ADD.L D2,D1" produce the original input value. For each instruction, output the result using HEXOUT_LONG.

37. A long word is stored at address L. In memory, exchange the low-order and high-order bytes of the long word. Assign the 32-bit contents of address L to register D0, and output the result using HEXOUT_LONG.

38. Output as a decimal number the 16-bit two's complement number $FFFF. Using long operations, output the decimal equivalent for the unsigned number $FFFF.

39. Enter a 16-bit decimal number. Write out the remainder MOD 16. For instance, an input of 77 will produce decimal output 13.

40. Write a test program to illustrate overflow. Add the decimal numbers 20,000 and 30,000. Output the sum as a 16-bit decimal number and then as a 32-bit decimal number.

41. Enter the full name of a country using STRIN. Output the first and last letter of the name as an abbreviation, followed by a period. For instance, with input "FRANCE", the output is "FE.".

42. The constant string 'My sign of the zodiac is' is stored in memory using a constant directive. First prompt the user to enter an input string containing his or her sign. Combine the constant and input string, and output them as a complete sentence.

43. Your program should contain the following two directives:

    A: DC.L   N,NUM_L1,NUM_2, . . . , NUM_N
    B: DS.W   1

    The value N is a count, and NUM_1, NUM_2, . . . , NUM_N are N long words. Write a program that outputs the address A and the address B. Then use the value of N and your knowledge of the address A to compute the address B. Output the result of this computation. Use HEXOUT_LONG to output all addresses as long words.

44. Using Appendix B, determine the code for the following instruction:

    MOVE.W   D3, D5

    Write a program that contains the instruction, reads that opcode word, and prints it using HEXOUT.

45. (This exercise requires absolute addressing.)
    Suppose that the data declaration section of a program contains four strings. Write code that will read in an integer from 0–3 and output the corresponding string. A skeleton of the code is shown here. Your code should first prompt for and then read the string number, 0 to 3, into register D0.

```
        ADD.W      D0,D0            ; COMPUTE 4 * D0
        ADD.W      D0,D0
        LEA        STRINGS,A1
                                    ASSIGN A1 THE STRINGS LABEL.
            .                       USING A1 AND D0 PLACE.
            .                       THE NUMBER OF CHARS IN D0.
            .                       AND THE STRING ADDRESS IN A0.
        JSR        STROUT
        JSR        STOP

        DATA

STRINGS:
        DC.L       STR0,STR1,STR2,STR3
STR0:   DC.B       18, 'This is Chapter 4',$0A
STR1:   DC.B       32, 'This code is not very efficient',$0A
STR2:   DC.B       16, 'A little string',$0A
STR3:   DC.B       6, 'Done!',$0A
```

CHAPTER 5

INTRODUCTION TO BRANCHING

Most computer algorithms contain decision points where code is conditionally executed depending on the status of program variables. Conditional execution and loop constructs are available in high-level languages. The equivalent constructs in assembly language use branch instructions. This chapter introduces the MC68000 branch instructions and covers the assembly language implementation of high-level language control constructs.

|5.1| THE CONDITION CODE REGISTER

When an MC68000 instruction executes, a CPU register keeps a record of arithmetic indicators such as sign and the presence of overflow. This record is kept in the **condition code register (CCR)**, the low-order byte of the status register. The high-order byte of the status register holds information for systems programming and is discussed in Chapters 12 to 15. The CCR contains five single-bit flags that monitor the algebraic sign, the presence of overflow and carry, and whether a zero resulted from the operation (see Figure 5.1).

All or a portion of the CCR bits may be set, cleared, or unaffected during execution of an MC68000 instruction. The term **set** implies that the bit is assigned value 1. The bit is **cleared** if it is assigned value 0. In some cases, a bit is **unaffected**, which implies that it retains its former value. Table 5.1 gives the meaning of each of the CCR bits.

Generally, the X bit is set to the value of the C bit for arithmetic operations. Otherwise, it is not affected by an instruction. The MC68000

FIGURE 5.1   16-Bit Status Register with CCR

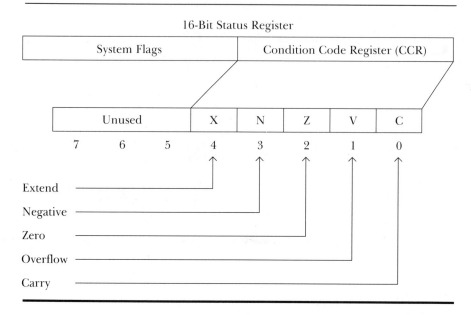

separates the functions of the C and X bits to simplify the programming of multiprecision arithmetic routines. The X bit is treated in Chapter 8 with the extended arithmetic instructions and is mostly ignored in the next three chapters.

EXAMPLE 5.1

The ADD instruction demonstrates the assigning of condition codes. Each bit in the CCR is affected by the operation. Assume initially that (D0.W) is $FFFE ($-2_{10}$).

(a) ADDI. W   #1, D0   Result: (D0.W) = $FFFF

CCR Information

Value of the result	Sum is not zero.	(Z = 0)
	Sum is negative.	(N = 1)
Overflow	No overflow occurs.	(V = 0)
Carry	No carry occurs.	(C = 0)
Extend	Same as the C bit.	(X = 0)

The resulting CCR is 0   1   0   0   0.

(b) ADDI. W   #$8001, D0   Result: (D0.W) = $7FFF

CCR Information

Value of the result	Sum is not zero.	(Z = 0)
	Sum is positive.	(N = 0)

Overflow	Overflow occurred.	(V = 1)
Carry	A carry occurs.	(C = 1)
Extend	Same as the C bit.	(X = 1)

The resulting CCR is 10011.

Motorola includes the assignment of CCR bits in each instruction specification. You can often deduce by simple logic the effect of an instruction on the CCR. A MOVE instruction never produces a carry or an overflow; consequently, C = 0 and V = 0. The MOVE instruction modifies the contents of the destination, and the result is reflected in the Z and N bits. In this text, the value of the CCR bits are given in the instruction description. Appendix B gives the full Motorola specifications of the MC68000 instruction set, including the CCR bits. The chart of each bit includes the symbols: − (unaffected), U (undefined and meaningless), * (instruction specification describes the result), or 0 (bit cleared). The CCR specification for the MOVE instruction follows:

−	*	*	0	0
X	N	Z	V	C

C: Always cleared (C = 0).
V: Always cleared (V = 0).
Z: Set if the result is zero. Cleared otherwise.
N: Set if the result is negative. Cleared otherwise.
X: Not affected.

TABLE 5.1 CCR Bits

NAME	SYMBOL	MEANING
Zero	Z	Set if the result is zero. Cleared if the result is nonzero.
Negative	N	Set if the result is negative. Cleared if the result is zero or positive.
Carry	C	Set if a carry or borrow is generated. Cleared if no carry or borrow is generated.
Overflow	V	Set if a signed overflow occurs. Cleared if no signed overflow occurs.
Extend	X	Retains information from the carry bit for multiprecision arithmetic.

EXAMPLE 5.2   Notice the change in the value of the CCR for different instructions. Initial CCR codes are given to highlight any changes that occur.

(a) MOVE.W   #−1, D0
Assume that (D0.W) = $4400. After the MOVE instruction, (D0.W) = $FFFF.

CCR Before					CCR After			
0	1	1	0		1	0	0	0
N	Z	V	C		N	Z	V	C

(b) ADD.W   D3, D7
Assume that (D3.W) = $FF00 and that (D7.W) = $8000. After the ADD instruction, (D7.W) = $7F00. The result in D7 is positive and nonzero. There is a carry and an overflow.

CCR Before					CCR After			
0	0	1	0		0	0	1	1
N	Z	V	C		N	Z	V	C

(c) CLR.L   D0
The CLR instruction clears the V, N, and C bits and sets the Z bit. The resulting CCR is

CCR			
0	1	0	0
N	Z	V	C

Note: If the result is 0, the Z bit is 1; if the result is not 0, the Z bit is 0. You can think of the Z bit as a Boolean variable. If Z = 1 (TRUE), a result of 0 occurred.

Subtraction and the Carry Bit

With subtraction, the MC68000 processor performs the subtraction $M - N$ by adding with the two's complement of N.

Subtraction: $M - N$
Operation: $M + 2\text{comp}(N)$

The programmer may be interested in identifying the presence of a borrow. However, the operation is inverted to be an addition. Fortunately, the carry bit assigned by the addition specifies a borrow. The following example reveals the relationship.

$M - N$	$M + 2\text{comp}(N)$	*Observe*
28AF − B408 74A7	28AF + 4BF8 0 74A7	In the subtraction operation, a borrow occurs. The corresponding addition has no carry.
8206 − 3A0F 47F7	8206 + C5F1 1 47F7	In the subtraction operation, no borrow occurs. The corresponding addition has a carry.

These examples demonstrate a pattern. A carry occurs in the two's complement addition if and only if no borrow is required in the corresponding subtraction operation. Using the formal definitions of two's complement numbers and subtraction, this pattern applies to a general subtraction problem.

Assume that the binary numbers have fixed length n.

$$M - N = M + 2\text{comp}(N) \quad \text{Definition of subtraction}$$
$$= M + (2^n - N) \quad \text{Definition of 2comp}(N)$$
$$= 2^n + (M - N) \quad \text{Result}$$

Focus on the result $2^n + (M - N)$.

1. If $M \geq N$, then no borrow occurs in the subtraction $M - N$. The term 2^n is unaffected, and this identifies a carry in the addition operation.

2. The opposite is true in the case of $M < N$. A borrow is required when subtracting $M - N$, and this is provided by the term 2^n. The corresponding addition has no resulting carry.

The MC68000 uses the C bit to indicate whether a borrow occurs during a subtraction operation. If $C = 1$, a borrow occurs. If $C = 0$, no borrow occurs. The processor implements this flag by inverting the value of the C bit obtained from the corresponding addition operation.

5.2 | SIMPLE BRANCH INSTRUCTIONS

The MC68000 supports a set of conditional branch instructions that test the status of the Z, N, V, and C bits in the CCR. It also provides for unconditional transfer of program control using the BRA "branch always" instruction. This branch is equivalent to a GOTO statement in a high-level language. In this section, the branch instructions are interspersed with new instructions and applications.

INSTRUCTION	*Syntax*				
Single CCR Bit	Z Bit	BEQ	⟨label⟩	"Branch on equal to zero"	$(Z = 1)$
Branches		BNE	⟨label⟩	"Branch on not equal to zero"	$(Z = 0)$
	N Bit	BMI	⟨label⟩	"Branch on minus"	$(N = 1)$
		BPL	⟨label⟩	"Branch on plus"	$(N = 0)$
	V Bit	BVS	⟨label⟩	"Branch on overflow set"	$(V = 1)$
		BVC	⟨label⟩	"Branch on overflow clear"	$(V = 0)$
	C Bit	BCS	⟨label⟩	"Branch on carry set"	$(C = 1)$
		BCC	⟨label⟩	"Branch on carry clear"	$(C = 0)$

Action   For the specific branch, assume that a previous instruction has already assigned the relevant CCR bit. If the condition is true, the branch is taken with the contents of the PC set to the value of the label. Program execution continues at the new address. Otherwise, the next instruction is executed.

Notes

1. The MC68000 requires that ⟨label⟩ be a symbolic label and not a constant. The branch jumps to the new address measured as a offset from the current PC.

2. The relative distance, in bytes, from the program counter location to the new location is called the **displacement**. The MC68000 permits only a 16-bit displacement. The MC68020/30/40 processors permit a 32-bit displacement.

3. The programmer's branch condition and the system's branch test have a different focus. Consider the instruction "BMI TESTNEG". The MC68000 tests if $N = 1$. The programmer is testing whether the result of the previous instruction was negative.

EXAMPLE 5.3   We assume that (D0.W) has the value $F000. For each example, the action of the branch instruction is specified.

(a) ADDI.W   #$1000,D0
    The result in (D0.W) after the ADDI instruction is $0000, and the CCR bits are

xxxx	0000						
D0.W			N	Z	V	C	

		CCR	
0	1	0	1
N	Z	V	C

Instruction		Branch Test	Action
BEQ	ALPHA	Result is 0 (Z = 1).	Branch to ALPHA
BVS	ALPHA	No overflow occurred (V = 0).	No branch
BCC	ALPHA	A carry occurred (C = 1).	No branch
BPL	ALPHA	Result is positive (N = 0).	Branch to ALPHA

(b) ADDI.B #$10,D0

The result in (D0.B) after the ADDI instruction is $10, and the CCR bits are

	CCR			
xxxx xx10	0	0	0	0
D0.W	N	Z	V	C

Instruction		Branch Test	Action
BMI	ALPHA	Result is positive (N = 0).	No branch
BVC	ALPHA	No overflow occurred (V = 0).	Branch to ALPHA

The unconditional branch instruction, BRA, assigns to the program counter the value ⟨label⟩ and causes direct transfer of program control to that value. The BRA branch, along with some conditional branches, is used to code high-level language control constructs.

INSTRUCTION

BRA (Unconditional Branch)

Syntax BRA ⟨label⟩

Action Program control passes directly to the instruction located at the address ⟨label⟩.

EXAMPLE 5.4

The unconditional branch causes program execution to continue at the value LOOP.

```
LOOP:                    ; BRA RETURNS CONTROL HERE
       .
       .
       .
       BRA   LOOP        ; SET PC TO VALUE LOOP
```

Testing and Branching

The conditional branch instructions use the current value of the CCR to determine whether a branch is required. In the logic of a program, a designated instruction assigns the CCR bits before executing the branch. The following simple example illustrates an error that can occur when the assignment of CCR bits is not monitored. Assume that you intend to have the BPL branch respond to the value in D0 after the ADDI instruction.

```
ADDI.W      #$6000,D0
JSR         DECOUT
BPL         THERE
```

If the result of the ADDI instruction is positive, the branch should execute. The processor tests the status of the N bit. However, the intervening call to DECOUT causes execution of a sequence of instructions that independently alter the CCR and cause the branch to execute incorrectly.

To deal with this situation, the MC68000 provides a TST instruction that tests the value in a data location and sets or clears the N and Z bits. The BEQ, BNE, BMI, and BPL branch instructions respond to the results of the TST instruction.

INSTRUCTION

TST
(Test)

Syntax   TST.⟨size⟩   ⟨ea⟩

Action   The value in location ⟨ea⟩ is tested. The sign of the number is determined and stored in the N bit. The Z bit indicates if the number is 0. The C and V bits are always cleared. The test does not affect the data.

Notes

1. The size parameter can be "B", "W", or "L".

2. The effective address of the operand is a data register or a memory reference.

EXAMPLE 5.5

Assume (D0.L) = $80F6 0000 and (A) = $A602.

80F6 0000		A602
D0		A

(*a*) TST.W   A   The CCR bits are N = 1 and Z = 0.
       BMI   ⟨label⟩   Execute a branch to ⟨label⟩.

(*b*) TST.W   D0   The CCR bits are N = 0 and Z = 1.
       BNE   ⟨label⟩   No branch is executed.

(*c*) In the preceding section, a call to DECOUT caused a possible error in executing the BPL instruction. The TST instruction reassigns the correct N-bit value.

```
ADDI.W      #$6000,D0
JSR         DECOUT
TST.W       D0
BPL         THERE
```

A complete program that computes the quotient and remainder for integer division illustrates the use of branch instructions. The algorithm is first implemented with equivalent Pascal code.

PROGRAM 5.1

Long Division Using Repeated Subtraction

Input the number $M \geq 0$ and $N > 0$. Test for valid input and re-enter if necessary. The program implements the Pascal operators "M DIV N = quotient" and "M MOD N = remainder" using repeated subtraction.

Algorithm   Repeatedly subtract the divisor N from M ($M := M - N$). Count the number of iterations Q until $M < 0$. This is one too many iterations, and the quotient is $Q - 1$. The remainder is $M + N$, the last positive value of M.

Pascal Code

```
PROGRAM longdivide (input, output);
    VAR
        m, n: integer;          { n is the divisor }
        quotient: integer;
        remainder: integer;
BEGIN
    quotient := 0;
        readln (m);
    WHILE (m < 0) DO            { test for M >= 0 }
        readln(m);
    readln(n);
    WHILE (n <= 0) DO           { test for N > 0 }
        readln(n);

    REPEAT
        quotient := quotient + 1;
        m := m - n;
    UNTIL m < 0;

    quotient := quotient - 1;
    remainder := m + n;
    writeln(quotient);
    writeln(remainder);
END.
```

MC68000 Code

```
          xref    decin,decout,stop,newline

start:    move.w  #0,d2      ; quotient in d2; set to 0
getm:     jsr     decin      ; read m
          tst.w   d0         ; test for m >= 0
          bmi     getm       ; if not, reenter m
          move.w  d0,d1      ; copy m to d1
getn:     jsr     decin      ; read n
          tst.w   d0         ; test for n > 0
          bmi     getn       ; if negative, reenter n
          beq     getn       ; if zero, reenter n
loop:     addi.w  #1,d2      ; increment the quotient
          sub.w   d0,d1      ; compute m - n
          bpl     loop       ; branch back if m not negative
setresult:
          subi.w  #1,d2
          add.w   d0,d1      ; set remainder
          move.w  d2,d0      ; move quotient to d0
          jsr     decout
          move.w  d1,d0      ; move the remainder to d0
          jsr     decout
          jsr     newline
          jsr     stop

          end
```

⟨Run of Program 5.1⟩

45   10
4   5

Computing 2comp(*N*)

The two's complement of a number can be computed from its definition using simple MC68000 instructions. Assume that N represents the value (D0.W).

Definition	*MC68000 Code*
$2\text{comp}(N) = 1\text{comp}(N) + 1$	NOT.W D0
	ADDI.W #1,D0

The MC68000 provides the NEG instruction to compute the two's complement of a number directly. The instruction is described and then used to compute the absolute value of a 16-bit integer. The absolute value of a number is its magnitude and is defined by

$$\text{Absolute value } (N) = \begin{cases} -N & \text{if } N < 0 \\ N & \text{if } N \geqslant 0 \end{cases}$$

INSTRUCTION

NEG (Negate)

Syntax NEG.⟨size⟩ ⟨ea⟩

Action The value of the operand is subtracted from 0.
$(2\text{comp}(N) = 0 - N)$. The CCR bits are set by the subtraction operation.

Notes

1. The size parameter can be "B", "W", or "L".

2. The operation uses subtraction. A borrow is required $(C = 1)$ unless the operand is 0.

3. Overflow does not occur unless $\text{NEG}(N) = N$. This case exists only when N is the most negative two's complement number. For example, if the size if "W", $\text{NEG}(\$8000) = \$8000$ and the V bit is set.

EXAMPLE 5.6

Assume that $(D0.L) = \$8FD6\ FF80$. The NEG instruction is illustrated for different size parameters.

(*a*) NEG.W D0
    The result $(D0.W) = \$0080$ and $(D0.L) = \$8FD6\ 0080$.

(*b*) NEG.L DO
    The result $(D0.L) = \$7029\ 0080$.

(*c*) NEG.B D0
    The result $(D0.B) = \$80$ and $(D0.L) = \$8FD6\ FF80$. The V bit is set.

PROGRAM 5.2

Absolute Value

Enter a 16-bit signed number N, and print its absolute value. The corresponding Pascal code is given to highlight the algorithm.

Pascal Code

```
PROGRAM absvalue (input, output);
   VAR
      n: integer;
BEGIN
   readln(n);
   IF n < 0 then
   n := -n;
   writeln(n);
END.
```

MC68000 Code

```
              xref      decin, decout, newline, stop

start:        jsr       decin    ; read n
              tst.w     d0
              bpl       print    ; n is positive. go print
              neg.w     d0       ; make it positive
print:        jsr       decout
              jsr       newline
              jsr       stop
              end
```

⟨Run of Program 5.2⟩

   −50
   50

5.3 | SHIFT OPERATIONS

The MC68000 provides a series of bit-shift operations that have important applications in arithmetic routines. The operations affect all the CCR bits and provide good applications for this chapter. The shift operations also implement multiplication and division by powers of 2 and are used extensively from this point on. The shift operations apply to both signed numbers (*arithmetic shift*) and unsigned numbers (*logical shift*).

This section defines the shift operations and discusses their effect on the value of a number with several examples.

EXAMPLE 5.7

The arithmetic shift operations perform multiplication and division by powers of 2. This example illustrates the arithmetic shift operations for 4-bit two's complement numbers ($-8 \leq x \leq 7$) using a variety of shift counts.

(a) *Arithmetic Shift Left:* We assume that X is the 4-digit two's complement number 0011_2. For a count of N, the number X is shifted to the left by N bits, and the vacated bits are filled with 0's.

   Shift X left by 1. Result: $X = 0110_2$.
   Shift X left by 3. Result: $X = 1000_2$.

An arithmetic shift to the left is equivalent to multiplication by 2^N. Consider the shift left of X by $N = 1$.

$$X = 0011_2 = 1(2^1) + 1(2^0) = 3_{10}$$
$$\text{Result:} \quad X = 0110_2 = 1(2^2) + 1(2^1) = 6_{10}$$

The power of 2 corresponding to each bit is increased by $N = 1$. The result is a multiplication by 2. The case of a shift by 3 has the effect of multiplying by $2^3 = 8$. The resulting 4-bit value of 8 reflects overflow.

(b) *Arithmetic Shift Right:* For a count of N, a number is shifted to the right by N bits, and the sign bit is replicated in the vacated bits.

Assume $X = 0110_2$. Shift right by 1. Result $X = 0011_2$.
Assume $X = 1100_2$. Shift right by 1. Result $X = 1110_2$.
Assume $X = 1010_2$. Shift right by 3. Result $X = 1111_2$.

Arithmetic shift to the right is the inverse of a left shift and implements signed division by 2^N. In the preceding examples,

$X = 0110_2 = 6$. The shift right by 1 gives $0011_2 = 3$.
$X = 1100_2 = -4$. The shift right by 1 gives $1110_2 = -2$.
$X = 1010_2 = -6$. The shift right by 3 gives $1111_2 = -1$.

The arithmetic right shift uses sign extension to implement integer division correctly. Assuming that the vacated bits are filled with 0, the result of dividing $X = 1100 = -4$ by 2 would be $0110 = 6$ and not $1110 = -2$.

EXAMPLE 5.8

Logical shift operations implement unsigned multiplication and division. The operations closely resemble arithmetic shifts. However, for both logical shift to the left and logical shift to the right, the vacated bits are replaced with 0's. No sign extension applies.

(a) *Logical Shift Left:* For a count of N, a number is shifted left by N bits and the vacated bits are filled with 0's.
Assume $X = 4F2C_{16}$ and $N = 4$. The result is $F2C0_{16}$.

(b) *Logical Shift Right* For a count of N, a number is shifted right by N bits, and the vacated bits are filled with 0's.
Assume $X = 1000_{16} = 4096_{10}$. A logical shift to the right by 8 is equivalent to division by $2^8 = 256$. The result after the shift is $0010_{16} = 16_{10}$.

INSTRUCTION

ASL/ASR

LSR/LSL

Shift

Syntax Arithmetic Shift

ASL.⟨size⟩	#N,Dn	ASR.⟨size⟩	#N,Dn
ASL.⟨size⟩	Dm,Dn	ASR.⟨size⟩	Dm,Dn
ASL	⟨ea⟩	ASR	⟨ea⟩

Syntax   Logical Shift

LSR.⟨size⟩	#N,D*n*	LSL.⟨size⟩	#N,D*n*
LSR.⟨size⟩	D*m*,D*n*	LSL.⟨size⟩	D*m*,D*n*
LSR ⟨ea⟩		LSL ⟨ea⟩	

Action   The results of the operations are given in Examples 5.7 and 5.8. The shift count is contained in the source operand. The immediate operand (#N) may be used only for a shift count in the range 1–8. A shift count in a data register is restricted to the range 0–63. The low-order 6 bits of D*m* are used.

Notes

1. The size parameter can be "B", "W", or "L". If the desired shift count is greater than 8, it must be stored in a data register D*m*.

2. The destination operand must be a data value contained either in a data register or in memory. A data register permits a byte, word, or long-word operation. The contents of memory may be shifted 1 bit only, and the operand size is restricted to a word.

3. A shift count can be loaded into register D*m* during program execution. This allows variable shift counts in loops.

4. All the CCR bits are affected by a shift instruction. For an arithmetic shift, the V bit indicates whether a sign change occurred at any time during the shift. The V bit is cleared for the logical shifts. The C and X bits contain the last bit shifted out of the operand. They are cleared when the shift count is 0. The Z and N bits indicate whether the result is zero or negative.

EXAMPLE 5.9

(a) ASL.W   #4, D0
Assume (D0.W) = $7653. Arithmetic shift left by 4. Result (D0.W) = $6530.

CCR Bit Assignment

Not zero	(Z = 0)
Positive	(N = 0)
Sign change	(V = 1)
Last shifted bit	(C = 1) and (X = 1)

(b) MOVE.B   #24, D1
ASR.L   D1, D2

Assume (D2.L) = $A885 66FF. Arithmetic shift right by 24. Result (D2.L) = $FFFF FFA8.

CCR Bit Assignment

Not zero	(Z = 0)
Negative	(N = 1)
No sign change	(V = 0)
Last shifted bit	(C = 1) and (X = 1)

(c) LSR.W #4, D0

Assume (D0.W) = $2194. Logical shift right by 4. Result (D0.W) = $0219.

CCR Bit Assignment

Not zero	(Z = 0)
Positive	(N = 0)
Always cleared	(V = 0)
Last shifted bit	(C = 0) and (X = 0)

(d) LSL $1000

Assume that the 16-bit contents at memory location $1000 are $40F3. The logical shift of a memory location implies a shift count of 1. The result is $81E6.

Before	After
0 1 0 0 0 0 0 0 1 1 1 1 0 0 1 1	1 0 0 0 0 0 0 1 1 1 1 0 0 1 1 0

PROGRAM 5.3

Count Ones

Enter a 16-bit number *N* using HEXIN. By successively logical-shifting the bits left, the number of 1's in the binary representation of *N* is computed and printed.

```
              xref       hexin,decout,newline,stop

start:        clr.w      d1              ; d1 will hold the count
              jsr        hexin           ; input n into d0
again:        lsl.w      #1,d0           ; shift 1 bit to the left
              bcc        testzero
              addi.w     #1,d1           ; increment (d1) if c = 1
testzero:
              tst.w      d0
              bne        again           ; repeat loop if (d0.w) not 0
              move.w     d1,d0           ; move count to d0 for output
              jsr        decout
```

```
jsr        newline
jsr        stop
end
```

⟨Run of Program 5.3⟩

AF29 (1010 1111 0010 1001)
9

5.4 | THE SIGNED COMPARISON BRANCHES

Branch instructions allow the assembly language programmer to construct conditional and loop statements. Most readers recognize the high-level arithmetic relations that create Boolean expressions, such as "equal," "greater than," and "less than or equal," and so forth. These same relations are available to assembly language in signed branches.

The MC68000 instruction CMP ("Compare") is used to assign the CCR bits for a subsequent branch test. The branch tests use the CCR bits assigned by CMP to determine the truth of an arithmetic relation.

INSTRUCTION

CMP/CMPI
(Compare)

Syntax   CMP.⟨size⟩   ⟨ea⟩,Dn
CMPI.⟨size⟩   #N,⟨ea⟩

Action   The contents of the source operand are subtracted from the destination operand without changing the destination. The subtraction operant, destination − source, determines the condition codes.

Notes

1. The size parameter may be "B", "W", or "L".

2. The source operand for CMP can be any addressing mode.

EXAMPLE 5.10

The following CMP instruction determines the CCR bits. Assume (D2.W) = $000A.

CMPI.W   #$10, D2

The subtraction 000A − 0010 = FFFA is executed. The result is negative (N = 1) and nonzero (Z = 0). A borrow occurs (C = 1), and the operation "positive − positive = negative" implies no overflow (V = 0).

CCR

1	0	0	1
N	Z	V	C

As an inequality, the destination is less than the source. The condition is equivalent to "destination $-$ source < 0".

$$(000A < 0010) \quad \text{if and only if} \quad (000A - 0010 < 0)$$

INSTRUCTION

Signed Comparison Branches

Syntax		Description	Action
BGE	⟨label⟩	Greater or equal	Branch if destination $\geq$ source
BGT	⟨label⟩	Greater than	Branch if destination $>$ source
BLE	⟨label⟩	Less or equal	Branch if destination $\leq$ source
BLT	⟨label⟩	Less than	Branch if destination $<$ source

Note Use BEQ and BNE combined with the signed comparison branches to handle all arithmetic inequalities.

EXAMPLE 5.11

(a) CMPI.W #$A, D5   Assume (D5.W) = $0006.
   BLT   LABEL

The BLT instruction causes a branch because the destination ($0006) is less than the source ($000A).

(b) CMP.W D3, D4   Assume (D3.W) = $7000 and (D4.W) = $A000.
   BGE   LABEL

The BGE instruction does not cause a branch because the destination ($A000) is not greater than or equal to the source ($7000).

The following program anticipates a study of high-level language control structures. Both a Pascal "REPEAT . . UNTIL" and an "IF . . THEN . . ELSE" construct are used.

PROGRAM 5.4

Sum the Positives

Enter a sequence of 16-bit signed numbers. A positive number is added to a running sum, whereas a number that is 0 or negative is rejected. Stop when the sum exceeds 100. Output the final sum and the number of rejected entries.

Pascal Code

```
PROGRAM sum_positives (input, output);
  VAR
    n: integer;
    sum: integer;
    reject_count: integer;

BEGIN
  sum := 0;
  reject_count := 0;
  repeat
    read(N);
    IF (n <= 0) THEN
      reject_count := reject_count + 1
    ELSE
      sum := sum + N
  UNTIL sum > 100;
  write (sum);
  writeln(reject_count : 6);
END.
```

MC68000 Code

```
; data register usage:
; d0        holds the input value from decin
; d1        holds the sum of the positive values.
; d2        holds number of rejected (non-positive) input values.

            xref      decin,decout,newline,stop
start:      move.w    #0,d1      ; clear the registers
            move.w    #0,d2
loop:       jsr       decin
; begin the "if..then..else"
            cmpi.w    #0,d0      ; test for input > 0
            bgt       addsum     ; branch to addsum if true
            addi.w    #1,d2      ; increment reject_count
            bra       loop       ; branch to loop continue test
addsum:
            add.w     d0,d1      ; add to the sum
testsum:
; begin the "until sum > 100" test
            cmpi.w    #100,d1    ; test if sum > 100
            ble       loop       ; if not, return for new input
            move.w    d1,d0      ; setup output of sum
            jsr       decout     ; output the sum
            move.w    d2,d0      ; setup output of reject_count
            jsr       decout     ; output reject_count
            jsr       newline
            jsr       stop
            end
```

⟨Run of Program 5.4⟩

35 20 −2 −3 50
105 2

Signed Branches and the CCR

The signed branches test the V, N, and Z bits in the CCR. By including the V bit, signed branches are correctly executed even when an operation may produce overflow. For instance, assume that (D0.W) = $7FFA. The following branch instructions "look" equivalent:

CMPI.W # − 8, D0	CMPI.W # − 8, D0
BPL LABEL	BGE LABEL

The CMPI instruction computes the difference $7FFA − (−8) = $8002. The result should have been positive; hence, overflow occurred (V = 1).

CCR

1	0	1	1
N	Z	V	C

The BPL instruction does not produce a branch because $N = 1$. The BGE instruction, however, causes a branch because the destination is greater than or equal to the source.

Let us examine the BGE branch more closely to see how the V bit is used. Assume that a CMP instruction assigns the CCR bits. We can make a geometric argument using the number line and the fact that the CMP instruction evaluates destination − source. A BGE branch occurs if the destination is greater than or equal to the source. On the number line, the destination is to the right of the source.

Test Case 1   Source and destination are positive.

Destination − source is positive with no overflow.

CCR

0		0	
N	Z	V	C

Test Case 2   Source and destination are negative.

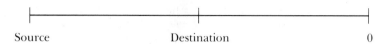

Source   Destination   0

Destination − source is positive with no overflow.

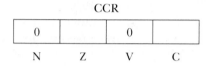

CCR

0		0	
N	Z	V	C

Test Case 3   Source is negative, and destination is positive.

Source   0   Destination

Overflow occurs if destination − source is negative.

CCR

1		1	
N	Z	V	C

No overflow occurs if destination − source is positive.

CCR

0		0	
N	Z	V	C

Note that the N and V bits are the same in all the cases.

An algebraic argument can be used to determine tests for the BGE branch. The BGE branch executes provided the CMP instruction recognizes

$$\text{destination} - \text{source} \geq 0$$

Under ordinary conditions (no overflow, or $V = 0$), the N bit is assigned 0. However, if overflow occurs ($V = 1$), the sign of the result is opposite what it should be. $N = 1$.

Summary   In all the cases resulting in a branch, the N and V bits have the same value. Hence, either (NOT N AND NOT V) or (N AND V) equals 1. To complete the analysis, it is necessary to show that in all cases where

TABLE 5.2 Signed Branch Test Condition

MNEMONIC	NAME	CONDITION
BGE	Greater than or equal	(NOT N AND NOT V) OR (N AND V)
BGT	Greater than	(NOT N AND NOT V AND NOT Z) OR (N AND V AND NOT Z)
BLE	Less than or equal	Z OR (N AND NOT V) OR (NOT N AND V)
BLT	Less than	(N AND NOT V) OR (NOT N AND V)

the source is greater than the destination, the V and N bits have opposite values and so both (NOT N AND NOT V) and (N AND V) equal 0.

BGE Test Condition

$$(\text{NOT N AND NOT V}) \text{ or } (\text{N AND V}) = \begin{cases} 1 \text{ branch occurs} \\ 0 \text{ no branch occurs} \end{cases}$$

Table 5.2 shows a complete set of CCR test conditions for the signed branches.

EXAMPLE 5.12

The branch instructions from Example 5.11 are executed using the test conditions in Table 5.2.

(a) CMPI.W   #$A, D5   Assume (D5.W) = $0006.
    BLT   LABEL

The CMPI instruction executes a subtraction ($6 - 10 = -4$). The resulting CCR bits are

CCR

1	0	0	1
N	Z	V	C

The BLT condition is (N AND NOT V) or (NOT N AND V).

(1 AND NOT 0) OR (NOT 1 AND 0) = 1

The branch to LABEL is executed.

(b) CMP.W   D3, D4   Assume (D3.W) = $7000 and (D4.W) = $A000.
    BGE   LABEL

The CMP instruction computes $A000 − $7000 = $3000. The CCR bits are

CCR

0	0	1	0
N	Z	V	C

The BGE condition is (NOT N AND NOT V) OR (N AND V)

(NOT 0 AND NOT 1) OR (0 AND 1) = 0

The branch to LABEL is not executed.

5.5 | STRUCTURED PROGRAMMING

High-level languages provide constructs for conditional code execution and loops. These constructs translate into test and branch instructions in assembly language. Sample programs have already used the basic control structures. This experience provides the foundation for a more formal analysis of the control constructs.

IF .. THEN

The IF .. THEN construct is the basic conditional statement in a high-level language. A condition is given in the form of a Boolean expression. If it evaluates TRUE, the code block [denoted Code(T)] is executed. Otherwise, program control passes to the first statement following the code block.

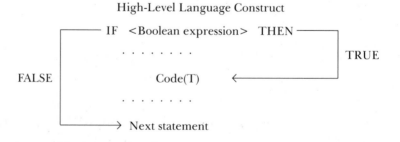

High-Level Language Construct

To understand the assembly language code for IF .. THEN, note that Code(T) is not executed if the expression evaluates to FALSE. In this case, program control passes to "Next statement." In assembly language, use a branch instruction to test the expression (NOT ⟨Boolean expression⟩) and branch to "Next statement" if it evaluates to TRUE. The following code outline gives the assembly language implementation. The notation "B$\overline{cc}$" means branch on "NOT condition cc". For instance, if cc = GE, the NOT condition cc is LT and the branch BLT is used.

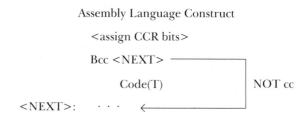

IF .. THEN .. ELSE
=====

Frequently, program logic requires an "either or" choice. If the condition is TRUE, take one line of action [Code(T)]; otherwise, select an alternative action [Code(F)]. Most high-level languages have an IF .. THEN .. ELSE statement.

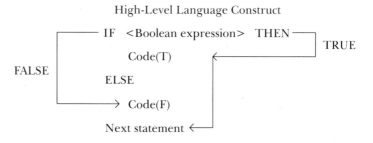

The corresponding assembly language construct requires two branches. A conditional branch directs program control to the Code(F) block. In case the Code(T) block is executed, an unconditional BRA branch transfers control to the "next statement."

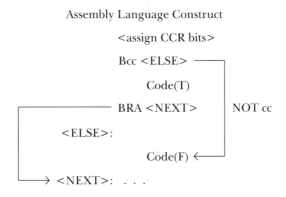

WHILE .. DO

A program loop is an extension of simple conditionals. In this case, however, a branch returns program control to previously executed instructions. The WHILE .. DO construct gives a general form of a loop. The WHILE clause tests a condition. If it is TRUE, program control enters the loop and executes Code(T). Before returning to the WHILE test, some variable is modified so that the test eventually fails. The following diagram shows the structure of the WHILE loop:

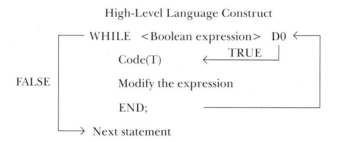

High-Level Language Construct

In an assembly language program, a conditional branch tests the Boolean expression. An unconditional BRA branch implements the return.

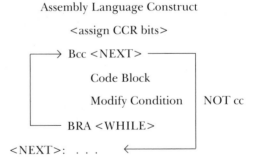

Assembly Language Construct

LOOP .. EXIT

High-level languages generally provide a variety of loop constructs. The modern trend in languages is to unify these constructs in a single, all-purpose LOOP .. EXIT statement. The "exit" condition can be tested at any appropriate point in the code block. If it is TRUE, an exit from the loop is performed.

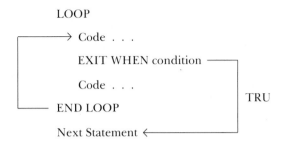

Assembly language code implements the "EXIT WHEN" test with a branch. The LOOP .. EXIT construct is the simplest way to implement an assembly language loop.

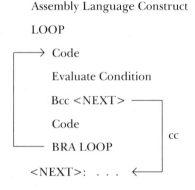

The FOR Loop

A special case of the WHILE .. DO construct is a loop with a fixed number of iterations. In many high-level languages, a FOR .. DO instruction, which carries out a series of steps to initialize and test a counter and execute a block of code, is available. In Pascal, the FOR .. DO loop has the syntax

FOR Counter := InitialValue TO UpperLimit DO ⟨Code⟩

The following sequence of steps implements the construct.

Step 1: Initialize the counter.

Step 2: Compare the counter with the upper limit.

Step 3: Exit if the value of the counter is greater than the upper limit; otherwise, execute the loop code.

Step 4: Increment the counter.

Step 5: Return to Step 2.

The following assembly language program implements the high-level language FOR .. DO statement. Trace the code and identify the five steps to implement the loop construct.

PROGRAM 5.5

The FOR .. DO Loop in Assembly Language

Enter a positive number N and evaluate the series

$$1 + 2 + 3 + \cdots + N$$

by emulating a FOR .. DO loop. Print the sum.

```
                xref        stop,decin,decout,newline
start:   jsr        decin
         move.w     d0,d2        ; copy n to d2
         clr.w      d0           ; d0 holds the sum
         move.w     #1,d1        ; initialize the counter
loop:    cmp.w      d2,d1        ; compare against n
         bgt        done         ; exit loop at (d1) = 11
         add.w      d1,d0
         addi.w     #1,d1        ; increment the counter
         bra        loop         ; return for next iteration
done:    jsr        decout       ; output the sum
         jsr        newline
         jsr        stop
         end
```

⟨Run of program 5.5⟩

```
5
15
```

The Quick Instructions

Most loops with a fixed number of iterations are executed more efficiently in assembly language by decrementing the counter to 0. No CMP statement is required because the loop terminates when the counter reaches 0. A BNE branch tests this condition. In this section, Program 5.5 is recoded to use a FOR .. DOWNTO loop. The program also motivates introduction of the MC68000 "QUICK" instructions. These instructions have a source operand in immediate mode. They are implemented as one-word instructions with an immediate mode constant included as part of the opcode word.

INSTRUCTION

The MOVEQ
(Move Quick)

Syntax MOVEQ #N, Dn

Action Stores the value N as the 32-bit contents of data register Dn.

Notes

1. The data must be an 8-bit two's complement number in the range $-128 \leq N \leq 127$.

2. The number N is part of the opcode word; hence, this is a one-word instruction.

3. The number N is sign-extended to a long word before being stored in Dn.

4. MOVEQ is used to initialize counters if the value is in the proper range. The instruction is significantly faster than "MOVE.L   #N, Dn".

EXAMPLE 5.13

(a) MOVEQ   #0, D0
Clears all 32 bits of D0.

(b) MOVEQ   #$FF, D6
Sets (D6) to -1.

(c) MOVEQ   #255, D0
Invalid because the data is out of range.

Warning   In case (c), your assembler may silently accept $255 = FF_{16}$. The value -1 would be stored in D0.

INSTRUCTION

ADDQ/SUBQ
(Add Quick and
Subtract Quick)

Syntax   ADDQ.⟨size⟩   #N, ⟨ea⟩
SUBQ.⟨size⟩   #N, ⟨ea⟩

Action   This is an optimized form of the ADD (or SUB) instruction. The source is immediate data in the range 1–8.

Note

1. The size parameter can be "B", "W", or "L".

2. The destination may be any non-PC-relative addressing mode. PC-relative mode is discussed in Chapter 6.

3. The destination may be an address register.

EXAMPLE 5.14

(a) ADDQ.W   #1, D0
Adds 1 to the LSW in D0.

(b) SUBQ.L   #3, A5
Subtracts 32-bit value 3 from (A5).

(c) ADDQ.L   #10, D3

Invalid because the data is out of range.

PROGRAM 5.6

A FOR ..
DOWNTO Loop
in Assembly
Language

This program evaluates the series

$$N + (N - 1) + \cdots + 3 + 2 + 1$$

using the "Quick" instructions.

```
          xref     decin, decout, newline, stop

start:    jsr      decin
          move.w   d0,d1        ; store the counter in (d1)
          moveq    #0,d0        ; initialize (d0) to 0
loop:     add.w    d1,d0        ; add counter to the sum
          subq.w   #1,d1        ; decrement (d1)
          bne      loop         ; go to loop if (d1) not yet zero
          jsr      decout       ; output sum
          jsr      newline
          jsr      stop
          end
```

⟨Run of Program 5.6⟩

5
15

5.6 | UNSIGNED BRANCHES

The discussion of branching so far has emphasized signed branches used with arithmetic operations. With addresses, characters, and unsigned numbers, a new set of comparison branches is required.

The MC68000 provides four unsigned branches that test the relative location of the source (*S*) and destination (*D*) on the number line. The options parallel the signed branches that test arithmetic inequalities.

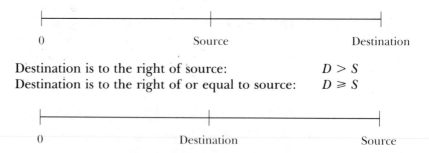

Destination is to the right of source: $D > S$

Destination is to the right of or equal to source: $D \geqslant S$

Destination is to the left of or equal to source: $D \leqslant S$

Destination is to the left of source: $D < S$

Because unsigned numbers are only positive and their operations do not generate signed overflow, the N and the V bits are not used to test any unsigned branch condition.

INSTRUCTION	Syntax	Description	Relative Location
Unsigned	BHI ⟨label⟩	Higher	$D > S$
Comparison	BHS ⟨label⟩	Higher or same	$D \geqslant S$
Branches	BLS ⟨label⟩	Lower or same	$D \leqslant S$
	BLO ⟨label⟩	Lower	$D < S$

Note

1. The unsigned branches test the Z and C bits. Table 5.3 shows the logical relations.

2. Technically, a standard Motorola assembler does not support the BHS and BLO mnemonics. Rather, it uses the equivalent BCC and BCS mnemonics in the unsigned branches.

MNEMONIC	CONDITION	TEST
BCC⟨label⟩	Higher or same	$D \geqslant S$
BCS ⟨label⟩	Lower	$D < S$

However, most assemblers recognize the BHS and BLO mnemonics and equate them with the corresponding branch on carry instruction. If your assembler uses only the BCC and BCS instruction mnemonics, you need some technique to relate unsigned comparison with values for the C bit. If $S \leqslant D$, then the result of the comparison operation $(D - S)$ is positive,

TABLE 5.3 Unsigned Branch Tests

MNEMONIC	CONDITION	TEST
BHS	Higher or same	$C = 0$
BHI	Higher	$C = 0$ AND $Z = 0$
BLO	Lower	$C = 1$
BLS	Lower or same	$C = 1$ OR $Z = 1$

and no borrow occurs (C = 0). Hence, BCC = BHS. Conversely, if D < S, then the result of the comparison operation (D − S) is negative, and a borrow occurs (C = 1). Hence, BCS = BLO.

Comparing Addresses

The CPMA instruction is designed for unsigned comparison of a source operand with an address register. The instruction is frequently used to test the relative location of addresses prior to an unsigned branch.

INSTRUCTION

CMPA
(Compare Address)

Syntax   CMPA.⟨size⟩   ⟨ea⟩,An

Action   Subtract the contents of the source operand from the 32-bit long word in the address register. The subtraction operation determines the C, V, Z, and N bits in the CCR.

Note

1. The size parameter is word or long word. A word-length source operand is sign-extended to 32 bits before the subtraction is executed.

2. All addressing modes are allowed for the source operand.

EXAMPLE 5.15

(a) CMPA.W   #$3A, A3
    Assume that (A3.L) = $0000902C. The immediate data $3A is sign-extended before the subtraction operation

$$0000902C - 0000003A = 00008FF2$$

As a 32-bit unsigned number, the result is positive with no borrow required. The destination is "higher or same" as the source.

(b) CMPA.L   A0, A1
    Assume that (A0.L) = $00008554 and (A1.L) = $000040FE. In the subtraction operation, a borrow is required:

$$000040FE - 00008554 = FFFFBBAA$$

The destination is "lower" than the source.

EXAMPLE 5.16

The scanning of elements in a list provides an application for unsigned branches. Assume that (A0) points at successive elements in the list and ADDR points to the end of the list. The scan of elements in the list continues as long as (A0) is less than or equal to ADDR.

(A0)   ADDR

EXAMPLE 5.17

Assume that ADDR = \$008554 and (A0) = \$000004FE. After executing the instruction "CMPA.W #ADDR, A0", the CCR bits are N = 0, V = 0, Z = 0, and C = 1. You must use an unsigned branch for the address comparison. Consider the following:

```
LABEL:          · · ·          LABEL:           · · ·
      CMPA.W   #ADDR,A0              CMPA.W   #ADDR,A0
      BLE      LABEL                 BLS      LABEL
```

The signed branch BLE does not cause a branch because N = 0 and no overflow occurred. However, the unsigned BLS will correctly result in a branch. *Warning:* Never use signed branches when comparing addresses.

PROGRAM 5.7

Address Range

Enter an address range in two steps. Using HEXIN—LONG, the first input is the lower bound, and the second input is the upper bound. The program determines if a test address is within the address range using the CMPA instruction. The output includes either an "out of range" message or the inequality

$$\langle \text{lower bound} \rangle \leq \langle \text{test address} \rangle \leq \langle \text{upper bound} \rangle$$

```
        xref     hexin_long, hexout_long, strout, newline, stop

start:  jsr      hexin_long           ; enter lower address bound
        movea.l  d0,a0
        jsr      hexin_long           ; enter upper address range
        movea.l  d0,a1
        jsr      hexin_long           ; enter test address
        cmpa.l   d0,a0
        bhi      off_range            ; test addr below lower bound
        cmpa.l   d0,a1
        blo      off_range            ; test addr above upper bound
        move.l   d0,d1                ; store addr in d1

        move.l   a0,d0                ; print lower bound
        jsr      hexout_long

        lea      less_equalmsg,a0     ; print "<=" symbols
        move.w   #4,d0
        jsr      strout
```

```
          move.l    d1,d0              ; print test address
          jsr       hexout_long

          move.w    #4,d0              ; print "<=" symbols
          jsr       strout

          move.l    a1,d0              ; print upper bound
          jsr       hexout_long
          bra       quit

off_range: lea      off_addrmsg,a0     ; print "out of range message"
          move.w    #12,d0
          jsr       strout
quit:     jsr       newline
          jsr       stop

          data
less_equalmsg:
          dc.b      '<= '
off_addrmsg:
          dc.b      'out of range'
          end
```

⟨Run of Program 5.7⟩

8000 C000
B000
00008000 <= *0000B000* <= *0000C000*

| 5.7 | ADDITIONAL BRANCH INSTRUCTIONS

Assembly language implements loops most efficiently by decrementing a counter. In some applications, a second condition (other than the counter) is involved in determining the number of iterations. You may execute the loop a fixed number of times N or until a condition becomes TRUE. For instance, in the sequential search algorithm, the list is searched until the key is found or until the list is exhausted. The MC68000 provides a family of decrement and branch instructions to treat loops with such exit conditions.

INSTRUCTION

DBCC
(Decrement and Branch)

Syntax   DBcc   D*n*, ⟨LABEL⟩   ("cc" is a condition code)

Action   The instruction executes conditional tests described by the following algorithm.

Algorithm

IF cc is TRUE then
Execution continues at the next instruction.
ELSE
Decrement the register counter by 1 [(Dn.W) = (Dn.W) − 1] and
test the resulting (Dn.W).
IF (Dn.W) ≠ −1, then
Program control passes to ⟨LABEL⟩
ELSE
Execution continues at the next instruction.

Summary   DBcc   Dn, ⟨LABEL⟩ implements the Pascal REPEAT .. UNTIL loop. The test condition can be stated as "REPEAT the loop UNTIL the condition (cc) is TRUE or (Dn.W) = −1."

Notes

1. Table 5.4 provides a list of "cc" tests. Most assemblers recognize the DBHS and DBLO tests. Standard Motorola uses DBCC ("Higher or Same") and DBCS ("Lower").

2. Most assemblers accept DBRA in place of DBF. Since the condition "F" is never TRUE, the loop terminates only when (Dn.W) = −1. This text consistently uses DBRA.

3. With the DBcc branch, iteration continues when the data register index reaches 0. Hence, the data register must be initialized to one less than the number of loop iterations.

4. The condition codes are not affected by the decrement operation.

TABLE 5.4   Decrement and Branch Codes

CODE	DESCRIPTION	CODE	DESCRIPTION
CC	Carry clear	LS	Lower or same
CS	Carry set	LT	Less than
EQ	Equal	MI	Minus
F	False	NE	Not equal
GE	Greater than or equal	PL	Plus
GT	Greater than	T	True
HI	Higher	VC	Overflow clear
LE	Less than or equal	VS	Overflow set
HS	Higher or same	LO	Lower

EXAMPLE 5.18

The code segments contrast a loop using the DBcc construct with a loop using standard branch instructions. In each case, the loop executes six iterations. Notice that the DBcc code initializes the counter to 5, one less than the number of interations.

<table>
<tr><td colspan="3">DBcc Code</td><td colspan="3">Bcc Code</td></tr>
<tr><td></td><td>MOVEQ</td><td>#5,D0</td><td></td><td>MOVEQ</td><td>#6,D0</td></tr>
<tr><td>LOOP:</td><td>·</td><td></td><td>LOOP:</td><td>·</td><td></td></tr>
<tr><td></td><td>·</td><td></td><td></td><td>·</td><td></td></tr>
<tr><td></td><td>·</td><td></td><td></td><td>SUBQ.W</td><td>#1,D0</td></tr>
<tr><td></td><td>DBRA</td><td>D0,LOOP</td><td></td><td>BNE</td><td>LOOP</td></tr>
</table>

Decrement and branch tests find applications with lists, search/sort algorithms, and so forth. The following program uses the DBEQ instruction to implement a sequential search for a key in a list. A list of *N* items is scanned until the key is found (EQ) or the list is exhausted (decrement counter $= -1$).

PROGRAM 5.8

Sequential Search

Six 16-bit signed numbers are stored in a list. A target value (KEY) is entered using DECIN, and the sequential search looks for the first occurrence of the KEY in the list.

Algorithm   The KEY is stored in D1. Using a DBEQ loop, the code looks for the first occurrence of (D1) in the list. If the KEY is found, its index in the list is returned. Otherwise, the index -1 is returned.

```
            xref      decin,decout,strout,newline,stop

start:      jsr       decin
            move.w    d0,d1          ; move key to (d1)
            lea       list-2,a0      ; set (a0) 1 word before the
;                                    ; start of the list
            moveq     #5,d2          ; list has 6 elements
checknext:  addq.w    #2,a0          ; move to next word
            cmp.w     (a0),d1
            dbeq      d2,checknext
            bne       return         ; cmp.w tested false
            subi.w    #5,d2          ; find index of the key
            neg.w     d2
return:     lea       returnmsg,a0
            moveq     #13,d0
            jsr       strout
            move.w    d2,d0          ; copy index to d0
            jsr       decout         ; output return value in d0
            jsr       newline
            jsr       stop
```

```
               data

list:          dc.w      -2000, -6, 100, 800, 3000, 10000
returnmsg:     dc.b      'return index '

               end
```

⟨Run of Program 5.8⟩

800
return index 3

Long Branches

MC68000 branch instructions have some restrictions. The target address of the branch must be a label. This target address is given relative to the PC with an offset limited to the range −32768 to 32766. To provide a more general branch instruction, the MC68000 introduces the JMP ("Jump") instruction.

INSTRUCTION

JMP
(Jump)

Syntax JMP ⟨ea⟩

Action Program control passes to the specified memory address.

Notes

1. The branch instruction requires a label as an operand. The JMP instruction allows any addressing mode that can be used to access memory. For instance, the data and address register direct modes cannot be used, but absolute long and address register indirect modes can be used.

2. The branch can be to any word in memory.

EXAMPLE 5.19

(a) JMP AGAIN
    Program control passes to address AGAIN.

(b) JMP (A2)
    Jump to the address identified by the contents of memory location (A2).

The JMP instruction is equivalent to the unconditional BRA branch. For short branches, the JMP instruction is less efficient because the machine code requires one or two extension words.

Some MC68000 assemblers implement a full family of conditional jump instructions that parallel the conditional branch instructions. For instance,

JEQ LOOP   JLT CONTINUE

Even though these are not standard MC68000 instructions, each is implemented by combining the complementary conditional branches and the JMP instruction. You can use the same logic if conditional jump instructions are not available. If the label is within the range of an ordinary branch instruction, use it. Otherwise, use the following logic:

Conditional *Jump Logic*	*MC68000* *Implementation Logic*
JNE LABEL	BEQ NEXT
Next Statement	JMP LABEL
	NEXT: Next Statement
.	.
.	.
.	.
LABEL:	LABEL:

5.8 | Bcc INSTRUCTION MACHINE CODE

The branch instruction has a 4-bit opcode (0110), a 4-bit condition code, and an 8-bit displacement field. An 8- or 16-bit two's complement offset from the PC defines the target address.

0 1 1 0	Condition	8-Bit Displacement
16-Bit Displacement if 8-Bit Displacement = $00		

8-bit: $-128 \le$ offset ≤ 126

16-bit: $-32768 \le$ offset ≤ 32766

Table 5.5 shows the 4-bit condition code for the branches.

Offsets are computed relative to the program counter. Recall that the PC is incremented by 2 on the read cycle of the instruction. Thus if a branch instruction is located at address A, the PC will have value A + 2 after reading the opcode word.

During the second pass of the assembler, the offset is computed with the following equation:

$$\text{Offset} = \text{LABEL} - (\text{Loc} + 2)$$

TABLE 5.5 Bcc Condition Codes

BRANCH	CONDITION	CODE	BRANCH	CONDITION	CODE
BHI	High	0010	BVS	Overflow set	1001
BLS	Lower than or same	0011	BPL	Plus	1010
BCC	Carry clear	0100	BMI	Minus	1011
BCS	Carry set	0101	BGE	Greater than or equal	1100
BNE	Not equal	0110	BLT	Less than	1101
BEQ	Equal	0111	BGT	Greater than	1110
BVC	Overflow clear	1000	BLE	Less than or equal	1111
BHS	Higher than or same	0100	BLO	Lower	0101

Loc is the value of the location counter at the branch instruction, and LABEL is the operand in the branch instruction. During execution, if the branch is taken, the CPU adds the offset to PC + 2 to obtain the address LABEL. The offset is a constant independent of the program counter.

If the offset is in the range -128 to 126, it can be stored as an 8-bit displacement in the opcode word. Otherwise, the opcode displacement is set to 0, and the offset is stored in the extension word. Most MC68000 assemblers will default to a 16-bit displacement for all forward branches unless you explicitly designate an 8-bit offset or "short" branch. Such a branch is specified by adding a suffix ".S" to the mnemonic.

BGT.S AGAIN   BRA.S OUTPUT

EXAMPLE 5.20

Branch Machine Code

Assume that the assembler defaults to a 16-bit displacement unless you specify short branch. Using a skeleton code segment, the example illustrates machine code with both a forward and a backward branch.

Address	*Instruction*
000100	BGE.S LABEL
	.
	.
	.
00011A LABEL:	.
	.
	.
000136	BEQ LABEL

(*a*) Forward Branch Code: BGE.S

$$\text{Offset} = \text{LABEL} - (\text{Loc} + 2) = 011A - (0100 + 2) = 0018$$

With the short branch reference, the displacement is given as an 8-bit number $0018. The condition code for BGE is 1100.

Machine Code

0 1 1 0	1 1 0 0	0 0 0 1 1 0 0 0	= $6C18
Branch Code	GE Code	Displacement	

(b) **Backward Branch: BEQ**

Offset = LABEL − (Loc + 2) = 011A − (0136 + 2) = FFE2

The displacement is given as a 16-bit number $FFE2. The condition code for BEQ is 0111.

Machine Code

0 1 1 0	0 1 1 1	0 0 0 0 0 0 0 0	= $6700
Branch Code	EQ Code	Null Displacement	

1 1 1 1	1 1 1 1	1 1 1 0 0 0 1 0	= $FFE2

Computing the Offset: An Algorithm

Assemblers compute the most efficient storage of the offset by using a simple algorithm. The process determines whether an 8-bit offset may be used or a 16-bit offset is required.

Algorithm   Perform the subtraction as a 16-bit operation. Offset = Target label − (Loc + 2). Table 5.6 shows a list of 16-bit numbers with partitioning blocks around the numbers in the range −128 ≤ Offset ≤ 127.

The numbers in Block A are in the range 0–127 and have the form $00XY_{16}$, where X ≤ 7. The numbers in Block B are in the range −1 to −128 and have the form $FFXY_{16}$, where X ≥ 8. An offset may be stored in 1 byte if it passes either of the following test conditions:

Test 1: If the offset is of the form 00XY and X ≤ 7, then XY is a valid 8-bit offset.

Test 2: If the offset is of the form FFXY and X ≥ 8, then XY is a valid 8-bit offset.

Any other combination requires a 16-bit offset.

TABLE 5.6   16-Bit Two's Complement Number Blocks

	Block B
0111111111111111 = 32767	1111111111111111 = −1
0111111111111110 = 32766	1111111111111110 = −2
. . . .	. . . .
. . . .	. . . .
. . . .	. . . .
0000000010000000 = 128	1111111110000000 = −128
Block A	
0000000011111111 = 127	
0000000011111110 = 126	1111111011111111 = −129
. . . . .	. . . . .
. . . . .	
0000000000000010 = 2	
0000000000000001 = 1	1000000000000001 = −32767
0000000000000000 = 0	1000000000000000 = −32768

EXAMPLE 5.21

Using the test conditions generates the most efficient code for a branch instruction. Assume label ALPHA is at location $05F0.

$$000600 \text{ BEQ ALPHA}$$

Using 16-bit subtraction,

$$\text{Offset} = 05F0 - (0600 + 2) = FFEE$$

From Test 2, the offset can be stored using 1 byte. The BEQ branch has condition code 0111.

Machine Code

0 1 1 0	0 1 1 1	1 1 1 0 1 1 1 0	= $67EE
Bcc Code	EQ Code	Displacement	

5.9 | MULTIPLICATION AND DIVISION

The MC68000 provides a set of multiplication and division instructions. They replace slower shift and add algorithms and increase the efficiency of applications. This section also includes the SWAP and "Sign-Extend" instructions to support division.

Multiplication with Shifts

Some microprocessors do not provide a hardware multiplication instruction. The operation must be performed with a software routine using repeated shift and add steps. An example using the familiar indent and multiply illustrates the method.

EXAMPLE 5.22

Using the binary numbers $A = 1101_2 = 13$ and $B = 1010_2 = 10$, compute the product $A \times B$ using shift and add.

Algorithm   This multiplication is a four-step process. For each digit of B, a partial product is generated.

$$
\begin{array}{r}
\text{(A)} \quad 1101 \\
\text{(B)} \quad \times\ 1010 \\
\hline
0000 \\
1101 \\
0000 \\
1101 \\
\hline
10000010 \quad \text{Add the partial products}
\end{array}
$$

The final result $10000010_2 = 130_{10}$ is the sum of the two partial products

$$
\begin{array}{r}
11010 \\
+\,1101000 \\
\hline
10000010
\end{array}
$$

Note   A partial product is required for each 1 in multiplier (B). The value of the partial product is the multiplier (A) shifted left by a shift count equal to the index of the bit in (B). For example, (B) has a 1 in bits b_1 and b_3. The corresponding partial products are 11010 (shift A by 1) and 1101000 (shift A by 3).

PROGRAM 5.9

Software
Multiplication Using
Shift and Add

The shift and add algorithm is implemented in assembly language code. The sample program 13×10 is used as a test case. The result is stored in (D0.L).

Algorithm   Use Example 5.22 to trace the steps of the algorithm.

1. Shift the low-order bit of multiplier (B) into the C bit. If the result is 1, the contents of multiplier (A) is added to the product in D0. If the result is 0, the partial product is 0, and no addition to the product is required.

2. Shift the multiplier (A) left 1 bit. The new contents of (A) is the partial product corresponding to the low-order bit of (B). Return to step 1.

The iterative process terminates when multiplier (B) becomes 0.

```
        xref     decout_long, newline, stop

start:  move.w   #13,d1          ; compute 13 × 10
        move.w   #10,d2
        moveq    #0,d0           ; set product to 0
        andi.l   #$0000ffff,d1   ; set msw of d1 to 0
mul1:   lsr.w    #1,d2           ; check the low bit of (b)
        bcc.s    mul2            ; branch if 0 found
        add.l    d1,d0           ; 1 was present. add.
mul2:   lsl.l    #1,d1           ; shift multiply (a) left 1 bit
        tst.w    d2              ; check if (b) is 0
        bne.s    mul1            ; if not, do it again
        jsr      decout_long     ; print product from d0
        jsr      newline
        jsr      stop

        end
```

⟨Run of Program 5.9⟩

130

Hardware Multiplication and Division

The MC68000 instructions MULU and MULS perform unsigned and signed multiplication. Note, however, the size constraints on the operands.

INSTRUCTION

MULU/MULS
(Multiply)

Syntax

MULU	⟨ea⟩,Dn	Unsigned multiplication
MULS	⟨ea⟩,Dn	Signed multiplication

Action Multiplies two unsigned (signed) 16-bit operands, yielding a 32-bit unsigned (signed) product. The product is stored in the data register Dn.

Note Since the instructions multiply two 16-bit operands, the product will not exceed 32 bits, and so no overflow can occur. The V and C bits are cleared. The value of the product is indicated by the N and Z bit.

EXAMPLE 5.23   Multiplication Examples

(a) Let (D0.W) = $FFFF and (D1.W) = $FFFE.
     MULS D1,D0   Result: (D0.L) = $00000002.
     MULU D1,D0   Results: (D0.L) = $FFFD0002.

(b) Let (D4.W) = $FFFF.
     MULU #4,D4   Result: (D4.L) = $0003FFFC.
     MULS #4,D4   Result: (D4.L) = $FFFFFFFC.

Like multiplication, the MC68000 system has two instructions that perform unsigned division (DIVU) and signed division (DIVS). The dividend is always a 32-bit data register, and the divisor is limited to 16 bits. The results are given in the form of a 16-bit quotient and a 16-bit remainder. The quotient is the LSW of the data register, and the remainder is the MSW of the data register.

Remainder	Quotient

INSTRUCTION

DIVU/DIVS
(Divide)

Syntax

DIVU	⟨ea⟩,Dn	Unsigned divide
DIVS	⟨ea⟩,Dn	Signed divide

Action Divide the 32-bit destination operand (dividend) by the 16-bit source operand, and store the remainder in the MSW and the quotient in the LSW of the destination.

Notes

1. Division by 0 generates an exception, usually causing a return to the operating system. Chapter 13 examines the topic of exceptions.

2. Overflow is detected and flagged before completion of the instruction. In this case, the operands are not affected.

3. In signed division (DIVS), the sign of the remainder is always the same as that of the dividend, unless the remainder is 0.

EXAMPLE 5.24 Division Examples

(a) Divide the unsigned number $FFFF ($65535_{10}$) by 6.

MOVE.L #$FFFF,D0
DIVU #6,D0

Result: Quotient   = $2AAA
Remainder = $0003

0003	2AAA

(b) Divide the 16-bit signed number -11 by 4.

MOVE.W #-11,D1
DIVS #4,D1

Result: Quotient   = $FFFE = -2
Remainder = $FFFD = -3

FFFD	FFFE

(c) Divide the 32-bit unsigned number $AAAA6667 by 2.

MOVE.L #$AAAA6667,D0
DIVU #2,D0

The division produces overflow because the quotient ($55553333) cannot be contained in a 16-bit number. The V bit is set, and the contents of D0 are unchanged.

The division operation returns two values in the same register. The quotient is stored in the LSW of Dn, and the remainder is stored in the MSW of Dn. The MC68000 system provides a SWAP instruction that switches the contents of these words, giving access to each of the division results.

INSTRUCTION

SWAP
(Swap)

Syntax SWAP Dn

Action The contents of the MSW and LSW of Dn are switched.

Note The Z and N bits reflect the full 32-bit result in the data register.

EXAMPLE 5.25   Assume (D3.L) = $87B0 D2F8.

SWAP D3

Before	After
87B0 D2F8	D2F8 87B0
D3	D3

Often it is necessary to sign-extend word data to a long word prior to division. The MC68000 system provides an instruction to do this directly. The "Sign-Extend" instruction allows users to extend a byte to a word and a word to a long word. The MC68020/30/40 systems also permit extending a byte to a long word.

INSTRUCTION

EXT
(Sign-Extend)

Syntax   EXT.L D*n*
EXT.W D*n*
EXTB.L D*n*   (MC68020/30/40 Instruction Only)

Action   The EXT instructions permit word (.W) or long (.L) size. If size is word, the least significant byte of D*n* is sign-extended to a word in bits 0–15. If size is long, bits 0–15 of D*n* are sign-extended to a long word.
The EXTB.L instruction sign extends D*n* from an 8-bit to a 32-bit value. The instruction is equivalent to a pair of MC68000 instructions

EXT.W D*n*
EXT.L D*n*

Note   The MC68000 EXT instructions permit only the word and long sizes.

EXAMPLE 5.26   Sign-Extension Examples

(*a*) EXT.W D5

Before	After
2A3F 178B	2A3F FF8B
D5	D5

(*b*) EXT.L D3

Before	After
10F6 7D08	0000 7D08
D3	D3

(c) EXTB.L   D4 (MC68020/30/40 instruction)

Before	After
1030 90A0	FFFF FFA0
D4	D4

PROGRAM 5.10

Prime Factorization

Enter a positive integer N greater than 1, and print out its prime factorization.

The Fundamental Theorem of Arithmetic states that any positive integer ($N > 1$) can be written as a product of powers of primes—that is,

$$N = p_1^{e_1} p_2^{e_2} \cdots p_n^{e_n}$$

where each p_i is a distinct prime.

Algorithm   Test each successive integer 2, 3, 4, . . . to determine whether it divides N. If it does, it is a factor of N and can be output. In this case, carry out the division and assign to N the quotient that can then be retested to see whether the same factor divides it. Multiple occurrences of a factor are identified in this way.

This process will produce only prime factors. Consider the case of a composite integer $k = 1_1 * 1_2$. If k is a factor of N then both 1_1 and 1_2 are factors, and they would have been treated by the algorithm at an earlier stage.

Integer	Factors
40	2 2 2 5
36	2 2 3 3
19	19

Step 1: Initialize $I = 2$.

Step 2: Compute $Q = N$ DIV I and $R = N$ MOD I. If $R = 0$, I is a factor. Output it. Set $N = Q$ and keep I. If $R \neq 0$, keep N and set $I = I + 1$.

Step 3: Return to Step 2, stopping when $N = 1$.

```
              xref                    decout,decin,newline,stop

    start:    jsr       decin        ; read n into d1
              move.w    d0,d1
              cmpi.w    #2,d1        ; prime factorization only if n >= 2
              blt.s     xit
              moveq     #2,d2        ; trial divisor

    factor:   ext.1     d1           ; extend n to long word
              move.1    d1,d3        ; save n in d3
              divu      d2,d1        ; check for factor
```

```
            divu      d2, d1      ; check for factor
            swap      d1          ; load remainder in (d1.w)
            tst.w     d1          ; factor present if remainder 0
            bne.s     reset_n     ; remainder is not 0
            move.w    d2, d0      ; write out the divisor
            jsr       decout
            swap      d1          ; get quotient back
            cmpi.w    #1, d1      ; test quotient for 1
            beq.s     xit
            bra.s     factor
reset_n:    addq.w    #1, d2      ; get next divisor
            move.1    d3, d1      ; restore n in d1
            bra.s     factor
xit:        jsr       newline
            jsr       stop

            end
```

⟨Run of Program 5.10⟩

36
2 2 3 3

|5.10| ADVANCED APPLICATIONS

The introductory programs in this chapter focused on branch instructions and simple program control logic. This section develops more advanced algorithms and application programs.

Testing for Signed and Unsigned Overflow

Signed overflow is flagged by the V bit, and unsigned overflow is flagged by the C bit. These facts are highlighted in the following program. A new MOVE instruction allows for a reading of the contents of the CCR.

INSTRUCTION

MOVE
(Move from Status Register)

Syntax MOVE.W SR,⟨ea⟩   MC68000 instruction
          MOVE.W CCR,⟨ea⟩   MC68010/20/30/40

Action The 16-bit (8-bit) contents of the status register SR (CCR) are moved into the data register or memory location specified by the destination operand. Only word size is permitted. For the CCR version of the instruction, the CCR is copied to the LSB of the destination. The MSB of the destination is set to 0.

Note The instruction "MOVE.W   SR, ⟨ea⟩" is a privileged instruction on the MC68010/20/30/40 systems and requires that the user be in supervisor mode (system manager status). Be aware of the processor you are using.

PROGRAM 5.11

Enter two 16-bit numbers, and compute their sum. The addition operation sets the CCR bits, which are then read from the status register (SR) into (D0.W) using the "MOVE FROM STATUS REGISTER" instruction. Unsigned overflow is detected in the C bit, and signed overflow is detected in the V bit. A message listing overflow conditions is printed.

```
        xref            hexin, hexout, strout, newline, stop
start:
;       initialize the ovrflstr array of addresses
        lea     ovrflstr, a0
        lea     no_ovrfl, a1
        move.w  #4, d1
init:   move.l  a1, (a0)
        adda.w  #28, a1
        adda.w  #4, a0
        sub.w   #1, d1
        bne.s   init

        jsr     hexin               ; enter m
        move.w  d0, d1              ; store m in d1
        jsr     hexin               ; enter n

        add.w   d0, d1              ; compute the sum n + m

;       On the MC68020/30, move.w sr, d0 is privileged.
;       Use move.w ccr, d0

        move.w  sr, d0              ; MC68000 instruction
        andi.w  #$0003, d0          ; clear bits #2 - #15
        jsr     hexout              ; output values for v and c bits
        lea     ovrflstr, a1
        asl.w   #2, d0              ; multiply (d0) by 4
        adda.l  d0, a1              ; set (a1) to address of string
        move.l  (a1), a0            ; set (a0) to start string
        move.w  #28, d0             ; each string has 28 characters
        jsr     strout
        jsr     newline
        jsr     stop

        data
ovrflstr:    ds.l  4
no_ovrfl:    dc.b  'no overflow                '
unsignovrfl: dc.b  'only unsigned overflow     '
signovrfl:   dc.b  'only signed overflow       '
dualovrfl:   dc.b  'unsigned and signed overflow'

        end
```

⟨Run of Program 5.11⟩

9000 A000
`0003 unsigned and signed overflow`

Bit Operations

The MC68000 system provides **bit-level instructions** to test and modify the contents of a single bit in a register or in memory. This section introduces the bit operations and applies them to a parity check routine for character transmission. The bit instructions are used extensively in the chapters on I/O programming and exception processing.

The MC68000 system has four bit instructions that act on a data register or memory. The BTST (bit test) instruction merely tests the value of a bit. Like the TST instruction, it assigns a value to the Z bit. The other bit instructions first test the bit and then potentially modify it. The BSET, BCLR, and BCHG instructions have actions that parallel the logical OR, AND, and NOT operations.

INSTRUCTION

BTST/BSET
BCLR/BCHG
(Test and Change)

Syntax   BTST   Dn, ⟨ea⟩   BSET   Dn, ⟨ea⟩
            BTST   #N,⟨ea⟩   BSET   #N,⟨ea⟩

            BCLR   Dn,⟨ea⟩   BCHG   Dn,⟨ea⟩
            BCLR   #N,⟨ea⟩   BCHG   #N,⟨ea⟩

Action   For the BTST instruction, a bit in the destination operand is tested, and its state is reflected in the Z bit. The other instructions (BSET, BCLR, and BCHG) first perform a test of the specified bit and assign the Z bit. Then the action of the instruction is performed. The referenced bit is set to 1 (BSET), set to 0 (BCLR), or inverted (BCHG) by the respective instruction.

Notes

1. The source operand specifies the bit to be tested. It can be given in the immediate data (#N) or in a data register.

2. If the destination is a data register, bits 0–31 can be tested. If the destination operand is a memory location, only bits 0–7 may be tested.

EXAMPLE 5.27

Bit Instructions

(a) BTST   #2,D0   ; ASSUME (D0.L) = $F564 3896

F564   3896

D0

Bit 2 of (D0.L) is 1 ($6 = 0110_2$); hence, Z = 0. Recall that the Z bit is set (Z = 1) when a 0 is found.

(b) BTST   #7,MEM   ; ASSUME THE CONTENTS OF MEM IS $758F

75
MEM

8F
MEM + 1

Bit 7 of MEM is 0 ($75 = 0111 0101$_2$); hence, Z = 1.

(c) MOVE.W   #16,D3   ; ASSUME (D1.W) = $F561 B875
    BCHG   D3,D1   ; BIT 16 OF (D1.W) IS 1

Before

F561   B875
D1

After

F560   B875
D1

Parity Checks

The binary representation of an ASCII character is defined with seven significant bits. Often a character is stored with the high-order bit set to 0. During data transmission, however, you can use the eighth bit for error checking with a parity algorithm. The transmitting device checks the number of 1's in the 7-bit ASCII representation and then sets (or clears) the high-order bit so that the resulting sum of the 1's is even (**even parity**) or odd (**odd parity**). If a data transmission error occurs and results in an odd number of bits being inverted, the receiving device can detect the error.

EXAMPLE 5.28

Parity Testing

Assume that the receiving device performs even parity checking.

(a) Character "c"

    ASCII code   1100011 = $63   (even number of 1's)
Code with parity   01100011 = $63   (bit 7 = 0)

(b) Character "4"

    ASCII code   0110100 = $34   (odd number of 1's)
Code with parity   10110100 = $B4   (bit 7 = 1)

You can set the parity bit for data transmission and then clear it for internal storage in memory.

PROGRAM 5.12

Even Parity
Transmission

Read in a string of up to 80 characters. Adjust each character to have even parity, and then print the 8-bit result using HEXOUT. The bit instructions BCLR, BTST, and BSET are used.

```
            xref      strin, hexout, newline, stop

start:      lea       string, a0
            move.w    #82, d0
            jsr       strin           ; read a string
            subq.w    #1, d0          ; delete line termination char
            beq.s     finish          ; test for empty input line
            move.w    d0, d2          ; copy # chars in string to d2
            move.w    d0, d3          ; save again for later
            subq.w    #1, d2          ; d2 is main loop counter
main_loop:  move.b    (a0), d0        ; get current character
            bclr      #7, d0          ; delete any parity setting
            move.b    d0, d1          ; work on d1
            moveq     #0, d4          ; clear bit counter
loop:       lsr.b     #1, d1          ; shift bit 0 into C and X
            bcc.s     tstzero
            addq.w    #1, d4
tstzero:    tst.b     d1              ; anymore 1's left?
            bne.s     loop            ; if yes, keep counting 1's
            btst      #0, d4          ; check for an odd no of 1's
            beq.s     printchar       ; if even, then print char now
            bset      #7, d0          ; make num 1's in char even
printchar:  jsr       hexout
            addq.l    #1, a0
            dbra      d2, main_loop
finish:     jsr       newline
            jsr       stop

            data
string:     ds.b      82

            end
```

⟨Run of Program 5.12⟩

ABC 012
0041 0042 00C3 00A0 0030 00B1 00B2

Binary Search

Binary search is a classical algorithm to find an item in a sorted list. A key represents the item. The algorithm iteratively uses the following test. Find the midpoint of the list and compare the entry against the key. If they are equal, return the index of the entry, and terminate the search. If the key is greater than the item, search the upper-half list; otherwise, search the lower-half list. The search fails when a sublist of length zero is found. In this case, return index -1.

PROGRAM 5.13

Binary Search

A sorted list contains eight 32-bit unsigned numbers. A key is read from the keyboard. The variables low (D1.W) and high (D2.W) are the lower and upper bounds of the sublist that is searched. Initially, these limits are the bounds of the list. If the key is not found, a message to that effect is printed.

```
            xref    decin, decout, newline, strout, stop

start:      jsr     decin           ; input key
            moveq   #0, d1          ; (d1) is low
            moveq   #7, d2          ; (d2) is high
srch:       lea     list, a0
            cmp.l   d1, d2
            blt.s   notfound        ; failure if high < low
            move.l  d1, d3          ; move low offset to d3
            add.l   d2, d3          ; form low + high
            asr.l   #1, d3          ; form (low + high) div 2
            move.l  d3, d4          ; copy index to d4
            asl.w   #2, d4          ; mult by 4; d4 is an offset
            adda.w  d4, a0          ; (a0) is list[mid]
            cmp.l   (a0), d0        ; compare key and list entry
            beq     printindex
            bgt     gohigh          ; search upper half list
            subq.l  #1, d3
            move.l  d3, d2          ; set new high = mid - 1
            bra     srch
gohigh:     addq.l  #1, d3
            move.l  d3, d1          ; set new low = mid + 1
            bra.s   srch
printindex: lea     foundmsg, a0
            moveq   #19, d0
            jsr     strout
            move.w  d3, d0
            jsr     decout
            jsr     newline
            bra.s   done
notfound:   lea     notfoundmsg, a0
            moveq   #13, d0
            jsr     strout
            jsr     newline
done:       jsr     stop

            data

list:         dc.l  10, 20, 30, 40, 50, 60, 70, 80
foundmsg:     dc.b  'key found at index '
notfoundmsg:  dc.b  'key not found'

            end
```

⟨Run of Program 5.13⟩

60
key found at index 5

Null-Terminated String

A **string** is an array of characters that is treated as a single data item for input, output, and operations. Strings are covered in detail in Chapter 9. Application Program 5.14 uses concepts from high-level language strings and introduces the EQU directive.

DIRECTIVE

EQU
(Equate)

Syntax   ⟨LABEL⟩:   EQU   ⟨constant expression⟩

Action   The expression in the operand field is assigned to the label. The label cannot be defined elsewhere in the program.

Note   The EQU directive is similar to the CONST declaration in Pascal and the "#define" directive in C.

EXAMPLE 5.29

```
NULL:    EQU      $00
         CMPI.B   #NULL, (A0)    ; SETS NULL = $00
```

PROGRAM 5.14

Null-Terminated String

A string is input using STRIN. The end of line character, which is initially stored in the string, is replaced by the null character. The string is then output using single character output [STROUT with (D0.W) = 1]. Recall that on the Macintosh, the end of line character is $0D = 13. On input with STRIN, the return character ($0D) is read and stored without conversion. On a UNIX system, the end of line character is $0A = 10. The return character is converted to $0A and stored as the end of line character.

```
NULL:        equ     0
MAC_NL:      equ     13
UNIX_NL:     equ     10
MSG_LENGTH:  equ     26

             xref  strin, strout, stop

start:       lea      line, a0  ; input the string
             move.w   #82,d0
             jsr      strin
             movea.l  a0,a1      ; use a1 to point at the CR
             adda.l   d0,a1
             subq.w   #1,a1
```

```
                 cmpi.b     #MAC_NL, (a1)      ; are you on a Macintosh system?
                 beq        print_mac
                 lea        unix_msg, a0       ; you are on a UNIX system
                 bra        printmsg
print_mac:       lea        mac_msg, a0
                 move.w     #MSG_LENGTH, d0
printmsg:        jsr        strout

                 move.b     #NULL, (a1)        ; null terminate the string
                 lea        line, a0           ; reset a0 to the input string
                 move.w     #1, d0             ; using single char output
printloop:       tst.b      (a0)               ; found NULL yet?
                 beq.s      done
                 jsr        strout             ; print the character
                 addq.w     #1, a0             ; move on to next char
                 bra        printloop
done:            jsr        stop

                 data

line:            ds.b  82
mac_msg:         dc.b  'Found a Macintosh Return  ', MAC_NL
unix_msg:        dc.b  'Found a UNIX Return       ', UNIX_NL
                 end
```

⟨Run of Program 5.14⟩

This is a sample string
Found a Macintosh Return
This is a sample string

5.11 MC68020/30/40 BRANCH AND COMPARE INSTRUCTIONS

The MC68020/30/40 systems extend the Bcc instructions by permitting 8-bit, 16-bit, and 32-bit displacements. Each assembler uses an algorithm to determine the size of the offset. In some cases, the assembler optimizes all backward references and chooses the minimum displacement. The same assembler may permit a forced 32-bit displacement using the "⟨Branch⟩.L" syntax. Check your assembler documentation for details. For instance, the BGE.L branch forces a 32-bit displacement.

```
LABEL_1:    BGE.L    FAR_AWAY
FAR_AWAY: . . . . .   ; OFFSET FROM LABEL_1 > $10000
```

MC68020/30/40 systems permit a 32-bit offset in the range $-2^{31} \leq$ offset $\leq 2^{31} - 1$. The branch instructions still permit only a label in the operand but expand the use of branch for large code files.

EXAMPLE 5.30

For MC68020/30/40 systems, if you use a 16-bit offset, a 0 is stored in the LSB of the opcode, and a single extension word holds the displacement. If you use a 32-bit offset, $FF is stored in the LSB of the opcode, and two extension words contain the displacement.

HERE: BHS.L   FAR_LABEL

Assume HERE = $00001000 and FAR_LABEL = $2000000

$$\text{offset} = \text{FAR\_LABEL} - (\text{HERE} + 2)$$
$$= 2000000 - (01000 + 2) = 1\text{FFFFFE}$$

The displacement is given as a 32-bit number $01FFFFFE. The condition code for BHS is 0100.

Machine Code

0 1 1 0	0 1 0 0	1 1 1 1 1 1 1 1
Branch Code	HS Code	32-Bit Displacement

0 0 0 0	0 0 0 1	1 1 1 1 1 1 1 1

1 1 1 1	1 1 1 1	1 1 1 1 1 1 1 0

MC68020/30/40 CMP2 Instruction

The MC68000 CMP instruction compares the contents of a data register with a source operand. When executing the subtraction, the CCR bits are set. The MC68020/30/40 provides a CMP2 instruction that compares an address or data register with both a signed or unsigned lower and upper bound contained in the source operand.

INSTRUCTION

CMP2
(Compare)

Syntax   CMP2.⟨size⟩   ⟨ea⟩,Rn (MC68020/30/40)

Action   The CMP2 instruction compares either an address or a data register Rn against a pair of bounds. The lower bound is the contents in memory specified by the effective address of the source operand. The upper bound is the contents in memory at locations ⟨ea⟩ + 1, 2, or 4, depending on the size of the operation.

If Rn is less than the lower bound or greater than the upper bound, the C bit is set; otherwise, it is cleared. If Rn equals either the upper or the lower bound, the Z bit is set.

Notes

1. The data being compared may be signed or unsigned. In either case, the lower bound must be the smaller of the two bounds. The processor evaluates upper bound − lower bound. If the result is negative, unsigned comparison is performed.

2. If the destination is an address register and the size is a byte or a word, the bounds are sign-extended before the comparison is made.

3. The register type and register number for the destination operand are contained in an extension word.

EXAMPLE 5.31

Assume that (D0.W) = $0050 and the contents of address A = $0000 0100.

(a) CMP2.W   A, D0
Test 0 ≤   (D0.W) ≤ $100. The C and Z bits are cleared.

(b) CMP2.B   A, D0
(D0.B) = $50. The 16-bit contents of A, $0000, are used for the lower and upper bounds. Test 0 ≤ (D0.B) ≤ 0. The C bit is set, and the Z bit is cleared.

Assume that (D0.W) = $AA00 and the contents of address A is $0000 AA00.

(c) CMP2.W   A,D0   ; UNSIGNED TEST
Since $AA00 − $0000 is negative, an unsigned test is performed with 0 ≤ (D0.W) ≤ $AA00. Because (D0.W) equals the upper bound, the C bit is cleared, and the Z bit is set.

PROGRAM 5.15

Bound Comparison
Test

An input routine expects a 16-bit number between 1 and $100. If the input is not in the specified range, an error message is given, and the input routine is repeated.

```
nl:          equ        13

             xref       hexin, hexout, strout, stop
```

```
start:      jsr       hexin
            cmp2.w    a,d0            ; the two word contents hold
                                      ; the lower and upper bound
   ;
            bcc       done            ; branch if d0 is within range
            jsr       hexout
            lea       errormsg,a0     ; print an 'out of range' message
            moveq     #27,d0
            jsr       strout
            bra       start
done:       jsr       stop

            data
a:          dc.w      1,$100
errormsg:   dc.b      'is out of range. re-enter',nl,0
            end
```

⟨Run of Program 5.15⟩

400
0400 is out of range.   re-enter
200
0200 is out of range.   re-enter
50

EXERCISES

1. Assume (D0.W) = $4A7B and (D2.W) = $D6AF for each of the following instructions. The CCR bits are X = 1, N = 0, Z = 1, C = 1, V = 0. Give the value of the CCR bits after executing the instruction.
   (a) ADD.W   D2,D0   (b) AND.B   D2,D0
   (c) MOVEA.W   D0,A2   (d) EOR.W   D2,D0

2. If (D0.L) = $45325587 and (D3.L) = $17843215, what are the values of the condition code bits after each subtraction?
   (a) SUB.W   D3,D0   (b) SUB.W   D0,D3
   (d) SUB.B   D0,D3   (d) SUB.L   D3,D0

3. Let (D0.L) = $00003485. For each pair of instructions, determine if the branch will occur.
   (a) TST.W   D0   (b) TST.B   D0
       BPL   ALPHA   BMI   ALPHA
   (c) TST.L   D0
       BEQ   ALPHA

4. Assume (D0.L) = $A7433590. For each shift, determine the value in D0 and the value of X N Z V C.
   (a) ASR.W   #4,D0   (b) LSR.W   #4,D0
   (c) ASR.L   #8,D0   (d) LSR.L   #8,D0
   (e) ASR.B   #2,D0   (f) MOVE.W #28,D1
                                 LSR.L   D1,D0

5. Let (D0.W) = $67C5 and (D1.W) = $D29E. Execute the following instruction:

   CMP.W D1,D0

   (a) What are the resulting values in the CCR?

   $$X \quad N \quad Z \quad V \quad C$$

   (b) With "YES" or "NO", indicate whether the following branches to ⟨label⟩ will execute:
   - (i) BPL ⟨label⟩
   - (ii) BLE ⟨label⟩
   - (iii) BGT ⟨label⟩
   - (iv) BCS ⟨label⟩
   - (v) BMI ⟨label⟩

6. Give an example of values for D0.W and D1.W where (D0.W) < (D1.W) but the sequence

   $$\text{CMP.W} \qquad \text{D0, D1}$$
   $$\text{BPL} \qquad \text{⟨label⟩}$$

   may fail to cause a branch when (D0) and (D1) are considered signed numbers.

7. Use a geometric or algebraic argument to show that

   $$\text{(NOT N AND NOT V AND NOT Z) OR (N AND V AND NOT Z)}$$

   is a test for BGT.

8. Draw a block diagram to show how the Pascal construct

   $$\text{REPEAT . . UNTIL}$$

   is implemented in assembly language.

9. Assume (D0.W) = $4A7B and (D1.W) = $D6AF. The values in the CCR are

   $$X = 1, \quad N = 0, \quad Z = 1, \quad V = 0, \quad C = 1$$

   Using these values for each of the instructions, give the resulting contents of the CCR after each instruction.
   - (a) TST.W D1
   - (b) CMP.W D0,D1
   - (c) BNE ⟨label⟩
   - (d) SUB.B D1,D0
   - (e) AND.W D0,D1
   - (f) ASL.W #6,D0

10. Change the operands of each of the following instructions to give an instruction that is syntactically correct:
    - (a) MOVEQ.W #35,D0
    - (b) ADDQ.W #22,D3
    - (c) BMI D4
    - (d) ASL.L D3,MEM
    - (e) ASR.W #16,D3
    - (f) CMP.W D2,B
    - (g) NEG.L A3
    - (h) TST.L A6

11. The machine code for a "move quick" instruction is 7C9A. Interpret the code, and give the corresponding MC68000 instruction.

12. Let (D0.W) = $8924, (D1.W) = $5527, and (D2.W) = $0000. Execute the following instruction:

CMP.W   D1, D0

(a) What are the resulting values in the CCR?

X   N   Z   V   C

(b) With "YES" or "NO", indicate whether the following branches to ⟨label⟩ will execute:

(i)	BCS	⟨label⟩	(ii) BHI	⟨label⟩
(iii)	BLS	⟨label⟩	(iv) BVC	⟨label⟩
(v)	BMI	⟨label⟩	(vi) DBHI	D2,⟨label⟩

13. A list of long words begining at address L is sorted in descending order. Write a code segment that implements a loop to find the position in which to insert a new entry in the same order. Assume the new entry is contained in D2. Use a DBcc instruction other than DBRA.

14. If (D3.W) = 1 and (D4.W) = 6, determine the value of D3.W and the PC after executing the DBGT instruction in the sequence

```
LOOP:      . . .
           CMPI.W     #3, D4
           DBGT       D3, LOOP
ENDL:      . . .
```

15. What is the standard Motorola assembly language code that will implement the conditional jump instruction

JHI   FAR_LABEL

16. Assume the label LOOP is at address $001006. Construct the machine language code for the branch instructions. (*Hint:* Compute the number of bytes for each instruction.)

```
LOOP:      SUB.L      D5, D3
           BPL.S      CONTINUE
           ADDQ.W     #1, D4
           BNE.S      LOOP
CONTINUE: . . .
```

17. Each of the following is an opcode word for a branch instruction. Assume the branch instruction occurs at location $010A. Give the assembly language form of the branch and the address of the ⟨label⟩.
(a) 66F4   (b) 6B08   (c) 6E06

18. The following are machine code instructions including the opcode word and extension word. The instruction mnemonic is given. Find the corresponding MC68000 instruction.
(a) 59CB   FFFA   "DECREMENT AND BRANCH"
(b) 66F8   "BRANCH"
(c) B090   "CMP"

19. From the machine code, determine the branch instruction and the displacement (in bytes) relative to the PC.
    (a) 65E8   (b) 6B08

20. Assume each branch instruction occurs at location $000550. Let ALPHA be address $000500 and BETA be address $000600. Generate the machine code, using the smallest possible displacement size.
    (a) BCC ALPHA   (b) BGT BETA

21. Hand-calculate the following products:
    (a) 11011 (Binary)   (b) FE (Hex)
        10011   72

22. Assume (D0.W) = $FFFE and (D1.W) = $0002. Show the contents of D1 after executing each of the following instructions:
    (a) MULS D0, D1   (b) MULU D0, D1

23. Show the contents of D0.L after executing each of the following instructions and indicate if overflow will occur:
    (a) Assume (D0.L) = $00000105
        (i) DIVS #5, D0   (ii) DIVU #5, D0
    (b) Assume (D0.L) = $FFFF FFA0
        (i) DIVS #4, D0   (ii) DIVU #4, D0

24. Assume (D0.L) = $0000 012A. Execute the following two instructions sequentially. After each, give the 32-bit contents (in hex) of D0.

    DIVU   #10, D0
    MULU   #10, D0

25. Execute the sequence of statements for each of the following pairs of numbers N and M. Give the resulting 32-bit contents of D0.

    MOVE.W   #N, D1
    MOVE.L   #M, D0
    DIVS   D1, D0

    (a) N = −4   M = 9
    (b) N = 4   M = −9
    (c) N = −4   M = −9

26. Change each of the following instructions to give an instruction that is syntactically correct:
    (a) MULU   #35,A3   (b) SWAP.W D2
    (c) EXT.W (A4)   (d) DIVS.B   D2,D7

27. Examine the following instruction sequence. What is the resulting value of ALPHA?

    MOVE.L   #109, D5
    DIVU   #7, D5
    SWAP   D5
    MOVE.W   D5, ALPHA

28. If (D3.L) = $87539076, what is the value of D3 after each instruction?
    (a) EXT.W D3   (b) EXT.L D3   (c) SWAP D3

29. Write a code sequence to sign-extend a byte in D1 to a long-word in each of the following ways:
    (a) Using the EXT instruction
    (b) Using ASL/ASR

30. Assuming odd parity, give the ASCII representation of each of the following characters:
    (a) HT   (b) LF   (c) A   (d) 3
    (e) e   (f) 4   (g) %

31. Assuming (D0.W) = $A568, give the value of D0 after executing each of the following instructions:
    (a) BTST   #7,D0   (b) BCHG   #7,D0
    (c) BCLR   #5,D0   (d) BSET   #2,D0

32. (MC68020/30/40) The PC is $6000 and a branch to target address DISTANT = $100000 is to be made on the condition HI.
    (a) Give the MC68000 code to implement the branch.
    (b) Give an MC68020/30/40 branch instruction to do this.
    (c) Give the machine code for the branch in (b).

33. (MC68020/30/40) If memory is initialized at address A by

    A: DC.W $500, $9000

    Determine whether a branch will occur for each value of D0.W.
    (a) (D0.W) = $800

        CMP2.W   A, D0
        BCC   ⟨label⟩

    (b) (D0.W) = $77

        CMP2.W   A, D0
        BCS   ⟨label⟩

PROGRAMMING EXERCISES

34. Write and run a complete program that inputs a 16-bit signed number N and prints out the following values:

    N $2 * N$ $16 * N$ N DIV 2 N DIV 16

35. Enter ten signed 16-bit numbers using DECIN. Output the largest and then the smallest of these numbers.

36. Input a sequence of positive numbers and maintain a running sum. Provide error correction so that a negative number is rejected with the error message

"Only positive numbers. Enter again." Terminate the input when the sum of the numbers exceeds $1000, and write out the sum.

37. Enter a 16-bit number N using HEXIN. View N as a base-4 number. As such, it has eight digits. By using the ASL and AND instructions, determine the number of digits that are 3's in the base-4 representation of N. For example, if N = \$E37A = 1110 0011 0111 1010, then in base-4 N = 32031322 and the output is 3.

38. Write a program to read in a 16-bit number using DECIN and determine whether it is divisible by 5. If it is, print out the factor; if not, print out the note "Not divisible by 5."

39. Enter a number representing time in minutes. Output the time in hours and minutes.

40. Enter a sequence of numbers stopping on an input of 0. Compute the integer average of the positive numbers and of the negative numbers. Output each value using DECOUT. Use DIVS.

41. The Fibonacci sequence $F_1, F_2, F_3, \ldots$ is defined recursively as follows:

$$F_1 = 1, \quad F_2 = 1, \quad F_n = F_{n-1} + F_{n-2}, \quad n \geq 3$$

Output the first 20 terms of the Fibonacci sequence. Use long-word arithmetic.

42. A static list of ten numbers is defined using DC.W declarations. A target number is input using DECIN. Read through the list and output the number of list items less than the target number.

43. Enter an initial hex digit using HEXIN. Generate the 32-bit value in D0 whose digits are the eight successive hex digits beginning with the given hex digit. For example,

Initial digit: A.   Resulting value: (D0.L) = ABCDEF01.
Initial digit: E.   Resulting value: (D0.L) = EF012345.

44. Show in a program that the two's complement of the most negative 16-bit number is the number itself. Verify that the overflow bit (V bit) is set.

45. Write a program to implement a Sequential Search algorithm, defined as follows: Given an N element list of 16-bit numbers and a KEY, store the key in the $N + 1$st element of the list. Execute a sequential search of the list for the KEY. It will be found. If the address of the matching location is not the $N + $ 1st element's address, the KEY was in the list. Otherwise, it is not present. Your program should enter N, the elements in the list, and the KEY. You should output one of the following messages:

⟨value of key⟩ IS IN THE LIST
⟨value of key⟩ IS NOT IN THE LIST

You must use the instruction DBEQ to construct your search loop.

46. Read a list UNSNO of ten unsigned 32-bit numbers. Scan the list and output the largest value.

47. Initialize two lists beginning at addresses A and B, respectively. Each list should contain six 16-bit signed numbers in sorted order. Scan the two lists and output the numbers in sorted order. For instance, assume

    A: DC.W   2,5,6,9,10,55
    B: DC.W   5,8,9,11,33,64
    ⟨Output⟩
          2   5   5   6   8   9   9   10   11   33   55   64

48. Read a 32-bit number using **HEXIN-LONG**. Rotate the number left 1 bit by shifting the number left 1 bit and storing the shifted bit in bit 0. Write out the new number.

49. Read number using **HEXIN_LONG** and count the number of 0's in the number using a loop constructed with
    (a) LSR
    (b) ASR
    Which approach is more efficient?

50. Enter a sequence of five powers of 2 using DECIN_LONG (e.g., 64, 16, 4, 1, 1024). Clear D1.
    (a) For each power of 2, determine the exponent by shifting right until the 1 is found. Set the bit in D1 corresponding to the exponent using BSET.
    (b) Write out your value in D1 using DECOUT_LONG. Compare this value to the sum of the numbers you input.

CHAPTER 6

ARRAYS AND STACKS

An address register points at a memory location. It is used with a variety of addressing modes to access the contents of the memory location. The address register indirect mode was covered in Chapter 4. This chapter introduces new modes for array and record processing. These new modes provide for sequential access and indexed direct access to memory. PC-relative modes are then introduced to develop position-independent code. PC-relative and base-relative addressing describe the structure of the Macintosh code structure in its run-time environment. Finally, two additional addressing modes available for the MC68020/30/40 are presented in Section 6.7. Four additional modes are presented in Chapter 8.

6.1 SEQUENTIAL MEMORY ACCESS

An **array** is a list of data items of the same type and size stored in consecutive memory locations. It is defined by a starting address, the size (in bytes) of each data item, and the total number of items in the array. High-level languages provide a means to declare and access items in an array.

Pascal Array Declaration

A: array [0 . . 5] of integer

1. A is the array name. It is the starting address of the list.

2. The size of an item is specified by the "integer" type declaration. With 16-bit integers, space for an item occupies 2 bytes.

3. The array contains six items with the index of the first element being 0. Items in the array are accessed by offsets from the starting address.

ITEMS	OFFSET	MEMORY LOCATION	CONTENTS
A[0]	0	A + 0	0001
A[1]	2	A + 2	0002
A[2]	4	A + 4	0013
A[3]	6	A + 6	0016
A[4]	8	A + 8	002D
A[5]	10	A + 10	0066

In general, $A[n]$ has an offset $n *$ (item size).

Array A

0001	0002	0013	0016	002D	0066
1000	1000 + 2	1000 + 4	1000 + 6	1000 + 8	1000 + A
A[0]	A[1]	A[2]	A[3]	A[4]	A[5]

Assembly language uses data directives to declare arrays. If the "Define Constant" (DC) or "Define Constant Block" (DCB) directive is used, the array is simultaneously declared and initialized, an action not available in Pascal.

Assembly Language Array Declaration

1. The memory storage directives DC, DCB, and DS allocate memory for an array. The DC and DCB directives initialize an array of memory with data values. The DS directive allocates data space into which the program can assign values during execution.

2. The label for the data directive is the value of the starting address of the list.

3. The first element in the list has offset of 0 from the starting address.

EXAMPLE 6.1

(a) A: DS.W   6
The "Define Storage" directive corresponds to the declaration of the Pascal array

A: array [0 . . 5] of integer

(b) A: DC.W $0001, $0002, $0013, $0016, $002D, $0066
Label A is the starting address for an initialized array of six words.

(c) A: DCB.W   6,0
The six-element array A is initialized to 0.

(d) MEMBLOCK: DCB.B   100,0
MEMBLOCK points at 100 null bytes of memory.

Sequential Access Addressing Modes

You can directly access individual elements in an array by computing an offset from the starting address. The MC68000 provides addressing modes to support this access method, and these are covered in the next section. For now, consider the array as a sequential list. The MC68000 has two addressing modes designed specifically for sequential access. Many applications, including searching and sorting algorithms, use these modes.

ADDRESSING MODE

Address Register Indirect with Postincrement

Syntax   (A*n*) +

Action   The operand specifies the contents of memory at location (A*n*). After the memory access (read or write), the value of the address register A*n* is automatically incremented by 1, 2, or 4 bytes, depending on the size parameter of the instruction; hence the name postincrement.

EXAMPLE 6.2

(a) ADD.W   (A0) + ,D0
The 16-bit contents at location (A0) are added to register D0, and the value of A0 is incremented by 2; that is, (A0) = (A0) + 2. Assume that (A0) = $000500.

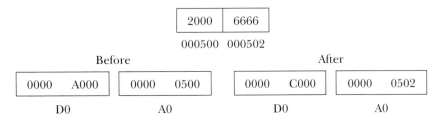

(b) MOVE.L   (A2) + ,(A2)
Assume that (A2) = $000500. The execution of this instruction requires three steps.

Step 1: Read the long-word contents at memory location $000500 (Read $44556688).

Step 2: Increment register A2 by 4, because the operation is ".L". (A2) is now $000504.

Step 3: Store the long word $44556688 in location $000504.

	Before				After		
4455	6688	1234	5789	4455	6688	4455	6688
00500		00504		00500		00504	

PROGRAM 6.1

Array I/O

Read *N* 16-bit numbers into the array LIST. Reset the starting address and output the array. This is an assembly language version of high-level language READARRAY and WRITEARRAY routines.

```
            xref    decin, decout, newline, stop

start:      jsr     decin           ; load array count n in d0
            move.w  d0, d1          ; d1 is counter for readarray
            move.w  d0, d2          ; save a copy for writearray
            subq.w  #1, d1          ; use dbra loop test
            lea     list, a0        ; initialize a0 to start of list

readarray:  jsr     decin           ; input a value into d0
            move.w  d0, (a0)+        ; load in the list and incr a0
            dbra    d1, readarray

            move.w  d2, d1          ; load the array count in d1
            subq.w  #1, d1          ; use dbra loop test
            lea     list, a0        ; initialize a0 to start of list
writearray: move.w  (a0)+, d0        ; set array element in d0 and
;                                   ; increment a0 by 2

            jsr     decout
            dbra    d1, writearray
            jsr     newline
            jsr     stop

            data

list:       ds.w    25
            end
```

⟨Run of Program 6.1⟩

```
3
25 −2 40
25 −2 40
```

Postincrement mode is used to traverse an array in the forward direction. Its counterpart, **predecrement mode**, can be used to move through an array in reverse order from higher to lower addresses.

**ADDRESSING
MODE**

Address Register
Indirect with
Postincrement

Syntax $-(An)$

Action   The value of address register A*n* is first decremented by 1, 2, or 4 bytes, specified by the size parameter of the operation. Then the contents of memory at the new location (A*n*) are accessed. The ordering is reflected in the name *predecrement*.

EXAMPLE 6.3

(a) MOVE.W $-(A2),D0$
The address register (A2) = \$000502 is first decremented by 2, since the size of the MOVE instruction is "W". The contents of (A2) are stored in D0.

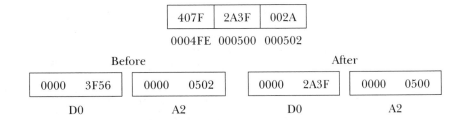

(b) MOVE.W $-(A0), -(A0)$
Assume that (A0) = \$00000502.

	Before		
00000502	407F	2A3F	002A
A0	0004FE	000500	000502

The operation requires a sequence of four steps:

Step 1: Decrement (A0) by 2 to its new value \$000500.

Step 2: Read the contents \$2A3F of address \$000500.

Step 3: Decrement the destination operand (A0) by 2 to the new value \$0004FE.

Step 4: The value $2A3F is stored in memory address (A0).

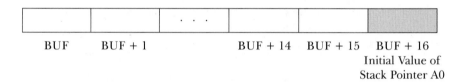

	After		
000004FE	2A3F	2A3F	002A
A0	0004FE	000500	000502

PROGRAM 6.2

Binary Number
Output

A 16-bit number is read into D0. Using successive right shifts, a character
('0' or '1'), corresponding to the shifted bit, is stored in a string buffer. The
buffer is filled right to left using address register indirect with predecrement
mode. The contents of the buffer are printed using STROUT.

		. . .			

BUF   BUF + 1   BUF + 14   BUF + 15   BUF + 16

Initial Value of
Stack Pointer A0

```
          xref     hexin, strout, newline, stop

start:    lea      buf+16, a0       ; set up 16 character buffer
          moveq    #15, d1          ; loop 16 times with dbra
          jsr      hexin
next:     asr.w    #1, d0           ; shift 1 bit right
          bcc.s    putzero          ; 1 was shifted out from d0
          move.b   #'1', -(a0)      ; store '1' in buffer
          bra.s    testcount
putzero:  move.b   #'0', -(a0)      ; store '0' in buffer
testcount: dbra    d1, next
          move.w   #16, d0
          jsr      strout
          jsr      newline
          jsr      stop

          data
buf:      ds.b     16
          end
```

⟨Run of Program 6.2⟩

a3f8
1010001111111000

|6.2| STACKS

A **stack** is a linear list of data items that is accessible at only one end of the list, called the Top. Items are added or deleted from the stack at the top. Food trays in a dining hall are a good model for this type of list. The operation of removing an element from the stack is called **popping** the stack. A **push** operation adds an item to the stack. In the list ordering, the last item entered is the first one removed. For this reason, a stack is said to have LIFO (last-in, first-out) ordering. Figure 6.1 illustrates a sequence of push and pop operations.

In high-level languages, stacks are frequently implemented with an array and an index Top. Assume LIST is the name of the array with index range 1–20. In one model, the stack grows in the direction of increasing array indices. In the diagram, the index Top = 3, and the element at the top of the stack is LIST[TOP] = C. Initially, the stack is empty, and Top = 0.

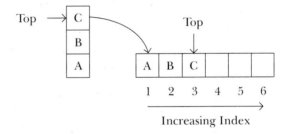

FIGURE 6.1 Models Illustrating Pushing and Popping Elements

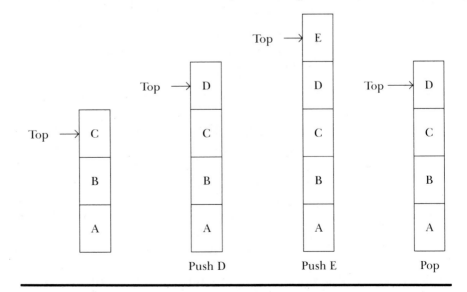

Pascal Implementation—Model 1

```
CONST
    Stackend = 20;
TYPE
    Stack = RECORD
        List : ARRAY[1 . . Stackend] OF Stacktype;
        TOP : 0 . . Stackend;
    END; {RECORD}
```

{Initialize Top to be 0}

In a second model, the stack grows in the direction of decreasing array indices. In the diagram, the index Top = 18, and the element at the top of the stack is LIST[TOP] = C. Initially, the stack is empty, and Top = 21.

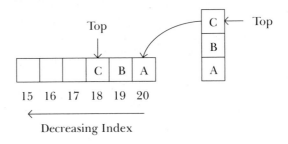

Pascal Implementation—Model 2

```
CONST
    Stackend = 20;
    Stackendp1 = 21;
TYPE
    Stack = RECORD
        List : Array[0 . . Stackend] OF Stacktype;
        TOP : 0 . . Stackendp1;
    END; {RECORD}
```

{Initialize Top to be Stkendp1}

In Model 1, the index Top increases on each PUSH operation. The stack grows out into the array. In Model 2, the stack grows in the opposite direction, with the index Top decreasing on each PUSH operation. Figure 6.2 shows the two models for a stack.

In MC68000 systems, it is most convenient to use Model 2 to implement stacks. This takes full advantage of the predecrement and postincrement addressing modes to implement the push and pop operations. To better

FIGURE 6.2 Stack Implementation Models

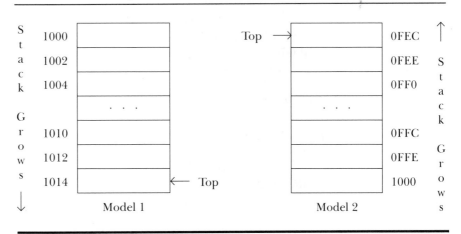

understand these ideas, compare code for Pascal PUSH and POP procedures with equivalent assembly language code. Assume that an integer is
16-bits.

Stack Declarations

Pascal Declaration

```
TYPE
    Stack = RECORD
        List : ARRAY[0 . . 9] OF Integer;
        Top : 0 . . 10;
    END; {RECORD}

Top := 10;
```

MC68000 Declaration

```
        LEA    LIST+20,A0
          .
          .
          .
LIST:   DS.W   10
```

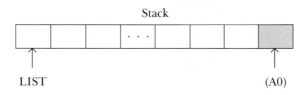

PUSH Routine

Pascal Code

```
PROCEDURE Push(Item : Integer; VAR S :Stack);
BEGIN
    S. Top := S.Top − 1;
    S.List[S.Top] := Item
END;
```

MC68000 Code

```
MOVE.W D0,−(A0)   ; Push from D0
```

Assume that (D0.W) = $700A is pushed on the stack.

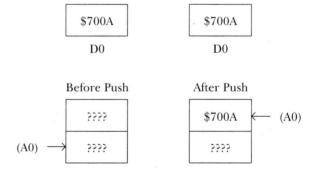

POP Routine

Pascal Code

```
PROCEDURE Pop (VAR Item : Integer; VAR S :Stack);
BEGIN
    Item := S.List[S.Top]
    S.Top := S.Top + 1;
END;
```

MC68000 Code

```
MOVE.W (A0)+,D0   ; POP to D0
```

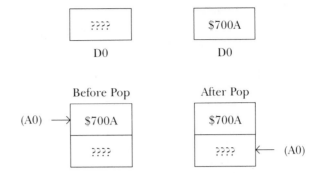

EXAMPLE 6.4

The following operations define and modify a stack.

Pascal Code	*MC68000 Code*
INITIALIZE THE STACK	LEA STACK + 20,A0
PUSH 25	MOVE.W #25, − (A0)
PUSH 10	MOVE.W #10, − (A0)
POP	MOVE.W (A0) + ,D0

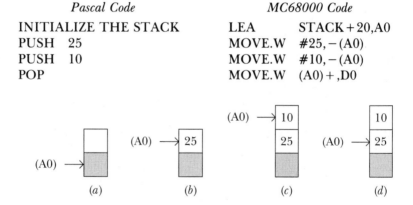

Stacks are of fundamental importance in dealing with subroutines and exception processing. Chapter 7 covers the use of stacks in subroutines, and Chapter 10 discusses the use of stacks to implement high-level language procedures and functions. Chapter 13 introduces exception processing.

PROGRAM 6.3

Evaluate Logical
Expressions

Logical expressions with operands 0 and 1 and operators * (AND) and + (OR) are entered in reverse Polish notation, and then each character in the input string is scanned. For example,

       1 AND 1 is input as 11*   1 OR 0 is input as 10+

1. When an operand is found, it is pushed onto a stack.

2. When an operator (+ or *) is found, two operands are popped from the stack, and the operation is performed. The result is pushed back onto the stack.

At the end of the input string, the value of the expression is on top of the stack, and the final value of the logical expression is printed. No error checking is done.

Algorithm

STRIN is used for the input, and thus the number of characters read is known. A DBcc loop manages the scanning of characters.

The operands '0' and '1' have ASCII values $30 and $31, respectively. The corresponding binary value is computed by subtracting '0' and storing it on the operand stack.

The operations * and + are executed by the AND and OR instructions. The result is printed as an ASCII character by adding '0' to the element at the top of the stack.

```
AND_op:      equ        '*'
OR_op:       equ        '+'
CHAR_0:      equ        '0'

             xref       strin, strout, newline, stop

start:       lea        inputbuf, a0
             moveq      #80, d0
             jsr        strin
             jsr        strout          ; echo input expression
             subq.w     #2, d0          ; skip newline and use dbra
             lea        opandstk+20, a1 ; opstk is the operand stack
scannext:
             cmpi.b     #CHAR_0, (a0)   ; test if char is '0' or '1'
             blt.s      evaluate        ; no! input is an operator
             move.b     (a0)+, (a1)     ; push input on stack
             subi.b     #CHAR_0, (a1)   ; convert to binary
             bra.s      chkcounter      ; test for another input
evaluate:    move.b     (a1)+, d2       ; pop the operands
             move.b     (a1)+, d1
             cmpi.b     #AND_op, (a0)+  ; test operator * or +
             beq.s      found_and       ; the operator is * (and)
             or.b       d1, d2
             bra.s      pushop
found_and:   and.b      d1, d2
pushop:      move.b     d2, -(a1)       ; push result on the stack
chkcounter:  dbra       d0, scannext
putans:      addi.b     #CHAR_0, (a1)   ; convert result to ASCII
             movea.l    a1, a0          ; a0 points to the result
             move.w     #1, d0          ; output 1 character
             jsr        strout
             jsr        newline
             jsr        stop

             data
opandstk:    ds.b       20
```

```
inputbuf:     ds.b        80

              end
```

⟨Run of Program 6.3⟩

```
01 + 0001 + + * +
01 + 0001 + + * +
1
```

6.3 | INDEXED DIRECT-MEMORY ACCESS

The MC68000 has addressing modes that allow indexed access to arrays and records. These addressing modes are fundamental to implementing arrays and records in high-level languages. With the release of the MC68020 processor, a new syntax was used for these indexed direct modes. Most MC68000 assemblers recognize the new syntax and it is used exclusively in this book.

ADDRESSING MODE

Address Register Indirect with Displacement

Syntax (d, An) where d is a 16-bit two's complement number

Action The constant d is sign-extended to 32 bits and added to address register An. The operand accesses the contents of address $(An) + d$.

Notes

1. The displacement d is stored as an extension word. Its range is -32768 to $+32767$ bytes.

2. The original MC68000 syntax was $d(An)$.

EXAMPLE 6.5

(a) MOVE.W (6,A2),D4
   The word at location (A2) + 6 is moved to register D4. The value of A2 is not affected.

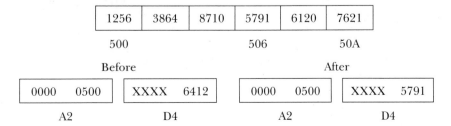

(b) Given an array of words starting at location $500, let (A4) = $000500.

$$\text{MOVE.W} \quad (A4),(-2,A4)$$

Move the value (A4) to the previous word in the sequence at address (A4) − 2.

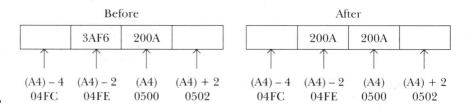

Records in Assembly Language

A Pascal record is a block of memory partitioned into fields that are stored in consecutive memory locations. In assembly language, a record is declared with "Define Storage" (DS) to allocate memory and EQU to name field offsets.

Pascal Declaration

```
TYPE
  Myrecord = RECORD
    Field0 : PACKED ARRAY[1 . . 10] OF Char;     { 10-byte field }
    Field1 : Integer;                            {  2-byte field }
    Field2 : Boolean;                            {  1-byte field }
  END { RECORD };
```

MC68000 Declaration

```
Field0:   EQU   0
Field1:   EQU   10
Field2:   EQU   12
REC:      DS.B  14   ; ALLOCATES 14 BYTES FOR A RECORD
                     ; MAINTAIN EVEN BYTE BOUNDARY
```

Field0	Field1	Field2	

REC　　　　　　　　　　　　　　　REC + 10　　REC + 12

EXAMPLE 6.6

Pascal and
MC68000 Record
Code

The following equivalent Pascal and MC68000 assembly language code
initialize the fields of a record.

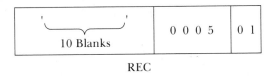

REC

Pascal Code

    VAR REC : Myrecord;

    REC.Field0[I] := '   '; {Blank out all chars of Field0}
    REC.Field1 := 5;
    REC.Field2 := True;

MC68000 Code

```
True:   EQU     1
False:  EQU     0

        LEA     REC,A3
        LEA     (Field0,A3),A0      ; A0 POINTS TO FIELD0
        MOVEQ   #9,D1
LOOP:   MOVE.B  #' ',(A0)+          ; PUT BLANKS IN THE
                                        STRING
        DBRA    D1,LOOP
        MOVE.W  #5, (Field1,A3)     ; CONTENTS OF FIELD1
        MOVE.B  #True,(Field2,A3)   : CONTENTS OF FIELD2
```

Note The fields of the 13-byte record REC are accessed using offsets to
address register A3, which is initialized to REC, the base address of the
record. It is good programming practice to use EQU directives to give
symbolic names to such offsets.

PROGRAM 6.4

32-Bit Signed-
Magnitude Addition

This program simulates 32-bit addition of signed-magnitude numbers. Each
number is stored in 6 bytes with the first word containing the sign ("+" =
0; "−" = 1) and the remaining long word containing the unsigned magnitude. The following familiar rules of signs apply when adding two numbers.

  Like Signs: Add the numbers and choose the common sign.
  Unlike Signs: Subtract the smaller from the larger and choose the
    sign of the larger.

Two numbers are entered into memory locations A and B using STRIN (sign) and DECIN__LONG (magnitude). For each number, the sign is stored in the SIGN FIELD, and the absolute value is stored in the MAGNITUDE FIELD. The addition B := A + B is executed, and the result is printed in signed-magnitude format.

	A	
Sign	Magnitude	

| (A1) − 6 | (A1) − 4 |

	B	
Sign	Magnitude	

| (A1) | (A1) + 2 |

```
                xref      strin,strout,decin__long,decout__long,newline,stop

SIGN:         equ             0
MAGNITUDE:    equ             2
BSIGN:        equ             0
BMAGNITUDE:   equ             2
ASIGN:        equ            -6
AMAGNITUDE:   equ            -4
NUMBERSIZE:   equ             6

start:   moveq   #1,d1                    ; loop to input 2 numbers
         lea     a,a1

read:    lea     signch,a0
         moveq   #1,d0                    ; read only the sign
         jsr     strin
         cmpi.b  #'+',(a0)                ; was it positive
         bne.s   neg                      ; no!
         move.w  #0,(SIGN,a1)             ; set sign bit to 0
         bra     getmagnitude
neg:     move.w  #1,(SIGN,a1)             ; set sign bit to 1

getmagnitude:
         jsr     decin_long
         move.l  d0,(MAGNITUDE,a1)        ; store the magnitude
         addq.l  #NUMBERSIZE,a1           ; set (a1) to address b
         dbra    d1,read
; begin the addition. store the signs for a and b in d0 and d1,
; the magnitudes in d2 and d3 respectively
         subq.w  #NUMBERSIZE,a1           ; reset a1 to point at b
         move.w  (ASIGN,a1),d0            ; get sign of a
         move.w  (BSIGN,a1),d1            ; sign of b
         move.l  (AMAGNITUDE,a1),d2       ; magnitude of a
         move.l  (BMAGNITUDE,a1),d3       ; magnitude of b
         eor.w   d0,d1                    ; test for like signs
         bne.s   testmagnitude           ; unlike signs. more testing
         add.l   d2,d3
         move.w  d0,(BSIGN,a1)            ; put correct sign back
```

```
        move.l   d3,(BMAGNITUDE,a1)        ; assign correct magnitude
        bra      donecomputing

testmagnitude:
        cmp.l    d2,d3                     ; find bigger magnitude
        bcc.s    b_bigger                  ; branch if b >= a
        move.w   (ASIGN,a1),(BSIGN,a1)     ; put sign of a in result
        sub.l    d3,d2                     ; subtract a - b
        move.l   d2,(BMAGNITUDE,a1)        ; put result in b
        bra      donecomputing
b_bigger:
        sub.l    d2,d3                     ; subtract b - a
        move.l   d3,(BMAGNITUDE,a1)        ; put result in b

donecomputing:
; the sum in now in b. it is time to output the result
        tst.w    (BSIGN,a1)
        bne.s    putneg
        move.b   #'+',(a0)                 ; store "+" in signchar
        bra.s    printnum
putneg: move.b   #'-',(a0)                 ; store "-" in signchar

printnum:
        move.w   #1,d0                     ; output only the sign
        jsr      strout
        move.l   (BMAGNITUDE,a1),d0        ; move magnitude to d0
        jsr      decout_long
        jsr      newline
        jsr      stop

        data
a:      ds.w     3
b:      ds.w     3
signch: ds.b     1


        end
```

⟨Run of Program 6.4⟩

```
-55-33
-88
```

The address register indirect with displacement mode permits only a constant displacement. Motorola provides a more general mode that allows the addition of a register offset. The new mode, address register indirect with index and displacement, allows direct memory access to arrays and records.

**ADDRESSING
MODE**

Address Register
Indirect with
Index and
Displacement

Syntax   (d,A*n*,Ri.W) or (d,A*n*,Ri.L)

Action   The mode specifies indirect addressing. The parameters d (displacement) and Ri.⟨size⟩ (index register) are used to compute the effective address of the operand.

$$\langle ea \rangle = (An) + (Ri.\langle size \rangle) + d$$

Notes

1. The base address A*n* can be held fixed, while the index register can be adjusted to provide variable access to elements in a data structure.

2. The displacement d is an 8-bit signed constant in the range −128 to 127.

3. Ri.⟨size⟩ is a 16-bit ("W") or a 32-bit ("L") index stored in either a data or an address register. If the index size is "W" the value is sign-extended to a long word.

4. The original syntax for the MC68000 was

   d(A*n*,Ri.size)

5. This mode requires a 16-bit extension word that contains information on the index and displacement. Information on the address register A*n* is contained in the opcode word. The format of the extension word is as follows:

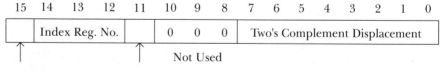

15	14	13	12	11	10	9	8	7	6	5	4	3	2	1	0
	Index Reg. No.				0	0	0	Two's Complement Displacement							

↑   ↑
                              Not Used

Index Type   Index Size
0 = Data Register   0 = Word
1 = Addr Register   1 = Long Word

EXAMPLE 6.7

Assume (A0) = \$00001000 and (D1.L) = \$00A32174.

(a) MOVE.W   (2,A0, D1.W), D0
    The effective address for the source operand is

         00001000 + 00002174 + 00000002 = 00003176
         (A0)   (D1.W)   d

    The instruction moves the 16-bit contents of location \$003176 to D0.

(b) ADD.L   D0,(16,A0,D1.L)

The effective address of the destination operand is

$$00001000 + 00A32174 + 00000010 = 00A33184$$
$$\;\;\;\text{(A0)}\qquad\text{(D1.L)}\qquad\qquad\text{d}$$

The instruction adds the 32-bit contents of D0 to the contents of location $A33184.

(c) MOVE.L   A,(18,A4,D2.W)   Assume A = $3000.

The extension word for the addressing mode follows the address A and is

Destination Extension	0	010	0	000	0001 0010
	Dn	D2	.W	Unused	18 = $12

The machine code for the instruction is

$$29B8\;\;0000\;\;3000\;\;2012$$

EXAMPLE 6.8

(a) Let A be an array of integers (2 bytes) with index I in the range $0 \leq I \leq$ upperbound. The element A[I] has offset I $*$ 2 from the starting address. The following MC68000 code implements indexed direct array access for A[I].

MC68000 Code

```
LEA       A,A0
MOVE.W  I,D0               ; SET INDEX I IN D0
ASL.W    #1,D0             ; OFFSET D0 = I * 2
MOVE.W  (0,A0,D0.W),ITEM   ; PUT A[I] IN ITEM
```

(b) Address register indirect with index and displacement is used to its fullest generality when accessing an array of records. Let A be an array of records structured as follows:

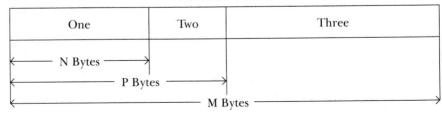

Individual Record

The offsets to the three fields are 0, N, and P, and the size of the record is M. Array element A[I] and its fields can be accessed in assembly language by using

```
LEA       A,A0       ; SET A0 TO START OF RECORDS
MOVE.W    I,D0
MULU      #M,D0      ; MULTIPLY I * M = I * SIZEOF(RECORD)
```

to assign the base address in A0 and the offset from the base of the array to the Ith record in D0.W. The three fields are accessed as follows:

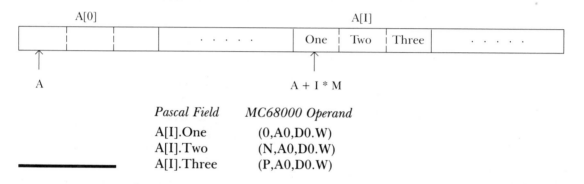

Pascal Field	MC68000 Operand
A[I].One	(0,A0,D0.W)
A[I].Two	(N,A0,D0.W)
A[I].Three	(P,A0,D0.W)

PROGRAM 6.5

Powers-of-2 Table

Powers of 2 are frequently used in applications. For exponent value N, 2^N can be computed using the ASL instruction or it can be accessed from a table using N as an index. Assume that the powers-of-2 table starts at address P2TABLE and contains the following values:

$$1 = 2^0, 2 = 2^1, 4 = 2^2, \quad \ldots, \quad 32768 = 2^{15}$$

Read the value N from the keyboard, and use it as an index to find and output 2^N.

```
          xref        decout,decin,newline,stop

start:    lea         p2table,a0
          jsr         decin            ; obtain a number
          bmi         out              ; number must be in the range
;                                      ; 0 <= n <= 15
          cmpi.w      #15,d0
          bgt         out
          asl.w       #1,d0
          move.w      (0,a0,d0.w),d0   ; get the table entry for 2 ** n
          jsr         decout           ; print the table entry
          jsr         newline
out:      jsr         stop
```

```
              data
p2table:      dc.w      1, 2, 4, 8, 16, 32, 64, 128, 256, 512, 1024
              dc.w      2048, 4096, 8192, 16384, 32768
              end
```

⟨Run of Program 6.5⟩

8
256

|6.4| THE PC-RELATIVE MODES

The branch instructions and the decrement and branch instructions are position independent. That is, the target address is specified as an offset to the program counter. For any load address, these instructions execute correctly without relocation. The MC68000 provides two addressing modes that can extend this position independence to a class of other instructions. The syntax is quite simple. Use address register indirect with displacement or address register indirect with index and displacement, and replace the "address register A*n*" with "program counter" PC. With the addition of these modes, it is now possible to explain the basic structure of a program in the Macintosh run-time environment.

ADDRESSING MODE

Program Counter with Displacement

Syntax (d,PC)   where d is a 16-bit two's complement number
          (label,PC) where "label" references a symbolic label

Action The displacement d is sign-extended to 32 bits and added to the program counter. The operand accesses the contents of address

$$\langle ea \rangle = (PC) + d$$

The use of a label reference causes the assembler to emit an offset to the program counter.

$$\text{Offset} = \text{label} - \text{PC}$$

The operand accesses the contents at location "label".

Notes

1. The value used for the PC is the address of the extension word containing d.

2. In the (d,PC) form, the constant d is stored as an extension word with a range of -32768 to $+32767$ bytes. In the (label,PC) form, the offset is stored as a 16-bit extension.

3. The original syntax for the MC68000 was

$$d(PC) \quad or \quad label(PC)$$

EXAMPLE 6.9

(a) MOVE.W ($500,PC),D4

If the value of the PC at the start of the instruction is $1000, then the effective address of the source operand is

$$1002 + 500 = 1502$$

The MOVE instruction stores the 16-bit contents at location $001502 in register D4

(b)   MOVEA.L   (CASE,PC),A0

.
.
.

CASE: DC.L   CASE_CODE

If the value of the PC at the start of the instruction is $005000 and CASE has value $006000, the computed offset is

$$6000 - 5002 = 0FFE$$

The MOVEA instruction stores the 32-bit long word CASE_CODE at location CASE in register A0.

(c) For the older MC68000 syntax, the PC instructions in this example are

$$\$500(PC) \quad and \quad CASE(PC)$$

(d) Label CONTINUE is referenced in PC-relative mode. Consider the following JMP instruction:

$$\text{JMP} \quad \text{(CONTINUE,PC)}$$

.

.

.

CONTINUE: MOVE.W   (A0)+,D0

Assume that the PC at the JMP instruction is \$000600 and that the address CONTINUE is equal to \$001000. The offset for the JMP instruction code is given by

$$(PC) + 2 + \text{Offset} = 1000$$
$$0602 + \text{Offset} = 1000$$
$$\text{Offset} = 09FE$$

The machine code for the JMP instruction is

0	1	0	0	1	1	1	0	1	1	1	1	1	0	1	0	4EFA

JMP   (d, PC)

0	0	0	0	1	0	0	1	1	1	1	1	1	1	1	0	09FE

Note The address CONTINUE is always \$09FE bytes from the instruction "JMP CONTINUE(PC)", no matter where the program is ultimately loaded. Thus the instruction will always jump to address CONTINUE.

Address register indirect with displacement mode was extended to include an index for applications involving arrays and records. This same generalization can be performed for program counter with displacement mode.

ADDRESSING MODE

Program Counter with Index and Displacement

Syntax (d,PC,Ri.⟨size⟩)
(label,PC,Ri.⟨size⟩)

Action The parameters d (displacement) and Ri.⟨size⟩ (index register) are used to compute the effective address of the operand.

$$\langle ea \rangle = (PC) + Ri.\langle size \rangle + d$$

If the "LABEL" parameter is used, the assembler emits an offset to the program counter.

$$\text{offset} = \text{label} - PC$$

The effective address of the operand is

$$\langle ea \rangle = (PC) + offset + Ri.\langle size \rangle = label + Ri.\langle size \rangle$$

Notes

1. The value used for the PC is the address of the extension word.

2. The displacement d or the offset to the label is an 8-bit number in the range -128 to $+127$.

3. $Ri.\langle size \rangle$ is a 16-bit ("W") or a 32-bit ("L") index stored in either a data or an address register.

4. This mode has a 16-bit extension word identical in format to that for address register indirect with index and displacement.

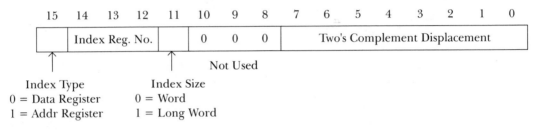

15	14	13	12	11	10	9	8	7	6	5	4	3	2	1	0
	Index Reg. No.				0	0	0	Two's Complement Displacement							

Index Type
0 = Data Register
1 = Addr Register

Index Size
0 = Word
1 = Long Word

Not Used

EXAMPLE 6.10

(a) Assume that (D1.L) = $0000 0008, (PC) = $002000, and (A0) = $00001000.

　　　MOVEA.L (6,PC,D1.W),A0

The effective address for the source operand is

$$\begin{array}{ccc} 002002 + & 000008 + & 000006 = 002010 \\ (PC) & (D1.W) & d \end{array}$$

Move the long word at location $002010 to A0.

Before

002000
PC

00001000
A0

0000	3000
2010	2012

002004
PC

00003000
A0

(b)   MULU   #4,D0
                  MOVEA.L   (CASES,PC,D0.W),A0
                                  .

                                  .

                                  .

      CASES: DC.L   CASE0__CODE
                  DC.L   CASE1__CODE

                  DC.L   CASE2__CODE

                  DC.L   CASE3__CODE

Assume that (D0.W) = 2 represents an index. After the MULU instruction, (D0.W) = 8 is an offset into the CASE list. The effective address of the source is

$$CASES + D0.W = CASES + 8$$

The MOVEA instruction stores the 32-bit long word CASE2__CODE in register A0.

(c) Generate the machine code for MOVE.B   (18,PC,D2.W),(A3).

Operand	0 0	0 1	0 1 1	0 1 0	1 1 1	0 1 1
	MOVE	.B	(A3)		(d, PC, Ri)_	

0	0 1 0	0	0 0 0	0 0 0 1	0 0 1 0
Dn	D2	.W	Unused	18 = $12	

Machine Code: 16BB   2012

Only a subset of MC68000 instructions permits the PC-relative mode. For two operand instructions, the PC-relative mode may not be used in the destination operand, with the sole exception of the BTST instruction. For instance, the following is valid:

BTST #0, (4,PC)

A PC-relative reference is considered a program reference and not a data reference. A **program reference** is a reference to a portion of a program that contains instructions and read-only data. The data portion contains read-write and, possibly, read-only data. No data modification is permitted for a memory address accessed by one of the PC-relative modes. Although the TST and CMPI instructions do not modify memory, their references to memory are not considered to be program references, and they may not use PC-relative mode. However, BTST is allowed to test program memory by using PC-relative mode. On the newer Motorola processors, these restrictions are removed for TST and CMPI.

EXAMPLE 6.11

(a) OR.W   (500,PC),D0
A valid instruction. Data is read from the contents of the source operand.

(b) OR.W   D0, (500,PC)
An invalid instruction. Data may not be written into instruction space with a PC-relative mode.

(c) BTST   #3, (LIST,PC,D0.L)
The special case. BTST only tests the destination operand and does not alter its contents.

Some assemblers provide a directive that forces the use of PC-relative modes whenever possible. An example of such a directive is

OPT   PCS   ; PC Relative Option

If such a directive were used, then the machine code for the JMP instruction

JMP CONTINUE

would automatically assemble into code for the instruction

JMP (CONTINUE, PC)

PROGRAM 6.6

PC-Relative
Demonstration
Program

A simple algorithm is implemented using both address register indirect with index and displacement mode and the equivalent PC-relative modes. A machine code listing is included to illustrate the PC-relative offsets.

Algorithm   The code is assumed to be loaded at $2000, with the code for subroutine STOP at address $5000. An INDEX is read from a memory location and then multiplied by 2 to represent an offset into an array LIST. The absolute value of LIST(INDEX) is written to memory location VALUE.

The algorithm includes a fetch from memory INDEX, access to the array LIST, and a store of data in memory location VALUE. Each of these memory accesses must be modified for PC-relative mode.

In the PC-relative case, data used by the program is not placed into a data segment by using the DATA directive. On systems where the program segment and data segment are in separate areas of memory, the origin of the data segment might be sufficiently far from the program segment that a 16-bit offset in the PC modes is not sufficient to reach the label.

Address Register Indirect Code

```
          xref    stop
start:    move.w  index,d0
          asl.w   #1,d0
          lea     list,a0
          move.w  (0,a0,d0.w),d1
          bge.s   putback
          neg.w   d1
putback:  move.w  d1,value
          jsr     stop

          data
list:     dc.w    5,3,55,-7,65,85,105,88,-43,-18,0
value:    ds.w    1
index:    dc.w    3

          end
```

PC Relative Code

```
          xref    stop
start:    move.w  (index,pc),d0
          asl.w   #1,d0
          lea     (list,pc),a0
          move.w  (0,a0,d0.w),d1
          bge.s   putback
          neg.w   d1
putback:
          lea     (value,pc),a0
          move.w  d1,(a0)
          jsr     (stop,pc)

list:     dc.w    5,3,55,-7,65,85,105,88,-43,-18,0
value:    ds.w    1
index:    dc.w    3

          end
```

PC Relative Modes Listing

```
 1  0000                         xref      stop
 2  0000

 3  0000  303A    start          move.w   (index,pc),d0
          0032
 4  0004  E340                   asl.w  #1,d0
 5  0006  41FA                   lea    (list,pc),a0
          0014
 6  000A  3230                   move.w   (0,a0,d0.w),d1
          0000
 7  000E  6C02                   bge.s putback
 8  0010  4441                   neg.w d1
 9  0012           putback:
10  0012           ;             move.w   d1,(value,pc)
11  0012           ; Replace with the next two instructions
12  0012  41FA                   lea    (value,pc),a0
          001E
13  0016  3081                   move.w   d1,(a0)
14  0018  4EBA                   jsr    (stop,pc)
          FFE6
15  001C
16  001C  0005    list:          dc.w  5,3,55,-7,65,85,105,88,-43,-18,0
17  0032          value:         ds.w  1
18  0034  0003    index:         dc.w  3
19  0036
20  0036                         end
```

|6.5| MACINTOSH CODE STRUCTURE

In the Macintosh run-time code structure, a program is composed of one or more code segments and a single data segment. Each is located in a separate area of memory. A set of constraints governs the structure of references to code and data in order to allow the code and data segments to be loaded at any available location in memory. The following analysis assumes a small assembly language program with a single code segment. This analysis demonstrates the use of PC-relative and base-relative addressing and includes critical information for a Macintosh assembly language programmer.

The Macintosh uses address register A5 as a pointer to the data segment. Each label in the data space is an offset from A5. The code is located in a separate segment loaded into memory by the segment loader. All labels in the code segment are identified as offsets to the PC. Consider the following code segments assembled in absolute address format and in Macintosh format. Listing files are included for both formats.

Absolute Address Format

```
START:          MOVE.W      CLABEL_1, DLABEL_1
                ADD.W       D1,D0
CLABEL_1:       LEA         START,A3
                CLR.W       DLABEL_2

                DATA
DLABEL_1:       DS.W        1
DLABEL_2:       DC.W        5
                END
```

Absolute Addressing Listing File

```
1   000000    33F9   START:      MOVE.W     CLABEL_1,   DLABEL_1
              0000
              000C
              0000
              0018
2   00000A    D041               ADD.W      D1,D0
3   00000C    47F9   CLABEL_1:   LEA        START,A3
              0000
              0000
4   000012    4279               CLR.W      DLABEL_2
              0000
              001A
5
6                                DATA
7   000018           DLABEL_1:   DS.W       1
8   00001A    0005   DLABEL_2:   DC.W       5
9   00001C                       END
                     SYMBOL  TABLE
              * * * * * * * * * * *
    CLABEL_1   00000C       START       000000
    DLABEL_1   000018       DLABEL_2    00001A
```

All labels have a value relative to a starting address of 0, and all label references are 32-bit absolute long. For example, in the CLR instruction, the label operand is assembled as the absolute long value $0000001A.

Macintosh Format

```
START:          MOVE.W      CLABEL_1, DLABEL_1
                ADD.W       D1,D0
CLABEL_1:       LEA         START,A3
                CLR.W       DLABEL_2

                DATA
DLABEL_1:       DS.L        1
DLABEL_2:       DC.W        5
                END
```

Macintosh Format Listing File

```
1  0000  3B7A  START:          MOVE.W      CLABEL_1,  DLABEL_1
         0006
         0000
2  0006  D041                  ADD.W       D1,D0
3  0008  47FA  CLABEL_1:       LEA         START,A3
         FFF6
4  000C  426D                  CLR.W       DLABEL_2
         0002
5  0010
6  0000                        DATA
7  0000        DLABEL_1:       DS.W        1
8  0002  0005  DLABEL_2:       DC.W        5
9  0004                        END
```

```
                        SYMBOL  TABLE
                  * * * * * * * * * * * *
                              CODE
            CLABEL_1    000008       START       000000

                              DATA
            DLABEL_1    000000       DLABEL_2    000002
```

The code segment begins with label START and contains a second label CLABEL__. The labels have values $000000 and $000008. In the Macintosh environment, however, the operand references in the code segment have values relative to the program counter. The value of a data label is its offset from the start of the data segment. For example, the reference to START in the LEA instruction is assembled as $FFF6 ($-10$), the displacement from the program counter to START. The reference to CLABEL__1 is also assembled PC-relative with displacement $0006. In the CLR instruction, the operand is a data label. Its reference is assembled as 2, the offset from the start of the data segment to the label. Using address register indirect with displacement, this offset is used with A5 to access DLABEL 2.

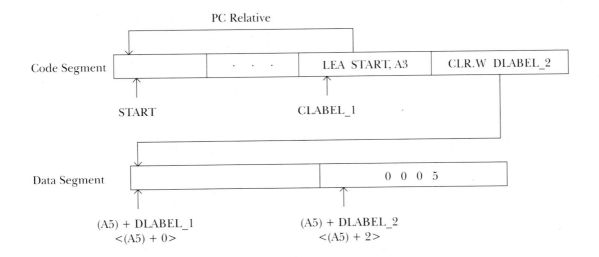

Notes

1. The Macintosh does not support absolute addressing mode for labels because they are assembled as a relative reference to either the PC or A5. Absolute constant addresses are permitted.

2. The data labels have a fixed offset from A5. If the programmer uses A5 as a scratch register and changes its value, the data items are lost because references are made relative to the new A5.

3. Attempts to reference a code label in a destination operand are invalid because the label is a PC-relative reference, and this is not permitted on the MC68000. The following is invalid.

MOVE.W   #$3039, CLABEL_1

CLABEL_1 must be referenced relative to an address register. The MOVE instruction can be implemented using the following:

LEA   CLABEL_1,A0
MOVE.W   #$3039,(A0)

EXAMPLE 6.12   A set of cases describes some of the restrictions that apply to a Macintosh programmer.

(*a*) The source operand is invalid.

MOVEA.L #LABEL,A0
 ...
DATA

LABEL: ...

Problem: Since LABEL must be expressed as an offset to A5, #LABEL makes no sense. You must replace the MOVEA instruction with

LEA LABEL,A0

(b) If data is to be placed into an address in the code segment, the following code sequence is not valid:

```
            MOVE.L   D0, CODETARGET
            . . .
CODETARGET:  DS.L        1
```

Problem: The destination of an instruction cannot be in PC-relative mode. Use the instructions

```
LEA         CODETARGET,A3
MOVE.L   D0,(A3)
```

(c) Unless an address is a constant or an equated constant, all absolute long (e.g., A.L) or absolute short (e.g., A.W) references are not acceptable. For example,

MOVE.L   A.W,D0

is unacceptable.

(d) A commonly used technique in assembly language programming is to access strings dynamically by reading a desired string address from an array of addresses.

```
            LEA         STRINGS,A0
            ASL.W       #2,D1               ; INDEX
            MOVE.L   0(A0,D1.W),A0
            JSR         STRLEN
                         . . .
            DATA
STRINGS:   DC.L        ONE, TWO, THREE, FOUR, FIVE
ONE:        DC.B        'HERE IS STRING ONE', 0
TWO:        DC.B        'STRING TWO', 0
```

Problem: Without modification, this code will not work on the Macintosh. The reason is that absolute long addresses are not placed to array "strings" but A5 relative offsets are. Recall that absolute long addressing for labels is not available.

Programming Examples

Techniques for programming with the Macintosh are illustrated with an example. The data declaration section of a program contains four strings. Each string begins with a byte that contains the length of the string. An input in the range 0–3 is sought, and the corresponding string is output. A non-Macintosh implementation accesses the strings using an array of absolute long addresses. The equivalent Macintosh code references the labels using A5-relative offsets.

PROGRAM 6.7

Non-Macintosh Form

The addresses for the strings are stored in the array of labels "strings."

```
        xref    decin, strout, newline, stop

start:  jsr     decin               ; load the index
        asl.w   #2, d0              ; compute offset to string
        lea     strings, a1         ; set a1 to string addresses
        movea.l (0, a1, d0.w), a0   ; store string address in a0
        move.b  (a0), d0            ; load string count in d0
        adda.l  #1, a0              ; set a0 to start of string
        jsr     strout              ; print the string
        jsr     newline
        jsr     stop

        data
strings: dc.l   str0, str1, str2, str3
str0:   dc.b    22, 'This code as it stands'
str1:   dc.b    22, 'will not work properly'
str2:   dc.b    6, 'on the'
str3:   dc.b    10, 'Macintosh!'
        end
```

PROGRAM 6.7

Macintosh Form

Identify the strings with run-time computed addresses.

```
        xref    decin, strout, newline, stop

start:  lea     strings, a0         ; initialize array strings
        lea     str0, a1
        moveq   #0, d0
        moveq   #3, d1
init:   move.l  a1, (a0)+           ; place an address into strings
        move.b  (a1), d0            ; get string length
        adda.l  d0, a1              ; move a1 to next string
        addq.w  #1, a1
        dbra    d1, init
        jsr     decin               ; load the index
        asl.w   #2, d0              ; compute offset to string
        lea     strings, a1         ; set a1 to string addresses
        movea.l (0, a1, d0.w), a0   ; store string address in a0
        move.b  (a0), d0            ; load string count in d0
        adda.l  #1, a0              ; set a0 to start of string
        jsr     strout              ; print the string
        jsr     newline
        jsr     stop
```

```
                data
strings:    ds.l    4
str0:       dc.b    22,'This code as it stands'
str1:       dc.b    18,'will work properly'
str2:       dc.b    6,'on the'
str3:       dc.b    10,'Macintosh! '
                end
```

6.6 APPLICATION PROGRAMS

The following application programs use the address register indirect modes presented in this chapter.

PROGRAM 6.8

Binary Digit Input

An unsigned number N is input as a string of up to 16 binary digits. The digits are scanned, and, using a powers of 2 table, the value of N is stored in D0 and output using hexout.

$$N = b_{15}b_{14} \cdots b_2 b_1 b_0$$

Note Each character b_i is a '0' or '1' and corresponds to the table value 2^i. The value for N is its expanded notation form.

```
            xref        hexout, strin, newline, stop

start:      lea         p2table, a1     ; set list pointers
            lea         bin, a0
            moveq       #80, d0
            jsr         strin           ; load the string of bits
            subq.w      #2, d0          ; skip cr and set dbra
            move.w      d0, d1          ; move counter to d1
            moveq       #0, d0          ; d0 holds the decimal sum
loop:       move.b      (a0)+, d2       ; move binary digit to d2
            andi.b      #$01, d2        ; mask all but bit #0
            beq.s       ltest           ; if 0, go to loop test code
            move.w      d1, d2          ; move index to d2
            asl.w       #1, d2          ; double d2 for word size
            add.w       (0, a1, d2), d0 ; add power of two
ltest:      dbra        d1, loop
            jsr         hexout
            jsr         newline
            jsr         stop
```

```
          data

p2table:
          dc.w        1, 2, 4, 8, 16, 32, 64, 128, 256, 512, 1024
          dc.w        2048, 4096, 8192, 16384, 32768
bin:      ds.b        80
          end
```

⟨Run of program 6.8⟩

```
10101
0015
```

The straight selection sort is one of the basic algorithms for ordering a list. Iteratively, a sublist is scanned to select the smallest element, which is then stored at the low index (ascending order) or high index (descending order) of the sublist. Sequential access modes are used for the code.

PROGRAM 6.9

Straight Selection Sort

Assume that A is an array with N elements and that the elements of A are to be sorted in ascending order.

Sort Algorithm   Begin by scanning the sublist A[1] $\cdots$ A[N] and place the smallest element in A[1]. To do this, scan the elements A[2] $\cdots$ A[N], comparing each to A[1]. If an element is less than A[1], exchange it with A[1]. The smallest entry of the sublist is A[1]. In the second pass, scan the sublist A[2] $\cdots$ A[N] by comparing each element with A[2]. The second smallest element in list is stored in A[2]. If the algorithm continues for $N - 1$ passes, the list is ordered. For example,

List:	18	37	9	21	4	($N = 5$)
Pass 1:	4	37	18	21	9	
Pass 2:	4	9	37	21	18	
Pass 3:	4	9	18	37	21	
Pass 4:	4	9	18	21	37	

Code Algorithm   DBRA is used for loop control. For $N - 1$ passes, the loop counter is initialized to $N - 2$ to set up the DBRA branch check.

Address register A0 points to the starting element in the sublist. The smallest element in the sublist is stored in (A0). Address register A1 scans the sublist. For each pass, initialize A1 = A0 + 2 using the instruction

LEA   (2,A0),   A1

```
          xref        hexout, newline, stop

start:    lea         list, a0
```

```
           move.w    size,d0          ; d0 = number of elements in list
           move.w    d0,d2            ; copy n to d2 for loop counter
           move.w    d0,d4            ; copy n to d4 for output of list
    ;
           subq.w    #2,d2            ; make n-1 passes, using dbra
    oloop:  move.w    d2,d3            ; d3 will be counter for inner loop
           lea       (2,a0),a1        ; initialize a1 for upper list scan
    iloop:  move.w    (a1)+,d0         ; stores (a1). move to next element
           cmp.w     (a0),d0          ; compares (a0) and (a1)
           bge       noexg            ; branch if (a1)≥(a0). no exchange
           move.w    (a0),(-2,a1)     ; do an exchange
           move.w    d0,(a0)
    noexg:  dbra      d3,iloop         ; end inner comparison loop
           addq.l    #2,a0            ; bump pointer by two bytes
           dbra      d2,oloop         ; end outer loop
           lea       list,a0          ; print sorted list
           subq.w    #1,d4            ; set counter for dbra
    ploop:  move.w    (a0)+,d0
           jsr       hexout
           dbra      d4,ploop
           jsr       newline
           jsr       stop

           data

    size:  dc.w      7                ; number of elements in list
    list:  dc.w      $0a00, $0080, $00f0, $5000, $0007, $c000, $0400
           end
```

⟨Run of Program 6.9⟩

C000 0007 0080 00F0 0400 0A00 5000

PROGRAM 6.10

Array of Records

A Pascal-like record has four fields in its structure. The total size of the record is 26 bytes.

DATE	DATE COUNT	LOW TEMP	HIGH TEMP
21 Bytes	1 Byte	2 Bytes	2 Bytes

The date field contains a date in the form: MONTH XX, XXXX. The number of characters in the date field is held in the DATE COUNT field. For example,

DECEMBER 7, 1941	16	33	55

Use STRIN and DECIN to initialize an array of three such records. Scan the array, and print the date with the lowest temperature and the date with the highest temperature.

```
; date and temperature record offsets

date:       equ        0
dcount:     equ        21
lowtemp:    equ        22
hightemp:   equ        24
recsize:    equ        26              ; total size in bytes
numrecs:    equ        3               ; number of records

            xref       decin, strin, decout, strout, newline, stop

start:      lea        recordpool, a0
            moveq      #numrecs-1, d1
            move.w     #$7fff, d2       ; (d2) holds lowest temp;
                                        ; (a2) address of temp
            move.w     #$8000, d3       ; (d3) holds highest temp;
;                                       ; (a3) address of temp
loadrec:
            moveq      #21, d0          ; set date buffer
            jsr        strin            ; enter the record
            move.b     d0, (dcount, a0) ; move char count into field
            jsr        decin            ; read low temp
            move.w     d0, (lowtemp, a0) ; move low temp into field
            cmp.w      d0, d2           ; check lowest previous temp
            ble.s      hitemp
            move.w     d0, d2           ; set new lowest temp
            lea        (date, a0), a2   ; set (a2) to new record
hitemp:     jsr        decin
            move.w     d0, (hightemp, a0) ; move high temp into field
            cmp.w      d0, d3
            bge.s      nextrecord
            move.w     d0, d3           ; set new highest temp
            lea        (date, a0), a3   ; set (a3) to new record
nextrecord:
            adda.l     #recsize, a0     ; set (a0) to next record
            dbra       d1, loadrec

; write the lowest and highest temperature
            lea        lowtempmsg, a0
            moveq      #24, d0
            jsr        strout
            movea.l    a2, a0
            move.b     (dcount, a2), d0 ; data count to d0
            andi.w     #$00ff, d0       ; clear msb of d0
            jsr        strout
            jsr        newline
            lea        hightempmsg, a0
            moveq      #24, d0
            jsr        strout
```

```
          movea.l     a3,a0
          move.b      (dcount,a3),d0
          andi.w      #$00ff,d0
          jsr         strout
          jsr         newline
          jsr         stop

          data

recordpool:
          ds.b        numrecs*recsize  ; storage for records
lowtempmsg:
          dc.b        'lowest temperature on  '
hightempmsg:
          dc.b        'highest temperature on '
          end
```

⟨Run of Program 6.10⟩

```
March 23, 1946
20 50
January 3, 1923
10 30
July 18, 1978
76 102
lowest temperature on   January 3, 1923
highest temperature on July 18, 1978
```

───────────

PROGRAM 6.11

String Pool Access

You are prompted to enter *N* strings using STRIN. For each input, delete the terminating newline character, and place the string in a consecutive array of bytes called a *string pool*. This data structure is an efficient method for storing variable-length strings.

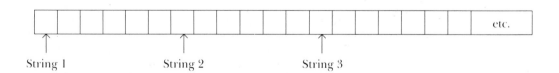

String 1   String 2   String 3

In addition to the string pool, maintain in array of records that holds the starting address of a string in the pool and the number of bytes in the string. This array, called an **access table**, allows access to the individual strings in the string pool.

Address (String 1)	Count (String 1)	Address (String 2)	Count (String 2)	etc.

4 Bytes   2 Bytes

After entering the N strings, you will be prompted to request the output of one of the strings in the range 1–N. Note the use of the EQU directive to assign meaningful names to record parameters.

```
;   string record parameters
stradr            equ  0          ; string address
strcnt:           equ  4          ; character count
recsize:          equ  6          ; total size of record in bytes
maxrecs:          equ  5          ; maximum number of strings

          xref    strin, strout, decin, decout, newline, stop

start:    lea     input_prompt,a0   ; prompt for number of strings
          move.w  #47,d0
          jsr     strout
          jsr     decin             ; get number of strings
          move.w  d0,d2             ; (d2) = n
          move.w  d0,d1
          subq.w  #1,d1             ; (d1) = loop counter = n-1
          lea     spool,a0          ; sequentially load strings
          lea     strecs,a1         ; create an array of records
inputs:   move.w  #81,d0            ; get a string
          jsr     strin
          subq.w  #1,d0             ; delete newline character
          move.l  a0,(a1)+          ; set string pool pointer
          move.w  d0,(a1)+          ; initialize string char count
          adda.w  d0,a0             ; new pointer to string pool
          dbra    d1,inputs
          lea     num_prompt,a0     ; request a record number
          move.w  #32,d0
          jsr     strout
          move.w  d2,d0
          jsr     decout
          jsr     decin
          subq.w  #1,d0             ; record is at address
                                    ; strecs + (recno-1); recsize
          mulu    #6,d0
          lea     strecs,a1
          movea.l stradr(a1,d0.w),a0
          move.w  strcnt(a1,d0.w),d0
          jsr     strout            ; output the requested string
          jsr     newline
          jsr     stop

          data
```

```
num_prompt:
            dc.b        'Enter a string number from 1 to  '
input_prompt:
            dc.b        'Enter the number of strings you wish to input:  '
            even

strecs:     ds.b        30                      ; recsize * maxrecs
spool:      ds.b        500                     ; maxrecs * 100
            end
```

⟨Run of Programs 6.11⟩

Let's get on with it and move on to the next chapter
You know we will output string 2
Enter a string number from 1 to 3 *2*
Let's get on with it and move on to the next chapter

6.7 | MC68020/30/40 ADDRESSING MODES

The MC68020/30/40 processors support 18 addressing modes, which include 6 new modes that expand memory access. The address register indirect with index and PC indirect with index modes now permit the index register to be scaled by a factor of 1, 2, 4, or 8 to allow access to byte, word, long-word, and 64-bit data, which in turn facilitates direct access of array elements. Address register indirect with index and PC indirect with index have been extended to a more general syntax that allows a 32-bit displacement. In the addressing mode syntax, the displacement, the address register, and the index register may be missing. This mode gives rise to data register indirect addressing and is called **base displacement**. The MC68020/30/40 also introduce memory indirect addressing, which allows intermediate access to the contents of a pointer field. The contents are then used as the base address for subsequent memory access. The memory indirect modes will be presented in Chapter 10.

Extended Address Register Indirect with Index Mode

Address register indirect with index mode specifies the effective address of an operand by adding the contents of an address register, displacement, and index. The displacement and index are sign extended to 32 bits during the calculation. The MC68020/30/40 support a **scale factor** in conjunction with the index register. This eliminates the need for an additional multiply instruction to scale the index register.

ADDRESSING MODE

MC68020/30/40 Address Register Indirect with Index (8-Bit Displacement d_8)

Syntax $(d_8, An, Rm.Size * Scale)$

Action   The operand specifies the effective address in memory.

$$\langle ea \rangle = (An) + d_8 + (Rm) * Scale$$

Notes

1. The index may be a data register or an address register.

2. The scale allows the contents of the index register to be multiplied by 1, 2, 4, or 8.

3. The displacement d_8 and index operand $(Rm) * Scale$ are sign extended to 32 bits in computing the effective address.

4. The comparable MC68000 syntax (d, An, Rm) uses a scale factor of 1.

EXAMPLE 6.13

(a) Assume that $(A0) = \$00001000$ and $(D1.W) = \$0100$. The effective address for the following operand is $\$00001420$:

$$(\$20, A0, D1.W * 4)$$

$$\langle ea \rangle = \$00001000 + \$00000100 * 4 + \$00000020 = \$00001420$$

(b) Assume that LIST is an array of long words. If (A0) is the address LIST and $(D1.W) = 7$ is an index into the array, then

$$\text{MOVE.L} \quad (0, A0, D1.W * 4), D0$$

directly accesses the contents of LIST[7] and stores it in D0.

(c) In Program 6.5, the power-of-2 table was read using the two statements

$$\text{ASL.W} \qquad \#1, D0$$
$$\text{MOVE.W} \qquad (0, A0, D0.W), D0$$

Using this MC68020/30/40 variant, the single statement

$$\text{MOVE.W} \quad (0, A0, D0.W * 2), D0$$

is sufficient.

Address register indirect with base displacement and index is a new mode for the MC68020/30/40. The displacement can be either 16 or 32 bits, and specification of all three items is optional.

ADDRESSING MODE

MC68020/30/40
Address
Register Indirect
with Index (Base
Displacement)

Syntax   (bd,An,Rm.Size * Scale)

Action   The operand specifies a computed effective address. An optional 16- or 32-bit base displacement bd is used in computing the effective address.

$$\langle ea \rangle = (An) + bd + (Rm) * Scale$$

Notes

1. The index may be a data register or an address register.

2. Each of the components is optional. If none is specified, the effective address of 0 is used.

3. The use of a 32-bit displacement allows an offset of $-2^{31} \leq bd \leq 2^{31} - 1$ from the base address (An), a large improvement over the MC68000.

4. When the operand may be confused with the MC68000 displacement or index mode, the notation "L" and "W" as a size specifier for the displacement is used to force the assembler to generate this mode. If the size is omitted and an address and index register are present, an 8-bit displacement is assumed. Some assemblers optimize by using an 8-bit displacement in place of a 16-bit one if it is in range.

EXAMPLE 6.14

(a) The following syntax forms are valid for the addressing mode:
Default scale factor of 1

$$(bd.L,An,Dm.W) \qquad \langle ea \rangle = (An) + bd + (Dm)$$

Suppress the address register

$$(bd.W,Dm.W * 4) \qquad \langle ea \rangle = bd + (Dm) * 4$$

Equivalent to absolute long mode

$$(bd.L) \qquad \langle ea \rangle = bd$$

Data register indirect access

$$(Dm.L) \qquad \langle ea \rangle = (Dm)$$

The effective address of 0 is used

$$() \qquad \langle ea \rangle = 0$$

(b) LIST is an array of long words, and (D1.W) = 7 is an index into the array. The following instruction stores the 32-bit value LIST[7] in D0:

MOVE.L (LIST.L, D1.W * 4), D0

(c) If LIST is a data segment label, on the Macintosh the code

$$\text{MOVE.L (LIST.L,A5,D1.W } * 4),D0$$

can be used to access LIST[7].

PROGRAM 6.12

Print Matrix (Base Displacement Test Program)

A 6 × 4 matrix of 16-bit data is located at address MAT.

MAT: ARRAY[0 . . 5] OF ARRAY[0 . . 3] OF INTEGER;

The row length is 8 bytes. Using address register indirect with index and base displacement, the contents of the matrix are printed. The base displacement is the value MAT.

```
        xref      hexout,newline,stop

start:  moveq     #5,d1                     ; use dbra for the rows
        lea       0,a0                      ; initialize a0 to 0 offset
        clr.w     d2                        ; clear column count
        clr.l     d0                        ; clear output register
print0: cmpi.w    #3,d2                     ; is index in column range
        bgt       print1                    ; go to next row
        move.w    (mat.l,a0,d2.w*2),d0      ; fetch mat(row)(col)
        jsr       hexout
        addq.w    #1,d2                     ; go to next column
        bra.s     print0                    ; add row length to a0
print1: addq.l    #8,a0                     ; add row length to a0
        clr.w     d2                        ; reset column index to 0
        jsr       newline
        dbra      d1,print0
        jsr       stop

        data

mat:    dc.w      $020,$040,$060,$080
        dc.w      $120,$140,$160,$180
        dc.w      $220,$240,$260,$280
        dc.w      $320,$340,$360,$380
        dc.w      $420,$440,$460,$480
        dc.w      $520,$540,$560,$580

        end
```

⟨Run of Program 6.12⟩

```
0020    0040    0060    0080
0120    0140    0160    0180
0220    0240    0260    0280
0320    0340    0360    0380
0420    0440    0460    0480
0520    0540    0560    0580
```

An adjustment must be made for this program to run on a Macintosh. Replace the statement

$$\text{MOVE.W} \quad \text{(MAT.L, A0, D2.W} * 2\text{), D0}$$

with the two statements

```
LEA (MAT.L, A0, D2.W * 2),A1 ; FETCH MAT [ROW] [COL]
MOVE.W (A5, A1.L), D0
```

Using the beginning of the data segment as a base address, the first statement places the offset of the desired matrix element into A1, and the second accesses the actual address of the element by adding the offset to the base address of the data segment.

Program Counter Indirect with Index Modes

Position-independent code is implemented using the program counter. The MC68020 provides two PC-relative modes similar to the address register indirect modes.

ADDRESSING MODE

MC68020 PC Indirect with Index Modes

Syntax (d8,PC,Rm.Size * Scale)   (8-bit displacement)
          (bd,PC,Rm.Size * Scale)   (base displacement)

Action The operand specifies an effective address relative to the program counter.

$$\langle ea \rangle = (PC) + d_8 + (Rm) * \text{Scale} \quad \text{(8-bit displacement)}$$
$$\langle ea \rangle = (PC) + bd + (Rm) * \text{Scale} \quad \text{(base displacement)}$$

Notes

1. With base displacement, each component of the computed effective address is optimal. If the PC is not specified, the assembler notation "ZPC" must be used, for which the corresponding value is 0. This notation allows the assembler to distinguish between address register and PC indirect with index modes.

2. If the base displacement is a label, assemblers compute the base displacement as an offset to the PC.

3. The PC used to compute the effective address is the address of the extension word.

EXAMPLE 6.15   Use PC-relative mode in the following code segment:

Address		Instruction
001000		. . .
001004		MOVE.L (HERE,PC,D2.W*4),D0
		. . .
001020	HERE:	. . .
		. . .
001028		DC.L $5000

Compute the displacement HERE as an offset to the PC with value $00001006 (2 bytes past the start of the instruction). The offset to HERE is $1020 − $1006 = $1A.

Assuming that (D2.W) = 2, the MOVE instruction fetches the 16-bit contents that are located 8 bytes (2 * 4) past the label HERE. In this example, the value $5000 is stored in D0.

Extension Word Format

The new MC68020/30/40 addressing modes have new extension words to specify the effective address. Figure 6.3 gives the one-word brief format. The full format code uses one to five extension words and is illustrated in Figure 6.4.

Brief Format Address or PC Indirect with Index (8-Bit Displacement)

This extension word is identical to that for the index mode on the MC68000, except for the use of bits 9 and 10 to specify the scale factor.

Full Format Address or PC Indirect with Index (Base Displacement)

The MSB of the first extension word differs from the brief format only in bit 8, which contains a 1. The LSB specifies the base and index

FIGURE 6.3 Brief Format Extension Word

	Index Register			0	Displacement
15	14–12	11	10–9	8	7–0

Index Type
0 = Dm
1 = Am

Index Size
0 = Word
1 = Long

Scale Factor
00 = 1
01 = 2
10 = 4
11 = 8

FIGURE 6.4 Full-Format Extension Word

Rm Type	Reg #	Index Size	Scale Factor	1	Base Suppress	Index Suppress	Base Size	0	0 0 0
15	14–12	11	10–9	8	7	6	5–4	3	2–0

Base Displacement 0 to 2 Words

parameters. Note that bits 0–2 take on additional values when the memory indirect modes are used. Memory indirect modes are presented in Chapter 10.

Base suppress:	0	Base register (An) added
	1	Base register (An) suppressed

Index suppress:	0	Evaluate and add index operand
	1	Suppress index operand

Base displacement size:	00	Reserved
	01	Null displacement
	10	Word displacement
	11	Long displacement

EXAMPLE 6.16

For the operand ($20,A3,D2.L*4), brief format is used for the extension word. The register A3 is stored in the opcode word. The brief format extension word is

0	010	1	10	0	00100000	$2C20
Dm	Reg 2		.L	*4	$20	

EXAMPLE 6.17

(a) For the instruction

OR.L   D3,(FLAGS.L, A2, D5.W)

because the displacement is a long word, full format is required, and there are three extension words. Assume that the value of FLAGS is $80000. The machine code is

87B2	5130	0008 0000
Opcode Word	Full-Format Extension Word	Base Displacement

(b) The instruction

TST.B   (A1, D4.L * 4)

illustrates the omission of a base displacement. In this case, the base displacement size field of the full-format extension word must be set to 01 to designate omission of the displacement.

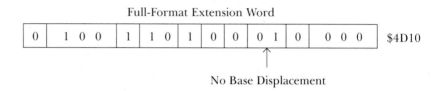

Full-Format Extension Word

The machine code for the instruction is then 4A31   4D10.

(c) Data register indirect mode is developed by omitting the base displacement and the base register. Here the base register is suppressed, and the base displacement is null. In the case of the instruction

MULU   (D5.W),D1

the machine code is C2F0   5190.

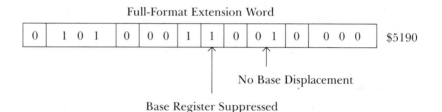

Full-Format Extension Word

6.8 MOTOROLA ADDRESSING CATEGORIES

The MC68000 supports 12 addressing modes that access an operand in immediate mode, in a register, at a memory address, and at a location specified relative to the PC. The MC68020/30/40 family adds an additional 6 addressing modes. The modes are listed according to the following four addressing categories that Motorola uses to specify the permissible addressing modes for the source or destination operands of an instruction. An addressing mode may appear in two or more categories. Table 6.1 lists addressing modes and categories.

Data: A *data addressing mode* may be used to refer to data operands. All addressing modes except address register direct are data modes.

Memory: A *memory addressing mode* may be used to refer to data in memory. All addressing modes except data and address register direct are memory modes.

Alterable: An *alterable addressing mode* may be used to alter the referenced data. All addressing modes except PC relative and immediate modes are alterable modes.

Control: A *control addressing mode* may be used to refer to memory operands without an associated size. The control addressing modes are a subset of the memory addressing modes. Predecrement, postincrement, and immediate modes are excluded.

Address register direct mode does not refer to data operands. Within families of instructions, certain forms permit the MC68000 to initialize and modify the address register. Examples of these instructions are ADDA,

TABLE 6.1 Addressing Mode Categories

	CATEGORY			
ADDRESSING MODE	DATA	MEMORY	ALTERABLE	CONTROL
Data register direct	X		X	
Address register direct			X	
Address register indirect	X	X	X	X
Address register indirect with postincrement	X	X	X	
Address register indirect with predecrement	X	X	X	
Address register indirect with displacement	X	X	X	X
Address register indirect with index (8-bit displacement)	X	X	X	X
Address register indirect with index (base displacement)	X	X	X	X
Memory indirect post-indexed	X	X	X	X
Memory indirect pre-indexed	X	X	X	X
Absolute short	X	X	X	X
Absolute long	X	X	X	X
Program counter indirect with displacement	X	X		X
Program counter indirect with index (8-bit displacement)	X	X		X
PC memory indirect post-indexed	X	X		X
PC memory indirect pre-indexed	X	X		X
Immediate	X	X		X

CMPA, MOVEA, and so forth. They are specifically designed to sign-extend source operands and access an address register in the destination operand.

Clearly, an operand in immediate mode is not memory alterable because it can be used only as a source. The PC-relative modes are a program reference and not a data reference. No data modification is permitted for a memory address accessed by one of the PC-relative modes.

Some instructions, including LEA and JMP, do not specify data size for the operands and require only control modes for their operands.

EXERCISES

1. (a) Declare an array A of five 16-bit numbers initially containing 1, 2, 3, 4, 5.
   (b) Declare an array B of 100 long words initially all zeros.
   (c) Consider the Pascal array declaration

   > TYPE ARR = ARRAY[0 . . 99] OF INTEGER;
   > VAR   C:ARR;

   (i) Declare C in assembly language, assuming each array element is 16-bits.
   (ii) Compute the addresses of C[5], C[18], and C[86] as the base address C plus an offset (e.g., C[1] is at address C + 2).

2. Suppose that (A2) = $001078 and the initial contents of memory are given as follows. Give the value of A2 and the contents of memory after executing the instruction.

1106	1074	1072	1106	1104	1100	1072
1072	1074	1076	1078	107A	107C	107E

   (a) CLR.W   (A2)+
   (b) MOVE.W   −(A2),−(A2)
   (c) MOVE.L   A2,(A2)+
   (d) MOVE.B   (A2)+,(A2)+
   (e) MOVE.W   (A2)+,−(A2)

3. A MOVE instruction is said to be an identity operation if it does not change memory. Indicate whether the given MOVE instruction serves as the identity.
   (a) MOVE.W   (A0)+,−(A0)
   (b) MOVE.W   −(A0),(A0)+
   (c) MOVE.L   (A1)+,(A1)+

4. Given that A2 contains the value (A2) = 0000FF76 and that the label BETA has value BETA = 00007F0C

what is the effective address of the operand in each of the following instructions?

(a) CLR.W   BETA   (b) CLR.L   BETA+$24
(c) CLR.W   −(A2)   (d) CLR.W   (A2)
(e) CLR.L   (A2)+

5. For each of the following instructions, find the number of words in the machine code, including extension words. Identify the addressing mode for the source and destination operands and the final effect on registers and memory. Assume

$$ALPHA = \$00456C \qquad (A0) = \$0000456A,$$

$$(\$00456A) = \$6 \qquad (\$00456C) = \$18 \qquad (\$00456E) = \$22$$

(a) MOVE.W   ALPHA.W, (A0)+
(b) MOVE.W   (A0)+,(A0)+

6. What is the effect of the program fragment

```
          JSR        DECIN
          LEA        A+40,A3
          MOVEQ      #19,D1
LOOP:     MOVE.W     −(A3),(2,A3)
          DBRA       D1,LOOP
          MOVE.W     D0,(A3)
                     . . .

          DATA
A:        DS.W       20
```

7. Assume the following data is available for each of the indicated instructions. Give the resulting 32-bit contents of registers D2 and A3 and the contents of memory after executing the instruction.

Address	Contents
001018	0007
00101A	0006
00101C	FFFD
00101E	01A3
001020	000E

(D2) = $FFFF 0004
(A3) = $0000 101A

(a) MOVE.L   #$A3,(A3)+
(b) LEA   (A3),A3
(c) MOVE.L   (A3)+,(A3)
(d) ADD.W   −(A3),D2
(e) ADD.L   D2,(A3)+

8. An array LIST contains ten long words, $N_1, N_2, \ldots, N_{10}$. Using postincrement mode, complete the code segment that computes the sum of the following series and outputs the final sum:

$$\frac{N_1}{2^1} + \frac{N_2}{2^2} + \frac{N_3}{2^3} + \cdots + \frac{N_{10}}{2^{10}}$$

```
        XREF        HEXOUT,STOP
        LEA         LIST,A0
        MOVE.W      #9,D1
        MOVEQ       #0,D0
        MOVE.W      #1,D2
LOOP:
        ⟨code⟩
        JSR         HEXOUT
        JSR         STOP

        DATA
LIST:   DC.L    · · ·
        END
```

9. You are given an array of up to 25 long words in memory beginning at address LONGARR. The end of the data is distinguished by the presence of a long word containing 0. Write a code segment that counts the number of data elements in the array and prints it out to the screen. Use a decrement and branch instruction other than DBRA.

10. Give code to initialize A2 as a stack pointer under the conditions given:
    (a) Array S1: DS.W 50 used for a stack or words.
    (b) Array S2: DS.B 20 used for a stack of bytes.
    (c) Array S3: DS.L 10 used for a stack of long words.

11. Show how to perform stack PUSH/POP operations in assembly language if stacks grow toward higher addresses. The routines in Pascal are given as follows:

PUSH Routine

```
PROCEDURE Push( Item : Integer; VAR S : Stack);
BEGIN
    S.Top := S.Top + 1;
    S.List[S.Top] := Item
END;
```

POP Routine

```
PROCEDURE Pop ( VAR Item : Integer; VAR S : Stack);
BEGIN
    Item := S.List[S.Top];
    S.Top := S.Top − 1
END;
```

12. In Program 6.3, logical expressions were given in reverse Polish notation.
    (a) Using the notation OR = +, AND = *, 1 = TRUE, AND 0 = FALSE, find the reverse Polish equivalent of the expression

    (TRUE OR FALSE) AND (FALSE OR TRUE AND FALSE)

    (b) Draw the operand stack as it changes when evaluating the expression $10 + 11 + *$.

13. For each of the following instructions, state the mode of the source and the mode of the destination operands. Construct the machine code including extension words.
    (a) LEA OUTPUT,A0   OUTPUT=$001000
    (b) MOVE.L (A0),(−8,A2)
    (c) MOVE.L $721A,(4,A2,D3.L)
    (d) CLR.L (A4)+
    (e) CMPI.B #$0A,−(A2)
    (f) AND.B D5,($26,A6,D1.W)

14. Given that A0, A1, and A2 contain the values

$$(A0) = 00000000$$
$$(A1) = 00000124$$
$$(A2) = 0000FF76$$

what is the effective address of the operand in each of the following instructions?
    (a) CLR.L (20,A1)   (b) CLR.W (56,A0)
    (c) CLR.W ($24,A2,A1.L)

15. For each of the following instructions, find the number of words in the machine code including extension words. Identify the addressing mode for the source and destination operands and the final effect on registers and memory. Assume (A0) = $0000456C and

($00456A) = $6 ($00456C) = $18 ($00456E) = $22 ($00$4570) = $33

    (a) MOVE.W − (A0),(2,A0)
    (b) MOVE.W (A0)+,(2,A0)

16. Assume the following data is available for each of the indicated instructions. Give the resulting 32-bit contents of registers D2 and D3 and the contents of memory after executing the instruction.

Address	Contents
001018	0007
00101A	0006
00101C	FFFD
00101E	01A3
001020	000E

$$(D2) = \$FFFF\ 0004$$
$$(A3) = \$0000\ 101A$$

    (a) ADD.W (−2,A3,D2.W),D2
    (b) MOVE.W −(A3),(6,A3)
    (c) SUBQ.W #5, (4,A3)

17. Suppose that (A2) = $001078 and the initial contents of memory are given as follows. Give the value of A2 and the contents of memory after executing the instruction.

1106	1074	1072	1106	1104	1100	1072
1072	1074	1076	1078	107A	107C	107E

(a) MOVE.L   (−4,A2),(A2)+
(b) MOVE.W   −(A2),(−4,A2)
(c) MOVEA.L   (−2,A2),A2

18. Generate the machine code including extension words for the following instructions:

  (a) AGE: EQU 26
            MOVE.L (AGE,A4,D1.W),(A0)+

  (b) LEA   BUF,A4   (BUF=$000500)
  (c) MOVEA.L   (A0),A2
  (d) MOVE.L   ($28,A2,D3.W),−(A4)

19. The following sequence forms the sum of the one's complement of the entries in a 20-word array of 16-bit integers beginning at address ARR. Rewrite the code so that it is more efficient. Use postincrement mode and one of the decrement and branch instructions.

```
        MOVEA.L    #ARR,A0
        MOVEQ      #0,D1
        MOVEQ      #19,D2
        MOVEQ      #0,D0
LOOP:   MOVE.W     (0,A0,D1.W),D3
        NOT.W      D3
        ADD.W      D3,D0
        ADDI.W     #2,D1
        SUBQ.W     #1,D2
        BNE.S      LOOP
```

20. Explain what the following program does. Do not simply specify the action of each individual instruction.

```
        XREF       DECOUT,STOP
START:  LEA        LIST,A0
        MOVEQ      #0,D0
        MOVEQ      #9,D1
LOOP:   CMP.W      (A0)+,D0
        BCC.S      CHECK
        MOVE.W     (−2,A0),D0
CHECK:  DBRA       D1,LOOP
        DATA
        JSR        DECOUT
        JSR        STOP
        DATA
LIST:   DC.W       $1055,$F890,$FFFE,$0845,$6435
        DC.W       $8F06,$1234,$FFFF,$5465,$5555
        END
```

21. An array of records has the Pascal declaration

    TYPE REC = RECORD
                    NAME :   ARRAY[1. . .20] OF CHAR;
                    DEPT: INTEGER;
                    CLASS: INTEGER
               END; {RECORD}

    VAR   A :   ARRAY[1 . . 50] OF REC;

    In assembly language, each record is stored in the format

    A[I]

NAME	DEPT	CLASS
20 Bytes	2 Bytes	2 Bytes

    and the array is declared by

    A: DS.B 50∗24

    Using the EQU directive to name record offsets, write code to initialize record A[I]. The name is to be Null terminated.

22. A MOVE instruction is said to be an identity operation if it does not change memory. Indicate whether the given MOVE instructions serve as the identity.
    (a) MOVE.W   − (A0),(2,A0)
    (b) MOVE.W   (− 2,A0),− (A0)

23. If ARR is an array of long words, which element of the array does the code move to D5?

    ```
    LEA        ARR,A0
    MOVEQ      #6,D1
    MOVE.L     (2,A0,D1.L),D5
    ```

24. What is the output of the following program if you input the number 8?

    ```
                XREF       HEXIN, HEXOUT, NEWLINE, STOP
    START:      JSR        HEXIN
                LEA        LST,A0
                MOVEQ      #7,D1
    SLOOP:      CMP.W      (A0)+,D0
                DBLE       D1,SLOOP
                BLE.S      IL
                MOVE.W     D0,(A0)
                BRA.S      PR
    IL:         MOVEA.L    A0,A1
                SUBQ.W     #2,A1
                LEA        LST+16,A0
    ```

```
MLOOP:   MOVE.W   -(A0),(2,A0)      ; COPY TO ADJOINING WORD
         CMPA.L   A0,A1
         BCS      MLOOP
         MOVE.W   D0,(A1)
PR:      LEA      LST,A0
         MOVEQ    #8,D1
PLOOP:   MOVE.W   (A0)+,D0
         JSR      HEXOUT
         DBRA     D1,PLOOP
         JSR      NEWLINE
         JSR      STOP
         DATA

LST:     DC.W     1, 3, 5, 7, 9, 11, 13, 15
         DS.W     1
         END
```

In problems 25–28, assume the assembler treats all source operands of the form

(Label,PC)

so that the displacement is the offset from the PC to Label.

25. If (D3.L) = $00000008, the PC at the start of the instruction is $008000, and ALPHA = $8800, what is the effective address of the source operand for each of the following instructions?
    (a) MOVE.L   (6,PC),D3
    (b) MOVE.B   (2,PC,D3.W),D5
    (c) CMP.W   (ALPHA,PC,D3.L),D2

26. Indicate if an instruction is in error and if so explain why.
    (a) JMP   (4,PC)   (d) BTST   #7,(88,PC)
    (b) MOVE.B   (8,PC),D0   (e) TST.L   (20,PC)
    (c) MOVE.L   D0,(6,PC)   (f) CMPI.W #7,(ALPHA,PC)

27. Is the following code position independent?

```
         MOVEQ    #0,D0
         MOVEQ    #99,D1
         LEA      (A,PC),A2
         LEA      (B,PC),A3
LOOP:    ADD.W    (A2)+,D0
         DBRA     D1,LOOP
         MOVE.W   D0,(A3)
```

28. If the PC at the start of the instruction is $3000 and NEXT has value $4500, give the machine code for the instruction

JMP   (NEXT,PC)

29. (MC68020/30/40) Assume

(A0.L) = $00001000   (A2.L) = $00008000
(D2.L) = $00000008   (D3.L) = $00000010

Give the effective address of the operand in each TST instruction.
(a) TST.W   (4,A0,D3.W*4)
(b) TST.W   (8,D2.L*8)
(c) TST.W   ($100000.L,A2,D2.W)
(d) TST.W   (D3.W*2)
(e) TST.W   ()

30. (MC68020/30/40) Give machine code for each instruction.
(a) MOVE.L ($88000.L,A3,D4.L*8),D0
(b) MOVE.W (D1.L),D2
(c) Assume label TARGET = $220000 and PC = $1000 for the instruction
CMPI.L #5, (TARGET.L,PC,D3.W*4)

PROGRAMMING EXERCISES

31. Read in the number of elements in a list of 16-bit integers followed by the list. Scan the list and replace each element by its absolute value. Print the list.

32. Write a program that reads any string of up to 80 characters, changes all uppercase characters to lowercase, and prints the new string. Use both the address register postincrement mode and address register indirect with displacement mode.

33. This exercise implements a simple calculator.

Setup: Initialize A3 as a stack pointer.
Input Format: Enter numbers using HEXIN with the format 0CXX where C = 0, 1, 2, 3, and XX is an 8-bit two's complement number.

Processing:
If $C = 0$, sign-extend XX to a word, and push it on the stack.
If $C = 1$, pop the top two numbers off the stack, and add them. Push the resulting sum on the stack.
If $C = 2$, pop the top two numbers off the stack, and subtract them. Push the resulting difference on the stack.
If $C = 3$, pop the stack, print the value in decimal, and exit the program.

For instance, the sequence

0003 0019 0100 0006 0200 0300

prints 22_{10}. (*Hint:* Use the EXT instruction for the sign extension.)

34. Read in a list of ten 16-bit integers. Prompt for any index N between 1 and 10. You are to move the value at that index to the front of the list in the following way:

> Push all elements from index 1 to $N - 1$ on a stack. Relocate the element at index N to index 1. Pop the stack and restore its elements into locations $N, N - 1, \ldots, 2$.

35. Read in 25 long words from the keyboard, and place them in array DAT. Read a 32-bit number from the keyboard, and search the array for the last occurrence of the number in the array. Print either of the following messages:

LAST OCCURRENCE WAS FOUND AT INDEX   ⟨INDEX FROM 1. .25⟩
THE NUMBER WAS NOT FOUND IN THE ARRAY

36. Write code to read in any string of up to 80 characters from the keyboard. Loop through the string and copy all nonblank characters to another string. Determine if the compressed string is a palindrome. A palindrome is any sequence of characters that reads the same forward as backward. For instance, the following are some palindromes:

MADAMIMADAM   DID   TOT   LEVEL

37. Set up a powers of 4 table in a list POWFOUR using DC.W. Using STRIN, enter a string of eight base 4 digits. Scan the input string, converting each character to the corresponding 4-bit number. Use the POWFOUR table to convert the base 4 number to binary. Store the result in D0, and output the result using HEXOUT. For example,

Input   10232001
(D0) =   1(16384) + 0(4096) + 2(1024) + 3(256) + 2(64)
            + 0(16) + 0(4) + 1(1)
Output 4B81

38. Enter a ten-element list, A, of 16-bit unsigned integers. Then, enter an index N from 1–10, and delete the Nth element from the list by moving each element

$$A(I) \text{ to } A(I - 1), \qquad N + 1 \le I \le 10$$

Print the new list.

39. A table of prime factors is stored in an array PFACTS of variable length records, each of which has the format

Number N	Number of Prime Factors	Prime Factors of N

A sample declaration for PFACTS is

```
PFACTS:    DC.W    9
           DC.W    2
           DC.W    3,3
```

```
DC.W      36
DC.W      4
DC.W      2,2,3,3

DC.W      30
DC.W      3
DC.W      2,3,5
```

Declare an array of five records in this format. Prompt for an integer, and search your list for it. If it is found, use the information in the record to print all the prime factors of the number. Use EQU's to define field offsets.

40. (MC68020/30/40) Rewrite Program 6.5 to use a scale factor for the index register.

41. Suppose that a record has the following three fields:

Symbol Length	Address of Start of Symbol in String Pool	Value of Symbol
2 Bytes	4 Bytes	2 Bytes

Suppose that Symrecs is an array of such records. Read in an integer N, and then execute the following code:

```
Value  := 0;
FOR I  := 1 TO N DO  BEGIN
    Input (symbol) into string pool;
    Place symbol length into Symrecs[I];
    Place symbol address into Symrecs[I];
    Place value into Symrecs[I];
    Value := Value + 1
END { FOR };
```

Now read a symbol S, and search the array Symrecs to see if the symbol exists in the list. If it does, print out the value of the symbol. To compare symbols, use the following algorithm:

```
IF Length(S) = Symrecs[I] THEN
        Compare symbols character by character

ELSE

        Reject equality
{ END IF }
```

CHAPTER 7

SUBROUTINES

Good high-level-language program design is based on the concept of modularity, the partitioning of code into subprograms. A main module contains the logical structure of the algorithm, whereas small program units consisting of procedures and functions execute many of the details. Parameters can be passed to procedures and functions, enabling them to operate on any data of the given types.

What is true of program design in high-level languages applies even more to the design of assembly language code. You begin with a simple main program whose steps clearly outline the logical flow of the algorithm, and then you assign the execution details to subprograms. Of course, the subprograms may themselves call other subprograms. Figure 7.1 illustrates the partitioning of structured program code.

The study of subprograms is fundamental to assembly language and is the subject of this chapter. In addition, this chapter will give you a better understanding and appreciation of high-level language subprograms, give you the tools to modularize your assembly language programs, and introduce you to new MC68000 instructions that support the use of subprograms.

7.1 SUBROUTINE CALL AND RETURN

In assembly language, a **subprogram** or a **subroutine** is a sequence of instructions stored in memory at a specified address. It can be called from any place in the code by a jump instruction that saves the address of the next instruction and passes program control to the first instruction of the subroutine. Upon completion, a "return" instruction directs program control back to the next instruction in the calling code. Figure 7.2 illustrates the process.

FIGURE 7.1   Structured Program Format

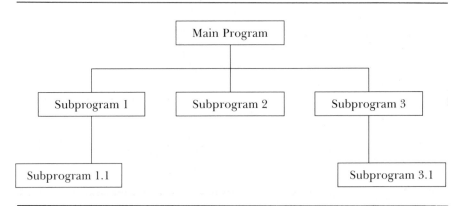

Subroutines are implemented using a stack that holds the address of the next instruction, parameters, and local variables. The MC68000 provides access to a **run-time stack** using address register A7, also called the **stack pointer** or **SP**. From now on, the run-time stack is referred to simply as the stack.

When a program starts under the control of an operating system, an area of memory is assigned for the stack, and the stack pointer is initialized. The stack grows toward lower memory addresses. When an operating system does not set up a stack, it is the user's responsibility to allocate memory and initialize the stack pointer. Figure 7.3 shows the resulting stack.

Calling a Subroutine

The MC68000 provides two instructions, JSR and BSR, for calling a subroutine. In terms of program control, they are similar to the "Jump" (JMP) and "Unconditional Branch" (BRA) instructions and have the same syntax

FIGURE 7.2   Subroutine Processing

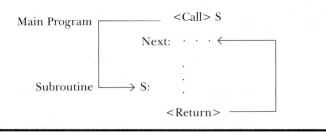

FIGURE 7.3 The Run-Time Stack

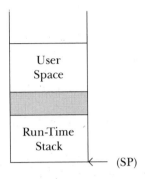

and available operands. The instructions, however, push the contents of the PC on the stack, which has the effect of saving the address of the next instruction. Upon return from the subroutine, the address is popped off the stack into the PC and is used to continue program execution. In this book, the JSR instruction is used for most examples.

INSTRUCTIONS

JSR/BSR
(Jump/Branch to
Subroutine)

Syntax JSR ⟨ea⟩   BSR   ⟨label⟩
                      BSR.S ⟨label⟩

Action

(a) The address of the next instruction is saved on the stack.

(b) Program control is passed to the address specified by the operand.

Consider the following general case:

$$
\begin{array}{l}
\text{JSR} \;\; \langle\text{ea}\rangle \\
\langle\text{next instruction}\rangle
\end{array}
$$

⟨ea⟩:   ⟨First subroutine instruction⟩

(a) The address of the next instruction ("Return Address") is pushed on the stack.

$$\text{Move PC} \rightarrow -(\text{SP})$$

(b) The PC is assigned ⟨ea⟩.

$$\text{Move } \langle ea \rangle \rightarrow PC$$

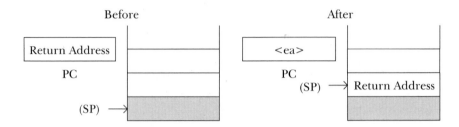

Notes

1. The operand for the JSR instruction must be a mode that specifies a memory address.

2. The operand for the BSR instruction must be a label. The opcode contains an 8-bit offset to the PC or a 16-bit two's complement offset stored in an extension word.

3. In this book, we will use the phrase "push the PC on the stack" when explaining the action of the JSR instruction. This describes the technical fact that the contents of the PC are pushed on the stack.

EXAMPLE 7.1

(a) JSR   OUTPUT
Program control passes to the instruction label OUTPUT.

(b) JSR   (2,A3)
The first instruction of the subroutine is located at address (A3) + 2. If (A3) = $0022080E, then control is passed to the instruction at memory location $220810.

$220810   ⟨first instruction of subroutine⟩
.
.
.

⟨return⟩

(c) BSR.S   READDATA
This is a one-word instruction that passes program control to the subroutine at address READDATA.

EXAMPLE 7.2

Assume that the label GETCHAR is address $001000 and that (SP) = $2000. Figure 7.4 illustrates the change of contents on the stack for the following subroutine call:

FIGURE 7.4 Subroutine Stack Contents

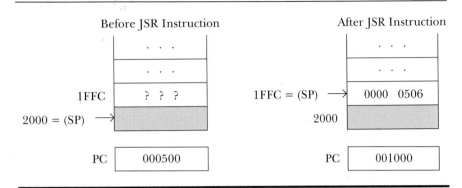

```
000500              JSR       GETCHAR     ; SUBROUTINE CALL
000506              MOVE.W    D0,VAL      ; NEXT INSTRUCTION
                      .
                      .
                      .

001000   GETCHAR:
```

Return From Subroutine

After program control transfers to a subroutine, execution follows the usual ordering of instructions. The subroutine contains a final instruction, RTS, that implements the return of control to the main program at the instruction that follows the call to the subroutine.

INSTRUCTION

RTS
(Return from
Subroutine)

Syntax   RTS

Action   A long word is popped off the stack and stored in the PC. Program execution then continues at the new address in the program counter. This new value is normally the return address placed on the stack by JSR/BSR.

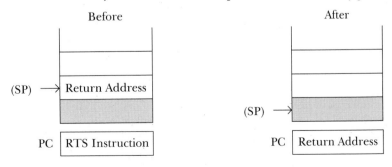

Notes

1. When RTS is executed, if the stack pointer does not point to the return address, program control may pass to an invalid address or to an unwanted or invalid instruction.

2. The phrase "pop the PC off the stack" describes the action of the RTS instruction. Technically, the RTS instruction pops a long word off the stack and puts it in the PC. This book will use similar references when saying "push the SR on the stack," "pop the SR off the stack," and so on.

EXAMPLE 7.3

Figure 7.5 describes the contents of the stack for the "Return from Subroutine" process. Assume that a program segment occupies the following addresses:

```
000500          JSR       GETCHAR     ; SUBROUTINE CALL
000506          MOVE.W    D0,VAL      ; NEXT INSTRUCTION
                  .
                  .
                  .
001000          GETCHAR:              ; SUBROUTINE
                  .
                  .
                  .
001018          RTS                   ; RETURN BACK
```

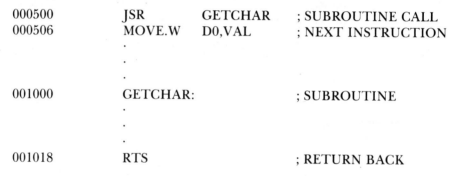

FIGURE 7.5 Return from Subroutine Stack

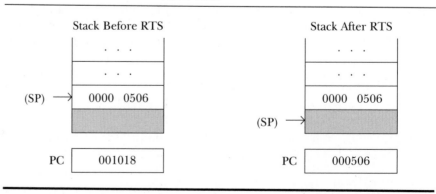

Structure of a Subroutine

A subroutine functions as a self-contained block of code. However, it is embedded in a larger block of code and must interact with the calling program. The most obvious interaction occurs in parameter passing. An equally important interaction occurs when the subroutine modifies data or address registers used by the calling program.

The following case illustrates a typical situation. Consider the subroutine COMPUTE, which takes (D0.W) as input and returns in D0 the square of the input plus the original value. The subroutine implements the algebraic function

$$COMPUTE(x) = x^2 + x$$

MC68000 code for COMPUTE is

```
COMPUTE:    MOVE.W    D0,D1     ; D1 IS A SCRATCH REGISTER
            MULU      D0,D1     ; GENERATE X * X
            ADD.W     D1,D0     ; STORE IN D0 X * X + X
            RTS
```

A main program calls COMPUTE and then prints out the value of the function for several inputs.

```
            XREF      DECOUT, NEWLINE, STOP
START:      MOVEQ     #6,D1     ; LOOP 7
                      TIMES
            MOVEQ     #1,D2
LOOP:       MOVE.W    D2,D0
            JSR       COMPUTE
            JSR       DECOUT
            JSR       NEWLINE
            ADDQ.W    #1,D2
            DBRA      D1,LOOP
            JSR       STOP
COMPUTE:    (subroutine code)
              ⋮
            END
```

The counter D1 in the calling code is destroyed by the subroutine COMPUTE. For instance, at the point marked by (*) in the first iteration of the loop, D1 has been changed from 6 to 1. In COMPUTE the register D1 is used to hold temporary data and hence is referred to as a "scratch" register. This use conflicts with its use as a counter in the main program. To use D1 properly, it must be saved on entry into COMPUTE and then restored before returning to the calling code. In general, a subroutine may use registers for parameter passing and "scratch" space, but except for an output parameter, it must do so without destroying the original values of the registers. The subroutine must save and restore register values to prevent unwanted destruction of data. The stack is a natural place to save registers, using the PUSH operation to save the original value and the POP operation to restore the value.

The subroutine COMPUTE can be modified to save D1.

```
COMPUTE:   MOVE.L    D1,-(SP)      ; PUSH D1 ON THE STACK
           MOVE.W    D0,D1
           MULU      D0,D1
           ADD.W     D1,D0
           MOVE.L    (SP)+,D1      ; RESTORE D1 WITH A POP
           RTS
```

If more than one register must be saved and restored, then the PUSH and POP operations must be repeated. For instance, to use registers D1, D2, and A0,

```
SAVE:      MOVE.L    A0,-(SP)
           MOVE.L    D2,-(SP)
           MOVE.L    D1,-(SP)


RESTORE:   MOVE.L    (SP)+,D1
           MOVE.L    (SP)+,D2
           MOVEA.L   (SP)+,A0
```

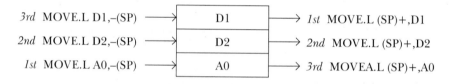

The process is tedious because the registers must be individually saved and then popped off in the opposite order. The MC68000 provides a "Move Multiple Registers" (MOVEM) instruction to efficently implement these save and restore operations. The instruction transfers data between a set of registers and memory. It has application in any situation where data must be transferred between memory and registers. However, its primary application is for saving and restoring registers in subroutines.

INSTRUCTION

MOVEM
(Multiple Move)

Syntax   (1) MOVEM.⟨size⟩   ⟨register list⟩,⟨ea⟩
           (2) MOVEM.⟨size⟩   ⟨ea⟩,⟨register list⟩

Action   Form 1 causes a transfer of word or long-word data from selected registers to consecutive memory locations beginning at the effective address specified by ⟨ea⟩.

Form 2 causes transfer of consecutive words or long words from memory beginning at effective address ⟨ea⟩ to selected registers specified in the list.

Notes

1. The register list differentiates individual registers with a slash (/) delimiter. A range of registers is specified by the hyphen (-). For instance,

Registers:	D0, D2, D3, D4, A0, A1, A6
Register list:	D0/D2–D4/A0–A1/A6

2. In Section 6.8, addressing modes were placed in categories. A memory-addressing mode may be used to refer to data in memory. All addressing modes except immediate, data register direct, and address register direct are memory addressing modes. A control addressing mode may be used to refer to memory operands without an associated size. The control addressing modes are a subset of the memory addressing modes. Predecrement, postincrement, and immediate modes are excluded. The effective address in a MOVEM may include control modes, the predecrement mode, or the postincrement mode. If the effective address is a control mode, the order of transfer is from data registers D0 to D7 and then address registers A0 to A7.

   For the postincrement mode, only a memory-to-register operation is allowed. The memory locations are accessed from the starting address through higher addresses and are stored in the data registers in the order D0 to D7 and then A0 to A7.

   For the predecrement mode, only a register-to-memory operation is allowed. The registers are stored in the order A7 to A0 and then D7 to D0.

3. The size parameter can be "L" or "W". When words are transferred from memory to registers, however, they are first sign extended and then stored in the registers.

EXAMPLE 7.4

Register List

(a) The registers to be saved or restored are D1, D2, and A0. The register list is D1–D2/A0.

(b) For register list D3–D5/A0/A2–A4, the set of designated registers is D3, D4, D5, A0, A2, A3, and A4.

EXAMPLE 7.5

(a) MOVEM.L   D0-D2/A5,A
The instruction copies the 32-bit contents of data registers D0, D1, D2, and A5 into memory beginning at address A.

Registers	F567 5555	1267 FDE3	0000 DEAE	· · ·	0001 0101
	D0	D1	D2		A5

Memory	F567 5555	1267 FDE3	0000 DEAE	0001 0101
	A	A + 4	A + 8	A + 12

(b) MOVEM.W   LOC,D0/D3/A0

The instruction copies the three words beginning at address LOC to registers D0, D3, and A0. Each word is sign extended before it is stored in the register.

6743	A4FD	176C		0000 6743		FFFF A4FD		0000 176C
LOC				D0		D3		A0

The opcode for the MOVEM instruction requires a *register list mask* that specifies the registers and the order of data transfer. The register list mask is a 16-bit word corresponding to the 16 MC68000 address and data registers. The form of the mask is determined by the mode used to specify the effective address ⟨ea⟩.

Mask Form 1   Effective address ⟨ea⟩ is a control mode or postincrement mode.

Register List Mask

Register Bit	A7	A6	A5	A4	A3	A2	A1	A0	D7	D6	D5	D4	D3	D2	D1	D0
	15	14	13	12	11	10	9	8	7	6	5	4	3	2	1	0

Action   For each register in the list, the corresponding bit in the list mask is set to 1. Registers are stored in memory or retrieved in order D0 to D7 and A0 to A7.

Mask Form 2   Effective address ⟨ea⟩ is predecrement mode.

Register List Mask

Register Bit	D0	D1	D2	D3	D4	D5	D6	D7	A0	A1	A2	A3	A4	A5	A6	A7
	15	14	13	12	11	10	9	8	7	6	5	4	3	2	1	0

Action   The instruction implements the pushing of multiple registers onto the stack. The registers are pushed on the stack in the order A7 to A0 and D7 to D0.

EXAMPLE 7.6

(a) MOVEM.W   D0/D3–D5/A1/A2,LIST
The destination operand is the memory reference and is absolute mode.
The register list mask uses Form 1.

Register List Mask

0	0	0	0	0	1	1	0	0	0	1	1	1	0	0	1
A7	A6	A5	A4	A3	A2	A1	A0	D7	D6	D5	D4	D3	D2	D1	D0

(b) MOVEM.L   D0/D3/A0, – (SP)
The destination operand is predecrement mode. The register list mask
uses Form 2.

Register List Mask

1	0	0	1	0	0	0	0	1	0	0	0	0	0	0	0
D0	D1	D2	D3	D4	D5	D6	D7	A0	A1	A2	A3	A4	A5	A6	A7

Assume that (D0.L) = $4A70 2FF3, (D3.L) = $001A 882C, and (A0)
= 19AE 0004. The registers are pushed on the stack in the order A0,
D3, and D0, as shown in Figure 7.6.

(c) MOVEM.L   (SP)+,D0/D3/A0
The source operand is predecrement mode. The register list mask uses
Form 1.

FIGURE 7.6   Long Words Pushed from Registers to Stack

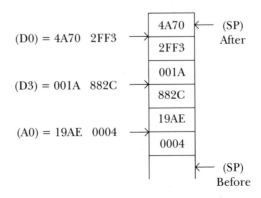

Register List Mask

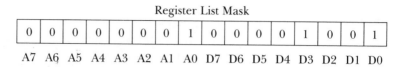

0	0	0	0	0	0	0	1	0	0	0	0	1	0	0	1
A7	A6	A5	A4	A3	A2	A1	A0	D7	D6	D5	D4	D3	D2	D1	D0

Figure 7.7 illustrates how three consecutive long words are popped from the stack and loaded into registers D0, D3, and A0.

By using predecrement mode for pushing registers on the stack and postincrement mode for popping the registers, data can be moved from registers to the stack and then restored. Thus, the instructions

MOVEM.L ⟨register list⟩, (SP)   ; SAVE REGISTERS
  .
  .
  .
MOVEM.L   (SP)+,⟨register list⟩   ; RESTORE REGISTERS

can be used to save registers upon subroutine entrance and to restore them prior to return.

EXAMPLE 7.7   MOVEM.L   D0–D2/A0–A1,(SP)   ; SAVE D0,D1,D2,A0,A1

⟨subroutine instructions⟩

MOVEM.L   (SP)+,D0–D2/A0–A1   ; RESTORE D0,D1,D2,A0,A1

FIGURE 7.7   Long Words Popped from Stack to Registers

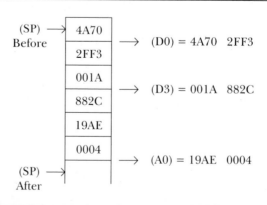

Machine code for the MOVEM instruction places the register list mask as the first extension word regardless of whether the mask is used for a source or destination operand. Some MC68000 assemblers require this extension word to be placed in the code file explicitly by using immediate mode.

EXAMPLE 7.8

The machine code for each MOVEM instruction is listed. Assume that A has value $4000.

	Instruction	*Machine Code*
(a)	MOVEM.L D0–D2/D4/A0–A2,A	48F9 0717 0000 40000
	Register list mask = $0717	
(b)	MOVEM.W A.W,D0/A0	4CB8 0101 4000
	Register list mask = $0101	

Demonstration Programs

The following two relatively simple, complete programs focus on the structure of a subroutine and its interaction with a main program. For each subroutine, parameters are passed using registers, and the MOVEM instruction is used to save and restore registers. The following general rules for register handling apply:

SAVE: Save each register used for input or scratch calculations, provided the contents of the register are changed within the subroutine.

RESTORE: Restore the saved registers before the return from subroutine.

The first example is a test-grading program that uses a new instruction CMPM that directly compares data in memory.

INSTRUCTION

CMPM
(Compare
Memory)

Syntax CMPM.⟨size⟩ (Ay)+,(Ax)+

Action The instruction executes the "compare" (CMP) operation.

Notes

1. The data size may be "B", "W", or "L".

2. The source and destination operand must be in postincrement mode.

EXAMPLE 7.9

The CMP instruction compares the contents of an effective address to a data register. To compare characters in memory pointed to by registers A0 and A1, the CMP instruction would require an assignment to a scratch data register. For example,

```
MOVE.B     (A0)+,D0
CMP.B      (A1)+,D0
```

The CMPM instruction more efficiently compares data in memory provided both operands are given in postincrement mode.

```
CMPM.  B  (A1)+,  (A0)+
```

PROGRAM 7.1

Test Grading

A test consisting of six true/false questions is to be graded for each of three students. The answer key is stored in the array KEY, and a student's response is stored in array ANSWER. For each test, call a subroutine GRADE that passes as input parameters the address KEY, the address ANSWER, and the number of questions N. The number of correct responses in the test is returned as an output parameter. A Pascal function GRADE is presented as a model for the assembly language code.

Pascal Code

```
FUNCTION grade(VAR key,answers:arraytype; numques:integer):integer;
   VAR    i     : integer;
          score : integer;
BEGIN
   score := 0;
   FOR i := 1 TO numques DO
      IF key [i] = answers [i] THEN
         score := score + 1;
   grade := score;
END;
```

Assembly Language Algorithm   In the main program, register A0 is the address of the KEY, A1 is the address of ANSWER, and (D1.W) is the number of questions to be graded. In subroutine GRADE, registers A0, A1, and D1 are input parameters, and register D0 is an output parameter, returning the number of correct answers. Using the CMPM instruction, each student's response is compared to the corresponding KEY value, and matches are recorded as a correct response.

MC68000 Code

```
            xref       strin, decout, strout, newline, stop

NumQues:    equ        5
```

```
start:        moveq      #2, d2              ; grade three tests

gradetests:   lea        answers, a0         ; input test
              move.w     #NumQues+1, d0
              jsr        strin
              lea        msg, a0             ; print score prompt
              move.w     #16, d0
              jsr        strout
              lea        answers, a0         ; grade the test
              lea        key, a1
              move.w     #NumQues, d1
              jsr        grade
              jsr        decout              ; number right in d0
              jsr        newline
              dbra       d2, gradetests
              jsr        stop

grade:        movem.l    d1/a0-a1, -(sp)     ; save input registers
              moveq      #0, d0              ; d0 = number right
              subq.w     #1, d1              ; d1 = NumQues
score:        cmpm.b     (a0)+, (a1)+        ; compare answer/key
              bne.s      nextscore
              addq.w     #1, d0
nextscore:    dbra       d1, score
              movem.l    (sp)+, d1/a0-a1     ; restore registers
              rts

              data

key:          dc.b       'TFFTT'
answers:      ds.b       NumQues
              ds.b       1                   ; space for newline
msg:          dc.b       'Number correct: '
              end
```

⟨Run of Program 7.1⟩

```
TFTTF
Number correct: 3
FTFFT
Number correct: 2
TFFTT
Number correct: 5
```

PROGRAM 7.2

Delete KEY

All occurrences of a value KEY are removed from a list. The program introduces three subroutines:

READLIST: Reads *N* 16-bit integers into an array.
WRITELIST: Outputs an *N* element array.
RMKEY: Removes all occurrences of the key word from
                 the array. The remaining elements in the array
                 are shifted left to replace the deleted elements.

Sample: Original list   1   7   7   5   N = 4   KEY = 7
            Deleted list   1   5   N = 2

Algorithm All the subroutines use register A0 for the starting address of
the array and D1 for the array count. Subroutine RMKEY uses D0 for the
KEY value and register D1 as an output parameter containing the possibly
reduced size of the list. Register A1, is used as a scratch variable to scan
the list. A0 is the address of the next insertion in the deleted list. The two
address registers work in tandem.

If a match is found [contents at address A1 = (D0.W)], increment A1
to the next item.
For a nonmatch, replace the list value at address (A0) by the list value
at address (A1), and increment both registers to the next entries in
the list.
Sample scan: List   1   7   7   5   N = 4   KEY = 7
List length = (D1.W) = 4   Key = (D0.W) = 7

Initialize
Registers

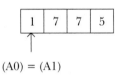

(A0) = (A1)

Scan List[0] = 1
No Match
Assign (A1) to (A0)
Increment A0 and A1

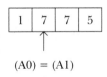

(A0) = (A1)

Scan List[1] = 7
Match
Increment only A1

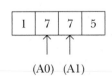

(A0)   (A1)

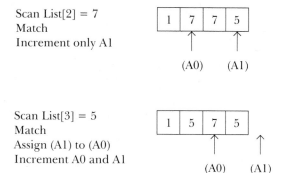

Scan List[2] = 7
Match
Increment only A1

Scan List[3] = 5
Match
Assign (A1) to (A0)
Increment A0 and A1

The new length of the list is computed using address calculations. Because each item is word length, the distance between the final address A0 and the starting address LIST is divided by 2.

$$\text{Length} = \frac{\text{final(A0)} - \text{original (A0)}}{2}$$

```
;   The demonstration program includes three subroutines.
;       First enter N, the number of elements in a list.
;       Call readlist to input the list elements; The routine
;       writelist prints the elements in the list.
;       Enter a key. By calling rmkey all elements matching
;       the input key are removed from the list. The resulting
;       list is printed using writelist

            xref        decin,decout,newline,stop

start:
            lea         list,a0         ; set a0 as pointer to array
            jsr         decin           ; enter # of elements in array
            move.w      d0,d1           ; save # of elements in d1
            jsr         readlist        ; enter array
            jsr         writelist       ; output original array
            jsr         decin           ; enter key
            jsr         rmkey           ; remove all occurrences of key
            jsr         writelist       ; output edited array
            jsr         stop

readlist:
            movem.l     d0-d1/a0,-(sp)  ; save registers
            subq.w      #1,d1           ; subtract 1 for dbra
loopin:     jsr         decin           ; read element
            move.w      d0,(a0)+        ; store in array
            dbra        d1,loopin
            movem.l     (sp)+,d0-d1/a0  ; restore registers
            rts
```

```
writelist:
            movem.l   d0-d1/a0,-(sp)      ; save registers
            subq.w    #1,d1               ; subtract 1 for dbra
            bmi.s     rtn                 ; test for empty list
loopout:    move.w    (ao)+,d0
            jsr       decout
            dbra      d1,loopout
            jsr       newline
rtn:        movem.l   (sp)+,d0-d1/a0
            rts


rmkey:      movem.l   d0/a0-a2,-(sp)
            movea.l   a0,a1               ; set a1 to scan the list
            movea.l   a0,a2               ; save original (a0)
            subq.w    #1,d1
next:       cmp.w     (a1)+,d0            ; look for occurrence of key
            beq.s     go_on
            move.w    (-2,a1),(a0)+       ; insert non-key in lower list
go_on:      dbra      d1,next             ; continue if data remaining

;   compute the new length of the list
            move.l    a0,d1               ; copy final (a0) into d1
            sub.l     a2,d1               ; subt original (a0) from d1
            asr.l     #1,d1               ; divide by two (bytes)
            movem.l   (sp)+,d0/a0-a2
            rts

            data
list:       ds.w      25
            end
```

⟨Run of Program 7.2⟩

```
4
1 7 7 5
1 7 7 5
7
1 5
```

An assembly language main program is typically short. It passes control to a series of subroutines that execute the algorithm. This philosophy is in keeping with structured high-level language programming. It also greatly simplifies the finding and correcting of run-time errors, the nemesis of assembly language programmers.

7.2 | PARAMETER PASSING

Parameters are typically passed to a subroutine in one of two ways: using registers or using the stack. The two demonstration programs in Section 7.1 pass parameters using registers. This method is limited by the number of available registers and does not take advantage of the wide variety of addressing modes for accessing parameters in program memory.

Parameter passing using the stack is efficient and is the technique employed by most high-level language compilers. The concepts are demonstrated here with simple examples to highlight the method. More complex examples are given in Section 7.3.

Passing Parameters on the Stack

High-level language subroutines are a good model for understanding parameter passing on the stack. The Pascal procedure READARR illustrates the declaration of a parameter list and the steps involved with executing a subroutine.

```
PROCEDURE readarr (VAR list : arraytype; listcount : integer)
VAR i : integer;
BEGIN
    FOR i := 1 TO listcount DO
        read(list[i]);
END;    { readarr }
```

The parameter list is given in the procedure declaration. In Pascal, a VAR variable is termed a **call by reference parameter**, and the address of the data location is passed to the subroutine. Otherwise, the variable is termed a **call by value parameter**, and the actual data value is passed to the subroutine. Figure 7.8 illustrates the parameter-passing protocol.

FIGURE 7.8 Parameter-Passing Protocol

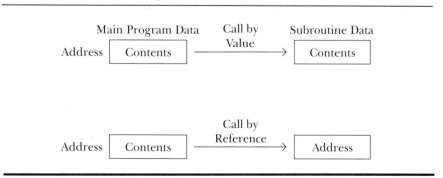

The mechanism of writing and calling a subroutine that accepts its parameters on the stack follows a carefully structured sequence of steps.

Step 1: Subroutine Calling Process

(a) Push the parameters on the stack—this book adopts the high-level language compiler convention of pushing subroutine parameters on the stack in the order right to left. For instance,

Pascal Code

        PROCEDURE READARR (VAR LIST:ARRAYTYPE; LISTCOUNT:INTEGER);

Assembly Language Parameters

        MOVE.W   LISTCOUNT, – (SP)   Push the LISTCOUNT value
                                                              (call by value parameter)
        MOVE.L   #LIST, – (SP)   Push the address of LIST
                                                              (call by reference parameter)

The convention is useful since the parameters on the stack have the same ordering as given in the procedure declaration.

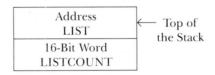

The convention simplifies the linking of high-level and assembly language routines.

(b) Call the subroutine.

        JSR   READARR   Put the return address on the stack.

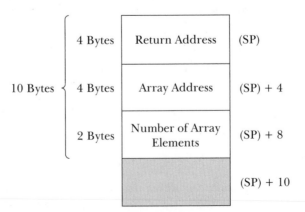

Step 2: Subroutine Execution Process

(*a*) Save registers as necessary.

   MOVEM.L   D0–D1/A0, – (SP)

(*b*) Execute the subroutine code. Each subroutine parameter can be referenced as a positive offset to the stack pointer (SP). The set of parameters, registers, and return address is called the **stack frame** and must be clearly understood before designing the subroutine code. Figure 7.9 shows the stack frame for READARR.

(*c*) To execute a return to the calling code, the saved registers must be restored.

   Restore the registers   MOVEM.L (SP)+,D0–D1/A0

Assume that the subroutine is responsible for clearing its parameters from the stack before returning to the calling code. Some high-level languages leave this task to the calling code. In general, if there were N bytes of parameters pushed on the stack, they reside just underneath the return address. Within this space of $N + 4$ bytes, relocate the return address with the instruction

   MOVE.L   (SP), (N,SP)

N bytes of space is now free at the top of the stack and is cleared with the instruction

   ADDA.L   #N,SP

FIGURE 7.9   READARR Stack Frame

	Stack Frame
(SP)	(D0)
(SP) + 4	(D1)
(SP) + 8	(A0)
(SP) + 12	Return Address
(SP) + 16	Address of LIST
(SP) + 20	LISTCOUNT

or ADDQ if appropriate. This situation is illustrated in Figure 7.10 for READARR.

| Relocate the return address | MOVE.L | (SP),(6,SP) |
| Adjust the stack pointer | ADDQ.L | #6,SP |

Step 3: Return from the Subroutine

The RTS instruction pops the stack and moves the long word pointed to by the SP into the PC. If the stack has not been cleared properly, the RTS may cause a jump to an invalid address with a resulting program error.

The code for READARR uses parameters passed on the stack and follows the convention of assigning names to all stack offsets in a subroutine. This practice makes it easier to understand the meaning of the data located in the stack frame.

```
RADDR:      EQU       16              ; USE NAMES FOR STACK
                                      ;   OFFSETS
RCOUNT:     EQU       20
RSTKSIZE:   EQU        6              ; NUMBER OF BYTES OF PARMS

READARR:    MOVEM.L   D0-D1/A0,-(SP)  ; SAVE REGISTERS
            MOVEA.L   (RADDR,SP),A0   ; SET (A0) TO ADDRESS OF
                                      ;   ARRAY
            MOVE.W    (RCOUNT,SP),D1  ; SET (D1) TO LIST LENGTH

            SUBQ.L    #1,D1           ; SET (D1) FOR DBRA
GETVAL:     JSR       HEXIN           ; READ IN A WORD
            MOVE.W    D0,(A0)+        ; STORE IN THE ARRAY
            DBRA      D1,GETVAL

            MOVEM.L   (SP)+,D0-D1/A0      ; RESTORE REGISTERS
            MOVE.L    (SP),(RSTKSIZE,SP)  ; RESET RETURN ADDRESS
            ADDQ.L    #RSTKSIZE,SP        ; RESET (SP)
            RTS
```

FIGURE 7.10 Clearing the READARR Stack

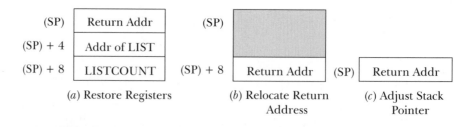

(a) Restore Registers   (b) Relocate Return Address   (c) Adjust Stack Pointer

PEA: The Call-by-Reference Instruction

With a call-by-reference parameter, the address of the data's memory location is pushed on the stack. The MC68000 provides an instruction, PEA, to automate this method of parameter passing. The syntax is similar to that of the LEA instruction.

INSTRUCTION

PEA
(Push Effective
Address)

Syntax   PEA   ⟨ea⟩

Action   The stack pointer is first decremented by 4, and then the effective address of the operand is copied onto the stack. The mode of the operand may include any of the address indirect modes or absolute memory access modes.

EXAMPLE 7.10

(a) PEA   LIST
     This is equivalent to the instruction "MOVE.L #LIST, −(SP)".

(b) PEA   (4,An)
     This stores the value (An) + 4 on the stack.

The LINK/UNLK Instructions for Parameter Passing

In the READARR example, the SP is used to reference the parameters. This is a dynamic pointer that changes as registers are saved and restored. Each parameter must be carefully computed as an offset to the SP. If you decide to use another scratch register in the subroutine code, you must change all the offsets. The MC68000 provides LINK and UNLK instructions that create a fixed reference point for access to parameters in the stack frame.

INSTRUCTION

LINK
(Link)

Syntax   LINK   An,#⟨displacement⟩

Action

1. The current contents of address register An are pushed onto the stack. This saved value becomes part of the stack frame.

2. The contents of the stack pointer are assigned to An.

3. The 16-bit displacement is added to the stack pointer.

Notes

1. The condition codes are not affected.

2. Normally, the displacement is zero or negative in order to provide scratch space on the stack above the return address.

3. An is left pointing at the stack frame. In fact, it points to its previous value. The return address is 4 bytes below An and the parameter list is 8 bytes below An. An is referred to as the **frame pointer**. All parameters can be accessed by positive offsets from (An). Figure 7.11 details the general picture of a stack frame.

The parameters are located at fixed offsets from An, with the first parameters always at address (8,An). The N bytes of stack space can be used for local storage or eliminated by using a displacement of 0. In this case, the stack frame assumes the form in Figure 7.12.

If registers are pushed onto the stack, it should be done immediately after the LINK statement. The offsets from (An) to the parameters remain the same, as illustrated in Figure 7.13.

The fixed position of the parameters relative to (An) eliminates the need to count byte offsets from the stack pointer to the parameters. This book

FIGURE 7.11   Stack Frame Produced by LINK with Displacement −N

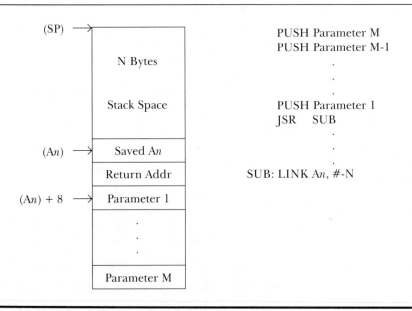

FIGURE 7.12 Stack Frame Produced by LINK with Displacement 0

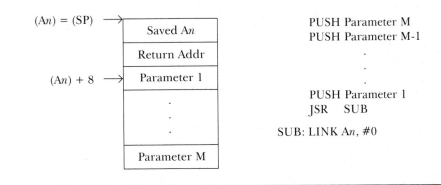

uses LINK in subsequent examples. Initially, the displacement will be zero. Chapter 10 presents stack frames for the coding of high-level language procedures and functions, and the use of a nonzero displacement for local variables.

The UNLK instruction performs the inverse of LINK when it is time to return from the subroutine. UNLK is called after restoring the saved registers. It copies the contents of A*n* into the stack pointer and pops the

FIGURE 7.13 Stack Frame After Pushing Registers on the Stack

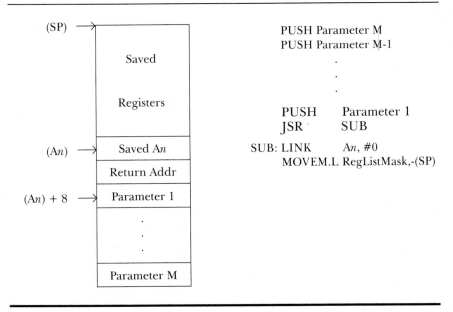

original value of A*n* from the stack back into A*n*. The stack is returned to the state existing prior to the LINK statement. Before returning to the calling program, the subroutine parameters must be flushed from the stack, and RTS is then executed. Figure 7.14 illustrates the action of clearing the stack.

INSTRUCTION

UNLK
(Unlink)

Syntax   UNLK   A*n*

Action   Two operations reset the address registers.

1. The value of address register A*n* is copied into the stack pointer.

2. The long word that (SP) points to is popped off the stack and stored in A*n*.

Notes

1. The condition codes are not affected.

2. The UNLK instruction is paired with the LINK instruction.

The procedure READARR is recoded using the LINK and UNLK instructions. A small main program illustrates the use of the subroutine.

PROGRAM 7.3

READARR using LINK/UNLK

```
          xref     decin, decout, newline, stop

start:    move.w   #5,-(sp)           ; read five numbers
          pea      a                  ; push array address
          jsr      readarr            ; call the subroutine
          lea      a,a0               ; print out the array
          moveq    #4,d1
print:    move.w   (a0)+,d0
          jsr      decout
          dbra     d1,print
          jsr      newline
          jsr      stop

raddr:    equ      8                  ; use names for stack offsets
rcount:   equ      12
rbytes:   equ      6                  ; number of bytes of parms

readarr:  link     a6,#0              ; set up frame pointer a6
          movem.l  d0-d1/a0,-(sp)     ; save registers
          movea.l  (raddr,a6),a0      ; set (a0) to address of array
          move.w   (rcount,a6),d1     ; set (d1) to list length

          subq.w   #1,d1              ; set (d1) for dbra
getval:   jsr      decin              ; read in a word
          move.w   d0,(a0)+           ; store in the array
```

FIGURE 7.14 Clearing the Stack

Stack After Saving Registers

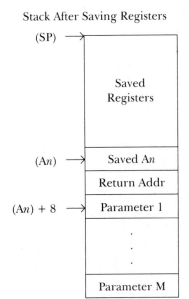

Stack After Restoring Registers

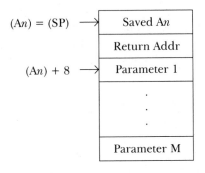

Stack After UNLK Instruction

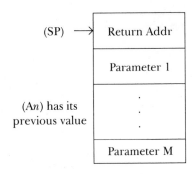

```
dbra      d1,getval
movem.l   (sp)+,d0-d1/a0      ; restore registers
unlk      a6
move.l    (sp),(rbytes,sp)    ; reset return address
addq.l    #rbytes,sp          ; reset (sp)
rts
```

```
                data
a:              ds.w        5

                end
```

⟨Run of Program 7.3⟩

20 −3 80 100 −10
20 −3 80 100 −10

Four demonstration programs use most of the concepts introduced in this chapter. The subroutine READARR is used in conjunction with a bubble sort algorithm. A second example gives formatted output of the general-purpose registers as well as the status register. You can use such a routine for program debugging. The third example will extend your understanding of subroutines. Here, a function is passed as a parameter. This is implemented by passing the address of a subroutine that serves as the function. The final example introduces an application of random number generation. It emulates a coin toss and prints a simple graph of the results.

PROGRAM 7.4

The Bubble Sort

An array of *N* integers is entered using READARR. The list is sorted using the bubble sort and then output using the subroutine WRITEARR. All parameters are passed on the stack. A Pascal version of the bubble sort is given as a model.

Bubble Sort Code in Pascal

```
CONST
  n = 20;
TYPE
  index = 1. .n;
  arrtype = array [index] of integer;

PROCEDURE bubblesort (var a: arrtype; n: index);
  var
    pass, i: index;
    inorder: Boolean;
    temp: integer;
BEGIN
  pass := 1;
  repeat
    inorder := true;
```

```
        for i := 1 to n - pass do
          IF a[i] > a[i + 1] then
                    BEGIN
                       temp := a[i];
                       a[i] = a[i + 1];
                       a[i + 1] = temp;
                       inorder := false
                    END;
            pass := pass + 1
          UNTIL inorder or (pass = n)
    END; { bubble }
```

MC68000 Code

```
              xref      decin, decout, strout, newline, stop

start:        jsr       decin                 ; read list count n
              move.w    d0, listct
              move.w    listct, -(sp)         ; pass list count
              pea       list                  ; pass list address
              jsr       readarr

; sort the array
              move.w    listct, -(sp)         ; pass list count
              pea       list                  ; pass list address
              jsr       bubblesort            ; sort!

; output the sorted list
              lea       sortmsg, a0
              move.w    #14, d0
              jsr       strout
              move.w    listct, -(sp)
              pea       list
              jsr       writearr              ; write the sorted list
              jsr       stop

; procedure to enter n integers into an array

raddr:        equ       8
rcount:       equ       12
rbytes:       equ       6

readarr:
              link      a6, #0                ; set up frame pointer
              movem.l   d0-d1/a0, -(sp)       ; save registers
              movea.l   raddr(a6), a0         ; set (a0) to array address
              move.w    rcount(a6), d1        ; set (d1) to list length
              subq.l    #1, d1                ; set (d1) for dbra
getval:       jsr       decin                 ; read in a word
              move.w    d0, (a0)+             ; store in the array
              dbra      d1, getval
              movem.l   (sp)+, d0-d1/a0       ; restore registers
```

```
            unlk      a6                      ; restore a6
            move.l    (sp),rbytes(sp)         ; reset return address
            addq.l    #rbytes,sp              ; reset (sp)
            rts


; bubble sort subroutine. sorts a list in ascending order
baddr:      equ       8
bcount:     equ       12
bbytes:     equ       6
previous:   equ       -2
true:       equ       1
false:      equ       0


bubblesort:
            link      a6,#0
            movem.l   d0-d3/a0-a2,-(sp)       ; save registers
            move.w    bcount(a6),d1           ; d1 holds the array count
            subq.w    #2,d1                   ; dbra for n-1 iterations
ploop:      moveq     #true,d0                ; assume inorder = true
            movea.l   baddr(a6)a0             ; put list address in a0
            lea       2(a0),a1                ; (a1) points at location
            move.w    d1,d2                   ; d2 is array counter
cloop:      cmpm.w    (a0)+,(a1)+             ; compare a[j] and a[j1]
            bge       looptest                ; branch if a[j+1] >= a[j]
            move.w    prev(a0),d3             ; swap the two locations
            move.w    (a0),prev(a0)
            move.w    d3,(a0)
            moveq     #false,d0               ; inorder = false
looptest:
            dbra      d2,cloop
            tst.w     d0                      ; did a swap occur?
            dbne      d1,ploop                ; if not the sort is over
            movem.l   (sp),d0-d3/a0-a2
            unlk      a6
            move.l    (sp),bbytes(sp)
            addq.l    #bbytes,sp
            rts


waddr:      equ       8
wcount:     equ       12
wbytes:     equ       6


writearr:
            link      a6,#0
            movem.l   d0-d1/a0,-(sp)
            movea.l   waddr(a6),a0            ; set (a0) to array address
            move.w    wcount(a6),d1           ; set (d1) to the array count
            subq.l    #1,d1                   ; prepare d1 for dbra
putval:     move.w    (a0)+,d0
            jsr       decout
```

```
        dbra      d1,putval
        jsr       newline
        movem.l   (sp)+,d0-d1/a0
        unlk      a6
        move.l    (sp),(wbytes,sp)
        addq.l    #wbytes,sp
        rts

        data
;  set up the data area
list:      ds.w    20
listct:    ds.w    1
sortmsg:   dc.b    'sorted list: '
        end
```

⟨Run of Program 7.4⟩

```
5
-99 25 333 45 -71
sorted list: -99 -71 25 45 333
```

Printing Registers: The RTR Instruction

A subroutine PRINTREGS is developed to print the contents of the internal MC68000 registers. Such a routine is useful in debugging run-time errors. It prints the current value of the data and address registers (D0–D7/A0–A6), the stack pointer (SP), the status register (SR), and the program counter (PC). Upon return from the subroutine, the status register has the same value it had when entering the routine. This is accomplished by pushing the SR on the stack and introducing a new instruction, "Return and Restore Condition Codes" (RTR). The instruction RTR pops the status register off the stack, placing its low 8 bits into the CCR, and then pops the return address into the PC. In this way, the original value of the CCR is restored (see Figure 7.15).

FIGURE 7.15 Popping the Stack Using RTR

INSTRUCTION

RTR
(Return and
Restore Condition
Codes)

Syntax   RTR

Action   Six bytes are cleared from the stack.

1. A word is popped from the stack, and the LSB is placed into the condition codes.

2. A long word is popped from the stack and placed into the program counter.

Note   If the instruction "MOVE.W   SR, − (SP)" is executed at the start of a subroutine, then RTR will cause a return to the calling program with the CCR unchanged.

EXAMPLE 7.11

Before execution of an RTR instruction, the stack contains the following 6 bytes of data:

$$(SP) = \$0400 \qquad (2,SP) = \$0001 \qquad (4,SP) = \$5000$$

The 16-bit word at location (SP) is popped from the stack, and the LSB is written into the CCR. The 32-bit long word at location (SP) + 2 is written into the PC.

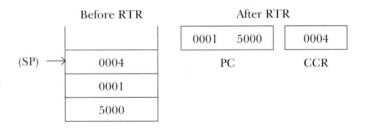

PROGRAM 7.5

Print Registers

The subroutine PRINTREGS requires no parameters. The SR, followed by the general-purpose data and address registers, are first pushed on the stack and then printed six to a line. The routine allows you to examine the values and then press Return to continue. This code includes a simple main program that makes two calls to the subroutine.

```
          xref      stop

start:
          movem.l   testregs, d0-d7/a0-a4/a6
          move.l    #−1,−(sp)          ; use stack
          jsr       printregs          ; print the registers
```

```
                move.l      (sp)+,d0              ; prepare for another call
                addq.l      #1,d0
                jsr         printregs
                jsr         stop

        xref    strout, strin, hexout, hexout_long, newline


savedsp:        equ         60                    ; offset to (sp) on stack

printregs:
; On an MC68020/30/40 system, use ''move.w ccr,-(sp)''
                move.w      sr,-(sp)
                pea         (6,sp)                ; save orig stack pointer
                movem.l     d0-d7/a0-a6,-(sp)     ; save gen registers
                moveq       #2,d1                 ; 3 rows of registers
                movea.l     sp,a1                 ; saved regs. begin at (sp)
                lea         regmsgs,a2
mloop:          movea.l     a2,a0
                move.w      #55,d0
                jsr         strout                ; print a row header
                jsr         newline
                moveq       #5,d2                 ; count 6 values per line
rploop:         tst.w       d1                    ; check to see if reg = sr
                bne.s       notsr
                cmp.w       #1,d2
                bne.s       notsr
                moveq       #2,d0
                lea         spaces,a0
                jsr         strout                ; spaces for alignment
                move.w      (a1)+,d0              ; sr is word
                jsr         hexout
                move.w      #2,d0
                jsr         strout                ; two spaces for alignment
                bra.s       endrpl
notsr:          move.l      (a1)+,d0              ; print a register
                jsr         hexout_long
endrpl:         dbra        d2,rploop
                jsr         newline               ; set for new table entry
                adda.l      #55,a2                ; point at next header
                dbra        d1,mloop
                move.w      #1,d0                 ; delay until <cr> struck
                lea         ch,a0
                jsr         strin
                movem.l     (sp)+,d0-d7/a0-a6     ; restore gen registers
                addq.w      #4,sp                 ; flush saved orig sp
                rtr                               ; return and restore ccr

                data
regmsgs:
                dc.b        '    d0      d1      d2      '
                dc.b        '    d3      d4      d5'
                dc.b        '    d6      d7      a0      '
                data
```

```
            dc.b      '     a1        a2        a3'
            dc.b      '     a4        a5        a6
            dc.b      '     sp        sr        pc'
spaces:     dc.b      '   '
ch:         ds.b      1
            even      0
testregs:   dc.l      1, 2, 3, 4, 5, 6, 7, 8, $a, $aa, $aaa
            dc.l      , $aaaa, $aaaaa, $aaaaaa

            end
```

⟨Run of Program 7.5⟩

d0	d1	d2	d3	d4	d5
00000001	00000002	00000003	00000004	00000005	00000006
d6	d7	a0	a1	a2	a3
00000007	00000008	0000000A	000000AA	00000AAA	0000AAAA
a4	a5	a6	sp	sr	pc
000AAAAA	0011E4C4	00AAAAAA	00164ABA	2008	00122AEC

d0	d1	d2	d3	d4	d5
00000000	00000002	00000003	00000004	00000005	00000006
d6	d7	a0	a1	a2	a3
00000007	00000008	0000000A	000000AA	00000AAA	0000AAAA
a4	a5	a6	sp	sr	pc
000AAAAA	0011E4C4	00AAAAAA	00164ABE	2015	00122AF4

Parameter Passing with Functions

The concept of parameter passing is extended to include a function that is the starting address of a block of code. The topic is straightforward after you understand that function passing is essentially the same as call-by-reference data passing. A Pascal program is provided to illustrate function passing.

The subroutine SUMVALS takes the following input parameters:

1. The address of A, an array of integers.

2. The value N, the number of elements in A.

3. An address of F, a function that takes an integer argument and returns an integer value. F is any arithmetic operation on integers.

The Pascal function SUMVALS outputs the sum

$$SUM = F(A[1]) + F(A[2]) + \cdots + F(A[N])$$

where F is a function passed to SUMVALS. Assembly language code that mirrors the Pascal implementation is given.

PROGRAM 7.6

In a test program, an array list of five elements is passed to the subroutine SUMVALS along with a function SQUARE [SQUARE $(x) = x^2$]. The address of array LIST, the number of elements in LIST, and the address of a subroutine SQUARE are passed on the stack. The subroutine SUM-VALS passes an argument on the stack to the function SQUARE, which returns its output value in D0. The result from SUMVALS is output using DECOUT.

Pascal Code

```
PROGRAM function_parameter (input, output);
   TYPE
      shortarray = array [1..5] of integer;
   VAR
      i: integer;
      a shortarray;

   FUNCTION square (x: integer): integer;
   BEGIN
      square := x * x
   END; { function square }

   FUNCTION sumvals (VAR a: shortarray; n: integer;
                            function f (x: integer): integer):
                            integer;
   VAR
      i: integer;
      sum: integer;
   BEGIN
      sum := 0;
      FOR i := 1 to n do
      sum := sum + f(a[i]);
      sumvals := sum
    END;        { function sumvals }
BEGIN    { main program }
   FOR i := 1 to 5 do
    read(a[i]);
    writeln(sumvals(a, 5, square))
END.

INPUT: 1 2 3 4 5

OUTPUT: 55
```

MC68000 Code

```
            xref        decout, newline, stop
start:
            pea         square                      ; push function address
            move.w      #5,-(sp)                    ; push array size
            pea         list                        ; push array address
            bsr         sumvals                     ; call the subroutine
            jsr         hexout
            jsr         newline
            jsr         stop



x:          equ         8
xsize:      equ         2
square:
            link        a6, #0
            move.w      (x,a6),d0                   ; get parameter x
            muls        d0,d0                       ; square the parameter
            unlk        a6
            move.l      (sp),(xsize,sp)             ; clean the stack
            adda.l      #xsize,sp
            rts                                     ; return value in d0.w



aaddr:      equ         8
acount:     equ         12
funcaddr:   equ         14
stacksize:  equ         10



sumvals:
            link        a6, #0
            movem.l     d1-d2/a0-a1,-(sp)
            moveq       #0,d1                       ; accumulator ''lans''
            movea.l     (aaddr,a6),a1               ; get array address ''a''
            move.w      (accout,a6),d2              ; get array size n
            subq.w      #1,d2                       ; (d2) = n - 1
            movea.l     (funcaddr,a6),a0            ; get funct address ''f''
oploop:     move.w      (a1)+,-(sp)                 ; push entry on stack
            jsr         (a0)                        ; call the function ''f''
            add.w       d0,d1
            dbra        d2,oploop
            move.w      d1,d0                       ; set return value in d0
            movem.l     (sp)+,d1-d2/a0-a1
            unlk        a6
            move.l      (sp),(stacksize,sp)         ; clean up the stack
            adda.l      #stacksize,sp
            rts
```

```
              data

list:         dc.w        1, 2, 3, 4, 5
              end
```

⟨Run of Program 7.6⟩

55

Random Number Generation

Random number generation has a great many applications in probability, statistics, and computer simulation. Most computer systems provide a function to generate a random number. In most cases, the generator creates the same sequence each time unless it is "seeded" first. A seed is used to determine the sequence of random numbers obtained by successively calling the generator. When the seed is changed, the sequence is changed. This program assumes that two subroutines are available for seeding and generating random numbers.

SEED: Seeds the random number generator RAND.
      Parameters
        Input: If (D0.W) is nonzero, a random seed is
               generated; otherwise, a fixed seed is used.
        Output: None
RAND: Generates a 16-bit random integer. RAND assumes an
      initial call to SEED.
      Parameters
        Input: None
        Output: (D0.W) is a 16-bit random integer.

PROGRAM 7.7

Random Numbers

A subroutine TOSS simulates tossing a coin by returning 1 if heads is tossed and 0 if tails is tossed. This routine is used to write a subroutine TOSS5, which simulates tossing five coins. TOSS5 is called in a loop 10,000 times. For each call to TOSS5, the number of heads is noted, and the corresponding entry in array COUNT is incremented by 1. If K heads are tossed, COUNT [K] is incremented. At the conclusion of the loop, you know how many times 0 heads occurred, 1 head occurred, and so on. A simple graph is printed to illustrate the relative number of times each of the possible outcomes occurred. This is done by scaling each of the sums in COUNT to print a '*' within a field of 20 character positions. To do this, each entry of COUNT is multiplied by 20 and then divided by 10,000 to reflect a portion of 20 character positions. Subroutine PRINTSTAR prints leading blanks followed by a "*" in the character position indicated by the computation. The graph illustrates what is known as the binomial distribution.

```
        xref        seed, rand, strout, newline, stop
        xref        decout


start:  moveq       #1,d0
        jsr         seed                ; create a random seed
        move.w      #9999,d1            ; 1000 tosses of 5 coins
        lea         counts,a0
tossloop:
        jsr         toss5
        asl.w       #1,d0               ; use d0.w as index into counts
        addi.w      #1,(0,a0,d0.w)      ; increment head count
        dbra        d1,tossloop

        moveq       #5,d1
        lea         counts,a0
        moveq       #0,d2               ; number of heads being graphed
graphloop:
        move.w      d2,d0
        jsr         decout              ; print number of heads
        move.w      (a0)+,d0
        mulu        #20,d0              ; scale within 20 positions
        divu        #10000,d0
        addq.w      #1,d0               ; guarantees char position >= 1
        jsr         printstar
        addq.w      #1,d2               ; increment number of heads
        dbra        d1,graphloop

        jsr         stop


; toss a single coin. return 1 for heads, 0 for tails
toss:
        jsr         rand
        andi.w      #1,d0
        rts


; toss five coins. return number of heads in (d0.w)
toss5:
        movem.l     d1/d2,-(sp)
        moveq       #4,d1
        moveq       #0,d2
throw:  jsr         toss
        add.w       d0,d2
        dbra        d1,throw
        move.w      d2,d0
        movem.l     (sp)+,d1/d2
        rts
```

```
printstar:
        movem.l    d0/a0,-(sp)
        subq.w     #1,d0              ; number of blanks to print
        beq.s      pstar             ; maybe '*' goes in column 1
        lea        blanks,a0         ; print blanks
        jsr        strout
pstar:  lea        star,a0           ; print '*'
        moveq      #1,d0
        jsr        strout
        jsr        newline
        movem.l    (sp)+,d0/a0
        rts

        data
counts: dcb.w      6,0               ; six zero words
blanks: dc.b       '         '       ; 20 blanks
star:   dc.b       'q*'
        even
        end
```

⟨Run of Program 7.7⟩

```
0      *
1           *
2                *
3                *
4           *
5      *
```

EXERCISES

1. Correct the following syntax errors by giving a similar instruction that is syntactically correct:
   (a) MOVEM.B   D1; D7; A0–A4,MEM
   (b) BSR   (A0)
   (c) JSR   A2
   (d) PEA   A5,–(SP)
   (e) MOVEM.L   –(SP),D0–D7/A6

2. Assume (A2) = $00011C, (D2) = $0004, and (D1) = $FF00. What are the values in memory after the MOVEM instruction is executed?

   MOVEM.W   D1–D2/A2, (A2)

3. Give the opcode and extension word for the following instructions:
   (a) MOVEM.L   D0–D3/A3–A5,–(SP)
   (b) MOVEM.L   (SP)+,D0–D3/A3–A5
   (c) MOVEM.W   D2–D6/A1–A3,$6000.W

4. Give the equivalent assembly language instructions for the two MOVEM instructions

$$
\begin{array}{ll}
\text{48E7} & \text{2F85} \\
\text{4CDF} & \text{3807}
\end{array}
$$

5. A subroutine ROUT is called with parameters passed in D0 and A0. D0 is an output parameter. The subroutine uses registers D1, D2, A0, and A1 as scratch registers. Assume that the return address from ROUT is $1000.
   (a) Draw a picture of the stack upon entrance to the subroutine.
   (b) What MOVEM instruction should be used to save registers?
   (c) Draw a picture of the stack after executing the MOVEM instruction.
   (d) What MOVEM instruction should be used to restore registers?

6. A subroutine SUB passes/receives its parameters to/from the stack. A total of 20 bytes is used for the parameters. Show how to:
   (a) Flush the parameters prior to a return from the subroutine.
   (b) Flush the parameters after a return to the calling code.

7. A main program passes the parameters PARM1, PARM2, and PARM3 to subroutine EXAMPLE by placing the values immediately after the subroutine call. The code for EXAMPLE must obtain the return address from the stack and use it to access the parameters. Upon accessing the parameters, the return address on the stack must be updated so that it becomes the address of the next instruction.

```
JSR     EXAMPLE
DC.W    PARM1
DC.L    PARM2
DC.W    PARM3
⟨NEXT   Inst⟩ . . .
```

Assume that EXAMPLE must save registers D0–D2/A0–A1. Write a code segment for EXAMPLE that will copy PARM1 into D0, PARM2 into A1, and PARM3 into D1, and will update the return address.

8. Suppose you are given the following Pascal procedure:

```
FUNCTION SAMPLE (A,B : INTEGER) : INTEGER;
VAR N,M : INTEGER;
BEGIN
        .
        .
        .
    CODE
        .
        .
        .
END; { SAMPLE }
```

The Pascal compiler implements integers as 16-bit two's complement numbers. Assume that the two parameters are passed using the stack. The order of placement on the stack is B followed by A. Assume that the function will need to save registers D1–D2/A0–A1, with the value being returned in D0. Storage is created for the local variables N and M by using LINK with a displacement of -4. Compute the offsets to the frame pointer for the following variables:

(a) Call-by-value parameter A
(b) The return address
(c) Local variables M and N
(d) Register A0

Write code that will clear the stack prior to the subroutine return (RTS).

9. Trace the code and state what output is produced.

```
         XREF        HEXOUT, STOP
         PEA         LIST1
         MOVE.W      #4,-(SP)
         JSR         TEST
         JSR         HEXOUT
         PEA         LIST2
         MOVE.W      #2,-(SP)
         JSR         TEST
         JSR         HEXOUT
         JSR         STOP


TEST:    LINK        A6,#0
         MOVEM.L     D1/A0,-(SP)
         MOVEA.L     (10,A6),A0
         MOVE.W      (8,A6),D1
         MOVE.W      (0,A0,D1.W),D0
         MOVEM.L     (SP)+,D1/A0
         UNLK        A6
         MOVE.L      (SP),(6,SP)
         ADDA.L      #6,SP
         RTS


         DATA
LIST1:   DC.W        2,3,5,7,9
LIST2:   DC.W        10,11,13,15
         END
```

10. Write assembly language code for the following program. Use the LINK and UNLK instructions, and pass the parameter on the stack.

```
PROGRAM LINK(OUTPUT);

VAR I : INTEGER;

PROCEDURE P (VAR I : INTEGER);
BEGIN
     I := I * I + 3
END;
```

```
BEGIN
    I := 4;
    P(I);
    WRITELN(I)
END.
```

11. Write assembly language code for the following Pascal procedure. Use the LINK and UNLK instructions, and pass parameters on the stack. Implement the local variables I and LSUM using registers.

```
TYPE ARR = ARRAY[1 . . 50] OF INTEGER;

PROCEDURE SUMSQ(VAR A: ARR; N: INTEGER; VAR SUM: INTEGER);
VAR I, LSUM : INTEGER;
BEGIN
    LSUM := 0;
    FOR I := 1 TO N DO
        LSUM := LSUM + SQR(A[I]);
    SUM := LSUM:
END { SUMSQ };
```

12. Label ARR is the address of a 25-element array of words. Trace the following code segment, and describe what the subroutine TESTSUB does.

```
            LEA         ARR,A0
            MOVE.W      #25,D1
            JSR         TESTSUB

                        .
                        .
                        .

TESTSUB:    MOVEM.L     D1/A0,-(SP)
            MOVE.W      (A0)+,D0
            SUBQ.W      #2,D1
AGAIN:      CMP.W       (A0)+,D0
            BLE.S       GO
            MOVE.W      (-2,A0),D0
GO:         DBRA        D1,AGAIN
            MOVEM.L     (SP)+,D1/A0
            RTS
```

13. Trace the following code, and describe its action:

```
SUB:
        LINK        A6,#0
        MOVEM.L     D0/A0,-(SP)
        MOVE.W      (12,SP),D0
        ADD.W       D0,D0
        MOVEA.L     (8,SP),A0
        MOVE.L      D0,(A0)
        MOVEM.L     (SP)+,D0/A0
        UNLK        A6
        MOVE.L      (SP),(6,SP)
        ADDQ.W      #6,SP
        RTS
```

14. Trace the following code, and give the output:

```
            XREF        HEXOUT, STOP
START:      PEA         LIST1
            MOVE.W      #4, - (SP)
            JSR         SUB
            JSR         HEXOUT
            PEA         LIST2
            MOVE.W      #2, - (SP)
            JSR         SUB
            JSR         HEXOUT
            PEA         LIST3
            MOVE.W      #5, - (SP)
            JSR         SUB
            JSR         HEXOUT
            JSR         STOP


SUB:        LINK        A6, #0
            MOVEM.L     D1/A0, - (SP)
            MOVEA.L     (10, A6) , A0
            MOVE.W      (8, A6) , D1
            MOVE.B      (0, A0, D1.W) , D0
            ANDI.W      #$00FF, D0
            MOVEM.L     (SP) +, D1/A0
            UNLK        A6
            MOVE.L      (SP) , (6, SP)
            ADDA.L      #6, SP
            RTS


LIST1:      DC.W        $FA20, $0A77, $2070, $C0A0, $7F0A
LIST2:      DC.W        $0110, $FF11, $A013, $5015
LIST3:      DC.W        $0000, $A327, $FF13, $0010
            END
```

15. Trace the following code:

```
            XREF        HEXOUT, STOP
START:      LEA         ARR, A0
            MOVE.L      #10, D1
            JSR         TESTSUB
            JSR         HEXOUT
            JSR         STOP


TESTSUB:    MOVEM.L     D1-D3/A0, - (SP)
            MOVEQ       #1, D0
            MOVE.L      D0, D2
            MOVE.B      (A0) +, D3
AGAIN:      ADDQ.L      #1, D2
            CMP.L       D2, D1
            BLT.S       DONE
            CMP.B       (A0) +, D3
            BLS.S       GO
            MOVE.B      (-1, A0) , D3
            MOVE.L      D2, D0
```

```
GO:        BRA.S      AGAIN
DONE:      MOVEM.L    (SP)+,D1-D3/A0
           RTS
ARR:       DC.B       < DATA LIST>
           END
```

(a) For the data list $A0,$30,$77,$0F,$50,$C0,$00,$01,$80,$7F, what is the output?

(b) For the data list $7F,$0F,$00,$A0,$00,$01,$00,$7F,$80,$30, what is the output?

(c) If the instruction "BLS.S GO" is replaced by "BLE.S GO", answer (a) and (b).

16. Trace the following code:

```
           XREF       DECIN,DECOUT,STOP
START:     JSR        DECIN
           MOVE.W     D0,-(SP)
           MOVE.W     #10,-(SP);
           PEA        LIST
           JSR        FINDIT
           JSR        DECOUT
           JSR        STOP

FINDIT:    LINK       A6,#0
           MOVEM.L    D1-D2/A0,-(SP)
           MOVEA.L    (8,A6),A0
           MOVE.W     (12,A6),D2
           MOVE.W     (14,A6),D1
           MOVE.W     D2,D0
           ASL.W      #1,D2
           ADDA.W     D2,A0
LOOP:      CMP.W      -(A0),D1
           BEQ.S      RETURN
           SUBQ.W     #1,D0
           BNE.S      LOOP
RETURN:    MOVEM.L    (SP)+,D1-D2/A0
           UNLK       A6
           MOVE.L     (SP),(8,SP)
           ADDQ.L     #8,SP
           RTS

LIST:      DC.W       0,1,2,3,4,5,6,7,8,9
           END
```

(a) For input 6, what is the output?

(b) For input 10, what is the output?

17. The following subroutine is passed the starting address of a list in A0, a 32-bit integer in D0, a 16-bit integer in D1, and another 16-bit integer in D2 giving the list length in units of long words. What is the action of the subroutine?

```
Q17:
           MOVEM.L    D1-D2/A1-A2,-(SP)
```

```
              TST.W      D2
              BNE        CONT
              MOVEA.L    A0,A2
              BRA        DOIT
     CONT:    SUBQ.W     #1,D1
              ASL.W      #2,D1
              ASL.W      #2,D2
              LEA        (0,A0,D2.W),A1
              LEA        (0,A0,D1.W),A2
     QLOOP:
              MOVE.L     -(A1),(4,A1)
              CMPA.L     A1,A2
              BCS.S      QLOOP
     DOIT:    MOVE.L     D0,(A2)
              MOVEM.L    (SP)+,D1-D2/A1-A2
              ADDQ.W     #1,D2
              RTS
```

PROGRAMMING EXERCISES

18. A subroutine SWAP takes the addresses of two long words and interchanges their values. A Pascal implementation is

    PROCEDURE SWAP (VAR X, Y : INTEGER);
    VAR TEMP: INTEGER;
    BEGIN
        TEMP := X;
        X := Y;
        Y := TEMP
    END; {SWAP}

    (a) Implement SWAP by passing the parameters using registers. Use a register for the local variable TEMP. Test your code by incorporating SWAP in a main program.
    (b) Do (a), but pass parameters using the stack.

19. Write a program that includes the following steps. Pass all parameters using registers.
    (a) Reads a number N from the keyboard.
    (b) Calls a subroutine ARRIN to fill an array with N 16-bit integers.
    (c) Calls a subroutine ARRPRINT to print the array.
    (d) Calls subroutine ABSVAL to replace each element in the array with its absolute value.
    (e) Prints out the modified array using ARRPRINT.

20. Rewrite exercise 19 to pass the array address and the array count N using the stack.

21. C is a label in data space. Write a subroutine COMPUTE that takes 16-bit input parameters *M* and *N* and returns the long-word value 2 * (*M* + *N*) in the memory address C. All parameters are to be passed using the stack. Thus two parameters are passed by value and one by reference. Create a main program to test COMPUTE. It is to read five sets of values *M* and *N* and print the computed value at address C.

22. Write a subroutine that takes as input parameters an array X of 16-bit words and the array count N. The subroutine returns in D0 the index of the minimum element in the array. Pass X and N using registers. Test using a main program.

23. Using subroutines SEED/RAND, write a subroutine that simulates tossing a pair of dice. Play the following game: Enter a target number using DECIN in the range 4–6 or 8–12. Toss the dice until you roll either your target number or a 7. If your target appears first, your win; otherwise, you lose. Print out the results for each roll as you are playing the game.

24. A list L of *N* elements is to be sorted from low to high. Consider the following algorithm.

Select the largest element in the list L(1) · · ·L(*N*), and exchange it with the contents of L(*N*).
Select the largest element in the list L(1) · · · L(*N* − 1), and exchange it with the contents of L(*N* − 1).
Continue the process. The final iteration will select the largest element in the list L(1) · · · L(2).

Write a subroutine that will implement this selection sort. Pass the address of the list in A0 and the list count in D0. Test using a main program that should include the printing of the list both before and after calling the sort routine.

25. Write a subroutine SKIPBLANK that takes in A0 an address of a string and returns in A0 the address of the next nonblank character. Write a second subroutine UPPERCASE that takes the address of a character in A0 and changes the character to uppercase if it lies in range 'a'–'z'. Write a third subroutine SKIPWORD that takes a string address in A0 and returns the address of the next blank or newline character. Using the subroutines, enter a string of words and capitalize the first letter of every word. Print the modified string.

26. This exercise will create a test corrector program. Enter a string containing up to 25 multiple choice answers in the range A–E. This is the test key. Write a subroutine called CORRTEST that is passed a string of answers. It is to
    (a) Print the input string.
    (b) Compute and print the number of correct answers.
    (c) Print a third line that contains a * if the answer is correct or prints the correct answer. For example,

    KEY   ACBDA
    ANSWERS   ABBDC   Correct 3
              * C * *A

    Verify the subroutine by correcting five tests.

27. Write a subroutine MAX that takes input parameters as follows:

> A—Array address
> N—Number of elements in the array
> SIZE—Number of bytes in each array element
> GREATER—Function that takes array elements X, Y and returns the address of the larger element

MAX is to return the address of the largest element in the array. This is a generic subroutine that handles variable-sized data types. Now write a program that uses MAX with arrays and functions defined in pseudoPascal as follows:

(a) VAR A: ARRAY[1 . . 10] OF INTEGER;

```
FUNCTION GREATERINT(X,Y : INTEGER) : ADDRESS;
BEGIN
  IF X < Y THEN
    GREATERINT : = Y.ADDRESS
  ELSE
    GREATERINT : = X.ADDRESS
END { GREATERINT };
```

(b) TYPE REC = RECORD
```
        ID : INTEGER;
        NAME : PACKED ARRAY [1 . . 20] OF CHAR;
        SCORE : INTEGER;
END;
VAR R: ARRAY[1 . . 5] OF REC;
```

```
FUNCTION GREATERREC (X,Y : REC) : ADDRESS;
BEGIN
  IF X.SCORE < Y.SCORE THEN
    GREATERREC : = X.ADDRESS
  ELSE
    GREATERREC : = Y. ADDRESS
END { GREATERREC };
```

For array (a), print out the largest value. For array (b), print all the fields of the record with the largest SCORE.

CHAPTER 8

EXTENDED ARITHMETIC ON THE MC68000

*P*revious chapters covered the basic MC68000 arithmetic operators and shift instructions. The operations are limited to byte, word, or long-word data. In many applications, greater precision is required, and the operations must be extended to data exceeding 32 bits. The MC68000 provides a series of extend instructions to support the programming of these operations. This chapter develops a library of extended arithmetic routines for 64-bit signed numbers.

Financial applications use binary coded decimal (BCD) numbers to represent currency. The numbers provide for precise fixed-point decimal arithmetic. Other applications include data encoding for electronic instruments. The MC68000 provides a set of arithmetic BCD instructions that are used for number conversion and calculation routines. The development of arithmetic routines extends to an optional section on floating-point numbers. The format of IEEE floating-point number representation is introduced along with a small library of arithmetic routines. The floating-point coprocessor is introduced in Chapter 15.

The MC68020/30/40 processors have 64-bit multiplication and division instructions. Quad, or 64-bit, numbers are stored in two data registers and are used in the extended operations. The processors also use bit fields, which allow access to a contiguous block of bits. Bit field instructions permit bit packing, extended bit tests, and access. The instructions are used to simplify some floating-point routines.

This chapter also develops a series of libraries—ArithmeticLib.i, and FloatingPointLib.i—that are used in most of the demonstration programs. The libraries are supported by two assembler directives. The source code is brought in using the INCLUDE directive. Depending on where the INCLUDE statement occurs within the application program, the assembler may need to use the ENTRY directive to identify the starting address of the program. Some assemblers support these directives. The following represents a typical syntax.

DIRECTIVE

INCLUDE

Syntax   INCLUDE   ⟨library⟩

Action   The assembler searches specified directories within the file system for the library and assembles the include files as part of the host program's code file.

Notes

1. Because included text is assembled along with the main body of text, all labels in the included text must be unique.

2. A program can have only one END directive, which the main program provides. There can be no END directive in any of the included files.

DIRECTIVE

ENTRY

Syntax   ENTRY   ⟨label⟩

Action   The directive specifies the starting address for program execution.

In Chapter 9, separately assembled coded files will be linked into the main program. This technique eliminates reassembly of the source text and, in most cases, is used instead of include files.

|8.1| EXTENDED ADDITIVE OPERATIONS

Because the basic MC68000 arithmetic operations are restricted to 32-bit data, greater precision requires software routines. The next two sections describe a series of 64-bit multiprecision arithmetic algorithms, including addition, subtraction, negation, and shift. The algorithms use MC68000 "Extend" instructions that utilize the X bit. Subroutine code is developed and the routines are included in a library.

Extended Addition

A 64-bit integer can be stored in memory using two consecutive long words, and the range of such numbers is

$$2^{-63} \leq N \leq 2^{63} - 1$$

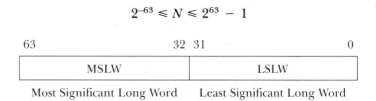

Most Significant Long Word   Least Significant Long Word

The addition of 64-bit numbers is implemented with a pair of long-word adds. The algorithm, however, requires special attention to the carry from one long word to another.

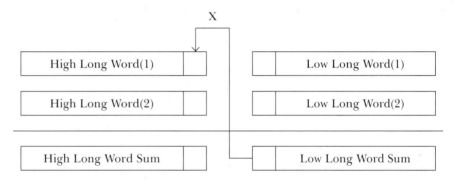

The carry from the sum of the low-order long words is stored in the C bit and the X (extend) bit. The addition of the high-order long words must include the addition of the X bit. The MC68000 ADDX instruction is designed for this situation.

INSTRUCTION

ADDX
(ADD with
Extend)

Syntax   ADDX.⟨size⟩   Dm,Dn
ADDX.⟨size⟩   −(Am),−(An)

Action   The contents of the two operands along with the value of the X bit are added. The sum is stored in the destination operand.

Notes

1. This instruction requires that the source and destination be either data registers or memory locations with predecrement mode.

2. The Z bit is cleared if the result is nonzero; otherwise, it is unchanged. This is important in applications where ADDX is applied to a series of memory locations. If the Z bit is initially set to 1, then the Z bit will have a final value of 0 only if it was cleared by one of the ADDX operations. In this case, the result of the addition is nonzero.

EXAMPLE 8.1

64-Bit Addition

(a) Add the 64-bit signed integer in (D2,D3) to that in (D0,D1).

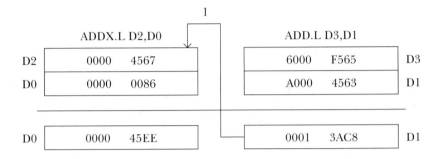

Step 1:   ADD.L   D3,D1
   The ADD is done first and produces a carry of 1, which is stored in both the C and X bits.

Step 2:   ADDX.L   D2,D0
   The X bit (carry) is added to the long-word contents in registers D0 and D1. The 64-bit sum is contained in registers D0 and D1

(b) Assume that the data from (a) is stored in memory. The 64-bit sum of the two terms can use the ADDX instruction with both the source and the destination operands with predecrement mode. Registers A0 and A1 are set 8 bytes past the address of the terms. The addition is a two-step process.

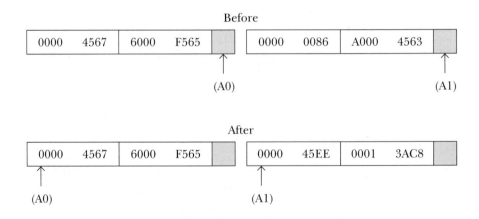

Step 1:   The instruction "ADD.L − (A0), − (A1)" is not valid because neither operand is a data register. However, if the X bit is 0, the ADDX and ADD instructions are equivalent. Assume X = 0, the sum of the low-order 32 bits is

ADDX.L −(A0),−(A1)

Step 2: From Step 1, the new register's values are (A0) = (A0) − 4 and (A1) = (A1) − 4. The add in Step 1 produces a carry and X = 1. A second ADDX instruction adds the high-order 32-bit values.

ADDX.L −(A0),−(A1)

In the preceding example, the X bit was assumed to be 0 so that the ADDX instruction could be used. A subroutine cannot presume this is true. The MC68000 provides you with a variant of the MOVE instruction to initialize the bits in the condition code register. This fact is used in developing algorithms for multiprecision addition.

INSTRUCTION

CCR
Instructions

Syntax MOVE.W ⟨ea⟩,CCR
ANDI.B #N,CCR
ORI.B #N,CCR
EORI.B #N,CCR

Action For the MOVE instruction, the contents of the source operand are moved to the CCR.
For the ANDI, ORI, and EORI instructions, the logical operations use the immediate data N as a mask. The CCR bits are modified by the operations.

Notes

1. CCR is a predefined symbol.

2. The "MOVE TO CCR" instruction is a word operation. However, only the LSB of the source operand is used. The high-order byte is ignored.

3. The logical instructions are byte operations.

EXAMPLE 8.2

The location of the CCR bits are shown here for reference.

*	*	*	*	*
X	N	Z	V	C

(a) MOVE #$04,CCR   Sets the Z bit; clears all others.

(b) MOVE #$1F,CCR   Sets all CCR bits.

(c) The mask $F7 isolates the N bit.

```
ANDI.B    #$F7,CCR
```

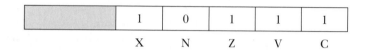

The 0 is used to clear the N bit. The 1's leave the other bits in the CCR unchanged.

(d) The mask $11 isolates the C and X bits.

```
ORI.B    #$11,CCR
```

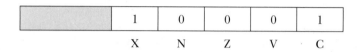

The X and C bits are set. All other bits are unchanged.

In this chapter extended arithmetic operations are placed in a library of included files, ArithmeticLib.i. The routines operate on data in memory, and parameters are passed using the stack. In order to maintain unique label names, labels within a subroutine are given by ⟨SubroutineName⟩_N. For example, in the subroutine ASR64, labels have names ASR64_1, ASR64_2.

The first subroutine in the library, ADD64(SOURCE,DEST), performs 64-bit two's complement addition in memory. If the first number is at address SOURCE and the second is at address DEST, then the two numbers are added, and the sum replaces the contents of DEST.

Contents(SOURCE) + Contents(DEST) → Contents(DEST)

The routine is designed in such a way that the condition codes upon return reflect only the action of the two ADDX instructions. Thus any appropriate branch instruction can be used directly following the call to ADD64. In particular, if the sum of the two numbers is zero, then Z = 1, and BEQ will branch. The subroutine effectively extends the instruction set of the machine by adding the new instruction ADD64. This is done by saving the CCR immediately after the last ADDX. It is placed 6 bytes into the stack area at an offset 10 bytes from the address given by the frame pointer A6.

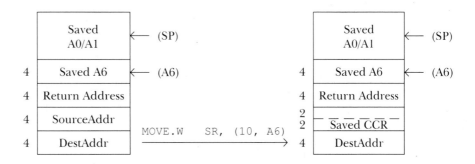

After restoring registers and doing an UNLK, the return address is then relocated below the saved CCR bits.

The SP is incremented by 6, and an RTR is executed.

ADD64   64-Bit Addition

Parameters passed
  Address of the source term on the stack.
  Address of the destination term on the stack.
Parameters returned
  The sum is stored in the destination term.

```
srcterm:        equ   8
desterm:        equ   12
ccrloc10:       equ   10
param8:         equ   8

add64:    link    a6,#0
          movem.1 a0/a1,-(sp)
          movea.1 (srcterm,a6),a0
          movea.1 (desterm,a6),a1
          addq.w  #8,a0                 ; point past 1st term
```

```
addq.w    #8,a1                    ; point past 2nd term
move w    #$04,ccr                 ; set z and clear x
addx.l    -(a0),-(a1)              ; add low order 32 bits + 0
addx.l    -(a0),-(a1)              ; add high order 32 bits + x
move.w    sr,(ccrloc10,a6)
movem.l   (sp)+,a0/a1
unlk      a6
move.l    (sp),(param8,sp)
addq.w    #param8-2,sp
rtr
```

Extended Subtraction

Subroutines for extended subtraction are similar to those for extended addition, except that the borrow must be carried across boundaries. Consider the case of two 16-bit numbers partitioned into bytes.

Subtraction in byte 1 requires a borrow. The result is $4A and X = C = 1. The borrow must be applied to byte 2, subtracting 1 from $8A. The subtraction in byte 2 is $89 − $23 = $66.

The SUBX instruction implements extended subtraction. A carryover borrow is identified by the X bit and is used in the subtraction.

INSTRUCTION

SUBX

(Sub with Extend)

Syntax   SUBX.⟨size⟩   D*m*,D*n*
           SUBX.⟨size⟩   −(A*m*),−(A*n*)

Action   The value of the X bit is subtracted from the difference of the destination and source operands.

$$(\text{destination}) = (\text{destination}) - (\text{source}) - X$$

Notes

1. The instruction requires that the source and destination be either data registers or memory locations with predecrement mode.

2. The Z bit is cleared if the result is nonzero; otherwise, it is unchanged. In applications where SUBX is applied to a series of memory locations, set the Z bit to be 1 initially. If the final value of the Z bit is 0, it was cleared by one of the SUBX operations, and the result is nonzero.

EXAMPLE 8.3

Extended
Subtraction

The 64-bit subtraction combines the two 32-bit operations

SUB.L   D3,D1
SUBX.L   D2,D0

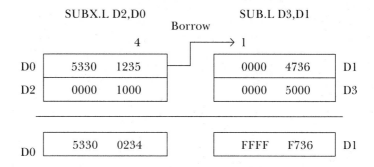

A borrow is required for the SUB.L   D3,D1 operation. The X bit is set. The SUBX.L   D2,D0 operation is

$$53301235 - 00001000 - 1 = 53300234$$

SUB64 64-Bit Subtraction

Parameters passed
    Address of the source term on the stack.
    Address of the destination term on the stack.
Parameters returned
    The difference is stored in the destination term.

```
srcterm:        equ   8
desterm:        equ   12
ccrloc10:       equ   10
param8:         equ   8

sub64:    link    a6,#0
          movem.1 a0/a1,-(sp)
          movea.1 (srcterm,a6),a0
          movea.1 (desterm,a6),a1
          addq.w  #8,a0             ; point past 1st term
          addq.w  #8,a1             ; point past 2nd term
          move w  #$04,ccr          ; set z and clear x
```

```
subx.1    -(a0),-(a1)           ; sub low order 32 bits - 0
subx.1    -(a0),-(a1)           ; sub high order 32 bits -
                                x
move.w    sr,(ccrloc10,a6)
movem.1   (sp)+,a0/a1
unlk      a6
move.1    (sp),(param8,sp)
addq.w    #param8-2,sp
rtr
```

Extended Negation

Using the definition of two's complement, an extended arithmetic algorithm computes the negative of a 64-bit number. The implementation of the algorithm is provided by the MC68000 NEGX instruction, described here with an example. Consider an N-bit number A in memory having low and high halves AL and AH, respectively.

A

AH	AL

Compute the two's complement directly by subtracting the contents of A from 0. It also can be done by considering each half of the number.

Unless AL is 0, subtraction in the low half will require a borrow. Subtraction in the high half will require another subtraction of 1 to account for the borrow. As with other extend instructions, the NEGX instruction includes an additional subtraction of the X bit. If a borrow has occurred, the X bit = 1. If no borrow has occurred, the NEGX and NEG instructions are equivalent.

2comp(A)

0	0
– AH	– AL

NEGX(AH)	NEGX(AL)

$$\text{NEGX (AL)} \;=\; 0 \;-\; AL \;-\; X \;=\; 0 \;-\; (AL + X)$$

$$\text{NEGX (AH)} \;=\; 0 \;-\; AH \;-\; X \;=\; 0 \;-\; (AH + X)$$

2comp(A) is computed by setting X = 0 and applying NEGX first to the lower half of A and then to the upper half of A.

$$2\mathrm{comp}(A) = \boxed{\begin{array}{c|c} \mathrm{NEGX(AH)} & \mathrm{NEGX(AL)} \\ (0 - AH - X) & (0 - AL) \end{array}}$$

INSTRUCTION

NEGX
(Negate with
Extend)

Syntax   NEGX.size ⟨ea⟩

Action   The X bit and the contents of the operand are subtracted from 0.

Notes

1. The size may be "B," "W," or "L."

2. The Z bit is cleared if the result is nonzero; otherwise, it is unchanged. Hence, if the Z bit is initially 1, its final value will indicate if the result is 0. If the Z bit is initially 0, it provides no information for the final result. The N bit indicates if the result is negative. Test program 8.2 demonstrates these facts.

3. If X = 0 and the operand is 0, then no borrow is necessary and the X and C bits are cleared. In all other cases, X = C = 1.

The NEGX instruction is used to implement extended 64-bit negation and extended 64-bit absolute value. In a fashion similar to ADD64/SUB64, the CCR after negation is stored on the stack and placed into the status register upon return from the subroutine using RTR.

NEG64   64-Bit Negation

Parameters passed
    Address of the operand is passed on the stack.
Parameters returned
    The 64-bit number in memory is negated.

```
srcterm:   equ      8
ccrloc6:   equ      6
param4:    equ      4
neg64:     link     a6,#0
           move.1   a0,-(sp)
           movea.1  (srcterm,a6),a0
           move.1   (4,a6),(src,a6)
           addq.w   #8,a0              ; set a0 for predecrement mode
           move.w   #$04,ccr           ; clear x and set z
```

```
            negx.1   -(a0)
            negx.1   -(a0)
            move.w   sr,(ccrloc6,a6)        ; save ccr for RTR
            movea.1  (sp)+,a0               ; restore register
            unlk     a6
            addq.w   #param4-2,sp
            rtr
```

ABS64   64-Bit Absolute Value

Parameters passed
   Address of the operand is passed on the stack.
Parameters returned
   The 64-bit number in memory is modified.

```
scrterm:    equ      8
ccrloc:     equ      6
param4:     equ      4

abs64:      link     a6,#0
            movem.1  d0/a0,-(sp)
            move.w   sr,d0                  ; temp save CCR
            movea.1  (srcterm,a6),a0
            move.1   (4,a6),(srcterm,a6)    ; relocate PC for RTR
            move.w   d0,(ccrloc6,a6)        ; save CCR on the stack
            tst.b    (a0)                   ; test for negative
            bpl.s    abs64_1                ; no just return
            adda.1   #8,a0                  ; compute the negative
            move.w   #$04,ccr
            negx.1   -(a0)
            negx.1   -(a0)
            move.w   sr,(ccrloc6,a6)        ; update CCR on stack
abs64_1:    movem.1  (sp)+,d0/a0
            unlk     a6
            addq.w   #param4-2,sp
            rtr
```

PROGRAM 8.1

**64-Bit Division
with Repeated
Subtraction**

The divisor (N) and dividend (M) are 64-bit unsigned numbers stored in memory. The algorithm uses repeated subtraction and the ADD64 and SUB64 routines.

Algorithm   Repeatedly compute $M = M - N$ until $M < 0$. The number of iterations is stored in Q. Because the process executes one too many subtracts, the quotient is $Q - 1$, and the remainder is $M + N$.

```
            xref     hexout_long,newline,stop

entry       start
            include  ArithmeticLib.i
```

```
start:
loop:       pea     quot            ; compute quot = quot + 1
            pea     inc_1
            jsr     add64
            pea     m               ; assign dividend address to a0
            pea     n               ; assign divisor address to a1
            jsr     sub64           ; compute m = m - n
            bmi.s   setans          ; test if m is negative
            bra     loop            ; return for another iteration
setans:     pea     m
            pea     n
            jsr     add64
            pea     quot
            pea     inc_1
            jsr     sub64
            lea     quot,a0         ; print quotient
            jsr     print
            lea     m,a0            ; print remainder
            jsr     print
            jsr     stop

print:      move.l  (a0)+,d0
            jsr     hexout_long
            move.l  (a0),d0
            jsr     hexout_long
            jsr     newline
            subq.w  #4,a0
            rts

            data
m:          dc.l    $00000000,$fffffffe
n:          dc.l    $00000000,$0000ffff
quot:       dc.l    $00000000,$00000000  ; initialize quotient to 0
incl_1:     dc.l    $00000000,$00000001  ; 64 bit value 1

            end
```

⟨Run of Program 8.1⟩

```
00000000  00010000
00000000  0000FFFE
```

PROGRAM 8.2

Z-Bit Test—NEGX

With the NEGX instruction, a 0 result occurs in only the following two cases:

Case 1: The operand is 0, and the X bit is 0.
Case 2: The operand is -1, and the X bit is 1.

$$\text{NEGX}(-1) = 0 - (-1) - 1 = 0$$

These two cases are tested under the assumption that the Z bit is assigned a value 1 and then under the assumption that the Z bit is assigned a value

0. In each case, the CCR bits are printed. The results demonstrate the importance of initially setting the Z bit to 1 if it is going to give valid information after executing an extend instruction.

```
NL:       equ       13
          xref      stop,hexout,strout,newline

start:    lea       header,a0
          move.w    #22,d0
          jsr       strout
          move.w    #0,dl            ; assign 0 to the operand
          move.w    #$04,d0
          jsr       printCCR
          move.w    #$04,ccr         ; set x = 0 and z = 1
          negx.w    dl
          jsr       printCCR         ; print test diagnostics
          jsr       newline

          move.w    #0,dl            ; assign 0 to the operand
          move.w    #$04,d0
          jsr       printCCR
          move.w    #$0,ccr          ; set x = 0 and z = 0
          negx.w    dl
          jsr       printCCR
          jsr       newline
          move.w    #-1,dl           ; assign -1 to the operand
          move.w    #$15,ccr
          jsr       printCCR
          move.w    #$14,ccr         ; set x = 1 and z = 1
          negx.w    dl
          jsr       printCCR
          jsr       newline
          move.w    #-1,dl           ; assign -1 to the operand
          move.w    #$15,ccr
          jsr       printCCR
          move.w    #$10,ccr         ; set x = 1 and z = 0
          negx.w    dl
          jsr       printCCR
          jsr       newline
          jsr       stop

; the subroutine prints the ccr bits and the final result
; the instruction move.w sr,d0 is privileged on an MC68020/30/40
; processor. Use the alternative, move.w ccr,d0
printCCR:
          move.w    sr,d0
          andi.w    #$1f,d0          ; mask ccr bits
          jsr       hexout           ; print ccr bits

          data
header:   dc.b      'Valid final', NL, 'CCR     CCR',NL
          end
```

⟨Run of Program 8.2⟩

Valid CCR	Final CCR
0004	0004
0004	0000
0015	0015
0015	0011

8.2 EXTENDED MULTIPLICATION OPERATIONS

The basic MC68000 multiply, divide, and shift instructions have restricted size requirements for their operands. Software is needed to extend the operations. This section implements extended shifts and multiplication and division operations using rotate-with-extend instructions.

Extended Shifts

The basic MC68000 arithmetic and logical-shift instructions are limited to long words. With larger numbers, the shifted bit must be transferred to an adjacent block of bits. The problem is handled with extend instructions that involve the X bit in the shift operation. After these instructions are introduced, 64-bit arithmetic shift routines are developed. The corresponding logical shift routines are given in the exercises at the end of the chapter.

INSTRUCTION

ROXL/ROXR
(Rotate with
Extend)

Syntax

ROXL.⟨size⟩	Dm,Dn	ROXR.⟨size⟩	Dm,Dn
ROXL.⟨size⟩	#N,Dn	ROXR.⟨size⟩	#N,Dn
ROXL	⟨ea⟩	ROXR	⟨ea⟩

Action   Rotate the bits of the destination operand in the specified direction with the X bit included in the rotation. The shift count is given as immediate data or in a data register.

For ROXL, a series of 1-bit shifts is executed up to the shift count. For each shift, the high-order bit shifts into both the C and X bits. The current value of the X bit is shifted into the low-order bit. The operation implements

FIGURE 8.1 Rotate Left with Extend

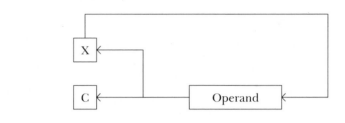

a circular rotation with the X bit dynamically included in the shift. Figure 8.1 diagrams the shift.

For ROXR, bits are shifted right. The low-order bit shifts into the C and X bits. The original value of the X bit is shifted into the high-order bit. This rotation of the X bit into the high-order bit occurs with each succeeding shift. Figure 8.2 shows the action.

Notes

1. Immediate data may be in the range 1 to 8.

2. If a data register is used, the shift count may be in the range 0–63. The low-order 6 bits of Dm are used as the unsigned shift count.

3. In the single-operand case, the destination must be in memory. The size defaults to "W," and the shift count is 1.

4. The V bit is always cleared. The Z and N bits are set by the results of the operations.

FIGURE 8.2 Rotate Right with Extend

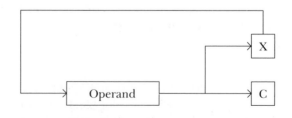

EXAMPLE 8.4

Rotate with Extend
Examples

(a) Assume that (D0.L) = \$F654   8001 and X = 0.

ROXR.W   #1,D0

After the Rotate

| F654   4000 | X = 1   C = 1 |

D0

The low-order 1 is shifted out of bit 0 into both the X and C bits.

(b) Assume that (D0.L) = \$0000   0004, (D1.L) = \$1685   3535, and X = 0.

ROXL.L   D0,D1

After the Rotate

| 6853   5350 | X = 1   C = 1 |

D1

Extended shift routines are implemented by combining the rotate-with-extend instructions and the arithmetic shift or logical shift instructions. The basic concept of extended shifts is illustrated with an arithmetic shift right of an 8-bit signed number composed of two 4-bit numbers.

EXAMPLE 8.5

Extended
Arithmetic Shift

Assume the 8-bit number A is initially 10110110_2. Shift A right 1 bit. The result is 11011011_2.

Invalid Algorithm   Consider A as two 4-bit numbers AH and AL. Using ASR on each 4-bit number, the result is incorrectly computed as 11010011_2. The problem occurs when the 1, shifted out of the low-order bit of AH, is not placed in the high-order bit of AL.

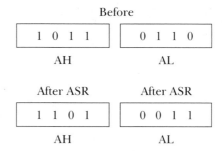

Valid Algorithm   Perform the shift on the two 4-bit numbers, but this time use ROXR on AL. The low-order bit of AH (located in the X bit) is shifted into the high-order bit of AL.

<table>
<tr><td>After ASR</td><td>After ROXR</td></tr>
<tr><td>1 1 0 1</td><td>1 0 1 1</td></tr>
<tr><td>AH</td><td>AL</td></tr>
</table>

In the right shift, AH is shifted using ASR in order to maintain the correct sign. Then, ROXR is used to shift AL. In a left shift, ASL is used on AL, followed by ROXL on AH. If ShiftCount > 1, the extended shift is implemented by executing the single-bit shift routine ShiftCount times. The example is generalized to 64-bit operations ASR64 (ShiftCount,N) and ASL64 (ShiftCount,N), which shift a number N stored in memory by ShiftCount.

ASR64   64-Bit Arithmetic Shift

Parameters passed
   The shift count is passed as a long word on the stack.
   The address of N is passed on the stack.
Parameters returned
   The 64-bit number N in memory is modified.

```
srcterm:     equ     8
desterm:     equ     12
ccrloc10:    equ     10
param8:      equ     8

asr64:       link     a6,#0
             movem.l  d0/a0,-(sp)
             move.l   (srcterm,a6),d0
             movea.l  (desterm,a6),a0
             andi.w   #$3f,d0            ; shift range 0 - 63
             subq.w   #1,d0             ; use dbra on shift count
             bmi.s    asr64_2           ; bail out if count = 0
             move.w   #$04,ccr
asr64_1:     asr.w    (a0)              ; shift 64 bits 16 at a time
             roxr.w   (2,a0)
             roxr.w   (4,a0)
             roxr.w   (6,a0)
             dbra     d0,asr64_1
             move.w   sr,(ccrloc10,a6)  ; save the ccr
; on MC68020/30/40 use move.w ccr,(ccrloc10,a6)
asr64_2:     movem.l  (sp)+,d0/a0       ; restore registers
             unlk     a6
```

```
            move.l    (sp),(param8,sp)
            addq.w    #param8-2,sp
            rtr                              ; return with ccr you want
```

ASL64   64-Bit Arithmetic Shift

Parameters passed
  The shift count is passed as a long word on the stack.
  The address of *N* is passed on the stack.
Parameters returned
  The 64-bit number *N* in memory is modified.

```
srcterm:    equ       8
desterm:    equ       12
ccrloc10:   equ       10
param8:     equ       8

asl64:      link      a6,#0
            movem.l   d0/a0,-(sp)
            move.l    (srcterm,a6),d0
            movea.l   (desterm,a6),a0
            andi.w    #$3f,d0              ; shift range 0 - 63
            subq.w    #1,d0                ; use dbra on shift count
            bmi.s     asl64_2              ; bail out if count = 0
            move.w    #$04,ccr
asl64_1:    asl.w     (6,a0)               ; shift 64 bits 16 at a time
            roxl.w    (4,a0)
            roxl.w    (2,a0)
            roxl.w    (0,a0)
            dbra      d0,asl64_1
            move.w    sr,(ccrloc10,a6)     ; save the ccr
;               on MC68020/30/40 use move.w ccr,(ccrloc10,a6)
asl64_2:    movem.l   (sp)+,d0/a0          ; restore registers
            unlk      a6
            move.l    (sp),(param8,sp)
            addq.w    #param8-2,sp
            rtr                            ; return with ccr you want
```

PROGRAM 8.3

64-Bit Count Ones

A test program uses ASL64 to count the number of 1's in a 64-bit number. Enter the number into location *N* using two calls to the 32-bit HEXIN_ LONG routine. A loop executes 64 times, each time shifting the number left 1 bit and then testing the status of the C bit. The number of 1's is printed with DECOUT.

```
xref      hexin_long,decout, stop

include   ArithmeticLib.i
entry     start
```

```
start:        jsr       hexin_long   ; input the MSLW of N
              move.l    d0,N
              jsr       hexin_long   ; input the LSLS of N
              move.l    d0,N+4
              moveq     #0,d0        ; clear the count
              moveq     #63,d1       ; set up the loop
test_1:       pea       N            ; pass parameters to asl64
              move.l    #1,-(sp)
              jsr       asl64
              bcc.s     next_shift   ; test the C bit
              addq.w    #1,d0        ; add + 1 if C = 1
next_shift:   dbra      d1,test_1
              jsr       decout
              jsr       stop

              data
N:            ds.l      2            ; allocate 2 long words

              end
```

⟨Run of Program 8.3⟩

C0000000
0000000F
6

Extended Multiplication

Chapter 5 introduced the instructions MULU and MULS to multiply 16-bit numbers. For extended multiplication, the MC68000 programmer needs a library of software routines. The MC68020/30/40 processors provide a series of instructions that include full 32-bit multipliers and 64-bit product. This section presents two 32-bit multiplication algorithms that are designed for the MC68000. The simple shift and add algorithm is extended to 32-bit numbers. A more efficient partial-products algorithm using MULU is also given. The MC68020/30/40 instructions are introduced in Section 8.5.

Assume that A and B are two 32-bit numbers. The subroutine UMUL32 (A,B) implements the shift and add algorithm. A loop tests the successive bits of B and shifts left the term A as a 64-bit number. The shift operation creates a doubling of the value, or multiplication by 2. For each nonzero bit of B, the corresponding shifted A is added to the partial sum. The final sum is the 64-bit product A × B.

UMUL32   32-Bit Unsigned Multiplication
(Shift and Add)

Parameters passed
    The 32-bit factors A and B are passed on the stack.

Parameters returned

The 64-bit product is returned in D0 and D1 (high-order 32 bits in D0; low-order 32 bits in D1).

```
multA:      equ     8
multB:      equ     12
param8:     equ     8

umul32:     link        a6,#0
            movem.l     d2-d4,-(sp)
            move.l      (multB,a6),d4       ; d4 contains B
            move.l      (multA,a6),d3       ; d3 contains A
            moveq       #0,d2               ; d2 used with addx
            moveq       #0,d0
            moveq       #0,d1
mul_shift1: lsr.l       #1,d4               ; look for 1 in multiplier
            bcc.s       mul_shift2          ; branch if 0 is found
            add.l       d3,d1               ; add shifted A to product
            addx.l      d2,d0               ; add carry if found
mul_shift2: lsl.l       #1,d3               ; shift for next iteration
            roxl.l      #1,d2
            tst.l       d4                  ; any 1's left?
            bne.s       mul_shift1
            movem.l     (sp)+,d2-d4
            unlk        a6
            move.l      (sp),(param8,sp)    ; clean stack
            addq.l      #param8,sp
            rts
```

A 32-bit number can be considered as two 16-bit words. The 32-bit × 32-bit product then becomes a paired multiplication of 16-bit factors much like the multiplication of two 2-digit base-10 numbers. In this form, the MULU instruction is efficiently applied. Some simple mathematics provide insight into the approach.

Algorithm   Partition the 32-bit number A into two words, the high half named AH and the low half AL. Similarly, B can be partitioned into BH and BL.

The product A × B is the sum of four 32-bit partial products, each computed using MULU.

Partial product 1: BL × AL
Partial product 2: BL × AH × (2^{16})
Partial product 3: BH × (2^{16}) × AL
Partial product 4: BH × 2^{16} × AH × 2^{16}

FIGURE 8.3 Partial-Product Grid

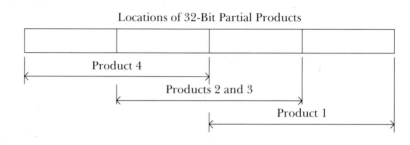

Locations of 32-Bit Partial Products

In UMUL32 (A,B), each of the four partial products accumulate in their own 32-bit portion of the 64-bit product. Note the overlap where carries will have to be considered (see Figure 8.3).

UMUL32   32-Bit
Unsigned Multiplication (MULU)

The subroutine multiplies two 32-bit unsigned numbers stored on the stack. The 64-bit result is returned in registers D0 and D1.

Parameters passed
  A—Passed on the stack.
  B—Passed on the stack.
Parameters returned
  D0 and D1—High and low portion of the 64-bit product.

```
multA:     equ     8
multB:     equ     12
param8:    equ     8

umul32:    link      a6,#0
           movem.l   d2-d4,-(sp)
           move.l    (multA,a6),d1
           move.l    (multB,a6),d0
           move.l    d1,d2              ; copy a to d2 and d3
           move.l    d1,d3
           move.l    d0,d4              ; copy b to d4
           swap      d3                 ; (d3) = al || ah
           swap      d4                 ; (d4) = bl || bh
           mulu      d0,d1              ; (d1) = al * bl
           mulu      d3,d0              ; (d0) = bl * ah
           mulu      d4,d2              ; (d2) = bh * al
           mulu      d4,d3              ; (d3) = bh * ah

; add up the partial products
           moveq     #0,d4              ; used with addx to add the carry
```

```
        swap     d1             ; (d1) = low(al;bl) || high(al;bl)
        add.w    d0,d1          ; (d1) = low(al;bl) || high(al;bl)
;                               ;              + low(bl;ah)
        addx.l   d4,d3          ; add carry from previous add
        add.w    d2,d1          ; (d1) = low(al;bl) || high(al;bl)
;                               ;              + low(bl;ah) + low(bh;al)
        addx.l   d4,d3          ; add carry from previous add
        swap     d1             ; put (d1) into its final form
        clr.w    d0             ; (d0) = high(bl;ah) || 0
        swap     d0             ; (d0) = 0 || high(bl;ah)
        clr.w    d2
        swap     d2             ; (d2) = 0 || high(bh;al)
        add.l    d2,d0          ; carry is stored in msw of d0
        add.l    d3,d0          ; (d0) = high(ah;bh) + carry ||
;                               ;        low(bh;ah) + high(bl;ah)
;                               ;              + high(bh;al)
        movem.l  (sp)+,d2-d4
        unlk     a6
        move.l   (sp),(param8,sp)
        addq.w   #param8,sp
        rts
```

PROGRAM 8.4

Multiplication Test
Program

This is a main program to test the two versions of UMUL32. The program
is run with both versions, and the total running time is determined in each
case.

```
        xref     hexout_long,newline,stop
        entry    start
        include  ArithmeticLib.i

start:  move.l   #100000,d2      ; repeat 100,000 times
tloop:  move.l   #$ffffffff,-(sp) ; pass b
        move.l   #$ffffffff,-(sp) ; pass a
        jsr      umul32
        subq.l   #1,d2
        bne.s    tloop
        jsr      hexout_long
        move.l   d1,d0
        jsr      hexout_long
        jsr      newline
        jsr      stop

        end
```

⟨Run of Program 8.4 (Shift-and-Add version)⟩

FFFFFFFE 00000001

⟨Run of Program 8.4 (MULU-based version)⟩

FFFFFFFE 00000001

The results are interesting. On a 25-MHz MC68030-based Macintosh IIci system, the shift-and-add version took approximately 1.7 times as long as the MULU-based version. The partial-products algorithm is significantly more efficient.

Extended Division

This section includes an extended-division algorithm that implements 32-bit unsigned division. The UDIV32 routine uses shift-and-subtract operations, the inverse of the multiplication shift-and-add algorithm. A simple example illustrates the key concepts.

Algorithm Assume that the dividend is $11101_2 = 29_{10}$ and the divisor is $101_2 = 5$.

$$101 \overline{)11101}$$

For Step 1, initialize the quotient to 0 and the X bit to 1. Shift the divisor left until its value is greater than the dividend. For each shift of the divisor, shift the quotient left using ROXL. Because the X bit is initially 1, the quotient will represent increasing powers of 2. For example,

Shift 1: Dividend   11101
          Divisor   1010   Quotient 001

Shift 2: Dividend   11101
          Divisor   10100   Quotient 010

Shift 3: Dividend   11101
          Divisor   101000   Quotient 100

          Stop

The divisor from the previous shift (Shift 2) is used, and the remainder is obtained by subtracting the shifted divisor from the dividend.

$$
\begin{array}{r}
100 \\
101 \overline{)11101} \\
10100 \\
\hline
1001
\end{array}
$$

The quotient is $100_2 = 4$ and the remainder is $1001_2 = 9_{10}$.

For Step 2, you need to repeat the division process for additional steps until the remainder is less than the divisor. The new dividend is $1001_2 = 9_{10}$ and the divisor is $101_2 = 5_{10}$.

$$
\begin{array}{r}
1 \\
101\,\overline{)1001} \\
101 \\
\hline
100
\end{array}
$$

The division step results in a partial quotient of 1 and a remainder of 4 and the process stops. For the final answer, the quotient is $100 + 1_2 = 101_2\ (4 + 1) = 5$ and the remainder is $100_2 = (4)$.

The preceding algorithm does not handle the situation where a 1 appears in bit 31 of the divisor, and the dividend is still greater than the divisor. In this case, another shift would not increase the value of the divisor. This is a stopping condition, and the quotient is found. The division algorithm is implemented in the subroutine UDIV32 (Divisor,Dividend) and tested in a subsequent complete program.

UDIV32   32-Bit Unsigned Division
(Shift and Subtract)

Parameters passed
Divisor—32-bit number passed on the stack.
Dividend—32-bit number passed on the stack.
Parameters returned
D0—32-bit quotient.
D1—32-bit remainder.

```
divisor:      equ    8
dividend:     equ    12
param8:       equ    8

udiv32:  link     a6,#0
         movem.l  d2-d4,-(sp)        ; save scratch registers
         move.l   (dividend,a6),d1
         move.l   (divisor,a6),d0
         clr.l    d3                 ; clear (d3) the quotient
udiv1:   cmp.l    d0,d1              ; test divisor > dividend
         blo.s    udiv5              ; if yes, done
         move.l   d0,d2              ; set divisor in temp register
         clr.l    d4                 ; clear partial quotient
         move.w   #$10,ccr           ; set x bit to 1
udiv2:   cmp.l    d2,d1              ; test divisor > dividend
         blo.s    udiv3              ; if yes, this step is done
         roxl.l   #1,d4              ; shift temp quotient left
         tst.l    d2                 ; test for another shift
         bmi.s    udiv4              ; if bit31 = 1, don't undo shift
```

```
            lsl.l    #1,d2              ; shift divisor to next test
            bra.s    udiv2             ; keep going
    udiv3:  lsr.l    #1,d2             ; undo the last shift
    udiv4:  sub.l    d2,d1             ; subtract shifted divisor
            add.l    d4,d3             ; add temp quoteint to d3
            bra.s    udiv1             ; go back for another division
    udiv5:  move.l   d3,d0             ; put the quotient in d0
            movem.l  (sp)+,d2-d4
            unlk     a6
            move.l   (sp),(param8,sp)
            addq.w   #param8,sp
            rts
```

PROGRAM 8.5

UDIV32 Test
Program

A long division problem tests the UDIV32 routine. First the dividend and
then the divisor are entered as decimal numbers. The quotient and remainder are output.

```
            xref     decin_long, decout_long, newline, stop

            entry    start
            include  ArithmeticLib.i

    start:  jsr      decin_long        ; enter the dividend
            move.l   d0,-(sp)          ; pass the dividend
            jsr      decin_long        ; enter the divisor
            move.l   d0,-(sp)          ; pass the divisor

            jsr      udiv32
            jsr      decout_long       ; print the quotient
            move.l   d1,d0
            jsr      decout_long       ; print the remainder
            jsr      newline
            jsr      stop

            end
```

⟨Run of Program 8.5⟩

555557
5
111111 2

8.3 | DECIMAL ARITHMETIC

The basic MC68000 arithmetic instructions assume that numbers have a
two's complement binary representation. This assumption is adequate for

integer calculations because precision is ensured. For business applications, the binary representation of numbers does not extend well to fixed-point numbers, where accuracy to two decimal places is required. For example, the fraction 1/10 cannot be represented exactly in binary, just as 1/3 cannot be represented exactly in decimal. To handle such applications, most high-level business languages implement a decimal representation of numbers. The representation uses 4 bits for each digit. The MC68000 provides three BCD instructions to implement addition, subtraction, and negation. The instructions can be used to construct a library of routines for implementation of a full range of arithmetic operations for BCD numbers.

BCD Digits

A BCD digit is in the range 0–9 and is represented by a 4-bit code. Each BCD digit has the value

$$D = B_3(2^3) + B_2(2^2) + B_1(2^1) + B_0(2^0)$$

where B_i is a binary digit 0 or 1.

BCD DIGITS			
Digit	BCD Form	Digit	BCD Form
0	0000	5	0101
1	0001	6	0110
2	0010	7	0111
3	0011	8	1000
4	0100	9	1001

BCD digits can be combined to represent a k-digit decimal number.

$$N = D_k(10^k) + D_{k-1}(10^{k-1}) + \cdots + D_0(10^0)$$

EXAMPLE 8.6

The decimal number is represented with BCD digits.

(a) $48 = 0100\ 1000$

(b) $391 = 0011\ 1001\ 0001$

(c) A 16-bit unsigned binary number N is in the range

$$0 \leqslant N \leqslant 2^{16} - 1 = 65535$$

A corresponding 16-bit BCD number is in the range

$$0 \leqslant N \leqslant 9999$$

Internal BCD Representation

Because a BCD digit requires four binary digits, two BCD digits can be stored in a single byte. This is called **packed BCD notation**. The MC68000 BCD instructions assume this packed form. An equivalent representation has a single BCD digit stored in a byte where all the high-order 4 bits are 0. This is called **unpacked BCD notation**. Algorithms for multiplication and division of BCD numbers typically use this unpacked representation.

EXAMPLE 8.7

Let $N = 8304$ be a 4-digit BCD number.

Unpacked notation	00001000 00000011 00000000 00000100
Packed notation	10000011 00000100

Pure BCD numbers represent unsigned decimal numbers. A variety of representations are available for signed BCD numbers. By appending a sign byte to the number, the BCD integer has a signed-magnitude representation. Recalling the discussion of the base 10 odometer numbers from Chapter 2, a BCD integer N also can be represented in ten's complement notation [10comp (N)].

Definition   For a k-digit BCD integer N, the ten's complement of N is

$$10\text{comp}\ (N) = 10^k - N$$

EXAMPLE 8.8

Assume that a 4-digit BCD number is stored with packed notation in 2 bytes.

(a) Signed-magnitude representation:

$-175 =$	00000001	0000	0001	0111	0101
	Sign (−)		Magnitude		

$8175 =$	00000000	1000	0001	0111	0101
	Sign (+)		Magnitude		

The range of such numbers is $-9999 \leqslant N \leqslant 9999$. They require 3 bytes.

(b) Ten's complement representation:

$$10\text{comp}\ (175) = 10000 - 175 = 9825 =$$

1001	1000	0010	0101

$$8175 =$$

1000	0001	0111	0101

The range of such numbers is $-5000 \leq N \leq 4999$. They require only 2 bytes.

MC68000 BCD Instructions

The MC68000 provides three hardware instructions to implement addition, subtraction, and negation with BCD numbers. Each instruction assumes byte-length operands that permit the addition (subtraction, negation) of two BCD digits stored in packed notation. Each instruction also includes the X bit, permitting extension to multiprecision BCD numbers.

INSTRUCTION

ABCD
(BCD Addition)

Syntax   ABCD   Dm,Dn
          ABCD $-(\text{A}m), -(\text{A}n)$

Action   The 8-bit source is added as packed BCD digits to the 8-bit destination along with the value of the X bit. The result is stored in the destination operand.

Notes

1. The C and X bits are set if a decimal carry occurs.

2. The operation is a byte operation only.

3. The Z bit is cleared if the result is nonzero; otherwise, it is unaffected.

EXAMPLE 8.9

BCD Addition
Example

Add two 4-digit BCD numbers.

ABCD $-(\text{A}2), -(\text{A}3)$
ABCD $-(\text{A}2), -(\text{A}3)$

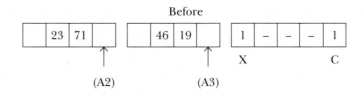

After

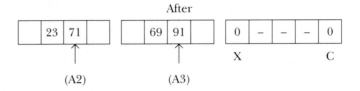

	23	71			69	91		0	–	–	–	0

(A2)   (A3)   X   C

INSTRUCTION

SBCD

BCD Subtraction

Syntax   SBCD   Dm,Dn
SBCD   – (Am), – (An)

Action   The 8-bit source plus the value of the extend bit are subtracted as BCD digits from the 8-bit destination. The result is stored in the destination operand.

Note

1. The X and C bits are set if a decimal borrow occurs.

2. The Z bit is cleared if the result is nonzero; otherwise, it is unaffected.

EXAMPLE 8.10

BCD Subtraction
Examples

Subtract two 4-digit BCD numbers.

SBCD   – (A2), – (A3)
SBCD   – (A2), – (A3)

Before

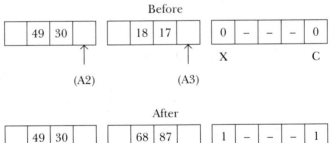

	49	30			18	17		0	–	–	–	0

(A2)   (A3)   X   C

After

	49	30			68	87		1	–	–	–	1

(A2)   (A3)   X   C

INSTRUCTION

NBCD

BCD Negation

Syntax   NBCD   ⟨ea⟩

Action   The contents of the destination location and the extend bit are subtracted from 0, and the result is stored in the destination location. That is, ⟨destination⟩ is replaced by

$$0 - \langle\text{destination}\rangle - X$$

The operation is performed using decimal arithmetic.

Notes

1. If the X bit is 0, NBCD computes the ten's complement. If X = 1, NBCD subtracts from 99 (the nine's complement).

2. The X and C bits are set if a decimal borrow occurs. In fact, X and C are 0 only if the contents of the destination and the incoming value of X are both 0.

3. The Z bit is cleared if the result is nonzero; otherwise, it is unchanged.

EXAMPLE 8.11

BCD Negate Example

Execute the instruction NBCD D0 for different values of D0.

D0 BEFORE		D0 AFTER	
BCD Digits	X Bit	BCD Digits	X Bit
61	1	38	1
77	0	23	1
99	0	01	1
00	0	00	0
99	1	00	1

BCD Library Routines

This section develops two internal conversion routines, PACK and UNPACK, for the BCD library. A four-digit BCD number is stored in 2 bytes using packed notation. In unpacked notation, the BCD number is stored in a 4-byte long word. The routines introduce the MC68000 rotate instructions ROL and ROR. An application program uses these routines and the ABCD instruction to emulate a "point of sales" cash register.

INSTRUCTIONS

ROL/ROR
(Rotate Left and Right)

Syntax

ROL.⟨size⟩	#N,D*n*		ROR.⟨size⟩	#N,D*n*
ROL.⟨size⟩	D*m*,D*n*		ROR.⟨size⟩	D*m*,D*n*
ROL	⟨ea⟩		ROR	⟨ea⟩

Action The bits of the destination operand are rotated (left or right). The extend bit is not included in the rotation. The number of bits rotated is determined by the source operand.

Notes

1. For ROL, bits are rotated left, with bits rotated out of the high-order bit going to both the carry bit and the low-order bit.

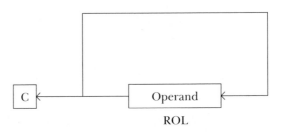

ROL

2. For ROR, bits are rotated right, with bits rotated out of the low-order bit going to both the carry bit and the high-order bit.

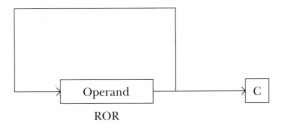

ROR

3. Rotate count in the range 1–8 may use immediate data.

4. Rotate count in the range 1–63 must use data register Dm. The low-order 6 bits of the unsigned value in Dm are used as the rotate count.

5. Memory is rotated only 1 bit, and the operand size must be "W".

EXAMPLE 8.12

Rotate Examples

(a) ROL.W   #8,D3

Before			After	
2A3F	174B		2A3F	4B17

D3 (Before)   D3 (After)

(b) MOVE.W   #24,D5
    ROR.L   D5,D2

Before			After	
10F6	2D08		F62D	0810

D2 (Before)   D2 (After)

The low-order 3-bytes (24 bits) in D2 are rotated clockwise to the high-order 3 bytes.

(c) ROR   MEM

Before	After
F804	7C02
MEM	MEM

The PACK Routine

A BCD routine PACK (UnpackedNumber,PackedNumber) passes the address of a 4-byte unpacked BCD number on the stack. The bytes are processed with a sequence of shift and rotate instructions, and the equivalent packed number is returned in memory. The address of this memory location is passed on the stack.

Parameters passed
  Address of the unpacked four-digit BCD number on stack.
  Address of the resulting packed BCD number on the stack.
Parameters returned
  The packed number is stored in the destination location.

```
srcterm:    equ     8
desterm:    equ     12
param8:     equ     8

pack:   link      a6,#0
        movem.l   d0-d2/a0-a1,-(sp)
        movea.l   (srcterm,a6),a0
        movea.l   (desterm,a6),a1
        move.l    (a0),d0            ; store unpacked number in d0
        clr.w     d1                 ; clear word in d1
        moveq     #3,d2              ; look at four bytes
pack1:  add.b     d0,d1
        lsr.l     #8,d0              ; shift to next byte
        ror.w     #4,d1              ; rotate bcd digit
        dbra      d2,pack1
        move.w    d1,(a1)            ; store packed number in memory
        movem.l   (sp)+,d0-d2/a0-a1  ; clean up stack
        unlk      a6
        move.l    (sp),(param8,sp)
        addq.w    #param8,sp
        rts
```

The UNPACK Routine

A BCD routine UNPACK(PackedNumber,UnpackedNumber) passes the address of a 2-byte packed BCD number on the stack. The bytes are expanded with a sequence of shift-and-rotate instructions, and the equivalent unpacked number is returned in memory. The address of this memory location is passed on the stack.

Parameters passed
    Address of packed four-digit BCD number on stack.
    Address of resulting unpacked BCD number on the stack.
Parameters returned
    The unpacked number is stored in the destination location.

```
srcterm:    equ     8
desterm:    equ     12
param8:     equ     8

unpack:     link    a6,#0
            movem.l d0-d2/a0-a1,-(sp)
            movea.l (srcterm,a6),a0
            movea.l (desterm,a6),a1
            move.w  (a0),d0             ; store packed number in d0
            clr.l   d1                  ; clear word in d1
            moveq   #3,d2               ; look at four bcd digits
unpack1:    move.b  d0,d1
            andi.b  #$0f,d1             ; extend bcd digit to a byte
            ror.l   #8,d1               ; store unpacked digit
            lsr.w   #4,d0               ; shift to next bcd digit
            dbra    d2,unpack1
            move.l  d1,(a1)
            movem.l (sp)+,d0-d2/a0-a1
            unlk    a6
            move.l  (sp),(param8,sp)
            addq.w  #param8,sp
            rts
```

A demonstration program gives a simple example of BCD arithmetic. A cash register accepts ASCII decimal input for sales receipts in the range $00.00–99.99. Items are entered and a total is output in the same ASCII decimal format. The code conversions are outlined to assist you.

Assume that 74.59 is the ASCII input string.

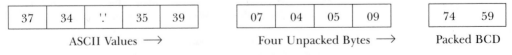

ASCII Values $\longrightarrow$ Four Unpacked Bytes $\longrightarrow$ Packed BCD

For output, the conversions are reversed.

PROGRAM 8.6

Point-of-Sales Cash
Register

Enter a series of cash amounts in the form xx.xx where each digit x is in
the range 0–9. The form represents a dollar amount $XX.XX with decimal
places giving the cents. Terminate the input with the amount 00.00. This
program will convert the ASCII digits into four unpacked BCD bytes. After
packing the digits, the amount is added to a running total, which on conclusion of input, is then unpacked, reconverted to ASCII digits, and output.

```
            xref      strin, strout, stop
            entry     start
            include   BCDLib.i
start:
            clr.w     sum                 ; clear initial value of sum
            lea       sum,a1              ; a1 points to the total
getsale:    jsr       loadamt             ; read and pack 4 digit input
            tst.w     (a0)                ; test for 0.00 input
            beq.s     printsum
            move.w    #$04,ccr            ; set x clear z
            addq.l    #2,a0               ; set up to add two bcd bytes
            addq.l    #2,a1
            abcd      -(a0),-(a1)
            abcd      -(a0),-(a1)
            bra       getsale
printsum:
            pea       unpknum
            move.l    a1,-(sp)            ; a0 points to the total
            jsr       unpack              ; unpack into 4 bytes
            lea       unpknum,a1
            jsr       outsum
            jsr       stop

; enter the amount in the input buffer and then convert into
; 4 packed bcd digits. set a0 to point at the packed digits

loadamt:    movem.l   d0/a1,-(sp)
            lea       unpknum,a1
            lea       buf,a0
            moveq     #6,d0
            jsr       strin
            clr.l     (a1)                ; set 4 bcd bytes to 0
            addq.l    #5,a0               ; skip the null terminator
            addq.l    #4,a1
            move.b    -(a0),-(a1)         ; move the cents into
            move.b    -(a0),-(a1)         ; the unpacked bytes
            subq.l    #1,a0               ; skip the decimal point
            move.b    -(a0),-(a1)         ; move the dollars into
            move.b    -(a1),-(a1)         ; the unpacked bytes
; convert ascii to decimal
            andi.l    #$0f0f0f0f,(a1)
            pea       pknum               ; push address of packed bytes
            move.l    a1,-(sp)            ; push unpacked number on stack
```

```
              jsr       pack
              lea       pknum, a0        ; set a0 to the packed bytes
              movem.l   (sp)+, d0/a1
              rts

outsum:       movem.l   d0/a0-a1, -(sp)
              lea       buf, a0
; convert decimal to ascii
              ori.l     #$30303030, (a1)
              addq.l    #6, a0           ; set a0 to end of buffer
              addq.l    #4, a1           ; set a1 to end of unpacked bytes
              move.b    #$0a, -(a0)      ; put newline at end of buffer
              move.b    -(a1), -(a0)     ; move "cents" into the next
              move.b    -(a1), -(a0)     ; bytes of the buffer
              move.b    #'.', -(a0)      ; put a "." in the buffer
              move.b    -(a1), -(a0)     ; move dollars into the buffer
              move.b    -(a1), -(a0)
              move.w    #5, d0
              jsr       strout
              movem.l   (sp)+, d0/a0-a1
              rts

              data
buf:          ds.b      6
unpknum:      ds.b      4
pknum:        ds.b      2
sum:          ds.b      2

              end
```

⟨Run of Program 8.6⟩

```
44.48
10.64
09.21
00.00
64.33
```

8.4 | FLOATING-POINT NUMBERS

In scientific notation, a **floating-point number** is a number consisting of digits (mantissa) and an exponent that defines the location of a decimal point. You are familiar with base-10 floating-point numbers written using fixed-point form. They are partitioned into a whole-number part and a fractional part split by a decimal point. The positional value of the fractional digits are 1/10, 1/100, 1/1000, and so forth, computed left to right from the decimal point.

$$-25638 \times 10^{-3} = -25.638$$

As with whole numbers, there are corresponding binary floating-point representations. The binary floating-point numbers contain a whole-number part, a binary-fraction part, and a binary point, with the fraction digits having positional value 1/2, 1/4, 1/8, and so forth. The general form of such a representation is

$$N = b_n \cdots b_0 . b_{-1} b_{-2} \cdots = b_n 2^n + \cdots + b_0 + b_{-1} 2^{-1} + b_{-2} 2^{-2} + \cdots$$

The conversion between decimal and binary floating-point numbers uses algorithms similar to those developed for whole numbers. Conversion to decimal numbers is accomplished by creating the decimal expansion of a binary floating-point number. The reverse process is more complex, because even simple decimal numbers may require an infinite binary representation to create the equivalent floating-point number. On a computer, the number of digits is limited because only floating-point numbers with a fixed number of bits are used.

EXAMPLE 8.13

Floating-Point Number Examples

Using expanded notation, convert the binary floating-point number to a decimal number.

(a) $1101.101_2 = 8 + 4 + 1 + 1/2 + 1/8 = 13.625$
$= 8 + 4 + 1 + 0.5 + 0.125 = 13.625$

(b) $0.01101_2 = 1/4 + 1/8 + 1/32$
$= 0.25 + 0.125 + 0.03125 = 0.40625$

Convert the decimal number to a binary floating-point number.

(c) $4.3125 = 4 + 0.25 + 0.0625 = 100.0101_2$

(d) The decimal number 0.15 does not have an equivalent fixed-length binary fraction. The partial sum in an infinite binary expansion is an approximation to the decimal value.

$$0.15 = 1/8 + 1/64 + 1/128 + 1/1024 + \cdots = 0.0010011001 \ldots_2$$

Most computers store floating-point numbers in binary form using scientific notation, with a sign, mantissa, and exponent.

$$N = \pm D_n D_{n-1} \cdots D_1 D_0 . d_1 d_2 \cdots d_n \times 2^e$$

The familiar rules for decimal numbers in scientific notation apply to binary numbers.

$$\text{Decimal numbers} \quad 103870.\,67 = 0.10387067 \times 10^6$$
$$= 103870670.0 \times 10^{-3}$$
$$\text{Binary numbers} \quad 1101.101 = 0.1101101 \times 2^4$$
$$= 0.01101101 \times 2^5$$

In the binary representation, numbers to the right of the "binary point" have decimal value 0.5, 0.25, 0.125, 0.06125, and so forth.

Over the years, computer vendors have implemented a variety of formats to store floating-point numbers. With the growth of third-party hardware and software, there is a strong movement to standardize the format. The Institute of Electrical and Electronics Engineers (IEEE) standard has been adopted by Motorola for some of its hardware. It creates compact memory storage for a number and is referred to as an **internal format**. An equivalent expanded representation is introduced as an external format in the next section.

Floating-Point Internal Format

The IEEE format uses a signed-magnitude representation and stores the exponent as an unsigned number. A standardized or normalized form permits a unique representation for each floating-point number.

Normalized Form   The floating-point number is adjusted to have a single nonzero digit to the left of the binary point.

$$N = \pm 1 . d_1 d_2 \cdots d_{n-1} \times 2^e$$

The floating-point number 0.0 is stored with sign, exponent, and mantissa of 0.

EXAMPLE 8.14   Binary numbers are converted to a normalized form representation.

Binary Number	*Normalized Form*
1101.101×2^1	1.1011010×2^4
0.0011×2^6	1.1×2^3
1.1×2^0	1.1×2^0

The normalized binary floating-point representation has a 1 in the most significant digit unless the number is 0.

Internal IEEE Format

Length   A number is stored in 32-bit (single-precision) or 64-bit (double-precision) length.

Sign The high-order bit (bit 31 or bit 63) is used for the sign. A "+" has 0 sign bit, and a "−" has a 1 sign bit.

Exponent The exponent is stored in 8 bits for 32-bit numbers or 11 bits for 64-bit numbers. For a 32-bit number, the exponent falls in the range $-127 \leq \text{exp} \leq 127$. In order to ensure that all exponents are stored as positive (unsigned) numbers, the IEEE format specifies using "excess-n" notation for the exponent. A stored exponent, Exp_s, is created by adding n to the real exponent. With excess 127 notation,

$$\text{Exp}_s = \text{Exp} + 127$$

The new exponent is said to have a **bias** of 127, where bias implies a shift to the range of positive numbers. A 32-bit number has a bias of 1023.

Size	True Exponent Range	Stored Exponent Range
32 bits	$-127 \leq \text{Exp} \leq 128$	$0 \leq \text{Exp}_s \leq 255$
64 bits	$-1023 \leq \text{Exp} \leq 1024$	$0 \leq \text{Exp}_s \leq 2047$

Mantissa A number has normalized form $1.f \times 2^e$ when $1.f$ is the significant part of the number and f is the fractional digits. The leading digit is 1. When storing the number, the leading digit is hidden and the fractional digits are stored in the mantissa.

Size	Mantissa Size	Significant Digits
32 bits	23	$23 + 1 = 24$
64 bits	52	$52 + 1 = 53$

Sign	Exponent	Mantissa
1 Bit	8 or 11 Bits	23 or 52 Bits

EXAMPLE 8.15

Internal Floating-Point Number Examples

(a) The internal format representation of 1.0 is \$3F800000.
Normalized Form: 1.00000×2^0
Sign: Positive with sign bit = 0
Exponent: $\text{Exp}_s = 0 + 127 = 127 = 01111111_2$
Mantissa: $\langle 1 \rangle\, 000000000 \ldots 00$

0	0111 1111	000 0000 0000 0000 0000 0000

$$1.0 = 0\ 01111111\ 000\ 0000 \ldots 0000 = 3F800000_{16}$$

(b) The internal representation of -0.1875 is \$BE400000.
Normalized Form: $(-)\ 1.100 \times 2^{-3}$
Sign: 1
Exponent: $\text{Exp}_s = -3 + 127 = 124 = 01111100_2$
Mantissa: $\langle 1 \rangle\ 1000000 \ldots 0$

1	0111 1100	100 0000 0000 0000 0000

(c) The internal representation of 12.5 is

$$0\ 1000\ 0010\ \langle 1 \rangle\ 100100 \ldots 0 = \$41480000$$

Floating-Point External Format

The compact storage of floating-point numbers does not permit efficient use of MC68000 instructions to implement the arithmetic operations. The "hidden 1," the excess-127 storage of the exponent, signed-magnitude representation, and the compact storage of the mantissa are but a few of the problems. Similar to BCD numbers, a corresponding unpacked representation of floating-point numbers must be used. This section develops such a representation and refers to it as **external format**. The internal and external formats are also referred to as **packed** and **unpacked** representations, respectively.

In practice, floating-point numbers are stored in memory in packed representation. They are read from memory and unpacked prior to implementing an arithmetic operation. The result is then normalized and packed before it is stored in memory. Assuming IEEE 32-bit internal format, subroutines PACK, UNPACK, and NORMALIZE are implemented in this section. These will be used in subsequent sections to implement subroutines to add, subtract, and multiply floating-point numbers. Typically these subroutines would be included in a library.

External Format
Unpacked Representation

Sign   A 16-bit word with value 0 or 1.

Exponent   A 16-bit signed integer in the range $-127 \leq \text{Exp} \leq 128$.

Mantissa   A 24-bit unsigned integer stored in a long word; the most significant digit 1 is stored in bit 23.

Sign		Exponent		0000 0000	1	Mantissa
15	0	15	0	31	24 23 22	0

EXAMPLE 8.16

Floating-Point
Numbers

Binary floating-point numbers are given in equivalent IEEE internal and external formats. The latter format is given as a triple.

Number	Internal Format	External Format		
3.0	40400000	0000	0001	00C00000
−0.1875	BE400000	0001	FFFD	00C00000
12.5	41480000	0000	0003	00C10000

Floating-Point Storage Routines

The initial routines for a floating-point library are created in this section. The utility routines UNPACKFLOAT, PACKFLOAT, SHIFT, and NORMALIZE are used extensively by the other library routines and pass parameters using registers.

An algorithm to convert (unpack) a floating-point number from internal to external format involves a series of shifts and masks. The unpacked representation is a three-field record. Assuming that address register A0 points to the record, each field is accessed as an offset to this base address.

```
SIGN:   EQU   0
EXP:    EQU   2
MANT:   EQU   4
```

Unpack Float Algorithm

Assuming that the floating-point number is stored in packed format as a long word in D0, the following steps convert the number to unpacked representation. The subroutine UNPACKFLOAT is the MC68000 code for the algorithm.

Sign   Test the sign bit in D0 with TST.L D0. Depending on the value of the Z bit, store a 0 or a 1 in the sign field.

Mantissa   Copy D0 to D1 and mask the low-order 23 bits in D1. Restore the hidden 1 in bit 23. The result in D1 is then stored in the mantissa field.

```
MOVE.L   D0,D1
ANDI.L   #$7FFFFF,D1
ORI.L    #$800000,D1
```

Exponent   Swap the exponent to (D0.W).

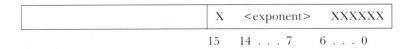

	X	\<exponent\>	XXXXXX
	15	14 . . . 7	6 . . . 0

Shift bits 14–7 to the LSB of D0 and clear the MSB of D0. Derive the real exponent by subtracting 127 from the stored exponent. The result is stored in the exponent field.

```
SWAP     D0
LSR.W    #7,D0
ANDI.W   #$FF,D0
SUBI.W   #127,D0
```

UNPACKFLOAT

Parameter passed
   (D0.W) contains the packed representation.
   (A0) points to the unpacked representation.
Parameter returned
   The unpacked representation is stored in memory at (A0).

```
sign:         equ     0
exp:          equ     2
mant:         equ     4

unpackfloat:  movem.l  d0-d1,-(sp)
              clr.w    (sign,a0)       ; clear sign
              tst.l    d0              ; test sign of internal
              bne.s    unpack0
              clr.w    (sign,a0)       ; clear sign
              clr.w    (exp,a0)        ; clear exponent
              clr.l    (mant,a0)       ; clear mantissa
              bra.s    unpack2
unpack0:      bpl.s    unpack1         ; set sign 0(+), 1(-)
              move.w   #1,(sign,a0)
unpack1:      move.l   d0,d1
              andi.l   #$7fffff,d1     ; mask the mantissa
              ori.l    #$800000,d1     ; add hidden high order bit
              move.l   d1,(mant,a0)    ; save high 1+23 bits of mant
              swap     d0
              lsr.w    #7,d0           ; move exponent to lsb
              andi.w   #$ff,d0         ; isolate exponent
              subi.w   #127,d0         ; convert from excess 127
              move.w   d0,(exp,a0)     ; store exponent
unpack2:      movem.l  (sp)+,d0-d1
              rts
```

Pack Float Algorithm

The algorithm takes a floating-point number stored in unpacked format in memory and returns the corresponding packed form in D0. The MC68000 code is given in the subroutine PACKFLOAT. Assume that A0 points at the unpacked floating-point number.

Exponent   The exponent is copied into D0, and the bias $+127$ is added.

```
        MOVE.W   (EXP,A0),D0
        ADDI.W   #127,D0
```

Sign   Store the sign as bit B_8 in D0. For a negative number, the sign bit is set using the OR operator.

```
        TST.W   (SIGN,A0)
            ⋮                 ; IF NEGATIVE
        ORI.W   #$100,D0
```

Now relocate the sign and exponent into the high-order 9 bits of D0.

```
        SWAP   D0         ; SHIFT LEFT 16 BITS
        LSL.L   #7,D0      ; SHIFT 7 MORE BITS
```

Mantissa   The mantissa with a hidden 1 is stored in the low-order 23 bits of D0.

```
        MOVE.L   (MANT,A0),D1
        ANDI.L   #$7FFFFF,D1   ; HIDE THE 1
        OR.L     D1,D0         ; COPY TO D0
```

PACKFLOAT

Parameters passed
(A0) points to the unpacked representation.
Parameters returned
D0 contains the packed representation.

```
sign:       equ     0
exp:        equ     2
mant:       equ     4

packfloat:  move.l  d1,-(sp)
            clr.l   d0
            tst.w   (exp,a0)        ; test for zero
            bne.s   pack0
            tst.l   (mant,a0)
            beq.s   pack2
```

```
pack0:      clr.l     d1                    ; clear (d0),(d1)
            move.w    (exp,a0),d0           ; get exponent
            addi.w    #127,d0               ; convert to excess 127
            tst.w     (sign,a0)             ; set sign
            beq.s     pack1                 ; sign bit 0(+), 1(−)
            ori.w     #$100,d0
pack1:      swap      d0                    ; align sign and exponent
            lsl.l     #7,d0                 ; in high part of d0
            move.l    (mant,a0),d1          ; get mantissa
            andi.l    #$7fffff,d1           ; delete high order hidden bit
            or.l      d1,d0                 ; put high 23 bits of mantissa
pack2:      move.l    (sp)+,d1
            rts                             ; return
```

The unpacked representation assumes that the floating-point number is stored in external format. In many cases, the mantissa may not have a leading 1 in bit 23. In such a case, use the subroutine NORMALIZE, which takes a mantissa stored as a long word and shifts the bits so that the most significant digit has value 1 in bit 23. Depending on the direction of shift, the exponent is adjusted.

Shift Left: Add 1 to the exponent. For instance,

$$11.0 \times 2^0 = 1.1 \times 2^1$$

Shift Right: Subtract 1 from the exponent. For instance,

$$0.11 \times 2^4 = 1.1 \times 2^3$$

The subroutine SHIFT is called by NORMALIZE to perform the actual shift.

SHIFT

Parameters passed
(A0) points at the unpacked representation.
D0 contains the shift count.

```
sign:       equ       0
exp:        equ       2
mant:       equ       4

shift:      movem.l   d1/d2,−(sp)
            clr.l     d1
            move.l    (mant,a0),d2          ; load mantissa
            move.w    d0,d1                 ; examine exponent correction
            bmi.s     shift1                ; shift left
            bne.s     shift0                ; shift right
            bra.s     shift3                ; no shift
```

```
shift0:    asr.l     #1,d2          ; shift mantissa right
           subq.w    #1,d1          ; repeat until count is zero
           bne       shift0
           and.l     #$ffffff,d2    ; clear high order byte
           bra       shift2         ; prepare to return
shift1:    asl.l     #1,d2          ; shift mantissa left
           addq.w    #1,d1          ; repeat until count is zero
           bne       shift1
shift2:    move.l    d2,(mant,a0)   ; store mantissa
shift3:    movem.l   (sp)+,d1/d2
           rts
```

NORMALIZE

Parameter passed
(A0) points at the unpacked representation.

```
sign:      equ       0
exp:       equ       2
mant:      equ       4
normalize: movem.l   d0/d1,-(sp)    ; use (d0) for offset/shift
           moveq     #1,d0
           move.l    (mant,a0),d1
           bne.s     normal0
           clr.w     d0             ; zero shift count
           bra.s     normal1
normal0:   subq.w    #1,d0          ; find most significant bit
           asl.l     #1,d1
           bcc.s     normal0
           addq.w    #8,d0          ; d0 contains exp correction
normal1:   add.w     d0,(exp,a0)    ; adjust exponent
           jsr       shift          ; shift mantissa
           movem.l   (sp)+,d0/d1
           rts
```

Floating-Point I/O Routines

Two basic I/O routines, READFLOAT and PRINTFLOAT, demonstrate floating-point numbers stored in both packed and unpacked format. The I/O routines are used to test the floating-point routines and are not intended to be of general use. For input, data is read into the fields of an unpacked number whose address is stored in A0. The routine assumes that the sign, exponent, and mantissa are entered in that order, each on a separate line. The binary point is assumed to be located immediately to the right of the 24th bit of the mantissa. For instance, you can enter the number 1 in any of the following ways:

Sign	Exponent	Mantissa
0	0	800000
0	2	200000
0	17	1

READFLOAT normalizes and packs the floating-point number before returning the value in D0. PRINTFLOAT assumes that a packed number is stored in D0 and prints the unpacked representation of the number.

READFLOAT

Parameter returned
D0—The packed floating-point number.

```
sign:        equ     0
exp:         equ     2
mant:        equ     4
unpkarea2:   equ     8

readfloat:   link     a6,#0
             suba.w   #unpkarea2,sp
             move.l   a0,(sp)
             lea      (unpkarea2,a6),a0    ; set a0 to point at record
             jsr      hexin               ; input sign
             move.w   d0,(sign,a0)
             jsr      hexin               ; input exponent
             move.w   d0,(exp,a0)
             jsr      hexin_long          ; input mantissa
             move.l   d0,(mant,a0)
             jsr      normalize
             jsr      packfloat
             move.l   (sp)+,a0
             unlk     a6                  ; clear the 8 bytes on stack
             rts
```

PRINTFLOAT

Parameters passed
D0 contains the packed floating-point number.

```
sign:        equ     0
exp:         equ     2
mant:        equ     4
unpkarea2:   equ     8

printfloat:  link     a6,#0               ; create unpack space on stack
             subq.w   #unpkarea2,sp
             movem.l  d0/a0,-(sp)
```

```
lea       (-unpkarea2,a6),a0
jsr       unpackfloat     ; unpack (d0) in the space
move.w    (sign,a0),d0    ; write out sign
jsr       hexout
move.w    (exp,a0),d0     ; write out exponent
jsr       hexout
move.l    (mant,a0),d0    ; write out mantissa as long word
jsr       hexout_long
jsr       newline
movem.l   (sp)+,d0/a0
unlk      a6              ; clean out unpack area
rts
```

Floating-Point Addition/Subtraction

Floating-point operations assume that the numbers are stored in unpacked representation. Given that sign magnitude is used, the algorithms apply the usual base-10 arithmetic rule of signs. Base-10 arithmetic examples motivate the algorithms. From experience, you could anticipate that the addition algorithm involves a shifting of the mantissa to align the decimal point. Subtraction is performed by changing signs and adding. Before examining the MC68000 code, consider a base-10 example.

EXAMPLE 8.17   Add the decimal floating-point numbers

$$-200.005 + 17.5$$

Assume that -200.005 is stored in scientific notation as -2.00005×10^2 and that 17.5 is stored as 1.75×10^1.

(a) Select the term with the smaller exponent and then shift its mantissa so that the exponents are equal. Select 1.75 and shift one position to the left.

(b) Add the mantissas using the usual rule of signs.

$$
\begin{array}{r}
(-) \quad 2.00005 \times 10^2 \\
+ \quad 0.17500 \times 10^2 \\
\hline
(-1)\ 1.82505 \times 10^2 = -182.505
\end{array}
$$

The following code implements the algorithm for binary floating-point numbers. The two terms are passed on the stack in packed format. (A0) and (A1) are set to point to the unpacked representations. The sum is normalized, packed, and then returned in D0.

In comparing exponents, (A0) is set to point to the smaller term. The new "Exchange Register" (EXG) instruction allows a simple switch of pointers (A0) and (A1).

INSTRUCTION

EXG
(Exchange
Registers)

Syntax   EXG   R*m*,R*n*   R represents a DATA or ADDRESS Register.

Action   The 32-bit contents of registers R*m* and R*n* are exchanged.

Note   The CCR bits are not affected.

EXAMPLE 8.18

Exchange Register
Example

EXG   A1,A0

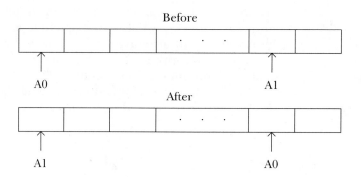

The pointers (A0) and (A1) are exchanged.

FADD

Parameters passed
    The terms A and B are on the stack in packed format.
Parameter returned
    The sum is returned in D0.

```
sign:          equ      0
exp:           equ      2
mant:          equ      4

a:             equ      8
b:             equ      12
addsize:       equ      8
unpkareas1:    equ      16

fadd:   link     a6,#0                    ; get space to unpack a and b
        suba.w   #unpkarea1,sp
        movem.l  d1/a0-a1,-(sp)
```

```
         lea        (-unpkarea1+8,a6),a0   ; set a0 to 8 byte record
         move.l     (b,a6),d0              ; unpacked b
         jsr        unpackfloat
         movea.l    a0,a1                  ; a1 points at unpacked b
         lea        (-unpkarea1,a6),a0     ; now (a0) points at the 8 byte
         move.l     (a,a6),d0              ; record unpacked a
         jsr        unpackfloat
         move.w     (exp,a0),d0            ; compare exponents
         move.w     (exp,a1),d1
         sub.w      d1,d0
         bmi.s      fadd0                  ; exp(a0) < exp(a1)
         exg        a1,a0                  ; (a0) points to smaller value
         jsr        shift                  ; shift mant(a0)
         add.w      d0,(exp,a0)            ; adjust exp(a0) after shift
         bra.s      fadd1
fadd0:   neg.w      d0                     ; make (d0) positive
         jsr        shift
         add.w      d0,(exp,a0)
; test the signs-- represent (-)n as neg(n)
fadd1:   tst.w      (sign,a0)
         beq.s      fadd2
         neg.l      (mant,a0)
fadd2:   move.l     (mant,a0),d0
         tst.w      (sign,a1)
         beq.s      fadd3
         neg.l      (mant,a1)
fadd3:   move.l     (mant,a1),d1
         add.l      d0,d1                  ; add the mantissas
; test the sign. if negative, both terms are negative or the negative
; term had larger mantissa. similarly for positive sum
         neg.l      d1
         move.w     #1,(sign,a0)           ; set sign of sum negative
         bra.s      fadd5
fadd4:   move.w     #0,(sign,a0)           ; set sign of sum positive
fadd5:   move.l     d1,(mant,a0)
         jsr        normalize
         jsr        packfloat
         movem.l    (sp)+,d1/a0-a1
         unlk       a6
         move.l     (sp),(addsize,sp)
         addq.l     #addsize,sp
         rts
```

FSUB

Parameters passed
    A and B are on the stack.
Parameter returned
    The difference is returned in D0.

Note: The algorithm computes A − B = A + (−B).

```
sign:     equ        0
exp:      equ        2
mant:     equ        4

a:        equ        8
b:        equ        12
subsize equ          8

fsub:     link       a6,#0
          bchg       #7,(b,a6)            ; reverse sign of b
          move.l     (a,a6),-(sp)         ; push a on stack
          move.l     (b,a6),-(sp)         ; push negated b on stack
          jsr        fadd
          unlk       a6                   ; perform addition
          move.l     (sp),(subsize,sp)
          addq.l     #subsize,sp
          rts
```

Floating-Point Multiplication

The algorithm to multiply floating-point numbers follows a simple set of rules. The main problem involves determining the mantissa of the product.

Sign   Use the rule of signs for multiplication.

>   The product of like signs is positive.
>   The product of unlike signs is negative.

Exponent   The exponent of the product is the sum of the exponents of the factors.

Mantissa   The mantissas for the two factors are multiplied as unsigned numbers. The product must be truncated to 24-bit precision.
   Note: A mantissa is a 24-bit unsigned number with most significant digit 1 representing 2^{23}. If neither number is 0, the minimal product is

$$\underbrace{1000\ldots000}_{24} \times \underbrace{1000\ldots000}_{24} = 2^{46} = \underbrace{01000\ldots000}_{48}$$

and the maximum product is

$$\underbrace{1111\ldots111}_{24} \times \underbrace{1111\ldots111}_{24} = 2^{48} - 2^{25} + 1$$

$$= \underbrace{111\ldots111}_{23}\underbrace{000\ldots0001}_{25}$$

The 47- or 48-bit product must be truncated to a 24-bit mantissa. Significant digits and precision are lost in the process.

MANT(A)   MANT(B)

0000	0000	1xxxx ..	X	0000	0000	1xxxx ..

64-Bit Product

0000	0000	0000	0000	X1xxxxxxxxxxx ..

X = 0 or 1 Depending on the Numbers Multiplied

The FMUL algorithm uses the 32-bit-by-32-bit unsigned multiplication routine UMUL32. The high-order 32 bits of the product are stored in D0, whereas the low-order 32 bits are stored in D1. Nine bits are shifted out of the high end of D1 to form MANT(Product) in D0.

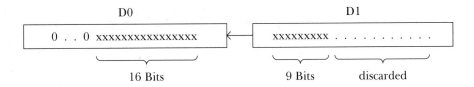

D0	D1
0 .. 0 xxxxxxxxxxxxxxx	xxxxxxxxx . . . .

16 Bits   9 Bits   discarded

FMUL

Parameters passed
   A and B are on the stack in packed format.
Parameter returned
   The product is returned in D0.

```
sign:       equ     0
exp:        equ     2
mant:       equ     4

a:          equ     8
b:          equ     12
mulsize:    equ     8
unpkarea1:  equ     16

fmul:       link    a6,#0                  ; allocate 16 bytes
            suba.l  #unpkarea1,sp
            movem.l d1-d2/a0-a1,-(sp)
            lea     (-unpkarea1+8,a6),a0   ; address for unpacked b
            move.l  (b,a6),d0
            jsr     unpackfloat            ; unpack b
            movea.l a0,a1                  ; set a1 at unpacked b
            lea     (-unpkarea1,a6),a0     ; address for unpacked a
            move.l  (a,a6),d0
```

```
          jsr      unpackfloat              ; unpack a
          move.w   (sgn,a1),d0
          eor.w    d0,(sign,a0)             ; set sign for the product
          move.w   (exp,a1),d0
          add.w    d0, (exp,a0)             ; add exponents
          move.l   (mant,a0),-(sp)          ; move mant(a) and mant(b)
          move.l   (mant,a1),-(sp)          ; to the stack for umul32
          jsr      umul32
          moveq    #8,d2
; the minimum product has a 1 in bit 46 (2**23 × 2**23)
; to ensure truncated exp has a 1 in bit 23 shift 9 bits into d0
fmul_1:   lsl.l    #1,d1
          roxl.l   #1,d0
          dbra     d2,fmul_1
          move.l   d0,(mant,a0)             ; pass significant bits
          jsr      normalize                ; normalize result
          jsr      packfloat
          movem.l  (sp)+,d1-d2/a0-a1        ; restore registers
          unlk     a6
          move.l   (sp),(mulsize,sp)        ; reset return address
          addq.l   #mulsize,sp
          rts
```

Floating-Point Test Program

A driver program is designed to test the floating-point routines. It allows the user to input a number N in the range 0–3 that is used to select a test routine.

Number N	Driver Routine	Test Routine
0	TESTFREAD	PACK and UNPACK
1	TESTFADD	FADD
2	TESTFSUB	FSUB
3	TESTFMUL	FMUL

Each routine inputs its parameters with READFLOAT and outputs a result using PRINTFLOAT.

PROGRAM 8.7

Floating-Point Test Program

The program tests the nine floating-point routines READFLOAT, PRINT FLOAT, SHIFT, NORMALIZE, UNPACKFLOAT, PACKFLOAT, FADD, FSUB, and FMUL that are stored in a library of floating-point routines.

Note To run the program you must determine the test routine and input the sign, exponent, and mantissa of a floating-point number. The sign is entered as a 0 or 1. The exponent may be any two's complement number in the range $-127 \leq exp \leq 127$. The mantissa may be any 32-bit unsigned number. The READFLOAT routine will store the input in unpacked representation. For example, to enter the binary floating-point number

$$1 = 1.0 \times 2^0$$

and run the READ/WRITE test routine, the following input can be used:

Enter 0	Calls a routine to test FREAD
Enter 0	Sign is 0
Enter 0	Exponent is 0
Enter 800000	Mantissa is 800000

1. The following inputs test the READFLOAT, FADD, and PRINTFLOAT routines. Comments are added to the input values.

   INPUT

0	Tests FREAD routine
0	Sign
0	Exponent
800000	Mantissa

   OUTPUT
   Read/write floating-point number
   3F800000 0000 0000 00800000

2. Test FADD with the following sum: $-13.25 + 8.5 = -4.75$

   $$-13.25 = 0.110101 \times 2^4$$
   $$+8.5 = 1.0001 \times 2^3$$
   $$-4.75 = 1.0011 \times 2^2$$

   INPUT

1	Tests FADD
1	Sign A
4	Exponent A
6A0000	Mantissa A
0	Sign B
3	Exponent B
880000	Mantissa B

   OUTPUT
   Add floating-point numbers
   0001 0002 00980000

3. Test FMUL with the following product: $2.5 \times (-5.0) = 12.50$

   $$2.5 = 1.01 \times 2^1$$
   $$(-5.0) = -1.01 \times 2^2$$
   $$-12.5 = -1.1001 \times 2^3$$

INPUT

3	Tests FMUL
0	Sign A
1	Exponent A
A00000	Mantissa A
1	Sign B
2	Exponent B
A00000	Mantissa B

OUTPUT

Multiply floating-point numbers

0001   0003   00C80000

```
xref strout,hexin,hexin_long,hexout,hexout_long,newline,stop
     entry main

        include  FloatingPointLib.i
        include  ArithmeticLib.i

NewLine: equ      13

main:
; initialize the list of drivers
        lea      stub,a0
        lea      sfread,a1
        move.l   a1,(a0)+
        lea      sfadd,a1
        move.l   a1,(a0)+
        lea      sfsub,a1
        move.l   a1,(a0)+
        lea      sfmul,a1
        move.l   a1,(a0)


; initialize the list of prompts
        lea      stubmsg,a0
        lea      read_prmsg,a1
        move.w   #3,d1
init:   move.l   a1,(a0)+
        adda.w   #36,a1
        dbra     d1,init

        lea      stub,a1        ; load list of drivers
        lea      stubmsg,a0     ; load list of driver prompts
        jsr      hexin          ; get driver# in range 0 - 3
        mulu     #4,d0          ; set 4*(d0) for lookup
        move.l   d0,d1
        movea.l  (0,a1,d1.w),a1 ; load driver address in a1
        movea.l  (0,a0,d1.w),a0 ; load prompt address in a0
        move.w   #36,d0
        jsr      strout         ; print the prompt
```

```
              jsr      (a1)                  ; call the driver routine
              jsr      stop

; driver routines
sfread:       jsr      readfloat             ; into a packed format
              move.l   d0,x                  ; store value in x
              jsr      hexout_long
              jsr      printfloat            ; test printfloat by writing
                                             ; x in unpacked format
              rts

sfadd:        jsr      readfloat
              move.l   d0,x                  ; load first term in x
              jsr      readfloat
              move.l   d0,y
              move.l   y,-(sp)               ; push x and y on the stack
              move.l   x,-(sp)               ; in packed format
              jsr      fadd                  ; add them
              jsr      printfloat            ; print result in d0 in
                                             ; unpacked format
              rts

sfsub:        jsr      readfloat
              move.l   d0,x                  ; load first term in x
              jsr      readfloat
              move.l   d0,y
              move.l   y,-(sp)               ; push x and y on the stack
              move.l   x,-(sp)               ; in packed format
              jsr      fsub                  ; subtract them
              jsr      printfloat            ; print result in d0 in
                                             ; unpacked format
              rts

sfmul:        jsr      readfloat
              move.l   d0,x                  ; load first term in x
              jsr      readfloat
              move.l   d0,y
              move.l   y,-(sp)               ; push x and y on the stack
              move.l   x,-(sp)               ; in packed format
              jsr      fmul                  ; multiply them
              jsr      printfloat            ; print result in d0 in
                                             ; unpacked format
              rts

              data

stub:         ds.l  4
stubmsg:

              ds.l  4

x:            ds.b  8
y:            ds.b  8
read_prmsg:
              dc.b  ' read/write floating point number  ',NewLine
```

```
addmsg:    dc.b  ' adding floating point numbers      ',NewLine
submsg:    dc.b  ' subtracting floating point numbers ',NewLine
mulmsg:    dc.b  ' multiplying floating point numbers ',NewLine

           end
```

⟨Run of Program 8.7⟩

```
3
multiplying floating point numbers
0 1 a00000
1 2 a00000
0001 0003 00C80000
```

This section has provided a relatively complete discussion of software routines to implement floating-point arithmetic. However, on many systems, a coprocessor handles floating-point numbers. A **floating-point coprocessor** is a separate processor for floating-point computation that resides on the system bus and communicates with the primary processor to pass floating-point data. The floating-point coprocessor performs a variety of floating-point computations at a high rate of speed. The MC68881 floating-point coprocessor can be used with the MC68020/30 processors, and the MC68040 processor contains a built-in floating-point coprocessor, the MC68882. A coprocessor effectively extends the instruction set of the MC68020/30/40 processors to do floating-point computations. Section 15.7 discusses the MC68881.

8.5 | MC68020/30/40 BIT FIELD INSTRUCTIONS

The Motorola 68020/30/40 systems have new instructions and data types that take advantage of the 32-bit data bus. The systems also include new instructions that speed up routines for floating-point processing and other applications and BCD number conversion. This section introduces the bit field data type along with the bit field instructions.

Bit Field Operations

The instructions BTST, BSET, BCLR, and BCHG operate on a single bit. The MC68020 has a family of instructions

BFTST	BFEXTS
BFCHG	BFEXTU

BFCLR   BFFFO
BFSET   BFINS

that perform operations on a range of bits specified by an offset and a width. Such a data structure is called a **bit field**. In a data register, the bit field offset is measured from the leftmost bit. Offset 0 identifies the most significant bit (bit 31) in the data register, and offset 31 identifies the least significant bit (bit 0). The offset specifies the number of bits to skip measured from the leftmost bit of the register. The width, a value in the range 1–32, specifies how many bits to include in the field.

The notation {offset:width} is used to designate a bit field.

31	Dn		0
	XXX . . . X		
Offset	Width		

For example, bits 23–20 of Dn correspond to the bit field {8:4} with offset 8 and width 4. The full 32-bit long word in a register corresponds to bit field {0:32}.

Bit field operations can be applied to data in memory. Three parameters specify the field:

1. The address of a byte in memory is referred to as the base address.

2. A bit field offset is measured relative to the most significant bit of the base address. Thus offset 0 corresponds to bit 7 of the base address. In memory, the offset is in the range -2^{31} to $2^{31} - 1$.

3. A bit field width determines the number of bits in the field. The width may range from 1 to 32.

EXAMPLE 8.19

Assume that the base address is specified by B and that the following data is stored in memory:

(*a*) The bit field B{−12:8} contains hex digits $BC.

(*b*) The bit field B{32:12} contains hex digits $123.

(*c*) The bit field B{−2:5} contains binary digits %01011.

Bit Field Instructions

The MC68020/30/40 provide eight instructions for bit field data. Four single-operand instructions (BFCHG, BFCLR, BFSET, and BFTST) are analogous to the MC68000 bit instructions. The other bit field instructions require two operands. The BFFFO instruction finds the index of the first 1 in the bit field. It is used in conjunction with the BFEXTS, BFEXTU, and BFINS instructions, which copy bit fields to and from data registers.

INSTRUCTION

MC68020/30/40
Single-Operand
Bit Field
Instructions

Syntax

BFCHG	⟨ea⟩{offset:width}	Bit field test and change
BFCLR	⟨ea⟩{offset:width}	Bit field test and clear
BFSET	⟨ea⟩{offset:width}	Bit field test and set
BFTST	⟨ea⟩{offset:width}	Bit field test

Action   Each instruction first tests the bit field and sets the CCR bits. The N bit is set if the most significant bit in the field is 1. The Z bit is set if all bits in the field are 0. The offset specifies the start bit of the field; the width specifies the number of bits in the field.

> BFCHG complements the bits in the field.
>
> BFCLR sets all bits in the field to 0.
>
> BFSET sets all bits in the field to 1.
>
> BFTST tests the field and leaves the bits unchanged.

Notes

1. Only data register direct and control addressing modes may be used for the operand.

2. All instructions clear the C and V bits and leave the X bit unchanged.

3. The offset can be either a constant in the range 0–31 or a data register containing a 32-bit two's complement offset. The width field is either a constant in the range 1–32 or the value of the low-order five bits of a data register.

EXAMPLE 8.20

(*a*) Assume that (D0.L) = $FCA4 0078.
    BFTST   D0{4:8}

> Bit field: %11001010 (bits 4–11)
> CCR bits: C = 0, V = 0, Z = 0, N = 1

(*b*) Assume that (D0.L = $8000   0078.
    BFCHG   D0{24:6}

Bit field: %011110 (bits 24–29)
CCR bits: C = 0, V = 0, Z = 0, N = 0
Result: (D0.L) = $8000 0084

Before				After		
1 . . . 0	0111 10	0 0		1 . . . 0	1000 01	0 0
0 . . . 23	24–29	30 . . . 31		0 . . . 23	24–29	30 . . . 31
	Bits				Bits	

(c) Assume that (D1.L) = $FFFFFFFA (−6) and that the 6-byte contents in memory starting at address A is $FA00 7707 8833.
BFSET A+4{D1:6}

Bit field: %000111 in A + 2

Before				After		
FA00	7707	8833		FA00	773F	8833
A	A + 2	A + 4		A	A + 2	A + 4

INSTRUCTION

MC68020/30/40
Two-Operand
Bit Field
Instructions

Syntax

BFEXTS	⟨ea⟩{offset:width},Dn	Signed extract
BFEXTU	⟨ea⟩{offset:width},Dn	Unsigned extract
BFFFO	⟨ea⟩{offset:width},Dn	Find first one
BFINS	Dn, ⟨ea⟩{offset:width}	Insert

Action

1. The BFEXTS and BFEXTU instructions extract the bit field from the source operand location, extend (signed or unsigned) this field to 32 bits, and store the result in the destination data register.

2. For BFFFO, the bit offset of the most significant 1 in the bit field is stored in the data register. If no 1 is found in the bit field, the sum of the offset and field width is stored in Dn.

3. For BFINS, the low-order w bits in the data register Dn are copied to the bit field specified by the source operand, where w = width.

Notes

1. The N and Z bits of the CCR are set from the value of the bit field. The C and V bits are cleared.

2. The offset field is an immediate operand (range 0–31) or a data register (range -2^{31} to $2^{31} - 1$). The width field is an immediate operand or a data register that can take a value from 1 to 32. The data register numbers and offset/width parameters are specified in an extension word.

EXAMPLE 8.21

(a) Assume that (D0.L) = \$0000008A.
    BFEXTS   D0{24:8},D1

> Bit field in D0: %10001010 (bits 24–31)
> CCR bits: C = 0, V = 0, Z = 0, N = 1
> Result: (D1.L) = \$FFFF FF8A

BFEXTU   D0{24:6},D1

> Bit field in D0: %100010 (bits 24–29)
> CCR bits: C = 0, V = 0, Z = 0, N = 1
> Result: (D1.L) = \$0000 0022

(b) Let (D3) = \$C01F0000 and (D0) = \$0008.
    BFFFO   D3{D0:4},D1

> Bit field in D3: %0001 (bits 8–11)
> CCR bits: C = 0, V = 0, Z = 0, N = 0
> Result: (D1.L) = \$0000 000B (bit 11)

BFFFO   D3{D0:2},D1

> Result: (D1.L) = \$0000 000A

(c) Let (D0.L) = \$000010FA and (D1.L) = \$0007 7F00.
    BFINS   D0,D1{4:8}

> Bit field in D0: \$FA (bits 0–7)
> Result: (D1.L) = \$0FA7 7F00

Floating-point number routines are used to demonstrate the bit field instructions. The pack and unpack routines are rewritten using the new instructions.

Program 8.8 converts a floating-point number from unpacked to packed representation. Program 8.9 reverses the process. It also introduces the MC68020 "Return and Deallocate Parameters" (RTD) instruction, in which a displacement factor may be used to simplify the clearing of the stack.

INSTRUCTION

RTD
(Return and
Deallocate
Parameters)

Syntax   RTD   #⟨displacement⟩

Action   The instruction extends the action of RTS. The program counter is popped from the stack. The 16-bit displacement is sign-extended and added to the stack pointer. The adjustment is used to clear the parameters that are passed on the stack by the calling program.

Assume that N is the size of the parameter list and that the address of the next instruction is stored as "Return Address" on the stack.

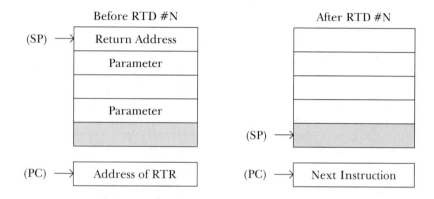

Notes

1. The condition codes are not affected.

2. The displacement is stored in a 16-bit extension word.

PROGRAM 8.8

Pack Floating-Point
Numbers

The I/O routines HEXIN and HEXIN_LONG input values into the three fields of a floating-point number in unpacked format. The equivalent packed representation is stored in D0 using calls to the routines NORMALIZE and PACK. The normalized unpacked representation and final packed representation are printed.

```
norm_exp:    equ      2
norm_mant:   equ      4
pack_sign:   equ      0
pack_exp:    equ      4
f_offset:    equ      8

             xref     hexin, hexin_long, newline, hexout_long, stop

start:       jsr      hexin             ; enter the sign
             move.w   d0, a
```

```
            jsr       hexin              ; enter the exponent
            move.w    d0,a+2
            jsr       hexin_long         ; enter the mantissa
            move.l    d0,a+4
            pea       a                  ; push unpacked float stack
            jsr       normalize          ; normalized number
            clr.l     d0                 ; clear register for output
            move.w    a,d0               ; output the sign
            jsr       hexout_long
            move.w    a+2,d0             ; output revised exponent
            jsr       hexout_long
            move.l    a+4,d0             ; output normalized mantissa
            jsr       hexout_long
            jsr       newline
            pea       a                  ; push addr unpacked number
            jsr       pack               ; packed form returned in d0
            jsr       hexout_long        ; output packed number
            jsr       newline
            jsr       stop

normalize:  link      a6,#0
            movem.l   d5-d7/a0,-(sp)
            movea.l   (f_offset,a6),a0
            move.l    (norm_mant,a0),d5  ; store mantissa on d5
            beq       norm1              ; mantissa is 0; quit
            bfffo     d5{0:32},d6        ; find most significant 1
            cmp.w     #8,d6              ; test against offset 8
            beq       norm1              ; mantissa is ok as is; quit
            bpl       norm0              ; will shift left
            moveq     #8,d7
            sub.w     d6,d7              ; bits to shift right
            lsr.l     d7,d5              ; shift 1 to bit 23
            add.w     d7,(norm_exp,a0)   ; update the exponent
            bra       norm1
norm0:      sub.w     #8,d6
            lsl.l     d6,d5
            sub.w     d6,(norm_exp,a0)   ; update the exponent
norm1:      move.l    d5,(norm_mant,a0)  ; store revised mantissa
            movem.l   (sp)+,d5-d7/a0
            unlk      a6
            rtd       #4                 ; pop pc and clear stack

pack:       link      a6,#0
            movem.l   d1/d2/a0,-(sp)
            clr.l     d0
            movea.l   (f_offset,a6),a0
            move.l    (pack_sign,a0),d1  ; store sign and exp in d1
            move.l    (pack_exp,a0),d2
            beq       pack0
            add.w     #127,d1            ; excess 127 notation
            bfins     d1,d0{1:8}         ; store exp in bits 30-23 d0
            swap      d1                 ; place sign in lsw of d1
            bfins     d1,d0{0:1}         ; store sign in bit 31 of d0
            bfins     d2,d0{9:23}        ; store low 23 bits of the
                                         ; mant in d0 (drop hidden 1)
```

```
pack0:        movem.l   (sp)+,d1/d2/a0
              unlk      a6
              rtd       #4                    ; pop the pc and clear stack

              data

a:            ds.b      8                     ; space for unpacked form
              end
```

⟨Run of Program 8.8⟩

1 0 80000000
00000001 00000008 00800000
C3800000

PROGRAM 8.9

Unpack Floating-
Point Numbers

A floating-point number in packed format is read in D0 using HEX-IN_LONG. The three fields of the corresponding unpacked normalized presentation are printed in hex.

```
              xref      hexin_long, hexout, hexout_long, newline, stop

start:  jsr       hexin_long       ; read the packed number
        move.l    d0,d1
        bfextu    d1{0:1},d2       ; copy the sign to d2
        bfextu    d0{1:8},d0       ; copy the exp to d0
        subi.w    #127,d0          ; compute the true exponent
        swap      d2               ; store sign in msw of d2
        or.l      d2,d0            ; move sign to msw of d0
        bfextu    d1{9:23},d1      ; copy mantissa to d1
        or.l      #$00800000,d1    ; add the hidden 1
        movem.l   d0/d1,a          ; copy the fields to a
        jsr       print_a          ; print the fields
        jsr       stop

print_a:
        lea       a,a0
        clr.l     d0               ; clear the output register
        move.w    (a0)+,d0
        jsr       hexout           ; print the sign
        move.w    (a0)+,d0
        jsr       hexout           ; print the exponent
        move.l    (a0)+,d0
        jsr       hexout_long      ; print the mantissa
        jsr       newline
        rts

        data
a:      ds.b      8
        end
```

⟨Run of Program 8.9⟩

```
BE400000
0001 FFFD 00C00000
```

8.6 | MC68020/30/40 MULTIPLY AND DIVIDE INSTRUCTIONS

Data registers support byte, word, and long-word operations. Quad word (8-byte) data is also permitted with data registers and is used by multiply and divide instructions. The notation Dn:Dm is used, where (Dn) is the most significant 32 bits and (Dm) is the least significant 32 bits. No order is implied for indices n and m. The high-order 32 bits of a quad word are called the **most significant long word (MSLW)**. The low-order 32 bits constitute the **least significant long word (LSLW)**.

MSLW		LSLW
Dn		Dm

For example, the quad-word integer \$55553333 FCDE1553 is represented by D6:D3.

5555 3333		FCDE 1553
D6		D3

The MC68020 provides extended multiplication (MULU/MULS) and division (DIVU/DIVS) instructions, including 64-bit products and 32-bit quotients and remainders.

INSTRUCTION

MULU/MULS
(MC68020/30/40
Multiplication)

Syntax

Unsigned		*Signed*		*Operand Size*
MULU.W	⟨ea⟩, Dn	MULS.W	⟨ea⟩, Dn	$16 \times 16 \rightarrow 32$
MULU.L	⟨ea⟩, Dl	MULS.L	⟨ea⟩, Dl	$32 \times 32 \rightarrow 32$
MULU.L	⟨ea⟩, Dh:Dl	MULS.L	⟨ea⟩, Dh:Dl	$32 \times 32 \rightarrow 64$

Action

1. MULU.W and MULS.W are the basic MC68000 instructions. The product of two unsigned (signed) 16-bit operands is stored as a long word in the data register Dn.

2. The long multiplication instructions take 32-bit operands and generate a 64-bit product.

Notes

1. If a single-destination operand is used, the low-order 32 bits of the product are stored in D*l*. Overflow occurs if the high-order 32 bits are nonzero.

2. If two destination operands are used, the factors are contained in the source operand and D*l*, respectively. The high-order 32 bits of the product are stored in D*h;* the low-order 32 bits are stored in D*l*.

EXAMPLE 8.22

Assume that (D0) = $A0000000 and (D1) = 0.

(a) MULS.L   #2,D0   Result: (D0.L) = $4000 0000   (V = 1)

(b) MULU.L   #2,D1:D0   Result: (D1.L) = $0000 0001
                                      (D0.L) = $4000 0000

(c) MULS.L   #4,D0:D1   Result: (D0.L) = $0000 0000
                                      (D1.L) = $0000 0000

PROGRAM 8.10

MC68020
Multiplication
Efficiency

In this example, Program 8.4 has been modified to use long multiplication. The product $FFFFFFFF × $FFFFFFFF is computed 100,000 times. A comparison is made with an algorithm that uses the UMUL32 routine.

```
            xref     hexout_long,newline,stop

start:      move.l   #100000,d2         ; repeat 100,000 times
tloop:      move.l   #$ffffffff,-(sp)   ; pass a
            move.l   #$ffffffff,-(sp)   ; pass b
            jsr      umul32             ; form a * b
            subq.l   #1,d2
            bne      tloop
            jsr      hexout_long        ; print high and low halves
            move.l   d1,d0
            jsr      hexout_long
            jsr      newline
            jsr      stop

a:          equ      8
b:          equ      4
psize:      equ      8

umul32:
            move.l   (a,sp),d0          ; fetch a
            move.l   (b,sp),d1          ; fetch b
            mulu.l   d0,d0:d1           ; 32 × 32 multiply
```

```
move.l   (sp),(psize,sp)
addq.l   #psize,sp
rts

end
```

⟨Run of Program 8.10⟩

FFFFFFFE 00000001

On a Macintosh IIci with an MC68030 processor running at 25 MHz, Program 8.4 ran in 4 seconds, and Program 8.10, in 3 seconds.

INSTRUCTION

DIVU/DIVS
(MC68020/30/40
Division)

Syntax

Unsigned		Signed		Operand Size
DIVU.W	⟨ea⟩,Dn	DIVS.W	⟨ea⟩,Dn	$32/16 \rightarrow 16r{:}16q$
DIVU.L	⟨ea⟩,Dq	DIVS.L	⟨ea⟩,Dq	$32/32 \rightarrow 32q$
DIVU.L	⟨ea⟩,D$r{:}$Dq	DIVS.L	⟨ea⟩,D$r{:}$Dq	$64/32 \rightarrow 32r{:}32q$
DIVUL.L	⟨ea⟩,D$r{:}$Dq	DIVSL.L	⟨ea⟩,D$r{:}$Dq	$32/32 \rightarrow 32r{:}32q$

Action

1. The word form is the basic MC68000 instruction. The 32-bit contents of the data register are divided by the LSW in the source operand. The quotient is stored in the LSW of Dn, the remainder in the MSW of Dn.

2. In the long form with a single destination register, the divisor is a 32-bit value in the source operand. The quotient is stored in Dq, and the remainder is discarded.

3. In the long form with a quad-word destination, the dividend for DIVU.L and DIVS.L is a quad word (Dr = MSLW, Dq = LSLW). The dividend for DIVUL.L and DIVSL.L is a long word (Dq). The divisor is a 32-bit value. The result is a long-word quotient and a long-word remainder.

Notes

1. Division by zero results in an exception.

2. If overflow occurs, the V bit is set and the operands remain unchanged.

3. For operand size of 32132, the result is exact. In the other two cases, overflow is possible.

EXAMPLE 8.23

(a) Assume that (D0) = $80000000.
DIVU.W   #2,D0

Result: (D0.L) = $80000000   32/16 → 16
Overflow occurs and (D0) is unchanged.

(b) Assume that (D0) = $06664441.
DIVS.L   #2,D0

Result: (D0.L) = $03332220   32/32 → 32

The quotient is stored in D0, and the remainder 1 is discarded.

(c) Assume that (D1.L) = $00000002 and (D0.L) = $00008882.
DIVU.L   #4,D1:D0

Result: (D0.L) = $80002220 (quotient)
        (D1.L) = $00000002 (remainder)
        64/32 → 32r:32q

The MSLW of the dividend is stored in D1; the LSLW of the dividend
is stored in D0.

(d) Let (D0.L) = $FFFFFFF9 (−7).
DIVSL.L   #2,D1:D0

Result (D0.L) = $FFFFFFFD (−3) (quotient)
                (D1.L) = $FFFFFFFF (−1) (remainder)
                32/32 → 32r:32q

The dividend is stored in D0.

PROGRAM 8.11

Long-Word
Decimal Output

The routine DECOUT_LONG is rewritten to use DIVUL.L. The number
to be output is stored in D0.

```
            xref    strout,hexin_long,newline,stop

start:      jsr     hexin_long
            lea     decbuf+12,a0    ; set a0 past last char of buffer
decloop:
            divul.l #10,d1:d0       ; long divide
            add.b   #'0',d1         ; convert to character digit
            move.b  d1,-(a0)
            tst.l   d0
            bne     decloop
            lea     endbuf,a1
            move.l  a1,d0
            sub.l   a0,d0
            jsr     strout
            jsr     newline
            jsr     stop
```

```
              data
decbuf:       ds.b      12
              dc.b      '  '
endbuf:
              end
```

⟨Run of Program 8.11⟩

ffffffff
4294967295

MC68020/30/40 BCD Instructions

For the MC68000, subroutines implement packing and unpacking of BCD data. The MC68020 has two instructions, PACK and UNPK, that are equivalent to these routines. An application program demonstrates the use of these instructions.

INSTRUCTION

PACK/UNPK
(BCD Format)

Syntax   PACK $-(An), -(Am), \#\langle \text{adjustment} \rangle$
           PACK $Dn, Dm, \#\langle \text{adjustment} \rangle$

           UNPK $-(An), -(Am), \#\langle \text{adjustment} \rangle$
           UNPK $Dn, Dm, \#\langle \text{adjustment} \rangle$

Action

1. The PACK instruction acts on consecutive bytes of data in memory or in a data register.

   In memory, 2 consecutive bytes from the source are used. Each byte is fetched after first decrementing the source address register 1 byte. The final result is stored in memory at address (Am). The 2 bytes are joined into a word, the adjustment is added, and bits [11:8] and [3:0] are concatenated to form a byte.

   In data registers, the adjustment is added to the LSW of the source register. Then bits [11:8] and bits [3:0] are concatenated and placed in the LSB of the destination register.

2. The UNPK instruction works on a single byte in memory or a data register. The unpacking process separates the two nibbles of the byte into a pair of bytes stored in the destination. Each nibble in the source byte is copied as the low-order nibble of the destination with the high-order nibble set to 0. The adjustment is added as a word to the adjacent bytes in the destination.

In memory, each nibble of the source byte is copied to a byte designated by A*m*. This address register is first decremented by 1 before the copy is made.

In data registers, the consecutive nibbles are selected from the LSB of the source register. The unpacked bytes are in the LSW of the destination register.

Notes

1. The condition codes are not affected.

2. The adjustment is stored as a 16-bit extension word.

3. The adjustment can be used for BCD scaling.

To convert BCD ASCII digits to BCD digits, use the PACK instruction with adjustment 0. To convert BCD digits to BCD ASCII digits, use the UNPK instruction with adjustment $3030 (add '0' to each byte in the result).

EXAMPLE 8.24   (*a*) BCD ASCII digits '5' and '7' are stored in memory with pointer A1. The packed digits are placed in a second array with pointer A2. The adjustment converts the ASCII digits to the BCD digits '5' and '7'.

$$\text{PACK} \quad -(A1), -(A2), \#0$$

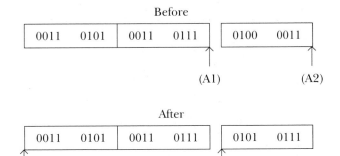

(*b*) Assume that (D0) = $53. For the instruction

$$\text{UNPK D0,D0,\#303}$$

0011	0101	0011	0011

D0

PROGRAM 8.12

BCD PACK/UNPK
Test Program

Two pairs of BCD ASCII digits are stored in memory at addresses A and B, respectively. These addresses are passed on the stack to the subroutine BCDADD20 as two long words. Each pair of ASCII digits is stored in data registers and then packed. A BCD add is performed, with the result stored as ASCII digits at address B using the UNPK routine. The contents of B are printed.

```
a_offset:    equ       8
b_offset:    equ       12
psize:       equ       8

             xref      strout,newline,stop

start:       pea       b
             pea       a
             jsr       bcdadd20
             lea       b,a0
             moveq     #2,d0
             jsr       strout
             jsr       newline
             jsr       stop

bcdadd20:    link      a6,#0
             movem.l   d0/d1/a0,-(sp)
             movea.l   (a_offset,a6),a0
             move.w    (a0),d0
             movea.l   (b_offset,a6),a0
             move.w    (a0),d1
             pack      d0,d0,#0
             pack      d1,d1,#0
             abcd      d0,d1
             unpk      d1,d1,#$3030
             move.w    d1,(a0)
             movem.l   (sp)+,d0/d1/a0
             unlk      a6
             rtd       #psize

             data
a:           dc.b      '27'
b:           dc.b      '52'

             end
```

⟨Run of Program 8.12⟩

EXERCISES

1. Write instructions to alter the CCR as requested in the following:
   (a) Set the Z and C bits; leave other bits unchanged.
   (b) Clear the Z and V bits; leave other bits unchanged.
   (c) Change the sense of the V and C bits; leave other bits unchanged.
   (d) Initialize the CCR with the following bit values, $Z = 1$, $V = 0$, $C = 0$, $X = 1$, and $N = 1$.

2. Trace the instructions in the following subroutine.

```
ADDEM:    MOVE.L    D1,-(SP)
          ADD.W     D1,D0
          SWAP      D1
          SWAP      D0
          ADD.W     D1,D0
          SWAP      D0
          MOVE.L    (SP)+,D1
          RTS
```

   (a) Assume that (D0.L) = \$4A20 8B10 and that (D1.L) = \$2FF3 A489. What is the value of (D0.L) after a return from the subroutine?
   (b) Describe the action of the subroutine. Why is it incorrect?
   (c) Using an extend instruction, how would you modify the subroutine to compute the sum (D0.L) + (D1.L)?
   (d) Assume that the MC68000 does not provide the appropriate extend instruction for (c). Modify the routine using the CCR bits and a branch instruction to compute the sum (D0.L) + (D1.L).

3. Describe the action of the following code segment:

```
ADDQ.W    #8,A0
ADDQ.W    #8,A1
MOVE.W    #4,CCR
SUBX.L    -(A0),-(A1)
SUBX.L    -(A0),-(A1)
RTS
```

4. Assume that the 32-bit number \$12FF00AA is stored in memory at location N. Assume each of the following code segments is run:

```
NEGATE1:              NEGATE2:              NEGATE3:
   LEA     N,A0          LEA     N,A0          LEA     N,A0
   ADDQ.L  #4,A0         ADDQ.L  #4,A0         ADDQ.L  #4,A0
   MOVE.W  #0,CCR        MOVE.W  #0,CCR        MOVE.W  #0,CCR
   NEG.B   -(A0)         NEG.W   -(A0)         NEGX.B  -(A0)
   NEG.B   -(A0)         NEG.W   -(A0)         NEGX.B  -(A0)
   NEG.B   -(A0)                               NEGX.B  -(A0)
   NEG.B   -(A0)                               NEGX.B  -(A0)
   RTS                   RTS                   RTS
```

   (a) Explain why the value of N after executing the routine NEGATE1 is \$EE010056.

(b) Explain why the value of N after executing the routine NEGATE2 is $ED01FF56.

(c) What is the value of N after executing the routine NEGATE3?

5. Describe the action of the following code segment:

```
MOVEM.L    D0-D1,-(SP)
MOVEM.L    (A0),D0-D1
LSR.L      #1,D0
ROXR.L     #1,D1
MOVEM.L    D0-D1,(A0)
MOVEM.L    (SP)+,D0-D1
RTS
```

6. Assume that (D1.L) = $AF047138, (D2.L) = $00A4A2FE, and CCR = $15.

(a) What is the value of (D2.L) after executing the instruction "ROXR.W #8,D2"?

(b) What is the value of (D1.L) after executing the instruction "ROXL.L #8,D1"?

(c) After executing the instruction "ADDX.L D2,D2", determine the value of (D2.L).

7. Trace the following code:

```
ADDA.L  #8,A0          ; A0 POINTS TO ALPHA
ADDA.L  #8,A1          ; A1 POINTS TO BETA
NEG.L   (-4,A1)
NEGX.L  (-8,A1)
MOVE.W  #0,CCR
ADDX.L  -(A0),-(A1)
ADDX.L  -(A0),-(A1)
RTS
```

(a) Indicate why the subroutine computes the equation

$$BETA := -BETA + ALPHA$$

(b) Rewrite the subroutine to compute the equation

$$BETA := -BETA - ALPHA$$

8. Assume that (D0.W) = $45 and (D1.W) = $30 and that each contains two BCD digits. After executing the individual instructions, give the 8-bit value of the following specified data registers:

(a) ABCD D1,D0   (D0.W) =

(b) SBCD D1,D0   (D0.W) =

(c) SBCD D0,D1   (D1.W) =

(d) NBCD D0   (D0.W) =

9. Assume that (D0.W) = $2743 is a 4-digit BCD number in packed notation. What would be the two's complement representation of this same value?

10. Data is stored in packed BCD notation as currency with two decimal places. The sign ("+" = 0, "−" = 1) is stored in the high-order 4 bits of the number.

Sign	Dollar Amount	2-Place Decimal
4 Bits	20 Bits	8 Bits

Assume values A and B use this representation and are stored in (D0.L) and (D1.L), respectively. Write a subroutine MONEY__ADD that computes A + B and returns the sum in D0. Include this subroutine in a main program to test your code.

11. Record the following as binary floating-point numbers in PACKED 32-bit IEEE representation:
    (a) 7.5   (b) $-1/4$ (c) -120.3125 (d) 17/64

12. The following floating-point numbers are given in base 2 scientific notation. First normalize the numbers and then convert them to packed floating-point representation.
    (a) 100110.011×2^5 (b) $(-)0.001101 \times 2^{-6}$
    (c) $(-)110.11 \times 2^{-16}$ (d) 0.111001×2^8

13. Each of the following numbers is given in packed floating-point representation. Write out the number in unpacked floating-point representation and also as a decimal number.
    (a)   C1800000   (b)   419E0000
    (c)   C0E00000   (d)   44640000

14. Write a subroutine FCMP that compares two floating-point numbers. Assume the calling program passes the values of A and B on the stack in packed form. The N and Z bits of the CCR are to be set appropriately. If B < A, then N = 0 and Z = 0. If A < B, then N = 1 and Z = 0. If A = B, then N = 0, Z = 1.

15. (MC68020/30/40) Assume that (D0.L) = \$4FA2789C. Give the binary digits for each of the following bit fields:
    (a)   D0 {8:4}   (b)   D0 {24:2}
    (c)   D0 {12:3}   (d)   D0 {1:1}

16. (MC68020/30/40) Assume that (D0.L) = \$4FA2789C. Give the hex value of (D0.L) after executing the instruction.
    (a)   BFCHG   D0 {8:4}   (b)   BFSET   D0 {24:2}
    (c)   BFCLR   D0 {12:3}   (d)   BFCHG   D0 {1:3}

17. (MC68020/30/40) Assume that (D2.L) = \$7038AF17. Give the hex value of (D3.L) after executing the instruction.
    (a)   BFEXTS   D2 {20:8},D3   (b)   BFEXTS   D2 {20:8},D3
    (c)   BFFFO   D2 {24:4},D3   (d)   BFFFO   D2 {4:6},D3

18. (MC68020/30/40) Assume that (D1.L) = \$7038AF17 and that (D0.L) = \$00001234. Give the hex value of (D1.L) after executing the instruction.
    (a) BFINS D0,D1{20:8}   (b) BFINS D0,D1{8:16}

19. (MC68020/30/40) Assume that (D0.L) = \$66444 and that (D2.L) = \$40000000.
    (a)   MULS.L   #4,D2   (D2.L) =

(b) Assume that D1 = $2
MULU.L   #4,D1:D0   (D1.L) =   (D0.L) =
(c) MULS.L   #4,D0:D2   (D0.L) =   (D2.L) =

20. (MC68020/30/40)
(a) Assume that (D0.L) = $4A008000.
DIVU.W   #4,D0   (D0.L) =
(b) Assume that (D0.L) = $4A008005.
DIVS.L   #−2,D0   (D0.L) =
(c) Assume that (D1.L) = $00000888 and (D0.L) = $000068A3
DIVU.L   #4,D1:D0   (D1.L) =   (D0.L) =
(d) Let (D0.L) = $FFFFFFF9 (−7).
DIVSL.L   #4,D1:D0   (D1.L) =   (D0.L) =

21. (MC68020/30/40) Write a code segment that will divide a 64-bit number in
D2:D3 by 10.

22. (MC68020/30/40)
(a) Consider the memory picture

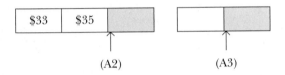

(A2)   (A3)

If the instruction

PACK   −(A2),−(A3),#0

is executed, show the final picture of memory.
(b) Consider the memory picture

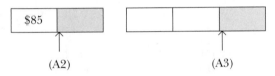

(A2)   (A3)

If the instruction

UNPK   −(A2),−(A3),#$3030

is executed, show the final picture of memory.

PROGRAMMING EXERCISES

23. Write code for subroutines LSL64 (ShiftCount,N) and LSR64 (ShiftCount,N).
Pass the address of the number N and the ShiftCount on the stack.

Test program. Rewrite Program 8.3 "64-bit Count Ones" using LSR64. Enter a number into location N using two calls to the 32-bit HEXIN_LONG routine. Print out the number of 1's using DECOUT.

24. Write a subroutine CMP64(A,B) that compares two 64-bit signed numbers A and B. Assume the two numbers are stored in memory. Return in D0 the value −1 ($FFFF) if A < B, the value 0 if A = B, and the value 1 if A > B.

    Test program. Initialize the value B to 0. Using two calls to HEXIN_LONG, enter a 64-bit number and store it at location A. Using CMP64, print a string indicating whether A is negative, zero, or positive.

25. Suppose numbers are stored in 64 bits with the high-order bit serving as a sign bit (0 is positive, 1 is negative).

    Sign   63-Bit Unsigned Magnitude

    Write a subroutine that adds two numbers stored in this signed-magnitude representation. Assume that the numbers are stored in memory and that their addresses are passed on the stack to the subroutine. Write a program to test the subroutine.

    Hint: After storing the sign in a register, clear the sign bit. Use the routines ADD64 and NEG64 on the resulting numbers. Your logic must implement the rules for adding signed numbers with ordinary base 10 integers.

26. Data for this problem uses the currency representation of Exercise 10.

Sign	Dollar Amount	2-Place Decimal
4 Bits	20 Bits	8 Bits

    (a) Write a routine PRINTMONEY to print out a number in BCD currency representation with the following form: [+/−]$[Dollars].[Cents]. For instance, 10398725_{16} is printed as −$3987.25.

    (b) Write a routine GETMONEY to enter a dollar amount from the keyboard in the form ⟨Sign⟩⟨Dollars⟩.⟨Cents⟩. Each field is required in the input. For instance, the input +476.91 has the BCD representation $00047691.

    (c) Use the routine MONEY_ADD from Exercise 10 to simulate integer multiplication. Write a subroutine MONEYMUL that multiplies a number in D0 by the unsigned integer value in (D1.B). Multiplication is implemented with repeated addition. Return the result in D0.

    Test program. Enter a dollar amount in D0 using GETMONEY. Using MONEYMUL, compute 6 × (D0) Write out the result using PRINT-MONEY.

    Advanced Program. Suppose that your city has a 6 percent sales tax on food. How would you adjust the last value in (D0) to represent the sales tax? Using the routines in (a)–(c), modify the test program to enter a food bill and then print out both the sales tax and the total bill.

27. Write a family of routines
    (a) PACK   (b) UNPACK   (c) BCDADD   (d) BCDSUB   (e) BCDNEG

to handle 8-digit BCD numbers. Test the routines in a main program similar to Program 8.7.

28. The Russian Peasant method of multiplication computes the product of two unsigned numbers by doubling/halving the factors. The algorithm is described through the example of multiplying 30 × 25. Put the factors in two columns. On each iteration, double the value in column 1 and divide the value in column 2 by 2. The process terminates when the quotient reaches 1. The product is formed by adding the terms in column 1 whose corresponding term in column 2 is odd.

Column 1	Column 2	
30	25	Add 30
60	12	
120	6	
240	3	Add 240
480	1	Add 480

The product of 3025 = 30 + 240 + 480 = 750.

Write a subroutine that implements the Russian Peasant multiplication algorithm. Assume the factors are passed as 32-bit data in (D0.L) and (D1.L). Write a main program to test the subroutine.

29. (MC68020/30/40) Using DIVUL.L, write a subroutine BINBCD32, that converts a 32-bit binary number *N* to an 8-digit BCD number in packed representation. You will need to divide by 10 repeatedly and store the remainder as a 4-bit BCD digit. The initial value is passed to the subroutine in register D0. The same register holds the returned BCD number.

Test program. Enter a 32-bit number in D0 using DECIN__LONG. After calling BINBCD32, print out the BCD number using HEXOUT__LONG.

30. (M68020/30/40) Modify Program 8.6 so it uses the machine instructions PACK/UNPK.

CHAPTER 9

CHARACTER HANDLING

*T*his chapter covers string-handling routines and data conversion. Section 9.1 provides a general discussion of external subroutines, picking up on the material presented in Chapter 8. Section 9.2 defines Null-terminated and byte-count string formats and presents routines for converting between the formats. Section 9.3 develops a standard string library for Null-terminated strings. One of the major topics is the design and implementation of an I/O library of routines for decimal, hex, and string input and output. Section 9.4 provides algorithms and code for conversion between ASCII number strings and binary numbers as well as conversion between binary and packed BCD numbers. Section 9.5 presents a complete keyboard/screen I/O library that is built from two primitive single-character routines GET-CHAR and PUTCHAR. The library can be ported to any system that provides these routines. Character-handling concludes in Section 9.6 with an illustration of algorithms for encrypting and decrypting code files.

The routines in this chapter are presented as external code files. A linker is required to combine the individual object modules and code libraries into an executable program. This is an efficient method now commonly used by most high-level languages. As with include files, discussed in Chapter 8, the ENTRY directive indicates the starting address of a linked program. The method of defining external code files and calling a linker differs from system to system. The first section of this chapter presents a specific example of the MC68000 ASM assembler running on UNIX. Similar principles are used with other assemblers and operating systems.

| 9.1 | EXTERNAL SUBROUTINES

Within a source file, the XDEF directive identifies those subroutines that may be used as assembled code modules by an external program. The I/O utilities HEXIN, HEXOUT__LONG, STOP, and so forth, are examples of **external subroutines** that reside in a subroutine library. They reside as assembled code in the library and must be linked into the main program before execution can occur.

A **linker** is used to merge external code with the main program. Most linkers use a **two-pass process**. In the first pass, the linker reads through each code file and, knowing the cumulative length of all previously read code files, maintains a location counter for what will be the final merged code file. During this pass, it constructs a **global symbol table**, which gives the value of each external symbol that may be referenced in one or more of the files. Assuming no undefined symbols, the linker performs a second pass of the code files. Whenever it encounters a reference to an external symbol, the linker looks up its value in the global symbol table and resolves all label references. Figure 9.1 illustrates the process for a MAIN program of 350 bytes and three assembled subroutines A, B, and C of length 100,

FIGURE 9.1   Linking External Routines

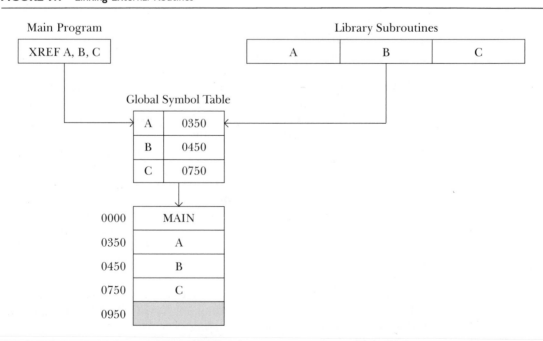

300, and 200 bytes, respectively. The XREF directive in the main program specifies references to the subroutines. The linked code file contains 950 bytes with routines combined in the order MAIN, A, B, and C.

The global symbol table refers to the subroutines A, B, and C available to the linker. During the assembling process, a reference to each subroutine is made with the XDEF directive, which marks the label as a globally defined symbol.

DIRECTIVE

XDEF

Syntax XDEF ⟨label⟩, ⟨label⟩, . . .

Action The assembler marks each label as a global symbol in the code file so that each can be used by other program units. Two or more labels, separated by commas, may be included in an XDEF directive.

EXAMPLE 9.1

(*a*) The subroutine ABS64, from Chapter 8, is modified for separate assembling into an external code file. The XDEF directive is used at the beginning of the code, and an END is added to terminate the assembly process.

```
srcterm:    equ     8
ccrloc6:    equ     6
param4:     equ     4


            xdef    abs64

abs64:      link    a6,#0
            movem.l d0/a0,-(sp)
            move.w  sr,d0               ; temporarily save CCR
            movea.l (srcterm,a6),a0
            move.l  (4,a6),(srcterm,a6) ; relocate PC for RTR
            move.w  d0,(ccrloc6,a6)     ; save CCR on the stack
            tst.b   (a0)                ; test for negative
            bpl.s   abs64_1             ; no just return
            adda.l  #8,a0               ; compute the negative
            move.w  #$04,ccr
            negx.l  -(a0)
            negx.l  -(a0)
            move.w  sr,(ccrloc6,a6)     ; update CCR on stack
abs64_1:    movem.l (sp)+,d0/a0
            unlk    a6
            addq.w  #param4-2,sp
            rtr

            end
```

(*b*) For demonstration purposes, assume that the subroutine is stored in a file ABS64.S with assembler ASM. The source file is assembled using the "−C" option, which creates an unlinked object file called ABS64.0.

Command: ASM   −C   ABS64.S

(c) Assume that a main program is named MAIN.S and has been assembled into an object code file MAIN.O. In the UNIX environment, the system linker "LD" creates a single executable code file called MAIN.OUT.

Command: LD −O MAIN.OUT MAIN.O ABS64.O

Use of a linker is system dependent, and you should consult your assembler manual for details.

9.2 | STRING FORMATS

A string is an array of characters. In some applications, the size of a string is predictable, and a fixed-length array is used. In cases involving text processing, variable-length strings are often more efficient. These are nonstandard data structures that high-level languages implement with different formats. This section introduces the null-terminated format used by the C language and the byte-count format used by Pascal. In each case, the string is an array of bytes stored in a buffer.

Null-Terminated Format

The string buffer is declared as a byte array, and the null character ($00) terminates the string.

STRINGBUF: DS.B   256

STRINGBUF

Notes

1. The null character is a good choice for the terminator because it is normally not used as a character in a string.

2. The length of a string must be computed by an array scan that terminates at the null character.

3. A property of null-terminated strings that is very useful in applications is the fact that any character position in the string defines a substring that is null-terminated. For example, consider the string

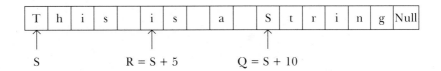

$$S \qquad\qquad R = S + 5 \qquad\qquad Q = S + 10$$

The whole string S is 'This is a String', the substring starting at address R has value 'is a String' and that at Q is 'String'.

Byte-Count Format

The string buffer is declared as a byte array, and byte 0 is reserved for the string count. Assuming that the buffer is a 256 byte array, the count is in the range 0–255.

STRINGBUF: DS.B   256

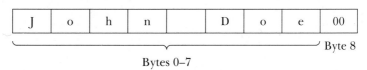

Count	String	Unused
Byte 0	Bytes 1–N	

STRINGBUF

EXAMPLE 9.2

String Formats

The string "John Doe" (8 characters) is stored in a string buffer.

(a) Null-terminated format

J	o	h	n		D	o	e	00

Bytes 0–7   Byte 8

(b) Byte-count format

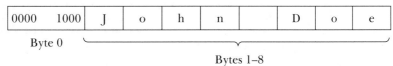

0000 1000	J	o	h	n		D	o	e

Byte 0

Bytes 1–8

9.3 | STRING ROUTINES

This section introduces basic string-handling routines, and Table 9.1 presents a string routine library that will be used to develop the concepts presented in this section. The MC68000 code assumes Null-terminated strings. The routines include I/O procedures, functions that return a single

TABLE 9.1 String Routine Library

ROUTINE NAME	FUNCTION
String Input/Output	
GETSTR (S)	Reads characters from the keyboard into the buffer pointed to by A0 and then appends a Null character. The read terminates on a carriage return, which is then deleted from the input string.
PUTSTR (S)	Writes to the screen a null-terminated strings pointed to by A0.
String Functions	
STRLENGTH(S)	Returns the length of a string S.
STRCOMPARE(S,T)	Given strings S and T, returns a negative value if S < T, 0 if S = T, or a positive value if S > T. Usual dictionary (alphabetical) ordering is assumed.
STRCHAR(S,CH)	Given string S and character CH, returns the address of the first occurrence of CH in S or returns $FFFFFFFF if CH is not found.
STRRCHAR(S,CH)	Given string S and character CH, returns the address of the last occurrence of CH in S or returns $FFFFFFFF if CH is not found.
String Operators	
STRCAT(S,T)	Joins string T to the end of string S.
STRCOPY(S,T)	Copies string T to string S.
STRINSERT(S,T,I)	Inserts string T in string S beginning at position I.
STRDELETE(S,I,J)	Deletes J characters in string S starting at location I.

value, and operators that update strings. The exercises include routines using the byte-count format.

String I/O Routines

The procedures STRIN and STROUT are used as primitive I/O routines for the development of the string routines. Using calls to the operating system, they read characters from the keyboard and write them to the screen. STRIN stores the characters in a string buffer with the character count located in D0. STROUT does not assume a specific string format and merely writes a specified number of characters to the terminal.

The routine GETSTR requires a buffer to hold the input string. The buffer is pointed to by A0. The routine reads characters from the keyboard into S until a carriage return is typed. The end-of-line character is replaced by the Null character. The output routine PUTSTR prints a Null-terminated string to the screen. Both I/O procedures use A0 to point to the strings.

String Input: GETSTR(S)

Parameters passed
    The address of the input string S is in A0
Parameters returned
    None.

```
        x def     getstr
        x ref     strin
Null:   equ       0

getstr:
        movem.l   d0/a0,-(sp)
        move.w    #255,d0            ; set an input count
        jsr       strin
        subq.w    #1,d0
        move.b    #Null,(0,a0,d0.w)  ; append a Null char
        movem.l   (sp)+,d0/a0
        rts
        end
```

String Output: PUTSTR(S)

Parameters passed
    The address of the output string S.
Parameters returned
    None.

PUTSTR introduces the use of **redefinable labels**. When subroutines are bundled in a library, it is necessary to maintain unique label names. In Chapter 8, the naming technique placed an "__N" after the subroutine name—for example, PUTSTR__1 and PUTSTR__2. Redefinable labels are a convenient alternative. They are defined with format N$:, where N is an integer in the range 0–99. A **redefinable label reference** is a reference of the form N$. Within reasonable restrictions, a label name may be used as often as desired. The rules are as follows:

1. The beginning of the module being assembled opens up a scope for redefinable labels. The scope continues until the occurrence of a standard label or the end of the program. Within this scope, any label N$ may be uniquely defined.

2. The occurrence of a standard label causes the current scope for redefinable labels to be closed. No labels outside the currently active scope are accessible. For example, consider the program segment:

```
1$:         . . .
        BRA.S   1$
    2$:     . . .
NEXT:       . . .
(*)     JMP     2$
            . . .

    2$:
```

The label NEXT closes the scope of the redefinable labels. The reference 2$ in the JMP instruction at location (*) refers to the label 2$: appearing after the label NEXT.

```
        xdef    putstr
        xref    strout

putstr:
        movem.l  d0/a0-a1,-(sp)
        movea.l  a0,a1          ; store string address in a1
        moveq    #0,d0          ; d0 will hold the string count
1$:     tst.b    (a1)+          ; test for a null byte in memory
        beq.s    2$
        addq.w   #1,d0
        bra.s    1$
2$:     jsr      strout         ; call primitive routine
        movem.l  (sp)+,d0/a0-a1
        rts
        end
```

String Functions

The function STRLENGTH(S) finds the length of a Null-terminated string S and returns the value in D0. The function STRCOMPARE(S,T) uses alphabetical order to compare two Null-terminated strings. The result of the comparison is returned to D0 as a Boolean flag that can be tested to see if it is negative, zero, or positive. The function STRCHAR(S,CH) finds the address of the first occurrence of CH in S. The value is returned in D0. By modifying the STRCHAR routine, the last (rightmost) occurrence of CH in S can be found. This routine, called STRRCHAR, is used to identify the pathname for a file in Program 9.1.

STRLENGTH(S) String Length

To find the length of a null-terminated string, scan the characters until the null character is found, and keep a running total of the number of nonnull characters.

STRLENGTH(S)
Parameters passed
Address of string S.
Parameters returned
The length of the string in (D0.W).

```
            xdef      strlength

buf:        equ       8
param4:     equ       4

strlength:
            link      a6,#0
            move.l    a0,-(sp)        ; save a0. do not use movem
            movea.l   (buf,a6),a0     ; get str address from stack
            moveq     #0,d0           ; initialize length to 0
1$:         tst.b     (a0)+           ; test if byte is null
            beq.s     2$
            addq.w    #1,d0           ; increment length
            bra.s     1$
2$:         movea.l   (sp)+,a0        ; restore a0
            unlk      a6
            move.l    (sp),(param4,sp)
            addq.w    #param4,sp
            rts

            end
```

STRCOMPARE(S,T) String Compare

To compare two Null-terminated strings, start at the first character of each string and compare byte for byte, exiting the loop under one of the following two conditions:

Condition 1   Corresponding characters in S and T differ.
   Result: The strings are not equal, and a number should be returned indicating which string is larger in alphabetical ordering. Subtract the ASCII value of the character in T from the one in S. Return the difference as an output value.

If the difference is negative, then S < T.
If the difference is positive, then S > T.

Condition 2   Two null characters are compared.
   Result: The two strings are equal. Return the value 0 as an output value.

The STRCOMPARE routine uses CMPM with byte operations. This instruction was introduced in conjunction with Program 7.1. Its use in string handling is one of its most important applications.

STRCOMPARE(S,T)

Parameters passed
Address of string S.
Address of string T.
Parameters returned
D0.W (positive if S > T; 0 if S = T; negative if S < T).

```
            xdef      strcompare

buf1:       equ       8
buf2:       equ       12
param8:     equ       8

strcompare:
            link      a6#0
            movem.l   a0-a1,-(sp)
            movea.l   (buf1,a6),a0      ; get address of string s
            movea.l   (buf2,a6),a1      ; get address of string t
1$:         cmpm.b    (a0)+,(a1)+       ; compare strings byte for byte
            bne.s     2$
            tst.b     (-1,a0)           ; comparing two nulls
            bne.s     1$                ; if not, keep comparing
            move.w    #0,d0             ; strings are equal
            bra.s     3$
2$:         move.b    (-1,a0),d0        ; form diff of non-equal chars
            sub.b     (-1,a1),d0
            ext.w     d0
3$:         movem.l   (sp)+,a0-a1
            unlk      a6
            move.l    (sp),(param8,sp)
            addq.w    #param8,sp
            rts
            end
```

STRCHAR(S,CH) STRRCHAR(S,CH) Substring Index

The STRCHAR function is a basic pattern-matching routine. Given the base string S, the function looks for the first occurrence of the character CH in S. The address of this position is the returned value. If no match occurs, the address $FFFFFFFF (invalid address) is returned. A more general problem is to find the first occurrence of a string T in S. The routine SUBSTR(S,T) is often included in a string library.

EXAMPLE 9.3

Substring Index

Assume that S = "Common Cause" located at address $001000.

(a) If CH = 'a', STRCHAR(S,CH) returns the address $001008.

(b) If CH = 't', STRCHAR(S,CH) returns the address $FFFFFFFF.

(c) If T = "on", SUBSTR(S,T) returns the address $001004. This is the general pattern-matching function.

STRCHAR(S,CH)
>   Parameters passed
>   Address of string S.
>   Character CH is pushed on the stack as a word.
>   Parameters returned
>   A0—Address of the first location of CH in S. A0 = $FFFFFFFF
>   if CH is not found in S.

```
            xdef      strchar

char:       equ       12
buf:        equ        8
param6:     equ        6
nomatch:    equ       $FFFFFFFF

strchar:    link      a6,#0
            movem.l   d0-d1/a1,-(sp)
            movea.l   (buf,a6),a1       ; get string s
            move.w    (char,a6),d0      ; get character ch
            movea.l   #nomatch,a0       ; assume ch is not present
1$:         move.b    (a1)+,d1          ; search for c
            beq.s     3$                ; stop if null character
            cmp.b     d0,d1
            beq.s     2$
            bra       1$
2$:         lea       (-1,a1),a0        ; ch found back one byte
3$:         movem.l   (sp)+,d0-d1/a1
            unlk      a6
            move.l    (sp),(param6,sp)
            adda.l    #param6,sp
            rts
            end
```

The routine STRCHAR finds the first occurrence of a character CH in string S. In some applications, it is important to find the last (or rightmost) occurrence of CH. This operation is denoted by STRRCHAR(S,CH). To modify the STRCHAR routine, simply assign the address of a match and then continue with another iteration. The process terminates only when the null character is read.

STRRCHAR(S,CH)

>   Parameters passed
>   Address of string S.
>   Character CH is pushed on the stack as a word.
>   Parameters returned
>   A0—Address of the last location of CH in S. A0 = $FFFFFFFF if
>   CH is not found in S.

```
            xdef      strrchar

char:       equ       12
buf:        equ        8
param6:     equ        6
nomatch:    equ       $FFFFFFFF

strrchar:   link      a6,#0
            movem.l   d0-d1/a1,-(sp)
            movea.l   (buf,a6),a1        ; get string s
            move.w    (char,a6),d0       ; get character ch
            movea.l   #nomatch,a0        ; assume ch is not present
1$:         move.b    (a1)+,d1           ; search for c
            beq.s     2$                 ; stop if null character
            cmp.b     d0,d1
            bne.s     1$
            lea       (-1,a1),a0         ; ch found back one byte
            bra.s     1$                 ; scan to end of string
2$:         movem.l   (sp)+,d0-d1/a1
            unlk      a6
            move.l    (sp),(param6,sp)
            addq.w    #param6,sp
            rts
            end
```

String Operators

The string operators STRCAT(S,T) and STRCOPY(S,T) are passed the addresses of the strings on the stack. The routines create a new Null-terminated string S. The routines STRINSERT(S,T,I) and STRDE-LETE(S,I,J) are implemented using other string-handling routines.

STRCAT(S,T) String Concatenation

An important, but simple, string operation is the joining of one string onto the end of another. This process is called **concatenation**. Some high-level languages include concatenation as part of their basic syntax. Other languages provide access to a string routine.

EXAMPLE 9.4

String
Concatenation
Example

Some Pascal compilers supply the operator "+". Let

$$A = \text{``THE GREAT STATE OF''}$$
$$B = \text{``HAWAII''}$$

Concatenation operation: A := A + B.

Result: A = "THE GREAT STATE OF HAWAII"

In the code, it is assumed that the addresses are pushed on the stack by the calling code in the order right to left. String T is concatenated with string S.

STRCAT(S,T)

Parameters passed (Assume that the two strings do not overlap in memory.)
Address of string S.
Address of string T.
Parameters returned
None.

```
            xdef     strcat

buf1:       equ      8
bug2:       equ      12
param8:     equ      8

strcat:     link     a6,#0
            movem.l  a0-a1,-(sp)
            movea.l  (buf1,a6),a0      ; let a0 point to s
            movea.l  (buf2,a6),a1      ; let a1 point to t
1$:         tst.b    (a0)+             ; find the end of s
            bne.s    1$
            subq.l   #1,a0             ; reset prior to null char
2$:         move.b   (a1)+,(a0)+       ; copy t to end of s
            bne.s    2$
            movem.l  (sp)+,a0-a1
            unlk     a6
            move.l   (sp),(param8,sp)  ; clean up the stack
            addq.w   #param8,sp
            rts
            end
```

Note that the algorithm will copy the Null character from string T to the end of string S, so that the new string is also Null-terminated.

STRCOPY(S,T) String Copy

The string T is copied to a string at address S. The parameter S need not be the starting address of a string but may be some intermediate address within a longer string. In this way, STRCOPY can create a Null-terminated substring within a string.

EXAMPLE 9.5

String Copy
Example

Assume that

STR = "COPY.X",
S   = STR + 5 (address of character "X" stored in STR), and
T   = "OUT"

STRCPY(Q,T) assigns the string "OUT" to Q.
STRCPY(S,T) results in the string STR = "COPY.OUT".

STRCOPY(S,T)

Parameters passed
    Assume the two strings do not overlap in memory.
    Address of string S.
    Address of string T.
Parameters returned
    None

```
        xdef    strcopy

buf1:   equ     8
bug2:   equ     12
param8: equ     8

strcopy: link    a6,#0
         movem.l a0-a1,-(sp)
         movea.l (buf2,a6),a0        ; put t into a0
         movea.l (buf1,a6),a1        ; put s into a1
1$:      move.b  (a0)+,(a1)+         ; move a character from t to s
         bne.s   1$                  ; branch back if no null yet
         movem.l (sp)+,a0-a1
         unlk    a6
         move.l  (sp),(param8,sp)    ; clean up the stack
         addq.w  #param8,sp
         rts
         end
```

STRINSERT(S,T,I) String Insert

The string T is copied into string S starting at Index I. If I is greater than the length of S, the insert is not implemented.

Algorithm   The Null-terminated substring beginning at index I is copied to an array SCRATCHBUF. The string T is copied over the characters in S beginning at index I. Finally, the tail of S previously saved in SCRATCH-BUF is concatenated onto S.

EXAMPLE 9.6

String Insert

Assume that S = 'ABC' and T = '1234'.

STRINSERT(S,T,1) yields the resulting string S = 'A1234BC'.
STRINSERT(S,T,3) yields the resulting string S = 'ABC1234'.
STRINSERT(S,T,5) yields the resulting string S = 'ABC'.

STRINS(S, T, 2)

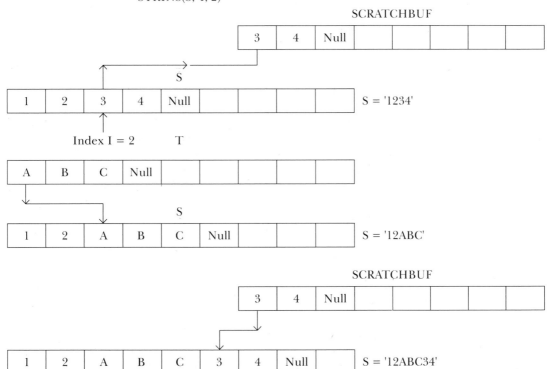

STRINSERT(S,T,I)

Parameters passed
  Address of string S.
  Address of string T.
  Index I in string S.
Parameters returned
  None

```
buf1:       equ       8
buf2:       equ       12
insindex:   equ       16
param10:    equ       10
```

```
              xdef     strinsert
strinsert:    link     a6,#0
              movem.l  d0-d1/a0-a1,-(sp)
              move.w   (insindex,a6),d0    ; get index in d0
              move.w   d0,d1               ; save copy in d1
              movea.l  (buf2,a6),a0        ; put T into a0
              movea.l  (buf1,a6),a1        ; put S into a1
              move.l   a1,-(sp)            ; get length of s
              jsr      strlength
              cmp.w    d0,d1               ; compare length with index
              bgt      1$                  ; abandon ins if i > length
              move.w   d1,d0               ; restore index in d0
              pea      (0,a1,d0.w)
              pea      scratchbuf
              jsr      strcopy
              move.b   #Null,(0,a1,d0.w)
              move.l   a0,-(sp)            ; pass address of T
              pea      (0,a1,d0.w)         ; copy T to S at address
              jsr      strcopy
              pea      scratchbuf
              move.l   a1,-(sp)
              jsr      strcat              ; copy tail of S onto S
1$:           movem.l  (sp)+,d0-d1/a0-a1
              unlk     a6
              move.l   (sp),(param10,sp)   ; clean up the stack
              adda.w   #param10,sp
              rts

              data
scratchbuf:   ds.b    256
              end
```

STRDELETE(S,I,J) String Delete

A sequence of J characters is deleted from string S starting at index I. If I + J is greater than or equal to the length of S, the end of the string is removed starting at index I.

EXAMPLE 9.7

String Delete
Example

Assume that S = "ABCDE".

STRDELETE(S,1,3) yields the resulting string S = 'AE'.
STRDELETE(S,0,2) yields the resulting string S = 'CDE'.
STRDELETE(S,3,5) yields the resulting string S = 'ABC'.

Algorithm   If the index I is greater than the length of the string, then no characters are deleted.

If the deletion would go beyond the end of the string, the tail of the string is deleted. Insert the Null character at the index.

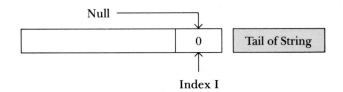

Index I

If the deletion occurs in the middle of the string, set off the substring starting at index I for J characters. Concatenate the tail section of the string to the head section of the string.

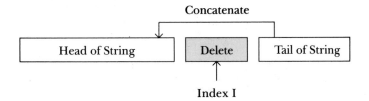

Index I

STRDELETE(S, I, J)

Parameters passed
    Address of string S.
    Index I.
    Delete count J.
Parameters returned
    None

```
            xdef    strdelete

buf:        equ     8
delindex:   equ     12
delcount:   equ     14
param8:     equ     8
Null:       equ     0

strdelete:  link    a6,#0
            movem.l d0-d3/a0,-(sp)
            move.w  (delindex,a6),d0   ; get index in d0
            move.w  (delcount,a6),d1   ; get del count in d1
            movea.l (buf,a6),a0        ; put s into a0
            move.w  d0,d2
            move.w  d0,d3              ; save index in d3
            add.w   d1,d2
            move.l  a0,-(sp)           ; get length of s
            jsr     strlength
            cmp.w   d0,d3              ; compare length with index
```

```
              bge       2$                    ; index >= length?
              cmp.w     d0,d2                 ; delete past string?
              bgt       1$                    ; cut the tail of the string
              move.w    d3,d0                 ; restore index in d0
              pea       (0,a0,d2.w)
              pea       (0,a0,d0.w)
              jsr       strcopy
              bra       2$
      1$:     move.w    d3,d0
              move.b    #Null,(0,a0,d0.w)
      2$:     movem.l   (sp)+,d0-d3/a0
              unlk      a6
              move.l    (sp),(param8,sp)      ; clean up the stack
              adda.w    #param8,sp
              rts
              end
```

Demonstration String Programs

String Program: File Names

Many operating systems permit files to be organized in a tree of directories and subdirectories. In such a system, file names are given by a path from the root directory to the host directory of the file. Here, we use the UNIX operating system to illustrate naming conventions for directories, subdirectories, and files.

EXAMPLE 9.8

A file is specified by a pathname that consists of a string of names separated by a slash (/). Each name prior to the last name is a directory, and the last name is the file name. All UNIX files are found by starting at a common directory, designated as the **root.** The root directory is specified by a leading slash.

> Pathname: class/jones/firstfile.t
> Directories: class, jones
> File Name: firstfile.t

> Pathname: /usr/users/class/testdata/
> Directories: root(/), usr, users, class, testdata
> Note: The pathname specifies a directory. No filename is specified.

> Pathname: firstfile.t
> Directories: No directories are listed.
> Filename: firstfile.t

In programming situations, it is often necessary to perform an analysis of file names. Such an analysis serves as an application of string handling.

Assume in the following program that the string-handling routines are present in a library and are linked into the main program code.

PROGRAM 9.1

String Handling with Directories

Read a pathname from the terminal.

1. If it contains directories, list the path of directories.

2. If the file name is present and ends with ".s", replace the substring ".s" with the substring ".out". Otherwise, append the string ".out" onto the end of the file name.

Print the new string.

Algorithm   To search for an ending substring ".s", first call STRRCHAR to see if "." is present. If it is, the address of "." is used for a terminating ".s".

```
            xref      newline,stop, getstr, putstr
            xref      strrchar, strcat

null:       equ       $00
nl:         equ       $0d
slash:      equ       '/'
dot:        equ       '.'
fail:       equ       $ffffffff

            entry     start

start:      lea       pathname,a0     ; read pathname
            jsr       getstr          ; get filename
            tst.b     pathname        ; check input string is null
            beq       outd

; find directories
            move.w    #slash,-(sp)    ; push '/'
            pea       pathname,a0     ; push string address
            jsr       strrchar        ; find last occurrence of '/'
            cmpa.l    #fail,a0        ; see if '/' is present
            bne.s     foundslash
            lea       pathname,a0
            bra.s     startappend

; print the directory path
foundslash:
            move.b    #null,(a0)      ; place null at last '/'
            lea       pathname
            jsr       putstr
            jsr       newline
            move.b    #slash,(a0)     ; put '/' back in
            lea       (1,a0),a0       ; advance over '/'
            tst.b     (a0)            ; see if pathname ends with '/'
            beq.s     outd
```

```
; append ".out" find last occurrence of ".s"
startappend:
                movea.l  a0,a1            ; save addr of 1st char in name
                move.w   #dot,-(sp)
                pea      (a0)             ; push addr of 1st char in name
                jsr      strrchar
                cmpa.l   #fail,a0         ; is '.' present
                beq.s    notfound         ; no '.' found. append '.out'
                cmpi.b   #'s',(1,a0)      ; check if next char is 's'
                bne.s    notfound
                move.b   #null,(a0)       ; replace '.' with null
                bra.s    append

notfound:       pea      dotout           ; string ".out"
                pea      (a1)             ; push address for strcat
                bra.s    catenate
append:         pea      dotout           ; string ".out"
                pea      (a0)             ; push address of null
catenate:       jsr      strcat           ; do the replace
; print out the adjusted file
                lea      pathname,a0
                jsr      putstr
                jsr      newline
outd:           jsr      stop

                data
pathname:       ds.b     256
dotout:         dc.b     '.out',null
                end
```

⟨Run of Program 9.1⟩

/usr/public/mc68000/demo.s
/usr/public/mc68000
/usr/public/mc68000/demo.out

PROGRAM 9.2

Find and Replace

The user initially enters a string T that is used as a replacement and then a second string that contains one or more asterisks (*). At each occurrence of "*", replace the "*" by the string T. For example, the replacement T = "GOOD" updates the string "* CHILDREN CAN BE REALLY *" to become "GOOD CHILDREN CAN BE REALLY GOOD". The new string is printed to the screen.

Algorithm The routine STRCHAR is called repeatedly to locate "*". At each such character, STRDELETE is called to remove the "*", and STRIN-SERT is called to insert the replacement string.

```
                    xref    getstr, strchar, putstr, strdelete
                    xref    stop, strlength, strinsert

null:               equ     $00
star:               equ     '*'
fail:               equ     $ffffffff

                    entry   start

start:              lea     replace_str,a0    ; read replacement string
                    jsr     getstr
                    lea     buffer,a0         ; read template
                    jsr     getstr

; find each occurrence of '*' and replace string
                    lea     buffer,a0
findstar:           move.w  #star,-(sp)       ; look for '*'
                    move.l  a0,-(sp)
                    jsr     strchar
                    cmpa.l  #fail,a0          ; see if '*' is present
                    beq.s   printstr

                    move.w  #1,-(sp)          ; first delete '*'
                    move.w  #0,-(sp)
                    move.l  a0,-(sp)
                    jsr     strdelete

                    move.w  #0,-(sp)
                    pea     replace_str
                    move.l  a0,-(sp)
                    jsr     strinsert
                    bra     findstar

printstr:                                     ; print out the adjusted file
                    lea     buffer,a0
                    jsr     putstr
                    jsr     stop

                    data
buffer:             ds.b    256
replace_str:
                    ds.b    256

                    end
```

⟨Run of Program 9.2⟩

```
good
* children can be really *
good children can be really good
```

String Program:
C and Pascal Strings

The C programming language uses Null-terminated strings, whereas the Pascal language uses byte-count strings. In applications, a programmer may be required to convert strings between the two formats. Both algorithms and code for the utility routines CtoPstr and PtoCstr are included along with test programs.

A C string of length N is stored in N + 1 bytes with a terminating Null character. Similarly, a Pascal string is stored in N + 1 bytes with a leading byte holding the length of the string. The conversion of strings between the two formats requires a shifting of bytes.

C to Pascal

This conversion shifts each character to the right 1 byte. The first byte is free to hold the length.

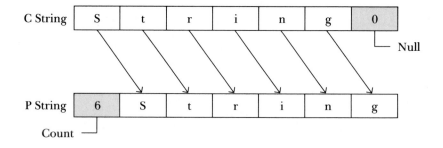

```
          xdef     CtoPstr

CtoPstr:  link     a6,#0
          move.l   d0-d1/a0,-(sp)
          movea.l  (8,a6),a0           ; put C string ptr in a0
          move.l   a0,-(sp)            ; find length
          jsr      strlength
          move.w   d0,d1               ; use d1 as counter
          subq.w   #1,d1
          lea      (0,a0,d0.w),a0      ; reposition a0 at end of str
CtoP_1:   move.b   -(a0),(1,a0)        ; shift each char right 1 byte
          dbra     d1,CtoP_1
          move.b   d0,(a0)             ; put the length at start of str
          movem.l  (sp)+,d0-d1/a0
          unlk     a6
          move.l   (sp)+,(sp)
          rts
          end
```

PROGRAM 9.3

C-to-Pascal Test
Conversion

A C string is created using GETSTR. After conversion to a Pascal string, the byte count in stored in D0, and output is generated using STROUT.

```
        xref    getstr,strout,stop
        xref    CtoPstr

        entry   start

start:  lea     buffer,a0   ; enter a null-terminated (C) string
        jsr     getstr
        pea     buffer      ; convert to a byte count (P) string
        jsr     CtoPstr
        lea     buffer,a0   ; output using strout
        move.b  (a0)+,d0    ; find string length in byte #0
        ext.w   d0
        jsr     strout
        jsr     stop

        data
buffer: ds.b    256
        end
```

⟨Run of Program 9.3⟩

String
String

Pascal to C

This conversion shifts each character to the left 1 byte and appends a terminating Null character.

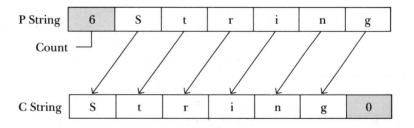

```
        xdef    PtoCstr

PtoCstr: link    a6,#0
         movem.l d0/a0,-(sp)
         movea.l (8,a6),a0       ; put P string ptr in a0
         moveq   #0,d0
```

```
                move.b    (a0),d0            ; get length from byte #0
                subq.w    #1,d0
      PtoC_1:   move.b    (1,a0),(a0)+       ; shift each char left 1 byte
                dbra      d0,PtoC_1
                move.b    #0,(a0)            ; null terminate the string
                movem.l   (sp)+,d0/a0
                unlk      a6
                move.l    (sp)+,(sp)
                rts
                end
```

PROGRAM 9.4

Pascal-to-C Test
Conversion

A string is input using STRIN. The byte count, returned in D0, is stored at the first byte of the string. After conversion to a C string, output is generated using PUTSTR.

```
                xref      PtoCstr,strin, putstr, stop
                xref      PtoCstr

                entry     start

      start:    lea       buffer+1,a0    ; enter a string using strin
                move.w    #255,d0
                jsr       strin
                move.b    d0,-(a0)       ; make it a byte count (P) string
                pea       buffer
                jsr       PtoCstr        ; convert to C-string
                lea       buffer, a0     ; output using putstring
                jsr       putstr
                jsr       stop

                data
      buffer:   ds.b  256
                end
```

⟨Run of Program 9.4⟩

String
String

9.4 | INTERNAL CONVERSION

The conversion of data between a string of digits in printable ASCII form and internal binary form is an important systems programming topic. For instance, a routine such as STRIN inputs a string of ASCII digits from a keyboard and produces a string in memory that can be converted to equivalent binary form. Assume that the decimal digits 265 are read from the keyboard into an input buffer.

Input Buffer

0011 0010	0011 0110	0011 0101
'2'	'6'	'5'

An internal ASCII decimal to binary conversion routine translates the characters in the input buffer to the binary data $0109 stored in N.

N | 0000 0001 0000 1001 |

16-Bit Value $0109

Reversing the process, assume that N is the integer 243_{10} with internal data representation as a 16-bit two's complement number.

$N =$ | 0000 0000 1111 0011 | = $00F3

An internal binary to ASCII decimal conversion routine must convert the binary number $00F3 into a sequence of ASCII characters '2', '4', '3' stored in an output buffer.

Output Buffer

0011 0010	0011 0100	0011 0011
'2'	'4'	'3'

The ASCII string can be transmitted from the output buffer to the screen using STROUT.

This section introduces the conversion routines between ASCII digit strings and their binary value. Section 9.5 develops an I/O library of routines that use internal conversion.

Internal Conversion: ASCII to Binary

The input subroutines HEXIN and HEXIN—LONG are used extensively in this book. The basis of the code is an algorithm that converts a string of ASCII hex digits to internal binary format.

HEXSTRTOBIN ASCII Hex-to-Binary Conversion

A simple example illustrates the conversion algorithm. Assume that a string of ASCII hex digits is Null-terminated. The routine HEXSTRTOBIN scans the characters in the string from left to right. Subtraction is used to convert an ASCII hex digit to its equivalent 4-bit hex number.

Character	Range	Action	Result
'0'–'9'	($30–39)	Subtract '0'	0–9
'A'–'F'	($41–45)	Subtract 'A'–10	10–15
'a'–'f'	($61–65)	Subtract 'a'–10	10–15

For example, assume that the input buffer contains the Null-terminated string '4B' and (D0.W) = 0.

$$\text{'4' 'B'} = 00110100\ 01000010$$

Step 1: Scan '4': Convert Ch = '4' = 0011 0100 to the hex digit 4 by subtracting '0' ('4' − '0' = $04). Add the result to D0.

$$(D0.W) = \$0000 + \$04 = \$0004$$

Shift the result in D0 left 4 bits to "open" the next hex digit.

Step 2: Scan 'B': Convert CH = 'B' = 0100 0010 to the hex digit B by subtracting 'A' − 10 ('B' − ('A' − 10) = 'B' − 'A' + 10 = $0B). Add to D0.

$$(D0.W) = \$0040 + \$0B = \$004B$$

HEXSTRTOBIN(S) ASCII Hex-to-Binary Conversion

Parameters passed
   Null-terminated string S of ASCII hex digits.
Parameters returned
   Hex number in (D0.L)

```
            xdef  hexstrtobin

straddr:    equ     8
param4      equ     4
savedd0:    equ     2

hexstrtobin:
            link    a6,#0
            movem.l d0-d1/a0,-(sp)
            movea.l (straddr,a6),a0
            moveq   #0,d0               ; accumulate ans in d0
```

```
htoi_1:      move.b    (a0)+,d1          ; get a character
             tst.b     d1                ; check for end of string
             beq.s     htoi_2
             jsr       htobin            ; convert digit to binary
             asl.l     #4,d0             ; prepare for next hex digit
             add.l     d1,d0             ; add in new low digit
             bra.s     htoi_1            ; get next hex digit
htoi_2:      move.w    d0,(savedd0,sp)   ; restore high half of D0
             movem.l   (sp)+,d1/a0
             unlk      a6
             move.l    (sp),(param4,sp)
             addq.w    #param4,sp
             rts

; Convert the character in d1.b to binary

htobin:
             cmpi.b    #'9',d1           ; check '0'-'9' range
             bgt.s     htobin_1
             subi.b    #'0',d1
             bra.s     htobin_3
htobin_1:
             cmpi.b    #'F',d1           ; check 'A'-'F' range
             bgt.s     htobin_2
             subi.b    #'A'-10,d1
             bra.s     hotbin_3
htobin_2:
             subi.b    #'a'-10,d1
htobin_3:
             rts
             end
```

DECSTRTOBIN ASCII Decimal-to-Binary Conversion

You can use the conversion DECSTRTOBIN for input routines DECIN and DECIN__LONG. It scans a Null-terminated string of ASCII decimal digits with an optional '−' and stores the binary equivalent in (D0.L). The algorithm uses repeated multiplication by powers of 10. Scan the characters in the input buffer from left to right. If the first character is '−', set a flag to indicate that the number is negative. Each ASCII decimal digit is converted to the corresponding binary value by subtracting '0'. The binary value in D0 is updated by first multiplying the current value by 10 and then adding the new decimal digit. After all digits have been scanned, negate the result if the number is negative.

For example, assume that the input buffer contains the ASCII digits 251 and (D0.L) = 0.

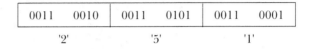

0011	0010	0011	0101	0011	0001

'2'   '5'   '1'

Step 1: Scan '2': The value 2 is obtained by subtracting '0' ('2' − '0' = 2). Multiply (D0.L) by 10, and add the new digit value.

$$(D0.L) = (D0.L) * 10 + 2 = 0 * 10 + 2 = 2$$

Step 2: Scan '5': First subtract '0' to obtain the value 5. The value of (D0.L) is updated.

$$(D0.L) = (D0.L) * 10 + 5 = 2 * 10 + 5 = 25 \qquad ((D0.L) = \$0019)$$

Step 3: Scan '1': Convert to digit 1 and update the result (D0.L).

$$(D0.L) = (D0.L) * 10 + 1 = 25 * 10 + 1 = 251 \qquad ((D0.L) = \$00FB)$$

DECSTRTOBIN(S): ASCII Decimal-to-Binary

Parameters passed
Null-terminated string S of ASCII decimal characters.
Parameters returned
Signed binary value in (D0.L).

```
          xdef    decstrtobin
          xref    umul32

straddr:  equ     8
param4:   equ     4

decstrtobin:
          link    a6,#0
          movem.l d1-d4/a0,-(sp)
          movea.l (straddr,a6),a0   ; get address of string
          moveq   #0,d3             ; put abs value in d3
          move.b  (a0),d4
          cmp.b   #'-',d4           ; see if the number is negative
          bne.s   dtol_1
          moveq   #1,d4             ; set d4 to indicate negative
          addq.w  #1,a0             ; skip over '-'
          bra.s   dtol_2
dtol_1:   moveq   #0,d4             ; number is nonnegative
dtol_2:   move.b  (a0)+,d2          ; get a character
          beq.s   dtol_3            ; quit if null char reached
          subi.b  #'0',d2           ; convert char to binary
          move.l  d3,-(sp)          ; compute 10 * CurrentValue
          pea     10
          jsr     umul32
          move.l  d1,d3             ; relevent 32 bits in d1.l
          ext.w   d2                ; convert char to long
          ext.l   d2
```

```
                add.l    d2,d3              ; add in the new digit
                bra.s    dtol_2
dtol_3:         move.l   d3,d0              ; answer returned in d0
                tst.w    d4                 ; test for negative number
                beq.s    dtol_4
                neg.l    d0                 ; negate it
dtol_4:         movem.l  (sp)+,d1-d4/a0
                unlk     a6
                move.l   (sp),(param4,sp)
                addq.w   #param4,sp
                rts
                end
```

Internal Conversion: Binary to ASCII

If it is necessary to have a printable form for a binary number in memory or a register, you must convert from binary to ASCII. For instance, the 32-bit value (D0.L) = $0000 018A ($394_{10}$) has the following ASCII hex and decimal strings:

Hex	0011	0001	0011	1000	0100	0001	'18A'
Decimal	0011	0011	0011	1001	0011	0100	'394'

The routine BINTOHEXSTR(S) takes a 16-bit integer in (D0.L) and generates a NULL-terminated string S containing the ASCII hex representation for the number. In its assembly language code, a table lookup scheme converts each 4-bit hex digit to HS equivalent ASCII hex digit. The routine pads with leading zeros so that eight hex digits are always output. A second routine, BINTODECSTR(S), formats the 32-bit contents of (D0.L) as an ASCII decimal string in S. It does not pad with leading zeros.

BINTOHEXSTR Binary-to-ASCII Hex Conversion

Binary-to-ASCII hex conversion uses the simple relation between a hex digit and four binary bits. The value in N is partitioned into eight hex digits. The algorithm uses an iterative process to scan the hex digits from left to right.

For example, assume that (D0.L) = $5E380000.

Step 1: Rotate (D0.L) 4 bits to the left using the instruction "ROL.L #4, D0". The result (D0.L) = $E3800005 allows for a scan of the hex digit 5. Move (D0.L) to (D2.L), and mask the high-order three hex digits in D2.

$$(D2.L) = \$00000005_{10}$$

(D2.L) is used as an index to access character '5' in the lookup table. The character is stored in the output buffer.

Steps 2–8: Continue the process by rotating left 4 bits and isolating the digit E. For index E = 14_{10} in the lookup table, there corresponds character 'E', which is placed in the output buffer. The process continues with '3' and '8' output, followed by four zeros. The Null character is then placed in the string S.

BINTOHEXSTR(S) *Binary-to-ASCII Hex*

Parameters passed
  32-bit integer in (D0.L).
  Address of string S on the stack.
Parameters returned
  The output buffer is stored in the Null-terminated string S.

```
            xdef   bintohexstr

s:            equ    8
null:         equ    0
binarytohsize: equ   4

bintohexstr:
            link    a6,#0
            movem.l d0-d2/a0-a1,-(sp)
            movea.l (straddr,a6),a0
            lea     hexdigits,a1        ; 4-bit conv table
            moveq   #7,d1               ; output four hex digits
itoh_1:     rol.w   #4,d0               ; output left to right
            move.b  d0,d2
            andi.w  #$000f,d2
            move.b  (0,a1,d2.w),a0)+    ; convert to ascii
            dbra    d1,itoh_1
            move.b  #Null,(a0)
            movem.l (sp)+,d0-d2/a0-a1
            unlk    a6
            move.l  (sp),(param4,sp)
            adda.w  #param4,sp
            rts

            data
hexdigits:
            dc.b    '0123456789ABCDEF'
            end
```

BINTODECSTR: 32-Bit Binary-to-ASCII
Decimal Conversion

The decimal output routine is based on the "repeated division" algorithm for converting a binary number to a decimal number. The algorithm, given in Chapter 2, is reviewed with an example. Assume that (D0.L) = $0000018A

(394_{10}). The digits '4', '9', and '3' are identified in that order and placed in buffer DECBUF.

Step 1: Divide (D0.L) by 10 using the 32-bit × 32-bit unsigned division subroutine UDIV32 presented in Chapter 8. The remainder is the units digit 4 in (D1.L) and the quotient is 39 in (D0.L). By adding $30 = '0'$, the remainder $0004 is converted to the equivalent ASCII decimal digit '4', which is stored in the last character of buffer DECBUF.

Steps 2–3: The subsequent steps identify digits 9 and 3. The equivalent characters are stored in DECBUF.

Copy step: The iteration stops when the quotient is 0. The routine is completed by copying the characters from DECBUF to string S.

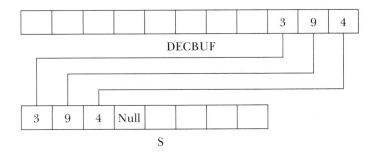

Note: If the number (D0.L) is negative, place a '–' in the output string S and use NEG to create the absolute value. Then convert (D0.L) to ASCII.

BINTODECSTR(N,S) *Binary-to-ASCII Decimal*

Parameters passed
   32-bit integer in (D0.L).
   Address of string S on the stack.
Parameters returned
   S is assigned a Null-terminated string containing the ASCII decimal equivalent of (D0.L).

```
        xdef    bintodecstr
        xref    undiv32

s:      equ     8
null:   equ     0
parm4:  equ     4

bintodecstr:
        link    a6,#0
        movem.l d0-d1/a0-a2,-(sp)
```

```
           movea.l   (straddr,a6),a0
           tst.l     d0
           bpl       btol_1
           move.b    #'-',(a0)+        ; move '-' into output string
           neg.l     d0
btol_1:    lea       decbuf+12,a1      ; set a1 past buffer
btol_2:    move.l    d0,-(sp)
           move.l    #10,-(sp)
           jsr       udiv32
           addi.b    #'0',d1           ; convert to character digit
           move.b    d1,-(a1)
           tst.l     d0
           bne.s     btol_2
           lea       decbuf+12,a2      ; copy from buffer to string
btol_3:    move.b    (a1)+,(a0)+
           cmpa.l    a2,a1
           bcs.s     btol_3            ; copy until hit "decbuf+12"
           move.b    #Null,(a0)        ; null terminate the string
           movem.l   (sp)+,d0-d1/a0-a2
           unlk      a6
           move.l    (sp),(param4,sp)
           adda.w    #param4,sp
           rts

           data
decbuf:    ds.b      12

           end
```

Internal Conversion: Binary to BCD

Some internal conversions do not involve ASCII strings. High-level languages frequently support decimal-based arithmetic for accounting applications. This involves conversion of numbers from binary to an internal decimal representation. Chapter 8 covers the MC68000 BCD instructions. This section presents algorithms to convert binary data to and from packed BCD format.

Binary/BCD Conversions

Assume that you are dealing with four-digit decimal numbers in the range 0–9999. Decimal arithmetic can be performed using the BCD instructions ABCD, SBCD, and NBCD. These routines operate on two BCD digits stored as 8-bit data. Extended arithmetic for four BCD digits (16 bits) and eight BCD digits (32 bits) is described in Chapter 8.

1001	0111	0001	0101	= 9715
4 Bits	4 Bits	4 Bits	4 Bits	

Multiplication and division algorithms for BCD numbers often use the corresponding binary representation to gain access to the MC68000 multiply and divide operations. The results are then converted back to the BCD format. The following routines implement the binary/BCD conversions.

BINBCD(B,N) Binary-to-BCD Conversion

Parameters passed
  B contains the 16-bit binary value.
  The address of the resulting BCD number N.
Parameters returned
  The equivalent BCD number is returned in N.

```
        xdef      binbcd

binbcdbparm:      equ    8
binbcdnparm:      equ    10
param6:           equ    6

binbcd:
        link      a6,#0
        movem.l   d0-d2/a0,-(sp)
        move.w    (binbcdbparm,a6),d0    ; get binary number
        movea.l   (binbcdnparm,a6),a0    ; get packed BCD number
        moveq     #0,d1                  ; build the bcd value in d1
        moveq     #3,d2                  ; only compute 4 decimal digits
        andi.l    #$ffff,d0              ; create equiv. long word
binbcd_0:
        divu      #10,d0                 ; divide to find a digit
        swap      d0                     ; get the remainder in view
        add.w     d0,d1                  ; put digit in d1
        ror.w     #4,d1                  ; rotate d1 to bring clear
                                         ; "nibble" in range
        swap      d0
        andi.l    #$ffff,d0              ; mask off old remainder
        dbra      d2,binbcd_0
        move.w    d1,(a0)                ; place bcd number in memory
        movem.l   (sp)+,d0-d2/a0
        unlk      a6
        move.l    (sp),(param6,sp)
        adda.w    #param6,sp
        rts

        end
```

BCDBIN(N,B) BCD-to-Binary Conversion

Parameters passed
  N is the four-digit BCD number.
  The address of the converted binary number.

Parameters returned
The 16-bit binary value is returned in B.

```
        xdef        bcdbin

bcdbinnparm:        equ     8
param6:             equ     10
bcdbinsize:         equ     6

bcdbin:
        link        a6,#0
        movem.l     d0-d3/a0,-(sp)
        move.l      (bcdbinnparm,a6),d3     ; packed BCD number
        movea.l     (bcdbinbparm,a6),a0     ; address of binary number
        moveq       #0,d0                   ; binary value will be in d0
        moveq       #3,d2                   ; look at four digits
bcdbin_0:
        mulu        #10,d0                  ; multiply value by 10
        rol.w       #4,d3                   ; get next significant digit
        move.w      d3,d1                   ; isolate the digit
        andi.w      #$000f,d1
        add.w       d1,d0                   ; accumulate the total
        dbra        d2,bcdbin_0
        move.w      d0,(a0)                 ; put number into memory
        movem.l     (sp)+,d0-d3/a0
        unlk        a6
        move.l      (sp),(param6,sp)
        adda.w      #param6,sp
        rts

        end
```

The binary/BCD routines are used in the following test program. It is assumed that the subroutines are separately assembled in a library and linked into the main code file.

PROGRAM 9.5

I/O Test Program

Subroutine DECIN reads a 16-bit decimal number from the keyboard, and HEXOUT prints it in hex. The result is converted to BCD using BINBCD. The BCD representation is printed in hex and then reconverted to binary using BCDBIN. The final value is printed using DECOUT.

```
        xref    decin, decout, hexout, newline, stop
        xref    binbcd, bcdbin

        entry   start

start:  jsr     decin               ; read a decimal number
        jsr     hexout              ; output it in hex
```

```
        pea     bcdnumber
        move.w  d0,-(sp)        ; convert the number to bcd
        jsr     binbcd
        move.w  bcdnumber,d0
        jsr     hexout          ; print the converted number
        pea     binnumber
        move.w  d0,-(sp)
        jsr     bcdbin          ; convert back to binary
        move.w  binnumber,d0
        jsr     decout          ; print the number in decimal
                                ; note that the last two numbers
                                ; printed should be the same

        jsr     newline
        jsr     stop

        data
bcdnumber:      ds.w  1
binnumber:      ds.w  1
        end
```

⟨Run of Program 9.5⟩

1234
04D2 1234 1234

9.5 | INPUT/OUTPUT LIBRARY

Chapter 4 presented a library of I/0 routines, including STRIN, HEXOUT, and DECOUT__LONG. For the material presented in this section, it is assumed that you have access to these routines. This section covers the design and implementation of such an I/0 library. Using single-character input from the keyboard (GETCHAR) and single-character output to the screen (PUTCHAR) as primitive routines, we develop a complete library based on the I/0 specifications from Chapter 4. In order to distinguish the new library routines from those used in previous chapters, the names have been changed (see Table 9.2). If the routines developed here are used, a linker will find no name conflicts.

The design of the I/O library is based on the primitive routines GET-CHAR and PUTCHAR. Typically, the routines are supplied by the operating system. When a "standalone" system is used, the user must write the primitive input and output routines. Chapter 12 develops I/O for a standalone Motorola system. In this section, it is assumed that the GETCHAR

TABLE 9.2 I/O Library Routines

TEST I/O LIBRARY	NEW I/O LIBRARY	REGISTERS
	GETCHAR	Use (D0.B)
	PUTCHAR	Use (D0.B)
STRIN	GETSTRIN	Use A0 and (D0.W)
	GETSTRING	Use A0
STROUT	PUTSTROUT	Use A0 and (D0.W)
	PUTSTRING	Use A0
DECIN	GETDECIN	Use (D0.W)
DECIN__LONG	GETDECIN__LONG	Use (D0.L)
DECOUT	PUTDECOUT	Use (D0.W)
DECOUT__LONG	PUTDECOUT__LONG	Use (D0.L)
HEXIN	GETHEXIN	Use (D0.W)
HEXIN__LONG	GETHEXIN__LONG	Use (D0.L)
HEXOUT	PUTHEXOUT	Use (D0.W)
HEXOUT__LONG	PUTHEXOUT__LONG	Use (D0.L)

and PUTCHAR routines can be written using operating system primitives. Repeated use of these routines creates the string routines PUTSTROUT and GETSTRIN, as well as the Null-terminated string I/O routines PUTSTRING and GETSTRING. The internal format conversion routines from Section 9.4 combine with these string-handling routines to produce the number routines GETHEXIN, PUTDEC__LONG, and so forth. The new I/O library can be ported to any system by implementing the GET-CHAR and PUTCHAR routines.

The specifications for input add some details to the library design. If you wish to allow multiple inputs from the same line, the number routines must skip over leading **white space** (blanks, tabs, and the end-of-line character) and terminate a scan on a character that is not a digit. String input must have available a "putback" utility that allows for the rescanning of characters. An example illustrates the problems for the following sequence of input.

Code JSR GETDECIN
      JSR GETHEXIN
      JSR GETSTRIN

Input 9875 A5F7MC68000⟨CR⟩

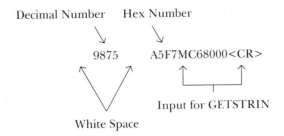

Rule 1 A decimal or hex input routine must skip leading white space and then test for a valid first character.

Examples

(a) The routine GETDECIN must skip white space at the beginning of the line and test that the first non–white-space character '9' is a valid decimal digit.

(b) The routine GETHEXIN must skip white space between the numbers and test that the first non–white-space character 'A' is a valid hex digit in the range

'0'–'9', 'A'–'F', 'a'–'f'

Rule 2 A decimal or hex input routine reads digits until a nonvalid digit (including end of line) is encountered. The nonvalid digit creates a stopping condition and not an error.

Example

GETHEXIN reads ASCII digits 'A', '5', 'F', and '7'. The process terminates after GETHEXIN reads the 'M' in MC68000. Code conversion applies to the string of valid digits.

Rule 3 When a non–"end-of-line" character terminates a number routine, the character should be available as input for a subsequent routine. The character may be an invalid digit for the specific number base and not be invalid for the next input.

Example

The character 'M' is read from the input stream and terminates the scan in GETHEXIN. For the subsequent call to GETSTRIN, the character must be returned to the input string and rescanned as part of the string 'MC68000'. The new library develops two routines GETC and UNGETC that complement each other to "unget" characters.

Input

Input is based on the primitive routine GETCHAR that reads a single character from the keyboard. An input routine must handle the end-of-file (EOF) condition that occurs when the user transmits a character indicating that no more keyboard input is to be entered. On UNIX systems, the character is normally ⟨*control*⟩D and on DOS systems it is ⟨*control*⟩Z. When EOF is transmitted, GETCHAR must return a value indicating this fact. The value must not be confused with any valid ASCII input character. Because input on some systems can be redirected from another device such as a disk, it is possible that a legitimate 8-bit character such as $FF may be input. Thus no 8-bit character can be used to indicate that the end of file has occurred. The standard solution is to have GETCHAR return an integer value. In a case in which an actual character was typed, bits 8–15 of the return value are clear. EOF is then designated as $FFFF $= -1$.

GETCHAR Read a Single Character from the Keyboard

Parameters passed
  None
Parameter returned
  The character is returned as an integer value in D0.W. EOF is
    indicated by (D0.W) $= -1$.

Example   The following routine outlines the reading of a string of characters. The routine GETCHAR reads individual characters and identifies EOF.

```
LOOP:   JSR     GETCHAR
        TST.W   D0            ; TEST FOR (D0.W) = -1 (EOF)
        BMI     XIT
                  .
                  .
                  .
        BRA     LOOP
XIT:              .
                  .
                  .
        END
```

Algorithms to read hex and decimal numbers scan the input stream of characters. They terminate the scan on a nonvalid digit. In order to have multiple inputs on the same line, the terminating character must be returned to the input stream and made available for the next read. The pair of routines GETC/UNGETC implement a one-character push-back buffer and are used to manage the input stream. The idea is very simple. A single byte in memory is set aside as a buffer that is initially empty. Whenever a character must be pushed back, UNGETC places the character into the buffer. On each request to read a character, the buffer is first checked by GETC. If the buffer is empty, no character has been pushed back, and a character is read from the input stream using GETCHAR. If the buffer is full, the most recently read character has been pushed back and is now available for rescanning. The routine GETC sets the buffer to empty and returns this character. The routine GETC becomes the operative routine for single character input.

GETC Read a Single Character from the Keyboard with Character Pushback

Parameters passed
None
Parameter returned
The character is returned as an integer value in (D0.W). EOF is indicated by (D0.W) = −1.

UNGETC Push a Single Character Back into the Input Stream

Parameters passed
The character to be pushed back is in (D0.B).
Parameter returned
None

```
        xdef    getc
        xref    getchar

getc:   tst.b   pushbackbuf     ; was a character pushed back?
        beq.s   getc_1          ; if not, call _getchar
        move.b  pushbackbuf,d0  ; get the push-back character
        andi.w  #$ff,d0         ; getc returns 16 bits
        clr.b   pushbackbuf     ; indicate pushbackbuf empty
        bra.s   getc_2          ; exit
getc_1: jsr     getchar         ; make primitive input call
getc_2: rts

        xdef    ungetc

ungetc: move.b  d0,pushbackbuf  ; save character in pushbackbuf
        rts

        data
```

```
pushbackbuf:
        dc.b  0                      ; char pushed back
        even

        end
```

The routine GETSTRIN uses GETC to implement string input. Characters are read into the string pointed to by A0. Input terminates on a carriage return or after (D0.W) characters have been read. The number of characters that are read is returned in (D0.W).

GETSTRIN Read a String from the Keyboard

Parameters passed
    The address of the input buffer is given in A0.
    The maximum number of characters permitted in the read is
       stored in (D0.W).
Parameters returned
    The number of characters actually read. 0 is returned if EOF is
       encountered.

```
        xdef      getstrin
        xref      getc

NewLine: equ      13                 ; macintosh newline

getstrin:
        movem.l   d0-d2/a0,-(sp)
        move.w    d0,d1              ; loop counter
        move.w    d0,d2              ; save max char count
        subq.w    #1,d1
        bmi.s     getstrin_4         ; requested null string
getstrin_1:
        jsr       getc
        tst.w     d0
        bpl.s     getstrin_2         ; end of file??
        moveq     #0,d0              ; return 0 upon EOF
        bra.s     getstrin_4
getstrin_2:
        move.b    d0,(a0)+
        cmpi.b    #NewLine,d0        ; has end of line been found?
        dbeq      d1,getstrin_1
        bne.s     getstrin_3         ; if cmp gave 0, we read EOLN
        sub.w     d1,d2              ; char read = max - (d1)
getstrin_3:
        move.w    d2,d0              ; d0 is output register
```

```
getstrin_4:
        move.w   d0,(2,sp)           ; give original d0 a new low half
        movem.l  (sp)+,d0-d2/a0
        rts

        end
```

GETSTRIN is now used to generate the Null-terminated string routine GETSTRING, which is identical to the routine GETSTR given in the last section.

GETSTRING Read a Null-Terminated String

Parameters passed
    The address of the input buffer is given in A0.
Parameters returned
    None.

```
xdef     getstring
xref     getstrin

getstring:
        movem.l  d0/a0,-(sp)
        move.w   #255,d0             ; set an input count
        jsr      getstrin
        subq.w   #1,d0
        move.b   #Null,(0,a0,d0.w)
        movem.l  (sp)+,d0/a0
        rts
        end
```

All the tools are in place to write input routines GETHEXIN and GETDECIN_LONG. These are more detailed than the output routines PUTHEXOUT and PUTDECOUT_LONG and include the following additional factors:

1. Initially, white space is skipped, which is done by repeated calls to GETC, until a character is found that is not a blank, tab, or newline. The current character must be a valid digit; otherwise, an error message is printed and a value of zero is returned. Characters are then read and placed into a string buffer until a character is found that is not a valid digit.

2. The routines define an external variable EOF that is set to -1 if GETC returns EOF. Immediately after calling the procedure, the user can test EOF as a Boolean flag. Because GETHEXIN can return any 16-bit value in (D0.W), no return value can be used to indicate the end of file.

3. The last character read is checked. If it is not a newline, it is placed back in the input stream using UNGETC. If a newline were left in the input stream, a subsequent call to GETSTRIN would return only the newline. To avoid this, the newline is discarded.

4. The string buffer is passed to HEXSTRTOBIN or DECSTRTOLBIN for conversion to binary form.

GETHEXIN Read a 16-Bit Hex Number

Parameters passed
   None
Parameters returned
   (D0.W) is the number read.

```
        xdef    gethexin
        xref    getc, ungetc, hexstrtobin, putstring

NewLine: equ    13
Tab:     equ    9
Null:    equ    0
savedd0: equ    2

gethexin:
        movem.l  d0-d2/a0,-(sp)
        clr.w    eof            ; end of file marker clear

; call getc until have skipped all "white space"
gethex_1:
        jsr      getc           ; get a character
        tst.w    d0             ; check for end of file
        bpl.s    gethex_2
        move.w   #-1,eof
        bra.s    gethex_7       ; end of file found
gethex_2:
        cmpi.b   #' ',d0
        beq.s    gethex_1
        cmpi.b   #NewLine,d0
        beq.s    gethex_1
        cmpi.b   #Tab,d0
        beq.s    gethex_1
; end skipping "white space"

        jsr      ishexdigit     ; test for non-hex 1st char
        tst.w    d2
        bmi.s    gethex_6       ; first digit must be hex digit
        lea      hexstrbuf,a0   ; build hex string in hexstrbuf

; loop, reading ascii hex chars until a non hex character is found
gethex_3:
        move.b   d0,(a0)+       ; load char into string buffer
```

```
            jsr      getc             ; get next ascii hex digit
            tst.w    d0               ; check for end of file
            bpl.s    gethex_4         ; stop input on eof
            move.w   #-1,eof
            bra.s    gethex_7
gethex_4:
            jsr      ishexdigit
            tst.w    d2
            bmi.s    gethex_5         ; stop input on a non hex digit
            bra.s    gethex_3         ; get next hex digit

gethex_5:
            cmpi.b   #NewLine,d0      ; do not put back newline
            beq.s    gethex_7
            jsr      ungetc           ; put back terminating char
            bra.s    gethex_7

; error reporting
gethex_6:
            pea      hex_errmsg       ; 1st digit incorrect
            jsr      putstring
            lea      hexstrbuf,a0     ; return null string on error

gethex_7:
            move.b   #Null,(a0)       ; Null terminate the string
            pea      hexstrbuf
            jsr      hexstrtobin
            tst.w    d6
            bne.s    gethex_8
            move.w   d0,(savedd0,sp)  ; save high word of D0
            bra.s    gethex_9
            rts

; Return 0 if char in D0.B is hex digit; else return -1

ishexdigit:
            clr.w    d2
            cmpi.b   #'0',d0          ; check '0'-'9' range
            blt.s    ishex_3          ; quit on a non-hex digit
            cmpi.b   #'9',d0
            bgt.s    ishex_1
            bra.s    ishex_4
ishex_1:    cmpi.b   #'A',d0          ; check 'A'-'F' range
            blt.s    ishex_3
            cmpi.b   #'F',d0
            bgt.s    ishex_2
            bra.s    ishex_4
ishex_2:    cmpi.b   #'a',d0          ; check 'a'-'f' range
            blt.s    ishex_3
            cmpi.b   #'f',d0
            bgt.s    ishex_3
            bra.s    ishex_4
ishex_3:    move.w   #-1,d2           ; not a hex digit
ishex_4:    rts
```

```
          data

          xdef      eof

eof:      ds.w      1
hexstrbuf:
          ds.b      20
hex_errmsg:
          dc.b      'Invalid hex digit begins the number', NewLine
          even

          end
```

The routine GETDECIN_LONG is very similar to GETHEXIN. It assumes that the external variable EOF has already been defined and tests for decimal digits rather than hex digits. A leading minus sign is handled as a special case of the first character. If present, it is copied into the string buffer passed to DECSTRTOLBIN.

GETDECIN_LONG Read a 32-Bit Decimal Number

Parameters passed
  None
Parameter returned
  (D0.L) is the number read.

```
          xdef      getdecin_long
          xref      getc, ungetc, desctrtolbin, putstring

NewLine:  equ       13
Tab:      equ       9                    ; macintosh newline
Null:     equ       0

getdecin_long:
          movem.l   d1-d2/a0,-(sp)
          clr.w     eof                  ; end of file marker clear

; call getc until have skipped all "white space"
getdecin_long_1:
          jsr       getc                 ; get a character
          tst.w     d0                   ; check for end of file
          bpl.s     getdecin_long_2
          move.w    #-1,eof
          bra.s     getdecin_long_8      ; end of file found
getdecin_long_2:
          cmpi.b    #' ',d0
          beq.s     getdecin_long_1
          cmpi.b    #NewLine,d0
          beq.s     getdecin_long_1
          cmpi.b    #Tab,d0
          beq.s     getdecin_long_1
; end skipping "white space"
```

```
            lea         decstrbuf,a0      ; build in hexstrbuf
            cmpi.b      #'-',d0
            bne.s       getdecin_long_3
            move.b      d0,(a0)+
            jsr         getc
getdecin_long_3:
            jsr         isdecdigit        ; test for non-decimal 1st char
            tst.w       d2
            bmi.s       getdecin_long_7   ; look for decimal digit

; loop, reading ascii decimal chars until a non-
decimal character is found
getdecin_long_4:
            move.b      d0,(a0)+          ; load char into string buffer
            jsr         getc              ; get next ascii decimal digit
            tst.w       d0                ; check for end of file
            bpl.s       getdecin_long_5   ; stop input on eof
            move.w      #-1,eof
            bra.s       getdecin_long_8
getdecin_long_5:
            jsr         isdecdigit
            tst.w       d2
            bmi.s       getdecin_long_6   ; stop on non-decimal digit
            bra.s       getdecin_long_4   ; get next decimal digit

getdecin_long_6:
            cmpi.b      #NewLine,d0       ; do not put back newline
            beq.s       getdecin_long_8
            jsr         ungetc            ; put back terminating char
            bra.s       getdecin_long_8
; error reporting
getdecin_long_7:
            pea         dec_errmsg        ; 1st digit incorrect
            jsr         putstring
            lea         decstrbuf,a0      ; return null string on error

getdecin_long_8:
            move.b      #Null,(a0)        ; null terminate the string buffer
            pea         decstrbuf
            jsr         decstrtolbin
            movem.l     (sp)+,d1-d2/a0
            rts

; Return 0 if char in D0.B is decimal digit; else return -1

isdecdigit:
            clr.w       d2
            cmpi.b      #'0',d0           ; check '0'-'9' range
            blt.s       isdec_1           ; quit on a non-hex digit
            cmpi.b      #'9',d0
            ble.s       isdec_2
isdec_1:
            move.w      #-1,d2
```

```
isdec_2:
        rts

        data

        xref    eof

decstrbuf:
        ds.b    20
dec_errmsg:
        dc.b    'Invalid decimal digit begins the number', NewLine
        even

        end
```

Output

A low-level routine PUTCHAR provides single-character output to the screen. The routines PUTSTROUT, PUTSTRING, PUTHEXOUT, and PUTDECOUT__LONG use PUTCHAR and format conversion. All output routines use registers for parameter passing.

PUTCHAR(C) Write a Single Character to the Screen

> Parameters passed
>   Character C is passed in (D0.B).
> Parameter returned
>   None

PUTCHAR is used to write PUTSTROUT, which is identical to routine STROUT.

PUTSTROUT(S) Print a String

> Parameters passed
>   Address of the string S is in A0.
>   Output length in (D0.W).
> Parameter returned
>   None

```
        xdef    putstrout
        xref    putchar
putstrout:
        movem.l  d0-d1/a0,-(sp)
        subq.w   #1,d0
        bmi.s    putstrout_2        ; exit if char count = 0
        move.w   d0,d1              ; use d1 as the loop count
```

```
putstrout_1:
        move.b    (a0)+,d0
        jsr       putchar              ; call library routine putchar
        dbra      d1,putstrout_1
        jsr       flushOutput
putstrout_2:
        movem.l   (sp)+,d0-d1/a0
        rts
        end
```

PUTSTROUT is now used to generate the Null-terminated string output routine PUTSTRING, which is identical to the routine PUTSTR given in the last section.

PUTSTRING(S) Print a Null-Terminated String

Parameters passed
Address of the string S is in A0.
Parameters returned
None

```
        xdef      putstring
        xref      putstrout

putstring:
        movem.l   d0/a0-a1,-(sp)
        movea.l   a0,a1                ; store string address in a1
        moveq     #0,d0                ; d0 holds the string count
puts_1: tst.b     (a1)+                ; test for a null byte
        beq.s     puts_2
        addq.w    #1,d0
        bra.s     puts_1
puts_2: jsr       putstrout
        movem.l   (sp)+,d0/a0-a1
        rts
        end
```

Numerical output is demonstrated by developing routines PUTHEXOUT and PUTDECOUT_LONG. In the case of PUTHEXOUT, the routine BINTOHEXSTR is called to convert the binary value in (D0.W) to a Null-terminated string, which is then output to the screen using PUTSTRING. PUTDECOUT_LONG uses LBINTODECSTR.

PUTHEXOUT(N) Output a 16-Bit Hex Number

Parameters passed
(D0.W) is the binary number N to output.

Parameter returned
   None

```
          xdef        puthexout
          xref        bintohexstr, putstring

Null:     equ         0

puthexout:
          movem.l     d0/a0,-(sp)
          move.w      #1,d0
          pea         puthexbuf
          jsr         bintohexstr
          lea         puthexbuf+4,a0
          jsr         putstring
          lea         blanks,a0
          jsr         putstring
          movem.l     (sp)+,d0/a0
          rts

          data
puthexbuf:
          ds.b        10
blanks:
          dc.b        ' ', Null
          even
          end
```

PUTDECOUT__LONG(N) Write a Long Word to the Screen in Decimal

Parameters passed
   D0.L is the binary number N to output.
Parameter returned
   None

```
          xdef        putdecout_long
          xref        bintodecstr, putstring

Null:     equ         0

putdecout_long:
          move.l      a0,-(sp)
          pea         putdecbuf
          jsr         bintodecstr
          lea         putdecbuf,a0
          jsr         putstring
          lea         blanks,a0
          jsr         putstring
          move.l      (sp)+,a0
          rts
```

```
                    data
putdecbuf:          ds.b        12
blanks:             dc.b        ' ', Null
                    even

                    end
```

PROGRAM 9.6

Looking for
End-of-File

This program first exercises PUTSTRING and GETSTRING by asking
whether the user really wants to continue. By setting bit 5 of the first
character of the string, it ensures that a response of 'Y' is converted to 'y',
so only a comparison with 'y' need be done. If the user wants to continue,
the program reads a series of 32-bit decimal integers until the end of file
is encountered at the keyboard. The 16-bit number in the external variable
EOF is checked for a value of −1, which indicates the end of file. Each
value is printed in hex by using PUTHEXOUT first on the most significant
word of D0.L and then on the least significant word. The machine instruction SWAP is used to bring the correct half of D0 into position.

```
            xref        getdecin_long, puthexout, newline, putstrout
            xref        putstring, getstring, stop
            entry       start

Null:       equ         0

start:      lea         contmsg, a0
            jsr         putstring
            lea         ans, a0
            jsr         getstring
            bset        #5, ans         ; if 'Y', convert to 'y'
            move.b      ans, d0
            cmpi.b      #'y', d0
            bne.s       out
read:       jsr         getdecin_long
            tst.w       eof
            bmi.s       out
            lea         mswmsg, a0
            jsr         putstring
            swap        d0              ; print MSW of D0 in hex
            jsr         puthexout
            lea         lswmsg, a0
            move.w      #34, d0
            jsr         putstrout
            swap        d0              ; print LSW of D0 in hex
            jsr         puthexout
            jsr         newline
            bra.s       read
out:        jsr         stop

            data
```

```
                    xref      eof
contmsg:     dc.b      'Do you wish to continue ', Null
ans:         ds.b      2
mswmsg:      dc.b      'The most significant word is ', Null
lswmsg:      dc.b      'and the least significant word is '

             end
```

⟨Run of Program 9.6⟩

```
Do you wish to continue? Y
55
The most significant word is 0000  and the least significant word is
0037
5533
The most significant word is 0000  and the least significant word is
159D
−1
The most significant word is FFFF  and the least significant word is
FFFF
⟨End of File Character⟩
```

9.6 | DATA ENCRYPTION

Typical data encryption algorithms require the user to enter a key that is used to transform a sequence of characters into "unreadable" form. The key is also used to restore the text to its original form. A study of modern algorithms used for encryption is beyond the scope of this text. The concepts are demonstrated with two encrypting schemes for ASCII code files. The casual "code breaker" would have difficulty discovering how to reconstruct the original file in each case.

EXAMPLE 9.9   The following scheme encrypts an 8-bit ASCII character.

Rule

Change the sense of bits 7 and 0 using BCHG.
Interchange bits 2 and 5.
Replace the original character with the encrypted character.

(*a*) a = $61 = %01100001   Encrypted (a) = %11000100 = $C4

(*b*) 7 = $37 = %00110111   Encrypted (7) = %10110110 = $B6

This encryption scheme is **invertible**. That is, if the same algorithm is applied to the encrypted byte, the original character is returned. An encryption scheme must allow for a decryption algorithm that is the inverse function or the original data cannot be restored. The encryption scheme is implemented by the following subroutine.

CRYPT1(S) Data Encryption Routine

Parameters passed
A0 contains the address S of a Null-terminated string.
Parameters returned
None (The string is encrypted in memory.)

```
            xdef      crypt1

crypt1:
            movem.l   d0-d2/a0,-(sp)
crypt_0:
            move.b    (a0),d0      ; get a string character
            beq.s     crypt_1      ; bail out if end of string reached
            bchg      #7,d0        ; change bits 7 and 0
            bchg      #0,d0
            move.b    d0,d1
            move.b    d0,d2
            andi.b    #$db,d0      ; clear bits 2 and 5
            andi.b    #$04,d1      ; move bit 2 to position 5
            lsl.b     #3,d1
            andi.b    #$20,d2      ; move bit 5 to position 2
            lsr.b     #3,d2
            add.b     d2,d0        ; put exchanged bits back in d0
            add.b     d1,d0
            move.b    d0,(a0)+     ; put transformed char into memory
            bra.s     crypt_0      ; loop to the null character
crypt_1:
            movem.l   (sp)+,d0-d2/a0
            rts
            end
```

PROGRAM 9.7

Testing CRYPT1

The result of running CRYPT1 on an ASCII input string is illustrated by this short program:

```
            xref      getstring, putstring, newline, crypt1, stop

            entry     start

start:      lea       str,a0
            jsr       getstring
            lea       str,a0
            jsr       crypt1
```

```
            lea     str,a0
            jsr     putstring    ; put out the crypted string
            jsr     newline
            lea     str,a0
            jsr     crypt1       ; decrypt the crypted string
            lea     str,a0
            jsr     putstring
            jsr     newline
            jsr     stop

            data
str:        ds.b    80
            end
```

⟨Run of Program 9.7⟩

```
Here is a string to crypt
...  ◊  ÖÃ÷OfÖ÷l◊ÃOEÖlOÖ△<'l
Here is a string to crypt
```

Another scheme for data encryption is to use a table that maps each ASCII character into another unique character. For instance, 'A' might be mapped into '^' and 'M' mapped into 'T'. Of course, an inverse table can be developed such that '^' maps to 'A' and 'T' maps to 'M'. Program 9.8 provides an example of such an encryption scheme. It reads a string, encrypts it using a transformation table, and prints the resulting encrypted string. Then the inverse mapping is applied to decrypt the string. The original string is printed. Table access is implemented by converting a character to an offset from 0 and using this offset in conjunction with the base address of the desired table. For instance, the transformation for 'C' is at location 'C' − 'A' = 2 in the table.

PROGRAM 9.8

Crypt/Decrypt a
String Using Tables

A string is input using GETSTRING and then encrypted using cryptable (D7 = 1). The encrypted string is first printed and then decrypted using decryptable (D7 = 0). The inverting process yields the original string for output.

```
            xref    getstring, putstring, newline, stop

            entry   begin

cryptext:           equ     1
decryptext:         equ     0
```

```
start:   lea      msg,a0
         jsr      getstring
         move.w   #cryptext,d7
         lea      msg,a0
         jsr      crypt2
         lea      msg,a0
         jsr      putstring
         jsr      newline
         move.w   #decryptext,d7
         lea      msg,a0
         jsr      crypt2
         lea      msg,a0
         jsr      putstring
         jsr      newline
         jsr      stop


crypt2:
         movem.l  d0-d1/d7/a0-a2,-(sp)
         tst.w    d7                    ; do we crypt or decrypt?
         bne.s    crypt2_5
         lea      decryptable,a2
         bra.s    crypt2_0
crypt2_5:
         lea      cryptable,a2
crypt2_0:
         movea.l  a2,a1                 ; set table address
         move.b   (a0),d0               ; read the character
         beq.s    crypt2_1              ; done when null character found
         jsr      isalpha               ; map 'A' . . 'Z', 'a' . . 'z'
         tst.w    d1
         bne.s    crypt2_4
         addq.w   #1,a0
         bra.s    crypt2_0
crypt2_4:
         cmpi.b   #'a',d0               ; which half of the table?
         bge.s    crypt2_2
         subi.b   #'A',d0               ; transform uppercase character
         bra.s    crypt2_3
crypt2_2:
         adda.w   #26,a1                ; move to upper half of table
         subi.b   #'a',d0               ; transform lowercase character
crypt2_3:
         ext.w    d0                    ; need a word index
         move.b   (0,a1,d0.w),(a0)+
         bra.s    crypt2_0
crypt2_1:
         movem.l  (sp)+,d0-d1/d7/a0-a2
         rts


; determine if (D0.B) is a letter by returning
;  (D1.W) = 1 for letter, (D1.W) = 0 if not
```

```
isalpha:
        cmpi.b      #'A',do
        bge.s       isalpha_0
        moveq       #0,d1
        bra.s       isalpha_4
isalpha_0:
        cmpi.b      #'Z',d0
        bgt.s       isalpha_1
        moveq       #1,d1
        bra.s       isalpha_4
isalpha_1:
        cmpi.b      #'a',d0
        bge.s       isalpha_2
        moveq       #0,d1
        bra.s       isalpha_4
isalpha_2:
        cmpi.b      #'z',d0
        bgt.s       isalpha_3
        moveq       #1,d1
        bra.s       isalpha_4
isalpha_3:
        moveq       #0,d1
isalpha_4:
        rts


        data
cryptable:
        dc.b        'N','G','Z','Q','T','C','O','B','M','U','H','E','L',
        dc.b        'K','P','D','A','W','X','F','Y','I','V','R','S','J'
        dc.b        's','a','r','z','c','i','u','e','o','b','x','q','n'
        dc.b        'd','v','f','w','l','g','k','y','h','t','m','p','j'


decryptable:
        dc.b        'Q','H','F','P','L','T','B','K','V','Z','N','M','I'
        dc.b        'A','G','O','D','X','Y','E','J','W','R','S','U','C'
        dc.b        'b','j','e','n','h','p','s','v','f','z','t','r','x'
        dc.b        'm','i','y','l','c','a','w','g','o','q','k','u','d'


msg:    ds.b        100

        end
```

⟨Run of Program 9.8⟩

```
Encrypt and then decrypt.
Tdrlpfk sdz kecd zcrlpkf.
Encrypt and then decrypt.
```

9.7 | MC68040 BLOCK MOVE INSTRUCTION

The MC68040 processor introduces the instruction MOVE16 for the block move of data. The instruction can be used for memory initialization, fast copy operations, and coprocessor communication.

INSTRUCTION

Move16
Block Move

Syntax   MOVE16   (A*x* +, (A*y*) +
MOVE16   xxx.L, (A*n*)
MOVE16   xxx.L, (A*n*) +
MOVE16   (A*n*),xxx.L
MOVE16   (A*n*) +,xxx.L

Action   Addresses for both the source and destination are aligned to 16-byte boundaries (mask off the low-order 4 bits). A line of 16 bytes or 4 long words is copied from the aligned source address to memory at the aligned destination address. An address register in the postincrement addressing mode is incremented by 16.

Notes

1. Operands are restricted to absolute and postincrement mode.

2. The machine code for the MOVE16 instruction with postincrement source and destination uses two words. The opcode word uses a 2-bit opmode to distinguish the other four forms of the instruction.

EXAMPLE 9.10

Assume that (A2) = $72004 and (A3) = $8067E.

$$MOVE16 (A2) +,(A3) +$$

For the instruction, the memory addresses are aligned at 16-byte boundaries. (A2) is aligned to $72000, and (A3) is aligned to $80670. The 4 long words at location $72000 are copied to location $80670. The resulting value of A2 is $72014, and the resulting value of A3 is $8068E.

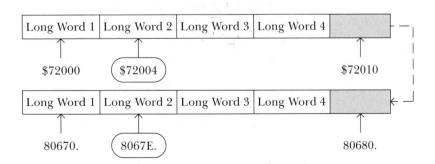

1. Compare and contrast the meaning of XDEF and XREF directive.

2. Use the byte-count format to store a string. Write out each of the following giving the hex value for each character:
   (a) 'BAD'   (b) 'ASCII'   (c) '1776'

3. Use the Null-terminated format to store a string. Write out each of the following, and give the hex value for each character:
   (a) 'BAD'   (b) 'ASCII'   (c) '1776'

4. A main program "MAIN" calls three external subroutines—CREATE, SEARCH, and INSERT. Assume further that SEARCH calls the external subroutine HASH. If the sizes of the code files are

   Code Library

MAIN	CREATE	SEARCH	INSERT	HASH
1000	0100	0200	0150	080

   convert each of the following local labels to labels on a possible global symbol table:
   (a) Label "INSERTQ" with value $50 in subroutine INSERT.
   (b) Label "LOOP" with value $500 in subroutine MAIN.
   (c) Label "HASH" with value $0 in subroutine HASH.
   (d) Label "REPLACE" with value $150 in subroutine SEARCH.
   (e) Label "MAKE" with value $10 in subroutine CREATE.

5. Assume that a string is to be stored in a "start/end" format where the string begins with the ASCII character STX and ends with the character ETX. Write a data constant directive that creates the string 'STX String Format ETX'.

6. The following string is stored in memory at location STR.

   STR: 07 41 61 20 00 30 31 65 70 31 00

   (a) Assume that the string is given in byte-count format and registers D0 and A0 contain the byte count and address STR, respectively. What is the output from the subroutine PUTSTROUT?
   (b) Assume that the string is given in Null-terminated format and register A0 contains the address STR. What is the output from the subroutine PUTSTRING?

7. Describe the action of the following subroutine. Null-terminated strings are used with parameters passed in A0/A1.

```
          MOVEM.L    A0-A1,-(SP)
LOOP1:    TST.B      (A0)+
          BNE.S      LOOP1
          SUBQ.W     #1,A0
```

```
LOOP2:      MOVE.B       (A1)+,(A0)+,
            BNE.S        LOOP2
            MOVEM.L      (SP)+,A0-A1
            RTS
```

8. The subroutine performs format conversion. What type of numbers does the subroutine deal with?

```
CONVERT:
            MOVEM.L      D1-D2/A0,-(SP)
            MOVEQ        #9,D0
            LEA          INBUF,A0
            JSR          GETSTRIN
            SUBQ.W       #2,D0
            BPL.S        CONT
            CLR.W        D0
            BRA.S        DONE
CONT:       MOVE.W       D0,D2
            MOVEQ        #0,D0
            MOVEQ        #0,D1
LOOP:       MOVE.B       (A0)+,D1
            SUBI.W       #'0',D1
            ASL.W        #2,D0
            ADD.W        D1,D0
            DBRA         D2,LOOP
DONE:       MOVEM.L      (SP)+,D1-D2/A0
            RTS
            DATA
INBUF:      DS.B         10
            EVEN
```

9. Assume Null-terminated strings. What is the action of the following subroutine?

```
Q9:
            MOVEM.L      D0/A0,-(SP)
            MOVEQ        #0,D0
            MOVE.B       (A0)+,D0
            BEQ          DONE
            SUBQ.W       #1,D0
LOOP:       CMPI.B       #'.',(A0)+
            DBEQ         D0,LOOP
            BNE          DONE
            MOVE.B       #'!',-(A0)
            SUBQ.W       #1,D0
            CMPI.W       #-1,D0
            BNE          LOOP
DONE:       MOVEM.L      (SP)+,D0/A0
            RTS
            DATA
INBUF:      DS.B         10
            EVEN
```

10. What is the action of the following subroutine?

```
Q10:
              MOVEM.L     D1-D2/A0,-(SP)
              LEA         INBUF,A0
              MOVE.W      #7,D0
              JSR         STRIN
              SUBQ.W      #2,D0
              BPL.S       CONT
              CLR.W       D0
              BRA.S       DONE
      CONT:   MOVE.W      D0,D2
              LEA         INBUF,A0
              MOVEQ       #0,D0
              MOVEQ       #0,D1
      LOOP:   MOVE.B      (A0)+,D1
              SUBI.W      #'0',D1
              ASL.W       #3,D0
              ADD.W       D1,D0
              DBRA        D2,LOOP
      DONE:   MOVEM.L     (SP)+,D1-D2/A0
              RTS
              DATA
      INBUF:  DS.B        7
              EVEN
```

11. A code encryption algorithm rotates the low- and high-order 4 bits of each byte.
    (a) Give the resulting encryption of the string '453' using the ASCII value of each character.
    (b) What three ASCII characters correspond to the encrypted string?

PROGRAMMING EXERCISES

12. The following routines implement byte-count string input/output.
    (a) Write a subroutine GETS_BCF that reads a string from the keyboard and stores the result in byte-count format. Pass the string input buffer in A0.
    (b) Write a subroutine PUTS_BCF that writes to the screen a string given in byte-count format. Pass the address of the string in A0.
        Test Program 1: Input a string STR using GETS_BCF and then echo it to the screen using PUTS_BCF.
        Test Program 2: Input a string using GETS_BCF. Print out the string using PUTS_BCF. Now modify the length byte of the string so PUTS_BCF prints out only the first half of the string. Set a byte count at the last character position of the first half of the original string in such a way that PUTS_BCF prints the second half of the string. Test your code by printing the first and then the second half of the string.
13. (a) Write a subroutine STRCAT(S1,S2) to concatenate two strings S1 and S2, assuming the strings are stored in byte-count format. Be sure to update the character count of the concatenated string.

(b) Using byte-count format, write a subroutine STRINS(S,T,I) that inserts string T into string S beginning at character position I.

Test Program: Initialize two byte-count strings with the time labels 'A.M.' and 'P.M.', respectively. Enter the hour of the day in military time (range 0–23) using DECIN and the day of the week using GETS_BCF. Using STRINS and STRCAT, form a string that contains the hour of the day in standard time (range 0–11) followed by the suffix A.M. or P.M. and ending with the day in the week abbreviated to three letters. Use PUTS_BCF to output the new string. For example,

Input: 20
              Friday
Output: 8 P.M. Fri

14. Write a program that reads a Null-terminated string S from the keyboard and, using the routine STRCHAR, replaces all occurrences of the character '.' in the character by '!'. Print the modified string.

15. Input a string and then convert it to Pig Latin. If the word begins with a consonant, move the first character of the word to the last position and append "ay". If the word begins with a vowel, simply append "ay". Print out the modified string. For example,

Input: this is simple
Output: histay isay implesay

16. Consider a chessboard whose rows and columns are numbered 0–7. Write a program that accepts an input of the form ij ($0 \le i \le 7$, $0 \le j \le 7$) and prints out all the possible positions of a bishop starting at the intersection of row i and column j. For example, when the input is 22, the output should be

```
   0  1  2  3  4  5  6  7
0  *           *
1     *     *
2        *
3     *     *
4  *           *
5              *
6                 *
7                    *
```

To help you, let (I_0, J_0) be the starting position. Then, if (I,J) is an arbitrary point on the board, it is on the bishop's path if either $J - J_0 = I - I_0$ or $J - J_0 = -(I - I_0)$.

17. Initialize four strings stored at addresses NAME1, NAME2, NAME3, and NAME4 in Null-terminated format. The four string addresses are stored in NAMELOC. Write a complete program to find and output the longest string in the list. For example,

Input: NAME1:   DC.B 'THOMAS JEFFERSON',0
                          DS.W   0

```
            NAME2:        DC.B 'ALLEN TALBOT',0
                          DS.W  0
            NAME3:        DC.B 'MARYLYN MONTGOMERY',0
                          DS.W  0
            NAME4:        DC.B 'STEVE ROSS',0
                          DS.W  0
            NAMELOC:      DC.L NAME1,NAME2,NAME3,NAME4
```

Output: MARYLYN MONTGOMERY

18. Write a complete program that reads two strings using GETSTRING. Each string is echoed back to the screen using PUTSTRING. Apply the subroutine STRCMP, and print out the outcome: "Match" or "Not a match".

19. This exercise develops a base-2 I/O package.
    (a) Write a subroutine BINSTRTOBIN that takes a Null-terminated string of ASCII binary digits ('0', '1') and returns the 16-bit binary equivalent.
    (b) Write a subroutine BININ that reads a string of ASCII binary digits from the keyboard and converts the input to the equivalent binary number in D0 using BINSTRTOBIN. Do error checking, test for the end of file, and do character push-back as necessary.
    (c) Write a subroutine BINTOBINSTR that takes a 16-bit binary number and returns a null-terminated string of ASCII binary digits ('0', '1') representing the number.
    (d) Write a subroutine BINOUT that outputs a 16-bit binary number to the screen in binary. Use BINTOBINSTR.
    Test Program: Write a complete program to enter a binary number from the keyboard, multiply it by 4 using ASL, and print the result as a binary number.

20. This exercise develops an octal (base 8) I/O package.
    (a) Write a subroutine OCTSTRTOBIN that takes a Null-terminated string of ASCII octal digits ('0' . . '7') and returns the 16-bit binary equivalent.
    (b) Write a subroutine OCTIN that reads a string of ASCII octal digits from the keyboard and converts the input to the equivalent binary number in D0 using OCTSTRTOBIN. Do error checking, test for the end of file, and do character push-back as necessary.
    (c) Write a subroutine BINTOOCTSTR that takes a 16-bit binary number and returns a Null-terminated string of ASCII octal digits ('0' . . '7') representing the number.
    (d) Write a subroutine OCTOUT that outputs a 16-bit binary number to the screen in octal. Use BINTOOCTSTR.
    Test Program: Write a complete program to enter an octal number from the keyboard, multiply it by 5 using MULU, and print the result as an octal number.

21. Modify the subroutine DECOUT to allow for printing the number right justified in the print field. Pass the number of print positions for the field in D1. If the number of positions is less than the number of significant digits in the number, expand the output to include all significant digits. This is the Pascal WRITE(N:size) procedure.

22. Write encryption and decryption subroutines for the following encryption algorithm. Test your code in a main program that reads and then writes a Null-terminated string.

    Assume the input file is composed of ASCII characters with bit 7 set to 0. The following are the encryption rules:
    1. If bit 5 is 1, set bit 7. If bit 5 is 0, clear bit 7.
    2. Set bit 5.
    3. Change the sense of bits 0 and 3.

23. Refer to exercise 11. The encryption algorithm rotates the low- and high-order 4 bits of each byte.
    (a) Write a subroutine that implements this encryption algorithm. Assume the string address is passed in register A0.
    (b) Write a subroutine BYTE_PRINT that outputs a byte to the screen as 2 ASCII hex digits followed by a blank.
    (c) Write a test program that enters a null-terminated string and calls the encryption algorithm. Write out the encrypted string using the BYTE_PRINT routine in (b).

CHAPTER 10

HIGH-LEVEL LANGUAGE RUN-TIME ENVIRONMENT

*T*his chapter focuses on code generated by a compiler to implement high-level language constructs. It also describes the high-level language run-time environment. The first three sections cover jump tables, stack frames for subroutine calls, and recursion. Section 10.4 introduces code that can be shared by two or more programs to make efficient use of memory. This code, called reentrant code, uses independent stack frames and separation of instruction and data space. In certain cases, position-independent code is generated to allow for the relocation of code to different areas of memory. This is the subject of Section 10.5. The Macintosh always uses position-independent code, as is noted in Chapter 6. The MC68020/30/40 systems support a series of memory indirect modes that have application with jump tables and table lookup. Section 10.6 discusses these modes, and demonstration programs highlight their applications.

10.1 JUMP TABLES

The JMP statement causes transfer of program control to a different location. When a jump must be made to one of several locations, the addresses of the code locations are often stored either directly or indirectly in a jump table. A **jump table** is an array of addresses, offsets, or instructions that permit reference to the selected code segment. On systems allowing absolute addressing, a jump table may be the list of addresses for the code segments. If only relative addressing is used, a jump table is a list of relative offsets or a list of statements, each of which directly implements a jump. This section illustrates three different jump table formats. The first example uses absolute addresses. The other examples use relative addressing and contain valid code for a Macintosh system.

Jump Format 1: Table of Absolute Addresses

The jump table is set up as an array of absolute addresses in either code or data space. An application fetches the address of a routine from the table and then jumps to that address.

```
LEA        JMPTABLE,A1      ; A1 POINTS TO THE TABLE
            .
            .
            .
ASL.W      #2,D0            ; D0 IS AN OFFSET INTO THE TABLE
MOVEA.L    (0,A1,D0.W),A0   ; MOVE ABSOLUTE CODE ADDR TO A0
JMP        (A0)             ; JUMP TO START OF CODE ROUTINE
            .
            .
            .
JMPTABLE:  DC.L    ROUTINE_0
           DC.L    ROUTINE_1
            .
            .
            .
```

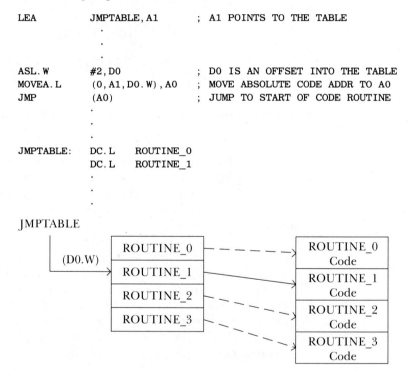

JMPTABLE

PROGRAM 10.1

Jump Table with Absolute Addresses

Enter a number *N* between 0 and 3. A jump table is used to execute a code segment that prints 'Executing in Routine #N'. The jump table is constructed using absolute addresses.

```
xref    decin, putstr, stop, newline

entry   start
```

```
start:   lea      jmptable,a1      ; set up access to the table
         jsr      decin            ; enter a index to the table
         asl.w    #2,d0            ; each table entry is 4 bytes
         movea.l  (0,a1,d0.w),a0   ; fetch the routine address
         jmp      (a0)             ; jump to the routine
jmptable:
         dc.l     routine_0        ; a jump table in code segment
         dc.l     routine_1
         dc.l     routine_2
         dc.l     routine_3
routine_0:
         lea      msg0,a0
         jsr      putstr
         bra      return
routine_1:
         lea      msg1,a0
         jsr      putstr
         bra      return
routine_2:
         lea      msg2,a0
         jsr      putstr
         bra      return
routine_3:
         lea      msg3,a0
         jsr      putstr
         bra      return
return:
         jsr      newline
         jsr      stop

         data
msg0:    dc.b     'Executing in Routine #0',0
msg1:    dc.b     'Executing in Routine #1',0
msg2:    dc.b     'Executing in Routine #2',0
msg3:    dc.b     'Executing in Routine #3',0
         end
```

⟨Run of Program 10.1⟩

```
2
```
───────────────
```
Executing in Routine #2
```

Jump Format 2: Table of Relative Offsets

Each entry in the jump table is a relative offset of a code segment from the base location of the jump table. An application sets the base address of the jump table in an address register and uses the index into the table to fetch the offset to the desired code segment. In the following code, each routine is expressed as an offset from base address JMPTABLE.

```
Code:
      LEA       JMPTABLE, A0
                  .
                  .
                  .
      ASL.W     #2,D0                  ;  INDEX -> TABLE OFFSET
      MOVE.L    (0,A0,D0.W),D0         ;  FETCH OFFSET FROM JMPTABLE
      JMP       (0,A0,D0.W)            ;  JUMP TO JMPTABLE + OFFSET
JMPTABLE:
      DC.L      ROUTINE_0-JMPTABLE     ;  OFFSET TO ROUTINE_0
      DC.L      ROUTINE_1-JMPTABLE     ;  OFFSET TO ROUTINE_1
                  .
                  .
```

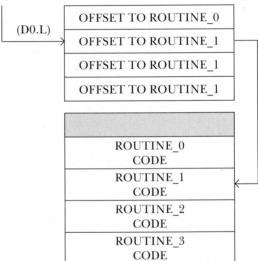

PROGRAM 10.2

Jump Table with
Relative
Offsets

Enter a number N between 0 and 3. A jump table is used to execute a code segment that prints 'Executing in Routine #N'. The jump table is constructed using a table of jump instructions.

```
        xref      decin, putstr, stop, newline

        entry     start

start:  lea       jmptable,a0          ; initialize the base address
        jsr       decin               ; enter index
        asl.w     #2,d0               ; long offsets are used
        move.l    (0,a0,d0.w),d0      ; fetch the offset
        jmp       (0,a0,d0.w)         ; jump to routine at base+offset
```

```
jmptable:
            dc.l        routine_0-jmptable   ; offsets from jmptable
            dc.l        routine_1-jmptable
            dc.l        routine_2-jmptable
            dc.l        routine_3-jmptable
routine_0:
            lea         msg0,a0
            jsr         putstr
            bra         return
routine_1:
            lea         msg1,a0
            jsr         putstr
            bra         return
routine_2:
            lea         msg2,a0
            jsr         putstr
            bra         return
routine_3:
            lea         msg3,a0
            jsr         putstr
            bra         return
return:     jsr         newline
            jsr         stop

            data
msg0:       dc.b        'Executing in Routine #0',0
msg1:       dc.b        'Executing in Routine #1',0
msg2:       dc.b        'Executing in Routine #2',0
msg3:       dc.b        'Executing in Routine #3',0
            end
```

⟨Run of Program 10.2⟩

0

Executing in Routine #0

Jump Format 3: Table of Jump Instructions

The jump table is an array of jump instructions. An application jumps to an instruction within the table. The instruction is itself a jump instruction to the specified routine. The process uses a "jump to a jump." The Macintosh operating system uses this type of jump table. In the following code, the index (D0.W) is multiplied by 4 because it is assumed that each jump instruction in the table is 4 bytes. This is the case for instructions that are assembled PC relative.

Code:

```
        LEA     JMPTABLE,A0
                .
                .
```

```
          ASL.W   #2,D0                    : INDEX → TABLE OFFSET
          JMP     (0,A0,D0.W)              ; FETCH OFFSET FROM JMPTABLE
JMPTABLE:
          DC.L    JMP     (ROUTINE_0,PC)   ; OFFSET TO ROUTINE_0
          DC.L    JMP     (ROUTINE_1,PC)   ; OFFSET TO ROUTINE_1
                          .
                          .
                          .
```

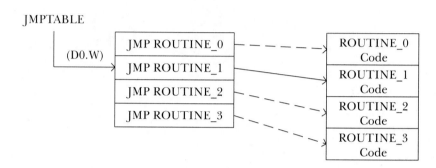

PROGRAM 10.3

Jump Table with
Jump
Instructions

Enter a number *N* between 0 and 3. A jump table is used to execute a code segment that prints 'Executing in Routine #N'. The jump table is constructed using a table of jump instructions.

```
          xref    decin, putstr, stop, newline

          entry   start

start:    lea     jmptable,a0        ; reference the jump table
          jsr     decin              ; enter index
          asl.w   #2,d0              ; each instruction is 4 bytes
          jmp     (0,a0,d0.w)        ; jump into the table
jmptable:
          jmp     (routine_0,pc)     ; a table of jump instructions
          jmp     (routine_1,pc)
          jmp     (routine_2,pc)
          jmp     (routine_3,pc)
routine_0:
          lea     msg0,a0
          jsr     putstr
          bra     return
routine_1:
          lea     msg1,a0
          jsr     putstr
          bra     return
```

```
routine_2:
        lea     msg2,a0
        jsr     putstr
        bra     return
routine_3:
        lea     msg3,a0
        jsr     putstr
        bra     return
return: jsr     newline
        jsr     stop

        data
msg0:   dc.b    'Executing in Routine #0',0
msg1:   dc.b    'Executing in Routine #1',0
msg2:   dc.b    'Executing in Routine #2,0
msg3:   dc.b    'Executing in Routine #3',0
        end
```

⟨Run of Program 10.3⟩

```
3
Executing in Routine #3
```

The CASE Statement

Most structured programming languages provide a CASE statement (or an equivalent construct) to implement multiway selection. One of several statements is executed, depending on the value of a discrete selector expression. The statements are labeled by one or more values that fall in the range of the selector. In addition, many languages allow for an "otherwise" statement that is executed if the selector does not evaluate to any of the labels. Assuming that the OTHERWISE option executes the ALTERNATIVE statement, the general form of the CASE statement follows:

```
CASE SELECTOR OF
    VALUE₀:              Statement₀
    VALUE₁:              Statement₁
         .
         .
         .
    VALUEₙ₋₁:            Statementₙ₋₁
    OTHERWISE:           ALTERNATIVE Statement
END CASE
NEXT STATEMENT
```

Action   If SELECTOR equals $VALUE_i$ ($0 \le i \le N - 1$), then execute $Statement_i$, and pass program control to the NEXT STATEMENT after

END CASE. Otherwise, execute the OTHERWISE statement. The CASE construct is the equivalent of a series of nested IF . . THEN . . ELSE statements. It can be implemented with a jump table.

Step 1: Create a table of addresses (one address for each of the possible alternatives in the CASE statement). Each table entry is the starting address of code for the statement labeled by the selector. Each of the code segments must contain a branch to NEXT STATEMENT as an exit from the CASE statement.

Step 2: Given a SELECTOR value, determine if it is out of range. If it is, execute an OTHERWISE statement. If not, use the SELECTOR as an index into the jump table, and use a JMP instruction to transfer to the appropriate address in the table.

The CASE statement maps (or translates) the set of possible SELECTOR values so that the first value has an offset of 0 in the jump table. For instance, SELECTOR values 2, 4, 5, and 7 are shifted by 2 and mapped to 0, 2, 3, and 5. For SELECTOR values outside the range 0–5 or with nonselectable values 1 and 4, the CASE statement executes an OTHERWISE statement.

A CASE statement for DAYS_IN_MONTH is implemented in MC68000 code. The Pascal CASE statement is a model.

Pascal Code   The SELECTOR is the value of a month (Jan = 1, Feb = 2, and so on). The CASE statements assigns to DAYS_IN_MONTH the number of days in the month for the SELECTOR value. Leap year is not treated by the CASE statement. The ALTERNATIVE statement prints the message "NOT A VALID MONTH."

```
CASE MONTH OF
     1:          DAYS_IN_MONTH := 31;
     2:          DAYS_IN_MONTH := 28;
     3:          DAYS_IN_MONTH := 31;
     4:          DAYS_IN_MONTH := 30;
     5:          DAYS_IN_MONTH := 31;
     6:          DAYS_IN_MONTH := 30;
     7:          DAYS_IN_MONTH := 31;
     8:          DAYS_IN_MONTH := 31;
     9:          DAYS_IN_MONTH := 30;
    10:          DAYS_IN_MONTH := 31;
    11:          DAYS_IN_MONTH := 30;
    12:          DAYS_IN_MONTH := 31;
  OTHERWISE: WRITELN('NOT A VALID MONTH');
END CASE;
```

Note: Pascal can combine labels with a common statement as illustrated in the following code segment:

```
CASE MONTH OF
  1,3,5,7,8,10,12   :    DAYS_IN_MONTH := 31;
  2    :                 DAYS_IN_MONTH := 28;
```

```
        4,6,9,11    :              DAYS_IN_MONTH := 30;
        OTHERWISE   :              WRITELN('NOT A VALID MONTH');
    END CASE;
```

For the corresponding assembly language code, the range of SELECTOR values is 1–12. By subtracting 1, the translated set of SELECTOR values has range 0–11. When a comparison with 11 is made, the BHI branch identifies both out-of-range conditions (SELECTOR > 11 and SELECTOR < 0). For a SELECTOR < 0, its signed value is $FFFF, $FFFE, and so forth. The corresponding unsigned values are 65535, 65534, and so forth. As an unsigned number, SELECTOR > 11.

PROGRAM 10.4

CASE Test: Days in the Month

The decimal value of the month is entered using DECIN. The number of days in the month is printed using DECOUT. An input that is out of range is flagged with an error message. The jump table is created as an array of jump statements (Format 3). The code runs on all MC68000 systems.

```
NewLine:    equ     13
            xref    decin, decout, newline, strout, stop

            jsr     decin       ; input month (1-12)
            subq.w  #1,d0       ; translate range
            cmpi.w  #11,d0      ; check for out of range
            bhi     otherwise   ; error if month <= 0 or month >= 13
            asl.w   #2,d0       ; multiply by 4 to get jump

            lea     cases,a0
            jmp     0(a0,d0.w)  ; jump to the table entry

cases:      jmp     load31      ; month = 1
            jmp     load28      ; month = 2
            jmp     load31      ; month = 3
            jmp     load30      ; month = 4
            jmp     load31      ; month = 5
            jmp     load30      ; month = 6
            jmp     load31      ; month = 7
            jmp     load31      ; month = 8
            jmp     load30      ; month = 9
            jmp     load31      ; month = 10
            jmp     load30      ; month = 11
            jmp     load31      ; month = 12

otherwise:  lea     errmsg,a0
            move.w  #18,d0
            jsr     strout
            bra.s   exit

load28:     move.w  #28,days_in_month
            bra     next
load30:     move.w  #30,days_in_month
            bra     next
```

```
load31:      move.w   #31,days_in_month
next:        lea      msg,a0
             move.w   #36,d0
             jsr      strout
             move.w   days_in_month,d0
             jsr      decout
             jsr      newline
exit:        jsr      stop

             data

days_in_month:
             ds.w     1
msg:         dc.b     'The number of days in that month is'
errmsg:      dc.b     'Not a valid month'
             end
```

⟨Run of Program 10.4⟩

3
The number of days in that month is 31

The jump table implementation of a CASE construct is more efficient than nested branches, but it requires additional memory to store the table. For values within the SELECTOR range that are treated as OTHERWISE cases, a branch to the ALTERNATIVE statement is included in the table.

PROGRAM 10.5

CASE Test:
Football Scores

In a football game, a score can be made from an extra point (1 point), a safety (2 points), a field goal (3 points), or a touchdown (6 points). For an input value, a CASE statement recognizes whether the value corresponds to an invalid score or one of the point-producing plays. The code uses jump table Format 2 and runs on all MC68000 systems.

```
Null:        equ      0

             xref     decin, putstr, newline, stop
             entry    start

start:       lea      cases,a1            ; set pointer to cases
             jsr      decin
             subq.w   #1,d0               ; translate range 1-6 to 0-5
             cmpi.w   #5,d0               ; score in range?
             bls      call_cases
             move.w   #6,d0
call_cases:  asl.w    #2,d0               ; offset is long word
             move.l   (0,a1,d0.w),d0      ; fetch offset
             jmp      (0,a1,d0.w)         ; jump to routine
```

```
cases:          dc.l    extrapt-cases   ; one point
                dc.l    safety-cases    ; two points
                dc.l    fieldgoal-cases ; three points
                dc.l    otherwise-cases ; four points (invalid)
                dc.l    otherwise-cases ; five points (invalid)
                dc.l    touchdown-cases ; six points
                dc.l    otherwise-cases ; general otherwise case

extrapt:        lea     extrapt_str, a0
                bra     print
safety:         lea     safety_str, a0
                bra     print
fieldgoal:      lea     fieldgoal_str, a0
                bra     print
touchdown:      lea     touchdown_str, a0
                bra     print
otherwise:      lea     noscore_str, a0
print:          jsr     putstr
                jsr     newline
                jsr     stop

                data
extrapt_str:    dc.b    'Extra Point', Null
safety_str:     dc.b    'Safety', Null
fieldgoal_str:  dc.b    'Field Goal', Null
touchdown_str:  dc.b    'Touchdown', Null
noscore_str:    dc.b    'Not a Valid Score', Null

                end
```

⟨Run of Program 10.5⟩

6
Touchdown

|10.2| STACK FRAMES IN HIGH-LEVEL LANGUAGES

The concept of a stack frame was introduced in Chapter 7. The MC68000 LINK instruction creates a fixed reference point for the frame and allows base-relative stack offsets for the parameters. Most modern languages are block structured, with local variables allocated and deallocated as the code enters and exits a program block. In Pascal, a **block** is the main program or the body of a procedure or function. This section describes how high-level languages implement storage for local variables in block structures. Some high-level languages, such as C, allow a call to a subprogram that has a variable number of parameters. This section explains how the subroutine knows what the parameters are and how the parameters are flushed from the stack. Code- and source-level debuggers are invaluable tools in program development. The last portion of this section defines them and presents a simple application for a code-level debugger.

The concepts are introduced with a Pascal procedure PRINTBASE that writes out a binary number in a designated base. The binary number N and BASE are input parameters for the subroutine. The variables defined within the subroutine are local variables stored on the stack. The algorithm uses repeated division by the BASE to identify the digits from right to left. The value of the digit is the remainder after division and is used as an index into the string OUTLIST containing the ASCII equivalent of each digit. The ASCII digits are placed on the stack called DIGITS. As the stack is popped, the digits are printed in the order left to right. The following Pascal implementation assumes a STRING type.

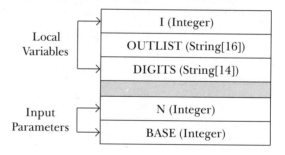

PROGRAM 10.6

PRINTBASE Test

Many Pascal compilers implement the integer data type using a long word. This is assumed here. The routine PRINTBASE, which is called with N and BASE as input parameters, prints out N in the BASE number system. The base is restricted to the range $2 \leq \text{BASE} \leq 16$. For two test cases, integers N and BASE are read by the main program.

Pascal Version of PRINTBASE

```
PROGRAM test (input, output);
VAR
    N, BASE: integer;

PROCEDURE printbase (N, BASE: integer);
var
    i: integer;
    outlist: string[16];
    Digits: string[14];
BEGIN
    outlist := '0123456789ABCDEF';
    i := 15;
    { use repeated division }
```

```
    WHILE (N > 0) DO BEGIN
      i := i - 1;
      Digits[i] := outlist[N mod base + 1];
      N := N div base
    END;
    WHILE (i < 15) DO BEGIN
      write(Digits[i]);
      i := i + 1
    END;
    writeln
END;

BEGIN
    readln(N, BASE);
    printbase(N, BASE);
    readln(N, BASE);
    printbase(N, BASE)
END.
```

⟨Run of Pascal Program 10.6⟩

100 4
1210
100 8
144

The stack, which is referenced by A7 = SP, is used to hold the parameters that are passed either by value or by reference. The stack is also used for local variables and for saving registers.

The order in which parameters are placed on the stack depends on the language and the compiler. Most languages place parameters on the stack in reverse order (right to left). In this way, the first parameter is on the top of the stack when the subroutine is called.

Memory can be allocated for the local variables I, OUTLIST, and DIGITS by decrementing the stack pointer (SUBA.L #34,SP). After saving registers, all variables, parameters, and register values are referenced by positive offsets from the stack pointer. Assuming that K is the number of bytes required to save register data, Figure 10.1 contains the stack entries and offsets for the local variables and parameters in procedure PRINTBASE.

Using the LINK instruction, parameters and local variables can be accessed as fixed offsets from an address register. This eliminates the need to worry about the saved registers when computing offsets. The LINK instruction, with its displacement, also can be used to allocate space for local variables.

LINK An, #−N

FIGURE 10.1   Stack Offsets Relative to Stack Pointer

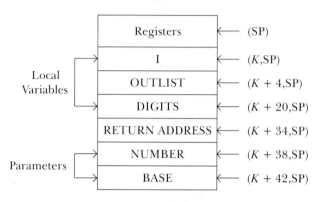

The negative displacement reserves N bytes of memory on the stack by decrementing the SP. The displacement serves the same purpose as the instruction

$$\text{SUBA.L} \quad \#N,SP$$

Assuming that LINK uses register A6, the value of the frame pointer A6 is used as a fixed point from which to reference the parameters with a positive offset and the local variables with a negative offset.

The following program converts the Pascal code to MC68000 code. It represents typical high-level language compiler code. With a few exceptions,

FIGURE 10.2   Stack Frame for PRINTBASE

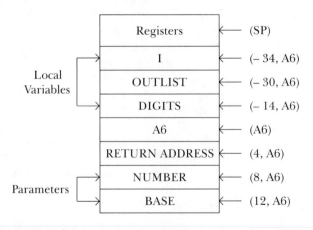

it is the assembly language code produced by a Pascal compiler. The routines DECIN__LONG and STROUT are used for I/O. Figure 10.2 gives the stack frame for the MC68000 code.

MC68000 Version of PRINTBASE

The offsets to the frame pointer A6 are given as EQU values. Equivalent Pascal statements are recorded in some comment fields.

Note that routine PRINTBASE does not clear the parameter N from the stack. That task is left to the calling program that originally placed the 8 bytes of parameters on the stack. After return from PRINTBASE, the stack is cleared with

ADDQ.W　#8,SP　; CLEAR N,　BASE FROM THE STACK

Because the calling program is responsible for placing parameters on the stack, it knows the number of bytes and can easily clear them upon return from the subroutine. This is typical of most high-level language code.

```
Null:           equ                 0
var_N:          equ                 8
var_Base:       equ                12
var_I:          equ               -34
var_Outlist:    equ               -30
var_Digits:     equ               -14

        xref    decin_long, strcopy, strout, newline, stop
        entry   start

start:
        jsr     decin_long      ; readln(N, BASE)
        move.l  d0,N
        jsr     decin_long
        move.l  d0,BASE
        move.l  BASE,-(sp)
        move.l  N,-(sp)         ; call printbase(N,BASE)
        jsr     printbase
        addq.w  #8,sp           ; clear N from the stack
        jsr     decin_long      ; readln(N,BASE)
        move.l  d0,N
        jsr     decin_long      ; repeat the process one more time
        move.l  d0,BASE
        move.l  BASE,-(sp)
        move.l  N,-(sp)
        jsr     printbase
        addq.w  #8,sp
        jsr     stop

printbase:
        link    a6,#-34         ; 34 bytes of local var
        movem.l d0-d2/a0,-(sp)
        pea     outlist         ; stat outlist :=
                                  ""0123456789ABCDEF'
```

```
          pea       (var_Outlist, a6)
          jsr       strcopy
          move.l    #14, (var_I, a6)    ; i := 14
printbase_1:
          tst.l     (var_N, a6)
          ble       printbase_2
          subq.l    #1, (var_I, a6)     ; i := - 1
          move.l    (var_N, a6), d2     ; compute N mod base; store in d2
          move.l    (var_Base, a6), d1
          divs      d1, d2
          swap      d2
          move.l    (var_I, a6), d0     ; fetch i

                                        ; digits[i] := outlist[N mod base]
          move.b    (var_Outlist, a6, d2.w), (var_Digits, a6, d0.1)

          move.l    (var_N, a6), d0     ; N := N div base
          move.l    (var_Base, a6), d1
          divs      d1, d0
          ext.l     d0
          move.l    d0, (var_N, a6)
          bra       printbase_1
printbase_2:
          cmpi.l    #14, (var_I, a6)    ; test i < 14
          bge       printbase_3
          move.l    (var_I, a6), d0     ; write(digits[i])
          lea       (var_Digits, a6, d0.1), a0
          move.w    #1, d0
          jsr       strout
          addq.l    #1, (var_I, a6)     ; i := i + 1
          bra       printbase_2
printbase_3:
          jsr       newline
          movem.l   (sp)+, d0-d2/a0
          unlk      a6
          rts


          data
N:        ds.l      1
BASE:     ds.l      1
outlist:
          dc.b      '0123456789ABCDEF', Null


          end
```

⟨Run of MC68000 Program 10.6⟩

100 4
1210
100 8
144

Subroutines with a Variable Number of Arguments

All the subroutines presented thus far have had a fixed number of parameters. In certain applications (such as high-level language I/O routines), it is desirable to call a subroutine that accepts a varying number of parameters.

EXAMPLE 10.1

The Pascal procedures WRITE and WRITELN accept a varying number of arguments. Consider instances of the following output statements:

WRITE('A AND B ARE', A, B);
WRITELN('THE MAXIMUM OF A AND B IS ', MAX);

The code for WRITELN is implemented by pushing on the stack user-supplied parameters followed by a template

PROCEDURE WRITELN(VAR T : TEMPLATE; ⟨PARAMETERS⟩);

The template is hidden from the user. It points to a string or record containing information necessary to print the required data.

The screen output routine PRINTF, supplied with C language compilers, provides a second example:

PRINTF ("A AND B ARE %D %D ", A, B);
PRINTF ("THE MAXIMUM OF A AND B IS %D\N ", MAX);

The first parameter is a string that contains an embedded format specification. A C compiler places parameters on the stack in reverse order; thus the format specification string is located on the top of the stack. PRINTF executes by scanning this string. Output occurs character by character until the format indicator "%" is recognized. The next character is a format specifier (d: decimal, x: hex, o: octal, s: string, and so forth). The code accesses a variable of that type from the stack and prints it. A C compiler leaves the flushing of parameters from the stack to the calling code. This is convenient, because only the calling program conveniently knows how many bytes of parameters were pushed on the stack.

A6
Return Address
Specification String Address
Output Parameter #1
Output Parameter #2
<etc.>

To demonstrate the use of a varying number of parameters, a subroutine PUT implements a simple variant of the C PRINTF routine. A format specification string contains the designator "%" to indicate output of a long-word integer from the stack. The integer parameters followed by the address of the specification string are pushed on the stack. The code for the PUT routine uses the LINK instruction to create a frame pointer, which provides convenient access to the parameters.

Subroutine PUT

Notes

1. Recall that DECOUT_LONG places two blank spaces after the decimal number. This is not acceptable in the routine, so the backspace character ($08) is output twice after the call to DECOUT_LONG. This causes the cursor to be placed in the position immediately after the last digit.

2. PUT leaves the flushing of parameters from the stack to the calling code because the calling code knows the number of parameters passed to PUT. PUT would have to compute the number of '%' format specifiers in order to flush the stack properly before returning from the subroutine.

```
fmtstring:   equ        8
firstint:    equ        12
BackSpace:   equ        8

             xref       decout_long, strout
             xdef       put

put:         link       a6,#0
             movem.l    d0-d1/a0-a2,-(sp)
             movea.l    (fmtstring,a6),a1
             lea        (firstint,a6),a2
formatloop:  move.b     (a1)+,d1
             beq.s      putisdone
             cmp.b      #'%',d1
             beq.s      foundint
             lea        (-1,a1),a0
             moveq      #1,d0
             jsr        strout
             bra.s      formatloop
foundint:    move.l     (a2)+,d0
             jsr        decout_long
             lea        clearSpaces,a0
             move.w     #2,d0
             jsr        strout
             bra.s      formatloop
putisdone:   movem.l    (sp)+,d0-d1/a0-a2
             unlk       a6
             rts
```

```
                    data
          clearSpaces:
                    dc.b  BackSpace, BackSpace

                    end
```

PROGRAM 10.7

Print Test

Two long words A and B are input using DECIN—LONG. The PUT routine outputs the string.

The sum of A and B is A + B.

The 32-bit values for A, B, and A + B are passed to the subroutine along with the format string. The calling program clears the parameters off the stack after returning from PUT.

```
Newline:       equ 13          ; Macintosh new line
          xref    stop, decin_long, put
          entry   start

start:
          jsr     decin_long
          move.l  d0, d2          ; save first number in d2
          jsr     decin_long
          move.l  d0, d1          ; save second number in d1
          add.l   d2, d0          ; compute the sum in d0
          move.l  d0, -(sp)       ; pass the sum
          move.l  d1, -(sp)       ; pass the second number
          move.l  d2, -(sp)       ; pass the first number
          pea     msg             ; pass format string on the stack
          jsr     put
          adda.w  #16, sp         ; clear the stack
          jsr     stop

          data
msg:      dc.b    'the sum of % and % is %', Newline, 0

          end
```

⟨Run of Program 10.7⟩

24 35
the sum of 24 and 35 is 59

Debuggers

Most systems provide the user with a **code-level debugger**. This software package disassembles machine instructions and thus allows you to look at the machine code in mnemonic form. By using a set of commands, you can display instructions beginning at a specific address, run code that "breaks" at a specified address, print the contents of registers and memory addresses, and so forth. To use a code-level debugger with a high-level language, you must know how the language generates code for procedures and functions. You have some of the necessary background with the LINK and UNLK instructions.

Some systems provide a **source-level debugger**. Such a program is normally provided with a high-level language compiler. The compiler emits information in the code file that allows blocks of code to be identified with particular lines in the source file. The debugger reads this information and allows you to view the source file during debugging. If an error occurs, the offending source line is displayed. This type of software is not usually available with assemblers. For Macintosh systems, the Macintosh Assembly System provides a source-level debugger. The construction of a code-level debugger is quite complex and will not be presented here.

An interesting systems programming application uses a code-level debugger. Suppose you have received a piece of software that does not work correctly. You run tests and manage to isolate the problem to a specific subroutine containing some incorrect code. Consider the following hypothetical situation:

Incorrect Code	Desired Code
ADDI.W #1,D0 ASL.W #1,D0	ADDI.W #1,D0
MOVE.W D0, (4,A0,Dl.L)	MOVE.W D0, (4,AO,D1.L)

The multiplication by 2 was not correct. Because you do not have source code, you cannot recompile the program. You need to remove the ASL instruction without altering memory references and PC-relative offsets. The solution lies with the instruction, NOP, that does nothing at all—it just occupies space in memory.

INSTRUCTION

NOP
(No Operation)

Syntax   NOP

Action   No operation occurs.

Note   None of the condition codes are affected, but the program counter is advanced 2 bytes.

EXAMPLE 10.2

(a) Consider the "dirty" code file in the hypothetical situation. Using the debugger, replace the ASL   #1,D0 instruction by the NOP instruction.

```
ADDI.W    #1,D0
NOP
MOVE.W    D0,(4,A0,D1.L)
```

The NOP occupies the same number of bytes as the original instruction. The modified code file will execute correctly.

(b) Your applications package contains a subroutine call to test for the presence of a piece of hardware. You do not have the hardware and do not need it. Using the debugger, you isolate the 6-byte instruction

```
JSR    FINDIT
```

The code file can be patched by replacing the subroutine call with three NOP instructions.

_____

|10.3| **RECURSION**

A subroutine is **recursive** if its execution involves calling itself. Many interesting problems in computer science are inherently recursive, such as tree scanning and recursive descent parsing of high-level language source code. A recursive routine calls itself, passing parameters using the stack just like any ordinary subroutine, and then carries out another "instance of execution" of its own code. The self-calls eventually end because the routine must contain conditions that cause a return rather than a continuation of the recursion. When a return is made, previous recursive calls complete.

High-level languages make the writing of recursive code straightforward. Unfortunately, they also hide the underlying stack manipulation and produce code that is difficult to trace. By looking at recursion in assembly language, you can develop a clearer understanding of a recursive process. The concepts are introduced using the function FACTORIAL. For a nonnegative integer N, N-FACTORIAL has both an iterative and a recursive definition. These definitions are used in two Pascal functions.

Iterative Definition

Special case $0! = 1$

General case

$$N! = N * (N - 1) * (N - 2) * \cdots * (2) * (1) \qquad N \geq 1$$

Pascal Function FACTORIAL (Iterative Form)

```
FUNCTION factorial(n : integer) : integer;
VAR prod, i : integer;
BEGIN
  prod := 1;
  IF n <= 1 THEN
    factorial := 1
  ELSE BEGIN
    FOR i:= 1 TO n DO
      prod := prod * i;
    factorial := prod
  END
END { factorial };
```

Recursive Definition

Return conditions $0! = 1$
$1! = 1$

Recursive step $N! = N * (N - 1)!$ $(N \geq 2)$

Pascal Function FACTORIAL (Recursive Form)

```
FUNCTION factorial (n : integer) : integer;
BEGIN
  IF n <= 1 THEN
    factorial := 1
  ELSE
      factorial := n * factorial (n - 1)
  END { factorial };
```

Address
  P

Pascal Main Program

```
PROGRAM main (input,output);
VAR m : integer;

      .
      .
      .

BEGIN.

    .
    .
    .
```

nfact := factorial(m);   { call from main program }

┌→ ⟨Next Statement⟩
│
Address
   A

In the recursive form of the function, the simple IF . . THEN . . ELSE statement permits execution of either the stopping condition or another recursive call. In the case where $N = 0$ or $N = 1$, the FACTORIAL value is assigned and the function returns. The alternative case (ELSE) makes a recursive subroutine call with a modified parameter "$N - 1$". When $N = 0$ or $N = 1$, a return is made to the instructions in the most recent recursive call that implements the product $N * \text{FACTORIAL} (N - 1)$. The successive products $2 * 1$, $3 * 2$, $4 * 6$, and so on, are computed. The final result is then output to the main program and stored in NFACT.

For a series of recursive calls, Table 10.1 describes the parameter, return address, and actions performed within the subroutine code. Note that the iterative implementation of the function is much more efficient and would be used in practice. However, the recursive implementation is simple and illustrates the recursive process.

Assume that P is the return address from the recursive call and A is the return address in the main program. The statements beginning at address P execute the product

$$N * \text{FACTORIAL} (N - 1)$$

TABLE 10.1 Factorial (N)

PARAMETER	SUBROUTINE ACTION	RETURN ADDRESS	ACTION OF CALL
N	Call FACTORIAL $(N - 1)$	A	Compute $N * \text{FACTORIAL} (N - 1)$
$N - 1$	Call FACTORIAL $(N - 2)$	P	Compute $(N - 1) * \text{FACTORIAL} (N - 2)$
	.		
	.		
	.		
4	Call FACTORIAL(3)	P	Compute $4 * 6$
3	Call FACTORIAL(2)	P	Compute $3 * 2$
2	Call FACTORIAL(1)	P	Compute $2 * 1$
1	FACTORIAL := 1	P	Return 1

The subroutine parameters are pushed on the stack in the order N, $N-1$, ..., 2, 1. The return code is executed as the stack is popped with products computed in the order 2 * 1, 3 * 2, 4 * 6, and so on.

Recursion is implemented in assembly language by having each instance of execution of a recursive subroutine have its own stack frame containing a copy of its own parameters and local variables. The stack frames keep the "environment" of each recursive call distinct. In Figure 10.3 A6 is the frame pointer used with the LINK instruction.

Stack frames on the top of the stack return program control to the "calling recursive code." The last stack frame returns program control to the "main calling program." A recursive process must have a "stopping condition." This instance of execution returns without making a recursive call. The most recent instance of execution is then restarted, with all its local variables and parameters saved on the stack. When it finishes, it returns to the next most recent instance of the recursive procedure, and so on. Eventually, the original call executes and returns to the main calling program.

The MC68000 code returns the function value of FACTORIAL in D0. If $N = 0$ or $N = 1$, the value 1 is placed in D0. If $N \geq 2$, N is saved in D1. A recursive call is made, and after the return, the product (D1.L) * (D0.L)

FIGURE 10.3 Instances of Execution

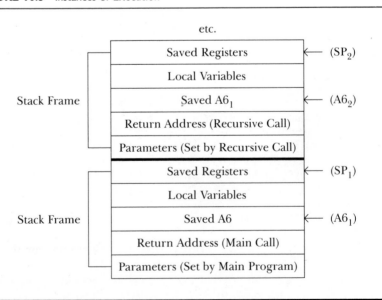

is found. The subroutine FACTORIAL takes a 32-bit unsigned integer as its parameter and returns the 32-bit factorial. The code uses the routine UMUL32 developed in Chapter 8. Recall that this routine takes two 32-bit unsigned numbers on the stack and returns the 64-bit product in D0 − D1. If the factorial calculation exceeds $2^{32} - 1$, it is truncated to 32 bits (there is no error message).

MC68000 Factorial Code

```
n:          equ     8               ; stack offset to parm n
parmsize:   equ     4


            xdef    factorial
            xref    umul32


factorial:  link    a6,#0           ; set up frame pointer
            move.l  d1,-(sp)        ; save d1 locally in this frame
            move.l  (n,a6),d0       ; fetch n
            cmpi.l  #1,d0           ; if n = 0 or n = 1, return 1
            bhi.s   factrecur
            moveq   #1,d0
            bra.s   return
factrecur:  move.l  d0,d1           ;  (d0) = n-1 and (d1) = n
            subq.l  #1,d0
            move.l  d0,-(sp)        ; compute (n-1)!
            bsr     factorial
            move.l  d1,-(sp)        ; compute n * (n-1)!
            move.l  d0,-(sp)
            jsr     umul32
            move.l  d1,d0           ; quitely truncate to 32 bits
return      move.l  (sp)+,d1
            unlk    a6              ; deallocate frame pointer
            move.l  (sp),(parmsize,sp)
            addq.w  #parmsize,sp
            rts


            end
```

Figure 10.4 describes the stack frames for the simple case of $N = 3$. The initial stack begins with $N = 3$ and the return address from a primary call to FACTORIAL. Execution requires two recursive calls to FACTORIAL with parameters $N = 2$ and $N = 1$, respectively.

FIGURE 10.4   FACTORIAL(3)

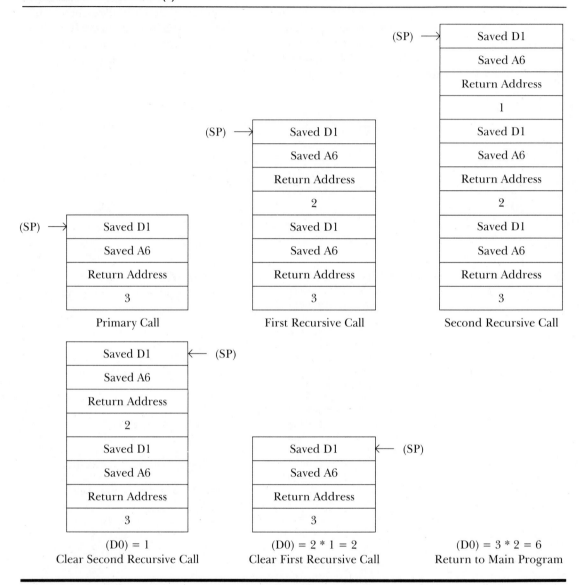

Primary Call

First Recursive Call

Second Recursive Call

(D0) = 1
Clear Second Recursive Call

(D0) = 2 * 1 = 2
Clear First Recursive Call

(D0) = 3 * 2 = 6
Return to Main Program

PROGRAM 10.8

FACTORIAL

Using DECIN__LONG, 32-bit numbers are entered until −1 is input. For each number, the corresponding factorial value is output. The routine FACTORIAL truncates values to 32 bits and is accurate for input in the range 0–13.

```
           xref     decin_long, decout_long, newline, stop
           xref     factorial
           entry    start

start:  jsr     decin_long    ; read in a 32 bit number n
        tst.l   d0            ; stop if n < 0
        bmi.s   out
        move.l  d0,-(sp)      ; push n on the stack
        jsr     factorial     ; compute n! recursively
        jsr     decout_long   ; print n! in decimal, noting that
;                             ; any result which exceeds 32 bits
;                             ; will have been truncated to 32 bits
        jsr     newline
        bra.s   start
out:    jsr     stop

        end
```

⟨Run of Program 10.8⟩

```
0     1
3     6
9     362880
10    3628800
12    479001600
13    1932053504
14    1278945280
-1
```

Tower of Hanoi

The classical puzzle "Tower of Hanoi" is an example of a recursive problem. Although a relatively simple case may require a large number of recursive calls, the simplicity of the code gives a clear picture of using the stack. This section begins with an explanation of the puzzle followed by a Pascal solution. The high-level language code is used as a model for the corresponding MC68000 solution.

Puzzle Directions *N* disks are stacked on a peg in increasing order of size with the largest at the bottom. The board contains two additional pegs. The object of the puzzle is to move all *N* disks from the *starting peg* to another peg called the *terminal peg*. Disks are moved one at a time, and a larger disk may never be placed on top of a smaller disk.

Figure 10.5 shows the movement of pegs for the case of *N* = 3. The pegs are labeled L, M, and R, with L being the starting peg and R being the terminal peg. The solution requires two recursive steps. First, move the top two disks from peg L to peg M. Then, after moving the large disk from peg L to peg R, complete the puzzle by moving the two-disk Tower of Hanoi from peg M to peg R.

FIGURE 10.5   Tower of Hanoi *(N = 3)*

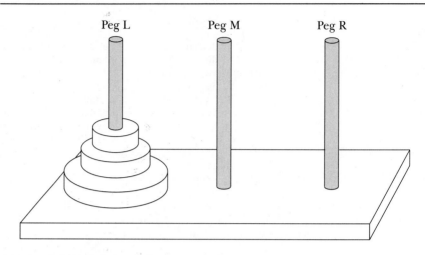

Step 1: Original three-disk tower on L.

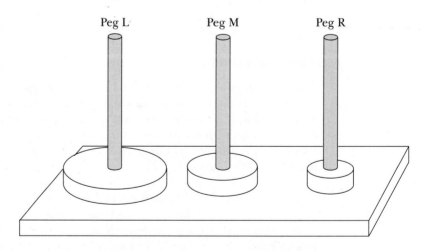

Step 2: Move small disk to R. Move medium disk to M.

FIGURE 10.5 Continued

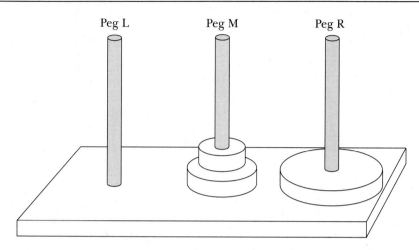

Step 3: Move R disk to M. Move L disk to R.
Note: The large disk is now on the terminal peg and the two-disk Tower of Hanoi is located on peg M.

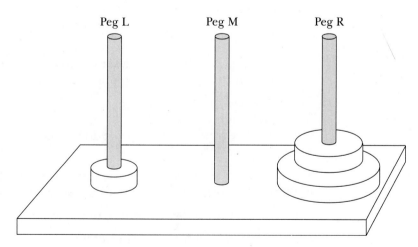

Step 4: Move small disk to L. Move M disk to R.

(continued)

FIGURE 10.5   Continued

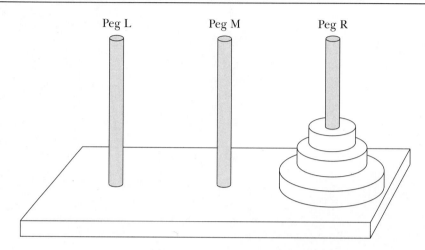

Step 5: The stopping condition occurs when a single disk (small disk) is moved to the $N - 1$ Tower of Hanoi. In this example, move L to R. The three-disk tower is complete.

The example can be generalized to a three-step recursive algorithm with the case of one disk being the stopping condition.

Tower of Hanoi Algorithm
Stopping Condition $N = 1$
Move the disk from the starting peg to the terminal peg.
Recursive Step $N > 1$

Step 1: Move $N - 1$ disks from the starting peg to the intermediate peg, using the final peg for temporary disk placement.

Step 2: Move the bottom (Nth) disk to the terminal peg.

Step 3: Move $N - 1$ disks from the intermediate peg to the final peg, using the starting peg for temporary disk placement.

Using mathematical induction, the algorithm requires $2^N - 1$ moves. The algorithm is now implemented in both Pascal and MC68000 assembler code. Study the Pascal solution first then compare it with the assembler solution. Basically, all that needs to be done is to implement the procedure calls of Pascal by using stack frames.

PROGRAM 10.9

Tower of Hanoi

Pascal Version

```
PROGRAM hanoi(input, output);
VAR n : integer;

    PROCEDURE hanoi (n : integer; startpeg,
                        endpeg, intpeg : char);
    BEGIN
        IF n = 1 THEN
            writeln( 'move' , startpeg, 'to' , endpeg)
        ELSE BEGIN
            { move n − 1 disks to intermediate peg }
            hanoi(n − 1, startpeg, intpeg, endpeg);
            { move bottom disk to final position }
            writeln(move , startpeg, to , endpeg);
            { move n − 1 disks from intermediate to final }
            hanoi(n − 1, intpeg, endpeg, startpeg)
        END
    END; { hanoi }

BEGIN
    write( 'enter the number of disks desired:' );
    readln(n);
    writeln;
    hanoi(n, 'l', 'r', 'm')
END.
```

MC68000 Assembly Language Version

```
n:          equ     8
stpeg:      equ     10          ; starting peg
endpeg:     equ     12          ; ending peg
intpeg:     equ     14          ; intermediate peg
parmsize:   equ     8

Newline:    equ     13

            xref    decin, strout, newline, stop

start:      lea     prompt,a0
            move.w  #35,d0
            jsr     strout
            jsr     decin
            jsr     newline
            move.w  #'m',−(sp)  ; move n pegs from l to r using m
                                ; note that each character is right
                                ; justified with leading null byte

            move.w  #'r',−(sp)
            move.w  #'l',−(sp)
```

```
                move.w    d0,-(sp)
                jsr       hanoi
                jsr       stop


hanoi:          link      a6,#0          ; create a frame pointer
                movem.l   d0-d1/a0,-(sp)
                move.w    (n,a6),d1      ; get n
                cmpi.w    #1,d1          ; is n = 1 ?
                bne.s     recur          ; if not, we must perform recursion
                                         ; set up the move string
                move.b    (stpeg+1,a6),src
                move.b    (endpeg+1,a6),dest
                lea       movemsg,a0
                move.w    #16,d0
                jsr       strout
                bra       endhanoi       ; clear the stack with unlk
recur:          subq.w    #1,d1          ; compute n-1


; call hanoi with parameter n-1, current,intermediate,final pegs
                move.w    (endpeg,a6),-(sp)
                move.w    (intpeg,a6),-(sp)
                move.w    (stpeg,a6),-(sp)
                move.w    d1,-(sp)
                bsr       hanoi
                                         ; move string bottom disk
                move.b    (stpeg+1,a6),src
                move.b    (endpeg+1,a6),dest
                lea       movemsg,a0
                move.w    #16,d0
                jsr       strout
; call hanoi use parameters n-1, intermediate,final,current pegs
                move.w    (stpeg,a6),-(sp)
                move.w    (endpeg,a6),-(sp)
                move.w    (intpeg,a6),-(sp)
                move.w    d1,-(sp)
                jsr       hanoi
endhanoi:
                movem.l   (sp)+,d0-d1/a0
                unlk      a6
                move.l    (sp),(parmsize,sp)
                addq.w    #parmsize,sp
                rts

                data


prompt:         dc.b      'enter the number of disks desired: '
movemsg:        dc.b      'move    '
src:            ds.b      1
                dc.b      ' to '
```

```
dest:          ds.b      1
               dc.b      Newline

               end
```

⟨Run of Program 10.9⟩

enter the number of disks desired: *3*

```
move  l to r
move  l to m
move  r to m
move  l to r
move  m to l
move  m to r
move  l to r
```

Recursive code is seldom written in assembly language. A high-level language is more easily used to implement a recursive algorithm. However, assembly language code allows greater understanding of the recursion process. Chapter 11 introduces trees and develops a series of recursive subroutines to initialize and scan a binary tree. They are difficult to understand, even in a high-level language, because they use call-by-reference parameters. By tracing the corresponding assembly language code, the parameter passing and recursive steps are clarified.

10.4 | REENTRANT CODE

A multiuser system runs two or more programs with a **time-slicing scheme** that switches the CPU from one program to another. Each program receives a quantum of time, and then an interrupting clock signal causes a switch to another program. During this **context switch**, the general-purpose registers and the PC, SP, and SR of the suspended process must be saved, and register values for the new program restored. (See Chapter 15 for more details.) On a multiuser system, it is often the case that two or more users are running the same piece of software. If the software is a compiler, editor, or assembler, typically 1 to 2M of memory are required. If each user had to execute a separate copy of the software, memory would become saturated, and the operating system would have to swap code to disk continually in order to make room for copies of the large software package, resulting in a frustratingly slow system.

It is desirable for systems to implement shared code. One copy of the

FIGURE 10.6   Memory Storage in Shared and Nonshared Code

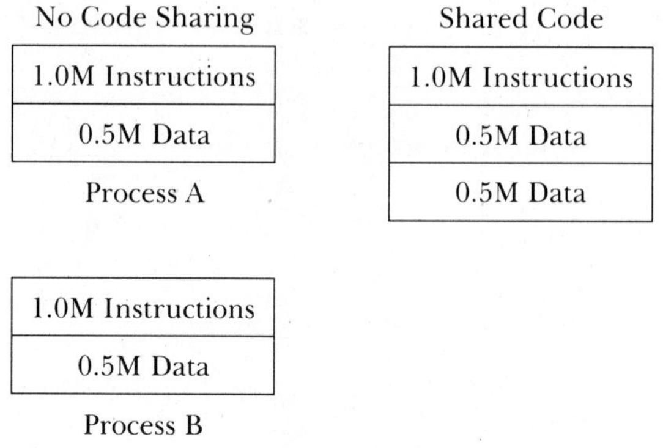

No Code Sharing

1.0M Instructions
0.5M Data

Process A

1.0M Instructions
0.5M Data

Process B

Shared Code

1.0M Instructions
0.5M Data
0.5M Data

machine instructions is shared by two or more programs in memory. In the time-slicing scheme, a program executes the shared code for a quantum, and another program is then permitted to have access to the code. Such shared code is said to be **reentrant**. For reasons discussed later, instructions and read-only data can be shared, whereas memory containing read/write data cannot be shared. Each instance of execution of the program must maintain its own copy of such data. In a multiuser environment, a program in memory competing with other programs is called a **process**.

Figure 10.6 illustrates the memory efficiency of reentrant code. To better understand the concept, assume that a compiler requires 1M of code space and 0.5M of data space and that processes A and B execute the compiler.

Summary: Processes A and B are running
Total memory required: With shared code   2.0M
                         Without shared code   3.0M

Conditions for Reentrant Code

The writing of reentrant code follows a carefully established set of guidelines, which can be summarized in a set of four rules. Consider the subroutine SUMARR whose parameters are passed on the stack and are an array address and the number of 16-bit elements in the array. The subroutine returns the sum of the array elements in D0.

```
ADDRARR:        EQU     8
ARRCOUNT:       EQU     12
PARAM6:         EQU      6
```

```
SUMARR:
        LINK        A6,#0                    ; SET UP THE FRAME POINTER
        MOVEM.L     D1/A0,-(SP)              ; SAVE REGISTERS
        MOVEA.L     (ADDRARR,A6),A0          ; GET ARRAY ADDRESS INTO A0
        MOVE.W      (ARRCOUNT,A6),D1         ; GET ARRAY COUNT INTO D1
        SUBQ.W      #1,D1                    ; USE D1 AS LOOP COUNTER
        MOVEQ       #0,D0                    ; ACCUMULATE SUM IN D0
LOOP:
        ADD.W       (A0)+,D0                 ; PERFORM THE SUMMATION
        DBRA        D1,LOOP
        MOVEM.L     (SP)+,D1/A0              ; POP REGISTERS OFF STACK
        UNLK        A6                       ; RESTORE ORIGINAL FRAME PTR
        MOVE.L      (A0),(PARAM6,SP)         ; CLEAN PARAMETERS OFF STACK
        ADDQ.W      #PARAM6,SP
        RTS
```

Issue 1

Assume that the code containing SUMARR is used by processes A and B sharing a common copy of the program in which SUMARR resides and that a call to SUMMAR takes the following form:

```
(1)                 MOVE.W      D0,NELTS
                        .
                        .
                        .
(2)                 MOVE.W      NELTS,-(SP)
(3)                 PEA         S
(4)                 JSR         SUMARR
                        .
                        .
                        .
(5)     S:          DS.W        100
(6)     NELTS:      DS.W        1
```

It is assumed that the programmer has placed S and NELTS in the code segment of the program. Under certain conditions, process switching could destroy parameters. Trace the following sequence of process switches:

Assume that the array for process A contains 7 active elements and the array for process B contains 77 active elements.
Process A executes instruction (1) with (D0.W) = 7. Variable NELTS has value 7.
Switch to process B before A gets to (2), and execute instructions (1)–(4). Variable NELTS has value 77.
Interrupt process B and switch to process A.
With the value of NELTS being 77 instead of 7, the results of SUMARR will be incorrect.

Rule 1 The segment of the code in which the machine instructions lie cannot be modified in any way.

Normally, S and NELTS would be placed in the data segment of the program. However, the same problem would exist if the processes shared the data segment. Issue 4 will discuss the data segment in more detail.

Issue 2

Each process must have access to its own register data (D0 − D7/A0 − A6 PC, SR, and SP). Otherwise this data acts like global variables and can be incorrectly modified by process switching.

Rule 2 At a context switch, all registers, including the status register SR, must be saved. Upon resumption of the process, the original register values must be restored.

Issue 3

Each process that shares code for subroutine SUMARR pushes parameters on the stack and calls SUMARR.

    (1)   MOVE.W   NELTS, − (SP)
    (2)   PEA   S
    (3)   JSR   SUMARR

If each process running on the system has its own unique area of memory for its stack, then each instance of SUMARR will access a distinct set of parameters. In general, each subroutine using the stack for its parameters and local variables will maintain its integrity (see Figure 10.7).

FIGURE 10.7   Unique Areas of Memory for Individual Stacks

		Stack Area for B			Stack Area for B
Process A		RETADDR	Process B		RETADDR
MOVE.W NELTS,–(SP)		S	MOVE.W NELTS,–(SP)		S
PEA S			PEA S		
JSR SUMARR		NELTS	JSR SUMARR		NELTS

Rule 3 Each process must have its own distinct stack area. In this way, all local variables and subroutine parameters remain distinct.

Issue 4

Several program units use global data. Each instance of process execution must maintain a unique copy of its global variables. The operating system can do this by maintaining a separation between the instructions/read-only data, the read-write data, and the stack. This is normally done by system hardware called the *memory management unit* or by means of software control. This will solve the problem presented in Issue 1, where S and NELTS were stored in the code segment with instructions. If they are placed in the data segment, and the data segments of separate processes sharing the code segment are kept distinct, then the problem described will not occur. At a process switch, the read-write data area of the new process becomes active (see Figure 10.8).

Rule 4 Each process must be given its own unique area of memory for global read-write data.

The rules are applied to an example in which a program contains subroutine calls to implement high-level file handling. The routines call lower-level operating system interfaces such as "OPEN" and "WRITE."

Suppose that a global file variable "SOURCEFILE" is shared by several routines in the program. Figure 10.9 outlines the run-time storage organization for the program containing subroutines "OPENF" and "WRITEF". Each process executing the code has its own stack and global data area. There is no possibility that any instance of execution of one can affect the other.

FIGURE 10.8 Unique Data for Separate Processes

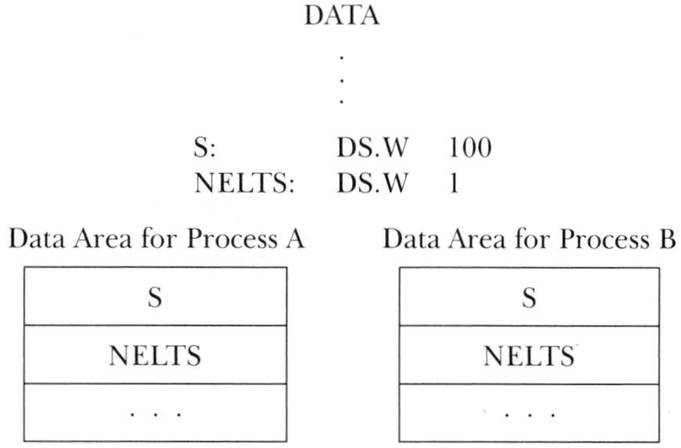

DATA

.
.
.

S:	DS.W	100
NELTS:	DS.W	1

Data Area for Process A | Data Area for Process B

S
NELTS
. . .

S
NELTS
. . .

FIGURE 10.9   Code Executed by A and B

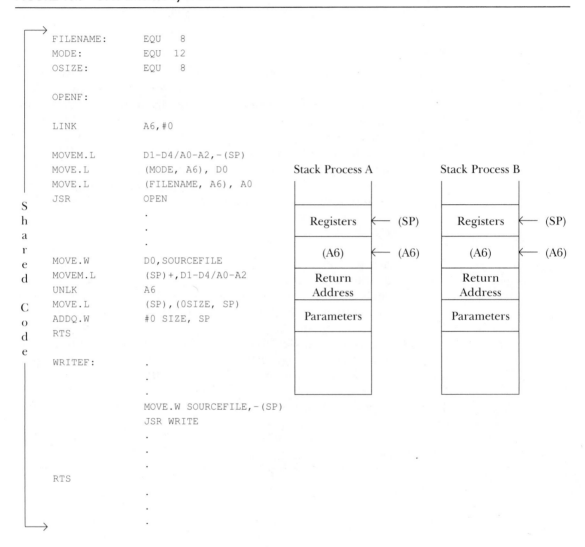

```
FILENAME:        EQU    8
MODE:            EQU    12
OSIZE:           EQU    8

OPENF:

LINK             A6,#0

MOVEM.L          D1-D4/A0-A2,-(SP)
MOVE.L           (MODE, A6), D0
MOVE.L           (FILENAME, A6), A0
JSR              OPEN
                 .
                 .
                 .
MOVE.W           D0,SOURCEFILE
MOVEM.L          (SP)+,D1-D4/A0-A2
UNLK             A6
MOVE.L           (SP),(OSIZE, SP)
ADDQ.W           #0 SIZE, SP
RTS

WRITEF:          .
                 .
                 .
MOVE.W SOURCEFILE,-(SP)
JSR WRITE
                 .
                 .
                 .
RTS
                 .
                 .
                 .
```

Shared Code

Stack Process A · Stack Process B

Registers ← (SP)
(A6) ← (A6)
Return Address
Parameters

```
SOURCEFILE: Data
            DS.W 1
            .
            .
            .
```

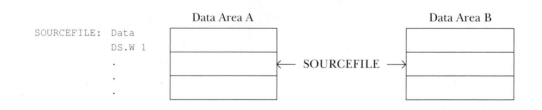

Data Area A   Data Area B

← SOURCEFILE →

POSITION-INDEPENDENT CODE

Chapter 6 introduced position-independent code in connection with the PC-relative addressing modes. This section expands on those ideas and presents a scheme that you can use to write such code. Historically, the writing of code that executes in the same way regardless of position in memory was very important. In a multiuser system, it is necessary to swap programs in and out of memory as the number of processes increases. When a process comes back in memory, its original location may be occupied, so it has to be relocated. The Macintosh operating system runs processes that are designed to be position-independent, as long as the operating system maintains address register A5. "Bare" systems are supplied with a monitor. This monitor provides a user with the ability to examine and modify memory, load code from a larger host system, cause a program to run to a designated location called a **breakpoint**, and so on. Monitors are covered in some detail in Chapters 12 and 13. It is common for monitors to be written in a position-independent fashion.

The two types of position-independent code (PIC) are **static** and **dynamic**. A program is statically position-independent if it can be loaded as a whole at a different starting address and then be executed to conclusion with no change in function. Dynamic position independence implies that the program can be interrupted at any point, moved to another location, and restarted with no change in function. This feature is mandatory in a time-sharing environment, in which programs are swapped to disk to allow other programs access to memory. Upon return, the program may be placed in a different area of memory. The following code has static, but not dynamic, position-independence.

Assume that TARGET has value $004000.

```
(1)              MOVEQ     #99,D1
(2)              LEA       (TARGET,PC),A2
(3)   LOOP:      CLR.W     (A2)+
(4)              DBRA      D1,LOOP
                    .
                    .
                    .

      TARGET:    DS.W      100
```

After instruction (2) has finished, (A2) = $004000. Assume that execution is suspended at this point and that the entire program is moved to a new area of memory. When the program is restarted at instruction (3), the contents of A2 are not relocated, and the block of memory in the old program location will be cleared.

Dynamic position-independent code will not be covered in detail in this section. Such code requires support by memory management hardware and an operating system and is discussed in Chapter 15.

"Pure" static PIC is difficult to write and requires great care. It requires a different "art of programming." Each instruction must execute in the same way, regardless of where it is loaded in memory, and must require no support from the operating system. Writing PIC requires a restricted use of addressing modes. The MC68000 modes and their availability for PIC are summarized here:

Data Register/Address Register Direct: This is always position independent.

Immediate: A numerical constant is position independent, but you must avoid addresses.

MOVE.W	#55,D0	Position-independent
MOVEA.L	#ARR,A0	Not position-independent

Absolute Long and Short: Constant addresses are position independent. Do not utilize user-defined labels.

MOVE.B	D0,$10040	Position-independent
MOVE.L	D3,A	Not position-independent

PC-Relative: May be used at any time. This includes all branch and decrement and branch instructions.

Address Register Indirect Modes: Can be used only if the address register has been loaded in a position-independent fashion.

	Position-Independent			*Not Position-Indenpendent*	
	LEA	(A,PC),A0	LEA	C,A2	
LOOP:	ADD.W	(A0)+,D0	MOVE.L	(0,A2,D1.W),D4	

Program 10.5 is a CASE statement example that selects football scoring plays for point values, 1, 2, 3, and 6. The following program introduces PC-relative mode to implement the CASE statement. The actions of the key instructions are as follows:

1. The mode (CASES,PC) accesses location CASES. The value of CASES is computed relative to the PC. The LEA instruction assigns the address of CASES in A0

    LEA   (CASES,PC),A0

2. The subroutines are specified as offsets to label CASES.

CASES:	DC.L	EXTRAPT-CASES
	DC.L	SAFETY-CASES
	DC.L	FIELDGOAL-CASES
		ETC

3. Assuming that (D0.W) is a long-word offset into the CASES table, the sum of the CASES address and the offset is the address of the subroutine. For instance, assume that (D0.W) = 8, the "Field Goal" offset.

> ADDA.L   (0,A0,D0.W),A0

The resulting value of A0 is

> CASES Address + Offset to FIELDGOAL = FIELDGOAL address

4. Program control is passed to the specific subroutine address. The following instruction transfers program control to the FIELDGOAL routine.

> JMP   (A0)

PROGRAM 10.10

PC-Relative Code:
Football Scores

```
Null:           equ     0

                xref    decin, putstr, newline, stop
                entry   start


start:          jsr     (decin,pc)
                subq.w  #1,d0               ; translate range 1-6 to 0-5
                cmpi.w  #5,d0               ; score in range?
                bls     call_cases
                move.w  #6,d0               ; set offset to 6
call_cases:     asl.w   #2,d0               ; offset is long word
                lea     (cases,pc),a0       ; get address of cases
                adda.l  (0,a0,d0.w),a0      ; add offset for subroutine
                jmp     (a0)                ; jump to routine


cases:          dc.l    extrapt-cases       ; one point
                dc.l    safety-cases        ; two points
                dc.l    fieldgoal-cases     ; three points
                dc.l    otherwise-cases     ; four points
                dc.l    otherwise-cases     ; five points
                dc.l    touchdown-cases     ; six points
                dc.l    otherwise-cases     ; general otherwise case


extrapt:        lea     extrapt_str,a0
                bra     print
safety:         lea     safety_str,a0
                bra     print
fieldgoal:      lea     fieldgoal_str,a0
                bra     print
touchdown:      lea     touchdown_str,a0
                bra     print
otherwise:      lea     noscore_str,a0
```

```
print:          jsr     (putstr,pc)
                jsr     (newline,pc)
                jsr     (stop,pc)
                data
extrapt_str:
                dc.b    'Extra Point', Null
safety_str:
                dc.b    'Safety', Null
fieldgoal_str:
                dc.b    'Field Goal', Null
touchdown_str:
                dc.b    'Touchdown', Null
noscore_str:
                dc.b    'Not a Valid Score', Null

                end
```

⟨Run of Program 10.10⟩

```
2
Safety
```

Base-Relative Addressing

The MC68000 does not support the general use of PC-relative addressing for the destination operand. Only the branch instructions (BRA, Bcc, DBcc, and BSR) and instructions BTST, JMP, and JSR allow a PC-relative destination operand. This complicates the writing of position-independent code and gives rise to base-relative addressing. The following rule applies.

Rule The operating system loads an address register with the starting address of the data area. Access all variables as offsets to this base register. The assembler must assemble data labels as offsets from the start of the data area.

Figure 10.10 illustrates a program using a base register to access data.

The displacement in PC-relative mode is limited to the range -32768 to 32767.

FIGURE 10.10 Base-Relative Addressing

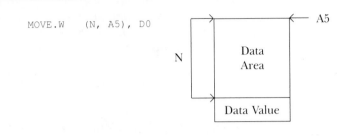

```
MOVE.W   (N, A5), D0
```

On the Macintosh, data references are A5 base-relative addresses. Without compiler or assembler support for 32-bit addressing, the data segment of a Macintosh application cannot exceed 32K.

10.6 MC68020/30/40 MEMORY INDIRECT MODES

Memory indirect modes enable the processor to compute an intermediate effective address whose contents become a base address for access to memory. The modes involve a two-phase computation of the effective address of the operand. Two MC68020 memory indirect modes are specified. In the pre-indexed mode, the contents of the intermediate effective address are added to an outer displacement to compute the final address of the operand. With the post-indexed mode, an outer displacement and scaled index are added to the contents of the intermediate effective address. These memory indirect modes allow for efficient access to tables of pointers.

ADDRESSING MODE

MC68020 Memory Indirect

Syntax   ([bd,An,Rm.Size * Scale],od)   Pre-indexed form
            ([bd,An],Rm.Size * Scale,od)   Post-indexed form

Action

1. For memory indirect pre-indexed mode, an intermediate effective address is computed using the base displacement, address register, and index operand. The 32-bit contents at this memory location are fetched, and the outer displacement is added to compute the effective address of the operand.

$$\langle ea \rangle = \text{contents}(bd + An + Rm * Scale) + od$$

2. For memory indirect post-index mode, an intermediate effective address is computed using the base displacement and address register. The 32-bit contents at this location are fetched, and the effective address of the operand is determined by adding the contents of the intermediate address, the index operand, and the outer displacement.

$$\langle ea \rangle = contents(bd + An) + Rm * Scale + od$$

Notes

1. The square brackets specify the intermediate effective address. The final effective address is computed by taking the 32-bit contents at the intermediate effective address and adding the outer displacement and scaled index (post-indexed form).

2. All four user-specified values in the operand are optional.

3. Both the base and the outer displacements may be 16- or 32-bit values. 16-bit values are sign extended.

EXAMPLE 10.3

The following contents are stored in memory starting at address $1000.

0000	1006	0000	100C	0000	3000	0000	3000
1000	1002	1004	1006	1008	100A	100C	100E

Assume that (A1) = $00000004 and (D0.L) = $00000002.

(a) ([$1000,A1,D0.L * 2],$20)   (Pre-indexed form)
The intermediate effective address is

$$\$1000 + \$0004 + \$0004 = \$1008$$

The contents at address $1008 is $00003000. The effective address of the operand is

$$\$3000 + \$0020 = \$3020$$

(b) ([$1000,A1],D0.L * 2,$20)   (Post-indexed form)
The intermediate effective address is

$$\$1000 + \$0004 = \$1004$$

The contents at address $1004 are $0000100C. The effective address of the operand is

$$\$100C + \$0004 + \$0020 = \$1030$$

PROGRAM 10.11

The CASE
Statement with
Memory Indirect
Mode

A modified version of an assembly language CASE routine is implemented using memory indirect pre-indexed mode. When you input a football score in the range 1–6, the play that produces that score is printed. The program assumes absolute addressing is valid.

```
Null:       equ     0

            xref    putstr,newline,decin,stop
            entry   start

start:      jsr     decin
            subq.w  #1,d0             ; translate range
            cmpi.w  #5,d0             ; score in range?
            bhi     otherwise
            jmp     ([cases,d0.w*4])  ; jump to selected code
; case table
cases:      dc.l    extrapt           ; one point
            dc.l    safety            ; two points
            dc.l    fieldgoal         ; three points
            dc.l    otherwise         ; four points
            dc.l    otherwise         ; five points
            dc.l    touchdown         ; six points
extrapt:    lea     extrapt_str,a0
            bra     print
safety:     lea     safety_str,a0
            bra     print
fieldgoal:  lea     fieldgoal_str,a0
            bra     print
touchdown:  lea     touchdown_str,a0
            bra     print
otherwise:  lea     noscore_str,a0
print:      jsr     putstr
            jsr     newline
            jsr     stop


            data
extrapt_str:
            dc.b    'Extra Point ', Null
safety_str:
            dc.b    'Safety ', Null
fieldgoal_str:
            dc.b    'Field Goal ', Null
touchdown_str:
            dc.b    'Touchdown ', Null
noscore_str:
            dc.b    'Not a Valid Score ', Null

            end
```

⟨Run of Program 10.11⟩

6
Touchdown

PROGRAM 10.12

Powers Table

Enter the base B and exponent e using DECIN. The value B^e is printed in decimal and hex by looking up a value in the table for the base B. This program assumes that absolute addressing is available.

Algorithm   TABLE contains an array of addresses for base 2, 3, 4, and 5 tables. A valid exponent for each entry in the table is in the range 0–10. The exponent is stored in an index register. Each entry in a table is a record with two long-word fields containing the decimal and hex result. Using memory indirect with post-indexed mode, the record corresponding to value B^e is fetched. The outer displacement of 0 (decimal) or 4 (hex) accesses the corresponding field in the record.

```
        xref    decin, decout_long, hexout_long, newline, stop

start:  jsr     decin                       ; load the base
        subq.w  #2,d0                       ; set base as index
        lea     (d0.w*4),a0                 ; (a0) = (d0.w)*4
        jsr     decin                       ; load the power
        move.w  d0,d1
        move.l  ([table,a0],d1.w*8),d0      ; fetch the decimal field
        jsr     decout_long
        move.l  ([table,a0],d1.w*8,4),d0    ; fetch the hex field
        jsr     hexout_long
        jsr     newline
        jsr     stop

        data

table:  dc.l    twotable, threetable, fourtable, fivetable
twotable:
        dc.l    1,$1,2,$2,4,$4,8,$8,16,$10,32,$20,64,$40
        dc.l    128,$80,256,$100,512,$200,1024,$400

threetable:
        dc.l    1,$1,3,$3,9,$9,27,$1b,81,$51,243,$f3,729
        dc.l    $2d9,2187,$88b,6561,$19a1,19683
        dc.l    $4ce3,59049,$e6a9
fourtable:
        dc.l    1,$1,4,$4,16,$10,64,$40,256,$100
        dc.l    1024,$400,4096,$1000
        dc.l    16384,$4000,65536,$10000,262144,$40000,1048576
        dc.l    $100000
fivetable:
        dc.l    1,$1,5,$5,25,$19,125,$7d,625,$271,3125
        dc.l    $c35,15625
```

```
        dc.1    $3d09, 78125, $1312d, 390625, $5f5e1, 1953125, $1dcd65
        dc.1    9765625, $9502f9

        end
```

⟨Run of Program 10.12⟩

```
2    8
256  00000100
```

PROGRAM 10.13

Powers Table
(Macintosh
Version)

In this version of the powers program, the array TABLE must contain run-time computed addresses. These are assigned in a loop at the start of the program. The value of TABLE used by the assembler is an offset to A5. The actual run-time value of TABLE is TABLE + A5. The post-indexed mode instruction must have A5 added to the value in A0.

```
        xref    decin, decout_long, hexout_long, newline, stop

start:  ; initialize "table" to be an array of runtime addresses
        moveq   #3, d1
        lea     twotable, a1
        lea     table, a0
initabs: move.l a1, (a0)+
        adda.w  #88, a1
        dbra    d1, initabs

        jsr     decin                           ; load the base
        subq.w  #2, d0                          ;· set base as index
        lea     (d0.w*4), a0                    ;  (a0) = (d0.w)*4
        jsr     decin                           ; load the power
        move.w  d0, d1
        adda.l  a5, a0                          ; table is an offset to a5
        move.l  ([table, a0], d1.w*8), d0       ; fetch the decimal field
        jsr     decout_long
        move.l  ([table, a0], d1.w*8, 4), d0    ; fetch the hex field
        jsr     hexout_long
        jsr     newline
        jsr     stop

        data

table:  ds.l    4
twotable:
        dc.l    1, $1, 2, $2, 4, $4, 8, $8, 16, $10, 32, $20, 64, $40
        dc.l    128, $80, 256, $100, 512, $200, 1024, $400
```

```
threetable:
        dc.l    1, $1, 3, $3, 9, $9, 27, $1b, 81, $51, 243, $f3, 729
        dc.l    $2d9, 2187, $88b, 6561, $19a1, 19683
        dc.l    $4ce3, 59049, $e6a9
fourtable:
        dc.l    1, $1, 4, $4, 16, $10, 64, $40, 256, $100
        dc.l    1024, $400, 4096, $1000
        dc.l    16384, $4000, 65536, $10000, 262144, $40000, 1048576
        dc.l    $100000
fivetable:
        dc.l    1, $1, 5, $5, 25, $19, 125, $7d, 625, $271, 3125
        dc.l    $c35, 15625
        dc.l    $3d09, 78125, $1312d, 390625, $5f5e1, 1953125, $1dcd65
        dc.l    9765625, $9502f9

        end
```

⟨Run of Program 10.13⟩

```
2    8
256  00000100
```

Program Counter Memory Indirect Modes

For the memory indirect modes, an address register is used to compute the intermediate effective address. The MC68020 extends this concept to the PC, which permits position-independent code. Two program counter memory indirect modes are available, and all user-specified values in the addressing modes are optional. If the PC is suppressed, the notation "ZPC" is used in the syntax. This enables the assembler to distinguish memory indirect and program counter memory indirect modes.

ADDRESSING MODE

MC68020 Program Counter Memory Indirect

Syntax   ([bd,PC,R*m*.Size ∗ Scale],od)   Pre-indexed form
             ([bd,PC],R*m*.Size ∗ Scale,od)   Post-indexed form

Action   The modes are similar to memory indirect with an address register. The intermediate effective address is computed relative to the program counter. On most assemblers, if the base displacement is a label, it is computed as a relative offset to the program counter.

⟨ea⟩ = contents (bd + PC + R*m* ∗ Scale) + od   Pre-indexed form
⟨ea⟩ = contents (bd + PC) + R*m* ∗ Scale + od   Post-indexed form

EXAMPLE 10.4

The following three instructions compare syntax for memory indirect and PC memory indirect mode. The address of the instruction is included in order to compute the PC-relative offset. Assume that (D0.W) = $0020.

(a) 005000   MOVE.L   ([$1000,D0.W]),D1

The address register is suppressed. The intermediate effective address is $1020. The contents of address $1020 is the effective address of the source operand.

(b) 005000   MOVE.L   ([$1000,PC,D0.W]),D1

The PC has the base address $5002. The intermediate effective address is $1000 + $5002 + $0020 = $6022. The contents of address $6022 is the effective address of the source operand.

(c) 005000   MOVE.L   ([$1000,ZPC,D0.W]),D1

The PC is suppressed. The intermediate effective address is $1000 + $0020 = $1020. The contents of address $1020 is the effective address of the source operand.

PROGRAM 10.14

The CASE Statement with PC Memory Indirect Mode

The football CASE program is rewritten to use PC memory indirect mode. When you input a football score, the program prints the play that produced the score.

```
Null:        equ      0

             xref     strout,newline,stop,decin

start:       jsr      decin
             subq.w   #1,d0                        ; translate range
             cmpi.w   #5,d0                        ; score in range?
             bhi      otherwise
             lea      ([cases,pc,d0.w*4]),a1       ; read offset from cases
             jmp      (cases,pc,a1.1)              ; jump to selected code
; case table
cases:       dc.1     extrapt-cases               ; one point
             dc.1     safety-cases                ; two points
             dc.1     fieldgoal-cases             ; three points
             dc.1     otherwise-cases             ; four points
             dc.1     otherwise-cases             ; five points
             dc.1     touchdown-cases             ; six points
extrapt:     lea      extrapt_str,a0
             bra      print
safety:      lea      safety_str,a0
             bra      print
fieldgoal:   lea      fieldgoal_str,a0
             bra      print
```

```
touchdown:    lea      touchdown_str,a0
              bra      print
otherwise:    lea      noscore_str,a0
print:        jsr      putstr
              jsr      newline
              jsr      stop

extrapt_str:
              dc.b     'Extra Point', Null
satefy_str:
              dc.b     'Safety', Null
fieldgoal_str:
              dc.b     'Field Goal', Null
touchdown_str:
              dc.b     'Touchdown', Null
noscore_str:
              dc.b     'Not a Valid Score', Null

              end
```

⟨Run of Program 10.14⟩

```
2
Safety
```

EXERCISES

1. (a) To map the selector (D0.W) in the CASE statement below into a jump table, what value must be subtracted?

```
CASE L OF
    5          :    M := 1;
    9          :    M := 2;
    4          :    M := 3;
    16         :    M := 4;
    OTHERWISE:      M := 7
END;
```

(b) The following code sequence is intended to implement the CASE statement:

```
CASE I OF
    2          :    J := J + 1;
    3          :    J := J + 2;
    5          :    J := J + 3;
    OTHERWISE:      J := J + 7
END;
```

```
(1)                --------------------------------
(2)                CMP.W      #3,D0
```

(3)		BHI	OTHERWISE
(4)		-----------------------------------	
(5)		LEA	CASES,A0
(6)		-----------------------------------	
(7)		JSR	(A0)
(8)	CASES:	DC.L	TWO
(9)		DC.L	THREE
(10)		-----------------------------------	
(11)		DC.L	FIVE
(12)	TWO:	ADDQ.W	#1, J
(13)		BRA.S	NEXT
(14)	THREE:	ADDQ.W	#2, J
(15)		BRA.S	NEXT
(16)	FIVE:	ADDQ.W	#3, J
(17)		BRA.S	NEXT
(18)	OTHERWISE:		
(19)		ADDQ.W	#7, J
(20)	NEXT:	. . .	

Fill in the statements that must be inserted at lines 1,4,6, and 10.

2. Code the following CASE statement in assembly language:

```
CASE     (I + 2) OF
  3  :        J := 1;
  5  :        J := 2;
  7  :        J := 3;
  8  :        J := 4;
  OTHERWISE  :
               J := 5
END CASE
```

3. Consider the following Pascal procedure and its equivalent assembly language:

**** Pascal ****

TYPE arrtype = ARRAY[0 . . 99] OF integer;

PROCEDURE q3(VAR a : arrtype;n : integer; VAR avg : integer);
VAR lavg,i : integer;
BEGIN
  lavg := 0;
  FOR I := 0 TO n − 1 DO
    lavg := lavg + a[i];
  lavg := lavg / n;
  avg := larg;
END {q3};

****Assembly Language ****

(1)	A:	EQU	8
(2)	N:	EQU	12

(3)	AVG:	EQU	14
(4)	PARSIZE:	EQU	10

(5)	Q3:		
(6)		---
(7)		MOVEM.L	D0/A0, − (SP)
(8)		CLR.W	(− 4,A6)
(9)		CLR.W	(− 2,A6)
(10)		MOVEA.L	(A,A6),A0
(11)	LP:	MOVE.W	(− 2,A6),D0
(12)		---
(13)		BGE	OUT
(14)		MOVE.W	(− 2,A6),D0
(15)		ASL.W	#1,D0
(16)		---
(17)		ADD.W	D0,(− 4,A6)
(18)		ADDQ.W	#1,(− 2,A6)
(19)		BRA	LP
(20)	OUT:	---
(21)		EXT.L	D0
(22)		DIVS	(N,A6),D0
(23)		MOVEA.L	(AVG,A6),A0
(24)		MOVE.W	D0,(A0)
(25)		MOVEM.L	(SP) + ,D0/A0
(26)		UNLK	A6
(27)		MOVE.L	(SP),(PARSIZE,SP)
(28)		ADDA.W	#PARSIZE,SP
(29)		RTS	

Fill in the instructions on lines 6, 12, 16 and 20.

4. The following code was generated by a high-level language compiler. The code performs some operation with an array of long words. Determine what is being done and code the subroutine as a Pascal function.

```
     XDEF      FNCT

FNCT:

     LINK      A6,# − 8
     MOVE.L    (8,A6),A0
     MOVE.L    (A0),( − 8,A6)
     MOVEQ     #1,D1
     MOVE.L    D1,( − 4,A6)
     BRA       L0

L1:
     MOVE.L    ( − 4,A6),D0
     ASL.L     #2,D0
     MOVE.L    (8,A6),A0
```

```
        MOVE.L      (0,A0,D0.L).D0
        CMP.L       (−8,A6),D0
        BLE         L2
        MOVE.L      (−4,A6),D0
        ASL.L       #2,D0
        MOVE.L      (0,A0,D0.L),(−8,A6)

L2:
    ADDQ.L      #1,(−4,A6)

L0:
    MOVE.L      (−4,A6),D0
    CMP.L       (12,A6),D0
    BLT         L1
    MOVE.L      (−8,A6),D0
    UNLK        A6
    RTS

        END
```

5. The following code was generated by a high-level language compiler. It performs an operation on an array of long words. What function does it perform?

```
Q5:
                LINK        A6,#−4
                CLR.L       (−4,A6)
                BRA         POINT2
POINT1:
                MOVE.L      (−4,A6),D0
                MOVE.L      (8,A6),A0
                ASL.L       #2,D0
                MOVE.L      (0,A0,D0.L),D0
                CMP.L       (16,A6),D0
                BNE         CONT
                MOVEQ       #1,D0
                BRA         XIT
CONT:
                ADDQ.L      #1,(−4,A6)
POINT2:
                MOVE.L      (−4,A6),D0
                CMP.L       (12,A6),D0
                BLT         POINT1
                MOVEQ       #0,D0
XIT:
                UNLK        A6
                RTS
```

6. Write assembly language code for the following program. Use the LINK/UNLK instructions.

```
PROGRAM link;
VAR i : integer;

PROCEDURE P (VAR i : integer);
  VAR j : integer;
  BEGIN
    j := 3;
    i := j + i + 1
  END;

BEGIN
  i := 4;
  P(i);
  writeln(i)
END.
```

7. Write assembly language code for the following Pascal procedure. Use the LINK/ UNLK instructions.

```
TYPE arr = ARRAY[1 .. 50] of integer;

PROCEDURE SumSq(var a : arr; n : integer;
    VAR sum: integer);
VAR i, lsum : integer;

BEGIN
  lsum := 0;
  FOR i := 1 TO n DO
    lsum := lsum + sqr(a[i]);
  sum := lsum;
END { SumSq };
```

8. Consider the following PRINTF statement from C:

$$\text{printf(``x = \%d y = \%d and String = \%s\textbackslash n'',x,y,s);}$$

Assume the format specifier is stored at address FS, x and y are labels containing long words, and s is the address of a Null-terminated string.
   (a) Show how to call the subroutine PRINTF.
   (b) Explain how PRINTF produces the required output. In particular, how does it know there are three variables to print?
   (c) Upon return, show how the calling code flushes the parameters off the stack.

9. In the following code segment from a large program, you want to return (D0.L) = $686 instead of the value currently computed. Show how a code-level debugger can be used to patch the code to do this:

```
ADD.L     (−6,A6),D0
ADD.L     (−10,A6),D0
ADDQ.L    #1,D0
```

```
MOVEM.L     (SP)+,D1-D3/A0-A2
UNLK        A6
RTS
```

10. The recurrence relation for the binomial coefficients is given by

$$C(n, k) \quad = \quad C(n - 1, k - 1) + C(n - 1, k)$$
$$C(n, 0) \quad = \quad 1$$
$$C(n, n) \quad = \quad 1$$

Is it more efficient to compute these coefficients using iteration or recursion?

11. The following Pascal program calls a recursive procedure REVPRINT to print *N* elements of an array of integers in reverse:

```
PROGRAM RecurTest (output);

  TYPE
    ArrType = array[1 .. 5] of integer;
  var
    a: ArrType;
    i: integer;

  PROCEDURE RevPrint (VAR List: ArrType; n, i: integer);
  BEGIN
    IF i <= n THEN BEGIN
        RevPrint (List, n, i + 1);
        writeln(List[i])
      END
  END; {RevPrint}

BEGIN
  FOR i := 1 TO 5 DO
    a[i] := i;
  RevPrint(a, 5, 1);
  readln
END.
```

In order to understand how the recursion works, draw the sequence of stack frames that are generated by the recursive calls.

12. The following recursive subroutine performs a string-handling function. What statement best describes the action of the subroutine?

```
PSIZE:   EQU       4
PARM:    EQU       8

         XDEF      Q12

Q12      LINK      A6,#0
         MOVE.L    A0,-(SP)
```

```
              MOVE.L      (PARM,A6),A0
              TST.B       (A0)+
              BEQ.S       P1
              PEA         (A0)
              JSR         Q12
              ADDQ.W      #1,D0
              BRA.S       OUT
P1:           MOVEQ       #0,D0
OUT:          MOVE.L      (SP)+,A0
              UNLK        A6
              MOVE.L      (SP),(PSIZE,SP)
              ADDA.W      #PSIZE,SP
              RTS
              END
```

13. Which of the following is not a requirement for writing reentrant code?
    (a) May not write into the code segment.
    (b) Maintain a separate stack area for each instance of execution.
    (c) All subroutine calls must be done in a position-independent fashion.
    (d) All registers must be saved at a context switch.
    (e) Each process must have its own data area.

14. In Chapter 3, the concept of self-modifying code was introduced. Why are programs that execute self-modifying code not reentrant?

15. The following code segment is not reentrant. Show how it can be made so and still pass parameters using program memory.

```
              MOVE.W      #3,NBYTES
              MOVE.L      #A,ADDR
              JSR         WRITE
NBYTES:       DS.W        1
ADDR:         DS.L        1

                  . . . .

                  . . . .

RETADDR:      EQU         8

WRITE:        MOVEM.L     D0/A0,-(SP)
              MOVE.L      (RETADDR,SP),A0
              MOVE.W      (A0)+,D0
              MOVEA.L     (A0)+,A0
              MOVE.L      A0,(RETADDR,SP)
              JSR         OSWRITE      ; CALL OPERATING SYSTEM
              MOVEM.L     (SP)+,D0/A0  ; WRITE ROUTINE
              RTS
```

Hint: Consider passing the address of a record containing the two parameters.

16. Which of the following statements can be used in code that is to be position independent?
    - (a) MOVEA.L   #A,A1
    - (b) LEA   A,A3
    - (c) BNE   ALPHA
    - (d) LEA   (A,PC),A1
    - (e) DC.L   ADDR0,ADDR1
    - (f) LEA   Q,A3

          MOVE.B   (0,A3,D6.L),D3
    - (g) LEA   (Q,PC),A3

          MOVE.B   (0,A3,D6.L),D3

17. Show that the following code is statically, but not dynamically, position independent:

    ```
               DS.B    1024
    START:     LEA     (START,PC),SP
               JSR     (INIT,PC)
    ```

18. Consider the code segment

    ```
               MOVEQ   #0,D0
               MOVEQ   #99,D1
               LEA     (ARR,PC),A0
    SLOOP:     ADD.W   (A0)+,D0
               DBRA    D1,SLOOP
    ```

    - (a) Is it statically position independent?
    - (b) Is it dynamically position independent? If not, what is necessary to make it so?

19. Is the following implementation of a CASE statement position independent?

    ```
               MOVE.W   I,D0
               SUBQ.W   #2,D0
               ASL.W    #2,D0
               MOVE.L   (CASES,PC,D0.W),A0
               JSR      (A0)

    CASES:     DC.L     ONE
               DC.L     TWO
                     . . .
               DC.L     LAST
    TWO:             . . .
    ```

20. The following program uses absolute addresses. Rewrite it so that each data reference is made relative to base register A5.

```
          xref        decout, newline, stop

start:    move.w      a,d0
          add.w       b,d0
          add.w       c,d0
          addi.w      #5,d0
          jsr         decout
          jsr         newline
          jsr         stop

          data
a:        dc.w        3
b:        dc.w        5
c:        dc.w        33
          end
```

21. (MC68020/30/40) Assume that labels and registers have values as follows:

$$A = \$1000 \quad (D0.L) = \$4 \quad (A0.L) = \$100$$

and that the following pictures of memory apply:

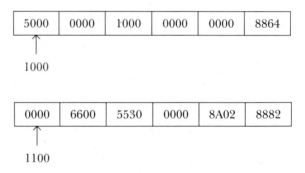

Compute the effective address of each operand. Assure that each instruction is located at address $5000.
(a) BTST #5,([A,A0,D0.W*2],$500)
(b) BTST #5,([A,A0],D0.L*4,$500)
(c) BTST #5,([A,PC,D0.W*2],$500)
(d) BTST #5,([A,PC],D0.L*4,$500)

22. (MC68020/30/40)
    (a) A table HASH consists of pointers to linked lists of nodes. Each node consists of a 4-byte data field and a field containing the address of the next node in the list.

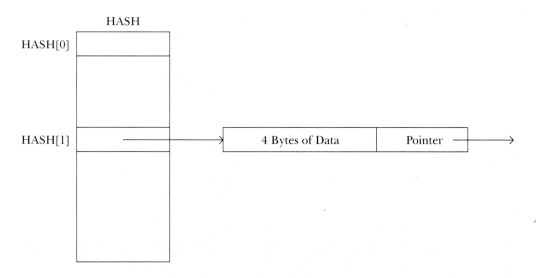

If (D1.W) is the index I, show how to use a memory indirect mode to read the data field of the first node of the list into D1 and the pointer field into A2.

(b) Assume that A is an array of pointers to an array of 16-bit integers. If A1 is set to the offset from A to a particular pointer in A, show how to use post-indexed memory indirect mode to access an element of the array pointed to.

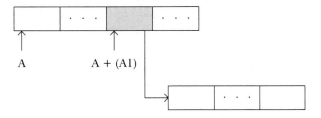

PROGRAMMING EXERCISES

23. Write a program that reads a number N from the keyboard and prints the following, depending on the value of N (use DECOUT):

$N = 1,$	→ "Ace"
$2 <= N <= 10$	→ N
$N = 11$	→ "Jack"
$N = 12$	→ "Queen"

$$N = 13 \qquad\qquad \rightarrow \text{``King''}$$
$$\text{Otherwise} \qquad \rightarrow \text{``Out of Range''}$$

24. Write a recursive routine to output the first 10 numbers in the Fibonacci sequence 1, 1, 2, 3, 5, 8, 13, and so on. The *n*th term of the sequence is recursively defined by the following:

    Stopping conditions $F(0) = 1, F(1) = 1$
    Recursive step· $F(n) = F(n - 1) + F(n - 2) \qquad n \geq 2$

25. Code the Pascal program of exercise 11 in assembly language and test it.

26. A palindrome is a "deblanked" string that reads the same forward and backward. Write an MC68000 code segment that recursively tests to see if a string is a palindrome. Use an algorithm described by the following example:

    Initial string is ABBCBBA of length 7

    (a) Recursively test the first and last characters and then discard them. In this case, the stages will be: ABBCBBA, BBCBB, BCB.
    (b) Stop if the first and last characters are not the same or the string length is < 2.

    Pass the address of the string and its length on the stack. Your routine should print out the original string and a message indicating whether it is a palindrome.

27. Write the program described in exercise 19 in such a way that the implementation of the CASE statement is position independent.

28. The following Pascal program computes all the permutations of the integers from 1–*N*. Using the Pascal code as a model, generate the equivalent MC68000 code. Use the LINK and UNLK instructions to create the stack frames. Note that the procedure PERMUTE has an array argument that is passed by value.

    Example: $N = 3$
    Permutations: 123   132   213   231   312   321

```
PROGRAM permutation (input, output);
TYPE arrtype = ARRAY[1 . . 5] OF integer;
VAR   a          :  arrtype;
        n          :  integer;
        i          :  integer;

PROCEDURE permute (a : arrtype; k, n : integer);
  VAR    temp    :  integer;
          i        :  integer;
BEGIN
  IF k = n THEN BEGIN
        FOR I := 1 TO n DO
            write(a[i] : 3);
        writeln
  END
```

```
        ELSE BEGIN
            FOR I := k TO n DO BEGIN
              temp := a[i];
              a[i] := a[k];
              a[k] := temp;
              permute(a, k + 1, n)
            END
    END
END;

BEGIN
  writeln( enter an n between 1 and 5');
  readln(n);
  FOR I := 1 TO n DO
        a[i] := i;
  permute(a, 1, n)
END.
```

CHAPTER 11

DATA STRUCTURES

Many data structures were already covered in our introduction to the MC68000 instructions and addressing modes. Unsigned and signed numbers, floating-point numbers, and characters were highlighted in separate sections. The structured data types, arrays, records, and stacks were introduced with the addressing modes.

This chapter covers the classical user-defined data structures. Section 11.1 interprets sets as an array of bits, and the operations are implemented with bit-handling instructions. A sample program uses random numbers. Section 11.2 then extends simple arrays to two-dimensional arrays and matrices. The main topics in the chapter focus on list processing, and Sections 11.3 through 11.6 discuss stacks, queues, linked lists, and binary trees. Each structure contains a package of operators that load, update, and retrieve data. Section 11.7 introduces hashing functions as a means of accessing elements in a list.

Programming languages use data structures for large application programs and for systems programming. Equivalent assembly language applications give an indepth understanding of the algorithms.

| 11.1 | SETS

A **set** is a mathematical structure used to represent a collection of objects. An object in a set is called a **member** of the set. You should be familiar with the mathematical operations of set union, intersection, difference, and complement, as well as the designations "is a subset" and "is a member." This section describes the Pascal SET type and syntax. The structure is represented in a data register as an array of bits with the set operations

517

implemented with MC68000 bit instructions. The set size is limited to 32 bits. Larger sets can be represented as an array of Booleans.

Pascal Declaration

```
TYPE
    DAYS_IN_WEEK = SET OF (SUN, MON, TUE, WED,
                                    THU, FRI, SAT);
VAR
    S : DAYS_IN_WEEK;
```

Assembly Language Implementation   Allocate the low-order 7 bits of data register D0. Let SUN correspond to bit 0, MON to bit 1, and so forth. An element is in the set if its corresponding bit is "on" in D0.

Bit Representation of DAYS_IN_WEEK

Sat	Fri	Thu	Wed	Tue	Mon	Sun
6	5	4	3	2	1	0

Pascal Assignment Statement

```
S := [SUN, WED, FRI, SAT];
```

Assembly Language Assignment

```
MOVE.L  #$69,D0     ; INITIALIZE A SET
```

Sat	Fri	Thu	Wed	Tue	Mon	Sun
1	1	0	1	0	0	1
6	5	4	3	2	1	0

```
BSET  #1,D0      ; ADD MON (BIT 1) TO THE SET
                 ; IN PASCAL, THIS REQUIRES A UNION
```

Sat	Fri	Thu	Wed	Tue	Mon	Sun
1	1	0	1	0	1	1
6	5	4	3	2	1	0

The MC68000 logical instructions are used for set operations. Assume that sets S and T are stored in registers D1 and D2, respectively, and that D0 (set U) is used to assign the result of the operations.

SET OPERATION	PASCAL NOTATION	MC68000 INSTRUCTION	
S union T	U := S + T	MOVE.L	D2,D0
		OR.L	D1,D0
S intersect T	U := S * T	MOVE.L	D2,D0
		AND.L	D1,D0
S complement	U := [SUN .. SAT] − S	MOVE.L	D1,D0
		NOT.L	D0
		ANDI.L	#$7F,D0
S minus T	U:= S − T	MOVE.L	D2,D0
		NOT.L	D0
		AND.L	D1,D0

EXAMPLE 11.1

Assume that the universal set is DAYS__IN__WEEK and that set S = {Mon, Wed, Fri} and set T = {Mon, Tue, Wed, Thu}. The MC68000 implementation uses the following set values. In assembly language, the value of set S is $002A, and the value of T is $001E.

Universal Set	1	1	1	1	1	1	1
	Sat	Fri	Thu	Wed	Tue	Mon	Sun

Set S	0	1	0	1	0	1	0
	Sat	Fri	Thu	Wed	Tue	Mon	Sun

Set T	0	0	1	1	1	1	0
	Sat	Fri	Thu	Wed	Tue	Mon	Sun

The assembly language value is computed for each of the set operations.

(a) S union T = {Mon, Tue, Wed, Thu, Fri}
The value is $002A OR $001E = $3E = 0111110_2.

(b) S intersect T = {Mon, Wed}
The MC68000 value is $002A AND $001E = $000A = 0001010_2.

(c) S complement = {Sun, Tue, Thu, Sat}
The MC68000 value is NOT($002A) AND $007F = $FFD5 AND $007F = $55 = 1010101_2.

(d) S minus T = {Fri}

The MC68000 value is \$002A AND NOT(\$001E) = \$002A AND \$FFE1 = \$20 = 01000000_2.

The set relations "is a subset" and "is a member" have simple implementations in MC68000 assembly language.

Set Relation	Pascal Notation	MC68000 Instructions	
S is a subset of T	S < T	AND.L	D0,D1
(TRUE if S * T = S)		CMP.L	D1,D0
X (Bit N) is a member of S	X in S	BTST	#N,D0

In Pascal, the value of the Boolean expression "is a member of" can be assigned to a Boolean variable using the IN operator. For example,

GOT_WED : = WED IN S;

assigns to the Boolean variable GOT_WED the value TRUE if the element WED is in the set and the value FALSE if the element WED is not in the set. The corresponding assembly language implementation might select an 8-bit variable GOT_WED using the "Define Storage" directive "GOT_WED: DS.B 1". The value of the Boolean expression is stored in GOT_WED with 1 representing TRUE and 0 representing FALSE.

The MC68000 provides the Scc ("Set On Condition") instructions to assign a Boolean value. The instructions use both memory and registers.

INSTRUCTION

Scc
(Set On Condition)

Syntax Scc ⟨ea⟩

Action The condition code is tested. If TRUE, the LSB of the operand specified by ⟨ea⟩ is set to all 1's ("TRUE"), otherwise, the LSB is set to all 0's ("FALSE").

Notes

1. The same condition codes used for DBcc instructions may be used with Scc instructions.

2. The bits in the CCR are not affected.

EXAMPLE 11.2

(a) SVS D2

The SVS instruction sets the LSB of D2 to all 1's if the overflow condition is TRUE (V bit is 1). If the V bit is cleared, the LSB of D2 contains all 0's, and the overflow condition is FALSE.

Note: The data register D2 stores information on the status of the V bit. This information is also contained in the V bit of the CCR but can be retained in the data register for later reference after executing subsequent instructions.

(b) SCC   D4

.

.

.

TST.B D4
BNE   ⟨label⟩

The logical value "C bit is 0" is stored in D4. The TST and BNE instructions provide a simple technique for testing the condition. After executing the TST instruction:

If the C bit is clear, (D4.B) = $FF, and the TST instruction sees non zero (TRUE). The BNE instruction (branch on TRUE) results in a branch.
If the C bit is not clear, (D4.B) = $00, and the TST instruction sees zero (FALSE). The BNE instruction does not result in a branch.

(c) Assume that DAYS__IN__WEEK is the universal set. The Scc instructions are used to implement the assembly language assignment GOT__WED : = WED IN S.

                 BTST   #3,D0   ; TEST FOR WED IN S
                 SNE   GOT__WED

.

.

.

GOT__WED: DS.B   1

The resulting value of GOT__WED is $FF (TRUE) or $00 (FALSE).

Demonstration Program: Sets

The following programs use many of the set operations. Program 11.1 illustrates the set operations in Example 11.1. Program 11.2 uses the random function (RAND) that returns a 16-bit unsigned number in D0. The random number generator is initially seeded by a subroutine SEED.

PROGRAM 11.1

Set Operations

Subroutines UNION, INTERSECTION, COMPLEMENT, and MINUS implement the set operations. Set S and set T are passed to the subroutines in registers D1 and D2, respectively. Each subroutine returns the resulting set in D0. The subroutine SUBSET tests the condition "S is a subset of T" and uses the Scc instruction SEQ to assign the result $FF (TRUE) or $00

(FALSE) to the variable IS__SUBSET. The test program inputs sets S and T using HEXIN__LONG and, after each operation, prints out the 32-bit representation of the resulting set using HEXOUT__LONG. The program is run with different test data.

Test 1: Input 2A   S = [SUN, WED, FRI, SAT];
             1E   T = [MON, TUE, WED, THU]

Test 2: Input 2A   S = [SUN, WED, FRI, SAT];
             3E   T = [MON, TUE, WED, THU, FRI]

```
        xref    hexin_long, hexout_long, strout, newline, stop

start:  move.l  #$7F,d7         ; universal set in d7
        jsr     hexin_long
        move.l  d0,d1           ; store set S in d1
        jsr     hexin_long
        move.l  d0,d2           ; store set T in d2

        lea     setHeaders,a0   ; print set op headers
        move.w  #47,d0
        jsr     strout
        jsr     newline

        jsr     union           ; S union T
        jsr     hexout_long
        jsr     intersect       ; S intersect T
        jsr     hexout_long
        jsr     complement      ; S complement
        jsr     hexout_long
        jsr     minus           ; S minus T
        jsr     hexout_long

        jsr     subset          ; test S subset of T
        move.b  isSubset,d0
        jsr     hexout_long
        jsr     newline

        jsr     stop

union:
        move.l  d2,d0           ; move T to d0
        or.l    d1,d0           ; union S and T
        rts

intersect:
        move.l  d2,d0           ; move T to d0
        and.l   d1,d0           ; intersect S and T
        rts

complement:
        move.l  d1,d0           ; move S to d0
```

```
              not.l   d0              ; complement S
              and.l   d7,d0           ; intersect compS and universal set
              rts

minus:
              move.l  d2,d0           ; move T to d0
              not.l   d0              ; complement T
              and.l   d1,d0           ; intersect S and compT
              rts

subset:
              move.l  d2,d0           ; move T to d0
              and.l   d1,d0           ; intersect S and T
              cmp.l   d0,d1           ; compare S and intersect with T
              seq     isSubset        ; TRUE if S >= S and T
              rts

              data

setHeaders:
              dc.b   ' Union Intersect Complement  Minus  Subset'
isSubset:
              ds.b  1
              end
```

⟨Run #1 of Program 11.1⟩

2A 1E

Union	Intersect	Complement	Minus	Subset
0000003E	0000000A	00000055	00000020	00000000

⟨Run #2 of Program 11.1⟩

2A 3E

Union	Intersect	Complement	Minus	Subset
0000003E	0000002A	00000055	00000000	000000FF

PROGRAM 11.2

Random Set

A 16-element set S = 0 . . 15 is defined in (D1.W). Initially, the set is empty. A series of random numbers in the range 0–15 is generated, and each element is added to the set (BSET) if it is not already there. The newly updated set is printed using hexout. The number of random draws required to store all the elements in the set is output using DECOUT.

```
              xref    decout,hexout,newline,seed,rand,stop

start:  moveq   #0,d1                   ; (d1) represents set 0 . . 15;
```

```
                                    ; (d1) = 0 is the empty set
            moveq    #0,d2          ; number of draws
            moveq    #1,d3          ; put 8 items per line
            move.w   #1,d0          ; initial seed
            jsr      seed           ; seed the random number generator

getnum:     cmpi.w   #$ffff,d1      ; test if set is full
            beq.s    printdraws     ; if so, write number of draws
            addq.w   #1,d2          ; increment the counter
            jsr      random         ; get item in range 0-15
            jsr      memberInSet    ; test to see if item in set
            tst.b    haveInSet
            bne      getnum
            bset     d0,d1          ; assign item to set
            jsr      hexout         ; write out the new set
            move.w   d3,d4
            andi.w   #$0007,d4      ; have we just put out an 8th item?
            bne.s    inc_draws
            jsr      newline
inc_draws:
            addq.w   #1,d3
            bra      getnum

printdraws:
            move.w   d2,d0          ; move number of draws to d0
            jsr      newline
            jsr      decout         ; print number of draws
            jsr      newline
            jsr      stop

random:     jsr      rand           ; get 16-bit random number in d0
            andi.l   #$0000ffff,d0  ; unsigned extension to 32 bits
            divu     #16,d0         ; get remainder in range 0-15
            swap     d0             ; move remainder to lsw of d0
            rts

memberInSet:
            movem.l  d0/d1,-(sp)
            btst     d0,d1          ; test for element in set
            sne      haveInSet
            movem.l  (sp)+,d0/d1
            rts

            data
haveInSet:      dc.b  0

            end
```

⟨Run of Program 11.2⟩

0100	0104	1104	1144	1944	1946	1947	1B47
1B57	3B57	3B77	3BF7	BBF7	FBF7	FBFF	FFFF

50

11.2 | MATRICES

An array is a list of equal-sized data items stored in consecutive memory locations. A **matrix** is an array of arrays, with storage in memory specified by rows or columns. As an array, elements of a matrix are read or written using an access function that allows for direct addressing. This section considers only matrices or two-dimensional arrays. The concepts can be extended to cover general multidimensional arrays, in which elements are accessed by three or more indices. The relationship between high-level language compiler code and assembly language code is illustrated with a Pascal example using a two-row by four-column matrix.

Pascal Declaration

VAR A : ARRAY[0 . . 1] OF ARRAY[0 . . 3] OF INTEGER;

	Column 0	Column 1	Column 2	Column 3
Row 0	20	5	-30	0
Row 1	-40	15	100	80

The array name and the row and column indices specify an element in the matrix—that is A[row][column]. Most compilers also accept the notation A[row,column]. For instance,

$$A[1][2] = A[1,2] = 100;$$

Pascal only supports run-time initialization of a matrix. Data is stored in elements of a matrix either by an assignment statement or by an input statement. For instance,

A[0][0] := 20; A[0][1] := 5; A[0][2] := $-$A[0][1] * 6;
READ(A[0][3] and so on

MC68000 Declaration Assembly language allocates memory for a matrix as an extended array. Assuming that an integer is stored as a 16-bit value, the number of memory locations for the Pascal matrix A is the product of the rows and columns.

```
ROWSIZE:     EQU    2
COLSIZE:     EQU    4
             .
             .
             .
A:           DS.W   ROWSIZE * COLSIZE
```

A matrix is stored in memory using either row-major ordering or column-major ordering. Pascal and most modern languages store matrices by row. Using the "Define Constant" directive, the array A can be initialized.

A: DC.W   20, 5, -30, 0, -40, 15, 100, 80

Matrix Storage by Rows

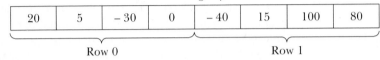

| 20 | 5 | -30 | 0 | -40 | 15 | 100 | 80 |

Row 0   Row 1

The FORTRAN language stores matrices in column-major order. The MC68000 data directive corresponding to an equivalent FORTRAN matrix is

A: DC.W   20, -40, 5, 15, -30, 100, 0, 80

Matrix Access Functions

Elements in a matrix are accessed as an offset to its starting address. An access function AF takes the row and column indices of an element and returns the address of the element.

$$AF(row,column) = \text{Address of matrix } [row,column]$$

For a given matrix, the function requires several parameters.

S—The starting address of the matrix in memory
L—The number of bytes required to store a row of elements
M—The number of bytes required to store a single element

The address of matrix [row,column] is computed from the row index and column index and the parameters S, L, and M.

$$S + (L * row) + (M * column)$$

Most high-level languages permit a lower bound for the row or column index to be other than 0. Assume R_0 and C_0 are the lower bounds for the respective indices. The general access function becomes

$$AF (row,column) = S + [L * (row - R_0)] + [M * (column - C_0)]$$

EXAMPLE 11.3

(a) In the Pascal matrix A, the parameters are $L = 8$ and $M = 2$. Assume that the starting address S of the matrix is \$001100. For element A[1,2], the value of the access function is

$$AF(1,2) = 1100 + (8 * 1) + (2 * 2) = \$110C$$

(b) Matrix B has Pascal declaration

VAR B : ARRAY[-2 . . 5] OF ARRAY[10 . . 20] OF INTEGER;

Assume that the starting address in memory is \$20450. The parameters for the access function are

$$S = \$20450$$
$$L = 22_{10} = \$16$$
$$M = 2$$

The value of the access function for B[2,15] is

$$AF(2,15) = \$20450 + [22 * (2-(-2)] + [2 * (15 - 10)]$$
$$= \$20450 + \$58 + \$0A = \$204B2$$

A matrix descriptor, called a **dope vector**, can be used to store key parameters for the access function. The descriptor, which is implemented as a record, assumes that the lower bounds for the row and column indices are 0.

Matrix Descriptor

Row Upper Bound	Column Upper Bound	Row Size L	Element Size M	Row Index	Column Index

A subroutine PRINTMAT uses the address of a matrix and its dope vector to write out the elements of a matrix. The subroutine assumes that the address of the matrix and the address of the dope vector are passed as parameters on the stack. Address register A1 points at the matrix descriptor. Using a series of EQU directives, the fields of the descriptor are defined as offsets relative to A1. The assembly language is modeled after typical Pascal compiler code for the following procedure.

```
PROCEDURE printmat (VAR M: matrix; row: integer; column: integer);
  var
    i, j: integer;
BEGIN
  FOR i := 0 TO row DO BEGIN
        FOR j := 0 TO column DO
          write(M[i, j] : 4);
          writeln;
  END;
END;
```

MC68000 PRINTMAT Code

```
rowbd:      equ     0               ; offset for row bound
colbd:      equ     2               ; offset for column bound
rowsize:    equ     4               ; offset for row size
eltsize:    equ     6               ; offset for element size
row:        equ     8               ; offset for row index
col:        equ     10              ; offset for column index
mataddr:    equ     8               ; offset to matrix on stack
```

```
matdesptor:  equ      12                ; offset to descriptor on stack
param8:      equ      8

             xdef     printmat
             xref     decout, newline

printmat     link     a6,#0
             movem.l  d0-d2/a0-a1,-(sp)
             movea.l  (mataddr,a6),a0   ; assign registers
             movea.l  (matdesptor,a6),a1
             move.w   #0,(row,a1)       ; set row = 0
print0:      move.w   (rowbd,a1),d1
             cmp.w    (row,a1),d1       ; compare row and rowbound
             blt.s    print3            ; if rowbd < row, print done
             move.w   #0,(col,a1)       ; set col = 0 for row print
print1:      move.w   (colbd,a1),d2
             cmp.w    (col,a1),d2       ; compare col and colbound
             blt.s    print2            ; if colbd < col row
;                                       ; print newline
; compute matrix offset
             move.w   (row,a1),d1
             mulu     (rowsize,a1),d1   ; (d1) = 1 ; row
             move.w   (col,a1),d2
             mulu     (eltsize,a1),d2   ; (d2) = m ; col
             add.w    d2,d1             ; (d1) = access offset

; assign element of matrix to d0
             move.w   (0,a0,d1.w),d0    ; use direct access to element
             jsr      decout
             addq.w   #1,(col,a1)       ; col = col + 1
             bra      print1            ; return to new col element
print2:      jsr      newline           ; end of row. print newline
             addq.w   #1,(row,a1)       ; row = row + 1
             bra      print0            ; go to next row print
print3:      movem.l  (sp)+,d0-d2/a0-a1
             unlk     a6
             move.l   (sp),(param8,sp)  ; reset the stack
             addq.l   #param8,sp
             rts

             end
```

PROGRAM II.3

Matrix Print Test

A 3 × 4 matrix MAT is stored in memory using the "Define Constant" directive. The address of the matrix and its descriptor are put on the stack as input parameters for the subroutine PRINTMAT. The equivalent Pascal code is given. Note that Pascal must use rather tedious run-time initialization of the matrix.

Pascal Test Code

```
PROGRAM test_printmat (input, output);
TYPE
    matrix = array[0..2, 0..3] of integer;
VAR
    mat: matrix;
    i, j: integer;

BEGIN
    mat[0][0] := 10;  mat[0][1] := 19;
    mat[0][2] := 22;  mat[0][3] := 45;
    mat[1][0] := 14;  mat[1][1] := 78;
    mat[1][2] := 30;  mat[1][3] := 18;
    mat[2][0] := 83;  mat[2][1] := 19;
    mat[2][2] := 20;  mat[2][3] := 42;
    printmat(mat, 2, 3);
END.
```

MC68000 Test Code

```
          xref    stop
          xref    printmat
          entry   start

start:    pea     matdesc          ; descriptor on the stack
          pea     mat              ; push address of matrix mat
          jsr     printmat
          jsr     stop

          data
mat:      dc.w    10,19,22,45
          dc.w    14,78,30,18
          dc.w    83,19,20,42

matdesc:  dc.w    2,3,8,2          ; initialize descriptor fields
          ds.w    2                ; index fields

          end
```

⟨Run of Program 11.3⟩

```
    10   19   22   45
    14   78   30   18
    83   19   20   42
```

|11.3| STACKS

A stack is a data structure that stores elements in a list and permits access at only one end of the list. The elements are loaded ("pushed") on the stack and removed ("popped") in LIFO (last-in, first-out) order.

In the context of subroutines, a stack is introduced as temporary storage for parameters, return addresses, local variables, and registers. Other applications use a stack to reverse the order of items and perform pattern matching. The use of stacks for subroutines has been demonstrated. The following two assembly language applications illustrate other uses of a stack.

I/O Routine STKDECOUT

The I/O routine STKDECOUT prints (D0.W) in decimal form. The main part of the algorithm uses repeated division to extract the decimal digits from right to left (units, tens, hundreds, and so on) and places the equivalent ASCII digit on a stack. Initially, the sign of the number is determined, and if it is negative, the character '−' is placed at the top of the stack. By popping elements from the stack, the decimal number is printed.

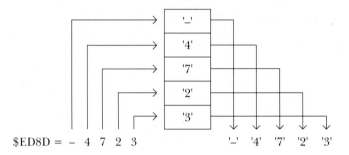

$ED8D = − 4 7 2 3   '−' '4' '7' '2' '3'

Code

```
          xdef     stkdecout
          xref     strout

stkdecout:  movem.l  d0/d7,-(sp)
            clr.b    d7              ; use d7 for the minus sign
            tst.w    d0
            bpl      stkdecout_1
            move.b   #'-', d7        ; move '-' into d7
            neg.w    d0              ; compute absolute value of d0
stkdecout_1: jsr     stkoutput
            movem.l  (sp)+,d0/d7
            rts

stkoutput:  movem.l  d0-d1/a0-a1,-(sp)
            lea      stack+10,a0     ; set a0 past last char of buffer
            movea.l  a0,a1           ; set a1 as end of stack mark
stkoutput_1: divu    #10,d0
            swap     d0              ; store remainder in (d0.w)
            move.w   d0,d1
```

```
              swap     d0                ; restore quotient in (d0.w)
              ext.l    d0
              ori.b    #$30,d1           ; convert remainder to ascii
              move.b   d1,-(a0)          ; push digit on stack
              tst.w    d0                ; more digits to process?
              bne.s    stkoutput_1

              tst.b    d7                ; was number negative?
              beq      stkoutput_2
              move.b   d7,-(a0)
stkoutput_2:  move.w   #1,d0             ; set for single character output
stkoutput_3:  cmpa.l   a0,a1             ; test for stackempty
              beq.s    stkoutput_4
              jsr      strout
              adda.w   #1,a0             ; pop stack by incr a0
              bra      stkoutput_3
stkoutput_4:  movem.l  (sp)+,d0-d1/a0-a1
              rts

              data

stack:        ds.b     10
              end
```

PROGRAM 11.4   A test program uses the subroutine.

Test STKDECOUT
with Stack

```
              xref     decin, stkdecout, newline, stop
              entry    begin

begin:        jsr      decin
              jsr      stkdecout
              jsr      newline
              jsr      stop
              end
```

⟨Run of Program 11.4⟩

−5050
−5050

A second application of stacks determines whether the left and right parentheses in an expression match. The algorithm illustrates the concepts used by the compiler for expression evaluation. Each left parenthesis is pushed on the stack, and each right parenthesis should identify a match and pop a left parenthesis off the stack. The algorithm identifies error conditions as it scans the expression.

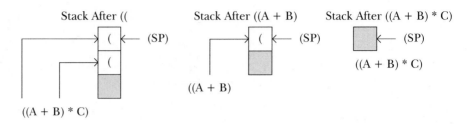

Stack After ((Stack After ((A + B)   Stack After ((A + B) * C)

((A + B) * C)   ((A + B)

Error checking is done by testing the "StackEmpty"" condition.

1. If a right parenthesis finds an empty stack, there is a missing left parenthesis.

2. If the stack is not empty after scanning the expression, there is a missing right parenthesis.

PROGRAM 11.5

Matching
Parentheses

An expression is entered using STRIN. The expression is scanned, and a CASE statement pushes a left parenthesis on the stack and pops a left parenthesis when scanning a right parenthesis. The number of characters in the expression is a counter for a loop. An output string places a '*' at the location of an error and indicates whether the expression is valid or is missing a parenthesis.

```
star:       equ         '*'              ; flags location of an error
blank:      equ         ' '
null:       equ         0
nl:         equ         13

            xref        getstr, putstr, strlength, stop
            entry       start

start:      lea         exprout,a1       ; output expression buffer
            lea         stack+20,a2      ; initialize the stack
            lea         cases,a3         ; address of case statements

            lea         expr,a0          ; input expression buffer
            jsr         getstr
            pea         expr             ; get string length
            jsr         strlength
            subq.w      #1,d0
            bmi         quit             ; entered a null string
            lea         expr,a0

nextchar:   move.b      (a0)+,d1         ; scan a character
            move.b      d1,d2            ; d2 is the case selector
            ext.w       d2
            subi.w      #'(',d2          ; set selector to 0
            cmpi.w      #1,d2            ; "(" has ascii value $28
                                         ; ")" has ascii value $29
```

```
;
                  bhi.s     otherwise
                  mulu      #4,d2            ; 4*(d2) is offset to cases
                  lea       (0,a3,d2.w),a4
                  jmp       (a4)

cases:            jmp       leftparen        ; case '('
                  jmp       rightparen       ; case ')'
                  jmp       otherwise        ; case otherwise

leftparen:        move.b    d1,-(a2)         ; push the character on stack
                  clr.w     stackempty       ; set stackempty to false
                  move.b    #blank,(a1)+     ; char ok; move blank for output
                  bra       decrct           ; branch to end of case statement

rightparen:       tst.w     stackempty
                  beq.s     popstack         ; if false pop stack
                  move.w    #1,exprstatus    ; found error 1, missing "("
                  move.b    #star,(a1)+      ; identify error with "*"
                  bra       decrct
popstack:         adda.l    #1,a2            ; pop stack
                  move.b    #blank,(a1)+     ; char ok; move blank for output
                  jsr       teststack        ; set stackempty flag
                  bra       decrct

otherwise:        move.b    #blank,(a1)+     ; move blank for output

decrct:           tst.w     exprstatus       ; is exprstatus > 0 (error found)
                  dbne      d0,nextchar      ; no or not end of expr continue
                  tst.w     stackempty       ; is stackempty true (= 1)
                  bne.s     printresult      ; if yes print output
                  move.w    #2,exprstatus    ; found error 2; missing ")"
                  move.b    #star,(a1)+      ; identify error with "*"
printresult:
                  move.b    #null,(a1)       ; terminate output expressing
                  lea       exprout,a0       ; print it
                  jsr       putstr
                  lea       errortbl,a0      ; a0 points at prompt table
                  move.w    exprstatus,d0    ; errorstatus is 0,1,or 2
                  mulu      #2,d0            ; get word offset
;                                            ; push prompt on stack
                  move.w    0(a0,d0.w),d3
                  lea       0(a5,d3.w),a0
                  jsr       putstr
quit:             jsr       stop

teststack:        move.l    a3,-(sp)
                  lea       stack+20,a3
                  cmpa.l    a3,a2            ; test (a2) = init stack value
                  bne       return           ; stack empty is false
                  move.w    #1,stackempty    ; if yes stackempty is true
return:           movea.l   (sp)+,a3
                  rts

                  data
```

```
expr:        ds.b    80
exprout:     ds.b    80
stack:       ds.b    20
exprstatus:  dc.w     0              ; initially valid expression
stackempty   dc.w     1              ; initialize stackempty true
errortbl:    d.cw    validexpr,missleft,missright
validexpr:   dc.b    ' Valid expression ',nl,null
             even
missleft:    dc.b    ' error: Missing left parenthesis ',nl,null
             even
missright:   dc.b    ' error: Missing right parenthesis',nl,null
             even

             end
```

⟨Run of Program 11.5⟩

```
((A + B)
       *    Missing right parenthesis
(A + B))
       *    Missing left parenthesis
```

|11.4| QUEUES

A **queue** is a data structure that stores elements in a linear list and permits data access at only the two ends of the list. An element is inserted at the rear of the list and is deleted from the front of the list. Most applications of queues use the structure for an orderly storage of items until they are required for processing. Because the first element stored in a queue is the first element to be removed, the data structure has first-in, first-out (**FIFO**) ordering. The buffering of printer jobs and the orderly backup of patrons awaiting service are classic applications of queues.

Storing and removing elements are the key operations in a queue. The list is stored in an array. The concept is illustrated for a fixed-length list with four cells. The first element in the queue has index FRONT. The location for inserting the next entry in the queue has index REAR. Figure 11.1 shows the contents of the queue during a series of insert and delete operations.

Some strategy must be used to insert an element E into the queue. The index REAR is out of range; thus the queue is technically "full" even though empty cells exist. If the queue were a waiting line, customers would gladly move forward, a strategy that could be used for an algorithm. The shifting of the list is inefficient, however, because this requires that you use CPU cycles simply to relocate the list in memory. A more efficient strategy at-

FIGURE 11.1   Queue Insertions and Deletions

Insert A, B, C	A	B	C	
	Front			Rear

Delete A, B,	xxx	xxx	C	
			Front	Rear

Insert D, E	xxx	xxx	C	D
			Front	Rear ?

tempts to insert the item in the empty cells at the front of the list. The queue then become a circular list.

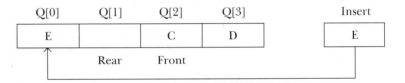

The circular queue strategy is also employed when deleting items from the list. After deleting both C and D, the index FRONT rotates to cell E, the original first cell in the list. The INSERT and DELETE algorithms implement the circular queue with a MOD operator as follows:

$$\text{FRONT} = (\text{FRONT} + 1) \text{ MOD SIZE}$$

$$\text{REAR} = (\text{REAR} + 1) \quad \text{MOD SIZE}$$

In the example, SIZE = 4. Cell E is inserted at

$$Q[(3 + 1) \text{ MOD } 4] = Q[0]$$

As with stacks, the conditions queue full and queue empty should be tested before inserting or deleting an item. When an insert to a full queue is attempted, an error flag must be available to the calling program indicating that the operation has not been performed. Similarly, a queue empty condition is tested prior to a deletion.

A queue can be defined in several ways. One technique defines a queue as a record. A COUNT field is used to test for the queue-full or queue-empty conditions. The queue-empty condition is true when COUNT = 0, and the queue-full condition is true when COUNT = SIZE. The following Pascal record is a model.

Pascal Declaration   Note that SIZE and LIMIT are defined with a CONST declaration. The value of LIMIT is SIZE − 1.

```
CONST   SIZE = 100;
        LIMIT =  99;

TYPE
QUEUE = RECORD
   QFRONT          :  0 .. LIMIT;
   QREAR           :  0 .. LIMIT;
   QCOUNT          :  0 .. SIZE;
   QSIZE           :  0 .. SIZE;
   QENTRIES        :  ARRAY[0 .. LIMIT] OF
                         ⟨QUEUETYPE⟩
END;  { QUEUE RECORD }
```

QFRONT	QREAR	QCOUNT	QSIZE	QENTRIES

Queue Operations

A package of routines—QINIT, QINSERT, QDELETE, QFULL, and QEMPTY—is implemented in MC68000 code to support queue handling. The queue stores only long words. The user passes parameters to the queue routines as long words on the stack. Because the queue holds 32-bit data, the user may pass byte, word, or long word data. Only QDELETE returns a value, and this is a long word in D0. The QINIT routine initializes to 0 the indices QFRONT, QREAR, and QCOUNT. The routine also passes the number of items in queue as a parameter that is then used to initialize the QSIZE field. It is assumed that the calling program will test QEMPTY before deleting an item and test QFULL before inserting an item. If the test is not made, the queue may be destroyed. Both QEMPTY and QFULL set the Z bit as a Boolean Flag and return the result in the CCR by using the RTR instruction.

Queue-Handling Routines
QINIT

Parameters passed
   Address of the queue record is passed on the stack.

The number of items in the queue is passed as a word on the stack.
Parameters returned
None

QINSERT

Parameters passed
Address of the queue record is passed on the stack.
The item to insert is passed on the stack as a long word.
Parameters returned
None

QDELETE

Parameters passed
Address of the queue record is passed on the stack.
Parameters returned
(D0.L) contains the item retrieved from the queue.

QEMPTY

Parameters passed
Address of the queue record is passed on the stack.
Parameters returned
The Z-bit is set to return TRUE or FALSE.

QFULL

Parameters passed
Address of the queue record is passed on the stack.
Parameters returned
The Z-bit is set to return TRUE or FALSE.

```
; offsets to the fields of the queue record
qfront:         equ     0
qrear:          equ     2
qcount:         equ     4
qsize:          equ     6
qdata:          equ     8

qaddr:          equ     8
qsizeparam:     equ     12
itemparam:      equ     12
param4:         equ     4
param6:         equ     6
param8:         equ     8

        xdef    qinit
```

```
        ; initialize the queue before use
qinit:  link      a6,#0
        move.l    a0,-(sp)
        movea.l   (qaddr,a6),a0            ; a0 points at queue
        move.w    (qsizeparam,a6),(qsize,a0)
        clr.w     (qfront,a0)              ; clear front and rear
        clr.w     (qrear,a0)
        clr.w     (qcount,a0)              ; set queue count to 0
        movea.l   (sp)+,a0
        unlk      a6
        move.l    (sp),(param6,sp)
        addq.w    #param6,sp
        rts


        xdef   qinsert

        ; circular queue insert algorith
qinsert:
        link      a6,#0
        movem.l   d0-d3/a0,-(sp)
        movea.l   (qaddr,a6),a0
        move.l    (itemparam,a6),d0        ; fetch the item to push
        move.w    (qsize,a0),d3
        move.w    (qrear,a0),d1            ; get the index of rear
        move.w    d1,d2
        lsl.w     #2,d2                    ; mult by 4 for long offset
        move.l    d0,(qdata,a0,d2.w)       ; store the item
        addq.w    #1,d1                    ; update the rear index
        ext.l     d1                       ; prepare for divu
        divu      d3,d1                    ; compute index mod qsize
        swap      d1
        move.w    d1,(qrear,a0)            ; store the new rear index
        addi.w    #1,(qcount,a0)           ; add to queue count
        movem.l   (sp)+,d0-d3/a0
        unlk      a6
        move.l    (sp),(param8,sp)
        adda.l    #param8,sp
        rts


        xdef   qdelete

        ; circular queue deletion algorithm
qdelete:
        link      a6,#0
        movem.l   d1-d3/a0,-(sp)
        movea.l   (qaddr,a6),a0
        move.w    (qsize,a0),d3
        move.w    (qfront,a0),d1           ; get index of front
        move.w    d1,d2
        lsl.w     #2,d2                    ; mult by 4 for long offset
        move.l    (qdata,a0,d2.w),d0       ; retrieve the entry
        addq.w    #1,d1
        ext.l     d1                       ; prepare for divu
        divu      d3,d1                    ; compute index mod qsize
```

```
            swap     d1
            move.w   d1,(qfront,a0)        ; store the new front index
            subi.w   #1,(qcount,a0)        ; subtract from qcount
            movem.l  (sp)+,d1-d3/a0
            unlk     a6
            move.l   (sp),(param4,sp)
            adda.l   #param4,sp
            rts


            xdef     qempty
; test for queue empty;  value returned in Z bit
qempty:     move.w   sr,-(sp)              ; save calling code's SR
            link     a6,#0
            move.l   a0,-(sp)
            movea.l  (qaddr+2,a6),a0       ; a0 points at queue
            tst.w    (qcount,a0)
            bne.s    qempty_1
            andi.w   #$fffb,(4,a6)         ; clear Z bit return TRUE
            bra.s    qempty_2
qempty_1:
            ori.w    #$0004,(4,a6)         ; set Z bit return FALSE
qempty_2:
            move.l   (sp)+,a0
            unlk     a6
            move.l   (2,sp),(param4+2,sp)
            move.w   (sp),(param4,sp)
            addq.w   #param4,sp
            rtr                            ; restore modified SR


            xdef  qfull


; test for queue empty;  value returned in Z bit
qfull:      move.w   sr,-(sp)
            link     a6,#0
            movem.l  d0/a0,-(sp)
            movea.l  (qaddr+2,a6),a0       ; a0 points at queue
            move.w   (qsize,a0),d0
            cmp.w    (qcount,a0),d0
            bne.s    qfull_1
            andi.w   #$fffb,(4,a6)         ; clear Z bit return TRUE
            bra.s    qfull_2
qfull_1:
            ori.w    #$0004,(4,a6)         ; set Z bit return FALSE
qfull_2:
            movem.l  (sp)+,d0/a0
            unlk     a6
            move.l   (2,sp),(param4+2,sp)
            move.w   (sp),(param4,sp)
            addq.w   #param4,sp
            rtr                            ; restore the modified SR


            end
```

The queue routines are used in the following test program. An artificially small three-element queue is used to test QFULL and QEMPTY conditions.

PROGRAM 11.6

Queue Test

The user inputs a queue operator (I = insert; D = delete). For an insert, a 16-bit word is entered using DECIN. The corresponding subroutine is called, and the operation is performed with the resulting contents of the queue printed. If the queue is empty or full, an error message is printed.

```
             xref      strin, strout, hexin, hexout, newline, stop
             xref      qinit, qinsert, qdelete, qempty, qfull

             entry     start

queue_size:  equ       3
front:       equ       0
rear:        equ       2
count:       equ       4
size:        equ       6
data:        equ       8

start:       move.w    #queue_size,-(sp)
             pea       queuerec          ; push addr of queue rec
             jsr       qinit             ; initialize the stack
             moveq     #9,d1             ; test routines with 10 inputs

nexttest:    jsr       getqueueop        ; input the char (i' or 'd')
             ori.b     #$20,queueop      ; uppercase to lower
             cmpi.b    #'i',queueop      ; is operator an insert
             bne.s     deleteop          ; no; then it is a delete
             jsr       hexin             ; input the item to insert
             pea       queuerec          ; test for queue full
             jsr       qfull
             bne.s     full              ; test for qfull exception
             move.l    d0,-(sp)          ; push item
             pea       queuerec          ; push the queue
             jsr       qinsert
             bra       decrct
full:        jsr       printful          ; print qfull message
             bra       decrct

deleteop:    pea       queuerec
             jsr       qempty
             bne.s     empty             ; test for qempty exception
             pea       queuerec          ; push the queue
             jsr       qdelete
             bra.s     decrct
empty:       jsr       printempty
```

```
decrct:      jsr       printqueue           ; print out items in the queue
             jsr       newline
             dbra      d1,nexttest
             jsr       stop

getqueueop:  movem.l   d0/a0,-(sp)          ; routine to input operation
             lea       queueop,a0
             move.w    #2,d0
             jsr       strin
             movem.l   (sp)+,d0/a0
             rts

printqueue:  movem.l   d0-d4/a0-a1,-(sp)
             lea       queuerec,a1
             move.w    (count,a1),d1        ; store qcount in d1
             beq.s     nolist               ; no output; list is empty
             lea       (data,a1),a0         ; store addr of queue in a0
             move.w    (front,a1),d2        ; store index of front in d2
             move.w    (size,a1),d4
             subq.w    #1,d1                ; will use dbra
ploop:       move.w    d2,d3
             lsl.w     #2,d3                ; mul by 4 for 32-bit entries
             move.l    (0,a0,d3.w),d0       ; fetch the item
             jsr       hexout
             addq.w    #1,d2                ; go to next item in the queue
             ext.l     d2                   ; using the circular queue
             divu      d4,d2                ; algorithm
             swap      d2
             dbra      d1,ploop
nolist:      movem.l   (sp)+,d0-d4/a0-a1
             rts

printful:    movem.l   d0/a0,-(sp)          ; print qfull prompt
             lea       fullmsg,a0
             moveq     #16,d0
             jsr       strout
             movem.l   (sp)+,d0/a0
             rts

printempty:  movem.l   d0/a0,-(sp)          ; print qempty prompt
             lea       emptymsg,a0
             moveq     #16,d0
             jsr       strout
             movem.l   (sp)+,d0/a0
             rts

             data
queuerec:    ds.w      1                    ; qfront field
             ds.w      1                    ; qrear field
             ds.w      1                    ; qcount field
             ds.w      1                    ; qsize field
             ds.l      queue_size           ; qlist field
fullmsg:     dc.b      'queue full:    '
emptymsg:    dc.b      'queue empty:   '
```

```
queueop:      ds.b      2                    ; buffer to hold operation
              end
```

⟨Run of Program 11.6⟩

```
i 9
0009
i 6
0009  0006
d
0006
i 2
0006  0002
i 5
0006  0002  0005
i 7
queue full:      0006  0002  0005
d
0002  0005
d
0005
d

d
queue empty:
```

|11.5| LINKED LISTS

Frequently, a sequential list of data items is stored in a logical order. If the list does not require frequent updates, an array is a simple and efficient storage structure. However, if frequent updates are required (including insertions and deletions), time-consuming data movement is required to maintain the logical order in the list.

Consider, for instance, a list of scores in ascending order in an array.

	60	65	74	82	

To insert score 68 into the list and maintain the ordering, at least two items must be moved to make room for the new entry. Deletions likewise can be time-consuming because periodic compacting of the list is required. To manage lists with frequent updates, a **linked list** is often used. An element in the linked list, called a **node**, is a record with a data field and a pointer field indicating the "next" item in the list. A pointer, called the

header, specifies the start of the list. The last item in the list is identified by a special value in the pointer field. The value can be given a generic name—Nil, for example—although the actual value is program dependent.

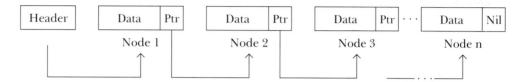

As an abstract structure, a linked list is a sequence of nodes. It can be implemented using an array of memory locations. Consider as a linked list the scores given previously. Each node occupies 6 bytes including a data field and a 32-bit address (pointer) field. After a few updates, the status of memory beginning at address 001000 could have the following contents:

	1006	65	001012	60	001000	82	FFFF FFFF	74	00100C
Header	1000	1002	1006	1008	100C	100E	1012	1014	

	Memory Address	*Data Field*	*Next Node Address*
Head	$001006	60	$001000
	$001000	65	$001012
	$001012	74	$00100C
	$00100C	82	NIL

In this example, the address $FFFFFFFF is used to represent Nil ("end of list").

The Node Allocation Function: NEW

Memory space must be allocated before a linked list can be stored. Either the user or the system can make this allocation. The user may declare a block of memory and then define an allocation procedure that is passed the number of bytes requested and returns the starting address of a block of that size. An operating system allocates memory in a similar way. When a request is made to allocate a node, the system extends memory space for the process and returns the starting address of the new block of memory.

Many high-level languages provide a data type, called a **pointer**, that contains the address for a node. The number of bytes for a node is specified from the declaration of the pointer. These same high-level languages provide a procedure to allocate memory dynamically. In Pascal, the procedure is called NEW(P).

EXAMPLE 11.4

Pascal Pointer
Declaration

```
TYPE NODEPTR =  ^NODE;
     NODE  = RECORD
        DATA  : INTEGER        { 2 bytes }
        PTR   : NODEPTR        { 4 byte address }
     END;

VAR P: NODEPTR;
```

A large block of memory, called a **heap,** is set aside to allocate nodes. Assume the system allocates the heap beginning at address $1000.

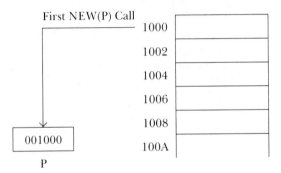

The initial call to NEW(P) returns the address $1000 in P. Pascal uses the size of the NODE type to identify the number of bytes to allocate. Subsequent calls to NEW(P) return addresses $1006, $100C, and so forth. Pascal accesses the data and pointer fields of a node with syntax P^.DATA and P^.PTR; respectively.

In this section, the Pascal function NEW is implemented in MC68000 assembly language. The subroutine, called *NEW,* returns the starting address of a node. To use the subroutine, pass on the stack the address of a pointer and the number of bytes in the node. The subroutine returns the starting address of the node, or it returns Nil (-1 = $FFFFFFFF), if insufficient space exists in the heap. Because this subroutine only simulates a system call, the NEW procedure allocates and manages the heap. On most systems, the operating system provides the heap. In our application, we set up heap space with a call to INITMEM and require that NEW update the variable HEAPPNT that points at the next free bytes of heap space.

INITMEM Function

Parameters passed
None

Parameters returned
  None

```
        xdef      initmem

initmem:
        move.l    a0,-(sp)
        lea       heap,a0
        move.l    a0,heappnt
        movea.l   (sp)+,a0
        rts
```

NEW Function

Parameters passed
  Pointer (32-bit address).
  Size of the node (32-bit long word).
Parameters returned
  An address from the heap is returned in the pointer.

```
byteaddr:  equ      8
memsize:   equ      12
param8:    equ      8

           xdef     new

new:       link     a6,#0
           movem.l  d1/a1-a3,-(sp)
           move.l   (memsize,a6),d1      ; store the node size in d1
           addq.l   #1,d1                ; round up to even number
           andi.l   #$0000fffe,d1
           movea.l  heappnt,a1           ; set both a1 and a2 to point
           movea.l  a1,a2                ; to the next open node
           adda.l   d1,a1
           lea      heaplimit,a3         ; check if space is available
           cmpa.l   a3,a1                ; on the heap
           bcc      new0                 ; if not return nil (-1)
           move.l   a1,heappnt           ; set heappnt for next call
           bra      new1
new0:      movea.l  #-1,a2
new1:      movea.l  (byteaddr,a6),a1     ; stores address of ptr in a1
           move.l   a2,(a1)              ; stores pointer in ptr
           movem.l  (sp)+,d1/a1-a3
           unlk     a6
           move.l   (sp),(param8,sp)
           addq.l   #param8,sp
           rts

           data
```

```
heappnt:    ds.l       1              ; initialize heappnt
heap:       ds.l       5000           ; heap space; system dependent
heaplimit:  ds.w       0

            end
```

EXAMPLE II.5

Updating Node
Fields

Offsets to the starting address of the nodes identify the fields of a node. For instance, a node with 16-bit data has offsets DATA = 0 and PTR = 2.

DATA	PTR

DATA EQU 0   PTR EQU 2

If the node has 20-byte data, the offsets are DATA = 0 and PTR = 20.

Call the NEW function to allocate a node with 16-bit data. Then assign the value 100 to the data field and Nil to the pointer field.

```
NIL:        EQU        -1
NODESIZE:   EQU        6
DATA:       EQU        0
PTR:        EQU        2

    MOVE.L    #NODESIZE,-(SP)    ; CALL NEW
    PEA       P
    JSR       NEW

    MOVEA.L   P,A2               ; ASSIGN NODE ADDR TO A2
    MOVE.W    #100,(DATA,A2)     ; STORE 100 IN DATA FIELD
    MOVE.W    #NIL,(PTR,A2)      ; INITIALIZE PTR TO NIL

    DATA
P:  DS.L      1                  ; HOLDS NODE ADDRESS
```

Inserting Nodes

A set of operations is used on linked lists. These operations include inserting and deleting nodes as well as updating fields within a node. Typically, a main program accesses the nodes of a linked list with a sequential scan that starts at the head and traverses the list's nodes by using the pointer field. When the program identifies a specific node, it performs an insert, delete, or update operation. We will develop insertion routines here, and present deletion algorithms in the exercises.

A new node is inserted in a linked list after a specified lead node. The INSERTNODE algorithm needs to know the address of this lead node and the address of the new node. The algorithm must distinguish between an insert of a node inside the list and an insert at the head of the list.

FIGURE 11.2 Inserting a Node and Changing the Pointers

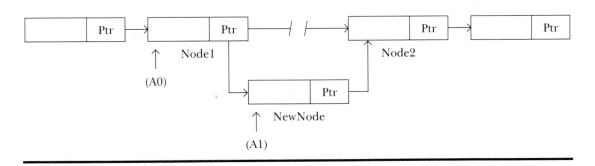

Case 1 Assume that a new node is inserted after the lead node NODE1, as shown in Figure 11.2. A call to the NEW function allocates the new node with address NEWNODE.

Initially, NODE1^.PTR points to node NODE2. Assume that the data field of NEWNODE has been initialized. The insert algorithm changes two pointers. The pointer field of NEWNODE is set to point at NODE2, and the pointer field in NODE1 is set to point at NEWNODE.

In MC68000 assembly language, two instructions implement the change in pointers. Assume that (A0) points at NODE1 and (A1) points at NEW-NODE.

```
MOVE.L   (PTR,A0),(PTR,A1)   ; NEWNODE POINTS TO NODE2
MOVE.L   A1, (PTR,A0)        ; NODE1 POINTS TO NEWNODE
```

Case 2 The insert algorithms must take into account the special cases of an empty list and an insert at the head of the list that requires an update to the header. This often requires separate logic. Figure 11.3 illustrates the redirection of pointers when inserting a node at the head of the list.

Assume that A1 points at NEWNODE and (A0) is the value of the header ([A0] is the address of the first node).

```
MOVE.L   (A0), (PTR,A1)   ; NEWNODE POINTS AT NODE 1
MOVE.L   A1,HEADER        ; RESET THE HEADER
```

The subroutine INSERTNODE is developed as a library routine. Assume that NEWNODE has been defined by a call to procedure NEW and its data field has been initialized by the calling program. The address of NEWNODE and the address of the lead node are passed as parameters on the stack. Two additional parameters are passed as 16-bit values on the

FIGURE 11.3   Insert at List Header

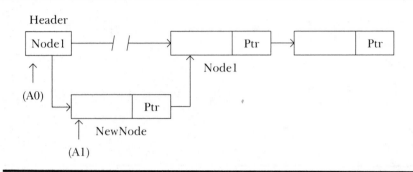

stack. The size of the DATA field gives the offset to the PTR field, and a Boolean flag AT_HEAD indicates whether the insert occurs at the head of the list. If the parameter is nonzero, AT_HEAD is TRUE; if not, AT_HEAD is FALSE.

INSERTNODE

Parameters passed
    The address of the designated lead node.
    The address of NEWNODE.
    The 16-bit size of the DATA field.
    Boolean flag AT_HEAD with value not zero (TRUE) or value zero (FALSE).
Parameters returned
    None

4 Bytes	Address of Lead Node
4 Bytes	Address of Newnode
2 Bytes	Data Size
2 Bytes	At_Head Flag

```
leadnode:     equ      8
newnode:      equ     12
data_size:    equ     16
at_headflag:  equ     18
param12:      equ     12

              xdef    insertnode
```

```
insertnode:  link      a6,#0
             movem.l   d0/d1/a0/a1,-(sp)
             movea.l   (leadnode,a6),a0
             movea.l   (newnode,a6),a1
             move.w    (data_size,a6),d0
             move.w    (at_headflag,a6),d1
             tst.w     d1
             bne.s     inserthead
             move.l    (0,a0,d0.w),(0,a1,d0.w)  ; assign ''next'' node
;                                                ; to newnode ptr
             move.l    a1,(0,a0,d0.w)           ; assign newnode to
;                                                ; first node ptr
             bra.s     cleanstack
inserthead:  move.l    (a0),(0,a1,d0.w)         ; set newnode ptr to header
             move.l    a1,(a0)                  ; reset header
cleanstack:  movem.l   (sp)+,d0/d1/a0/a1
             unlk      a6
             move.l    (sp),(param12,sp)
             adda.w    #param12,sp
             rts

             end
```

Demonstration Program

A list of 16-bit unsigned numbers is stored in array SCORE. Each number in the list is inserted into a linked list ORDERED_LIST in ascending order, using a scan algorithm. A node in the linked list contains two data fields, SCORE and COUNT, along with a pointer field. The COUNT field holds the number of occurrences of a score. After selecting a number N from the original list, the following tests define separate cases within the scan algorithm. For the sample code, assume the NEW function has been called and that P points at a new node with DATA value N and COUNT value 1.

Case 1 The header ORDERED_LIST is NIL, indicating that the linked list is empty. Insert the new node at the head of the list.

Case 2 Assuming that the list is not empty, a pair of node pointers is used, with CURR ("Current Pointer") being the address of the node being scanned and PREV being the address of the previous node in the list. Initially, CURR and PREV are set to the first node in the list. This pair of pointers are used to scan the linked list until a stop is required because CURR = Nil or CURR points at a node whose DATA value is greater than or equal to N. If the DATA value equals N, increment the COUNT field and continue. If this option does not apply, a new node must be inserted in the list. Three options apply and are treated separately.

Option 1   CURR = Nil. For instance, the elements 20 and 30 are in the linked list and $N = 40$. Insert the new node after the PREV node.

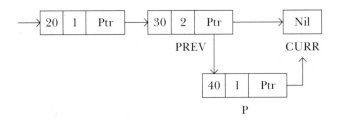

Option 2   CURR points at a node greater than N, and PREV is the header ORDERED__LIST. For instance, the elements 10 and 20 are in the linked list and $N = 5$. Insert the new node at the head of the list.

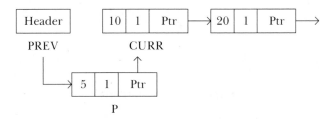

Option 3   CURR points at a node greater than N, and PREV is not the header. For instance, the elements 10 and 20 are in the linked list, and $N = 15$. Insert the new node after the PREV node.

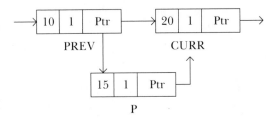

PROGRAM 11.7

Ordered Linked
List

Ten 16-bit unsigned numbers are stored in array SCORE. Each number is inserted into the linked list ORDERED__LIST using the scan algorithm. The resulting DATA and COUNT values for each node are printed.

```
        xref    decout,newline,stop
        xref    initmem, new, insertnode
        entry   start


data_offset:    equ        0                    ; the node fields
```

```
count_offset:    equ      2
ptr_offset:      equ      4

nodesize:        equ      8
nil:             equ     -1              ; value of nil pointer
false:           equ      0
true:            equ      1

start:      jsr      initmem             ; initialize the heap
            move.l   #nil,head           ; initialize head to nil
            lea      score,a2
            moveq    #9,d1               ; store 10 scores
getscore:   move.w   (a2)+,d0            ; get score
            jsr      update              ; store n in the list
            dbra     d1,getscore
            jsr      writelist           ; scan and output list
            jsr      stop

getnode:    move.l   a2,-(sp)            ; store scratch register
            move.l   #nodesize,-(sp)     ; get a new node
            pea      p
            jsr      new
            movea.l  p,a2
            move.w   d0,(data_offset,a2)  ; store n in the data field
            move.w   #1,(count_offset,a2) ; set count field to 1
            move.l   #nil,(ptr_offset,a2)
            movea.l  (sp)+,a2            ; restore scratch register
            rts

update:     cmpi.l   #nil,head           ; test for nil
            beq.s    update_5            ; insert at head of list
            movea.l  head,a1             ; a1 is ptr to current node
            movea.l  a1,a0               ; a0 is ptr to prev node
update_1:   cmp.w    (data_offset,a1),d0  ; compare score/data item
            ble.s    update_3            ; start insert
            movea.l  a1,a0               ; set prev to curr node
            movea.l  (ptr_offset,a1),a1  ; set current to next node
            cmpa.l   #nil,a1             ; test if current is nil
            beq.s    update_4            ; insert at end of list
            bra.s    update_1

update_3:   cmp.w    (data_offset,a1),d0  ; test for duplicate
            bne.s    update_4            ; no duplicate; insert node
            addq.w   #1,(count_offset,a1) ; duplicate inc count
            bra.s    update_6            ; we are ready to return

update_4:   cmpa.l   head,a1
            beq.s    update_5            ; insert at head of list
            jsr      getnode             ; get newnode p
            move.w   #false,-(sp)        ; not insert at front
            move.w   #ptr_offset,-(sp)   ; offset to ptr field
            move.l   p,-(sp)             ; newnode on stack
            move.l   a0,-(sp)            ; move prev node on stack
```

```
                    jsr       insertnode
                    bra.s     update_6
        update_5:   jsr       getnode
                    move.w    #true,-(sp)
                    move.w    #ptr_offset,-(sp)
                    move.l    p,-(sp)
                    pea       head
                    jsr       insertnode
        update_6:   rts

        writelist:  movem.l   d0/a0,-(sp)
                    movea.l   head,a0               ; set a0 to sentinel node
        write_1:    cmpa.l    #nil,a0               ; is there another node
                    beq.s     write_2               ; no! ok quit
                    move.w    (data_offset,a0),d0   ; write out the data and
                    jsr       decout                ; count fields
                    move.w    (count_offset,a0),d0
                    jsr       decout
                    jsr       newline
                    movea.l   (ptr_offset,a0),a0    ; move a0 to next node
                    bra       write_1               ; continue list scan
        write_2:    movem.l   (sp)+,d0/a0
                    rts

                    data
        score       dc.w      40,20,50,20,40,10,20,30,20,40
        head:       ds.l      1
        p:          ds.l      1
                    end
```

⟨Run of Program 11.7⟩

```
10   1
20   4
30   1
40   3
50   1
```

11.6 | BINARY TREES

The linked lists defined in the preceding section are more precisely called **linear linked lists**. The nodes have a linear ordering that permits sequential access to the list beginning at the header. Each node is followed by a single successor node (unless it is the last node). The concept of a linked list can be extended to a nonlinear structure called a **binary tree**. Its components are a set of nodes containing a data field and two pointer fields (see Figure 11.4). The name tree is derived from the layout of the nodes, which resembles an upside-down tree.

FIGURE 11.4 Binary Tree

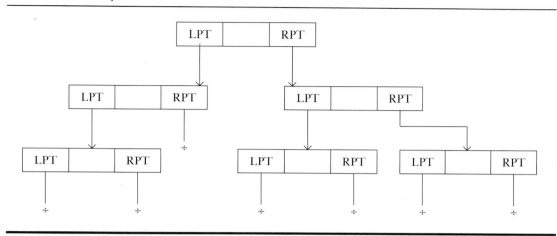

The starting node of the tree is called the **root**. The pointer fields of the node are referred to as the **left pointer** (**LPT**) and the **right pointer** (**RPT**). A binary tree is a recursive structure. Each node points to a pair of nodes, which are roots of trees, called the **left and right subtrees** of the node. Tree access routines are therefore naturally recursive.

A special kind of binary tree is called a **binary search tree**. For each node, the data values in its left subtree are less than or equal to the data value of the node. The data values in its right subtree are greater than the data value of the node. Figure 11.5 shows an example of a binary search tree.

FIGURE 11. 5 Binary Search Tree

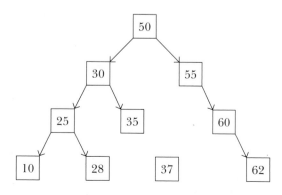

Binary Tree Scan Algorithms

A tree is a nonlinear list in the sense that there is no simple ordering that specifies a single "next" node. Hence it is necessary to define scanning orders to guarantee that all nodes are visited. Historically, three distinct scanning orders have been defined to use the recursive structure of the tree. Each scan ordering begins at the root node. Recursively, the program scans the left and right subtrees and visits each node. A "visit" is an operation that performs some analysis on the data field of the node. The ordering of the scan is determined by the occurrence of the "visit."

Preorder Scan

Recursively descend the tree, taking the following actions at each node:

1. Visit the node.

2. Descend to the root node of the left subtree.

3. Descend to the root node of the right subtree.

EXAMPLE 11.6

Assume that a "visit" means writing out the value in the data field of the node. For the binary search tree in Figure 11.5, a preorder scan results in the following list:

50   30   25   10   28   35   37   55   60   62

Inorder Scan

Recursively descend the tree, taking the following actions at each node:

1. Descend to the root node of the left subtree.

2. Visit the node.

3. Descend to the root node of the right subtree.

EXAMPLE 11.7

The inorder scan listing for the sample binary search tree is

10   25   28   30   35   37   50   55   60   62

Note: In the case of a binary search tree, the inorder scan will access elements in sorted order.

Postorder Scan

Recursively descend the tree, taking the following actions at each node:

1. Descend to the root node of the left subtree.

2. Descend to the root node of the right subtree.

3. Visit the node.

EXAMPLE 11.8

The postorder scan listing for the sample binary search tree is

    10 28 25 37 35 30 62 60 55 50

Clearly the prefixes *pre, in,* and *post* indicate when the "visit" occurs at each node. Algorithms that require scanning of the tree nodes are based on one of these recursive descent routines. They provide the equivalent of a sequential scan on an array or linked list. We will develop the MC68000 subroutine INORDER using Pascal as a model. We will first present the algorithm as a Pascal procedure and then in MC68000 code. The routine includes a call to an external "visit node" routine.

Pascal Tree Declaration

```
TYPE    TREEPTR       = ^TREENODE ;
        TREENODE      = RECORD
          LPT     :     TREEPTR;
          DATA    :     ⟨DATA TYPE⟩
          RPT     :     TREEPTR;
        END;


VAR     ROOT  :   TREEPTR;
```

Pascal Inorder Scan Procedure

```
PROCEDURE inorder (tree : treeptr);
  BEGIN
    IF tree ⟨ ⟩ nil THEN BEGIN
      inorder (tree^.lpt);
      ⟨visit the node⟩
      inorder(tree^.rpt)
      END
    END;
```

INORDER Scan Routine

Parameters passed
   The address of the root node.
Parameters returned
   None

```
lpt:        equ        0              ; left tree pointer
rpt:        equ        4              ; right tree pointer
```

```
root:        equ      8
param4:      equ      4
             xdef     inorder
             xref     visitnode

inorder:     move.l   a0,-(sp)
             tst.l    (root,sp)              ; test if pointer is nil
             bmi.s    inorder_1              ; if so quit with stack clear
             movea.l  (root,sp),a0           ; fetch "treeptr"
             move.l   (lpt,a0),-(sp)         ; go left with "treeptr^.lpt"
             jsr      inorder
             movea.l  (root,sp),a0           ; again fetch "treeptr"
             jsr      visitnode
             move.l   (rpt,a0),-(sp)         ; go right with "treeptr^.rpt"
             jsr      inorder
inorder_1:   movea.l  (sp)+,a0
             move.l   (sp),(param4,sp)
             addq.w   #param4,sp
             rts

             end
```

Demonstration Program

A complete program, using recursion, sets up a binary search tree. An INORDER scan routine writes out the elements of the tree in ascending order. Note that the parameter TREE is recursively passed by reference. Read the Pascal code carefully before tracing the corresponding MC68000 code.

PROGRAM 11.8

Binary Search Tree
Load and Scan

A list of ten words is stored in memory as an initialized array. After loading the elements into a binary search tree, an INORDER scan is used to print the list in sorted order.

Pascal Code

```
PROGRAM bintree (input, output);
TYPE
  treeptr  = ^treenode;
  treenode = record
       lpt : treeptr;
       data : integer;
       rpt : treeptr
    END;
VAR
     root, p : treeptr;
     n, i    : integer;

     PROCEDURE load(VAR tree : treeptr);
     BEGIN
       IF tree = nil THEN BEGIN
         new(p);
```

```
              p^.lpt := nil;
              p^.rpt := nil;
              p^.data := n;
              tree := p
            END
          ELSE IF tree^.data < n then
            load(tree^.rpt)
          ELSE
            load(tree^.lpt)
      END; { load }

  BEGIN
      root := nil;
      FOR i := 1 TO 10 DO BEGIN
        read(n);
        load(root)
      END
  END.
```

The Pascal program is now implemented in MC68000 assembly language. As with nodes in a linked list, offsets to the pointer address specify the fields of the tree node.

MC68000 Code

A tree node contains three fields. The items are loaded from the array into a binary search tree using the tree load algorithm.

```
lpt:    equ     0              ; left tree pointer
rpt:    equ     4              ; right tree pointer
data:   equ     8              ; offset to node data field
nil:    equ     -1             ; definition of nil pointer

        xref    decout,newline,stop
        xref    initmem, inorder, new

        xdef    visitnode
        entry   start

start:  jsr     initmem
        lea     list,a0        ; set a0 to start of data list
        moveq   #9,d1          ; input 10 elements using dbra
getn:   move.w  (a0)+,d0
        pea     head           ; call by reference parameter
        jsr     load           ; call the load recursively
        dbra    d1,getn

        move.l  head,-(sp)     ; call by value parameter pass
        jsr     inorder
```

```
                    jsr     newline
                    jsr     stop
        ;                                    ; fetch the address of "treeptr"
        load:
                    movea.l (4,sp),a1
                    tst.l   (a1)             ; test the pointer "treeptr"
                    bpl.s   load0            ; branch if pointer is not nil
                    move.l  #10,-(sp)
                    pea     p                ; get a new 10 byte node
                    jsr     new
                    movea.l p,a2             ; load the contents of the node
                    move.l  #nil,(lpt,a2)    ; left pointer field is nil
                    move.w  d0,(data,a2)     ; data field contains new entry
                    move.l  #nil,(rpt,a2)    ; right pointer field is nil
                    movea.l (4,sp),a1
                    move.l  p,(a1)           ; store the new node pointer
                    bra.s   load2
        load0:      movea.l (a1),a1          ; a1 points at "treeptr" node
                    cmp.w   (data,a1),d0
                    beq.s   load2            ; the item is already there
                    blt.s   load1            ; scan the left subtree
                    pea     (rpt,a1)         ; addr of "treeptr^.rpt"
                    jsr     load             ; make recursive call
                    bra.s   load2
        load1:      pea     (lpt,a1)         ; addr of "treeptr^.lpt"
                    jsr     load             ; make recursive call
        load2:      move.l  (sp)+,(sp)
                    rts

        visitnode:  move.l  d0,-(sp)
                    move.w  (data,a0),d0
                    jsr     decout
                    move.l  (sp)+,d0
                    rts

                    data
        head:       dc.l    -1
        p:          ds.l    1
        list:       dc.w    45,20,38,55,20,50,47,9,40,30
                    end
```

⟨Run of Program 11.8⟩

9   20   30   38   40   45   47   50   55

11.7 HASHING

In an array, an element is associated with its index, which is used to provide direct access to the element. In some applications, a data field of the array element may be used to identify the index of the element. Such a field, called a **key**, defines a mapping from the element to its index. For example, student records at a university contain a Social Security Number field. This key can be used to access the student record. One simple, though impractical, method would be to declare an array of 1 billion records with the Social Security Number serving as the index.

The problem is handled more realistically by using a function that maps the key into a smaller range of indices and then uses the mapped key to access the item. The function, referred to as a **hash function**, is the basic component of an important data structure concept called **hashing**. It is used in commercial applications and systems programming to facilitate list access and update procedures. Most assembler and compiler symbol tables use hashing to load and access labels.

The concept of a hash function is first defined and then applied to several hashing techniques. Algorithms to implement linear probe open addressing and chaining with linked lists are presented and then coded in MC68000 assembly language. A demonstration program compares average search time for each of these algorithms.

Definition   Assume that ITEM specifies a record and TABLE is an array of elements of type ITEM with INDEXRANGE = 0 . . N.

```
CONST N = 9;
TYPE INDEXRANGE = 0 . . N;
   ITEM = RECORD
      KEY        :   KEYTYPE;
      DATA       :   DATATYPE
   END;
VAR  TABLE  :   ARRAY[INDEXRANGE] OF ITEM;
```

A hash function is a mapping of KEYTYPE to INDEXRANGE.

$$\text{HASH(KEY)} \rightarrow \text{INDEXRANGE}$$

EXAMPLE 11.9   Assume that KEY is a positive integer with HASH(KEY) assigned the value of the ones digit of the KEY. The INDEXRANGE is 0 . . 9.

For the following KEY values, the result of the HASH function is given:

KEY	HASH(KEY)
31	HASH(31) = 1
49	HASH(49) = 9
71	HASH(71) = 1

FIGURE 11.6   Mapping of Ten-Element Array TABLE

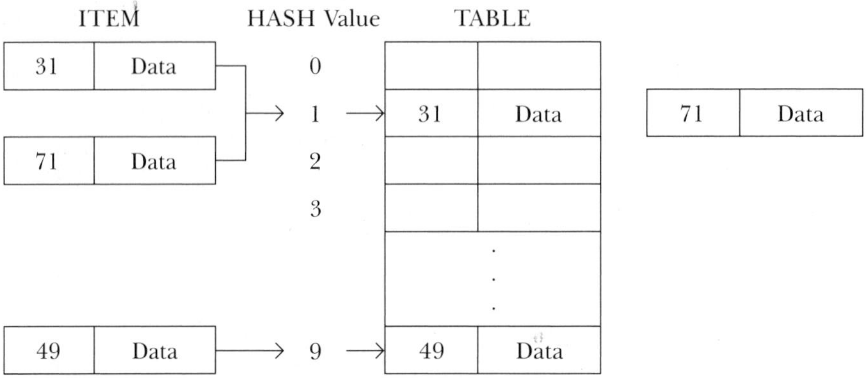

Unfortunately, a hash function is frequently "many to one," resulting in collisions. In Example 11.9, the "hashing to the ones digit" causes collisions for all numbers that have the same first digit. Given that TABLE is a ten-element array in Figure 11.6, the hashed KEY does not provide a unique index to store the ITEM.

When collisions occur, two or more records map to the same location in TABLE. Some resolution scheme must be adopted to permit the ITEM to occupy another location in the TABLE or be placed in an overflow area linked to the TABLE. We will discuss these schemes after an introduction to several types of hashing functions.

Hashing Functions

A hash function should be designed to limit collisions, and its evaluation should be efficient. Because the range of the hash function is an INDEXRANGE (0 .. N), it will typically use some MOD operation. Other operations, including multiplication and addition, may be used in the hash function. Less frequently, a random number generator is used.

EXAMPLE 11.10   The hash function is defined and then evaluated using MC68000 code.

(a) The KEY is a five-digit number. The hash function masks all but the low-order two digits. For instance, if the number is 56389, then HASH(56389) = 89.

$$\text{HASH(KEY)} = \text{KEY} \quad \text{MOD} \quad 100$$

Assume that the KEY is stored in D0. The MC68000 code is

```
        DIVU   #100,D0
        SWAP   D0
```

(b) The KEY is a label name. The hash function takes the sum of the first character and last character MOD 101.

In Pascal, the hash function is defined as follows:

$$HASH(LABEL) := (ORD(LABEL[1]) + ORD (LABEL [LENGTH(LABEL)]) \ MOD \ 101$$

Assume that the label is entered using STRIN. A0 points at the label name, and D0 contains the length. The following MC68000 code implements the HASH function with the result returned in D0.

```
HASH:   MOVE.L   D1,–(SP)
        SUBQ.W   #1,D0            ; DELETE LINEFEED
        CLR.L    D1
        MOVE.B   (A0),D1          ; MOVE CHAR TO D1
        ADD.B    (0,A0,D0.W),D1   ; ADD LAST CHADIVU
        DIVU     #101,D1          ; MOD 101
        SWAP     D1               ; PUT RESULT IN (D1.W)
        MOVE.W   D1,D0
        MOVE.L   (SP)+,D1
        RTS
```

Overflow-Handling Strategies

Collisions caused by hashing create overflow. A simple strategy stores the first ITEM in the list at the hashed index. For storing any subsequent collision, the item is placed in the TABLE at the next available location. The scheme is referred to as **open probe addressing**. The hash function targets an index in TABLE. If a record is already present, continue in a circular fashion to look for the next available location. The iterative routine implements "probing" to find the first open record, hence the name for the algorithm. If the size of TABLE is large relative to the number of items, the process works well because collision is unlikely and ample open records are provided. As the ratio of table size to records approaches 1, the inefficiencies of the process are apparent.

EXAMPLE 11.11   Store a list of seven integers in a table using the following hash function:

$$HASH(KEY) = KEY \ MOD \ 10$$

Annotate table entries with the number of probes required to place the elements in the table.

List: 54 77 94 89 14 45 76

76(5)				54(1)	94(2)	14(3)	77(1)	45(4)	89(1)
0	1	2	3	4	5	6	7	8	9

Even with this strategy, the number of probes is large because of the number of collisions and the resulting searches for open locations.

The list has three collisions (54, 94, and 14) that force the items to go on an extended search to find a home. For instance, the array element 76 should be located in TABLE index 6. However, previous entries and collisions have filled all indices in the range 6–9. Five probes are required to find the first open location at index 0.

The total number of probes to store all the items in the list is 17, or an average of 2.4 probes per item. This is also the average number of probes required to search for an item in the table.

A simple algorithm implements open probe addressing. Initially, set all table locations to be "vacant." After computing the hash function, try to place the data item in the table at the hashed index. If the slot is not vacant, increment the index until an open location is found. Be sure to MOD the index by the TABLESIZE to form a circular list.

The obvious problem with this strategy is the overflow from one location to the next. A more efficient algorithm treats TABLE as an array of pointers to linked lists. The entries in each linked list are the items that hash to the given index in the table. A colliding element is simply placed as another node in the list, usually at the front or rear of the list. This collision resolution strategy is referred to as **chaining with linked lists**.

EXAMPLE 11.12

List: 54   77   94   89   14   45   76
Function: HASH(KEY) = KEY MOD 10
Storage: TABLE is an array of heads of linked lists.

Initialize each pointer in the hash TABLE to NIL. In order to compute the average number of probes required to search for an item, place an element of the array at the rear of its list. In Figure 11.7, each data value is annotated by the number of probes to store it in the table. The total number of probes to store the list is 10, or an average of 1.4 probes per item.

The algorithms of the examples are implemented in a complete MC68000 program that uses both open probe addressing and chaining with linked lists. The number of probes required to store the elements in the list are computed for each collision resolution strategy.

FIGURE 11.7   Probes in HASH TABLES

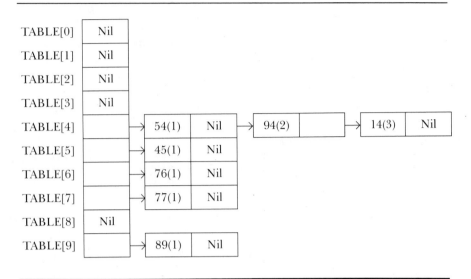

PROGRAM 11.9

Evaluating Collision
Resolution
Strategies

A list of 500 random numbers is stored in a 1000-element TABLE. The
same list of numbers is also stored using a TABLE of 1000 pointers to
linked lists. The hash function is

$$\text{HASH (KEY)} = \text{KEY MOD 1000}$$

```
              xref       strout, decout, newline, seed, rand, stop
              xref       initmem, new, insertnode
              entry      start

data_offset:   equ       0
ptr_offset:    equ       2
hashval:       equ       1000 hash function
nil:           equ       -1
loadAtHead:    equ       1
noloadAtHead:  equ       0

start:        jsr        initmem
              move.w     #499,d2            ; fetch 500 numbers
              lea        hashtable,a0       ; a0 points at the hash table
              jsr        inittable          ; initialize table entries
              lea        headlist,a1        ; a1 points at the heads
              jsr        initheads          ; each head to nil
              move.w     #1,d0
              jsr        seed
getitem:      jsr        rand               ; get 16 bit random number
              andi.l     #$7fff,d0
```

```
                    jsr        hash                ; get number mod 1000 in d1
                    jsr        loadhashtable
                    jsr        loadchainlist
                    dbra       d2,getitem
                    jsr        outputprobes        ; print number of table and
;                                                  ; number of chaining probes
                    jsr        stop


inittable:
                    movem.l    d2/a0,-(sp)
                    move.w     #999,d2             ; 1000 entry table
inittable0:
                    move.w     #-1,(a0)+           ; set table values -1
                    dbra       d2,inittable0
                    movem.l    (sp)+,d2/a0
                    rts


initheads:
                    moveml.    d2/a1,-(sp)
                    move.w     #999,d2             ; 1000 heads
inithead0:
                    move.l     #-1,(a1)+           ; set array of heads to nil
                    dbra       d2,inithead0
                    movem.l    (sp)+,d2/a1
                    rts

hash:               move.l     d0,d1               ; copy entry to d1
                    divu       #hashval,d1         ; compute d1/1000
                    swap       d1                  ; return d1 mod 1000
                    andi.l     #$7fff,d1
                    rts


loadhashtable:
                    movem.l    d1-d2,-(sp)
loadhash0:
                    addq.w     #1,tableprobe       ; increment table probe count
                    move.w     d1,d2
                    lsl.w      #1,d2               ; double d2 for a byte offset
                    tst.w      (0,a0,d2.w)         ; is table entry empty
                    bmi.s      loadhash1           ; if not store value
                    addq.w     #1,d1               ; go to next index
                    divu       #hashval,d1         ; use a circular table
                    swap       d1
                    andi.l     #$7fff,d1
                    bra        loadhash0           ; return; probe next location
loadhash1:
                    move.w     d0,(0,a0,d2.w)      ; store the entry
                    movem.l    (sp)+,d1-d2
                    rts


loadchainlist:
                    movem.l    d1/a0-a2,-(sp)
                    addq.w     #1,chainprobe       ; increment chain probe count
```

```
                    move.l    #6,-(sp)                    ; want 6 byte node
                    pea       p                           ; set parameters for new
                    jsr       new
                    movea.l   p,a1                        ; a1 points at newnode
                    move.w    d0,(0,a1)                   ; store d0 in p^.data
                    move.l    #nil,(ptr_offset,a1)        ; set p^.ptr to nil
                    lea       headlist,a2                 ; a1 points at the heads
                    lsl.w     #2,d1                       ; set d1 * 4 as offset
                    lea       (0,a2,d1.w),a0              ; load address of head
                    cmpi.l    #$FFFFFFFF,(a0)             ; test if head is nil
                    beq.s     loadchain_3
                    movea.l   (a0),a0                     ; set a0 to head of list
loadchain_1:                                              ; scan end of list
                    addq.w    #1,chainprobe
                    tst.l     (ptr_offset,a0)             ; test for nil pointer
                    bmi.s     loadchain_2                 ; if node nil, end found
                    movea.l   (ptr_offset,a0),a0          ; get next node
                    bra       loadchain_1
loadchain_2:
                    move.w    #noloadAtHead,-(sp)
                    move.w    #2,-(sp)
                    move.l    p,-(sp)
                    move.l    a0,-(sp)
                    jsr       insertnode
                    bra.s     loadchain_4
loadchain_3:
                    move.w    #loadAtHead,-(sp)
                    move.w    #2,-(sp)
                    move.l    p,-(sp)
                    move.l    a0,-(sp)
                    jsr       insertnode
loadchain_4:
                    movem.l   (sp)+,d1/a0-a2
                    rts


outputprobes:
                    lea       tablemsg,a0                 ; set message on table probes
                    move.w    #24,d0
                    jsr       strout
                    move.w    tableprobe,d0               ; output the number
                    jsr       decout                      ; of table probes
                    jsr       newline
                    lea       chainmsg,a0                 ; set message on chain probes
                    move.w    #24,d0
                    jsr       strout
                    move.w    chainprobe,d0               ; output the number
                    jsr       decout                      ; of chain probes
                    jsr       newline
                    rts

                    data
hashtable:
                    ds.w      1000                        ; table has 1000 locations
 headlist:
                    ds.l      1000                        ; 1000 heads
```

```
p:
        ds.1        1                    ; pointer to a node
tableprobe:
        dc.w        0                    ; set probe counts to 0
chainprobe:
        dc.w        0
tablemsg:
        dc.b        'number of table probes: '
chainmsg:
        dc.b        'number of chain probes: '
        even
        end
```

⟨Run of Program 11.9⟩

number of table probes: 744
number of chain probes: 616

EXERCISES

1. Assume that the universal set is the months of the year. The assembly language representation is given in D0.

   (a) Give the assembly language presentation in D0 for each of the following sets:

      i. {Jan, Feb, Mar, Oct, Nov, Dec}
      ii. {Jan, Jun, Jul}
      iii. The set of months containing only 30 days
      iv. The months of summer vacation

   (b) Write out the set for each of the following data register values:

      i. $00000FFF   ii. $00000111   iii. $0000003F
      iv. $00000070   v. $00000C00

   (c) Describe the action for each of the following:

      i. BSET   #7,D0
      ii. OR.L   #$7F,D0
      iii. BTST   #11,D0
      iv. NOT   D0
          ANDI.L   #$FFF,D0
      v. AND.L   #$3F,D0
          CMPI.L   #$3F,D0

2. Assume MAT is an m × n matrix with row indices in the range 0 to $(m - 1)$ and column indices in the range 0 to $(n - 1)$. Generate an access function that computes the offset of MAT(row,col) assuming that the elements are stored in column-major format.

3. Write a subroutine that forms the maximum norm of an $N \times N$ matrix A, defined as follows:

$$A = \max\{|A[i, j]|, 1 \leq i, j \leq N\}$$

where $|A[i, j]|$ is the absolute value of $A[i, j]$. Thus the maximum norm of a matrix A is the maximum of the absolute values of its entries.

4. The trace of an $N \times N$ matrix is defined as the sum of the diagonal elements of A.

$$\text{Trace } (A) = A[1, 1] + A[2, 2] + \cdots + A[N, N]$$

Write a subroutine that computes the trace.

5. Assume that (D2.L) = $00000001. Trace the following code segment:

```
MOVEQ     #0,D0
CMPI.L    #1,D2
SEQ       D0
NEG.B     D0
MOVEQ     #0,D1
CMPI.L    #2,D2
SEQ       D1
```

(a) What is the value of D0 after executing the instruction "SEQ D0"?
(b) What is the value of D1 after executing the instruction "SEQ D1"?

6. The procedure NEW allocates N bytes of memory from a heap and returns the starting address of the memory block. N is a constant for all allocations. Assuming the heap is declared, write a subroutine to implement a procedure FREE. The code should take the address of a deallocated node and place it on a stack of pointers. Then it should modify NEW so that it first searches the availability stack for a free node before seeking additional memory from the heap.

7. Linked lists can be implemented using an availability stack of free nodes. The following routines assume that a node has a 32-bit data field and a 32-bit pointer field. The routine INIT initializes the availability stack of nodes. After tracing the code, you will be asked to indicate the action of several instructions.

```
              XDEF        INIT

INIT:         MOVEM.L     D0/A0,-(SP)
              LEA         AVAILSTACK,A0
              MOVEQ       #99,D0
INIT1:        LEA         (8,A0),A0
              MOVE.L      A0,(-4,A0)
              DBRA        D0,INIT1
              MOVE.L      #0,(4,A0)
              MOVEM.L     (SP)+,D0/A0
              RTS

              DATA

AVAIL:        DC.L        AVAILSTACK
AVAILSTACK:   DS.L        200

              END
```

(a) After executing the LEA instruction at INIT1, describe the resulting value in A0.

(b) What is the value of the pointer field of the last node in the availability stack?

8. The following GETNODE routine fetches the address of a node from the availability stack and returns it in A0.

```
              XDEF       GETNODE
GETNODE:      MOVEA.L    AVAIL,A0
              TST.L      A0
              BEQ.S      GET1
              MOVE.L     (4,A0),AVAIL
GET1:         RTS
```

(a) What address is returned if the availability stack is empty?

(b) Describe the action of the instruction "MOVE.L (4,A0),AVAIL".

9. The routine PUTNODE takes a free node from a list and returns it to the availability stack. The address of the node is in A0.

```
              XDEF       PUTNODE
PUTNODE:      MOVE.L     AVAIL,_____
              _____  ; UPDATE AVAIL
              RTS
```

(a) Which of the following operands can complete the MOVE statement?
   i. (A0)   ii. AVAIL + 4   iii. (4,A0)   iv. A0

(b) Which statement could be used to update the contents of AVAIL?

10. Write subroutines to implement the PREORDER and the POSTORDER scan of a binary tree.

11. Assume that the list $20,$10,$70,$50,$30,$40 is stored in a binary search tree. The resulting tree is scanned using INORDER.

(a) Assume that the following routine implements "VISITNODE".

```
LPT:          EQU        0
RPT:          EQU        4
DATA:         EQU        8
NIL:          EQU        -1

              XDEF       VISITNODE
VISITNODE:    ADD.W      (DATA,A0),D0
              RTS
              END
```

What is the resulting value of D0

(b) Which list of nodes is output by the following "VISITNODE" routine.

```
              XDEF       VISITNODE
              XREF       HEXOUT
```

```
VISITNODE:
            CMPI.L      #NIL,(LPT,A0)
            BNE.S       RETURN
            CMPI.L      #NIL,(RPT,A0)
            BNE.S       RETURN
            MOVE.W      (DATA,A0),D0
            JSR         HEXOUT
RETURN      RTS
            END
```

(c) Which list of nodes is output by the following "VISITNODE" routine?

```
            XDEF        VISITNODE
            XREF        HEXOUT
VISITNODE:  CMPI.L      #NIL,(LPT,A0)
            BEQ.S       RETURN
            CMPI.L      #NIL,(RPT,A0)
            BEQ.S       RETURN
            MOVE.W      (DATA,A0),D0
            JSR         HEXOUT
RETURN      RTS
            END
```

(d) Which list of nodes is output by the following "VISITNODE" routine?

```
            XDEF        VISITNODE
            XREF        HEXOUT
VISITNODE:  MOVEM.L     D0/D1,-(SP)
            MOVE.L      (RPT,A0),D1
            CMP.L       (LPT,A0),D1
            BGE.S       RETURN
            MOVE.W      (DATA,A0),D0
            JSR         HEXOUT
RETURN      MOVEM.L     (SP)+,D0/D1
            RTS
            END
```

12. Trace the following code, which implements a hash function. Then select the hash value for each N passed to the hash function in D0.

```
HASH:       MOVE.L      D1,-(SP)
            MOVE.W      D0,D1
            ROR.W       #8,D1
            ADD.W       D1,D0
            ANDI.W      #$000F,D0
            MOVE.L      (SP)+,D1
            RTS
```

(a) For $N = \$68AB$, the hash value is?
(b) For $N = \$617A$, the hash value is?

PROGRAMMING EXERCISES

13. A small cafe has ten tables. You are going to use sets to manage the available tables for the hostess. Use a bit representation in the range 0–9 for the set of tables, and set a bit when the table is occupied.

    (a) Write a subroutine LIST_OCCUPIED that prints out the table numbers of the occupied tables. Write a second subroutine LIST_EMPTY to print out the table numbers of the empty tables.

    (b) At the start of business, some of the tables are reserved. Initialize your set with a list of reserved tables using HEXIN, and then print out the list of occupied tables and the list of empty tables.

    (c) A series of four customers arrive at the cafe. For each arrival, give the customer the list of empty tables and request that he or she select a table. After verifying that the request is valid, seat the customer.

    (d) After the four customers arrive, some of the initial group is finished eating and leave. Enter a list of departing customer using HEXIN. Print out the list of empty tables.

14. A stack can be implemented as a linked list with the TOP of the stack being the head of the linked list. Using the linked-list implementation, write a package of stack routines that include PUSH, POP, ISEMPTY, and ISFULL. Write a program to test the package.

15. A linked list can be used to implement a queue. The header points at the front of the queue and is referred to as FRONT. A second pointer, REAR, is used to access the rear of the queue. Declare a queue as an 8-byte record containing addresses for FRONT and REAR.

Front	Rear

Write code to implement the operations QINSERT and QDELETE. The delete operation should first test for a QEMPTY condition. Write a program to test the routines.

16. An array A can be accessed with tree operations. This is the principle behind the heap sort. For each index i, define the root of the left and right subtrees of A[i] as A[2 * i + 1] and A[2 * i + 2], respectively. For an array A with indices in the range 0 . . 8, the corresponding tree has the following nodes and indices:

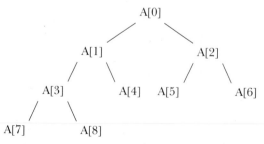

Modify the INORDER scan code to work with an array modeled as a tree. Test the scan routine on an array.

17. Use the INORDER scan to count the number of leaf nodes. A leaf node has left and right pointer fields that are both NIL. Your code should contain a subroutine COUNT_LEAF that increments a counter when a leaf node is found.

18. Write a program to enter strings using STRIN. For each string, apply the following function:

$$HASH(STR) = (STR(1) + STR(2)) \; MOD \; 11$$

The strings are to be stored in a StringPool. Using chaining with linked lists and the given HASH function, place the string in the linked list by creating a node with the address of the string in the StringPool and the length of the string.

Address in the StringPool	String Length	Ptr

Write a complete program that reads 15 strings and stores them in the StringPool. For each string, place a node in the linked list that identifies the address of the string and its length. Write out the strings in the order of their hash values.

CHAPTER 12

COMMUNICATION INTERFACE PROGRAMMING

*T*he I/O routines given in previous chapters use operating system calls to transfer data to and from a keyboard and monitor. This chapter focuses on direct data transfer using a hardware interface between the computer system and peripheral devices. In particular, this chapter introduces details of serial communication with a console and host system and parallel communication with a printer. The topics are ordered to present general concepts of data communication first and then programming principles. However, an understanding of the general concepts requires an ability to apply them to real devices. This chapter also describes in detail the MC6850 ACIA (Asynchronous Communication Interface Adapter) and the MC68230 PI/T (Parallel Interface/Timer) devices. The MC68230 includes a digital timer that can be used to time events or monitor process switching. Library-support routines are developed to initialize the devices and implement communication. A full listing of the routines is given in Appendix D. All the peripheral interface devices in this chapter are revisited in Chapter 14 as illustrations for interrupt processing.

12.1 | PERIPHERAL INTERFACES

A peripheral device (such as a monitor or disk) is connected to the CPU through the data, address, and control buses. Each type of device has its own communication protocol and external circuitry. A keyboard transmits

FIGURE 12.1   Peripheral Interface (Controller)

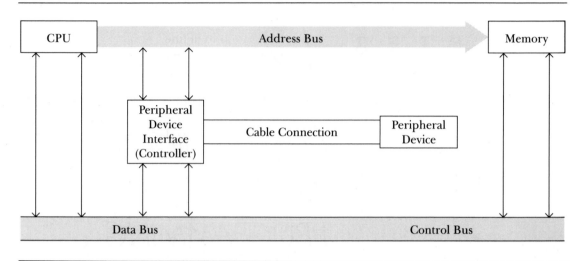

ASCII characters. A disk or tape drive transmits large blocks of binary data that may represent machine instructions or data. For the CPU and peripheral devices to interact, intermediate hardware, called a **peripheral interface** or **controller**, is used. The controller communicates with the device using a particular communication protocol (see Figure 12.1).

A peripheral interface, or simply **interface**, is a device that resolves timing and format differences between the CPU and the peripheral device. It processes commands and data and passes them to and from the device

FIGURE 12.2   Typical Interface Register Structure

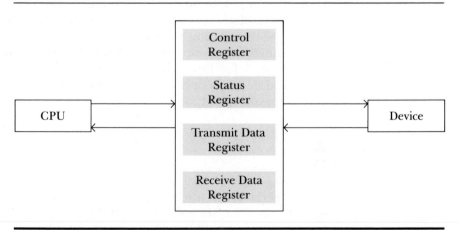

in an electronic form recognizable by the device. The interface circuitry consists of one or more chips and is located on the mother board or on a separate board in a bus extension slot. Like the CPU, the interface has a series of registers that hold information to define the communication protocol (control register), to monitor the peripheral device (status register), and to hold data for transfer (receive/transmit registers). On a write cycle, data is read from memory and stored in the transmit register. The interface is responsible for passing the data to the peripheral device. On a read cycle, data from the peripheral device is stored in the receive register and then is fetched and placed in memory by the interface. Figure 12.2 gives a diagram of a simple I/O interface with four registers.

DMA Interfaces

Interfaces use different techniques to communicate between the peripheral devices and the processor. A disk or tape drive transfers data in blocks. To keep from tying up the CPU during these data transfers, the tape or disk device is allowed to take control of the address and data bus (*bus mastery*) and perform the data transfer. The CPU can break in during the slow transfer and reestablish access to memory. The interface can place data into memory directly without CPU intervention and thus is referred to as a *direct memory access* (DMA) interface. The DMA interface transfers data independent of the CPU. The hardware of such interface devices is often sophisticated, and its study is beyond the goals of this book. We consider only interface devices that use the CPU to initiate and perform the data transfer.

I/O Interfaces

Two basic CPU architectures perform I/O data transfer: *isolated I/O* and *memory-mapped I/O*. With isolated I/O, an array of up to 256 8-bit input ports and 256 8-bit output ports may be accessed using specific instructions, typically "IN" and "OUT". The data transfer occurs on a separate I/O bus that connects the I/O device with internal CPU registers. Even though system input has 256 possible port numbers and a like number for output, a typical small PC uses 5–25 ports. On an Intel 80-series system, AX is a data register whose low-order byte is named AL. The instructions

    IN   AL, portnum
    OUT   portnum,AL

transfer a byte of data to and from AL.

For memory-mapped I/O, the interface registers are just addresses on the bus and can be accessed using the processor's memory access instructions. Both memory and peripheral devices share the same address space. The programmer identifies the address of a device and accesses its registers through their addresses. The Motorola family of processors, use this method of I/O communication. We will assume memory-mapped I/O for the development of topics in Chapters 12–15.

System Memory Map

With memory-mapped I/O, each peripheral device register has what appears to be an ordinary memory address. In most cases, these addresses are set at the high end of memory, separate from the user RAM addresses. Figure 12.3 shows a typical memory map scheme.

To access a peripheral interface and transfer data, you may use the full MC68000 instruction set with all its memory reference addressing modes. However, you must know the specific register addresses. This information is usually provided in a system documentation manual. The following section introduces the Motorola Educational Computer Board (ECB). It has an address range $000000–$01FFFF and contains a variety of peripheral devices, including two serial ports, a timer, and a printer port. The ECB represents a typical small computer system. The concepts in this chapter apply to any standalone system. You can substitute the devices and memory map from your own system.

The Educational Computer Board

The ECB is a single-board MC68000 system with a monitor called **TUTOR.** The monitor is a resident firmware package that allows the user to modify or display memory and registers, to execute programs, and to control access to the peripheral devices on the board. The ECB has two MC6850 serial interface adapters that link the processor to a console and a host system, respectively. A multifunction MC68230 interface device includes a timer and a parallel interface for a printer. The ECB system contains 32K of RAM and a 4-MHz clock. Figure 12.4 gives a diagram of the system.

The ECB memory map is partitioned into system and user RAM, monitor EPROMs, and peripheral device registers. A block of memory in the address range $OOC000–$00FFFF is not available to the user.

FIGURE 12.3 System Memory Map

Low Address	System RAM
	User Memory
	System ROM
High Address	I/O Interface Registers

FIGURE 12.4 ECB System Components

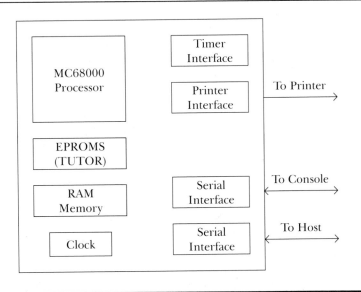

$000000–$0008FF	System Memory
$000900–$007FFF	User Memory
$008000–$00BFFF	Monitor EPROM
$00C000–$00FFFF	Not Available
$010000–$01FFFF	Peripheral Devices

Programming an Interface Device

A peripheral interface contains a series of 8-bit registers that are used for control, data, and status information. Each register has a specific memory address. The MC6850 serial interface from the ECB system has four registers that are used as an example (see Figure 12.5).

The control register and status register occupy numerically the same address value. The user is responsible for initializing the control register. When a write cycle accesses address $10040, the 8-bit data on the bus is stored in the control register. When the CPU requests data from address $10040 (read bus cycle), the status register is placed on the data bus. Put simply, the control register is a write-only register, and the status register is a read-only register. A similar distinction is made with the transmit and

FIGURE 12.5   Sample Interface Registers/Addresses

$010040	Control Register
$010040	Status Register
$010042	Receive Data Register
$010042	Transmit Data Register

receive data registers. The base address of the interface is $010040. Using relative addressing, the registers can be defined as offsets to the base.

```
CONTROL_REG:    EQU   0
STATUS_REG:     EQU   0
RECEIVE_REG:    EQU   2
TRANSMIT_REG:   EQU   2
```

The following MC68000 instructions are typically used to access or modify the contents of the registers. Assume that A0 is used as the base pointer.

```
LEA   $010040,A0
```

1. *Control register:* The control register is initialized with a write cycle.

```
MOVE.B   #⟨init value⟩, (CONTROL_REG,A0)
```

2. *Status register:* Individual bits in the status register are accessed in a read cycle. The bits represent flags monitoring the status of the device. Assume that the condition "receive register full" is maintained in bit 0. This Boolean flag is tested with the instruction

```
BTST   #0, (STATUS_REG,A0)
```

The BEQ instruction transfers program control on FALSE ("register not full"). The BNE instruction transfers program control on TRUE ("register full").

3. *Receive data register:* On a read cycle, data is fetched from the 8-bit receive register and placed in a system register or in memory.

```
MOVE.B   (RECEIVE_REG,A0),D0
```

4. *Transmit data register:* On a write cycle, the CPU stores data in the 8-bit transmit register.

```
MOVE.B   D0, (TRANSMIT_REG,A0)
```

The CPU can respond to a peripheral interface either by **polling** the device or by responding to an interrupt signal from the peripheral device.

In the case of polling, the CPU is placed in a loop waiting on a flag in the status register of the interface. When the flag becomes TRUE, the CPU leaves the loop and continues program execution. Polling can be inefficient in a multiprocessing environment because the CPU is not free to service other processes. In interrupt mode, the CPU executes instructions without any concern for the peripheral device. When the device becomes active, it signals the CPU, which then suspends execution of the current process and services the device. Interrupt-driven programming of interface devices is covered in Chapter 14.

Consider polling with the sample serial device. The subroutine GET-CHAR waits for the status register to identify the presence of a character and then retrieves it from the receive register into (D0.W). The following code within the subroutine tests for a character and reads it from the device. Assume that A0 contains the base address and the RXFULL bit (bit 0) is the flag indicating the presence of a character in the receive register.

```
RXFULL:   EQU      0

IPOLL:    BTST     #RXFULL, (STATUS_REG,A0)    ; TEST CHAR PRESENT
          BEQ.S    IPOLL                       ; IF NOT KEEP POLLING
          MOVE.B   (RECEIVE_REG,A0),D0         ; READ THE CHARACTER
```

The first two lines are the polling loop, which causes a wait until the RXFULL bit of the status register is set. This occurs when a character has arrived in the receive data register. The character is immediately read from the register by the MOVE instruction. This action causes the RXFULL bit to be cleared so that the arrival of a new character can be detected.

Entering and Running Standalone ECB Code

The ECB system has a monitor (TUTOR) that allows users to directly enter programs into memory. Program entry requires a fairly tedious word-by-word input of machine code or the line-by-line assembling of MC68000 instructions using an absolute assembler. The TUTOR assembler permits only constant addresses and no symbolic labels, hence the name **absolute assembler**. A simpler method for entering programs on an ECB system involves downloading code from a host machine into user memory, as shown in Figure 12.6.

Motorola has designed an S-record format for the purpose of converting machine code into a printable format for transmission between computer systems. Each S-record is composed of ASCII hex digits that includes a line of data and the load address for the data. Many MC68000 assemblers have an option to produce an S-record file that contains a sequence of Motorola

FIGURE 12.6 Host to ECB download

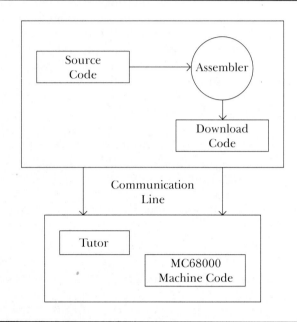

S-records. The TUTOR monitor on the ECB is capable of reading an S-record, converting ASCII hex digits back to binary, and storing the data at the specified load address.

In order for S-record generation to be effective, the host system must set a load address for the downloaded code so that it can be placed within the range of user memory ($000900–$007FFF). In most cases, the linker on the host system can be used to set the load address of the code. Many MC68000 assemblers provide a directive, called *ORG*, that can be used to set the load address for the assembled code.

The *ORG* Directive

Syntax   ORG ⟨fixed address⟩

Action   The ORG directive places a new value in the location counter during the assembly process.

Note   The directive RORG may be available. It functions like the ORG directive, except that all the code following RORG is assembled using PC-relative addressing if possible.

EXAMPLE 12.1   ORG $900   ; SET AS STARTING ADDRESS $000900

If the assembler were producing code to be downloaded from a host system to a standalone system, the resulting machine code would be located at the starting address $900 on the standalone system.

|12.2| SERIAL TRANSMISSION

An example of a serial communication port is the computer interface that connects a CRT terminal or a modem to a microprocessor. With **serial communication**, data is transmitted along a pair of lines; one carries the signal and the other returns the current and acts as ground. When both transmit and receive circuitry is active, the ground may be shared, resulting in a three-wire connect. Other wires may be involved for signal handshaking, which is a coordinated exchange of information across signal lines.

As a peripheral interface device, the serial controller has a link with the CPU through the data, address, and control buses. It has a link with the peripheral device through a multiwire cable. This section introduces many of the details of this twofold link. It begins by introducing some general properties of serial transmission.

Two types of serial transmission, synchronous and asynchronous, are used in computer systems. In synchronous transmission, a clock line, which is always active, connects the transmitting and receiving devices as a master/slave. The clock is used to synchronize the flow of data between the transmitter and receiver. Data transfer from either side is synchronized to be in rhythm with the clock pulse. The transmitter sends special synchronization characters that the receiver recognizes and then transfers a block of data (see Figure 12.7). For large blocks of data, the synchronization characters may be repeated periodically to reaffirm proper synchronization between transmitting and receiving devices. This type of communication is used for high-speed data transfer and the connection of a terminal with a mainframe host. Synchronous communication is not covered in this text.

Asynchronous transmission occurs without the use of a clock line. Synchronization is achieved by using special bits at the beginning and end of each character. Bits are transmitted in a data packet that has a specified format. A 1 is represented by a positive voltage and is called a *mark*. A 0 is

FIGURE 12.7 Synchronous Data Communication

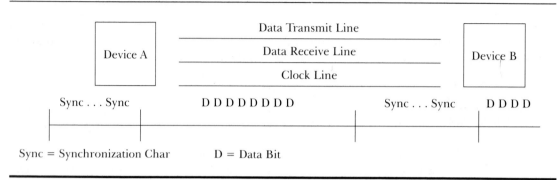

The initial line diagram shows:

Device A ——— Data Transmit Line ——— Device B
Data Receive Line
Clock Line

Sync ... Sync   D D D D D D D D   Sync ... Sync   D D D D

Sync = Synchronization Char   D = Data Bit

represented by negative voltage and is referred to as a **space**. Serial data transmission is accomplished by changing voltage levels.

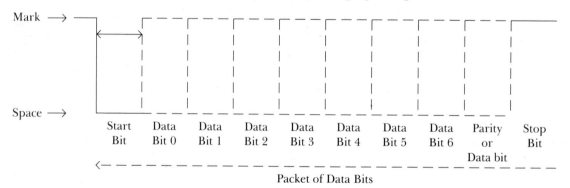

Mark →

Space →

| Start Bit | Data Bit 0 | Data Bit 1 | Data Bit 2 | Data Bit 3 | Data Bit 4 | Data Bit 5 | Data Bit 6 | Parity or Data bit | Stop Bit |

Packet of Data Bits

The initial bit (or **start bit**) indicates the beginning of transmission of a bit packet and must be a space (0). The actual data is then transmitted from the low-order bit to the high-order bit. Transmission concludes with one, one and one-half, or two **stop bits**, which are always a mark (1). The actual data is transmitted with 7 or 8 bits and an optional **parity bit**. Chapter 5 introduced the concept of a parity bit. Both the interface and the peripheral device must know what format and what speed to expect. A hardware switch setting on the peripheral device and the proper initialization of the control register in the interface determine the exact format for asynchronous serial transmission.

EXAMPLE 12.2

Sample
Transmission
Formats

(*a*) Send 7 data bits (B), 1 parity bit (P), and 1 stop bit.

-(Start)-B-B-B-B-B-B-B-P-(Stop)-

(*b*) Send 8 data bits (B), no parity bit, and 2 stop bits.

-(Start)-B-B-B-B-B-B-B-B-(Stop)-(Stop)-

(c) Send the character 'C' with 7 data bits, 1 even parity bit, and 1 stop bit.

-0-1-1-0-0-0-0-1-1-1

A clock pulse synchronizes transmission rates. The clock is called a **baud rate generator**. Bits are put on the line in rhythm with the clock pulse. The rate at which data transmission occurs is called the **signaling speed** or *baud rate*. Signaling speed refers to the number of times in each second the line condition changes. If the line can be in only two states, then the speed of the baud rate generator in ticks per second is the number of bits transmitted per second. If the line can be in one of four possible states, then 2 bits per second can be transmitted. The term *baud rate* has been used in data communications literature to mean the rate in bits per second. This is only true if the line uses two-state signaling. For instance, with two-state signaling, the clock pulses 9600 times per second and 9600 bits are sent per second. The receiving unit must be set to process the same 9600 bits per second. Assuming that the total character format contains 10 bits, 960 characters are transmitted per second.

RS232 Control Lines

A serial interface and a peripheral device are connected by a series of signal lines. Typically, the serial port (referred to in this section simply as the *Port*) is an RS232 interface, which is defined as a standard by the Electronic Industries Association (EIA) for asynchronous serial communication with I/O devices. The RS232 standard defines a 25-pin connection between the port and peripheral device. In general, only 3–9 signal lines are connected; hence a smaller 9-pin connection can be used. Table 12.1 lists the most significant signal lines and the direction of information flow.

Pin 2 Transmit Data (TD)   On the transmit line, data is transmitted serially to the device.

TABLE 12.1   RS232 Signal Lines

SIGNAL	PIN	DIRECTION
Transmit data (TD)	2	Port to Device
Receive data (RD)	3	Device to Port
Request to send (RTS)	4	Port to Device
Clear to send (CTS)	5	Device to Port
Data set ready (DSR)	6	Device to Port
Signal ground	7	
Carrier detect (DCD)	8	Device to Port
Data terminal ready (DTR)	20	Port to Device

Pin 3 Receive Data (RD)   Like the transmit line, data is passed serially to the Port receive register.

Pin 4 Request to Send (RTS)   The Port requests permission to transmit data. The peripheral device sends a response to this signal, "Clear to Send".

Pin 5 Clear to Send (CTS)   A signal sent by the peripheral device in response to an RTS signal.

Pin 6 Data Set Ready (DSR)   A signal sent by the peripheral device to the Port indicating that the device is *on-line,* or ready for communication.

Pin 7 Signal Ground   The pin sets a base reference for voltage level (level 0). Signals are measured as high (positive) or low (negative) against this ground level.

Pin 8 Carrier Detect (DCD)   A **modem**, an interface that translates analog signals to and from digital signals, uses pin 8 to indicate that a proper phone signal is present and that the modem device is configured to transmit data.

Pin 20 Data Terminal Ready (DTR)   A signal sent by the Port to the peripheral device, indicating that the Port is on-line.

Data transmission between the peripheral device and the Port requires a coordinated exchange of information across the signal lines, a process referred to as **handshaking protocol**. Assume that control signals RTS, CTS, DCD, DSR, and DTR are used. Figure 12.8 shows a sample protocol

FIGURE 12.8   Port/Modem Handshaking Protocol

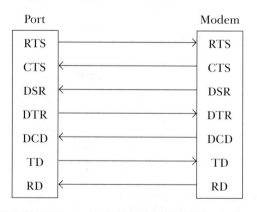

for transmission between a modem and the Port. In this example, control lines are connected so that CTS, DSR, and DCD are input lines to the Port, with RTS and DTR designated as output lines. The actual transfer of data occurs on the transmit data (TD) and receive data (RD) lines.

To transmit data from the Port to the modem, the interface issues an RTS output signal that the modem recognizes as a request to send from the Port. When ready, the modem responds with a CTS signal, granting the Port a CTS signal. With the communication protocol established, data is sent on the transmit data line. The modem receives data on the TD pin, so named because it receives data sent from the Port TD pin. For the modem to transmit data to the Port, it needs only to assert DCD, indicating that a data carrier is present, and to transmit the data. The Port must be prepared to receive data any time DCD is asserted.

Often in terminal transmission, pins on the Port and peripheral device are found to be constantly active by making the connecting pins a constant 0 or 1 level. The handshake protocol is thus eliminated, and transmission flows freely across the transmit and receive lines.

12.3 | THE MC6850 ACIA

The MC6850 ACIA (Asynchronous Communications Interface Adapter) was the first serial I/O controller for the MC6800 family of processors. The MC68000 architecture allows upward compatible use of most older MC6800 peripheral interfaces. The MC6850 is still used, and its relatively simple register structure makes it a good starting point for understanding assembly language programming of I/O devices. The MC6850 ACIA contains separate receive and transmit registers, along with 8-bit control and status registers. This section describes the action of each bit in these registers and gives values that apply to the ECB system.

Control Register

The control register, an 8-bit write-only register, determines the format of the serial transmission.

Receive Interrupt Enable	Transmit Control	Format Select	Counter Select
Bit 7	Bits 6–5	Bits 4–2	Bits 1–0

MC6850 Control Register

Counter Divide Select Field   The MC6850 receives a clock pulse from a baud rate generator. It uses all or a portion of the clock's frequency as follows:

BIT 1	BIT 0	FRACTION
0	0	1/1
0	1	1/16 ←
1	0	1/64
1	1	Master reset

The ECB system uses an MC14411 baud rate generator to permit transmission speeds in the range 110–9600 baud. The MC14411 generates clock pulses that are actually 16 times higher in frequency than the desired serial baud rates. Hence the ECB uses the fraction 1/16 (divide by 16), so that the counter divide select field is set to 0 1. The counter divide select field can provide a master reset for the ACIA. By setting the 2 bits, the status register is cleared, except for the externally set condition bits CTS and DCD. This action initializes both the receiver and the transmitter.

Format Select Field   This field determines the format used for serial transmission. Eight possible format settings specify the number of stop bits, the number of data bits, and the presence of a parity bit as follows:

BIT 4	BIT 3	BIT 2	FORMAT
0	0	0	7 bits + even parity + 2 stop bits
0	0	1	7 bits + odd parity + 2 stop bits
0	1	0	7 bits + even parity + 1 stop bit
0	1	1	7 bits + odd parity + 1 stop bit
1	0	0	8 bits + no parity + 2 stop bits
1	0	1	8 bits + no parity + 1 stop bit
1	1	0	8 bits + even parity + 1 stop bit
1	1	1	8 bits + odd parity + 1 stop bit

The ECB system normally transmits and receives with 8 data bits, no parity, and 1 stop bit. The format select field is set to 1 0 1.

Transmit Control Field   The transmit control field controls the RTS line and determines whether an interrupt is generated when the ACIA is ready to transmit a character to the peripheral device. In general, an interrupt causes the CPU to stop after executing its current instruction and transfer program control to an interrupt service routine. A transmit interrupt can be generated if the transmit register is empty.

BIT 6	BIT 5		ACTION
0	0	RTS = low	Transmit interrupt disabled
0	1	RTS = low	Transmit interrupt enabled
1	0	RTS = high	Transmit interrupt disabled
1	1	RTS = low	Transmit interrupt disabled
			Transmit a break level on output.

Chapter 14 presents interrupts. For now, assume that the RTS line is low with interrupts disabled. The transmit control field is set to 0 0.

Receive Interrupt Enable Field If the receive interrupt enable field bit is set to 1, the ACIA will interrupt the CPU when the receive data register is full. For now, assume that this bit is 0.

If interrupts are not used, the control register for each port on the ECB board should be set to $15.

Status Register

The 8-bit status register monitors data transmission. It tests the receive and transmit registers, input signals, and data transmission errors. The register is read-only.

Interrupt Request	Parity Error	Receiver Overrun	Framing Error	Clear to Send	Data Carrier Detect	Transmit Data Register Empty	Receive Data Register Full
7	6	5	4	3	2	1	0

Status Register

Receive Data Register Full When a character arrives from the terminal, the bit is set to 1. It remains set until the character is read from the ACIA data receive register. The bit then reverts to 0.

Transmit Data Register Empty If the transmit data register is empty, the transmit data register bit (bit 1) is set to 1. If a character is in the transmit register or the ACIA is in the process of transmitting a character, the bit is 0.

Data Carrier Detect This bit is used for an ACIA connected to a modem. If the modem loses the telephone signal, this bit becomes 1.

Clear to Send   The ACIA will not transmit a character unless this bit is 0. Most serial devices are capable of activating the "Clear to Send" signal on the corresponding RS232 line. The connecting cable must be wired to transmit this signal, or the ACIA must be wired so that the pin is constantly made active.

Framing Error   A **framing error** occurs when the start of a character is detected but the proper number of stop bits is not detected. This error can occur because of a synchronization error, faulty transmission, or a break condition normally caused by pressing the BREAK key on a terminal. The BREAK key causes the transmission of a continuous stream of null characters for a period of 250–500 milliseconds (ms). Generation of a framing error has various applications, including sensing the need for a speed change in multispeed modems and signaling the desire to terminate a running program. When a framing error occurs, this bit is set to 1.

Receiver Overrun   An **overrun condition** occurs when a character is not read before another character arrives. The incoming character will overwrite the existing contents of the receive data register. The overrun condition is flagged, and this bit is set to 1. Overrun occurs primarily when higher baud rates (such as 19,200 baud or higher) are being used and the CPU is busy with other tasks. If interrupt processing is used, this problem can be avoided by using a buffer to store characters not yet processed. Chapter 14 develops this technique.

Parity Error   If the ACIA is configured to test for even or odd parity and a parity error is detected, this bit becomes 1. Parity, overrun, and framing errors can be tested before reading a character from the receive data register. If an error is discovered, the I/O routine can report the error.

Interrupt Request   The ACIA can be set to interrupt the CPU when a character is received from the terminal or when the transmitter is ready to send another character. One of these interrupt requests is active when this bit is set to 1.

Receive Data Register

When a character is received from a terminal or other serial device, the ACIA places it into this 8-bit read-only register. Upon receipt of a character, bit 0 of the status register is set to 1.

Transmit Data Register

This register is loaded with the character to be transmitted. The transmit register empty bit (bit 1) of the status register is set to 1 when the register is empty and the ACIA is ready to transmit a character.

MC6850 ACIA Demonstration Programs

The ECB system has two ACIA ports. The base address for the console port is $10040, and the base address for the host port is $10041. A library of I/O routines is created in the next section. The package accesses both ACIAs and is available to users in Appendix D. We begin with simple programs that directly access the ACIA registers.

PROGRAM 12.1

Convert to Uppercase

Characters are received at the console port and then echoed to the screen in uppercase. The test program returns to the TUTOR monitor on ⟨control⟩Z, which is treated as end-of-file.

Notes

1. The four fields of the control register are initialized with the bit pattern: 0 00 101 01 = $15.

   > MOVE.B   #$15, (CONTROLREG,A0)

2. Polling is used to implement the GETCHAR and PUTCHAR routines. The PUTCHAR code is enhanced to include **newline expansion**, in which a linefeed character is appended as a second output after a carriage return. Newline expansion is standard with most operating systems.

3. For standalone programming under the control of a monitor, the user must initialize the stack. In general, an operating system startup routine sets the stack address.

4. The program was written and assembled on a UNIX system with the ASM assembler. The object code was converted to S-records and stored in the file CAP.SOUT. The TUTOR load command (LO) on the ECB system is used to download code from the UNIX host system to the standalone system. On the host system, the command "cat" copies the S-record file to the console port. The program is loaded at location 900 and begins execution with the Tutor command GO 900.

```
TermBase:      equ    $10040
controlreg:    equ    0
statusreg:     equ    0
receivereg:    equ    2
transmitreg:   equ    2
tutor:         equ    $8146

carr_return:   equ    $0d          ; carriage return
linefeed:      equ    $0a          ; linefeed
lowcase_A:     equ    $61          ; lowercase A
lowcase_Z:     equ    $7a          ; lowercase Z
ctrl_Z:        equ    $1A          ; returns to monitor
```

```
start:     lea       $8000, sp                    ; initialize stack pointer
           lea       TermBase, a0
           move.b    #$15, (controlreg, a0)       ; initialize the acia

getchar:   btst      #0, (statusreg, a0)
           beq       getchar                      ; poll for a character
           move.b    (receivereg, a0), d0
           cmpi.b    #ctrl_Z, d0                  ; test for control Z to quit
           beq.s     endit
           cmpi.b    #lowcase_A, d0               ; test for small A
           blt.s     putchar
           cmpi.b    #lowcase_Z, d0
           bgt.s     putchar
           subi.b    #3' '2, d0                   ; convert to uppercase

putchar:   btst      #1, (statusreg, a0)
           beq       putchar
           move.b    d0, (transmitreg, a0)        ; echo char received
           cmpi.b    #carr_return, d0             ; newline expansion
           bne.s     getchar                      ; if not CR, loop back
           move.b    #linefeed, d0
           bra       putchar                      ; append a LINEFEED
           bra.s     getchar                      ; go for another character

endit:     jmp       tutor                        ; reset the monitor

           end
```

⟨Run of Program 12.1⟩

```
THIS IS ALL LOWERCASE INPUT
WITH 12345 #^$% ADDED⟨ctrl Z⟩
```

Program 12.1 illustrates the typical structure of a standalone program. A beginning code segment ("START") initializes the interface device, and a final code segment ("ENDIT") exits the program and returns to the monitor or operating system. The main program uses routines to access the device. The code segments are ordinarily application independent and can be efficiently included in a library. For the MC6850, a series of subroutines such as SETUPTERM, GETCHAR, PUTCHAR, and STOP are placed in the library file "TermLib.i". This file isolates the system-dependent routines to initialize the ECB console port and implement the primitive I/O routines GETCHAR and PUTCHAR. The utility routine STOP, which returns to TUTOR, is included. The library is used as an include file in

Programs 12.2 and 12.3. In the next section, the complete I/O library from
Chapter 9 is ported to the ECB system and adapted to both the host and
console ports. This expanded library is used for programs in Chapters 13–
15. For now, the relatively simple TermLib package is developed to focus
on the process of developing a library of routines for a standalone device.

TermLib Library

```
TermBase:       equ       $10040
ctrlreg:        equ       0
statreg:        equ       0
receivereg:     equ       2
transmitreg:    equ       2
rxfull:         equ       0
txempty:        equ       1

cr:             equ       $0d                 ; carriage return
lf:             equ       $0a                 ; linefeed
tutor:          equ       $8146               ; tutor address

                xdef      setupTerm, getchar, putchar, stop

setupTerm:      move.l    a0,-(sp)
                lea       TermBase,a0          ; initialize acia
                move.b    #$15, (ctrlreg,a0)
                movea.l   (sp)+,a0
                rts

getchar:        move.l    a0,-(sp)
                lea       TermBase,a0
ipoll:          btst      #rxfull, (statreg,a0)
                beq.s     ipoll                ; polling loop
                move.b    (receivereg,a0),d0   ; fetch the character
                andi.w    #$7F,d0              ; mask off parity bits
                movea.l   (sp)+,a0
                rts

; the output char is in d0. it is
; transmitted to the port using polling

putchar:        movem.l   d0/a0,-(sp)
                jsr       putc
                cmpi.b    #cr,d0               ; newline expansion
                bne.s     finished             ; if not CR, return
                move.b    #lf,d0
                jsr       putc                 ; append a LINEFEED
finished:       movem.l   (sp)+,d0/a0
                rts

putc:           lea       TermBase,a0
opoll:          btst      #txempty, (statreg,a0)
```

```
              beq       opoll
              move.b    d0, (transmitreg, a0)
              rts

stop:         jmp       tutor
```

PROGRAM 12.2

Convert to
Uppercase (with
Subroutines)

Program 12.1 is rewritten using subroutines from the include file "TermLib.i". The labels READCHAR and WRITECHAR set off the reading and echoing of a character.

```
lowcase_A:    equ       'a'              ; lowercase A
lowcase_Z:    equ       'z'              ; lowercase Z
ctrl_Z:       equ       $1A              ; returns to monitor

start:        lea       $8000,sp         ; initialize stack pointer
              jsr       setupTerm        ; initialize the ACIA

readchar:     jsr       getchar
              cmpi.b    #ctrl_Z,d0       ; test for control Z to quit
              beq.s     endit
              cmpi.b    #lowcase_A,d0    ; test for small A
              blt.s     writechar
              cmpi.b    #lowcase_Z,d0
              bgt.s     writechar
              subi.b    #' ',d0          ; convert to uppercase
writechar:    jsr       putchar
              bra.s     readchar         ; go for another character

endit:        jsr       stop             ; return to tutor

              include   TermLib.i

              end
```

⟨Run of Program 12.2⟩

ALL IO ACCESS IS PROVIDED IN A SIMPLE TERMLIB ⟨*control*⟩ Z

PROGRAM 12.3

Echo Mode

A Boolean flag ECHOMODE is allocated in memory. When the condition is TRUE (bit 0 = 1), an input character is echoed to the screen; when it is FALSE, the user is typing invisibly. On input, the code tests the flag and then calls PUTCHAR if TRUE. The ECHOMODE flag is inverted (toggled) on input of ⟨*control*⟩E. The program terminates upon receipt of ⟨*control*⟩Z.

```
ctrl_E:       equ       $05
ctrl_Z:       equ       $1A
```

```
main:           lea       $8000,sp     ; initialize
                jsr       setupTerm
                bset      #0,echomode  ; initialize echomode on

process_char:   jsr       getchar
                cmpi.b    #ctrl_Z,d0
                beq.s     quit
                cmpi.b    #ctrl_E,d0
                bne.s     test_echo
                bchg      #0,echomode  ; reverse echomode
                bra       process_char

test_echo:      btst      #0,echomode
                beq.s     process_char
                move.w    d0,-(sp)
                jsr       putchar
                bra.s     process_char

quit:           jsr       stop

                include   TermLib.i

                data
echomode:       ds.w      1
                end
```

⟨Run of Program 12.3⟩

Now you see it ⟨*control*⟩ E now you don't ⟨*control*⟩ E!!!

A Standalone I/O Library

This section presents a complete standalone I/O library using the two ACIA ports on the ECB. The main routines were presented in Chapter 9, including one-character pushback using GETC and UNGETC. With the standalone library, the user has subroutines ECHON, ECHOFF, NLON, and NLOFF to select echo mode and newline expansion. For the ECB system, the routines INITPORT, CHARPRESENT, and STOP have been added. A list of primitive routines is given in Table 12.2. For each routine that deals with a port, data register D7 is a parameter containing the port number of the ACIA (0 = console, 1 = host). The higher-level routines are listed in Table 12.3 and are a duplicate of those given in Chapter 9. A complete listing of the system-dependent primitive routines is included under IO-PRIMITIVES in Appendix D. You can substitute this file for the primitive routines assumed in Chapter 9 and create a library that can be assembled separately and linked into application programs.

TABLE 12.2   ACIA Primitive Routines

ROUTINE	ACTION
INITPORT	Initializes the ACIA control register.
GETCHAR	Returns a character in D0 from the ACIA receive data register.
PUTCHAR	Takes the 8-bit character in (D0.B) and places it in the transmit data register.
GETC	Returns a character in D0 from either the pushback buffer or the keyboard using GETCHAR.
CHARPRESENT	If a character is found in the ACIA receive-data register, the CCR Z bit is cleared; otherwise, the Z bit is set. A BNE will branch when a character is present.
STOP	Returns the running program to the monitor.
ECHON	Causes characters to be echoed on input from the specified port (the default).
ECHOFF	Eliminates character echo on input from the specified port.
NLON	On input, replaces a carriage return with a linefeed. On output, expands a linefeed to a carriage return and a linefeed (the default).
NLOFF	Turns off newline expansion.

TABLE 12.3   ACIA IO Utilities

ROUTINE	ACTION
GETSTRING	Inputs a string that is terminated by a Null character. The string address is passed in A0.
GETSTRIN	Reads a string of up to (D0.W) characters from the keyboard into a buffer at address A0. Input is halted on a CR. The number of characters read is returned in (D0.W)
PUTSTRING	Outputs a Null-terminated string whose address is passed in A0.
PUTSTROUT	Outputs a string of (D0.W) characters. The address of the string is in A0.
PUTNEWLINE	Outputs a CR/LF.
GETHEXIN	Reads a hex number from the ACIA port and stores the result in (D0.W).
GETHEXIN_LONG	Reads a hex number from the ACIA port and stores the result in (D0.L)
PUTHEXOUT	Prints the 16-bit contents of D0 using 4 hex digits.
PUTHEXOUT_LONG	Prints the 32-bit contents of D0 using 8 hex digits.
GETDECIN	Reads a 16-bit decimal number from the ACIA port and stores the result in (D0.W).
GETDECIN_LONG	Reads a 32-bit decimal number from the ACIA port and stores the result in (D0.L).
PUTDECOUT	Prints the 16-bit contents of D0 as a decimal number.
PUTDECOUT_LONG	Prints the 32-bit contents of D0 as a decimal number.

The following code gives a listing of the routines GETCHAR, PUT-CHAR, CHARPRESENT, and relevant constant definitions. For a full listing of the package, see Appendix D. The routine SETA0 is used internally in the package and sets A0 to point to the base of the ACIA referenced by D7.

Partial Listing of I/O Primitives

```
; package for performing polled i/o at the ecb serial ports
; fundamental constants

aciasr:            equ     0          ; status register offset
aciardr:           equ     2          ; receiver reg offset
aciatdr:           equ     2          ; transmitter reg offset
rxfull:            equ     0          ; reciever full bit
txempty:           equ     1          ; transmitter empty
frerr:             equ     4          ; framing error

carr_return:       equ     $0d        ; ascii carriage return
linefeed:          equ     $0a        ; ascii linefeed
eolnchar           equ     10
param_2:           equ     2

        xdef       initPort, getchar, charpresent, putchar, monitor
        xdef       getc, ungetc
        xdef       echon, echoff, nlon, nloff

; the character in d0 is transmitted to the acia whose port
; number is in d7. the newline character <lf> is expanded into
; the newline sequence <lf>/<cr>.

putchar:
        movem.l    d0/a0-a1,-(sp)
        jsr        seta0                  ; set acia base address
opoll:
        btst       #txempty,(aciasr,a0)   ; test for tdr reg empty
        beq.s      opoll                  ; if not keep polling
        move.b     d0,(aciatdr,a0)        ; transmit character
        cmp.b      #eolnchar,d0           ; check for linefeed
        bne.s      putxit                 ; if no, restore reg
        lea        nlexpansion,a1         ; check for end-of-line
        tst.b      (0,a1,d7.w)
        beq.s      putxit                 ; if no expansion, exit
        move.b     #carr_return,d0        ; send cr
;       bra.s      opoll                  ; return to polling
putxit:                                   ; to transmit the cr char
        movem.l    (sp)+,d0/a0-a1         ; restore registers
        rts

; read a charcter from the acia port designated by (d7).
; the char is returned in d0, with any parity bit masked off
; a framing error (break) is indicated by returning the null
; character. if character echo is on, the input character is
```

```
; echoed back to the terminal and <cr> causes a <cr>/<lf> to be
; sent. a <cr> is replaced by the "newline" character <lf>

getchar:
                move.l   a0,-(sp)
                jsr      seta0              ; set acia base address
ipoll:          btst     #rxfull,(aciasr,a0) ; test for char in acia
                beq.s    ipoll              ; if not keep polling
                move.b   (aciardr,a0),d0    ; read the character
                btst     #frerr,(aciasr,a0) ; test for framing error
                beq.s    noferr
                clr.b    d0                 ; return null char
                bra.s    exitgetc           ; return
noferr:
                bclr     #7,d0              ; mask off any parity
                lea      nlexpansion,a0     ; do no convert <cr> to <lf>
;                                           ; if newline expansion is off
                tst.b    (0,a0,d7.w)
                beq.s    techo
                cmpi.b   #carr_return,d0
                bne.s    techo

                move.b   #linefeed,d0       ; <cr> -> <lf>
techo:          lea      echochars,a0       ; check echo on
                tst.b    (0,a0,d7.w)
                beq.s    exitgetc           ; bypass char echo
                jsr      putchar            ; echo back the char
exitgetc:
                andi.w   #$00FF,d0
                movea.l  (sp)+,a0           ; restore a0 and return
                rts
; the routine charpresent determines if a character is
; presnt in the acia port designated by (d7). if present, the
; z bit of the ccr register is cleared (TRUE). if not, the
; z bit is set (FALSE). use this routine if the program cannot poll
; waiting for a charcter to arrive

zbit:           equ      2                  ; z bit is bit 2 of ccr
savedsr:        equ      5                  ; low byte of sr

charpresent:
                move.w   sr,-(sp)           ; save ccr bits
                move.l   a0,-(sp)
                jsr      seta0              ; set acia base address
;                                           ; test for char present
                btst     #rxfull,(aciasr,a0)
                beq.s    setz               ; no char present
                bclr     #zbit,(savedsr,sp)
                bra.s    retc
setz:           bset     #zbit,(savedsr,sp)
retc:           movea.l  (sp)+,a0
                rtr
```

Standalone Library Test Program: Echoing Characters

Serial devices communicate in full-duplex or half-duplex mode. With **full-duplex communication**, data can be simultaneously sent and received. Characters can be transmitted from the terminal while characters are being received. When communicating over serial lines in full-duplex mode, two signal lines connect the transmitting and receiving devices. Each line is dedicated to one data transfer direction. In this communication mode, a character received from the keyboard is echoed back to the screen only if the receiving system explicitly transmits the character to the screen.

The computer system or the application program must determine whether to echo a character back to the console. In most cases, it is very important that characters be echoed so that you can see the character received by the computer. In limited cases, echo is turned off. For instance. system security turns off echo while receiving a user password.

In **half-duplex communication**, a single line of communication connects the transmitting and receiving devices. Data is transferred in one direction at a time. In this communication mode, characters are echoed back to the screen by the terminal or modem and not by the receiving system. This mode of transmission is inappropriate for such things as screen editors and is seldom used.

A sample program uses full-duplex communication on the ECB system and tests the routines in the I/O package.

PROGRAM 12.4

I/O Library Test Program: Login/ Password

This program calls many of the routines in the package.

1. PUTSTRING: A prompt "**** Welcome to the Tutor System ****" is printed.

2. GETSTRING/ECHOFF: Input a password with character echo turned off. Only the valid password "TUTOR" will permit further program execution.

3. PUTHEXOUT/CHARPRESENT: A counter is initially set to 0. The program prints out the count 1, 2, 3, and so forth until a character is input from the keyboard. When CHARPRESENT is TRUE, output halts.

4. GETCHAR/STOP/GETHEXIN: If the character is a ⟨control⟩Z, the program terminates, and control passes to the monitor. For any other character, a new base for the count is entered and program execution continues.

```
lf:      equ     $0a
ctrl_Z:  equ     $1A

         xref    getstring, putstring, echon, echoff, puthexout
```

```
            xref      charpresent, putnewline, initPort, strcompare
            xref      gethexin, getchar, stop

start:      lea       $8000,sp
            moveq     #0,d7
            jsr       initPort            ; initialize console port
            lea       welcomemsg,a0       ; send welcome message
            jsr       putstring

enterlogin:
            lea       passwdmsg,a0        ; request password
            jsr       putstring
            jsr       echoff              ; don't display password
            lea       buf,a0              ; get password
            jsr       getstring
            jsr       putnewline          ; with echoff, <cr> <lf>
;                                         ; not sent to console
            jsr       putnewline          ; double space
            pea       buf                 ; load parms for string compare
            pea       passwd
            jsr       strcompare
            tst.w     d0                  ; 0 means they are same
            bne.s     enterlogin          ; if not =, request passwd again

            moveq     #0,d0               ; start base at 0
loop:       jsr       charpresent
            beq.s     addone              ; no char present => add 1
            jsr       getchar             ; char present. check for ctrl t
            cmpi.b    #ctrl_Z,d0
            bne.s     getnumber           ; if not = ctrl_Z, get new base
            jsr       stop                ; return to monitor
getnumber:
            jsr       putnewline          ; put out two blank lines
            jsr       putnewline
            jsr       echon               ; view number as it is typed
            jsr       gethexin            ; read new base
            jsr       putnewline
            jsr       echoff              ; turn echo back off
            jsr       puthexout           ; output the base
addone:     addq.l    #1,d0
            jsr       puthexout           ; output n := n + 1
            bra.s     loop                ; keep going

            data
welcomemsg:
            dc.b      '**** Welcome to the Tutor System ****',lf,lf,0
passwdmsg:
            dc.b      'Enter the password: ',0
passwd:
            dc.b      'tutor',0
buf:
            ds.b      82
            end
```

⟨Run of Program 12.4⟩

```
**** Welcome to the Tutor System ****

Enter the password: <invisibly: tutor>

0001 0002 0003 0004 0005 0006 0007 0008 0009 000A 000B 000C 000D
000E 000F 0010 0011 0012 0013 0014 0015 0016 0017 0018 0019 001A
<a character is input here. execution pauses>

500
0500 0501 0502 0503 0504 0505 0506 0507 0508 0509 050A 050B 050C
050D 050E 050F 0510 0511 0512 0513 0514 0515 0516 0517 0518 0519
051A 051B 051C 051D 051E 051F 0520 0521 0522 0523 0524 0525 0526
0527 0528 0529 052A 052B 052C 052D 052E 052F 0530 0531 0532 0533
<enter the halt character <control>Z here>
```

12.4 TIMER FEATURE

The MC68230 PI/T is a versatile parallel interface and timer. Section 12.5 focuses on the PI/T as a printer interface. In this section, we examine the PI/T's digital timer feature. It is capable of signaling when a given amount of time has elapsed. It acts much like an oven timer, setting a bit in the status register or generating an interrupt when a timeout signal becomes active. Numerous applications exist for such a timer. It can provide an interrupt signal for process switching in a multiuser operating system. It can monitor devices under computer control. For instance, the TUTOR LOAD command causes downloading of code from a host computer. However, if data transmission does not begin within a specified time, the download request is terminated and control returns to TUTOR. The alternative would be a system locked in an infinite polling loop.

The MC68230 timer contains nine registers serving a range of functions. A control register configures the timer, and a status register contains a flag that identifies the timeout condition. Three internal 8-bit registers are preloaded with a 24-bit count (measured in ticks) corresponding to the desired time setting. On the ECB system, the timer is configured to tick 125,000 times per second. When the timer is running, the count in these internal registers is decremented once every tick (1/125,000 of a second). When the counter is in transition from 1 to 0, a bit in the status register is set to indicate zero detect, which simply means that time has expired. Depending on action specified in the control register, the device can be reloaded with the original count and can continue running through another cycle. The following subsection introduces the timer registers in greater detail, along with programming techniques to initialize and run the timer.

EXAMPLE 12.3

(a) For a 5-second timer, load the count registers with

$$5 * 125000 = 625000 \text{ ticks}$$

(b) For a time duration of 1/60 of a second, load the count registers with

$$125000/60 = 2083 \text{ ticks}$$

Timer Registers

Table 12.4 is a list of MC68230 timer registers. Except for the counter registers, all have read-write access, although the data may be unreliable when the timer is running. A write to the status register performs a reset operation.

Counter Preload Registers

The counter preload registers are a group of three 8-bit registers used for storing a time unit measured in number of ticks. The stored time unit in the preload registers is moved to the counter registers where the actual decrement operation is performed. The preload registers collectively hold a 24-bit count in the range from 1 to $(2^{24} - 1)$ ticks. Assuming that a tick occurs at the rate of 125,000 per second, the time range is

$$1/125,000 \text{ second} \leq \text{Time} \leq 134.22 \text{ seconds}$$

The registers are located at consecutive odd or consecutive even addresses. Because the registers occupy only 24 bits, the memory map for the timer provides a special null register whose address is 2 bytes below the most significant byte of the preload registers (CPRH). This permits the

TABLE 12.4 MC68230 Timer Registers

REGISTER	MNEMONIC	ACCESS
Timer control register	TCR	R/W
Timer interrupt vector register	TIVR	R/W
Counter preload register high	CPRH	R/W
Counter preload register middle	CPRM	R/W
Counter preload register low	CPRL	R/W
Counter register high	CNTRH	R
Counter register middle	CNTRM	R
Counter register low	CNTRL	R
Timer status register	TSR	R/W

counter preload registers to be loaded with the MOVEP instruction described in the next subsection. A read from the null register returns all 0's for data. A write to the null register results in a normal bus cycle, but no write occurs.

EXAMPLE 12.4

Assume that the address of the null register is A. The LSB of the 24-bit time value is stored in CPRL, and the MSB of the value in CPRH.

Null		CPRH		CPRM		CPRL
A		A + 2		A + 4		A + 6

Counter Preload Register

Initializing the Counter Preload Register

The preload registers can be initialized by three successive MOVE.B instructions, each providing 1 byte in the 24-bit tick count. This is awkward, so the MC68000 employs an instruction, MOVEP, for performing multiple byte moves to peripheral registers.

INSTRUCTION

MOVEP

Move Peripheral

Syntax   MOVEP.size   Di,(d,Aj)
MOVEP.size   (d,Aj),Di

Action   Data is transferred between a data register and alternate bytes of memory, starting at the address specified by (d,Aj) and incrementing by 2. Address register indirect with displacement is the only addressing mode allowed.

Notes

1. The size parameter is restricted to "L" or "W". If a long-word operation is specified, 4 data bytes are transferred. A word operation transfers 2 data bytes.

2. The high-order byte of the data register is transferred first, and the low-order byte is transferred last.

3. The condition codes are not affected.

4. The MOVEP instruction makes it convenient for MC68000 systems to be compatible with peripheral devices designed for MC6800-based systems.

EXAMPLE 12.5   *(a)* MOVEP.L   D0,(5,A0)   Assume that (A0) = $001000
The operation performs a long-word transfer to memory.

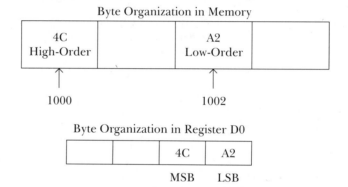

Byte Organization in Register D0

40	F0	3A	60
High-Order	Mid-Upper	Mid-Lower	Low-Order

Byte Organization in Memory

	40		F0		3A		60
	1005		1007		1009		100B

(b) MOVEP.W   (0,A0),D0   Word transfer from memory
Assume that (A0) = $001000.

Byte Organization in Memory

4C High-Order		A2 Low-Order	
↑		↑	
1000		1002	

Byte Organization in Register D0

		4C	A2
		MSB	LSB

The null register of the timer combines with the three 8-bit preload registers to permit a long-word operation with MOVEP because they are located at consecutive odd memory locations. On the ECB system, the base address of the timer is $10021. The null register and the counter preload registers are located at addresses $10025–1002B. Assuming that A0 contains the timer base address, the offset to the null register is 4. To initialize the preload registers, place the tick count in a data register Dn, and use the MOVEP instruction.

```
MOVE.L     #⟨tick count⟩,D0
MOVEP.L    D0,(4,A0)
```

EXAMPLE 12.6   Initialize the preload registers to 3 seconds. For timing, 125,000 ticks equate to 1 second. Store 375000 in data register D0, and use MOVEP. Assume Tpreload is the offset of the preload registers from the timer's base address.

```
TimerBase:    EQU        $10021
Tpreload:     EQU        4

              LEA        TimerBase,A0
                .
                .
                .

              MOVE.L     #375000,D0
              MOVEP.L    D0,(Tpreload,A0)
```

Timer Control Register

The timer has an 8-bit control register in which four fields determine the operations of the timer.

7	6	5	4	3	2	1	0
Action on Zero Detect			Counter Load	*	Clock Control		Timer Enable

Timer Control Register

Timer Enable (bit 0)   The timer enable bit turns the timer on and off. The timer is disabled when the bit is cleared; it is enabled when set. To start the timer, place a 1 in the bit; to stop the timer, place a 0 in the bit.

Clock Control (bits 1–2)   The PI/T timer permits different clock pulse options. When the field is 0 0, every 32 CPU clock cycles become 1 timer tick. The ECB system runs at 4 MHz. The timer decrements at the following:

$$4,000,000 \text{ DIV } 32 = 125,000 \text{ ticks per second}$$

Counter Load (bit 4)   After completing its countdown, the tick count is either reset from the counter preload register or it rolls over, reverting to all 1's. The reset condition is affirmed by placing a 0 in the counter load bit. A 1 causes rollover of the tick count. Assume that the field is 0.

Action on Zero Detect (bits 5–7)   The timer can select from a series of actions when the tick count reaches 0. Because the device is part of the PI/T, it may combine with registers in the parallel interface to output a digital pulse to an audio cassette. This is one of the actions available to the timer on zero detect. Interrupts are specified by this field and are introduced in Chapter 14. Table 12.5 lists the possible actions.

TABLE 12.5 Action on Zero Detect

BIT 7	BIT 6	BIT 5	TIMER RESPONSE
0	0	x	Use timer pins for the operation of I/O port C.
0	1	x	Toggle a square wave with each expiration of the timer.
1	0	0	No vectored interrupt generated on a count of 0.
1	0	1	Generate a vectored interrupt on a count of 0.
1	1	0	No autovectored interrupt generated on a count of 0.
1	1	1	Generate an autovectored interrupt on a count of 0.

This chapter does not discuss interrupts. Assume that the zero detect field is set to 1 0 0.

EXAMPLE 12.7 The timer control register on the ECB system is initialized by storing byte $80 in the register. Interrupts are not generated, and the timer is off.

1 0 0	0	0	0 0	0
Action on Zero Detect	Counter Load	Unused	Clock Control	Timer Enable

(a) The timer is started by turning on the timer enable bit. Assume that TCTRL is the offset of the control register from the timer's base address.

```
LEA       TIMERBASE,A0
          ⋮
MOVE.B  #$80,(TCTRL,A0)     ; INIT CONTROL REG


          ⋮
BSET      #0,(TCTRL,A0)      ; TURN ON THE TIMER
```

(b) During program execution, the clock may be reset by turning off the timer (clear timer enable bit), loading the preload register (if necessary), and restarting the timer.

```
BCLR      #0,(TCTRL,A0)          ; TURN OFF THE TIMER
MOVE.L  #NEW__TIME,D0)          ; SET NEW TICK COUNT
MOVEP.L D0,(TPRELOAD,A0)
BSET      #0,(TCTRL,A0)          ; TURN ON THE TIMER
```

Timer Status Register

Only bit 0 of the timer status register is used. The bit is called *ZDS,* which stands for "**Zero Detect Status**." If ZDS = 1, the count has reached 0; otherwise, the timer is still running or is not enabled. This register can, therefore, be polled to determine when the count reaches 0 in exactly the same way that the ACIA status register can be polled for the reception of a character from a keyboard. However, the ZDS bit must be manually cleared after a 1 is detected. To clear the bit, a 1 must be written to the status register. This is called a **direct clear operation**.

```
BSET    #0,(TSTATUS,A0)
```

Note: If you fail to reset the timer, the ZDS bit will remain 1. A program that repeatedly checks the timer will constantly "discover" that time has elapsed.

EXAMPLE 12.8

Most applications use a timer to switch processes or to monitor events. Each algorithm uses the ZDS bit in the status register.

(a) Process Switching: The application tests the timer to verify that a process may continue.

```
BTST    #0,(TSTATUS,A0)      ; TEST ZDS BIT
BNE.S   SWITCH_PROC          ; ON TIMEOUT, SWITCH PROCESSES
```

(b) Event Monitor: Assume that the preload register has been set and the timer started. To wait for timeout, poll the status register.

```
T_POLL:
        BTST #0,(TSTATUS,A0)      ; TEST ZDS BIT
        BEQ.ST_POLL               ; IF NO TIMEOUT, WAIT
        ⟨take action⟩
```

Once timeout occurs, the program takes some action. The timer can be reset using the direct clear.

```
BSET    #0,(TSTATUS,A0)      ; CLEAR ZDS TO RESET TIMER
```

Note: This code can be used to put a delay of "TIME_AMT" ticks into a process.

Programming the Timer on the ECB

The timer's base address (TimerBase) is $010021. The register offsets include the control register, status register, and counter preload register. Table 12.6 shows the relative addresses of the registers.

TABLE 12.6 Timer Register Offsets

TIMER REGISTER	OFFSET
Control register	0
Timer interrupt vector register	2
Null register	4
Counter preload register high	
Counter preload register middle	
Counter preload register low	
Status register	$14

PROGRAM 12.5

Countdown

This program uses the timer as a countdown clock. Starting at 9, the countdown time is printed each second. At 0, the message "Blast Off" is printed. The timer is set to 125,000 ticks (1 second) and polling the ZDS bit is used to wait for each 1-second count.

```
TimerBase:  equ     $010021             ; timer base address
Tctrl:      equ     0                   ; timer control register
Tpreload:   equ     4                   ; timer counter preload register
Tstatus:    equ     $14                 ; timer status register

lf:         equ     10
cr:         equ     13
            xref    initPort, putchar, putstring, stop

start:      movea.l #$8000,sp           ; set stack pointer

            jsr     initPort            ; initialize the acia port
            lea     TimerBase,a1
            move.l  #125000,d0          ; load timer for 1 second
            movep.l d0,(Tpreload,a1)
            move.b  #$80,(Tctrl,a1)     ; initialize timer protocol

countdown:  moveq   #9,d1               ; set the countdown to 9
            bset    #0,(Tctrl,a1)       ; turn on the timer
countloop:  btst    #0,(Tstatus,a1)     ; poll for 1 second time out
            beq.s   countloop
            move.b  d1,d0               ; action print the watch time
            add.b   #$30,d0             ; as an ascii digit
            jsr     putchar
            bset    #0,(Tstatus,a1)     ; reset the timer and go
            dbra    d1,countloop

            moveq   #13,d1              ; print 14 char msg
                                        ; ' Blast Off!',cr,lf
;
            lea     msg,a0
            jsr     putstring

            jsr     stop
```

```
            data
msg:        dc.b        ' Blast Off!',cr,lf

            end
```

⟨Run of program 12.5⟩

```
9876543210 Blast Off!
```

A Standalone Timer Library

A library of timer routines is developed for the ECB. The package isolates the details for the system-dependent calls from the user. If the timer is changed, a simple modification of the library is sufficient to port application programs. A complete list of timer routines is given in Table 12.7. The timer preload tick count is passed as a parameter on the stack to the procedure INITTIMER. Each routine calls TIMERADDR, which sets A1 to the TIMERBASE ($10021) of the ECB.

TABLE 12.7   Timer Routines

ROUTINE	ACTION
INITTIMER	The timer preload register is loaded with the input parameter "tickcount".
STARTTIMER	The timer is started by setting the timer enable bit.
RESETTIMER	The timer is reset using a direct clear of the ZDS bit.
TESTTIMEOUT	A Boolean value is set in the Z bit after testing the ZDS bit. If Z = 0 (TRUE), the timeout condition is in effect. If Z = 1 (FALSE), the timer continues to run.
RESTARTTIMER	The timer is restarted by turning it off and then on.
STOPTIMER	The timer is turned off by clearing the timer enable bit.

TimerLib

```
TimerBase:  equ         $010021         ; timer base address
Tctrl:      equ         0               ; timer control register
Tpreload:   equ         4               ; timer preload register
Tstatus:    equ         20              ; timer status register

ccr_loc:    equ         5
tickcount:  equ         8
```

```
param4:       equ      4
              xdef     initTimer

initTimer:
              link     a6,#0
              movem.l  d0/a1,-(sp)
              jsr      timerAddr
              move.l   (tickcount,a6),d0   ; fetch tick count
              movep.l  d0,(Tpreload,a1)
              move.b   #$80,(Tctrl,a1)     ; init timer protocol
              movem.l  (sp)+,d0/a1
              unlk     a6
              move.l   (sp),(param4,sp)
              addq.w   #param4,sp
              rts


              xdef     startTimer
startTimer:
              move.l   a1,-(sp)
              jsr      timerAddr
              bset     #0,(Tctrl,a1)       ; start the timer
              move.l   (sp)+,a1
              rts


              xdef     stopTimer
stopTimer:
              move.l   a1,-(sp)
              jsr      timerAddr
              bclr     #0,(Tctrl,a1)       ; stop the timer
              move.l   (sp)+,a1
              rts


              xdef     resetTimer
resetTimer:
              move.l   a1,-(sp)
              jsr      timeAddr
              bset     #0,(Tstatus,a1)     ; direct write to status reg
              move.l   (sp)+,a1
              rts


              xdef     restartTimer
restartTimer:
              move.l   a1,-(sp)
              jsr      timerAddr
              bclr     #0,(Tctrl,a1)       ; pulse signal line
              bset     #0,(Tctrl,a1)       ; with clear/set
              move.l   (sp)+,a1
              rts


              xdef     testTimeout
testTimeout:
              move.w   sr,-(sp)            ; push sr on stack
              link     a6,#0
              move.l   a1,-(sp)
```

```
                jsr       timerAddr
                btst      #0,(Tstatus,a1)    ; test status bit
                beq.s     setFalse
                bclr      #2,(ccr_loc,a6)    ; clear Z bit (TRUE)
                bra.s     cleanup
setFalse:       bset      #2,(ccr_loc,a6)    ; set Z bit (FALSE)
cleanup:        move.l    (sp)+,a1
                unlk      a6
                rtr                          ; pop both SR and PC

timerAddr:
                lea       TimerBase,a1       ; utility routine
                rts
                end
```

PROGRAM 12.6

Timer Control
Device

This program uses the timer library and the ACIA I/O library. It simulates a daily calendar. Each hour, the time is printed along with a schedule of activities. The clock time is used as an index into the activity table.

```
null:           equ       0

                xref      initPort, putdecout, putstring, putnewline, stop
                xref      initTimer, testTimeout, startTimer, resetTimer

start:          lea       $8000,sp           ; initialize the sp
                lea       schedule,a2
                moveq     #0,d7              ; initialize console port
                jsr       initPort
                move.l    #125000,-(sp)      ; initialize timer to 1 second
                jsr       initTimer
                moveq     #4,d1
                jsr       startTimer

clock:          jsr       testTimeout
                beq.s     clock              ; poll for 1 second timeout
                cmpi.w    #22,d1             ; quit after 10:00pm
                beq.s     quit
                addq.w    #1,d1              ; increment the hour count
                move.w    d1,d0
                jsr       putdecout          ; print the time in hours
                asl.w     #2,d0              ; compute index into activity
                movea.l   (0,a2,d0.w),a0 ;   push activity address on stack
                jsr       putstring
                jsr       putnewline
                jsr       resetTimer
                bra.s     clock

quit:           jsr       stop

                data
```

```
schedule:    dc.l     null,null,null,null,null,alarm,coffee,null
             dc.l     breakfast,null,null,null,lunch,null,computer,null
             dc.l     null,happyhour,null,supper,null,null,tv,null,null

alarm:       dc.b     'Wake up and shower',0
coffee:      dc.b     'Enjoy coffee and the morning paper',0
breakfast:   dc.b     'Breakfast meeting',0
lunch:       dc.b     'Brown bag lunch',0
computer:    dc.b     'Attend computer sales conference',0
happyhour:   dc.b     'Meet client for happy hour',0
supper:      dc.b     'Quiet dinner',0
tv:          dc.b     'News sports and then bed',0

             end
```

⟨Run of Program 12.6⟩

```
 5  Wake up and shower
 6  Enjoy coffee and the morning paper
 7
 8  Breakfast meeting
 9
10
11
12  Brown bag lunch
13
14  Attend computer sales conference
15
16
17  Meet client for happy hour
18
19  Quiet dinner
20
21
22  News sports and then bed
```

PROGRAM 12.7

Typing Speed

The timer is used to test your typing speed. The program uses both a timer and a character counter. The system waits for an initial input of ⟨*control*⟩Q, which then activates the timer and the fetching of characters from the keyboard. The timer is incremented each second, and characters are echoed to the screen. The speed test stops when ⟨*control*⟩S is pressed, and the results are printed in characters per minute.

Algorithm   The main loop RUNTEST must repeatedly test for both a character at the keyboard and for the timeout condition. First, test for timeout, and increment the clock if it occurs. Then test for a character. If a character is present, read it and look for Ctrl__S that terminates the test. For any

other character, increment the count, and continue the testing cycle on the
timer.

```
ctrl_Q:      equ      17
ctrl_S:      equ      19


             xref     initPort, charpresent, getchar, echoff, echon
             xref     putdecout, putstring, putnewline, stop
             xref     initTimer, startTimer, testTimeout,resetTimer

start:       moveq    #0,d7           ; initialize the terminal port
             jsr      initPort
             move.l   #125000,-(sp)   ; initialize timer for 1 second
             jsr      initTimer
             moveq    #0,d1           ; clear the time count
             moveq    #0,d2           ; clear the character count
             jsr      echoff          ; initially echo is turned off

waitforstart:
             jsr      getchar         ; get character
             cmpi.b   #ctrl_Q,d0      ; test for ctrl_Q
             bne.s    waitforstart    ; if not keep waiting
             jsr      echon
             jsr      startTimer      ; found ctrl_Q; start timing


runtest:     jsr      testTimeout     ; check for 1 second timeout
             beq.s    testchar        ; if no time out, look for char
             addq.w   #1,d1           ; timer went off; incr count
             jsr      resetTimer      ; start timer again
testchar:    jsr      charpresent     ; look for char
             beq.s    runtest         ; if not present; check timer
             jsr      getchar         ; if present, get it
             cmpi.b   #ctrl_S,d0      ; ctrl_S (quit test)?
             beq.s    printspeed      ; if yes, print char/minute
             addq.l   #1,d2           ; add 1 to char counter
             bra.s    runtest         ; keep going


; char/minute = d2/(chars) * 60/d1 (secs)
printspeed:
             mulu     #60,d2
             divu     d1,d2
             ext.l    d2
             jsr      putnewline
             lea      printmsg,a0
             jsr      putstring
             move.l   d2,d0
             jsr      putdecout
             jsr      stop
```

```
                 data
printmsg:        dc.b     'Characters per minute: ',0

                 end
```

⟨Run of Program 12.7⟩

not very fast
Characters per minute: 240

|12.5| COMMUNICATING WITH A PARALLEL PRINTER

Section 12.4 examined the MC68230 PI/T as a timer. This section focuses on its use as a **parallel interface adapter (PIA)** for a printer. This section describes only the registers and functions in the PI/T that support communication with a parallel printer and outlines the key principles for programming a printer. The handshaking and transfer of data are the most important parts of the section.

The PI/T has three 8-bit data ports (Port A, Port B, Port C) that provide 24 I/O lines and 4 programmable handshake lines (H1–H4) to implement I/O handshaking protocols. Only Port A and Port B are used with a printer. Port C is used for I/O to a cassette tape. While each of the ports permits bidirectional communication, the I/O port pins cannot simultaneously function as both input and output pins. Each port must be preconfigured as

TABLE I2.8   PI/T Registers

REGISTER	MNEMONIC	ACCESS	ECB ADDRESS
Port general control register	PGCR	R/W	$10001
Port service request register	PSRR	R/W	$10003
Port A data direction register	PADDR	R/W	$10005
Port B data direction register	PBDDR	R/W	$10007
Port C data direction register	PCDDR	R/W	$10009
Port interrupt vector register	PIVR	R/W	$1000B
Port A control register	PACR	R/W	$1000D
Port B control register	PBCR	R/W	$1000F
Port A data register	PADR	R/W	$10011
Port B data register	PBDR	R/W	$10013
Port C data register	PCDR	R/W	$10019
Port status register	PSR	R/W	$1001B

either an input or an output port. The PI/T has three data direction registers corresponding to each of its data ports. Three control registers allow the user to configure the general functions of the PI/T and specific actions of Port A and Port B. This device also uses a status register, a service request register, and an interrupt vector register. Table 12.8 shows a complete listing of the PI/T registers. The timer registers were covered previously and are not repeated.

Printer Port Interface

The Centronix interface has become a standard for communication with a parallel printer. This interface includes eight data lines and several control lines. On the ECB, the Centronix lines are connected to Port A, Port B, and the handshake lines of the PI/T. The Port A data lines (D0–D7) are buffered to provide 8-bit parallel data transmission to the printer. The Port B data lines and the handshake lines H1–H4 are also connected to the Centronix interface to monitor data transmission. Figure 12.9 shows the specific communication lines and their functions.

FIGURE 12.9 Centronix Interface-PI/T Lines

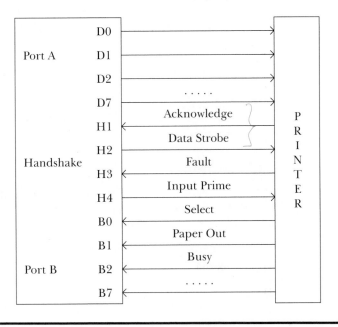

The following list examines each of the interface lines:

D0–D7:	The 8-bit character data is transmitted in parallel to the printer along the eight data lines.
ACKNOWLEDGE:	After accepting a character, the printer activates this line.
DATA STROBE:	A PIA does not use a clock line. The program using the PIA must cause the PIA to emit a state transition (pulse). This pulse notifies the printer that a character is coming and causes the PIA to send the character. This pulse is sent down the data strobe line, and the process is called strobing the printer.
FAULT:	When an error occurs, the printer will assert the fault line, if it is connected. The PIA can be initialized to interrupt the CPU in this case.
INPUT PRIME:	Some parallel printers require initialization before use. This line is provided so that an initialization pulse can be sent to the printer.
SELECT:	This indicates whether the printer is on-line or off-line. If a character has been sent and the printer is not on-line, the character must be sent again when the printer comes back on-line.
PAPER OUT:	This indicates whether the paper in the printer has run out.
BUSY:	This indicates whether the printer is busy. If it is busy, the printer will not accept data.

PI/T Registers

This subsection introduces programming details for initializing and using the PI/T as a printer interface.

Port General Control Register

Port Mode Control	H3/H4 Enable	H1/H2 Enable	H4–H1 Sense
7–6	5	4	3–0

This register contains a 2-bit mode control field that specifies one of four operational modes involving Port A and Port B. For modes 0 and 2, the ports are used separately for 8-bit unidirectional and bidirectional data transfer. In the other modes, the ports are combined to allow 16-bit unidirectional or bidirectional data transfer. For printer use, this field is initially set to 0 0.

Bit 7	Bit 6	Mode
0	0	Mode 0, unidirectional 8-bit
0	1	Mode 1, unidirectional 16-bit
1	0	Mode 2, bidirectional 8-bit
1	1	Mode 3, bidirectional 16-bit

Bits 5–4 enable and disable the handshake lines. Initially, the lines are disabled with a value of 0 0. After initializing the other device registers, the handshake lines are enabled.

The sense of the H1–H4 lines indicates the active logic level. By clearing bits 3–0, low voltage is the active state.

Port Service Request Register

The port service request register enables the user to specify whether activity on the ACKNOWLEDGE and FAULT lines will generate interrupts or DMA requests. Chapter 14 details the bits of this register. Because we are not using interrupts, the register is set to $00.

Port A Data Direction Register

Data is transmitted to the printer from Port A. Each PI/T port is capable of transmitting or receiving data on each of its eight pins. The direction of transmission for each bit must be explicitly set in the ports direction register. A bit set to 1 specifies output; a bit set to 0 specifies input. Because Port A is used to transmit data to the printer, each bit in this register must be 1. Thus $FF is written to the register.

Port B Data Direction Register

The status signals from the printer are sent to Port B. Each bit is an input bit, and $00 is written to the register.

Port A Control Register

Setting this register to $60 disables interrupts and selects the initial sense of the DATA STROBE line. Once a character is placed in the Port A data register, it is sent to the printer by causing a pulse on the DATA STROBE line to strobe the printer. This is accomplished by first setting and then clearing bit 3 of the Port A control register.

Port B Control Register

This register controls handshaking on the INPUT PRIME line for initializing the printer. Setting the register to $A0 disables interrupts and selects the initial sense of the INPUT PRIME line. The line is pulsed by setting and clearing bit 3 of the Port B control register.

Port A Data Register

For a character to be transmitted to the printer, it must be placed in this register. The MC68230 is *double buffered,* permitting a second character to be placed in the device while an earlier character is being processed. The position in the PI/T where a character is kept is called a *latch*. With at least one character in a latch, the printer is then strobed to send the character.

Port B Data Register

Bits 0–2 monitor the status of the SELECT, PAPER OUT, and BUSY lines.

    If bit 0 is 1, the printer is on-line.
    If bit 1 is 1, the printer is out of paper.

The BUSY bit is not used in the printer routines. The normal state for this register is thus xxxxxx01.

After a character is sent to the printer, this register is tested to verify that bit $0 = 1$ and bit $1 = 0$. If not, the printer status must be polled until it returns to normal. At that time, the character must be sent to the printer again.

Port Status Register

This register monitors the status of the four handshake lines H1–H4. Specifically, bit 0 tests the ACKNOWLEDGE line and indicates whether a character can be placed in the latch for transmission to the printer. If set, a "latch empty" condition is TRUE, and a character can be placed in the PI/T. If clear, the latches are full. The bit resembles the transmit register empty bit in the MC6850 ACIA status register.

A Standalone Printer Library

On the ECB system, the PI/T is located at $010001. Nine registers are used for non-interrupt driven parallel data transmission. The register offsets and the basic routines INITPRINTER, PRINTCHAR, and PRINTDELAY are included in a library. The action of each routine is given in some detail along with its code. The library also includes the routine PRINTNEWLINE for applications.

INITPRINTER

The register offsets are defined with the EQU directive.

```
piabase:   equ   $10001      ; pi/t address (ecb system)
pgcr:      equ   0           ; port general control reg
psrr:      equ   2           ; port service request reg
paddr:     equ   4           ; port a data direction reg
pbddr:     equ   6           ; port b data direction reg
pacr:      equ   $c          ; port a control register
pbcr:      equ   $e          ; port b control register
padr:      equ   $10         ; port a data register
pbdr:      equ   $12         ; port b data register
psr:       equ   $1a         ; port status register
lf         equ   $0a

initPrinter:
        move.l   a2,-(sp)
        lea      piabase,a2
        move.b   #$00,(pgcr,a2)    ; disable handshake lines
        move.b   #$00,(psrr,a2)    ; interrupts not used
        move.b   #$ff,(paddr,a2)   ; port a pins for output
        move.b   #$00,(pbddr,a2)   ; port b pins for input
        move.b   #$60,(pacr,a2)    ; port a: data strobe
        move.b   #$a0,(pbcr,a2)    ; port b: input prime
        move.b   #$30,(pgcr,a2)    ; enable handshake lines
        bset     #3,(pbcr,a2)      ; pulse input prime by a set
        bclr     #3,(pbcr,a2)      ; and clear of bit #3
        movea.l  (sp)+,a2
        rts
```

Initialize Registers For relative addressing, the base address of the PI/T is stored in A2.

   LEA   PIABASE,A2

Set unidirectional 8-bit data transmission, and set all handshake lines inactive. This resets the PI/T.

   MOVE.B   #$00,(PGCR,A2)   ; DISABLE HANDSHAKE LINES

Disable all interrupts and determine the function of the ACKNOWLEDGE and FAULT handshake lines.

   MOVE.B   #$00,(PSRR,A2)   ; INTERRUPTS NOT USED

Set Port A for output. Set Port B for input.

```
        MOVE.B   #$FF,(PADDR,A2)   ; PORT A PINS FOR OUTPUT
        MOVE.B   #$00,(PBDDR,A2)   ; PORT B PINS FOR INPUT
```

Set the Port A control register so that the sense of the DATA STROBE line is properly selected and interrupts are disabled. Set the Port B control register so that the sense of the INPUT PRIME line is properly selected and interrupts are disabled.

```
        MOVE.B   #$60,(PACR,A2)    ; PORT A: DATA STROBE
        MOVE.B   #$A0,(PBCR,A2)    ; PORT B: INPUT PRIME
```

Initialize Handshaking   Enable all handshake lines.

```
        MOVE.B   #$30,(PGCR,A2)    ; ENABLE HANDSHAKE LINES
```

Enable the printer by pulsing the INPUT PRIME line.

```
        BSET     #3,(PBCR,A2)      ; PULSE INPUT PRIME
        BCLR     #3,(PBCR,A2)      ; WITH SET/CLEAR
```

PRINTCHAR

The subroutine PRINTCHAR sends a character in (D0.B) to the printer. It tests the "latch empty" condition and then puts the character in the data register prior to strobing the DATA STROBE line. The printer status is tested by CHECKSTATUS, which returns a Boolean value in (D1.W). In this routine, an error occurs if the printer is off-line or out of paper. If (D1.W) ≠ 0 is TRUE, the character is sent again.

```
printchar:
            movem.l   d1/a2,-(sp)
            lea       piabase,a2
printch_1:
            btst      #0,(psr,a2)      ; check if latch available
            beq.s     printch_1        ; if not keep polling
            move.b    d0,(padr,a2)     ; write out the character
            bset      #3,(pacr,a2)     ; strobe the printer
            bclr      #3,(pacr,a2)
            jsr       checkstatus      ; test printer status
            tst.w     d1               ; d1 is flag "found_error"
            bne.s     printch_1        ; if a problem, retransmit
            movem.l   (sp)+,d1/a2
            rts

checkstatus:  move.l  d2,-(sp)         ; save scratch register
            clr.w     d1               ; assume printerror is false
testprinter:  move.b  (pbdr,a2),d2     ; read status lines
```

```
                andi.b     #$03,d2          ; mask all but low 2 bits
                cmpi.b     #$01,d2          ; should be 01
                beq.s      exitcheck        ; exit when no problem
                move.w     #1,d1            ; set printerror true
                bra.s      testprinter      ; poll until printer ready
exitcheck:      move.l     (sp)+,d2
                rts
```

PRINTNEWLINE

The newline routine sends only the linefeed character ($0A). Most printers
have an option to set newline expansion.

```
lf:             equ        $0A

printnewline:
                move.l     d0,-(sp)
                move.b     #lf,d0
                jsr        printchar
                move.l     (sp)+,d0
                rts
```

PRINTDELAY

Most printers require some action to ensure that their local buffer is flushed.
Some printers look for a CR character, and others need a delay to flush
characters before the system sends a reset signal. A printer's technical manual gives details. The PRINTDELAY routine is included for applications.
The number of seconds is passed in (D0.W).

```
printdelay:
                movem.l    d1-d3,-(sp)
                move.l     #125000,d1
                move.w     d1,d2
                mulu       d0,d2            ; multiply D0 by LSW of D1
                swap       d1
                mulu       d0,d1            ; multiply D0 by MSW of D1
                moveq      #16,d3
                asl.l      d3,d1
                add.l      d2,d1            ; add partial products
                move.l     d1,-(sp)         ; push tick count on stack
                jsr        initTimer
                jsr        startTimer       ; start the timer

delay_1:        jsr        testTimeout
                beq.s      delay_1
                jsr        stopTimer
                movem.l    (sp)+,d1-d3
                rts
```

PROGRAM 12.8

PRINTLIB Test

The characters "1" and "A" are printed on separate lines. The program was run on an ECB system and uses PRINTDELAY to flush the printer buffer before TUTOR issues a reset.

```
        xref      initPrinter, printchar, printnewline, stop,
        xref      printdelay

start:  lea       8000,sp
        jsr       initPrinter
        move.b    #'1',d0
        jsr       printchar
        jsr       printnewline
        move.b    #'A',d0         ; printable character
        jsr       printchar       ; print the character
        jsr       printnewline    ; one more newline
        move.w    #2,d0           ; delay 2 seconds
        jsr       printdelay
        jsr       stop

        end
```

⟨Printer Run of Program 12.8⟩

```
1
A
```

PROGRAM 12.9

Printstring Test

Printing a single character with PRINTCHAR is extended to a string. The output "Testing the print routine PRINTSTRING" is repeated five times.

```
        xref      initPrinter, printchar, printdelay

start:  lea       $8000,sp
        jsr       initPrinter
        moveq     #4,d6              ; print a string 5 times
        lea       msg,a0
loop:   jsr       printstring
        dbra      d6,loop
        move.w    #2,d0
        jsr       printdelay
        jsr       stop               ; return to Tutor

printstring:
        move.l    d0/a0,-(sp)
send:   move.b    (a0)+,d0
        beq.s     exit
        jsr       printchar
```

```
                 bra.s     send
                 movem.l   (sp)+,d0/a0
exit:            rts

                 data

msg:             dc.b  'Testing the print routine PRINTSTRING', 10,0

                 end
```

⟨Printer Run of Program 12.9⟩

```
Testing the print routine PRINTSTRING
Testing the print routine PRINTSTRING
Testing the print routine PRINTSTRING
Testing the print routine PRINTSTRING
Testing the print routine PRINTSTRING
```

|12.6| APPLICATION PROGRAMS

A series of application programs is given to advance your understanding of interface devices. The applications use more advanced algorithms and are coded with routines from the I/O library, timer library, and printer library.

ACIA Application: ECB Transparent Mode

On the ECB board, one ACIA is connected to the console port, and a second is connected to the host port. Normally, the host port is connected to another computer system. In order for a user (working on a console terminal) to connect with the host computer system, a program is necessary to pass characters back and forth between the terminal and the computer system (see Figure 12.10). In this environment, the ECB board is running in **transparent mode**.

The following program emulates the TUTOR TM ("Transparent Mode") command that permits console characters to be passed through to the host and vice versa. Transmission is terminated when a Ctrl⎽A is entered at the console. When a character arrives from the host, it must be sent to the console, and when a character is typed on the console, it must be sent to the host system. The program algorithm alternates a testing of the two ACIA ports.

FIGURE 12.10   ECB Transparent Mode

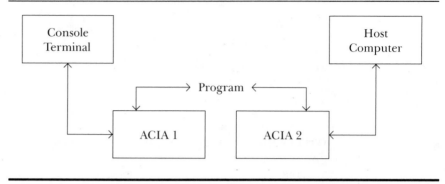

Console Port

See whether a character has arrived from the console.
If no character has arrived, test the host port.
If a character has arrived, test it.
If it is a CTRL__A, exit to the monitor.
If it is not CTRL__A, send it through to the host port and switch to
the host port test.

Host Port

See if a character has arrived from the host port.
If no character has arrived, test the console port.
If a character has arrived, send it through to the console and switch
to the console port test.

PROGRAM 12.10

Transparent Mode
with Polling

This program establishes a transparent interface between a console and a
computer system connected through the host port. Characters are passed
back and forth until a CTRL__A is typed at the console. At this time,
program control returns to the monitor. The program executes with NLOFF.
The host system typically implements the newline expansion.

Note: The transparent mode program with interrupts is presented in
Chapter 14.

```
ctrl_A:   equ     $01            ; char for return to monitor
console:  equ     0
host:     equ     1              ; starting address of monitor

          xref    initPort,charpresent,getchar,putchar
          xref    echoff, nloff, stop
```

```
tm:         lea     $8000,sp        ; initialize stack pointer
            moveq   #console,d7     ; initialize console acia
            jsr     initPort        ; default is echo on
            jsr     echoff          ; host system does echoing
            jsr     nloff           ; <lf> and <cr> must be passed
;                                   ; through without change
            moveq   #host,d7        ; initialize host acia
            jsr     initPort
            jsr     echoff          ; no echo both ports
            jsr     nloff           ; no newline conversion at
;                                   ; either port

terminal:   moveq   #console,d7     ; test for char at console
            jsr     charpresent     ; d0 has the char or is 0
            beq     hostline        ; if no char, check host
            jsr     getchar         ; read char from console
            cmpi.b  #ctrl_A,d0      ; test for return to monitor
            beq     return          ; if ctrl a, exit to monitor
            moveq   #host,d7        ; send char to host port
            jsr     putchar
hostline:   moveq   #host,d7        ; test for char from the host
            jsr     charpresent
            beq     terminal        ; if no char, check console
            jsr     getchar         ; read char from host port
            moveq   #console,d7     ; send char to console port
            jsr     putchar
            bra     terminal        ; go back to test terminal
return:     jsr     stop            ; return to the monitor

            end
```

⟨Run of Program 12.10⟩

```
%> echo We have contact with the UNIX system
   We have contact with the UNIX system
%> ls /usr/local
   bin/    emacs/   games/   include/   lib/    man/
   public/   src/
%> echo logging off the system
   logging off the system
```

Timer Application: Download Record Format

Motorola S-records were described in Section 12.1 while introducing the downloading of code from a host computer to an ECB system. The S-record format encodes programs and data files in a printable form prior to their transfer between computer systems. Many compilers and assemblers on Motorola systems are capable of generating an S-record code file that contains only ASCII data to avoid sending 8-bit data on serial lines. S-records are organized as lines of data. Each line contains its load address, data bytes, and a check-sum byte. The check sum serves as a test of data transmission accuracy. In the S-record format, each byte is represented as two ASCII digits. For example,

Binary Data	*S-Record Format*	
01011110 ($5E)	00110101	01000101
	'5'	'E'

A receiving system must contain a routine to initiate the download transfer, convert the S-records back to binary data, and load the resulting code into memory at the specified load address.

This application illustrates the creation of ASCII download records and the code to download the records. The application concludes with a run of a sample program on a UNIX system to create download records and then run on an ECB system. To avoid the complexity of S-records, we introduce SZ-format, a simplified format for ASCII download records. On the host system, a C program SZ_MAKE translates a binary file to an SZ-format file. The source code for SZ_MAKE is given in Appendix D. The MC68000 program SZ_DOWNLOAD runs on the ECB system (see Figure 12.11).

SZ-Format   The character "S" specifies start of transmission. The SZ-format file splits each byte of machine code into two ASCII hex digits. The file consists of ASCII character pairs. The end of transmission sequence is

FIGURE 12.11   ASCII Record Download

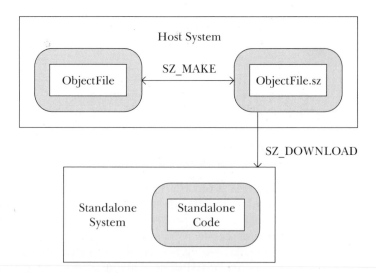

specified by the character "Z". Note that the file is one long line with a newline only after the character "Z".

Binary File	SZ-Record File (ASCII characters)
2A 10 3F 69	S 2A 10 3F 69 Z

SZ-Format Generator Program (SZ—MAKE) If you are familiar with the C programming language and the UNIX system, you may wish to look at the program SZ_MAKE.C in Appendix D. It reads a code file in UNIX codefile format, performs SZ-format translation, and writes to the UNIX standard output. Using redirection, output can be stored in the file LOAD_DEMO.SZ. The compiled codefile for SZ.MAKE.C is called SZ.MAKE.

EXAMPLE 12.9

An MC68000 assembly language file on a UNIX host system illustrates the output of the SZ—MAKE program. An MC68000 file LOAD_DEMO.S is assembled to an unlinked code file LOAD_DEMO.O in UNIX code file format. The program SZ_MAKE translates the binary data in LOAD_DEMO.O to the SZ-format file LOAD_DEMO.SZ. A listing of LOAD_DEMO.SZ is given to illustrate an SZ-format file.

MC68000 Code (Host Program LOAD_DEMO.S)

```
        xref    putdecout, putnewline, stop

start:  move.w  #3,d0
        addi.w  #2,d0       ; Value 5 in d0
        mulu    d0,d0       ; square d0
        jsr     putdecout   ; output result 25
        jsr     putnewline
        jsr     stop

        end
```

Assembling Process (Using host assembler ASM)

asm −c load_demo.s   ⟨creates UNIX code file load_demo.o⟩

UNIX Code

```
0001 0107 0000 001c 0000 0000 0000 0000     UNIX header
0000 0030 0000 0000 0000 0018 0000 0000

303c 0003 0640 0002 c0c0 4eb9 0000 0000     Code
4eb9 0000 0000 4eb9 0000 0000
... and other relocation, symbol table, and string pool information
```

Generate SZ-Record File   (Run host program MAKE__SZ)

make__sz load__demo.o > load__demo.sz

SZ__Format

S303C000306400002C0C04EB9000000004EB9000000004EB900000
000Z

Program 12.11 SZ-Format Download Program (SZ__DOWNLOAD)   The load program, running on the standalone system, prompts the user to pass a command string to the host system. The command should direct the host to pass characters to the console port. SZ__DOWNLOAD reads downloaded data sent in SZ-format and places the extracted bytes in memory starting at address $4000.

During the download, the timer monitors delay in transmission. If a delay of 10 seconds occurs, the download is halted, and a TIMEOUT message is given. This prevents the standalone system from being locked as a result of problems at the host system. For instance, an error may occur in opening the code file on the host system. The SZ__DOWNLOAD command may reference a nonexistent file and leave the standalone system in an infinite loop waiting for the "start of transmission" character.

The SZLOAD program calls the routine WAITFORSTART to look for the start character "S". The subroutine GETBYTE reads the ASCII data, echoes it to the screen, and converts it to binary. HEXBIN is responsible for the conversion and returns to the monitor if it finds a nonhex ASCII digit. Each code byte is loaded into memory. The character "Z" terminates the download and causes a DOWNLOAD COMPLETE message to be printed.

The routine TGETCHAR reads characters from the host port. A time check is done, if TIMEOUT occurs, the download is terminated and control passed to the monitor.

```
null:     equ     0
lf:       equ     $0a
cr:       equ     $0d
set_Z:    equ     4               ; z bit of ccr is bit 4
clear_Z:  equ     $1b             ; clear z bit keep other bits

          xref    initTimer, startTimer, restartTimer, testTimeout
          xref    initPort, charpresent, getchar, putchar, stop
          xref    getstring, putstring, putnewline, echoff, nloff

start:    lea     $8000, sp
          lea     $4000, a1       ; code starts at $4000
          moveq   #1, d7          ; initialize host port
          jsr     initPort
          jsr     echoff          ; echo downloaded chars
          jsr     nloff           ; no newline expansion
```

```
                moveq      #0,d7              ; initialize console port
                jsr        initPort

                move.l     #1250000,-(sp)     ; set timer for 10 seconds
                jsr        initTimer

                jsr        entercmd           ; sent download request to host
                jsr        waitforstart       ; wait for startup 'S' character

loadloop:
                jsr        getbyte            ; convert ascii chars to byte
                beq.s      endload            ; getbyte returns "stop" flag
                move.b     d0,(a1)+           ; put code byte into memory
                bra        loadloop           ; get next pair
endload:        moveq      #0,d7              ; print "download complete"
                lea        endmsg,a0
                jsr        putstring
                jsr        stop               ; exit back to monitor
```

```
; Conversion routine reads pair of ascii hex characters and
; compresses them into a single byte in d0. The end of download flag
; is set using the z-bit. If the character 'Z' is read, the download
; is complete and the ccr bit z = 1; otherwise, return with z = 0.
```

```
getbyte:
                movem.l    d1/d7,-(sp)
                moveq      #1,d7              ; read chars from host
                jsr        restartTimer       ; start 10 second timer
                jsr        tgetchar           ; get char within the time
                cmpi.b     #'Z',d0            ; end of download?
                beq.s      endfound
                jsr        echoTerm
                jsr        hexbin             ; convert hex char to binary
                move.b     d0,d1              ; store value in d1
                asl.b      #4,d1              ; shift value to bits 7-4
                jsr        restartTimer       ; get second char in pair
                jsr        tgetchar
                jsr        echoTerm
                jsr        hexbin             ; convert 2nd digit to binary
                add.b      d0,d1              ; store in bits 3-0
                move.b     d1,d0              ; d0 is output register
                andi.b     #clear_Z,ccr       ; clear z bit and return
                bra.s      xit
endfound:
                ori.b      #set_Z,ccr         ; set the z bit and return
xit:            movem.l    (sp)+,d1/d7
                rts
```

```
; convert the ascii hex character in d0 to binary. if the char
; is not a valid digit, return to monitor.
```

```
hexbin:
                cmpi.b     #'0',d0            ; error if digit < '0'
                blt.s      error
```

```
               cmpi.b    #'9',d0
               bgt.s     atof              ; is digit in '0' . . '9'?
               subi.b    #'0',d0           ; convert to binary and return
               rts
atof:          cmpi.b    #'A',d0           ; digit > '9' but < 'A' is error
               blt.s     error
               cmpi.b    #'F',d0           ; digit 'A' . . 'F' ?
               bgt.s     error
               subi.b    #'A'-10,d0        ; convert to binary
               rts

error:         moveq     #0,d7             ; print error message to console
               lea       badchar,a0
               jsr       putstring
               jsr       stop              ; quit and return to monitor

echoTerm:
               move.l    d7,-(sp)
               moveq     #0,d7
               jsr       putchar           ; putchar to console
               addq.w    #1,linelimit
               btst      #4,linelimit
               beq.s     continue
               jsr       putnewline
               clr.b     linelimit
continue:      move.l    (sp)+,d7
               rts


; ignore characters until an 'S' is found. this subroutine is
; used to ignore any command line chars echoed back by the host.

waitforstart:
               move.l    d7,-(sp)
               moveq     #1,d7
               jsr       startTimer
waitchar:      jsr       tgetchar          ; timed char read from host line
               cmpi.b    #'S',d0           ; have we read an 'S'?
               bne.s     waitchar
               move.l    (sp)+,d7
               rts


tgetchar:      movem.l   d7/a0,-(sp)
               moveq     #1,d7
tryagain:      jsr       charpresent       ; look for character
               bne.s     rtn               ; if present, get it
               jsr       testTimeout       ; check for time out
               beq.s     tryagain          ; if time remains, try again
               moveq     #0,d7
               lea       timeoutmsg,a0     ; fatal timeout print message
               jsr       putstring
               jsr       stop
rtn:           jsr       getchar
               movem.l   (sp)+,d7/a0
               rts
```

```
entercmd:  move.l    a0,-(sp)
           moveq     #0,d7           ; send prompt to console
           lea       cmdprompt,a0    ; request command for host system
           jsr       putstring
           lea       cmdstring,a0    ; read command from console
           jsr       getstring
           moveq     #1,d7           ; send download command to host
           lea       cmdstring,a0
           jsr       putstring
           move.b    #13,d0
           jsr       putchar
           ;jsr      putnewline      ; host must see <lf> or <cr>
           movea.l   (sp)+,a0
           rts

           data
linelimit:
           dc.w      0
timeoutmsg:
           dc.b      'Timeout'cr,lf,null
endmsg:
           dc.b      cr,lf,'Download complete',cr,lf,null
cmdprompt:
           dc.b      'Enter download command: ',null
badchar:
           dc.b      cr,lf,'Invalid download charcter',cr,lf,null
cmdstring:
           ds.b      80

           end
```

PROGRAM 12.11

Download Test

The following steps are executed on the host and ECB systems in order to download and then run the program LOAD—DEMO.S on the ECB system.

Step 1: On the UNIX system, the code file LOAD—DEMO.O is linked with the standalone I/O library TUTORIO. The "-T" option sets the load address of the linked code file.

    ld -N -o load_demo.out -T 4000 load_demo.o -1tutorio

Step 2: SZ.MAKE converts the code file LOAD—DEMO.OUT to the SZ-format file LOAD—DEMO.OUT.SZ.

    sz_make load_demo.out > load_demo.out.sz

Step 3: On the ECB system, the program SZ—DOWNLOAD initiates file transfer from the host system and the reading of SZ-format data. After completing the downloading, we run the program LOAD—DEMO, residing at address 4000. It produces the single output 25.

Note that the code for SZ_DOWNLOAD was downloaded by the TUTOR download program LOAD and starts at address $900.

⟨Run of Program 12.11⟩

```
TUTOR 1.3 > G 900
PHYSICAL ADDRESS=00000900
Enter download command: cat load_demo.out.sz

303C000306400002C0C04EB90000401C4EB9000040B64EB9000081462F0048C048
79000045A84EB9000041AA4879000045A84EB90000408E4879000045B44EB90000
408E201F4E754879000045A84EB9000041AA4879000045A84EB90000408E487900
..................................................................
4F4E7500000000000000000000000000000000202000000A000000000000000000
00000000000000000000303132333435363738394142434445460000000000000
0100400001004100000000000000
Download complete

TUTOR 1.3 > G 4000
PHYSICAL ADDRESS=00004000
25
```

Timer Application: Screen Blank

The timer is used in a screen-blanking program. The main code continuously waits for a character to arrive from the keyboard and then echoes it back to the screen. However, if a sufficient delay occurs before a character is typed, the screen is turned off (dimmed). The typing of a character turns the screen back on. The control characters necessary to dim and brighten the screen are a function of the terminal hardware.

PROGRAM 12.12

Screen Blank

Characters are echoed to the terminal. If a 1-minute delay occurs before a character is typed, the screen is dimmed. By pressing a key, which is discarded, the user reactivates the screen. The test program terminates with a ⟨*control*⟩Z.

Note This program was run on a terminal that uses ESC-o and ESC-n to turn the screen video off and on. Check your own terminal manual for similar escape sequences.

```
console:    equ    0              ; parameter for term IO library
ctrl_Z:     equ    26
esc:        equ    $1b            ; screen video esc o (screen off)
;                                 ; esc n (screen on)

            xref   initPort,getchar,putchar,charpresent,echon,echoff
            xref   initTimer, startTimer, testTimeout, restartTimer,
                   stop
```

```
start:      lea         #$8000,sp           ; set stack pointer
            moveq       #console,d7         ; set console for acia package
            move.b      #1,haveScrOn        ; assume screen starts on
            jsr         initPort            ; initialize console acia
            move.l      #7500000,-(sp)      ; set timer to 60 seconds
            jsr         initTimer
            jsr         startTimer

scanchar:   jsr         charpresent         ; test for console character
            bne.s       gotchar             ; take action
            jsr         testTimeout         ; test for time out
            beq.s       scanchar            ; no! keep polling for character
            jsr         turnScrOff          ; timeout turn off screen
            bra.s       scanchar            ; return to poll for character

gotchar:    jsr         getchar
            cmpi.b      #ctrl_Z,d0          ; look for control_Z to quit
            bne.s       continue
            jsr         stop
continue:   jsr         restartTimer
            btst        #0,haveScrOn        ; test the screen status
            bne.s       scanchar            ; if lighted echo and keep going
            jsr         turnScrOn           ; it was off turn it on
            bra.s       scanchar            ; return to poll for character

turnScrOn:  jsr         echon               ; want to see chars as typed
            move.b      #esc.d0             ; transmit esc n
            jsr         putchar
            move.b      #'n',d0
            jsr         putchar
            bset        #0,haveScrOn        ; set ScreenOn TRUE
            rts

turnScrOff: jsr         echoff
            move.b      #esc,d0             ; transmit esc o
            jsr         putchar
            move.b      #'o',d0
            jsr         putchar
            bclr        #0,haveScrOn        ; set ScreenOn FALSE
            jsr         stopTimer
            rts

            data
haveScrOn:  ds.b        1                   ; flag for screen status
            end
```

Timer Application: Process Switching

Time sharing in a multiuser environment is frequently implemented by process timeslicing. A user or system process is given access to the CPU for a short period of time while other processes are held waiting in a queue. Using a scheduling algorithm, one of the waiting processes is given access to the CPU, and the process presently running goes back to the queue for subsequent return to a running state. Critical information about the process is saved so that the process can resume execution. The scheduling algorithm uses a timer to decide when to make a switch. Chapter 15 covers this topic in greater detail.

The following complete program simulates timeslicing with a simple case of two processes:

Process 1: Sends a stream of 1's to the screen for 5 seconds.
Process 2: Sends a stream of 2's to the screen for 3 seconds.

The scheduling algorithm uses the timer to switch between the processes so that they run alternately. Two key subroutines, which access a global variable NEXTPROCADDR, implement the scheduling algorithm. The PROCESSMGR routine is called just prior to executing a process. The PROC–SWITCHER routine is called periodically by the main processes or to test for timeout.

PROCESSMGR

Input Parameters

SECS:	The number of seconds allocated to the presently running process. The value is passed as a word on the stack.
NEXTADDRESS:	The address of the next process that will run. The value is passed as a long word on the stack.

The address of the next process is read from the stack and stored in the global variable NEXTPROCADDR. The value will be used later by the subroutine PROC—SWITCHER to dispatch the next process. In this program, there are only two processes. Each is responsible for pushing the address of the other process on the stack. It is a 2-element circular queue. In a multiprocessing environment, a process manager would manage a larger queue.

The value of SECS is read from the stack and used to initialize the timer preload register.

PROC—SWITCHER

The subroutine fetches the address of the next process from the global variable NEXTPROCADDR. This value replaces the return address on the stack. The next process is dispatched when RTS is executed.

PROGRAM 12.13
_____

Process Switching

Two timed processes execute alternately, sending a stream of 1's to the console (5 seconds) and a stream of 2's to the console (3 seconds), respectively. The ACIA subroutine package is used for output, and the timer package is used for the process switching.

```
; ascii characters
one:          equ         '1'
two:          equ         '2'

console:      equ         0               ; console acia
nextproc:     equ         8
proctime:     equ         12
retaddr:      equ         4

              xref        initPort, putchar
              xref        initTimer, startTimer, testTimeout, stopTimer

start:        lea         $8000,sp        ; set stack pointer
              moveq       #console,d7     ; set acia parameter
              jsr         initPort        ; initialize terminal acia

;             process 1

proc1:        move.l      #625000,-(sp)   ; proc1 runs for 5 seconds
              pea         proc2           ; push addr of proc2 on stack
              jsr         processmgr      ; setup process handling
              move.b      #one,d0         ; proc1 prints "1"
ploop1:       jsr         putchar         ; use standard acia routine
              jsr         proc_switcher   ; check for timeout
              bra.s       ploop1          ; if no switch print the '1's

;             process 2

proc2:        move.l      #375000,-(sp)   ; proc2 runs for 3 seconds
              pea         proc1           ; push addr of proc1 on stack
              jsr         processmgr      ; setup process handling
              move.b      #two,d0
ploop2:       jsr         putchar         ; proc2 prints "2"
              jsr         proc_switcher   ; check for timeout
              bra.s       ploop2          ; if no switch print the '2's

processmgr:
              link        a6,#0
              movem.l     d0/a0,-(sp)
              move.l      (nextproc,a6),nextprocaddr
                                          ; get time measure in ticks
;
              move.l      (proctime,a6),d0
              move.l      d0,-(sp)        ; set timer to process length
              jsr         initTimer
              jsr         startTimer
              movem.l     (sp)+,d0/a0
              unlk        a6
              move.l      (sp),(8,sp)     ; clean up the stack
              addq.w      #8,sp
              rts                         ; go back and execute proc

proc_switcher:
              link        a6,#0
              jsr         testTimeout
              beq         cret            ; if time remains, return
;                                         ; set next process as return address
```

```
               jsr        stopTimer
               move.l     nextprocaddr,(retaddr,a6)
cret:          unlk       a6
               rts                            ; this dispatches new proc

               data

nextprocaddr:
               ds.l       1

               end
```

⟨Run of Program 12.13⟩

```
111111111111111111111111111111111111111111111111111111111111111111111
111111111111111111111111111111111111111111111111111111111111111111111
111111111111111111111111111111111111111111111111111111111111111111111
1111111111111 ⟨etc⟩ 11111111111111111111111111111111111111222222222
222222222222222222222222222222222222222222222222222222222222222222222
222222222222222222222222222222222222222222222222222222222222222222222
2222222222222222222222222 ⟨etc⟩ 22222222222222222222222222222222222
222222211111111111111111111111111111111111111111111111111111111111111
111111111111111111111111111111111111111111111111111111111111111111111
1111111111111111111111111111 ⟨etc⟩ 111111111111111111111111111111111
111111111111111111111111111111111111111111111111111111111111111111
```

Printer Application: Printing ASCII Characters

This sample program initializes the PI/T and sends all the printable ASCII characters to the printer.

PROGRAM 12.14

Printing ASCII
Characters

The range of printable ASCII characters is $20 (Space)-$7E (~). The program prints all characters in this range, limiting output to ten characters per line. Upon completion, control passes to the monitor.

```
               xref       initprinter, printchar, printdelay
               xref       printnewline, stop

space:         equ        $20
delete:        equ        $7f

start:         lea        $8000,sp
               jsr        initprinter
```

```
                moveq   #10, d2              ; d2 counts 10 chars per line
                move.b  #space, d0           ; first printable character
loop:           jsr     printchar            ; print the character
                subq.w  #1, d2               ; one more char on the line
                bne.s   nextchar             ; end of line yet;
                moveq   #10, d2              ; reset char/line count
                jsr     printnewline         ; send the line
nextchar:       addq.b  #1, d0               ; go to next character
                cmpi.b  #delete, d0          ; test last printable char
                beq.s   return               ; at "delete", quit
                bra.s   loop
return:         jsr     printnewline         ; one more newline
                jsr     printdelay
                jsr     stop

                end
```

⟨Printer Run of Program 12.14⟩

```
! #$%&' ()
*+,-. /0123
456789: ; <=
>?@ABCDEFG
HIJKLMNOPQ
RSTUVWXYZ[
\]^_`abcde
fghijklmno
pqrstuvwxy
z{|}~
```

EXERCISES

1. Compare and contrast isolated and memory-mapped I/O programming.

2. A computer connects several output ports to a multiplexor, which buffers the data. Could the multiplexor be a DMA device? Explain.

3. Assuming 1 start bit, 1 stop bit, 7 data bits, and even parity, give the complete bit sequence for serial transmission of the following characters:
   (a) a   (b) 0   (c) @

4. The character '1' = $31. Show how '1' is transmitted with two stop bits and odd parity.

5. Which ASCII character, transmitted with 7 bits and 1 stop bit, has bit pattern -start-1-0-0-0-0-1-stop?

6. On the Motorola ECB system, the receive and transmit data registers have address $10042. Explain how two different registers can have the same memory address.

7. With the directive ORG $1000 in the code segment, what is the value of label B?

      ORG $1000

  A: DS.L   40
  B: DC.L   5

8. Can the selective turning on and off of character echo be done on a system running in full duplex? Explain. What about a system running in half duplex?

9. How is a parity error detected with MC6850 ACIA data transmission? What is the effect of putting a 111 in the format select field of the MC6850 ACIA control register?

10. Assume that (D0.L) = $56783344; give the memory contents starting at location $10000 after executing the following instructions. Use X to indicate UN-KNOWN contents.

      LEA $10000,A0
      MOVEP.L   D0,(0,A0)

11. Describe how a character is transmitted from register D0 to the printer. Use the ECB MC68230 interface for details.

12. What is the action of the following program? Assume that the standalone I/O library is available.

```
              xref      getchar,putchar,initPort,stop

    space:    equ      $20              ; blank character
    delete:   equ      $7f              ; delete character
    conport:  equ      0

    start:    lea      $8000,sp         ; initialize stack pointer
              moveq    #conport,d7
              jsr      initPort         ; initialize acia
    main:     jsr      getchar          ; wait for a character
              cmpi.b   #space,d0
              blt.s    endit
              cmp.b    #delete,d0
              bge.s    endit
              jsr      putchar
              bra.s    main             ; keep going
    endit:    jsr      stop
              end
```

13. What is the action of the following program? Assume that the standalone I/O library is available.

```
    tbase:    equ      $010021          ; timer base address
    tcon:     equ      0                ; timer control register
    tcpr:     equ      4                ; timer preload register
    tsr:      equ      20               ; timer status register
```

```
        bell        equ         $07                   ; terminal bell character

                    xref        initPort, charpresent, putchar, getchar
        start:
                    movea.l     #$8000,sp             ; set stack pointer
                    move.w      #0,d7
                    jsr         initPort
                    lea         tbase,a0
                    move.l      #250000,d0
                    movep.l     d0,tcpr(a0)
                    move.b      #$80,tcon(a0)

                    bset        #0,tcon(a0)

        mloop:
                    jsr         charpresent
                    beq.s       ttest
                    jsr         getchar
                    jsr         putchar
        ttest:
                    btst        #0,tsr(a0)
                    beq.s       mloop
                    bset        #0,tsr(a0)
                    move.b      #bell,d0
                    jsr         putchar
                    bra.s       mloop

                    end
```

Rewrite the preceding program using TimerLib routines.

14. A character is present in the ACIA transmit register. Can you force this character to be sent to the peripheral device by placing a second character in the transmit register, an action similar to strobing a printer port? Explain.

15. What is the action of the following code?

```
        console:    equ         0

                    xref        initPort,charpresent,getchar,putchar, stop


        start:      moveq       #console,d7
                    jsr         initPort
        st1:        jsr         charpresent
                    beq.s       st1
                    jsr         getchar
                    cmpi.b      #4,d0
                    beq.s       st2
                    move.w      #7,d0
                    jsr         putchar
                    bra.s       st1
        st2:        jsr         stop
                    end
```

16. What is the action of the following code?

```
tbase:      equ         $10021
tcr:        equ         0
tcpr:       equ         4
tsr:        equ         20

ctrl_D:     equ         4

            xref        initPort,charpresent,getchar,putchar,putnewline
            xref        initTimer,startTimer,testTimeout, stop

start:      moveq       #0,d7
            jsr         init
            move.l      #25000,-(sp)
            jsr         initTimer
loop1:      jsr         charpresent
            beq.s       loop1
            jsr         getchar
            cmpi.b      #ctrl_D,d0
            beq.s       loop3
            cmpi.b      #' ',d0
            bne.s       loop1
            jsr         startTimer
loop2:      move.b      #'.',d0
            jsr         putchar
            jsr         testTimeout
            beq.s       loop2
            jsr         putnewline
            bra.s       loop1
loop3:      jsr         stop
            end
```

17. A MC6850 ACIA is connected to a modem. Trace the code and indicate the actions outlined in subroutine TESTCODE.

```
TermBase:       equ         $10040
status_reg:     equ         0
receive_reg:    equ         2

                xref        stop
                            .
                            .
                            .
                lea         termBase,a0
                jsr         testcode
                            .
                            .
                            .
testcode:       btst        #2,(status_reg,a0)
                bne         moff
```

```
                        btst        #0, (status_reg, a0)
                        beq         back
                        move.b      (receive_reg, a0), d0
                        moveq       #1, d1
                        rts
        back:           mo.eq       #0, d1
                        rts


        moff:           jsr         stop
```

18. In the TUTORIO library (see Appendix D), modify the subroutine GETCHAR so that if an overrun occurs, an error message is printed on the console and program control returns to the calling program with (D0.B) = $FF.

19. Write a code segment that moves the most significant bytes of the four words beginning at address $1000 to the least significant bytes of the four words beginning at address $2000. Use the MOVEP instruction.

20. Trace the following code and indicate what it does:

```
        TimerBase:      equ         $10021
        timercontrol:   equ         0
        timerpreload:   equ         4
        timerstatus:    equ         $14

                        xref        initPort, puthex, putstring, stop

                        moveq       #0, d7
                        jsr         initPort
                        lea         TimerBase, a0
                        move.b      #$80, (timercontrol, a0)
                        move.l      #1125000, d1
                        movep.l     d1, (timerpreload, a0)
                        bset        #0, (timercontrol, a0)
                        moveq       #9, d0
        wait:           btst        #0, (timerstatus, a0)
                        beq         wait
                        bclr        #0, (timercontrol, a0)
                        divu        #2, d1
                        andi.l      #$FFFF, d1
                        movep.l     d1, (timerpreload, a0)
                        jsr         puthexout
                        bset        #0, (timercontrol, a0)
                        dbra        d0, b
                        lea         msg, a0
                        jsr         putstring
                        jsr         stop

                        data
        msg:            dc.b        'Done', 0
                        end
```

PROGRAMMING EXERCISES

21. Use the standalone library for character handling at a serial port.
    (a) Write a subroutine PUTHEXBYTE that writes out the 8-bit contents of (D0.B) as two ASCII hex digits followed by one blank.
    (b) Write a main program that reads characters from the keyboard and writes out their ASCII value using PUTHEXBYTE. Control characters in the range 0–31 use the following input format:

    Put a ' ^ ' followed by a character. The resulting control character is the ASCII value modulo 32. To enter the character ' ^ ' as itself, preceed it by '\'. For instance, ^D is ASCII $04, ^Z is ASCII $1A, and \^D is ^D.

22. Modify the subroutine GETCHAR so that it tests a global variable "TABEXP".

    If TABEXP = 0, do not expand tabs.
    If TABEXP = 1, expand a tab character to a sequence of blanks that implement tab stops. Assume tab stops occur at character positions 1, 9, 17, 25, and so forth.

23. Use the timer to implement the following countdown process:

    Initially, the message "5 Seconds" is written to the screen and remains there for 5 seconds. Then "4 Seconds" is printed to the screen and remains there for 4 seconds. This sequence continues until the message "1 Second" has remained visible for 1 second.

24. This program will use the ACIA and TIMER interfaces. Write a program that implements the following algorithm:

    Step 1: Initialize each device.

    Step 2: Begin a process PRINTNAME that successively writes your name to the screen. At the same time, start up the timer and use the timer to measure the length of time the program has been running. Measure the time in units of 1 second.

    Step 3: During execution of PRINTNAME, respond to keyboard input. When ⟨*control*⟩T is entered from the keyboard, the program time should be output in the following form:

    Running XX seconds

    When ⟨*control*⟩D is entered from the keyboard, the process should halt.

25. Extend Program 12.13 to switch among three processes. The third process should print a stream of 3's to the screen for 2 seconds.

26. Read a sequence of characters into an array until the end-of-file character ⟨*control*⟩Z is input. Print the text received to the printer.

CHAPTER 13

EXCEPTION PROCESSING

---

*T*he MC68000 processor provides instructions that interrupt ordinary program execution and create access to system utilities. The CPU also interrupts the program to report internal system errors (such as an address error) or to implement the debugging of programs. Peripheral devices can interrupt the CPU by activating control lines. Thereby permitting the CPU to carry out independent processing while the device is not in use. Instructions and conditions interrupting ordinary program execution are called **exceptions**. Exception processing is one of the most important and fundamental topics in assembly language programming. Many of its applications are drawn from the field of systems programming.

During ordinary execution, a program runs under the control of an **executive program**. The executive program is responsible for starting and monitoring subordinate code. Examples of executive programs are monitors and full-scale operating systems such as UNIX. A monitor is a program to perform basic command processing for a standalone system. It allows the display and modification of registers, the setting of breakpoints, and the loading and running of user programs. A monitor processes commands in a nonterminating main loop. When the user requests that a program be executed, the monitor passes control to the starting address of the user program. If an error occurs, the monitor must print diagnostic information and return to command processing in its main loop. Exceptions cause transfer to the executive program so that a service can be performed. Exception processing implies a deviation from the CPU's ordinary mode of execution. For example, a user program can request a file operation by executing an MC68000 TRAP instruction. The program is suspended, the file service is performed, and the program continues execution after the TRAP instruction. During this process, the CPU shifts from ordinary program execution to the exception-processing state. This chapter describes in detail the exception state and the exception-processing cycle. MC68020/30/40 exceptions are covered in Section 13.8. Peripheral device interrupts are covered in Chapter 14.

13.1 | CPU STATES

The MC68000 processor is always in one of three states. The **normal state** is the default state, consisting of sequential execution of instructions in a user program. Up to this point in the text, programs have been running in the normal state.

A second state, called the **exception state**, is entered after an exception occurs. Exceptions cause the CPU to stop after the current instruction, save program status information on the stack, and then transfer control to a specified block of code in the executive program called an **exception service routine**. The actions that take place to save program status information

FIGURE 13.1   State Transitions in a Running Program

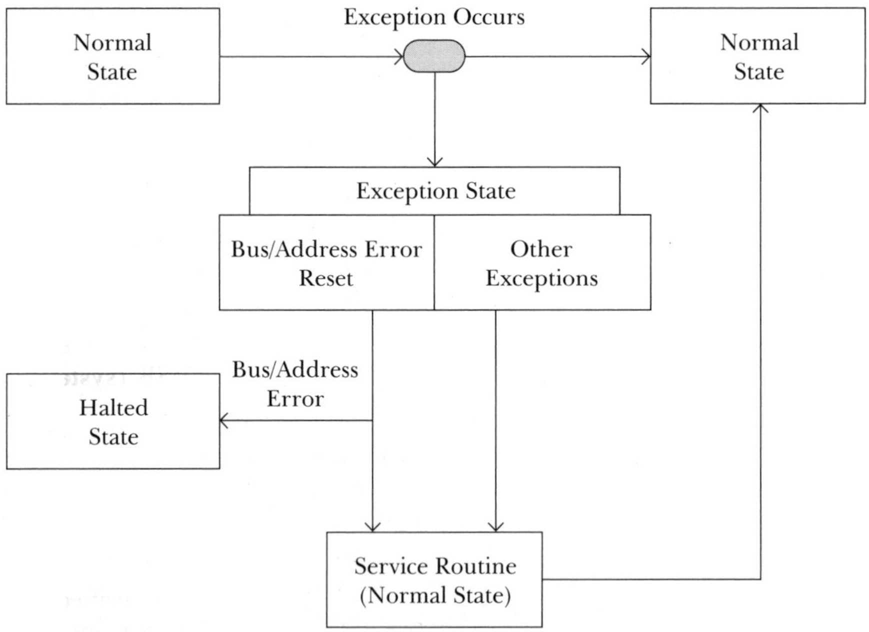

and transfer control to the service routine constitute the exception state. The instructions in the service routine are again executed in the normal state. The service routine contains the code necessary to respond to the exception. The exception state is entered when a special instruction causes an exception, when an instruction error occurs, or when the CPU is interrupted by a peripheral device. If the exception is not caused by an error, control can be returned from the service routine to the original program. If an error caused the exception, the service routine usually terminates the program.

The third possible state of the CPU is the **halted state**. If a program running in normal state attempts to access a word or long word at an odd byte address, an **address error exception** occurs. Similarly, if a program attempts to address a nonexistent memory location, a **bus error exception** occurs. A system reset is an exception that causes the system to "reboot." The halt state is entered when a bus or address error occurs while the CPU is in an exception state caused by a bus error, address error, or system reset. The system cannot reliably continue execution, and some externally generated reset is required.

Figure 13.1 illustrates the possible state transitions in a running program.

13.2 THE STATUS REGISTER AND SYSTEM STACK

Frequent references have been made to the status register and its low-order byte, the condition code register. The CCR byte holds the C, V, Z, N, and X bits. The high-order byte of the status register is used for exception processing. The full status register is now introduced, and a distinction is made between a user and a supervisor stack pointer.

Status Register

The status register is a 16-bit register whose contents reflect the state of the CPU. The LSB (the CCR) reflects the arithmetic and logical conditions resulting from CPU execution. The MSB (**system byte**) uses 5 bits that define the mode and interrupt level of the system. Figure 13.2 illustrates each field and the corresponding system condition.

Trace Mode

For run-time debugging, it is useful to interrupt program execution after each instruction (single stepping) or at specified points (breakpoints) to examine registers and data values. This post-instruction review of system data is called **tracing**. Setting bit 15 of the status register enables the trace

FIGURE 13.2   Status Register Fields

Status Register

T		S			Interrupt Level			X	N	Z	V	C
15	14	13	12	11	10–8	7	6	5	4	3	2	1	0

$\longleftarrow$————— System Byte ————— $\times$ ——————— CCR ———————$\longrightarrow$

CONDITION	STATUS REGISTER BIT(S)	BIT NUMBER(S)
Trace mode	T	15
Supervisor mode	S	13
Interrupt level	$I_2 \, I_1 \, I_0$	10–8

exception after each instruction. The topic is discussed thoroughly in Section 13.6.

Supervisor Mode

The MC68000 processor can operate in one of the two modes, supervisor mode or user mode. In **supervisor mode**, all MC68000 instructions are available, including those that modify the status register. In **user mode**, the program has access to a subset of the instructions. The instructions that are excluded, called **privileged instructions**, can alter the environment of the system (such as turning on tracing or changing the priority bits in the status register). The need for a privileged mode is obvious in a multiuser environment. The operating system must deal with peripheral devices, control tracing, oversee memory management, and so on. The operating system must run in supervisor mode. A user program, on the other hand, should have only restricted access to the system environment. It would be a serious problem if a user within a multiuser environment could turn on tracing without knowledge of the operating system. The distinction between user and supervisor modes is generally of importance only in a multiuser environment. Single-user operating systems or monitors normally run all programs in supervisor mode. Exception service routines execute in supervisor mode. Thus after an exception occurs, the full range of MC68000 instructions is available to the service routine.

Interrupt Level

An **interrupt** is a signal sent by a peripheral device to the CPU indicating that the device is in a state that requires attention. When the signal arrives, the CPU has the option of servicing the request immediately or postponing service. If two or more devices request service at the same time, the operating system must arbitrate the two requests.

The MC68000 uses the interrupt-level field in the status register to arbitrate CPU responses to interrupt requests from peripheral devices. Seven levels of interrupt (001_2–111_2) can be asserted by a device. If the interrupt-level field of the status register has value $N < 7$, the CPU will respond only to interrupts with a level greater than N. During service, the interrupt-level field is set to the level of the current interrupt, and the CPU is shielded from responding to requests unless they are at a higher level ("more significant"). Level-7 interrupts are treated differently. A level-7 interrupt will be serviced no matter what the value of the interrupt-level field. When the interrupt level has value 7, the CPU will ignore all interrupt requests of levels 1–6. In this case, the CPU is said to be running with "interrupts disabled." Chapter 14 covers the subject of peripheral-device interrupts.

Status Register Access

The high-order byte of the status register can be modified by a program only when the system is running in supervisor mode. Four privileged instructions serve this purpose. In each case, the instruction is a simple variant of a basic instruction.

INSTRUCTIONS

MOVE/ANDI
ORI/EORI
(Access SR)

Syntax MOVE.W ⟨ea⟩,SR

ANDI.W #N,SR   ORI.W #N,SR   EORI.W #N,SR

Action In each case, the source operand is applied to the 16-bit contents of the status register.

Notes

1. Each of the instructions is privileged.

2. In each case, only word operations are allowed.

3. For the "MOVE to SR" instruction, all data modes may be used for the source operand.

EXAMPLE 13.1

(a) ORI.W #$8000,SR
   Sets the trace mode (bit 15) of the SR. The remaining status bits are unaffected.

(b) ANDI.W #$7FFF,SR
   Trace mode is turned off.

(c) ANDI.W   #$F0FF,SR
Sets the interrupt level to 0.

(d) MOVE.W   #$2700,SR
Initializes the status register with tracing off, supervisor mode on, and interrupt level at 7 (interrupts disabled). The condition code bits are cleared.

An MC68000 program running in user mode or supervisor mode can read the contents of the entire status register using the "MOVE from SR" instruction presented in Chapter 5. Note that this instruction is privileged on the MC68020/30/40 processors. On these processors, you must use the instruction "MOVE.W CCR,⟨ea⟩" in user mode.

INSTRUCTION

MOVE
(Move From)

Syntax   MOVE.W   SR,⟨ea⟩

Action   The contents of the status register are moved to the destination location.

Notes

1. The operand size is a word.

2. The condition codes are not affected.

3. The destination must be in a data-alterable mode.

4. The instruction is privileged on the MC68020/30/40 processors.

EXAMPLE 13.2

To read the contents of the CCR in user mode, use one of the following nonprivileged instructions on a Motorola processor:

MOVE.W   SR,D0   (MC68000)
MOVE.W   CCR,D0   (MC68020/30/40)

Supervisor and User Stack Pointers

Chapter 7 introduced the stack pointer (SP) for subroutine calls. There are actually two stack registers. One is used when the processor is in supervisor mode (**supervisor stack pointer**), and one is used when the processor is in user mode (**user stack pointer**). Although they share a common register name (A7 or SP), each stack register references a distinct stack. When running in supervisor mode, SP is the supervisor stack pointer and is used for all instructions involving the stack. In supervisor mode, the user stack

FIGURE 13.3 Supervisor Mode/User Mode Stacks

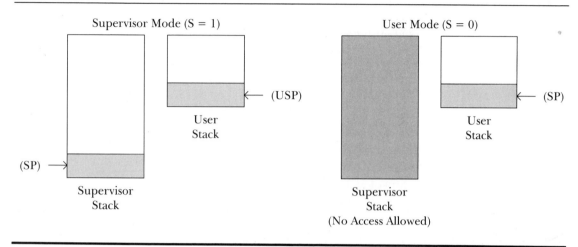

pointer is accessed under the mnemonic USP and can be accessed only by two privileged instructions. In supervisor mode, USP is not a general-purpose address register. In user mode, SP is the user stack pointer, and no access to the supervisor stack pointer is permitted. Figure 13.3 illustrates the two stacks and their access permissions.

Whenever an exception occurs, the CPU enters supervisor mode with the PC and SR saved on the supervisor stack. The corresponding exception service routine executes in supervisor mode while the user program is suspended. Because there are two stack pointers, data for both the service routine and the user program may be kept separate on the two stacks. At times, the service routine may need to access the user stack for data. Two MC68000 instructions are available for accessing the user stack while in supervisor mode.

INSTRUCTION

MOVE
(Move USP)

Syntax   MOVE.L   USP,An
MOVE.L   An,USP

Action   The contents of the user stack pointer are transferred to or from the specified address register A*n*.

Notes

1. Both instructions are privileged.

2. A full 32 bits are transferred.

EXAMPLE 13.3

(a) Assume that $S = 1$ (supervisor mode)

The user stack pointer is initialized to $6000 by using an intermediate move to the address register A0.

```
LEA      $6000,A0
MOVE.L   A0,USP
```

The supervisor stack pointer is initialized to $8000.

```
LEA   $8000,SP
```

(b) Assume that $S = 0$ (user mode). A MOVEM instruction saves all data registers and address registers A0–A6 on the user stack.

```
MOVEM.L   D0–D7/A0–A6, − (SP)
```

Assume that $S = 1$ (supervisor mode). The following code saves all data registers, address registers A0–A6, and the user stack pointer on the system stack:

```
MOVEM.L   D0–D7/A0–A6, − (SP)
MOVE.L    USP,A0
MOVE.L    A0, − (SP)
```

(c) ADDA.L   D0,USP

This is an invalid instruction because USP is not a general-purpose address register; it is an internal register that can be accessed only with the two user-stack instructions.

13.3 | THE EXCEPTION-PROCESSING CYCLE

This section discusses the actions taken by the MC68000 processor while servicing an exception. A common set of activities occurs for each exception. For some exceptions, additional details must be added, and these are provided in subsequent sections as the individual exceptions are defined.

Action 1: Identifying the Exception

An exception is initiated by an internal CPU event (such as a divide by zero) or by an external signal on the control bus. In the case of an **external exception**, the signal lines identify the specific exception for the CPU. **Internal exceptions** are identified by the CPU itself.

Action 2: Saving the Current Status Register

Key information for the currently running process must be saved so that program execution can continue upon return from the exception service routine. Initially, a copy of the SR is saved in an internal CPU register.

Action 3: Initializing the Status Register

In the status register, the S bit is set (supervisor mode on) and the T bit is cleared (trace mode off). **Trace** is one of the exceptions and causes a break after each instruction of a program. You do not want to trace the exception service routine. The S bit is set to 1 to ensure that exceptions are executed in supervisor mode. Thus the entire MC68000 instruction set is available to the service routine. When a peripheral-device interrupt is generated, the interrupt-level bits are set to the level of the interrupt so that the service routine is protected from an interrupt of lower or equal priority.

Action 4: Determining the Vector Number

An operating system is responsible for specifying the starting address of the exception service routines. Uniformity across MC68000 systems is provided by allocating the first 1K of memory for a table, called the **exception vector table**. Each type of execution is assigned a unique position in the table. The 255 entries in the table are loaded by the operating system during its startup routine. A table entry is called an **exception vector**. A vector has a fixed address in the table and contains the 32-bit starting address of the corresponding service routine. The first exception vector, numbered 0, is special, occupying two long words of memory. The next vector is numbered 2 and begins at address $000008. Subsequent vectors are numbered 3–255. Once the CPU identifies the exception, it also identifies the **exception vector number**. The address of the exception vector is obtained by multiplying the exception vector number by 4.

Action 5: Saving the Return Address and Status Register

After identifying the exception vector, the system is ready to execute the service routine. Key information from the running program is stored on the stack. The PC is pushed on the supervisor stack, and then the original value of the SR (stored in an internal register) is pushed on the stack.

Action 6: Loading the Service Routine Starting Address

In action 4, the CPU identifies the address of the exception vector containing the starting address of the exception service routine. This starting address is placed in the PC, and execution of the service routine begins.

The exception service routines are system dependent. Each monitor or operating system contains a series of routines to service the individual exceptions. In some cases, you may choose to create your own service routines for a particular application. In this case, you are responsible for placing the new starting address of the service routine in the exception vector table entry at the address identified by the exception vector number.

After completing the service routine, program control normally returns to the user program. The saved status register and program counter are restored by popping them from the supervisor stack. The MC68000 processor provides an instruction to do this.

INSTRUCTION

RTE
(Return From
Exception)

Syntax   RTE

Action   The status register and program counter are popped from the supervisor stack. The previous status register and program counter are lost. All bits of the status register are affected.

Notes

1. The RTE instruction reverses the effect of action 5. If the service routine has not modified the PC or SR on the stack, the original values are restored, permitting the suspended process to continue with the same status as when the exception occurred.

2. The instruction is privileged.

3. RTE restores only SR/PC. It is the programmer's responsibility to save and restore any of the registers D0–D7/A0–A6 that are modified by the exception service routine.

Summary of the Exception-Processing Cycle

1. The specific exception is identified by the CPU.

2. The present contents of the SR are saved in an internal system register.

3. The T bit is cleared, and the S bit is set to 1. For an interrupt, the interrupt level bits are set to the level of the interrupt.

Status Register

0		1			Interrupt Level		CCR Bits (Unchanged)					
15	14	13	12	11	10–8	7	6	5	4	3	2	1	0

4. The CPU has identified the exception vector number. This is used to compute the corresponding address of the exception vector containing the starting address of the service routine. Because each exception vector table entry (excluding the RESET exception) is a 32-bit address, its location in the table is computed by multiplying the exception vector number by 4. The actual calculation is carried out by adding two trailing 0's to the vector number and filling the high-order bits with 0 to form a long-word address. For instance,

Exception
Number *Table Location*
$6 = \%00000110$ $6 * 4 = 24$ $= \%0000 \ldots 011000 = \$000018$
$64 = \%01000000$ $64 * 4 = 256 = \%0000 \ldots 0100000000$
$= \$000100$

5. Push the PC and the original SR onto the stack. The address and bus error exceptions push additional information onto the stack.

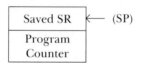

6. Load the contents of the exception vector in the PC, and begin execution of the service routine.

7. Upon completion of the service routine, the RTE instruction restores the PC and SR from the stack.

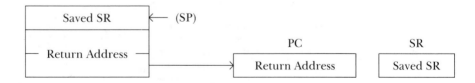

EXAMPLE 13.4

Assume that the following code is executing in user mode with tracing on. After executing the MOVE.W instruction, the trace exception occurs. The contents of the supervisor stack are identified during exception processing (see Figure 13.4).

FIGURE 13.4 Exception-Processing Cycle

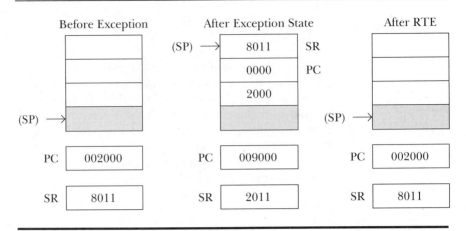

$001FFC   MOVE.W   D0,(16,A0)
$002000   ADD.W   D2,D3

Assume the following:

1. The starting address of the trace service routine is $9000.

2. The internally stored SR has value $8011.

All MC68000 systems share common exception vector numbers and locations in the exception vector table. Table 13.1 shows the memory map for the exception vector table. This table is used throughout this chapter. It is possible for the entire table to be stored in ROM if neither the monitor nor a user program will alter a vector entry. Otherwise, except for an 8-byte entry for the reset vector, the table entries must be initialized by the monitor.

TABLE 13.1 Exception Vector Table

VECTOR NUMBER DECIMAL	ADDRESS HEX	ASSIGNMENT
0	0000	Reset: initial supervisor stack pointer (SSP)
	0004	Reset: initial program counter (PC)
2	0008	Bus error
3	000C	Address error
4	0010	Illegal instruction
5	0014	Zero divide
6	0018	CHK, CHK2 instruction
7	001C	TRAPV, cpTRAPcc, TRAPcc instruction
8	0020	Privilege violation

TABLE 13.1 Continued

VECTOR NUMBER DECIMAL	ADDRESS HEX	ASSIGNMENT
9	0024	Trace
10	0028	A-Line exception
11	002C	F-Line exception
12*	0030	Not assigned, but reserved by Motorola
13 +	0034	Coprocessor protocol violation
14 +	0038	Format error
15	003C	Initialized interrupt vector
	0040	
	·	
16–23*	·	Not assigned, but reserved by Motorola
	·	
	005F	
24	0060	Spurious interrupt
25	0064	Level 1 interrupt autovector
26	0068	Level 2 interrupt autovector
27	006C	Level 3 interrupt autovector
28	0070	Level 4 interrupt autovector
29	0074	Level 5 interrupt autovector
30	0078	Level 6 interrupt autovector
31	007C	Level 7 interrupt autovector
	0080	
	·	
32–47	·	TRAP instruction vectors
	·	
	00BF	
48 +	00C0	FPCP branch or set on unordered condition
49 +	00C4	FPCP inexact result
50 +	00C8	FPCP divide by zero
51 +	00CC	FPCP underflow
52 +	00D0	FPCP operand error
53 +	00D4	FPCP overflow
54 +	00D8	FPCP signaling NAN
55 +	00DC	Not assigned, but reserved by Motorola
56 +	00E0	PMMU configuration
57 +	00E4	PMMU illegal configuration
58 +	00E8	PMMU access level violation
	·	
59–63*	·	Not assigned, but reserved by Motorola
	·	
	·	
64–255	·	User interrupt vectors
	·	
	03FF	

* No peripheral devices should be assigned these numbers.
+ MC68020/20/40 exceptions.
TRAP #N uses vector number 32 + N.

Programming an Exception Service Routine

A program illustrates the initialization of the exception vector table and the writing of a service routine. The TRAPV instruction is used as an example. It generates an exception whenever $V = 1$. The exception vector number for TRAPV is 7, so the address of the exception vector is $7 * 4 = 28_{10} = \$1C$. The program "plants" the address of the TRAPV service routine in the long word at address $\$00001C$. The service routine prints a message indicating that arithmetic overflow has occurred and returns back to the monitor. The test phase of the program causes an overflow using a DIVS instruction. The operation "DIVS D1,D0" results in overflow for the following data, because the quotient $\$2C87BB$ exceeds 16 bits.

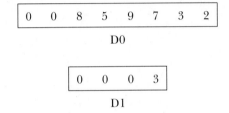

0	0	8	5	9	7	3	2

D0

0	0	0	3

D1

PROGRAM 13.1

Illustrating an
Exception Service
Routine

A 32-bit dividend is input using GETHEXIN__LONG. A 16-bit divisor is stored in D1 using GETHEXIN. If a zero divisor is entered, the program terminates. If the "DIVS D1,D0" instruction causes an overflow condition, the TRAPV instruction generates an exception (see Section 13.5). While reading the program, note the use of defined constants for exception vector addresses and the use of absolute short addressing when initializing exception vectors. Because the vectors lie in the low 1K of memory, this mode saves 2 bytes of storage in each instruction.

```
vtrapv:    equ       $1c      ; trap on overflow exception vector addr

null:      equ       0
startsp:   equ       $8000

           xref      initPort, stop
           xref      putstring,puthexout,putnewline
           xref      gethexin, gethexin_long

start:     movea.l   #startsp,sp           ; init supervisor stack
           move.l    #ovrflerr,vtrapv.w    ; init exception vector

; initialize console port
           moveq     #0,d7
           jsr       initPort
```

```
; main body of program
loop:       jsr       gethexin
            tst.w     d0
            beq.s     exit
            move.w    d0,d1
            jsr       gethexin_long
            divs      d1,d0
            trapv
            jsr       puthexout          ; print quotient
            swap      d0
            jsr       puthexout          ; print remainder
            jsr       putnewline
            bra.s     loop
exit:       jsr       stop

; exception service routine for trap on overflow
ovrflerr:   lea       ovrflmsg,a0
            jsr       putstring
            jsr       stop


            data
ovrflmsg:   dc.b      'overflow ',null
            end
```

⟨Run of Program 13.1⟩

```
67      3456
0082    0008
55      12345
036D    0014
0
```


⟨Run⟩

```
3       00859732
overflow
```

13.4 SYSTEM INITIALIZATION

An executive program was defined as a monitor or operating system. Each type uses similar code for initialization. A monitor is a simpler program, and this section presents its initialization. When a monitor begins, certain critical software actions must be performed. These include allocating a region of memory for the supervisor stack, initializing the peripheral-device interfaces and the exception vector table. These routines are part of the

FIGURE 13.5 Monitor Memory Map

0000	Reset Vector
0008	Remainder of Vector Table
0400	Monitor Read-Write Data
	Monitor Stack Area
0900	User Code
008000	Monitor Code (Read-Only)
010000	Peripheral Devices

monitor's initial code segment. The full monitor code is usually located in an EPROM to prevent accidental modification by a user program. Figure 13.5 depicts the memory map for the ECB. It is typical of most systems.

System Initialization: Hardware

An MC68000 system is started by activating the **reset input control line**. External circuitry supplies this signal. It causes the reset exception and sets in motion a sequence of events that cause the monitor to "boot up."

1. The status register is set to supervisor mode with tracing off. The interrupt level bits of the status register are set to 111 (7 = interrupts disabled). The CPU is thus immune to all peripheral-device interrupt requests except those asserting a level-7 interrupt.

2. The supervisor SP is loaded with the contents of the long word at address $000000 (the first half of the reset vector).

3. The PC is loaded with the contents of the long word at address $000004 (the second half of the reset vector).

4. Instruction execution is started at the address in the PC.

EXAMPLE 13.5

The following are events in the reset exception cycle. Assume that the contents of the reset exception vector are as follows:

0000 0500	0000 8146
000000	000004

(a) $S = 1$ Initialize the SR with \$2700.
$T = 0$
$I_2 I_1 I = 111$

(b) (SP) = 000500   Initialize the SP with the long-word contents of address \$000000.

(c) (PC) = 008146   Initialize the PC with the long-word contents of address \$000004.

(d) Execute the monitor's initialization routine at the starting address in the PC.

The reset exception is intended to restart the system. Because this restart must occur whenever an external event asserts the reset input line, the 8-byte reset vector is saved in ROM. This is done by hardware that translates addresses 000000–000007 into the first 8 bytes of the ROM, which contains code for the monitor. In most systems, the remaining portion of the exception vector table (from addresses 000008 to 0003FF) is held in RAM and initialized under program control.

When the **reset output control line** is asserted, peripheral devices on the system initialize their internal circuitry. For instance, a timer will go to the halt state; an ACIA (capable of changing baud rates) will return to its default rate. An MC68000 privileged instruction, RESET, will cause the reset signal to be asserted without causing the reset exception.

INSTRUCTION

RESET
(Software Reset)

Syntax RESET

Action The reset signal line is asserted, causing all external devices to return to their default states. The processor status register is unaffected, and execution resumes with the next instruction.

Note The instruction is privileged.

System Initialization: Software

When reset exception processing is completed, the monitor begins a system software initialization routine. Code to initialize the supervisor and user stack pointers, as well as peripheral devices (such as a timer, ACIA and PIA), has been introduced. We now present the structure of code used by a monitor to initialize the exception vector table.

A monitor contains exception service routines whose starting addresses are loaded into the exception vector table at memory locations $000008–$0003FF. A monitor must be able to handle any exception occurring on the system. Typically, the monitor will service such key exceptions as the bus or address errors and divide by zero with specific service routines. The other exceptions are handled with a generic service routine. The following code initializes the exception vector table at startup. Assume that the five exceptions listed in Table 13.2 have distinct service routines, whereas the others are serviced by a generic exception service routine XHANDLE.

Monitor Initialization   Assume that the system reset exception places the PC at address INIT.

```
startsp:        equ    10000  ; initial sp value

; exception vector addresses
vbuserr:        equ    $08    ; user-generated bus error
vaddrerr:       equ    $0c    ; user-generated address error
villeginst:     equ    $10    ; user-generated illegal instruction
vzerodiv:       equ    $14    ; following three exceptions mapped
                              ; to a generic exception service routine
vchk:           equ    $18
vtrapv:         equ    $1c
vprivinst:      equ    $20    ; user-generated privilege violation
vtrace:         equ    $24    ; for single stepping

xhandlebase:    equ    $28    ; complete table with
                              ; generic exception survive routine

endvectors:     equ    $3FC   ; vector range $000000-$0003FF
```

TABLE 13.2   Monitor Exception Handling

EXCEPTION	VECTOR ADDRESS
Bus error	000008
Address error	00000C
Illegal instruction	000010
Privilege violation	000020
Trace	000024

```
        xref      puthexout, putstring, putnewline

; store exception vectors in the vector table

init:   lea       startsp, sp
        move.l    #buserr, vbuserr.w          ; exc #2 (Bus Error)
        move.l    #addrerr, vaddrerr.w        ; exc #3 (Address Error)
        move.l    #illinstruct, villeginst.w  ; exc #4 (Illegal
                                              ;          Instruction)
        move.l    #xhandle, vzerodiv.w        ; exc #5 (Divide by Zero)
        move.l    #xhandle, vchk.w            ; exc #6 (CHK exception)
        move.l    #xhandle, vtrapv.w          ; exc #7 (Trap on Overflow)
        move.l    #priviol, vprivinst.w       ; exc #8 (Privilege
                                              ;          Violation)
        move.l    #trace, vtrace.w            ; exception #9 (Trace)
        lea       xhandlebase, a0             ; load rest of table
                                              ; address of routine xhandle
tabinit:
        move.l    #xhandle, (a0)+
        cmpa.l    #endvectors, a0
        bls.s     tabinit

main:
        . . .                                 ; main command processing
        . . .
        bra       main                        ; read next command
; exception service routines
buserr:                                       ; bus error routine
        . . .

addrerr:                                      ; address error routine
        . . .

illinstruct:                                  ; illegal instr routine
        . . .

priviol:                                      ; privilege viol routine
        . . .

trace                                         ; trace exception routine
        . . .


xpcaddr: equ  2
xsize:   equ  6

xhandle:
        move.l    (xpcaddr, sp), d0           ; load pc from stack into d0
        moveq     #0, d7                      ; generic exception handler
        lea       exceptmsg, a0               ; print error msg
        jsr       putstring
        jsr       puthexout                   ; print pc in hex
        jsr       putnewline
        addq.w    #xsize, sp                  ; flush the stack
        bra       main                        ; continue processing

exceptionmsg:
        dc.b      'unexpected exception at ', 0
        end
```

|13.5| PROGRAM TRAP EXCEPTIONS

A class of exceptions is caused by an instruction executing in either user or supervisor mode. These internal exceptions are called **program traps** and are generated by specific MC68000 instructions. They cause entry to the operating system for execution of the service routines. Other than the divide-by-zero exception, specific MC68000 instructions are required to generate this class of exceptions. Each instruction is introduced with its corresponding exception. Table 13.3 lists theses program traps.

The TRAP Exception

The TRAP exception is used to make a system call from a user program. The TRAP instruction is used to request that the operating system perform a task. The user program is suspended until the task is performed and then continues normal execution when the operating system returns from the exception.

The TRAP instruction has one operand in immediate mode. The operand is the trap number in the range 0–15. Each trap number generates a unique exception vector number in the range 32–47. The corresponding exception vectors lie in the address range $000080–$0000BF of the exception vector table.

INSTRUCTION

TRAP

Syntax   TRAP   #N $0 \leq N \leq 15$

Action   The processor initiates exception processing. The corresponding trap vector number is generated from the #N parameter.

$$\text{Trap vector number} = 32 + N$$

The TRAP exception follows the usual stages in the exception-processing cycle. The address of the next instruction and the status register of the currently running program are placed on the supervisor stack. The actions of the trap service routines are system dependent and are specified by the operating system.

Programming TRAP Service Routines

Two programs are given to illustrate the use and programming of system TRAP calls. Each program assumes that the TRAP service routine is contained in an executive program.

A small executive program demonstrates the use of system TRAP calls. The executive starts with a stack pointer at $8000 and launches a user

TABLE 13.3 Program Trap Exceptions

EXCEPTION	INSTRUCTION	VECTOR ADDRESS	TYPICAL SERVICE ROUTINE ACTION
Trap	TRAP #N	$80–$BC	Call monitor or operating system.
Unimplemented instruction	DC.W $Axxx DC.W$Fxxx	$28 or $2C	Emulate an instruction using software. Call monitor or operating system.
Divide by 0	DIVS/DIVU	$14	Fatal error; abort program.
Trap on overflow	TRAPV	$1C	Fatal error; abort program.
Range out of bounds	CHK	$18	Fatal error; abort program.

program that is located at $2000 with stack pointer at $5000. The program runs in user mode. During execution, the user program may make TRAP #0 and TRAP #1 systems calls, which are serviced by routines in the executive program. The TRAP #0 exception prints a string to the screen. The number of characters and the address of the string are passed as parameters on the stack. The TRAP #1 exception is handled by the executive program, which returns to the monitor. The program is partitioned into code blocks that are detailed in the following section.

Code Block 1: Setup for the Exception Vector Table   The executive program contains service routines for the TRAP calls. It is responsible for loading the addresses of these routines in the exception vector table. The program uses the standalone I/O library and must initialize the console.

```
MOVE.L   #TRAP0,VTRAP0.W      ; SET EXCEPTION VECTORS

MOVE.L   #TRAP1,VTRAP1.W
MOVE Q   #CONSOLE,D7          ; INITIALIZE ACIA
JSR      INITPORT
```

Code Block 2: Launch of the User Program   The stack pointer of the user program is set to $5000 by using the MOVE-to-USP instruction.

```
LEA      STARTUSP,A0
MOVE.L   A0,USP
```

The starting address of the user program ($002000) and the initial value of the SR ($0000) are stored on the stack. The user program is launched with RTE.

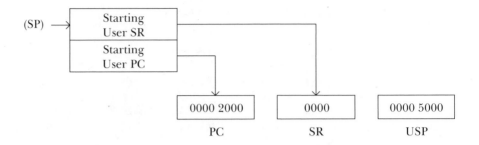

```
; START PROGRAM AT ADDRESS "USERPC" IN SUPERVISOR MODE
MOVE.L    #USERPC, – (SP)     ; PUT STARTING PC ON STACK
MOVE.W    #INITSR, – (SP)     ; PUT STARTING SR ON STACK
RTE                           ; LAUNCH USER PROGRAM
```

Code Block 3: TRAP #0 Service Routine   The TRAP #0 service routine calls the library routine PUTSTROUT. The address of the string and the number of characters are popped from the user stack and placed in registers A0 and D0, respectively. This is done by copying the user stack pointer into address register A1 using the MOVE from USP instruction. A1 is used to access the two items on the stack using postincrement mode. At this point, A1 has the value that the USP must have after the data is popped off. Using MOVE to USP then adjusts the user stack pointer.

```
MOVE.L    USP,A1
MOVE.L    (A1) + ,A0
MOVE.W    (A1) + ,D0
MOVE.L    A1,USP
```

Code Block 4: TRAP #1 Service Routine   The TRAP #1 service routine returns to the monitor. The routine implements a program EXIT. Note that if the user program executes a direct "JSR STOP", the monitor would be entered in user mode. Any privileged instructions it needed to execute would cause an exception, and any subsequent program it launched would start up in user mode. In particular, any executive program it launched would not have access to privileged instructions.

```
TRAP1:
          JSR   STOP     ; RETURN TO MONITOR
```

PROGRAM 13.2

TRAP Calls

A sample user program tests the executive program and the trap service routines. Using five TRAP #0 calls, a portion of the string "Testing!!!" is printed.

```
        MOVE.W  #NUMCHARS, - (SP)      ; PRINT STRING
        PEA     BUF
        TRAP    #0
```

The first call prints all 10 characters. On subsequent calls, the first 8, 6, 4, and 2 letters are printed. The two parameters NUMCHARS and BUF are flushed from the stack prior to a return from the TRAP service routine. An EXIT is made with TRAP#1.

```
vtrap0:   equ     $80              ; trap #0 exception address
vtrap1:   equ     $84              ; trap #1 exception address

userpc:   equ     $2000            ; load address of user program
startsp:  equ     $8000            ; initial sp value
          equ     $5000            ; initial usp value
startusp:
initsr:   equ     $0000            ; initial user status register

console:  equ     0                ; console port
straddr:  equ     10
charcnt:  equ     14

          xref    initPort,putstrout,stop

main:     lea     startsp,sp       ; initialize stack pointer

; ************ Code Block 1 ************
          move.l  #trap0,vtrap0.w  ; initialize exception vectors
          move.l  #trap1,vtrap1.w

          moveq   #console,d7      ; initialize acia
          jsr     initPort

; ************ Code Block 2 ************
; start program at address "userpc" in user mode
          lea     startusp,a0
          move.l  a0,usp
          move.l  #userpc,-(sp)
          move.w  #initsr,-(sp)
          rte
; ************ Code Block 3 ************
; output string whose address and char count was placed
; on the user stack by the calling program

trap0:
          movem.l d0/a0-a1,-(sp)
          move.l  usp,a1           ; pop the parms off user stack
          move.l  (a1)+,a0         ; string address
          move.w  (a1)+,d0         ; character count
          move.l  a1,usp           ; updata user stack pointer
          jsr     putstrout        ; print the string
          movem.l (sp)+,d0/a0-a1
          rte
```

```
; ************ Code Block 4 ************
trap1:
          jsr       stop              ; return to monitor
          end
```

⟨Run of Program 13.2⟩

The test program is assembled and loaded at address $2000. The executive program initiates execution of the test program:

```
NewLine:   equ       10

start:
           moveq     #4,d1
           moveq     #10,d0
loop:      move.w    d0,-(sp)
           pea       msg
           trap      #0                ; print (d0.w) chars of msg
           move.w    #1,-(sp)          ; write out a newline
           pea       nl
           trap      #0
           subq.w    #2,d0
           dbra      d1,loop
           trap      #1                ; exit

           data
msg:       dc.b      'Testing!!!'
nl:        dc.b      NewLine
           even
           end
```

⟨Run of Program 13.2⟩

```
Testing!!!
Testing!
Testin
Test
Te
```

Unimplemented Instruction Exception

All instructions for which bits 15–12 of the opcode word are either 1010_2 ($Axxx) or 1111_2 ($Fxxx) are recognized by the processor as **unimplemented instructions**. These instructions generate internal exceptions, referred to as **A-line** and **F-line exceptions**, respectively. These instructions enable the operating system to emulate instructions not available in the hardware and can be used by an operating system as an alternative to TRAP for making system calls. Typical applications are emulation of floating-point hardware, vector operations, and fast Fourier transform algorithms. The Macintosh operating system calls are done using A-line exceptions. Only the high-order 4 bits of the opcode word are used by the processor. The remaining 12 bits are available as parameters for the service routine.

The exception-processing cycle for the A-line and F-line exceptions follows the usual pattern, except that the PC placed on the exception stack is the address of the A-line or F-line opcode word. The service routine can use the saved PC to read the opcode word and extract the low-order 12 bits to identify the operation that is to be performed. Thus before returning from the service routine, the PC saved on the stack must be set to the address of the next valid instruction. The A-line or F-line instruction is 2 bytes long, so as long as no data was placed after the instruction, the program counter must be advanced 2 bytes. If the LINK instruction has been used as a frame pointer for the status register and program counter, then the instruction

$$\text{ADDQ.L} \quad \#2,(6,A6)$$

will cause the PC to advance to the next instruction.

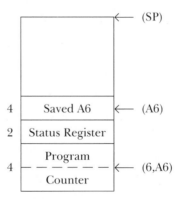

As an application, use of the A-line exception for system calls is illustrated. If you are familiar with the Macintosh operating system, you will recognize that the A-line exception is used to make ToolBox calls. The calls are of the Form $AXXX, where XXX is the number assigned to the particular system routine. Parameters are passed using the stack, and the operating system flushes the parameters from the stack before returning to the user program. On the Macintosh, the procedure *SelectWindow(W)* makes W the active window. It is called if the user presses the mouse within an inactive window. The routine takes a single parameter W, which is a pointer to a window data structure in memory.

PROCEDURE SelectWindow (theWindow: WindowPtr);

The routine is executed by an assembly language A-line TRAP call. Assume that W is a long word containing a pointer to a window structure.

```
MOVE.L   W, - (SP)      ; PLACE WINDOW POINTER ON STACK
DC.W     $A91F          ; MACINTOSH CALL TO "SELECTWINDOW"
```

The use of A-line or F-line exceptions to implement system calls is emulated with a simple example. The general concepts are emphasized. If you are interested in a particular operating system, you may want to use the example as background for understanding an actual set of system calls.

PROGRAM 13.3

The Use of A-Line Traps for System Calls

An executive program supports four different bit-handling operations that can be called from a user program. Parameters are passed on the stack, and the return value is found in (D0.L). Because the A-line exception is used, the service routine must determine the operation to be performed by looking at the low-order 12 bits, fetch any necessary parameters, and perform the operation. The return is made with the user stack flushed. Table 13.4 lists the set of available bit-handling operations and corresponding A-line opcode words.

For a user program, the Pascal statement RESULT := BITAND(X,Y) can be executed with the following assembly language code:

```
MOVE.L   Y, - (SP)          ; PUSH PARAMS ON STACK
MOVE.L   X, - (SP)
DC.W     $A000              ; MAKE THE SYSTEM CALL
MOVE.L   D0,RESULT          ; ASSIGN THE ANSWER TO RESULT
```

The executive program launches a user program at address $2000. The program is running in user mode. The executive program includes the A-line exception service routine BITOPS, which takes the parameters off the user stack, identifies the operation, and performs the necessary action. The specific bit operator is called using a jump table with index computed from the low-order 12 bits of the $AXXX opcode word. The user program exits back to the executive program by executing TRAP #1.

TABLE 13.4   Bit-Handling Operations/Opcode Word

FUNCTION	OPERATION	OPCODE WORD
BITAND(X,Y)	X AND Y	$A000
BITOR(X,Y)	X OR Y	$A001
BITXOR(X,Y)	X EOR Y	$A002
BITNOT(X)	NOT X	$A003

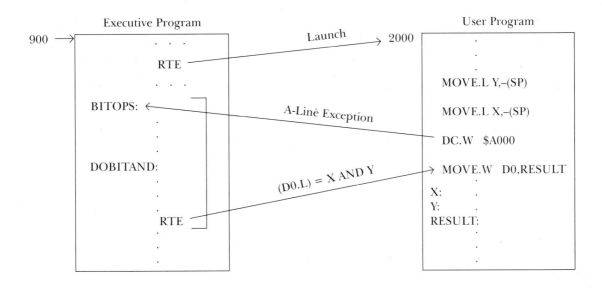

```
vAline:    equ      $28              ; A-line exception address
vTrap1:    equ      $84              ; TRAP #1 vector address
userpc:    equ      $2000            ; load address of user program
startsp:   equ      $8000            ; initial sp value
startusp:  equ      $5000            ; initial usp value
initsr:    equ      $0000            ; initial user status register

console:   equ      0                ; console port

           xref     initPort,putstrout,stop

main:      lea      startsp,sp       ; initialize stack pointer

           move.l   #bitops,vAline.w ; initialize exception vectors
           move.l   #Exit,vTrap1.w

           moveq    #console,d7       ; initialize acia
           jsr      initPort

; start program at address "userpc" inuser mode
           lea      startusp,a1
           move.l   a1,usp
           move.l   #userpc,-(sp)
           move.w   #initsr,-(sp)
           rte
; ************** A-Line Service Routine BitOps **************

alinepc:   equ      6

bitops:
           link     a6,#0
           movem.l  d1/a0-a1,-(sp)
```

```
                move.l    usp,a1                  ; get user stack pointer

                movea.l   (alinepc,a6),a0         ; get saved PC
                move.w    (a0),d1                 ; get opcode word $AXXX
                addi.l    #2,(alinepc,a6)         ; patch return address
                andi.w    #$0fff,d1               ; isolate low 12 bits

                asl.w     #2,d1                   ; (D0.W) index into case table
                lea       opsaddr,a0
                movea.l   (0,a0,d1.w),a0          ; get code address to jump to
                jmp       (a0)
opsaddr:
                dc.l      doBitAnd
                dc.l      doBitOr
                dc.l      doBitXor
                dc.l      doBitNot

doBitAnd:
                move.l    (a1)+,d0
                and.l     (a1)+,d0
                bra       xit

doBitOr:
                move.l    (a1)+,d0
                or.l      (a1)+,d0
                bra       xit

doBitXor:
                move.l    (a1)+,d0
                move.l    (a1)+,d1                ; eor requires data reg source
                eor.l     d1,d0
                bra       xit

doBitNot:
                move.l    (a1)+,d0
                not.l     d0

xit:            move.l    a1,usp                  ; flush the user stack
                movem.l   (sp)+,d1/a0-a1
                unlk      a6
                rte

Exit:           addq.w    #6,sp
                jsr       stop
                end
```

⟨Run of Program 13.3⟩

A user program is assembled and loaded at address $2000. The executive program launches a user program that uses the service routine BITOPs, to verify the equation

$$(X \text{ EOR } Y) = (X \text{ AND } \text{ NOT } Y) \text{ OR } (\text{NOT } X \text{ AND } Y)$$

is verified for the case X = $AC5533 and Y = $67CF7633.

```
BitAnd:     equ         $0000
BitOr:      equ         $0001
BitXor:     equ         $0002
BitNot:     equ         $0003
Aline:      equ         $a000

            xref        initPort, puthexout_long, putnewline


start:      moveq       #0,d7
            jsr         initPort

            move.l      x,-(sp)
            dc.w        Aline+BitNot  ;  (D0) = not x

            move.l      y,-(sp)
            move.l      d0,-(sp)
            dc.w        Aline+BitAnd  ;  (D0) = (not x and y)

            move.l      d0,d1

            move.l      y,-(sp)
            dc.w        Aline+BitNot  ;  (D0) = not y

            move.l      d0,-(sp)
            move.l      x,-(sp)
            dc.w        Aline+BitAnd  ;  (D0) = (x and not y)

            move.l      d0,-(sp)
            move.l      d1,-(sp)
            dc.w        Aline+BitOr   ;  (D0) = (not x and y) or (x and not y)


            jsr         puthexout_long
            jsr         putnewline


    ; compute x eor y by directly calling BitXor
            move.l      y,-(sp)
            move.l      x,-(sp)
            dc.w        Aline+BitXor


            jsr         puthexout_long
            jsar        putnewline


            trap        #1                      ; exit to monitor


            data
x:          dc.l        $a98C5533
y:          dc.l        $67cf7633


            end
```

The Divide-by-Zero and TRAP-on-Overflow Exceptions

Signed division (DIVS) and unsigned division (DIVU) instructions generate an exception with vector number 5 when the divisor is 0. The exception-processing cycle stores the PC of the next instruction on the stack. Typically, the service routine treats "division by 0" as a fatal error and returns program control to the monitor.

If an operation causes the V bit to be set, the program must overflow and make the necessary response. There is no automatic hardware response to signed overflow. The BVC and BVS branch instructions can be used to transfer program control to a labeled location. The MC68000 provides the TRAPV instruction to generate an exception if the V bit is set. Program control is passed to a service routine, where the operating system typically aborts the program.

INSTRUCTION

TRAPV
(Trap on
Overflow)

Syntax   TRAPV

Action   If the overflow bit V in the CCR is 1, the processor generates an internal exception with the exception vector number 7. If the overflow bit is 0, no operation is performed, and execution continues with the next instruction in sequence.

Both the divide-by-zero and trap-on-overflow exception service routines typically give an error message and abort program execution. The following code implements both trap-on-overflow and divide-by-zero service routines.

PROGRAM 13.4

Error Handler

The code initiates execution of a program at address $2000. For demonstration, the TRAPV service routine prints a message and returns control to the user program. The divide-by-zero service routine prints the PC saved on the supervisor stack and passes control to the monitor.

```
vdiv:     equ      $14                 ; divide by 0 exception addr
vtrapv:   equ      $1c                 ; trap on overflow exc addr

null:     equ      0
rtnaddr:  equ      2                   ; offset to return address
startsp:  equ      $8000

          xref     initPort,putstring,puthexout_long,putnewline,stop

start:    movea.l  #startsp,sp         ; initialize supervisor stack

          move.l   #diverr,vdiv.w      ; initialize exception vectors
          move.l   #ovrflerr,vtrapv.w
```

```
; initial acia console port
          moveq      #0,d7
          jsr        initPort

; start up a user program at address $2000 in supervisor mode
          move.l     #$2000,-(sp)
          move.w     #$2000,-(sp)
          rte

; exception service routines
diverr:   moveq      #0,d7              ; the acia is the terminal
          lea        divmsg,a0
          jsr        putstring
          move.l     (2,sp),d0          ; load return address in d0
          jsr        puthexout_long     ; print return address
          jsr        putnewline
          jsr        stop               ; return user to monitor
; rte is not done here. just abort the program


ovrflerr: moveq      #7,d1
          lea        ovrflmsg,a0
          jsr        putstring
          jsr        putnewline
          rte


          data
divmsg:   dc.b       'divide by zero: pc = ',null
overflmsg:dc.b       'overflow ',null

          end
```

⟨Run of Program 13.4⟩

The following program is assembled and loaded at address $2000. Program 13.4 initiates execution of the program and produces the following output:

```
start:    move.w     #$5000,d0
          addi.w     #$4000,d0          ; v will be set
          trapv
          divs       #0,d0              ; divide by zero
          end
<output>
overflow:
divide by zero: pc = 0000200E
```

The CHK Exception

In high-level languages, array declaration statements specify the lower and upper bounds of the indices. Assigning to array elements out of the index range likely indicates a logical error and produces aberrant program behavior by overwriting data. The MC68000 provides an instruction, CHK, explicitly designed for array index checking. The instruction is often not used in assembly language programs but is generated by some high-level language compilers to assist in debugging.

INSTRUCTION

CHK
(Check Bounds)

Syntax   CHK ⟨ea⟩,D*n*

Action   The source operand specifies a 16-bit two's complement integer called the upper bound. The low-order 16 bits of the data register is a two's complement integer representing an index. The data register is compared to the upper bound and to 0. If the register value is less than 0 or greater than the upper bound, the CHK exception is generated, with the exception vector at address $18.

> D*n* < 0   Generate the CHK exception
> D*n* > ⟨ea⟩   Generate the CHK exception
> 0 ≤ D*n* ≤ ⟨ea⟩   No action; continue with next instruction

---

Note   The source may have any data addressing mode.

EXAMPLE 13.6

Assume that (D1.W) = $0003, (D2.W) = $0040, and (D0.W) = $0031. In application, (D0.W) may represent the upper bound for an array

> A: array[0 . . 49] of ⟨data type⟩

(a) CHK   D0,D1
   No action is taken. A[3] is a valid array element.

(b) CHK   D0,D2
   Generates an exception. A[64] is not declared in the array list.

Some compilers generate code to check array bounds at run-time. It is usually possible to turn off this feature after a program has been debugged, thus eliminating the storage and execution time consumed by the checking code. A program compiled with index checking can be run under the control of a debugger that intercepts the CHK exception and generates diagnostic information.

As an example of index checking, sample code is given for a Pascal program fragment.

Algorithm   The index is computed by first decrementing I by 1 and checking to see if I is in the range 0–99. If the CHK instruction does not generate an exception, I − 1 is multiplied by 2 and used as an offset to the base address A.

Pascal Fragment	*MC68000 Code*	

VAR   A : ARRAY[1 .. 100] OF INTEGER;

     I : INTEGER:

```
BEGIN                                    MOVE.W   I,D0
    .                                    SUBI.W   #1,D0
    .                                    CHK      #99,D0
    .                                    ASL.W    #1,D0
    WHILE LOOPINFORCE DO BEGIN           LEA      A,A1
    .                                    MOVE.W   I,D1
    .                                    MULS     I,D1
    .                                    MOVE.W   D1, (0,A1,D0.W)
    A[I] := I * I;                       ADDI.W   #1,I
    I := I + 1;
    .
    .
    .

END;
```

This example represents the kind of code generated by a complier for array handling.

13.6   THE TRACE EXCEPTION

The MC68000 processor includes a facility for instruction-by-instruction tracing called **single stepping**. When the trace bit is set, a trace exception is asserted after execution of an instruction. This causes transfer to an exception service routine that prints key information. The trace exception does not occur if the instruction is illegal or privileged or if the instruction is aborted by a reset, bus error, or address error exception. Because the trace exception is not caused by external hardware, it is classified as an internal exception.

The trace vector number is 9, with an exception vector located at address $24 in the exception vector table. Because the trace exception occurs after the execution of an instruction, the PC on the stack contains the address of the next instruction. The service routine normally prints the contents of registers D0–D7/A0–A6, the supervisor stack pointer (SSP), the user stack pointer (USP), and the SR and PC. If you wish, you can use the PC to print the opcode word of the next instruction.

Most monitors provide a trace command that initiates program execution in trace mode. A simple code segment can be used for this purpose. Assume that the PC of the code to be traced is located in (D0.L) and the initial status register in (D1.W). Push the PC on the stack followed by the SR with the T bit set. The RTE instruction will pop the stack and begin program execution.

```
TRACE:   MOVE.L   D0, – (SP)     ; PUSH PC ONTO STACK
         BSET     #15,D1         ; TURN ON THE TRACE BIT
         MOVE.W   D1, – (SP)
         RTE                     ; POP THE STACK
```

If at some point you decide to terminate single stepping, you must return from the exception service routine with the T bit in the status register off. It is a common error to write the code

ANDI.W   #$7FFF,SR

in an attempt to turn off the T bit prior to RTE. However, when the RTE is executed, the original value of SR is pulled from the system stack and placed into the status register, overwriting the assignment done by ANDI. The saved status register value must be modified on the stack so that the changes will be incorporated into the SR when RTE executes.

EXAMPLE 13.7

The trace bit is on during execution of the ADD instruction. Assume that the SR has value $8011 corresponding to user mode with tracing on.

```
$002000    ADD.W   D2,D3
$002002    ⟨NEXT INSTRUCTION⟩
```

PC │ 002000 │   SR │ 8011 │

Prior to Executing ADD.W D2,D3

Assume that the address of the trace service routine is $009000. The PC on the stack is the address of the next instruction. The SR has tracing off and supervisor mode on.

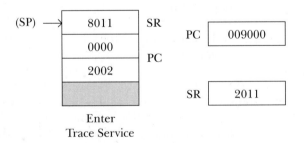

Enter
Trace Service

The service routine can turn tracing off by masking the T bit of the saved status register. Assume that SAVEDSR is the offset to the saved status register relative to A6. Tracing is turned off with a simple ANDI instruction.

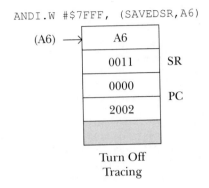

```
ANDI.W #$7FFF, (SAVEDSR,A6)
```

(A6) ⟶

A6	
0011	SR
0000	
2002	PC

Turn Off
Tracing

After returning from the trace service routine through the RTE instruction, the program executes ⟨next instruction⟩ in user mode with tracing off.

| PC | 002002 | SR | 0011 |

After Return from Service Routine

Program 13.5 is an example of simple tracing. The program initializes the trace exception vector and then turns on tracing by directly writing a 1 into the T bit of the status register.

ORI.W #$8000,SR

For demonstration, the program somewhat artificially allows the exception routine to be called three times before turning off tracing. The variable "ninstructions" is a global variable used to count instructions. A complete single-stepping program is presented in Section 13.8.

PROGRAM 13.5

Simple Tracing

```
vTrace:        equ    $24          ; trace exception vector addr
opcodeaddr:    equ    6            ; a6 offset to PC
savedsr:       equ    4            ; a6 offset to SR
startsp:       equ    $8000

        xref    initPort, puthexout, putnewline, stop

start:  movea.l  #startsp,sp        ; initialize supervisor stack
        move.l   #trace,vTrace.w    ; initialize exception vector

; initialize console port
        moveq    #0,d7
        jsr      initPort

; main body of program
        move.w   #1,ninstructions    ; instruction count
```

```
          ori.w    #$8000,sr          ; turn on tracing
          move.w   a,d0
          add.w    b,d0               ; 1st trace before add
          move.w   d0,c               ; 2nd trace before move
          jsr      stop               ; 3rd trace before jsr

; exception service routine for trace
trace:
          link     a6,#0
          movem.l  d0/a0,-(sp)
          cmpi.w   #3,ninstructions
          ble.s    printopcode
          andi.w   #$7fff,(savedsr,a6)  ; turn off T bit in saved SR
          bra.s    xitrace
; print out opcode word of next instruction
printopcode:
          movea.l  (opcodeaddr,a6),a0
          move.w   (a0),d0
          jsr      puthexout
          jsr      putnewline
          addi.w   #1,ninstructions     ; update instruction count
xitrace:
          movem.l  (sp)+,d0/a0
          unlk     A6
          rte

          data

a:        dc.w     3
b:        dc.w     5
c:        ds.w     1
ninstructions:
          ds.w     1
          end
```

⟨Run of Program 13.5⟩

```
D079
33C0
4EB9
```

|13.7| ERROR CONDITIONS CAUSING EXCEPTIONS

The MC68000 processor is designed to signal a number of errors caused by abnormal program behavior. Table 13.5 lists the errors, along with descriptions and examples.

The customary action taken when one of these errors occurs is to abort the program with a message sufficient to aid in debugging.

TABLE 13.5 Exceptions Caused by Errors

ERROR	CAUSE	EXAMPLE
Illegal instruction	Opcode word does not correspond to a valid MC68000 instruction	MOVE.W D0,D1 DC.W $4AFC
Privilege violation	Execution of privileged instruction while in user mode	ORI.W #$8000,SR (with $S = 0$)
Address error	Access a word or long word at an odd address	MOVE.W #7, (A0) (with (A0) = $00F02B)
Bus error	Improper use of the system bus	MOVE.W #$FFFE,$8000 (with only 32K of RAM)

Illegal Instruction Exception

An **illegal instruction** is an instruction whose opcode word does not correspond to a valid MC68000 instruction. If an opcode word is read and cannot be decoded to a legal instruction, the illegal instruction exception occurs.

In many cases, incorrect handling of the stack during a subroutine results in an illegal instruction violation. The program may return within data space or outside the bounds of the code space. In some cases, an invalid instruction is used to force access to a service routine. Motorola reserves three bit patterns ($4AFA, $4AFB, and $4AFC) as predefined illegal instructions on the MC68000 CPU. One of these, $4AFC, is intended for customer use. The others are reserved by Motorola for its own use.

INSTRUCTION

Illegal

Syntax ILLEGAL or DC.W $4AFC

Action The mnemonic ILLEGAL or the generation of the bit pattern $4AFC causes an illegal instruction exception.

Note All other illegal instruction bit patterns are reserved for further expansion of the instruction set.

EXAMPLE 13.8

(a) HERE: ILLEGAL   ; ILLEGAL INSTRUCTION

(b) Some assemblers do not recognize the code ILLEGAL. In such cases, the DC.W directive must be used.

     HERE: DC.W $4AFC   ; ILLEGAL INSTRUCTION

The exception-processing sequence saves the PC of the illegal instruction. The normal action of the service routine is to abort the program. However, if return from the exception is to occur, the PC on the stack must be incremented appropriately.

PROGRAM 13.6

Illegal Instruction
Test

An illegal instruction is often generated when the user inadvertently omits critical code when writing a program. A mistake in coding the simple routine STRLENGTH is used to illustrate the illegal instruction. The input register A0 contains the address of the string. It is used to step through the string, counting the nonnull characters. In the subroutine, A0 is saved on the stack and should be restored before the RTS. When this last step is skipped, an illegal instruction likely occurs.

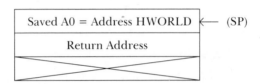

The RTS causes return to address HWORLD, which is in the data segment. The CPU is asked to execute the "instruction" at HWORLD, which is in an ASCII string. The opcode word of the instruction is $4865, the value of the letters 'He'. This opcode word does not correspond to a valid MC68000 instruction.

```
            xref      putdecount, putnewline, stop

start:      lea       hworld, a0
            jsr       strlength
            jsr       putdecout
            jsr       putnewline
            jsr       stop

strlength:
            move.l    a0, -(sp)
            moveq     #0, d0
loop:       tst.b     (a0)+
            beq.s     out
            addq.w    #1, d0
            bra.s     loop
out:        rts

            data
hworld:
            dc.b      'Hello world! ', 0
            end
```

⟨Run of Program 13.6⟩

```
ILLEGAL INSTRUCTION
PC=00001130 SR=2004=.S0..Z..  US=00005000 SS=00000782
D0=0000000C D1=00000002 D2=000320B0 D3=00005D7F
D4=00000000 D5=00000000 D6=00000006 D7=00000000
A0=0000113D A1=00008348 A2=00000414 A3=00010041
A4=00000782 A5=00000540 A6=00000547 A7=00000782
-------------------001130    4865                    DC.W    $4865
```

Privilege Violation Exception

If code running in user mode attempts to execute a privileged instruction, an internal **privilege violation exception** is generated. The PC saved on the stack is the address of the opcode word of the offending instruction. The following program deliberately generates and handles a privilege violation by quietly returning to the monitor:

```
vpriviolation:    equ    $20
progcounter:      equ    2
monitor:          equ    $8146

        xref      puthexout, putnewline, stop

move.l #priviolation,vpriviolation.w
        andi.w    #$dfff,sr                ; enter user mode
        ori.w     #$2000,sr                ; privilege violation

priviolation:
        move.l    (progcounter,sp),A0      ; get pc of priv instruction
        move.w    (A0),D0
        moveq     #0,D7                    ; set console acia
        jsr       puthexout                ; print opcode word
        jsr       putnewline
        jsr       stop
```

Address Error Exception

An **address error exception** occurs when the processor attempts to access a word or a long word at an odd address. This internal exception is recognized by the processor during instruction execution and causes an extended exception-processing cycle. Additional information is stored on the stack to identify the status of the instruction at the time of the address error. The revised cycle has the following steps:

1. A status information word is pushed on the stack. This word provides specific information about the access taking place at the time of the address error. The low-order 5 bits of the word are used.

15	14	13	12	11	10	9	8	7	6	5	4	3	2	1	0

Unused	R/W	I/N	Function Code

Status Information Word

(a) R/W access (read = 1/write = 0): Indicates whether the processor was doing a read or write access when the address error occurred.

(b) I/N instruction status (instruction = 0/not instruction = 1): Specifies whether the CPU was processing an instruction or involved in exception processing when the error occurred.

(c) Function code: Three **function code** output control lines classify the type of reference during execution. These allow a memory management unit to perform address translation and control access to instructions and data. The function codes also allow differentiation of certain processor states (such as a peripheral-device interrupt acknowledge). The 3-bit field, listed in Table 13.6, classifies the eight function codes.

The function code lines provide some clues to reconstructing the status of the instruction at the point where the error occurred. For example, if the PC is set to an odd address and the processor is in supervisor mode, then an address error occurs during the attempted read of the opcode word. In this case, the function code bits are set to 110. If the error occurs during a data operand read or write, the bits are 101. Similar actions take place while in user mode.

2. The address being accessed when the error occurred is pushed on the stack.

3. The CPUs internal copy of the instruction opcode word is pushed on the stack.

TABLE 13.6 Function Code Output Lines

FUNCTION CODE OUTPUT			
FC2	FCI	FC0	REFERENCE CLASS
0	0	0	Unassigned
0	0	1	User data
0	1	0	User program
0	1	1	Unassigned
1	0	0	Unassigned
1	0	1	Supervisor data
1	1	0	Supervisor program
1	1	1	Interrupt acknowledge

4. The status register is pushed on the stack.

5. The program counter is pushed on the stack. Because of instruction prefetch (see Section 15.1), the resulting value of the program counter will occupy some address between the opcode word and the next instruction. The PC on the stack may be advanced anywhere from 2 to 10 bytes beyond the start of the instruction.

In summary, when an address error occurs, seven words are pushed on the supervisor stack. Figure 13.6 illustrates the contents on the supervisor stack at the start of the exception service routine.

EXAMPLE 13.9

	Address		Instruction
(a)	00090E	LEA	$1005,A0
	000914	MOVE.W	(2,A0),$7000
(b)	00090E	LEA	$1001,A0
	000914	JMP	(A0)

In each case, the address error occurs during execution of the instruction at address $000914. The contents of the stack are as follows:

	PC	SR	Opcode Word	Address	Status
(a)	0916	2000	33E8	1007	0015
(b)	0916	2000	4ED0	1001	0016

In case (a), the PC is left midway into the instruction, the offending effective address is $1007, and the function code bits indicate a supervisor data reference. In case (b), the offending address is $1001, and the function code bits indicate a bad supervisor program reference.

An address error service routine typically treats the problem as a fatal error, printing some diagnostic information from the stack, and then returns to the executive. The following sample program deliberately generates an address error using case (a) from Example 13.9. The case (b) error is listed in the code but commented out. The service routine prints the PC of the offending instruction by fetching the saved PC and scanning backward through memory from that address until the contents of memory match the opcode word saved on the stack. The service routine prints this value of the PC and the other items from the supervisor stack.

FIGURE 13.6   Supervisor Stack during Address Error

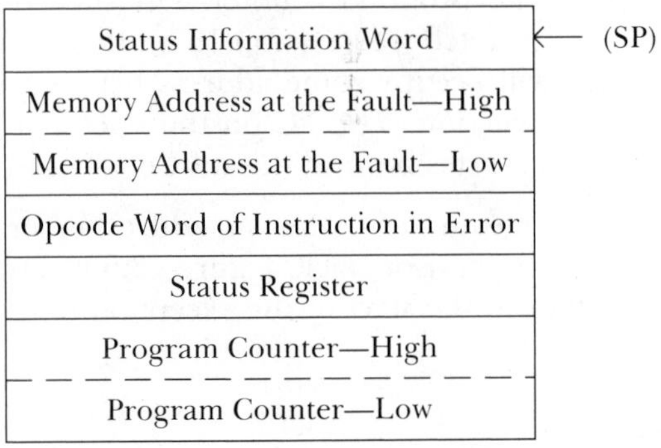

Status Information Word	← (SP)
Memory Address at the Fault—High	
Memory Address at the Fault—Low	
Opcode Word of Instruction in Error	
Status Register	
Program Counter—High	
Program Counter—Low	

PROGRAM 13.7

Address Error Test

```
consoleport:     equ    0
endofline:       equ    $0a
null:            equ    $00
vadderr:         equ    $0c

        xref     initPort, puthexout, puthexout_long
        xref     putnewline, putstring, stop

; initialize registers and console port
start:  lea      $8000,sp
        move.l   #addrerror,vadderr.w
        moveq    #consoleport,d7
        jsr      initPort

; test program
        lea      $1005,a0
        move.w   (2,a0),$7000        ; addr error - data ref
;       lea      $1001,a0
;       jmp      (a0)                 ; addr error - program ref

; address error service routine
progcounter:     equ    10
statusreg:       equ    8
opcodeword:      equ    6
faultaddr:       equ    2
statusword:      equ    0
asize:           equ    14

addrerror:
        moveq    #consoleport,d7
        lea      adderrmsg,a0
        jsr      putstring
        move.w   (opcodeword,sp),d2
```

```
            movea.l  (progcounter,sp),a0   ; get value of pc saved on the
;                                          ; stack and search for the
;                                          ; opcode word in memory
again:  cmp.w    -(a0),d2
        bne.s    again
        move.l   a0,d0                     ; print pc at instruction start
        jsr      puthexout_long
        bsr      spaces
        move.w   (statusreg,sp),d0         ; print sr
        jsr      puthexout
        bsr      spaces
        move.w   (opcodeword,sp),d0        ; print opcode word
        jsr      puthexout
        bsr      spaces
        move.l   (faultaddr,sp),d0         ; print address accessed when
;                                          ; the fault occurred
        jsr      puthexout_long
        bsr      spaces
        move.w   (statusword,sp),d0        ; print status word
        andi.w   #$1f,d0                   ; mask off all unused bits
        jsr      puthexout
        jsr      putnewline
        adda.w   #asize,sp
        jsr      stop

spaces: move.l   a0,-(sp)
        lea      blanks,a0
        jsr      putstring
        movea.l  (sp)+,a0
        rts

        data
adderrmsg:
        dc.b     'Address Error:',endofline
        dc.b     '    PC        SR      Opcode Word '
        dc.b     'Bad Addr     Status Word',endofline,null
blanks: dc.b     '        ',null

        end
```

⟨Run of Program 13.7⟩

```
Address Error:
   PC            SR          Opcode Word      Bad Addr      Status Word
  0000091C      2704          33E8           00001007         0015
```

Bus Error Exception

A **bus error exception** occurs when external logic asserts the processor's BERR control line. The typical cause of a bus error is placing an invalid address on the address bus. Assume that a system has 32K of RAM in the range 0—$7FFF and peripheral devices and ROM addresses greater than $10000. The instruction

MOVE.B   #1,(A0)   with (A0) = $0008555

will produce a bus error. The bus error exception-processing cycle parallels that of the address error with the opcode, address, and status information word pushed on the stack. In a virtual memory system using paging, a memory management unit translates logical addresses into real memory addresses. At any point, it is not necessary for all the program to have been loaded into memory. If a reference is made to a logical address whose page has not yet been loaded, a bus error occurs. The needed page must be brought from disk into memory. At this point, the instruction executing at the time of the fault must be continued. This means that all previous work of the CPU in decoding the instruction and fetching operands must have been retained in the bus error stack frame so that RTE will restore the state of the processor. Although the bus error stack frame of the MC68000 has been extended with additional information, it is insufficient to allow the CPU to continue an instruction upon the RTE. The MC68010/20/30/40 processors are capable of doing this correctly. To do so, they create a much larger stack frame when a bus error occurs. The problem of bus fault recovery with these more advanced processors is presented in Chapter 15.

If the external logic is present to create the BERR signal, the size of RAM can be determined by using the bus error exception. The idea is simple. Start at any even address following the last word of the sizing program and begin writing data into successive words of memory until a bus error occurs. If the offending address is N, then the available RAM is in the range

$$8 \leq \text{RAM SIZE} \leq N - 1$$

Note that the first 8 bytes are the reset vector and are not normally in RAM. Thus the system contains $N - 8$ bytes of RAM. The following program performs this memory-sizing function, with the program assumed to be loaded at address $900.

PROGRAM 13.8

Sizing Memory

This program starts at the word whose address follows the program and writes one word at a time until a bus error is generated. The size of the available RAM is then printed. Because the size of memory is not known, the stack is allocated within the data segment of the testing program. The memory allocated for the stack need only be large enough to accommodate a 14-byte bus error stack frame and a few subroutine calls. The end of the program is found by having a data label ENDPROG linked into the program after the main program and all the support subroutines. Its value is the address of the memory location immediately following the program.

```
vbuserror:      equ     $08
null:           equ     $00

        xref    initPort,putdecout_long,putstring,putnewline,stop

; initialize registers, exception vector, and console port
start:
        lea     buserrstack,sp   ; used for bus error processing
        move.l  #endmem,bvuserror.w
        moveq   #0,d7            ; output to console acia
        jsr     initPort
        lea     endprog,a0

; routine to test memory size and generate a bus error
size:   move.w  #7,(a0)+         ; write data into memory
        bra.s   size             ; loop until bus error

; bus error exception service routine
endmem:
        move.l  a0,d0            ; store first address past
;                                ; ram memory in a0
        lea     msg,a0
        jsr     putstring
        subq.l  #8,d0            ; delete storage for reset vector
        jsr     putdecout_long
        jsr     putnewline
        jsr     stop

        data

        xref    endprog

msg:    dc.b    'bytes of available ram: ',null
        even
        ds.b    100              ; space for small stack
buserrstack:
        end

<Module used to define ENDPROG -- linked in last>

        data
        xdef    endprog
endprog:
        end
```

⟨Run of Program 13.8⟩

```
bytes of available ram: 32760
```

A final comment about address and bus errors is necessary. If an address
or bus error occurs during exception processing for a bus error, address

error, or reset, the processor is halted. Only the external RESET signal can restart a halted processor.

13.8 | APPLICATION PROGRAMS

The material from preceding sections is enhanced by three reasonably sophisticated complete programs. Each deals with situations presented earlier but does so under more general conditions. The first discusses a technique for writing a trap handler for system calls, the second presents a single-stepping scheme, and the third demonstrates setting and handling breakpoints.

Trap Handler

Programs running under the control of an operating system make system calls by executing trap or A-line exceptions. The user places parameters on the stack or in registers prior to making the system call. The exception service routine is called a **trap handler** and is responsible for identifying the system call and invoking an operating system routine. The trap handler makes the user parameters available to the routine.

EXAMPLE 13.10

Assume the following conditions:

- A user program running under an operating system may use file operations CREATE, OPEN, READ, WRITE, and CLOSE.
- The actual file operations are performed by the operating system in the TRAP #0 service routine.
- The user program is responsible for placing parameters on the stack to be used by the operating system to identify the file operation, the file, and so forth. All parameters are long words.

In this example, file operations are identified by the following numbers: 0 (CREATE), 1 (OPEN), 2 (READ), 3 (WRITE), 4 (CLOSE). To read a file, the user program must push a sequence of parameters on the stack containing file-handling information.

PARAM #1: A file number assigned to identify the file. The file number is returned from a previous CREATE or OPEN operation on the file.

PARAM #2: The address of a buffer to store the data being read.

PARAM #3: The number of bytes to read.

PARAM #4: The file operation number 2.

Sample Case: The following user code segment reads 512 bytes of data from a file into the buffer BUF. The file has a number 3. A complete handler would include routines for WRITE and CLOSE. In this example only the labels "write" and "close" are included.

```
MOVE.L    #3,-(SP)          ; FILE NUMBER
PEA       BUF,-(SP)         ; INPUT BUFFER
MOVE.L    #512,-(SP)        ; READ 512 CHAR
MOVE.L    #2,-(SP)          ; READ OPERATION
TRAP      #0
```

PROGRAM 13.9

Trap Handler

This program is a trap handler that simulates the file operations in Example 13.10. The trap handler initializes the TRAP #0 and TRAP #1 exception vectors and includes code for the service routines.

The program initiates execution of a user program at address $2000 running in user mode. The user program loads parameters on the user stack for the READ operation. A TRAP #0 exception causes the service routine to call the subroutine READ and then return from exception.

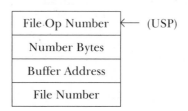

The executive program pops the parameters off the user stack by using the instructions

```
MOVE.L    USP,A1
MOVE.L    A1,USP
```

When the user program is ready to return, a jump to monitor would leave the monitor in user mode. To ensure that the command processor is running in supervisor mode, a TRAP #1 call is made.

```
vtrap0:     equ     $80               ; trap #0 exception address
vtrap1:     equ     $84               ; trap #1 exception address

startsp:    equ     $8000             ; initial sp value
startusp:   equ     $4000             ; initial usp value

null:       equ     0
console:    equ     0                 ; console port

            xref    initPort,putdecount,puthexout_long
            xref    putstring,putnewline, stop
```

```
main:       lea         startsp,sp          ; initial stacks
            lea         startusp,a0
            move.l      a0,usp

            move.l      #trap0,vtrap0,w     ; initialize exception vectors
            move.l      #trap1,vtrap1.w

            moveq       #console,d7         ; initialize acia
            jsr         initPort

; start program at address $2000 in user mode
            move.l      #$2000,-(sp)
            clr.w       -(sp)
            rte

; service routine for trap #0. only a "file read" routine
; is simulated.
trap0:
            movem.l     d0/a0-a1,-(sp)
            move.l      usp,a1             ; a1 points at user stack
            move.l      (a1)+,d0           ; get the operation number
            asl.l       #2,d0              ; 4 byte index to i/o calls
            lea         iocalls,a0
            movea.l     (0,a0,d0.l),a0     ; (a0) is addr of the routine
            jsr         (a0)               ; make the system call
            move.l      a1,usp             ; reset user stack pointer
            movem.l     (sp)+,d0/a0-a1
            rte

; routines to create and open a file are placed here
create:

open:

; read routine dumps and prints the parameters on the user stack
; a1 points at the parameters

read:       lea         bytestoread,a0     ; give the bytes to be read
            jsr         putstring
            move.l      (a1)+,d0
            jsr         putdecout
            jsr         putnewline
            lea         bufaddr,a0         ; give address of input buffer
            jsr         putstring
            move.l      (a1)+,d0
            jsr         puthexout_long
            jsr         putnewline
            lea         filenumber,a0      ; give the system file number
            jsr         putstring
            move.l      (a1)+,d0
            jsr         putdecout
            jsr         putnewline
            rts
```

```
; routines to write to a file and close a file are placed here
write:

close:

trap1:      jsr     stop               ; go to the monitor in
;                                      ; supervisor mode

            data
iocalls:
            dc.l    create, open, read, write, close
bytestoread:
            dc.b    'bytes to read: ',null
bufaddr:
            dc.b    'address of input buffer: ',null
filenumber:
            dc.b    'file number: ',null

            end
```

⟨Run of Program 13.9⟩

The following program is assembled and loaded at address $2000. Program 13.9 initiates execution of the program and produces the following output:

```
start:      move.l  #3,-(sp)           ; file number is 3
            pea     buf                ; address of input buffer
            move.l  #512,-(sp)         ; number of bytes to read
            move.l  #2,-(sp)
            trap    #0                 ; read is z
            trap    #1                 ; exit

            data
buf:        ds.b    512
            end

TUTOR 1.3 > G 900
bytes to read: 512
address of input buffer: 00002020
file number: 3
```

Single Stepping

A monitor must be able to handle single stepping a program. When the user requests this option, the monitor must turn on the T bit and begin executing the program. In the trace-service routine, the monitor must dump all the machine registers and indicate what the next instruction will be. This can be done by printing out the opcode word of the next instruction. A sophisticated monitor will disassemble the next instruction. The effect of single stepping is to enable the user to "see" the program execute.

PROGRAM 13.10

Single Stepping a
User Program

A user program previously loaded at address $3C00 is launched with a user stack pointer of $4000. The executive program traces each instruction of the user program. At the >> prompt, the trace is continued if a carriage return is typed and discontinued if any other character is typed.

The following two system calls are implemented using TRAP:

TRAP #0 causes (D0) to be printed to the terminal in hex.
TRAP #1 causes return to the monitor.

The bus error, address error, illegal instruction, and privilege violation exceptions cause an error message to be printed, and the user program is aborted.

```
; control characters
linefeed:                     equ    $0a
null:                         equ    $00

; exception vectors
vtrace:                       equ    $24
vbuserror:                    equ    $08
vaddresserror:                equ    $0c
villegalinstruction:          equ    $10
vprivilegeviolation:          equ    $20
vtrap0:                       equ    $80
vtrap1:                       equ    $84

        xref     initPort, puthexout, puthexout_long, getchar
        xref     putnewline, echoff, putstring, getstring, stop

; initialize the supervisor and user stack pointers
start:  lea      $8000,sp
        lea      $4000,a0
        move.l   a0,usp

; initialize the exception vectors
        move.l   #trace,vtrace.w
        move.l   #fatalerror, vbuserror.w
        move.l   #fatalerror,vaddresserror.w
        move.l   #fatalerror,villegalinstruction.w
        move.l   #fatalerror,vprivilegeviolation.w
        move.l   #output,vtrap0,w
        move.l   #exit,vtrap1.w

; initialize the acia
        moveq    #0,d7
        jsr      initPort
        jsr      echoff
```

```
; start the program at address 3c00
        move.l    #$3c00,-(sp)        ; starting address is 3c00
        move.w    #$8000,-(sp)        ; tracing on, user mode
;                                     ; interrupt level 0
        rte                           ; start the program
endrun:
        jsr       stop                ; return to main monitor

; bus/address error, illegal instruction, privilege violation,
; trap service routines

fatalerror:
        moveq     #0,d7
        lea       fatalmsg,a0
        jsr       putstring
        bra       endrun              ; return to monitor

; user program executing trap #1 causes trap to here
exit:
        bra       endrun              ; return to monitor

; user program executing trap #0 causes trap here for hex output
output:
        move.l    d7,-(sp)
        moveq     #0,d7
        jsr       putnewline
        jsr       puthexout_long      ; output (d0)
        jsr       putnewline
        move.l    (sp)+,d7
        rte

; primary routine - catches trace trap, displays registers, and
; handles prompt for another instruction

progcounter:    equ    6
statreg:        equ    4
tsize:          equ    10               ; subtracted from SP

trace:
        link      a6,#0
        movem.l   d0-d7/a0-a6,genregs.w
        move.l    (progcounter,a6),d0  ; get pc
        move.w    (statreg,a6),d1      ; get sr
        lea       (tsize,sp),a0        ; original value of sp
        move.l    usp,a1               ; get usp
        movem.l   d0-d1/a0-a1,regs.w   ; load pc/sr/ssp/usp to print
        moveq     #0,d7                ; output to console port
        moveq     #1,d2                ; allow four regs. per line
        moveq     #18,d3               ; 19 entries to print
        lea       regs.w,a1            ; saved regs. begin at
;                                      ; address (sp)
        lea       regmsgs.w,a2
regpl:  movea.l   a2,a0
        jsr       putstring
```

```
                move.l    (a1)+,d0
                cmpi.w    #17,d3              ; 16 bits in SR
                bne.s     long
                lea       spaces,a0
                jsr       putstring           ; pad SR field with blanks
                jsr       puthexout
                bra.s     cont
        long:   jsr       puthexout_long
        cont:   adda.l    #8,a2
                addq.w    #1,d2               ; count four regs. per line
                cmpi.w    #4,d2
                ble.s     next
                moveq     #1,d2
                jsr       putnewline
        next:   dbra      d3,regpl
                lea       opmsg,a0            ; print msg about opcode word
                jsr       putstring
                movea.l   (progcounter,a6),a0 ; get opcode word of next inst
                moveq     #0,d0
                move.w    (a0),d0
                jsr       puthexout           ; print it
                lea       prompt,a0           ; ">>" prompt
                jsr       putstring
                jsr       getchar             ; read a char from keyboard
                cmpi.b    #linefeed,d0        ; carriage return, continue
                beq.s     ret
                andi.w    #$7fff,(statreg,a6) ; turn tracing off
        ret:    jsr       putnewline
                movem.l   genregs,d0-d7/a0-a6
                unlk      a6
                rte                           ; back to user program


                data
        regs:
                ds.l      4                   ; to contain pc/sr/ssp/usp/
        ;                                     ; do-d7/a0-a6
        ;                                     ; at each trace exception.
        genregs:
                ds.l      15


        regmsgs:
                dc.b      ' pc = ',null,' sr = ',null' ssp = ',null
                dc.b      ' usp= ',null,' d0 = ',null,' d1 = ',null
                dc.b      ' d2 = ',null,' d3 = ',null,' d4 = ',null
                dc.b      ' d5 = ',null,' d6 = ',null,' d7 = ',null
                dc.b      ' a0 = ',null,' a1 = ',null,' a2 = ',null
                dc.b      ' a3 = ',null,' a4 = ',null,' a5 = ',null
                dc.b      ' a6 = ',null
        opmsg:  dc.b      linefeed,'opcode word next instruction = ',null
        prompt: dc.b      linefeed,linefeed,'>> ',null
        fatalmsg:
                dc.b      linefeed,'fatal error has occurred',linefeed,null
```

```
spaces:   dc.b      '       ',null
          end
```

⟨Run of Program 13.10⟩

The following program is assembled and loaded at address $3c00. Program 13.10 initiates execution of the program and produces the following output:

```
003c00              start:
003c00    2f3c               move.l  #5,-(sp)
          0000
          0005
003c06    7a05               moveq   #5,d5
003c08    47fa               lea     (output,pc),a3
          0006
003c0c    44fc               move.w  #$001f,ccr
          001f
003c10    203c    output:    move.l  #$55553333,d0
          5555
          3333
003c16    4e40               trap    #0
003c18    4e41               trap    #1
003c1a              end
```

```
TUTOR 1.3 > G 900
    pc = 00003C06  sr =      8000  ssp = 00008000  usp = 00003FFC
    d0 = 00300020  d1 = 00000001  d2 = 00000000  d3 = 00000000
    d4 = 00000030  d5 = 00000003  d6 = 00430000  d7 = 00000000
    a0 = 00004000  a1 = 00004000  a2 = 00010001  a3 = 00000408
    a4 = 00008902  a5 = 00000568  a6 = 00007FF6
opcode word next instruction = 7A05


>>
    pc = 00003C08  sr =      8000  ssp = 00008000  usp = 00003FFC
    d0 = 00300020  d1 = 00000001  d2 = 00000000  d3 = 00000000
    d4 = 00000030  d5 = 00000005  d6 = 00430000  d7 = 00000000
    a0 = 00004000  a1 = 00004000  a2 = 00010001  a3 = 00000408
    a4 = 00008902  a5 = 00000568  a6 = 00007FF6
opcode word next instruction = 47FA


>>
    pc = 00003C0C  sr =      8000  ssp = 00008000  usp = 00003FFC
    d0 = 00300020  d1 = 00000001  d2 = 00000000  d3 = 00000000
    d4 = 00000030  d5 = 00000005  d6 = 00430000  d7 = 00000000
    a0 = 00004000  a1 = 00004000  a2 = 00010001  a3 = 00003C10
    a4 = 00008902  a5 = 00000568  a6 = 00007FF6
opcode word next instruction = 44FC
```

```
 >>
      pc = 00003C10   sr =       801F   ssp = 00008000   usp = 00003FFC
      d0 = 00300020   d1 = 00000001   d2 = 00000000   d3 = 00000000
      d4 = 00000030   d5 = 00000005   d6 = 00430000   d7 = 00000000
      a0 = 00004000   a1 = 00004000   a2 = 00010001   a3 = 00003C10
      a4 = 00008902   a5 = 00000568   a6 = 00007FF6
 opcode word next instruction = 203C

 >>
      pc = 00003C16   sr =       8010   ssp = 00008000   usp = 00003FFC
      d0 = 55553333   d1 = 00000001   d2 = 00000000   d3 = 00000000
      d4 = 00000030   d5 = 00000005   d6 = 00430000   d7 = 00000000
      a0 = 00004000   a1 = 00004000   a2 = 00010001   a3 = 00003C10
      a4 = 00008902   a5 = 00000568   a6 = 00007FF6
 opcode word next instruction = 4E40

 >>
      pc = 00000978   sr =       2010   ssp = 00007FFA   usp = 00003FFC
      d0 = 55553333   d1 = 00000001   d2 = 00000000   d3 = 00000000
      d4 = 00000030   d5 = 00000005   d6 = 00430000   d7 = 00000000
      a0 = 00004000   a1 = 00004000   a2 = 00010001   a3 = 00003C10
      a4 = 00008902   a5 = 00000568   a6 = 00007FF0
 opcode word next instruction = 2F07
 >>

 55553333
      pc = 00000976   sr =       2010   ssp = 00007FFA   usp = 00003FFC
      d0 = 55553333   d1 = 00000001   d2 = 00000000   d3 = 00000000
      d4 = 00000030   d5 = 00000005   d6 = 00430000   d7 = 00000000
      a0 = 00004000   a1 = 00004000   a2 = 00010001   a3 = 00003C10
      a4 = 00008902   a5 = 00000568   a6 = 00007FF0
 opcode word next instruction = 60E8

 >>
```

Breakpoints

The illegal instruction exception is used to implement breakpoints. A **breakpoint** is a predetermined address at which program execution will be interrupted. A breakpoint is chosen to be a key point in the program being debugged, such as the branch point of a loop that is not functioning correctly. Key information, such as a dump of all registers, is output at the breakpoint. A monitor stores breakpoints in the **breakpoint table**. Breakpoints can be implemented by an efficient algorithm that uses illegal instructions along with tracing.

Algorithm for Initialization

1. Create a breakpoint table as an array of records.

PC at Breakpoint	Opcode Word at Breakpoint

The table can be searched sequentially if only a small number of breakpoints are to be handled. If the number of breakpoints is potentially large, entries can be loaded into the table using a hash function whose key is the program counter at which the breakpoint occurs. Unused entries in the table are identified by the impossible address $FFFFFFFF.

2. For each breakpoint, copy the PC and opcode word into the table. Replace the opcode word in the actual code by the illegal instruction $4AFC, forcing an illegal instruction exception when the code is executed.

Algorithm for the Service Routine

The breakpoint occurs: During program execution, the illegal instruction service routine will be entered to handle the breakpoint.

(a) Us the PC on the stack to see if the exception was caused by $4AFC. If not, a "real" invalid instruction has occurred, and the program should be aborted. If LINK is used in the exception service routine and PROGCOUNTER is the offset from A6 to the saved program counter, then the instruction sequence below will determine if $4AFC caused the exception.

```
MOVEA.L    (PROGCOUNTER,A6),A2
CMPI.W     #$4AFC,(A2)
```

(b) Search the breakpoint table for the current program counter. If the PC is not found in the table, the illegal instruction occurred for some other reason, so abort the program. Otherwise, a breakpoint has been found. At this point, it is customary to dump all the CPU registers and return to the monitor command loop. The user can view memory locations relevant to the current status of the program. When the user is ready to continue the program, a GO command is issued. The monitor must resume execution of the program from the breakpoint.

Algorithm for Program Resumption: The original instruction must be executed. However, it is not sufficient merely to replace the illegal instruction by the original opcode word and let the CPU execute the instruction. If this is done, no more breakpoints would occur at that location, a situation not desired if the breakpoint occurs in a loop. The original instruction must be executed, and a break in execution must occur so that the $4AFC opcode can be placed back in the code stream. A precise sequence of steps is required:

(a) Place a new trace exception vector in the vector table so that a trace exception will transfer to a new service routine.

(b) Turn on the trace bit ($T = 1$) and execute the instruction, which now contains the original opcode word. The trace exception is generated with its new service routine address in the exception vector table.

(c) The new service routine must replace the trace exception vector with the address of the original trace service routine. The current trace service routine is used only for this one instruction trace. The opcode word of the breakpoint instruction is again loaded with the illegal instruction code $4AFC, and program execution continues with tracing off.

EXAMPLE 13.11

We will use the MOVE instruction to illustrate the breakpoint service routine.

Address	Machine Code	Instruction
$002000	1390 1000	MOVE.B (A0),(0,A1,D1.W)

(a) When the breakpoint is set, the opcode word and PC are placed in the breakpoint table, and the illegal instruction is put in the code stream.

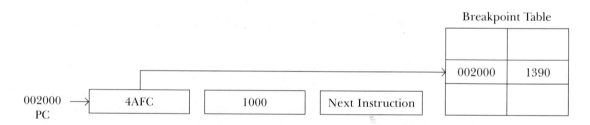

(b) Within the resumption routine, place the original opcode word back in the code at the breakpoint address, and store a new trace service routine address in the exception vector table. Program execution continues with tracing turned on.

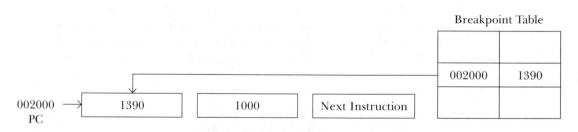

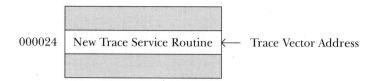

000024   New Trace Service Routine ⟵ Trace Vector Address

(c) With the T bit on, program execution falls into the new trace service routine. Continue program execution with the original trace service routine restored, the illegal instruction replacing the breakpoint opcode word, and tracing off.

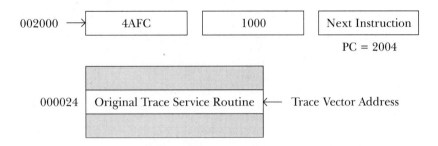

002000 ⟶   4AFC   1000   Next Instruction

PC = 2004

000024   Original Trace Service Routine ⟵ Trace Vector Address

---

PROGRAM 13.11

Breakpoints

A user program was previously loaded at address \$4000. The user is prompted for two addresses A_1 and A_2 in hex. These addresses are placed into a breakpoint table with two entries in the following format:

A_1	Opcode Word at Address A_1

A_2	Opcode Word at Address A_2

The program then replaces the original opcode words with the illegal instruction and runs the code at \$4000 in user mode with a user stack pointer of \$5000. When a breakpoint is hit, the illegal instruction exception service routine prints the value of the PC, SR, USP, D0, D1, and A0 and continues the program after a carriage return is typed. The user program can print the contents of (D0.L) by executing TRAP #14 and exits by means of TRAP #15.

```
vTrace:         equ     $024
vIllegal:       equ     $010
vTrap14:        equ     $080+4*14
vTrap15:        equ     $080+4*15
```

```
NewLine:        equ    10
Null:           equ    0

        xref    initPort,gethexin_long,getstring
        xref    putstring,puthexout, puthexout_long,putnewline, stop

start:  lea     $8000,sp                ; initialize SSP
        moveq   #0,d7                   ; initialize ACIA port #0
        jsr     initPort

        move.l  #TraceOne,vTrace.w      ; initialize vectors
        move.l  #Bkpt,vIllegal.w
        move.l  #Print,vTrap14.w
        move.l  #Exit,vTrap15.w

        lea     Prompt,a0               ; request the two addresses
        jsr     putstring
        lea     BkptTable,a1
        moveq   #1,d1
tloop:  jsr     gethexin_long           ; get instruction addr
        move.l  d0,(Breakaddress,a1)    ; put in table field 1
        movea.l d0,a0
        move.w  (a0),(OpcodeWord,a1)    ; place in table field 2
        move.w  #$4afc,(a0)             ; replace by ILLEGAL
        addq.w  #6,a1                   ; advance to next record
        dbra    d1,tloop

        pea     $4000                   ; start address of $4000
        clr.w   -(sp)                   ; user mode, CCR clear
        lea     $5000,a0                ; user stack pointer $5000
        move.l  a0,usp
        rte                             ; start the program

; Print (d0) in hex

Print:  move.l  d7,-(sp)
        moveq   #0,d7
        jsr     puthexout_long
        jsr     putnewline
        move.l  (sp)+,d7
        rte

; Exit to monitor

Exit:
        ; restore opcode words before exit
        lea     BkptTable,a1
        moveq   #1,d1
xitloop:
        movea.l (BreakAddress,a1),a0    ; grab addr of breakpoint
        move.w  (OpcodeWord,a1),(a0)    ; restore opcode word
        addq.w  #6,a1                   ; advance to next record
        dbra    d1,xitloop
        jsr     stop
```

```
ProgCounter:      equ    6
StatusReg:        equ    4

Bkpt:    link     a6,#0
         movem.l  d0-d2/a0-a2,-(sp)
         movea.l  (ProgCounter,a6)a2       ; get PC of illegal inst
         cmpi.w   #$4afc,(a2)              ; verify opcode word = $4AFC
         bne      realillegal
         moveq    #1,d2                    ; verify breakpoint address
         lea      BkptTable-6,a1
cktable:
         addq.w   #6,a1
         cmpa.l   (BreakAddress,a1),a2     ; does PC match table entry
         dbeq     d2,cktable
         bne      realillegal              ; should have found a match
         lea      FormatTable+24,a2
         movem.l  d0-d1/a0,-(a2)           ; prepare to print d0-d1/a0
         move.l   usp,a0                   ; prepare USP
         move.l   a0,-(a2)
         moveq    #0,d0                    ; prepare SR
         move.w   (StatusReg,a6),d0
         move.l   d0,-(a2)
         move.l   (BreakAddress,a1),-(a2)  ; prepare PC
         lea      RegStrings,a0            ; print label for reg
         jsr      putstring
         moveq    #5,d1                    ; print registers
print:   move.l   (a2)+,d0
         cmpi.w   #4,d1
         bne.s    long
         jsr      puthexout                ; SR is 16 bits
         bra.s    cont
long:    jsr      puthexout_long
cont:    dbra     d1,print
         jsr      putnewline
         lea      opcodemsg,a0
         jsr      putstring
         move.w   (OpcodeWord,a1),d0
         jsr      puthexout
         jsr      putnewline
         lea      wait,a0                  ; wait until [cr] typed
         jsr      getstring
         move.l   a1,ActiveTableEntry.w    ; save ptr to table entry
; place correct opocode word back in instruction stream
         movea.l  (BreakAddress,a1),a0
         move.w   (OpcodeWord,a1),(a0)
         movem.l  (sp)+,d0-d2/a0-a2
         unlk     a6
         ori.w    #$8000,(sp)              ; trace the instruction
         rte

; get here when we trace instruction at breakpoint

TraceOne:
         move.l   a1,-(sp)
```

```
                move.l    ActiveTableEntry.w,a1    ; get active table entry
                move.l    (BreakAddress,a1),a1     ; put illegal into code
                move.w    #$4afc,(a1)
                move.l    (sp)+,a1
                andi.w    #$7fff,(sp)              ; tracing off
                rte

; oops! found a real illegal instruction

realillegal:
                lea       IllegalMsg,a0
                jsr       putstring
                move.l    a2,d0                    ; print PC
                jsr       puthexout_long
                jsr       putnewline
                jsr       stop

                data

Prompt: dc.b    'Enter the two breakpoint addresses: ',Null
RegStrings:
        dc.b    '  PC    SR    SP    D0    D1    A0'
        dc.b    NewLine,Null
wait:   ds.b    2
IllegalMsg:
        dc.b    'Illegal instruction at ',Null
opcodemsg:
        dc.b    'Opcode word: ',Null
        even

BreakAddress:    equ    0                          ; PC at breakpoint
OpcodeWord:      equ    4                          ; opcode word at breakpoint

BkptTable:
        ds.b    12                                 ; room for two breakpoints
FormatTable:
        ds.l    6                                  ; holds regs. to be printed
ActiveTableEntry:
        ds.l    1                                  ; ptr to active table entry

        end
```

⟨Run of Program 13.11⟩

The following program is assembled and loaded at address $4000. Program 13.11 initiates execution of the program and produces the following output:

```
4000    7202    start:  moveq  #2,d1
4002    41F9            lea    a,a0
        0000
        0014
```

```
      4008    7000            moveq   #0,d0
      400A    D098    loop:   add.l   (a0)+,d0
      400C    4E4E            trap    #14
      400E    51C9            dbra    d1,loop
              FFFA
      4012    4E4F            trap    #15
      4014

                              data

      4014    0000    a:      dc.l    1,2,3,4,5
              0001
      4028                    end
```

```
Enter the two breakpoint addresses:  400e 4012
00000001
    PC      SR      SP        D0        D1        A0
0000400E  0000  00005000  00000001  00000002  0000401C
Opcode word: 51C9


00000003
    PC      SR      SP        D0        D1        A0
0000400E  0000  00005000  00000003  00000001  00004020
Opcode word: 51C9


00000006
    PC      SR      SP        D0        D1        A0
0000400E  0000  00005000  00000006  00000000  00004024
Opcode word: 51C9


    PC      SR      SP        D0        D1        A0
00004012  0000  00005000  00000006  0000FFFF  00004024
Opcode word: 4E4F
```

13.9 MC68020/30/40 EXCEPTION PROCESSING

Before reading this section, you may wish to reread Section 3.5 for additional details on the architecture of the MC68020/30/40 processors. Many of the details of exception processing for the MC68000 apply to the MC68020/30/40 processors. However, new features have been added. Two additional bits in the status register are used. The number of exceptions has been increased, along with the number of instructions that cause exceptions. The stack frame is extended to provide additional information for the service routines and permit recovery from bus and address errors. Each exception stack frame contains the offset of the exception vector from the base of the exception vector table, permitting generic exception handlers.

Status Registers

The status register uses 2 additional bits in the high-order byte, as shown in Figure 13.7.

1. *Trace enable bits:* Tracing is defined by bits 15 and 14. Like the MC68000 processor, the MC68020/30/40 processors permit tracing of every instruction. They also allow selective tracing for change of program flow instructions (branch, jump, and so forth). The details are given in association with Program 13.15.

2. *Supervisor mode:* The processor executes in user mode ($S = 0$) or supervisor mode ($S = 1$). All instructions can be executed in supervisor mode. Only nonprivileged instructions can be executed in user mode.

3. *Master interrupt mode:* The master interrupt bit M (bit 12) allows a multitasking operating system to maintain two separate stacks.

    (a) With $M = 1$, the CPU is in master mode and uses the master stack pointer (MSP) for all references to A7 = SP. When an exception generated by a peripheral device (peripheral-device interrupt) occurs, the processor executes the interrupt service routine using a second supervisor stack referenced by the interrupt stack pointer (ISP). The use of two supervisor stacks allows complete separation between the stack area used for interrupt processing and the stack area used for process control.

    (b) With $M = 0$, the MC68020/30/40 processors use the interrupt stack pointer for all stack accesses occurring in supervisor mode. M is set to 0 on system reset.

MSP	ISP	USP
Master Stack	Interrupt Stack	User Stack

MSP: Supervisor stack pointer for exception processing when $M = 1$ and exception is not a peripheral-device interrupt.
ISP: Supervisor stack pointer for exception processing when $M = 0$ or for interrupt service routines when $M = 1$.
USP: User stack pointer in supervisor mode.

Interrupt processing on the MC68020/30/40 processors is presented in Chapter 14. Assume that the M bit is 0 for the remainder of this chapter.

FIGURE I3.7　MC68020 Status Register

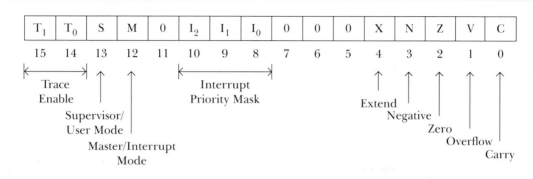

Exception-Processing Sequence

The MC68020/30/40 exception-processing sequence occurs in four distinct steps:

1. *Save and then alter the status register:* The status register is saved in an internal register. The S bit is set, placing the processor in supervisor mode. The two trace bits T1/T0 are cleared. For an interrupt exception, the interrupt mask is updated to the interrupt level.

2. *Generate the vector number of the exception:* For a peripheral device, the interrupt acknowledge cycle is performed by using CPU space bus cycles (FC2 − FC0 = 111). Chapter 15 defines and presents applications of CPU space.

3. *Save the current processor context:* An exception stack frame is created. The standard stack frame for the MC68020/30/40 processors contains an additional word not available to the MC68000 processor. The structure of exception stack frames is presented in the next subsection.

4. Execute the service routine: The location of the exception vector is computed using base-relative addressing. The base address of the exception vector table is defined by the vector base register (VBR). The vector address is computed by multiplying the vector number by 4 and adding the contents of the internal VBR. On the MC68020/30/40 systems, programmers may place the exception vector table anywhere in memory and even maintain multiple tables. With the VBR-assigned address $000000 (default on system reset), the exception vector table occupies addresses $000–$3FF, identical to the MC68000 processor.

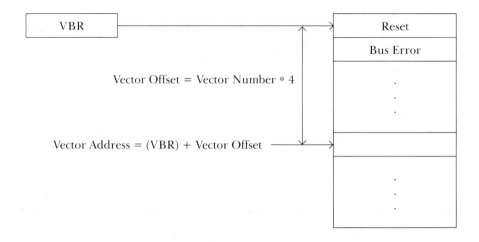

The MC68020/30/40 processors have several **control registers**, in contrast to only the status register present on the MC68000. The VBR is a member of the control register set. The MC68020/30/40 processors provide a privileged instruction, MOVEC, to access the contents of the VBR and other control registers. The use of this instruction is expanded in Chapters 14 and 15.

INSTRUCTION

MOVEC
(MC68020 "Move
Control Register")

Syntax   MOVEC Rc,Rn
            MOVEC Rn,Rc

Action   Copy the contents of the control register Rc to the data or address register Rn, or copy the contents of the data or address register to the control register.

The following control registers may be specified:

SFC—Source function code register
DFC—Destination function code register
CACR—Cache control register
CAAR—Cache address register
USP—User stack pointer
VBR—Vector base register
MSP—Master stack pointer
ISP—Interrupt stack pointer

Notes

1. Only long-word data transfer is performed, even if the specified control register is not 32 bits in size. The unused bits are ignored on a write cycle and are stored as 0 on a read cycle.

2. The MSP/ISP control registers are presented in detail in Chapter 14. The control registers SFC/DFC and CACR/CAAR are presented along with other advanced topics in Chapter 15.

3. Additional control registers are present on the MC68030/40 processors.

EXAMPLE 13.12   *(a)* The MOVEC instruction allows you to initialize the vector base register. To load the exception vector table in the address range $FFFF0000–$FFFF03FF, set the VBR as follows:

```
TBLBASE:  EQU         $FFFF0000
          .
          .
          .
          LEA         TBLBASE,A0
          MOVEC       A0,VBR
```

(b) Assignments to the table are made relative to the new base. The TRACE exception vector is initialized to TRACESERV.

```
VTRACE:   EQU         $024
          .
          .
          .
          LEA         TBLBASE,A0
          MOVE.L      #TRACESERV,(VTRACE,A0)
```

Exception Stack Frames

The MC68020/30/40 systems use one of six different stack frames, depending on the type of exception. The expanded information better enables the service routine to extract the condition that caused the exception. Figure 13.8 illustrates the basic stack format. The first three words on the stack

FIGURE 13.8   Four-Word Stack

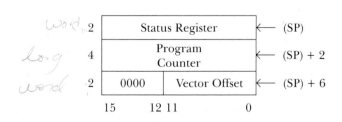

contain the status register and the program counter, exactly as found with the MC68000 processor. The fourth word of each frame contains a format number and a vector offset.

Format Type	Vector Offset

15   12 11   0

The format field specifies the type of stack frame. Valid frame types are 0, 1, 2, 9, 10, and 11. Types 10 and 11 handle bus and address error faults and are covered with those exceptions. Type 9 occurs with coprocessor instructions. Coprocessing is covered in Chapter 15. Type 1 defines throwaway stacks used with interrupts. They are covered in Chapter 14. The vector offset is the number of bytes from the beginning of the exception vector table to the vector. In cases in which two or more exceptions use the same service routine, the vector offset permits the service routine to determine which exception occurred. Such a service routine is referred to as a **generic exception handler**.

The six-word stack has format type 2, as shown in Figure 13.9. It contains the address of the instruction being processed at the time of the exception as well as the format word, the PC and the SR.

The RTE instruction is used to return from the exception. When RTE is executed, the processor determines the frame type from the format field and restores data as specified for that frame type. For instance, with the normal four-word stack having format 0, the processor loads the SR and PC from the stack, increments the SP by 8, and resumes normal execution.

FIGURE 13.9   Six-Word Stack

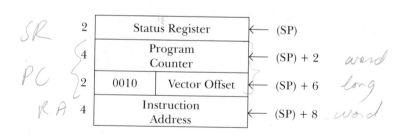

EXAMPLE 13.13

MC68020/30/40
Stack Frame
Examples

(a) The simple four-word stack has format type 0. The TRAP #N instructions use the four-word stack frame. Their vector offset begins at $80.

$002000   TRAP #2

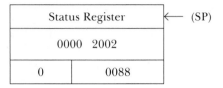

(b) The six-word stack has format type 2. It contains the address of the instruction being processed at the time of the exception as well as the format word, the PC, and the SR. The divide-by-zero exception uses the six-word stack. Its vector address is $14.

$002000   DIVS #0,D0

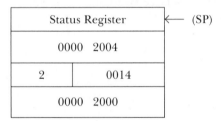

Program Trap Exceptions

This section introduces a class of exceptions generated by specific MC68020/30/40 instructions. These internal exceptions, called **program traps**, cause entry to the monitor or operating systems for execution of service routines. The exceptions are listed in Table 13.7.

Divide-by-Zero Exception

The MC68020/30/40 DIVS and DIVU instructions will generate an exception on division by zero. The exception uses a six-word stack with vector offset $14.

TRAP Exceptions

The MC68000 instructions TRAP and TRAPV can initiate exception processing. The MC68020 extends the TRAPV instruction to include the other

TABLE 13.7 Program Trap Exceptions

EXCEPTION	MC68020 INSTRUCTION	VECTOR OFFSET
Divide by zero	DIVS, DIVU	$14
Trap	TRAP #N	$80–$BC
	TRAPcc, TRAPV	$1C
	cpTRAPcc	$1C
Line emulator trap	DC.W $Axxx	$28
	DC.W $Fxxx	$2C
Range check	CHK, CHK2	$18

condition codes and coprocessor operations. These new trap exceptions are used to detect run-time errors. The new TRAPcc instructions are introduced in this section. The cpTRAPcc instructions deal with a coprocessor. The TRAP instruction is a carryover from the MC68000 machine. It allows a parameter in the range 0–15. The exceptions use a four-word stack frame with vector offset in the range $80–$BC.

INSTRUCTION

TRAPV/TRAPcc
(MC68020/30/40
TRAP on
Condition)

Syntax   TRAPV
TRAPcc
TRAPcc.W   #N
TRAPcc.L   #N

Action   If the selected condition is true, the processor executes exception processing with a six-word stack frame. The program counter points at the next instruction. If the selected condition is not true, the next instruction is executed. The vector offset is $1C.

Note   A word or long-word immediate operand may be used in the instruction. It is stored as an extension word and is used as a parameter by the exception service routine. The conditions used by DBcc instructions are available to this instruction.

PROGRAM 13.12

Trap Tests

The trap condition for a TRAPcc instruction is located in bits 8–11 of the opcode word.

0 1 0 1	Condition	1 1 1 1 1	Mode

11 ⟵⟶ 8   2 ⟵⟶ 0

The mode selects the instruction form, indicating whether it has 0, 1, or 2 extension words. The following sample program forces two TRAPcc exceptions:

```
                MOVE.L          #$100000,A1
    COMPARE:    CMPA.L          #$8000,A1
                TRAPHI.L        #0
                MOVE.L          #$44444444,D2
    DIVIDE:     DIVS.W          #2,D2
                TRAPVS.L        #1
```

The service routine fetches the condition bits and uses them as an index into a string table to identify the code mnemonic. The TRAPcc instructions use the long size and have two extension words that are printed.

```
vtrapcc:        equ     $1c
inst_off:       equ     12                      ; offset to addr field

        xref    hexout_long, newline, strout, stop

start:
        lea     traptest,a0
        move.l  a0,vtrapcc.w
        movea.l #$100000,a1
compare:
        cmpa.l  #$8000,a1                        ; a1 is higher than $8000
        traphi.l #0
        move.l  #$44444444,d2
divide: divs.w  #2,d2                            ; v bit is set
        trapvs.l #1
        jsr     stop

traptest:
        link    a6,#0
        movem.l d0/a0,-(sp)
        lea     ccmsg,a0                         ; print 'trap on '
        move.w  #8,d0
        jsr     strout
        bfextu  ([inst_off,a6]){4:4},d0  ; extract the condition
        lea     cclist,a0
        lea     (a0,d0.1*2),a0                   ; print the mnemonic
        move.w  #2,d0
        jsr     strout
        lea     addrmsg,a0                       ; print ' with parameter'
        move.w  #16,d0
        jsr     strout
; add 2 to advance past opcode word to immediate operand
        move.l  ([inst_off,a6],2),d0     ; fetch TRAP parameter
        jsr     hexout_long                      ; print TRAP parameter
        jsr     newline
```

```
                    movem.l    (sp)+,d0/a0
                    unlk       a6
                    rte

                    data

        trapparms:
                    ds.l       2

        cclist: dc.b      't', 'f', 'hi','ls','cc'
                dc.b      'cs','ne','eq','vc','vs'
                dc.b      'pl','mi','ge','lt','gt'
                dc.b      'le'
        ccmsg:  dc.b      'trap on '
        addrmsg:
                dc.b      ' with parameter '
                end
```

⟨Run of Program 13.12⟩

```
trap on hi with parameter 00000000
trap on vs with parameter 00000001
```

Line Emulator Trap Exception

Any instruction whose opcode bits 15–12 are "1010" is considered an un-implemented instruction; the instruction is termed an **A-line code.** A-line codes are typically used for instruction emulation or system calls. **F-line codes** have "1111" in bits 15–12 and are used for the coprocessor interface on the MC68020/30/40 processors. When the processor encounters an F-line opcode, it runs a bus cycle designed to communicate with one of eight possible coprocessors. If the bus cycle terminates in a bus error, the F-line exception is taken. A four-word stack frame is generated for the A-line and F-line exceptions. A trace exception does not occur for an unimplemented instruction. The unimplemented instruction service routine must check the SR on the stack and test to see if tracing is enabled. In this case, the unimplemented instruction service routine would have to call routines to execute a trace.

PROGRAM 13.13

Line Emulation Test Program

A code sequence contains an A-line and an F-line trap. The same service routine handles both the exceptions and illustrates the use of a generic exception handler. The type of exception is identified by looking at the vector offset, which is saved in the fourth word of the exception stack frames. ($28 = A-line offset; $2C = F-line offset.) The type of exception and the 12-bit parameter in the opcode word are printed.

Assume that the program is running on a system that uses A-line exceptions to make operating system calls. In this case, the original system A-line exception vector must be saved prior to the program initializing the vector. During the service routine, the original exception vector must be restored to allow for operating system calls. Prior to RTE, the program's A-line exception vector is again copied to the exception table.

```
va_line:     equ       $28
vf_line:     equ       $2c
pc_off:      equ         6
vector_off:  equ        10

             xref      newline, strout, decout, stop

start:       lea       a_fline, a0
             move.l    va_line.w, savedALine    ; save A-line vector
             move.l    a0, vf_line.w
             move.l    a0, va_line.w
             dc.w      $a010                    ; a-line exception
             dc.w      $f111                    ; f-line exception
             move.l    savedALine, va_line.w    ; A-line vector
             jsr       stop


a_fline:     link      a6, #0
             movem.l   d0-d1/a0, -(sp)
             move.l    savedALine, va_line.w    ; A-line vector
             move.w    #34, d0
; get vector offset from fourth word on stack
             befextu   (vector_off, a6) {4:12}, d1
             cmpi.w    #va_line, d1
             bne.s     fline
             lea       alinemsg, a0             ; was A-line exception
             bra.s     print
fline:       lea       flinemsg, a0             ; was F-line exception
print:       jsr       strout
             bfextu    ([pc_off, a6]) {4:12}, d0
             jsr       decout
             jsr       newline
             lea       a_fline, a0
             move.l    a0, va_line.w            ; A-line vector
             addq.l    #2, (pc_off, a6)
             movem.l   (sp)+, d0-d1/a0
             unlk      a6
             rte

             data
savedALine:
             ds.l      1
alinemsg:    dc.b      'A-Line Exception: Parameter is : '
```

```
flinemsg:    dc.b      'F-Line Exception: Parameter is : '
             end
```

⟨Run of Program 13.13⟩

```
A-Line Exception: Parameter is : 16
F-Line Exception: Parameter is : 273
```

Check Bounds Exceptions

The MC68000 processor provides a CHK instruction to test array bounds. If the data value is out of bounds, a CHK exception is generated. The MC68020/30/40 processors provide a CHK2 instruction similar to CMP2. The destination operand may be a general register.

INSTRUCTION

CHK/CHK2
(MC68020/30/40
Check
Register
Against
Bounds)

Syntax   CHK.⟨size⟩   ⟨ea⟩,Dn
           CHK2.⟨size⟩   ⟨ea⟩,Rn

Action   The CHK instruction is a carryover from the MC68000. The CHK2 instruction compares either an address or a data register Rn against a pair of bounds. The lower bound is the contents in memory specified by the effective address of the source operand. The upper bound is the contents in memory at locations ⟨ea⟩ + 1, 2, or 4, depending on the size of the operation. If Rn is less than the lower bound or greater than the upper bound, a CHK exception is generated.

The CHK and CHK2 exceptions use a six-word stack frame with a vector offset $18.

PROGRAM 13.14

CHK2 Exception
Test

In this program, an input routine expects data in the range 64–128. Data that is out of range cause CHK2 to generate an exception. The exception service routine returns to the operating system.

```
vchk2:    equ       $18

          xref      strout, decin_long, decout_long, newline, stop

start:    lea       chk2test,a0
          move.l    a0,vchk2.w
loop:     jsr       decin_long
          chk2.l    a,d0
          jsr       decout_long
          lea       inbound,a0
          move.l    #20,d0
```

```
          jsr     strout
          jsr     newline
          bra     loop

chk2test: jsr     decout_long
          lea     outbound,a0
          move.w  #16,d0
          jsr     strout
          jsr     newline
          adda.w  #12,sp              ; fix stack before return OS
          jsr     stop

          data

a:        dc.l    64, 128
inbound:  dc.b    'is within the bounds'
outbound: dc.b    'is out of bounds'
          end
```

⟨Run of Program 13.14⟩

```
80
80  is within the bounds
99
99  is within the bounds
128
128  is within the bounds
129
129  is out of bounds
```

Trace and Breakpoint Exceptions

The MC68020/30/40 processors use two trace bits, T_1 and T_0 (bits 15–14).
If both bits are clear, the trace exception is not active. If $T_1 = 1$ and
$T_0 = 0$, full tracing from the MC68000 processor is implemented. If
$T_1 = 0$ and $T_0 = 1$, the trace exception occurs only after an instruction
that alters program control (**control change point tracing**). These instructions include

- All branches (Bcc, DBcc, BRS)
- JMP, JSR
- Instruction traps (TRAP, TRAPcc, and so forth)
- Returns (RTD, RTE, RTR, RTS)
- Status register modifications
- Coprocessor instructions that modify program flow

Note: The case of status register modifications requires an explanation.
Suppose that $T_1 = 0$ and $T_0 = 1$. The instruction

ANDI.W   #$DFFF,SR

changes the processor from supervisor to user mode. If a memory-management unit is used, subsequent instructions cause the function code bits to indicate user space references. This involves fetching instructions from new absolute memory locations. Instruction words that have been prefetched must be discarded, and new fetches must be made.

The trace exception takes place after an instruction has run properly. If an instruction is aborted because of a bus or address error, the trace exception is left pending until the service routine performs software or hardware repair of the faulty bus cycle and executes RTE.

EXAMPLE 13.14

With $T_1 = 0$ and $T_0 = 1$, the following test code will trace the DBRA and TRAP instructions. A listing file with starting address at $11000 is included. The code is used to test the single-stepping trace routine in Program 13.15.

ADDRESS	OPCODE		MC68020 INSTRUCTION	
110000	7201		MOVEQ	#1,D1
110002	4240	LOOP:	CLR.W	D0
110004	4E71		NOP	
110006	51C9		DBRA	D1,loop
	FFFA			
11000A	4E40		TRAP	#0
11000C	4E41		TRAP	#1
11000E			END	

The trace exception uses a six-word stack. Unlike the MC68000, the service routine can access the opcode word of the instruction that caused the trace exception.

A complete program illustrates the use of tracing, as well as TRAP #0 and TRAP #1. The program runs under the Macintosh Assembly System (MAS) and was tested on a Macintosh IIx with an MC68030 processor. The RTE instruction is used to launch a user program with full tracing enabled. The user program is assembled along with the executive and begins at address PROG. In the trace exception service routine, the user is prompted to toggle between full and control change point tracing. The TRAP #0 routine prints the contents of D0. The TRAP #1 routine returns control to the system monitor.

PROGRAM 13.15

MC68020/30/40
Single-Step Tracing

The trace exception routine prints out the SR, PC, format type, vector offset, and the opcode word for the instruction that just executed. At the prompt, the user may signal the end of execution by typing "Q". A response "C" reverses the type of tracing. The test code from Example 13.14 located at address PROG is executed. Output from the trace is included.

(a) The first instruction is traced (full tracing on).

(b) Control change point tracing is turned on. The DBRA instruction is traced.

(c) The DBRA instruction is not traced on the second and last iteration because no change in program control is required. The TRAP #0 instruction is traced.

(d) The TRAP #1 instruction is traced.

```
; exception vectors
vtrace:             equ     $24
vtrap0:             equ     $80
vtrap1:             equ     $84

; stack offsets
sr_offset:          equ     4
progctr_offset:     equ     6
vector_offset:      equ     10
inst_offset:        equ     12

Null:               equ     0

        xref        hexout,hexout_long,getchar,newline
        xref        putstr,stop

        entry       main

; initialize the exception vectors
main:   lea         trace,a0
        move.l      a0,vtrace.w
        lea         output,a0
        move.l      a0,vtrap0.w
        lea         exit,a0
        move.l      a0,vtrap1.w
        move.l      sp,origsp           ; save original sp for exit
                                        ; under all circumstances
; start the program at address "prog"
        clr.w       -(sp)               ; 4 word stack, format = 0
        lea         prog,a0
        move.l      a0,-(sp)            ; starting address is prog
        move.w      #$8000,-(sp)        ; full tracing on, user mode
        rte                             ; start the program

endrun: movea.l     origsp,sp           ; restore original sp
        jsr         stop                ; return to main system

; trap service routines
; user program executing trap #1 cause strap to here
exit:
        addi.w      #$3fff,sr           ; clean off the stack
        bra         endrun              ; return to system
```

```
                ; user program executing trap #0 causes trap here for hex output
                output:
                        andi.w      #$3fff,sr
                        jsr         newline
                        jsr         hexout_long                 ; output (d0)
                        jsr         newline
                        rte

                ; primary trace routine displays the status register, program
                ; counter, vector offset and stack format and the opcode word
                ; the user is prompted for a change in the trace exception type
                ; enter q quit and return to system
                ; enter c change between full and control change trace

        trace:  link        a6,#0
                movem.l     d0-d1/a0,-(sp)
                lea         srmsg,a0                    ; set to sr message
                jsr         putstr
                move.w      (sr_offset,a6),d0
                jsr         hexout                      ; print the status register

                lea         pcmsg,a0                    ; set to pc message
                jsr         putstr
                move.l      (progctr_offset,a6),d0
                jsr         hexout_long                 ; print the program counter
                jsr         newline

                lea         fmtmsg,a0                   ; set to format message
                jsr         putstr
                bfextu      (vector_offset,a6){0:4},d0
                jsr         hexout                      ; print the stack format
                lea         vctmsg,a0                   ; set to vector message
                jsr         putstr
                bfextu      (vector_offset,a6){4:12},d0
                jsr         hexout                      ; print the vector offset
                lea         instmsg,a0                  ; pointer to opcode message
                jsr         putstr
                move.w      ([inst_offset,a6]),d0
                jsr         hexout
                jsr         newline

                lea         prompt,a0                   ; set prompt >>
                jsr         putstr
                jsr         getchar                     ; char input
                cmpi.b      #'q',d0                     ; test for quit
                bne.s       cont
                bra         endrun
        cont:   cmpi.b      #'c',d0                     ; test to change trace type
                bne.s       return
                bfchg       (sr_offset,a6){0:2}         ; reverse tracing
                jsr         getchar                     ; flush end of line character
        return: movem.l     (sp)+,d0-d1/a0
                unlk        a6
                rte                                     ; back to user program
```

```
            data

origsp:   ds.l        1
srmsg:    dc.b        'status reg = ',Null
pcmsg:    dc.b        'prog count = ',Null
fmtmsg:   dc.b        'format type = ',Null
vctmsg:   dc.b        'vector off = ',Null
instmsg:
          dc.b        'opcode word = ',Null
prompt:   dc.b        '>> ',Null

            code
prog:
          moveq       #1,d1
          moveq       #0,d0
loop:     addq.l      #1,d0
          dbra        d1,loop
          trap        #0
          trap        #1
          end
```

⟨Run of Program 13.15⟩

```
status reg  = 8000  prog count = 0043495A
format type = 0002  vector off = 0024  opcode word = 7201
>> c
status reg  = 4000  prog count = 0043495C
format type = 0002  vector off = 0024  opcode word =51C9
>>
status reg  = 2000  prog count = 004348B8
format type = 0002  vector off = 0024  opcode word = 4E40
>>
00000002
status reg  = 2000  prog count = 004348B4
format type = 0002  vector off = 0024  opcode word = 4E41
>>
```

Software routines implement breakpoints by placing an illegal instruction in the code at the breakpoint address. When the illegal instruction is executed, control is returned to the monitor. When the user requests that the program be continued, the correct opcode word is placed into the instruction stream, the instruction is traced, and the illegal instruction is copied back into the code.

The BKPT instruction allows the MC68020/30 processors to communicate with a hardware device for breakpoint handling. The device sends the correct opcode word, which is placed by the CPU in the instruction stream in place of BKPT. On the MC68040, this instruction just causes the illegal instruction exception to take place.

INSTRUCTION

BKPT
(MC68020/30
Breakpoint)

Syntax   BKPT   #N

Action   The instruction supports breakpoint processing using external hardware such as a debug monitor and a real-time hardware emulator. Execution causes the processor to perform a bus cycle known as a **breakpoint acknowledge bus cycle**. The immediate data *N* is limited to 3 bits and is passed to the device during the bus cycle. If the device acknowledges the cycle by responding with a 16-bit opcode word, the word replaces BKPT as the opcode word, and the resulting instruction is executed. The entire breakpoint process is handled in hardware. If the bus cycle results in a bus error signal, no hardware is present, and the illegal instruction exception is taken.

EXAMPLE 13.15

The instruction BKPT #6 (code $484E), when executed at address $1050, causes any external hardware present to recognize breakpoint 6.

If opcode $303C is returned during the breakpoint acknowledge bus cycle, the word is placed in the instruction stream, and the corresponding MOVE.W ⟨address⟩, D0 instruction is executed.

Error Conditions Causing Exceptions

The MC68020/30/40 processors detect abnormal instruction execution and generate error exceptions. The list of exceptions is given in Table 13.8.

Illegal-Instruction Exception

An illegal instruction is an opcode word bit pattern that does not correspond to a valid MC68020/30/40 instruction or a MOVEC instruction that does not reference a valid control register. Exception processing generates a

TABLE 13.8   Exceptions Caused by Errors

ERROR	CAUSE
Illegal instruction	Opcode does not correspond to a valid instruction.
Privilege violation	Execution of a privileged instruction while in user mode.
Format error	Invalid stack format number is detected by an RTE instruction or invalid data used for CALLM/RTM, cpRESTORE.
Address error	Attempt to fetch instruction opcode word at an odd address.
Bus error	Improper use of the system bus.

normal four-word stack frame. The instruction ILLEGAL, with opcode $4AFC, generates an illegal instruction exception. All other unused bit patterns are reserved by Motorola for future expansion of the instruction set. The vector offset is $10, and the PC on the stack is the address of the illegal instruction.

Privilege Violation Exception

The MC68020/30/40 processors have 13 privileged instructions. An attempt to use a privileged instruction in user mode generates a privilege violation exception with a four-word stack. The vector offset is $20, and the PC on the stack is the address of the privileged instruction.

MC68020/30/40 PRIVILEGED INSTRUCTIONS			
ANDI to SR	MOVE from SR	RESET	cpRESTORE
EORI to SR	MOVE to SR	RTE	cpSAVE
ORI to SR	MOVE USP	STOP	
MOVEC	MOVES		

Format Error

The RTE instruction detects an invalid stack frame format number and causes the format error exception. It generates a four-word stack frame. The vector offset is $38, and the stacked PC is the address of the instruction that generated the format error. The cpRESTORE, CALLM, and RTM instructions test data formats before execution. cpRESTORE is a copro-

FIGURE 13.10   Format Error Stack Frame

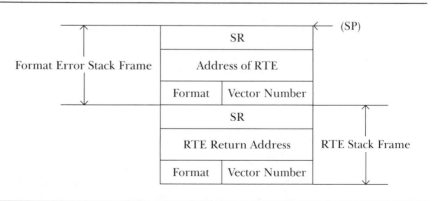

cessor instruction, and coprocessing is discussed in Chapter 15. The MC68030/40 processors have deimplemented the CALLM/RTM instructions. As a result, they are not presented in this text. In the case of RTE, the original stack frame is left unchanged, and the format error stack frame is placed on top of the faulty frame with the PC pointing to RTE (see Figure 13.10). The format error service routine can attempt to repair the faulty stack and then return from the format error, which causes the RTE to execute again.

PROGRAM 13.16

Faulty Stack Frame Recovery

A faulty stack frame is set with format number 15. The RTE causes a format exception. The service routine resets the format number on the faulty frame to 0 and causes the RTE to be re-executed.

```
vformat:   equ      $038
patch:     equ      14

           xref     strout, newline, stop

start:     lea      format, a0            ; init format exception vector
           move.l   a0, vformat.w
           move.w   #$f000, -(sp)         ; format number 15 (invalid!)
           lea      rte_ok, a0
           move.l   a0, -(sp)             ; just return to ourselves
           move.w   #$2000, -(sp)         ; have a valid SR on the stack
           rte                            ; generate the format error
rte_ok:    lea      rtemsg, a0            ; print the outcome
           move.w   #17, d0
           jsr      strout
           jsr      newline
           jsr      stop

format:    moveq    #0, d0               ; set format number to 0
           bfins    d0, (patch, sp) {0: 4}
           rte

           data
rtemsg:    dc.b     'stack is repaired'
           end
```

⟨Run of Program 13.16⟩

```
stack is repaired
```

Bus/Address Error Exceptions

An MC68020/30/40 address error occurs when the processor attempts to prefetch an instruction from an odd address. On the MC68000 processor, an address error also occurs when a word or long-word data access is at-

FIGURE 13.11 Bus and Address Error Stack Frames

	15	0
+0	Status Register	← (SP)
+2	Program Counter	
+4		
+6	1010	Vector Offset
+8	Internal Register	
+10	Special Status Word	
+12	Instruction Pipe Stage C	
+14	Instruction Pipe Stage B	
+16	Data Cycle Fault Address	
+18		
+20	Internal Register	
+22	Internal Register	
+24	Data Output Buffer	
+26		
+28	Internal Register	
+30	Internal Register	

Short Bus Cycle Fault Stack Frame (16 Words)

	15	0
+0	Status Register	← (SP)
+2	Program Counter	
+4		
+6	1011	Vector Offset
+8	Internal Register	
+10	Special Status Word	
+12	Instruction Pipe Stage C	
+14	Instruction Pipe Stage B	
+16	Data Cycle Fault Address	
+18		
+20	Internal Register	
+22	Internal Register	
+24	Data Output Buffer	
+26		
+28	Internal Registers, Four Words	
+36	Stage B Address	
+40	Internal Registers, Two Words	
+44	Data Input Buffer	
+48	Internal Registers	
	22 Words	
+90		

Long Bus Cycle Fault Stack Frame (46 Words)

tempted at an odd address. The MC68020/30/40 processors do not have data alignment restrictions.

A bus error can occur during an instruction prefetch if the processor attempts to fetch an instruction from a nonexistent address. An instruction prefetch bus error occurs naturally on a system with a memory management unit when the block of logical memory containing the instruction has not been mapped to physical memory. In addition, a bus error can occur on a data space access when an operand has a nonexistent effective address.

Bus error exception processing occurs immediately if a data access caused the fault. For an instruction prefetch fault, exception processing is delayed until instruction execution begins. The exception-processing sequence is similar to that on the MC68000. However, an extended exception stack frame is generated to provide for error recovery from the fault. This feature is absolutely necessary for a virtual memory system using paging. The additional information stored in the stack frame includes internal registers of the processor that are not visible to the user, such as the words in stages B and C of the instruction stream. Because the processor was probably in the middle of an instruction when the bus error occurred, the additional information is necessary to recover from the error. The value of the PC on the stack is the address of the instruction that was executing at the time the bus error was detected. This may not be the PC of the instruction that generated the bus error. The topic of bus fault recovery is presented in Chapter 15.

Two distinct bus error stack frames are generated, depending on the point at which the bus error occurs. If the fault occurs at the beginning of the instruction, a 16-word **short bus cycle fault stack frame** is created with format number 10. If the fault occurs during execution of the instruction, a 46-word **long bus cycle fault stack frame** is created with format number 11 (see Figure 13.11). The larger frame contains information on the effective address calculations and the bus controller interface.

On the MC68000 processor, the system enters the halt state if a bus or an address error occurs during the processing of a bus error, an address error, or a system reset. On the MC68020/30/40 processors, this also happens if a bus or an address error occurs while the processor is reading the stack frame during execution of the RTE instruction.

EXERCISES

1. Does the exception state end when the service routine executes RTE?

2. Classify each of the following exceptions as internal or external:
   (a) Trace
   (b) Address error
   (c) TRAP
   (d) Divide by zero
   (e) Bus error

(f) Reset

(g) CHK

3. Indicate what action is being performed. Assume that (SR) = $2000.

(a) ORI.W   #$8000,SR

(b) ANDI.W   #$DFFF,SR

(c) MOVE.W   SR,D0

      ANDI.W   #$F8FF,D0

      ORI.W   #$0500,D0

      MOVE.W   D0,SR

(d) MOVE.L   USP,A3

      MOVE.L   (A3)+,D0

      MOVE.L   (A3)+,D1

4. Assume that

$$(PC) = \$001000 \text{ and } (SR) = \$0502$$

The indicated instruction is the next to be executed. Draw a picture of the exception stack frame, which is active at entrance to the exception service routine.

(a) TRAP #7

(b) $A005

5. Assuming that the CPU is in supervisor mode, write short code segments to perform the following actions:

(a) Turn off tracing.

(b) Turn on tracing.

(c) Change from supervisor to user mode.

(d) Load $6000 into the USP.

(e) Read and print the long word on the top of the user stack.

(f) Without altering any other portion of the status register, set the CPU to level 7.

(g) Change the processor to run at level 5 with the X and C bits cleared. Make no assumptions about the current level of the processor.

6. Assuming that the CPU is running in user mode, give an instruction sequence that will generate a privilege violation. Do not use the following instruction:

MOVE.W   #n,SR

7. Each of the following instructions is located at address $1004, with (SR) = $0000 and (SP) = $7FFE. Give a picture of the stack, including the value of the supervisor stack pointer and the contents of the SR after each of the following instructions is processed:

(a) TRAP   #5

(b) CHK   #10,D1 and (D1) = $0B

(c) DC.W $F000

(d) MOVE.W   #$2000,SR

(e) MOVE.W   #7,$5001

(f) MOVE.L   #77,(4,A)   with (A0) = $100002 on a system with 1M of RAM.

8. (a) This code segment is designed to begin a supervisor mode program at address $10000 with initial status register $2000 and a user stack pointer of $20000. Is it correct? If not, what does it do?

```
LEA        $8000,SP
MOVE.W     #$2000,-(SP)
MOVE.L     #$10000,-(SP)
LEA        $20000,A0
MOVE.L     A0,USP
RTE
```

   (b) If the processor is in supervisor mode, the code segment is designed to start a user mode program at address S with an initial status register of 0. Is it correct? If not, what is the result of executing it?

```
ANDI.W     #$DFFF,SR
MOVE.L     #S,-(SP)
CLR.W      -(SP)
RTE
```

9. The CPU is running in supervisor mode. Write a code segment to start a program with a load address of $10000 executing in user mode with all bits of the status register cleared and a stack pointer of $20000.

10. Indicate the effect of the following instructions:
   (a) ANDI.W   #$70FF,SR
   (b) EORI.W   #$8000,SR
   (c) EORI.W   #$0011,SR
   (d) ORI.W   #$0700,SR
   (e) MOVE.W   #$2400,SR

11. (a) Given the Pascal declarations

```
A : ARRAY[1 . . 50] OF INTEGER;
I : INTEGER;
```

   will the following sequence correctly determine if I is in bounds? Explain.

```
MOVE.W   I,D0
CHK      #50,D0
SUBQ.W   #1,D0
ASL.W    #1,D0
```

   (b) In a system with 1M RAM and EPROM starting at $F70000, the RESET exception vector has the 8-byte contents

   $00001000 $00F76000

   What are the SP/PC/SR when the RESET exception service routine begins execution?

12. Present detailed steps to solve the following problem: You are using a monitor called UNFORTUNATEMON that executes a user program in user mode. However, your program must run in supervisor mode. Show how you can use a TRAP instruction in order to get the CPU into supervisor mode. Remember, you can plant any exception vectors you wish.

13. Given the Pascal array definition

    VAR A : ARRAY[0 . . 49] OF INTEGER;

    and the code segment

    WHILE MORE DO
    BEGIN
       .
       .
       .
      I := I + 1;
      A[I] := I
    END;

    write code that will generate an exception if A goes out of bounds.

14. The CPU is in user mode ($S = 0$). What happens when the following code segment is executed?

```
VTRAP3: EQU        $80 + 3*4
        MOVE.L     #N,VTRAP3.W
        MOVE.L     #1, – (SP)
        MOVE.L     #5, – (SP)
        TRAP       #3
        ADDQ.W     #8,SP
H:      BRA.S      H

N:      MOVE.L     (6,SP),D0
        JSR        PUTHEXOUT__LONG
        MOVE.L     (10,SP),D0
        JSR        PUTHEXOUT__LONG
        JSR        PUTNEWLINE
        RTE
```

15. What happens in the following code sequence with the given input?

```
JSR        GETHEXIN__LONG
DIVU       #3,D0
TRAPV
JSR        PUTHEXOUT
SWAP       D0
JSR        PUTHEXOUT
JSR        NEWLINE
```

    (a) $50005533
    (b) $10000

16. What is the result of running the following program?

```
VLINE1010:     EQU     $0028
VTRACE:        EQU     $0024
```

```
                XREF       PUTHEXOUT, PUTNEWLINE, INITPORT, STOP

MAIN:           LEA        $8000,SP
                MOVEQ      #0,D7
                JSR        INITPORT
                MOVE.L     #Q,VLINE1010.W
                MOVE.L     #TR,VTRACE.W
                MOVE.W     #$A000,EXSR
                MOVEQ      #5,D1
LOOP:           JMP        EXSR
NEXT:           ORI.W      #$8000,SR
                NOP        ; NOP INSTRUCTION DOES NOTHING
                DBRA       D1,LOOP
                JSR        PUTNEWLINE
                JSR        STOP

Q:              MOVE.L     (2,SP),A0
                MOVE.W     (A0),D0
                ANDI.W     #$0FFF,D0
                JSR        PUTHEXOUT
                ADDQ.L     #2,(2,SP)
                RTE

TR:             ADDQ.W     #1,EXSR
                BCLR       #7,(SP)
                RTE

EXSR:           DS.W       1
                JMP        NEXT
                END
```

17. Consider the following program:

```
V1111EMULATOR:  EQU  $2C
VTRACE:         EQU  $24
VADDRESS:       EQU  $0C


                XREF       INITPORT,PUTHEXOUT,PUTHEXOUT_
                           LONG,PUTNEWLINE

START:
                LEA        $8000,SP
                MOVEQ      #0,D7
                JSR        INITPORT
                LEA        S1111,A0
                MOVE.L     A0,V1111EMULATOR.W
                LEA        TRACE,A0
                MOVE.L     A0,VTRACE.W
                LEA        ADDRESSERROR,A0
                MOVE.L     A0,VADDRESS.W

                DC.W       $FFFF

                ORI.W      #$8000,SR
```

```
                          MOVE.W       D0,D1
                          ANDI.W       #$F000,D1
                          ANDI.W       #$7FFF,SR

                          MOVE.W       #7,$7FFF

PCOUNTER:                 EQU          6

S1111:
                          LINK         A6,#0
                          MOVEM.L      D0/D7/A0,-(sp)
                          MOVEA.L      (PCOUNTER,A6),A0
                          MOVE.W       (A0),D0
                          ANDI.W       #$0FFF,D0
                          MOVEQ        #0,D7
                          JSR          PUTHEXOUT
                          JSR          PUTNEWLINE
                          ADDI.L       #2,(PCOUNTER,A6)
                          MOVEM.L      (SP)+,D0/D7/A0
                          UNLK         A6
                          RTE


TRACE:
                          LINK         A6,#0
                          MOVEM.L      D0/D7/A0,-(SP)
                          MOVEA.L      (PCOUNTER,A6),A0
                          MOVE.W       (A0),D0
                          MOVEQ        #0,D7
                          JSR          PUTHEXOUT
                          JSR          PUTNEWLINE
                          MOVEM.L      (SP)+,D0/D7/A0
                          UNLK         A6
                          RTE


PROGCOUNTER:       EQU 14
STATUSREGISTER:    EQU 12
OPCODEWORD:        EQU 10
FAULTADDRESS:      EQU  6
STATUSWORD:        EQU  4


ADDRESSERROR:
                          LINK         A6,#0
                          MOVEQ        #0,D7
                          MOVE.L       (FAULTADDRESS,A6),D0
                          JSR          PUTHEXOUT_LONG
                          JSR          PUTNEWLINE
                          MOVE.W       (OPCODEWORD,A6),D0
                          JSR          PUTHEXOUT
                          JSR          PUTNEWLINE
                          MOVE.W       (STATUSREGISTER,A6),D0
                          JSR          PUTHEXOUT
                          JSR          PUTNEWLINE
                          MOVE.L       (PROGCOUNTER,A6),D0
```

```
                        JSR         PUTHEXOUT_LONG
                        JSR         PUTNEWLINE
        IDLE:           BRA.S       IDLE
                        END
```

Trace the program, and state precisely what will happen when the program executes.

18. What is the output of the following program? Does it ever terminate?

```
V1010EMULATOR:          EQU     $28
VTRAP0:                 EQU     $80
VTRACE:                 EQU     $24

            XREF        INITPORT, PUTHEXOUT, PUTNEWLINE, STOP


START;      LEA         $8000,SP
            MOVE.L      #EMU,V1010EMULATOR.W
            MOVE.L      #PR,VTRAP0.W
            MOVE.L      #TRACE,VTRACE.W

            MOVE.Q      #0,D7
            JSR         INITPORT

            DC.W        $A000

            ORI.W       #$8000,SR
            MOVE.W      #1,D0
            MOVE.W      #2,D0
            MOVE.W      #3,D0
            ANDI.W      #$7FFF,SR
            JSR         STOP

ID:         BRA.S       ID


PROGCOUNTER:            EQU     6

EMU:        LINK        A6,#0
            MOVEM.L     D0/D7/A0,-(SP)
            MOVEQ       #0,D7
            MOVE.L      (PROGCOUNTER,A6),A0
            MOVE.W      (A0),D0
            JSR         PUTHEXOUT
            JSR         PUTNEWLINE
            ADDI.L      #2,(PROGCOUNTER,A6)
            MOVEM.L     (SP)+,D0/D7/A0
            UNLK        A6
            RTE

TRACE:      TRAP        #0
            RTE
```

```
PR:        MOVE.L     D7,-(SP)
           JSR        PUTHEXOUT
           JSR        PUTNEWLINE
           MOVE.L     (SP)+,D7
           RTE

           END
```

19. Suppose that tracing is on when the instruction

    TRAP #5

    begins execution at address $3300. If the trace service routine prints the PC, it will not be $3302! The TRAP exception has priority over the trace exception and is processed first. This means that the exception-processing state is executed first for trap and then for trace. At that point, normal execution begins in an exception service routine. Draw a stack diagram to determine what PC will be printed by the trace service routine.

20. The code segment below is taken from a service routine for the bus error. What does it appear to be doing?

```
* ADDRESSS ERROR SERVICE ROUTINE
PROGCOUNTER:    EQU      14
STATUSREG:      EQU      12
OPCODEWORD:     EQU      10
FAULTADDR:      EQU       6
STATUSWORD:     EQU       4

ADDRERROR:
                . . .
           MOVE.W     (OPCODEWORD,A6),D2
           MOVE.L     (PROGCOUNTER,A6),A0
AGAIN:     CMP.W      -(A0),D2
           BNE.S      AGAIN
           MOVE.L     A0,D0
           JSR        PUTHEXOUT
                . . .
```

21. Specify what happens when the following code segment runs on a 32K system:

```
BUSERROR:    EQU      $08

START:       MOVE.L   #BERR,BUSERROR.W
             LEA      $8000,SP
             MOVE.W   #7,(6,SP)

BERR:        LEA      (26,SP),SP
             RTE
```

22. (a) What is the effect of the following program?

```
VADDRERR:    EQU      $000C

             XREF     STOP
```

```
START:      LEA      $8000, SP
            MOVE. L  #QA, VADDRERR. W
            LEA      $10001, A1
INST:       JMP      (A1)
            JMP      STOP

QA:         ADDA. L  #14, SP
            MOVE. L  #INST+1, − (SP)
            MOVE. W  #$2000, − (SP)
            RTE

            END
```

(b) What is the effect of the following program?

```
VADDRERR:   EQU      $000C

            XREF     STOP

START:      LEA      $8000, SP
            MOVE. L  #QB, VADDRERR. W
INST:       MOVE. L  #7, $10001
            JMP      STOP

QB:         ADDA. L  #14, SP
            ADDQ. L  #1, VADDRERR. W
            MOVE. L  #INST+1, − (SP)
            MOVE. W  #$2000, − (SP)
            RTE

            END
```

23. The processor is in supervisor mode and the instruction

    MOVE.W $5000,D0

    is to be executed. What are the values of the function code lines when:
    (a) The opcode word is read from memory.
    (b) The contents of $5000 are read.

24. (MC68020/30/40) Assume that

    $$(PC) = \$001000 \quad \text{and} \quad (SR) = \$0502$$

    The indicated instruction is the next to be executed. Draw a picture of the exception stack frame that is active at entrance to the exception service routine.
    (a) TRAPGT.L #5
    (b) CHK2.W $1000,d3

25. (MC68020/30/40)
    (a) Show how to initialize the VBR to $500.
    (b) Assuming the VBR is $500, what is the exception vector address for the TRAPcc instruction?
    (c) Assuming the VBR is $500, what is the format and vector offset for the BKPT instruction?

26. (MC68020/30/40) The instruction

    BFINS   D0,$2000{4:8}

    is located at address $10000. $T_1 T_0 = 10_2$ at the start of the instruction. Show the contents of the stack at the start of the service routine.

PROGRAMMING EXERCISES

27. Write a program that does the following: For your standalone system, write out the exception vector number, exception vector address, and starting address of the exception service routine for the exceptions:

    Illegal Instruction
    Zero Divide
    CHK Instruction
    TRAPV Instruction
    Privilege Violation

28. Write a program that does the following:

    Step 1: Plants a generic service routine GENSERV for all exceptions whose vector number is in the range 4–11. GENSRV prints out the PC and SR from the exception stack.

    Step 2: Tests the service routine by generating a TRAP, CHK, divide-by-zero, and TRAPV exception.

29. Create a service routine GENSRV__PC that prints the opcode word of the instruction that caused the exception. Before executing the RTE, the service routine should increment the program counter on the stack to that of the next instruction. Plant the service routine address in the exception vectors for Illegal Instruction, Privilege Violation, and A-Line and F-Line exceptions. Test the service routine by generating those exceptions.

30. Load the simple program at address $2000.

```
              XREF      GETDECIN, PUTDECOUT, PUTNEWLINE, STOP

    START:    JSR       GETDECIN
              ASL.W     #2,D0
              JSR       PUTDECOUT
              JSR       PUTNEWLINE
              JSR       STOP
              END
```

    Write an executive program that contains the instruction JMP $2001, causing an address error. The executive program should provide an address error service routine that flushes the exception stack and causes the program at $2000 to be run correctly upon RTE.

31. Suppose a user program may add or subtract two 32-bit numbers N1 and N2 by pushing the addresses of the numbers onto the stack and then executing an A-line trap call

    DC.W $A000   ; ADD   N2 + N1

    or

    DC.W $A001   ; SUB   N2 − N1

    The service routine pops the addresses off the stack, does the calculation, and stores the sum, or difference, in N2.

    Implement an executive program that starts a program at load address $2000 in user mode with a stack pointer of $5000 and handles all A-line traps as described. Furthermore, if the user program wishes to output a 32-bit number, it can do so by placing the address of the number in D0 and executing TRAP #0. A TRAP #1 causes a return to the primary monitor. Text the executive program by writing a user program that adds and subtracts two numbers and then uses TRAP #10 to print each result.

CHAPTER 14

PERIPHERAL DEVICE INTERRUPTS

Chapter 13 introduced the concept of an exception. This chapter focuses on exceptions caused when a peripheral device issues an interrupt request. The exceptions are called **peripheral-device interrupts**, and they assert that the device is ready to transfer data or has identified an error condition. Unlike polling, in which the CPU waits on the device, interrupts permit the CPU to execute other code between requests. The CPU services the peripheral device only on request and when some meaningful action is needed. The keyboard is a good example. When the user strikes a key, the CPU halts its current execution, completes the transfer, and then returns. Each of the peripheral interfaces studied in Chapter 12 is capable of generating an interrupt, provided certain bits are set in the control register. Table 14.1 lists each device, its interrupts, and the corresponding action in the service routines.

Interrupts are essential in a multiprocessing environment. They enable the CPU to switch from process to process as devices request resources. They also can be used in a standalone system to buffer input so data is not lost and to buffer output for more efficient throughput. This chapter introduces interrupts for the ECB and creates applications for the MC6850 ACIA and the MC68230 PI/T. Programs include a complete interrupt-driven I/O driver, a transmit-interrupt printer driver, and a timer-interrupt program. A summary of exception priority classes is given to cover cases in which two or more exceptions are pending at the same time. Finally, Section 14.8 covers interrupts for the MC68020/30/40 processors.

TABLE 14.1   ECB Peripheral Device Interrupts

DEVICE	INTERRUPT SOURCE	SERVICE ROUTINE ACTION
ACIA	Receive register full	Read the character from the input buffer.
ACIA	Transmit register empty	If a character is ready to send, transmit it; otherwise, turn off the transmit interrupt.
Timer	Timeout occurs	Take specified action on timeout and reset the timer, if desired.
PI/T	Latch available	If a character is ready to print, transmit it; otherwise, turn off the transmit interrupt.

| 14.1 | PRIORITY INTERRUPTS

An efficiently running system must make effective use of its resources. The operating system must adapt to devices running at different speeds. The performance of a software system is often dictated by how well it handles disk resources. A disk access request should receive almost immediate attention and be serviced before a slower ACIA data transfer request. In order to manage the service of resources, priority-based interrupts are used. An MC68000 system can rank interrupts by their "access rights" to the CPU. Such systems are classified as **priority interrupt systems**. The processor status register contains three bits (I_0–I_2) that determine the level of an interrupt. The bits, referred to as the **interrupt mask**, control the processor's response to an interrupt request from an external device.

15	14	13		10	9	8		4	3	2	1	0
T		S		I_2	I_1	I_0		X	N	Z	V	C

Status Register

On MC68000 systems, peripheral devices are connected to one of seven input lines leading to a priority encoder. Each input line corresponds to an interrupt level in the range 1–7. Any number of devices can be connected to the encoder. The encoder continuously passes interrupt requests through to the CPU on a set of three control lines called the **interrupt request lines**, IPL0–IPL2 (see Figure 14.1). A description of the MC68000 signal lines and hardware details of the interrupt acknowledge cycle are given in Section 14.8. You will understand interrupts better if you study the interrupt signal handshaking.

FIGURE 14.1   Priority Encoder

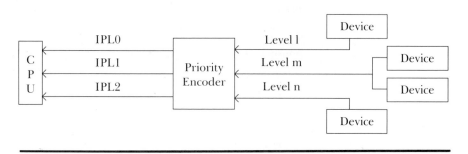

When inactive, the interrupt request lines have value 0. When peripheral devices generate interrupts, the corresponding signal lines to the encoder are activated. The encoder, a hardware device connected to seven interrupt-level signal lines, identifies the highest level interrupt and passes this value through to the CPU. It is entirely possible that two or more devices are connected to the encoder along the same line, so there will be more than one possible interrupt source at that level.

The CPU's response to an interrupt request depends on the interrupt mask in the status register. The following conditions summarize the action.

Condition 1   The mask has value N, $0 \leq N \leq 6$. A peripheral device asserting an interrupt with a priority greater than N will interrupt the CPU. Exception processing begins upon completion of the present instruction. An interrupt with a priority level less than or equal to N is left pending.

Condition 2   The mask has value 7. All interrupts are disabled except for the case of an interrupt of priority level 7. An interrupt of level 7 will always be serviced immediately and hence is called a **nonmaskable interrupt**. This feature has been added so that the operating system can recover control from the currently running program. Often a standalone system has a software reset switch that generates a level 7 interrupt. When pressed, the service routine prints diagnostic information and aborts the program.

EXAMPLE 14.1

Interrupt Service
Priority

This example illustrates interrupt service priority, which is given for a sequence of device interrupts. The value of the interrupt request lines (IPL0–IPL2) and the CPU interrupt acknowledge status are included.

SR INTERRUPT MASK (I_0–I_2)	ACTIVE INTERRUPT REQUESTS	PRIORITY ENCODER LEVEL (IPL0–IPL2)	INTERRUPT ACKNOWLEDGED
3	Inactive	0	No
5	1, 3, 5	5	No
7	1, 4, 6	6	No
3	1, 4, 6	6	Yes
7	3, 7	7	Yes

14.2 THE INTERRUPT PROCESSING CYCLE

If the priority of an interrupt is greater than the current value of the interrupt mask, or if a level 7 interrupt is asserted, the exception-processing sequence begins upon completion of the current instruction. The sequence of events follows the usual pattern for exceptions. However, additional handshaking is required, so that the CPU can identify the interrupting device and the appropriate exception vector number.

Stage 1: Status Register Setup

The initial phase of the exception-processing cycle is executed. The SR is saved in an internal register, the supervisor bit is set ($S = 1$) and the trace bit is cleared ($T = 0$). The interrupt mask in the status register is set to the priority level of the interrupt request. This ensures that the exception service routine will not be preempted by an interrupt request of the same or lower priority.

Status Register

0		1			Priority Level		X	N	Z	V	C

15   13   10   8

Stage 2: Interrupt-Acknowledge Bus Cycle

The interrupt-acknowledge bus cycle is detailed in Section 14.8. During this stage, the CPU identifies the type of interrupt, autovectored or vectored, and the interrupt vector number.

In the interrupt-acknowledge bus cycle, the CPU sends an output signal that identifies the interrupt level that the CPU will respond to. A device, asserting that level of interrupt request, recognizes that it will be serviced. The device that receives the interrupt acknowledge will then communicate an exception vector number to the CPU. This process depends on the hardware configuration of the device. In **autovectored mode**, the exception vector is derived from the interrupt level of the requesting device. In **vectored mode**, the exception vector is defined when the device is initialized and supplied to the CPU during the acknowledge cycle.

Autovector Interrupt Mode   The MC68000 provides seven exception vectors corresponding to the different interrupt levels. The CPU recognizes that the device is asserting an autovectored interrupt and uses the priority level of the interrupt as an index into the exception vector table.

EXCEPTION	NUMBER	ADDRESS
Level 1: Interrupt autovector	25	$64
Level 2: Interrupt autovector	26	$68
Level 3: Interrupt autovector	27	$6C
Level 4: Interrupt autovector	28	$70
Level 5: Interrupt autovector	29	$74
Level 6: Interrupt autovector	30	$78
Level 7: Interrupt autovector	31	$7C

If p is the priority level of the interrupt, the interrupt exception address is

$$\text{Interrupt autovector}(p) = \$064 + (p - 1) * 4$$

Older MC6800 peripheral devices are configured to request interrupt service in autovector mode. They require less complicated interface circuitry and can be used with the newer MC68000 processors. Autovectored interrupts require additional code when two or more devices have the same interrupt level. The service routine must scan the devices to determine which one is causing the interrupt.

Vectored Interrupt Mode   The MC68000 processor has left addresses $100–$3FC (vector numbers 64–255) unassigned. Some peripheral devices can generate a vectored interrupt that uses these unassigned addresses. When a vectored device recognizes that the CPU acknowledges it, the device sends an 8-bit vector number down the data bus. The processor multiplies this vector number by 4 and reads the address of the service routine from the exception vector table. It is the responsibility of the programmer to plant the 8-bit vector number in a device register before the device asserts an interrupt.

Vectored interrupt mode is more flexible than autovectored mode. Devices can assign a vector number from among 192 different choices, providing a unique vector for each device or function of a device, as in the case of the multifunction MC68230 PI/T.

Stage 3: Exception Service

Once the exception vector has been identified, the exception-processing cycle continues. The PC and SR are pushed on the supervisor stack, and the PC is loaded from the exception vector table and interrupt service begins.

It is the responsibility of the service routine to ensure that the interrupt is turned off. For many devices, the service routine clears the interrupt by reading or writing data. For instance, an ACIA receive interrupt is turned off by reading the character. In the case of a timer, a bit is cleared to turn off the interrupt.

The interrupt mask in the status register ensures that the CPU can be interrupted only by higher-level devices. If warranted, the service routine can reserve exclusive access to the CPU by disabling all but level-7 interrupts.

```
MOVE.W   #$2700,SR     ; DISABLE INTERRUPTS
```

The service routine may want to raise the interrupt mask in the status register saved on the stack so that a driver will be immune to interrupts. The following code disables all interrupts upon execution of the RTE:

```
ORI.W   #$0700, (SAVED_SR,A6)     ; INTERRUPT LEVEL 7
RTE
```

Interrupt Error Exceptions

Two error exceptions, the **spurious interrupt** and the **uninitialized interrupt**, can occur with device interrupts. If no device responds during the interrupt acknowledge cycle, board circuitry asserts the bus error (BERR) signal. The processor recognizes that this signal occurred during the interrupt acknowledge cycle and reads the spurious interrupt vector (vector number 24) at address $60 instead of the bus error. A peripheral device generating vectored interrupts must assign an exception vector to a designated interrupt register. If the program fails to initialize the register, during an interrupt the device returns the uninitialized interrupt exception (vector number 15) with address $3C.

14.3 | MC6850 ACIA INTERRUPTS

This section begins the development of interrupt processing for peripheral devices on the Motorola ECB. With the MC6850 ACIA, both receive and transmit interrupts can be used. Two sample programs illustrate programming techniques for receive interrupts. An I/O driver featuring both receive and transmit interrupts concludes this section. The principles applied to the MC6850 ACIA can be adapted to run on other ACIA devices.

Interrupts and the ACIA Registers

The three high-order bits of the MC6850 control register are used to enable receive and transmit interrupts, as illustrated in Figure 14.2. Bit 7 is the **receive interrupt enable bit**. When this bit is set, the arrival of a character in the receive data register causes the ACIA to generate an interrupt and set bit 7 of the status register. Bits 5 and 6 are the **transmit interrupt enable bits**. The transmit interrupts are enabled if the respective bits in the control register are 0 and 1 (see Figure 14.2). In this case, whenever the transmit data register is empty, the ACIA interrupts the CPU and indicates that it is free to send a character. In Chapter 12 the four fields in the control register were initialized with $15. To enable receive interrupt, set the fields to $95.

Bit 7 of the status register is called the *interrupt request bit* (IRQ). When the ACIA is requesting interrupt service, this bit becomes 1. When two or more autovectored devices assert an interrupt request at the same level, this bit is read to determine if the particular device is the source of the interrupt. See Figure 14.3.

Initializing the ACIA

On the ECB, the console ACIA generates a level-5 autovectored interrupt, and the host port generates a level-6 interrupt. During program initialization, the exception vectors must be assigned the address of the autovector service routine, and interrupts must be enabled in the control register. While

FIGURE 14.2   Interrupts and the ACIA Control Register

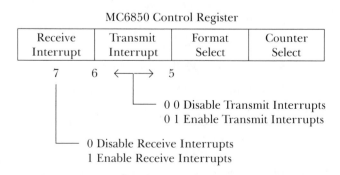

FIGURE 14.3 MC6850 Status Register

MC6850 Status Register

Console Interrupt Request		Receive Register Full
7		1

└── 0 No Interrupt Request
     1 Interrupt Request

the initialization code is executing, interrupts are disabled by setting the interrupt mask to 7. When initialization is complete, interrupts are enabled by changing the mask in the status register. The following code initializes the console port with receive interrupts enabled:

```
TERMBASE:      EQU  $10040
CTRLREG:       EQU  0
STATREG:       EQU  0
RXREG:         EQU  2
RXFULL:        EQU  0
DISABLEINTS:   EQU  $2700      ; INTERRUPT MASK = 7
ENABLEINTS:    EQU  $2000      : INTERRUPT MASK = 0
CONTROLVAL:    EQU  $95        ; CONTROL REG FIELDS
VAUTOV5:       EQU  $74        ; LEVEL 5 AUTOVECTOR
```

Initialization Code

```
MOVE.W  #DISABLEINTS,SR           ; DISABLE INTERRUPTS
LEA     TERMBASE,A0               ; SET BASE ADDRESS
MOVE.B  #CONTROLVAL,(CTRLREG,A0)  ; INITIALIZE CONTROL REG
MOVE.L  #CONSOLE,VAUTOV5.W        ; CONSOLE SERVICE ROUTINE
MOVE.W  #ENABLEINTS,SR            ; ENABLE INTERRUPTS
```

ACIA Interrupt Programming

Two sample programs illustrate the coding of interrupt service routines for the MC6850 ACIA. In the first program, receiver interrupts are enabled so that each character input from the keyboard generates an interrupt. The service routine reads the character into (D0.B). The second example is a repeat of the transparent mode program, this time running with receiver interrupts.

PROGRAM 14.1

Character Print

The main program is an infinite loop printing out the character in (D0.W) and then incrementing the register value to the next character. For output, characters are truncated to the range $00–$7F. A delay loop of one half second is included to slow output. When the user enters a character, it becomes the base for subsequent output. The "delay" routine contains inefficient code. However, the routine is a simple illustration of problems that interrupts can cause.

```
TermBase     equ     $10040
ctrlreg:     equ     0
statreg:     equ     0
rxreg:       equ     2
txreg:       equ     2
rxfull:      equ     0
txempty:     equ     1
TimerBase:   equ     $10021          ; timer base address
Tctrl:       equ     0               ; timer control register
Tpreload:    equ     4               ; timer preload register
Tstatus:     equ     20              ; timer status register

disableints: equ     $2700           ; interrupt mask = 7
enableints:  equ     $2000           ; interrupt mask = 0
controlval:  equ     $95             ; control reg fields
vautov5:     equ     $74             ; Level 5 autovector

start:
        lea     $8000, sp            ; set up a stack pointer
        move.w  #disableints, sr     ; disable interrupts
        lea     TermBase, a0         ; initialize control reg
        move.b  #controlval, (ctrlreg, a0)
        move.l  #keyboard, vautov5.w ; keyboard service routine
        lea     TimerBase, a1
        move.b  #$80, (Tctrl, a1)    ; init timer protocol
        move.b  #'A', d0
        move.w  #enableints, sr      ; enable interrupts

main:   jsr     outchar
        addq.b  #1, d0
        andi.b  #$7f, d0
        jsr     delay
        bra.s   main

outchar:
        btst    #txempty, (statreg, a0)  ; wait for empty register
        beq.s   outchar                  ; use polling for output
        move.b  d0, (txreg, a0)
        rts

; service routine for the console receiver interrupt.
console:
        move.w  #disableints, sr         ; disable interrupts
```

```
              move.b    (rxreg,a0),d0
              andi.w    #$7F,d0
              rte                              ; restore interrupt level

delay:
              move.l    d0,-(sp)
              move.l    #62500,d0              ; load tick count
              movep.l   d0,(Tpreload,a1)
              bclr      #0,(Tctrl,a1)          ; turn off the timer
              bset      #0,(Tctrl,a1)          ; turn on the timer
wait:         btst      #0,(Tstatus,a1)        ; test for timeout
              beq.s     wait
              move.l    (sp)+,d0
              rts

              end
```

⟨Run of Program 14.1⟩

Note: Output begins with the character 'A'. During execution, the user enters 'j' and then '4'. The program is predominantly in the DELAY look. Hence, input from the keyboard is overwritten when the register D0 is restored. Typically, the program outputs the sequence A,B,C, (etc.) without a break. This is not the intended result.

```
Typical Output: ABCDEFGHIJKLMNOPQRSTUVWXYZ[\]
Intended Output: ABCDEFGHIJKjklmnopqrs456789:
```

The user must carefully diagnose interrupt-driven programs. Because interrupts can occur at random instructions within a code block, it is important to ensure that an interrupt is not allowed to go off and inadvertently modify data. The DELAY routine in Program 14.1 illustrates a problem that can occur.

Assume that you type a character during execution of the statement "MOVE.L #62500,D0". An interrupt is asserted, and the CPU enters the service routine and reads the character into D0. That new value is then stored in the timer preload register and used in the delay. This code is vulnerable to interrupts. In general, interrupts require strict programming principles.

1. Make sure that an interrupt service routine saves and restores registers so that a random interrupt will not contaminate register data.

2. Disable interrupts during a code block if an interrupt could destroy key data used by the block. For instance, the following modified DELAY would not be affected by typing at the keyboard:

3. Disable interrupts when a routine will overwrite the effect of a keyboard input.

```
DELAY:
    MOVE.W   #DISABLEINTS,SR     ; DISABLE INTERRUPTS
    MOVE.L   D0,-(SP)
    MOVE.L   #62500,D0           ; LOAD TICK COUNT
    MOVEP.L  D0,(TPRELOAD,A1)
    BCLR     #0,(TCTRL,A1)       ; TURN OFF THE TIMER
    BSET     #0,(TCTRL,A1)       ; TURN ON THE TIMER
WAIT:
    BTST     #0,(TSTATUS,A1)     ; TEST FOR TIMEOUT
    BEQ.S    WAIT
    MOVE.L   (SP)+,D0
    MOVE.W   #ENABLEINTS,SR      ; ENABLE INTERRUPTS
    RTS
```

Demonstration Program: Transparent Mode with Interrupts

A transparent mode example in Chapter 12 passes characters back and forth between the host and console ACIA ports by using polling. This example implements transparent mode using receive interrupts at both ports. The terminal is made to appear as though it is connected directly to the host system.

Think of the program as the following three active processes:

1. The main program waiting for ⟨control⟩-A to be input.

2. A console interrupt service routine to read characters from the keyboard and write them to the host port.

3. A host interrupt service routine to read characters from the host system and write them to the console port.

PROGRAM 14.2

Transparent Mode with Interrupts

The main program loops, waiting for a ⟨control⟩-A to be input at the console. Two exception service routines at addresses CONSOLE and HOST take care of reading the character received and sending it to the other port (see Figure 14.4). The memory location CRTLARECEIVED acts like a Boolean variable with values 0 (CTRL-A not present) and 1 (CTRL-A present).

```
TermBase    equ  $10040
HostBase:   equ  $10041
ctrlreg:    equ  0
statreg:    equ  0
rxreg:      equ  2
txreg:      equ  2
rxfull:     equ  0
```

```
txempty:      equ  1
disableints:  equ  $2700         ; interrupt mask = 7
enableints:   equ  $2000         ; interrupt mask = 0
controlval:   equ  $95           ; control reg fields
vautov5:      equ  $74           ; Level 5 autovector

vautov6:      equ  $78           ; Level 6 autovector
ctrl_A:       equ  1
monitor:      equ  $8146

tm:      move.w  #disableints,sr     ; disable interrupts
;                                    ; during acia init routine
         lea     $8000,sp            ; set up a stack pointer
         lea     TermBase,a0         ; initialize the two acia's
         bsr     init
         lea     HostBase,a0
         bsr     init
         move.l  #console,vautov5.w  ; initialize acia vectors
         move.l  #host,vautov6.2
         clr.w   ctrlareceived       ; should be false initially
         move.w  #enableints,sr      ; enable interrupts


; main program

wait:    tst.w   ctrlareceived       ; main program
         beq.s   wait
         jmp     monitor             ; back to monitor


; initialize acia whose base address is in a0

init:
;        move.b  #mastereset,ctrlreg(a0)
         move.b  #controlval,ctrlreg(a0)
         rts


; read the char from the acia whose base address is in a0
getchar: move.b  (rxreg,a0),d0       ; read the character
         bclr    #7,d0               ; mask off any parity
         rts


; send the char in d0 to the acia whose base address is in a0
putchar: btst    #txempty,statreg(a0) ; wait for empty tdr
         beq.s   putchar             ; use polling for transmit
         move.b  d0,txreg(a0)
         rts


; service routine for the console receiver interrupt.
; disable interrupts
; get the character received and check if it is ctrl a.
; if not ctrl a, send the char to the opposite acia and return
```

```
; if ctrl a, set ctrlareceived to 1 and return. the main
; program, waiting for this event, will terminate.

console:
        move.w  #disableints,sr
        lea     TermBase,a0           ; read char from keyboard
        bsr     getchar
        cmpi.b  #ctrl_A,d0
        bne.s   cont
        move.w  #1,ctrlareceived
        bra.s   xit
cont:   lea     HostBase,a0           ; send char to host
        bsr     putchar
xit:    rte


; service routine for the host receive interrupt.
; just send the character received to the console port and return
; from the exception.

host:
        move.w  #disableints,sr
        lea     HostBase,a0          ; read character from host
        bsr     getchar
        lea     TermBase,a0          ; send char to console
        bsr     putchar
        rte

        data

ctrlareceived:
        dc.w    0

        end
```

FIGURE 14.4 Transparent Mode with Interrupts

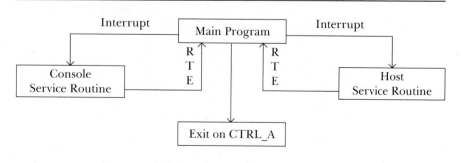

14.4 | SERIAL I/O DRIVER

A library illustrating the main components of an interrupt-driven I/O driver is presented in this section. An I/O driver is code that communicates with an I/O device and passes data to and from the device. In an operating system, drivers must be written so that they work efficiently, because the performance of the system is linked to the efficiency with which it deals with its peripheral devices. A driver is designed around the interrupt service routines for the device. When an interrupt occurs, the driver issues a command to a device and then waits until the service routine notifies it that the device has responded.

I/O transfers are often **buffered**; that is, for input, data is read from a device by the interrupt service routine and placed into a list (called a *buffer*) maintained as a queue. When a code segment needs data, it is retrieved from the buffer. In this way, data loss is prevented when the program is not attending to the device. If the program must perform significant work when a character is read, this technique avoids data overruns. For serial devices, buffering is frequently used at higher baud rates. For output, data is placed in the buffer. Waiting is necessary only if the buffer fills up. When the output device is free to transmit a character, it generates an interrupt, and the service routine takes a character out of the buffer and writes it to the device. This technique is used in the writing of print spoolers and greatly improves data throughput.

Program Description: ACIA Receive/Transmit Interrupts

Complete code for the serial driver is found in Appendix D. In this section the routines GETCHAR, PUTCHAR, and CHARPRESENT are described with the accompanying code. The routines were developed in Chapter 12 for a standalone system using polling. Now the routines are modified to use interrupts and buffering. The interrupt service routine TERMINAL handles the I/O. The GETCHAR and PUTCHAR routines use their own 16-character buffer and enable both receive and transmit interrupts for the console port.

The driver implements the XON/XOFF protocol. When XOFF (⟨*control-S*⟩) is received, all output to the screen is stopped until XON (⟨*control-Q*⟩) is received. Normal output then resumes. This protocol has many applications. It is used to assist you in viewing your output so that lines do not scroll off the screen. It is also used for **flow control** in which the receiving system sends XOFF when its internal buffer is in danger of overflowing and sends XON when the danger has passed. Most systems have the option of allowing output to resume when any character except XOFF is received.

The driver emulates part of an operating system and contains techniques to suspend or block processes. Each buffer has an associated flag. When a GETCHAR routine is called and the input buffer is empty, the variable SUSPEND__INPUT is set TRUE, and the input process suspends itself and enters a polling loop until a character is typed at the keyboard. The receive interrupt service routine sets and clears the flag. The same technique is used if the output buffer is full.

The input and output buffers are implemented as queues. The routines INITQUEUE, QDELETE, QINSERT, QEMTPY, and QFULL were developed in Chapter 11. A queue is designed to store only long words. In this way, the same structure can be used for byte, word, and long-word data. An item is inserted in the queue by placing it as a long word on the stack. An item is deleted from the stack and placed as a long word in D0. Recall that the queue parameters FRONT, REAR, COUNT, and SIZE are four 16-bit fields in the queue record. For convenience, the action of each routine is summarized in Table 14.2 It is assumed that the QueueLib code is linked into the user program along with the driver.

Front	Rear	Count	Size = 16	16-Bit Long Word Buffer

InputBuffer

Front	Rear	Count	Size = 16	16-Bit Long Word Buffer

OutputBuffer

The two subroutines GETCHAR and PUTCHAR use the QDELETE and QINSERT routines to process characters in the input and output buffers. This gives rise to the critical data problem that can occur when one process, while performing an update to data in a queue, is interrupted and

TABLE 14.2 Character Queue Routines

ROUTINE	ACTION
QINIT	The address of the queue record and its SIZE are passed on the stack. The queue record is initialized with Front = 0, Rear = 0, Count = 0, and Size = parameter SIZE.
QINSERT	Address of the queue record and the item to insert are placed on the stack as long words.
QDELETE	Address of the queue record is passed on the stack. The returned item is stored in (D0.L).
QEMPTY	Address of the queue record is passed on the stack. The Z bit indicates TRUE (Z = 0) or FALSE (Z = 1).
QFULL	Address of the queue record is passed on the stack. The Z bit indicates TRUE (Z = 0) or FALSE (Z = 1).

a second routine attempts to access the same data. Upon return from the exception, the original routine may leave critical data (such as queue pointers) in an incorrect state. The problem is addressed in the I/O driver by disabling interrupts during critical data access. This works for the driver but is not a general solution to the problem. A more complete presentation of the critical data problem appears in Chapter 15.

Driver Routine GETCHAR

The queue INPUTQUEUE is used to maintain a 16-character receiver buffer. GETCHAR and the interrupt service routine TERMINAL maintain this structure. When a character is requested, interrupts are disabled, and QEMPTY is called to check if any characters are available.

> If at least one character is available, the character is fetched from the buffer using the routine READINPUTQUEUE, which calls QDELETE. Interrupts are enabled and the routine returns.
>
> If the input queue is empty, the SUSPEND_FOR_INPUT flag is assigned TRUE, and interrupts are enabled. The GETCHAR routine enters an idle loop waiting until SUSPEND_FOR_INPUT becomes FALSE. This is done by the routine TERMINAL while servicing a character at the keyboard. When a key is struck, the interrupt service routine gets the character, places it in the input buffer, and sets the SUSPEND_FOR_INPUT flag FALSE. The service routine disables interrupts so that GETCHAR can be unblocked and can fetch the character from the queue. GETCHAR removes the character by calling READINPUTCHAR, enables interrupts, and returns to the calling program.

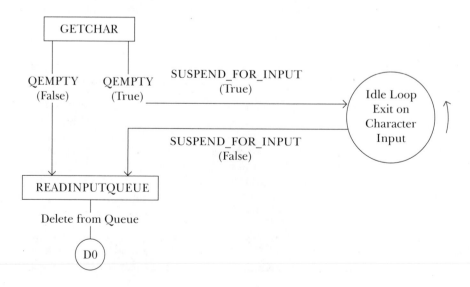

By looping while waiting for input, the process simulates an operating system call to block until the arrival of a character causes the interrupt service routine to wake up the "sleeping" driver.

GETCHAR Code

```
GETCHAR:
        MOVE.W  #DISABLEINTS,SR
        PEA     INPUTQUEUE          ; TEST FOR INPUT QUEUE EMPTY
        JSR     QEMPTY
        BEQ.S   UNLINKCHAR          ; IF FALSE, READ FROM QUEUE
        JSR     WAITFORINPUT
UNLINKCHAR:

        JSR     READINPUTQUEUE
        MOVE.W  #ENABLEINTS,SR      ; RE-ENABLE INTERRUPTS
        RTS


; UNLINK THE CHARACTER FROM THE INPUT BUFFER AND RETURN IN (D0)
READINPUTQUEUE:
        PEA     INPUTQUEUE
        JSR     QDELETE
        RTS


; BLOCK UNTIL THE ACIA INTERRUPT SERVICE ROUTINE HAS BUFFERED A CHAR
WAITFORINPUT:
        BSET    #0,SUSPEND_FOR_INPUT  ; SET TRUE; WAITING FOR CHAR
        MOVE.W  #ENABLEINTS,SR        ; ALLOW RECEIVE INTERRUPTS

GETCWAIT:
        BTST    #0,SUSPEND_FOR_INPUT  ; SIMULATE OPERATING SYS BLOCK
        BNE.S   GETCWAIT
        RTS
```

Driver Subroutine PUTCHAR

A 16-byte queue OUTPUTBUFFER holds characters for output. When PUTCHAR is called, interrupts are disabled, and QFULL is called to see if there is room for another character in the buffer.

> If space is available, the character is placed in the buffer. Interrupts are enabled, and the routine returns.
>
> If space is not available, SUSPEND_FOR_OUTPUT is assigned TRUE, CPU interrupts are enabled, and PUTCHAR loops until the SUSPEND_FOR_OUTPUT flag becomes FALSE, at which time the character is placed in the buffer. SUSPEND_ FOR_OUTPUT is set FALSE by the routine TERMINAL which handles transmit interrupts. Before returning, the service routine checks the status of the SUSPEND_FOR_OUTPUT flag to determine whether PUTCHAR is waiting for the buffer. If PUTCHAR is waiting in an idle loop, the service routine returns to PUTCHAR with interrupts

disabled so that PUTCHAR can insert the character in the output buffer. Prior to return, PUTCHAR enables interrupts.

PUTCHAR Code

```
; WRITE A CHARACTER. BLOCK IF THE OUTPUT BUFFER IS FULL
PUTCHAR:
        MOVE.W    #DISABLEINTS,SR
        MOVE.L    A0,-(SP)
        PEA       OUTPUTQUEUE
        JSR       QFULL
        BEQ.S     ADDTOQUEUE            ; IF QUEUE NOT FULL, ADD CHAR
        JSR       WAITFOROUTPUT
ADDTOQUEUE:

        JSR       ADDTOOUTPUTQUEUE
        LEA       TERMBASE,A0
        MOVE.B    #REC_TRINT,(CTRLREG,A0)  ; TURN TRANSMITINTS BACK ON
        MOVEA.L   (SP)+,A0
        MOVE.W    #ENABLEINTS,SR       ; RE-ENABLE INTERRUPTS
        RTS

; ADD A CHARACTER TO THE OUTPUT BUFFER
ADDTOOUTPUTQUEUE:
        MOVE.L    D0,-(SP)
        PEA       OUTPUTQUEUE
        JSR       QINSERT
        RTS

; BLOCK UNTIL INTERRUPT SERVICE HAS UNLINKED A CHAR FROM THE OUTPUT
BUFFER WAITFOROUTPUT:
        BSET      #0,SUSPEND_FOR_OUTPUT  ; WAIT FOR FREE SLOT
        MOVE.W    #ENABLEINTS,SR         ; WAIT WITH INTERRUPTS ENABLED
PUTCWAIT:
        BTST      #0,SUSPEND_FOR_OUTPUT
        BNE.S     PUTCWAIT
        RTS
```

Driver Subroutine CHARPRESENT

If an element is present in the input buffer, CHARPRESENT returns TRUE by clearing the Z bit. If the buffer is empty (QEMPTY is TRUE), the Z bit is set.

CHARPRESENT Code

```
; CHARACTER ARRIVED - RECEIVED BUFFER EMPTY?
CHARPRESENT:
        MOVE.W    SR,-(SP)             ; SAVE SYSTEM SR
        PEA       INPUTQUEUE
        JSR       QEMPTY
```

```
        BEQ.S     HAVECHAR
        ORI.W     #$0004, (SP)          ; NO  CHAR - SET  Z  BIT
        BRA.S     XIT
HAVECHAR:
        ANDI.W    #$FFFB, (SP)          ; HAVE CHAR - CLEAR  Z  BIT
XIT:    RTR                             ; RETURN WITH INFO IN Z BIT
```

Interrupt Service Routine TERMINAL

This service routine is entered if the receive interrupt, the transmit interrupt, or both, become active. During execution, interrupts are disabled, and the service routine must test the receive-full and transmit-empty bits of the ACIA status register to determine which condition has caused the interrupt. The testing follows this sequence:

1. The ACIA has received a new character. The receive register full bit (RX) is set to 1.

   (a) The character is read from the receive-data register, and the parity bit is cleared.

   (b) The driver implements the XON/XOFF protocol. When XOFF (CTRL-S) is received, all output to the screen is stopped until XON (CTRL-Q) is received. When a character is input, the Boolean flag XOFF_TYPED is checked.

   > If the XOFF condition is in effect (XOFF_TYPED is TRUE), all characters except XON are discarded. The XON character, however, turns XOFF_TYPED to FALSE and returns.
   > If the XOFF condition is not in effect, the character is checked. If it is XOFF, XOFF_TYPED is set to TRUE, and the service routine returns.

   (c) Assuming that the XON/XOFF protocol is handled in (b), the character is placed into the input buffer unless the buffer is full. If this is the case, the routine BEEP is called to send a bell and return.

   (d) At this point in the algorithm, at least one character is available in the input buffer. GETCHAR may be looping, waiting for input from a previously encountered empty buffer. The SUSPEND_FOR_INPUT flag is set to FALSE. If GETCHAR is waiting for input, a return is made to GETCHAR with interrupts disabled. If GETCHAR is not waiting, the transmitter is checked to see if it needs service. If not, a return is made.

2. The ACIA is ready to transmit a character with the transmit register empty bit (TX) set to 1.

(a) The output buffer is checked. If it is empty, the transmit interrupt must be turned off or it will continue to interrupt the system. A value of $95 (receive interrupt on; transmit interrupt off) is placed in the control register, and a return is made.

(b) If the output buffer is not empty, delete a character from the output queue and prepare to transmit it. The variable XOFF_TYPED is checked.

> If it is FALSE, the character is sent. If it is TRUE, the character cannot be sent. The transmit interrupt is disabled, the CPU interrupt mask is cleared (set to level 0), and an idle loop is entered until XOFF_TYPED becomes FALSE. Recall that XOFF_TYPED becomes FALSE when the XON charactered is input. Hence the idle loop is waiting for the service routine to assign XOFF_TYPED FALSE in response to processing the XON character. When XOFF_TYPED becomes FALSE and the loop is exited, CPU interrupts are disabled, and the transmit interrupt is enabled.

(c) The character has been removed from the buffer and is now sent. The SUSPEND_FOR_OUTPUT flag is set to FALSE. If the previous value was TRUE, the PUTCHAR was looping waiting on a full output buffer. In this case, a return is made to PUTCHAR with interrupts disabled. If the previous value was FALSE, a normal RTE is done.

```
; Acia interrupt service routine

statusreg:  equ     4               ; offset to sr saved by interrupt

terminal:
    move.w   #disableints,sr
    link     a6,#0
    movem.l  d0-d1/a0-a1,-(sp)
    lea      TermBase,a1            ; point at the acia
    btst     #0,(statreg,a1)       ; determine interrupt source
    beq.s    transint              ; transmitter caused interrupt?
    move.b   (rxreg,a1),d0         ; get the character received
    bclr     #paritybit,d0         ; mask off parity bit
    tst.w    xoff_typed            ; was Xoff typed previously?
    beq.s    notoff
    cmpi.b   #Xon,d0               ; char must be Xon
    bne      ret                   ; clear Xoff hold flag
    clr.w    xoff_typed
    bra      ret
notoff:
    cmpi.b   #Xoff,d0              ; did new Xoff arrive?
    bne.s    queue
    move.w   #1,xoff_typed         ; flag reception of Xoff
    bra      ret
queue:                             ; put char received in queue
```

```
        pea     inputqueue
        jsr     qfull               ; is input queue full?
        beq.s   cont
        jsr     beep                ; ring bell if queue overflow
        bra     ret                 ; discard character
cont:                               ; add char to the input queue
        move.l  d0,-(sp)
        pea     inputqueue
        jsr     qinsert
        bclr    #0,suspend_for_input
        bne.s   rxdrivewaiting      ; driver waiting for char?
;                                   ; if not test transmitter
        btst    #txempty,(statreg,a1)
        bne.s   transint            ; if empty, service it
        bra.s   ret                 ; return with char queued


rxdriverwaiting:
        ori.w   #level7,(statusreg,a6)
        bra.s   ret                 ; return with ints disabled


; code to handle the transmitter interrupt
transint:
        pea     outputqueue
        jsr     qempty
        beq.s   charbuffered
        move.b  #recOnlyInt,(ctrlreg,a1)
        bra.s   ret
charbuffered:
        pea     outputqueue
        jsr     qdelete
        tst.w   xoff_typed          ; check for Xoff
        beq.s   send
        move.b  #recOnlyInt,(ctrlreg,a1) ; clear tx interrupt and poll
        move.w  #enableints,sr
holdit:
        tst.w   xoff_typed          ; loop until Xoff cleared
        bne.s   holdit
        move.w  #disableints,sr     ; disable cpu interupts
        move.b  #rec_trInt,(ctrlreg,a1) ; re-enable transmit interrupts
send:
        move.b  d0,(txreg,a1)       ; send the character
        bclr    #0,suspend_for_output
        bne.s   txdriverwaiting     ; output driver waiting?
        bra.s   ret


txdriverwaiting:
        ori.w   #level7,(statusreg,sp)
ret:
        movem.l (sp)+,d0-d1/a0-a1
        unlk    a6
        rte
```

The serial driver includes two important utility routines INITPORT and CHECKOUTPUTBUF. The INITPORT routine initializes the ACIA to assert interrupts for both input and output, to set up the input and output buffers, and to clear critical variables. The CHECKOUTPUTBUF routine flushes the output buffer, discards any pending input, and turns off all ACIA interrupts.

PROGRAM 14.3

Buffered
Interrupt-Driven
Serial I/O

This program uses the interrupt-driven I/O library to read characters and echo each back to the screen 50 times, followed by a carriage return/linefeed. The multiple echoing of a character ensures that output buffering is used. It also allows additional characters to be typed while the program is busy producing output ("type ahead"). This utilizes input buffering. After outputting 50 characters, the input buffer is checked by calling CHARPRESENT. The routine returns TRUE if a character arrives during output, and Program 14.3 acknowledges this condition by outputting a '*'. The process continues until the user presses ⟨*control*⟩-Z (end of file).

```
ctrl_Z:       equ     26
cr:           equ     13
lf:           equ     10

        xref    initPort, putchar, getchar, charpresent, stop
        xref    clearOutputQueue

        movea.l #$8000,sp
        jsr     initPort

main:   jsr     getchar          ; get a char from the console
        cmpi.b  #ctrl_Z,d0       ; eof signals program termination
        beq.s   done
        moveq   #49,d1
ploop:  move.w  d0,-(sp)
        jsr     putchar          ; echo character back to console
;                                ; and fill one terminal line
        dbra    d1,ploop
        jsr     newline
        jsr     charpresent
        beq.s   main
        move.b  #'*',d0          ; type adhead has occurred
        jsr     putchar
        jsr     newline
        bra.s   main             ; do it again
done:   jsr     clearOutputQueue
        jsr     stop             ; done
```

⟨During execution, the user rapidly types "abc" and so forth.⟩

```
newline:
        move.l    d0,-(sp)
        move.b    #cr,d0              ; send newline sequence
        jsr       putchar
        move.b    #lf,d0
        jsr       putchar
        move.l    (sp)+,d0
        rts

        end
```

⟨Run of Program 14.3⟩

```
TUTOR 1.3 > G 900
PHYSICAL ADDRESS -00000900
aaaaaaaaaaaaaaaaaaaaaaaaaaaaaaaaaaaaaaaaaaaaaaaaaaaaaaaaaaaaaaaa
aaaaaaaaaaaaaaaa
bbbbbbbbbbbbbbbbbbbbbbbbbbbbbbbbbbbbbbbbbbbbbbbbbbbbbbbbbbbbbbbb
bbbbbbbbbbbbbbbb
*
cccccccccccccccccccccccccccccccccccccccccccccccccccccccccccccccc
cccccccccccccccccccc
1111111111111111111111111111111111111111111111111111111111111111
11111111111111111
*
2222222222222222222222222222222222222222222222222222222222222222
22222222222222222
*
3333333333333333333333333333333333333333333333333333333333333333
333333333333333
```

PROGRAM 14.4

Memory Display

The program dumps bytes in memory from $900 to $A000. Output sets off 16 bytes to the line. At any time during the memory dump, a CTRL_S (XOFF) halts output to enable viewing of the data. The CTRL_Q (XON) character causes output to resume. The code is loaded on the ECB system at address $900. The run dumps the code file similar to the TUTOR Memory Display (MD) command.

```
monitor:        equ     $8146
cr:             equ     13
lf:             equ     10

        xref    initPort, putchar, getchar, clearOutputQueue

        movea.l #$8000,sp
        jsr     initPort

main:   lea     $900,a0
```

```
            moveq     #0,d1
            move.l    a0,d0
            jsr       printaddress
dump:       addq.w    #1,d1
            move.b    (a0)+,d0
            jsr       hexbyteout
            cmpi.w    #16,d1
            blt.s     cont
            jsr       newline
            move.l    a0,d0
            jsr       printaddress
            moveq     #0,d1
cont:       cmpa.l    #$a00,a0
            bcs       dump

            jsr       getchar          ; pause for final input character
            jsr       clearOutputQueue
            jsr       stop

hexbyteout:
            movem.l   d0/d7,-(sp)
            move.w    #1,d7
            jsr       printhex
            move.b    #' ',d0
            jsr       putchar
            jsr       putchar
            movem.l   (sp)+,d0/d7
            rts


printaddress:
            movem.l   d0/d7,-(sp)
            move.w    #3,d7
            jsr       printhex
            move.b    #':',d0
            jsr       putchar
            move.b    #' ',d0
            jsr       putchar
            jsr       putchar
            movem.l   (sp)+,d0/d7
            rts


printhex:
            movem.l   d0-d3/a0,-(sp)
            move.w    d7,d1
            lea       hexdigits,a0
            move.w    d0,d2
pr:         cmpi.w    #1,d7
            beq.s     byte
            rol.w     #4,d2
            bra.s     print
byte:       rol.b     #4,d2
print:      move.w    d2,d3
            andi.w    #$0f,d3
            move.b    (0,a0,d3.w),d0
```

```
            jsr        putchar
            dbra       d1,pr
            movem.l    (sp)+,d0-d3/a0
            rts

newline:
            move.l     d0,-(sp)
            move.b     #cr,d0          ; send newline sequence
            jsr        putchar
            move.b     #lf,d0
            jsr        putchar
            move.l     (sp)+,d0
            rts

stop:       jmp        monitor

            data
hexdigits:
            dc.b       '0123456789ABCDEF'

            end
```

⟨Run of Program 14.4⟩

```
TUTOR 1.3 > G 900
PHYSICAL ADDRESS-00000900
0900:  2E  7C  00  00  80  00  4E  B9  00  00  09  FC  41  F9  00  00
0910:  09  00  72  00  20  08  4E  B9  00  00  09  7A  52  41  10  18
0920:  4E  B9  00  00  09  56  0C  41  00  10  6D  10  4E  B9  00  00
0930:  09  DC  20  08  4E  B9  00  00  09  7A  72  00  B1  FC  00  00
0940:  0A  00  65  D8  4E  B9  00  00  0A  90  4E  B9  00  00  0A  66
0950:  4E  B9  00  00  09  F6  48  E7  81  00  3E  3C  00  01  4E  B9
0960:  00  00  09  A8  10  3C  00  20  4E  B9  00  00  0A  DA  4E  B9
0970:  00  00  0A  DA  4C  DF  00  81  4E  75  48  E7  81  00  3E  3C
0980:  00  03  4E  B9  00  00  09  A8  10  3C  00  3A  4E  B9  00  00
0990:  0A  DA  10  3C  00  20  4E  B9  00  00  0A  DA  4E  B9  00  00
09A0:  0A  DA  4C  DF  00  81  4E  75  48  F7  F0  80  32  07  41  F9
09B0:  00  00  0D  68  34  00  0C  47  00  01  67  04  E9  5A  60  02
09C0:  E9  1A  36  02  02  43  00  0F  10  30  30  00  4E  B9  00  00
09D0:  0A  DA  51  C9  FF  E2  4C  DF  01  0F  4E  75  2F  00  10  3C
09E0:  00  0D  4E  B9  00  00  0A  DA  10  3C  00  0A  4E  B9  00  00
09F0:  0A  DA  20  1F  4E  75  4E  F9  00  00  81  46  46  FC  27  00
0A00:
```

14.5 THE TIMER INTERRUPT

The timer is a useful tool for measuring elapsed time, monitoring process switching in a multiprocessing environment, and other time-dependent applications. Repeated testing of the timer to check for timeout is a wasteful use of processor cycles. In most applications, the timer should be interrupt driven. By setting bits in the control register, an interrupt is generated when the counter is in transition from 1 to 0.

Timer Control Register

Action on Zero Detect			Counter Load	*		Clock Control	Timer Enable
7	6	5	4	3	2	1	0

In Chapter 12, the fields of the timer control register were specified. The clock control field is set to 00, the counter load field is 0, and the timer enable field turns the timer on and off. Interrupts are specified by the action on zero detect field.

100   Vectored interrupts disabled
101   Vectored interrupt generated on zero detect

The corresponding settings for the control register are

$80   No interrupt
$A0   Vectored interrupt on zero detect

The timer generates a vectored interrupt on the ECB system. The vector number, asserted during the interrupt acknowledge cycle, is determined by the value in the **timer interrupt vector register (TIVR)**. Select an 8-bit number from the user vector number range 64–255.

EXAMPLE 14.2

The TIVR has address $10023 on the ECB system. This address has offset 2 from the timer base. Assume that A0 is the base address for the timer registers. To assign vector number 68 to the timer interrupt, execute the following:

```
TIVR:  EQU     2
       MOVE.B  #68,(TIVR,A0)
```

Demonstration Program: Clock

A complete program illustrates the use of a timer interrupt. The service routine maintains the elapsed time since the program was started. Note that the timer interrupt service routine CLOCK disables the timer interrupt during execution. The interrupt is enabled by the RTE. If this is not done, the timer will still be generating an interrupt request, and the program will be locked into continuous service of the interrupt. The TimerLib package from Chapter 12 has an alternative initialization routine INITINTTIMER for use with timer interrupts.

Parameters passed
The vector number and the tick count are passed as long words on
the stack.
Parameters returned
None

```
TimerBase:      equ     $010021     ; timer base address
Tctrl:          equ     0           ; timer control register
Tivr:           equ     2           ; timer interrupt register
Tpreload:       equ     4           ; timer counter preload register

tickcount:      equ     8
tivrval:        equ     12
param_4:        equ     4

        xdef    initIntTimer

initIntTimer:
        link        a6,#0
        movem.l     d0/a1,-(sp)
        jsr         timerAddr
        move.l      (tickcount,a6),d0   ; fetch tick count
        movep.l     d0,(Tpreload,a1)
        move.w      (tivrval,a6),d0     ; set TIVR
        move.b      d0,(Tivr,a1)
        move.b      #$A0,(Tctrl,a1)     ; init timer protocol
        movem.l     (sp)+,d0/a1
        unlk        a6
        move.l      (sp),(param_4,sp)
        addq.w      #param_4,sp
        rts

timerAddr:
        lea         TimerBase,a1        ; utility routine
        rts

        end
```

PROGRAM 14.5

Elapsed Time

The timer is set to interrupt every second and to update the elapsed time
of the program by maintaining a clock count. The main program reads
characters from the keyboard and writes them to the screen. However,
when a user presses ⟨control⟩-T, the time in seconds is printed in the form
"⟨time⟩". Note that the PUTDECOUT routine appends two blank characters
to the number. These characters are removed with the backspaces in the
BACKMARK string.

```
consoleport:    equ     0
disableints:    equ     $2700
enableints:     equ     $2000
ctrl_T:         equ     20
TvecNum:        equ     64
vClock:         equ     TvecNum*4
```

```
backspace:      equ    8

        xref    initPort,putstring,charpresent
        xref    getchar,putdecout
        xref    initIntTimer, startTimer, resetTimer

start:

        move.w   #disableints,sr  ; disable interrupts for now
        movea.l  #$8000,sp        ; set stack pointer at end of 32k
        move.l   #clock,vClock.w
        move.w   #TvecNum,-(sp)   ; set up interrupt vector for ptm
        move.l   #125000,-(sp)    ; load tcpr for 1 second
        jsr      initIntTimer
        moveq    #consoleport,d7  ; initialize the console port
        jsr      initPort
        clr.w    seconds          ; ensure times cleared
        move.w   #enableints,sr   ; enable interrupts
        jsr      startTimer       ; enable the timer


    loop:

        jsr      charpresent      ; see if character typed on console
        beq.s    loop
        jsr      getchar          ; get character with no echo
        cmpi.b   #ctrl_T,d0
        bne.s    loop
        jsr      reporttime       ; print elapsed time since startup
        bra.s    loop             ; go do it again
;                                 ; subroutine to print elapsed time


reporttime:
```

⟨*Note:* During the run, CONTROL = T is entered after the words "clocked," "T," and "plus".⟩

```
        move.l   d0,-(sp)
        lea      frontmark        ; print two blanks each iteration
        jsr      putstring        ; print two (2) blanks
        move.w   seconds,d0
        jsr      putdecout        ; print it
        lea      backmark         ; print two blanks each iteration
        jsr      putstring        ; print two (2) blanks
        move.l   (sp)+,d0
        rts

; interrupt service routine for the timer
clock:  move.w   #disableints,sr  ; disable interrupts
        movem.l  d0/a0,-(sp)
```

```
        addq.w   #1,seconds
        jsr      resetTimer
        movem.l  (sp)+,d0/a0
        rte                        ; original SR is reset
        data

seconds:   ds.w  1

frontmark: dc.b  ' <'
           dc.b  0
backmark:  dc.b  backspace,backspace,' >'
           dc.b  0

        end
```

⟨Run of Program 14.5⟩

```
TUTOR 1.3 > G 900
PHYSICAL ADDRESS = 00000900
This text is being clocked <15> The typing is slow to
illustrate time delay to a <control>T <56> Done after
one minute plus ⟨73⟩
```

14.6 | MC68230 PI/T INTERRUPTS

The parallel interface provided with the MC68230 PI/T is capable of generating four vectored interrupts on its handshake lines H1–H4. When the interface is used with a printer, the ACKNOWLEDGE and FAULT interrupts are relevant. The ACKNOWLEDGE interrupt is generated when a latch is available for a new character. This section presents a complete program that implements transmit interrupts for a parallel printer. Many of the principles used for the serial driver are applied to the printer, including the buffering of output.

PI/T Interrupt Registers

In order to enable PI/T interrupts, the interface device must be initialized appropriately. This involves giving a more detailed analysis of the port service request register and the use of the interrupt vector register.

Port Service Request Register

The port service request register (PSRR) is used to specify whether interrupt or direct memory access (DMA) requests are to be generated from the use of the H1 and H3 handshake lines. The register also specifies the priority among the four possible interrupts, in case two or more interrupt conditions are present at the same time. The condition with the highest priority has precedence in asserting its vector number. With the ECB system, a value of $18 initializes the register. It places the ACKNOWLEDGE interrupt with highest priority. All PI/T interrupts on the ECB are generated at level 3.

Port Interrupt Vector Register

The port interrupt vector register (PIVR) contains the high-order 6 bits of the four exception vector numbers for the device. When an interrupt is generated, the PI/T adds the 2 low-order bits and uses the resulting value in the interrupt acknowledge cycle. This results in four distinct and consecutive vector numbers. The ordering of the low-order bits is

ACKNOWLEDGE   Interrupt—00
DATA STROBE   Interrupt—01
FAULT   Interrupt—10
INPUT PRIME   Interrupt—11

Port Interrupt Vector Register

High 6 Bits of Vector Number						*	*
7	6	5	4	3	2	1	0

Initialize the PIVR with a number divisible by 4 (low-order 2 bits are 00). For example, by using the initial number of 64, the resulting four interrupt vector numbers are 64, 65, 66, and 67. In this case, the ACKNOWLEDGE interrupt vector address is

$$4 * 64 = 256 = \$100$$

The PI/T initialization process is completed by setting bits in the Port A control register to enable interrupts. Bit 1 of this register controls the generation of the ACKNOWLEDGE interrupt. When the bit is 0, no interrupt is generated when a latch is empty. When it is 1, a vectored interrupt results when the PI/T will accept another character. The following code initializes the printer as an interrupt driven device with vectored interrupt 64 planted in the PIVR.

```
NPRINTER:       EQU     64              ; USER SELECTED VECTOR
VPRINTER:       EQU     4*NPRINTER      ; TRANSMIT INTERRUPT

INITPRINTER:
        MOVE.L  A0,-(SP)
        LEA     PIABASE,A0
        MOVE.B  #$00,(PGCR,A0)          ; DISABLE HANDSHAKE LINES
        MOVE.B  #$18,(PSRR,A0)          ; SET FOR PI/T INTERRUPTS
        MOVE.B  #$FF,(PADDR,A0)         ; ALL PORT A PINS FOR OUTPUT
        MOVE.B  #$00,(PBDDR,A0)         ; ALL PORT B PINS FOR INPUT
```

```
        MOVE.B   #$60, (PACR, A0)         ; INIT PORT A, NO INTERRUPTS
        MOVE.B   #$A0, (PBCR, A0)         ; INIT PORT B, NO INTERRUPTS
        MOVE.B   #NPRINTER, (PIVR, A0)    ; IVEC NUMBER = NPRINTER
        MOVE.B   #$30, (PGCR, A0)         ; ENABLE THE HANDSHAKE LINES
        BSET     #3, (PBCR, A0)           ; PULSE INPUT PRIME;
        BCLR     #3, (PBCR, A0)
        MOVE.L   (SP)+, A0
        RTS
```

Demonstration Program: PRINTSTRING

This sample program demonstrates printer transmit interrupts. The program logic is similar to that for serial transmit interrupts. Characters are sent to the printer with ACKNOWLEDGE interrupts enabled. The techniques for strobing the printer and checking the status of the printer after transmission were developed in Chapter 12.

The print routine uses a 256-character output queue. The main program called PRINTCHAR, which takes a character in (D0.B) and sends it to the output queue. The routine executes with interrupts disabled, so that it can correctly update the output queue without interruption.

If the output queue is not full, the character is inserted in the queue using routine OUTPUT.

If the queue is full, PRINTCHAR sets the WAITFORSLOT flag and goes into an idle loop that tests the Boolean variable until a slot in the queue is available.

The transmit interrupt service routine handles the printing of characters and the blocking of transmit interrupts if no characters are available to print. After entering the service routine, the queue is tested. If it is empty, transmit interrupts are turned off by clearing bit 1 of the Port A control register. Failure to do this would result in a locked system endlessly responding to the availability of the printer. The interrupt is turned back on by PRINTCHAR. If a character is available in the output queue, it is sent to the printer with the strobe signals. Before exiting the service routine with RTE, test to see if any output request is pending (WAITFORSLOT is TRUE). If output is pending, disable interrupts and return to the idle loop in PRINTCHAR.

PROGRAM 14.6

PI/T Printer with Interrupts

The string "Testing the printer" is printed 16 times. The main program uses PRINTSTRING, which extends the primitive PRINTCHAR routine.

```
piabase:        equ      $10001
pgcr:           equ      0              ; port general control register
```

```
psrr:              equ    2           ; port service request register
paddr:             equ    4           ; port a data direction register
pbddr:             equ    6           ; port b data direction register
pivr:              equ    10          ; port interrupt vector register
pacr:              equ    12          ; port a control register
pbcr:              equ    14          ; port b control register
padr:              equ    16          ; port a data register
pbdr:              equ    18          ; port b data register
psr:               equ    26          ; port status register
latchavailable:    equ    0


nprinter:          equ    64          ; user selected vector number
vprinter:          equ    4*nprinter  ; transmit interrupt service


disableintr:       equ    $2700
enableintr:        equ    $2000
level7:            equ    $0700


cr:                equ    $0d
lf:                equ    $0a
null:              equ    $00



        xref    qinit, qempty, qfull, qinsert, qdelete, stop
        xref    initTimer, startTimer, testTimeout, stopTimer



start:
        move.w   #disableintr,sr     ; disable interrupts for now
        movea.l  #$8000,sp
        jsr      initPrinter
        clr.w    waitforslot
        move.l   #printr,vprinter.w  ; initialize printer ivec
        move.w   #printbuffersize,-(sp)
        pea      printbuffer
        jsr      qinit


main:   moveq    #15,d2              ; print a string 16 times
        jsr      checkstatus         ; make sure printer ready
        move.w   #enableintr,sr      ; allow interrupts to the cpu
        lea      piabase,a0
        bset     #1,(pacr,a0)        ; enable printer interrupts
        lea      msg,a0
loop:   jsr      printstring
        dbra     d2,loop
        move.w   #5,d0
        jsr      printdelay          ; delay Tutor reset
        jsr      stop                ; return to tutor
```

```
initPrinter:
        move.l    a0,-(sp)
        lea       piabase,a0
        move.b    #$00,(pgcr,a0)      ; temp disable handshake lines
        move.b    #$18,(psrr,a0)      ; configure pi/t interrupts
        move.b    #$ff,(paddr,a0)     ; port a pins for output
        move.b    #$00,(pbddr,a0)     ; all port b pins for input
        move.b    #$60,(pacr,a0)      ; init port a, no interrupts
        move.b    #$a0,(pbcr,a0)      ; init port b, no interrupts
        move.b    #nprinter,(pivr,a0) ; ivec number = nprinter
        move.b    #$30,(pgcr,a0)      ; enable the handshake lines
        bset      #3,(pbcr,a0)        ; pulse input prime;
        bclr      #3,(pbcr,a0)
        move.l    (sp)+,a0
        rts


printstring:
        movem.l   d0/a0,-(sp)
printloop:
        move.b    (a0)+,d0
        beq.s     exit
        jsr       printchar
        bra.s     printloop
exit:   movem.l   (sp)+,d0/a0
        rts


printdelay:
        movem.l   d1-d3,-(sp)
        move.l    #125000,d1
        move.w    d1,d2
        mulu      d0,d2              ; multiply D0 by LSW of D1
        swap      d1
        mulu      d0,d1              ; multiply d0 by MSW of D1
        moveq     #16,d3
        asl.l     d3,d1
        add.l     d2,d1              ; add partial products
        move.l    d1,-(sp)           ; push tickcount on stack
        jsr       initTimer
        jsr       starttimer         ; start the timer
delay_1:
        jsr       testTimeout
        beq.s     delay_1
        jsr       stopTimer
        movem.l   (sp)+,d1-d3
        rts


printchar:
        move.w    #disableintr,sr    ; disallow interrupts
        move.l    a0,-(sp)
        lea       piabase,a0
```

```
            pea       printbuffer
            jsr       qfull
            beq.s     output
            bset      #0,waitforslot      ; sleep waiting for interrupt
            move.w    #enableintr,sr      ; wake up when latch available

idle:       btst      #0,waitforslot
            bne.s     idle
;                                         ; after idle, run at level 7
output:
            move.l    d0,-(sp)
            pea       printbuffer
            jsr       qinsert
            bset      #1,(pacr,a0)        ; interrupts when latch available
            move.l    (sp)+,a0
            move.w    #enableintr,sr
            rts


checkstatus:
            move.l    a0,-(sp)
            lea       piabase,a0
            clr.w     printfail           ; assume all is ok
wait:       move.b    (pbdr,a0),d1        ; read status lines
            andi.b    #$03,d1
            cmpi.b    #$01,d1             ; should be 01
            beq.s     chkleave            ; exit when no problem indicated
            move.w    #1,printfail        ; set problem flag
            bra.s     wait
chkleave:
            tst.w     printfail           ; if failure, exit with (d1) = 1
            bne.s     xit
            moveq     #0,d1
xit:        move.l    (sp)+,a0
            rts


savedsr:              equ       4


printr:
            move.w    #disableintr,sr
            link      a6,#0
            movem.l   d0-d1/a0,-(sp)
            lea       piabase,a0
            pea       printbuffer
            jsr       qempty
            beq.s     print
            bclr      #1,(pacr,a0)        ; turn off printer interrupts
            bra.s     ret
print:      pea       printbuffer
            jsr       qdelete
```

```
send:
          move.b   d0,(padr,a0)
          bset     #3,(pacr,a0)
          bclr     #3,(pacr,a0)
          jsr      checkstatus
          tst.w    d1
          bne.s    send                    ; resend until it gets there
          bclr     #0,waitforslot
          beq.s    ret                     ; is printchar waiting?
          ori.w    #level7,(savedsr,a6)    ; rte with interrupts disabled
ret:      movem.l  (sp)+,d0-d1/a0
          unlk     a6
          rte


          data

printbuffersize:
                            equ      256
waitforslot:
          ds.w     1
printfail:
          ds.w     1


printbuffer:
          ds.w     1                       ; queue head
          ds.w     1                       ; queue tail
          ds.w     1                       ; queue count
          ds.w     1                       ; queue size
          ds.l     printbuffersize         ; data buffer


msg:      dc.b     'Testing the printer.',lf,cr,null


          end
```

⟨Run the Program 14.6⟩

```
Testing the printer.
Testing the printer.
Testing the printer.
Testing the printer.
Testing the printer.
Testing the printer.
Testing the printer.
Testing the printer.
Testing the printer.
Testing the printer.
Testing the printer.
```

```
Testing the printer.
Testing the printer.
Testing the printer.
Testing the printer.
Testing the printer.
```

14.7 MULTIPLE EXCEPTIONS

The MC68000 processor establishes a priority structure for its exceptions to handle a case in which two or more exceptions occur simultaneously. In the ordering, exceptions with higher priority enter the exception-processing state before those of lower priority. Note that the exception-processing state ends when the PC is assigned the address of the first instruction of the service routine. Because the processing cycle uses the stack for the PC and SR parameters, the last exception cycle executed (lower-priority exception) passes program control to the service routine of the lower-priority exception. The resulting order of execution is counterintuitive. That is, the higher priority exception is processed first, but the service routine of the lower

FIGURE 14.5 Priority Stacking of Exceptions

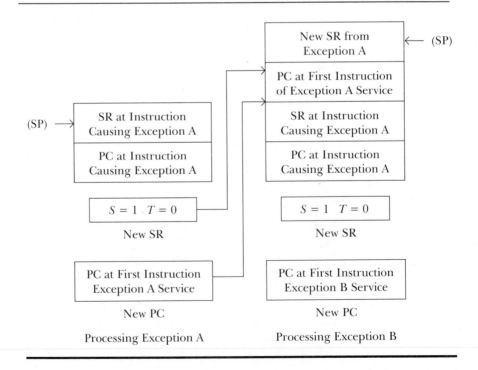

priority exception is executed first. Figure 14.5 illustrates the process for exceptions A and B with A of higher priority.

In a case in which B is a trace exception, tracing occurs at the current PC. Because the exception A cycle has completed, the current PC is the first instruction in the exception A service routine. Originally, the trace was intended to trace an instruction in the user program.

Exceptions are grouped into three categories. Table 14.3 summarizes the priority structure. The following discussion describes each group.

Group 0: The highest-priority exceptions are contained in this group, which consists of the reset, address error, and bus error exceptions. Within this group, the exceptions have priority in the order of their listing. These exceptions cause the instructions currently executing to be aborted, and exception processing begins within two CPU clock cycles. It is likely that the instruction involved would not have completed execution and the PC would be pointing at an address prior to the end of the instruction.

Group 1: These exceptions are (in order of priority) trace, interrupt, illegal instruction, and privilege violation. The current instruction is allowed to complete execution before the exception forces the next instruction to be preempted in favor of exception processing. The trace and interrupt exceptions occur before the next instruction begins execution. Privilege violations and illegal instructions are detected when the opcode word is fetched. The program counter does not advance.

Group 2: This group includes the TRAP, TRAPV, CHK, and divide-by-zero exceptions. These exceptions are caused by normal program

TABLE 14.3 Interrupt Priority Structure

GROUP	EXCEPTION	PROCESSING
0	Reset Address error Bus error	Exception processing begins within 2 clock cycles.
1	Trace Interrupt Illegal instruction Privilege violation	Exception processing starts before the next instruction begins execution.
2	TRAP TRAPV CHK Divide by zero	Exception processing is started by normal instruction execution.

highest priority [handwritten annotation]

execution. Because only one instruction can execute at a time, there are no priorities within this group.

EXAMPLE 14.3

The priority structure specifies the order in which exceptions are processed when two or more occur simultaneously.

(a) A bus error occurs during the exception-processing cycle for the CHK instruction. The bus error is processed, and CHK is aborted.

(b) The T bit is on, and the next instruction is TRAP. If a trace is on while executing an instruction that causes an exception, that exception has priority. The TRAP exception has priority in this case, so the trace service routine executes first. The first instruction of the trap service routine is traced.

(c) The processor executes the following instruction with the T bit set:

    MOVE.L   (A3),(A5)+

If a peripheral-device interrupt occurs, the trace exception is processed first, followed by the interrupt. Normal execution continues in the service routine for the interrupt.

PROGRAM 14.7

Multiple Exception
Test Program

Three exceptions (trace, trap, and timer interrupt) are generated. Each service routine prints the contents of the PC and SR on the stack along with a message identifying the exception.

1. The CPU is set to level 7 and the timer is turned on. A delay is executed to make sure that a timer interrupt is asserted.

2. The trap exception occurs with the trace bit on. The trap exception has priority. The PC on the stack for the trace service routine is the address of the first instruction of the trap service routine. While executing this service routine, the SR for the TRAP #0 exception is on the stack with $T = 1$.

SR = 2704	Trace Exception
PC First Instruction Trap Service Routine	
SR = A704	Trap Exception
PC Next Instruction After Trap #0	

3. Upon return from the trap service routine, the trace bit is on. The trace exception is asserted after executing MOVE.B #$2000,SR. A timer interrupt is also asserted at this point and has lower priority than the trace exception. The service routine for the interrupt is executed first.

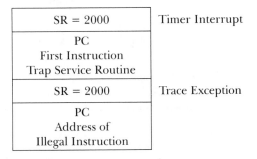

SR = 2000	Timer Interrupt
PC First Instruction Trap Service Routine	
SR = 2000	Trace Exception
PC Address of Illegal Instruction	

```
; exception vector addresses
vtimer:    equ      256
vtrace:    equ      36
vtrap0:    equ      128

; acia and timer parameters
console:   equ      0
aciacr:    equ      $10040
timerbase: equ      $10021
tcon:      equ      0
tivr:      equ      2
tcpr:      equ      4

; character constants
nl:        equ      $0a
cr:        equ      $0d
null:      equ      $00

monitor:   equ      $8146          ; ecb monitor address
progct:    equ      14             ; stack offset to pc
statreg:   equ      12             ; stack offset to sr

           xref     initPort,putstring,puthexout

start:     lea      $8000,sp

; initialize exception vectors
           move.l   #timer,vtimer.w
           move.l   #trace,vtrace.w
           move.l   #trap0,vtrap0,w

; initialize acia and timer registers
           move.w   #console,d7
           jsr      initPort
           lea      timerbase,a1   ; initialize the timer
           move.b   #$a0,(tcon,a1)
```

```
            move.b    #64, (tivr,a1)
            move.l    #5,d0                    ; 5/125000 secs will
;                                              ; allow a timer interrupt
            movep.l   d0, (tcpr,a1)
            move.w    #$2700,sr                ; mask interrupts
            bset      #0, (tcon,a1)            ; start timer

            move.l    #250000,d2               ; delay so timer goes off
delay:      subi.l    #1,d2
            bne.s     delay
            ori.w     #$8000,sr                ; turn tracing on
            trap      #0                       ; make trap call
            move.w    #$2000,sr                ; allow timer interrupt
            jmp       monitor

timer:      jsr       printstk                 ; print the stack
            lea       timermsg,a0
            jsr       putstring                ; timer message
            bclr      #0, (tcon,a1)            ; turn off timer
            rte

trace:      jsr       printstk
            lea       tracemsg,a0
            jsr       putstring                ; trace message
            bclr      #7, (sp)                 ; turn off tracing
            rte

trap0:      jsr       printstk
            lea       trapmsg,a0
            jsr       putstring                ; trap message
            rte

; print out the value of the pc and sr on the stack
printstk:   movem.l   d0/a0,-(sp)
            move.l    (progct,sp),d0
            jsr       puthexout
            lea       spaces,a0
            jsr       putstring
            move.w    (statreg,sp),d0
            andi.l    #$ffff,d0
            jsr       puthexout
            movem.l   (sp)+,d0/a0
            rts

            data

label:
            dc.b      ' PC    SR    Exception',nl
            dc.b      '_____',nl,null
timermsg:   dc.b      ' timer ',cr,nl,null
tracemsg:   dc.b      ' trace ',cr,nl,null
trapmsg:    dc.b      ' trap ',cr,nl,null
spaces:     dc.b      '  ',null

            end
```

⟨Run of Program 14.7⟩
All addresses are given relative to the load address $000900.

```
TUTOR 1.3 > G 900
PHYSICAL ADDRESS = 00000900
   PC        SR        Exception

  09AA      2704         trace
  096E      A704         trap
  092       2000         timer
  0972      2000         trace
```

14.8 MC68000 SIGNAL LINES AND INTERRUPT ACKNOWLEDGE

The MC68000 processor contains 64 signal lines linking components of a system. These include address, data, and control signal lines. This section includes a diagram of the lines and a brief description of their use. The information applies to exception processing, interrupts, the design of memory management schemes, and so forth. The information also contributes to a deepened understanding of assembly language programming.

The use of function code lines was used in Chapter 13 to describe the bus and address error exceptions. In this chapter, the lines are used during the interrupt cycle acknowledge, along with the interrupt control signals

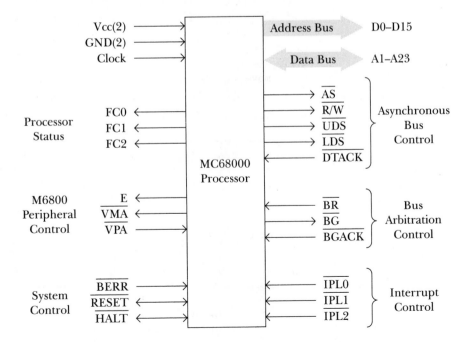

and the peripheral device VPA and DTACK control signals. Chapter 15 uses the function control lines to describe an MMU coprocessor. Additional details on the signal lines are found in the Motorola product information publication *MC68000 16-Bit Microprocessor.*

The operation for each group of signal lines is outlined. The term *assert* implies that a signal is active and *negate* implies that a signal is inactive.

Address Bus (A1 through A23)   This 23-bit unidirectional bus can address up to 16M (8 megawords) of data. It provides the address for a bus operation during all cycles except interrupt cycles. During interrupt cycles, address lines A1, A2, and A3 provide information about the interrupt level that is being serviced.

Data Bus (D0 through D15)   This 16-bit, bidirectional bus is used for general-purpose data transfer. It can transfer and accept data in either word or byte length. During an interrupt acknowledge cycle, the external device supplies the vector number on data lines D0–D7.

Asynchronous Bus Control   Asynchronous data transfers are handled using the address strobe, read/write, upper and lower data strobes, and data transfer acknowledge signals.

ADDRESS STROBE (AS) is a signal indicating that there is a valid address on the address bus.

READ/WRITE (R/W) is a signal defining the data bus transfer as a read or write cycle. The R/W signal also works in conjunction with the data strobes.

UPPER AND LOWER DATA STROBE (UDS, LDS) are signals that control the flow of data on the data bus. When the R/W line is high, the processor will read from the data bus. When the R/W is low, the processor will write to the data bus. The following signals specify access to the 16 lines of data.

UDS	LDS	R/W	D8–D15	D0–D7
High	High	—	No valid data	Valid data bits 0–7
Low	Low	High	Valid data bits 8–15	Valid data bits 0–7
High	Low	High	No valid data	Valid data bits 0–7
Low	High	High	Valid data bits 8–15	No valid data
Low	Low	Low	Valid data bits 8–15	Valid data bits 0–7
High	Low	Low	Valid data bits 0–7	Valid data bits 0–7
Low	High	Low	Valid data bits 8–15	Valid data bits 8–15

DATA TRANSFER ACKNOWLEDGE (DTACK) is input indicating that the data transfer is completed. When the processor recognizes

DTACK during a read cycle, data is latched, and the bus cycle is terminated. When DTACK is recognized during a write cycle, the bus cycle is terminated.

Bus Arbitration Control These three signals form a bus arbitration circuit to determine which device will be the bus master device.

BUS REQUEST (BR) is an input that is OR'ed with all other devices that could be bus masters. This input indicates to the processor that some other device desires to become the bus master.

BUS GRANT (BG) is an output signal that indicates to all other potential bus master devices that the processor will release bus control at the end of the current bus cycle.

BUS GRANT ACKNOWLEDGE (BGACK) is an input signal that indicates that some other device has become the bus master.

Interrupt Control (IPL0, IPL1, IPL2) These input pins indicate the encoded priority level of the device requesting an interrupt. The last significant bit is given in IPL0, and the most significant bit is contained in IPL2. These lines must remain asserted until the processor signals interrupt acknowledge (FC0 through FC2 are all high) to ensure that the interrupt is recognized.

System Control The system control inputs are used to either reset or halt the processor and to indicate to the processor that bus errors have occurred.

BUS ERROR (BERR) is an output that informs the processor that there is a problem with the cycle currently being executed. Problems may result from nonresponding devices, failure to acquire an interrupt vector number, or improper memory access. The bus error signal interacts with the halt signal to determine whether the current bus cycle should be re-executed or exception processing performed.

RESET (RESET) is a bidirectional signal line that acts to reset (start a system initialization sequence in) the processor in response to an external reset signal. An internally generated reset (the result of a RESET instruction) causes all external devices to be reset, and the internal state of the processor is not affected. A total system reset (processor and external devices) is the result of external HALT and RESET signals applied at the same time.

HALT (HALT) is a bidirectional line that is driven by an external device. It will cause the processor to stop at the completion of the current bus cycle. When the processor has been halted using this input, all control signals are inactive. When the halt state is entered because of major system failure, as described in Chapter 12, the HALT line is driven by the processor to indicate the condition to external devices.

M6800 Peripheral Control   These control signals are used to allow the interfacing of synchronous M6800 peripheral devices with the asynchronous MC68000.

ENABLE (E) is the standard enable signal common to all M6800-type peripheral devices. The period for this output is ten MC68000 clock periods (six clocks low, four clocks high). Enable is generated by an internal ring counter that may come up in any state (i.e., at power on, it is impossible to guarantee the phase relationship of E to Clock). E is a free-running clock and runs regardless of the state of the bus.

VALID PERIPHERAL ADDRESS (VPA) is an input signal that indicates that the device or region addressed is an M6800 family device and that data transfer should be synchronized with the enable (E) signal. This input also indicates that the processor should use automatic vectoring for an interrupt.

VALID MEMORY ADDRESS (VMA) is an output signal that is used to indicate to M6800-type peripheral devices that there is a valid address on the address bus and the processor is synchronized to enable. This signal only responds to a valid peripheral address (VPA) input, which indicates that the peripheral is an M6800 family device.

Processor Status (FC0, FC1, FC2)   These function code outputs indicate the state (user or supervisor) and the cycle type currently being executed. The information indicated by the function code outputs is valid whenever address strobe (AS) is active.

Interrupt Acknowledge Bus Cycle

The CPU places the interrupt level on address lines A1–A3. The three function code lines FC2–FC0 are set to 111_2, which is the code for interrupt acknowledge. Each device asserting an interrupt is looking for a function code of 111_2. It then looks for its interrupt level to appear on A1–A3. Assuming that devices are organized around a backplane, when two or more devices assert an interrupt at the same level, the one located on the bus in the "slot" closest to the processor is serviced. The device that receives the interrupt acknowledge will then communicate an exception vector number.

A device in autovectored interrupt mode asserts the valid peripheral address (VPA) signal to the processor. The CPU uses the priority level of the interrupt as an index into the exception vector table.

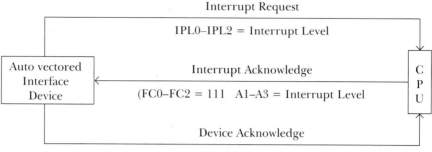

Interrupt Request

VPA Active

A device in vectored-interrupt mode sends an 8-bit vector number down the data bus, followed by assertion of the data transfer acknowledge (DTACK) signal. The processor multiplies this vector number by 4 and reads the address of the service routine from the exception vector table.

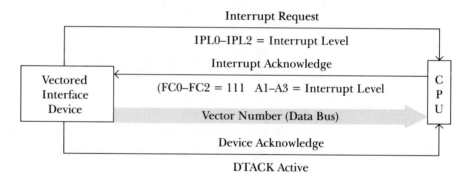

Interrupt Request

DTACK Active

If, during the interrupt acknowledge cycle, no device responds by asserting DTACK or VPA, board circuitry asserts the bus error (BERR) signal, which is recognized by the CPU as the spurious interrupt exception.

14.9 | MC68020/30/40 INTERRUPT PROCESSING

The MC68020/30/40 systems use two different stack pointers in supervisor mode. The traditional supervisor stack pointer (SSP) of the MC68000 system is called the **interrupt stack pointer (ISP)**. A second stack, the master stack, is associated with the master state bit (bit M = bit 12) of the status register and is used with exception processing. In a multitasking system, if $M = 1$, the two stacks allow all interrupt processing to be done using the ISP, whereas all other exceptions are done using the MSP. When $M = 0$, peripheral-device interrupts are identical to those on the MC68000. A four-word exception stack frame is generated with format 0 and vector offset equal to the autovectored interrupt or the vectored interrupt offset from the base address of the vector table. When $M = 1$, a normal four-word stack is created on the master stack and a second copy (a **throwaway stack frame**) is placed on the interrupt stack. The throwaway stack frame has the same PC and vector offset as the one created on the master stack, and has format number 1. The M and S bits are set in the SR that is saved in the new stack frame. The M bit is 0 in the SR, and hence interrupt processing uses the ISP stack.

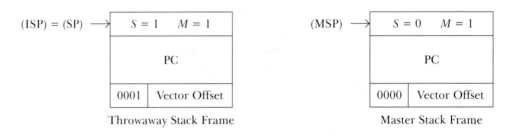

Throwaway Stack Frame   Master Stack Frame

When RTE is executed, the processor notes that it is using the throwaway stack frame and performs the following actions:

1. It reads the saved status register on the throwaway stack frame and assigns that value to the status register. Note that the M bit is set in the new SR, so the master stack is the active stack.

2. It increments the ISP by 8 to flush the throwaway stack.

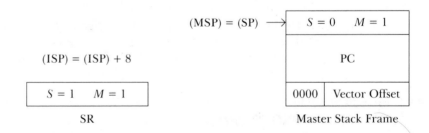

3. A second RTE is executed. Because the active stack pointer is now the master stack, the original SR and PC are pulled from the master stack.

$(MSP) = (MSP) + 8$ ┌─────────────────────┐
                     │ $S = 0$ $M = 1$ │
                     └─────────────────────┘
                               SR

An interrupt handler may have to modify the master stack frame. For instance, if the interrupt service routine returns to an I/O driver with interrupts disabled, the interrupt mask of the status register saved on the master stack must be changed. This is done using MOVEC. The following code disables interrupts for the master stack:

```
MOVEC   MSP,A0
ORI.W   #$0700,(A0)
```

When an RTE is executed with a throwaway stack frame, the second frame can be of any type, including another throwaway stack frame. Furthermore, the second frame can reside on any of the three stacks: interrupt, master, or user.

PROGRAM 14.8

Throwaway Stack
Frame Processing

An RTE is executed with the interrupt stack active. A second stack frame is another throwaway stack frame in master space, which in turn is followed by a normal four-word stack frame in user space. The RTE causes a return to the next instruction. The CPU is now in user mode. A return using JSR STOP would leave the operating system in user mode. To avoid this, a TRAP #15 is selected. The service routine is entered in supervisor mode and the S bit of the SR stored on the stack is set. The return from the trap service routine leaves the operating system in supervisor mode.

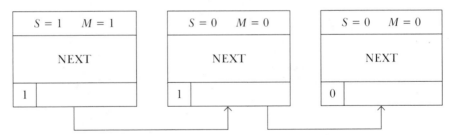

```
vTrap15:    equ    $00bc

            xref   strout, hexout, newline, stop

            move.w  #$2000,sr             ; s = 1, m = 0 - isp active stack
            lea     exit,a0
            move.l  a0,vTrap15.w          ; plant TRAP #15 vector
            lea     userstack+8,a0        ; create user stack frame
            clr.w   -(a0)                 ; format = 0
            lea     next,a1               ; pc = next
            move.l  a1,-(a0)
            move.w  #$0015,-(a0)          ; s = 0, ccr = $15
            move.l  a0,usp               ; initialize user stack pointer
            lea     masterstack+8,a0      ; create master stack frame
            move.w  #$1000,-(a0)          ; format = 1
            lea     next,a1
            move.l  a1,-(a0)
            clr.w   -(a0)                 ; user stack to be used
```

```
        movec    a0,msp              ; initialize master stack pointer
        move.w   #$1000,-(sp)        ; format = 1 for frame on intpt stack
        lea      next,a1
        move.l   a1,-(sp)
        move.w   #$3000,-(sp)        ; s = 1, m = 1
        rte

next:
        trap     #15                 ; go back to supervisor mode!
        jsr      stop

exit:
        lea      finished,a0
        move.w   #43,d0
        jsr      strout
        move.w   (sp),d0
        jsr      hexout
        jsr      newline
        ori.w    #$2000,(sp)         ; return in supervisor mode
        rte

        data
finished:
        dc.b     'Returned from two stack sequence with SR = '
        even

userstack:
        ds.b     8

masterstack:
        ds.b     8

        end
```

⟨Run of Program 14.8⟩

```
Returned from two stack sequence with SR = 0015
```

The distinction between the interrupt and master stack pointer is useful only in a multitasking environment. The concepts are used in the design of operating systems.

MC68020/30/40 Multiple Exceptions

Multiple exceptions are resolved by defining a priority scheme similar to that of the MC68000. The exception-processing sequences are executed in

TABLE 14.4 MC68020/30/40 Exception Priorities

GROUP PRIORITY	PRIORITY WITHIN THE GROUP
0	Reset
1	Address error
	Bus error
2	BKPT #*n*, CHK, CHK2
	Divide by zero, format
	TRAP #*n*, TRAPcc, TRAPV
3	Illegal instruction
	A-line, F-line, privilege
4	Trace, interrupt

the order of their priority. Before any service routine executes, all exception-processing sequences complete. As a result, the service routines for the exceptions are executed in the reverse order of their priorities. In general, the lower the priority of an exception, the more quickly its exception service routine will execute. For example, the trap exception has a higher priority than the trace. If a trap instruction executes with tracing on, the trace service routine executes first and sees as program counter the address of the first instruction in the trap service routine. The groupings and priorities of the exceptions are given in Table 14.4.

EXERCISES

1. The CPU interrupt mask is currently set at 5. At this time, two devices, one at level 5 and one at level 4, make an interrupt request.
   (a) What is the processor's response?
   (b) At what CPU level would only one of the two levels be acknowledged?

2. The CPU interrupt mask is currently set to level 7, at which time interrupt requests at levels 6 and 7 are made. Identify the processor's response.

3. Write a code segment to perform the following:
   (a) Set the CPU priority to 7.
   (b) Set the CPU priority to 5.
   (c) Change to user mode with all interrupts enabled.

4. How do you turn off the interrupt line for each of the following devices?
   (a) The ACIA   (b) the PI/T   (c) the timer

5. A level-2 interrupt occurs while a program is executing the instruction

   MOVEA.W   (6,PC,D2.W),A5

   at address $1000. The current content of the SR is $0007.

(a) What is the value of the PC that is pushed onto the stack?

(b) What is the value of the SR at the start of the service routine?

6. A level-5 interrupt occurs while a program is executing the instruction

MOVE.W   #$2600,SR

at address $8000. The current content of the SR is $0015.

(a) What is the action of the processor?

(b) What will happen if a level-6 interrupt occurs during the following instruction?

MOVE.W   #$2500,SR

7. (a) The level-1 autovector has vector number 25. A device asserts a level-5 autovectored interrupt. What is the exception vector address?

(b) A device asserts a vectored interrupt at level 6. During the interrupt acknowledge cycle, it identifies its vector number as 75. What is the exception vector address used by the processor?

8. (a) The programmer has failed to assign a vector number to a device that generates vectored interrupts. When the device makes an interrupt request, what exception will be asserted? What is its vector number?

(b) The CPU accepts an interrupt request and receives the BERR signal during the interrupt acknowledge cycle. What exception is generated? What is the exception vector number?

9. The T bit is set at the start of the instruction

MOVEA.W   (6,PC,D2.W),A5

at address $1000. The current content of the SR is $8007.

(a) What is the value of the PC that is pushed onto the stack?

(b) What is the value of the SR at the start of the service routine?

10. Write code to initialize the MC68230 timer to generate a vectored interrupt with vector number $66.

11. Suppose the following code is executed as the service routine for the timer.

TIMER: ADDQ.W   #1,TICKSELAPSED
         RTE

Program "death" will occur. Why?

12. The following is a timer interrupt service routine that maintains a count of elapsed time in a location ELTIME. What is the action of the routine?

```
BELL:     EQU       7

TIMER:    MOVEM.L   D0/D7,-(SP)
          MOVE.L    ELTIME,D0
          ADDQ.L    #1,D0
          MOVE.L    D0,ELTIME
          DIVU      #60,D0
```

```
                    SWAP       D0
                    TST. W     D0
                    BNE. S     OUT
                    MOVE. B    #BELL, D0
                    MOVEQ      #0, D7
                    JSR        PUTCHAR
          OUT:      MOVEM. L   (SP) +, D0/D7
                    RTE
```

13. (a) The trace exception has priority over an interrupt from a peripheral device. Which service routine is executed first?
    (b) A bus error occurs during the execution of an instruction with tracing on ($T = 1$). When is the trace exception processed?

14. Indicate the order of processing for each of the following combinations of exceptions:
    (a) While the instruction LEA (2,A0,D3.L),A5 is executing with tracing on ($T = 1$), an interrupt of priority 5 is asserted.
    (b) An address error occurs during a DIVU instruction that generates the divide-by-zero exception.
    (c) The trace bit is on while executing a CHK instruction that generates an exception.

15. Suppose that an MC68000 system has a switch that will generate a level-7 autovectored interrupt whenever it is pressed. Write a service routine for the switch that prints the following registers and then exits to a monitor:

    PC / SR/ SP/ USP/ D0/ A0

    Could this switch be a valuable diagnostic tool? Why?

16. The service routine L2 handles a device asserting a level-2 interrupt, and routine L3 services a device asserting a level-3 interrupt. In order to maintain data integrity, it is necessary for each service routine to execute completely without being interrupted. However, the following problem exists:
    The first instruction of the level-2 routine is

    L2:   MOVE.W   #$2700,SR

    but occasionally the CPU is interrupted before the instruction gets a chance to execute. Routine L3 executes and returns control to L2, leaving data corrupted. Propose a patch to L3 that will leave the level-3 interrupt pending and cause L2 to execute completely before reentrance to L3.

17. A problem with autovectored interrupts occurs when two or more sources of interrupt generate the same vector. For instance, two ACIA's both generate a level-5 autovectored interrupt. How does the exception service routine identify the source of the interrupt?

18. The following complete program runs and produces output. Carefully explain what it does.

```
          TBASE:    EQU  $010021    ; TIMER BASE ADDRESS
          TCON:     EQU  0          ; TIMER CONTROL REGISTER
```

```
TIVR:      EQU  2              ;  TIMER INTERRUPT VECTOR REGISTER
TCPR:      EQU  4              ;  TIMER COUNTER PRELOAD REGISTER
TSR:       EQU  20             ;  TIMER STATUS REGISTER
NCLOCK:    EQU  64             ;  TIMER INTERRUPT VECTOR NUMBER
VCLOCK:    EQU  NCLOCK*4       ;  TIMER INTERRUPT VECTOR

           XREF  INITPORT, PUTCHAR

START:
           MOVE.W    #$2700,SR
           MOVEA.L   #$8000,SP
           MOVE.L    #CLOCK,VCLOCK.W
           MOVEQ     #0,D7
           JSR       INIT
           LEA       TBASE,A0
           MOVE.B    #NCLOCK,(TIVR,A0)
           MOVE.L    #250000,D0
           MOVEP.L   D0,(TCPR,A0)
           MOVE.B    #$A0,(TCON,A0)
           MOVE.W    #1,SW
           MOVE.W    #$2000,SR
           BSET      #0,(TCON,A0)

P1:
           MOVE.B    #'A'D0
           JSR       PUTCHAR
           BRA.S     P1

P2:
           MOVE.B    #'B',D0
           JSR       PUTCHAR
           BRA.S     P2

CLOCK:
           MOVE.W    #$2700,SR
           LEA       TBASE,A0              ;  IMPORTANT!  WHY?
           TST.W.    SW
           BGT.S     SP2
           MOVE.L    #P1,(2,SP)
           BRA.S     CHG
SP2:       MOVE.L    #P2,(2,SP)
CHG:       NEG.W     SW
           BSET      #0,(TSR,A0)
           RTE

           DATA
SW:        DS.W      1

           END
```

19. The following program uses both the MC6850 ACIA and the MC68230 timer. Study the program and answer the questions.

```
              SP2         MOVE.L    #P2,(2,SP)
              ACIABSE:    EQU       $10040          ; ACIA BASE ADDRESS
              ACIASR:     EQU       0
              ACIACR:     EQU       0
              ACIARDR:    EQU       2
              ACIATDR:    EQU       2
              TBASE:      EQU       $010021         ; TIMER BASE ADDRESS
              TCON:       EQU       0               ; TIMER CONTROL REGISTER
              TIVR:       EQU       2
              TCPR:       EQU       4               ; TIMER COUNTER PRELOAD
                                                    REGISTER
              TSR:        EQU       20              ; TIMER STATUS REGISTER

              VAUTO5:     EQU       $74
              NTIMER:     EQU       64
              VTIMER:     EQU       NTIMER*4

              MONITOR:    EQU       $8146

              CTRLQ:      EQU       17


                          XREF      INIT, NEWLINE, PUTHEX


              START:
                          MOVE.W    #$2700,SR
                          MOVEA.L   #$8000,SP       ; SET STACK POINTER
                          BCLR      #0,DONE
                          MOVE.W    #0,CHARTOTAL
                          MOVE.W    #0,TIMETOTAL
                          MOVE.L    #TERMINAL,VAUTO5.W
                          LEA       ACIABASE,A0
                          MOVE.B    #$95(ACIACR,A0) ; TURN ON ACIA RECEIVE
                                                    INTERRUPT
                          LEA       TBASE,A0
                          MOVE.B    #$A0,(TCON,A0)  ; SET TIMER FOR INTERRUPTS
                          MOVE.B    #NTIMER,(TIVR,A0)
                          MOVE.L    #TIMER,$100     ; SET SERVICE ROUTINE ADDRESS
                          MOVE.L    #125000,D0
                          MOVEP.L   D0,(TCPR,A0)
                          BSET      #0,(TCON,A0)    ; START THE TIMER
                          MOVE.W    #$2000,SR

              MAIN:       BTST      #0,DONE
                          BEQ.S     MAIN
                          JMP       MONITOR


              TERMINAL;   MOVE.W    #$2700,SR
                          MOVEM.L   D0/D7/A0,-(SP)
                          LEA       ACIABASE,A0
                          MOVE.B    (ACIARDR,A0),D0
                          CMPI.B    #CTRLQ,D0
                          BEQ.S     QUIT
       (1)    WAIT:       BTST      #1,(ACIASR,A0)
                          BEQ       WAIT
                          MOVE.B    D0,(ACIATDR,A0) ; ECHO CHAR TO TERMINAL
```

```
                    ADDQ.W    #1, CHARTOTAL
                    BRA.S     RET


        QUIT:       MOVE.W    CHARTOTAL, D0
                    EXT.L     D0
                    DIVU      TIMETOTAL, D0
                    MOVEQ     #0, D7
                    JSR       PUTNEWLINE
                    ANDI.L    #$0000FFFF, D0
                    JSR       PUTHEXOUT
                    JSR       PUTNEWLINE
                    BSET      #0, DONE
                    LEA       TBASE, A0
  (2)               BCLR      #0, (TCON, A0)
        RET:        MOVEM.L   (SP)+, D0/D7/A0
                    RTE


        TIMER:      MOVE.W    #$2700, SR
                    MOVE.L    A0, -(SP)
                    ADDQ.W    #1, TIMETOTAL
                    LEA       TBASE, A0
  (3)               BSET      #0, (TSR, A0)
                    MOVE.L    (SP)+, A0
                    RTE


                    DATA
        CHARTOTAL:  DS.W      1
        TIMETOTAL:  DS.W      1
        DONE:       DS.B      1
                    END
```

(a) What is the vector number for the timer interrupt request?

(b) Failure to include which statement would prevent the CPU from acknowledging interrupts?

(c) When does the main program terminate?

(d) What is the purpose of the two statements beginning at (1)?

(e) What is the purpose of statement (2)?

(f) What is the purpose of statement (3)?

(g) What is the overall function of the program?

20. (MC68020/30/40) Indicate the order of processing for each of the following combinations of exceptions:

(a) While the instruction LEA ([$5000,A3,D3.W*8],$10),A5 is executing with $T = 1$, an interrupt of priority 5 is asserted.

(b) The CHK2 exception and an interrupt are pending at the same time.

21. (MC68020/30/40) Show how to construct a sequence of throwaway stacks so that a master mode stack returns to an interrupt throwaway stack, which returns to a user stack frame.

PROGRAMMING EXERCISES

22. This exercise uses the timer interrupt and ACIA receive interrupts. When ⟨*control*⟩*T* is entered, the timer is started running for 3 seconds, and the data register (D0.L) is set to 0. All other characters are simply echoed to the screen by the ACIA service routine. The timer service prints the value in D0 and turns off the timer. The main program should execute the following code:

```
MAINLOOP:   ADDQ.L   #1,D0
            BRA.S    MAINLOOP
```

Initially, type nothing after entering ⟨*control*⟩*T*. Subsequently, increase the number of characters typed in a 3-second period. Notice that the sum printed by the timer service routine becomes less the faster you type. Why?

23. Write a program that implements ACIA Reception Time Out, in which a timer interrupt is generated if no character is typed at the terminal for a 10-second period.

    Timer Service Routine: Prints the message "ACIA Time Out" and exits to the monitor.
    ACIA Receive Interrupt Service Routine: First turn off the timer and then load the character into D0 and echo it back to the terminal.

24. This exercise uses timer interrupts. Every 5 seconds, send to the screen the program's elapsed time followed by a bell character. In an infinite loop, the main program is to read a character using the standalone I/O package of Chapter 12. Whenever the XOFF character CTRL_S ($13) is input, echoing of characters is turned off, and the printing of the elapsed time is halted. Printing and echoing of characters is to resume when a character other than XOFF is input.

25. Modify the serial driver of Section 14.4 so that the interrupt service routine echoes back characters as they are received.

CHAPTER 15

ADVANCED M68000
SYSTEM TOPICS

*T*he chapter includes topics that apply primarily to the MC68020, MC68030, and MC68040 processors. These processors have advanced features that increase speed and efficiency, including pipelined architecture, indivisible instructions for concurrent programming, data and instruction cache, and a coprocessor interface. Introduced in their own sections, the topics generally apply to each of the processors because they are all similar to the MC68020. References to specific differences on the MC68030 or MC68040 processor will be made when they apply.

This chapter begins with a detailed explanation of the MC68000 prefetch used with the instruction execution cycle. Instruction fetching was introduced in Chapter 3 and is now presented with machine-specific details. The enhancement of instruction prefetch for the MC68020/30/40 processors involves pipeline architecture.

The interrupting digital timer was presented in Chapter 14. This chapter also presents some fundamental concepts in concurrent programming and provides a complete program illustrating the use of a timer to switch systematically between a series of processes, giving each the illusion that it has its own CPU and memory. In the case of shared memory, the process-switching program demonstrates an incorrect result that can occur when proper synchronization primitives are not used. This motivates introduction of the TAS instruction for the MC68000 processor and the CAS/CAS2 instructions for the MC68020/30/40 processors.

The MC68020/30/40 processors have built-in cache memory. Techniques for manipulating the cache are presented with a programming example.

One of the primary architectural features of the MC68020/30/40 processors is their ability to use the features of a coprocessor. The M68000 coprocessor interface is presented in a very basic fashion, and this is followed by a presentation of the MC68881/68882 floating-point coprocessors.

The basic elements of paging through the use of a memory management unit (MMU) are discussed. Chapter 13 presented the MC68000 bus error exception and illustrated that the processor is not capable of recovering properly from a bus fault. Thus paging systems are not implemented using the MC68000 processor. The MC68020/30/40 processors introduce bus fault recovery, which allows a system to return from a bus error exception and continue executing right at the point of the fault. The entire bus fault recovery process is described, along with a complete program implementing software recovery from a fault. The last section details the on-chip MMU of the MC68030 and concludes with a complete program using the MMU for memory mapping and memory protection.

15.1 INSTRUCTION PREFETCH ON THE MC68000

The MC68000 processor simultaneously fetches and decodes instructions to speed up program execution. The processor uses a two-word instruction prefetch queue that enables it concurrently to fetch opcode and extension words, to decode an instruction, and to begin instruction execution. The following steps describe the manipulation of this queue and the execution of an instruction.

Step 1: At the start of an instruction, the opcode word and the word following have already been fetched. The opcode word is in the portion of the CPU that decodes an instruction (the instruction decoder).

Decoder	Prefetch Queue	
Opcode Word	Opcode Word	Next Word

Step 2: In the case of instructions occupying more than one word, as each word of the instruction is moved from the prefetch queue and used internally, the next code word is read into the queue.

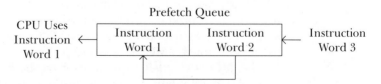

Step 3: At the point when the last code word of an instruction has been used, the queue contains the opcode word of the next instruction. As that opcode word is moved into the decoder, the code word following it is read into the queue.

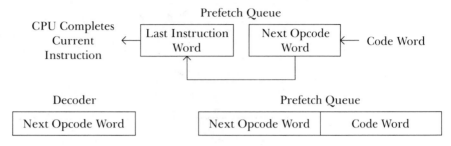

Step 4: If the instruction in the decoder is a single-word instruction causing a branch, the code word following the opcode word in the queue is not valid and is discarded. In the event of an interrupt or trace exception, both words in the queue are discarded.

```
              BNE.S    HERE        ; SHORT BRANCH
              MOVE     D0, $2000
                         ⋮
HERE →        ADDI     #5, D0
```

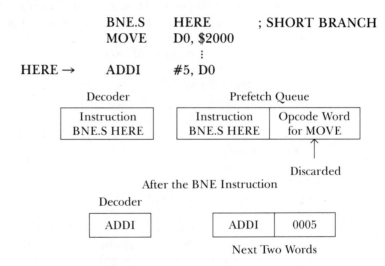

Step 5: The program counter usually points to the last word fetched from the instruction stream.

```
ADDI   #3,D0
```

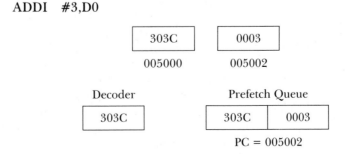

FIGURE 15.1   MC68020 Pipeline Architecture

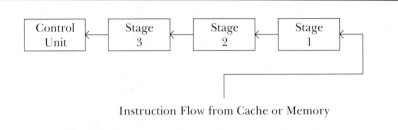

Instruction Flow from Cache or Memory

MC68020/30/40 Pipelined Architecture

A **pipeline** is a channel through which data flows. It performs much like an assembly line. At various stages within the pipeline, input data is received, processed, and then passed as output to the next stage of the pipeline. All stages within the pipeline operate concurrently. The MC68020/30/40 systems implements a three-stage pipeline, as shown in Figure 15.1. When one instruction has completed execution, the two 16-bit words after the code for that instruction will already have been loaded into the pipeline.

In the MC68020/30/40 pipeline architecture, instructions are loaded into stage 1 from memory or from the instruction cache. The instruction cache is a high-speed holding buffer for previously fetched instruction words. An instruction opcode has been completely decoded by the time it arrives at stage 3. In stages 1 and 2, extension words can be processed directly and passed on to the execution unit. The intermediate stages can compute effective addresses and request bus cycles to fetch data. After an extension word is processed, the stage is free, and a new word can be loaded for processing. When a bus error occurs, the contents of the pipeline stages are saved on the bus error stack frame to enable bus fault recovery. Bus fault recovery is presented in Section 15.7. The MC68020/30/40 processors require that an instruction be aligned on an even byte boundary, and if this requirement is violated, an address error occurs during the instruction prefetch.

15.2 | CONCURRENT PROGRAMMING

A **concurrent program** is one in which two or more separate code units called processes execute at the same time, share data in common memory, and synchronize their actions using tools provided by the programming environment. Such tools include busy-wait, semaphores, monitors, and rendezvous. Concurrent programming is a very important topic in modern computing, particularly in light of the increased use of multiprocessor systems. A number of programming languages, most notably Ada and Concurrent C++, have special constructs to facilitate concurrency.

On single-processor systems, the operating system uses an interrupting timer to implement **time sharing**. A process, with its process status information, is placed into a queue of processes waiting for access to the CPU. This is called the **ready queue**. The timer is set for a short period of time called the **time-sharing quantum**, and the process at the head of the ready queue is allowed to execute. If the process has not concluded before the timer expires, it moves to the tail of the queue, and the next process in the queue is given access to the CPU and either begins or continues execution.

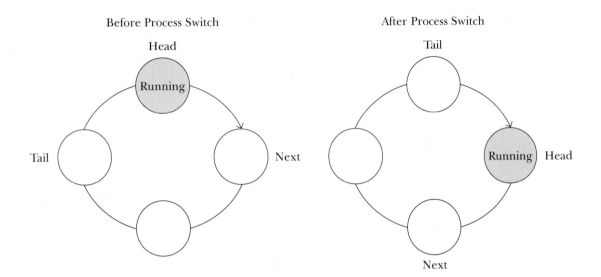

A process that is running in the system will go through a series of state changes before it issues an exit call and is deleted from the queue. The processes in the ready queue are either running or are in a ready state. The process at the head of the queue runs for its time quantum. The other processes are in ready state. At a time slice, the currently running process shifts to the ready state and is repositioned at the end of the queue. The next process then shifts to the running state. If a process requests I/O service by making a system call, it must wait on the device and not be involved in the time slice transitions. The process is deleted from the ready queue and placed on hold to wait for a response from the device. The process is said to be **blocked**. When the device interrupt signal is received, the blocked process is reinserted into the ready queue. These ideas are depicted in the state transition diagram of Figure 15.2.

FIGURE 15.2   Change of States for a Process

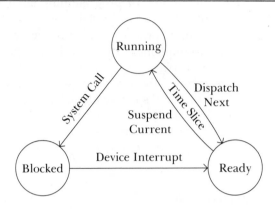

Demonstration Program: Process Switching

The concepts involved in writing operating system process-switching routines are illustrated in this complete program. A run-time environment supports three processes with time slicing every 1/20th of a second using the timer on the ECB. The program includes code to handle the ready queue and to handle process transition among the running, ready, and blocked states. Two pointers RQHEAD and PRQHEAD point to the current and previous ready queue entries, respectively (the process currently running is always pointed to by RQHEAD). The queue is illustrated in Figure 15.3.

When the timer expires, each pointer is advanced forward (clockwise), and the next process resumes (Process 3 in Figure 15.3). An **idle process** in an operating system is the process that is run when no other process requires the CPU. The idle process can perform routine bookkeeping chores. When RQHEAD advances to the idle process, both pointers are moved forward. If there are any other processes in the system, the running of the idle process is avoided. If the idle process is the only one left, both RQHEAD and PRQHEAD point to the idle process, and it is run.

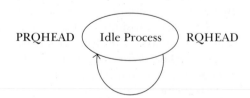

FIGURE 15.3 Ready Queue

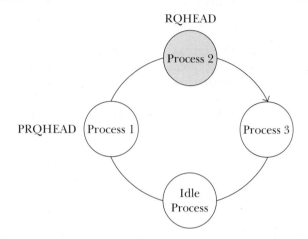

The idle process is run when all other processes have either finished or are waiting for I/O. In this program, the idle process leaves interrupts enabled but consumes no actual CPU time. This is accomplished by using the STOP instruction.

INSTRUCTION

STOP

Syntax STOP #*n*

Action The immediate operand is moved into the 16-bit SR, the PC is advanced to the next instruction, and the processor stops reading and executing instructions. Execution of instructions resumes when an interrupt of sufficiently high priority occurs or the reset exception is generated. If the trace bit is on when STOP is executed, the trace exception will occur.

Notes

1. The STOP instruction is privileged.

2. An external reset will always initiate exception processing.

EXAMPLE 15.1

(*a*) STOP #$2000
The processor is suspended with all interrupts enabled. Any interrupt will "wake it up."

(*b*) STOP #$2500
The processor will awaken only for interrupts of priority higher than 5.

(c) STOP   #$2700

Only a level-7 interrupt will wake up the CPU.

Processes 1 and 2 access a variable GLOBAL that is initialized to 0 in the data initialization section. Consider GLOBAL to represent a major resource—for instance, a shared buffer—that is updated by two or more routines. Each process runs in user mode and executes a loop in which it prepares to update GLOBAL, does the actual update, and executes follow-up action. Upon completion of the loop, termination code is executed.

Sequence of Actions Performed by Process 1 and Process 2

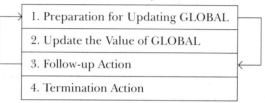

Each process executes Steps 1–3 a total of 16 times. At that point, each process executes its own termination code.

1. The preparation for updating GLOBAL is emulated by a delay loop.

2. Each process updates the value of GLOBAL with the assignment

$$\text{GLOBAL} := 2 * \text{GLOBAL} + 1$$

3. Follow-up action is emulated by a second delay loop.

The termination code for Process 1 is a loop that continues until the variable PROC2FINISHED becomes nonzero. At this point, Process 1 outputs the final value of GLOBAL and exits the process queue by executing TRAP #1. The termination code for Process 2 places a 1 (TRUE) in PROC2FINISHED and exits.

Process 3 enables console receive interrupts and enters a loop. Its first action is to disable CPU interrupts and check to see whether a character has arrived from the console. Interrupts are disabled throughout the process of reading a character. This is considered a critical activity. If no character is available, Process 3 turns interrupts back on and makes the system call TRAP #0. This causes the process to be removed from the ready queue and blocked until a receive interrupt occurs. At this point, it is immediately activated with interrupts disabled so that it can complete its task. No system resources are wasted with polling. The character is read, and the CPU interrupts are re-enabled. The character is checked to see if it is printable. If so, it is echoed to the terminal. If it is a control character, its two-digit hex code surrounded by angle brackets is printed. For instance, pressing

⟨Return⟩ will print ⟨0d⟩. When the character CTRL_Z is input, the process terminates by executing the exit system call TRAP #1.

PROGRAM 15.1

Process Switching

During program execution, Processes 1 and 2 should combine to compute the following sequence:

$$GLOBAL_0 = 0$$

$$GLOBAL_{n+1} = 2 * GLOBAL_n + 1 \qquad n = 0, 1, 2, \ldots, 32$$

The sequence of values is 0, 1, 3, 7, 15, 31, ... On the nth iteration, $GLOBAL_n = 2^n - 1$. After 32 iterations, GLOBAL should be \$FFFFFFFF $= 2^{32} - 1$. Process 3 allows the user to enter characters at the keyboard and write them to the screen.

The program is partitioned into blocks. The action of each block is summarized to assist you in tracing the code.

Hardware Initialization (Block 1)   The timer and the console serial ports are initialized. Vector number 68 is used for the timer. This places the exception vector within the area allocated for user vectors. The timer is set to generate an interrupt every 1/20th second (timer counter preload register = 6250).

Data Initialization (Block 2)   The program uses timer interrupts, console receive interrupts, and exceptions generated by TRAP #0 (wait for input) and TRAP #1 (exit). The exception vectors for each source are initialized.

The data initialization code places the idle process and three user processes in the ready queue. The first two user processes run in user mode, and the last executes in supervisor mode. Each has its own area of memory for its stack and a process descriptor with the following structure:

Time Slice

Program Counter	Status Register	Stack Pointer	Pointer to Next Process	Saved Registers D0–A6
4 Bytes	2 Bytes	4 Bytes	4 Bytes	60 Bytes

|← ———————————————— 74 Bytes ————————————————— →|

The process descriptors are nodes in the ready queue and are allocated from a memory pool. The routine GETNEWDESCRIPTOR allocates a new descriptor node.

Each field contains the values of an item at the point at which the process was suspended. The routine RQINSERT places a process descriptor at the head of the current queue. RQDELETE removes the process at the head of the queue.

System Startup (Block 3)   The timer is started by setting bit 0 of the timer control register. A branch is made to the code segment DISPATCH. This code segment restores the registers of the process at the head of the queue and starts the process running.

The Processes (Block 4)   The code for each process, including the idle process, is given in this block.

Exception Service Routines (Block 5)   The timer interrupt service routine, at address CLOCK, implements process switching. The interval of 1/20th second between process switches is the quantum for the time-slicing scheme. Registers for the interrupted process are saved, and the code at address DISPATCH is used to start the next process. Care must be taken to save/restore the correct stack pointer, depending on the mode of the process.

The service routine for TRAP #1 is executed when a process is finished. This causes transfer to the service routine EXIT that unlinks the process descriptor for the running process and causes the next one in the list to resume. All records of the deleted process are removed from the system.

The TRAP #0 instruction causes the service routine at address SLEEP to be entered. This code unlinks the calling process from the ready queue and retains a pointer to the process descriptor of the blocked process in the location SLEEPINGPROCESS. The next process in the queue is then resumed.

When a console receive interrupt occurs, the service routine at address CONRECEIVER is executed. If SLEEPINGPROCESS is not zero, a process was previously suspended via TRAP #0. That process is placed at the head of the ready queue and is dispatched with interrupts disabled. This implements a simple but effective mechanism for handling I/O with no polling. While the process is suspended, it consumes no CPU time.

Queue Maintenance (Block 6)   This block contains all the routines that manipulate the ready queue.

Data Declarations (Block 7)   All data is declared here.

```
tcon           equ     $10021      ; timer control register
tivr:          equ     $10023      ; timer interrupt vector reg
tcpr:          equ     $10025      ; timer preload register
tsr:           equ     $10035      ; timer status register
nclock:        equ     68          ; timer vector number
consreg:       equ     $10040      ; console status register
conctrlreg:    equ     $10040      ; console control register
conrecdreg:    equ     $10042      ; console input

vclock:        equ     nclock*4    ; interrupt vector for timer
vtrap0:        equ     $80         ; vector address for "trap #0"
vtrap1:        equ     $84         ; vector address for "trap #1"
```

```
vconsole:       equ     $74              ; console receiver interrupt
;                                        ; for autovec 5

consoleport     equ     0
nl:             equ     $0a
null:           equ     $00
bell:           equ     $07
backspace:      equ     $08              ; ctrl h
ctrlz:          equ     $1a
delete:         equ     $7f
space:          equ     ' '

disableintr:    equ     $2700
enableintr:     equ     $2000

        xref    initPort, putstring, puthexout_long, putchar

start:  move.w  #disableintr,sr
        lea     $8000,sp                 ; set stack pointer

; block 1 : hardware initialization

; initialize the console port so any
; process can use the i/o package
; note that the package is reentrant
        moveq   #consoleport,d7
        jsr     initPort
        move.b  #nclock,tivr             ; initialize timer vector reg
        move.l  #6250,d0                 ; preload register at 1/20th sec
        lea     tcpr,a0
        movep.l d0,(0,a0)
        move.b  #$a0,tcon                ; initialize timer control reg

; block 2 : initialize data

        move.l  #conreceiver,vconsole.w
        move.l  #clock,vclock.w          ; set timer exception vector
        move.l  #exit,vtrap1.w           ; process exit via trap #1
        move.l  #sleep,vtrap0.w          ; sleep awaiting a character

        ; initialize misc data
        clr.l   global                   ; global initially 0
        clr.w   proc2finished            ; false initially
        clr.l   sleepingprocess          ; no process sleeping yet

        ; initialize idle process descriptor
        lea     idleentry,a0
        move.l  #idleproc,(progctr,a0)
        move.w  #$2000,(statusreg,a0)
        move.l  #$7000,(stackptr,a0)
        move.l  #idleentry,(next,a0)

        ; initialize pointers
        move.l  #idleentry,rqhead
```

```
                move.l    #idleentry,prqhead
                move.l    #readyqueue,rqentryptr

; initialize the ready queue

; initialize process1 with s=0, (usp)=$6000, (pc)=process1
                jsr       getfreedescriptor
                move.l    #process1,(progctr,a0)
                clr.w     (statusreg,a0)
                move.l    #$6000,(stackptr,a0)
                jsr       rqinsert
; initialize process2 with s=0, (usp)=$5000, (pc)=process2
                jsr       getfreedescriptor
                move.l    #process2,(progctr,a0)
                clr.w     (statusreg,a0)
                move.l    #$5000,(stackptr,a0)
                jsr       rqinsert
; initialize process3 with s=1, (ssp)=$4000, (pc)=process3
                jsr       getfreedescriptor
                move.l    #process3,(progctr,a0)
                move.w    #$2000,(statusreg,a0)
                move.l    #$4000,(stackptr,a0)
                jsr       rqinsert

                move.w    #enableintr,sr

; block 3 : start the timer and run 1st process

                bset      #0,tcon          ; enable the timer
                bra       dispatch         ; start processes


; block 4 : first process

process1:
                moveq     #15,d1
mloop1:
                move.l    global,d0        ; obtain copy of shared variable
                move.w    #999,d2
work1:          dbra      d2,work1         ; act on data
                lsl.l     #1,d0            ; form global := 2 * global + 1
                addq.l    #1,d0
                move.l    d0,global
                move.w    #99,d2           ; other processing
rem1:           dbra      d2,rem1
                dbra      d1,mloop1
wait1:          tst.w     proc2finished    ; wait until proc 2 finished
                beq.s     wait1
                moveq     #consoleport,d7  ; print the value of "global"
                move.l    global,d0
                jsr       puthexout_long
                lea       msg,a0
                jsr       putstring
                trap      #1               ; exit system call
```

```
; block 4 : second process

process2:
        moveq     #15,d1
mloop2:
        move.l    global,d0            ; obtain copy of shared variable
        move.w    #999,d2
work2:  dbra      d2,work2            ; act on data
        lsl.l     #1,d0              ; form global := 2 * global + 1
        addq.l    #1,d0
        move.l    d0,global
        move.w    #99,d2             ; other processing
rem2:   dbra      d2,rem2
        dbra      d1,mloop2
        move.w    #1,proc2finished   ; let proc 1 know we're finished
        trap      #1                 ; exit system call

; block 4 : third process

process3:
        move.b    #$95,conctrlreg    ; enable console receive int
inputchar:
        move.w    #disablintr,sr     ; don't interrupt
        btst      #0,constreg        ; character already there?
        bne       readc
        trap      #0                 ; sleep waiting for wakeup
readc:  move.b    conrecdreg,d0      ; get the character
        move.w    #enableintr,sr     ; back to normal
        bclr      #7,d0
        cmpi.b    #ctrlz,d0
        beq.s     endproc3           ; ctrl z typed. exit.
        cmpi.b    #space,d0
        blt.s     controlchar
        cmpi.b    #delete,d0
        beq.s     controlchar
        jsr       putchar
        bra.s     inputchar
controlchar:
        move.w    d0,d2
        move.w    #'<',d0
        jsr       putchar
        move.w    2,d0
        jsr       hexbyte
        move.w    #'>',d0
        jsr       putchar
        bra.s     inputchar
endproc3:
        trap      #1

; block 4 : idle process

idleproc:
        stop      #enableintr
        bra.s     idleproc
```

```
; block 5: exception service routines

; timer service routine. save current process data and start
; the next process in the queue.

clock:
        move.w    #disableintr,sr
        bset      #0,tsr              ; negate timer interrupt request
        jsr       saveprocessdata     ; save regs before suspending
        jsr       rqadvance           ; get next process in queue

dispatch:
        cmpi.l    #idleentry,rqhead
;                                     ; run idle proc as last resort
        bne.s     restore
        jsr       rqadvance
restore:
        movea.l   rqhead,a0           ; restore regs for new proc
        btst      #5,(statusreg,a0)   ; restore which stack pointer?
        bne.s     supvprocess
        movea.l   (stackptr,a0),a1    ; restore usp
        move.l    a1,usp
        bra.s     fixstack
supvprocess:
        movea.l   (stackptr,a0),sp    ; restore ssp
fixstack:
        move.l    (progctr,a0),-(sp)
;                                     ; preapre for rte
        move.l    (statusreg,a0),-(sp)
        movem.l   (registers,a0),d0-d7/a0-a6
;                                     ; restore general regs
        rte                           ; return to the process

; system call a process uses to terminate itself

exit:
        move.w    #disableintr,sr
        addq.w    #6,sp               ; flush off pc/sr of exiting
;                                     ; process
        jsr       rqdelete            ; remove process descriptor
        jsr       freshslice          ; reset timer
        bra       dispatch            ; run next process in queue

; system call to wait for i/o

sleep:
        move.w    #disableintr,sr
        jsr       saveprocessdata     ; save process regs
        jsr       rqdelete            ; unlink for ready queue
        move.l    a0,sleepingprocess
        jsr       freshslice          ; start timer again from scratch
        bra       dispatch            ; start up next process
```

```
; handles a receiver interrupt. decides whether to dispath a
; driver waiting for a character or just throw the character
; away

conreceiver:
        move.w    #disableintr,sr
        tst.l     sleepingprocess     ; is process waiting for char?
        beq.s     nowaitingprocess    ; no. read char and throw away
;                                     ; to negate interrupt request
        jsr       saveprocessdata     ; activate waiting process now!
        movea.l   sleepingprocess,a0
        ori.w     #$0700,(statusreg,a0)
;                                     ; return to i/o process with
;                                     ; interrupts disabled
        jsr       rqinsert            ; put i/o process at queue head
        clr.l     sleepingprocess     ; nothing waiting any more
        bra       dispatch            ; run the i/o process
nowaitingprocess:
        tst.b     conrecdreg          ; turn off interrupt request
        rte

; block 6: maintenance routines

; allow the next process to have a full quantum by restarting
; the timer

freshslice:
        bclr      #0,tcon
        bset      #0,tcon
        rts

; save pc/sr/stack pointer/d0-a6 in the process descriptor prior
; to changing processes

sreg:           equ    8              ; stack offset to status reg
spc:            equ    10             ; stack offset to program counter
newstkdatasize: equ    14
addrsaveda0:    equ    46             ; stack offset to a0
pcplussr:       equ    6              ; stack size of pc and sr

saveprocessdata:
        move.l    a0,-(sp)            ; temp save a0 on stack
        movea.l   rqhead,a0           ; set (a0) to point to
;                                     ; current process descriptor
        move.w    (sreg,sp),(statusreg,a0)
;                                     ; save status register
        move.l    (spc,sp),(progctr,a0)
;                                     ; save program counter
        movem.l   d0-d7/a0-a6,(registers,a0)
;                                     ; all but (a0) is correct
        btst      #5,(statusreg,a0)   ; suspending supervisor or
;                                     ; user mode process?
```

```
              beq       usermode1
              move.l    sp, (stackptr, a0)
              addi.l    #newstkdatasize, (stackptr, a0)
;                                          ; 14 bytes on stack
              bra       savea0
usermode1:
              move.l    usp, a1
              move.l    a1, (stackptr, a0)    ; save stack pointer
savea0:  lea       (addrsaveda0, a0), a0
              move.l    (sp)+, (a0)           ; restore orig (a0)
              move.l    (sp), (pcplussr, sp)
;                                          ; flush stacked sr and pc
              addq.w    #pcplussr, sp
              rts


; allocate a free process descriptor for an array of empty
; descriptors by returning a pointer in a0

getfreedescriptor:
              movea.l   rqentryptr, a0
              addi.l    #processdesclen, rqentryptr
              rts


; insert process descriptor pointed to by (a0) into the ready list

rqinsert:
              move.l    a1, -(sp)
              movea.l   rqhead, a1            ; get current queue head
              move.l    a1, prqhead          ; it becomes the previous head
              move.l    (next, a1), (next, a0)
;                                          ; update pointers
              move.l    a0, (next, a1)       ; link old head to new one
              move.l    a0, rqhead           ; have a new queue head pointer
              movea.l   (sp)+, a1
              rts


; delete the process at the head of the ready list
; return a pointer to it in (a0)

rqdelete:
              move.l    a1, -(sp)
              movea.l   rqhead, a0           ; get queue head pointer
              movea.l   prqhead, a1          ; link previous node to the one
;                                          ; pointed at by the node being
;                                          ; deleted
              move.l    (next, a0), (next, a1)
              move.l    (next, a0), rqhead   ; new queue head
              movea.l   (sp)+, a1
              rts


; advance the queue forward one process
; leave (a0) pointing at the new queue head
```

```
rqadvance:
        movea.l    rqhead,a0
        move.l     a0,prqhead
        move.l     (next,a0),rqhead
        rts

hexbyte:
        movem.l    d0-d3/a0,-(sp)
        lea        hexdigits,a0
        moveq      #1,d1
        move.w     d0,d2
pr:     ror.b      #4,d2
        move.b     d2,d3
        andi.w     #$0f,d3
        move.b     (0,a0,d3.w),d3
        ext.w      d3
        move.w     d3,d0
        jsr        putchar
        dbra       d1,pr
        movem.l    (sp)+,d0-d3/a0
        rts

        data

; block 7 : data declarations

msg:    dc.b       ' is the final value of global'
        dc.b       nl,null
hexdigits:
        dc.b       '0123456789abcdef'
        even

; format for each process descriptor

progctr:        equ     0
statusreg:      equ     4
stackptr:       equ     6
next:           equ     10            ; pointer to next process
registers:      equ     14
processdesclen: equ     74
numberofprocs:  equ     3

idleentry:
        dc.l       idleproc          ; initial pc for idle process
        dc.w       $2000             ; initial sr
        dc.l       $7000             ; initial ssp
        dc.l       idleentry         ; linked to itself
        ds.l       15                ; scratch space for general regs
readyqueue:
        ds.b       numberofprocs*processdesclen
        even

rqhead: ds.l       1                 ; address of process descriptor
```

```
;                                      ; for the current process
prqhead: ds.l      1                   ; address of process descriptor
;                                      ; for previous process
rqentryptr:
         ds.l      1                   ; points to next decriptor
;                                      ; available for allocation
sleepingprocess:
         ds.l      1                   ; pointer to process blocked
;                                      ; on i/o
global:
         ds.l      1                   ; the shared variable
proc2finished:
         ds.w      1                   ; process 1 prints only after
;                                      ; process 2 has completed

         end
```

⟨Run of Program 15.1⟩

```
TUTOR 1.3 > G 900
PHYSICAL ADDRESS=00000900
1FFFFFFF is the final value of global
Control A <01> Control M <0d> Control Q <11> Delete <7f> and Control
Z
```

Mutual Exclusion with the MC68000

When the process-switching program is loaded and run, Process 1 outputs the final value of GLOBAL. The expected value for GLOBAL was $FFFFFFFF; however, the actual output is $1FFFFFFF. The problem stems from the way GLOBAL was computed. It is a variable shared by both Processes 1 and 2.

Suppose that Process 1 has just finished the instruction

ADDQ.L   #1,D0

and the value of D0 (potential value of GLOBAL) is $000FFFFF. If the timer interrupt occurs and causes a process switch, upon return the old value in D0 will be written to GLOBAL, and the work that was done by Process 2 will be lost. The following sequence of events would cause the results of Process 2 to be lost.

1. After completing the instruction "ADDQ.L #1,D0", the timer interrupt occurs, and $000FFFFF is saved in the process descriptor of Process 1 as part of the actions involved in suspending the process.

Process Descriptor for Process 1

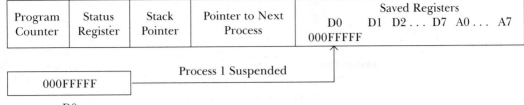

2. Process 2 executes until the timer goes off again. At this point, the value of D0 is $0FFFFFFF, which is the current value in GLOBAL. $0FFFFFFF is saved in the process descriptor of Process 2 as part of a switch to Process 1.

0FFFFFFF

GLOBAL

Process Descriptor for Process 2

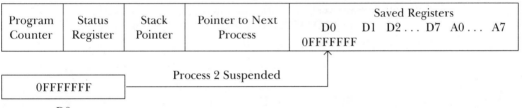

3. Process 1 is reactivated. The value $000FFFFF, saved in its process descriptor, is restored into (D0.L). The first instruction to be executed after restoration is "MOVE.L D0,GLOBAL". Execution now continues with this value, and all the work just done by Process 2 is lost!

000FFFFF

MOVE.L D0,GLOBAL

Process Descriptor for Process 1

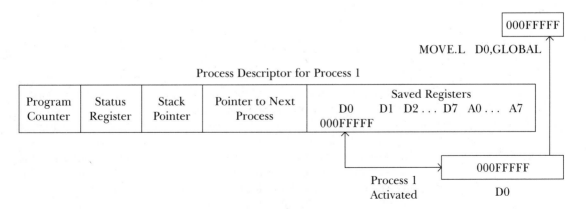

The preceding example illustrates a fundamental problem in concurrent programming, called the **mutual exclusion problem**. A block of code that accesses shared data is called a **critical section**. Mechanisms must be developed to protect shared data by allowing only one process at a time to access the critical section. One solution would be to disable interrupts at the start of a critical section and then turn them back on at the end. However, this would prohibit a process switch while executing a critical section. If the critical section is somewhat lengthy, this would slow down the entire system. Furthermore, requests for interrupt service from other devices would be delayed. For these reasons, this solution is rejected. The answer will be to create a loop mechanism that, when executed by two or more processes, will allow only one at a time to exit from the loop and proceed into the critical section.

Mutual Exclusion Code: Model I

Suppose Processes P1 and P2 wish to access critical data. To deal with the data, Process P1 executes code segment Crit1, and P2 executes code segment Crit2. The problem is to place code before and after critical sections, so that only one process at a time can execute its critical section. One solution is to let variable MUTEX be a shared byte of memory initialized to 0. Consider the following code segments:

Process P1		*Process P2*	
ENTER1:		ENTER2:	
	BSET #7,MUTEX		BSET #7,MUTEX
	BMI.S ENTER1		BMI.S ENTER2
	.		.
	.		.
	.		.
	Crit1		Crit2
	.		.
	.		.
	.		.
	BCLR #7,MUTEX		BCLR #7,MUTEX

Recall that BSET returns the state of the N bit before bit 7 is set and that a pending timer interrupt will not interfere with a currently executing BSET instruction. Only one process will see that the N bit is cleared as a result of executing BSET. The other process will see that the N bit is set and will wait in the loop until the BCLR instruction is executed.

In the case of several processors sharing a common bus to memory, this scheme does not work because the execution of BSET involves separate read and write cycles. After P1 reads the value of MUTEX into its processor, P2 may read the same value into its processor. Each processor will internally

FIGURE 15.4 Mutual Exclusion in Multiprocessor Systems

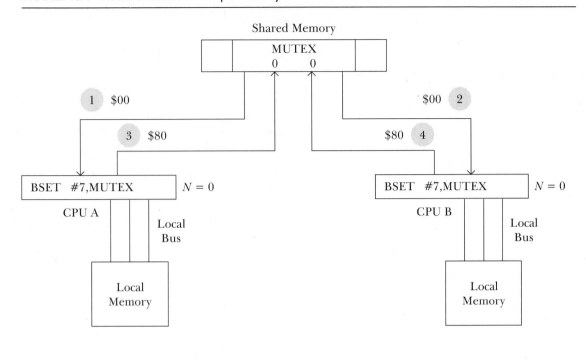

set bit 7 of MUTEX, set the N bit to 0 in its own CCR, and successively write the modified value to memory. Both P1 and P2 then proceed into their critical sections, and the scheme has failed, as illustrated in Figure 15.4. The circled numbers specify the order in which the bus cycles are executed.

Motorola recognized the problem of instructions having separate read and write cycles and designed the TAS instruction for precisely the critical section situation.

INSTRUCTION

TAS
(TEST and SET on
Operand)

Syntax   TAS   ⟨ea⟩

Action   The byte addressed by the operand is tested, and the N and Z bits of the CCR are set accordingly. The high-order bit (bit 7) of the operand is set. The operation is made indivisible by using a **read-modify-write bus cycle**.

Notes

1. The status register reflects the state of the memory byte before bit 7 is set.

2. The instruction can be used to synchronize the access of several processors to shared memory. The instruction can also be used to synchronize the action of two or more processes in the case of time slicing with a single processor.

3. No size attribute is given. It is assumed that ⟨ea⟩ addresses byte data.

4. A read-modify-write bus cycle causes all other requests for bus service to be denied until the TAS instruction has completely finished executing. TAS performs a read, sets the N and Z bits appropriately, sets the high-order bit of the byte in the arithmetic-logic unit, and writes the data back to the same address. This is all done in a noninterruptable fashion.

Mutual Exclusion Code: Model 2

With the TAS instruction, a correct solution to mutual exclusion is possible.

```
          Process P1                              Process P2
ENTER1:                                ENTER2:
          TAS     MUTEX                          TAS     MUTEX
          BMI.S   ENTER1                          BMI.S   ENTER2
                    .                                       .
                    .                                       .
                    .                                       .

               Crit1                                   Crit2

                    .                                       .
                    .                                       .
                    .                                       .

          BCLR    #7,MUTEX                        BCLR    #7,MUTEX
```

Program 15.1 can now be corrected. Simply declare a byte of data named MUTEX and initialize it to 0. Process 1 then executes the following code:

```
PROCESS1:
          MOVEQ     #15,D1
MLOOP1:

CRIT1:    TAS       MUTEX      ; ENTER CRITICAL SECTION
          BMI.S     CRIT1

          MOVE.L    GLOBAL,D0 ; COPY OF SHARED VAR
          MOVE.W    #999,D2
```

```
WORK1:    DBRA     D2,WORK1     ; ACT ON DATA
          LSL.L    #1,D0        ; FORM GLOBAL = 2*GLOBAL+1
          ADDQ.L   #1,D0
          MOVE.L   D0,GLOBAL

          BCLR     #7,MUTEX     ; END CRITICAL SECTION
```

Process 2 is repaired in the same way. You could use the BSET approach, but it is best to use a solution that is correct in every case. With these changes, the correct output for GLOBAL, namely $FFFFFFFF, is printed.

The CAS/CAS2 Instructions

The MC68020/30/40 processors provide two instructions that, like TAS, are used to maintain critical data in multiprocessor environments. The actions of the instructions are presented with a critical section example.

Processes 1 and 2 write to a global variable G. G could contain a sum, a pointer to a list, and so forth. Assume that Process 1 loads the current value of G into D0, copies it to D1, and then performs its update operations in D1. If the time slice for Process 1 expires before the updated value has been written to G and Process 2 updates G, the code in Process 1 must not write its instance of D1 to G. This can be avoided by comparing D0 against the current value of G.

If the values agree, then G has not been altered by Process 2, and D1 can be written to G.

If the two values do not agree, then Process 2 has altered G. The new value of G should be written to D0, and the update operations of Process 1 should be repeated.

In the same way, Process 2 should protect itself against updates by Process 1. The comparison and the writing of D1 to G must ensure that the other process does not intervene. This can be accomplished by using a read-modify-write bus cycle.

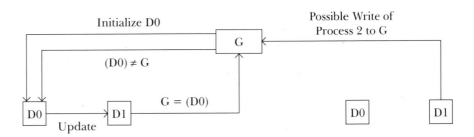

The MC68020 CAS instruction implements the comparison of register and a global data values as well as a data transfer using a read-modify-write bus cycle.

INSTRUCTION

CAS
(MC68020/30/40
Compare and Swap
with Operand)

Syntax   CAS.⟨size⟩   Dc,Du,⟨ea⟩

Action   The destination operand ⟨ea⟩ is compared to the contents of the compare operand data register Dc. If they are equal, the update data register Du is written to ⟨ea⟩; otherwise, the contents of the effective address ⟨ea⟩ are written to the compare operand Dc. The instruction uses a read-modify-write memory cycle to allow protection of critical data.

If ⟨ea⟩ and Dc are equal, the another process has not interfered, and Z = 1; otherwise, Z = 0. BNE can be used to construct a polling loop that will cycle until the value of ⟨eq⟩ has not changed from Dc.

EXAMPLE 15.2

Consider the mutual exclusion problem posed by Program 15.1. You can write the code to handle the critical sections with CAS. Recall that each of the two processes executes the following code segment:

```
MOVE.L   GLOBAL,D0      ; COPY OF SHARED VAR
LSL.L    #1,D0
ADDQ.L   #1,D0
MOVE.L   D0,GLOBAL      ; GLOBAL := 2 * GLOBAL + 1
```

To use CAS, read the value of GLOBAL into D0 and perform the update in D1. Then execute CAS with D0 as the compare data register and D1 as the update data register. The update is done only if D0 has remained unchanged during the update operation. If the value of D0 has changed, the update is not done, and the value of GLOBAL is loaded in D0. Another update is then prepared.

```
          MOVE.L GLOBAL,D0        ; COPY OF SHARED VAR
UPDLOOP:
          MOVE.L D0,D1
          LSL.L    #1,D1
          ADDQ.L #1,D1
          CAS.L    D0,D1,GLOBAL    ; GLOBAL := 2 * GLOBAL + 1
          BNE.S    UPDLOOP
```

INSTRUCTION	***Syntax*** CAS2.⟨size⟩ Dc1:Dc2,Du1:Du2, (Rn1):(Rn2)

INSTRUCTION

CAS2
MC68020/30/40
Compare and Swap
with Operand

Action   The instruction CAS2 is similar to CAS but performs comparisons and updates on two data values. Rn_i is any data or address register. The only mode allowed for the memory operands is address or data register indirect. Only if the contents of Dc1 equals (Rn1) and the contents of Dc2 equals (Rn2) will the contents of Du1 be assigned to (Rn1) and the contents of Du2 be assigned to (Rn2). This instruction is used to update pointers in linked queues, stacks, doubly linked lists, and so forth. For additional information, consult Section 1.2.1.2.1 of the *MC68000 Family Programmer's Reference Manual.*

15.3	**MC68020/30/40 CACHE**

Most programs implement algorithms that require a series of short loops. For instance, to compute the maximum value in a series of 100 positive numbers, each item is read and tested. The following code contains a loop that executes 100 times and determines the maximum value:

```
        MOVEQ   #0,D2       ; SET MAX VALUE IN D2 TO 0
        MOVEQ   #99,D1      ; SET D1 TO THE UPPER INDEX 99
        LEA     ARRAY,A0    ; LOAD ADDR TO POINT AT ARRAY
LOOP:   CMP.L   (A0)+,D2    ; COMPARE CURR VALUE AGAINST D2
        BGE.S   CONT        ; IF D2 > = CURR VALUE, CONTINUE
        MOVE.L  (-4,A0),D2  ; REPLACE THE MAXIMUM
CONT:   DBRA    D1,LOOP     ; DECREMENT D1 AND LOOP AGAIN
```

The loop contains four instructions (12 bytes) that are executed 100 times. In an MC68000 system, the processor must fetch the four instructions for each iteration. The MC68020/30/40 processors implement an instruction cache in which the last 64 long words (256 bytes) from the instruction stream are saved. During instruction prefetch, the cache is checked. If the instruction word specified by the program counter is present, a cache "hit" occurs. The word is copied from the cache and placed in the instruction pipeline. If the instruction word is not in the cache, a cache "miss" occurs, and the word is fetched from memory, copied to the cache, and sent into the instruction pipeline. Execution time is significantly improved for small loops through the use of an instruction cache, because use of the cache reduces the processor's external bus activity. The cache increases system throughput in two ways. First, the cache is accessed in 2 CPU clock cycles, as compared with a minimum of 3 required for external memory access. Second, the cache allows instruction fetches and operand accesses to proceed in parallel. For instance, if the processor requires an instruction word and a bus access to process an operand, the instruction may be fetched from the cache while the bus access occurs. The MC68030/40 processors implement a new data cache for higher performance. MC68030/40 cache memories are introduced in the next subsection.

MC68020 Instruction Cache

Each of the long words from the instruction stream is stored in a cache record that consists of three fields. The first field, a 25-bit tag field, consists of bits A08–A31 of the instruction address and the function code bit FC2 (introduced in Chapter 13). This function code bit distinguishes between supervisor program space and user program space in cases in which two instructions have the same address. This is needed when an MMU is running, because both the operating system running in supervisor mode and a user program may have an instruction word at the same virtual address. A 1-bit field, the valid bit, specifies whether the cache entry contains a valid long word. A third field contains the long word. There are 64 cache records located in a cache table with indices 0–63.

Tag Field	Valid	Instruction Data (1 long word)

FC2   A31–A08

Bits A07–A02 of the instruction address are used as a 6-bit index into the table. The algorithm also uses bit A01 to specify whether the high-order word (A01 = 0) or low-order word (A01 = 1) of the instruction data is referenced. The structure of the cache is given in Figure 15.5.

The index field of the current program counter is extracted, and that record is looked up in the cache. A hit occurs if the cache entry is "valid," bits 8–31 of the address agree with those of the cache entry, and the function code bit FC2 agrees with that recorded in the cache entry. The MSW or LSW from the instruction data field is passed to the pipeline for instruction processing, depending on the value of bit 1 of the address. If no hit occurs, a long word from the prefetch instruction stream is loaded into the cache. Under program control, the cache may be "frozen," and the cache load sequence is not executed. The "frozen" cache will be discussed under the topic of cache programming.

FIGURE 15.5 MC68020 Cache

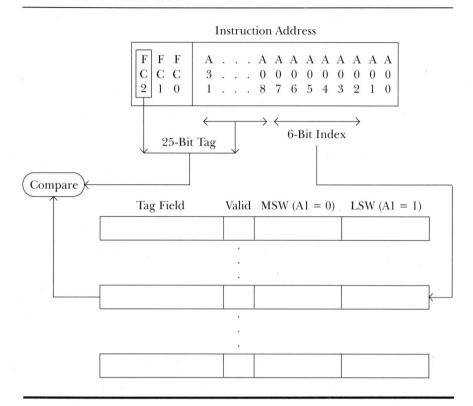

Instruction Address

25-Bit Tag

6-Bit Index

Compare

Tag Field   Valid   MSW (A1 = 0)   LSW (A1 = 1)

EXAMPLE 15.3

Assume that (PC) = $0A008046 and FC2 = 1.

(a) Bits A02–A07 (%010001) specify index 17 in the cache table.

(b) The tag field corresponding to index 17 is tested for the value $10A0080.

(c) Assume that there is a match and the "valid" flag is set. If the 32-bit cache data field contains the value $303CA279, the LSW $A279 is placed in the instruction stream (A01 = 1).

Cache on the MC68030/40 Processors

The 256-byte instruction cache of the MC68030/40 processors is organized as an array of 16 records, each containing a tag field and four long words. The tag field is constructed exactly as with the MC68020 processor. The tag field is followed by four "valid" bits, each representing one of the four long words in a cache entry. The index is formed from bits 4–7 of the address, with bits 2 and 3 determining which of the four long words is to be selected. As with the MC68020 processor, bit 1 is used to determine which word of the long word is to be supplied to the instruction pipeline. See Figure 15.6 for a diagram of the instruction cache.

A 256-byte data cache serves to reduce bus activity further and to decrease execution time. The instruction cache always contains words from the instruction stream. In general, the data cache contains words fetched from the program's data space but also may contain words from the instruction stream. Additional information is placed in each data cache entry in order to distinguish these two types of references. If a cache hit occurs during a write operation to memory, both the cache and memory are updated to contain the new value. With both an instruction and data cache, instruction fetches, data fetches, and a third external access can all occur simultaneously if the instruction and data caches are both hit.

FIGURE 15.6   MC68030/40 Instruction Cache

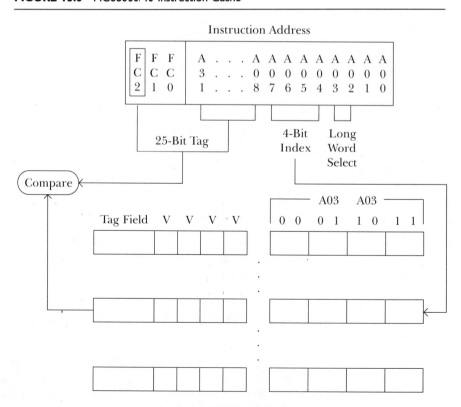

The data cache is structured in almost the same way as the instruction cache. Although most memory accesses caused by operands are to data space, operands can involve program space memory references. For instance, in the code segment

       MOVEA.L   (CASES,PC,D1.W),A0
       JMP   (A0)
CASES: .
               .
               .

the memory reference at address (CASES,PC,D1.W) is a program reference because all PC-relative modes generate program references only. In order to distinguish between an operand fetch in program or data space, all three function code bits are placed in the tag. The cache is diagrammed in Figure 15.7.

FIGURE 15.7 MC68030/40 Data Cache

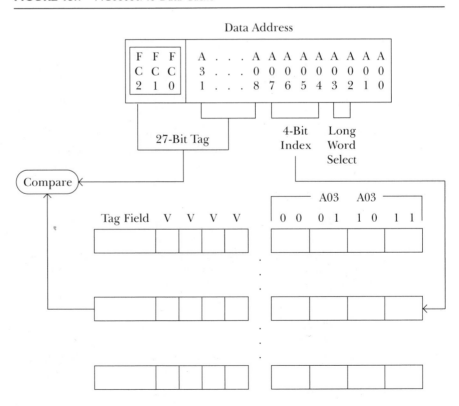

Cache Programming

The caches on the MC68020/30/40 processors are equipped with several options that can be set by a supervisor mode program. The caches can be enabled/disabled, an individual entry or the whole cache can be cleared, and a cache can be frozen to retain its data. The MC68030/40 cache memories have some additional features.

Programming the MC68020 Instruction Cache

The MC68020 instruction cache is accessible only by using the MOVEC instruction, which was introduced in Chapter 13. The programmer can address the **cache control register (CACR)** to utilize the features of the cache. The specific instructions used are

MOVEC   Register,CACR
MOVEC   CACR,Register

The CACR is a 32-bit register whose low-order 4 bits direct the cache's programmable features. The other bits always read as zeros.

31					8	7	6	5	4	3	2	1	0
0	0	0	0	· ·	· 0	0	0	0	0	C	CE	F	E

E = Enable Cache   F = Freeze Cache   CE = Clear Entry   C = Clear Cache

Cache Control Register

Bit 0: Enable Cache   On system reset, this bit is cleared, and the cache is disabled. In this situation, the processor uses external memory for all instruction stream fetches. The cache is enabled by setting the E bit. The cache should be enabled in normal programming situations.

Bit 1: Freeze Cache   When the F bit is set, the cache is checked for a hit on each instruction fetch. If the data is present in the cache, it is retrieved. However, if the data is not present, external memory is used, and the new data is not loaded into the cache. In this way, a short segment of code can be kept in the cache for frequent use.

Bit 2: Clear Entry   An individual cache entry can be cleared (made invalid) by writing to the CACR with the CE bit set. The bit always reads as 0. The entry to be cleared is determined by extracting the index from bits 2–7 of the **cache address register (CAAR)**. This 32-bit register is initialized by using MOVEC.

Cache Address Register

Bit 3: Clear Cache If the C bit is set, all entries in the cache are marked invalid. This function occurs only when MOVEC is used to write to the cache control register with the C bit set. This bit always reads as 0. Subsequent instruction addresses cause a cache miss and are placed in the cache. This action is needed when an operating system switches from one user process to another.

EXAMPLE 15.4

(a) The following code clears the cache entry at index 5.

```
MOVEA.L  #%00010100,A0    ; 101 IN BITS 2-7 OF CAAR
MOVEC    A0,CAAR
MOVEQ    #%101,D0         ; E = 1 and CE = 1
MOVEC    D0,CACR
```

(b) The instruction cache is placed between the CPU and the MMU, so it deals with virtual addresses, not physical addresses. The following situation demonstrates the need to clear the cache during process switching:

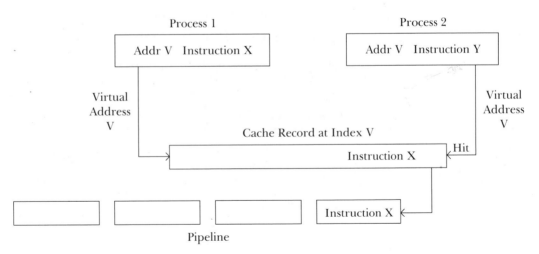

Assume that Process 1 is running in user mode and has just been suspended after executing an instruction at virtual address $00155566. The address $00155566 will tag data in the cache.

Process 2 then resumes execution in user mode at virtual address

$00155566. The two virtual addresses correspond to different real addresses. However, when Process 2 executes the instruction at address $00155566, a cache hit occurs and the wrong opcode word is passed into the instruction pipeline.

Programming the MC68030/40 Instruction and Data Caches

The caches on the MC68030/40 processors are also programmed by accessing the cache control and address registers through the MOVEC instruction. The cache control register has additional fields to handle the data cache separately from the instruction cache and to designate the method of loading long words into the caches. Figure 15.8 details the new fields of the cache control register.

Fields 0–3 have the same function as the corresponding fields in the cache control register of the MC68020 processor. The index field in the cache address register (CAAR) is used to clear one of the four long words in a cache entry when bit CEI is set. Fields ED, FD, CED, and CD independently perform those functions for the data cache. The IBE and DBE fields cause burst filling of a four long-word cache entry, and the WA field determines whether the data cache is filled when a write cycle causes a cache miss. These actions are unique to the MC68030/40 processors.

The cache can be loaded when a miss occurs in one of two ways:

1. One long word at a time as with the MC68020.

2. Four long words at once, called *burst-fill mode*.

The instruction cache is loaded one long word at a time when IBE = 0, and the data cache is loaded one word at a time when DBE = 0. When a

FIGURE 15.8   MC68030/40 Cache Control Register

31				14	13	12	11	10	9	8	7	6	5	4	3	2	1	0
0	0	0	0 . . . 0	WA	DBE	CD	CED	FD	ED	0	0	0	IBE	CI	CEI	FI	EI

MC68030/40 Cache Control Register

WA   =   Write Allocate
DBE =   Data Burst Enable
CD   =   Clear Data Cache
CED =   Clear Entry in Data Cache
FD   =   Freeze Data Cache
ED   =   Enable Data Cache

IBE   =   Instruction Burst Enable
CI   =   Clear Instruction Cache
CEI   =   Clear Entry in Instruction Cache
FI   =   Freeze Instruction Cache
EI   =   Enable Instruction Cache

cache is enabled and burst-fill mode is on, the bus controller requests burst-fill mode if

1. A read cycle is initiated, but the tag field of the address does not match the tag stored in the indexed cache entry.

2. A read cycle is initiated and the tag fields match, but all four long words in the cache entry are marked invalid.

The entire four long-word cache entry is filled using one burst operation, which takes less time than the four separate memory operations. This requires a main memory controller that can cooperate with the CPU to transfer data in this way.

The data cache on the MC68030/40 processors is said to be a **write-through cache**. This means that whenever a cache hit occurs on a write cycle, both the cache and memory are updated. A subsequent read operation will find the correct value in the cache. The WA bit determines the **write allocate policy** used by the cache. The setting of the WA bit in the cache control register determines what happens when a cache miss occurs on a write cycle. If WA = 0 and a cache miss occurs on a write cycle, the write to memory proceeds without updating the cache. A subsequent read operation will cause the cache to be updated, and then a write will cause a hit and a cache update. If WA = 1, the cache is updated on all write cycles, regardless of whether a hit or a miss occurs. The cache always contains the most up-to-date value possible. A side effect of this policy is that previously valid long words may be replaced, causing the running of subsequent memory operations in order to fill the invalidated items. The technical details of the write allocate policy are beyond the scope of this text. Consult the *MC68030 Enhanced 32-Bit Microprocessor User's Manual* for more information.

Programs 15.2 and 15.3 demonstrate the efficiency of using an instruction cache for loop processing. The actions of the programs are identical. However, one is run with cache enabled, and the other, with cache disabled. A loop consisting of a series of NOP instructions is executed 1 million times. The size of the code in the loop equals the cache size of 128 words. After one iteration, the cache is loaded with the NOP instruction data. With the cache enabled, the CPU will access the cache to fetch the instruction opcode word. With the cache disabled, each fetch of the NOP instruction is made from memory. The time of execution for each program is included. The programs were run on a Macintosh IIci with an MC68030 processor. The timing method used is unique to the Macintosh, but a similar method can be used on other systems.

PROGRAM 15.2

Cache Enabled Test

```
                    xref    decout_long, newline, stop
cache:  moveq   #%1001,d0
```

```
            movec   d0,cacr         ; clear and enable instruction cache
            move.l  #1000000,d1
            move.l  $16a,d0         ; number 1/60 secs. since startup
loop:       dcb.w   125,$4e71       ;125 nop's
            subq.l  #1,d1
            bne     loop
            sub.l   $16a,d0         ; compute loop time in 1/60th secs.
            neg.l   d0
            jsr     decout_long
            jsr     stop
            end
```

⟨Run of Program 15.2⟩

674 (11.2 seconds)

PROGRAM 15.3

Cache Disabled Test

```
            xref    decout_long, newline, stop
cache:      moveq   #%1001,d0
            ;movec  d0,cacr         ; clear and enable instruction cache
            dc.w    $4e7b
            dc.w    $0002
            move.l  #1000000,d1
            move.l  $16a,d0         ; number 1/60 secs. since startup
loop:       dcb.w   125,$4e71       ;125 nop's
            subq.l  #1,d1
            bne     loop
            sub.l   $16a,d0         ; compute loop time in 1/60th secs.
            neg.l   d0
            jsr     decout_long
            jsr     stop
            end
```

⟨Run of Program 15.3⟩

1126 (18.8 seconds)

15.4 | THE M68000 COPROCESSOR INTERFACE

For many applications, the general-purpose MC68020 CPU is sufficient. When specialized processing is required, efficiency is increased by using external computing hardware. A **coprocessor** is a separate computational device that resides on the system bus and is capable of executing its own instruction set. It can be thought of as a special-purpose CPU executing instructions using hardware that otherwise would be done using subroutines executed by the main processor. As much as possible, the activities occur in parallel with those of the master processor.

On many systems, a coprocessor handles floating-point computation. Chapter 8 discussed some of the complex software necessary to handle floating-point numbers. Section 15.5 introduces the MC68881 floating-point coprocessor that is provided by Motorola to implement IEEE floating-point arithmetic.

The MC68020 processor can use the MC68851 memory management coprocessor. The MMU is a hardware device that intercepts program addresses (virtual addresses) as they are put on the address bus and translates them to real memory locations, as shown in Figure 15.9. For instance, a Pascal program might be compiled with starting address $0000. If the operating system loads the code at location $1000, all memory addresses have to be relocated to the new range of addresses. The MMU chip intercepts each address as it goes out on the address bus and translates it to the correct real address. The MMU used by the MC68030 is covered in Section 15.8.

Only selected coprocessors can be placed on an M68020/30/40 system, because each must communicate with the processor through the protocol defined by the M68000 coprocessor interface. The MC68020/30/40 processors provide a set of "CP" instructions to implement communication between the main processor and coprocessors. The instructions have an opcode format $Fxxx. Typically, a Motorola assembler provides mnemonics that are translated by the assembler to the correct "CP" instruction.

Coprocessors require a communication protocol with the CPU for several reasons:

1. The CPU must recognize that a coprocessor instruction is to be executed, determine which coprocessor is involved, and then establish bus communication with that coprocessor.

2. The status of the coprocessor may need to be presented to the CPU.

3. The coprocessor may need data from memory.

FIGURE 15.9 MMU Translation

4. The coprocessor may need to transfer results of computations to memory or CPU registers.

5. The coprocessor may have detected an error condition, such as an illegal instruction or divide by zero, and it must request that the CPU initiate exception processing.

The protocol that enables this cooperation is called the **M68000 coprocessor interface**. A detailed knowledge of this protocol is necessary only for a designer who wishes to place a nonstandard coprocessor in systems driven by MC68020/30/40 processors or who wishes to use a Motorola coprocessor in a system not employing an MC68020/30/40 processor. Knowledge of this protocol is not necessary for the programmer who wishes to use the standard Motorola floating-point and memory management coprocessors, which are described in this chapter. For this reason, only a few basic details of the protocol are provided here. Consult Motorola technical documentation for additional information.

All coprocessor instructions are F-line instructions that have hex value F as the most significant 4 bits of the opcode word. The general format of a coprocessor instruction is shown in Figure 15.10. The 3-bit Cp-ID identifies the number of the coprocessor. Up to eight coprocessors can be present on a system. Motorola uses "000" for the MC68851 paged memory management unit and "001" for the MC68881/MC6882 floating-point coprocessors. The Type field identifies the kind of coprocessor instruction to be executed. There are four coprocessor instructions: general, conditional, context save, and context restore.

Every coprocessor must have a series of **coprocessor interface registers** that are used to communicate between the CPU and the coprocessor. The first of these is the **response coprocessor interface register**. This register directs the actions of the CPU while the coprocessor is executing an instruction. The **command coprocessor interface register** contains the com-

FIGURE 15.10   Coprocessor Instruction Format

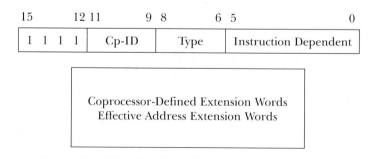

mand that the coprocessor is being asked to execute. The interface register set of a coprocessor occupies 32 bytes and is arranged as follows:

	31	15	0
00	Response*	Control*	
04	Save*	Restore*	
08	Operation Word	Command*	
0C	(Reserved)	Condition*	
10	Operand*		
14	Register Select	(Reserved)	
18	Instruction Address		
1C	Operand Address		

The registers marked by * must be present for a coprocessor

The coprocessor interface registers reside on the bus in what is called *CPU space*. A CPU space address is an address passed on the bus with all three function code bits set to 1. CPU space is used for interrupt acknowledge, breakpoint acknowledge, and coprocessor communication cycles. Only a subset of the possible CPU space addresses is used. In the case of interrupt and breakpoint acknowledge, the CPU space addresses are as follows:

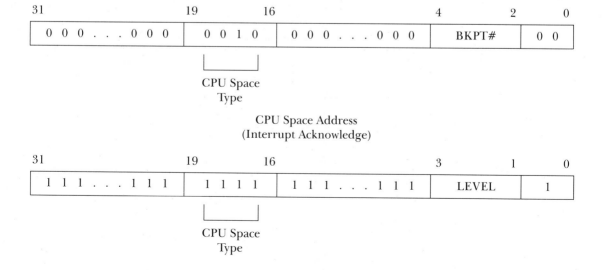

CPU Space Address
(Breakpoint Acknowledge)

31	19	16	4	2	0
0 0 0 . . . 0 0 0	0 0 1 0	0 0 0 . . . 0 0 0	BKPT#	0 0	

CPU Space
Type

CPU Space Address
(Interrupt Acknowledge)

31	19	16	3	1	0
1 1 1 . . . 1 1 1	1 1 1 1	1 1 1 . . . 1 1 1	LEVEL	1	

CPU Space
Type

In each case, bits 16–19 of the address identify the type of CPU space address, and lower-order bits specify additional information. This is how the interrupt level is sent on the bus during the MC68020/30/40 interrupt acknowledge bus cycle. The CPU space address for a coprocessor is similar.

Coproducer CPU Space Address
(Coprocessor Communication)

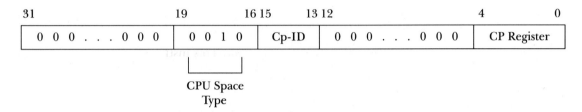

The set of eight possible coprocessor interface registers reside in CPU space at the base address $20000. The Cp-ID field of the CPU space address determines the starting address for the set of interface registers for the coprocessor being used, and the CP Register field contains the offset to the particular register.

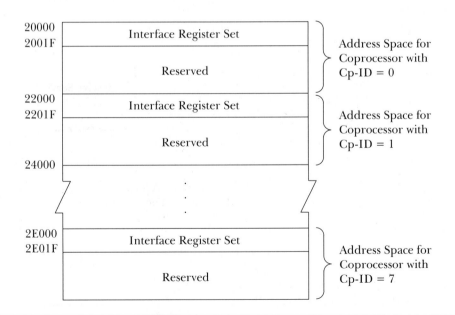

EXAMPLE 15.5 It is desired to address the command register of the floating-point coprocessor at Cp-ID = 1. The CPU space address is determined by using Cp-ID = 001_2 and CP Register = 01010_2.

$$\text{Command Register address} = 00000000000000100010000000001010_2$$
$$= \$2200A$$

When the CPU sees an F-line instruction, it does no further decoding but attempts to communicate with the coprocessor as determined by the value in bits 9–11 of the F-line opcode word. As indicated earlier, there are four types of coprocessor instructions. The most commonly used type is the **coprocessor general instruction**. This instruction has a type field of 000_2 in bits 6–8 of the F-line opcode word. The word following the F-line

FIGURE 15.11   Coprocessor Interface Protocol for Coprocessor General Instructions

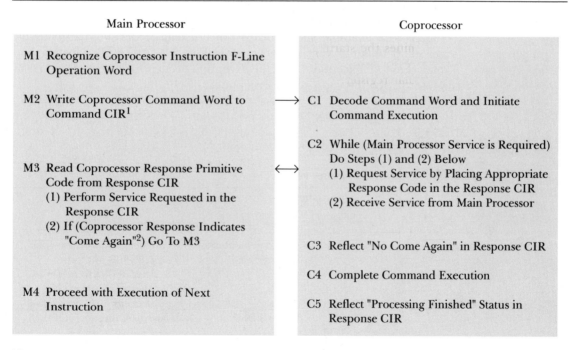

Notes:
1. CIR is short for "Coprocessor Interface Register."
2. "Come Again" indicates that further service of the
   main processor is being requested by the coprocessor.

instruction contains the actual coprocessor command to be executed. The CPU writes this command word to the command register of the coprocessor. If a bus error signal is received, then the coprocessor does not exist, and the F-line exception is taken. If the coprocessor is present, a communication sequence between the CPU and the coprocessor begins. The sequence is described in Figure 15.11. As execution proceeds, the coprocessor can request service from the CPU by placing a code in the response coprocessor interface register. When the coprocessor no longer needs the CPU, the coprocessor releases it by placing an appropriate value in the response register, and the CPU then continues by executing the next instruction in the program. If the coprocessor needs to do additional computation to complete the instruction, the CPU and the coprocessor execute in parallel.

A sequence like that in Figure 15.11 is defined for the other types of coprocessor instructions. Table 15.1 lists the specific coprocessor instructions along with a typical use of each. For further details on the M68000 coprocessor interface, consult the Motorola user manuals for the MC68020 or MC68030. Specific examples will be given in the next section for the MC68881/68882 floating-point coprocessor.

During execution of an instruction, a coprocessor may detect error conditions—for example, illegal instructions or data errors such as divide-by-zero and floating-point underflow/overflow. The cpTRAPcc instructions may cause an exception. Specific exception vectors have been reserved by Motorola for the coprocessor exceptions.

TABLE 15.1   Types of Coprocessor Instructions

TYPE	INSTRUCTION OPERAND	SYNTAX	FUNCTION
General	cpGen	Implementation defined	Implements data-processing instructions and other instructions defined for a particular coprocessor
Conditional	cpBcc	Label	Allows program flow control
	cpDBcc	Dn,Label	based on the operations
	cpScc	⟨ea⟩	of a coprocessor
	cpTRAPcc	none or #N	
Context Save	cpSAVE	⟨ea⟩	Saves the state of the coprocessor
Context Restore	cpRESTORE	⟨ea⟩	Restores the state of the coprocessor

|15.5| **FLOATING-POINT COPROCESSOR**

A floating-point coprocessor is used for scientific and engineering applications in which extensive floating-point computations must be done. Through its implementation as a coprocessor, it essentially extends the instruction set of the primary processor. A floating-point coprocessor includes instructions to add, subtract, multiply, and divide floating-point numbers at hardware speed. In addition, the coprocessor supplies a number of mathematical functions such as $\sin(x)$, $\cos(x)$, and e^x. Using the basic computational ability of the coprocessor and the mathematical functions it makes available, the programmer can apply techniques from numerical analysis to develop numerical solutions to problems in integration, root finding, linear algebra, and differential equations. The MC68020/30 processors can take advantage of the MC68881 floating-point coprocessor. The MC68882 floating-point coprocessor is located onboard the MC68040. The two coprocessors are identical in function, so only the MC68881 coprocessor is described in this section. The data formats used by the coprocessors are given, followed by a discussion of the basic architecture and instruction set. Two useful subroutines for floating-point I/O are presented and then used in a complete program that calculate the roots of a nonlinear equation.

Data Formats

The MC68881 coprocessor can read data in memory and write data to memory in any of the formats listed in Table 15.2. The byte, word, and long-word formats are used to convert integers to floating-point format. The single- and double-precision real formats are as defined by the IEEE standard. Each assumes a hidden 1 as the most significant bit of the mantissa. Single- and double-precision formats use excess-127 and excess-1023

TABLE 15.2 MC66881 Data Formats

DATA TYPE	INSTRUCTION EXTENSION	SIZE
Byte integer	.B	8 bits
Word integer	.W	16 bits
Long-word integer	.L	32 bits
Singe-precision real	.S	32 bits
Double-precision real	.D	64 bits
Extended-precision real	.X	96 bits
Packed-decimal string real	.P	96 bits

exponents, respectively. The single-precision format was discussed thoroughly in Chapter 8, and the double-precision format is a direct extension, so no more explanation will be added.

The MC68881 coprocessor actually performs all computations using 80-bit extended-precision real format, and its registers hold only extended-precision values. Extended-precision is like single- and double-precision, except that a hidden 1 is not used, so all digits are explicitly present. A 15-bit excess-16383 exponent is used. In order for extended-precision data in memory to be long-word aligned, the processor reads and writes extended-precision values using a 96-bit format, in which 16 bits containing zeros are added immediately following the exponent.

To facilitate the input and output of floating-point numbers, the processor provides a 96-bit packed-decimal real format. This represents a decimal number of the form

$$\pm D_{16} . D_{15} \cdots D_2 D_1 D_0 \times 10^{\pm e_2 e_1 e_0}$$

Each digit of the exponent and mantissa is a 4-bit packed BCD digit. Bits 68–79 are stored as zeros unless an attempt to convert an extended real number to decimal causes an overflow. Positive and negative infinity ($\pm \infty$) are signed numbers and represent real values that fall outside the range provided by the floating-point representation being used. A **NAN** (Not-A-Number) represents the result of an operation that has no mathematical validity, such as infinity divided by infinity. When an infinity or NAN is represented, bits 92–93 are both 1.

Figure 15.12 provides a summary of all the data formats used by the MC68881.

EXAMPLE 15.6   The number -25.53 is stored in packed-decimal real format as the equivalent number

$$-2.553 \times 10^1$$

The sign bit for the mantissa is 1 and that for the exponent is 0, the exponent is 001, and the mantissa is 2553. In hex, the number is

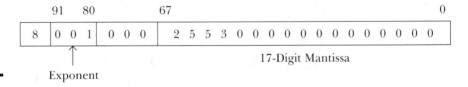

EXAMPLE 15.7   The floating-point number 1.1011×2^{-1} is stored in extended real form as

$$\$3FFE0000D800000000000000$$

FIGURE 15.12 MC68881 Data Formats

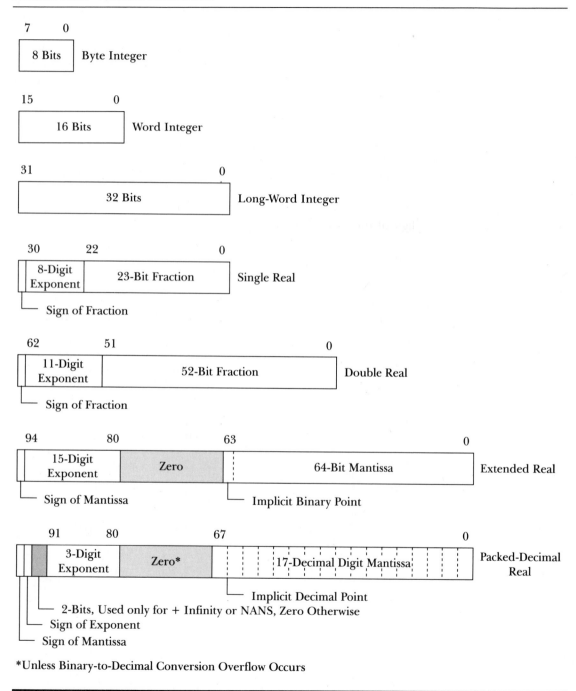

*Unless Binary-to-Decimal Conversion Overflow Occurs

The sign bit is 0 ($+$), the mantissa is 1.1011000 . . . 000, and the exponent field evaluates to 16382. Recalling that excess 16383 notation is used, the true exponent is -1.

A primary application of packed-decimal form is to simplify the output of floating-point numbers. The subroutine PACKDECOUT takes the address of a 96-bit packed-decimal real number in A0 and prints the most significant 9 decimal digits in the format

$$\pm D_8 . D_7 D_6 \cdots D_2 D_1 D_0 E \pm e_2 e_1 e_0$$

The sequence $E \pm e_2 e_1 e_0$ stands for $10^{\pm e_2 e_1 e_0}$ and is a standard notation for high-level language I/O routines. PACKDECOUT will be used later as part of a subroutine to output floating-point numbers stored in 64-bit double format.

PACKDECOUT Packed Decimal Output

Parameters passed:
Address of a 96-bit packed decimal real number in A0.

```
packdecout:
        link    a6,#-18               ; 16 char number and two blanks
        movem.l d0-d1/a0-a2,-(sp)
        move.w  #$2020,(-2,a6)        ; print two trailing blanks
        lea     (-2,a6)a1             ; build number right to left
        lea     (2,a0),a2             ; set just past exponent
        unpk    -(a2),-(a1),#$3030    ; 2 rightmost exponent digits
        bfextu  (a0){4:4},d0          ; get most sig exponent digit
        addi.b  #'0',d0
        move.b  d0,-(a1)              ; output most sig exponent digit
        btst    #6,(a0)               ; output sign of exponent
        beq.s   1$
        move.b  #'-',-(a1)
        bra.s   2$
1$:     move.b  #'+',-(a1)
2$:     move.b  #'E',-(a1)            ; put out E
        moveq   #3,d1
        lea     (8,a0),a2             ; output 4 pairs of digits
3$:     unpk    -(a2),-(a1),#$3030
        dbra    d1,3$
        move.b  #'.',-(a1)            ; output decimal point
        bfextu  (a0){28:4},d0         ; digit to right of dec point
        addi.b  #'0',d0
        move.b  d0,-(a1)
        btst    #7,(a0)               ; output sign of number
        beq.s   4$
        move.b  #'-',-(a1)
        bra.s   5$
```

```
4$:  move.b   #'+',-(a1)
5$:  move.w   #18,d0
     lea      (-18,a6),a0
     jsr      strout
     movem.l  (sp)+,d0-d1/a0-a2
     unlk     a6
     rts
```

MC68881 Registers

The MC68881 coprocessor contains eight general-purpose 80-bit floating-point data registers, a 32-bit control register, a 32-bit status register, and a 32-bit instruction address register.

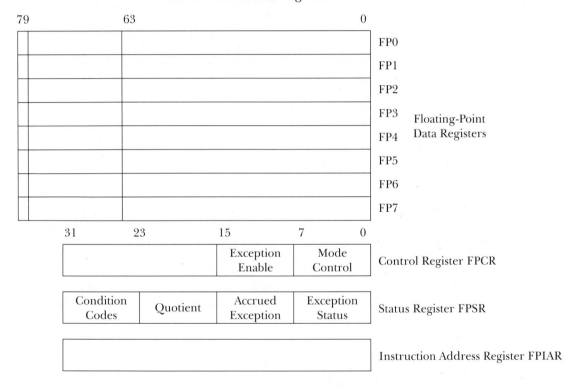

Floating-Point Data Registers

In assembly language, the floating-point registers are given the names FP0–FP7, analogous to the MC68000 data registers D0–D7. These registers always contain an 80-bit extended-precision number. Before data in any format is placed into a floating-point register or is used in a calculation, it is converted to extended-precision. For instance, the FMOVE instruction is used to transfer data in memory to a floating-point register. When the instruction

FMOVE.W   #1,FP0

is executed, the 16-bit integer value 1 is converted to 80-bit extended-precision floating-point format and placed into FP0. The floating-point registers are the focal point for all floating-point communications.

Floating-Point Control Register

The exception enable byte of the control register contains 1 bit for each of eight exceptions that can be generated by the MC68881 coprocessor. Setting or clearing a bit will enable/disable the corresponding exception. The mode control byte allows the user to control rounding modes and rounding precisions. A result can be rounded or chopped to either double, single, or extended precision. If single or double precision is selected, the bits of the mantissa following the number allocated to the given precision are filled with zeros. The most common setting for the mode control byte is to have both fields zero, which corresponds to rounding to the nearest extended-precision value.

Floating-Point Status Register

The condition code byte is analogous to the MC68000 CCR and reflects the status of a computation that involves a floating-point data register. The quotient byte is used in conjunction with floating-point remaindering operations. The exception status byte contains a bit for each floating-point exception and is used to determine whether an exception occurred during the last arithmetic instruction or move operation. The accrued exception byte contains a logical combination of bits in the exception status byte. It contains a history of all floating-point exceptions that have occurred since the user last cleared this byte.

Floating Point Instruction Address Register

It is possible for the MC68020/30/40 processors to execute an instruction while the MC68881 coprocessor is executing a floating-point instruction. For instance, if the CPU encounters the instruction

FDIV.D   X,FP0

that divides the number in register FP0 by the double floating-point number at address X, it is free to execute another instruction after it transfers X to the floating-point coprocessor. The next CPU instruction and the floating-point coprocessor division operation proceed in parallel. If an exception is caused by a floating-point coprocessor and the CPU has moved on to another instruction, the PC saved on the stack is not the address of the floating-point instruction that actually caused the exception. The floating-point instruction address register holds the address of the current floating-point instruction being executed. The exception service routine for the floating-point exception can read the address of the offending instruction from this register.

MC68881 Instructions

The instruction set for the MC68881 floating-point coprocessor can be divided into the five groups indicated in Table 15.3. The host addressing modes are used to access memory, because the MC68881 coprocessor performs no address calculations.

To indicate the power of the processor, Table 15.4 lists the complete instruction set for the MC68881 coprocessor. The next subsection contains sample code illustrating a number of MC68881 instructions. A short instruction description is presented for each instruction used in a programming example.

MC68881 Programming

For effective programming of the MC68881 coprocessor, an assembler that translates the set of mnemonics defined for the processor must be used. Fortunately, most assemblers recognize these mnemonics. Programming the MC68881 coprocessor is introduced by first writing two I/O routines, one for floating-point output and one for input. These routines can be added to the packed-decimal output routine already developed to form a useful library for floating-point I/O. This library is used to solve an interesting problem in numerical analysis that requires floating-point computation.

TABLE 15.3 MC68881 Instruction Types

GROUP	EXAMPLES
MOVE instructions	Genral move, move to/from control register
Instructions computing with one argument	sin, cos, e^x
Instructions computing with two arguments	$+$, $-$, $*$, $/$, compare
Program control operations	Branch on FP condition codes
System control operations	Trap conditionally, save/restore the internal state of the coprocessor

TABLE 15.4   Instruction Set of the MC68881

MNEMONIC	
MOVE Instructions	DESCRIPTION
FMOVE.⟨fmt⟩ ⟨ea⟩,FP*n*	Move to 68881
FMOVE.⟨fmt⟩ FP*m*,⟨ea⟩	Move from 68881
FMOVE.X FP*m*,FP*n*	Move within 68881
FMOVE.P FP*m*,⟨ea⟩{#*k*}	Move packed decimal with static *k*-factor
FMOVE.P FP*m*,⟨ea⟩{D*n*}	Move packed decimal with dynamic *k*-factor
FMOVE.L ⟨ea⟩,FPcr	Move to 68881 control register
FMOVE.L FPcr,⟨ea⟩	Move from 68881 control register
FMOVECR.X #ccc,FP*n*	Move constant from 68881 ROM
FMOVEM ⟨list⟩,⟨ea⟩	Move multiple from 68881
FMOVEM ⟨ea⟩,⟨list⟩	Move multiple to 68881
Conditional Instructions	
FBcc	Branch on 68881 condition
FDBcc	Decrement and branch on 68881 condition
FScc	Set according to 68881 condition
FTRAPcc	Trap on 68881 condition
Instructions Computing with One Argument	
FABS	Absolute value
FACOS	Arc cosine
FASIN	ARC sine
FATAN	Arc tangent
FATANH	Hyperbolic arc tangent
FCOS	Cosine
FCOSH	Hyperbolic cosine
FETOX	e to the x power
FETOXM1	e to the $(x - 1)$ power
FGETEXP	Get exponent
FGETMAN	Get mantissa
FINT	Integer part
FINTRZ	Integer part (truncated)
FLOG10	Logarithm to the Base 10
FLOG2	Logarithm to the Base 2
FLOGN	Logarithm to the Base e
FLOGNP1	Log to base e of $(x + 1)$
FNEG	Negate
FSIN	Sine
FSINCOS	Sine and cosine (simultaneous)
FSINH	Hyperbolic sine
FSQRT	Square root
FTAN	Tangent
FTANH	Hyperbolic tangent
FTENTOX	10 to the x power
FTST	Test
FTWOTOX	2 to the x power

TABLE 15.4 Continued

MNEMONIC	
MOVE Instructions	DESCRIPTION
Instructions Computing with Two Arguments	
FADD	Add
FCMP	Compare
FDIV	Divide
FMOD	Modulo remainder
FMUL	Multiply
FREM	IEEE remainder
FSCALE	Scale exponent
FSGLDIV	Single-precision divide
FSGLMUL	Single-precisions multiply
FSUB	Subtract
Miscellaneous Instructions	
FNOP	No operation
FSAVE ⟨ea⟩	Save state of coprocessor
FRESTORE ⟨ea⟩	Restore state of coprocessor

Floating-Point Output

The packed-decimal output routine already developed can be used to format floating-point output. The routine FLOATOUT prints a double format floating-point number to the screen by reading the number into a floating-point register, writing the number to memory in packed-decimal real format, and then calling PACKDECOUT. The only floating-point instruction the routine uses is FMOVE, which is used to move data to or from floating-point registers.

INSTRUCTION

FMOVE
(Move Floating-Point Data Register)

Syntax FMOVE.⟨fmt⟩ ⟨ea⟩,FPn
FMOVE.⟨fmt⟩ FPm,⟨ea⟩
FMOVE.X FPm,FPn
FMOVE.P FPm,⟨ea⟩{#k}
FMOVE.P FPm,⟨ea⟩{Dn}

Action Transfer data from memory to a floating-point register or from a floating-point register to memory.

Notes

1. Any of the formats B, W, L, S, D, X, and P are allowed. Data is rounded to 80-bit extended-precision when placed into a floating-point register and converted to the given precision when written to memory.

2. If the data format is byte, word, long word or single, ⟨ea⟩ may refer to an MC68020/30/40 data register.

3. When the format is packed-decimal real, the *k*-factor follows the destination effective address. The 7-bit *k*-factor can be static (#*k*) or dynamic {D*n*}. If the *k*-factor is in the range −64 to 0, it indicates the number of decimal digits to the right of the decimal point. If it is in the range 1–17, it indicates the number of significant decimal digits in the number. The output is rounded to conform to the requirements of the *k*-factor. Excess digits are filled with zeros.

EXAMPLE 15.8

(a) FMOVE.W   #1,FP0
(b) FMOVE.L   (A0),FP3
(c) FMOVE.X   FP3,FP5
(d) FMOVE.D   FP2, (2,A3)
(e) FMOVE.P   FP0,(A0) {#9}   ; RETAIN 9 SIGNIFICANT DIGITS

FLOATOUT   Double Floating-Point Output

Parameters passed
     Address of a 64-bit double format real number in A0.

```
; output a double format real number at address (a0)

floatout:
          link      a6,#-12
          move.l    a0,-(sp)
          fmove.x   fp0,-(sp)
          fmove.d   (a0),fp0
          lea       (-12,a6),a0
          fmove.p   fp0,(a0){#9}
          jsr       packdecout
          fmove.x   (sp)+,fp0
          move.l    (sp)+,a0
          unlk      a6
          rts
```

Floating-Point Input

Of course, floating-point input is more difficult than output. Leading blanks, tabs, and newlines must be skipped. A check is made for a sign ('+','−'), and then digits are read until a nondigit is encountered. As each new digit is found, the accumulated value is multiplied by 10, and the new digit is added. When the digit string is completed, a check must be made for a decimal point ('.'). If one is found, the process of accumulating digits continues, but a count is made of the number of digits to the right of the decimal point. When the number has been read, the accumulated value is divided by 10^m, where m is the number of digits to the right of the decimal point. This algorithm does not allow for the specification of an exponent, which is normally indicated by an E followed by a signed or unsigned exponent. This is left for the exercises. Pascal code that implements this algorithm is provided to make reading the assembly language code easier.

FLOATIN Pascal Code

```
{ Is c a blank, tab or end of line? }
FUNCTION whitespace (c: char): Boolean;
BEGIN
    IF eoln THEN
       whitespace := True
    ELSE
       whitespace := (c = ' ') or (c = chr(9))
END; {whitespace}

{ Is c a decimal digit? }
FUNCTION isdecdigit (c: char): Boolean;
BEGIN
    isdecdigit := ('0' <= c) and c <= '9')
END; {isdecdigit}

{ Read a floating-point number from keyboard }
PROCEDURE floatin(VAR x: real);
    VAR
       sign: integer;
       val, power: real;
       c: char;
BEGIN
    sign := 1;
    val := 0.0;
    power := 1.0;
    REPEAT      { skip leading white space }
       read(c);
    UNTIL not whitespace(c);
    IF c = '-' THEN
       sign := -1;
    IF (c = '+') or c = '-') THEN
       read(c);
```

```
    WHILE isdecdigit(c) DO { accumulate interger part }
        BEGIN
            val := val * 10.0 + (ord(c) - ord('0'));
            read(c)
        END;
    IF c = '.' THEN
        read(c);
    WHILE isdecdigit(c) DO { bring in fractional part }
        BEGIN
            val := val * 10.0 + (ord(c) - ord('0'));
            power := 10.0 * power;
            read(c)
        END;
    x := sign * val / power { final value }
END; {floatin}
```

This code indicates that we must be able to perform three floating-point operations to do the input conversion, multiplication, addition, and division. Subtraction is used in Program 15.4.

INSTRUCTIONS

FADD/FSUB/ FMUL/FDIV (Floating-Point Arithmetic)

Syntax

FADD.⟨fmt⟩	⟨ea⟩,FP*n*
FADD.X	FP*m*, FP*n*
FSUB.⟨fmt⟩	⟨ea⟩,FP*n*
FSUB.X	FP*m*,FP*n*
FMUL.⟨fmt⟩	⟨ea⟩,FP*n*
FMUL.X	FP*m*, FP*n*
FDIV.⟨fmt⟩	⟨ea⟩,FP*n*
FDIV.X	FP*m*, FP*n*

Action   Perform the designated floating-point computation and leave the result in FP*n*.

Notes

1. Any of the formats B, W, L, S, D, X, and P are allowed.

2. The source operand is converted to extended precision (if necessary), and the operation is performed using extended precision. The result replaces the contents of the destination register.

We must save data and address registers altered by a subroutine and then restore them prior to return. The same should be done for floating-point data registers. To do this, the MC68881 coprocessor provides an instruction FMOVEM, analogous to MOVEM on the MC68000 family.

<table>
<tr><td>

INSTRUCTION

FMOVEM
(Move Multiple
Floating-Point Data
Registers)

</td><td>

Syntax FMOVEM.X ⟨list⟩,⟨ea⟩

FMOVEM.X ⟨ea⟩,⟨list⟩

</td></tr>
</table>

Action Move one or more extended-precision values to or from a list of floating-point data registers.

Notes

1. The format for ⟨list⟩ is identical to that for MOVEM.

2. Unlike MOVEM, the list can contain only one floating-point register.

3. The list can be dynamic. In this case, it is contained in the low 8 bits of a CPU data register. For information on this feature, consult the *MC68881 Floating-Point Coprocessor User Manual*.

FLOATIN Double Floating-Point Input

Parameters passed
Address of a contiguous 64 bits of memory in A0.

Action A double-precision floating-point number is read from the keyboard and placed at address (A0). A leading sign can be given, but no exponent may be specified.

```
NewLine:  equ        13
Tab:      equ         9

; input a double-precision real number at address (a0)
floatin:
          movem.l    d0-d2,-(sp)
          fmovem.x   fp0/fp1,-(sp)   ; save floating-point registers
1$:       jsr        getchar         ; skip white space
          jsr        whitespace
          bne.s      1$
          moveq      #1,d1           ; sign initially positive
          cmpi.b     #'+',d0
          beq.s      2$
          cmpi.b     #'-',d0
          bne.s      3$
          moveq      #-1,d1          ; sign actually negative
2$:       jsr        getchar         ; get next char after + or -
3$:       fmove.w    #0,fp0          ; val initially 0.0
          fmove.w    #10,fp1         ; keep constant 10.0 in a register
4$:       jsr        isdecdigit      ; accumulate integer part
          beq.s      5$
          fmul.x     fp1,fp0         ; 10.0 * val
          subi.b     #'0',d0
          fadd.b     d0,fp0          ; val = 10.0*val+(Ord(c)-Ord('0'))
```

```
                jsr        getchar
                bra.s      4$
    5$:         cmpi.b     #'.',d0
                bne.s      6$
                jsr        getchar        ; get char after a decimal point
    6$:         fmove.w    #1,fp2         ; power initially 1.0
    7$:         jsr        isdecdigit     ; accumulate in fractional part
                beq.s      8$
                fmul.x     fp1,fp0
                subi.b     #'0',d0
                fadd.b     d0,fp0
                fmul.x     fp1,fp2
                jsr        getchar
                bra.s      7$
    8$:         fmul.w     d1,fp0         ; give it the right sign
                fdiv.x     fp2,fp0        ; account for any fractional part
                fmove.d    fp0,(a0)       ; output the value to memory
                fmovem.x   (sp)+,fp0/fp1  ; restore floating-point registers
                movem.l    (sp)+,d0-d2
                rts

; verify if a character is a blank, tab or newline
whitespace:
                move.w     ccr,-(sp)
                cmpi.b     #' ',d0
                beq.s      1$
                cmpi.b     #Tab,d0
                beq.s      1$
                cmpi.b     #NewLine,d0
                beq.s      1$
                ori.w      #4,(sp)
                bra.s      2$
    1$:         andi.w     #$fb,(sp)
    2$:         move.w     (sp)+,ccr
                rts

; verify if a character is a decimal digit
isdecdigit:
                move.w     ccr,-(sp)
                cmpi.b     #'0',d0
                blt.s      1$
                cmpi.b     #'9',d0
                bgt.s      1$
                andi.w     #$fb,(sp)
                bra.s      2$
    1$:         ori.w      #4,(sp)
    2$:         move.w     (sp)+,ccr
                rts
```

PROGRAM 15.4

Newton's Method

We are now in a position to give a complete program using the floating-point coprocessor. One of the many problems in numerical analysis for which a floating-point coprocessor is useful is in finding the roots of nonlinear functions. One of the oldest techniques is Newton's method. An initial guess x_0 is made for the root, and then the iteration

$$x_{n+1} = x_n - \frac{f(x_n)}{f'(x_n)}$$

is applied until the desired accuracy is achieved.

Newton's method applies to the solution of differential equations describing the problem of growth in two populations conflicting with one another. It is necessary to solve nonlinear equations of the form

$$xe^{-x} = \mu$$

It can be shown that if $\mu < 1/e$, there are exactly two roots, one in the range $0 < x < 1$ and the other in $x > 1$. When Newton's method is applied to this problem, the following iteration is computed.

$$x_{n+1} = \frac{\mu e^x - x_n^2}{1 - x_n}$$

This problem is solved in Pascal for $\mu = 1/\pi$.

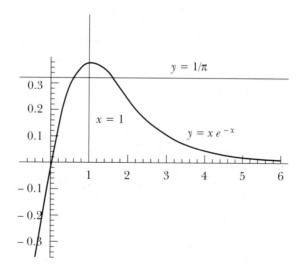

The program prompts for an initial approximation to the root, performs the iteration 20 times, and prints the approximation.

Pascal Code for Program 15.4: Roots of a Nonlinear Equation Using Newton's Method

```
PROGRAM Newton (input, output);

    CONST
        Pi = 3.14159265;

    VAR
        x: real;
        i: integer;

BEGIN
    write('Enter the initial approximation to the root: ');
    readln(x);
    FOR i := 1 TO 20 DO
        x := ((1.0 / Pi) * exp(x) - x * x) / (1.0 - x);
    writeln(x : 12 : 9);
    readln
END.
```

⟨Run of Pascal Program 15.4 (1)⟩

```
Enter the initial approximation to the root: .5
0.553827047
```

⟨Run of Pascal Program 15.4 (2)⟩

```
Enter the initial approximation to the root: 2.0
1.638528466
```

This program implements Newton's method in assembly languge. The I/O routines FLOATIN/FLOATOUT are assumed to be placed in a code library. The program was run on a Macintosh IIci using the Macintosh Assembly System. The calculation requires that e^x be computed, but fortunately the MC68881 coprocessor has a built-in instruction FETOX to compute this.

INSTRUCTION

FETOX
(Compute e^x)

Syntax   FETOX.⟨fmt⟩   ⟨ea⟩,FP*n*
           FETOX.X   FP*m*,FP*n*
           FETOX.X   FP*n*

Action   Perform the designated floating-point computation and leave the result in FP*n*.

Note   The source operand is converted to extended precision (if necessary), and e^x is left in the destination register. The constant π is used in many mathematical calculations, so it and other frequently used constants are stored in an MC68881 on-chip ROM. The constants are accessed by using the FMOVECR instruction.

INSTRUCTION

FMOVECR
(Move Constant
from ROM)

Syntax   FMOVECR.⟨fmt⟩   #ccc,FP*n*

Action   Move an extended-precision constant from the on-chip ROM, round it to the precision indicated by ⟨fmt⟩, and store it in FP*n*.

Note   ccc is a predefined offset into the ROM. A list of the offsets for frequently used constants follows:

Offset	*Constant*
$00	π
$0C	e
$0D	$Log_2(e)$
$30	$\ln(2)$

Program 15.4 uses FMOVECR to compute $1/\pi$.

```
        xref        floatin, floatout, strout, newline, stop
Pi:     equ         $00
        entry       main

main:   lea         prompt, a0
        moveq       #45, d0
        jsr         strout
        lea         x, a0
        jsr         floatin

        fmove.d     x, fp0       ;  (fp0) is current value of x
        fmovecr.x   #Pi, fp1     ;  (fp1) = π
        fmove.w     #1, fp2
        fdiv.x      fp1, fp2     ;  (fp2) = 1.0/π
        moveq       #19, d1
1$:     fmove.w     #1, fp1
        fsub.x      fp0, fp1
        fmove.x     fp0, fp3
        fetox       fp3
```

```
        fmul.x      fp2,fp3     ; (fp3) = (1.0/π) * exp(x)
        fmul.x      fp0,fp0
        fneg.x      fp0         ; (fp0) = -x*x
        fadd.x      fp3,fp0     ; (fp0) = (1.0/π)*exp(x) - x*x
        fdiv.x      fp1,fp0     ; (fp0) = (1.0/π*)exp(x)-x*x)/(1.0-x)
        dbra        d1,1$

        fmove.d     fp0,root
        lea         root,a0
        jsr         floatout
        jsr         newline
        jsr         stop

        data
x:      ds.b        8
root:   ds.b        8
prompt:
        dc.b        'Enter the initial approximation to the root: '
        even

        end
```

⟨Run of Program 15.4 (1)⟩

```
Enter the initial approximation to the root: .5
+5.53827037E-001
```

⟨Run of Program 15.4 (2)⟩

```
Enter the initial approximation to the root: 2.0

+1.63852842E+000
```

|15.6| MEMORY MANAGEMENT UNIT (MMU)

In a multiprocessing environment, several programs are loaded into memory and share the same processor. At times, the programs share data or execute a common code block. Despite this interaction, the programs must retain their integrity. The operating system is responsible for creating and maintaining an environment for efficient access to memory. The operating system uses memory management strategies that may include a hardware memory management unit. The primary goal of the section is to introduce basic concepts in memory management.

A memory management unit relocates absolute addresses and provides memory access protection for a user or systems program. A large contiguous block of memory, sufficient to hold the text or data space, may not be available when starting the program. A memory management unit is used to efficiently transform programmer address references to real memory space. The transformation will likely be made to disjoint blocks of real memory.

A memory management unit also provides memory protection. When two processes are executing, it is necessary that each process does not inadvertently alter memory used by the other process. The operating system is responsible for testing each memory access and ensuring that the code accesses only that memory space allocated to the process.

A memory management unit translates programmer addresses to real memory addresses. The program address is referred to as a logical or virtual address. The range of addresses used by the program is the virtual address space. This space is translated into real memory space by the MMU.

$$\text{MMU: virtual address space} \rightarrow \text{memory space}$$

Memory management systems are often built around the concept of **paging**. A program's virtual address space is partitioned into a sequence of equal-sized memory blocks called **pages**. At the same time, real memory space is partititioned into **page frames** of the same page size. A **page map table** specifies the correspondence between a virtual page and the associated real page frame (see Figure 15.13).

A simple form of the translation is implemented by using the high-order bits of the virtual address as an index into the page map table. Assume 24-bit addresses and 4K pages. An address in a page can be represented as a displacement relative to the starting address of the page. A displacement

FIGURE 15.13 Page Map Translation

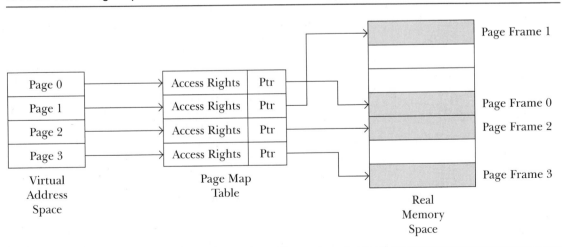

is in the range 0 to $2^{12} - 1$. The virtual address is partitioned into a 12-bit page number and a 12-bit displacement. Virtual address space contains $4096 = 2^{12}$ 4K pages. The page number is used as an index into the page map table.

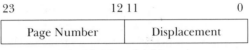

24-Bit Virtual Address

Assuming that the program is running on a 2M system, real memory contains 512 page frames. Often, a program will access pages that do not correspond to active page frames. When an inactive page frame is referenced, a bus fault occurs, and if possible, the data is retrieved from secondary storage and loaded into an active page frame.

EXAMPLE 15.9   Assume that a 2M system has a 24-bit address space with 4K pages. The following table gives four of the 512 entries. A simple page access field contains a V (valid) or I (Invalid) to indicate whether the corresponding page frame is active. For most MMU devices, the page access field also contains read/write protection bits.

This example illustrates the translation of three virtual addresses.

000888 → 002888 (page 000 maps to frame 002)
00140A → 00540A (page 001 maps to frame 005)
003FFE → 004FFE (page 003 maps to frame 004)

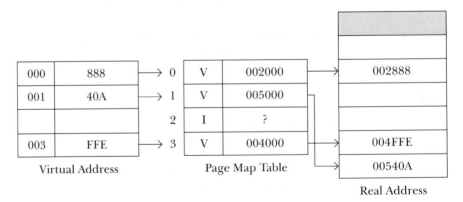

Virtual Address   Page Map Table   Real Address

The size of the page map table is inversely proportional to the size of a page and directly proportional to the size of the address space. If the page size is small, there is less waste in the user address space but more entries in the page map table (see Figure 15.14). In Example 15.9, with a

FIGURE 15.14 Small-Page Model

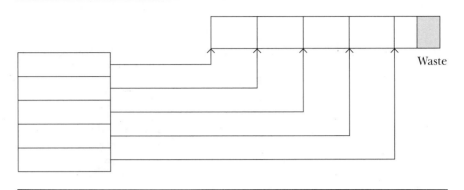

Waste

24-bit address bus and 4K page size, there are 2^{12} = 4096 pages. If the page size is reduced to 256 bytes, the number of pages expands to 64K, which is also the number of entries in the page table. With a 32-bit address space, a 4K page size results in 2^{20} = 1M page table entries. If the page size is large, there is more waste in the user address space but fewer entries in the page table (see Figure 15.15). In Example 15.9, with a 24-bit address bus, an increase in the page size to 2^{16} = 64K reduces the size of the page map table to 2^8 = 256 entries.

Associative Store

In practice, the entire address translation process is handled by hardware except when the page frame is not active. Access to a nonactive frame produces a page fault and begins the process of loading data from secondary storage. A page in memory may have to be replaced if there are no unused page frames. Page fault handling algorithms are covered in operating systems books and are not discussed in this text. We will focus on how an MMU performs address translation.

FIGURE 15.15 Large-Page Model

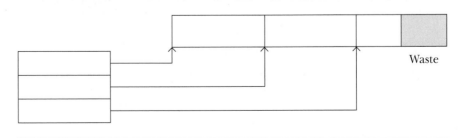

Waste

With a simple page map table, a memory access is required to look up the page frame address in the page table. To increase efficiency, the memory management hardware provides a series of registers that contain the most recently accessed page addresses. This device is called an *associative store* and contains a small subset of the active pages. Each register in the store contains a logical page address, page access rights, and corresponding page frame address. For each virtual address, the MMU simultaneously scans each entry in the associative store, looking for an entry with a matching logical page address. If no hit occurs, the MMU checks the page map table. When it finds the entry, it identifies whether the corresponding page frame is valid. If the frame is not valid, a bus error occurs. This topic is covered in Section 15.7. When no associative memory is used, two memory accesses are required for each virtual address. One access looks up the page frame address in the page map table and a second access fetches the actual data. There is a 100% penalty in using an MMU. Using the associative memory, the penalty can be reduced to as little as 25%.

EXAMPLE 15.10   Entries from the page map of Example 15.9 are included in an associative store. For virtual address 003FFE, a hit occurs, and the MMU uses the entry to translate the address to the real address 004FFE in page frame 4.

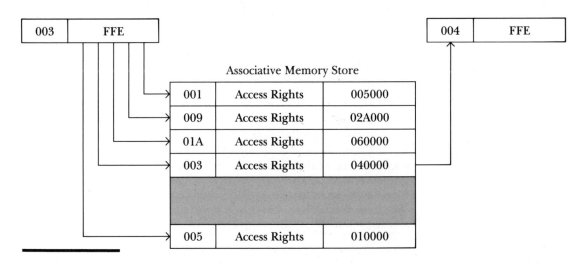

Address Translation Tree

For most address spaces, the range of page numbers is large. The operating system may have to store in memory a translation table that can map many possible pages. The table must be efficiently stored to save memory space for user programs. Modern MMU devices allow access with a multilevel address translation tree.

FIGURE 15.16 Three-Level Translation Tree

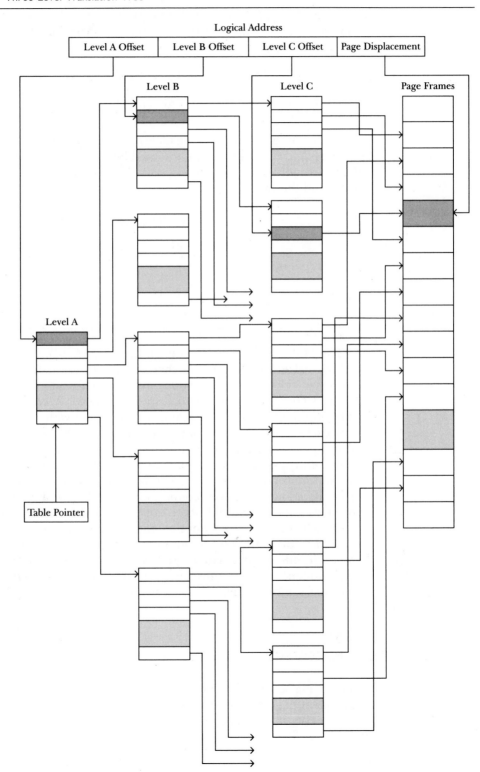

Figure 15.16, depicts a three-level tree. The MMU is set to identify the number of levels, and virtual addresses are partitioned into four fields, which serve as indices into multilevel tables.

Logical Address Fields

Level A Index	Level B Index	Level C Index	Displacement

At each level, an entry in the table contains an access field and a pointer to the next level. At Level C, if the valid bit is set, the pointer field contains the address of the corresponding active page frame. The simple page map scheme in the previous subsection represents a one-level tree.

Level A and Level B Table

Access Rights	Table Pointer

Level C Table

Access Rights	Page Frame

The MMU is initialized to contain the address of the Level A table. For each virtual address, associative memory is first scanned, and then the tree is accessed. The bits in the Level A index field are an index into the Level A table. The pointer in the corresponding Level A entry is the starting address of the Level B table. The search continues with the bits in the Level B index field serving as an index into the Level B table. In a three-level table, three references are required to locate the page frame address. If a table entry contains a nil pointer, the set of all tables emanating from that table entry need not be present in memory. Furthermore, it is possible to specify a lower or upper bound on valid indices at any given level. Any table entry not in the valid range can be omitted from the tree, along with all the tables emanating from that entry. Thus the size of the tree can be reduced to primarily only valid entries. If an invalid table entry is referenced, the address translation process results in a page fault and bus error fault handling begins. Figure 15.16 illustrates a three-level tree. The translation of a sample virtual address is given by tracing the shaded table entries.

| 15.7 | MC68020/30/40 BUS FAULT RECOVERY

In a paging scheme, it is not necessary for all logical pages to correspond to resident page frames. Entries in the page map table for which no page frame exists in memory are marked invalid. When the MMU receives a logical address for which the page map table entry is invalid, it generates a bus error. A bus fault service routine (bus error reception routine) can provide error recovery. The routine loads the page frame into memory and updates the page map table to reflect the presence of the new page. The instruction that generated the bus error must continue once the new page has been loaded. A system that uses paging requires a CPU that is capable of continuing an instruction right at the point of the fault without repeating any decoding activity, effective address calculations, or operand fetches.

The information necessary to recover from a bus error is stored in the long or short bus fault frame and is used in conjunction with the RTE instruction. Several internal registers are saved on each bus fault stack frame, including the special status word (SSW), which is located at offset 10. Figure 15.17 shows the fields of the special status word and briefly describes their function.

By executing an RTE, hardware completes the faulted bus cycles, allowing instruction execution to continue. Most operating systems use this type of bus fault handling.

The action of RTE in completing the faulted bus cycles may be emulated by software. By using the information saved on the bus error stack frame, the handler emulates the action of the bus cycle by fetching the instruction from program space, or the data from data space in the case of a data cycle bus error. The technique used by the handler to complete the cycles

FIGURE 15.17 The Special-Status Word

FC	FB	RC	RB	0	0	0	DF	RM	RW	SIZ	0	FC2-FC0

FC	Fault on stage C of the instruction pipe
FB	Fault on stage B of the instruction pipe
RC	Rerun flag for stage C of the instruction pipe*
RB	Rerun flag for stage B of the instruction pipe*
DF	Fault/Rerun flag for data cycle*
RM	Read-Modify-Write on data cycle
RW	Read-Write for data cycle: 1 = Read, 0 = Write
SIZ	Size code for the data cycle
	(0 = Long word, 1 = Byte, 2 = Word, 3 = Three Bytes)
FC0–FC2	Address space for the data cycle

———

* 1 = Rerun, 0 = Do not rerun

depends on the type of bus cycle that caused the fault. These faults include instances where

- a data read or write fault has occurred.
- a fault occurred during a read-modify-write bus cycle.
- an instruction stream fault has occured.

A complete discussion of bus fault repair is beyond the scope of this text, but techniques used to handle a data read or write fault are included as a demonstration. This case is identified when the DF bit in the SSW is set. The handler examines the RW bit to determine whether the fault was on a read or write bus cycle. The two SIZ bits specify the data size. For a write error, the data is taken from the data output buffer at offset 24 of the stack frame and written to the fault address contained at offset 16 of the stack frame. If a data read error occurs, the processor always generates a long bus cycle fault frame. The handler transfers data from the fault address at stack frame offset 16 to the data input buffer at stack frame offset 44. Byte, word, and 3-byte (generated by a bit field instruction) operands are right-justified within the data buffers of the exception stack frame. If memory management is in effect, the R/W operations are done in the space specified by the FC2–FC0 bits of the SSW. Before executing RTE, the handler clears the DF bit to indicate that the faulty bus cycle has been completed. The following program demonstrates the action of a bus error handler.

PROGRAM 15.5

Bus Fault Recovery

An executive program runs in supervisor mode and starts the execution of a test program located at address PROG. A series of four programs is run to test the service routine on different types of data read or write bus errors. The test programs refer to data at nonexistent addresses in the ranges $AAAA0000–$AAAA0FFF and $BBBB0000–$BBBB0FFF. These are considered to be virtual addresses. The handler repairs the bus fault by translating the range of virtual addresses to one of the real memory ranges

REAL1 to REAL1 + $0FFF
REAL2 to REAL2 + $0FFF

The read or write operation is performed and instruction execution continues. Only the starting address of the data is checked, and a word or long-word data value could exceed the upper bound of a virtual range. An instruction stream bus fault or a reference to a nonexistent address outside the two virtual ranges results in program termination. Each test program that runs to conclusion with no error terminates by executing TRAP #1. The code was run on a Macintosh IIX with an MC68030 processor.

```
; the following fields of the ssw are defined relative to the msb
; of the ssw on the exception stack. thus, bit field instructions
; can conveniently be used.
```

```
df:             equ   7
rw:             equ   9
siz:            equ   10

; bus fault stack offsets which are needed

ssw:            equ   14                ; special status word
faultaddr:      equ   20                ; data cycle fault address
outbuf:         equ   28                ; data output buffer
inbuf:          equ   48                ; data input buffer
pcounter:       equ   6                 ; saved program counter
vector:         equ   10                ; contains vector offset/format

format:         equ   0                 ; offset to format number
sfsize:         equ   32                ; size of short bus error stack
lfsize:         equ   92                ; size of long bus error stack

; exception vectors used

vbuserr:        equ   $08
vtrap1:         equ   $84

; ascii characters used

nl:             equ   10
null:           equ   0

                xref      strout, hexout_long, newline, stop

start:          lea       trap1, a0
                move.l    a0, vtrap1.w    ; init trap #1 vector
                lea       buserr, a0
                move.l    a0, vbuserr.w   ; bus error handler
                clr.w     -(sp)           ; set up type 0 stack frame
                                          ; to start user prog with rte.
                lea       prog, a0
                move.l    a0, -(sp)       ; pc = "prog"
                move.w    #$2000, -(sp)   ; initial sr
                rte

trap1:          addq.w    #8, sp          ; flush exception stack frame
                jsr       stop


buserr:         link      a6, #0
                movem.l   d0-d2/a0-a1, -(sp)


                ; determine the type of bus error stack frame
                bfextu    (vector, a6){format:4}, d0
                cmpi.w    #10, d0
                beq.s     short
                move.w    #lfsize+24, framesize ; includes saved regs and a6
                bra.s     cont
short:          move.w    #sfsize+24, framesize
```

```
cont:       bftst    (ssw,a6){df:1}          ; treat only data cycle errors
            bne.s    cont1
            lea      streamflt,a0            ; bail out if not data fault
            moveq    #39,d0
            jsr      strout
            move.l   (pcounter,a6),d0        ; print stacked pc
            jsr      hexout_long
            jsr      newline
            adda.w   framesize,sp
            jsr      stop
cont1:      move.l   (faultaddr,a6),a0       ; do address translation
            cmp2.l   range1,a0               ; see if in $aaaa0000-$aaaa0fff
            bcs.s    test2                   ; if c=1, test range2
            suba.l   #$aaaa0000,a0           ; range real1 - real1+$0fff
            lea      real1,a1
            adda.l   a1,a0
            bra.s    cont2
test2:      cmp2.l   range2,a0               ; see if in $bbbb0000-$bbbb0fff
            bcc.s    cont3                   ; if c=1, not in either range
            move.l   a0,d1                   ; data fault. exit to monitor
            lea      datafault, a0
            moveq    #39,d0
            jsr      strout
            move.l   d1,d0
            jsr      hexout_long
            jsr      newline
            adda.w   framesize,sp
            jsr      stop
cont3:      suba.l   #$bbbb0000,a0           ; range real2 - real2+$0fff
            lea      real2,a1
            adda.l   a1,a0
cont2:      bfextu   (ssw,a6){siz:2},d1      ; extract the size field
            bne.s    cont4
            moveq    #32,d1                  ; length of long = 32
            bra.s    doio
cont4:      lsl.w    #3,d1                   ; (d1.w) = length = size*8
doio:       moveq    #32,d0
            sub.w    d1,d0                   ; (d0.w) = offset = 32-length
            bftst    (ssw,a6){rw:1}          ; see if read or write cycle
            beq.s    write                   ; if rw=0 then write else read
            bfextu   (a0){0:d1},d2           ; get correct size data into d2
                                             ; place input data into buffer
            bfins    d2,(inbuf,a6){d0:d1}
            bra.s    exit
                                             ; get correct size data into d2
write:      bfextu   (outbuf,a6){d0:d1},d2
            bfins    d2,(a0){0:d1}           ; write data to memory
exit:       bfclr    (ssw,a6){df:1}          ; clear df and return
            movem.l  (sp)+,d0-d2/a0-a1
            unlk     a6
            rte                              ; bus cycle emulated. return

            data
```

```
range1:      dc.l       $aaaa0000,$aaaa0fff
range2:      dc.l       $bbbb0000,$bbbb0fff
framesize:   ds.w       1
streamflt:   dc.b       'instruction stream bus fault near pc = '
datafault:   dc.b       'data cycle bus fault. fault address = '
             even


; areas into which logical (virtual) addresses are mapped
real1:       ds.b       4096
filler:      ds.b       1024
real2:       ds.b       4096



             code
end
```

Testing Programs

Test A

```
prog:    lea      $aaaa0000,a0      ; generates a bus error
         moveq    #1,d1
loop1:   move.w   d1,(a0)+          ; write cycle gives bus error
         addq.w   #1,d1
         cmpa.l   #$aaaa1000,a0
         bcs.s    loop1


         lea      $aaaa0000,a0
         lea      $bbbb0000,a1
loop2:   move.w   (a0)+,(1)+        ; each copy gen. 2 bus faults
         cmpa.l   #$aaaa1000,a0
         bcs.s    loop2


         lea      $bbbb0000,a1
         moveq    #0,d0
         moveq    #0,d1
loop3:   move.w   (a1)+,d1          ; read cycle gives bus error
         add.l    d1,d0
         cmpa.l   #$bbbb1000,a1
         bcs.s    loop3


         jsr      hexout_long
         jsr      newline
         trap     #1
```

⟨Run of Program 15.5(A)⟩

00200400

Test B

```
prog:   move.l  #5555,$aaaa0000     ; valid instruction
        move.l  #3333,$bbbb0000     ; valid instruction
        jmp     $fffffff0           ; gen. inst. stream bus fault
```

⟨Run of Program 15.5(B)⟩

```
instruction stream bus fault near pc = 003341D4
```

Test C

```
prog:   move.b  #22,$aaaa0ffe       ; valid instruction
        move.b  #77,$aaaa1000       ; data cycle bus fault
```

⟨Run of Program 15.5(C)⟩

```
data cycle bus fault. fault address = AAAA1000
```

Test D

```
prog:   move.l  #22,$aaaa0ffc       ; in range
        move.l  #$303132,d2         ; puts string "123" in d2
        bfins   d2,$aaaa0ffd{0:24}  ; 3 byte write - no bus fault
        bfins   d2,$aaaa1000{0:24}  ; 3 byte write - with fault
```

⟨Run of Program 15.5(D)⟩

```
data cycle bus fault. fault address = AAAA1000
```

15.8 | THE MC68030 MEMORY MANAGEMENT UNIT

The MC68030 MMU resides onboard the chip and provides all the functions needed to implement a virtual memory-based operating system.

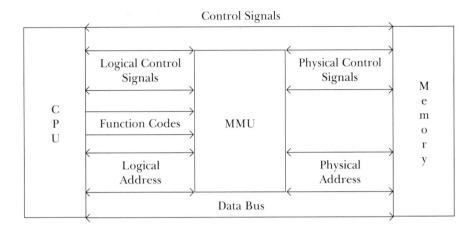

It implements the hierarchical translation tree structure already discussed and is driven by four MC68030 privileged instructions. Virtual memory management is a difficult topic, and so it is not surprising that the MMU is a complex device. This section discusses only the basics of MC68030 MMU use and includes a complete program illustrating a number of its features. For further information, consult Chapter 9 of the Motorola publication entitled *Enhanced 32-Bit Microprocessor User's Manual.*

Programming Model

The MMU contains six registers, which are controlled using MMU instructions, as shown in Figure 15.18.

CPU Root Pointer (CRP) (64 Bits)   This register contains a pointer to the root of the tree of address translation information for the currently executing task. Task switching can be accommodated by resetting the CRP to point to the translation tree of the next process that is to execute. As will be discussed later in this section, the supervisor address space can be translated by using a subset of each translation tree to which the CRP points, or the CRP can point to a table of pointers to translation trees indexed by the current function code value.

Supervisor Root Pointer (SRP) (64 Bits)   A separate address space translation can be configured for supervisor routines by having the SRP contain a pointer to the root of the tree of address translation information for the supervisor's address space.

Translation Control Register (TC) (32 Bits)   This register is the heart of the translation process. It consists of several fields that control address translation, including fields that allow the programmer to enable or disable

FIGURE 15.18 The MC68030 MMU Register Set

```
63                                                              32
┌──────────────────────────────────────────────────────────────┐
│                        CPU Root                                │
├──────────────────────────────────────────────────────────────┤
│                     Pointer (CRP)                              │
└──────────────────────────────────────────────────────────────┘
31                                                               0

63                                                              32
┌──────────────────────────────────────────────────────────────┐
│                     Supervisor Root                            │
├──────────────────────────────────────────────────────────────┤
│                     Pointer (SRP)                              │
└──────────────────────────────────────────────────────────────┘
31                                                               0

31                                                               0
┌──────────────────────────────────────────────────────────────┐
│                  Translation Control (TC)                      │
└──────────────────────────────────────────────────────────────┘

31                                                               0
┌──────────────────────────────────────────────────────────────┐
│              Transparent Translation 0 (TT0)                   │
└──────────────────────────────────────────────────────────────┘

31                                                               0
┌──────────────────────────────────────────────────────────────┐
│              Transparent Translation 1 (TT1)                   │
└──────────────────────────────────────────────────────────────┘

                            31                                   0
                            ┌────────────────────────────────────┐
                            │       MMU Status Register (PSR)     │
                            └────────────────────────────────────┘
```

address translation, define the size of memory pages, and control which bit fields of an address are used for the hierarchical mapping.

Transparent Translation Registers (TT0, TT1) (32 Bits)   These registers can be used to identify memory areas for direct addressing without address translation. This allows for the rapid movement of large amounts of data in memory without the overhead of translation table lookups. The use of these registers is not presented in this text.

MMU Status Register (PSR) (16 Bits)   This register contains memory management status information obtained from a search of the address translation cache or the translation tree for a particular logical address. The register is filled by execution of the PTEST instruction.

The MMU address translation is supported by a 22-entry associative cache memory called the *Address Translation Cache* (ATC). It contains up to 22 logical page addresses and the physical page addresses to which each is mapped. When a virtual address is placed on the bus, the ATC is searched. If the logical address mapping is found, a table search is avoided. If an ATC hit does not occur, the translation tree must be searched. The MC68030 is organized so that the translation time of the ATC is always completely overlapped by other operations, so no performance penalty is associated with ATC searches. The structure of ATC entries and details of the search process are given later in this section.

The MMU Translation Process

The configuration of the MMU is determined by the *translation control register*. This section presents the structure of the register along with the PMOVE instruction that initializes the register fields.

The Translation Control Register

The translation control (TC) register is a 32-bit register that contains control fields that direct address translation. It is analogous to the control register of an ACIA, which sets parameters such as baud rate, parity, and the number of stop bits for transmission. The fields of the translation control register are shown in Figure 15.19.

Enable (E) This bit enables and disables address translation:

0 Translation disabled
1 Translation enabled

FIGURE 15.19 Translation Control Register

31						25	24		20		16
E	0	0	0	0	0	SRE	FCL	PS		IS	
TIA			TIB			TIC		TID			
15		12			8			4			0

E	Enable MMU
SRE	Supervisor Root Pointer Enable
FCL	Function Code Lookup Enable
PS	Page Size
IS	Initial Shift
TIA, TIB, TIC, TID	Table Indices

A reset operation clears this bit, so at boot-up time the MMU is "turned off." When translation is disabled, logical addresses are used as physical addresses.

Table Indices (TIA, TIB, TIC, and TID)   These 4-bit fields specify the numbers of logical address bits used as the indices for the four possible levels of the translation tables. The index into the highest level table is specified by TIA, and the lowest level by TID. The fields contain integers 0–15. Thus no table in a hierarchical translation scheme can exceed 32,768 elements. When a zero value in a TI*x* field is encountered during a table search operation, the search is terminated unless the indexed descriptor is an indirect descriptor. We will not discuss indirect descriptors here.

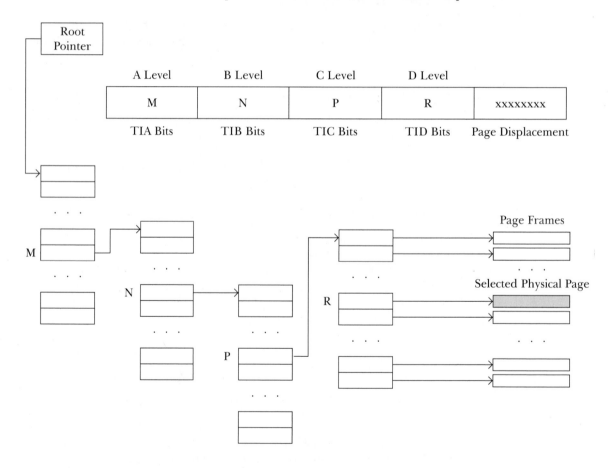

Supervisor Root Pointer Enable (SRE)   This bit controls the use of the supervisor root pointer register:

    0—SRP disabled
    1—SRP enabled

When the SRP is disabled, both user and supervisor accesses use the translation table defined by the CRP. When the SRE bit is enabled, user mode addresses use the CRP, and supervisor accesses use the SRP.

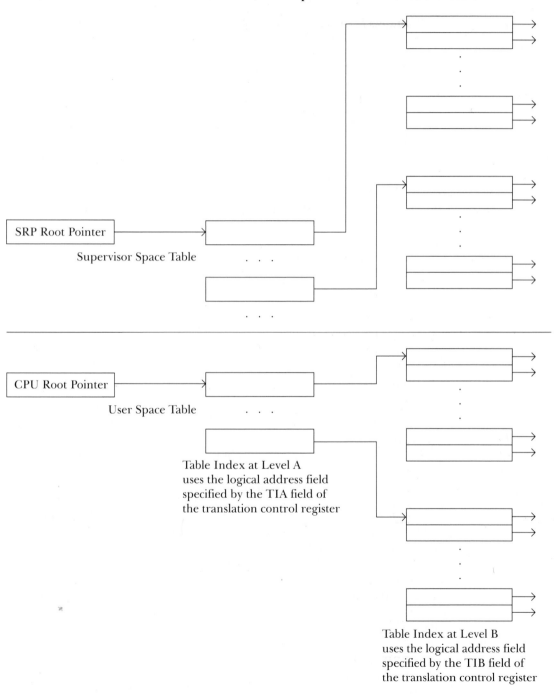

SRP Root Pointer

Supervisor Space Table   . . .

CPU Root Pointer

User Space Table   . . .

Table Index at Level A
uses the logical address field
specified by the TIA field of
the translation control register

Table Index at Level B
uses the logical address field
specified by the TIB field of
the translation control register

By setting the SRE bit, the operating system can maintain a completely separate translation table for supervisor mode that does not interact with any user mode tables.

Function Code Lookup (FCL)   This bit enables the use of function code lookup for searching the address translation tables:

0—Function code lookup disabled
1—Function code lookup enabled

When function code lookup is disabled, the first level of pointer tables within the translation table structure is indexed by the logical address field defined by TIA. When function code lookup is enabled, the CRP points to an array of pointers to translation tables indexed by function code. When function code lookup is used, the CRP is used, and the SRE bit has no effect. This feature provides maximum generality in construction of address space translation. Both the supervisor and user processes have translation trees for both program and data space. See the accompanying diagram on page 865.

Page Size (PS)   This 4-bit field specifies the system page size:

1000—256 bytes
1001—512 bytes
1010—1K bytes
1011—2K bytes
1100—4K bytes
1101—8K bytes
1110—16K bytes
1111—32K bytes

All other bit combinations are reserved by Motorola for future use. An attempt to load another value into this field of the TC register causes an MMU configuration exception. Note that the minimum page size of 256 bytes means that the maximum number of bits that can be used for indexing the translation tables is 24. Also note that the value of the bit pattern for each page size is the number of bits needed for the page displacement.

Initial Shift (IS)   This 4-bit field contains the number of high-order bits of the logical address that are ignored during table search operations. The field contains an integer 0–15, which sets the effective size of the logical address to 32–17 bits, respectively. Bits ignored due to initial shift cannot have random values. Because the ATC compares all bits not involved with the page displacement, including bits ignored in table access by specifying IS $\neq$ 0, ignored bits must be specified and be consistent in order to ensure that subsequent address translations match the corresponding entries in the ATC. As an example of using IS, the Macintosh II line of computers can run in 24-bit address mode or 32-bit mode. The 24-bit mode allows

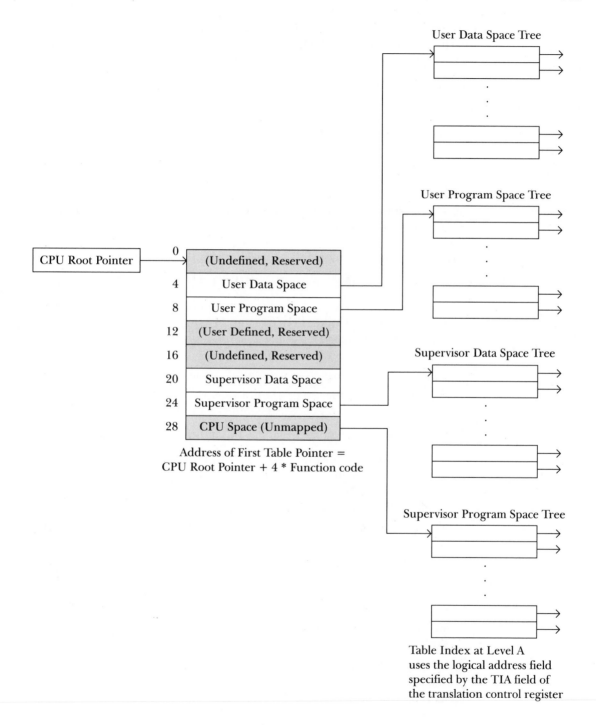

User Data Space Tree

User Program Space Tree

Supervisor Data Space Tree

Supervisor Program Space Tree

CPU Root Pointer

0	(Undefined, Reserved)
4	User Data Space
8	User Program Space
12	(User Defined, Reserved)
16	(Undefined, Reserved)
20	Supervisor Data Space
24	Supervisor Program Space
28	CPU Space (Unmapped)

Address of First Table Pointer =
CPU Root Pointer + 4 * Function code

Table Index at Level A
uses the logical address field
specified by the TIA field of
the translation control register

program compatibility with older Macintosh systems. This can be accomplished by setting IS = 8 when defining the memory map for the system. The TC is accessed by using the privileged PMOVE instruction.

INSTRUCTION

(PMOVE)
(MC68030 Move
To/From MMU
Registers)

Syntax   PMOVE   MR*n*,⟨ea⟩
           PMOVE   ⟨ea⟩,MR*n*
           PMOVEFD   ⟨ea⟩,MR*n*

Action   Moves the contents of the source effective address to the specified MMU register MR*n*, or moves the contents of the MMU register to the destination effective address.

Notes

1. The MMU registers are specified as TC, CRP, SRP, PSR, TT0, and TT1.

2. The instruction is a quad word (8-byte) operation for the CRP and SRP. It is a long-word operation for the TC register and the transparent translation registers (TT0 and TT1). It is a word operation for the MMU status register (PSR).

3. The PMOVEFD (PMOVE with flush disable) form of this instruction disables flushing the ATC when a new value is loaded into the SRP, CRP, TT0, TT1, or TC register (but not the PSR).

Writing to the following registers has the indicated side effects.

4. CRP/SRP: if PMOVEFD is not used, the instruction flushes the ATC. If the operand value is invalid for a root pointer descriptor, the instruction takes an MMU configuration error exception after moving the operand to the CRP. The MMU configuration exception has vector $0E0.

5. TC: if PMOVEFD is not used, the instruction flushes the ATC. If the E bit is set, a consistency check is performed on the PS, IS, and TI*x* fields. The values in the TI*x* fields are added until the first zero value is found. The values in the IS and PS fields are added to the sum of the TI*x* fields. If the sum is not 32 bits, the instruction causes an MMU configuration exception after moving the operand to the TC. The instruction also causes an exception if a reserved value 0–7 is placed in the PS field.

6. TTx: if PMOVEFD is not used, the instruction flushes the ATC. It enables or disables the transparent translation register according to whether its E bit is set (bit 15). If the E bit is set to 1, the transparent translation register is enabled. If the E bit is 0, the register is disabled.

EXAMPLE 15.11   Configure the MMU to use the SRP and the CRP, ignore the high 8 bits of each address, use a page size of 8K, and index the A-level table using 4 bits and the B-level table with 7 bits. The C and D levels are not used. This can be accomplished by using the instruction sequence

PMOVE   TCONFIG,TC
.
.
.

TCONFIG: DC.L $82D84700

The Root Pointers

The CRP and SRP are 64-bit registers that contain the address and related status information for the start of the translation table tree. The SRP, used for supervisor accesses only, is enabled or disabled by setting or clearing the SRE bit of the translation control register. The CRP corresponds to the current translation table for user space (when the SRP is enabled) or both user and supervisor space (when the SRP is disabled). When a new task begins execution, the operating system typically writes a new root pointer descriptor to the CRP. A new translation table address implies that the contents of the ATC may no longer be valid. Therefore, the PMOVE instruction that loads the CRP or SRP can optionally flush the ATC. The fields of the CRP and SRP are as follows:

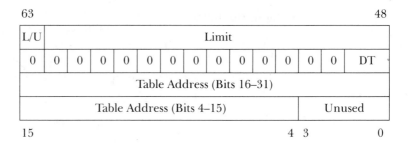

L/U	Limit
DT	
Table Address (Bits 16–31)	
Table Address (Bits 4–15)	Unused

L/U   Lower or upper index range
Limit   Limit on table index for this table address
DT   Descriptor type
Table Address   Address of table at next level or constant offset if DT = 1

Lower Upper (L/U)   It is possible to limit the indices that are present at the A level of the translation table. By doing so, the size of the translation table can be reduced. For instance, if the A level potentially contains 512 entries but only indices 510 and 511 correspond to valid addresses, the lower index can be limited to 510. Only two entries must then be present in the table. However, the table address placed in the root pointer must be set as if the entire table is present. When the L/U bit is set to 1, the value contained in the limit field is to be used as the unsigned lower limit of indices into the translation tables. When this bit is cleared, the limit field is the unsigned upper limit of the translation table indices.

Limit   This specifies a maximum or minimum value for the index to be used at the next level of table search. If the function code lookup (FCL) enable bit is set in the TC, the function code level cannot be limited. To suppress the limit function, the L/U bit is cleared and the limit field is set to ones ($7FFF in the high 16 bits), or the L/U bit is set and the limit field is cleared ($8000 in high 16 bits).

Descriptor Type (DT)   Specifies the type of descriptor contained in either the root pointer or the entries contained in the first level of the translation table identified by the root pointer. The values are:

   0 INVALID   This value is not allowed at the root pointer level. When a root pointer register is loaded with an invalid root pointer descriptor, an MMU configuration exception is taken.
   1 PAGE DESCRIPTOR   There is not a translation table for this root pointer. The MC68030 internally adds the value in the table address field to the incoming logical address. This results in direct mapping with a constant offset given by the table address. The supervisor can be given direct access to all of memory by setting DT = 1 in the root pointer and specifying a table address of 0.
   2 VALID 4 BYTE   The translation table at the root of the translation tree contains short-format descriptors (32 bits). The MC68030 accesses the descriptor at the A level by computing

   Table Address + TIA * 4

   3 VALID 8 BYTE   The translation table at the root of the translation tree contains long-format descriptors (64 bits). The MC68030 accesses the descriptor at the A level by computing

   Table Address + TIA * 8

Table Address   All translation tables must be located on 16-byte boundaries in memory. In other words, they must be 16-byte aligned. As a result, the physical base address of the translation table uses only bits 31–4, and bits 3–0 are ignored. When the DT field contains $1, the value in the table address field is the offset used to calculate the physical address for the page descriptor. The table address field can contain zero (for zero offset).

Unused Bits 3–0 of the root pointer are not used and are ignored when written. All other unused bits must always be zeros.

EXAMPLE 15.12

(a) Assume that the first level of the translation table is not to be limited, that its entries contain 8-byte descriptors, and that the table starts at physical address A_TABLE. The CRP can be initialized using the statements

```
        LEA      A_TABLE,A0
        MOVE.L   A0,CRPVAL+4
        PMOVE    CRPVAL,CRP
        . . .
        DATA
CRPVAL: DC.L     $7FFF0003, 0
```

(b) Assume the translation control register specifies that the SRP is to be used for supervisor accesses. The supervisor has access to all system memory directly by specifying DT = 1, a table address field of 0, and a limit field of $7FFF.

```
        PMOVE    SRPVAL,SRP
        . . .
        DATA
SRPVAL: DC.L     $7FFF0001,0
```

Translation Table Structure

The overall structure of hierarchical translation tables has already been discussed. Our purpose in this section is to specify the structure of the table entries at the various levels. The entries that can be placed in tables are either table descriptors, page descriptors, invalid descriptors, or indirect descriptors. Each of these descriptors can be specified using long format (64 bits) or short format (32 bits). The short-format descriptors save space but have less capability and are not discussed. There are various fields common to all of these descriptors, so we begin by defining the fields.

DT This bit field specifies the type of descriptor. The first two values apply to the descriptor itself, and the other two values to descriptors at the next level of the tree. The values are:

   0 INVALID   The descriptor is invalid. The table search ends, and a bus error will be generated.

   1 PAGE DESCRIPTOR   If a page descriptor occurs at the lowest level of the translation tree, it contains the base address of a page frame in memory. When a page descriptor occurs at a higher level,

it is termed an **early termination page descriptor** and maps memory contiguously. We will examine this case in more detail shortly. The translation table search ends when a page descriptor is encountered.

2 VALID 4 BYTE   The next translation table entries contain short-format descriptors.

3 VALID 8 BYTE   The next translation table entries contain long-format descriptors.

S   This one-bit field specifies that the table or page pointed to by the descriptor can be accessed only if the processor is in supervisor mode. When this bit is used judiciously, one translation tree entered through the CRP is adequate for both supervisor and user access. Each user mapping is appended to a fixed portion of every translation tree containing descriptors with the S bit set, as illustrated on page 871.

U   The processor sets this one-bit field when a descriptor is accessed. If a supervisor violation is detected (user mode access to a table entry with $S = 1$), the access is denied, and the U bit is not set. The processor never clears this bit. It is used in page replacement algorithms to determine which is the best page to replace.

WP   This one-bit field provides write protection. The real address space emanating from this descriptor cannot be written into. This protection is most commonly imposed at the last level of the translation table, that of the page descriptors.

CI   This one-bit field occurs only in a page descriptor. When the bit is set, data within the address range of the page is not placed in the on-chip instruction and data caches.

L/U and Limit   These fields are used to control the index limits for the next level of the table. They are defined as with the CRP/SRP.

M   This one-bit field is set when a page is written to, unless it is already set. M is unaffected in the case of a supervisor violation or when $WP = 1$.

Page Address   This 24-bit field contains the physical base address of a page in memory. Page displacement supplies the low-order bits of the address. If the page size is greater than 256 bytes, then the number of unused bits is the PS value in the TC register minus eight.

Table Address   This 28-bit field contains the physical base address of a table of descriptors. All tables must be 16-byte aligned, so the low-order four bits are not needed.

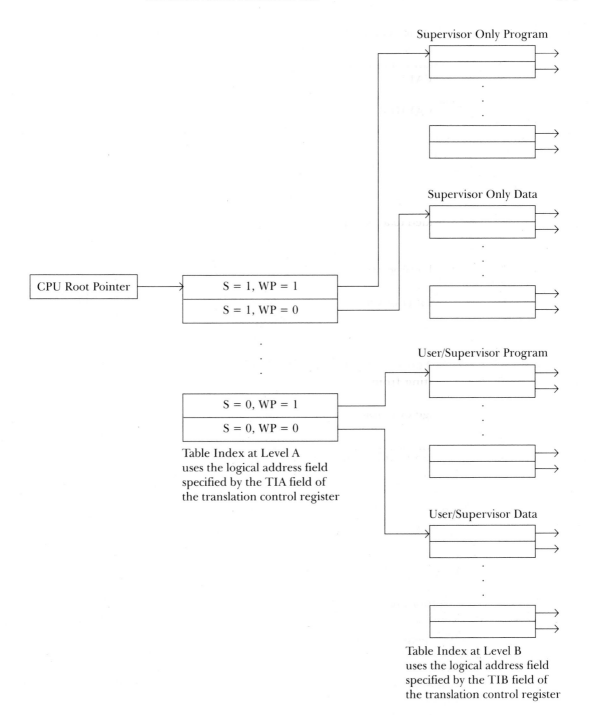

Supervisor Only Program

Supervisor Only Data

CPU Root Pointer

S = 1, WP = 1

S = 1, WP = 0

S = 0, WP = 1

S = 0, WP = 0

Table Index at Level A
uses the logical address field
specified by the TIA field of
the translation control register

User/Supervisor Program

User/Supervisor Data

Table Index at Level B
uses the logical address field
specified by the TIB field of
the translation control register

The structure of the actual descriptors can now be given. Only the format for descriptors actually used in the demonstration program at the end of this section will be given.

Long-Format Table Descriptor

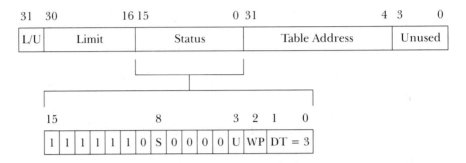

These descriptors are used at any level up to the last level to specify the base address of the next table and the type of descriptors it contains.

Long-Format Early Termination Page Descriptor

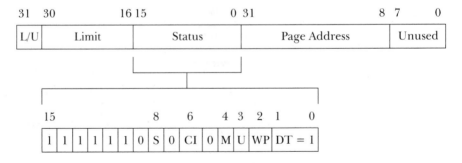

This descriptor is used to map memory in a contiguous block beginning at the address specified. This eliminates the need for all table and page descriptors that would be found in the tree at the next and all subsequent levels. The memory mapped is determined by letting the unused bits of the logical address vary from all 0's to all 1's and adding this range to the physical page address given. If n bits are unused, this descriptor contiguously maps 2^{PS+n} bytes. This technique is used to perform an identity mapping of the first 8M of memory in the sample program at the end of the section. Figure 15.20 should assist you in understanding this very important technique in MMU use.

FIGURE 15.20 Sample of Early Termination Page Descriptor

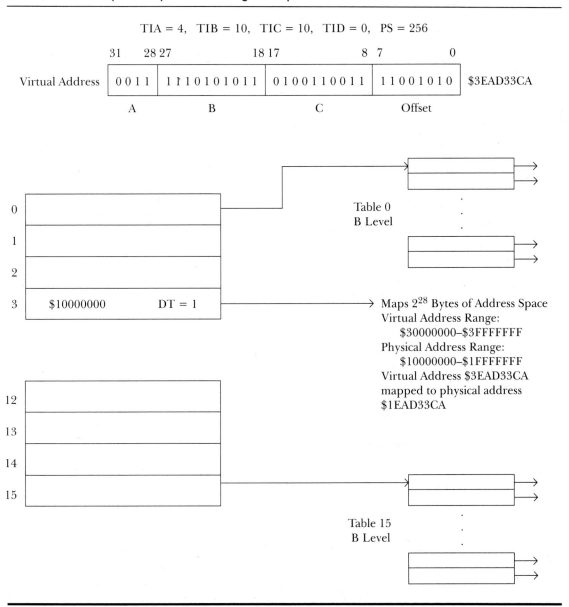

Long-Format Page Descriptor

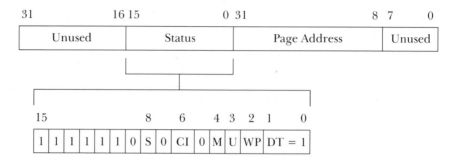

This descriptor is found in the lowest level of the translation tree and defines the physical page.

Long-Format Invalid Descriptor

31	2 1	0 31	0
Unused	DT = 0	Unused	

This descriptor is used to terminate address translation. When it is encountered, the address is not mapped, and a bus error will occur. It is essentially a premature Nil pointer in the tree.

The Address Translation Cache

It is instructive to see how the CPU implements the address translation process in some detail. Recall that a CPU space address (FC0–FC2 = $7) is generated for coprocessor instructions and interrupt acknowledge. A CPU space address is a special case that is immediately used as a physical address without translation. For other accesses, the translation process proceeds as follows:

1. Search the on-chip data and instruction caches for the required instruction word or operand for read accesses.

2. Compare the logical address and function code to the transparent translation parameters in the transparent translation registers, and use the logical address as a physical address for the memory access when one or both of the registers match.

3. Compare the logical address and function code to the tag portions of the entries in the ATC and use the corresponding physical address for the memory access when a match occurs.

4. When no on-chip cache hit occurs (on a read), no TT*x* register matches, and no valid ATC entry matches, initiate a table search operation to obtain the corresponding physical address from the corresponding translation tree, create a valid ATC entry for the logical address, and repeat the ATC search in Step 3.

If possible, when the ATC stores a new address translation, it replaces an entry that is no longer valid. When all entries in the ATC are valid, the ATC selects a valid entry to be replaced, using a pseudo least recently used algorithm. ATC hit rates are application dependent, but hit rates ranging from 98 percent to greater than 99 percent can be expected.

Each ATC entry consists of a logical address and a page descriptor that contains the physical address. The 28-bit logical (or tag) portion of each entry consists of three fields.

27	26	24 23		0
V	FC		Logical Address	

V—VALID   This bit indicates the validity of the entry. If V is set, this entry is valid. This bit is set when the MC68030 loads an entry. An ATC entry can be invalidated by a PMOVE instruction or the instruction PFLUSH.

FC—FUNCTION CODE   This 3-bit field contains the function code bits (FC0–FC2) corresponding to the logical address in this entry.

Each ATC entry has a 28-bit physical portion.

27	26	25	24 23		0
B	CI	WP	M	Physical Address	

B—BUS ERROR   This bit is set for an entry if a bus error, an invalid descriptor, a supervisor violation, or a limit violation is encountered during the table search corresponding to this entry. When B is set, a subsequent access to the logical address causes the MC68030 to take a bus error exception. Because an ATC miss causes an immediate retry of the access after the table search operation, the bus error exception is taken on the retry. The B bit remains set until it is invalidated or until the replacement algorithm for the ATC replaces it.

The CI, WP, and M bits of the ATC are as described for page descriptors.

The MC68030 has two instructions designed specifically for manipulating the ATC. The instruction PFLUSH is used to invalidate all or a portion of the ATC entries. The instruction PLOAD runs a table search for a given logical address and function code and loads the address translation into the ATC. We will not discuss these instructions further here.

Detecting Errors in Address Translation

When a bus error occurs, the bus fault handler must determine whether an address translation error occurred. This could include a page fault, an attempt of a user mode process to access a supervisor-only page or an attempt to write into a read-only page. The PTEST instruction is used to detect errors. The instruction runs a search for the virtual address and reflects the results by setting and clearing bits in the MMU Status Register (PSR). The structure of the MMU status register is as follows:

15	14	13	12	11	10	9		6				2			0
B	L	S	0	W	I	M	0	0	T	0	0	0	N		

B	Bus error		I	Invalid
L	Limit violation		M	Modified
S	Supervisor only		T	Transparent access
W	Write-protected		N	Number of levels

The instruction will search either the ATC or the translation tables but not both. The way PSR bits are set depends on what is searched. We discuss only the results from searching the translation tables.

B   set if a bus error occurs during a PTEST table search
L   set if a limit violation occurred
S   set if a supervisor violation occurred
W   set if any descriptor or page encountered had its WP bit set
I   set if mapping is invalid
M   set if the page descriptor for the address has its M bit set
T   set to 0
N   number of levels accessed during the search

INSTRUCTION

PTEST
(MC68030 Test
Address
Translation)

Syntax

PTESTR   ⟨function code⟩, ⟨ea⟩, #⟨level⟩
PTESTR   ⟨function code⟩, ⟨ea⟩, #⟨level⟩,An
PTESTW   ⟨function code⟩, ⟨ea⟩, #⟨level⟩
PTESTW   ⟨function code⟩, ⟨ea⟩, #⟨level⟩,An

Action   If ⟨level⟩ ≠ 0, the translation tables are searched up to the given level for the logical address ⟨ea⟩, and PSR bits are set to reflect the results of the search.

Notes

1. The 'R' and 'W' indicate whether a read or a write bus cycle is simulated during the search. Actually, it makes no difference for the MC68030 MMU.

2. When an address register An is present, upon completion it contains the physical address of the last descriptor searched.

3. The function code operand specifies what address space to search. For instance, to test an address in user data space, use a function code value of 1. The operand is normally specified using immediate mode but can also be specified using a data register or the source or destination function code register.

EXAMPLE 15.13

(a) To test the specific user data address ADDR in a three-level translation scheme and leave the address of the last descriptor searched in A2, execute

```
LEA      ADDR,A3
PTESTR   #1,(A3),#3,A2
```

(b) A bus fault handler can use the data cycle fault address stored in the bus error stack frame to determine whether the fault was caused by an error in address translation. The address is at an offset of 16 from the stack pointer.

```
            PTST     #1,([16,SP]),#5
            PMOVE    PMU,MMUSTATREG
            . . .
            DATA
MMUSTATREG:
            DS.W 1
```

The MOVES Instruction

If an operating system is running using the SRP or the function codes ($FCL = 1$ in the translation control register), the function code bits FC0–FC2 specify to the MMU the space in which to perform the read or write operation. For example, a program running in supervisor mode fetches instructions from supervisor program space. Its data bus cycles reference supervisor data space. However, the operating system may need to read or write data into user space accessed by user logical addresses. Without special consideration, the MMU would read the function codes and access only supervisor space. The problem is solved by temporarily changing the function code values with the MOVES instruction, which uses two control registers: the **source function code (SFC) register** and the **destination function**

code (DFC) register. Use the MOVEC instruction to set appropriate function code values in the SFC (used to read data) or DFC (used to write data). The MOVEC instruction modifies only the low-order 3 bits of these registers. The data access is performed by the MOVES instruction. For instance, if 32 bits are to be transferred from a register to user program space, the DFC must be set to 010_2.

FC2	FC1	FC0
	SFC	

FC2	FC1	FC0
	DFC	

INSTRUCTION

MOVES
(MC68020/30/40
Move Address
Space)

Syntax   MOVES.⟨size⟩   R*n*,⟨ea⟩   Write operation

MOVES.⟨size⟩   ⟨ea⟩,R*n*   Read operation

Action   Copy data to/from space given by the DFC/SFC.

Notes

1. For the write operation, data of the specified size is copied from the general register R*n* to the address ⟨ea⟩ in the address space defined by the 3-bit value in the DFC register.

2. For the read operation, data is copied from the address ⟨ea⟩ in the address space defined by the 3-bit value in the SFC register to the general register R*n*. If R*n* is a data register, the operation affects only the low-order bits defined by the size. If R*n* is an address register, the operand is sign-extended to 32 bits and then placed into the address register.

3. MOVES is a privileged instruction.

EXAMPLE 15.14

(a) The following code segment copies 2K of data from array BUFFER to user data space beginning at address $2000.

```
                MOVEQ    #%001,D0
                MOVEC    D0,DFC
                LEA      $2000,A1
                LEA      BUFFER,A0
                MOVE.W   #511,D1
     TLOOP:     MOVE.L   (A0)+,D0
                MOVES.L  D0,(A1)+
                DBRA     D1,TLOOP
```

(b) If the process is running in supervisor mode and a page fault occurs on an instruction stream fetch, any data specified in the destination of a MOVE instruction in the page fault handler will be placed into su-

pervisor data space. To move data into program space, the MOVES
instruction can be used.

```
MOVEQ    #%110,D0
MOVEC    D0,DFC
   .
   .
   .

MOVES.L  Register,⟨ea⟩
   .
   .
```

Demonstration Program

This section concludes with a complete program illustrating a number of
MMU features. The program was developed on a Macintosh SE/30 system
running the Macintosh Assembly System (MAS). The system was equipped
with an MC68030 processor and 5M RAM. The development of such a
program was complicated by the fact that the Macintosh operating system
on the SE/30 itself used memory management. In particular, the system
used a 24-bit address (IS = 8), four bits for level A, 5 bits for level B, and
pages of 32K. Fortunately, the area where user programs were loaded was
mapped into itself. Thus if a program loaded into this area changed the
MMU mapping but mapped its own program range as the identity, the PC
would remain at the same address after the mapping change. Also, the
operating system undergoes a periodic interrupt, when its own mapping is
reasserted. To deal with this, interrupts are masked off during the time
that the mapping is changed. Of course, all operating system calls, such as
those to print data, must be performed after a return to the native operating
system mapping. Unfortunately, the program will not run on any system
that maps memory for user programs to other areas of physical memory.
This excluded all Macintosh II series systems tested.

PROGRAM 15.6

MMU Mapping

This program sets up a mapping that uses the SRP to map all system
memory linearly in supervisor mode. This is done by defining the SRP to
be a page descriptor with a page address of 0. Defined is a user mapping
that ignores the high 8 bits of each address (IS = 8), uses 3 Level A bits,
9 Level B bits, and a page size of 4K. The first 8M of memory is mapped
using the identity mapping by defining the first four A-level descriptors to
be early termination page descriptors with properly chosen page addresses.
The next 6M of memory is marked as unmapped by loading invalid descriptors. The last Level A descriptor is set up so its limit field specifies only
indices 510 and 511 at the B level to be valid. Each of these B-level entries

defines a 4K page in memory. The first of these is marked read-only and contains 1024 long words having value 5. The program starts up a user mode program after setting up the mappings. Several user mode programs are presented. The first of these reads 1K long words from the read-only page, writes them to the read-write page, then reads them back and computes the sum. Other test programs illustrate using the PTEST instruction in a bus fault handler to determine the cause of an address translation error. The program will be easier to read if you study the mapping illustrated in Figure 15.21.

```
NewLine:            equ     13

vtrap1:             equ     $84
vmmuconfig:         equ     $0e0
vbuserr:            equ     $08

        xref        hexout_long, decout, decout_long, strout, newline, stop


start:  lea         mmuconfig, a0
        move. l     a0, vmmuconfig. w

        lea         ExitUserProg, a0
        move. l     a0, vtrap1. w

        lea         BusError, a0
        move. l     a0, vbuserr. l

;;;;;;;;;;;;;;;;;;; Save original TC and CRP ;;;;;;;;;;;;;;;;;;;;;;;;;;

        pmove       tc, origTCval

        pmove       crp, origCRPval

;;;;;;;;;;;;;;;;;;;;;;;;;;;;;;;;;;;;;;;;;;;;;;;;;;;;;;;;;;;;;;;;;;;;;;;;

;;;;;;;;;;;;;;;;;;;;; Prepare new CRP value ;;;;;;;;;;;;;;;;;;;;;;;;;;;;

        lea         ATable, a0              ; set to nearest 16-byte boundary
        move. l     a0, d0
        andi. l     #$0000000f, d0
        beq. s      1$
        adda. w     #16, a0
        suba. w     d0, a0
1$:     move. l     a0, CRPval+4

;;;;;;;;;;;;;;;;;;;;;;; and initialize A Level Table ;;;;;;;;;;;;;;;;;;;;;;;;;

        moveq       #3, d1
        move. l     #0, a1
2$:     move. l     earlytermpgdesc, (a0)+
        move. l     a1, (a0)+
```

FIGURE 15.21 Mapping Used in Program 15.6

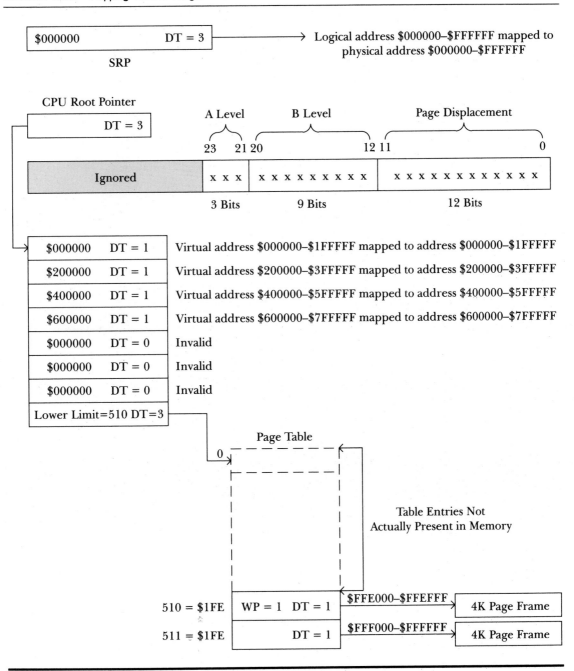

```
              adda.l     #$200000,a1
              dbra       d1, 2$
              moveq      #2,d1
              move.l     #0,a1
      3$:     move.l     invaliddesc,(a0)+
              move.l     a1,(a0)+
              dbra       d1, 3$
              move.l     tabledesc,(a0)+      ; load table desc at index 7
              movea.l    a0,a1
              suba.w     #4076,a1
              move.l     a1,(a0)+
;;;;;;;;;;;;;;;;;;;;;;;;;;;;;;;;;;;;;;;;;;;;;;;;;;;;;;;;;;;;;;;;;;;;;;;;;;;

;;;;;;;;;;;;;;;;;;;;  Initialize B Level Table - 2 Entries  ;;;;;;;;;;;;;;;;;;

              lea        RealPages,a1       ; set to nearest 4K-byte boundary
              move.l     a1,d0
              andi.l     #$00000fff,d0
              beq.s      4$
              adda.w     #4096,a1
              suba.w     d0,a1
      4$:     move.l     pagedesc,(a0)+     ; initialize PMT entry 510
              bset       #2,(-1,a0)         ; make page write protected
              move.l     a1,(a0)+           ; load page address
              movea.l    a1,a2              ; save base addr of read-only page
              adda.w     #4096,a1           ; (a1) = address of 2nd page
              move.l     pagedec,(a0)+      ; initialize PMT entry 511
              move.l     a1,(a0)

;;;;;;;;;;;;;;;;;;;;;;;;;;;;;;;;;;;;;;;;;;;;;;;;;;;;;;;;;;;;;;;;;;;;;;;;;;;

              pmove      SRPval,srp         ; initialize SRP

              move.w     #$2700,sr

              pmove      TCval,tc           ; initialize TC

              pmove      CRPval,crp         ; set CRP for user mode mapping

              move.w     #1023,d1           ; load 1024 long words of 5's
                                            ; into read-only page
loadpage:
              move.l     #5,(a2)+
              dbra       d1,loadpage

              move.w     #0,-(sp)           ; start user mode program
              pea        userprog
              move.w     #$0700,-(sp)
              rte

      exit:   jsr        decout_long        ; print d0.l
              jsr        newline
              jsr        stop
```

```
mmuconfig:
        jsr      restoreToOS
        lea      configexceptionmsg, a0
        moveq    #29, d0
        jsr      strout

        adda.w   #12, sp
        jsr      stop


BusError:
        link     a6, #-2                    ; two bytes for MMU status

        ptestw   #1, ([20, a6]), #2         ; test data address
        pmove    pmu, (-2, a6)

        jsr      restoreToOS

        lea      buserrmsg, a0
        moveq    #11, d0
        jsr      strout
        lea      faultaddr, a0             ; assume a data cycle fault
        moveq    #28, d0
        jsr      strout
        move.l   (20, a6), d0
        jsr      hexout_long
        jsr      newline
        jsr      newline


        lea      bitsheader, a0
        moveq    #24, d0
        jsr      strout
        bfextu   (-2, a6) {0:1}, d0        ; B
        jsr      decout
        bfextu   (-2, a6) {1:1}, d0        ; L
        jsr      decout
        bfextu   (-2, a6) {2:1}, d0        ; S
        jsr      decout
        bfextu   (-2, a6) {4:1}, d0        ; W
        jsr      decout
        bfextu   (-2, a6) {5:1}, d0        ; I
        jsr      decout
        bfextu   (-2, a6) {6:1}, d0        ; M
        jsr      decout
        bfextu   (-2, a6) {13:3}, d0       ; Level
        jsr      decout
        jsr      newline


        unlk     a6
        ; determine the type of bus error stack frame
        bfextu   (-6, sp) {0:4}, d0        ; check frame format number
        cmpi.w   #10, d0                   ; 10 short, 11 long bus cycle
                                           ; stack frame
```

```
                beq.s    1$
                adda.w   #92,sp                  ; long bus cycle fault frame
                bra.s    2$
        1$:     adda.w   #32,sp                  ; short bus cycle fault frame
        2$:     jsr      stop

ExitUserProg:
                jsr      restoreToOs
                move.w   #$2000,(sp)
                lea      exit,a0
                move.l   a0,(2,sp)
                rte

PrintTrap:

restoreToOS:
                ; restore MMU to operating system's original state
                pmove    origCRPval,crp

                pmove    origTCval,tc

                move.w   #$2000,sr               ; interrupts back on
                rts

userprog:
                lea      $ffe000,a0
                lea      fff000,a1
                move.w   #1023,d1
        copy:   move.l   (a0)+,(a1)+
                dbra     d1,copy

                moveq    #0,d0                   ; add 1K long words print sum
                lea      $fff000,a0
                move.w   #1023,d1
        addup:  add.l    (a0)+,d0
                dbra     d1,addup
                trap     #1                      ; exit to supervisor and print

                data


origTCval:
                ds.l     1
origCRPval:
                ds.l     2
TCval:   dc.l     $82c83900                      ; 24-bit addr, 4K pages, 8 entries
                                                 ; at A level, 512 entries at B level
CRPval:  dc.l     $7fff0003, $00000000
SRPval:  dc.l     $7fff0001, $00000000

earlytermpgdesc:
                dc.l     $7ffffc01, 0
invaliddesc:
                dc.l     $7ffffc00, 0
tabledesc:
                dc.l     $81fefc03, 0
```

```
pagedesc:
              dc.l        $0000fc01, 0

configexceptionmsg:
              dc.b        'MMU Configuration Exception!', NewLine
buserrmsg:
              dc.b        'Bus Error', NewLine, NewLine
bitsheader:
              dc.b        'B L S W I M Level', NewLine
faultaddr:
              dc.b        'Data Cycle Fault Address is '
              even

ATable:       ds.b        80                 ; A-level descriptor table
              ds.b        16                 ; space for B-level page table
RealPages:
              ds.b        12288              ; space for two 4K pages
              even

              end
```

⟨Run of user program 1⟩

```
5120
```

⟨Listing of user program 2⟩

```
userprog:
              move.w      $c00000, d0
              trap #1     ; exit back to supervisor and print
```

⟨Run of user program 2⟩

```
Bus Error

Data Cycle Fault Address is 00C00000

B L S W I M Level
0 0 0 0 1 0 1
```

⟨Listing of user program 3⟩

```
userprog:
              move.b      #77, $ffe007
              trap #1,    ; exit back to supervisor and print
```

⟨Run of user program 3⟩

```
Bus Error

Data Cycle Fault Address is 00FFE007

B L S W I M Level
0 0 0 1 0 0 2
```

⟨Listing of user program 4⟩

The line

```
TCval:    dc.l    $82c83900           ; 24-bit address, 4K pages, 8 entries
```

is changed to

```
TCval:    dc.l    $82783900           ; Invalid page size field (PS = 7)
```

The page size field is assigned 7, which is invalid. The CPU takes an MMU configuration exception.

⟨Run of user program 4⟩

```
MMU Configuration Exception!
```

EXERCISES

1. Consider the problem of dealing with transmit interrupts. Assume that we are dealing with a program controlling two or more processes that are executing using time slicing. The MC6850 will generate a Level 5 autovectored interrupt when the transmitter is ready if bit 5 of the control register is set. If receive and transmit interrupts are to be generated, the control register must be initialized to $B5. If only receive interrupts are to be allowed, the control register must be given the value $95. It is possible for the transmitter and the receiver to interrupt at the same time. The two signals are ORed into the Level 5 interrupt line. Thus the interrupt line is quiet only if neither the receiver or transmitter is requesting service. Below you will find a code segment for an interrupt service routine.

```
        ACIASR:      EQU      $10040
        ACIACR:      EQU      $10040
        ACIARDR:     EQU      $10042

    (1) TTY:         MOVE.W   #$2700,SR
    (2)              "SAVE ALL REGISTERS"
    (3)              BTST     #0,ACIASR
    (4)              BEQ      CONSOLEWRITER
    (5)              MOVE.B   ACIARDR,D0
    (6)              BTST     #4,ACIASR
```

```
(7)                    BEQ        NOFEC
(8)                    CLR.B      D0
(9)  NOFEC:            "BUFFER THE CHARACTER. SEE IF A PROCESS IS
                        WAITING FOR A CHARACTER"
(10)                   "IF NO PROCESS IS WAITING GO TO ENQUEUE1
                        ELSE
(11)                   ACTIVATE A PROCESS WHICH HANDLES INPUT"

(12) ENQUEUE1:
(13)                   BTST       #1,ACIASR
(14)                   "IF BIT 1 = 0 RETURN FROM INTERRUPT
                        ELSE CONTINUE EXECUTION AT
                           CONSOLEWRITER."

(15) CONSOLEWRITER:
                       "SEE IF A PROCESS IS WAITING TO TRANSMIT A
                        CHARACTER"
(16)                   "IF A PROCESS IS WAITING TO TRANSMIT, GO
                        TO ITS CODE"
(17)                   MOVE.B     #$95,ACIACR
(18)                   "RESUME EXECUTION OF THE PROCESSES"
```

(a) How many different combinations of receive and transmit interrupt requests are there?

(b) What is the purpose of line 1?

(c) If statement 4 causes a branch, what is the source of the interrupt?

(d) What interrupt request does statement 5 negate?

(e) If a character arrives and no process is waiting, the character is queued. At that point, does the service routine return or does it check the transmitter as another source of interrupt?

(f) If the code at address "ConsoleWriter" is reached, is the transmitter generating an interrupt?

(g) What is the purpose of line 17?

(h) What problem would be caused by the omission of line 17?

2. The following code updates the rear of a queue after an insert of long-word data into the queue:

```
MOVE.W    (QSIZE,A0),D3
MOVE.W    (QREAR,A0),D1
MOVE.W    D1,D2
LSL.W     #2,D2
MOVE.L    D0,(QDATA,A0,D2.W)
ADDQ.W    #1,D1
EXT.L     D1
DIVU      D3,D1
SWAP      D1
MOVE.W    D1,(QREAR,A0)
```

(a) Use TAS to protect the update of the queue rear.

(b) (MC68020/30/40) Use CAS to protect the update.

3. (MC68020/30/40)
   (a) List the advantages of an instruction cache. In particular, what type of parallelism does it provide?
   (b) What are the advantages of adding a data cache?

4. (MC68020/30/40) The instruction

   MOVE.L   (TABLE,A3,D2.L*8),D0

   encounters a data bus fault. Describe in detail how to complete the faulty bus cycle with software.

5. (MC68020/30) Assume that (PC) = $0500A530, $FC_2FC_1FC_0 = 101_2$ and that the MC68020 processor is being used.
   (a) Determine the index used to access the instruction cache.
   (b) What is the tag field?
   (c) Assume that the tag field matches and that the entry is "Valid." If the cache entry contains

   2A03 E785

   what opcode word is placed into the instruction stream?

6. (MC68020/30) Answer exercise 5 if the MC68030 processor is used. Assume the 4 long words at the indexed cache entry are

   2A18 E785 23C5 0002 0000 D7B9 0002 0000

7. (MC68020/30/40) Write code to
   (a) Clear the MC68020 instruction cache.
   (b) Clear the MC68020 instruction cache entry at index 32.
   (c) Clear the MC68030 instruction and data caches.
   (d) On the MC68030, clear the second long word in the data cache entry at index 7.
   (e) Enable burst filling of both the MC68030 instruction and data caches.

8. (MC68020/30) Given the F-Line opcode word

   $F22D

   (a) What is the coprocessor ID?
   (b) What is the type of instruction?

9. (MC68020/30)
   (a) What is the CPU space address for the control register of a coprocessor with ID 6?
   (b) The MOVES instruction can be used to generate CPU space bus cycles, although the practice is not recommended. Show how to use MOVES to write the 16-bit word $5500 to the command register of the coprocessor with ID 1.

10. (MC68020/30) For which instructions is the MC68030 free to work in parallel with the MC68881?

    FDIV.D   NUM,FP3
    FMOVE.D   FP3,NUM

11. (a) The number -107.85 is stored in memory in packed-decimal real format. Show its hex representation.

    (b) Determine the extended real representation for the number

$$0.101111 \times 2^4$$

12. (MC68020/30) Write code segments to do the following computations. All constants are assumed to be in double-precision; x is the double-precision number at address DAT.

    (a) $x + 6.08 * 0.9876$

    (b) $\pi * x^2$

    (c) e^x

    (d) $\sin(x^2)$

13. (a) Configure the MMU to use the function codes, only 28 bits of the address, and a page size of 16K bytes; index the A-level table using 5 bits and the B-level table using 9 bits. The C and D levels are not used.

    (b) Initialize the CRP so that all addresses are translated by adding $5000.

14. In a four-level translation scheme, give a PTEST instruction necessary to test the address X in user program space and leave the address of the last descriptor searched in A4.

15. Show how to copy 4K of data from BUFFER to address (A3) in supervisor program space.

PROGRAMMING EXERCISES

16. Add a third process to Program 15.1. It is to find the largest prime factor of 9135450. Use the techniques presented in Program 5.10.

17. (MC68020/30) Modify Program 15.2 so that it translates three sets of virtual addresses to the ranges

```
RANGE1   to   RANGE1 + $FF
RANGE2   to   RANGE2 + $FF
RANGE3   to   RANGE3 + $FF
```

Test it using programs similar to those used to test Program 15.2.

18. (MC68020/30) Consider the 256-byte loop

```
        move.l  #1000000,d1
        lea     addr,a0
loop:   dcb.w   125,$3410       ;125 "move.w (a0),d2" instructions
        subq.l  #1,d1
        bne     loop
          ⋮
        data
```

```
addr:   dc.w 5
        end
```

Write a program containing the loop that computes the amount of time it takes to execute the loop under the following conditions:
(a) MC68030 data and instruction cache cleared and enabled, burst mode fill on for each cache.
(b) MC68030 instruction cache cleared and enabled, burst mode fill enabled, data cache disabled.
(b) Both caches disabled.

19. (MC68020/30) Modify Program 15.5 so the iterations terminate under the condition

$$|x_n - x_{n-1}| < 10^{-14}$$

20. (MC68020/30) Write a program to compute and print e^π and π^e. Which is larger?

21. (MC68020/30) It is standard in a calculus course to show that

$$\lim_{x \to 0} \frac{\sin(x)}{x} = 1$$

Compute this function for the sequence

$$x = 1.0, 0.1, 0.01, 0.001, \ldots, 10^{-10}$$

to demonstrate this convergence.

22. (MC68030/40) Alter Program 15.6 so that it maps 8K pages and uses 3 A-level bits and 8 B-level bits.

APPENDIX A

M68000 FAMILY OF INTEGER INSTRUCTIONS

SECTION 1
INTRODUCTION

This manual contains detailed information about each of the software instructions used by the microprocessors and coprocessors in the M68000 Family. The M68000 Family includes:

MC68000	— 16-/32-Bit Microprocessor
MC68HC000	— Low Power 16-/32-Bit Microprocessor
MC68008	— 16-Bit Microprocessor with 8-Bit Data Bus
MC68010	— 16-/32-Bit Virtual Memory Microprocessor
MC68020	— 32-Bit Virtual Memory Microprocessor
MC68030	— Second Generation 32-Bit Enhanced Microprocessor
MC68040	— Third Generation 32-Bit Microprocessor
MC68851	— Paged Memory Management Unit
MC68881	— Floating-Point Coprocessor
MC68882	— Enhanced Floating-Point Coprocessor

1.1 INSTRUCTION FORMAT

This section briefly describes the M68000 instruction set in detail using the Motorola assembly language syntax and notation. It includes descriptions of the instruction format and the operands used by instructions, followed by a summary of the instruction set. The integer condition codes and floating-point details are discussed. This main instruction set listing, arranged in alphabetical order, gives detailed descriptions of the operation of each instruction. Programming examples for selected instructions are presented, followed by an instruction set summary arranged by opcode map.

All instructions consist of at least one word; some have as many as 11 words (see Figure 1-1). The first word of the instruction, called the operation word, specifies the length of the instruction and the operation to be performed. The remaining words, called extension words, further specify the instruction and operands. These words may be floating-point command words, conditional predicates, immediate operands, extensions to the effective address mode specified in the operation word, branch displacements, bit number or bit field specifications, special register specifications, trap operands, pack/ unpack constants, or argument counts.

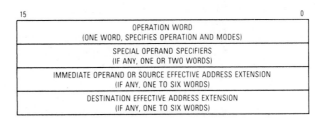

Figure 1-1. Instruction Word General Format

Besides the operation code, which specifies the function to be performed, an instruction defines the location of every operand for the function. Instructions specify an operand location in one of three ways:

- Register Specification — A register field of the instruction contains the number of the register.

- Effective Address — An effective address field of the instruction contains address mode information.

- Implicit Reference — The definition of an instruction implies the use of specific registers.

The register field within an instruction specifies the register to be used. Other fields within the instruction specify whether the register selected is an address or data register and how the register is to be used.

Effective address information includes the registers, displacements, and absolute addresses for the effective address mode.

Certain instructions operate on specific registers. These instructions imply the required registers.

The instructions form a set of tools to perform the following operations:

Data Movement	Binary Coded Decimal Arithmetic
Integer Arithmetic	Program Control
Floating-Point Arithmetic	System Control
Logical	Memory Management
Shift and Rotate	Cache Maintenance
Bit Manipulation	Multiprocessor Communications
Bit Field Manipulation	Dyadic Operation
	Monadic Operation

Each instruction type is described in detail in the following paragraphs.

The following notations are used in this section. In the operand syntax statements of the instruction definitions, the operand on the right is the destination operand.

An = any address register, A7–A0
Dn = any data register, D7–D0
Rn = any address or data register
CCR = condition code register (lower byte of status register)
cc = condition codes from CCR
ccc = index into the MC68881/MC68882 constant ROM
SR = status register
SP = active stack pointer
USP = user stack pointer
ISP = supervisor/interrupt stack pointer
MSP = supervisor/master stack pointer
SSP = supervisor (master or interrupt) stack pointer
DFC = destination function code register
SFC = source function code register
Rc = control register (VBR, SFC, DFC, CACR SRP, URP, TC, DTT0, DTT1, ITT0, ITT1, MMUSR)
MMUSR = MMU status register
B, W, L = specifies a signed integer data type (twos complement) of byte, word, or long word
S = single precision real data format (32 bits)
D = double precision real data format (64 bits)
X = extended precision real data format (96 bits, 16 bits unused)
P = packed BCD real data format (96 bits, 12 bytes)
FPm, FPn = any floating-point data register FP7–FP0
FPcr = floating-point system control register (FPCR, FPSR, or FPIAR)
k = a twos complement signed integer (-64 to $+17$) that specifies the format of a number be stored in the packed decimal format
d = displacement; d_{16} is a 16-bit displacement
<ea> = effective address
list = list of registers, for example D3–D0
#<data> = immediate data; a literal integer
{offset:width} = bit field selection
label = assemble program label
[m] = bit m of an operand

[m:n] = bits m through n of operand
X = extend (X) bit in CCR
N = negative (N) bit in CCR
Z = zero (Z) bit in CCR
V = overflow (V) bit in CCR
C = carry (C) bit in CCR
+ = arithmetic addition or postincrement indicator
− = arithmetic subtraction or predecrement indicator
× = arithmetic multiplication
÷ = arithmetic division or conjunction symbol
~ = invert; operand is logically complemented
Λ = logical AND
V = logical OR
⊕ = logical exclusive OR
Dc = data register, D7–D0 used during compare
Du = data register, D7–D0 used during update
Dr, Dq = data registers, remainder or quotient of divide
Dh, Dl = data registers, high or low order 32 bits of product
MSW = most significant word
LSW = least significant word
MSB = most significant bit
FC = function code
{R/W} = read or write indicator
[An] = address extensions

1.2 INSTRUCTION SET DETAILS

The following contains detailed information about each instruction in the M68000 Family instruction set. First a description of the notation and format of the instruction description is presented here. The instruction descriptions are arranged in alphabetical order by instruction mnemonic.

1.2.1 Notation and Format

The instruction descriptions use notational conventions for the operands, the subfields and qualifiers, and the operations performed by the instructions. In the syntax descriptions, the left operand is the source operand, and the right operand is the destination operand. The following lists contain the notations used in the instruction descriptions.

Notation for operands:

PC—Program counter

SR—Status register

V—Overflow condition code

Immediate Data—Immediate data from the instruction

Source—Source contents

Destination—Destination contents

Vector—Location of exception vector

+ inf—Positive infinity

− inf—Negative infinity

<fmt>—Operand data format: byte (B), word (W), long (L), single (S), double (D), extended (X), or packed (P).

FPm—One of eight floating-point data registers (always specifies the source register)

FPn—One of eight floating-point data registers (always specifies the detination register)

Notation for subfields and qualifiers:

<bit> of <operand>—Selects a single bit of the operand

<ea>{offset:width}—Selects a bit field

(<operand>)—The contents of the referenced location

<operand>10—The operand is binary coded decimal, operations are performed in decimal

(<address register>)—The register indirect operator

−(<address register>)—Indicates that the operand register points to the memory

(<address register>)+—Location of the instruction operand — the optional mode qualifiers are −, +, (d), and (d,ix)

#xxx or #<data>—Immediate data that follows the instruction word(s)

Notations for operations that have two operands, written <operand> <op> <operand>, where <op> is one of the following:

♦—The source operand is moved to the destination operand

♦♦—The two operands are exchanged

+ —The operands are added

− —The destination operand is subtracted from the source operand

× —The operands are multiplied

÷ —The source operand is divided by the destination operand

< —Relational test, true if source operand is less than destination operand

>—Relational test, true if source operand is greater than destination operand

V—Logical OR

⊕—Logical exclusive OR

Λ—Logical AND

shifted by, rotated by—The source operand is shifted or rotated by the number of positions specified by the second operand

Notation for single-operand operations:

~<operand>—The operand is logically complemented

<operand>sign-extended—The operand is sign extended, all bits of the upper portion are made equal to the high-order bit of the lower portion

<operand>tested—The operand is compared to zero and the condition codes are set appropriately

Notation for other operations:

TRAP—Equivalent to Format/Offset Word ♦ (SSP); SSP − 2 ♦ SSP; PC ♦ (SSP); SSP − 4 ♦ SSP; SR ♦ (SSP); SSP − 2 ♦ SSP; (vector) ♦ PC

STOP—Enter the stopped state, waiting for interrupts

If <condition> then—The condition is tested. If true, the operations <operations> else after "then" are performed. If the condition is <operations> false and the optional "else" clause is present, the operations after "else" are performed. If the condition is false and else is omitted, the instruction performs no operation. Refer to the Bcc instruction description as an example.

1.2.1.1 INSTRUCTION DESCRIPTIONS.   Figure 1-2 shows the format of the instruction descriptions. The attributes line specifies the size of the operands of an instruction. When an instruction can use operands of more than one size, a suffix is used with the mnemonic of the instruction:

.B — Byte operands

.W — Word operands

.L — Long-word operands

.S — Single-precision real operands

.D — Double-precision real operands

.X — Extended-precision real operands

.P — Packed BCD real operands

INSTRUCTION NAME ⟶

PROCESSOR THAT INSTRUCTION APPLIES TO ⟶

OPERATION DESCRIPTION ⟶

SYNTAX FOR THIS INSTRUCTION ⟶

SIZE ATTRIBUTE ⟶

TEXT DESCRIPTION OF INSTRUCTION OPERATION ⟶

RESULT OF OPERATION FOR INPUT OPERAND(S) AS APPLICABLE. (THIS TABLE DEFINES THE DATA TYPE OF THE RESULT THAT IS RETURNED FOR EACH COMBINATION OF INPUT OPERANDS FOR FLOATING-POINT INSTRUCTIONS.) ⟶

CONDITION CODE EFFECTS (FOR INTEGER INSTRUCTIONS) OR STATUS REGISTER EFFECTS (FOR FLOATING-POINT INSTRUCTIONS). ⟶

INSTRUCTION FORMAT (THIS SPECIFIES THE BIT PATTERN AND FIELDS OF THE OPERATION AND COMMAND WORDS, AND ANY OTHER WORDS THAT ARE ALWAYS PART OF THE INSTRUCTION. THE EFFECTIVE ADDRESS EXTENSIONS ARE NOT EXPLICITLY ILLUSTRATED. THE EXTENSION WORDS (IF ANY) FOLLOW IMMEDIATELY AFTER THE ILLUSTRATED PORTIONS OF THE INSTRUCTIONS.) ⟶

MEANINGS AND ALLOWED VALUES (FOR THE VARIOUS FIELDS REQUIRED BY THE INSTRUCTION FORMAT) ⟶

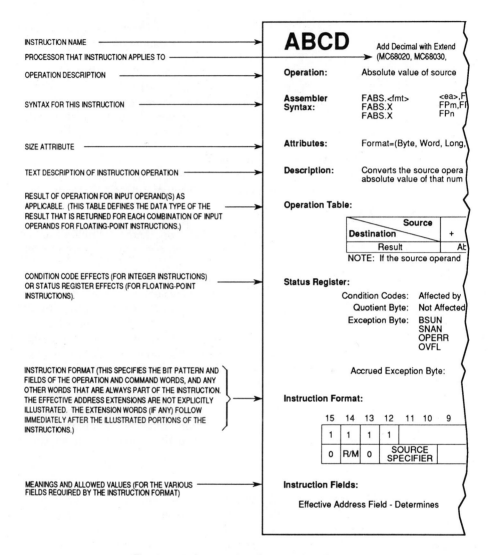

ABCD   Add Decimal with Extend (MC68020, MC68030,

Operation: Absolute value of source

Assembler Syntax: FABS.<fmt>   <ea>,F
FABS.X   FPm,F
FABS.X   FPn

Attributes: Format=(Byte, Word, Long,

Description: Converts the source opera
absolute value of that num

Operation Table:

Destination	Source	+
	Result	At

NOTE: If the source operand

Status Register:

Condition Codes: Affected by
Quotient Byte: Not Affected
Exception Byte: BSUN
SNAN
OPERR
OVFL

Accrued Exception Byte:

Instruction Format:

15	14	13	12	11	10	9
1	1	1	1			
0	R/M	0	SOURCE SPECIFIER			

Instruction Fields:

Effective Address Field - Determines

Figure 1-2. Instruction Description Format

INTEGER INSTRUCTIONS

This section contains detailed information about the integer instructions for the M68000 Family. Each instruction is described in detail and the instruction descriptions for arranged in alphabetical order by instruction mnemonic.

Any differences within the M68000 Family of instructions is identified in the instruction. If an instruction only applies to a certain processor or processors, the processor(s) that the instruction pertains to is identified under the title of the instruction. For example:

Test Bit Field and Change
(MC68030/MC68040)

If the instruction applies to all the M68000 Family but a processor or processors may use a different instruction field, instruction format, etc., the differences will be identified within the paragraph. For example:

MC68020, MC68030, AND MC68040 ONLY

(bd,An,Xn)∗	110	reg. number:An

∗Can be used with CPU32 processor

Appendix A provides a listing of all processors and the instructions that applied to them for quick reference.

The MC68HC000 is identical to the MC68000 except for power dissipation, therefore all instructions that apply to the MC68000 also apply to the MC68HC000.

ABCD

Add Decimal with Extend
(M68000 Family)

Operation: $Source_{10} + Destination_{10} + X \rightarrow Destination$

Assembler   ABCD Dy,Dx
Syntax: ABCD $-(Ay), -(Ax)$

Attributes: Size = (Byte)

Description: Adds the source operand to the destination operand along with the extend bit, and stores the result in the destination location. The addition is performed using binary coded decimal arithmetic. The operands, which are packed BCD numbers, can be addressed in two different ways:

1. Data register to data register: The operands are contained in the data registers specified in the instruction.
2. Memory to memory: The operands are addressed with the predecrement addressing mode using the address registers specified in the instruction.

This operation is a byte operation only.

Condition Codes:

X	N	Z	V	C
*	U	*	U	*

X   Set the same as the carry bit.
N   Undefined.
Z   Cleared if the result is nonzero. Unchanged otherwise.
V   Undefined.
C   Set if a decimal carry was generated. Cleared otherwise.

NOTE

Normally the Z condition code bit is set via programming before the start of an operation. This allows successful tests for zero results upon completion of multiple-precision operations.

Instruction Format:

15	14	13	12	11	10	9	8	7	6	5	4	3	2	1	0
1	1	0	0	REGISTER Rx			1	0	0	0	0	R/M	REGISTER Ry		

Instruction Fields:

Register Rx field — Specifies the destination register:
   If R/M = 0, specifies a data register
   If R/M = 1, specifies an address register for the predecrement addressing
            mode

ABCD

R/M field — Specifies the operand addressing mode:
  0 — the operation is data register to data register
  1 — the operation is memory to memory
Register Ry field — Specifies the source register:
  If R/M = 0, specifies a data register
  If R/M = 1, specifies an address register for the predecrement addressing
    mode

ADD

Add
(M68000 Family)

Operation: Source + Destination ⟶ Destination

Assembler   ADD ⟨ea⟩,Dn
Syntax: ADD Dn,⟨ea⟩

Attributes: Size = (Byte, Word, Long)

Description: Adds the source operand to the destination operand using binary
addition, and stores the result in the destination location. The size of the operation may be specified as byte, word, or long. The mode of the instruction
indicates which operand is the source and which is the destination as well as
the operand size.

Condition Codes:

X	N	Z	V	C
*	*	*	*	*

X Set the same as the carry bit.
N Set if the result is negative. Cleared otherwise.
Z Set if the result is zero. Cleared otherwise.
V Set if an overflow is generated. Cleared otherwise.
C Set if a carry is generated. Cleared otherwise.

Instruction Format:

15	14	13	12	11	10	9	8	7	6	5	4	3	2	1	0
1	1	0	1	REGISTER			OPMODE			EFFECTIVE ADDRESS					
										MODE			REGISTER		

ADD

Instruction Fields:

Register field — Specifies any of the eight data registers.

Opmode field:

Byte	Word	Long	Operation
000	001	010	$\langle ea \rangle + \langle Dn \rangle \blacklozenge \langle Dn \rangle$
100	101	110	$\langle Dn \rangle + \langle ea \rangle \blacklozenge \langle ea \rangle$

Effective Address Field — Determines addressing mode:

a. If the location specified is a source operand, all addressing modes are allowed as shown:

Addressing Mode	Mode	Register	Addressing Mode	Mode	Register
Dn	000	reg. number:Dn	(xxx).W	111	000
An*	001	reg. number:An	(xxx).L	111	001
(An)	010	reg. number:An	#⟨data⟩	111	100
(An)+	011	reg. number:An			
−(An)	100	reg. number:An			
(d_{16},An)	101	reg. number:An	(d_{16},PC)	111	010
(d_8,An,Xn)	110	reg. number:An	(d_8,PC,Xn)	111	011

MC68020, MC68030, AND MC68040 ONLY

Addressing Mode	Mode	Register	Addressing Mode	Mode	Register
(bd,An,Xn)**	110	reg. number:An	(bd,PC,Xn)**	111	011
([bd,An,Xn],od)	110	reg. number:An	([bd,PC,Xn],od)	111	011
([bd,An],Xn,od)	110	reg. number:An	([bd,PC],Xn,od)	111	011

*Word and Long only.
**Can be used with CPU32.

b. If the location specified is a destination operand, only memory alterable addressing modes are allowed as shown:

Addressing Mode	Mode	Register	Addressing Mode	Mode	Register
Dn	—	—	(xxx).W	111	000
An	—	—	(xxx).L	111	001
(An)	010	reg. number:An	#⟨data⟩	—	—
(An)+	011	reg. number:An			
−(An)	100	reg. number:An			
(d_{16},An)	101	reg. number:An	(d_{16},PC)	—	—
(d_8,An,Xn)	110	reg. number:An	(d_8,PC,Xn)	—	—

MC68020, MC68030, AND MC68040 ONLY

Addressing Mode	Mode	Register	Addressing Mode	Mode	Register
(bd,An,Xn)*	110	reg. number:An	(bd,PC,Xn)*	—	—
([bd,An,Xn],od)	110	reg. number:An	([bd,PC,Xn],od)	—	—
([bd,An],Xn,od)	110	reg. number:An	([bd,PC],Xn,od)	—	—

*Can be used with CPU32.

ADD

Notes:
1. The Dn mode is used when the destination is a data register; the destination ⟨ea⟩ mode is invalid for a data register.
2. ADDA is used when the destination is an address register. ADDI and ADDQ are used when the source is immediate data. Most assemblers automatically make this distinction.

ADDA

Add Address
(M68000 Family)

Operation: Source + Destination ⬧ Destination

Assembler
Syntax: ADDA ⟨ea⟩, An

Attributes: Size = (Word, Long)

Description: Adds the source operand to the destination address register, and stores the result in the address register. The size of the operation may be specified as word or long. The entire destination address register is used regardless of the operation size.

Condition Codes:
Not affected.

Instruction Format:

15	14	13	12	11	10	9	8	7	6	5	4	3	2	1	0
1	1	0	1	REGISTER			OPMODE			EFFECTIVE ADDRESS					
										MODE			REGISTER		

Instruction Fields:
Register field — Specifies any of the eight address registers. This is always the destination.
Opmode field — Specifies the size of the operation:
011 — Word operation. The source operand is sign-extended to a long operand and the operation is performed on the address register using all 32 bits.
111 — Long operation.

ADDA

Effective Address field — Specifies the source operand. All addressing modes are allowed as shown:

Addressing Mode	Mode	Register	Addressing Mode	Mode	Register
Dn	000	reg. number:Dn	(xxx).W	111	000
An	001	reg. number:An	(xxx).L	111	001
(An)	010	reg. number:An	#⟨data⟩	111	100
(An)+	011	reg. number:An			
−(An)	100	reg. number:An			
(d₁₆,An)	101	reg. number:An	(d₁₆,PC)	111	010
(d₈,An,Xn)	110	reg. number:An	(d₈,PC,Xn)	111	011

MC68020, MC68030, AND MC68040 ONLY

Addressing Mode	Mode	Register	Addressing Mode	Mode	Register
(bd,An,Xn)∗	110	reg. number:An	(bd,PC,Xn)∗	111	011
([bd,An,Xn],od)	110	reg. number:An	([bd,PC,Xn],od)	111	011
([bd,An],Xn,od)	110	reg. number:An	([bd,PC],Xn,od)	111	011

∗Can be used with CPU32.

ADDI

Add Immediate
(M68000 Family)

Operation: Immediate Data + Destination ⬎ Destination

**Assembler
Syntax:**   ADDI #⟨data⟩,⟨ea⟩

Attributes: Size = (Byte, Word, Long)

Description: Adds the immediate data to the destination operand, and stores the result in the destination location. The size of the operation may be specified as byte, word, or long. The size of the immediate data matches the operation size.

Condition Codes:

X	N	Z	V	C
∗	∗	∗	∗	∗

X   Set the same as the carry bit.
N   Set if the result is negative. Cleared otherwise.
Z   Set if the result is zero. Cleared otherwise.
V   Set if an overflow is generated. Cleared otherwise.
C   Set if a carry is generated. Cleared otherwise.

ADDI

Instruction Format:

15	14	13	12	11	10	9	8	7	6	5	4	3	2	1	0
0	0	0	0	0	1	1	0	\multicolumn{2}{c}{SIZE}	\multicolumn{4}{c}{EFFECTIVE ADDRESS}

0	0	0	0	0	1	1	0	SIZE		MODE			REGISTER		
WORD DATA (16 BITS)								BYTE DATA (8 BITS)							
LONG DATA (32 BITS)															

Instruction Fields:

Size field — Specifies the size of the operation:

00 — Byte operation.

01 — Word operation.

10 — Long operation.

Effective Address field — Specifies the destination operand.

Only data alterable addressing modes are allowed as shown:

Addressing Mode	Mode	Register
Dn	000	reg. number:Dn
An	—	—
(An)	010	reg. number:An
(An)+	011	reg. number:An
−(An)	100	reg. number:An
(d16,An)	101	reg. number:An
(d8,An,Xn)	110	reg. number:An

Addressing Mode	Mode	Register
(xxx).W	111	000
(xxx).L	111	001
#⟨data⟩	—	—
(d16,PC)	—	—
(d8,PC,Xn)	—	—

MC68020, MC68030, AND MC68040 ONLY

(bd,An,Xn)*	110	reg. number:An
([bd,An,Xn],od)	110	reg. number:An
([bd,An],Xn,od)	110	reg. number:An

(bd,PC,Xn)*	—	—
([bd,PC,Xn],od)	—	—
([bd,PC],Xn,od)	—	—

*Can be used with CPU32.

Immediate field — (data immediately following the instruction):

If size = 00, the data is the low-order byte of the immediate word.

If size = 01, the data is the entire immediate word.

If size = 10, the data is the next two immediate words.

ADDQ

Add Quick
(M68000 Family)

Operation: Immediate Data + Destination ♦ Destination

Assembler
Syntax: ADDQ #⟨data⟩,⟨ea⟩

Attributes: Size = (Byte, Word, Long)

Description: Adds an immediate value of one to eight to the operand at the destination location. The size of the operation may be specified as byte, word, or long. Word and long operations are also allowed on the address registers. When adding to address registers, the condition codes are not altered, and the entire destination address register is used regardless of the operation size.

Condition Codes:

X	N	Z	V	C
*	*	*	*	*

X   Set the same as the carry bit.
N   Set if the result is negative. Cleared otherwise.
Z   Set if the result is zero. Cleared otherwise.
V   Set if an overflow occurs. Cleared otherwise.
C   Set if a carry occurs. Cleared otherwise.

The condition codes are not affected when the destination is an address register.

Instruction Format:

15	14	13	12	11	10	9	8	7	6	5	4	3	2	1	0
0	1	0	1		DATA		0		SIZE		EFFECTIVE ADDRESS MODE			REGISTER	

Instruction Fields:

Data field — Three bits of immediate data, 0–7 (with the immediate value zero representing a value of eight).
Size field — Specifies the size of the operation:
   00 — Byte operation.
   01 — Word operation.
   10 — Long operation.
Effective Address field — Specifies the destination location.
   Only alterable addressing modes are allowed as shown:

ADDQ

Addressing Mode	Mode	Register
Dn	000	reg. number:Dn
An*	001	reg. number:An
(An)	010	reg. number:An
(An)+	011	reg. number:An
−(An)	100	reg. number:An
(d$_{16}$,An)	101	reg. number:An
(d$_8$,An,Xn)	110	reg. number:An

Addressing Mode	Mode	Register
(xxx).W	111	000
(xxx).L	111	001
#⟨data⟩	—	—
(d$_{16}$,PC)	—	—
(d$_8$,PC,Xn)	—	—

MC68020, MC68030, AND MC68040 ONLY

Addressing Mode	Mode	Register
(bd,An,Xn)**	110	reg. number:An
([bd,An,Xn],od)	110	reg. number:An
([bd,An],Xn,od)	110	reg. number:An

Addressing Mode	Mode	Register
(bd,PC,Xn)**	—	—
([bd,PC,Xn],od)	—	—
([bd,PC],Xn,od)	—	—

*Word and Long only.
**Can be used with CPU32.

ADDX

Add Extended
(M68000 Family)

Operation: Source + Destination + X ⧫ Destination

Assembler
Syntax:
ADDX Dy,Dx
ADDX −(Ay),−(Ax)

Attributes: Size = (Byte, Word, Long)

Description: Adds the source operand to the destination operand along with the extend bit and stores the result in the destination location. The operands can be addressed in two different ways:
1. Data register to data register: The data registers specified in the instruction contain the operands.
2. Memory to memory: The address registers specified in the instruction address the operands using the predecrement addressing mode.
The size of the operation can be specified as byte, word, or long.

Condition Codes:

X	N	Z	V	C
*	*	*	*	*

X   Set the same as the carry bit.
N   Set if the result is negative. Cleared otherwise.

ADDX

Z Cleared if the result is nonzero. Unchanged otherwise.
V Set if an overflow occurs. Cleared otherwise.
C Set if a carry is generated. Cleared otherwise.

NOTE

Normally the Z condition code bit is set via programming before the start of an operation. This allows successful tests for zero results upon completion of multiple-precision operations.

Instruction Format:

15	14	13	12	11	10	9	8	7	6	5	4	3	2	1	0
1	1	0	1	REGISTER Rx			1	SIZE		0	0	R/M	REGISTER Ry		

Instruction Fields:

Register Rx field — Specifies the destination register:
  If R/M = 0, specifies a data register.
  If R/M = 1, specifies an address register for the predecrement addressing mode.
Size field — Specifies the size of the operation:
  00 — Byte operation.
  01 — Word operation.
  10 — Long operation.
R/M field — Specifies the operand address mode:
  0 — The operation is data register to data register.
  1 — The operation is memory to memory.
Register Ry field — Specifies the source register:
  If R/M = 0, specifies a data register.
  If R/M = 1, specifies an address register for the predecrement addressing mode.

AND

AND Logical
(M68000 Family)

Operation: Source∧Destination ♦ Destination

Assembler   AND ⟨ea⟩,Dn
Syntax: AND Dn,⟨ea⟩

Attributes: Size = (Byte, Word, Long)

Description: Performs an AND operation of the source operand with the destination operand and stores the result in the destination location. The size of the

AND

operation can be specified as byte, word, or long. The contents of an address register may not be used as an operand.

Condition Codes:

X	N	Z	V	C
—	*	*	0	0

X   Not affected.
N   Set if the most significant bit of the result is set. Cleared otherwise.
Z   Set if the result is zero. Cleared otherwise.
V   Always cleared.
C   Always cleared.

Instruction Format:

15	14	13	12	11	10	9	8	7	6	5	4	3	2	1	0
1	1	0	0		REGISTER			OPMODE		EFFECTIVE ADDRESS					
										MODE			REGISTER		

Instruction Fields:

Register field — Specifies any of the eight data registers.
Opmode field:

Byte	Word	Long	Operation
000	001	010	$(\langle ea \rangle) \wedge (\langle Dn \rangle) \blacktriangleright Dn$
100	101	110	$(\langle Dn \rangle) \wedge (\langle ea \rangle) \blacktriangleright ea$

Effective Address field — Determines addressing mode:

a. If the location specified is a source operand only data addressing modes are allowed as shown:

Addressing Mode	Mode	Register
Dn	000	reg. number:Dn
An	—	—
(An)	010	reg. number:An
(An)+	011	reg. number:An
−(An)	100	reg. number:An
(d$_{16}$,An)	101	reg. number:An
(d$_8$,An,Xn)	110	reg. number:An

Addressing Mode	Mode	Register
(xxx).W	111	000
(xxx).L	111	001
#⟨data⟩	111	100
(d$_{16}$,PC)	111	010
(d$_8$,PC,Xn)	111	011

MC68020, MC68030, AND MC68040 ONLY

Addressing Mode	Mode	Register
(bd,An,Xn)*	110	reg. number:An
([bd,An,Xn],od)	110	reg. number:An
([bd,An],Xn,od)	110	reg. number:An

Addressing Mode	Mode	Register
(bd,PC,Xn)*	111	011
([bd,PC,Xn],od)	111	011
([bd,PC],Xn,od)	111	011

*Can be used with CPU32.

AND

AND Logical
(M68000 Family)

b. If the location specified is a destination operand only memory alterable addressing modes are allowed as shown:

Addressing Mode	Mode	Register	Addressing Mode	Mode	Register
Dn	—	—	(xxx).W	111	000
An	—	—	(xxx).L	111	001
(An)	010	reg. number:An	#⟨data⟩	—	—
(An)+	011	reg. number:An			
–(An)	100	reg. number:An			
(d_{16},An)	101	reg. number:An	(d_{16},PC)	—	—
(d_8,An,Xn)	110	reg. number:An	(d_8,PC,Xn)	—	—

MC68020, MC68030, AND MC68040 ONLY

(bd,An,Xn)*	110	reg. number:An	(bd,PC,Xn)*	—	—
([bd,An,Xn],od)	110	reg. number:An	([bd,PC,Xn],od)	—	—
([bd,An],Xn,od)	110	reg. number:An	([bd,PC],Xn,od)	—	—

*Can be used with CPU32.

Notes:

1. The Dn mode is used when the destination is a data register; the destination ⟨ea⟩ mode is invalid for a data register.
2. Most assemblers use ANDI when the source is immediate data.

ANDI

AND Immediate
(M68000 Family)

Operation: Immediate Data $\wedge$ Destination ➧ Destination

Assembler Syntax: ANDI #⟨data⟩,⟨ea⟩

Attributes: Size = (Byte, Word, Long)

Description: Performs an AND operation of the immediate data with the destination operand and stores the result in the destination location. The size of the operation can be specified as byte, word, or long. The size of the immediate data matches the operation size.

ANDI

Condition Codes:

X	N	Z	V	C
—	*	*	0	0

X   Not affected.
N   Set if the most significant bit of the result is set. Cleared otherwise.
Z   Set if the result is zero. Cleared otherwise.
V   Always cleared.
C   Always cleared.

Instruction Format:

15	14	13	12	11	10	9	8	7	6	5	4	3	2	1	0
0	0	0	0	0	0	1	0	SIZE		EFFECTIVE ADDRESS					

										MODE			REGISTER		
WORD DATA (16 BITS)								BYTE DATA (8 BITS)							
LONG DATA (32 BITS)															

Instruction Fields:

Size field — Specifies the size of the operation:

00 — Byte operation

01 — Word operation.

10 — Long operation.

Effective Address field — Specifies the destination operand.

Only data alterable addressing modes are allowed as shown:

Addressing Mode	Mode	Register	Addressing Mode	Mode	Register
Dn	000	reg. number:Dn	(xxx).W	111	000
An	—	—	(xxx).L	111	001
(An)	010	reg. number:An	#(data)	—	—
(An)+	011	reg. number:An			
−(An)	100	reg. number:An			
(d16,An)	101	reg. number:An	(d16,PC)	—	—
(d8,An,Xn)	110	reg. number:An	(d8,PC,Xn)	—	—

MC68020, MC68030, AND MC68040 ONLY

Addressing Mode	Mode	Register	Addressing Mode	Mode	Register
(bd,An,Xn)*	110	reg. number:An	(bd,PC,Xn)*	—	—
([bd,An,Xn],od)	110	reg. number:An	([bd,PC,Xn],od)	—	—
([bd,An],Xn,od)	110	reg. number:An	([bd,PC],Xn,od)	—	—

*Can be used with CPU32.

Immediate field — (data immediately following the instruction):

If size = 00, the data is the low-order byte of the immediate word.

If size = 01, the data is the entire immediate word.

If size = 10, the data is the next two immediate words.

ANDI
to CCR

AND Immediate to Condition Codes
(M68000 Family)

Operation: Source.\CCR ♦ CCR

**Assembler
Syntax:**   ANDI #⟨data⟩,CCR

Attributes: Size = (Byte)

Description: Performs an AND operation of the immediate operand with the condition codes and stores the result in the low-order byte of the status register.

Condition Codes:

X	N	Z	V	C
*	*	*	*	*

X   Cleared if bit 4 of immediate operand is zero. Unchanged otherwise.
N   Cleared if bit 3 of immediate operand is zero. Unchanged otherwise.
Z   Cleared if bit 2 of immediate operand is zero. Unchanged otherwise.
V   Cleared if bit 1 of immediate operand is zero. Unchanged otherwise.
C   Cleared if bit 0 of immediate operand is zero. Unchanged otherwise.

Instruction Format:

15	14	13	12	11	10	9	8	7	6	5	4	3	2	1	0
0	0	0	0	0	0	1	0	0	0	1	1	1	1	0	0
0	0	0	0	0	0	0	0	BYTE DATA (8 BITS)							

ASL,
ASR

Arithmetic Shift
(M68000 Family)

Operation: Destination Shifted by ⟨count⟩ ♦ Destination

**Assembler
Syntax:**   ASd Dx,Dy
ASd #⟨data⟩,Dy
ASd ⟨ea⟩
where d is direction, L or R

Attributes: Size = (Byte, Word, Long)

ASL,
ASR

Description: Arithmetically shifts the bits of the operand in the direction (L or R) specified. The carry bit receives the last bit shifted out of the operand. The shift count for the shifting of a register may be specified in two different ways:

1. Immediate — The shift count is specified in the instruction (shift range, 1–8).
2. Register — The shift count is the value in the data register specified in instruction modulo 64.

The size of the operation can be specified as byte, word, or long. An operand in memory can be shifted one bit only, and the operand size is restricted to a word.

For ASL, the operand is shifted left; the number of positions shifted is the shift count. Bits shifted out of the high-order bit go to both the carry and the extend bits; zeros are shifted into the low-order bit. The overflow bit indicates if any sign changes occur during the shift.

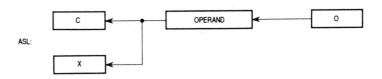

For ASR, the operand is shifted right; the number of positions shifted is the shift count. Bits shifted out of the low-order bit go to both the carry and the extend bits; the sign-bit (MSB) is shifted into the high-order bit.

Condition Codes:

X	N	Z	V	C
*	*	*	*	*

X   Set according to the last bit shifted out of the operand. Unaffected for a shift count of zero.
N   Set if the most significant bit of the result is set. Cleared otherwise.
Z   Set if the result is zero. Cleared otherwise.
V   Set if the most significant bit is changed at any time during the shift operation. Cleared otherwise.
C   Set according to the last bit shifted out of the operand. Cleared for a shift count of zero.

ASL, ASR

Instruction Format (Register Shifts):

15	14	13	12	11	10	9	8	7	6	5	4	3	2	1	0
1	1	1	0	COUNT/REGISTER			dr	SIZE		i/r	0	0	REGISTER		

Instruction Fields (Register Shifts):

Count/Register field — Specifies shift count or register that contains the shift count:

If i/r = 0, this field contains the shift count. The values 1–7 represent counts of 1–7; value of zero represents a count of eight.

If i/r = 1, this field specifies the data register that contains the shift count (modulo 64).

dr field — Specifies the direction of the shift:
0 — Shift right.
1 — Shift left.

Size field — Specifies the size of the operation:
00 — Byte operation.
01 — Word operation.
10 — Long operation.

i/r field:
If i/r = 0, specifies immediate shift count.
If i/r = 1, specifies register shift count.

Register field — Specifies a data register to be shifted.

Instruction Format (Memory Shifts):

15	14	13	12	11	10	9	8	7	6	5	4	3	2	1	0
1	1	1	0	0	0	0	dr	1	1	EFFECTIVE ADDRESS MODE			REGISTER		

Instruction Fields (Memory Shifts):

dr field — Specifies the direction of the shift:
0 — Shift right.
1 — Shift left.

Effective Address field — Specifies the operand to be shifted.

Only memory alterable addressing modes are allowed as shown:

Addressing Mode	Mode	Register
Dn	—	—
An	—	—
(An)	010	reg. number:An
(An)+	011	reg. number:An
−(An)	100	reg. number:An
(d$_{16}$,An)	101	reg. number:An
(d$_8$,An,Xn)	110	reg. number:An

Addressing Mode	Mode	Register
(xxx).W	111	000
(xxx).L	111	001
#⟨data⟩	—	—
(d$_{16}$,PC)	—	—
(d$_8$,PC,Xn)	—	—

ASL,
ASR

MC68020, MC68030, AND MC68040 ONLY

(bd,An,Xn)*	110	reg. number:An	(bd,PC,Xn)*	—	—
([bd,An,Xn],od)	110	reg. number:An	([bd,PC,Xn],od)	—	—
([bd,An],Xn,od)	110	reg. number:An	([bd,PC],Xn,od)	—	—

*Can be used with CPU32.

Bcc

Branch Conditionally
(M68000 Family)

Operation: If (condition true) then PC + d ♦ PC

Assembler
Syntax: Bcc ⟨label⟩

Attributes: Size = (Byte, Word, Long*)
*(MC68020/MC68030/MC68040 only)

Description: If the specified condition is true, program execution continues at location (PC) + displacement. The PC contains the address of the instruction word of the Bcc instruction plus two. The displacement is a twos complement integer that represents the relative distance in bytes from the current PC to the destination PC. If the 8-bit displacement field in the instruction word is zero, a 16-bit displacement (the word immediately following the instruction) is used. If the 8-bit displacement field in the instruction word is all ones ($FF), the 32-bit displacement (long word immediately following the instruction) is used. Condition code cc specifies one of the following conditions:

CC	carry clear	0100	$\overline{C}$
CS	carry set	0101	C
EQ	equal	0111	Z
GE	greater or equal	1100	$N{\cdot}V + \overline{N}{\cdot}\overline{V}$
GT	greater than	1110	$N{\cdot}V{\cdot}\overline{Z} + \overline{N}{\cdot}\overline{V}{\cdot}\overline{Z}$
HI	high	0010	$\overline{C}{\cdot}\overline{Z}$
LE	less or equal	1111	$Z + N{\cdot}\overline{V} + \overline{N}{\cdot}V$
LS	low or same	0011	$C + Z$
LT	less than	1101	$N{\cdot}\overline{V} + \overline{N}{\cdot}V$
MI	minus	1011	N
NE	not equal	0110	$\overline{Z}$
PL	plus	1010	$\overline{N}$
VC	overflow clear	1000	$\overline{V}$
VS	overflow set	1001	V

Condition Codes:
Not affected.

Bcc

Instruction Format:

15	14	13	12	11	10	9	8	7	6	5	4	3	2	1	0
0	1	1	0		CONDITION					8-BIT DISPLACEMENT					

16-BIT DISPLACEMENT IF 8-BIT DISPLACEMENT = $00

32-BIT DISPLACEMENT IF 8-BIT DISPLACEMENT = $FF

Instruction Fields:

Condition field — The binary code for one of the conditions listed in the table.

8-Bit Displacement field — Twos complement integer specifying the number of bytes between the branch instruction and the next instruction to be executed if the condition is met.

16-Bit Displacement field — Used for the displacement when the 8-bit displacement field contains $00.

32-Bit Displacement field — Used for the displacement when the 8-bit displacement field contains $FF.

NOTE

A branch to the immediately following instruction automatically uses the 16-bit displacement format because the 8-bit displacement field contains $00 (zero offset).

BCHG

Test a Bit and Change
(M68000 Family)

Operation: ~(⟨number⟩ of Destination) ⧫ Z;
~(⟨number⟩ of Destination) ⧫ ⟨bit number⟩ of Destination

Assembler   BCHG Dn,⟨ea⟩
Syntax: BCHG #⟨data⟩,⟨ea⟩

Attributes: Size = (Byte, Long)

Description: Tests a bit in the destination operand and sets the Z condition code appropriately, then inverts the specified bit in the destination. When the destination is a data register, any of the 32 bits can be specified by the modulo 32-bit number. When the destination is a memory location, the operation is a byte operation, and the bit number is modulo 8. In all cases, bit zero refers to the least significant bit. The bit number for this operation may be specified in either of two ways:

1. Immediate — The bit number is specified in a second word of the instruction.
2. Register — The specified data register contains the bit number.

BCHG

Condition Codes:

X	N	Z	V	C
—	—	*	—	—

X   Not affected.
N   Not affected.
Z   Set if the bit tested is zero. Cleared otherwise.
V   Not affected.
C   Not affected.

Instruction Format (Bit Number Dynamic, specified in a register):

15	14	13	12	11	10	9	8	7	6	5	4	3	2	1	0
0	0	0	0	REGISTER			1	0	1	EFFECTIVE ADDRESS					
										MODE			REGISTER		

Instruction Fields (Bit Number Dynamic):

Register field — Specifies the data register that contains the bit number.
Effective Address field — Specifies the destination location. Only data alterable addressing modes are allowed as shown:

Addressing Mode	Mode	Register
Dn*	000	reg. number:Dn
An	—	—
(An)	010	reg. number:An
(An)+	011	reg. number:An
−(An)	100	reg. number:An
(d_{16},An)	101	reg. number:An
(d_8,An,Xn)	110	reg. number:An

Addressing Mode	Mode	Register
(xxx).W	111	000
(xxx).L	111	001
#(data)	—	—
(d_{16},PC)	—	—
(d_8,PC,Xn)	—	—

MC68020, MC68030, AND MC68040 ONLY

Addressing Mode	Mode	Register
(bd,An,Xn)**	110	reg. number:An
([bd,An,Xn],od)	110	reg. number:An
([bd,An],Xn,od)	110	reg. number:An

Addressing Mode	Mode	Register
(bd,PC,Xn)**	—	—
([bd,PC,Xn],od)	—	—
([bd,PC],Xn,od)	—	—

*Long only; all others are byte only.
**Can be used with CPU32.

Instruction Format (Bit Number Static, specified as immediate data):

15	14	13	12	11	10	9	8	7	6	5	4	3	2	1	0
0	0	0	0	1	0	0	0	0	1	EFFECTIVE ADDRESS					
										MODE			REGISTER		
0	0	0	0	0	0	0	0	BIT NUMBER							

BCHG

Instruction Fields (Bit Number Static):

Effective Address field — Specifies the destination location.
Only data alterable addressing modes are allowed as shown:

Addressing Mode	Mode	Register	Addressing Mode	Mode	Register
Dn*	000	reg. number:Dn	(xxx).W	111	000
An	—	—	(xxx).L	111	001
(An)	010	reg. number:An	#⟨data⟩	—	—
(An)+	011	reg. number:An			
−(An)	100	reg. number:An			
(d$_{16}$,An)	101	reg. number:An	(d$_{16}$,PC)	—	—
(d$_8$,An,Xn)	110	reg. number:An	(d$_8$,PC,Xn)	—	—

MC68020, MC68030, AND MC68040 ONLY

Addressing Mode	Mode	Register	Addressing Mode	Mode	Register
(bd,An,Xn)**	110	reg. number:An	(bd,PC,Xn)**	—	—
([bd,An,Xn],od)	110	reg. number:An	([bd,PC,Xn],od)	—	—
([bd,An],Xn,od)	110	reg. number:An	([bd,PC],Xn,od)	—	—

*Long only; all others are byte only.
**Can be used with CPU32.

Bit Number field — Specifies the bit number.

BCLR

Test a Bit and Clear
(M68000 Family)

Operation: ~(⟨bit number⟩ of Destination) ▶ Z;
0 ▶ ⟨bit number⟩ of Destination

Assembler   BCLR Dn,⟨ea⟩
Syntax: BCLR #⟨data⟩,⟨ea⟩

Attributes: Size = (Byte, Long)

Description: Tests a bit in the destination operand and sets the Z condition code appropriately, then clears the specified bit in the destination. When a data register is the destination, any of the 32 bits can be specified by a modulo 32-bit number. When a memory location is the destination, the operation is a byte operation, and the bit number is modulo 8. In all cases, bit zero refers to the least significant bit. The bit number for this operation can be specified in either of two ways:

1. Immediate — The bit number is specified in a second word of the instruction.
2. Register — The specified data register contains the bit number.

BCLR

Condition Codes:

X	N	Z	V	C
—	—	*	—	—

X   Not affected.
N   Not affected.
Z   Set if the bit tested is zero. Cleared otherwise.
V   Not affected.
C   Not affected.

Instruction Format (Bit Number Dynamic, specified in a register):

15	14	13	12	11	10	9	8	7	6	5	4	3	2	1	0
0	0	0	0	REGISTER			1	1	0	EFFECTIVE ADDRESS MODE / REGISTER					

Row reads: `0 0 0 0 | REGISTER | 1 1 0 | EFFECTIVE ADDRESS (MODE | REGISTER)`

Instruction Fields (Bit Number Dynamic):

Register field — Specifies the data register that contains the bit number.

Effective Address field — Specifies the destination location.

Only data alterable addressing modes are allowed as shown:

Addressing Mode	Mode	Register	Addressing Mode	Mode	Register
Dn*	000	reg. number:Dn	(xxx).W	111	000
An	—	—	(xxx).L	111	001
(An)	010	reg. number:An	#⟨data⟩	—	—
(An)+	011	reg. number:An			
−(An)	100	reg. number:An			
(d₁₆,An)	101	reg. number:An	(d₁₆,PC)	—	—
(d₈,An,Xn)	110	reg. number:An	(d₈,PC,Xn)	—	—

MC68020, MC68030, AND MC68040 ONLY

Addressing Mode	Mode	Register	Addressing Mode	Mode	Register
(bd,An,Xn)**	110	reg. number:An	(bd,PC,Xn)**	—	—
([bd,An,Xn],od)	110	reg. number:An	([bd,PC,Xn],od)	—	—
([bd,An],Xn,od)	110	reg. number:An	([bd,PC],Xn,od)	—	—

*Long only; all others are byte only.
**Can be used with CPU32.

Instruction Format (Bit Number Static, specified as immediate data):

15	14	13	12	11	10	9	8	7	6	5	4	3	2	1	0
0	0	0	0	1	0	0	0	1	0	EFFECTIVE ADDRESS MODE / REGISTER					
0	0	0	0	0	0	0	0	BIT NUMBER							

Row 1 reads: `0 0 0 0 1 0 0 0 1 0 | EFFECTIVE ADDRESS (MODE | REGISTER)`
Row 2 reads: `0 0 0 0 0 0 0 0 | BIT NUMBER`

BCLR

Instruction Fields (Bit Number Static):

Effective Address field — Specifies the destination location.

Only data alterable addressing modes are allowed as shown:

Addressing Mode	Mode	Register	Addressing Mode	Mode	Register
Dn*	000	reg. number:Dn	(xxx).W	111	000
An	—	—	(xxx).L	111	001
(An)	010	reg. number:An	#(data)	—	—
(An)+	011	reg. number:An			
–(An)	100	reg. number:An			
(d$_{16}$,An)	101	reg. number:An	(d$_{16}$,PC)	—	—
(d$_8$,An,Xn)	110	reg. number:An	(d$_8$,PC,Xn)	—	—

MC68020, MC68030, AND MC68040 ONLY

(bd,An,Xn)**	110	reg. number:An	(bd,PC,Xn)**	—	—
([bd,An,Xn],od)	110	reg. number:An	([bd,PC,Xn],od)	—	—
([bd,An],Xn,od)	110	reg. number:An	([bd,PC],Xn,od)	—	—

*Long only; all others are byte only.
**Can be used with CPU32.

Bit Number field — Specifies the bit number.

BFCHG

Test Bit Field and Change
(MC68020/MC68030/MC68040)

Operation: ~(⟨bit field⟩ of Destination) ♦ ⟨bit field⟩ of Destination

**Assembler
Syntax:**   BFCHG ⟨ea⟩{offset:width}

Attributes: Unsized

Description: Sets the condition codes according to the value in a bit field at the specified effective address, then complements the field.

A field offset and a field width select the field. The field offset specifies the starting bit of the field. The field width determines the number of bits in the field.

BFCHG

Condition Codes:

X	N	Z	V	C
—	*	*	0	0

X   Not affected.
N   Set if the most significant bit of the field is set. Cleared otherwise.
Z   Set if all bits of the field are zero. Cleared otherwise.
V   Always cleared.
C   Always cleared.

Instruction Format:

15	14	13	12	11	10	9	8	7	6	5	4	3	2	1	0
1	1	1	0	1	0	1	0	1	1	EFFECTIVE ADDRESS					

15	14	13	12	11	10	9	8	7	6	5	4	3	2	1	0
1	1	1	0	1	0	1	0	1	1	MODE			REGISTER		
0	0	0	0	Do	OFFSET					Dw	WIDTH				

Instruction Fields:

Effective Address field — Specifies the base location for the bit field. Only data register direct or control alterable addressing modes are allowed as shown:

Addressing Mode	Mode	Register	Addressing Mode	Mode	Register
Dn	000	reg. number:Dn	(xxx).W	111	000
An	—	—	(xxx).L	111	001
(An)	010	reg. number:An	#⟨data⟩	—	—
(An) +	—	—			
– (An)	—	—			
(d$_{16}$,An)	101	reg. number:An	(d$_{16}$,PC)	—	—
(d$_8$,An,Xn)	110	reg. number:An	(d$_8$,PC,Xn)	—	—
(bd,An,Xn)	110	reg. number:An	(bd,PC,Xn)	—	—
([bd,An,Xn],od)	110	reg. number:An	([bd,PC,Xn],od)	—	—
([bd,An],Xn,od)	110	reg. number:An	([bd,PC],Xn,od)	—	—

Do field — Determines how the field offset is specified.
0 — The Offset field contains the bit field offset.
1 — Bits [8:6] of the extension word specify a data register that contains the offset; bits [10:9] are zero.
Offset field — Specifies the field offset, depending on Do.
If Do = 0, the Offset field is an immediate operand; the operand value is in the range 0–31.
If Do = 1, the Offset field specifies a data register that contains the offset. The value is in the range of -2^{31} to $2^{31} - 1$.

BFCHG

Dw field — Determines how the field width is specified.
  0 — The Width field contains the bit field width.
  1 — Bits [2:0] of the extension word specify a data register that contains the
     width; bits [3:4] are zero.
Width field — Specifies the field width, depending on Dw.
  If Dw = 0, the Width field is an immediate operand; an operand value in the
        range 1–31 specifies a field width of 1–31, and a value of zero
        specifies a width of 32.
  If Dw = 1, the Width field specifies a data register that contains the width.
        The value is modulo 32; values of 1–31 specify field widths of
        1–31, and a value of zero specifies a width of 32.

BFCLR

Test Bit Field and Clear
(MC68020/MC68030/MC68040)

Operation: 0 ♦ ⟨bit field⟩ of Destination

Assembler
Syntax: BFCLR ⟨ea⟩{offset:width}

Attributes: Unsized

Description: Sets condition codes according to the value in a bit field at the
specified effective address, and clears the field.

The field offset and field width select the field. The field offset specifies the
starting bit of the field. The field width determines the number of bits in the
field.

Condition Codes:

X	N	Z	V	C
—	*	*	0	0

X Not affected.
N Set if the most significant bit of the field is set. Cleared otherwise.
Z Set if all bits of the field are zero. Cleared otherwise.
V Always cleared.
C Always cleared.

BFCLR

Instruction Format:

15	14	13	12	11	10	9	8	7	6	5	4	3	2	1	0
1	1	1	0	1	1	0	0	1	1	— EFFECTIVE ADDRESS					

15	14	13	12	11	10	9	8	7	6	5	4	3	2	1	0
1	1	1	0	1	1	0	0	1	1	MODE			REGISTER		
0	0	0	0	Do		OFFSET				Dw		WIDTH			

Instruction Fields:

Effective Address field — Specifies the base location for the bit field. Only data register direct or alterable control addressing modes are allowed, as shown:

Addressing Mode	Mode	Register	Addressing Mode	Mode	Register
Dn	000	reg. number:Dn	(xxx).W	111	000
An	—	—	(xxx).L	111	001
(An)	010	reg. number:An	#⟨data⟩	—	—
(An)+	—	—			
−(An)	—	—			
(d$_{16}$,An)	101	reg. number:An	(d$_{16}$,PC)	—	—
(d$_8$,An,Xn)	110	reg. number:An	(d$_8$,PC,Xn)	—	—
(bd,An,Xn)	110	reg. number:An	(bd,PC,Xn)	—	—
([bd,An,Xn],od)	110	reg. number:An	([bd,PC,Xn],od)	—	—
([bd,An],Xn,od)	110	reg. number:An	([bd,PC],Xn,od)	—	—

Do field — Determines how the field offset is specified.

0 — The Offset field contains the bit field offset.

1 — Bits [8:6] of the extension word specify a data register that contains the offset; bits [10:9] are zero.

Offset field — Specifies the field offset, depending on Do.

If Do = 0, the Offset field is an immediate operand; the operand value is in the range of 0–31.

If Do = 1, the Offset field specifies a data register that contains the offset. The value is in the range of -2^{31} to $2^{31}-1$.

Dw field — Determines how the field width is specified.

0 — The Width field contains the bit field width.

1 — Bits [2:0] of the extension word specify a data register that contains the width; bits [3:4] are zero.

Width field — Specifies the field width, depending on Dw.

If Dw = 0, the Width field is an immediate operand; operand values in the range of 1–31 specify a field width of 1–31, and a value of zero specifies a width of 32.

If Dw = 1, the Width field specifies a data register that contains the width. The value is modulo 32; values of 1–31 specify field widths of 1–31, and a value of zero specifies a width of 32.

BFEXTS

Extract Bit Field Signed
(MC68020/MC68030/MC68040)

Operation: ⟨bit field⟩ of Source ◆ Dn

Assembler
Syntax: BFEXTS ⟨ea⟩{offset:width},Dn

Attributes: Unsized

Description: Extracts a bit field from the specified effective address location, sign extends to 32 bits, and loads the result into the destination data register.

The field offset and field width select the bit field. The field offset specifies the starting bit of the field. The field width determines the number of bits in the field.

Condition Codes:

X	N	Z	V	C
—	*	*	0	0

X   Not affected.
N   Set if the most significant bit of the field is set. Cleared otherwise.
Z   Set if all bits of the field are zero. Cleared otherwise.
V   Always cleared.
C   Always cleared.

Instruction Format:

15	14	13	12	11	10	9	8	7	6	5	4	3	2	1	0
1	1	1	0	1	0	1	1	1	1	EFFECTIVE ADDRESS					
										MODE			REGISTER		
0	REGISTER			Do	OFFSET					Dw	WIDTH				

Instruction Fields:

Effective Address field — Specifies the base location for the bit field. Only data register direct or control addressing modes are allowed as shown:

BFEXTS

Addressing Mode	Mode	Register
Dn	000	reg. number:Dn
An	—	—
(An)	010	reg. number:An
(An) +	—	—
– (An)	—	—
(d$_{16}$,An)	101	reg. number:An
(d$_8$,An,Xn)	110	reg. number:An
(bd,An,Xn)	110	reg. number:An
([bd,An,Xn],od)	110	reg. number:An
([bd,An],Xn,od)	110	reg. number:An

Addressing Mode	Mode	Register
(xxx).W	111	000
(xxx).L	111	001
#(data)	—	—
(d$_{16}$,PC)	111	010
(d$_8$,PC,Xn)	111	011
(bd,PC,Xn)	111	011
([bd,PC,Xn],od)	111	011
([bd,PC],Xn,od)	111	011

Register field — Specifies the destination register.

Do field — Determines how the field offset is specified.

    0 — The Offset field contains the bit field offset.

    1 — Bits [8:6] of the extension word specify a data register that contains the offset; bits [10:9] are zero.

Offset field — Specifies the field offset, depending on Do.

    If Do = 0, the Offset field is an immediate operand; the operand value is in the range of 0–31.

    If Do = 1, the Offset field specifies a data register that contains the offset. The value is in the range of -2^{31} to $2^{31} - 1$.

Dw field — Determines how the field width is specified.

    0 — The Width field contains the bit field width.

    1 — Bits [2:0] of the extension word specify a data register that contains the width; bits [4:3] are zero.

Width field — Specifies the field width, depending on Dw.

    If Dw = 0, the Width field is an immediate operand; operand values in the range of 1–31 specify a field width of 1–31, and a value of zero specifies a width of 32.

    If Dw = 1, the Width field specifies a data register that contains the width. The value is modulo 32; values of 1–31 specify field widths of 1–31, and a value of zero specifies a width of 32.

BFEXTU

Extract Bit Field Unsigned
(MC68020/MC68030/MC68040)

Operation: ⟨bit offset⟩ of Source ⬦ Dn

Assembler
Syntax: BFEXTU ⟨ea⟩{offset:width},Dn

BFEXTU

Attributes: Unsized

Description: Extracts a bit field from the specified effective address location, zero extends to 32 bits, and loads the results into the destination data register.

The field offset and field width select the field. The field offset specifies the starting bit of the field. The field width determines the number of bits in the field.

Condition Codes:

X	N	Z	V	C
—	*	*	0	0

X   Not affected.
N   Set if the most significant bit of the source field is set. Cleared otherwise.
Z   Set if all bits of the field are zero. Cleared otherwise.
V   Always cleared.
C   Always cleared.

Instruction Format:

15	14	13	12	11	10	9	8	7	6	5	4	3	2	1	0
1	1	1	0	1	0	0	1	1	1	EFFECTIVE ADDRESS MODE			REGISTER		
0	REGISTER			Do	OFFSET					Dw	WIDTH				

Instruction Fields:

Effective Address field — Specifies the base location for the bit field. Only data register direct or control addressing modes are allowed as shown:

Addressing Mode	Mode	Register	Addressing Mode	Mode	Register
Dn	000	reg. number:Dn	(xxx).W	111	000
An	—	—	(xxx).L	111	001
(An)	010	reg. number:An	#⟨data⟩	—	—
(An) +	—	—			
− (An)	—	—			
(d$_{16}$,An)	101	reg. number:An	(d$_{16}$,PC)	111	010
(d$_8$,An,Xn)	110	reg. number:An	(d$_8$,PC,Xn)	111	011
(bd,An,Xn)	110	reg. number:An	(bd,PC,Xn)	111	011
([bd,An,Xn],od)	110	reg. number:An	([bd,PC,Xn],od)	111	011
([bd,An],Xn,od)	110	reg. number:An	([bd,PC],Xn,od)	111	011

BFEXTU

Register field — Specifies the destination data register.

Do field — Determines how the field offset is specified.

    0 — The Offset field contains the bit field offset.

    1 — Bits [8:6] of the extension word specify a data register that contains the offset; bits [10:9] are zero.

Offset field — Specifies the field offset, depending on Do.

    If Do = 0, the Offset field is an immediate operand; the operand value is in the range of 0–31.

    If Do = 1, the Offset field specifies a data register that contains the offset. The value is in the range of -2^{31} to $2^{31} - 1$.

Dw field — Determines how the field width is specified.

    0 — The Width field contains the bit field width.

    1 — Bits [2:0] of the extension word specify a data register that contains the width; bits [4:3] are zero.

Width field — Specifies the field width, depending on Dw.

    If Dw = 0, the Width field is an immediate operand; operand values in the range of 1–31 specify a field width of 1–31, and a value of zero specifies a width of 32.

    If Dw = 1, the Width field specifies a data register that contains the width. The value is modulo 32; values of 1–31 specify field widths of 1–31, and a value of zero specifies a width of 32.

BFFFO

Find First One in Bit Field
(MC68020/MC68030/MC68040)

Operation: ⟨bit offset⟩ of Source Bit Scan ▶ Dn

Assembler
Syntax: BFFFO ⟨ea⟩{offset:width},Dn

Attributes: Unsized

Description: Searches the source operand for the most significant bit that is set to a value of one. The bit offset of that bit (the bit offset in the instruction plus the offset of the first one bit) is placed in Dn. If no bit in the bit field is set to one, the value in Dn is the field offset plus the field width. The instruction sets the condition codes according to the bit field value.

The field offset and field width select the field. The field offset specifies the starting bit of the field. The field width determines the number of bits in the field.

BFFFO

Condition Codes:

X	N	Z	V	C
—	*	*	0	0

X   Not affected.
N   Set if the most significant bit of the field is set. Cleared otherwise.
Z   Set if all bits of the field are zero. Cleared otherwise.
V   Always cleared.
C   Always cleared.

Instruction Format:

15	14	13	12	11	10	9	8	7	6	5	4	3	2	1	0
1	1	1	0	1	1	0	1	1	1	EFFECTIVE ADDRESS MODE			REGISTER		
0	REGISTER			Do	OFFSET					Dw	WIDTH				

Instruction Fields:

Effective Address field — Specifies the base location for the bit field. Only data register direct or control addressing modes are allowed as shown:

Addressing Mode	Mode	Register	Addressing Mode	Mode	Register
Dn	000	reg. number:Dn	(xxx).W	111	000
An	—	—	(xxx).L	111	001
(An)	010	reg. number:An	#(data)	—	—
(An) +	—	—			
−(An)	—	—			
(d$_{16}$,An)	101	reg. number:An	(d$_{16}$,PC)	111	010
(d$_8$,An,Xn)	110	reg. number:An	(d$_8$,PC,Xn)	111	011
(bd,An,Xn)	110	reg. number:An	(bd,PC,Xn)	111	011
([bd,An,Xn],od)	110	reg. number:An	([bd,PC,Xn],od)	111	011
([bd,An],Xn,od)	110	reg. number:An	([bd,PC],Xn,od)	111	011

Register field — Specifies the destination data register operand.
Do field — Determines how the field offset is specified.
   0 — The Offset field contains the bit field offset.
   1 — Bits [8:6] of the extension word specify a data register that contains the offset; bits [10:9] are zero.
Offset field — Specifies the field offset, depending on Do.
   If Do = 0, the Offset field is an immediate operand; the operand value is in the range of 0–31.
   If Do = 1, the Offset field specifies a data register that contains the offset. The value is in the range of -2^{31} to $2^{31} - 1$.
Dw field — Determines how the field width is specified.
   0 — The Width field contains the bit field width.

BFFFO

1 — Bits [2:0] of the extension word specify a data register that contains the width; bits [4:3] are zero.

Width field — Specifies the field width, depending on Dw.

If Dw = 0, the Width field is an immediate operand; operand values in the range of 1–31 specify a field width of 1–31, and a value of zero specifies a width of 32.

If Dw = 1, the Width field specifies a data register that contains the width. The value is modulo 32; values of 1–31 specify field widths of 1–31, and a value of zero specifies a width of 32.

BFINS

Insert Bit Field
(MC68020/MC68030/MC68040)

Operation: Dn ◗ ⟨bit field⟩ of Destination

**Assembler
Syntax:**   BFINS Dn,⟨ea⟩{offset:width}

Attributes: Unsized

Description: Inserts a bit field taken from the low-order bits of the specified data register into a bit field at the effective address location. The instruction sets the condition codes according to the inserted value.

The field offset and field width select the field. The field offset specifies the starting bit of the field. The field width determines the number of bits in the field.

Condition Codes:

X	N	Z	V	C
—	*	*	0	0

X   Not affected.
N   Set if the most significant bit of the field is set. Cleared otherwise.
Z   Set if all bits of the field are zero. Cleared otherwise.
V   Always cleared.
C   Always cleared.

Instruction Format:

15	14	13	12	11	10	9	8	7	6	5	4	3	2	1	0
1	1	1	0	1	1	1	1	1	1	EFFECTIVE ADDRESS					

15	14	13	12	11	10	9	8	7	6	5	4	3	2	1	0
1	1	1	0	1	1	1	1	1	1	MODE			REGISTER		
0	REGISTER		Do	OFFSET					Dw	WIDTH					

BFINS

Instruction Fields:

Effective Address field — Specifies the base location for the bit field. Only data register direct or control alterable addressing modes are allowed as shown:

Addressing Mode	Mode	Register	Addressing Mode	Mode	Register
Dn	000	reg. number:Dn	(xxx).W	111	000
An	—	—	(xxx).L	111	001
(An)	010	reg. number:An	#⟨data⟩	—	—
(An)+	—	—			
−(An)	—	—			
(d$_{16}$,An)	101	reg. number:An	(d$_{16}$,PC)	—	—
(d$_8$,An,Xn)	110	reg. number:An	(d$_8$,PC,Xn)	—	—
(bd,An,Xn)	110	reg. number:An	(bd,PC,Xn)	—	—
([bd,An,Xn],od)	110	reg. number:An	([bd,PC,Xn],od)	—	—
([bd,An],Xn,od)	110	reg. number:An	([bd,PC],Xn,od)	—	—

Register field — Specifies the source data register operand.

Do field — Determines how the field offset is specified.

   0 — The Offset field contains the bit field offset.

   1 — Bits [8:6] of the extension word specify a data register that contains the offset; bits [10:9] are zero.

Offset field — Specifies the field offset, depending on Do.

   If Do = 0, the Offset field is an immediate operand; the operand value is in the range of 0–31.

   If Do = 1, the Offset field specifies a data register that contains the offset. The value is in the range of -2^{31} to $2^{31}-1$.

Dw field — Determines how the field width is specified.

   0 — The Width field contains the bit field width.

   1 — Bits [2:0] of the extension word specify a data register that contains the width; bits [4:3] are zero.

Width field — Specifies the field width, depending on Dw.

   If Dw = 0, the Width field is an immediate operand; operand values in the range of 1–31 specify a field width of 1–31, and a value of zero specifies a width of 32.

   If Dw = 1, the Width field specifies a data register that contains the width. The value is modulo 32; values of 1–31 specify field widths of 1–31, and a value of zero specifies a width of 32.

BFSET

Test Bit Field and Set
(MC68020/MC68030/MC68040)

Operation: 1s ♦ ⟨bit field⟩ of Destination

BFSET

**Assembler
Syntax:**   BFSET ⟨ea⟩{offset:width}

Attributes: Unsized

Description: Sets the condition codes according to the value in a bit field at the specified effective address, then sets each bit in the field.

The field offset and the field width select the field. The field offset specifies the starting bit of the field. The field width determines the number of bits in the field.

Condition Codes:

X	N	Z	V	C
—	*	*	0	0

X   Not affected.
N   Set if the most significant bit of the field is set. Cleared otherwise.
Z   Set if all bits of the field are zero. Cleared otherwise.
V   Always cleared.
C   Always cleared.

Instruction Format:

15	14	13	12	11	10	9	8	7	6	5	4	3	2	1	0
1	1	1	0	1	1	1	0	1	1	EFFECTIVE ADDRESS					
										MODE			REGISTER		
0	0	0	0	Do		OFFSET			Dw		WIDTH				

Instruction Fields:

Effective Address field — Specifies the base location for the bit field. Only data register direct or control alterable addressing modes are allowed as shown:

Addressing Mode	Mode	Register	Addressing Mode	Mode	Register
Dn	000	reg. number:Dn	(xxx).W	111	000
An	—	—	(xxx).L	111	001
(An)	010	reg. number:An	#⟨data⟩	—	—
(An)+	—	—			
−(An)	—	—			
(d16,An)	101	reg. number:An	(d16,PC)	—	—
(d8,An,Xn)	110	reg. number:An	(d8,PC,Xn)	—	—
(bd,An,Xn)	110	reg. number:An	(bd,PC,Xn)	—	—
([bd,An,Xn],od)	110	reg. number:An	([bd,PC,Xn],od)	—	—
([bd,An],Xn,od)	110	reg. number:An	([bd,PC],Xn,od)	—	—

BFSET

Do field — Determines how the field offset is specified.

0 — The Offset field contains the bit field offset.

1 — Bits [8:6] of the extension word specify a data register that contains the offset; bits [10:9] are zero.

Offset field — Specifies the field offset, depending on Do.

If Do = 0, the Offset field is an immediate operand; the operand value is in the range of 0–31.

If Do = 1, the Offset field specifies a data register that contains the offset. The value is in the range of -2^{31} to $2^{31} - 1$.

Dw field — Determines how the field width is specified.

0 — The Width field contains the bit field width.

1 — Bits [2:0] of the extension word specify a data register that contains the width; bits [4:3] are zero.

Width field — Specifies the field width, depending on Dw.

If Dw = 0, the Width field is an immediate operand; operand values in the range of 1–31 specify a field width of 1–31, and a value of zero specifies a width of 32.

If Dw = 1, the Width field specifies a data register that contains the width. The value is modulo 32; values of 1–31 specify field widths of 1–31, and a value of zero specifies a width of 32.

BFTST

Test Bit Field
(MC68020/MC68030/MC68040)

Operation: ⟨bit field⟩ of Destination

Assembler
Syntax: BFTST ⟨ea⟩{offset:width}

Attributes: Unsized

Description: Sets the condition codes according to the value in a bit field at the specified effective address location.

The field offset and field width select the field. The field offset specifies the starting bit of the field. The field width determines the number of bits in the field.

Condition Codes:

X	N	Z	V	C
—	*	*	0	0

X   Not affected.

N   Set if the most significant bit of the field is set. Cleared otherwise.

BFTST

Z   Set if all bits of the field are zero. Cleared otherwise.
V   Always cleared.
C   Always cleared.

Instruction Format:

15	14	13	12	11	10	9	8	7	6	5	4	3	2	1	0
1	1	1	0	1	0	0	0	1	1	EFFECTIVE ADDRESS					

15	14	13	12	11	10	9	8	7	6	5	4	3	2	1	0
1	1	1	0	1	0	0	0	1	1	MODE			REGISTER		
0	0	0	0	Do	OFFSET					Dw	WIDTH				

Instruction Fields:

Effective Address field — Specifies the base location for the bit field. Only data register direct or control addressing modes are allowed as shown:

Addressing Mode	Mode	Register
Dn	000	reg. number:Dn
An	—	—
(An)	010	reg. number:An
(An) +	—	—
− (An)	—	—
(d$_{16}$,An)	101	reg. number:An
(d$_8$,An,Xn)	110	reg. number:An
(bd,An,Xn)	110	reg. number:An
([bd,An,Xn],od)	110	reg. number:An
([bd,An],Xn,od)	110	reg. number:An

Addressing Mode	Mode	Register
(xxx).W	111	000
(xxx).L	111	001
#(data)	—	—
(d$_{16}$,PC)	111	010
(d$_8$,PC,Xn)	111	011
(bd,PC,Xn)	111	011
([bd,PC,Xn],od)	111	011
([bd,PC],Xn,od)	111	011

Do field — Determines how the field offset is specified.
  0 — The Offset field contains the bit field offset.
  1 — Bits [8:6] of the extension word specify a data register that contains the offset; bits [10:9] are zero.
Offset field — Specifies the field offset, depending on Do.
  If Do = 0, the Offset field is an immediate operand; the operand value is in the range of 0–31.
  If Do = 1, the Offset field specifies a data register that contains the offset. The value is in the range of -2^{31} to $2^{31} - 1$.
Dw field — Determines how the field width is specified.
  0 — The Width field contains the bit field width.
  1 — Bits [2:0] of the extension word specify a data register that contains the width; bits [4:3] are zero.
Width field — Specifies the field width, depending on Dw.
  If Dw = 0, the Width field is an immediate operand, operand values in the range of 1–31 specify a field width of 1–31, and a value of zero specifies a width of 32.
  If Dw = 1, the Width field specifies a data register that contains the width. The value is modulo 32; values of 1–31 specify field widths of 1–31, and a value of zero specifies a width of 32.

BKPT

Breakpoint
(MC68010/MC68020/MC68030/MC68040/CPU32)

Operation: Run breakpoint acknowledge cycle;
TRAP as illegal instruction

**Assembler
Syntax:**   BKPT #⟨data⟩

Attributes: Unsized

Description: For the **MC68010**, a breakpoint acknowledge bus cycle is run with function codes driven high and zeros on all address lines. Whether the breakpoint acknowledge bus cycle is terminated with DTACK, BERR, or VPA, the processor always takes an illegal instruction exception. During exception processing, a debug monitor can distinguish different software breakpoints by decoding the field in the BKPT instruction. For the **MC68000** and **MC68008** the breakpoint cycle is not run but an illegal instruction exception is taken.

For the **MC68020**, **MC68030**, and **CPU32**, a breakpoint acknowledge bus cycle is executed with the immediate data (value 0–7) on bits 2–4 of the address bus and zeros on bits 0 and 1 of the address bus. The breakpoint acknowledge bus cycle accesses the CPU space, addressing type 0, and provides the breakpoint number specified by the instruction on address lines A2–A4. If the external hardware terminates the cycle with DSACKx or STERM, the data on the bus (an instruction word) is inserted into the instruction pipe and is executed after the breakpoint instruction. The breakpoint instruction requires a word to be transferred so, if the first bus cycle accesses an 8-bit port, a second bus cycle is required. If the external logic terminates the breakpoint acknowledge bus cycle with BERR (i.e., no instruction word available) the processor takes an illegal instruction exception.

For the **MC68040**, this instruction executes a breakpoint acknowledge bus cycle. Regardless of the cycle termination, the MC68040 takes an illegal instruction exception.

For more information on the breakpoint instruction refer to the appropriate processor user's manual on **BUS OPERATION**.

This instruction supports breakpoints for debug monitors and real-time hardware emulators.

BKPT

Condition Codes:
Not affected.

Instruction Format:

15	14	13	12	11	10	9	8	7	6	5	4	3	2	1	0
0	1	0	0	1	0	0	0	0	1	0	0	1		VECTOR	

Instruction Fields:
Vector field — Contains the immediate data, a value in the range of 0–7. This is the breakpoint number.

BRA

Branch Always
(M68000 Family)

Operation: PC + d ♦ PC

Assembler Syntax: BRA ⟨label⟩

Attributes: Size = (Byte, Word, Long*)
*(MC68020/MC68030/MC68040 only)

Description: Program execution continues at location (PC) + displacement. The PC contains the address of the instruction word of the BRA instruction plus two. The displacement is a twos complement integer that represents the relative distance in bytes from the current PC to the destination PC. If the 8-bit displacement field in the instruction word is zero, a 16-bit displacement (the word immediately following the instruction) is used. If the 8-bit displacement field in the instruction word is all ones ($FF), the 32-bit displacement (long word immediately following the instruction) is used.

Condition Codes:
Not affected.

Instruction Format:

15	14	13	12	11	10	9	8	7	6	5	4	3	2	1	0
0	1	1	0	0	0	0	0	8-BIT DISPLACEMENT							
16-BIT DISPLACEMENT IF 8-BIT DISPLACEMENT = $00															
32-BIT DISPLACEMENT IF 8-BIT DISPLACEMENT = $FF															

BRA

Instruction Fields:

8-Bit Displacement field — Twos complement integer specifying the number of bytes between the branch instruction and the next instruction to be executed.

16-Bit Displacement field — Used for a larger displacement when the 8-bit displacement is equal to $00.

32-Bit Displacement field — Used for a larger displacement when the 8-bit displacement is equal to $FF.

NOTE

A branch to the immediately following instruction automatically uses the 16-bit displacement format because the 8-bit displacement field contains $00 (zero offset).

BSET

Test a Bit and Set
(M68000 Family)

Operation: $\sim(\langle$bit number$\rangle$ of Destination$) \blacktriangleright$ Z;
$1 \blacktriangleright \langle$bit number$\rangle$ of Destination

Assembler   BSET Dn,$\langle$ea$\rangle$
Syntax: BSET #$\langle$data$\rangle$,$\langle$ea$\rangle$

Attributes: Size = (Byte, Long)

Description: Tests a bit in the destination operand and sets the Z condition code appropriately. Then sets the specified bit in the destination operand. When a data register is the destination, any of the 32 bits can be specified by a modulo 32-bit number. When a memory location is the destination, the operation is a byte operation, and the bit number is modulo 8. In all cases, bit zero refers to the least significant bit. The bit number for this operation can be specified in either of two ways:

1. Immediate — The bit number is specified in the second word of the instruction.
2. Register — The specified data register contains the bit number.

Condition Codes:

X	N	Z	V	C
—	—	*	—	—

BSET

X   Not affected.
N   Not affected.
Z   Set if the bit tested is zero. Cleared otherwise.
V   Not affected.
C   Not affected.

Instruction Format (Bit Number Dynamic, specified in a register):

15	14	13	12	11	10	9	8	7	6	5	4	3	2	1	0
0	0	0	0		REGISTER		1	1	1		EFFECTIVE ADDRESS				
											MODE			REGISTER	

Instruction Fields (Bit Number Dynamic):

Register field — Specifies the data register that contains the bit number.

Effective Address field — Specifies the destination location. Only data alterable addressing modes are allowed as shown:

Addressing Mode	Mode	Register
Dn*	000	reg. number:Dn
An	—	—
(An)	010	reg. number:An
(An)+	011	reg. number:An
–(An)	100	reg. number:An
(d$_{16}$,An)	101	reg. number:An
(d$_8$,An,Xn)	110	reg. number:An

Addressing Mode	Mode	Register
(xxx).W	111	000
(xxx).L	111	001
#(data)	—	—
(d$_{16}$,PC)	—	—
(d$_8$,PC,Xn)	—	—

MC68020, MC68030, AND MC68040 ONLY

Addressing Mode	Mode	Register
(bd,An,Xn)**	110	reg. number:An
([bd,An,Xn],od)	110	reg. number:An
([bd,An],Xn,od)	110	reg. number:An

Addressing Mode	Mode	Register
(bd,PC,Xn)**	—	—
([bd,PC,Xn],od)	—	—
([bd,PC],Xn,od)	—	—

*Long only; all others are byte only.
**Can be used with CPU32.

Instruction Format (Bit Number Static, specified as immediate data):

15	14	13	12	11	10	9	8	7	6	5	4	3	2	1	0
0	0	0	0	1	0	0	0	1	1		EFFECTIVE ADDRESS				
											MODE			REGISTER	
0	0	0	0	0	0	0				BIT NUMBER					

Instruction Fields (Bit Number Static):

Effective Address field — Specifies the destination location. Only data alterable addressing modes are allowed as shown:

BSET

Addressing Mode	Mode	Register	Addressing Mode	Mode	Register
Dn*	000	reg. number:Dn	(xxx).W	111	000
An	—	—	(xxx).L	111	001
(An)	010	reg. number:An	#(data)	—	—
(An)+	011	reg. number:An			
–(An)	100	reg. number:An			
(d16,An)	101	reg. number:An	(d16,PC)	—	—
(d8,An,Xn)	110	reg. number:An	(d8,PC,Xn)	—	—

MC68020, MC68030, AND MC68040 ONLY

Addressing Mode	Mode	Register	Addressing Mode	Mode	Register
(bd,An,Xn)**	110	reg. number:An	(bd,PC,Xn)**	—	—
([bd,An,Xn],od)	110	reg. number:An	([bd,PC,Xn],od)	—	—
([bd,An],Xn,od)	110	reg. number:An	([bd,PC],Xn,od)	—	—

*Long only; all others are byte only.
**Can be used with CPU32.

Bit Number field — Specifies the bit number.

BSR

Branch to Subroutine
(M68000 Family)

Operation: SP − 4 ⬧ SP; PC ⬧ (SP); PC + d ⬧ PC

**Assembler
Syntax:**   BSR ⟨label⟩

Attributes: Size = (Byte, Word, Long*)
*(MC68020/MC68030/MC68040 only)

Description: Pushes the long word address of the instruction immediately following the BSR instruction onto the system stack. The PC contains the address of the instruction word plus two. Program execution then continues at location (PC) + displacement. The displacement is a twos complement integer that represents the relative distance in bytes from the current PC to the destination PC. If the 8-bit displacement field in the instruction word is zero, a 16-bit displacement (the word immediately following the instruction) is used. If the 8-bit displacement field in the instruction word is all ones ($FF), the 32-bit displacement (long word immediately following the instruction) is used.

Condition Codes:
Not affected.

BSR

Instruction Format:

15	14	13	12	11	10	9	8	7	6	5	4	3	2	1	0
0	1	1	0	0	0	0	1			8-BIT DISPLACEMENT					

16-BIT DISPLACEMENT IF 8-BIT DISPLACEMENT = $00

32-BIT DISPLACEMENT IF 8-BIT DISPLACEMENT = $FF

Instruction Fields:

8-Bit Displacement field — Twos complement integer specifying the number of bytes between the branch instruction and the next instruction to be executed.

16-Bit Displacement field — Used for a larger displacement when the 8-bit displacement is equal to $00.

32-Bit Displacement field — Used for a larger displacement when the 8-bit displacement is equal to $FF.

NOTE

A branch to the immediately following instruction automatically uses the 16-bit displacement format because the 8-bit displacement field contains $00 (zero offset).

BTST

Test a Bit
(M68000 Family)

Operation: − (⟨bit number⟩ of Destination) ⟩ Z;

Assembler
Syntax: BTST Dn,⟨ea⟩
BTST #⟨data⟩,⟨ea⟩

Attributes: Size = (Byte, Long)

Description: Tests a bit in the destination operand and sets the Z condition code appropriately. When a data register is the destination, any of the 32 bits can be specified by a modulo 32-bit number. When a memory location is the destination, the operation is a byte operation, and the bit number is modulo 8. In all cases, bit zero refers to the least significant bit. The bit number for this operation can be specified in either of two ways:

1. Immediate — The bit number is specified in a second word of the instruction.
2. Register — The specified data register contains the bit number.

BTST

Condition Codes:

X	N	Z	V	C
—	—	*	—	—

X Not affected.
N Not affected.
Z Set if the bit tested is zero. Cleared otherwise.
V Not affected.
C Not affected.

Instruction Format (Bit Number Dynamic, specified in a register):

15	14	13	12	11	10	9	8	7	6	5	4	3	2	1	0
0	0	0	0		REGISTER		1	0	0		EFFECTIVE ADDRESS MODE			REGISTER	

Instruction Fields (Bit Number Dynamic):

Register field — Specifies the data register that contains the bit number.
Effective Address field — Specifies the destination location. Only data addressing modes are allowed as shown:

Addressing Mode	Mode	Register
Dn*	000	reg. number:Dn
An	—	—
(An)	010	reg. number:An
(An)+	011	reg. number:An
−(An)	100	reg. number:An
(d$_{16}$,An)	101	reg. number:An
(d$_8$,An,Xn)	110	reg. number:An

Addressing Mode	Mode	Register
(xxx).W	111	000
(xxx).L	111	001
#(data)	111	100
(d$_{16}$,PC)	111	010
(d$_8$,PC,Xn)	111	011

MC68020, MC68030, AND MC68040 ONLY

Addressing Mode	Mode	Register
(bd,An,Xn)**	110	reg. number:An
([bd,An,Xn],od)	110	reg. number:An
([bd,An],Xn,od)	110	reg. number:An

Addressing Mode	Mode	Register
(bd,PC,Xn)**	111	011
([bd,PC,Xn],od)	111	011
([bd,PC],Xn,od)	111	011

*Long only; all others are byte only.
**Can be used with CPU32.

Instruction Format (Bit Number Static, specified as immediate data):

15	14	13	12	11	10	9	8	7	6	5	4	3	2	1	0
0	0	0	0	1	0	0	0	0	0		EFFECTIVE ADDRESS MODE			REGISTER	
0	0	0	0	0	0	0	0				BIT NUMBER				

BTST

Instruction Fields (Bit Number Static):

Effective Address field — Specifies the destination location. Only data addressing modes are allowed as shown:

Addressing Mode	Mode	Register	Addressing Mode	Mode	Register
Dn	000	reg. number:Dn	(xxx).W	111	000
An	—	—	(xxx).L	111	001
(An)	010	reg. number:An	#⟨data⟩	—	—
(An)+	011	reg. number:An			
−(An)	100	reg. number:An			
(d$_{16}$,An)	101	reg. number:An	(d$_{16}$,PC)	111	010
(d$_8$,An,Xn)	110	reg. number:An	(d$_8$,PC,Xn)	111	011

MC68020, MC68030, AND MC68040 ONLY

Addressing Mode	Mode	Register	Addressing Mode	Mode	Register
(bd,An,Xn)*	110	reg. number:An	(bd,PC,Xn)*	111	011
([bd,An,Xn],od)	110	reg. number:An	([bd,PC,Xn],od)	111	011
([bd,An],Xn,od)	110	reg. number:An	([bd,PC],Xn,od)	111	011

*Can be used with CPU32.

Bit Number field — Specifies the bit number.

CALLM

CALL Module
(MC68020)

Operation: Save current module state on stack;
Load new module state from destination

**Assembler
Syntax:**   CALLM #⟨data⟩, ⟨ea⟩

Attributes: Unsized

Description: The effective address of the instruction is the location of an external module descriptior. A module frame is created on the top of the stack, and the current module state is saved in the frame. The immediate operand specifies the number of bytes of arguments to be passed to the called module. A new module state is loaded from the descriptor addressed by the effective address.

Condition Codes:
Not affected.

CALLM

Instruction Format:

15	14	13	12	11	10	9	8	7	6	5	4	3	2	1	0
0	0	0	0	0	1	1	0	1	1	\multicolumn{6}{c}{EFFECTIVE ADDRESS}

15	14	13	12	11	10	9	8	7	6	5	4	3	2	1	0
0	0	0	0	0	1	1	0	1	1	MODE			REGISTER		
0	0	0	0	0	0	0	0	\multicolumn{8}{c}{ARGUMENT COUNT}

Instruction Fields:

Effective Address field — Specifies the address of the module descriptor. Only control addressing modes are allowed as shown:

Addressing Mode	Mode	Register	Addressing Mode	Mode	Register
Dn	—	—	(xxx).W	111	000
An	—	—	(xxx).L	111	001
(An)	010	reg. number:An	#(data)	—	—
(An) +	—	—			
– (An)	—	—			
(d$_{16}$,An)	101	reg. number:An	(d$_{16}$,PC)	111	010
(d$_8$,An,Xn)	110	reg. number:An	(d$_8$,PC,Xn)	111	011
(bd,An,Xn)	110	reg. number:An	(bd,PC,Xn)	111	011
([bd,An,Xn],od)	110	reg. number:An	([bd,PC,Xn],od)	111	011
([bd,An],Xn,od)	110	reg. number:An	([bd,PC],Xn,od)	111	011

Argument Count field — Specifies the number of bytes of arguments to be passed to the called module. The 8-bit field can specify from 0 to 255 bytes of arguments. The same number of bytes is removed from the stack by the RTM instruction.

CAS
CAS2

Compare and Swap with Operand
(MC68020/MC68030/MC68040)

Operation: CAS Destination — Compare Operand ⬧ cc;
    if Z, Update Operand ⬧ Destination
    else Destination ⬧ Compare Operand
CAS2 Destination 1 — Compare 1 ⬧ cc;
    if Z, Destination 2 — Compare 2 ⬧ cc
    if Z, Update 1 ⬧ Destination 1; Update 2 ⬧ Destination 2
    else Destination 1 ⬧ Compare 1; Destination 2 ⬧ Compare 2

Assembler   CAS Dc,Du,(ea)
Syntax: CAS2 Dc1:Dc2,Du1:Du2,(Rn1):(Rn2)

CAS
CAS2

Attributes: Size = (Byte*, Word, Long)

Description: CAS compares the effective address operand to the compare operand (Dc). If the operands are equal, the instruction writes the update operand (Du) to the effective address operand; otherwise, the instruction writes the effective address operand to the compare operand (Dc).

CAS2 compares memory operand 1 (Rn1) to compare operand 1 (Dc1). If the operands are equal, the instruction compares memory operand 2 (Rn2) to compare operand 2 (Dc2). If these operands are also equal, the instruction writes the update operands (Du1 and Du2) to the memory operands (Rn1 and Rn2). If either comparison fails, the instruction writes the memory operands (Rn1 and Rn2) to the compare operands (Dc1 and Dc2).

Both operations access memory using locked or read-modify-write transfer sequences. This provides a means of synchronizing several processors.

Condition Codes:

X	N	Z	V	C
—	*	*	*	*

X   Not affected.
N   Set if the result is negative. Cleared otherwise.
Z   Set if the result is zero. Cleared otherwise.
V   Set if an overflow is generated. Cleared otherwise.
C   Set if a borrow is generated. Cleared otherwise.

---

*CAS2 cannot use byte operands

Instruction Format: (CAS):

15	14	13	12	11	10	9	8	7	6	5	4	3	2	1	0
											EFFECTIVE ADDRESS				
0	0	0	0	1	SIZE		0	1	1	MODE			REGISTER		
0	0	0	0	0	0	0	Du			0	0	0	Dc		

Instruction Fields:

Size field — Specifies the size of the operation.
   01 — Byte operation.
   10 — Word operation.
   11 — Long operation.

Effective Address field — Specifies the location of the memory operand. Only memory alterable addressing modes are allowed as shown:

CAS
CAS2

Addressing Mode	Mode	Register
Dn	—	—
An	—	—
(An)	010	reg. number:An
(An)+	011	reg. number:An
–(An)	100	reg. number:An
(d16,An)	101	reg. number:An
(d8,An,Xn)	110	reg. number:An
(bd,An,Xn)	110	reg. number:An
([bd,An,Xn],od)	110	reg. number:An
([bd,An],Xn,od)	110	reg. number:An

Addressing Mode	Mode	Register
(xxx).W	111	000
(xxx).L	111	001
#(data)	—	—
(d16,PC)	—	—
(d8,PC,Xn)	—	—
(bd,PC,Xn)	—	—
([bd,PC,Xn],od)	—	—
([bd,PC],Xn,od)	—	—

Du field — Specifies the data register that contains the update value to be written to the memory operand location if the comparison is successful.

Dc field — Specifies the data register that contains the value to be compared to the memory operand.

Instruction Format (CAS2):

15	14	13	12	11	10	9	8	7	6	5	4	3	2	1	0
0	0	0	0	1	SIZE		0	1	1	1	1	1	1	0	0
D/A1	Rn1			0	0	0	Du1			0	0	0	Dc1		
D/A2	Rn2			0	0	0	Du2			0	0	0	Dc2		

Instruction Fields:

Size field — Specifies the size of the operation.

    10 — Word operation.

    11 — Long operation.

D/A1, D/A2 fields — Specify whether Rn1 and Rn2 reference data or address registers, respectively.

    0 — The corresponding register is a data register.

    1 — The corresponding register is an address register.

Rn1, Rn2 fields — Specify the numbers of the registers that contain the addresses of the first and second memory operands, respectively. If the operands overlap in memory, the results of any memory update are undefined.

Du1, Du2 fields — Specify the data registers that contain the update values to be written to the first and second memory operand locations if the comparison is successful.

Dc1, Dc2 fields — Specify the data registers that contain the test values to be compared to the first and second memory operands, respectively. If Dc1 and Dc2 specify the same data register and the comparison fails, memory operand 1 is stored in the data register.

CAS
CAS2

NOTES

The CAS and CAS2 instructions can be used to perform secure update operations on system control data structures in a multiprocessing environment.

In the MC68040 if the operands are not equal, the destination or destination 1 operand is written back to memory to complete the locked access for CAS or CAS2, respectively.

CHK

Check Register Against Bounds
(M68000 Family)

Operation: If Dn < 0 or Dn > Source then TRAP

Assembler
Syntax: CHK ⟨ea⟩,Dn

Attributes: Size = (Word, Long*)
*(MC68020/MC68030/MC68040 only)

Description: Compares the value in the data register specified in the instruction to zero and to the upper bound (effective address operand). The upper bound is a twos complement integer. If the register value is less than zero or greater than the upper bound, a CHK instruction exception, vector number 6, occurs.

Condition Codes:

X	N	Z	V	C
—	*	U	U	U

X Not affected.
N Set if Dn < 0; cleared if Dn > effective address operand.
   Undefined otherwise.
Z Undefined.
V Undefined.
C Undefined.

Instruction Format:

15	14	13	12	11	10	9	8	7	6	5	4	3	2	1	0
0	1	0	0	REGISTER			SIZE		0	EFFECTIVE ADDRESS					
										MODE			REGISTER		

CHK

Instruction Fields:

Register field — Specifies the data register that contains the value to be checked.

Size field — Specifies the size of the operation.

11 — Word operation.

10 — Long operation.

Effective Address field — Specifies the upper bound operand. Only data addressing modes are allowed as shown:

Addressing Mode	Mode	Register	Addressing Mode	Mode	Register
Dn	000	reg. number:Dn	(xxx).W	111	000
An	—	—	(xxx).L	111	001
(An)	010	reg. number:An	#(data)	111	100
(An)+	011	reg. number:An			
−(An)	100	reg. number:An			
(d$_{16}$,An)	101	reg. number:An	(d$_{16}$,PC)	111	010
(d$_8$,An,Xn)	110	reg. number:An	(d$_8$,PC,Xn)	111	011

MC68020, MC68030, AND MC68040 ONLY

Addressing Mode	Mode	Register	Addressing Mode	Mode	Register
(bd,An,Xn)*	110	reg. number:An	(bd,PC,Xn)*	111	011
([bd,An,Xn],od)	110	reg. number:An	([bd,PC,Xn],od)	111	011
([bd,An],Xn,od)	110	reg. number:An	([bd,PC],Xn,od)	111	011

*Can be used with CPU32.

CHK2

Check Register Against Bounds
(MC68020/MC68030/MC68040/CPU32)

Operation: If Rn < lower bound or
           Rn > upper bound
       then TRAP

Assembler Syntax: CHK2 ⟨ea⟩,Rn

Attributes: Size = (Byte, Word, Long)

Description: Compares the value in Rn to each bound. The effective address contains the bounds pair: the lower bound followed by the upper bound. For signed comparisons, the arithmetically smaller value should be used as the lower bound. For unsigned comparisons, the logically smaller value should be the lower bound.

CHK2

The size of the data and the bounds can be specified as byte, word, or long. If Rn is a data register and the operation size is byte or word, only the appropriate low-order part of Rn is checked. If Rn is an address register and the operation size is byte or word, the bounds operands are sign extended to 32 bits and the resultant operands are compared to the full 32 bits of An.

If the upper bound equals the lower bound, the valid range is a single value. If the register value is less than the lower bound or greater than the upper bound, a CHK instruction exception, vector number 6, occurs.

Condition Codes:

X	N	Z	V	C
—	U	*	U	*

X   Not affected.
N   Undefined.
Z   Set if Rn is equal to either bound. Cleared otherwise.
V   Undefined.
C   Set if Rn is out of bounds. Cleared otherwise.

Instruction Format:

15	14	13	12	11	10	9	8	7	6	5	4	3	2	1	0
0	0	0	0	0	SIZE		0	1	1	_MODE_ EFFECTIVE ADDRESS			REGISTER		
D A.	REGISTER			1	0	0	0	0	0	0	0	0	0	0	0

Instruction Fields:

Size field — Specifies the size of the operation.

00 — Byte operation
01 — Word operation.
10 — Long operation.

Effective Address field — Specifies the location of the bounds operands. Only control addressing modes are allowed as shown:

Addressing Mode	Mode	Register
Dn	—	—
An	—	—
(An)	010	reg. number:An
(An)+	—	—
−(An)	—	—
(d₁₆,An)	101	reg. number:An
(d₈,An,Xn)	110	reg. number:An
(bd,An,Xn)	110	reg. number:An

Addressing Mode	Mode	Register
(xxx).W	111	000
(xxx).L	111	001
#(data)	—	—
(d₁₆,PC)	111	010
(d₈,PC,Xn)	111	011
(bd,PC,Xn)	111	011

CHK2

MC68020, MC68030, AND MC68040 ONLY

([bd,An,Xn],od)	110	reg. number:An	([bd,PC,Xn],od)	111	011
([bd,An],Xn,od)	110	reg. number:An	([bd,PC],Xn,od)	111	011

D A field — Specifies whether an address register or data register is to be checked.
 0 — Data register.
 1 — Address register.
Register field — Specifies the address or data register that contains the value to be checked.

CLR

Clear an Operand
(M68000 Family)

Operation: 0 ▶ Destination

Assembler
Syntax: CLR ⟨ea⟩

Attributes: Size = (Byte, Word, Long)

Description: Clears the destination operand to zero. The size of the operation may be specified as byte, word, or long.

Condition Codes:

X	N	Z	V	C
—	0	1	0	0

X Not affected.
N Always cleared.
Z Always set.
V Always cleared.
C Always cleared.

Instruction Format:

15	14	13	12	11	10	9	8	7	6	5	4	3	2	1	0
0	1	0	0	0	0	1	0	SIZE		EFFECTIVE ADDRESS					
										MODE			REGISTER		

CLR

Instruction Fields:
   Size field — Specifies the size of the operation.
      00 — Byte operation.
      01 — Word operation.
      10 — Long operation.
   Effective Address field — Specifies the destination location. Only data alterable addressing modes are allowed as shown:

Addressing Mode	Mode	Register	Addressing Mode	Mode	Register
Dn	000	reg. number:Dn	(xxx).W	111	000
An	—	—	(xxx).L	111	001
(An)	010	reg. number:An	#⟨data⟩	—	—
(An) +	011	reg. number:An			
– (An)	100	reg. number:An			
(d$_{16}$,An)	101	reg. number:An	(d$_{16}$,PC)	—	—
(d$_8$,An,Xn)	110	reg. number:An	(d$_8$,PC,Xn)	—	—

MC68020, MC68030, AND MC68040 ONLY

Addressing Mode	Mode	Register	Addressing Mode	Mode	Register
(bd,An,Xn)∗	110	reg. number:An	(bd,PC,Xn)∗	—	—
([bd,An,Xn],od)	110	reg. number:An	([bd,PC,Xn],od)	—	—
([bd,An],Xn,od)	110	reg. number:An	([bd,PC],Xn,od)	—	—

∗Can be used with CPU32.

NOTE

In the MC68000 and MC68008 a memory location is read before it is cleared.

CMP

Compare
(M68000 Family)

Operation: Destination — Source ⧫ cc

Assembler
Syntax: CMP ⟨ea⟩, Dn

Attributes: Size = (Byte, Word, Long)

Description: Subtracts the source operand from the destination data register and sets the condition codes according to the result; the data register is not changed. The size of the operation can be byte, word, or long.

CMP

Condition Codes:

X	N	Z	V	C
—	*	*	*	*

X Not affected.
N Set if the result is negative. Cleared otherwise.
Z Set if the result is zero. Cleared otherwise.
V Set if an overflow occurs. Cleared otherwise.
C Set if a borrow occurs. Cleared otherwise.

Instruction Format:

15	14	13	12	11	10	9	8	7	6	5	4	3	2	1	0
1	0	1	1	REGISTER			OPMODE			EFFECTIVE ADDRESS MODE			REGISTER		

Instruction Fields:

Register field — Specifies the destination data register.
Opmode field:

Byte	Word	Long	Operation
000	001	010	(⟨Dn⟩) − (⟨ea⟩)

Effective Address field — Specifies the source operand. All addressing modes are allowed as shown:

Addressing Mode	Mode	Register
Dn	000	reg. number:Dn
An*	001	reg. number:An
(An)	010	reg. number:An
(An)+	011	reg. number:An
−(An)	100	reg. number:An
(d$_{16}$,An)	101	reg. number:An
(d$_8$,An,Xn)	110	reg. number:An

Addressing Mode	Mode	Register
(xxx).W	111	000
(xxx).L	111	001
#⟨data⟩	111	100
(d$_{16}$,PC)	111	010
(d$_8$,PC,Xn)	111	011

MC68020, MC68030, AND MC68040 ONLY

(bd,An,Xn)**	110	reg. number:An
([bd,An,Xn],od)	110	reg. number:An
([bd,An],Xn,od)	110	reg. number:An

(bd,PC,Xn)**	111	011
([bd,PC,Xn],od)	111	011
([bd,PC],Xn,od)	111	011

*Word and Long only.
**Can be used with CPU32.

NOTE

CMPA is used when the destination is an address register. CMPI is used when the source is immediate data. CMPM is used for memory-to-memory compares. Most assemblers automatically make the distinction.

CMPA

Compare Address
(M68000 Family)

Operation: Destination − Source

Assembler
Syntax: CMPA ⟨ea⟩, An

Attributes: Size = (Word, Long)

Description: Subtracts the source operand from the destination address register and sets the condition codes according to the result; the address register is not changed. The size of the operation can be specified as word or long. Word length source operands are sign extended to 32 bits for comparison.

Condition Codes:

X	N	Z	V	C
—	*	*	*	*

X   Not affected.
N   Set if the result is negative. Cleared otherwise.
Z   Set if the result is zero. Cleared otherwise.
V   Set if an overflow is generated. Cleared otherwise.
C   Set if a borrow is generated. Cleared otherwise.

Instruction Format:

15	14	13	12	11	10	9	8	7	6	5	4	3	2	1	0
1	0	1	1	REGISTER			OPMODE			EFFECTIVE ADDRESS					
										MODE			REGISTER		

Instruction Fields:
Register field — Specifies the destination address register.
Opmode field — Specifies the size of the operation:
   011 — Word operation. The source operand is sign extended to a long operand and the operation is performed on the address register using all 32 bits.
   111 — Long operation.
Effective Address field — Specifies the source operand. All addressing modes are allowed as shown:

CMPA

Addressing Mode	Mode	Register
Dn	000	reg. number:Dn
An	001	reg. number:An
(An)	010	reg. number:An
(An)+	011	reg. number:An
−(An)	100	reg. number:An
(d16,An)	101	reg. number:An
(d8,An,Xn)	110	reg. number:An

Addressing Mode	Mode	Register
(xxx).W	111	000
(xxx).L	111	001
#⟨data⟩	111	100
(d16,PC)	111	010
(d8,PC,Xn)	111	011

MC68020, MC68030, AND MC68040 ONLY

Addressing Mode	Mode	Register
(bd,An,Xn)*	110	reg. number:An
([bd,An,Xn],od)	110	reg. number:An
([bd,An],Xn,od)	110	reg. number:An

Addressing Mode	Mode	Register
(bd,PC,Xn)*	111	011
([bd,PC,Xn],od)	111	011
([bd,PC],Xn,od)	111	011

*Can be used with CPU32.

CMPI

Compare Immediate
(M68000 Family)

Operation: Destination − Immediate Data

Assembler Syntax: CMPI #⟨data⟩,⟨ea⟩

Attributes: Size = (Byte, Word, Long)

Description: Subtracts the immediate data from the destination operand and sets the condition codes according to the result; the destination location is not changed. The size of the operation may be specified as byte, word, or long. The size of the immediate data matches the operation size.

Condition Codes:

X	N	Z	V	C
—	*	*	*	*

X   Not affected.
N   Set if the result is negative. Cleared otherwise.
Z   Set if the result is zero. Cleared otherwise.
V   Set if an overflow occurs. Cleared otherwise.
C   Set if a borrow occurs. Cleared otherwise.

CMPI

Instruction Format:

15	14	13	12	11	10	9	8	7	6	5	4	3	2	1	0
0	0	0	0	1	1	0	0	SIZE		EFFECTIVE ADDRESS					
										MODE			REGISTER		
WORD DATA (16 BITS)								BYTE DATA (8 BITS)							
LONG DATA (32 BITS)															

Instruction Fields:

Size field — Specifies the size of the operation:

00 — Byte operation.

01 — Word operation.

10 — Long operation.

Effective Address field — Specifies the destination operand. Only data addressing modes are allowed as shown:

Addressing Mode	Mode	Register
Dn	000	reg. number:Dn
An	—	—
(An)	010	reg. number:An
(An) +	011	reg. number:An
(An)	100	reg. number:An
(d$_{16}$,An)	101	reg. number:An
(d$_8$,An,Xn)	110	reg. number:An

Addressing Mode	Mode	Register
(xxx).W	111	000
(xxx).L	111	001
#(data)	—	—
(d$_{16}$,PC)	111	010
(d$_8$,PC,Xn)	111	011

MC68020, MC68030, AND MC68040 ONLY

Addressing Mode	Mode	Register
(bd,An,Xn)*	110	reg. number:An
([bd,An,Xn],od)	110	reg. number:An
([bd,An],Xn,od)	110	reg. number:An

Addressing Mode	Mode	Register
(bd,PC,Xn)*	111	011
([bd,PC,Xn],od)	111	011
([bd,PC],Xn,od)	111	011

*Can be used with CPU32.

Immediate field — (Data immediately following the instruction):

If size = 00, the data is the low-order byte of the immediate word.

If size = 01, the data is the entire immediate word.

If size = 10, the data is the next two immediate words.

CMPM

Compare Memory
(M68000 Family)

Operation: Destination — Source ♦ cc

Assembler
Syntax: CMPM (Ay) + ,(Ax) +

Attributes: Size = (Byte, Word, Long)

Description: Subtracts the source operand from the destination operand and sets
the condition codes according to the results; the destination location is not
changed. The operands are always addressed with the postincrement addressing mode, using the address registers specified in the instruction. The size of
the operation may be specified as byte, word, or long.

Condition Codes:

X	N	Z	V	C
—	*	*	*	*

X   Not affected.
N   Set if the result is negative. Cleared otherwise.
Z   Set if the result is zero. Cleared otherwise.
V   Set if an overflow is generated. Cleared otherwise.
C   Set if a borrow is generated. Cleared otherwise.

Instruction Format:

15	14	13	12	11	10	9	8	7	6	5	4	3	2	1	0
1	0	1	1	REGISTER Ax			1	SIZE		0	0	1	REGISTER Ay		

Instruction Fields:

Register Ax field — (always the destination) Specifies an address register in
the postincrement addressing mode.

Size field — Specifies the size of the operation:

00 — Byte operation.
01 — Word operation.
10 — Long operation.

Register Ay field — (always the source) Specifies an address register in the
postincrement addressing mode.

CMP2

Compare Register Against Bounds
(MC68020/MC68030/MC68040/CPU32)

Operation: Compare Rn < lower-bound or
Rn > upper-bound
and Set Condition Codes

**Assembler
Syntax:**   CMP2 ⟨ea⟩,Rn

Attributes: Size = (Byte, Word, Long)

Description: Compares the value in Rn to each bound. The effective address contains the bounds pair: the lower bound followed by the upper bound. For signed comparisons, the arithmetically smaller value should be used as the lower bound. For unsigned comparisons, the logically smaller value should be the lower bound.

The size of the data and the bounds can be specified as byte, word, or long. If Rn is a data register and the operation size is byte or word, only the appropriate low-order part of Rn is checked. If Rn is an address register and the operation size is byte or word, the bounds operands are sign extended to 32 bits and the resultant operands are compared to the full 32 bits of An.

If the upper bound equals the lower bound, the valid range is a single value.

NOTE
This instruction is identical to CHK2 except that it sets condition codes rather than taking an exception when the value in Rn is out of bounds.

Condition Codes:

X	N	Z	V	C
—	U	*	U	*

X   Not affected.
N   Undefined.
Z   Set if Rn is equal to either bound. Cleared otherwise.
V   Undefined.
C   Set if Rn is out of bounds. Cleared otherwise.

Instruction Format:

15	14	13	12	11	10	9	8	7	6	5	4	3	2	1	0
0	0	0	0	0	SIZE		0	1	1	EFFECTIVE ADDRESS					
										MODE			REGISTER		
D/A	REGISTER			0	0	0	0	0	0	0	0	0	0	0	0

CMP2

Instruction Fields:
  Size field — Specifies the size of the operation.
  00 — Byte operation.
  01 — Word operation.
  10 — Long operation.
  Effective Address field — Specifies the location of the bounds pair. Only control addressing modes are allowed as shown:

Addressing Mode	Mode	Register	Addressing Mode	Mode	Register
Dn	—	—	(xxx).W	111	000
An	—	—	(xxx).L	111	001
(An)	010	reg. number:An	#⟨data⟩	—	—
(An) +	—	—			
− (An)	—	—			
(d16,An)	101	reg. number:An	(d16,PC)	111	010
(d8,An,Xn)	110	reg. number:An	(d8,PC,Xn)	111	011
(bd,An,Xn)	110	reg. number:An	(bd,PC,Xn)	111	011

MC68020, MC68030, AND MC68040 ONLY

([bd,An,Xn],od)	110	reg. number:An	([bd,PC,Xn],od)	111	011
([bd,An],Xn,od)	110	reg. number:An	([bd,PC],Xn,od)	111	011

  D/A field — Specifies whether an address register or data register is compared.
  0 — Data register.
  1 — Address register.
  Register field — Specifies the address or data register that contains the value to be checked.

cpBcc

Branch on Coprocessor Condition
(MC68020/MC68030)

Operation: If cpcc true then scanPC + d ⬧ PC

Assembler
Syntax: cpBcc ⟨label⟩

Attributes: Size = (Word, Long)

Description: If the specified coprocessor condition is true, program execution continues at location scanPC + displacement. The value of the scanPC is the address of the first displacement word. The displacement is a twos complement integer that represents the relative distance in bytes from the scanPC to the

cpBcc

destination PC. The displacement can be either 16 bits or 32 bits. The coprocessor determines the specific condition from the condition field in the operation word.

Condition Codes:
Not affected.

Instruction Format:

15	14	13	12	11	10	9	8	7	6	5	4	3	2	1	0
1	1	1	1	CP-ID			0	1	SIZE	COPROCESSOR CONDITION					

OPTIONAL COPROCESSOR-DEFINED EXTENSION WORDS

WORD OR
LONG WORD DISPLACEMENT

Instruction Fields:

Cp-Id field — Identifies the coprocessor for this operation. Cp-Id of 000 results in an F-line exception for the MC68030.

Size field — Specifies the size of the displacement.

0 — The displacement is 16 bits.

1 — The displacement is 32 bits.

Coprocessor Condition field — Specifies the coprocessor condition to be tested. This field is passed to the coprocessor which provides directives to the main processor for processing this instruction.

16-Bit Displacement field — The displacement value occupies 16 bits.

32-Bit Displacement field — The displacement value occupies 32 bits.

cpDBcc

Test Coprocessor Condition
Decrement and Branch
(MC68020/MC68030)

Operation: If cpcc false then (Dn − 1 ⬦ Dn; If Dn ≠ −1 then scanPC + d ⬦ PC)

Assembler
Syntax: cpDBcc Dn,⟨label⟩

Attributes: Size = (Word)

Description: If the specified coprocessor condition is true, execution continues with the next instruction. Otherwise, the low-order word in the specified data register is decremented by one. If the result is equal to − 1, execution continues with the next instruction. If the result is not equal to − 1, execution continues at the location indicated by the value of the scanPC plus the sign extended 16-

cpDBcc

bit displacement. The value of the scanPC is the address of the displacement word. The displacement is a twos complement integer that represents the relative distance in bytes from the scanPC to the destination PC. The coprocessor determines the specific condition from the condition word which follows the operation word.

Condition Codes:
Not affected.

Instruction Format:

15	14	13	12	11	10	9	8	7	6	5	4	3	2	1	0
1	1	1	1		CP-ID		0	0	1	0	0	1		REGISTER	
0	0	0	0	0	0	0	0	0	0			COPROCESSOR CONDITION			
OPTIONAL COPROCESSOR-DEFINED EXTENSION WORDS															
DISPLACEMENT (16 BIT)															

Instruction Fields:
Cp-Id field — Identifies the coprocessor for this operation. Cp-Id of 000 results in an F-line exception for the MC68030.

Register field — Specifies the data register used as the counter.

Coprocessor Condition field — Specifies the coprocessor condition to be tested. This field is passed to the coprocessor which provides directives to the main processor for processing this instruction.

Displacement field — Specifies the distance of the branch (in bytes).

cpGEN

Coprocessor General Function
(MC68020/MC68030)

Operation: Pass Command Word to Coprocessor

Assembler Syntax: cpGEN ⟨parameters as defined by coprocessor⟩

Attributes: Unsized

Description: Transfers the command word that follows the operation word to the specified coprocessor. The coprocessor determines the specific operation from the command word. Usually a coprocessor defines specific instances of this instruction to provide its instruction set.

Condition Codes:
May be modified by coprocessor. Unchanged otherwise.

cpGEN

Instruction Format:

15	14	13	12	11	10	9	8	7	6	5	4	3	2	1	0
1	1	1	1		CP-ID		0	0	0		EFFECTIVE ADDRESS MODE			REGISTER	

COPROCESSOR-DEPENDENT COMMAND WORD

OPTIONAL EFFECTIVE ADDRESS OR COPROCESSOR-DEFINED EXTENSION WORDS

Instruction Fields:

Cp-Id field — Identifies the coprocessor for this operation. Note that Cp-Id of 000 is reserved for MMU instructions for the MC68030.

Effective Address field — Specifies the location of any operand not resident in the coprocessor. The allowable addressing modes are determined by the operation to be performed.

Coprocessor Command field — Specifies the coprocessor operation to be performed. This word is passed to the coprocessor, which in turn provides directives to the main processor for processing this instruction.

cpScc

Set on Coprocessor Condition
(MC68020/MC68030)

Operation: If cpcc true then 1s ◆ Destination
else 0s ◆ Destination

Assembler
Syntax: cpScc ⟨ea⟩

Attributes: Size = (Byte)

Description: Tests the specified coprocessor condition code; if the condition is true, the byte specified by the effective address is set to TRUE (all ones), otherwise that byte is set to FALSE (all zeros). The coprocessor determines the specific condition from the condition word that follows the operation word.

Condition Codes:
Not affected.

Instruction Format:

15	14	13	12	11	10	9	8	7	6	5	4	3	2	1	0
1	1	1	1		CP-ID		0	0	1		EFFECTIVE ADDRESS MODE			REGISTER	
0	0	0	0	0	0	0	0	0	0		COPROCESSOR CONDITION				

OPTIONAL EFFECTIVE ADDRESS OR COPROCESSOR-DEFINED EXTENSION WORDS

cpScc

Instruction Fields:

Cp-Id field — Identifies the coprocessor for this operation. Cp-Id of 000 results in an F-line exception for the MC68030.

Effective Address field — Specifies the destination location. Only data alterable addressing modes are allowed as shown:

Addressing Mode	Mode	Register	Addressing Mode	Mode	Register
Dn	000	reg. number:Dn	(xxx).W	111	000
An	—	—	(xxx).L	111	001
(An)	010	reg. number:An	#⟨data⟩	—	—
(An)+	011	reg. number:An			
−(An)	100	reg. number:An			
(d$_{16}$,An)	101	reg. number:An	(d$_{16}$,PC)	—	—
(d$_8$,An,Xn)	110	reg. number:An	(d$_8$,PC,Xn)	—	—
(bd,An,Xn)	110	reg. number:An	(bd,PC,Xn)	—	—
([bd,An,Xn],od)	110	reg. number:An	([bd,PC,Xn],od)	—	—
([bd,An],Xn,od)	110	reg. number:An	([bd,PC],Xn,od)	—	—

Coprocessor Condition field — Specifies the coprocessor condition to be tested. This field is passed to the coprocessor, which in turn provides directives to the main processor for processing this instruction.

cpTRAPcc

Trap on Coprocessor Condition
(MC68020/MC68030)

Operation: If cpcc true then TRAP

Assembler   cpTRAPcc
Syntax: cpTRAPcc #⟨data⟩

Attributes: Unsized or Size = (Word, Long)

Description: Tests the specified coprocessor condition code; if the selected co-processor condition is true, the processor initiates a cpTRAPcc exception, vector number 7. The program counter value placed on the stack is the address of the next instruction. If the selected condition is not true, no operation is performed, and execution continues with the next instruction. The coprocessor determines the specific condition from the condition word that follows the operation word. Following the condition word is a user-defined data operand specified as immediate data to be used by the trap handler.

Condition Codes:
Not affected.

cpTRAPcc

Instruction Format:

15	14	13	12	11	10	9	8	7	6	5	4	3	2	1	0
1	1	1	1		CP-ID		0	0	1	1	1	1		OPMODE	
0	0	0	0	0	0	0	0	0	0		COPROCESSOR CONDITION				
OPTIONAL COPROCESSOR-DEFINED EXTENSION WORDS															
OPTIONAL WORD															
OR LONG WORD OPERAND															

Instruction Fields:

Cp-Id field — Identifies the coprocessor for this operation. Cp-Id of 000 results in an F-line exception for the MC68030.

Opmode field — Selects the instruction form.

010 — Instruction is followed by one operand word.

011 — Instruction is followed by two operand words.

100 — Instruction has no following operand words.

Coprocessor Condition field — Specifies the coprocessor condition to be tested. This field is passed to the coprocessor, which provides directives to the main processor for processing this instruction.

DBcc

Test Condition, Decrement, and Branch
(M68000 Family)

Operation: If condition false then (Dn − 1 ▸ Dn;
If Dn ≠ −1 then PC + d ▸ PC)

**Assembler
Syntax:**   DBcc Dn,⟨label⟩

Attributes: Size = (Word)

Description: Controls a loop of instructions. The parameters are: a condition code, a data register (counter), and a displacement value. The instruction first tests the condition (for termination); if it is true, no operation is performed. If the termination condition is not true, the low-order 16 bits of the counter data register are decremented by one. If the result is − 1, execution continues with the next instruction. If the result is not equal to − 1, execution continues at the location indicated by the current value of the PC plus the sign-extended 16-bit displacement. The value in the PC is the address of the instruction word of the DBcc instruction plus two. The displacement is a twos complement integer that represents the relative distance in bytes from the current PC to the destination PC.

DBcc

Condition code cc specifies one of the following conditions:

CC	carry clear	0100	$\overline{C}$
CS	carry set	0101	C
EQ	equal	0111	Z
F	never equal	0001	0
GE	greater or equal	1100	$N{\cdot}V + \overline{N}{\cdot}\overline{V}$
GT	greater than	1110	$N{\cdot}V{\cdot}\overline{Z} + \overline{N}{\cdot}\overline{V}{\cdot}\overline{Z}$
HI	high	0010	$\overline{C}{\cdot}\overline{Z}$
LE	less or equal	1111	$Z + N{\cdot}\overline{V} + \overline{N}{\cdot}V$
LS	low or same	0011	$C + Z$
LT	less than	1101	$N{\cdot}\overline{V} + \overline{N}{\cdot}V$
MI	minus	1011	N
NE	not equal	0110	$\overline{Z}$
PL	plus	1010	$\overline{N}$
T	always true	0000	1
VC	overflow clear	1000	$\overline{V}$
VS	overflow set	1001	V

Condition Codes:
Not affected.

Instruction Format:

15	14	13	12	11	10	9	8	7	6	5	4	3	2	1	0
0	1	0	1		CONDITION			1	1	0	0	1		REGISTER	
DISPLACEMENT (16 BITS)															

Instruction Fields:
Condition field — The binary code for one of the conditions listed in the table.
Register field — Specifies the data register used as the counter.
Displacement field — Specifies the number of bytes to branch.

Notes:
1. The terminating condition is similar to the UNTIL loop clauses of high-level languages. For example: DBMI can be stated as "decrement and branch until minus".
2. Most assemblers accept DBRA for DBF for use when only a count terminates the loop (no condition is tested).
3. A program can enter a loop at the beginning or by branching to the trailing DBcc instruction. Entering the loop at the beginning is useful for indexed addressing modes and dynamically specified bit operations. In this case, the control index count must be one less than the desired number of loop executions. However, when entering a loop by branching directly to the trailing DBcc instruction, the control count should equal the loop execution count. In this case, if a zero count occurs, the DBcc instruction does not branch, and the main loop is not executed.

DIVS,
DIVSL

Signed Divide
(M68000 Family)

Operation: Destination/Source ◆ Destination

Assembler   DIVS.W ⟨ea⟩,Dn   32/16 ◆ 16r:16q
Syntax: *DIVS.L ⟨ea⟩,Dq   32/32 ◆ 32q
         *DIVS.L ⟨ea⟩,Dr:Dq   64/32 ◆ 32r:32q
         *DIVSL.L ⟨ea⟩,Dr:Dq   32/32 ◆ 32r:32q
         *Applies to MC68020/MC68030/MC68040/CPU32 only

Attributes: Size = (Word, Long)

Description: Divides the signed destination operand by the signed source operand and stores the signed result in the destination. The instruction uses one of four forms. The word form of the instruction divides a long word by a word. The result is a quotient in the lower word (least significant 16 bits) and the remainder is in the upper word (most significant 16 bits) of the result. The sign of the remainder is the same as the sign of the dividend.

The first long form divides a long word by a long word. The result is a long quotient; the remainder is discarded.

The second long form divides a quad word (in any two data registers) by a long word. The result is a long-word quotient and a long-word remainder.

The third long form divides a long word by a long word. The result is a long-word quotient and a long-word remainder.

Two special conditions may arise during the operation:
1. Division by zero causes a trap.
2. Overflow may be detected and set before the instruction completes. If the instruction detects an overflow, it sets the overflow condition code, and the operands are unaffected.

Condition Codes:

X	N	Z	V	C
—	*	*	*	0

X   Not affected.
N   Set if the quotient is negative. Cleared otherwise. Undefined if overflow or divide by zero occurs.
Z   Set if the quotient is zero. Cleared otherwise. Undefined if overflow or divide by zero occurs.
V   Set if division overflow occurs; undefined if divide by zero occurs. Cleared otherwise.
C   Always cleared.

DIVS, DIVSL

Instruction Format (word form):

15	14	13	12	11	10	9	8	7	6	5	4	3	2	1	0
1	0	0	0	REGISTER			1	1	1	EFFECTIVE ADDRESS MODE			REGISTER		

15	14	13	12	11	10	9	8	7	6	5	4	3	2	1	0
1	0	0	0	REGISTER	REGISTER	REGISTER	1	1	1	MODE	MODE	MODE	REGISTER	REGISTER	REGISTER

Instruction Fields:

Register field — Specifies any of the eight data registers. This field always specifies the destination operand.

Effective Address field — Specifies the source operand. Only data addressing modes are allowed as shown:

Addressing Mode	Mode	Register
Dn	000	reg. number:Dn
An	—	—
(An)	010	reg. number:An
(An) –	011	reg. number:An
– (An)	100	reg. number:An
(d16,An)	101	reg. number:An
(d8,An,Xn)	110	reg. number:An

Addressing Mode	Mode	Register
(xxx).W	111	000
(xxx).L	111	001
#⟨data⟩	111	100
(d16,PC)	111	010
(d8,PC,Xn)	111	011

MC68020, MC68030, AND MC68040 ONLY

Addressing Mode	Mode	Register
(bd,An,Xn)*	110	reg. number:An
([bd,An,Xn],od)	110	reg. number:An
([bd,An],Xn,od)	110	reg. number:An

Addressing Mode	Mode	Register
(bd,PC,Xn)*	111	011
([bd,PC,Xn],od)	111	011
([bd,PC],Xn,od)	111	011

*Can be used with CPU32.

NOTE

Overflow occurs if the quotient is larger than a 16-bit signed integer.

Instruction Format (long word form):

15	14	13	12	11	10	9	8	7	6	5	4	3	2	1	0
0	1	0	0	1	1	0	0	0	1	EFFECTIVE ADDRESS MODE	MODE	MODE	REGISTER	REGISTER	REGISTER
0	REGISTER Dq	REGISTER Dq	REGISTER Dq	1	SIZE	0	0	0	0	0	0	0	REGISTER Dr	REGISTER Dr	REGISTER Dr

Instruction Fields:

Effective Address field — Specifies the source operand. Only data addressing modes are allowed as shown:

DIVS, DIVSL

MC68020, MC68030, MC68040, AND CPU32 ONLY

Addressing Mode	Mode	Register	Addressing Mode	Mode	Register
Dn	000	reg. number:Dn	(xxx).W	111	000
An	—	—	(xxx).L	111	001
(An)	010	reg. number:An	#⟨data⟩	111	100
(An)+	011	reg. number:An			
−(An)	100	reg. number:An			
(d$_{16}$,An)	101	reg. number:An	(d$_{16}$,PC)	111	010
(d$_8$,An,Xn)	110	reg. number:An	(d$_8$,PC,Xn)	111	011
(bd,An,Xn)	110	reg. number:An	(bd,PC,Xn)	111	011

MC68020, MC68030, AND MC68040 ONLY

Addressing Mode	Mode	Register	Addressing Mode	Mode	Register
([bd,An,Xn],od)	110	reg. number:An	([bd,PC,Xn],od)	111	011
([bd,An],Xn,od)	110	reg. number:An	([bd,PC],Xn,od)	111	011

Register Dq field — Specifies a data register for the destination operand. The low-order 32 bits of the dividend comes from this register, and the 32-bit quotient is loaded into this register.

Size field — Selects a 32- or 64-bit division operation.

0 — 32-bit dividend is in Register Dq.

1 — 64-bit dividend is in Dr:Dq.

Register Dr field — After the division, this register contains the 32-bit remainder. If Dr and Dq are the same register, only the quotient is returned. If Size is 1, this field also specifies the data register that contains the high-order 32 bits of the dividend.

NOTE

Overflow occurs if the quotient is larger than a 32-bit signed integer.

DIVU, DIVUL

Unsigned Divide
(M68000 Family)

Operation: Destination/Source ♦ Destination

Assembler Syntax:

DIVU.W ⟨ea⟩,Dn	32/16 ♦ 16r:16q
*DIVU.L ⟨ea⟩,Dq	32/32 ♦ 32q
*DIVU.L ⟨ea⟩,Dr:Dq	64/32 ♦ 32r:32q
*DIVUL.L ⟨ea⟩,Dr:Dq	32/32 ♦ 32r:32q

*Applies to MC68020/MC68030/MC68040/CPU32 only

Attributes: Size = (Word, Long)

DIVU, DIVUL

Description: Divides the unsigned destination operand by the unsigned source operand and stores the unsigned result in the destination. The instruction uses one of four forms. The word form of the instruction divides a long word by a word. The result is a quotient in the lower word (least significant 16 bits) and the remainder is in the upper word (most significant 16 bits) of the result.

The first long form divides a long word by a long word. The result is a long quotient; the remainder is discarded.

The second long form divides a quad word (in any two data registers) by a long word. The result is a long-word quotient and a long-word remainder.

The third long form divides a long word by a long word. The result is a long-word quotient and a long-word remainder.

Two special conditions may arise during the operation:
1. Division by zero causes a trap.
2. Overflow may be detected and set before the instruction completes. If the instruction detects an overflow, it sets the overflow condition code, and the operands are unaffected.

Condition Codes:

X	N	Z	V	C
—	*	*	*	0

X   Not affected.
N   Set if the quotient is negative. Cleared otherwise. Undefined if overflow or divide by zero occurs.
Z   Set if the quotient is zero. Cleared otherwise. Undefined if overflow or divide by zero occurs.
V   Set if division overflow occurs; undefined if divide by zero occurs. Cleared otherwise.
C   Always cleared.

Instruction Format (word form):

15	14	13	12	11	10	9	8	7	6	5	4	3	2	1	0
1	0	0	0	REGISTER			0	1	1	EFFECTIVE ADDRESS					
										MODE			REGISTER		

Instruction Fields:
Register field — Specifies any of the eight data registers. This field always specifies the destination operand.
Effective Address field — Specifies the source operand. Only data addressing modes are allowed as shown:

DIVU, DIVUL

Addressing Mode	Mode	Register
Dn	000	reg. number:Dn
An	—	—
(An)	010	reg. number:An
(An)+	011	reg. number:An
−(An)	100	reg. number:An
(d$_{16}$,An)	101	reg. number:An
(d$_8$,An,Xn)	110	reg. number:An

Addressing Mode	Mode	Register
(xxx).W	111	000
(xxx).L	111	001
#(data)	111	100
(d$_{16}$,PC)	111	010
(d$_8$,PC,Xn)	111	011

MC68020, MC68030, AND MC68040 ONLY

Addressing Mode	Mode	Register
(bd,An,Xn)*	110	reg. number:An
([bd,An,Xn],od)	110	reg. number:An
([bd,An],Xn,od)	110	reg. number:An

Addressing Mode	Mode	Register
(bd,PC,Xn)*	111	011
([bd,PC,Xn],od)	111	011
([bd,PC],Xn,od)	111	011

*Can be used with CPU32.

NOTE

Overflow occurs if the quotient is larger than a 16-bit signed integer.

Instruction Format (long word form):

15	14	13	12	11	10	9	8	7	6	5	4	3	2	1	0
0	1	0	0	1	1	0	0	0	1	EFFECTIVE ADDRESS					
										MODE			REGISTER		
0	REGISTER Dq			0	SIZE	0	0	0	0	0	0	0	REGISTER Dr		

Instruction Fields:

Effective Address field — Specifies the source operand. Only data addressing modes are allowed as shown:

MC68020, MC68030, MC68040, AND CPU32 ONLY

Addressing Mode	Mode	Register
Dn	000	reg. number:Dn
An	—	—
(An)	010	reg. number:An
(An)+	011	reg. number:An
−(An)	100	reg. number:An
(d$_{16}$,An)	101	reg. number:An
(d$_8$,An,Xn)	110	reg. number:An
(bd,An,Xn)*	110	reg. number:An

Addressing Mode	Mode	Register
(xxx).W	111	000
(xxx).L	111	001
#(data)	111	100
(d$_{16}$,PC)	111	010
(d$_8$,PC,Xn)	111	011
(bd,PC,Xn)*	111	011

MC68020, MC68030, AND MC68040 ONLY

Addressing Mode	Mode	Register
([bd,An,Xn],od)	110	reg. number:An
([bd,An],Xn,od)	110	reg. number:An

Addressing Mode	Mode	Register
([bd,PC,Xn],od)	111	011
([bd,PC],Xn,od)	111	011

DIVU, DIVUL

Register Dq field — Specifies a data register for the destination operand. The low-order 32 bits of the dividend comes from this register, and the 32-bit quotient is loaded into this register.

Size field — Selects a 32- or 64-bit division operation.

 0 — 32-bit dividend is in Register Dq.

 1 — 64-bit dividend is in Dr:Dq.

Register Dr field — After the division, this register contains the 32-bit remainder. If Dr and Dq are the same register, only the quotient is returned. If Size is 1, this field also specifies the data register that contains the high-order 32 bits of the dividend.

NOTE
Overflow occurs if the quotient is larger than a 32-bit unsigned integer.

EOR

Exclusive-OR Logical
(M68000 Family)

Operation: Source $\oplus$ Destination $\blacktriangleright$ Destination

Assembler
Syntax: EOR Dn,⟨ea⟩

Attributes: Size = (Byte, Word, Long)

Description: Performs an exclusive-OR operation on the destination operand using the source operand and stores the result in the destination location. The size of the operation may be specified to be byte, word, or long. The source operand must be a data register. The destination operand is specified in the effective address field.

Condition Codes:

X	N	Z	V	C
—	*	*	0	0

X Not affected.
N Set if the most significant bit of the result is set. Cleared otherwise.
Z Set if the result is zero. Cleared otherwise.
V Always cleared.
C Always cleared.

Instruction Format (word form):

15	14	13	12	11	10	9	8	7	6	5	4	3	2	1	0
1	0	1	1	REGISTER			OPMODE			EFFECTIVE ADDRESS					
										MODE			REGISTER		

EOR

Instruction Fields:

Register field — Specifies any of the eight data registers.

Opmode field:

Byte	Word	Long	Operation
100	101	110	$(\langle ea \rangle) \oplus (\langle Dn \rangle) \blacklozenge \langle ea \rangle$

Effective Address field — Specifies the destination operand. Only data alterable addressing modes are allowed as shown:

Addressing Mode	Mode	Register
Dn	000	reg. number:Dn
An	—	—
(An)	010	reg. number:An
(An) +	011	reg. number:An
− (An)	100	reg. number:An
(d_{16},An)	101	reg. number:An
(d_8,An,Xn)	110	reg. number:An

Addressing Mode	Mode	Register
(xxx).W	111	000
(xxx).L	111	001
#⟨data⟩	—	—
(d_{16},PC)	—	—
(d_8,PC,Xn)	—	—

MC68020, MC68030, AND MC68040 ONLY

Addressing Mode	Mode	Register
(bd,An,Xn)∗	110	reg. number:An
([bd,An,Xn],od)	110	reg. number:An
([bd,An],Xn,od)	110	reg. number:An

Addressing Mode	Mode	Register
(bd,PC,Xn)∗	—	—
([bd,PC,Xn],od)	—	—
([bd,PC],Xn,od)	—	—

∗Can be used with CPU32.

NOTE

Memory-to-data register operations are not allowed. Most assemblers use EORI when the source is immediate data.

EORI

Exclusive-OR Immediate
(M68000 Family)

Operation: Immediate Data $\oplus$ Destination $\blacklozenge$ Destination

Assembler Syntax: EORI #⟨data⟩,⟨ea⟩

Attributes: Size = (Byte, Word, Long)

Description: Performs an exclusive-OR operation on the destination operand using the immediate data and the destination operand and stores the result in the destination location. The size of the operation may be specified as byte, word, or long. The size of the immediate data matches the operation size.

EORI

Condition Codes:

X	N	Z	V	C
—	*	*	0	0

X   Not affected.
N   Set if the most significant bit of the result is set. Cleared otherwise.
Z   Set if the result is zero. Cleared otherwise.
V   Always cleared.
C   Always cleared.

Instruction Format:

15	14	13	12	11	10	9	8	7	6	5	4	3	2	1	0
0	0	0	0	1	0	1	0	SIZE		EFFECTIVE ADDRESS					
										MODE			REGISTER		
WORD DATA (16 BITS)								BYTE DATA (8 BITS)							
LONG DATA (32 BITS)															

Instruction Fields:

Size field — Specifies the size of the operation:
00 — Byte operation.
01 — Word operation.
10 — Long operation.

Effective Address field — Specifies the destination operand. Only data alterable addressing modes are allowed as shown:

Addressing Mode	Mode	Register
Dn	000	reg. number:Dn
An	—	—
(An)	010	reg. number:An
(An)+	011	reg. number:An
−(An)	100	reg. number:An
(d$_{16}$,An)	101	reg. number:An
(d$_8$,An,Xn)	110	reg. number:An

Addressing Mode	Mode	Register
(xxx).W	111	000
(xxx).L	111	001
#⟨data⟩	—	—
(d$_{16}$,PC)	—	—
(d$_8$,PC,Xn)	—	—

MC68020, MC68030, AND MC68040 ONLY

Addressing Mode	Mode	Register
(bd,An,Xn)*	110	reg. number:An
([bd,An,Xn],od)	110	reg. number:An
([bd,An],Xn,od)	110	reg. number:An

Addressing Mode	Mode	Register
(bd,PC,Xn)*	—	—
([bd,PC,Xn],od)	—	—
([bd,PC],Xn,od)	—	—

*Can be used with CPU32.

Immediate field — (Data immediately following the instruction):
If size = 00, the data is the low-order byte of the immediate word.
If size = 01, the data is the entire immediate word.
If size = 10, the data is next two immediate words.

EORI
to CCR

**Exclusive-OR Immediate
to Condition Code**
(M68000 Family)

Operation: Source ⊕ CCR ♦ CCR

**Assembler
Syntax:**   EORI #⟨data⟩,CCR

Attributes: Size = (Byte)

Description: Performs an exclusive-OR operation on the condition code register
using the immediate operand and stores the result in the condition code register
(low-order byte of the status register). All implemented bits of the condition
code register are affected.

Condition Codes:

X	N	Z	V	C
*	*	*	*	*

X   Changed if bit 4 of immediate operand is one. Unchanged otherwise.
N   Changed if bit 3 of immediate operand is one. Unchanged otherwise.
Z   Changed if bit 2 of immediate operand is one. Unchanged otherwise.
V   Changed if bit 1 of immediate operand is one. Unchanged otherwise.
C   Changed if bit 0 of immediate operand is one. Unchanged otherwise.

Instruction Format:

15	14	13	12	11	10	9	8	7	6	5	4	3	2	1	0
0	0	0	0	1	0	1	0	0	0	1	1	1	1	0	0
0	0	0	0	0	0	0	0	BYTE DATA (8 BITS)							

EXG

Exchange Registers
(M68000 Family)

Operation: Rx ♦♦ Ry

**Assembler
Syntax:**   EXG Dx,Dy
EXG Ax,Ay
EXG Dx,Ay
EXG Ay, Dx

EXG

Attributes: Size = (Long)

Description: Exchanges the contents of two 32-bit registers. The instruction performs three types of exchanges:
1. Exchange data registers.
2. Exchange address registers.
3. Exchange a data register and an address register.

Condition Codes:
Not affected.

Instruction Format:

15	14	13	12	11	10	9	8	7	6	5	4	3	2	1	0
1	1	0	0	REGISTER Rx			1			OPMODE			REGISTER Ry		

Instruction Fields:
Register Rx field — Specifies either a data register or an address register depending on the mode. If the exchange is between data and address registers,
this field always specifies the data register.
Opmode field — Specifies the type of exchange:
01000 — Data registers.
01001 — Address registers.
10001 — Data register and address register.
Register Ry field — Specifies either a data register or an address register depending on the mode. If the exchange is between data and address registers,
this field always specifies the address register.

EXT, EXTB

Sign Extend
(M68000 Family)

Operation: Destination Sign-Extended ♦ Destination

Assembler   EXT.W Dn   extend byte to word
Syntax: EXT.L Dn   extend word to long word
                          EXTB.L Dn   extend byte to long word (MC68020/
                                               MC68030/MC68040/CPU32)

Attributes: Size = (Word, Long)

Description: Extends a byte in a data register to a word or a long word, or a word
in a data register to a long word, by replicating the sign bit to the left. If the
operation extends a byte to a word, bit [7] of the designated data register is

EXT, EXTB   copied to bits [15:8] of that data register. If the operation extends a word to a long word, bit [15] of the designated data register is copied to bits [31:16] of the data register. The EXTB form copies bit [7] of the designated register to bits [31:8] of the data register.

Condition Codes:

X	N	Z	V	C
—	*	*	0	0

X   Not affected.
N   Set if the result is negative. Cleared otherwise.
Z   Set if the result is zero. Cleared otherwise.
V   Always cleared.
C   Always cleared.

Instruction Format:

15	14	13	12	11	10	9	8	7	6	5	4	3	2	1	0
0	1	0	0	1	0	0		OPMODE		0	0	0		REGISTER	

Instruction Fields:

Opmode field — Specifies the size of the sign-extension operation:
010 — Sign extend low-order byte of data register to word.
011 — Sign extend low-order word of data register to long.
111 — Sign extend low-order byte of data register to long.
Register field — Specifies the data register is to be sign extended.

ILLEGAL

Take Illegal Instruction Trap
(M68000 Family)

Operation: *SSP − 2 ◆ SSP; Vector Offset ◆ (SSP);
SSP − 4 ◆ SSP; PC ◆ (SSP);
SSP − 2 ◆ SSP; SR ◆ (SSP);
Illegal Instruction Vector Address ◆ PC

*The MC68000 and MC68008 cannot write the vector offset and format code to the system stack.

Assembler Syntax: ILLEGAL

Attributes: Unsized

ILLEGAL

Description: Forces an illegal instruction exception, vector number 4. All other illegal instruction bit patterns are reserved for future extension of the instruction set and should not be used to force an exception.

Condition Codes:
Not affected

Instruction Format:

15	14	13	12	11	10	9	8	7	6	5	4	3	2	1	0
0	1	0	0	1	0	1	0	1	1	1	1	1	1	0	0

JMP

Jump
(M68000 Family)

Operation: Destination Address ⬦ PC

Assembler Syntax: JMP ⟨ea⟩

Attributes: Unsized

Description: Program execution continues at the effective address specified by the instruction. The addressing mode for the effective address must be a control addressing mode.

Condition Codes:
Not affected.

Instruction Format:

15	14	13	12	11	10	9	8	7	6	5	4	3	2	1	0
0	1	0	0	1	1	1	0	1	1	\multicolumn{3}{c}{MODE}	\multicolumn{3}{c}{REGISTER}

EFFECTIVE ADDRESS — MODE | REGISTER

Instruction Fields:
Effective Address field — Specifies the address of the next instruction. Only control addressing modes are allowed as shown:

JMP

Addressing Mode	Mode	Register
Dn	—	—
An	—	—
(An)	010	reg. number:An
(An)+	—	—
−(An)	—	—
(d$_{16}$,An)	101	reg. number:An
(d$_8$,An,Xn)	110	reg. number:An

Addressing Mode	Mode	Register
(xxx).W	111	000
(xxx).L	111	001
#⟨data⟩	—	—
(d$_{16}$,PC)	111	010
(d$_8$,PC,Xn)	111	011

MC68020, MC68030, AND MC68040 ONLY

Addressing Mode	Mode	Register
(bd,An,Xn)∗	110	reg. number:An
([bd,An,Xn],od)	110	reg. number:An
([bd,An],Xn,od)	110	reg. number:An

Addressing Mode	Mode	Register
(bd,PC,Xn)∗	111	011
([bd,PC,Xn],od)	111	011
([bd,PC],Xn,od)	111	011

∗Can be used with CPU32.

JSR

Jump to Subroutine
(M68000 Family)

Operation: SP − 4 ⬥ Sp; PC ⬥ (SP)
Destination Address ⬥ PC

**Assembler
Syntax**:   JSR ⟨ea⟩

Attributes: Unsized

Description: Pushes the long-word address of the instruction immediately following the JSR instruction onto the system stack. Program execution then continues at the address specified in the instruction.

Condition Codes:
Not affected.

Instruction Format:

15	14	13	12	11	10	9	8	7	6	5	4	3	2	1	0
0	1	0	0	1	1	1	0	1	0	EFFECTIVE ADDRESS					
										MODE			REGISTER		

JSR

Instruction Fields:

Effective Address field — Specifies the address of the next instruction. Only control addressing modes are allowed as shown:

Addressing Mode	Mode	Register	Addressing Mode	Mode	Register
Dn	—	—	(xxx).W	111	000
An	—	—	(xxx).L	111	001
(An)	010	reg. number:An	#⟨data⟩	—	—
(An) +	—	—			
−(An)	—	—			
(d$_{16}$,An)	101	reg. number:An	(d$_{16}$,PC)	111	010
(d$_8$,An,Xn)	110	reg. number:An	(d$_8$,PC,Xn)	111	011

MC68020, MC68030, AND MC68040 ONLY

Addressing Mode	Mode	Register	Addressing Mode	Mode	Register
(bd,An,Xn)∗	110	reg. number:An	(bd,PC,Xn)∗	111	011
([bd,An,Xn],od)	110	reg. number:An	([bd,PC,Xn],od)	111	011
([bd,An],Xn,od)	110	reg. number:An	([bd,PC],Xn,od)	111	011

∗Can be used with CPU32.

LEA

Load Effective Address
(M68000 Family)

Operation: ⟨ea⟩ ▶ An

Assembler
Syntax: LEA ⟨ea⟩,An

Attributes: Size = (Long)

Description: Loads the effective address into the specified address register. All 32 bits of the address register are affected by this instruction.

Condition Codes:
Not affected.

Instruction Format:

15	14	13	12	11	10	9	8	7	6	5	4	3	2	1	0
0	1	0	0	REGISTER			1	1	1	EFFECTIVE ADDRESS					

15	14	13	12	11 10 9	8	7	6	5 4 3	2 1 0
0	1	0	0	REGISTER	1	1	1	EFFECTIVE ADDRESS MODE	REGISTER

LEA

Instruction Fields:

Register field — Specifies the address register to be updated with the effective address.

Effective Address field — Specifies the address to be loaded into the address register. Only control addressing modes are allowed as shown:

Addressing Mode	Mode	Register
Dn	—	—
An	—	—
(An)	010	reg. number:An
(An)+	—	—
−(An)	—	—
(d₁₆,An)	101	reg. number:An
(d₈,An,Xn)	110	reg. number:An

Addressing Mode	Mode	Register
(xxx).W	111	000
(xxx).L	111	001
#⟨data⟩	—	—
(d₁₆,PC)	111	010
(d₈,PC,Xn)	111	011

MC68020, MC68030, AND MC68040 ONLY

Addressing Mode	Mode	Register
(bd,An,Xn)*	110	reg. number:An
([bd,An,Xn],od)	110	reg. number:An
([bd,An],Xn,od)	110	reg. number:An

Addressing Mode	Mode	Register
(bd,PC,Xn)*	111	011
([bd,PC,Xn],od)	111	011
([bd,PC],Xn,od)	111	011

*Can be used with CPU32.

LINK

Link and Allocate
(M68000 Family)

Operation: Sp − 4 ♦ Sp; An ♦ (SP);
SP ♦ An; SP+d ♦ SP

Assembler Syntax: LINK An, #⟨displacement⟩

Attributes: Size = (Word, Long*)
*(MC68020/MC68030/MC68040 only)

Description: Pushes the contents of the specified address register onto the stack. Then loads the updated stack pointer into the address register. Finally, adds the displacement value to the stack pointer. For word-size operation, the displacement is the sign-extended word following the operation word. For long-size operation, the displacement is the long word following the operation word. The address register occupies one long word on the stack. The user should specify a negative displacement in order to allocate stack area.

LINK

Condition Codes:
Not affected.

Instruction Format (Word):

15	14	13	12	11	10	9	8	7	6	5	4	3	2	1	0
0	1	0	0	1	1	1	0	0	1	0	1	0	REGISTER		
WORD DISPLACEMENT															

Instruction Format (Long):

15	14	13	12	11	10	9	8	7	6	5	4	3	2	1	0
0	1	0	0	1	0	0	0	0	0	0	0	1	REGISTER		
HIGH-ORDER DISPLACEMENT															
LOW-ORDER DISPLACEMENT															

Instruction Fields:
Register field — Specifies the address register for the link.
Displacement field — Specifies the twos complement integer to be added to the stack pointer.

NOTE
LINK and UNLK can be used to maintain a linked list of local data and parameter areas on the stack for nested subroutine calls.

LSL,LSR

Logical Shift
(M68000 Family)

Operation: Destination Shifted by ⟨count⟩ ◗ Destination

Assembler   LSd Dx,Dy
Syntax: LSd #⟨data⟩,Dy
LSd ⟨ea⟩
where d is direction, L or R

Attributes: Size = (Byte, Word, Long)

Description: Shifts the bits of the operand in the direction specified (L or R). The carry bit receives the last bit shifted out of the operand. The shift count for the shifting of a register is specified in two different ways:
1. Immediate — The shift count (1–8) is specified in the instruction.

LSL,LSR

2. Register — The shift count is the value in the data register specified in the instruction modulo 64.

The size of the operation for register destinations may be specified as byte, word, or long. The contents of memory, ⟨ea⟩, can be shifted one bit only, and the operand size is restricted to a word.

The LSL instruction shifts the operand to the left the number of positions specified as the shift count. Bits shifted out of the high-order bit go to both the carry and the extend bits; zeros are shifted into the low-order bit.

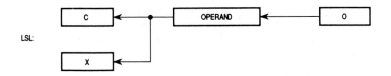

The LSR instruction shifts the operand to the right the number of positions specified as the shift count. Bits shifted out of the low-order bit go to both the carry and the extend bits; zeros are shifted into the high-order bit.

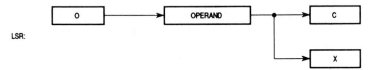

Condition Codes:

X	N	Z	V	C
*	*	*	0	*

X   Set according to the last bit shifted out of the operand. Unaffected for a shift count of zero.
N   Set if the result is negative. Cleared otherwise.
Z   Set if the result is zero. Cleared otherwise.
V   Always cleared.
C   Set according to the last bit shifted out of the operand. Cleared for a shift count of zero.

Instruction Format (Register Shifts):

15	14	13	12	11	10	9	8	7	6	5	4	3	2	1	0
1	1	1	0	COUNT/REGISTER			dr	SIZE		i/r	0	1	REGISTER		

Instruction Field (Register Shifts):

Count/Register field:
  If i/r = 0, this field contains the shift count. The values 1–7 represent shifts of 1–7; value of zero specifies a shift count of eight.

LSL,LSR

If i/r = 1, the data register specified in this field contains the shift count (modulo 64).

dr field — Specifies the direction of the shift:

0 — Shift right.

1 — Shift left.

Size field — Specifies the size of the operation:

00 — Byte operation.

01 — Word operation.

10 — Long operation.

i/r field:

If i/r = 0, specifies immediate shift count.

If i/r = 1, specifies register shift count.

Register field — Specifies a data register to be shifted.

Instruction Format (Memory Shifts):

15	14	13	12	11	10	9	8	7	6	5	4	3	2	1	0
1	1	1	0	0	0	1	dr	1	1	EFFECTIVE ADDRESS					
										MODE			REGISTER		

Instruction Fields (Memory Shifts):

dr field — Specifies the direction of the shift:

0 — Shift right.

1 — Shift left.

Effective Address field — Specifies the operand to be shifted. Only memory alterable addressing modes are allowed as shown:

Addressing Mode	Mode	Register	Addressing Mode	Mode	Register
Dn	—	—	(xxx).W	111	000
An	—	—	(xxx).L	111	001
(An)	010	reg. number:An	#⟨data⟩	—	—
(An)+	011	reg. number:An			
−(An)	100	reg. number:An			
(d16,An)	101	reg. number:An	(d16,PC)	—	—
(d8,An,Xn)	110	reg. number:An	(d8,PC,Xn)	—	—

MC68020, MC68030, AND MC68040 ONLY

Addressing Mode	Mode	Register	Addressing Mode	Mode	Register
(bd,An,Xn)*	110	reg. number:An	(bd,PC,Xn)*	—	—
([bd,An,Xn],od)	110	reg. number:An	([bd,PC,Xn],od)	—	—
([bd,An],Xn,od)	110	reg. number:An	([bd,PC],Xn,od)	—	—

*Can be used with CPU32.

MOVE

Move Data from Source to Destination
(M68000 Family)

Operation: Source ◆ Destination

Assembler
Syntax: MOVE ⟨ea⟩,⟨ea⟩

Attributes: Size = (Byte, Word, Long)

Description: Moves the data at the source to the destination location, and sets the condition codes according to the data. The size of the operation may be specified as byte, word, or long.

Condition Codes:

X	N	Z	V	C
—	*	*	0	0

X   Not affected.
N   Set if the result is negative. Cleared otherwise.
Z   Set if the result is zero. Cleared otherwise.
V   Always cleared.
C   Always cleared.

Instruction Format:

15	14	13	12	11	10	9	8	7	6	5	4	3	2	1	0
0	0	SIZE		DESTINATION						SOURCE					
				REGISTER			MODE			MODE			REGISTER		

Instruction Fields:

Size field — Specifies the size of the operand to be moved:
01 — Byte operation.
11 — Word operation.
10 — Long operation.
Destination Effective Address field — Specifies the destination location. Only data alterable addressing modes are allowed as shown:

MOVE

Addressing Mode	Mode	Register
Dn	000	reg. number:Dn
An	—	—
(An)	010	reg. number:An
(An)+	011	reg. number:An
−(An)	100	reg. number:An
(d16,An)	101	reg. number:An
(d8,An,Xn)	110	reg. number:An

Addressing Mode	Mode	Register
(xxx).W	111	000
(xxx).L	111	001
#⟨data⟩	—	—
(d16,PC)	—	—
(d8,PC,Xn)	—	—

MC68020, MC68030, AND MC68040 ONLY

Addressing Mode	Mode	Register
(bd,An,Xn)*	110	reg. number:An
([bd,An,Xn],od)	110	reg. number:An
([bd,An],Xn,od)	110	reg. number:An

Addressing Mode	Mode	Register
(bd,PC,Xn)*	—	—
([bd,PC,Xn],od)	—	—
([bd,PC],Xn,od)	—	—

*Can be used with CPU32.

Source Effective Address field — Specifies the source operand. All addressing modes are allowed as shown:

Addressing Mode	Mode	Register
Dn	000	reg. number:Dn
An*	001	reg. number:An
(An)	010	reg. number:An
(An)+	011	reg. number:An
−(An)	100	reg. number:An
(d16,An)	101	reg. number:An
(d8,An,Xn)	110	reg. number:An

Addressing Mode	Mode	Register
(xxx).W	111	000
(xxx).L	111	001
#⟨data⟩	111	100
(d16,PC)	111	010
(d8,PC,Xn)	111	011

MC68020, MC68030, AND MC68040 ONLY

Addressing Mode	Mode	Register
(bd,An,Xn)**	110	reg. number:An
([bd,An,Xn],od)	110	reg. number:An
([bd,An],Xn,od)	110	reg. number:An

Addressing Mode	Mode	Register
(bd,PC,Xn)**	111	011
([bd,PC,Xn],od)	111	011
([bd,PC],Xn,od)	111	011

*For byte size operation, address register direct is not allowed.
**Can be used with CPU32.

Notes:

1. Most assemblers use MOVEA when the destination is an address register.
2. MOVEQ can be used to move an immediate 8-bit value to a data register.

MOVEA

Move Address
(M68000 Family)

Operation: Source ♦ Destination

Assembler
Syntax: MOVEA ⟨ea⟩,An

Attributes: Size = (Word, Long)

Description: Moves the contents of the source to the destination address register. The size of the operation is specified as word or long. Word-size source operands are sign extended to 32-bit quantities.

Condition Codes:
Not affected.

Instruction Format:

15	14	13	12	11	10	9	8	7	6	5	4	3	2	1	0
0	0	SIZE		DESTINATION REGISTER			0	0	1	SOURCE					
										MODE			REGISTER		

Instruction Fields:

Size field — Specifies the size of the operand to be moved:

11 — Word operation. The source operand is sign extended to a long operand and all 32 bits are loaded into the address register.

10 — Long operation.

Destination Register field — Specifies the destination address register.

Effective Address field — Specifies the location of the source operand. All addressing modes are allowed as shown:

Addressing Mode	Mode	Register
Dn	000	reg. number:Dn
An	001	reg. number:An
(An)	010	reg. number:An
(An)+	011	reg. number:An
−(An)	100	reg. number:An
(d$_{16}$,An)	101	reg. number:An
(d$_8$,An,Xn)	110	reg. number:An

Addressing Mode	Mode	Register
(xxx).W	111	000
(xxx).L	111	001
#⟨data⟩	111	100
(d$_{16}$,PC)	111	010
(d$_8$,PC,Xn)	111	011

MC68020, MC68030, AND MC68040 ONLY

Addressing Mode	Mode	Register
(bd,An,Xn)*	110	reg. number:An
([bd,An,Xn],od)	110	reg. number:An
([bd,An],Xn,od)	110	reg. number:An

Addressing Mode	Mode	Register
(bd,PC,Xn)*	111	011
([bd,PC,Xn],od)	111	011
([bd,PC],Xn,od)	111	011

*Can be used with CPU32.

MOVE
from CCR

**Move from the
Condition Code Register
(MC68010/MC68020/MC68030/MC68040)**

Operation: CCR ⬦ Destination

**Assembler
Syntax:**   MOVE CCR,⟨ea⟩

Attributes: Size = (Word)

Description: Moves the condition code bits (zero extended to word size) to the destination location. The operand size is a word. Unimplemented bits are read as zeros.

Condition Codes:
Not affected.

Instruction Format:

15	14	13	12	11	10	9	8	7	6	5	4	3	2	1	0
0	1	0	0	0	0	1	0	1	1						

EFFECTIVE ADDRESS — MODE — REGISTER

Instruction Fields:

Effective Address field — Specifies the destination location. Only data alterable addressing modes are allowed as shown:

Addressing Mode	Mode	Register	Addressing Mode	Mode	Register
Dn	000	reg. number:Dn	(xxx).W	111	000
An	—	—	(xxx).L	111	001
(An)	010	reg. number:An	#⟨data⟩	—	—
(An)+	011	reg. number:An			
−(An)	100	reg. number:An			
(d₁₆,An)	101	reg. number:An	(d₁₆,PC)	—	—
(d₈,An,Xn)	110	reg. number:An	(d₈,PC,Xn)	—	—

MC68020, MC68030, AND MC68040 ONLY

(bd,An,Xn)*	110	reg. number:An	(bd,PC,Xn)*	—	—
([bd,An,Xn],od)	110	reg. number:An	([bd,PC,Xn],od)	—	—
([bd,An],Xn,od)	110	reg. number:An	([bd,PC],Xn,od)	—	—

*Can be used with CPU32.

NOTE

MOVE from CCR is a word operation. ANDI, ORI, and EORI to CCR are byte operations.

MOVE
to CCR

Move to Condition Codes
(M68000 Family)

Operation: Source ▶ CCR

Assembler
Syntax: MOVE ⟨ea⟩,CCR

Attributes: Size = (Word)

Description: Moves the low-order byte of the source operand to the condition code register. The upper byte of the source operand is ignored; the upper byte of the status register is not altered.

Condition Codes:

X	N	Z	V	C
*	*	*	*	*

X   Set to the value of bit 4 of the source operand.
N   Set to the value of bit 3 of the source operand.
Z   Set to the value of bit 2 of the source operand.
V   Set to the value of bit 1 of the source operand.
C   Set to the value of bit 0 of the source operand.

Instruction Format:

15	14	13	12	11	10	9	8	7	6	5	4	3	2	1	0
0	1	0	0	0	1	0	0	1	1	EFFECTIVE ADDRESS					

| | | | | | | | | | | MODE | | | REGISTER | | |

Instruction Fields:

Effective Address field — Specifies the location of the source operand. Only data addressing modes are allowed as shown:

MOVE
to CCR

Addressing Mode	Mode	Register
Dn	000	reg. number:Dn
An	—	—
(An)	010	reg. number:An
(An)+	011	reg. number:An
−(An)	100	reg. number:An
(d$_{16}$,An)	101	reg. number:An
(d$_8$,An,Xn)	110	reg. number:An

Addressing Mode	Mode	Register
(xxx).W	111	000
(xxx).L	111	001
#⟨data⟩	111	100
(d$_{16}$,PC)	111	010
(d$_8$,PC,Xn)	111	011

MC68020, MC68030, AND MC68040 ONLY

Addressing Mode	Mode	Register
(bd,An,Xn)∗	110	reg. number:An
([bd,An,Xn],od)	110	reg. number:An
([bd,An],Xn,od)	110	reg. number:An

Addressing Mode	Mode	Register
(bd,PC,Xn)∗	111	011
([bd,PC,Xn],od)	111	011
([bd,PC],Xn,od)	111	011

∗Can be used with CPU32.

NOTE

MOVE to CCR is a word operation. ANDI, ORI, and EORI to CCR are byte operations.

MOVE
from SR

Move from the Status Register
(MC68000/MC68008)

Operation: SR ⬧ Destination

**Assembler
Syntax:**   MOVE SR,⟨ea⟩

Attributes: Size = (Word)

Description: Moves the data in the status register to the destination location. The destination is word length. Unimplemented bits are read as zeros.

Condition Codes:
Not affected

Instruction Format:

15	14	13	12	11	10	9	8	7	6	5	4	3	2	1	0
0	1	0	0	0	0	0	0	1	1	EFFECTIVE ADDRESS					
										MODE			REGISTER		

MOVE
from SR

Instruction Fields:

Effective Address field — Specifies the destination location. Only data alterable addressing modes are allowed as shown:

Addressing Mode	Mode	Register
Dn	000	reg. number:Dn
An	—	—
(An)	010	reg. number:An
(An) +	011	reg. number:An
− (An)	100	reg. number:An
(d$_{16}$,An)	101	reg. number:An
(d$_8$,An,Xn)	110	reg. number:An

Addressing Mode	Mode	Register
(xxx).W	111	000
(xxx).L	111	001
#(data)	—	—
(d$_{16}$,PC)	—	—
(d$_8$,PC,Xn)	—	—

NOTE

Use the MOVE from CCR instruction to access only the condition codes. Memory destination is read before it is written to.

MOVE16

Move 16 Bytes Block
(MC68040)

Operation: Source Block > Destination Block

Assembler
Syntax:
MOVE16 (Ax) + ,(Ay) +
MOVE16 xxx.L,(An)
MOVE16 xxx.L,(An) +
MOVE16 (An),xxx.L
MOVE16 (An) + ,xxx.L

Attributes: Size = (Line)

Description: Moves the source line to the destination line. The lines are aligned to 16-byte boundaries. Applications for this instruction include coprocessor communications, memory initialization, and fast block copy operations.

MOVE16 has two formats. The postincrement format uses the postincrement addressing mode for both source and destination, while the absolute format specifies an absolute long address for either the source or destination.

Line transfers are performed using burst reads and writes which begin with the long word pointed to by the <ea> of the source and destination, respec-

MOVE16

tively. An address register used in the postincrement addressing mode is incremented by 16 after the transfer.

Example: MOVE16 (A0) + ,$FE802   A0 = $1400F

The line at address $14000 is read into a temporary holding register by a burst read transfer starting with long word $1400C. Address values in A0 of $14000–$1400F cause the same line to be read, starting at different long words. The line is then written to the line at address $FE800 beginning with long word $FE800. After the instruction A0 contains $1401F.

Source line at $14000

$14000	$14004	$14008	$1400C
LONG WORD 0	LONG WORD 1	LONG WORD 2	LONG WORD 3

Destination line at $FE8000

$FE800	$FE804	$FE808	$FE80C
LONG WORD 0	LONG WORD 1	LONG WORD 2	LONG WORD 3

Condition Codes:
Not affected.

Instruction Format (Postincrement source and destination):

15	14	13	12	11	10	9	8	7	6	5	4	3	2	1	0
1	1	1	1	0	1	1	0	0	0	1	0	0	REGISTER Ax		
1	REGISTER Ay		0	0	0	0	0	0	0	0	0	0	0	0	0

Instruction Fields (Postincrement source and destination):
Register Ax — Specifies a source address register for the postincrement addressing mode.
Register Ay — Specifies a destination address register for the postincrement addressing mode.

Instruction Format (Absolute Long Address source or destination):

15	14	13	12	11	10	9	8	7	6	5	4	3	2	1	0
1	1	1	1	0	1	1	0	0	0	0	OPMODE		REGISTER Ay		
HIGH-ORDER ADDRESS															
LOW-ORDER ADDRESS															

MOVE16

Instruction Fields (Absolute Long Address source and destination):

Opmode Field — Specifies the addressing modes used for source and destination:

Opmode	Source	Destination	Assembler Syntax
0 0	(Ay) +	xxx.L	MOVE16 (Ay) + ,xxx.L
0 1	xxx.L	(Ay) −	MOVE15 xxx.L.(Ay) −
1 0	(Ay)	xxx.L	MOVE16 (Ay),xxx.L
1 1	xxx.L	(Ay)	MOVE16 xxx.L,(Ay)

Register Ay — Specifies an address register for the indirect and postincrement addressing mode used as a source or destination.

32-Bit Address field — Specifies the absolute address used as a source or destination.

MOVEM

Move Multiple Registers
(M68000 Family)

Operation: Registers ♦ Destination
Source ♦ Registers

Assembler   MOVEM register list,⟨ea⟩
Syntax: MOVEM ⟨ea⟩,register list

Attributes: Size = (Word, Long)

Description: Moves the contents of selected registers to or from consecutive memory locations starting at the location specified by the effective address. A register is selected if the bit in the mask field corresponding to that register is set. The instruction size determines whether 16 or 32 bits of each register are transferred. In the case of a word transfer to either address or data registers, each word is sign extended to 32 bits, and the resulting long word is loaded into the associated register.

Selecting the addressing mode also selects the mode of operation of the MOVEM instruction, and only the control modes, the predecrement mode, and the postincrement mode are valid. If the effective address is specified by one of the control modes, the registers are transferred starting at the specified address, and the address is incremented by the operand length (2 or 4) following each transfer. The order of the registers is from data register 0 to data register 7, then from address register 0 to address register 7.

If the effective address is specified by the predecrement mode, only a register-to-memory operation is allowed. The registers are stored starting at the spec-

MOVEM

ified address minus the operand length (2 or 4), and the address is decremented by the operand length following each transfer. The order of storing is from address register 7 to address register 0, then from data register 7 to data register 0. When the instruction has completed, the decremented address register contains the address of the last operand stored. For the MC68020, MC68030, MC68040, and CPU32, if the addressing register is also moved to memory, the value written is the initial register value decremented by the size of the operation. The MC68000 and MC68010 write the initial register value (not decremented).

If the effective address is specified by the postincrement mode, only a memory-to-register operation is allowed. The registers are loaded starting at the specified address; the address is incremented by the operand length (2 or 4) following each transfer. The order of loading is the same as that of control mode addressing. When the instruction has completed, the incremented address register contains the address of the last operand loaded plus the operand length. If the addressing register is also loaded from memory, the memory value is ignored and the register is written with the postincremented effective address.

Condition Codes:

Not affected.

Instruction Format:

15	14	13	12	11	10	9	8	7	6	5	4	3	2	1	0
0	1	0	0	1	dr	0	0	1	SIZE	EFFECTIVE ADDRESS					

EFFECTIVE ADDRESS: MODE (bits 5-3), REGISTER (bits 2-0)

REGISTER LIST MASK

Instruction Field:

dr field — Specifies the direction of the transfer:
0 — Register to memory.
1 — Memory to register.
Size field — Specifies the size of the registers being transferred:
0 — Word transfer.
1 — Long transfer.
Effective Address field — Specifies the memory address for the operation. For register-to-memory transfers, only control alterable addressing modes or the predecrement addressing mode are allowed as shown:

MOVEM

Addressing Mode	Mode	Register
Dn	—	—
An	—	—
(An)	010	reg. number:An
(An) +	—	—
−(An)	100	reg. number:An
(d₁₆,An)	101	reg. number:An
(d₈,An,Xn)	110	reg. number:An

Addressing Mode	Mode	Register
(xxx).W	111	000
(xxx).L	111	001
#⟨data⟩	—	—
(d₁₆,PC)	—	—
(d₈,PC,Xn)	—	—

MC68020, MC68030, AND MC68040 ONLY

Addressing Mode	Mode	Register
(bd,An,Xn)*	110	reg. number:An
([bd,An,Xn],od)	110	reg. number:An
([bd,An],Xn,od)	110	reg. number:An

Addressing Mode	Mode	Register
(bd,PC,Xn)*	—	—
([bd,PC,Xn],od)	—	—
([bd,PC],Xn,od)	—	—

*Can be used with CPU32.

For memory-to-register transfers, only control addressing modes or the post-increment addressing mode are allowed as shown:

Addressing Mode	Mode	Register
Dn	—	—
An	—	—
(An)	010	reg. number:An
(An) +	011	reg. number:An
−(An)	—	—
(d₁₆,An)	101	reg. number:An
(d₈,An,Xn)	110	reg. number:An

Addressing Mode	Mode	Register
(xxx).W	111	000
(xxx).L	111	001
#⟨data⟩	—	—
(d₁₆,PC)	111	010
(d₈,PC,Xn)	111	011

MC68020, MC68030, AND MC68040 ONLY

Addressing Mode	Mode	Register
(bd,An,Xn)*	110	reg. number:An
([bd,An,Xn],od)	110	reg. number:An
([bd,An],Xn,od)	110	reg. number:An

Addressing Mode	Mode	Register
(bd,PC,Xn)*	111	011
([bd,PC,Xn],od)	111	011
([bd,PC],Xn,od)	111	011

*Can be used with CPU32.

Register List Mask field — Specifies the registers to be transferred. The low-order bit corresponds to the first register to be transferred; the high-order bit corresponds to the last register to be transferred. Thus, both for control modes and for the postincrement mode addresses, the mask correspondence is:

15	14	13	12	11	10	9	8	7	6	5	4	3	2	1	0
A7	A6	A5	A4	A3	A2	A1	A0	D7	D6	D5	D4	D3	D2	D1	D0

For the predecrement mode addresses, the mask correspondence is reversed:

15	14	13	12	11	10	9	8	7	6	5	4	3	2	1	0
D0	D1	D2	D3	D4	D5	D6	D7	A0	A1	A2	A3	A4	A5	A6	A7

MOVEP

Move Peripheral Data
(M68000 Family)

Operation: Source ⬧ Destination

Assembler   MOVEP Dx,(d,Ay)
Syntax: MOVEP (d,Ay),Dx

Attributes: Size = (Word, Long)

Description: Moves data between a data register and alternate bytes within the address space starting at the location specified and incrementing by two. The high-order byte of the data register is transferred first and the low-order byte is transferred last. The memory address is specified in the address register indirect plus 16-bit displacement addressing mode. This instruction was originally designed for interfacing 8-bit peripherals on a 16-bit data bus, such as the MC68000 bus.

Example: Long transfer to/from an even address.

Byte Organization in Register

31	24 23	16 15	8 7	0
HI ORDER	MID UPPER	MID LOWER	LOW ORDER	

Byte Organization in 16-Bit Memory (Low Address at Top)

15	8 7	0
HI ORDER		
MID UPPER		
MID LOWER		
LOW ORDER		

MC68040 Byte Organization in Memory

31	24 23	16 15	8 7	0
HI ORDER		MID UPPER		
MID LOWER		LOW ORDER		

MOVEP

Example: Word transfer to/from (odd address).

Byte Organization in Register

31	24	23	16	15	8	7	0
				HI ORDER		LOW ORDER	

Byte Organization in 16-Bit Memory (Low Address at Top)

15	8	7	0
		HI ORDER	
		LOW ORDER	

MC68040 Byte Organization in Memory

31	24	23	16	15	8	7	0
						HI ORDER	
		LOW ORDER					

Condition Codes:
Not affected.

Instruction Format:

15	14	13	12	11	10	9	8	7	6	5	4	3	2	1	0
0	0	0	0	DATA REGISTER			OPMODE			0	0	1	ADDRESS REGISTER		
DISPLACEMENT (16 BITS)															

Instruction Fields:

Data Register field — Specifies the data register for the instruction.

Opmode field — Specifies the direction and size of the operation:

100 — Transfer word from memory to register.

101 — Transfer long from memory to register.

110 — Transfer word from register to memory.

111 — Transfer long from register to memory.

Address Register field — Specifies the address register which is used in the address register indirect plus displacement addressing mode.

Displacement field — Specifies the displacement used in the operand address.

MOVEQ

Move Quick
(M68000 Family)

Operation: Immediate Data ♦ Destination

Assembler
Syntax: MOVEQ #⟨data⟩,Dn

Attributes: Size = (Long)

Description: Moves a byte of immediate data to a 32-bit data register. The data in an 8-bit field within the operation word is sign extended to a long operand in the data register as it is transferred.

Condition Codes:

X	N	Z	V	C
—	*	*	0	0

X Not affected.
N Set if the result is negative. Cleared otherwise.
Z Set if the result is zero. Cleared otherwise.
V Always cleared.
C Always cleared.

Instruction Format:

15	14	13	12	11	10	9	8	7	6	5	4	3	2	1	0
0	1	1	1	REGISTER			0	DATA							

Instruction Fields:
Register field — Specifies the data register to be loaded.
Data field — Eight bits of data, which are sign extended to a long operand.

MULS

Signed Multiply
(M68000 Family)

Operation: Source * Destination ♦ Destination

Assembler
Syntax:

MULS.W ⟨ea⟩,Dn   16x16 ♦ 32
*MULS.L ⟨ea⟩,Dl   32x32 ♦ 32
*MULS.L ⟨ea⟩,Dh:Dl 32 x 32 ♦ 64

*Applies to MC68020/MC68030/MC68040/CPU32

MULS

Attributes: Size = (Word, Long)

Description: Multiplies two signed operands yielding a signed result. This instruction has a word operand form and a long-word operand form.

In the word form, the multiplier and multiplicand are both word operands, and the result is a long-word operand. A register operand is the low-order word; the upper word of the register is ignored. All 32 bits of the product are saved in the destination data register.

In the long form, the multiplier and multiplicand are both long-word operands, and the result is either a long word or a quad word. The long-word result is the low-order 32 bits of the quad word result; the high-order 32 bits of the product are discarded.

Condition Codes:

X	N	Z	V	C
—	*	*	*	0

X   Not affected.
N   Set if the result is negative. Cleared otherwise.
Z   Set if the result is zero. Cleared otherwise.
V   Set if overflow. Cleared otherwise.
C   Always cleared.

NOTE

Overflow (V = 1) can occur only when multiplying 32-bit operands to yield a 32-bit result. Overflow occurs if the high-order 32 bits of the quad-word product are not the sign extension of the low-order 32 bits.

Instruction Format (word form):

15	14	13	12	11	10	9	8	7	6	5	4	3	2	1	0
1	1	0	0	REGISTER			1	1	1	EFFECTIVE ADDRESS MODE			REGISTER		

Instruction Fields:

Register field — Specifies a data register as the destination.

Effective Address field — Specifies the source operand. Only data addressing modes are allowed as shown:

MULS

Addressing Mode	Mode	Register	Addressing Mode	Mode	Register
Dn	000	reg. number:Dn	(xxx).W	111	000
An	—	—	(xxx).L	111	001
(An)	010	reg. number:An	#(data)	111	100
(An) –	011	reg. number:An			
– (An)	100	reg. number:An			
(d$_{16}$,An)	101	reg. number:An	(d$_{16}$,PC)	111	010
(d$_8$,An,Xn)	110	reg. number:An	(d$_8$,PC,Xn)	111	011

MC68020, MC68030, AND MC68040 ONLY

Addressing Mode	Mode	Register	Addressing Mode	Mode	Register
(bd,An,Xn)∗	110	reg. number:An	(bd,PC,Xn)∗	111	011
([bd,An,Xn],od)	110	reg. number:An	([bd,PC,Xn],od)	111	011
([bd,An],Xn,od)	110	reg. number:An	([bd,PC],Xn,od)	111	011

∗Can be used with CPU32.

Instruction Format (long form):

15	14	13	12	11	10	9	8	7	6	5	4	3	2	1	0
0	1	0	0	1	1	0	0	0	0	EFFECTIVE ADDRESS					
										MODE			REGISTER		
0	REGISTER Dl			1	SIZE	0	0	0	0	0	0	0	REGISTER Dh		

Instruction Fields:

Effective Address field — Specifies the source operand. Only data addressing modes are allowed as shown:

Addressing Mode	Mode	Register	Addressing Mode	Mode	Register
Dn	000	reg. number:Dn	(xxx).W	111	000
An	—	—	(xxx).L	111	001
(An)	010	reg. number:An	#(data)	111	100
(An) +	011	reg. number:An			
– (An)	100	reg. number:An			
(d$_{16}$,An)	101	reg. number:An	(d$_{16}$,PC)	111	010
(d$_8$,An,Xn)	110	reg. number:An	(d$_8$,PC,Xn)	111	011

MC68020, MC68030, AND MC68040 ONLY

Addressing Mode	Mode	Register	Addressing Mode	Mode	Register
(bd,An,Xn)∗	110	reg. number:An	(bd,PC,Xn)∗	111	011
([bd,An,Xn],od)	110	reg. number:An	([bd,PC,Xn],od)	111	011
([bd,An],Xn,od)	110	reg. number:An	([bd,PC],Xn,od)	111	011

∗Can be used with CPU32.

MULS

Register Dl field — Specifies a data register for the destination operand. The 32-bit multiplicand comes from this register, and the low-order 32 bits of the product are loaded into this register.

Size field — Selects a 32- or 64-bit product.

    0 — 32-bit product to be returned to Register Dl.

    1 — 64-bit product to be returned to Dh:Dl.

Register Dh field — If Size is one, specifies the data register into which the high-order 32 bits of the product are loaded. If Dh = Dl and Size is one, the results of the operation are undefined. Otherwise, this field is unused.

MULU

Unsigned Multiply
(M68000 Family)

Operation: Source * Destination ⬥ Destination

Assembler   MULU.W ⟨ea⟩,Dn   16x16 ⬥ 32
Syntax: *MULU.L ⟨ea⟩,Dl   32x32 ⬥ 32
          *MULU.L ⟨ea⟩,Dh:Dl   32x32 ⬥ 64

    *Applies to MC68020 MC68030 MC68040/CPU32 only.

Attributes: Size = (Word, Long)

Description: Multiplies two unsigned operands yielding an unsigned result. This instruction has a word operand form and a long-word operand form.

In the word form, the multiplier and multiplicand are both word operands, and the result is a long-word operand. A register operand is the low-order word; the upper word of the register is ignored. All 32 bits of the product are saved in the destination data register.

In the long form, the multiplier and multiplicand are both long-word operands, and the result is either a long word or a quad word. The long word result is the low-order 32 bits of the quad word result; the high-order 32 bits of the product are discarded.

Condition Codes:

X	N	Z	V	C
—	*	*	*	0

X Not affected.
N Set if the result is negative. Cleared otherwise.
Z Set if the result is zero. Cleared otherwise.
V Set if overflow. Cleared otherwise.
C Always cleared.

MULU

NOTE

Overflow (V = 1) can occur only when multiplying 32-bit operands to yield a 32-bit result. Overflow occurs if any of the high-order 32 bits of the quad-word product are not equal to zero.

Instruction Format (word form):

15	14	13	12	11	10	9	8	7	6	5	4	3	2	1	0
1	1	0	0	REGISTER			0	1	1	EFFECTIVE ADDRESS MODE			REGISTER		

Instruction Fields:

Register field — Specifies a data register as the destination.

Effective Address field — Specifies the source operand. Only data addressing modes are allowed as shown:

Addressing Mode	Mode	Register	Addressing Mode	Mode	Register
Dn	000	reg. number:Dn	(xxx).W	111	000
An	—	—	(xxx).L	111	001
(An)	010	reg. number:An	#⟨data⟩	111	100
(An) +	011	reg. number:An			
− (An)	100	reg. number:An			
(d$_{16}$,An)	101	reg. number:An	(d$_{16}$,PC)	111	010
(d$_8$,An,Xn)	110	reg. number:An	(d$_8$,PC,Xn)	111	011

MC68020, MC68030, AND MC68040 ONLY

Addressing Mode	Mode	Register	Addressing Mode	Mode	Register
(bd,An,Xn)∗	110	reg. number:An	(bd,PC,Xn)∗	111	011
([bd,An,Xn],od)	110	reg. number:An	([bd,PC,Xn],od)	111	011
([bd,An],Xn,od)	110	reg. number:An	([bd,PC],Xn,od)	111	011

∗Can be used with CPU32.

Instruction Format (long form):

15	14	13	12	11	10	9	8	7	6	5	4	3	2	1	0
0	1	0	0	1	1	0	0	0	0	EFFECTIVE ADDRESS MODE			REGISTER		
0	REGISTER Dl		0	SIZE	0	0	0	0	0	0	0	REGISTER Dh		

Instruction Fields:

Effective Address field — Specifies the source operand. Only data addressing modes are allowed as shown:

MULU

Addressing Mode	Mode	Register
Dn	000	reg. number:Dn
An	—	—
(An)	010	reg. number:An
(An)+	011	reg. number:An
−(An)	100	reg. number:An
(d$_{16}$,An)	101	reg. number:An
(d$_8$,An,Xn)	110	reg. number:An

Addressing Mode	Mode	Register
(xxx).W	111	000
(xxx).L	111	001
#⟨data⟩	111	100
(d$_{16}$,PC)	111	010
(d$_8$,PC,Xn)	111	011

MC68020, MC68030, AND MC68040 ONLY

Addressing Mode	Mode	Register
(bd,An,Xn)*	110	reg. number:An
([bd,An,Xn],od)	110	reg. number:An
([bd,An],Xn,od)	110	reg. number:An

Addressing Mode	Mode	Register
(bd,PC,Xn)*	111	011
([bd,PC,Xn],od)	111	011
([bd,PC],Xn,od)	111	011

*Can be used with CPU32.

Register Dl field — Specifies a data register for the destination operand. The 32-bit multiplicand comes from this register, and the low-order 32 bits of the product are loaded into this register.

Size field — Selects a 32- or 64-bit product.

0 — 32-bit product to be returned to Register Dl.

1 — 64-bit product to be returned to Dh:Dl.

Register Dh field — If Size is one, specifies the data register into which the high-order 32 bits of the product are loaded. If Dh = Dl and Size is one, the results of the operation are undefined. Otherwise, this field is unused.

NBCD

Negate Decimal with Extend
(M68000 Family)

Operation: $0 - (\text{Destination}_{10}) - X \rightarrow \text{Destination}$

Assembler
Syntax: NBCD ⟨ea⟩

Attributes: Size = (Byte)

Description: Subtracts the destination operand and the extend bit from zero. The operation is performed using binary coded decimal arithmetic. The packed BCD result is saved in the destination location. This instruction produces the tens complement of the destination if the extend bit is zero, or the nines complement if the extend bit is one. This is a byte operation only.

NBCD

Condition Codes:

X	N	Z	V	C
*	U	*	U	*

X   Set the same as the carry bit.
N   Undefined.
Z   Cleared if the result is nonzero. Unchanged otherwise.
V   Undefined.
C   Set if a decimal borrow occurs. Cleared otherwise.

NOTE

Normally the Z condition code bit is set via programming before the start of the operation. This allows successful tests for zero results upon completion of multiple precision operations.

Instruction Format:

15	14	13	12	11	10	9	8	7	6	5	4	3	2	1	0
0	1	0	0	1	0	0	0	0	0	EFFECTIVE ADDRESS					

| | | | | | | | | | | MODE | | | REGISTER | | |

Instruction Fields:

Effective Address field — Specifies the destination operand. Only data alterable addressing modes are allowed as shown:

Addressing Mode	Mode	Register	Addressing Mode	Mode	Register
Dn	000	reg. number:Dn	(xxx).W	111	000
An	—	—	(xxx).L	111	001
(An)	010	reg. number:An	#⟨data⟩	—	—
(An)+	011	reg. number:An			
−(An)	100	reg. number:An			
(d$_{16}$,An)	101	reg. number:An	(d$_{16}$,PC)	—	—
(d$_8$,An,Xn)	110	reg. number:An	(d$_8$,PC,Xn)	—	—

MC68020, MC68030, AND MC68040 ONLY

(bd,An,Xn)*	110	reg. number:An	(bd,PC,Xn)*	—	—
([bd,An,Xn],od)	110	reg. number:An	([bd,PC,Xn],od)	—	—
([bd,An],Xn,od)	110	reg. number:An	([bd,PC],Xn,od)	—	—

*Can be used with CPU32.

NEG

Negate
(M68000 Family)

Operation: 0 − (Destination) ▶ Destination

NEG

**Assembler
Syntax:**   NEG ⟨ea⟩

Attributes: Size = (Byte, Word, Long)

Description: Subtracts the destination operand from zero and stores the result in the destination location. The size of the operation is specified as byte, word, or long.

Condition Codes:

X	N	Z	V	C
*	*	*	*	*

X   Set the same as the carry bit.
N   Set if the result is negative. Cleared otherwise.
Z   Set if the result is zero. Cleared otherwise.
V   Set if an overflow occurs. Cleared otherwise.
C   Cleared if the result is zero. Set otherwise.

Instruction Format:

15	14	13	12	11	10	9	8	7	6	5	4	3	2	1	0
0	1	0	0	0	1	0	0	SIZE		EFFECTIVE ADDRESS					
										MODE			REGISTER		

Instruction Fields:

Size field — Specifies the size of the operation.
00 — Byte operation.
01 — Word operation.
10 — Long operation.
Effective Address field — Specifies the destination operand. Only data alterable addressing modes are allowed as shown:

Addressing Mode	Mode	Register
Dn	000	reg. number:Dn
An	—	—
(An)	010	reg. number:An
(An)+	011	reg. number:An
−(An)	100	reg. number:An
(d₁₆,An)	101	reg. number:An
(d₈,An,Xn)	110	reg. number:An

Addressing Mode	Mode	Register
(xxx).W	111	000
(xxx).L	111	001
#⟨data⟩	—	—
(d₁₆,PC)	—	—
(d₈,PC,Xn)	—	—

MC68020, MC68030, AND MC68040 ONLY

	Mode	Register
(bd,An,Xn)*	110	reg. number:An
([bd,An,Xn],od)	110	reg. number:An
([bd,An],Xn,od)	110	reg. number:An

	Mode	Register
(bd,PC,Xn)*	—	—
([bd,PC,Xn],od)	—	—
([bd,PC],Xn,od)	—	—

*Can be used with CPU32.

NEGX

Negate with Extend
(M68000 Family)

Operation: 0 − (Destination) − X ⬧ Destination

Assembler
Syntax: NEGX ⟨ea⟩

Attributes: Size = (Byte, Word, Long)

Description: Subtracts the destination operand and the extend bit from zero. Stores the result in the destination location. The size of the operation is specified as byte, word, or long.

Condition Codes:

X	N	Z	V	C
*	*	*	*	*

X   Set the same as the carry bit.
N   Set if the result is negative. Cleared otherwise.
Z   Cleared if the result is nonzero. Unchanged otherwise.
V   Set if an overflow occurs. Cleared otherwise.
C   Set if a borrow occurs. Cleared otherwise.

NOTE

Normally the Z condition code bit is set via programming before the start of the operation. This allows successful tests for zero results upon completion of multiple precision operations.

Instruction Format:

15	14	13	12	11	10	9	8	7	6	5	4	3	2	1	0
0	1	0	0	0	0	0	0	SIZE		EFFECTIVE ADDRESS					
										MODE			REGISTER		

Instruction Fields:

Size field — Specifies the size of the operation.
00 — Byte operation.
01 — Word operation.
10 — Long operation.
Effective Address field — Specifies the destination operand. Only data alterable addressing modes are allowed as shown:

NEGX

Addressing Mode	Mode	Register
Dn	000	reg. number:Dn
An	—	—
(An)	010	reg. number:An
(An)+	011	reg. number:An
−(An)	100	reg. number:An
(d$_{16}$,An)	101	reg. number:An
(d$_8$,An,Xn)	110	reg. number:An

Addressing Mode	Mode	Register
(xxx).W	111	000
(xxx).L	111	001
#⟨data⟩	—	—
(d$_{16}$,PC)	—	—
(d$_8$,PC,Xn)	—	—

MC68020, MC68030, AND MC68040 ONLY

Addressing Mode	Mode	Register
(bd,An,Xn)∗	110	reg. number:An
([bd,An,Xn],od)	110	reg. number:An
([bd,An],Xn,od)	110	reg. number:An

Addressing Mode	Mode	Register
(bd,PC,Xn)∗	—	—
([bd,PC,Xn],od)	—	—
([bd,PC],Xn,od)	—	—

∗Can be used with CPU32.

NOP

No Operation
(M68000 Family)

Operation: None

Assembler
Syntax: NOP

Attributes: Unsized

Description: Performs no operation. The processor state, other than the program counter, is unaffected. Execution continues with the instruction following the NOP instruction. The NOP instruction does not begin execution until all pending bus cycles are completed. This synchronizes the pipeline, and prevents instruction overlap.

Condition Codes:
Not affected.

Instruction Format:

15	14	13	12	11	10	9	8	7	6	5	4	3	2	1	0
0	1	0	0	1	1	1	0	0	1	1	1	0	0	0	1

NOT

Logical Complement
(M68000 Family)

Operation: $\sim$ Destination $\blacklozenge$ Destination

Assembler
Syntax: NOT $\langle$ea$\rangle$

Attributes: Size = (Byte, Word, Long)

Description: Calculates the ones complement of the destination operand and stores the result in the destination location. The size of the operation is specified as byte, word, or long.

Condition Codes:

X	N	Z	V	C
—	*	*	0	0

X   Not affected.
N   Set if the result is negative. Cleared otherwise.
Z   Set if the result is zero. Cleared otherwise.
V   Always cleared.
C   Always cleared.

Instruction Format:

15	14	13	12	11	10	9	8	7	6	5	4	3	2	1	0
0	1	0	0	0	1	1	0	SIZE		EFFECTIVE ADDRESS					
										MODE			REGISTER		

Instruction Fields:

Size field — Specifies the size of the operation.
00 — Byte operation.
01 — Word operation.
10 — Long operation.

Effective Address field — Specifies the destination operand. Only data alterable addressing modes are allowed as shown:

Addressing Mode	Mode	Register	Addressing Mode	Mode	Register
Dn	000	reg. number:Dn	(xxx).W	111	000
An	—	—	(xxx).L	111	001
(An)	010	reg. number:An	#$\langle$data$\rangle$	—	—
(An)	011	reg. number:An			
(An)	100	reg. number:An			
(d$_{16}$,An)	101	reg. number:An	(d$_{16}$,PC)	—	—
(d$_{8}$,An,Xn)	110	reg. number:An	(d$_{8}$,PC,Xn)	—	—

NOT

MC68020, MC68030, AND MC68040 ONLY

(bd,An,Xn)*	110	reg. number:An	(bd,PC,Xn)*	—	—
([bd,An,Xn],od)	110	reg. number:An	([bd,PC,Xn],od)	—	—
([bd,An],Xn,od)	110	reg. number:An	([bd,PC],Xn,od)	—	—

*Can be used with CPU32.

OR

Inclusive-OR Logical
(M68000 Family)

Operation: Source V Destination ▸ Destination

Assembler
Syntax: OR ⟨ea⟩,Dn
OR Dn,⟨ea⟩

Attributes: Size = (Byte, Word, Long)

Description: Performs an inclusive-OR operation on the source operand and the destination operand and stores the result in the destination location. The size of the operation is specified as byte, word, or long. The contents of an address register may not be used as an operand.

Condition Codes:

X	N	Z	V	C
—	*	*	0	0

X Not affected.
N Set if the most significant bit of the result is set. Cleared otherwise.
Z Set if the result is zero. Cleared otherwise.
V Always cleared.
C Always cleared.

Instruction Format:

15	14	13	12	11	10	9	8	7	6	5	4	3	2	1	0
1	0	0	0	REGISTER			OPMODE			EFFECTIVE ADDRESS					
										MODE			REGISTER		

Instruction Fields:
Register field — Specifies any of the eight data registers.
Opmode field:

Byte	Word	Long	Operation
000	001	010	(⟨ea⟩) V (⟨Dn⟩) ▸ ⟨Dn⟩
100	101	110	(⟨Dn⟩) V (⟨ea⟩) ▸ ⟨ea⟩

OR

Inclusive-OR Logical
(M68000 Family)

Effective Address field — If the location specified is a source operand, only data addressing modes are allowed as shown:

Addressing Mode	Mode	Register	Addressing Mode	Mode	Register
Dn	000	reg. number:Dn	(xxx).W	111	000
An	—	—	(xxx).L	111	001
(An)	010	reg. number:An	#(data)	111	100
(An)+	011	reg. number:An			
−(An)	100	reg. number:An			
(d$_{16}$,An)	101	reg. number:An	(d$_{16}$,PC)	111	010
(d$_8$,An,Xn)	110	reg. number:An	(d$_8$,PC,Xn)	111	011

MC68020, MC68030, AND MC68040 ONLY

(bd,An,Xn)*	110	reg. number:An	(bd,PC,Xn)*	111	011
([bd,An,Xn],od)	110	reg. number:An	([bd,PC,Xn],od)	111	011
([bd,An],Xn,od)	110	reg. number:An	([bd,PC],Xn,od)	111	011

*Can be used with CPU32.

If the location specified is a destination operand, only memory alterable addressing modes are allowed as shown:

Addressing Mode	Mode	Register	Addressing Mode	Mode	Register
Dn	—	—	(xxx).W	111	000
An	—	—	(xxx).L	111	001
(An)	010	reg. number:An	#(data)	—	—
(An)+	011	reg. number:An			
−(An)	100	reg. number:An			
(d$_{16}$,An)	101	reg. number:An	(d$_{16}$,PC)	—	—
(d$_8$,An,Xn)	110	reg. number:An	(d$_8$,PC,Xn)	—	—

MC68020, MC68030, AND MC68040 ONLY

(bd,An,Xn)*	110	reg. number:An	(bd,PC,Xn)*	—	—
([bd,An,Xn],od)	110	reg. number:An	([bd,PC,Xn],od)	—	—
([bd,An],Xn,od)	110	reg. number:An	([bd,PC],Xn,od)	—	—

*Can be used with CPU32.

Notes:

1. If the destination is a data register, it must be specified using the destination Dn mode, not the destination ⟨ea⟩ mode.
2. Most assemblers use ORI when the source is immediate data.

ORI

Inclusive OR
(M68000 Family)

Operation: Immediate Data V Destination ▶ Destination

Assembler
Syntax: ORI #⟨data⟩,⟨ea⟩

Attributes: Size = (Byte, Word, Long)

Description: Performs an inclusive-OR operation on the immediate data and the
destination operand and stores the result in the destination location. The size
of the operation is specified as byte, word, or long. The size of the immediate
data matches the operation size.

Condition Codes:

X	N	Z	V	C
—	*	*	0	0

X   Not affected.
N   Set if the most significant bit of the result is set. Cleared otherwise.
Z   Set if the result is zero. Cleared otherwise.
V   Always cleared.
C   Always cleared.

Instruction Format:

15	14	13	12	11	10	9	8	7	6	5	4	3	2	1	0
0	0	0	0	0	0	0	0	SIZE		EFFECTIVE ADDRESS					
										MODE			REGISTER		
WORD DATA (16 BITS)								BYTE DATA (8 BITS)							
LONG DATA (32 BITS)															

Instruction Fields:
Size field — Specifies the size of the operation.
00 — Byte operation.
01 — Word operation.
10 — Long operation.
Effective Address field — Specifies the destination operand. Only data alterable
addressing modes are allowed as shown:

ORI

Addressing Mode	Mode	Register	Addressing Mode	Mode	Register
Dn	000	reg. number:Dn	(xxx).W	111	000
An	—	—	(xxx).L	111	001
(An)	010	reg. number:An	#⟨data⟩	—	—
(An)+	011	reg. number:An			
−(An)	100	reg. number:An			
(d₁₆,An)	101	reg. number:An	(d₁₆,PC)	—	—
(d₈,An,Xn)	110	reg. number:An	(d₈,PC,Xn)	—	—

MC68020, MC68030, AND MC68040 ONLY

Addressing Mode	Mode	Register	Addressing Mode	Mode	Register
(bd,An,Xn)∗	110	reg. number:An	(bd,PC,Xn)∗	—	—
([bd,An,Xn],od)	110	reg. number:An	([bd,PC,Xn],od)	—	—
([bd,An],Xn,od)	110	reg. number:An	([bd,PC],Xn,od)	—	—

∗Can be used with CPU32.

Immediate field — (Data immediately following the instruction):
If size = 00, the data is the low-order byte of the immediate word.
If size = 01, the data is the entire immediate word.
If size = 10, the data is the next two immediate words.

ORI
to CCR

**Inclusive-OR Immediate
to Condition Codes
(M68000 Family)**

Operation: Source V CCR ⬧ CCR

**Assembler
Syntax:**   ORI #⟨data⟩,CCR

Attributes: Size = (Byte)

Description: Performs an inclusive-OR operation on the immediate operand and the condition codes and stores the result in the condition code register (low-order byte of the status register). All implemented bits of the condition code register are affected.

Condition Codes:

X	N	Z	V	C
∗	∗	∗	∗	∗

X   Set if bit 4 of immediate operand is one. Unchanged otherwise.
N   Set if bit 3 of immediate operand is one. Unchanged otherwise.
Z   Set if bit 2 of immediate operand is one. Unchanged otherwise.

ORI
to CCR

V Set if bit 1 of immediate operand is one. Unchanged otherwise.
C Set if bit 0 of immediate operand is one. Unchanged otherwise.

Instruction Format:

15	14	13	12	11	10	9	8	7	6	5	4	3	2	1	0
0	0	0	0	0	0	0	0	0	0	1	1	1	1	0	0
0	0	0	0	0	0	0	0	BYTE DATA (8 BITS)							

PACK

Pack
(MC68020/MC68030/MC68040)

Operation: Source (Unpacked BCD) + adjustment ♦ Destination (Packed BCD)

Assembler   PACK – (Ax), – (Ay),#⟨adjustment⟩
Syntax: PACK Dx,Dy,#⟨adjustment⟩

Attributes: Unsized

Description: Adjusts and packs the low four bits of each of two bytes into a single byte.

When both operands are data registers, the adjustment is added to the value contained in the source register. Bits [11:8] and [3:0] of the intermediate result are concatenated and placed in bits [7:0] of the destination register. The remainder of the destination register is unaffected.

Source (Dx):

15	14	13	12	11	10	9	8	7	6	5	4	3	2	1	0
x	x	x	x	a	b	c	d	x	x	x	x	e	f	g	h

Add Adjustment Word:

15	14	13	12	11	10	9	8	7	6	5	4	3	2	1	0
16-BIT EXTENSION															

Resulting in:

15	14	13	12	11	10	9	8	7	6	5	4	3	2	1	0
x'	x'	x'	x'	a'	b'	c'	d'	x'	x'	x'	x'	e'	f'	g'	h'

Destination (Dy):

15	14	13	12	11	10	9	8	7	6	5	4	3	2	1	0
u	u	u	u	u	u	u	u	a'	b'	c'	d'	e'	f'	g'	h'

PACK

When the predecrement addressing mode is specified, two bytes from the source are fetched and concatenated. The adjustment word is added to the concatenated bytes. Bits [3:0] of each byte are extracted. These eight bits are concatenated to form a new byte which is then written to the destination.

Source (Ax):

7	6	5	4	3	2	1	0
x	x	x	x	a	b	c	d
x	x	x	x	e	f	g	h

Concatenated Word:

15	14	13	12	11	10	9	8	7	6	5	4	3	2	1	0
x	x	x	x	a	b	c	d	x	x	x	x	e	f	g	h

Add Adjustment Word:

15	14	13	12	11	10	9	8	7	6	5	4	3	2	1	0
16-BIT EXTENSION																

Destination (Ay):

7	6	5	4	3	2	1	0
a'	b'	c'	d'	e'	f'	g'	h'

Condition Codes:

Not affected.

Instruction Format:

15	14	13	12	11	10	9	8	7	6	5	4	3	2	1	0
1	0	0	0	REGISTER Dy/Ay			1	0	1	0	0	R/M	REGISTER Dx/Ax			
16-BIT EXTENSION: ADJUSTMENT																

Instruction Fields:

Register Dy/Ay field — Specifies the destination register.

If R/M = 0, specifies a data register.

If R/M = 1, specifies an address register in the predecrement addressing mode.

R/M field — Specifies the operand addressing mode.

0 — The operation is data register to data register.

1 — The operation is memory to memory.

Register Dx/Ax field — Specifies the source register.

If R/M = 0, specifies a data register.

If R/M = 1, specifies an address register in the predecrement addressing mode.

PACK

Adjustment field — Immediate data word that is added to the source operand. This word is zero to pack ASCII or EBCDIC codes. Other values can be used for other codes.

PEA

Push Effective Address
(M68000 Family)

Operation: $Sp - 4 \rightarrow SP; \langle ea \rangle \rightarrow (SP)$

Assembler
Syntax: PEA ⟨ea⟩

Attributes: Size = (Long)

Description: Computes the effective address and pushes it onto the stack. The effective address is a long-word address.

Condition Codes:
Not affected.

Instruction Format:

15	14	13	12	11	10	9	8	7	6	5	4	3	2	1	0
0	1	0	0	1	0	0	0	0	1	EFFECTIVE ADDRESS					

| | | | | | | | | | | MODE | | | REGISTER | | |

Instruction Fields:

Effective Address field — Specifies the address to be pushed onto the stack. Only control addressing modes are allowed as shown:

Addressing Mode	Mode	Register
Dn	—	—
An	—	—
(An)	010	reg. number:An
(An) +	—	—
– (An)	—	—
(d16,An)	101	reg. number:An
(d8,An,Xn)	110	reg. number:An

Addressing Mode	Mode	Register
(xxx).W	111	000
(xxx).L	111	001
#⟨data⟩	—	—
(d16,PC)	111	010
(d8,PC,Xn)	111	011

MC68020, MC68030, AND MC68040 ONLY

Addressing Mode	Mode	Register
(bd,An,Xn)*	110	reg. number:An
([bd,An,Xn],od)	110	reg. number:An
([bd,An],Xn,od)	110	reg. number:An

Addressing Mode	Mode	Register
(bd,PC,Xn)*	111	011
([bd,PC,Xn],od)	111	011
([bd,PC],Xn,od)	111	011

*Can be used with CPU32.

PVALID

Validate a Pointer
(MC68851)

Operation: If (source AL bits) > (destination AL bits) then Trap

Assembler   PVALID VAL,⟨ea⟩
Syntax: PVALID an,⟨ea⟩

Attributes: Size = (Long)

Description: The upper bits of the source (VAL or An) are compared with the upper bits of the destination ⟨ea⟩. The number of bits compared is defined by the ALC field of the AC register. If the upper bits of the source are numerically greater than (less privileged than) the destination, they cause an MMU access level exception. Otherwise, execution continues with the next instruction. If the MC field of the AC register is zero, then this instruction always causes a PMMU access level exception.

PSR: Not affected.

Instruction Format 1 (VAL contains access level to test against):

15	14	13	12	11	10	9	8	7	6	5	4	3	2	1	0
1	1	1	1	0	0	0	0	0	0	MODE			REGISTER		
0	0	1	0	1	0	0	0	0	0	0	0	0	0	0	0

The row with MODE/REGISTER represents the EFFECTIVE ADDRESS field (bits 5–0).

Instruction Fields:

Effective Address field — Specifies the logical address to be evaluated and compared against the VAL register. Only control alterable addressing modes are allowed as shown:

Addressing Mode	Mode	Register	Addressing Mode	Mode	Register
Dn	—	—	(xxx).W	111	000
An	—	—	(xxx).L	111	001
(An)	010	reg. number:An	#⟨data⟩	—	—
(An) +	—	—			
− (An)	—	—			
(d$_{16}$,An)	101	reg. number:An	(d$_{16}$,PC)	—	—
(d$_8$,An,Xn)	110	reg. number:An	(d$_8$,PC,Xn)	—	—
(bd,An,Xn)	110	reg. number:An	(bd,PC,Xn)	—	—
([bd,An,Xn],od)	110	reg. number:An	([bd,PC,Xn],od)	—	—
([bd,An],Xn,od)	110	reg. number:An	([bd,PC],Xn,od)	—	—

PVALID

Validate a Pointer
(MC68851)

Instruction Format 2 (main processor register contains access level to test against):

15	14	13	12	11	10	9	8	7	6	5	4	3	2	1	0

15	14	13	12	11	10	9	8	7	6	5	4	3	2	1	0
1	1	1	1	0	0	0	0	0	0	\multicolumn3c(MODE)			\multicolumn3c(REGISTER)		
0	0	1	0	1	0	0	0	0	0	0	0	0	\multicolumn3c(REG)		

Top row right section header: EFFECTIVE ADDRESS — MODE | REGISTER

Instruction Fields:

Effective Address field — Specifies the logical address to be evaluated and compared against specified main processor address register. Only control alterable addressing modes are allowed as shown:

Addressing Mode	Mode	Register
Dn	—	—
An	—	—
(An)	010	reg. number:An
(An) +	—	—
– (An)	—	—
(d_{16},An)	101	reg. number:An
(d_8,An,Xn)	110	reg. number:An
(bd,An,Xn)	110	reg. number:An
([bd,An,Xn],od)	110	reg. number:An
([bd,An],Xn,od)	110	reg. number:An

Addressing Mode	Mode	Register
(xxx).W	111	000
(xxx).L	111	001
#⟨data⟩	—	—
(d_{16},PC)	—	—
(d_8,PC,Xn)	—	—
(bd,PC,Xn)	—	—
([bd,PC,Xn],od)	—	—
([bd,PC],Xn,od)	—	—

Note that the effective address field must provide the MC68851 with the effective address of the logical address to be validated, not the effective address describing where the PVALID operand is located. For example, in order to validate a logical address that is temporarily stored on the system stack, the instruction PVALID VAL,[(SP)] must be used since PVALID VAL,(SP) would validate the mapping on the system stack (i.e., the effective address passed to the MC68851 is the effective address of the system stack, not the effective address formed by the operand located on the top of the stack).

Reg field — Specifies the main processor address register to be used in the compare.

ROL, ROR

Rotate (Without Extend)
(M68000 Family)

Operation: Destination Rotated by ⟨count⟩ ♦ Destination

Assembler   ROd Dx,Dy
Syntax: ROd #⟨data⟩,Dy
                   ROd ⟨ea⟩
                   where d is direction, L or R

Attributes: Size = (Byte, Word, Long)

Description: Rotates the bits of the operand in the direction specified (L or R).
The extend bit is not included in the rotation. The rotate count for the rotation
of a register is specified in either of two ways:
   1. Immediate — The rotate count (1–8) is specified in the instruction.
   2. Register — The rotate count is the value in the data register specified in
      the instruction, modulo 64.

The size of the operation for register destinations is specified as byte, word,
or long. The contents of memory, ⟨ea⟩; can be rotated one bit only, and operand
size is restricted to a word.

The ROL instruction rotates the bits of the operand to the left; the rotate count
determines the number of bit positions rotated. Bits rotated out of the high-
order bit go to the carry bit and also back into the low-order bit.

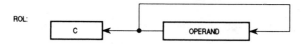

The ROR instruction rotates the bits of the operand to the right; the rotate count
determines the number of bit positions rotated. Bits rotated out of the low-
order bit go to the carry bit and also back into the high-order bit.

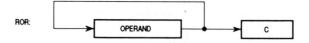

Condition Codes:

X	N	Z	V	C
—	*	*	0	*

ROL, ROR

X   Not affected.
N   Set if the most significant bit of the result is set. Cleared otherwise.
Z   Set if the result is zero. Cleared otherwise.
V   Always cleared.
C   Set according to the last bit rotated out of the operand. Cleared when the rotate count is zero.

Instruction Format (register rotate):

15	14	13	12	11	10	9	8	7	6	5	4	3	2	1	0
1	1	1	0	COUNT/ REGISTER			dr	SIZE		i/r	1	1	REGISTER		

Instruction Fields (register rotate):

Count/Register field:

If i/r = 0, this field contains the rotate count. The values 1–7 represent counts of 1–7, and zero specifies a count of eight.

If i/r = 1, this field specifies a data register that contains the rotate count (modulo 64).

dr field — Specifies the direction of the rotate:

0 — Rotate right.

1 — Rotate left.

Size field — Specifies the size of the operation:

00 — Byte operation.

01 — Word operation.

10 — Long operation.

i/r field — Specifies the rotate count location:

If i/r = 0, immediate rotate count.

If i/r = 1, register rotate count.

Register field — Specifies a data register to be rotated.

Instruction Format (memory rotate):

15	14	13	12	11	10	9	8	7	6	5	4	3	2	1	0
1	1	1	0	0	1	1	dr	1	1	EFFECTIVE ADDRESS					
										MODE			REGISTER		

Instruction Fields (memory rotate):

dr field — Specifies the direction of the rotate:

0 — Rotate right.

1 — Rotate left.

Effective Address field — Specifies the operand to be rotated. Only memory alterable addressing modes are allowed as shown:

ROL, ROR

Addressing Mode	Mode	Register
Dn	—	—
An	—	—
(An)	010	reg. number:An
(An) +	011	reg. number:An
−(An)	100	reg. number:An
(d$_{16}$,An)	101	reg. number:An
(d$_8$,An,Xn)	110	reg. number:An

Addressing Mode	Mode	Register
(xxx).W	111	000
(xxx).L	111	001
#⟨data⟩	—	—
(d$_{16}$,PC)	—	—
(d$_8$,PC,Xn)	—	—

MC68020, MC68030, AND MC68040 ONLY

Addressing Mode	Mode	Register
(bd,An,Xn)∗	110	reg. number:An
([bd,An,Xn],od)	110	reg. number:An
([bd,An],Xn,od)	110	reg. number:An

Addressing Mode	Mode	Register
(bd,PC,Xn)∗	—	—
([bd,PC,Xn],od)	—	—
([bd,PC],Xn,od)	—	—

∗Can be used with CPU32.

ROXL, ROXR

Rotate with Extend
(M68000 Family)

Operation: Destination Rotated with X by ⟨count⟩ ⬦ Destination

Assembler
Syntax: ROXd Dx,Dy
              ROXd #⟨data⟩,Dy
              ROXd ⟨ea⟩
              where d is direction, L or R

Attributes: Size = (Byte, Word, Long)

Description: Rotates the bits of the operand in the direction specified (L or R).
The extend bit is included in the rotation. The rotate count for the rotation of
a register is specified in either of two ways:
1. Immediate — The rotate count (1–8) is specified in the instruction.
2. Register — The rotate count is the value in the data register specified in
   the instruction, modulo 64.

The size of the operation for register destinations is specified as byte, word,
or long. The contents of memory, ⟨ea⟩, can be rotated one bit only, and operand
size is restricted to a word.

The ROXL instruction rotates the bits of the operand to the left; the rotate count
determines the number of bit positions rotated. Bits rotated out of the high-

ROXL, ROXR

order bit go to the carry bit and the extend bit; the previous value of the extend bit rotates into the low-order bit.

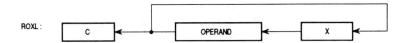

The ROXR instruction rotates the bits of the operand to the right; the rotate count determines the number of bit positions rotated. Bits rotated out of the low-order bit go to the carry bit and the extend bit; the previous value of the extend bit rotates into the high-order bit.

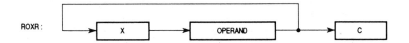

Condition Codes:

X	N	Z	V	C
*	*	*	0	*

X Set to the value of the last bit rotated out of the operand. Unaffected when the rotate count is zero.
N Set if the most significant bit of the result is set. Cleared otherwise.
Z Set if the result is zero. Cleared otherwise.
V Always cleared.
C Set according to the last bit rotated out of the operand. When the rotate count is zero, set to the value of the extend bit.

Instruction Format (register rotate):

15	14	13	12	11	10	9	8	7	6	5	4	3	2	1	0
1	1	1	0	COUNT/ REGISTER			dr	SIZE		i/r	1	0	REGISTER		

Instruction Fields (register rotate):
Count/Register field:
  If i/r = 0, this field contains the rotate count. The values 1–7 represent counts of 1–7, and zero specifies a count of eight.
  If i/r = 1, this field specifies a data register that contains the rotate count (modulo 64).
dr field — Specifies the direction of the rotate:
0 — Rotate right.
1 — Rotate left.

ROXL, ROXR

Rotate with Extend
(M68000 Family)

Size field — Specifies the size of the operation:
00 — Byte operation.
01 — Word operation.
10 — Long operation.
i/r field — Specifies the rotate count location:
If i/r = 0, immediate rotate count.
If i/r = 1, register rotate count.
Register field — Specifies a data register to be rotated.

Instruction Format (memory rotate):

15	14	13	12	11	10	9	8	7	6	5	4	3	2	1	0
1	1	1	0	0	1	0	dr	1	1	EFFECTIVE ADDRESS					

| | | | | | | | | | | MODE | | | REGISTER | | |

Instruction Fields (memory rotate):

dr field — Specifies the direction of the rotate:
0 — Rotate right.
1 — Rotate left.
Effective Address field — Specifies the operand to be rotated. Only memory alterable addressing modes are allowed as shown:

Addressing Mode	Mode	Register		Addressing Mode	Mode	Register
Dn	—	—		(xxx).W	111	000
An	—	—		(xxx).L	111	001
(An)	010	reg. number:An		#(data)	—	—
(An)+	011	reg. number:An				
−(An)	100	reg. number:An				
(d$_{16}$,An)	101	reg. number:An		(d$_{16}$,PC)	—	—
(d$_8$,An,Xn)	110	reg. number:An		(d$_8$,PC,Xn)	—	—

MC68020, MC68030, AND MC68040 ONLY

(bd,An,Xn)*	110	reg. number:An		(bd,PC,Xn)*	—	—
([bd,An,Xn],od)	110	reg. number:An		([bd,PC,Xn],od)	—	—
([bd,An],Xn,od)	110	reg. number:An		([bd,PC],Xn,od)	—	—

*Can be used with CPU32.

RTD

Return and Deallocate
(MC68010/MC68020/MC68030/MC68040/CPU32)

Operation: (SP) ⬇ PC; SP + 4 + d ⬇ SP

**Assembler
Syntax:**   RTD #⟨displacement⟩

Attributes: Unsized

Description: Pulls the program counter value from the stack and adds the sign-extended 16-bit displacement value to the stack pointer. The previous program counter value is lost.

Condition Codes:
Not affected.

Instruction Format:

15	14	13	12	11	10	9	8	7	6	5	4	3	2	1	0
0	1	0	0	1	1	1	0	0	1	1	1	0	1	0	0
DISPLACEMENT (16 BITS)															

Instruction Field:
Displacement field — Specifies the twos complement integer to be sign extended and added to the stack pointer.

RTM

Return from Module
(MC68020)

Operation: Reload Saved Module State from Stack

**Assembler
Syntax:**   RTM Rn

Attributes: Unsized

Description: A previously saved module state is reloaded from the top of stack. After the module state is retrieved from the top of the stack, the caller's stack pointer is incremented by the argument count value in the module state.

Condition Codes:
Set according to the content of the word on the stack.

RTM

Instruction Format:

15	14	13	12	11	10	9	8	7	6	5	4	3	2	1	0
0	1	0	0	1	1	1	0	0	1	1	1	D/A	REGISTER		

Instruction Fields:

D/A field — Specifies whether the module data pointer is in a data or an address register.

    0 — the register is a data register

    1 — the register is an address register

Register field — Specifies the register number for the module data area pointer which is to be restored from the saved module state. If the register specified in A7 (SP), the updated value of the register reflects the stack pointer operations, and the saved module data area pointer is lost.

RTR

Return and Restore Condition Codes
(M68000 Family)

Operation: (SP) ⬧ CCR; SP + 2 ⬧ SP;

                (SP) ⬧ PC; SP + 4 ⬧ SP

Assembler Syntax: RTR

Attributes: Unsized

Description: Pulls the condition code and program counter values from the stack. The previous condition codes and program counter values are lost. The supervisor portion of the status register is unaffected.

Condition Codes:

Set to the condition codes from the stack.

Instruction Format:

15	14	13	12	11	10	9	8	7	6	5	4	3	2	1	0
0	1	0	0	1	1	1	0	0	1	1	1	0	1	1	1

RTS

Return from Subroutine
(M68000 Family)

Operation: (SP) ♦ PC; SP + 4 ♦ SP

Assembler
Syntax: RTS

Attributes: Unsized

Description: Pulls the program counter value from the stack. The previous program counter value is lost.

Condition Codes:
Not affected.

Instruction Format:

15	14	13	12	11	10	9	8	7	6	5	4	3	2	1	0
0	1	0	0	1	1	1	0	0	1	1	1	0	1	0	1

SBCD

Subtract Decimal with Extend
(M68000 Family)

Operation: $Destination_{10} - Source_{10} - X$ ♦ Destination

Assembler   SBCD Dx,Dy
Syntax: SBCD $-(Ax), -(Ay)$

Attributes: Size = (Byte)

Description: Subtracts the source operand and the extend bit from the destination operand and stores the result in the destination location. The subtraction is performed using binary coded decimal arithmetic; the operands are packed BCD numbers. The instruction has two modes:
    1. Data register to data register: The data registers specified in the instruction contain the operands.
    2. Memory to memory: The address registers specified in the instruction access the operands from memory using the predecrement addressing mode.
This operation is a byte operation only.

SBCD

Condition Codes:

X	N	Z	V	C
*	U	*	U	*

X   Set the same as the carry bit.
N   Undefined.
Z   Cleared if the result is nonzero. Unchanged otherwise.
V   Undefined.
C   Set if a borrow (decimal) is generated. Cleared otherwise.

NOTE

Normally the Z condition code bit is set via programming before the start of an operation. This allows successful tests for zero results upon completion of multiple-precision operations.

Instruction Format:

15	14	13	12	11	10	9	8	7	6	5	4	3	2	1	0
1	0	0	0	REGISTER Dy/Ay			1	0	0	0	0	R/M	REGISTER Dx/Ax		

Instruction Fields:

Register Dy/Ay field — Specifies the destination register.
   If R/M = 0, specifies a data register.
   If R/M = 1, specifies an address register for the predecrement addressing
      mode.
R/M field — Specifies the operand addressing mode:
   0 — The operation is data register to data register.
   1 — The operation is memory to memory.
Register Dx/Ax field — Specifies the source register:
   If R/M = 0, specifies a data register.
   If R/M = 1, specifies an address register for the predecrement addressing
      mode.

Scc

Set According to Condition
(M68000 Family)

Operation: If Condition True
                    then 1s ◆ Destination
                    else 0s ◆ Destination

Assembler
Syntax: Scc ⟨ea⟩

Attributes: Size = (Byte)

Scc

Description: Tests the specified condition code; if the condition is true, sets the byte specified by the effective address to TRUE (all ones). Otherwise, sets that byte to FALSE (all zeros). Condition code cc specifies one of the following conditions:

CC	carry clear	0100	$\overline{C}$	LS	low or same	0011	$C + Z$	
CS	carry set	0101	C	LT	less than	1101	$N{\cdot}\overline{V} + \overline{N}{\cdot}V$	
EQ	equal	0111	Z	MI	minus	1011	N	
F	never true	0001	0	NE	not equal	0110	$\overline{Z}$	
GE	greater or equal	1100	$N{\cdot}V + \overline{N}{\cdot}\overline{V}$	PL	plus	1010	$\overline{N}$	
GT	greater than	1110	$N{\cdot}V{\cdot}\overline{Z} + \overline{N}{\cdot}\overline{V}{\cdot}\overline{Z}$	T	always true	0000	1	
HI	high	0010	$\overline{C}{\cdot}\overline{Z}$	VC	overflow clear	1000	$\overline{V}$	
LE	less or equal	1111	$Z + N{\cdot}\overline{V} + \overline{N}{\cdot}V$	VS	overflow set	1001	V	

Condition Codes:
Not affected.

Instruction Format:

15	14	13	12	11	10	9	8	7	6	5	4	3	2	1	0
0	1	0	1		CONDITION			1	1		EFFECTIVE ADDRESS				
											MODE			REGISTER	

Instruction Fields:
Condition field — The binary code for one of the conditions listed in the table.
Effective Address field — Specifies the location in which the true/false byte is to be stored. Only data alterable addressing modes are allowed as shown:

Addressing Mode	Mode	Register
Dn	000	reg. number:Dn
An	—	—
(An)	010	reg. number:An
(An)+	011	reg. number:An
−(An)	100	reg. number:An
(d_{16},An)	101	reg. number:An
(d_8,An,Xn)	110	reg. number:An

Addressing Mode	Mode	Register
(xxx).W	111	000
(xxx).L	111	001
#(data)	—	—
(d_{16},PC)	—	—
(d_8,PC,Xn)	—	—

MC68020, MC68030, AND MC68040 ONLY

(bd,An,Xn)*	110	reg. number:An
([bd,An,Xn],od)	110	reg. number:An
([bd,An],Xn,od)	110	reg. number:An

(bd,PC,Xn)*	—	—
([bd,PC,Xn],od)	—	—
([bd,PC],Xn,od)	—	—

*Can be used with CPU32.

NOTE

A subsequent NEG.B instruction with the same effective address can be used to change the Scc result from TRUE or FALSE to the equivalent arithmetic value (TRUE = 1, FALSE = 0). In the MC68000 and MC68008 a memory destination is read before it is written to.

SUB

Subtract

(M68000 Family)

Operation: Destination − Source ◆ Destination

Assembler   SUB ⟨ea⟩,Dn
Syntax: SUB Dn,⟨ea⟩

Attributes: Size = (Byte, Word, Long)

Description: Subtracts the source operand from the destination operand and stores the result in the destination. The size of the operation is specified as byte, word, or long. The mode of the instruction indicates which operand is the source, which is the destination, and which is the operand size.

Condition Codes:

X	N	Z	V	C
*	*	*	*	*

X Set to the value of the carry bit.
N Set if the result is negative. Cleared otherwise.
Z Set if the result is zero. Cleared otherwise.
V Set if an overflow is generated. Cleared otherwise.
C Set if a borrow is generated. Cleared otherwise.

Instruction Format:

15	14	13	12	11	10	9	8	7	6	5	4	3	2	1	0
1	0	0	1	REGISTER			OPMODE			EFFECTIVE ADDRESS					
										MODE			REGISTER		

Instruction Fields:
Register field — Specifies any of the eight data registers.
Opmode field:

Byte	Word	Long	Operation
000	001	010	(⟨Dn⟩) − (⟨ea⟩) ◆ ⟨Dn⟩
100	101	110	(⟨ea⟩) − (⟨Dn⟩) ◆ ⟨ea⟩

Effective Address field — Determines the addressing mode. If the location specified is a source operand, all addressing modes are allowed as shown:

SUB

Addressing Mode	Mode	Register
Dn	000	reg. number:Dn
An*	001	reg. number:An
(An)	010	reg. number:An
(An) +	011	reg. number:An
− (An)	100	reg. number:An
(d$_{16}$,An)	101	reg. number:An
(d$_8$,An,Xn)	110	reg. number:An

Addressing Mode	Mode	Register
(xxx).W	111	000
(xxx).L	111	001
#⟨data⟩	111	100
(d$_{16}$,PC)	111	010
(d$_8$,PC,Xn)	111	011

MC68020, MC68030, AND MC68040 ONLY

Addressing Mode	Mode	Register
(bd,An,Xn)**	110	reg. number:An
([bd,An,Xn],od)	110	reg. number:An
([bd,An],Xn,od)	110	reg. number:An

Addressing Mode	Mode	Register
(bd,PC,Xn)**	111	011
([bd,PC,Xn],od)	111	011
([bd,PC],Xn,od)	111	011

*For byte size operation, address register direct is not allowed.
**Can be used with CPU32.

If the location specified is a destination operand, only memory alterable addressing modes are allowed as shown:

Addressing Mode	Mode	Register
Dn	—	—
An	—	—
(An)	010	reg. number:An
(An) +	011	reg. number:An
− (An)	100	reg. number:An
(d$_{16}$,An)	101	reg. number:An
(d$_8$,An,Xn)	110	reg. number:An

Addressing Mode	Mode	Register
(xxx).W	111	000
(xxx).L	111	001
#⟨data⟩	—	—
(d$_{16}$,PC)	—	—
(d$_8$,PC,Xn)	—	—

MC68020, MC68030, AND MC68040 ONLY

Addressing Mode	Mode	Register
(bd,An,Xn)*	110	reg. number:An
([bd.An,Xn],od)	110	reg. number:An
([bd.An],Xn,od)	110	reg. number:An

Addressing Mode	Mode	Register
(bd,PC,Xn)*	—	—
([bd,PC,Xn],od)	—	—
([bd,PC],Xn,od)	—	—

*Can be used with CPU32.

Notes:

1. If the destination is a data register, it must be specified as a destination Dn address, not as a destination ⟨ea⟩ address.
2. Most assemblers use SUBA when the destination is an address register, and SUBI or SUBQ when the source is immediate data.

SUBA

Subtract Address
(M68000 Family)

Operation: Destination − Source ◆ Destination

Assembler
Syntax: SUBA ⟨ea⟩,An

Attributes: Size = (Word, Long)

Description: Subtracts the source operand from the destination address register and stores the result in the address register. The size of the operation is specified as word or long. Word size source operands are sign extended to 32-bit quantities prior to the subtraction.

Condition Codes:
Not affected.

Instruction Format:

15	14	13	12	11	10	9	8	7	6	5	4	3	2	1	0
1	0	0	1	REGISTER			OPMODE			EFFECTIVE ADDRESS					
										MODE			REGISTER		

Instruction Fields:

Register field — Specifies the destination, any of the eight address registers.
Opmode field — Specifies the size of the operation:
   011 — Word operation. The source operand is sign extended to a long operand and the operation is performed on the address register using all 32 bits.
   111 — Long operation.
Effective Address field — Specifies the source operand. All addressing modes are allowed as shown:

Addressing Mode	Mode	Register	Addressing Mode	Mode	Register
Dn	000	reg. number:Dn	(xxx).W	111	000
An	001	reg. number:An	(xxx).L	111	001
(An)	010	reg. number:An	#⟨data⟩	111	100
(An)+	011	reg. number:An			
−(An)	100	reg. number:An			
(d$_{16}$,An)	101	reg. number:An	(d$_{16}$,PC)	111	010
(d$_8$,An,Xn)	110	reg. number:An	(d$_8$,PC,Xn)	111	011

SUBA

MC68020, MC68030, AND MC68040 ONLY

(bd,An,Xn)*	110	reg. number:An		(bd,PC,Xn)*	111	011
([bd,An,Xn],od)	110	reg. number:An		([bd,PC,Xn],od)	111	011
([bd,An],Xn,od)	110	reg. number:An		([bd,PC],Xn,od)	111	011

*Can be used with CPU32.

SUBI

Subtract Immediate
(M68000 Family)

Operation: Destination − Immediate Data ♦ Destination

**Assembler
Syntax:**   SUBI #⟨data⟩,⟨ea⟩

Attributes: Size = (Byte, Word, Long)

Description: Subtracts the immediate data from the destination operand and stores the result in the destination location. The size of the operation is specified as byte, word, or long. The size of the immediate data matches the operation size.

Condition Codes:

X	N	Z	V	C
*	*	*	*	*

X   Set to the value of the carry bit.
N   Set if the result is negative. Cleared otherwise.
Z   Set if the result is zero. Cleared otherwise.
V   Set if an overflow occurs. Cleared otherwise.
C   Set if a borrow occurs. Cleared otherwise.

Instruction Format:

15	14	13	12	11	10	9	8	7	6	5	4	3	2	1	0
0	0	0	0	0	1	0	0	SIZE		EFFECTIVE ADDRESS					

										EFFECTIVE ADDRESS					
0	0	0	0	0	1	0	0	SIZE		MODE			REGISTER		
WORD DATA (16 BITS)								BYTE DATA (8 BITS)							
LONG DATA (32 BITS)															

Instruction Fields:
Size field — Specifies the size of the operation.
    00 — Byte operation.
    01 — Word operation.
    10 — Long operation.

SUBI

Effective Address field — Specifies the destination operand. Only data alterable addressing modes are allowed as shown:

Addressing Mode	Mode	Register	Addressing Mode	Mode	Register
Dn	000	reg. number:Dn	(xxx).W	111	000
An	—	—	(xxx).L	111	001
(An)	010	reg. number:An	#⟨data⟩	—	—
(An) +	011	reg. number:An			
– (An)	100	reg. number:An			
(d₁₆,An)	101	reg. number:An	(d₁₆,PC)	—	—
(d₈,An,Xn)	110	reg. number:An	(d₈,PC,Xn)	—	—

MC68020, MC68030, AND MC68040 ONLY

(bd,An,Xn)*	110	reg. number:An	(bd,PC,Xn)*	—	—
([bd,An,Xn],od)	110	reg. number:An	([bd,PC,Xn],od)	—	—
([bd,An],Xn,od)	110	reg. number:An	([bd,PC],Xn,od)	—	—

*Can be used with CPU32.

Immediate field — (Data immediately following the instruction)
If size = 00, the data is the low-order byte of the immediate word.
If size = 01, the data is the entire immediate word.
If size = 10, the data is the next two immediate words.

SUBQ

Subtract Quick
(M68000 Family)

Operation: Destination − Immediate Data ⬦ Destination

**Assembler
Syntax:**   SUBQ #⟨data⟩,⟨ea⟩

Attributes: Size = (Byte, Word, Long)

Description: Subtracts the immediate data (1–8) from the destination operand. The size of the operation is specified as byte, word, or long. Only word and long operations are allowed with address registers, and the condition codes are not affected. When subtracting from address registers, the entire destination address register is used, regardless of the operation size.

Condition Codes:

X	N	Z	V	C
*	*	*	*	*

X   Set to the value of the carry bit.
N   Set if the result is negative. Cleared otherwise.

SUBQ

Z   Set if the result is zero. Cleared otherwise.
V   Set if an overflow occurs. Cleared otherwise.
C   Set if a borrow occurs. Cleared otherwise.

Instruction Format:

15	14	13	12	11	10	9	8	7	6	5	4	3	2	1	0
0	1	0	1	DATA			1	SIZE		EFFECTIVE ADDRESS					

| | | | | | | | | | | MODE | | | REGISTER | | |

Instruction Fields:

Data field — Three bits of immediate data; 1–7 represent immediate values of 1–7, and zero represents eight.

Size field — Specifies the size of the operation:

00 — Byte operation.
01 — Word operation.
10 — Long operation.

Effective Address field — Specifies the destination location. Only alterable addressing modes are allowed as shown:

Addressing Mode	Mode	Register
Dn	000	reg. number:Dn
An*	001	reg. number:An
(An)	010	reg. number:An
(An) +	011	reg. number:An
(An)	100	reg. number:An
(d₁₆,An)	101	reg. number:An
(d₈,An,Xn)	110	reg. number:An

Addressing Mode	Mode	Register
(xxx).W	111	000
(xxx).L	111	001
#⟨data⟩	—	—
(d₁₆,PC)	—	—
(d₈,PC,Xn)	—	—

MC68020, MC68030, AND MC68040 ONLY

(bd,An,Xn)**	110	reg. number:An
([bd,An,Xn],od)	110	reg. number:An
([bd,An],Xn,od)	110	reg. number:An

(bd,PC,Xn)**	—	—
([bd,PC,Xn],od)	—	—
([bd,PC],Xn,od)	—	—

*Word and Long only.
**Can be used with CPU32.

SUBX

Subtract with Extend
(M68000 Family)

Operation: Destination − Source − X ⬥ Destination

Assembler
Syntax: SUBX Dx,Dy
SUBX −(Ax),−(Ay)

Attributes: Size = (Byte, Word, Long)

SUBX

Description: Subtracts the source operand and the extend bit from the destination operand and stores the result in the destination location. The instruction has two modes:
1. Data register to data register: The data registers specified in the instruction contain the operands.
2. Memory to memory: The address registers specified in the instruction access the operands from memory using the predecrement addressing mode.

The size of the operand is specified as byte, word, or long.

Condition Codes:

X	N	Z	V	C
*	*	*	*	*

X Set to the value of the carry bit.
N Set if the result is negative. Cleared otherwise.
Z Cleared if the result is nonzero. Unchanged otherwise.
V Set if an overflow occurs. Cleared otherwise.
C Set if a borrow occurs. Cleared otherwise.

NOTE

Normally the Z condition code bit is set via programming before the start of an operation. This allows successful tests for zero results upon completion of multiple-precision operations.

Instruction Format:

15	14	13	12	11	10	9	8	7	6	5	4	3	2	1	0
1	0	0	1	REGISTER Dy/Ay			1	SIZE		0	0	R/M	REGISTER Dx/Ax		

Instruction Fields:

Register Dy/Ay field — Specifies the destination register:
If R/M = 0, specifies a data register.
If R/M = 1, specifies an address register for the predecrement addressing mode.
Size field — Specifies the size of the operation:
00 — Byte operation.
01 — Word operation.
10 — Long operation.
R/M field — Specifies the operand addressing mode:
0 — The operation is data register to data register.
1 — The operation is memory to memory.
Register Dx/Ax field — Specifies the source register:
If R/M = 0, specifies a data register.
If R/M = 1, specifies an address register for the predecrement addressing mode.

SWAP

Swap Register Halves
(M68000 Family)

Operation: Register [31:16] ⬌ Register [15:0]

**Assembler
Syntax:**   SWAP Dn

Attributes: Size = (Word)

Description: Exchange the 16-bit words (halves) of a data register.

Condition Codes:

X	N	Z	V	C
—	*	*	0	0

X   Not affected.
N   Set if the most significant bit of the 32-bit result is set. Cleared otherwise.
Z   Set if the 32-bit result is zero. Cleared otherwise.
V   Always cleared.
C   Always cleared.

Instruction Format:

15	14	13	12	11	10	9	8	7	6	5	4	3	2	1	0
0	1	0	0	1	0	0	0	0	1	0	0	0	REGISTER		

Instruction Fields:

Register field — Specifies the data register to swap.

TAS

Test and Set an Operand
(M68000 Family)

Operation: Destination Tested ⬇ Condition Codes; 1 ⬇ bit 7 of Destination

**Assembler
Syntax:**   TAS ⟨ea⟩

Attributes: Size = (Byte)

Description: Tests and sets the byte operand addressed by the effective address
field. The instruction tests the current value of the operand and sets the N and

TAS

Z condition bits appropriately. TAS also sets the high-order bit of the operand. The operation uses a locked or read-modify-write transfer sequence. This instruction supports use of a flag or semaphore to coordinate several processors.

Condition Codes:

X	N	Z	V	C
—	*	*	0	0

X   Not affected.
N   Set if the most significant bit of the operand is currently set. Cleared otherwise.
Z   Set if the operand was zero. Cleared otherwise.
V   Always cleared.
C   Always cleared.

Instruction Format:

15	14	13	12	11	10	9	8	7	6	5	4	3	2	1	0
0	1	0	0	1	0	1	0	1	1	EFFECTIVE ADDRESS					

| | | | | | | | | | | MODE | | | REGISTER | | |

Instruction Fields:

Effective Address field — Specifies the location of the tested operand. Only data alterable addressing modes are allowed as shown:

Addressing Mode	Mode	Register	Addressing Mode	Mode	Register
Dn	000	reg. number:Dn	(xxx).W	111	000
An	—	—	(xxx).L	111	001
(An)	010	reg. number:An	#⟨data⟩	—	—
(An)+	011	reg. number:An			
−(An)	100	reg. number:An			
(d$_{16}$,An)	101	reg. number:An	(d$_{16}$,PC)	—	—
(d$_8$,An,Xn)	110	reg. number:An	(d$_8$,PC,Xn)	—	—

MC68020, MC68030, AND MC68040 ONLY

(bd,An,Xn)*	110	reg. number:An	(bd,PC,Xn)*	—	—
([bd,An,Xn],od)	110	reg. number:An	([bd,PC,Xn],od)	—	—
([bd,An],Xn,od)	110	reg. number:An	([bd,PC],Xn,od)	—	—

*Can be used with CPU32.

TRAP

Trap
(M68000 Family)

Operation: 1 ⬇ S Bit of SR
*SSP − 2 ⬇ SSP; Format/Offset ⬇ (SSP);
SSP − 4 ⬇ SSP; PC ⬇ (SSP); SSP − 2 ⬇ SSP;
SR ⬇ (SSP); Vector Address ⬇ PC

*The MC68000 and MC68008 do not write vector offset or format code to the system stack.

**Assembler
Syntax:**   TRAP #⟨vector⟩

Attributes: Unsized

Description: Causes a TRAP #⟨vector⟩ exception. The instruction adds the immediate operand (vector) of the instruction to 32 to obtain the vector number. The range of vector values is 0–15, which provides 16 vectors.

Condition Codes:
Not affected.

Instruction Format:

15	14	13	12	11	10	9	8	7	6	5	4	3	2	1	0
0	1	0	0	1	1	1	0	0	1	0	0	VECTOR			

Instruction Fields:
Vector field — Specifies the trap vector to be taken.

TRAPcc

Trap on Condition
(MC68020/MC68030/MC68040/CPU32)

Operation: If cc then TRAP

**Assembler
Syntax:**   TRAPcc
TRAPcc.W #⟨data⟩
TRAPcc.L #⟨data⟩

Attributes: Unsized or Size = (Word, Long)

TRAPcc

Description: If the specified condition is true, causes a TRAPcc exception. The vector number is seven. The processor pushes the address of the next instruction word (currently in the program counter) onto the stack. If the condition is not true, the processor performs no operation, and execution continues with the next instruction. The immediate data operand should be placed in the next word(s) following the operation word and is available to the trap handler. Condition code cc specifies one of the following conditions.

CC	carry clear	0100	$\overline{C}$
CS	carry set	0101	C
EQ	equal	0111	Z
F	never true	0001	0
GE	greater or equal	1100	$N \cdot V + \overline{N} \cdot \overline{V}$
GT	greater than	1110	$N \cdot V \cdot \overline{Z} + \overline{N} \cdot \overline{V} \cdot \overline{Z}$
HI	high	0010	$\overline{C} \cdot \overline{Z}$
LE	less or equal	1111	$Z + N \cdot \overline{V} + \overline{N} \cdot V$
LS	low or same	0011	$C + Z$
LT	less than	1100	$N \cdot \overline{V} + \overline{N} \cdot V$
MI	minus	1011	N
NE	not equal	0110	$\overline{Z}$
PL	plus	1010	$\overline{N}$
T	always true	0000	1
VC	overflow clear	1000	$\overline{V}$
VS	overflow set	1001	V

Condition Codes:
Not affected.

Instruction Format:

15	14	13	12	11	10	9	8	7	6	5	4	3	2	1	0
0	1	0	1		CONDITION			1	1	1	1	1		OPMODE	
OPTIONAL WORD															
OR LONG WORD															

Instruction Fields:
Condition field — The binary code for one of the conditions listed in the table.
Opmode field — Selects the instruction form.
   010 — Instruction is followed by word-size operand.
   011 — Instruction is followed by long-word-size operand.
   100 — Instruction has no operand.

TRAPV

Trap on Overflow
(M68000 Family)

Operation: If V then TRAP

Assembler
Syntax: TRAPV

Attributes: Unsized

Description: If the overflow condition is set, causes a TRAPV exception (vector number 7). If the overflow condition is not set, the processor performs no operation and execution continues with the next instruction.

Condition Codes:
Not affected.

Instruction Format:

15	14	13	12	11	10	9	8	7	6	5	4	3	2	1	0
0	1	0	0	1	1	1	0	0	1	1	1	0	1	1	0

TST

Test an Operand
(M68000 Family)

Operation: Destination Tested ⬥ Condition Codes

Assembler
Syntax: TST ⟨ea⟩

Attributes: Size = (Byte, Word, Long)

Description: Compares the operand with zero and sets the condition codes according to the results of the test. The size of the operation is specified as byte, word, or long.

TST

Condition Codes:

X	N	Z	V	C
—	*	*	0	0

X   Not affected.
N   Set if the operand is negative. Cleared otherwise.
Z   Set if the operand is zero. Cleared otherwise.
V   Always cleared.
C   Always cleared.

Instruction Format:

15	14	13	12	11	10	9	8	7	6	5	4	3	2	1	0
0	1	0	0	1	0	1	0	SIZE		EFFECTIVE ADDRESS					

EFFECTIVE ADDRESS — MODE | REGISTER

Instruction Fields:

Size field — Specifies the size of the operation:
00 — Byte operation.
01 — Word operation.
10 — Long operation.
Effective Address field — Specifies the addressing mode for the destination operand:

Addressing Mode	Mode	Register	Addressing Mode	Mode	Register
Dn	000	reg. number:Dn	(xxx).W	111	000
An*	001	reg. number:An	(xxx).L	111	001
(An)	010	reg. number:An	#⟨data⟩*	111	100
(An)+	011	reg. number:An			
−(An)	100	reg. number:An			
(d_{16},An)	101	reg. number:An	(d_{16},PC)	111	010
(d_8,An,Xn)	110	reg. number:An	(d_8,PC,Xn)	111	011

MC68020, MC68030, AND MC68040 ONLY

(bd,An,Xn)**	110	reg. number:An	(bd,PC,Xn)**	111	011
([bd,An,Xn],od)	110	reg. number:An	([bd,PC,Xn],od)	111	011
([bd,An],Xn,od)	110	reg. number:An	([bd,PC],Xn,od)	111	011

*MC68020, MC68030, MC68040, and CPU32. Address register direct allowed only for word and long.
**Can be used with CPU32.

UNLK

Unlink
(M68000 Family)

Operation: An ♦ SP; (SP) ♦ An; SP + 4 ♦ SP

Assembler
Syntax: UNLK An

Attributes: Unsized

Description: Loads the stack pointer from the specified address register then loads the address register with the long word pulled from the top of the stack.

Condition Codes:
Not affected.

Instruction Format:

15	14	13	12	11	10	9	8	7	6	5	4	3	2	1	0
0	1	0	0	1	1	1	0	0	1	0	1	1		REGISTER	

Instruction Fields:
Register field — Specifies the address register for the instruction.

UNPK

Unpack BCD
(MC68020/MC68030/MC68040)

Operation: Source (Packed BCD) + adjustment ♦ Destination (Unpacked BCD)

Assembler   UNPACK −(Ax), −(Ay),#⟨adjustment⟩
Syntax: UNPK Dx,Dy,#⟨adjustment⟩

Attributes: Unsized

Description: Places the two BCD digits in the source operand byte into the lower nibbles of two bytes, and places zero bits in the upper nibbles of both bytes. Adds the adjustment value to this unpacked value. Condition codes are not altered.

When both operands are data registers, the instruction unpacks the source register contents, adds the extension word, and places the result in the destination register. The high word of the destination register is unaffected.

UNPK

Source (Dx):

15	14	13	12	11	10	9	8	7	6	5	4	3	2	1	0
u	u	u	u	u	u	u	u	a	b	c	d	e	f	g	h

Intermediate Expansion:

15	14	13	12	11	10	9	8	7	6	5	4	3	2	1	0
0	0	0	0	a	b	c	d	0	0	0	0	e	f	g	h

Add Adjustment Word:

15	14	13	12	11	10	9	8	7	6	5	4	3	2	1	0
16-BIT EXTENSION															

Destination (Dy):

15	14	13	12	11	10	9	8	7	6	5	4	3	2	1	0
v	v	v	v	a'	b'	c'	d'	w	w	w	w	e'	f'	g'	h'

When the specified addressing mode is predecrement, the instruction extracts two BCD digits from a byte at the source address. After unpacking the digits and adding the adjustment word, the instruction writes the two bytes to the destination address.

Source (Ax):

7	6	5	4	3	2	1	0
a	b	c	d	e	f	g	h

Intermediate Expansion:

15	14	13	12	11	10	9	8	7	6	5	4	3	2	1	0
0	0	0	0	a	b	c	d	0	0	0	0	e	f	g	h

Add Adjustment Word:

15	14	13	12	11	10	9	8	7	6	5	4	3	2	1	0
16-BIT EXTENSION															

Destination (Ay):

7	6	5	4	3	2	1	0
v	v	v	v	a'	b'	c'	d'
w	w	w	w	e'	f'	g'	h'

UNPK

Condition Codes:
   Not affected.

Instruction Format:

15	14	13	12	11	10	9	8	7	6	5	4	3	2	1	0
1	0	0	0	REGISTER Dy/Ay			1	1	0	0	0	R/M	REGISTER Dx/Ax		
16-BIT EXTENSION: ADJUSTMENT															

Instruction Fields:
   Register Dy/Ay field — Specifies the destination register.
      If R/M = 0, specifies a data register.
      If R/M = 1, specifies an address register in the predecrement addressing
         mode.
   R/M field — Specifies the operand addressing mode.
      0 — The operation is data register to data register.
      1 — The operation is memory to memory.
   Register Dx/Ax field — Specifies the data register.
      If R/M = 0, specifies a data register.
      If R/M = 1, specifies an address register in the predecrement addressing
         mode.
   Adjustment field — Immediate data word that is added to the source operand.
      Appropriate constants can be used as the adjustment, to translate from BCD
      to the desired code. The constant used for ASCII is $3030; for EBCDIC, $F0F0.

APPENDIX B

M68000 FAMILY OF SUPERVISOR (PRIVILEGED) INSTRUCTIONS

ANDI
to SR

AND Immediate to the Status Register
(M68000 Family)

Operation: If supervisor state
                  then Source \SR ⬦ SR
                  else TRAP

**Assembler
Syntax:**   ANDI #⟨data⟩,SR

Attributes: Size = (Word)

Description: Performs an AND operation of the immediate operand with the contents of the status register and stores the result in the status register. All implemented bits of the status register are affected.

Condition Codes:

X	N	Z	V	C
·	·	·	·	·

X   Cleared if bit 4 of immediate operand is zero. Unchanged otherwise.
N   Cleared if bit 3 of immediate operand is zero. Unchanged otherwise.
Z   Cleared if bit 2 of immediate operand is zero. Unchanged otherwise.
V   Cleared if bit 1 of immediate operand is zero. Unchanged otherwise.
C   Cleared if bit 0 of immediate operand is zero. Unchanged otherwise.

Instruction Format:

15	14	13	12	11	10	9	8	7	6	5	4	3	2	1	0
0	0	0	0	0	0	1	0	0	1	1	1	1	1	0	0
WORD DATA (16 BITS)															

CINV

Invalidate Cache Lines
(MC68040)

Operation: If supervisor state
                  then invalidate selected cache lines
                  else TRAP

CINV

Assembler Syntax:	CINVL	<caches>,(An)
	CINVP	<caches>,(An)
	CINVA	<caches>

<caches> specifies either the instruction (IC), data (DC), or both caches.

Attributes: Unsized

Description: Invalidates selected cache lines. The data cache (DC), instruction cache (IC), both caches (BC), or neither cache (NC) can be specified. Any dirty data in data cache lines that are invalidated is lost; the CPUSH instruction must be used when dirty data may be contained in the data cache.

Specific cache lines can be selected in three ways:
1) CINVL invalidates the cache line (if any) matching the physical address in the specified address register.
2) CINVP invalidates the cache lines (if any) matching the physical memory page in the specified address register. For example, if 4K page sizes are selected and An contains $12345000, all cache lines matching page $12345000 are invalidated.
3) CINVA invalidates all cache entries.

Condition Codes:
Not affected.

Instruction Format:

15	14	13	12	11	10	9	8	7	6	5	4	3	2	1	0
1	1	1	1	0	1	0	0	CACHE		0	SCOPE		REGISTER		

Instruction Fields:
Cache field — Specifies the Cache:
00 — No Operation
01 — Data Cache
10 — Instruction Cache
11 — Data and Instruction Caches
Scope field — Specifies the Scope of the Operation:
00 — Illegal (causes illegal instruction trap)
01 — Line
10 — Page
11 — All
Register field — Specifies the address register for line and page operations. For line operations, the low order bits 3:0 of the address are don't cares. Bits 11:0 or 12:0 of the address are don't care for 4K or 8K page operations, respectively.

cpRESTORE

**Coprocessor Restore
Functions
(MC68020/MC68030)**

Operation: If supervisor state
then Restore Internal State of Coprocessor
else TRAP

**Assembler
Syntax:**   cpRESTORE ⟨ea⟩

Attributes: Unsized

Description: Restores the internal state of a coprocessor usually after it has been
saved by a preceding cpSAVE instruction.

Condition Codes:
Not affected.

Instruction Format:

15	14	13	12	11	10	9	8	7	6	5	4	3	2	1	0
1	1	1	1		CP-ID		1	0	1		EFFECTIVE ADDRESS MODE			REGISTER	

Instruction Field:

Cp-Id field — Identifies the coprocessor that is to be restored. Cp-Id of 000
results in an F-line exception for the MC68030.

Effective Address field — Specifies the location where the internal state of the
coprocessor is located. Only postincrement or control addressing modes are
allowed as shown:

Addressing Mode	Mode	Register	Addressing Mode	Mode	Register
Dn	—	—	(xxx).W	111	000
An	—	—	(xxx).L	111	001
(An)	010	reg. number:An	#⟨data⟩	111	100
(An)	011	reg. number:An			
(An)	—	—			
(d₁₆,An)	101	reg. number:An	(d₁₆,PC)	111	010
(d₈,An,Xn)	110	reg. number:An	(d₈,PC,Xn)	111	011
(bd,An,Xn)	110	reg. number:An	(bd,PC,Xn)	111	011
([bd,An,Xn],od)	110	reg. number:An	([bd,PC,Xn],od)	111	011
([bd,An],Xn,od)	110	reg. number:An	([bd,PC],Xn,od)	111	011

NOTE

If the format word returned by the coprocessor indicates "come again",
pending interrupts are not serviced.

cpSAVE

Coprocessor Save Function
(MC68020/MC68030)

Operation: If supervisor state
                  then Save Internal State of Coprocessor
                  else TRAP

**Assembler
Syntax:**   cpSAVE ⟨ea⟩

Attributes: Unsized

Description: Saves the internal state of a coprocessor in a format that can be restored by a cpRESTORE instruction.

Condition Codes:
    Not affected.

Instruction Format:

15	14	13	12	11	10	9	8	7	6	5	4	3	2	1	0
1	1	1	1	CP-ID			1	0	0	EFFECTIVE ADDRESS MODE / REGISTER					

Instruction Fields:

Cp-Id field — Identifies the coprocessor for this operation. Cp-Id of 000 results in an F-line exception for the MC68030.

Effective Address field — Specifies the location where the internal state of the coprocessor is to be saved. Only predecrement or control alterable addressing modes are allowed as shown:

Addressing Mode	Mode	Register	Addressing Mode	Mode	Register
Dn	—	—	(xxx).W	111	000
An*	—	—	(xxx).L	111	001
(An)	010	reg. number:An	#⟨data⟩	—	—
(An) ⁺	—	—			
−(An)	100	reg. number:An			
(d₁₆,An)	101	reg. number:An	(d₁₆,PC)	—	—
(d₈,An,Xn)	110	reg. number:An	(d₈,PC,Xn)	—	—
(bd,An,Xn)	110	reg. number:An	(bd,PC,Xn)	—	—
([bd,An,Xn],od)	110	reg. number:An	([bd,PC,Xn],od)	—	—
([bd,An],Xn,od)	110	reg. number:An	([bd,PC],Xn,od)	—	—

CPUSH

Push and Invalidate Cache Lines
(MC68040)

Operation: If supervisor state
       then
         if data cache then push selected dirty data cache lines
         invalidate selected cache lines
       else TRAP

Assembler   CPUSHL   <caches>,(An)
Syntax: CPUSHP   <caches>,(An)
              CPUSHA   <caches>

                     <caches> specifies either the instruction (IC), data (DC), or both caches.

Attributes: Unsized

Description: Pushes and then invalidates selected cache lines. The data cache (DC), instruction cache (IC), both caches (BC), or neither cache (NC) can be specified. When the data cache is specified, the selected data cache lines are first pushed to memory (if they contain dirty data) and then invalidated. Selected instruction cache lines are invalidated.

Specific cache lines can be selected in three ways:
1) CPUSHL pushes and invalidates the cache line (if any) matching the physical address in the specified address register.
2) CPUSHP pushes and invalidates the cache lines (if any) matching the physical memory page in the specified address register. For example, if 4K page sizes are selected and An contains $12345000, all cache lines matching page $12345000 are selected.
3) CPUSHA pushes and invalidates all cache entries.

Condition Codes:
Not affected.

Instruction Format:

15	14	13	12	11	10	9	8	7	6	5	4	3	2	1	0
1	1	1	1	0	1	0	0	CACHE		1	SCOPE		REGISTER		

Instruction Fields:
Cache field — Specifies the Cache:
00 — No Operation
01 — Data Cache
10 — Instruction Cache
11 — Data and Instruction Caches

CPUSH

Scope field — Specifies the Scope of the Operation:
  00 — Illegal (causes illegal instruction trap)
  01 — Line
  10 — Page
  11 — All
Register field — Specifies the address register for line and page operations. For line operations, the low order bits 3:0 of the address are don't care. Bits 11:0 or 12:0 of the address are don't care for 4K or 8K page operations, respectively.

EORI
to SR

Exclusive-OR Immediate to the Status Register
(M68000 Family)

Operation: If supervisor state
  then Source $\oplus$ SR $\blacktriangleright$ SR
  else TRAP

**Assembler
Syntax:**   EORI #⟨data⟩,SR

Attributes: Size = (Word)

Description: Performs an exclusive-OR operation on the contents of the status register using the immediate operand and stores the result in the status register. All implemented bits of the status register are affected.

Condition Codes:

X	N	Z	V	C
*	*	*	*	*

X Changed if bit 4 of immediate operand is one. Unchanged otherwise.
N Changed if bit 3 of immediate operand is one. Unchanged otherwise.
Z Changed if bit 2 of immediate operand is one. Unchanged otherwise.
V Changed if bit 1 of immediate operand is one. Unchanged otherwise.
C Changed if bit 0 of immediate operand is one. Unchanged otherwise.

Instruction Format:

15	14	13	12	11	10	9	8	7	6	5	4	3	2	1	0
0	0	0	0	1	0	1	0	0	1	1	1	1	1	0	0
WORD DATA (16 BITS)															

MOVE
from SR

Move from the Status Register
(MC68010/MC68020/MC68030/MC68040/CPU32)

Operation: If supervisor state
        then SR ♦ Destination
        else TRAP

Assembler
Syntax: MOVE SR,⟨ea⟩

Attributes: Size = (Word)

Description: Moves the data in the status register to the destination location. The destination is word length. Unimplemented bits are read as zeros.

Condition Codes:
Not affected.

Instruction Format:

15	14	13	12	11	10	9	8	7	6	5	4	3	2	1	0
0	1	0	0	0	0	0	0	1	1	EFFECTIVE ADDRESS				

| | | | | | | | | | | MODE | | | REGISTER | | |

Instruction Fields:

Effective Address field — Specifies the destination location. Only data alterable addressing modes are allowed as shown:

Addressing Mode	Mode	Register
Dn	000	reg. number:Dn
An	—	—
(An)	010	reg. number:An
(An) +	011	reg. number:An
(An)	100	reg. number:An
(d$_{16}$,An)	101	reg. number:An
(d$_8$,An,Xn)	110	reg. number:An

Addressing Mode	Mode	Register
(xxx).W	111	000
(xxx).L	111	001
#⟨data⟩	—	—
(d$_{16}$,PC)	—	—
(d$_8$,PC,Xn)	—	—

MC68020, MC68030, AND MC68040 ONLY

Addressing Mode	Mode	Register
(bd,An,Xn)∗	110	reg. number:An
([bd,An,Xn],od)	110	reg. number:An
([bd,An],Xn,od)	110	reg. number:An

Addressing Mode	Mode	Register
(bd,PC,Xn)∗	—	—
([bd,PC,Xn],od)	—	—
([bd,PC],Xn,od)	—	—

∗Available for the CPU32.

NOTE

Use the MOVE from CCR instruction to access only the condition codes.

MOVE to SR

Move to the Status Register
(M68000 Family)

Operation: If supervisor state
then Source ♦ SR
else TRAP

**Assembler
Syntax:** MOVE ⟨ea⟩,SR

Attributes: Size = (Word)

Description: Moves the data in the source operand to the status register. The source operand is a word and all implemented bits of the status register are affected.

Condition Codes:
Set according to the source operand.

Instruction Format:

15	14	13	12	11	10	9	8	7	6	5	4	3	2	1	0
0	1	0	0	0	1	1	0	1	1	EFFECTIVE ADDRESS				
										MODE			REGISTER		

Instruction Fields:
Effective Address field — Specifies the location of the source operand. Only data addressing modes are allowed as shown:

Addressing Mode	Mode	Register	Addressing Mode	Mode	Register
Dn	000	reg. number:Dn	(xxx).W	111	000
An	—	—	(xxx).L	111	001
(An)	010	reg. number:An	#⟨data⟩	111	100
(An)+	011	reg. number:An			
-(An)	100	reg. number:An			
(d₁₆,An)	101	reg. number:An	(d₁₆,PC)	111	010
(d₈,An,Xn)	110	reg. number:An	(d₈,PC,Xn)	111	011

MC68020, MC68030, AND MC68040 ONLY

Addressing Mode	Mode	Register	Addressing Mode	Mode	Register
(bd,An,Xn)*	110	reg. number:An	(bd,PC,Xn)*	111	011
([bd,An,Xn],od)	110	reg. number:An	([bd,PC,Xn],od)	111	011
([bd,An],Xn,od)	110	reg. number:An	([bd,PC],Xn,od)	111	011

*Available for the CPU32.

MOVE USP

Move User Stack Pointer
(M68000 Family)

Operation: If supervisor state
                       then USP ◆ An or An ◆ USP
                       else TRAP

Assembler   MOVE USP,An
Syntax: MOVE An,USP

Attributes: Size = (Long)

Description: Moves the contents of the user stack pointer to or from the specified address register.

Condition Codes:
Not affected.

Instruction Format:

15	14	13	12	11	10	9	8	7	6	5	4	3	2	1	0
0	1	0	0	1	1	1	0	0	1	1	0	dr	REGISTER		

Instruction Fields:
dr field — Specifies the direction of transfer:
    0 — Transfer the address register to the USP.
    1 — Transfer the USP to the address register.
Register field — Specifies the address register for the operation.

MOVEC

Move Control Register
(MC68010/MC68020/MC68030/MC68040/CPU32)

Operation: If supervisor state
                       then Rc ◆ Rn or Rn ◆ Rc
                       else TRAP

Assembler   MOVEC Rc,Rn
Syntax: MOVEC Rn,Rc

Attributes: Size = (Long)

Description: Moves the contents of the specified control register (Rc) to the specified general register (Rn) or copies the contents of the specified general register

MOVEC

to the specified control register. This is always a 32-bit transfer even though the control register may be implemented with fewer bits. Unimplemented bits are read as zeros.

Condition Codes:

Not affected.

Instruction Format:

15	14	13	12	11	10	9	8	7	6	5	4	3	2	1	0
0	1	0	0	1	1	1	0	0	1	1	1	1	0	1	dr
A D	REGISTER			CONTROL REGISTER											

Instruction Fields:

dr field — Specifies the direction of the transfer:

0 — Control register to general register.

1 — General register to control register.

A D field — Specifies the type of general register:

0 — Data register.

1 — Address register.

Register field — Specifies the register number.

Control Register field — Specifies the control register.

Hex	Control Register
MC68010/MC68020/MC68030/MC68040/CPU32	
000	Source Function Code (SFC)
001	Destination Function Code (DFC)
800	User Stack Pointer (USP)
801	Vector Base Register (VBR)
MC68020/MC68030/MC68040	
002	Cache Control Register (CACR)
802	Cache Address Register (CAAR)*
803	Master Stack Pointer (MSP)
804	Interrupt Stack Pointer (ISP)
MC68040	
003	MMU Translation Control Register (TC)
004	Instruction Transparent Translation Register 0 (ITT0)
005	Instruction Transparent Translation Register 1 (ITT1)
006	Data Transparent Translation Register 0 (DTT0)
007	Data Transparent Translation Register 1 (DTT1)
805	MMU Status Register (MMUSR)
806	User Root Pointer (URP)
807	Supervisor Root Pointer (SRP)

Any other code causes an illegal instruction exception.

*For the MC68020 and MC68030 only.

MOVES

Move Address Space
(MC68010/MC68020/MC68030/MC68040/CPU32)

Operation: If supervisor state
　　　　　　　then Rn ♦ Destination [DFC] or Source [SFC] ♦ Rn
　　　　　　　else TRAP

Assembler   MOVES Rn,⟨ea⟩
Syntax: MOVES ⟨ea⟩,Rn

Attributes: Size = (Byte, Word, Long)

Description: Moves the byte, word, or long operand from the specified general register to a location within the address space specified by the destination function code (DFC) register; or, moves the byte, word, or long operand from a location within the address space specified by the source function code (SFC) register to the specified general register.

If the destination is a data register, the source operand replaces the corresponding low-order bits of that data register, depending on the size of the operation. If the destination is an address register, the source operand is sign extended to 32 bits and then loaded into that address register.

Condition Codes:
Not affected.

Instruction Format:

15	14	13	12	11	10	9	8	7	6	5	4	3	2	1	0
0	0	0	0	1	1	1	0	_SIZE_		_EFFECTIVE ADDRESS MODE_			_REGISTER_		
A/D	_REGISTER_		dr	0	0	0	0	0	0	0	0	0	0	0	0

Instruction Fields:
　　Size field — Specifies the size of the operation:
　　　　00 — Byte operation.
　　　　01 — Word operation.
　　　　10 — Long operation.
　　Effective Address field — Specifies the source or destination location within the alternate address space. Only memory alterable addressing modes are allowed as shown:

MOVES

Addressing Mode	Mode	Register
Dn	—	—
An	—	—
(An)	010	reg. number:An
(An) -	011	reg. number:An
-(An)	100	reg. number:An
(d$_{16}$,An)	101	reg. number:An
(d$_8$,An,Xn)	110	reg. number:An

Addressing Mode	Mode	Register
(xxx).W	111	000
(xxx).L	111	001
#⟨data⟩	—	—
(d$_{16}$,PC)	—	—
(d$_8$,PC,Xn)	—	—

MC68020, MC68030, AND MC68040 ONLY

Addressing Mode	Mode	Register
(bd,An,Xn)*	110	reg. number:An
([bd,An,Xn],od)	110	reg. number:An
([bd,An],Xn,od)	110	reg. number:An

(bd,PC,Xn)*	—	—
([bd,PC,Xn],od)	—	—
([bd,PC],Xn,od)	—	—

*Available for the CPU32.

A/D field — Specifies the type of general register:

  0 — Data register.

  1 — Address register.

Register field — Specifies the register number.

dr field — Specifies the direction of the transfer:

  0 — From ⟨ea⟩ to general register.

  1 — From general register to ⟨ea⟩.

NOTE

For either of the two following examples with the same address register as both source and destination

    MOVES.x An,(An)+

    MOVES.x An,−(An)

the value stored is undefined. The current implementations of the MC68010, MC68020, MC68030, and MC68040 store the incremented or decremented value of An. Check the following code sequence to determine what value is stored for each case.

    MOVEA.L #$1000,A0

    MOVES.L A0,(A0)+

    MOVES.L A0,−(A0)

ORI
to SR

Inclusive-OR Immediate to the Status Register
(M68000 Family)

Operation: If supervisor state
      then Source V SR ◆ SR
      else TRAP

**Assembler
Syntax:**   ORI #⟨data⟩,SR

Attributes: Size = (Word)

Description: Performs an inclusive-OR operation of the immediate operand and
the contents of the status register and stores the result in the status register.
All implemented bits of the status register are affected.

Condition Codes:

X	N	Z	V	C
*	*	*	*	*

X   Set if bit 4 of immediate operand is one. Unchanged otherwise.
N   Set if bit 3 of immediate operand is one. Unchanged otherwise.
Z   Set if bit 2 of immediate operand is one. Unchanged otherwise.
V   Set if bit 1 of immediate operand is one. Unchanged otherwise.
C   Set if bit 0 of immediate operand is one. Unchanged otherwise.

Instruction Format:

15	14	13	12	11	10	9	8	7	6	5	4	3	2	1	0
0	0	0	0	0	0	0	0	0	1	1	1	1	1	0	0
WORD DATA (16 BITS)																

RESET

Reset External Devices
(M68000 Family)

Operation: If supervisor state
      then Assert $\overline{\text{RESET}}$ ($\overline{\text{RSTO}}$, MC68040 only) Line
      else TRAP

**Assembler
Syntax:**   RESET

RESET

Attributes: Unsized

Description: Asserts the $\overline{\text{RSTO}}$ signal for 512 (124 for MC68000, MC68008, and MC68010) clock periods, resetting all external devices. The processor state, other than the program counter, is unaffected and execution continues with the next instruction.

Condition Codes:
Not affected.

Instruction Format:

15	14	13	12	11	10	9	8	7	6	5	4	3	2	1	0
0	1	0	0	1	1	1	0	0	1	1	1	0	0	0	0

RTE

Return from Exception
(MC68000 Family)

Operation: If supervisor state
then (SP) ♦ SR; SP + 2 ♦ SP; (SP) ♦ PC;
SP + 4 ♦ SP;
restore state and deallocate stack according to (SP)
else TRAP

Assembler
Syntax: RTE

Attributes: Unsized

Description: Loads the processor state information stored in the exception stack frame located at the top of the stack into the processor. The instruction examines the stack format field in the format/offset word to determine how much information must be restored.

Condition Codes:
Set according to the condition code bits in the status register value restored from the stack.

Instruction Format:

15	14	13	12	11	10	9	8	7	6	5	4	3	2	1	0
0	1	0	0	1	1	1	0	0	1	1	1	0	0	1	1

RTE

Format/Offset Word (in stack frame) (MC68010/MC68020/MC68030/MC68040/CPU32):

15	14	13	12	11	10	9	8	7	6	5	4	3	2	1	0
	FORMAT			0	0					VECTOR OFFSET					

Format Field of Format/Offset Word:

Contains the format code, which implies the stack frame size (including the format/offset word).

0000 — Short Format, removes four words. Loads the status register and the program counter from the stack frame.

0001 — Throwaway Format, removes four words. Loads the status register from the stack frame and switches to the active system stack. Continues the instruction using the active system stack.

0010 — Instruction Error Format, removes six words. Loads the status register and the program counter from the stack frame and discards the other words.

0111 — Access Error Format, removes 30 words.

1000 — MC68010 Long Format, removes 29 words.

1001 — MC68020/MC68030 Mid-Instruction Format, removes 10 words.

1010 — MC68020/MC68030 Short Format, removes 16 word.

1011 — MC68020/MC68030 Long Format, removes 46 words.

1100 — CPU32 Bus Error Format, processor state is recovered from stack in addition to the SR and PC.

Format	Supported By				
	MC68010	MC68020	MC68030	MC68040	CPU32
0000	√	√	√	√	√
0001	—	√	√	√	—
0010	—	√	√	√	√
0111	—	—	—	√	—
1000	√	—	—	—	—
1001	—	√	√	—	—
1010	—	√	√	—	—
1011	—	√	√	—	—
1100	—	—	—	—	√

NOTE: An unsupported format causes the processor to take a format error exception.

STOP

Load Status Register and Stop
(M68000 Family)

Operation: If supervisor state
then Immediate Data ♦ SR; STOP
else TRAP

**Assembler
Syntax:**   STOP #⟨data⟩

Attributes: Unsized

Description: Moves the immediate operand into the status register (both user and supervisor portions), advances the program counter to point to the next instruction, and stops the fetching and executing of instructions. A trace, interrupt, or reset exception causes the processor to resume instruction execution. A trace exception occurs if instruction tracing is enabled (T0 = 0, T1 = 1) when the STOP instruction begins execution. If an interrupt request is asserted with a priority higher than the priority level set by the new status register value, an interrupt exception occurs; otherwise, the interrupt request is ignored. External reset always initiates reset exception processing.

Condition Codes:
Set according to the immediate operand.

Instruction Format:

15	14	13	12	11	10	9	8	7	6	5	4	3	2	1	0
0	1	0	0	1	1	1	0	0	1	1	1	0	0	1	0
IMMEDIATE DATA															

Instruction Fields:
Immediate field — Specifies the data to be loaded into the status register.

APPENDIX C

COPROCESSOR INSTRUCTIONS

|C.1| **FLOATING POINT INSTRUCTIONS**

FABS Floating-Point Absolute Value

Operation   Absolute Value of Source $->$ FPn

Syntax
FABS. ⟨fmt⟩	⟨ea⟩,FPn	
FABS.X	FPm,FPn	
FABS.X	FPn	
*FrABS. ⟨fmt⟩	⟨ea⟩,FPn	r is rounding precision, S or D
*FrABS.X	FPm,FPn	r is rounding precision, S or D
*FrABS.X	FPn	r is rounding precision, S or D

Attributes   Format = (Byte, Word, Long, Single, Double, Extended, Packed)

*Supported by MC68040 only

FACOS Arc Cosine

Operation   Arc Cosine of Source $->$ FPn

Syntax
FACOS.⟨fmt⟩	⟨ea⟩,FPn
FACOS.X	FPm,FPn
FACOS.X	FPn

Attributes   Format = (Byte, Word, Long, Single, Double, Extended, Packed)

FADD Floating-Point Add

Operation   Source + FPn $->$ FPn

Syntax
FADD.⟨fmt⟩	⟨ea⟩,FPn	
FADD.X	FPm,FPn	
*FrADD.⟨fmt⟩	⟨ea⟩,FPn	r is rounding precision, S or D
*FrADD.X	FPm,FPn	r is rounding precision, S or D

Attributes   Format = (Byte, Word, Long, Single, Double, Extended, Packed)

*Supported by MC68040 only

FASIN Arc Sine

Operation	Arc Sine of the Source −> FPn
Syntax	FASIN.⟨fmt⟩ ⟨ea⟩,FPn FASIN.X FPm,FPn FASIN.X FPn
Attributes	Format = (Byte, Word, Long, Single, Double, Extended, Packed)

FATAN Arc Tangent

Operation	Arc Tangent of Source −> FPn
Syntax	FA- TAN.⟨fmt⟩ ⟨ea⟩,FPn FTAN.X FPm,FPn FATAN.X FPn
Attributes	Format = (Byte, Word, Long, Single, Double, Extended, Packed)

FATANH Hyperbolic Arc Tangent

Operation	Hyperbolic Arc Tangent of Source −> FPn
Syntax	FA- TANH.⟨fmt⟩ ⟨ea⟩,FPn FATANH.X FPm,FPn FATANH.X FPn
Attributes	Format = (Byte, Word, Long, Single, Double, Extended, Packed)

FBcc Floating-Point Branch Conditionally

Operation	If floating-point condition TRUE, then PC + d −> PC
Syntax	FBcc.⟨size⟩ ⟨label⟩
Attributes	Size = (Word, Long)

FCMP Floating-Point Compare

Operation	Compute FPn − Source
Syntax	FCMP.⟨fmt⟩ ⟨ea⟩,FPn FCMP.X FPm,FPn
Attributes	Format = (Byte, Word, Long, Single, Double, Extended, Packed)

FCOS Cosine

Operation	Cosine of Source $->$ FPn

Syntax

FCOS.⟨fmt⟩	⟨ea⟩,FPn
FCOS.X	FPm,FPn
FCOS.X	FPn

Attributes Format = (Byte, Word, Long, Single, Double, Extended, Packed)

FCOSH Hyperbolic Cosine

Operation	Hyperbolic Cosine of Source $->$ FPn

Syntax

FCOSH.⟨fmt⟩	⟨ea⟩,FPn
FCOSH.X	FPm,FPn
FCOSH.X	FPn

Attributes Format = (Byte, Word, Long, Single, Double, Extended, Packed)

FDBcc Floating-Point Test Condition, Decrement and Branch

Operation

If condition TRUE then no operation;
else
{
   Dn $-$ 1 $->$ Dn;
   if Dn $\neq$ -1 then
     PC $+$ d $->$ PC;
}

Syntax FDBcc Dn,⟨label⟩

Attributes Unsized

FDIV Floating-Point Divide

Operation	FPn/Source $->$ FPn

Syntax

FDIV.⟨fmt⟩	⟨ea⟩,FPn	
FDIV.X	FPm,FPn	
*FrDIV.⟨fmt⟩	⟨ea⟩,FPn	r is rounding precision, S or D.
*FrDIV.X	FPm,FPn	r is rounding precision, S or D.

Attributes Format = (Byte, Word, Long, Single, Double, Extended, Packed)

*Supported by MC68040 only

FETOX e^x

Operation	$e^{(Source)} -> FPn$

Syntax

FETOX.⟨fmt⟩	⟨ea⟩,FPn
FETOX.X	FPm,FPn
FETOX.X	FPn

Attributes   Format = (Byte, Word, Long, Single, Double, Extended, Packed)

FGETEXP Get Exponent

Operation	Exponent of Source FPn

Syntax

FGETEXP.⟨fmt⟩	⟨ea⟩,FPn
FGETEXP.X	FPm,FPn
FGETEXP.X	FPn

Attributes   Format = (Byte, Word, Long, Single, Double, Extended, Packed)

FGETMAN Get Mantissa

Operation	Mantissa of Source $->$ FPn

Syntax

FGETMAN.⟨fmt⟩	⟨ea⟩,FPn
FGETMAN.X	FPm,FPn
FGETMAN.X	FPn

Attributes   Format = (Byte, Word, Long, Single, Double, Extended, Packed)

FINT Integer Part

Operation	Integer Part of Source $->$ FPn

Syntax

FINT.⟨fmt⟩	⟨ea⟩,FPn
FINT.X	FPm,FPn
FINT.X	FPn

Attributes   Format = (Byte, Word, Long, Single, Double, Extended, Packed)

FINTRZ Integer Part (Round-to-Zero)

Operation	Integer Part of Source $->$ FPn

Syntax

FINTRZ.⟨fmt⟩   ⟨ea⟩,FPn
FINTRZ.X   FPm,FPn
FINTRZ.X   FPn

Attributes   Format = (Byte, Word, Long, Single, Double, Extended, Packed)

FLOG10 Log_{10}

Operation	Log_{10} of Source $->$ FPn

Syntax

FLOG10.⟨fmt⟩   ⟨ea⟩,FPn
FLOG10.X   FPm,FPn
FLOG10.X   FPn

Attributes   Format = (Byte, Word, Long, Single, Double, Extended, Packed)

FLOG2 Log_2

Operation	Log_2 of Source $->$ FPn

Syntax

FLOG2.⟨fmt⟩   ⟨ea⟩,FPn
FLOG2.X   FPm,FPn
FLOG2.X   FPn

Attributes   Format = (Byte, Word, Long, Single, Double, Extended, Packed)

FLOGN Log_e

Operation	Log_e of Source $->$ FPn

Syntax

FLOGN.⟨fmt⟩   ⟨ea⟩,FPn
FLOGN.X   FPm,FPn
FLOGN.X   FPn

Attributes   Format = (Byte, Word, Long, Single, Double, Extended, Packed)

FLOGNP1 $Log_e(x + 1)$

Operation	Log_e of (Source $+1$) $->$ FPn
Syntax	FLOGNP1.⟨fmt⟩ ⟨ea⟩,FPn
	FLOGNP1.X FPm,FPn
	FLOGNP1.X FPn
Attributes	Format = (Byte, Word, Long, Single, Double, Extended, Packed)

FMOD Modulo Remainder

Operation	Modulo Remainder of (FPn/Source) $->$ FPn
Syntax	FMOD.⟨fmt⟩ ⟨ea⟩,FPn
	FMOD.X FPm,FPn
Attributes	Format = (Byte, Word, Long, Single, Double, Extended, Packed)

FMOVE Move Floating-Point Data Register

Operation	Source $->$ Destination
Syntax	FMOVE.⟨fmt⟩ ⟨ea⟩,FPn
	FMOVE.⟨fmt⟩ FPm,⟨ea⟩
	FMOVE.P FPm⟨ea⟩{#k}
	FMOVE.P FPM,⟨ea⟩{Dn}
	*FrMOVE.⟨fmt⟩ ⟨ea⟩,FPn r is rounding precision, S or D.
Attributes	Format = (Byte, Word, Long, Single, Double, Extended, Packed)

*Supported by MC68040 only

FMOVE Move Floating-Point System Control Register

Operation	Source $->$ Destination
Syntax	FMOVE.L ⟨ea⟩,FPcr
	FMOVE.L FPcr,⟨ea⟩
Attributes	Size = (Long)

FMOVECR Move Constant ROM

Operation	ROM Constant $->$ FPn
Syntax	FMOVECR.X #ccc,FPn
Attributes	Format = (Extended)

FMOVEM Move Multiple Floating-Point Data Registers

Operation	Register List $->$ Destination
	Source $->$ Register List
Syntax	FMOVEM.X ⟨list⟩,⟨ea⟩
	FMOVEM.X Dn,⟨ea⟩
	FMOVEM.X ⟨ea⟩,⟨list⟩
	FMOVEM.X ⟨ea⟩,Dn
Attributes	Format = (Extended)

FMOVEM Move Multiple Floating-Point Control Registers

Operation	Register List $->$ Destination
	Source $->$ Register List
Syntax	FMOVEM.L ⟨list⟩,⟨ea⟩
	FMOVEM.L ⟨ea⟩,⟨list⟩
Attributes	Size = (Long)

FMUL Floating-Point Multiply

Operation	Source * FPn $->$ FPn	
Syntax	FMUL.⟨fmt⟩ ⟨ea⟩,FPn	
	FMUL.X FPm,FPn	
	*FrMUL.⟨fmt⟩ ⟨ea⟩,FPn	r is rounding precision, S or D.
	*FrMUL.X FPm,FPn	r is rounding precision, S or D.
Attributes	Format = (Byte, Word, Long, Single, Double, Extended, Packed)	

*Supported by MC68040 only

FNEG Floating-Point Negate

Operation $-$ (Source) $->$ FPn

Syntax

FNEG.⟨fmt⟩	⟨ea⟩,FPn
FNEG.X	FPm,FPn
FNEG.X	FPn
*FrNEG.⟨fmt⟩	⟨ea⟩,FPn r is rounding precision, S or D
*FrNEG.X	FPm,FPn r is rounding precision, S or D
*FrNEG.X	FPn r is rounding precision, S or D

Attributes Format = (Byte, Word, Long, Single, Double, Extended, Packed)

*Supported by MC68040 only

FNOP No operation

Operation None

Syntax FNOP

Attributes Unsized

FREM IEEE Remainder

Operation IEEE Remainder of (FPn / Source) $->$ FPn

Syntax

FREM.⟨fmt⟩	⟨ea⟩,FPn
FREM.X	FPm,FPn

Attributes Format = (Byte, Word, Long, Single, Double, Extended, Packed)

FRESTORE Restore Internal Floating-Point State

Operation If in supervisor state then
    FPU State Frame $->$ Internal State
else
    TRAP

Syntax FRESTORE ⟨ea⟩

Attributes Unsized

FSAVE Save Internal Floating-Point State

Operation   If in supervisor state then
                    FPU Internal State $->$ State Frame
                else
                    TRAP

Syntax   FSAVE   ⟨ea⟩

Attributes   Unsized

FSCALE Scale Exponent

Operation   FPn * INT(2^{Source}) $->$ FPn

Syntax   FSCALE.⟨fmt⟩   ⟨ea⟩,FPn
                FSCALE.X   FPm,FPn

Attributes   Format = (Byte, Word, Long, Single, Double, Extended, Packed)

FScc Set According to Floating-Point Condition

Operation   If (condition TRUE) then
                    $111 \ldots 111_2$ $->$ Destination
                else
                    $000 \ldots 000_2$ $->$ Destination

Syntax   FScc.⟨size⟩   ⟨ea⟩

Attributes   Size = (Byte)

FSGLDIV Single Precision Divide

Operation   FPn / Source $->$ FPn

Syntax   FSGLDIV.⟨fmt⟩   ⟨ea⟩,FPn
                FSGLDIV.X   FPm,FPn

Attributes   Format = (Byte, Word, Long, Single, Double, Extended, Packed)

FSGLMUL Single Precision Multiply

Operation   FPn * Source $->$ FPn

Syntax   FSGLMUL.⟨fmt⟩   ⟨ea⟩,FPn
                FSGLMUL.X   FPm,FPn

Attributes   Format = (Byte, Word, Long, Single, Double, Extended, Packed)

FSIN Sine

Operation	Sine of Source − > FPn

Syntax   FSIN.⟨fmt⟩   ⟨ea⟩,FPn
FSIN.X   FPm,FPn
FSIN.X   FPn

Attributes   Format = (Byte, Word, Long, Single, Double, Extended, Packed)

FSINCOS Simultaneous Sine and Cosine

Operation   Sine of Source − > FPs
Cosine of Source − > FPc

Syntax   FSINCOS.⟨fmt⟩   ⟨ea⟩,FPc:FPs
FSINCOS.X   FPm,FPc:FPs

Attributes   Format = (Byte, Word, Long, Single, Double, Extended, Packed)

FSINH Hyperbolic Sine

Operation   Hyperbolic Sine of Source − > FPn

Syntax   FSINH.⟨fmt⟩   ⟨ea⟩,FPn
FSINH.X   FPm,FPn
FSINH.X   FPn

Attributes   Format = (Byte, Word, Long, Single, Double, Extended, Packed)

FSQRT Floating-Point Square Root

Operation   Square Root of Source − > FPn

Syntax   FSQRT.⟨fmt⟩   ⟨ea⟩,FPn
FSQRT.X   FPm,FPn
FSQRT.X   FPn
*FrSQRT.⟨fmt⟩   ⟨ea⟩,FPn   r is rounding precision, S or D
*FrSQRT   FPm,FPn   r is rounding precision, S or D
*FrSQRT   FPn   r is rounding precision, S or D

Attributes   Format = (Byte, Word, Long, Single, Double, Extended, Packed)

*Supported by MC68040 only

FSUB Floating-Point Subtract

Operation   FPn − Source −> FPn

Syntax   FSUB.⟨fmt⟩   ⟨ea⟩,FPn
              FSUB.X   FPm,FPn
              *FrSUB.⟨fmt⟩   ⟨ea⟩,FPn   r is rounding precision, S or D
              *FrSUB.X   FPm,FPn   r is rounding precision, S or D

Attributes   Format = (Byte, Word, Long, Single, Double, Extended, Packed)

*Supported by MC68040 only

FTAN Tangent

Operation   Tangent of Source −> FPn

Syntax   FTAN.⟨fmt⟩   ⟨ea⟩,FPn
              FTAN.X   FPm,FPn
              FTAN.X   FPn

Attributes   Format = (Byte, Word, Long, Single, Double, Extended, Packed)

Attributes   Format = (Byte, Word, Long, Single, Double, Extended,

FTANH Hyperbolic Tangent

Operation   Hyperbolic Tangent of Source −> FPn

Syntax   FTANH.⟨fmt⟩   ⟨ea⟩,FPn
              FTANH.X   FPm,FPn
              FTANH.X   FPn

Attributes   Format = (Byte, Word, Long, Single, Double, Extended, Packed)

FTENTOX 10^x

Operation 10^{Source} −> FPn

Syntax   FTENTOX.⟨fmt⟩   ⟨ea⟩,FPn
              FTENTOX.X   FPm,FPn
              FTENTOX.X   FPn

Attributes   Format = (Byte, Word, Long, Single, Double, Extended, Packed)

FTRAPcc Trap on Floating-Point Condition

Operation   If condition TRUE, then TRAP

Syntax   FTRAPcc
FTRAPcc.W   #⟨data⟩
FTRAPcc.L   #⟨data⟩

Attributes   Size = (Word, Long)

FTST Test Floating-Point Operand

Operation   Condition Codes for Operand − > FPCC

Syntax   FTST.⟨fmt⟩   ⟨ea⟩
FTST.X   FPm

Attributes   Format = (Byte, Word, Long, Single, Double, Extended, Packed)

FTWOTOX 2^x

Operation $2^{\text{Source}} >$ FPn

Syntax   FTWOTOX.⟨fmt⟩ ⟨ea⟩,FPn
FTWOTOX.X   FPm,FPn
FTWOTOX.X   FPn

Attributes   Format = (Byte, Word, Long, Single, Double, Extended, Packed)

|C.2| MC68030 MMU INSTRUCTIONS

PFLUSH Flush Entry in ATC

Operation   If supervisor state then
    invalidate ATC entries for destination address
else
    TRAP

Syntax   PFLUSHA
PFLUSH   ⟨function code⟩,#⟨mask⟩
PFLUSH   ⟨function code⟩,#⟨mask⟩,⟨ea⟩

Attributes   Unsized

PLOAD Load Entry into ATC

Operation   If supervisor state then
                search translation table and make ATC entry for effective
                address
            else
                TRAP

Syntax   PLOADR   ⟨function code⟩,⟨ea⟩
                PLOADW   ⟨function code⟩,⟨ea⟩

Attributes   Unsized

PMOVE Move to/from MMU Registers

Operation   If supervisor state then
                (Source) –> MRn or MRn –> (Destination)

Syntax   PMOVE   MRn,⟨ea⟩
                PMOVE   ⟨ea⟩,MRn
                PMOVEFD   ⟨ea⟩,MRn

Attributes   Size = (Word, Long, Quad)

PTEST Test a Logical Address

Operation   If supervisor state then
                logical address status –> PSR
            else
                TRAP

Syntax   PTESTR   ⟨function code⟩,⟨ea⟩,#⟨level⟩
                PTESTR   ⟨function code⟩,⟨ea⟩,#⟨level⟩,An
                PTESTW   ⟨function code⟩,⟨ea⟩,#⟨level⟩
                PTESTW   ⟨function code⟩,⟨ea⟩,#⟨level⟩,An

Attributes   Unsized

APPENDIX D

INPUT/OUTPUT LIBRARIES

*T*he text develops a series of input/output libraries for the demonstration programs. The routines for an assembler library are defined in Chapter 4 and used for all standard applications. A standalone library is defined in Chapter 12 for the Motorola Educational Computer Board (ECB) system. The primitive routines in the standalone library are rewritten as interrupt-driven routines in Chapter 14. All programs for the ECB system can be first compiled on a host system and downloaded to the standalone board. Motorola assumes that your assembler can produce S-Records for the download file. This text defines SZ-Records as a model. The SZ-Record generator, written in the programming language C, is included in this appendix.

D.1   THE ASM ASSEMBLER ROUTINES

The following routines are available with the ASM Assembler by Ramsoft, running Sun OS 4.1 or System V. The routines meet the text specifically from Chapter 4. All parameters are passed in registers.

Primitive Routines

GETCHAR	Inputs a character from the keyboard.
GETC	Inputs a character from the input stream (using a one character pushback buffer) or the keyboard.
UNGETC	Pushes a character back into the input stream.
PUTCHAR	Prints a characters to the screen.
STOP	Terminates the program.

String Routines

STRIN	Inputs a string from the keyboard.
STROUT	Outputs a string to the screen.
NEWLINE	Moves the cursor to the beginning of the next line.

Hexadecimal Number Routines

HEXIN	Inputs a 16-bit hexadecimal number from the keyboard.
HEXIN_LONG	Inputs a 32-bit hexadecimal number from the keyboard.
HEXOUT	Prints a 16-bit hexadecimal number to the screen.
HEXOUT_LONG	Prints a 32-bit hexadecimal number to the screen.

Decimal Number Routines

DECIN	Inputs a signed 16-bit decimal number from the keyboard.
DECIN__LONG	Inputs a signed 32-bit decimal number from the keyboard.
DECOUT	Prints a 16-bit signed decimal number to the screen.
DECOUT__LONG	Prints a 32-bit signed decimal number to the screen.

Random Number Routines

SEED	Seeds the random number generator RAND.
RAND	Generates a 16-bit random integer. RAND assumes an initial call to SEED.

The following code listings are given for the Sun OS 4.1 implementation. Only small changes are necessary for System V.

Primitive Routines

GETCHAR

Inputs a character from the keyboard

Parameters passed
  None
Parameters returned
  (D0.W) contains the character read. End of file has been reached if (D0.W) = −1

```
        xdef      getchar

        xref      _getchar

getchar:
        movem.l   d0-d1/a0-a1,-(sp)  ; compilers often use d0-d1/a0-a1
                                     ; as scratch registers
        jsr       _getchar
        move.w    d0,(2,sp)
        movem.l   (sp)+,d0-d1/a0-a1
        rts
        end
```

GETC

Inputs a character from the keyboard with one character pushback.

Parameters passed
  None
Parameters returned
  (D0.W) contains the character read. End of file has been reached if
  (D0.W) = −1

UNGETC

Pushes a character back into the input stream

Parameters passed
  (D0.W) contains the character to be pushed back
Parameters returned
  (D0.W) contains the character read

```
          xdef      getc, ungetc

          xref      getchar

getc:     move.l    d0,-(sp)
          andi.w    #$ff,d0           ; clear all but bits 0-7 of d0
          tst.b     pushbackbuf       ; was a character pushed back?
          beq.s     callget           ; if not, call getchar
          move.b    pushbackbuf,d0    ; get the put back character
          clr.b     pushbackbuf       ; indicate pushbackbuf empty
          bra.s     retgetc           ; exit
callget:
          jsr       getchar           ; make getchar call
retgetc:
          move.w    d0,(2,sp)         ; leave high half of d0 unchanged
          move.l    (sp)+,d0
          rts

ungetc:
          move.b    d0,pushbackbuf    ; save character in pushbackbuf
          rts

          data

          xdef      eof

pushbackbuf:
          dc.b      0                 ; char pushed back
          even                        ; create word alignment
```

```
eof:    ds.w        1                       ; variable used by numerical input
;                                           ; routines to indicate that end
;                                           ; of file has been found

        end
```

PUTCHAR

Prints a character to the screen.

Parameters passed
  (D0.W) contains the character to print
Parameters returned
  None

```
        xdef        putchar

        xref        _putchar

putchar:
        movem.l   d0-d1/a0-a1,-(sp)    ; compilers often use d0-d1/a0-a1
        ext.w     d0                   ; as scratch registers
        ext.l     d0
        move.l    d0,-(sp)
        jsr       _putchar
        addq.w    #4,sp
        movem.l   (sp)+,d0-d1/a0-a1
        rts

        end
```

STOP

Calls the C library routine *exit*, which flushes the standard I/O buffer and terminates the program

Parameters passed
  None
Parameters returned
  None

```
        xdef        stop

        xref        _exit

stop:   clr.l       -(sp)               ; make C call exit(0)
;                                       ; flushes any output remaining in the
```

```
                                      ; buffer, if output redirected
            jsr       _exit
            end
```

String Routines

STRIN

Inputs a string from the keyboard.

Parameters passed
   (A0)   address of the input buffer
   (D0.W) maximum number of characters expected.
Parameters returned
   (D0.W) number of characters actually read, including
               the terminating end-of-line character.

```
NewLine:  equ       10

          xdef      strin

          xref      getc

strin:    movem.l   d0-d2/a0,-(sp)
          move.w    d0,d1         ; loop counter
          move.w    d0,d2         ; save max char count
          subq.w    #1,d1
          bmi.s     out1          ; requested null string
iloop:    jsr       getc
          tst.w     d0
          bpl.s     cont          ; end of file??
          moveq     #0,d0         ; return 0 upon EOF
          bra.s     out2
cont:     move.b    d0,(a0)+
          cmp.b     #NewLine,d0   ; has end of line been found?
          dbeq      d1,iloop
          bne.s     out1          ; if cmp gave 0, we read EOLN

gotnl:    sub.w     d1,d2         ; chars read = max requested − (d1)
out1:     move.w    d2,d0         ; d0 is output register
out2:     move.w    d0,2(sp)      ; give original d0 a new low half
          movem.l   (sp)+,d0-d2/a0
          rts

          end
```

STROUT

Outputs a string to the screen.

Parameters passed
    (A0)   address of the output string
    (D0.W)   number of characters to output
Parameters returned
    None

```
         xdef      strout

         xref      putchar

strout:  movem.l   d0-d1/a0,-(sp)
         move.w    d0,d1             ; use d1 as loop counter
         subq.w    #1,d1
         bmi.s     out               ; exit if char count = 0
ouptut:  move.b    (a0)+,d0
         jsr       putchar
         dbra      d1,ouptut
out:     movem.l   (sp)+,d0-d1/a0
         rts
         end
```

NEWLINE

Moves the cursor to the beginning of the next line.

Parameters
    None

```
NewLine: equ       10

         xdef      newline

         xref      putchar

newline:
         move.l    d0,-(sp)
         move.w    #NewLine,d0
         jsr       putchar
         move.l    (sp)+,d0
         rts
         end
```

Hexadecimal Number Routines

HEXIN

Inputs a 16-bit hexadecimal number from the keyboard.

> *Parameters passed*
>   None
> *Parameters returned*
>   (D0.W)   contains the 16-bit number read.

HEXIN_LONG

Inputs a 32-bit hexadecimal number from the keyboard

> *Parameters passed*
>   None
> *Parameters returned*
>   (D0.L)   contains the 32-bit number read.

```
NewLine:          equ       10
Tab:              equ        9

        xdef      hexin
        xdef      hexin_long

        xref      getc, ungetc, strout

hexin:
        move.l    d7,-(sp)
        moveq     #0,d7
        jsr       hexinput
        move.l    (sp)+,d7
        rts

hexin_long:
        move.l    d7,-(sp)
        moveq     #1,d7
        jsr       hexinput
        move.l    (sp)+,d7
        rts

hexinput:
        movem.l   d0-d3/a0,-(sp)
        moveq     #0,d1           ; accumulate ans in d1
        clr.w     eof             ; end of file marker clear
1$:     jsr       getc            ; get a character
        tst.w     d0              ; check for end of file
        bpl.s     2$
        move.w    #-1,eof
        bra.s     7$
```

```
2$:         cmpi.b    #' ',d0
            beq.s     1$
            cmpi.b    #NewLine,d0
            beq.s     1$
            cmpi.b    #Tab,d0
            beq.s     1$
            jsr       ishexdigit          ; test for non-hex 1st char in d2
            tst.w     d2
            bmi.s     6$                  ; first digit must be hex digit
3$:         asl.l     #4,d1               ; prepare for next hex digit
            add.w     d2,d1               ; add in new low digit
            jsr       getc                ; get next ascii digit
            tst.w     d0                  ; check for end of file
            bpl.s     4$                  ; stop input on eof
            move.w    #-1,eof
            bra.s     7$
4$:         jsr       ishexdigit
            tst.w     d2
            bmi.s     5$                  ; stop input on a non hex digit
            bra.s     3$                  ; get next hex digit
5$:         cmpi.b    #NewLine,d0         ; do not put back newline
            beq.s     7$
            jsr       ungetc              ; put back terminating char
            bra.s     7$
6$:         lea       hex_errmsg,a0       ; 1st digit incorrect
            move.w    #36,d0
            jsr       strout
            moveq     #0,d0
7$:         move.l    d1,d0
            btst      #0,d7               ; test for hexin or hexin_long
            bne.s     8$
            move.w    d0,2(sp)            ; restore original high half D0
            bra.s     9$
8$:         move.l    d0,(sp)             ; store full 32 bits in d0
9$          movem.l   (sp)+,d0-d3/a0
            rts


ishexdigit:
            move.w    d0,d2
            ext.w     d2                  ; 16 bit value same as char
            cmpi.b    #'0',d0             ; check '0'-'9' range
            blt.s     3$                  ; quit on a non-hex digit
            cmpi.b    #'9',d0
            bgt.s     1$
            subi.b    #'0',d2
            bra.s     4$
1$:         cmpi.b    #'A',d0             ; check 'A'-'F' range
            blt.s     3$
            cmpi.b    #'F',d0
            bgt.s     2$
            subi.b    #'A'-10,d2
            bra.s     4$
```

```
2$:       cmpi.b    #'a',d0                  ; check 'a'-'f' range
          blt.s     3$
          cmpi.b    #'f',d0
          bgt.s     3$
          subi.b    #'a'-10,d2
          bra.s     4$
3$:       move.w    #-1,d2
4$:       rts

          data

          xref      eof

hex_errmsg:
          dc.b      'Invalid hex digit begins the number', NewLine
          even

          end
```

HEXOUT

Prints a 16-bit hexadecimal number to the screen

> *Parameters passed*
>   (D0.W)   contains the 16-bit number to print
> *Parameters returned*
>   None

HEXOUT__LONG

Prints a 32-bit hexadecimal number to the screen

> *Parameters passed*
>   (D0.L)   contains the 32-bit number to print
> *Parameters returned*
>   None

```
NewLine:          equ       10
Tab:              equ        9

          xdef      hexout
          xdef      hexout_long

          xref      strout

hexout:
          move.l    d7,-(sp)
          moveq     #4,d7
          jsr       hexoutput
          move.l    (sp)+,d7
          rts
```

```
hexout_long:
        move.l    d7,-(sp)
        moveq     #8,d7
        jsr       hexoutput
        move.l    (sp)+,d7
        rts

hexoutput:
        movem.l   d0-d2/a0-a1,-(sp)
        move.w    d7,d1
        subq.w    #1,d1
        lea       _bufhex+8,a0        ; find digits in reverse order
        lea       _hexdigits,a1       ; 4 bit binary->ascii conv table
1$:     move.b    d0,d2               ; isolate right-most four bits
        andi.w    #$000f,d2
        move.b    (0,a1,d2.w),-(a0)   ; convert to ASCII
        lsr.l     #4,d0               ; move next four bits in place
        dbra      d1,1$
        addq.w    #2,d7               ; print hexdigits + 2 blanks
        move.w    d7,d0               ; output the digits and 2 blanks
        jsr       strout
        movem.l   (sp)+,d0-d2/a0-a1
        rts

        data

_bufhex:
        ds.b      8
        dc.b      '  '

_hexdigits:
        dc.b      '0123456789ABCDEF'

        end
```

Decimal Number Routines

DECIN

Inputs a signed 16-bit decimal number from the keyboard

> *Parameters passed*
> None
> *Parameters returned*
> (D0.W)   contains the 16-bit number read.

DECIN_LONG

Inputs a signed 32-bit decimal number from the keyboard

> *Parameters passed*
> None

Parameters returned
(D0.L)   contains the 32-bit number read.

```
          (D0.L) contains the 32-bit number read.
NewLine:                equ     10
Tab:                    equ      9

          xdef    decin
          xdef    decin_long

          xref    getc, ungetc, strout

decin:
          move.l  d7,-(sp)
          moveq   #0,d7
          jsr     decinput
          move.l  (sp)+,d7
          rts

decin_long:
          move.l  d7,-(sp)
          moveq   #1,d7
          jsr     decinput
          move.l  (sp)+,d7
          rts

decinput:
          movem.l d0-d4/a0,-(sp)
          moveq   #0,d3           ; accumulate ans in d3
          clr.w   eof             ; end-of-file marker clear
          moveq   #0,d4           ; assume sign flag is positive
1$:       jsr     getc            ; get a charcter
          tst.w   d0              ; check for end of file
          bpl.s   2$
          move.w  #-1,eof
          bra.s   7$
2$:       cmpi.b  #' ',d0
          beq.s   1$
          cmpi.b  #NewLine,d0
          beq.s   1$
          cmpi.b  #Tab,d0
          beq.s   1$
          cmp.b   #'-',d0         ; test for minus sign
          bne     3$
          moveq   #1,d4           ; set d4 to be negative flag
          jsr     getc
3$:       jsr     isdecdigit      ; test for nondecimal 1st char in d2
          tst.w   d2
          bmi.s   7$              ; first digit must be decimal digit

4$:       move.l  d3,-(sp)
          pea     10
          jsr     mul32
```

```
                move.l     d1.d3
                ext.l      d2
                add.l      d2,d3
                jsr        getc              ; get next ascii digit
                tst.w      d0                ; check for end of file
                bpl.s      5$                ; stop input on eof
                move.w     #-1,eof
                bra.s      8$
5$:             jsr        isdecdigit
                tst.w      d2
                bmi.s      6$                ; stop input on a non decimal digit
                bra        4$                ; get next digit
6$:             cmpi.b     #NewLine,d0       ; do not put back newline
                beq.s      8$
                jsr        ungetc            ; put back terminating char
                bra.s      8$
7$:             lea        dec_errmsg,a0     ; 1st digit incorrect
                move.w     #40,d0
                jsr        strout
                moveq      #0,d0
                bra.s      10$
8$:             move.l     d3,d0
                tst.l      d4                ; test for negative number
                beq        10$               ; branch for a positive number
                btst       #0,d7             ; test for decin or decin_long
                beq.s      9$
                neg.l      d0                ; branch with decin
                bra.s      10$
9$:             neg.w      d0
10$             btst       #0,d7
                bne.s      11$               ; decin_long case
                move.w     d0,2(sp)          ; restore original high half D0
                bra.s      12$
11$:            move.l     d0,(sp)           ; store full 32 bits in d0
12$:            movem.l    (sp)+,d0-d4/a0
                rts


isdecdigit:
                move.w     d0,d2
                ext.w      d2                ; 16 bit value same as char
                cmpi.b     #'0',d0           ; check '0'-'9' range
                blt.s      1$                ; quit on a nonhex digit
                cmpi.b     #'9',d0
                bgt.s      1$
                subi.b     #'0',d2
                rts
1$:             move.w     #-1,d2
                rts


multA:      equ      8
multB:      equ      12
param8:     equ       8
```

```
mul32:    link      a6,#0
          movem.l   d2-d4,-(sp)
          move.l    (multA,a6),d1
          move.l    (multB,a6),d0
          move.l    d1,d2            ; copy a to d2 and d3
          move.l    d1,d3
          move.l    d0,d4            ; copy b to d4
          swap      d3               ; (d3) = al || ah
          swap      d4               ; (d4) = bl || bh
          mulu      d0,d1            ; (d1) = al * bl
          mulu      d3,d0            ; (d0) = bl * ah
          mulu      d4,d2            ; (d2) = bh * al
          mulu      d4,d3            ; (d3) = bh * ah


; add up the partial products
          moveq     #0,d4            ; used with addx to add the carry
          swap      d1               ; (d1) = low(al * bl) || high(al * bl)
          add.w     d0,d1            ; (d1) = low(al * bl)|| high(al * bl)
;                                    ;             + low(bl * ah)
          addx.l    d4,d3            ; add carry from previous add
          add.w     d2,d1            ; (d1) = low(al * bl)|| high(al * bl)
;                                    ;             + low(bl * ah) + low(bh * al)
          addx.l    d4,d3            ; add carry from previous add
          swap      d1               ; put (d1) into its final form
          clr.w     d0               ; (d0) = high(bl * ah) || 0
          swap      d0               ; (d0) = 0 || high(bl * ah)
          clr.w     d2
          swap      d2               ; (d2) = 0 || high(bh * al)
          add.l     d2,d0            ; carry is stored in msw of d0
          add.l     d3,d0            ; (d0) = high(ah * bh)+ carry||
;                                    ;        low(bh * ah) + high(bl * ah)
;                                    ;             + high(bh * al)
          movem.l   (sp)+,d2-d4
          unlk      a6
          move.l    (sp),(param8,sp)
          addq.w    #param8,sp
          rts

          data

          xref      eof

decbuf:   ds.b      12
          dc.b      ' '
          even


dec_errmsg:
          dc.b      'Invalid decimal digit begins the number', NewLine
          even

          end
```

DECOUT

Prints a 16-bit signed decimal number to the screen

Parameters passed
   (D0.W)   contains the 16-bit number to print
Parameters returned
   None

DECOUT__LONG

Prints a 32-bit signed decimal number to the screen

Parameters passed
   (D0.L)   contains the 32-bit number to print
Parameters returned
   None

```
NewLine:              equ     10
Tab:                  equ      9

        xdef        decout
        xdef        decout_long

        xref        strout

decout:
        movem.l   d0/d6-d7,-(sp)
        andi.l    #$0000ffff,d0
        clr.w     d6
        clr.b     d7                      ; use d7 for the minus sign
        tst.w     d0
        bpl       1$
        move.b    #'-',d7                 ; move '-' into d7
        neg.w     d0                      ; compute absolute value of d0
1$:     jsr       decoutput
        movem.l   (sp)+,d0/d6-d7
        rts


decout_long:
        movem.l   d0/d6-d7,-(sp)
        moveq     #1,d6
        clr.b     d7
        tst.l     d0
        bpl       1$
        move.b    #'-',d7                 ; move '-' into d7
        neg.l     d0
1$:     jsr       decoutput
        movem.l   (sp)+,d0/d6-d7
        rts
```

```
decoutput:
        movem.l    d0-d1/a0-a1,-(sp)
        lea        decbuf+12,a0          ; set a0 past last char of buffer
1$:     tst.w      d6
        bne.s      2$
        divu       #10,d0
        swap       d0
        move.w     d0,d1
        swap       d0
        andi.l     #$0000ffff,d0
        bra.s      3$
2$:     move.l     d0,-(sp)
        move.l     #10,-(sp)
        jsr        div32
3$:     add.w      #'0',d1               ; convert to character digit
        move.b     d1,-(a0)
        tst.l      d0
        bne.s      1$
        tst.b      d7
        beq        4$
        move.b     d7,-(a0)
4$:     lea        decbuf+14,a1
        move.l     a1,d0                 ; output digits and two blanks
        sub.l      a0,d0
        jsr        strout
        movem.l    (sp)+,d0-d1/a0-a1
        rts


divisor:            equ     8
dividend:           equ     12
param8:             equ     8


div32:  link       a6#0
        movem.l    d2-d4,-(sp)           ; save scratch registers
        move.l     (dividend,a6),d1
        move.l     (divisor,a6),d0
        clr.l      d3                    ; clear (d3) the quotient
udiv1:  cmp.l      d0,d1                 ; test divisor > dividend
        blo.s      udiv5                 ; if yes, done
        move.l     d0,d2                 ; set divisor in temp register
        clr.l      d4                    ; clear partial quotient
        move.w     #$10,ccr              ; set x bit to 1
udiv2:  cmp.l      d2,d1                 ; test divisor > dividend
        blo.s      udiv3                 ; if yes, this step is done
        roxl.l     #1,d4                 ; shift temp quotient left
        tst.l      d2                    ; test for another shift
        bmi.s      udiv4                 ; if bit31 = 1, don't undo shift
        lsl.l      #1,d2                 ; shift divisor to next test
        bra.s      udiv2                 ; keep going
udiv3:  lsr.l      #1,d2                 ; undo the last shift
udiv4:  sub.l      d2,d1                 ; subtract shifted divisor
        add.l      d4,d3                 ; add temp quotient to d3
        bra.s      udiv1                 ; go back for another division
```

```
udiv5:    move.l    d3,d0                ; put the quotient in d0
          movem.l   (sp)+,d2-d4
          unlk      a6
          move.l    (sp),(param8,sp)
          addq.w    #param8,sp
          rts

          data

decbuf:   ds.b      12
          dc.b      ' '
          even

          end
```

Random Number Routines

SEED

Seeds the random number generator RAND

> *Parameters passed*
> (D0.W)   If non-zero, a random seed is generated; otherwise, a
>   fixed seed is used
> *Parameters returned*
> None

RAND

Generates a 16-bit random integer; RAND assumes an initial call to SEED

> *Parameters passed*
> None
> *Parameters returned*
> (D0.W)16-bit random integer

```
          xdef      seed, rand

          xref      _time,_srandom, _random

seed:
          movem.l   d0-d1/a0-a1,-(sp)    ; compilers often use d0-d1/a0-a1
          tst.w     d0                   ; as scratch registers
          beq.s     1$
          clr.l     -(sp)                ; call _time(0) to get GMT time
;                                        ; to seed the generator
          jsr       _time
          addq.w    #4,sp                ; flush off the parameter
          bra.s     2$
```

```
1$:     moveq      #1,d0
2$:     move.l     d0,m-(sp)            ; call C library routine _srand to
;                                       ; seed the random generator
                                        ; _rand
        jsr        _srandom
        addq.w     #4,sp
        movem.l    (sp)+,d0-d1/a0-a1
        rts

rand:
        movem.l    d0-d1/a0-a1,-(sp)   ; compilers often use these
;                                       ; registers for scratch
        jsr        _random             ; make C call random()
;                                       ; random integer returned in d0
        andi.l     #$ffff00,d0
        lsr.l      #8,d0
        move.w     d0,(2,sp)
        movem.l    (sp)+,d0-d1/a0-a1
        rts
        data
        xdef       _environ
_environ:
        ds.l       1
        end
```

D.2 | THE STANDALONE I/O LIBRARY

The following is a listing of the primitive routines needed for the standalone serial I/O library developed in Chapter 12. It provides for I/O at the two serial ports on the ECB board. The code is easily modified to provide serial I/O for any standalone board. The remaining routines needed are the high level conversion and I/O routines of Chapter 9.

```
; package for performing polled i/o at the ecb serial ports

; fundamental constants

consoleacia:  equ  $10040   ; base address of console acia
hostacia:     equ  $10041   ; base address of host acia
aciacr:       equ  0        ; control register offset
aciasr:       equ  0        ; status register offset
aciardr:      equ  2        ; receiver data register offset
aciatdr:      equ  2        ; transmitter data register offset
rxfull:       equ  0        ; receiver data reg full bit
txempty:      equ  1        ; transmitter data register empty bit
frerr:        equ  4        ; status reg framing error bit
mastereset    equ  $03      ; acia master reset byte
ctrlregval:   equ  $15      ; acia control register value
```

```
carr_return:    equ     $0d         ; ascii carriage return
linefeed:       equ     $0a         ; ascii line feed
eolnchar        equ     10
tab:            equ     9
null:           equ     $00         ; ascii null character
tutor:          equ     $8146

        xdef    initPort, getchar, charpresent, putchar, stop
        xdef    getc, ungetc
        xdef    echon, echoff, nlon, nloff

; utility routine to set (a0) to the correct base address:
;       if (d7) = 0 then (a0) points to consoleacia
;       if (d7) = 1 then (a0) points to hostacia

seta0: lea      bases,a0              ; bases is a lookup table
       lsl.w    #2,d7                 ; mult by 4 for table offset
       movea.l  (0,a0,d7.w),a0        ; set address in a0
       lsr.w    #2,d7                 ; restore d7
       rts

; initialize acia whose port number is in d7
; clear the push back record for each port

initPort:
       move.l   a0,-(sp)
       jsr      seta0                 ; load in a0 the acia base
; the ecb system does not require a software reset
;      move.b   #mastereset,(aciacr,a0)
       move.b   #ctrlregval,(aciacr,a0)
       lea      echochars,a0          ; default is char echo on input
       move.b   #1,(0,a0,d7.w)
       lea      nlexpansion,a0        ; default is char echo on input
       move.b   #1,(0,a0,d7.w)
       lea      pushbackchars,a0
       clr.b    (0,a0,d7.w)           ; initially no pushed back
;                                     ; character
       movea.l  (sp)+,a0
       rts

; the character in d0 is transmitted to the acia whose port
; number is in d7. the newline character <lf> is expanded into
; the newline sequence <lf>/<cr>.

putchar:
       movem.l  d0/a0-a1,-(sp)
       jsr      seta0                 ; set acia base address
opoll: btst     #txempty,(aciasr,a0)  ; test for tdr reg empty
       beq.s    opoll                 ; if not keep polling
       move.b   d0,(aciatdr,a0)       ; transmit character
       cmp.b    #eolnchar,d0          ; check for linefeed
       bne.s    putxit                ; if no, restore reg
       lea      nlexpansion,a1        ; check to see if end of line
```

```
;  should be expanded to <lf> <cr>
        tst.b    (0,a1,d7.w)
        beq.s    putxit                 ;  if no expansion, just exit
        move.b   #carr_return,  d0      ;  send cr
        bra.s    opoll                  ;  return to polling
;                                       ;  to transmit the cr char
putxit:
        movem.l  (sp)+,d0/a0-a1         ;  restore registers
        rts


;  turn char echo on at the port whose number is in d7

echon:
        move.l   a0,-(sp)
        lea      echochars,a0
        move.b   #1,(0,a0,d7.w)         ;  echo on input = true
        movea.l  (sp)+,a0
        rts


;  turn off char echo at the port whose number is in d7

echoff:
        move.l   a0,-(sp)
        lea      echochars,a0
        clr.b    (0,a0,d7.w)            ;  echo on input = false
        movea.l  (sp)+,a0
        rts


;  on input, <cr> is converted to <lf> and on output <lf> is
;  expanded to <lf> <cr>

nlon:
        move.l   a0,-(sp)
        lea      nlexpansion,a0
        move.b   #1,(0,a0,d7.w)         ;  set newline feature
        movea.l  (sp)+,a0
        rts


;  no newline conversion is done.

nloff:
        move.l   a0,-(sp)
        lea      nlexpansion,a0
        clr.b    (0,a0,d7.w)            ;  clear newline feature
        movea.l  (sp)+,a0
        rts


;  read a character from the acia port designated by (d7).
;  the char is returned in d0, with any parity bit masked off
;  a framing error (break) is indicated by returning the null
;  character. if character echo is on, the input character is
;  echoed back to the terminal and <cr> causes ; a <cr>/<lf> to be
;  sent. a <cr> is replaced by the "newline" character <lf>
```

```
getchar:
        move.l  a0,-(sp)
        jsr     seta0              ; set acia base address
ipoll:  btst    #rxfull,(aciasr,a0) ; test for char in acia
        beq.s   ipoll              ; if not keep polling
        move.b  (aciardr,a0),d0    ; read the character
        btst    #frerr,(aciasr,a0) ; test for framing error
        beq.s   noferr
        clr.b   d0                 ; return null char
        bra.s   exitgetc           ; return
noferr:
        bclr    #7,d0              ; mask off any parity
        lea     nlexpansion,a0     ; do not convert <cr> to <lf>
;                                  ; if newline expansion is off
        tst.b   (0,a0,d7.w)
        beq.s   techo
        cmpi.b  #carr_return,d0    ; test if char return present
        bne.s   techo
        move.b  #linefeed,d0       ; <cr> --> <lf>
techo:  lea     echochars,a0       ; see if char echo is on or off
        tst.b   (0,a0,d7.w)
        beq.s   exitgetc           ; bypass char echo
        jsr     putchar            ; echo back the char
exitgetc:
        andi.w  #$00FF,d0
        movea.l (sp)+,a0           ; restore a0 and return
        rts

; the routine charpresent determines if a character is
; present in the acia port designated by (d7). if present, the
; z bit of the ccr register is cleared (TRUE). if not, the
; z bit is set (FALSE). use this routine if the program cannot poll
; waiting for a character to arrive

zbit:           equ     2          ; z bit is bit 2 of ccr
savedsr:        equ     5          ; low byte of sr at sp offset 5

charpresent:
        move.w  sr,-(sp)           ; save ccr bits
        move.l  a0,-(sp)
        jsr     seta0              ; set acia base address
;                                  ; test for char present
        btst    #rxfull,(aciasr,a0)
        beq.s   setz               ; no char present
        bclr    #zbit,(savedsr,sp)
        bra.s   retc
setz:   bset    #zbit,(savedsr,sp)
retc:   movea.l (sp)+,a0
        rtr

getc:   move.l  a0,-(sp)
        lea     pushbackchars,a0
        move.b  (0,a0,d7.w),d0
```

```
        beq.s getc_1                    ; if not, call _getchar
        andi.w  #$ff,d0                 ; getc returns 16 bits
        clr.b (0,a0,d7.w)               ; indicate pushbackbuf empty
        bra.s getc_2                    ; exit
getc_1: jsr  getchar                    ; make primitive input call
getc_2: move.l (sp)+,a0
        rts

ungetc:
        move.l   a0,-(sp)
        lea      pushbackchars,a0
        move.b   d0,(0,a0,d7.w)         ; save character in pushbackbuf
        move.l   (sp)+,a0
        rts

stop:
        jmp      tutor

        data

        xdef     eof

eof:    ds.w     1                      ; variable indicates eof found

bases: dc.l     consoleacia, hostacia
echochars:
        ds.b     2                      ; indicates whether echo on char
;                                       ; input
nlexpansion:
        ds.b     2                      ; indicates if <cr> is converted
pushbackchars:
        ds.b     2                      ; pushback buffers for ports

        code

        end
```

D.3 | THE INTERRUPT-DRIVEN I/O LIBRARY

The interrupt driven I/O library is presented in Chapter 14. It provides fully interrupt driven I/O for the console port on the ECB board. It is straightforward to modify the code to handle another standalone board.

```
; ACIA parameters
monitor:        equ $8146
TermBase        equ $10040
ctrlreg:        equ 0
statreg:        equ 0
rxreg:          equ 2
```

```
txreg:          equ   2
rxfull:         equ   0
txempty:        equ   1
controlval:     equ   $95      ; control reg fields
vconsole:       equ   $74      ; console level 5 autovector
rec_trInt:      equ   $B5      ; receive/transmit interrupts on
recOnlyInt:     equ   $95      ; just receiver interrupts on
allIntOff:      equ   $15

; Interrupt Mask Values
disbleints:     equ   $2700    ; interrupt mask = 7
enableints:     equ   $2000    ; interrupt mask = 0

; Misc constants
level7:         equ   $0700    ; driver return at level 7
paritybit:      equ   7
Bell:           equ   7
Xoff:           equ   $13
Xon:            equ   $11

        xdef      initPort, getchar, putchar
        xdef      charpresent, stop, clearOutputQueue
        xref      qinit, qempty, qfull, qdelete, qinsert
; Initializes all data used
initPort:
        move.w    #disableints,sr         ; disable interrupts
        move.l    a0,-(sp)
        move.l    #terminal, vconsole.w   ; setup console
        lea       TermBase,a0
        move.b    #rec_trInt,(ctrlreg,a0)
        move.w    #queuesize,-(sp)        ; setup 2 byte input queue
        pea       inputqueue
        jsr       qinit
        move.w    #queuesize,-(sp)        ; setup 32 byte output queue
        pea       outputqueue
        jsr       qinit
        clr.l     suspend_for_input       ; used for blocking on input
        clr.w     xoff_typed
        move.l    (sp)+,a0
        move.w    #enableints,sr          ; re-enable interrupts
        rts

; Character arrived - receive buffer empty?
charpresent:
        move.w    sr,-(sp)                ; save system sr
        pea       inputqueue
        jsr       qempty
        beq.s     havechar
        ori.w     #$0004,(sp)             ; no char - set Z bit
        bra.s     xit
havechar:

        andi.w    #$fffb,(sp)             ; have char - clear Z bit
xit:    rtr                               ; return with info in Z bit
```

```
; shut down the interrupt driven I/O system
clearOutputQueue:
        move.l    a0,-(sp)
        lea       TermBase,a0
        move.b    #rec_trInt,(ctrlreg,a0)   ; transmitter on
        move.w    #enableints,sr
checkoutputbuf:                             ; loop till output buffer empty
        pea       outputqueue
        jsr       qempty
        beq.s     checkoutputbuf
        move.b    #allIntOff,(ctrlreg,a0)
        move.l    (sp)+,a0
        rts


; Read a character. Block if no char in the input buffer
getchar:
        move.w    #disableints,sr
        pea       inputqueue                ; test for input queue empty
        jsr       qempty
        beq.s     unlinkchar                ; if FALSE, read char from queue
        jsr       waitforinput
unlinkchar:

        jsr       readinputqueue
        move.w    #enableints,sr            ; re-enable interrupts
        rts


; Unlink the character from the input buffer and return in (d0)
readinputqueue:
        pea       inputqueue
        jsr       qdelete
        rts


; Block until the ACI interrupt service routine has buffered a char
waitforinput:
        bset      #0,suspend_for_input      ; set TRUE; waiting for char
        move.w    #enableints,sr            ; allow receive interrupts
getcwait:

        btst      #0,suspend_for_input      ; simulate operating sys block
        bne.s     getcwait
        rts


; Write a character. Block if the output buffer is full
putchar:
        move.w    #disableints,sr
        move.l    a0,-(sp)
        pea       outputqueue
        jsr       qfull
        beq.s     addtoqueue                ; if queue not full, add char
        jsr       waitforoutput
addtoqueue:
```

```
        jsr       addtooutputqueue
        lea       TermBase, a0
        move.b    #rec_trInt, (ctrlreg, a0)    ; turn transmitints back on
        movea.l   (sp)+, a0
        move.w    #enableints, sr              ; re-enable interrupts
        rts

; Add a character to the output buffer
addtooutputqueue:
        move.l    d0, -(sp)
        pea       outputqueue
        jsr       qinsert
        rts

; Block until interrupt service has unlinked a char from the output buffer
waitforoutput:
        bset      #0, suspend_for_output       ; wait for free slot
        move.w    #enableints, sr              ; wait with interrupts enabled
putcwait:

        btst      #0, suspend_for_output
        bne.s     putcwait
        rts

; ACIA interrupt service routine

statusreg:   equ      4                         ; offset to sr saved by interrupt


terminal:
        move.w    #disableints, sr
        link      a6, #0
        movem.l   d0-d1/a0-a1, -(sp)
        lea       TermBase, a1                  ; point at the acia
        btst      #0, (statreg, a1)             ; determine interrupt source
        beq.s     transint                      ; transmitter caused interrupt?
        move.b    (rxreg, a1), d0               ; get the character received
        bclr      #paritybit, d0                ; mask off parity bit
        tst.w     xoff_typed                    ; was Xoff typed previously?
        beq.s     notoff
        cmpi.b    #Xon, d0                      ; char must be Xon
        bne       ret                           ; clear Xoff hold flag
        clr.w     xoff_typed
        bra       ret
notoff: cmpi.b    #Xoff, d0                     ; did new Xoff arrive?
        bne.s     queue
        move.w    #1, xoff_typed                ; flag reception of Xoff
        bra       ret
queue:                                          ; put char received in queue
        pea       inputqueue
        jsr       qfull                         ; is input queue full?
        beq.s     cont
```

```
            jsr      beep                         ; is input queue full?
            beq.s    cont
            jsr      beep                         ; ring bell if queue overflow
            bra      ret                          ; discard character
   cont:                                          ; add char to the input queue
            move.l   d0,-(sp)
            pea      inputqueue
            jsr      qinsert
            bclr     #0,suspend_for_input
            bne.s    rxdriverwaiting              ; driver waiting for char?
;                                                 ; if not test transmitter
            btst     #txempty,(statreg,a1)
            bne.s    transint                     ; if empty, service it
            bra.s    ret                          ; return with char queued

   rxdriverwaiting:
            ori.w    #level7,(statusreg,a6)
            bra.s    ret                          ; return with ints disabled

; code to handle the transmitter interrupt
transint:

            pea      outputqueue
            jsr      qempty
            beq.s    charbuffered
            move.b   #recOnlyInt,(ctrlreg,a1)
            bra.s    ret
   charbuffered:
            pea      outputqueue
            jsr      qdelete
            tst.w    xoff_typed                   ; check for Xoff
            beq.s    send
            move.b   #recOnlyInt,(ctrlreg,a1)     ; clear tx interrupt and poll
            move.w   #enableints,sr
   holdit:

            tst.w    xoff_typed                   ; loop until Xoff cleared
            bne.s    holdit
            move.w   #disableints,sr              ; disable cpu interrupts
            move.b   #rec_trInt,(ctrlreg,a1)      ; re-enable transmit interrupts
   send     move.b   d0,(txreg,a1)                ; send the character
            bclr     #0,suspend_for_output
            bne.s    txdriverwaiting              ; output driver waiting?
            bra.s    ret

   txdriverwaiting:
            ori.w    #level7,(statusreg,sp)
   ret:     movem.l  (sp)+,d0-d1/a0-a1
            unlk     a6
            rte
; Ring the bell if get receiver buffer overflow
beep:    move.l   a0,-(sp)
            lea      TermBase,a0
```

```
bell:           btst       #txempty, (statreg, a0)
                beq. s     bell
                move. b    #Bell, (txreg, a0)
                move. l    (sp)+, a0
                rts

stop:           jmp        monitor

                data

queuesize:      equ    16                          ; buffer up to sixteen characters


inputqueue:
                ds. w      1                        ; front index
                ds. w      1                        ; rear index
                ds. w      1                        ; count
                ds. w      1                        ; size
                ds. l      queuesize                ; input buffer

outputqueue:
                ds. w      1                        ; front index
                ds. w      1                        ; rear index
                ds. w      1                        ; count
                ds. w      1                        ; size
                ds. l      queuesize                ; output buffer

suspend_for_input:
                ds. w       1                       ; input queue empty

suspend_for_output:
                ds. w       1                       ; output queue full

xoff_typed:
                ds. w       1                       ; handle XON/XOFF

                end
```

D.4 | SZ RECORD GENERATOR (MAKE__SZ)

The C program MAKE__SZ reads a file in UNIX code file format ("a.out" format) and sends the corresponding SZ-records to the standard output. The SZ record format is used to download code from a host system to a standalone machine. The format is described in Chapter 12.

```
#include <stdio. h>
#include <a. out. h>
```

```
void outhex();

main(argc, argv)
int argc;
char **argv;
{
    FILE *in;                /* input code file */
    int c, i;
    struct exec header;      /* to contain codefile header */

    if (argc = 1)            /* allow code to be a filter */
        in = stdin;
    else
    if ((in = fopen(argv[1], "r")) == NULL)
    {
        perror(argv[1]);
        exit(1);
    }

    /* read header in the code file. system dependent */
    fread(&header, sizeof(header), 1, in);

    putchar('S');            /* start character */

    /* read and convert code bytes for the text and data segments
       of the code file */

    for (i = 1; i <= header.a_text + header.a_data; i++)
    {
        c = fgetc(in);
        outhex(c);           /* output char as two hex digits */
    }
    printf("Z\n");           /* indicate code end */
}

void outhex(c)
int c;
{
    putchar(hexdigit(c >> 4)); /* print bits 4-7 */
    putchar(hexdigit(c & 0x0f)); /* print bits 0-3 */
}

int hexdigit(i)
int i;
{
    if (i <= 9)
        return (i + '0');
    else
        return ('A' + (i- 10));
}
```

APPENDIX E

CONDITION CODE COMPUTATIONS

1.2.2 Condition Codes

The CCR portion of the SR contains five bits which are affected by many integer instructions to indicate the results of the instructions. Program and system control instructions use certain combinations of these bits to control program and system flow.

The first four bits represent a condition of the result of a processor operation. The X bit is an operand for multiprecision computations; when it is used, it is set to the value of the carry bit. The carry bit and the multiprecision extend bit are separate in the M68000 Family to simplify programming techniques that use them (refer to Table 1-18 as an example).

The condition codes were developed to meet two criteria:
- Consistency — across instructions, uses, and instances
- Meaningful Results — no change unless it provides useful information

Consistency across instructions means that all instructions that are special cases of more general instructions affect the condition codes in the same way. Consistency across instances means that all instances of an instruction affect the condition codes in the same way. Consistency across uses means that conditional instructions test the condition codes similarly and provide the same results whether the condition codes are set by a compare, test, or move instruction.

In the instruction set definitions, the CCR is shown as follows:

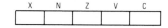

where:

X (extend)
Set to the value of the C bit for arithmetic operations. Otherwise not affected or set to a specified result.

N (negative)
Set if the most significant bit of the result is set. Cleared otherwise.

Z (zero)
Set if the result equals zero. Cleared otherwise.

V (overflow)
Set if arithmetic overflow occurs. This implies that the result cannot be represented in the operand size. Cleared otherwise.

C (carry)
Set if a carry out of the most significant bit of the operand occurs for an addition. Also set if a borrow occurs in a subtraction. Cleared otherwise.

1.2.2.1 CONDITION CODE COMPUTATION. Most operations take a source operand and a destination operand, compute, and store the result in the destination location. Single-operand operations take a destination operand, compute, and store the result in the destination location. Table 1-18 lists each instruction and how it affects the condition code bits.

Table 1-18. Condition Code Computations (Sheet 1 of 2)

Operations	X	N	Z	V	C	Special Definition
ABCD	*	U	?	U	?	C = Decimal Carry $Z = Z \setminus \overline{Rm} \setminus \dots \setminus \overline{R0}$
ADD, ADDI, ADDQ	*	*	*	?	?	$V = Sm \setminus Dm \setminus \overline{Rm}\ V\ \overline{Sm} \setminus \overline{Dm} \setminus Rm$ $C = Sm \setminus Dm\ V\ \overline{Rm} \setminus Dm\ V\ Sm \setminus \overline{Rm}$
ADDX	*	*	?	?	?	$V = Sm \setminus Dm \setminus \overline{Rm}\ V\ \overline{Sm} \setminus \overline{Dm} \setminus Rm$ $C = Sm \setminus Dm\ V\ \overline{Rm} \setminus Dm\ V\ Sm \setminus \overline{Rm}$ $Z = Z \setminus \overline{Rm} \setminus \dots \setminus \overline{R0}$
AND, ANDI, EOR, EORI, MOVEQ, MOVE, OR, ORI, CLR, EXT, NOT, TAS, TST	—	*	*	0	0	
CHK	—	*	U	U	U	
CHK2, CMP2	—	U	?	U	?	$Z = (R = LB)\ V\ (R = UB)$ $C = (LB \le UB) \setminus (\overline{(IR \ge LB)}\ V\ (R \ge UB))$ $V\ (UB < LB) \setminus (R < UB) \setminus (R > LB)$
SUB, SUBI, SUBQ	*	*	*	?	?	$V = \overline{Sm} \setminus Dm \setminus \overline{Rm}\ V\ Sm \setminus \overline{Dm} \setminus Rm$ $C = Sm \setminus \overline{Dm}\ V\ Rm \setminus \overline{Dm}\ V\ Sm \setminus Rm$
SUBX	*	*	?	?	?	$V = \overline{Sm} \setminus Dm \setminus \overline{Rm}\ V\ Sm \setminus \overline{Dm} \setminus Rm$ $C = Sm \setminus \overline{Dm}\ V\ Rm \setminus \overline{Dm}\ V\ Sm \setminus Rm$ $Z = Z \setminus \overline{Rm} \setminus \dots \setminus \overline{R0}$
CAS, CAS2, CMP, CMPI, CMPM	—	*	*	?	?	$V = \overline{Sm} \setminus Dm \setminus \overline{Rm}\ V\ Sm \setminus \overline{Dm} \setminus Rm$ $C = Sm \setminus \overline{Dm}\ V\ Rm \setminus \overline{Dm}\ V\ Sm \setminus Rm$
DIVS, DUVI	—	*	*	?	0	V = Division Overflow
MULS, MULU	—	*	*	?	0	V = Multiplication Overflow
SBCD, NBCD	*	U	?	U	?	C = Decimal Borrow $Z = Z \setminus \overline{Rm} \setminus \dots \setminus \overline{Ro}$
NEG	*	*	*	?	?	$V = Dm \setminus Rm$ $C = Dm\ V\ Rm$
NEGX	*	*	?	?	?	$V = Dm \setminus Rm$ $C = Dm\ V\ Rm$ $Z = Z \setminus \overline{Rm} \setminus \dots \setminus \overline{R0}$
BTST, BCHG, BSET, BCLR	—	—	?	—	—	$Z = \overline{Dn}$
BFTST, BFCHG, BFSET, BFCLR	—	?	?	0	0	$N = Dm$ $Z = \overline{Dm} \setminus \overline{DM-1} \setminus \dots \setminus \overline{D0}$
BFEXTS, BFEXTU, BFFFO	—	?	?	0	0	$N = Sm$ $Z = \overline{Sm} \setminus \overline{Sm-1} \setminus \dots \setminus \overline{S0}$
BFINS	—	?	?	0	0	$N = Dm$ $Z = \overline{Dm} \setminus \overline{DM-1} \setminus \dots \setminus \overline{D0}$

Table 1-18. Condition Code Computations (Sheet 2 of 2)

Operations	X	N	Z	V	C	Special Definition
ASL	*	*	*	?	?	$V = Dm \setminus (\overline{Dm-1} \lor \ldots \lor \overline{Dm-r}) \lor \overline{Dm} \setminus$ $(DM-1 \lor \ldots + Dm-r)$ $C = \overline{Dm-r+1}$
ASL (R = 0)	—	*	*	0	0	
LSL, ROXL	*	*	*	0	?	$C = Dm-r+1$
LSR (r = 0)	—	*	*	0	0	
ROXL (r = 0)	—	*	*	0	?	$C = X$
ROL	—	*	*	0	?	$C = Dm-r+1$
ROL (r = 0)	—	*	*	0	0	
ASR, LSR, ROXR	*	*	*	0	?	$C = Dr-1$
ASR, LSR (r = 0)	—	*	*	0	0	
ROXR (r = 0)	—	*	*	0	?	$C = X$
ROR	—	*	*	0	?	$C = Dr-1$
ROR (r = 0)	—	*	*	0	0	

— = Not Affected
U = Undefined, Result Meaningless
? = Other — See Special Definition
* = General Case
    $X = C$
    $N = \overline{Rm}$
    $Z = \overline{Rm} \setminus \ldots \setminus \overline{R0}$
Sm = Source Operand — Most Significant Bit
Dm = Destination Operand — Most Significant Bit

Rm = Result Operand — Most Significant Bit
R = Register Tested
n = Bit Number
r = Shift Count
LB = Lower Bound
UB = Upper Bound
\ = Boolean AND
V = Boolean OR
$\overline{Rm}$ = NOT Rm

A P P E N D I X F

ASCII CODE CHART

ASCII Code Chart

00 NUL	01 SOH	02 STX	03 ETX	04 EOT	05 ENG	06 ACK	07 BEL
08 BS	09 HT	0A LF	0B VT	0C FF	0D CR	0E S0	0F S1
10 DLE	11 DC1	12 DC2	13 DC3	14 DC4	15 NAK	16 SYN	17 ETB
18 CAN	19 EM	1A SUB	1B ESC	1C FS	1D GS	1E RS	1F US
20 SP	21 !	22 "	23 #	24 $	25 %	26 &	27 '
28 (	29)	2A *	2B +	2C ,	2D –	2E .	2F /
30 0	31 1	32 2	33 3	34 4	35 5	36 6	37 7
38 8	39 9	3A :	3B ;	3C <	3D =	3E >	3F ?
40 @	41 A	42 B	43 C	44 D	45 E	46 F	47 G
48 H	49 I	4A J	4B K	4C L	4D M	4E N	4F O
50 P	51 Q	52 R	53 S	54 T	55 U	56 V	57 W
58 X	59 Y	5A Z	5B [	5C \	5D]	5E ^	5F_
60 `	61 a	62 b	63 c	64 d	65 e	66 f	67 g
68 h	69 i	6A j	6B k	6C l	6D m	6E n	6F o
70 p	71 q	72 r	73 s	74 t	75 u	76 v	77 w
78 x	79 y	7A z	7B {	7C		7D }	7E ~	7F DEL

A N S W E R S

TO SELECTED EXERCISES

Chapter 1

1. IBM PC (Intel 80286, Intel 80386, Intel 80386SX, Intel 80486) Macintosh SE (MC68000); Macintosh IIci (MC68030); Next (MC68040)

3. Systems programs are software that enable users and the computer to make effective use of the system resources. These include the operating system itself, compilers, editors, etc. Applications programs are software that use existing system resources to solve problems.

5. (a) The compiler explicitly uses registers to store data, thus improving access time. Compound Boolean expressions are evaluated term by term, stopping once the value of the expression is known. Short branches and jumps are used when possible. Invariant code in a loop is moved outside the loop.
   (b) No. The assembly language code can better manage data access, better select a sequence of instructions to directly implement an algorithm, and uses the full range of instructions available with the processor.

7. (a) The user can list out the assembly language source code and determine what code the compiler is generating. Different machines, even ones having the same processor, use different code file formats. The assembly language text can be carried to a machine using a different format and assembled there into the correct format for the new machine.
   (b) The code generator for machine A can be modified to emit assembly language for machine B.

Chapter 2

1. (a) $10110_2 = 1(2)^4 + 0(2^3) + 1(2^2) + 1(2^1) + 0(2^0) = 22$
   (b) $302_4 = 3(4^2) + 0(4^1) + 2(4^0) = 50$
   (c) $4421_5 = 4(5^3) + 4(5^2) + 2(5^1) + 1(5^0) = 611$
   (d) $1670_8 = 1(9^3) + 6(9^2) + 7(9^1) + 0(9^0) = 1278$

3. (a) $22 = 16_{16}$ (e) $256 = 100_{16}$
   (b) $52 = 34_{16}$ (f) $991 = 3DF_{16}$
   (c) $96 = 60_{16}$ (g) $2000 = 7D0_{16}$
   (d) $190 = BE_{16}$

5. (a) $A06C = 41068$ (d) $42FA = 17146$
   (b) $5FFD = 24573$ (e) $FFFF = 65535$
   (c) $2847 = 10311$

7. $2365 = 6616_7$

9. (a) $A876 = 1010\ 1000\ 0111\ 0110_2$
   (b) $A8897 = 1010\ 1000\ 1000\ 1001\ 0110_2$
   (c) $FFFF = 1111\ 1111\ 1111\ 1111_2$
   (d) $7896 = 0111\ 1000\ 1001\ 0110_2$
   (e) $0167 = 0000\ 0001\ 0110\ 0111_2$
   (f) $5555 = 0101\ 0101\ 0101\ 0101_2$

11. (a) (i) $25 = 31_8$ (iii) $48 = 60_8$
        (ii) $87 = 127_8$ (iv) $101 = 148_8$
    (b) (i) $47 = 100111_2$
        (ii) $216 = 10001110_2$
        (iii) $646 = 110100110_2$
        (iv) $17221 = 111101001\ 0001_2$
    (c) (i) $11011011 = 333_8$
        (ii) $1010011 = 128_8$
        (iii) $100100111100 = 4474_8$
    (d) (i) $4F = 1001111 = 117_8$
        (ii) $A27 = 101000100111 = 5047_8$
        (iii) $1101 = 0001000100000001 = 10401_8$
        (iv) $FFFF = 1111111111111111 = 177777_8$

13. (a) 232 (to base 5) = 1412_5
   (b) 1523 (to base 7) = 6122_7
   (c) 194 (to base 3) = 21012_3
   (d) 3721 (to base 20) = 961_{20}

15. (a) 68AF   (e) 121
   (b) 1A7516   (f) 22D7
   (c) 5564A9   (g) 10A82
   (d) 1001133F   (h) 675D

17. (a) 10 miles backward = 990
   (b) 280 miles backward = 720
   (c) 102 miles backward = 898
   (d) 800 miles forward = 800
   Fewest number of miles to get the reading 650?
   650 miles. Fewest number of miles if pedaling
   backward? 350 miles. Fewest number of miles to
   get the reading 300? 450 miles backwards.

19. (a) Decimal: −2048 to 2047
       Binary: 100000000000_2 to
                    011111111111_2
       Hex: 800_{16} to $7FF_{16}$
   (b) Decimal: −524288 to 524287
       Binary: 100000000000000000000_2 to
                    011111111111111111111_2
       Hex: 80000_{16} to $7FFFF_{16}$

21. (a) 2comp(48_{16}) = $B8_{16}$
   (b) 2comp($FFF4_{16}$) = $000C_{16}$
   (c) 2comp(120_{16}) = $EE0_{16}$
   (d) 2comp($AB76_{16}$) = $548A_{16}$
   (e) 2comp(1_{16}) = $FFFF_{16}$
   (f) 2comp(0_{16}) = 0000_{16}
   (g) 2comp(8000_{16}) = 8000_{16}

23. (a) 10101011   (c) 11011111
   (b) 11001011   (d) 10001110

25. (a) 92_{16} = $FF92_{16}$ (c) $7F_{16}$ = $007F_{16}$
   (b) $A8_{16}$ = $FFA8_{16}$ (d) $E0_{16}$ = $FFE0_{16}$

27. (a) 97CE   (c) 9E7C
   (b) 18D0 (yes)   (d) 8001 (yes)

29. (a) 10 = 001010_2
   (b) −18 = 101101_2
   (c) 31 = 011111_2
   (d) −31 = 100000_2 Range: −31 to +31

31. (a) 50 61 73 63 61 6C 27   Pascal's CH
       73 20 43 48
   (b) 50 41 47 45 3D 0D   PAGE
                                     = ⟨cr⟩
       52 20 69 73 20 65 61   R is easier
       73 69 65 72

33. (a) U AND V = 6700_{16}
   (b) U OR V = $FFAB_{16}$
   (c) NOT U = $00FF_{16}$
   (d) U EOR V = $98AB_{16}$

35. Use the mask 11111111_2.
   01001110_2 EOR 11111111_2 = 10110001_2

37. Use the mask $000F_{16}$. 23_{10} = 0017_{16}
   0017_{16} AND $000F_{16}$ = 0007_{16}

Chapter 3

1. RAM can be read from and written to. However,
   you can only read from ROM.
   The program is lost and must be reloaded after
   the system is restarted.
   ROM retains its data with or without power and
   cannot be altered.

3. (a) A special piece of equipment must be used,
       called an EPROM "burner".
   (b) Place the EPROM under ultraviolet light.
   (c) Electrically erasable PROMs. An EEPROM can
       be programmed directly from the host system.
       A pernicious user could alter system code.

5. $8 * (1/25,000,000) = 8 * .04 * 10^{-6} = .32$ ms

7. PC–microchannel bus
   Macintosh–NuBus

9. 512K of memory contains $2^9 * 2^{10} = 2^3 * 16^4 =$
   \$80000 bytes. The highest addressable byte is
   \$7FFFF. If 128K of memory is added, there are
   \$20000 more bytes of memory available. The
   highest addressable byte is then \$9FFFF.

11. (a) The XYZ-784 is a byte addressable computer.
   (b) The data bus width is 24-bits. It is a 24-bit
       computer.
   (c) A word contains 24 bits, with bits numbered
       from 0 to 23. A long word consists of two
       adjacent words, with bits numbered from 0 to
       47.
   (d) The maximum number of bytes is $2^{20} = 1M$.
       The range of address is \$00000 to \$FFFFF.
   (e) 1M = 1024K

13. High speed backup of a large amount of data.

15. A printer which contains a microprocessor dedicated to interpreting postscript language commands sent from a host system.

17. The most significant word is the word at the address of the long word. The least significant word is the word at location address + 2.
223 = $000000DF. The most significant word is $0000 and the least significant word is $00DF.

19. (a) (D0.W) = $6AFA
    (b) (D0.L) = $207B6AFA
    (c) (D0.B) = $FA
    (d) LSB of D0 = $FA
    (e) MSW of D0 = $207B
    (f) LSW of D0 = $6AFA

21. (a) $3BD7
    (b) $61FC56FF
    (c) Offset 3 for $FC; Offset 5 for $FF

23. (a) D079 0001 0500
        ADD $010500,D0
    (b) 0679 0032 0002 0000
        ADDI #50,$020000

25.
Address	Machine Code	Instruction	
000200	3039 0000 0500	MOVE	$000500,D0
000206	9079 0000 0502	SUB	$000502,D0
00020C	D079 0000 0504	ADD	$000504,D0
000212	D079 0000 0506	ADD	$000506,D0
000218	4E42	TRAP	#2
00021E	4E40	TRAP	#0
⋮	⋮		
000500	000A		
000502	0007		
000504	0010		
000506	0025		

Writes out the value in D0 which is $0038

27.
Statement 1	TRAP	#1	4E41
Statement 2	MOVE	D0, $950	33C0 0000 0950
Statement 3	MOVE	#$FFFF,D0	303C FFFF
Statement 4	SUB	$950,D0	9070 0000 0950
Statement 5	ADDI	#1,D0	0640 0001
Statement 6	TRAP	#2	4E42
Statement 7	TRAP	#0	4E40

The output is 2comp(N)

29. (a) MOVE #1,D0   2 read 0 write
    (b) MOVE D0,$008000   3 read 1 write
    (c) ADDI #5,$002210   5 read 1 write
    (d) SUB $002000,D0   4 read 0 write
    (e) MOVE $006008,D0   4 read 0 write
    (f) MOVE #5,$3300   4 read 1 write

31. With PC = $002000, fetch opcode   0440
    With PC = $002002, fetch number   0007
    PC = $002004, pointing to the next
                  instruction

33. (a) 303C 8000   MOVE #8000,D0   Executes
    (b) 3039 0000 8000 MOVE $008000,D0 Address
                        out of range

35. The contents of $000518 is $33C0, opcode for MOVE D0,$1004. The value at location $518 resides in D0 at instruction (*). Hence, the final value in $1004 is $33C0

37. The contents of $512 = $0679; the contents of $774 = $1007.

Chapter 4

1. (a) ADD.W D0;Y   (c) ADDI.W #5A,D0
       is correct or   is correct or
       ADD.W D0,Y   ADDI.W #$5A,D0
   (b) MOVE.L X Y
       is correct or
       MOVE.L X,Y
   (d) GLOBAL STOP,HEXOUT
       is correct or
       XREF STOP,HEXOUT
   (e) LOOP: THIS IS A LABEL
       is correct or
       LOOP: ;THIS IS A LABEL
   (f) MOVE.L D0,#3A0F
       is correct or
       MOVE.L D0,$3A0F

3. (a) The directive allocates a single word of data with an initial value 7. The directive "DS.W 7" allocates the 7 words of memory.
   (b) DCB.W 7,0

5. A: DC.W   18, −32, 14, −1, 67, 162

7. C has value $000026

9. (a) MOVE.B #'f', D0 MOVE.B #$66,D0
   (b) MOVE.B #'[', D0 MOVE.B #$5B,D0

11. In a one-pass assembler, a symbol table is maintained as before, but each entry of the table contains a pointer to a "fixup" list. On the one pass, code is generated and when a label is found, the value of the label is placed within the code at all the places where it was previously referenced.

13. (a) MOVE.W #5,D0   The constant 5 is absolute

    (b) ADDI.W #$56,D0 The constant $56 is absolute

    (c) MOVE.W D0,I   The address I is relocatable

    (d) MOVE.W #8,J   The constant 8 is absolute and the address J is relocatable

15.

START: MOVE.W #ENDCODE, DO   Relocatable address

        SUBI.W   #START,D0   Relocatable address

17. *See below.*

19.
(a) ADD.W   D0,D1   (D1.L) = $7890EAD9
(b) SUB.B   D2,D1   (D1.L) = $7890EA95
(c) ADD.L   D0,D1   (D1.L) = $BDF8EAD9
(d) ORI.W   #$0F66,D1   (D1.L) = $7890EFFE
(e) ANDI.B   #$66,D1   (D1.L) = $7890EA64
(f) EORI.L   #$FFF084,D1 (D1.L) = $786F1A78

21. (a) LEA $5000,A5 Loads the address $005000 in A5

    (b) MOVEA.W A2,A5   Sign extends the LSW of A2 and places it in A5

    (c) LEA   (A2),A5 Loads the 32-bit value in A2 in register A5

    (d) MOVEA.L (A2),A5 Assigns the 32-bit contents at location A2 to register A5

23.
(a) LEA $4000,A2   A2 has value $00004000
(b) MOVEA.L $4000,A2   A2 has value $00F20052
(c) LEA   (A0),A2   A2 has value $00004000
(d) MOVEA.L #$4000,A2   A2 has value $00004000
(e) MOVEA.L (A0),A2   A2 has value $00F20052
(f) MOVEA.L #$A0,A2   A2 has value $000000A0

25. (a) MOVE.W   #1,D0   303C 0001
    (b) MOVEA.L A,A3   2679 0000 1000
    (c) LEA   A.W,A6   4DF8 0000 1000
    (d) MOVE.B   (A3),D1   3213
    (e) SUBA.L   (A0),A6   9DD0
    (f) SUB.B   D2,D3   9602
    (g) CLR.B   D3   4203
    (h) OR.W   D0,D1   8240

27.
(a) LEA $4000,A5   4BF9 0000 4000
(b) MOVE.L $3000.W,$4000   23F8 3000 0000 4000
(c) ANDI.L   #7,D0   0280 0000 0007
(d) NOT.B   D3   4603

29. (a) DC.B 50   (b) 82   (c) 15

31. (a) The label I begins at an odd address. The word instruction MOVE.W I,D0 would result in an address error.

    (b) A0 is set to be the location of the "jump" in the JSR STOP statement.
    If START is entered, the program does not jump to STOP but to START, causing the program to run as an infinite loop.

Chapter 5

1. (a) ADD.W D2,D0
       X = 1, N = 0, Z = 0, V = 0, C = 1
    (b) AND.B D2,D0
       X = 1, N = 0, Z = 0, V = 0, C = 1
    (c) MOVEA.W D0,A2
       X = 1, N = 0, Z = 1, V = 1, C = 0

---

17. (a) MOVE.W   #5,(A6)   Immediate   Address Indirect
    (b) ADD.L   LIST,D4   Absolute Long   Data Register
    (c) ANDI.B   #$80,D0   Immediate   Data Register
    (d) SUB.W   A.W,D3   Absolute Short   Data Register
    (e) MOVEA.L   T.W,A4   Absolute Short   Address Register
    (f) LEA   BUF,A5   Absolute Long   Address Register
    (g) MOVE.B   #'0',(A2)   Immediate   Address Indirect
    (h) ADD.L   #LIST,D3   Immediate   Data Register

(d) EOR.W D2,D0

   X = 1, N = 8, Z = 0, V = 0, C = 0

3. (a) Branch occurs.

   (b) Branch occurs.

   (c) Branch does not occur.

5. (a) X = 0, N = 0, Z = 0, V = 0, C = 0

   (b) (i)   BPL   ⟨label⟩   YES

      (ii)   BLE   ⟨label⟩   NO

      (iii) BGT   ⟨label⟩   YES

      (iv)   BCS   ⟨label⟩   YES

      (v)   BMI   ⟨label⟩   NO

7. Algebraic argument: The BGT branch executes provided the CMP instruction recognizes

$$\text{Destination} - \text{source} > 0$$

Under ordinary conditions (no overflow, or V = 0), the N bit is assigned 0 and the Z bit is 0. However, if overflow occurs (V = 1), the sign of the result is opposite what it should be. Thus if N = 1 and V = 1, the correct N should be N = 0 and the branch occurs. In this case Z must be 0.

9. (a) TST   D1

   X = 1 N = 1 Z = 0 V = 0 C = 0

   (b) CMP.W D0,D1

   X = 1 N = 1 Z = 0 V = 0 C = 0

   (c) BNE   ⟨label⟩

   X = 1 N = 1 Z = 0 V = 0 C = 1

   (d) SUB.B D1,D0

   X = 1 N = 1 Z = 0 V = 1 C = 1

   (e) AND.W D0,D1

   X = 1 N = 0 Z = 0 V = 0 C = 0

   (f) ASL.W #6,D0

   X = 1 N = 1 Z = 0 V = 0 C = 1

11. MOVEQ #−102,D6 or MOVEQ #$9A,D6

13. A complete program is included below

⟨Listing of Exercise 13 Ch 5.a⟩

```
    xref    decin_long, decout
    xref    stop, newline

    jsr     decin_long
    move.l  d0, d2
    lea     1-4, a0  ; set a0 1 long
                     word before
                     list 1
```

```
    moveq   #9, d1
loop: addq.l  #4, a0   ; go to the
                       ; next long word
    cmp.l   (a0), d2 ; compare against
                     ; key in d2
    dbge    d1, loop ; branch if key less
                     ; than array item
    neg.w   d1       ; compute index at
                     ; point to insert

    add.w   #9, d1
    move.w  d1, d0
    jsr     decout
    jsr     newline
    jsr     stop

    data
1:  dc.l  100, 90, 80, 70, 60, 50, 40, 30, 20, 10, 0
    end
```

⟨Run of Exercise 5.13⟩

   65

   4

15. MC68000 Code:

```
          BLS    AFTER_BRA
          BRA    FAR_LABEL

AFTER_BRA:      . . . . .
```

17. (a) 66F4 BNE ⟨LABEL⟩

            LABEL AT ADDRESS $000100

   (b) 6B08 BMI ⟨LABEL⟩

            LABEL AT ADDRESS $000114

   (c) 6E06 BGT ⟨LABEL⟩

            LABEL AT ADDRESS $000112

19. (a) 65E8 BCS ⟨LABEL⟩

            Displacement = E8 (−24)

   (b) 6B08 BMI ⟨LABEL⟩

            Displacement = 8

21. (a) 1000000001 (Binary)   (b) 711C (Hex)

23. (a) Assume (D0.L) = $0000 0105

      (i) DIVS #5,D0   (D0.L) = 0001 0034

      (ii) DIVU #5,D0   (D0.L) = 0001 0034

   (b) Assume (D0.L) = $FFFF FFA0

      (i) DIVS #4,D0   (D0.L) = FFFF FFED

      (ii) DIVU #4,D0 (D0.L) = FFFF FFA0 with
                                    overflow

25. (a) N = −4   M =   9   (D0.L) = 0001 FFFE
    (b) N =   4   M = −9   (D0.L) = FFFF FFFE
    (c) N = −4   M = −9   (D0.L) = FFFF 0002

27. The 16-bit contents at address ALPHA is $0004

29. (a) Using the EXT instruction
       EXT.W D1
       EXT.L D1
    (b) Using ASL/ASR   Assign (D2,W) = 24
       ASL.L D2,D1
       ASR.L D2,D1

31. (a) BTST #7,D0   (D0.W) = A568
    (b) BCHG #7,D0   (D0.W) = A5E8
    (c) BCLR #5,D0   (D0.W) = A548
    (d) BSET #2,D0   (D0.W) = A56C

33. (a) Yes   (b) Yes

Chapter 6

1. (a) DC.W 1,2,3,4,5
   (b) DCB.L   100,0
   (c) (i) C: DS.W   100
   (ii) Addr(C[5]) = C + 8
       General address: Addr(C[n]) = C + (n − 1) ∗ 2

3. (a) MOVE.W (A0)+,−(A0)   Identity
   (b) MOVE.W −(A0),(A0)+   Identity
   (c) MOVE.L (A1)+,(A1)+   Not identity

5. (a) MOVE.W ALPHA.W, (A0)+
      Instruction size = 2 words; source mode is
      absolute short; destination mode is address
      register indirect with postincrement; the 16-
      bit contents at location A0 = $00456A is as-
      signed the value $0018 from ALPHA; register
      A0 is incremented by 2 bytes to value
      $0000456C.
   (b) MOVE.W (A0)+,(A0)+
      Instruction size = 1 word; source mode and
      destination mode is address register indirect
      with postincrement; the 16-bit contents $0006
      at location A0 = $00456A is assigned to ad-
      dress $00456C; register A0 is incremented by
      4 bytes to value $0000456E.

7. (a) MOVE.L #$A3,(A3)+
      (A3) = $0000 101E
      The 32-bit contents at
      $00101A is $0000 00A3

(b) LEA   (A3),A3
    (A3) = $0000 101A
    Memory is not changed
(c) MOVE.L (A3)+,(A3)
    (A3) = $0000 101E
    The 32-bit contents at
    $00101E is $0006 FFFD
(d) ADD.W −(A3),D2
    (A3) = $0000 1018
    (D2.W) = $0007
    Memory is not changed
(e) ADD.L D2,(A3)+
    (A3) = $0000 101
    The 32-bit contents at
    $00101A is $FFFF 0004

9. A complete program is included.

```
        xref stop, decout

        lea   list,a0
        moveq#9, d0
loop:   tst.1 (a0)+
        dbeq d0, loop
        sub.w#9, d0
        neg.wd0
        jsr   decout
        jsr   stop

        data
list:   dc.1 00, 80, 70, 60, 50, 30, 20, 10, 0
        end
```

⟨Run of Exercise 6.9⟩

8

11. PUSH Routine

    ; Assume that A0 points at the Top of the stack
        ADDQ.W #2,A0
        MOVE.W D0,(A0) ; PUSH FROM D0

    POP Routine
    ; Assume that A0 points at the Top of the stack
        MOVE.W (A0),D0 ; POP TO DO
        SUBQ.W #2,A0

13. (a) LEA OUTPUT,A0   OUTPUT = $001000
       Source mode is absolute long
       Destination mode is address register direct
       Machine code is: 4179 0000 1000
    (b) MOVE.W (A0),(−8,A2)
       Source mode is address register indirect
       Destination mode is address register
         indirect with displacement.
       Machine code is: 3550 FFF8

(c) MOVE.L $721A.W,(4,A2,D3.L)
    Source mode is absolute short
    Destination mode is address register
      indirect with displacement and index.
    Machine code is: 25B8 721A 3804

(d) CLR.L   (A4)+
    Source mode is address register indirect with
      postincrement.
    Machine code is: 429C

(e) CMPI.B   #$0A,−(A2)
    Source mode is immediate
    Destination mode is address register
      indirect with predecrement.
    Machine code is: 0C22 000A

(f) AND.B   D5,($26,A6,D1.W)
    Source mode is data register direct
    Destination mode is address register
      indirect with displacement and index.
    Machine code is: CB36 1026

15. (a) MOVE.W   −(A0),(2,A0)
    Instruction size = 4 words; source mode is
    address register indirect with predecrement;
    destination mode is address register indirect
    with displacement; the 16-bit contents $0006
    at location (A0) − 2 = $00456A is assigned
    to location $00456C.

(b) MOVE.W   (A0)+,(2,A0)
    Instruction size = 4 words; source mode is
    address register indirect with postdecrement;
    destination mode is address register indirect
    with displacement; the 16-bit contents $0018
    at location (A0) = $00456C is assigned to lo-
    cation $004570.

17. (a) MOVE.L   (−4,A2),(A2)+
    (A2) = $0000 107A
    The 16-bits $1074 is assigned to location
    $001078

(b) MOVE.W   −(A2),(−4,A2)
    (A2) = $0000 1076
    The 16-bits $1072 is assigned to location
    $001072

(c) MOVEA.L   (−2,A2),A2
    (A2) = $10721106
    The 32-bits $10721106 is assigned to register
    A2

19. Rewritten code included in a complete program:

```
        xref    stop,  hexout
        lea     arr,a0
        moveq   #19,d2
        moveq   #0,d0
loop:   move.w  (a0)+,d3
        not.w   d3
        add.w   d3,d0
        dbra    d2,loop
        jsr     hexout

        data
arr:    dcb.w   10,−1
        dcb.w   10,0
        end
```

⟨Run of Exercise 6.19⟩

FFF6

21. NULL: EQU   0
    NAME: EQU   0
    DEPT: EQU   20
    CLASS: EQU   22

    LEA   A,A0
    MOVE.W   I,D0
    MULU   #24,D0

    MOVE.B   #NULL,(NAME,A0,D0.W)
    MOVE.W   #0,(DEPT,A0,D0.W)
    MOVE.B   #0,(CLASS,A0,D0.W)

23. The code moves A[2], the third element in the
    array, to D5

25. (a) Effective address of the source operand is
        $008008
    (b) Effective address of the source operand is
        $008004
    (c) Effective address of the source operand is
        $008808

27. Position independent.

29. (a) Effective address of the source operand is
        $001044
    (b) Effective address of the source operand is
        $000048
    (c) Effective address of the source operand is
        $108008
    (d) Effective address of the source operand is
        $000020
    (e) Effective address of the source operand is
        $000000

Chapter 7

1. (a) MOVEM.L   D1/D7/A0-A4,MEM
   (b) BSR LABEL
   (c) JSR (A2)
   (d) PEA (A5)
   (e) MOVEM.L   (SP)+,D0-D7/A6

3.
(a) MOVEM.L   D0-D3/A3-A5,−(SP)   48E7 F01C
(b) MOVEM.L   (SP)+,D0-D3/A3-A5   4CDF 380F
(c) MOVEM.W   D2-D6/A1-A3,$6000.W   48B8 0E7C 6000

5. (a)

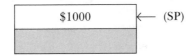

$1000   ←── (SP)

(b) MOVEM.L   D1-D2/A0-A1,−(SP)

(c)

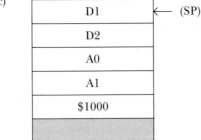

D1   ←── (SP)
D2
A0
A1
$1000

(d) MOVEM.L (SP)+,D1-D2/A0-A1

7. RETADDR: EQU   4

EXAMPLE:
```
LINK    A6,#0
MOVEM.L D0-D2/A0-A1,  −(SP)
MOVEA.L (RETADDR,A6)A0
MOVE.W  (A0)+,D0       ; GET 1st PARAM
MOVE.L  (A0)+,A1       ; GET 2nd PARAM
MOVE.W  (A0)+,D1       ; GET 3rd PARAM
MOVE.L  A0,(RETADDR,A6) ; RESET RETADDR
```

9. Output is: 0005   0008

11. Complete program

```
        xref    hexout, stop
        pea     sum
        move.w  #5,-(sp)
        pea     list1
        jsr     sumsq
        move.w  sum,d0
        jsr     hexout
        jsr     stop
sumsq:  link    a6,#0
        movem.l d0-d2/a0-a1,-(sp)
        move.l  (8,a6),a0
        move.w  (12,a6),d1
        movea.l (14,a6),a1
        subq.w  #1,d1
        moveq   #0,d0
loop:   move.w  (a0)+,d2
        mulu    d2,d2
        add.w   d2,d0
        dbra    d1,loop
        move.w  d0,(a1)
        movem.l (sp)+,d0-d2/a0-a1
        unlk    a6
        move.l  (sp),(10,sp)
        adda.l  #10,sp
        rts
        data
list1:  dc.w    2,3,5,7,9
sum:    ds.w    1
        end
```

⟨Run of Exercise 7.11⟩

a8

13. The routine assumes the calling program pushes an address followed by a 16-bit integer on the stack. The routine replaces the contents of the address by twice the integer value.

15. (a) Output is 0007
    (b) Output is 0003
    (c) Both print the value 0009

17. The following is a complete program demonstrating that the routine Q17 inserts the given long word in D0 at item number D1 in the list. All subsequent items in the list are shifted to the right by one item.

```
        xref        hexout_long, stop

start:  lea         arr, a0
        moveq       #-1, d0
        move.w      #3, d1
        move.l      #10, d2
        jsr         q17
        move.w      #10, d1

printagain:
        move.l      (a0)+, d0
        jsr         hexout_long
        dbra        d1, printagain
        jsr         stop


q17:
        movem.l     d1-d2/a1-a2, -(sp)
        tst.w       d2
        bne         cont
        movea.l     a0, a2
        bra         doit
cont:   subq.l      #1, d1
        asl.w       #2, d1
        asl.w       #2, d2
        lea         (0, a0, d2.W), a1
        lea         (0, a0, d1.W), a2

qloop:
        move.l      -(a1), (4, a1)
        cmpa.l      a1, a2
        bcs.s       qloop
doit:   move.l      d0, (a2)
        move.l      (sp)+, d1-d2/a1-a2
        addq.w      #1, d2
        rts


arr:    dc.l        $a0, $30, $77, $0f, $50,
        dc.l        $c0, $00, $01, $80, $7f
        ds.l        1
        end
```

⟨Run of Exercise 7.17⟩

```
000000A0   00000030   FFFFFFFF   00000077
0000000F   00000050   000000C0   00000000
00000001   00000080   0000007F
```

Chapter 8

1. (a) ORI.W #$05,CCR
   (b) ANDI.W #$19,CCR
   (c) EORI.W #$03,CCR
   (d) MOVE.W #$1C,CCR

3. Subtracts two (2) 64-bit numbers, leaving the result at the location of the second number.

5. Performs an unsigned division of a 64-bit number by 2.

7. (a) The routine negates the 64-bit number BETA and then adds ALPHA, leaving the result in BETA

   (b)
   ```
            XDEF    ADDEM
   ADDEM:   ADDA.L  #8,A0       ; A0 POINTS TO ALPHA
            ADDA.L  #8,A1       ; A1 POINTS TO BETA
            NEG.L   -4(A1)
            NEGX.L  -8(A1)
            MOVE.W  #0,CCR
            SUBX.L  -(A0),-(A1)
            SUBX.L  -(A0),-(A1)
            RTS
   ```

9. AB7

11. (a) 7.5   40F00000
    (b) −1/4   BE800000
    (c) −120.3125   C2F0A000
    (d) 17/64   3E880000

13. (a) C1800000   −16.0
    (b) 419E0000   19.75
    (c) C0E00000   −7.0
    (d) 44640000   912.0

15. (a) D0 {8:4}   1010
    (b) D0 {24:2}   10
    (c) D0 {12:3}   001
    (d) D0 {1:1}   1

17. (a) BFEXTS   D2 {20:8},D3   FFFFFFF1
    (b) BFEXTU   D2 {20:8},D3   000000F1
    (c) BFFFO   D2 {24;4},D3   0000001B
    (d) BFFFO   D2 {4:6},D3   0000000A

19. (a) (D2.L) = 00000000
    (b) (D1.L) = 00000000 (D0.L) = 01991110
    (c) (D0.L) = 00000001 (D2.L) = 00000000

21. MOVEM.L   (A0),D2-D3
    DIVU.L   #10,D2:D3

Chapter 9

1. Both represent global variables. The XREF directive specifies that the variable is contained in an external file. The XDEF directive specifies that the variable is defined within the file and may be accessed by other external files that use an XREF directive to request access.

3. (a) 'BAD'   42 41 44 00
   (b) 'ASCII'   41 53 43 49 49 00
   (c) '1776'   31 37 37 36 00

5. DC.B $02,'String Format start/end',$03

7. Concatenates the string pointed to by A1 onto the end of the string pointed to by A0.

9. The string is stored in byte count format. The routine replaces all occurrences of '.' by '!'.

11. (a) 43   53   33
    (b) CS3

Chapter 10

1. (a) Subtract 5 from the selector.
   (b) Line #1 : SUBQ.W   #2,D0
       Line #4 : ASL.W   #2,D0
       Line #6 : MOVEA.L (0,A0,D0.W),A0
       Line #10: DC.L   OTHERWISE

3. Line #6 : LINK   A6,#−4
   Line #12: CMP.W   (N,A6),D0
   Line #16: MOVE.W   (0,A0,D0.W),D0
   Line #20: MOVE.W   (−4,A6),D0

5. The routine determines whether a given KEY is in the list.

7. MC68000 Procedure: *See below.*

```
lsum:      equ       −8
i:         equ       −4
a:         equ        8
n:         equ       12
sumaddr:   equ       16

           xdef      sumsq

sumsq:     link      a6,#0
           movem.l   d0-d1/A0,−(sp)
           clr.l     (lsum,a6)          ; isum := 0
           move.l    #1,(i,a6)          ; i = 1
           move.l    (n,a6),d1          ; place n in d1 for
           movea.l   (a,a6),a0          ; let a0 point to the array
sloop:     move.l    (i,a6),d0          ; get I in d0
           cmp.l     d0,d1              ; i <= n?
           Blt.s     eloop
           subq.l    #1,d0              ; offset = 4*[(d0)−1]
           asl.l     #2,d0
           move.l    (0,a0,d0.l),d0     ; (d0) = a[i]
           muls      d0,d0              ; sqr (a[i]). Trunc to 16 bits
           add.l     d0,(lsum,a6)       ; isum := isum + squ(a[i])
           addq.l    #1(i,a6)           ; i: = i + 1
           bra.s     sloop
eloop:     movea.l   (sumaddr,a6),a0    ; get address of sum in a0
           move.l    (lsum,a6),a0)      ; sum := lsum
           movem.l   (sp)+,d0-d1/A0
           unlk      a6
           rts
           end
```

9. Rewrite using:

```
MOVE.L      #$686,D0
NOP
NOP
MOVEM.L     (SP)+,D1-D3/A0-A2
UNLK        A6
RTS
```

13. 1. May not write into the code segment. REQUIREMENT
    2. Maintain a separate stack area for each instance of execution. REQUIREMENT
    3. All subroutine calls must be done in a position independent fashion. NOT A REQUIREMENT
    4. All registers must be saved at a context switch. REQUIREMENT
    5. Each process must have its own data area. REQUIREMENT

15. Place a record WRITEREC in data space with the following fields:

Before calling the subroutine, place the buffer size and address into WRITEREC. Place the read-only data item

```
DC.L        WRITEREC
```

in memory after the call to WRITE. The subroutine then reads this address from program memory, accesses the two fields and performs the operation. This code is reentrant as long as any two processes have separate data areas.

```
NBYTES:     EQU         0
ADDR:       EQU         2

            LEA         WRITEREC,A0
            MOVE.W      #3,(NBYTES,A0)
            MOVE.L      #A,(ADDR,A0)
            JSR         WRITE
            DC.L        WRITEREC
             . . .
```

```
RETADDR:    EQU         12
WRITE:      MOVEM.L     D0/A0-A1,-(SP)
            MOVE.L      (RETADDR,SP),A0
            MOVE.L      (A0)+,A1
            MOVE.L      A0,(RETADDR,SP)
            MOVE.W      (A1)+,D0
            MOVE.L      (A1),A0
; CALL OPERATING SYSTEM WRITE ROUTINE
            JSR         OSWRITE
            MOVEM.L     (SP)+,D0/A0-A1
            RTS
            . . .

WRITEREC:
            DS.W        1           ; NBYTES
            DS.L        1           ; ADDR
```

17. If the program is interrupted immediately after

```
START: LEA (START,PC),SP
```

and is subsequently moved to another area of memory and restarted, the stack pointer will still refer to the area allocated prior to relocation.

19. No, since ONE, TWO, etc. are absolute long addresses.

21. Revised Text:

```
        xref     decout, newline, stop

start:  lea      a,a5
        move.w   (0,a5),d0
        add.w    (2,a5),d0
        add.w    (4,a5),d0
        addi.w   #5,d0
        jsr      decout
        jsr      newline
        jsr      stop

        data
a:      dc.w     3
b:      d.cw     5
c:      dc.w     33
        end
```

23. (MC68020/30/40)
    (a) MOVE.L ([HASH,D1.W*4]),D1
        MOVEA.L ([HASH],D1.W*4],4),A2
    (b) MOVE.W ([A,A1],D1.W*2]),D1

Chapter 11

1. (a) i. {Jan, Feb, Mar, Oct, Nov, Dec}
        (D0.W) = $0E07
    ii. {Jan, Jun, Jul} (D0.W) = $0061
    iii. The set of months containing only 30 days
        (D0.W) = $0528
    iv. The months of summer vacation.
        (D0.W) = $00E0
   (b) i. $00000FFF S = {Jan .. Dec}
       ii. $00000111 S = {Jan,Feb,Mar}
       iii. $0000003F S = {Jan .. Jun}
       iv. $00000070 S = {May,Jun,Jul}
       v. $00000C000 S = { }
   (c) i. BSET #7,D0 Puts month AUG in the set
       ii. OR.L #$7F,D0 Puts months JAN .. JUL in the set
       iii. BTST #11,D0 Tests if DEC is in the set
       iv. NOT D0 Complements the set
           ANDI.L #$0FFF,D0 Clears excess bits
       v. AND.L #$3F,D0 Tests if JAN .. JUN is a subset of
           CMPI.L #$3F,D0 the set

3. See page 229.

5. (a) $FF   (b) $00

7. (a) (A0) = address of next node on the availability stack.
   (b) Value is nil or 0

9. (a) (4,A0)   (b) MOVE.L A0,AVAIL

11. (a) (D0.W) = $0160 (c) $20
    (b) $10, $40   (d) $50, $70

Chapter 12

1. With isolated I/O, an array of up to 256 8-bit input ports and 256 8-bit output ports may be accessed using specific instructions, typically "IN" and "OUT". The data transfer occurs on a separate I/O bus that connects the I/O device with internal CPU registers.

   For memory-mapped I/O, the interface registers are just addresses on the bus and can be accessed using the processor's memory access instructions. Both memory and peripheral devices share the same address space.

3. Bit transmission is from left to right; ⟨start⟩ = 0; ⟨stop⟩ = 1
   (a) 'a' ⟨start⟩-1-0-0-0-1-1-⟨stop⟩
   (b) '0' ⟨start⟩-0-0-0-0-1-1-0-⟨stop⟩
   (c) '@' ⟨start⟩-0-0-0-0-0-1-⟨stop⟩

5. Character 'A'

7. Label B has value $10A0

9. The parity bit in the status register is set. Sets transmission to 8 data bits, odd parity, and 1 stop bit.

11. Step 1: Poll until a latch is available. Place the character in the latch.
    Step 2: Do a data strobe
    Step 3: Check the status lines to determine if the character has been received. If not, repeat the process beginning with step 1.

13. This program reads and echoes characters and rings the terminal bell every two seconds.

15. Characters are typed at the terminal and echoed until a ⟨control⟩D is typed. A bell rings for each character input.

17. The routine tests the status of carrier detect. If the carrier has dropped, the program is aborted; otherwise, the presence of a character is tested. If present the character is returned in D0 and D1 is set to 1. If no character is present, D1 is set to 0.

19. LEA $1000,A0
    LEA $2000,A1
    MOVEP.L (0,A0),D0
    MOVEP.L D0,(1,A1)

```
Rowbd:          equ       0           ; offset for row bound
colbd:          equ       2           ; offset for column bound
rowsize:        equ       4           ; offset for row size
eltsize:        equ       6           ; offset for element size
row:            equ       8           ; offset for row index
col:            equ      10           ; offset for column index

mataddr:        equ      12           ; offset to matrix on stack
matdesptor:     equ       8           ; offset to descriptor on stack
parsize:        equ       8           ; two 32 bit parameters on stack

                xdef     norm

norm:           link     a6,#0
                movem.L  d1-d3/a0-a1,-(sp)
                moveq    #0,d0                ; norm returned in d0
                movea.L  (matdesptor,a6),a1   ; set (a1) to matrix descr
                movea.L  (mataddr,a6),a0      ; assign (a0) to matrix addr
                move.W   #0,(row,a1)          ; set row = 0
                move.W   #0,(col,a1)          ; set col = 0
norm0:          move.W   (row,a1),d1
                cmp.W    (rowbd,a1),d1        ; compare row and rowbound
                bgt.S    norm5                ; if rowbd < row, trace done
norm1:          move.W   (row,a1),d1
                mulu     (rowsize,a1),d1      ; (d1) = 1 * row
                move.W   (col,a1),d2
                mulu     (eltsize,a1),d2      ; (d2) = m * col
                add.W    d2,d1                ; (d1) = access offset

; test matrix element against norm in d0
                move.W   (0,a0,d1.W),d3       ; use direct access to byte
                tst.W    d3                   ; is matrix element positive
                bpl.S    norm2
                neg.W    d3                   ; if not get absolute value
norm.2:         cmp.W    d0,d3
                ble.S    norm3
                move.W   d3,d0
norm3:          move.W   (colbd,a1),d2
                cmp.W    (col,a1),d2          ; found last column
                bgt.S    norm4
                move.W   #0,(col,a1)          ; if yes, set column to 0
                addq.W   #1,(row,a1)
                bra.S    norm0
norm4:          addq.W   #1,(col,a1)          ; if not, col = col + 1
                bra.S    norm1                ; go add next a[i,i]
norm5:          unlk     a6
                movem.L  (sp)+,d1-d3/a0-a1
                move.L   (sp),(parsize,sp)    ; reset the stack
                addq.L   #parsize,sp
                rts

                end
```

Chapter 13

1. No. The exception state ends at the point of executing the first instruction in the service routine.

3. (a) ORI.W   #$8000,SR   Turns on tracing
   (b) ANDI.W   #$DFFF,SR   Puts the processor in user mode
   (c) MOVE.W   SR,D0   Sets the interrupt level to 5

   ANDI.W   #$F8FF,D0
   ORI.W   #$0500,D0
   MOVE.W   D0,SR
   (d) MOVE.L   USP,A3   Reads two long words from the user stack

   MOVE.L   (A3)+,D0
   MOVE.L   (A3)+,D1

5. (a) ANDI.W   #$7FFF,SR
   (b) ORI.W   #$8000,SR
   (c) ANDI.W   #$DFFF,SR
   (d) LEA $6000,A0
   MOVE   A0,USP
   (e) MOVE   USP,A0
   MOVE.L   (A0)+,D0
   JSR   HEXOUT_LONG
   (f) ORI.W   #$0700,SR
   (g) ANDI.W   #$F8EE,SR
   ORI.W   #$0500,SR

7. (a) TRAP #5
   SR (on the stack) = $0000
   Current SP = $7FF8
   PC (on the stack) = $00001006
   Current SR = $2000
   (b) CHK #10,D1 and (D1) = $0B
   SR (on the stack) = $0008
   Current SP = $7FF8
   PC (on the stack) = $00001008
   Current SR = $2008
   (c) DC.W $F000
   SR (on the stack) = $0000
   PC (on the stack) = $00001004
   Current SP = $7FF8
   Current SR = $2000
   (d) MOVE.W #$2000,SR
   SR (on the stack) = $0000
   Current SP = $7FF8
   PC (on the stack) = $00001004
   Current SR = $2000

(e) MOVE.W #7,$5001
   SR (on the stack) = $0000
   Current SP = $7FF0
   PC (on the stack) is between $00001004 and $0000100C.
   Current SR = $2000
(f) MOVE.L #77,(4,A0) with (A0) = $100002 with 1MB of RAM.
   PC (on the stack) is between $00001004 and $0000100C.
   Current SR = $2000

9. LEA $20000,A3
   MOVE.L   A3,USP
   PEA $10000
   CLR.W   −(SP)
   RTE

11. (a) False. A one must be subtracted from I and the comparison to make 49.
   (b) The SP = $00001000   PC = $00F76000
                              SR = $2700

13.   LEA   A, A1
                MOVE.W   I, D0
   WHILE: TST.W   MORE
                BEQ   NEXT   ; CONDITION
                                ; IS FALSE

                . . .

                ADDI.W   #1, D0
                CHK   #49, D0
                MOVE.W   D0, D1
                ASL.W   #1, D1   ; SET INDEX
                                    ; FOR WORD
                                    ; DATA
                MOVE.W   D0, 0 (A0, D1. W)
                BRA   WHILE
   NEXT: . . .

15. (a) $50005533 A trap on overflow exception occurs
   (b) $10000 The output is 00015555 55550001

17. The main code causes five exceptions to be generated.
   (a) DC.W $FFFF causes an F-line exception. The service routine outputs 00000FFF, the low order 12 bits of the opcode word $FFFF.
   (b) Tracing is turned on by the ORI.W #$8000,SR instruction. Tracing begins with the MOVE.W D0,D1 instruction. The trace service routine

outputs the opcode word of the next instruction.

Traced Instruction	Next Instruction	Opcode Word
MOVE.W D0,D1	ANDI.W #$F000,D1	$0241
ANDI.W #$7000,D1	ANDI.W #$7FFF,SR	$027C
ANDI.W #$7FFF,SR	MOVE.W #7,$7FFF	$33FC

(c) The instruction MOVE.W #7,$7FFF causes an address error whose service routine accesses the seven word stack.

Fault Address $7FFF
Opcode Word $33FC
Status Register $2700
Program Counter $093E Assuming load address of $900

19. The subject of exception priorities is discussed in Chapter 14. For now, assume that a higher priority means that the service routine is executed after the service routine for a lower priority exception. Thus, the service routine for trace will execute first and "see" the PC of the first instruction in the service routine for TRAP. Anticipating discussion in Chapter 14, the following is a more technical explanation. When tracing is on at the start of an instruction which causes an exception, the exception has "priority" and its exception processing cycle is executed first, followed immediately by the cycle for trace. Thus, the trace service routine executes first and "sees" the PC for the first instruction of the TRAP service routine.

21. The RTE causes a bus error. A bus error occurs during the processing of this bus error. The system will go into the halt state.

23. (a) FC2 = 1 FC1 = 1 FC0 = 0
    (b) FC2 = 1 FC1 = 0 FC0 = 1

25. (a) LEA $500,A2
       MOVEC A2,VBR
    (b) Address is $500 + $1C
    (c) The normal response is for a debug monitor or real-time hardware emulator to return an opcode word on the data bus. If this does not occur, the illegal instruction exception is taken. The illegal instruction exception has format 0 and vector offset $10.

Chapter 14

1. (a) No response is made.
   (b) CPU interrupt level 4.

3. (a) ORI.W   #$0700,SR
   (b) ANDI.W   #$F8FF,SR
       ORI.W   #$0500,SR
   (c) MOVE.W #$0000,SR

5. (a) PC = $1004
   (b) SR = $2007

7. (a) 29 ∗ 4 = $74
   (b) 75 ∗ 4 = $12C

9. (a) PC = $1004
   (b) SR = $2007

11. The direct clear operation is not done and the timer continues to assert an interrupt.

13. (a) Interrupt occurs first.
    (b) On the MC68000, the trace exception is not processed.

15. *See page 232.*

17. 1. Disable interrupts
    2. Check the first ACIA to see if it is the source of the interrupt.
       (a) If it is the source, check to see if a character has arrived. If so, read it and return from interrupt.
       (b) If a character was not received check the transmit register. If it is empty and output is pending, send a character. If it is not empty, turn off the transmit and continue with (c).
    (c) Check the second ACIA to see if it is the source of the interrupt. The code should check the logic of (b).
    Note: It may be possible for all four interrupts to be asserted at the same time.

19. (a) $64
    (b) Statement 1
    (c) A special character is typed.
    (d) To transmit a character to the ACIA using polling.
    (e) To the monitor from inheriting an interrupting timer.
    (f) Negates the timer interrupt request.
    (g) Prints the number of characters typed per second.

```
monitor:     equ        $8146
vautov7:     equ        $007c

             xref       puthexout,puthexout_long,newline

start:       lea        $8000,sp
             move.L     #switch,vautov7.W
             movea.L    #$100000,a0
             move.L     a0,usp
             move.L     #1,d0
             movea.L    #2,a0
             move.W     #$2615,sr

idle:        bra.S      idle

; level 7 interrupt should cause the following to be printed
; 00000926  00002615  8000  00100000  00000001  00000002

switch:      movem.L    d0/A0,-(sp)
             move.L     (10,sp),d0          ; print pc
             jsr        puthexout_long
             moveq      #0,d0
             move.W     (8,sp),d0           ; print sr
             jsr        puthexout
             lea        (14,sp),a0          ; print original sp
             move.L     a0,d0
             jsr        puthextout_long
             move.L     usp,a0              ; print usp
             move.L     a0,d0
             jsr        puthexout_long
             move.L     (sp),d0             ; print d0
             jsr        puthexout_long
             move.L     (4,sp),d0           ; print a0
             jsr        puthexout_long
             jsr        newline
             jmp        monitor

             end
```

Chapter 15

1. (a) Three (3)
   (b) Disables interrupts for the duration of the service routine.
   (c) Transmitter
   (d) Receive
   (e) Checks the transmitter.
   (f) Yes
   (g) Turns off transmit interrupts.
   (h) Causes continuous service of the transmit interrupt.

3. (a) Execution time is significantly improved for small loops through the use of an instruction cache because use of the cache reduces the

processor's external bus activity. The cache increases system throughput in two ways. First, the cache is accessed in two CPU clock cycles, as compared with a minimum of three required for external memory access. Second, the cache allows instruction fetches and operand accesses to proceed in parallel. For instance, if the processor requires an instruction word and a bus access to process an operand, the instruction may be fetched from the cache while the bus access occurs in parallel.

(b) The data cache serves to reduce bus activity and decrease execution time. With both an instruction and data cache, instruction fetches, data fetches, and a third external access can all occur simultaneously if the instruction and data caches are both hit.

5. (a) Index = $0C = 12
   (b) Tag field is 10500A5
   (c) Opcode = 2A03

7. (a) Clear the MC68020 instruction cache.
```
MOVEQ #%1001,D0
MOVEC D0,CACR    ; CLEAR AND
                 ; ENABLE CACHE
```
   (b) Clear the MC68020 instruction cache entry at index 32.
```
MOVEA.L #%10000000,A0  ; 1000000 IN
                       ; BITS 2-7
                       ; OF CAAR

MOVEC   A0,CAAR
MOVEQ   #%101,D0       ; E = 1 AND
                       ; CE = 1

MOVEC   D0,CACR
```
   (c) Clear the MC68030 instruction and data caches.
```
MOVEQ #%100100001001,D0
MOVEC D0,CACR    ; CLEAR AND
                 ENABLE
                 INSTRUCTION
                 CACHE
```

(d) On the MC68030, clear the second long word in the data cache entry at index 7.
```
MOVEQ   #%01110100,D0
MOVEC   D0,CAAR
MOVEQ   #%10100000001,D0
MOVEC   D0,CACR
```
(e) Enable burst filling of both the MC68030 instruction and data caches.
```
MOVEC   CACR,D0
ORI.W   #$1010,D0
MOVEC   D0,CACR
```

9. (a) $0002C002
   (b)
```
MOVEC   #%111,DFC
MOVE.W  #$5500,D0
MOVES.W D0,$2200A
```

11. (a) $8002   0001   0785   0000   0000   0000
    (b) $4002   0000   BC00   0000   0000   0000

13. (a)
```
            PMOVE   TCVAL,TC
            . . .
TCVAL: DC.L     $81E45900
```
    (b)
```
            PMOVE   CRPVAL,CRP
            . . .
CRPVAL: DC.L     $07FF0001,$00005000
```

15.
```
            MOVEQ   #%110,D0
            MOVEC   D0,DFC
            LEA     BUFFER,A2
            MOVE.W  #1023,D1
COPY:  MOVE.L  (A2)+,D0
            MOVES.L D0,(A3)+
            DBRA    D1,COPY
```

INDEX